INTRODUCTION TO THE
SCIENCE OF SOCIOLOGY

THE HERITAGE OF SOCIOLOGY

A Series Edited by Morris Janowitz

Robert E. Park
and Ernest W. Burgess

INTRODUCTION TO THE
SCIENCE OF SOCIOLOGY

*including the original index to basic
sociological concepts*

Third Edition, Revised

With an Introduction by
MORRIS JANOWITZ

THE UNIVERSITY OF CHICAGO PRESS

CHICAGO AND LONDON

Library of Congress Catalog Card Number: 69-15366

The University of Chicago Press, Chicago 60637
The University of Chicago Press, Ltd., London W.C. 1

Published 1921. Third Edition published 1969

Printed in the United States of America

INTRODUCTION

For twenty years after its publication in 1921, *Introduction to the Science of Sociology* by Robert E. Park and Ernest W. Burgess was the leading textbook in the discipline. But it was a volume which conformed to the older format of a textbook and a treatise at the same time. There was no conscious effort at popularization of an academic specialty to reach a wider undergraduate audience. It contained no photographs or wide margins as has become the practice for social science textbooks. There was no doubt that it was designed for the classroom and the increasing numbers of undergraduates enrolled in courses offered by the Department of Sociology at the University of Chicago. As a treatise, it was simultaneously addressed to graduate students throughout the country for whom it became known as "the green bible" as they prepared for their doctoral examinations and research endeavors. Park and Burgess thought of it as a reasoned statement of the theoretical state of the discipline, and they were prepared to have it evaluated as such by mature scholars in the field. In fact, it also served to present sociological thinking to the related faculties of the social science community.

It is now over a quarter of a century since the book went out of print and became a collector's item. A great many of the specific selections included in the volume have, of course, become outdated. But the decision to reprint the volume in its entirety is thought to be more than a contribution to the history of the development of sociology. Many of the concepts presented and illustrated in the *Introduction to the Science of Sociology,* especially those concerning collective behavior (which has experienced a renewed interest in sociology), are remarkably up to date, and their presentation is indeed penetrating. For example, one is struck that the concept of "institutionalization," which plays such an important part in contemporary structural functional analysis, had by 1921 already sociological currency. Thus, the contemporary student of sociology will find in this treatise a wide range of concepts that remain viable because of their present utility, and he will be able to note how Park and Burgess sought to handle these concepts. Of particular relevance is the careful analytic index which supplies a guide to the conceptualizations in the volume.

v

The collaboration between Robert E. Park and Ernest W. Burgess was a fortunate and fruitful one. While there is no need to deprecate Burgess' contribution, it was clear to all including Burgess himself that the volume represented the theoretical impact of Robert E. Park, who, in effect, was drawing upon and modifying the ideas of W. I. Thomas. In responding to an inquiry from Ralph H. Turner shortly before his death, Ernest Burgess stated in a brief handwritten letter that "the leadership in the preparation of the book *Introduction to the Science of Sociology*" was taken on by Dr. Park. "He came to the project with a conceptual framework of sociology. He and I shared the task of looking up the reading selections, we went through hundreds of volumes to make the selections."

It does appear that the first draft of chapter 1 was under the sole authorship of Robert Park since it had appeared previously in the form of three articles in the *American Journal of Sociology*. For the bulk of the book, chapters 2 through 11, Burgess indicated that "in writing the introduction and the statements of further research for each chapter, we typically talked these over and I wrote the first draft which Dr. Park edited." From chapter 12 on, dealing with social control and collective behavior, Burgess stated that Robert Park wrote the introductions.

The *Introduction to the Science of Sociology* rapidly came to represent the Chicago school of sociology wherever sociology was taught or debated. The scope of the treatise is remarkably comprehensive in the range of the problems and concepts it presented. However, neither Park nor Burgess were system builders and were content to present a loose collection of concepts. In this sense, the volume is an unfortunate and unrepresentative perspective of the intellectual interests subsumed under the Chicago school of sociology. The work of W. I. Thomas or that of William Ogburn represented a much more systematic effort to present an integrated approach to sociology. No doubt the very eclecticism of the Park and Burgess volume made for its popularity as a textbook and its usefulness as a reference volume to the sociology fraternity concerned with developing empirical research.

Its impact and success were almost instantaneous. E. A. Ross, professor of sociology and social psychology at the University of Wisconsin, removed from the intellectual and social life of the Midway and in opposition to many of its social values, reviewed it for the *American Journal of Sociology* (November 1921) and declared "this handsome, wieldy volume will prove a Godsend to teachers of sociology. . . . This ripe and scholarly volume is the last word of perfection in source books for the classroom, no teacher of sociology can afford to be without it. No doubt it will contribute much to the expansion of social studies in our colleges."

At that time, to produce a book of over a thousand pages was a major enterprise for a university press if the book was devoted to sociological materials. However, from 1921 until it was declared out of print in June 1943, over thirty thousand copies were sold. By contemporary standards this seems modest. It was indeed impressive for that period. In the absence of planned obsolescence by continuous minor revisions, secondhand copies passed back and forth from student generation to student generation. It was translated into various foreign languages as foreign students completed their education at Chicago and returned home.

As a footnote in the changing social history of the university professor the income derived from royalties was not viewed by Park and especially by Ernest Burgess as a regular part of their standard of living. It was something extraordinary and special. In the case of Ernest W. Burgess it was carefully husbanded in order to underwrite research and ultimately after his death turned over to the Department of Sociology to make possible a generous scholarship fund.

The format of the treatise was a direct replication of W. I. Thomas' earlier influential volume which appeared in 1908 under the title *Source Book for Social Origins: Ethnological Materials, Psychological Standpoint, Classified and Annotated Bibliographies for the Interpretation of Savage Societies.* Both volumes represented the Chicago school's concern with fusing theory and empirical data. Each was not only a voluminous collection of essential source materials but included careful introductions and conceptual commentaries as well as bibliographic annotations. This format is still widely used in sociological textbooks, even though they are no longer treatises.

Park and Burgess were dedicated to the energetic application of the scientific method to those human phenomena which they saw as part of sociology. And yet, not for a moment did they believe that the generalizations being sought by the social scientists would dispense with the importance of concrete detail. It was out of this sensitivity that the tradition of interplay between concept and social detail developed, as represented in the research monographs about the urban community and the social worlds of the metropolis of their students. These men believed that sociology had to have a special genre, and subsequent generations of empirical researchers clung to this tradition.

At the conceptual level, Park and Burgess represented the view of the Chicago empirical school that fused sociology into the classical problems of social philosophy. They sought to understand the social order or, in their language, the processes of social control. There was no hesitation; it was abundantly evident that society, the social organism, was in a never-ending process of flux. As a result this volume reflects their underlying intellectual orientation. It focuses on categories of social processes. At the heart of their analysis is a set of process categories which have become classical in describing social change, namely, competition, conflict, and accommodation. All of these are elements of social control. For them collective behavior was not a distinct aspect of sociological analysis but an essential element in the processes of social change. They were interested in the study of social contagion, crowds, mass movements, and public opinion, topics which remain contemporary in a period of explosive social tensions.

But their very concern with social process limited their identification of the essential stratification features of an industrial society and weakened their analysis of social structure. Instead of examining the macrostructures of society, at points they used such vague formulations as "social forces." This is not to deny their awareness of the political process that penetrated the local community. Rather they viewed these political elements as derivative or epiphenomenological. They could not see political institutions as having independent consequences.

Nevertheless, this volume is a powerful refutation of the argument that the American sociological tradition avoided a concern with the analysis of conflict. In the approach that Park and Burgess were striving to construct, the notion of interaction is crucial. It is the counterpart of Parsons' theory of action. It is not merely a social psychological term connected with the subjective definition of the self, as derived from the writings of George Herbert Mead. Interaction is a process to be seen at all the levels of sociological analysis: ecological, social organizational, and the normative as well.

In turn, the more specific processes of competition, conflict, accommodation, and assimilation cut through the variety of structures that are to be found in organized society. The positive benefits of conflict which are so much at the core of contemporary conflict theory were already identified in an undifferentiated way by Park and Burgess. More precisely there is a Hobbesian overtone throughout the volume. The term social organization has come to be neutrally defined as an abstracted entity involving either patterns of roles or patterns of influence among social groups. There was no such academic attachment in the thinking of Park and Burgess. Their view of the ecological substructure of society led them to see an unending competition and conflict of interests. The development of forms of social organization was already essentially an accommodation of differences through the transformation or limitation of conflicts. "Social organization, with the exception of the order based on competition and adaptation, is essentially an accommodation of differences through conflicts" (p. 664).

Their interest in the ecological order led them to focus the bulk of their own writings at the community level. The human community was the object of analysis that interested them. But community was loosely fused with society. Through the fundamental processes of social transformation "a community assumes the form of a society" (p. 786). They did not highlight the structures and the mechanisms by which the parts related to the whole. The absence of an explicit macrosociology was a source of intellectual and analytic weakness. The collection of the statistical trend data about the national arena stimulated by their quantitative colleagues such as William F. Ogburn served to introduce a better balance but failed to stimulate them to concern with societal structures.

They were deeply aware of nationalism. Their frequent references to the collective representation stimulated by the writings of Emile Durkheim attest to their awareness of the social system level of analysis. But again national authority and legitimacy were not central concerns of theirs. This was seen by the relative absence of reference to the work of Max Weber.

It was not far-fetched to point out that much of what has come to be described as phenomenology is part of their concern. Repeatedly, page after page and section after section, whether one is reading the original contributions of Park and Burgess or included selections, there is an expression of the subjective definition of social behavior and social institutions. Thus, for example, the discussion of prestige encompasses the nonrational and mystical aspects of this concept. If in effect prestige can be reduced to the concrete measures of income and education then there is something subjective left over. In turn, contemporary analysis of the presentation of individual self has its earlier analogy in concepts dealing with ceremonialism, individual control, and the like. Furthermore, one has only to read the analysis of collective behavior and public opinion to realize the extent to which their categories are relevant in a period of rapid social change. They emphasized myth, ritual, dogma, and propaganda.

One of the most dramatic aspects of the volume is the concluding section on the idea of progress. The notion that Chicago sociology under the impact of empiricism was devoid of value concerns is hardly documented by the contents of this volume. The idea that American sociologists got their interests in social goals from Europe is simply incorrect. Of course, these men were aware of eighteenth- and nineteenth-century European social philosophers. For them, the study of human values was an essential part of the subject matter of sociology. And more important, they believed in the last analysis that sociology had to deal with policy and problem issues. Their terminology centered on definitions, including sociological definitions of progress and the conditions for achieving progress and its consequences.

Park and Burgess were men of great insight who sought to extend their knowledge by the use of specific concepts. Contemporary sociologists are more concerned with systems of concepts in order to present a more integrated overview.

There is no doubt that if they were alive today they would participate in the efforts at new formulations in sociology. But they would not have abandoned their commitment to concrete and specific data. Thus, it is well to point out their fundamental viewpoint: "It has been the dream of philosophers that theoretical and abstract science could and some day would succeed in putting into formulae and into general terms all that was significant in the concrete facts of life. It has been the tragic mistake of the so-called intellectuals, who have gained their knowledge from textbooks rather than from observation and research, to assume that science had already realized its dream. But there is no indication that science has begun to exhaust the sources or significance of concrete experience."

MORRIS JANOWITZ

TABLE OF CONTENTS

CHAPTER I. SOCIOLOGY AND THE SOCIAL SCIENCES

PAGE

I Sociology and "Scientific" History 1

II. Historical and Sociological Facts 6

III. Human Nature and Law . . . . ; 12

IV. History, Natural History, and Sociology 16

V. The Social Organism: Humanity or Leviathan? 24

VI. Social Control and Schools of Thought 27

VII. Social Control and the Collective Mind 36

VIII. Sociology and Social Research 43
Representative Works in Systematic Sociology and Methods of Sociological Research 57
Topics for Written Themes 60
Questions for Discussion 60

CHAPTER II. HUMAN NATURE

I. Introduction
   1. Human Interest in Human Nature 64
   2. Definition of Human Nature 65
   3. Classification of the Materials 68

II. Materials
  A. The Original Nature of Man
    1. Original Nature Defined. *Edward L. Thorndike* . 73
    2. No Separate Instincts. *John Dewey* 75
    3. Man Not Born Human. *Robert E. Park* 79
    4. The Natural Man. *Milicent W. Shinn* 85
    5. Sex Differences. *Albert Moll* 88
    6. Racial Differences. *C. S. Myers* 92
    7. Individual Differences. *Edward L. Thorndike* . . 95
  B. Human Nature and Social Life
    1. Human Nature and Its Remaking. *W. E. Hocking* 98
    2. Human Nature, Folkways, and the Mores. *William G. Sumner* 100

PAGE

3. Habit and Custom, the Individual and the General
   Will. *Ferdinand Tönnies*   103
4. The Law, Conscience, and the General Will. *Viscount Haldane*   105

C. Personality and the Social Self

1. The Organism as Personality. *Th. Ribot.* . . .   111
2. Personality as a Complex. *Morton Prince* . . .   113
3. The Self as the Individual's Conception of His Rôle.
   Alfred Binet   116
4. The Natural Person versus the Social and Conventional Self. *L. G. Winston*   120
5. The Divided Self and Moral Consciousness. *William James*   122
6. Personality of Individuals and of Peoples. *W. v. Bechterew*   126

D. Biological and Social Heredity

1. Nature and Nurture. *J. Arthur Thomson* . . .   129
2. Inheritance of Original Nature. *C. B. Davenport* .   131
3. Inheritance of Acquired Nature: Tradition. *Albert G. Keller*   137
4. Temperament, Tradition, and Nationality. *Robert E. Park*   138

III. Investigations and Problems

1. Conceptions of Human Nature Implicit in Religious
   and Political Doctrines   142
2. Literature and the Science of Human Nature . .   144
3. Research in the Field of Original Nature   146
4. The Investigation of Human Personality . . .   146
5. The Measurement of Individual Differences . . .   148
Selected Bibliography   150
Topics for Written Themes   157
Questions for Discussion   157

CHAPTER III. SOCIETY AND THE GROUP

I. Introduction

1. Society, the Community, and the Group   161
2. Classification of the Materials   164

PAGE

II. Materials

    A. Society and Symbiosis

        1. Definition of Society. *Alfred Espinas* 167

        2. Symbiosis (literally "living together"). *William M. Wheeler* 169

        3. The Taming and the Domestication of Animals. *P. Chalmers Mitchell*. 172

    B. Plant Communities and Animal Societies

        1. Plant Communities. *Eugenius Warming*. . . . 175

        2. Ant Society. *William M. Wheeler* 182

    C. Human Society

        1. Social Life. *John Dewey* 184

        2. Behavior and Conduct. *Robert E. Park* 187

        3. Instinct and Character. *L. T. Hobhouse*. . . . 192

        4. Collective Representation and Intellectual Life. *Émile Durkheim* 195

    D. The Social Group

        1. Definition of the Group. *Albion W. Small* . . . 198

        2. The Unity of the Social Group. *Robert E. Park* . 200

        3. Types of Social Groups. *S. Sighele* 202

        4. *Esprit de Corps*, Morale, and Collective Representations of Social Groups. *William E. Hocking* . . 207

III. Investigations and Problems

        1. The Scientific Study of Societies 210

        2. Surveys of Communities 211

        3. The Group as a Unit of Investigation. 212

        4. The Study of the Family 213

    Selected Bibliography 217

    Topics for Written Themes 223

    Questions for Discussion 223

CHAPTER IV. ISOLATION

I. Introduction

        1. Geological and Biological Conceptions of Isolation . 226

        2. Isolation and Segregation 228

        3. Classification of the Materials 230

II. Materials

    A. Isolation and Personal Individuality

        1. Society and Solitude. *Francis Bacon*. 233

        2. Society in Solitude. *Jean Jacques Rousseau*. . . 234

PAGE

3. Prayer as a Form of Isolation. *George Albert Coe* . 235
4. Isolation, Originality, and Erudition. *T. Sharper Knowlson* 237

B. Isolation and Retardation
1. Feral Men. *Maurice H. Small* 239
2. From Solitude to Society. *Helen Keller* 243
3. Mental Effects of Solitude. *W. H. Hudson* . . . 245
4. Isolation and the Rural Mind. *C. J. Galpin* . . 247
5. The Subtler Effects of Isolation. *W. I. Thomas* . 249

C. Isolation and Segregation
1. Segregation as a Process. *Robert E. Park* . . . 252
2. Isolation as a Result of Segregation. *L. W. Crafts and E. A. Doll* 254

D. Isolation and National Individuality
1. Historical Races as Products of Isolation. *N. S. Shaler* 257
2. Geographical Isolation and Maritime Contact. *George Grote* 260
3. Isolation as an Explanation of National Differences. *William Z. Ripley* 264
4. Natural versus Vicinal Location in National Development. *Ellen C. Semple* 268

III. Investigations and Problems
1. Isolation in Anthropogeography and Biology . . 269
2. Isolation and Social Groups 270
3. Isolation and Personality 271
Bibliography: Materials for the Study of Isolation. 273
Topics for Written Themes 276
Questions for Discussion 277

CHAPTER V. SOCIAL CONTACTS

I. Introduction
1. Preliminary Notions of Social Contact 280
2. The Sociological Concept of Contact 281
3. Classification of the Materials 282

II. Materials
A. Physical Contact and Social Contact
1. The Frontiers of Social Contact. *Albion W. Small* . 288
2. The Land and the People. *Ellen C. Semple* . . . 289
3. Touch and Social Contact. *Ernest Crawley* . . 291

PAGE

B. Social Contact in Relation to Solidarity and to Mobility

    1. The In-Group and the Out-Group. *W. G. Sumner* .   293

    2. Sympathetic Contacts versus Categoric Contacts. *N. S. Shaler*   294

    3. Historical Continuity and Civilization. *Friedrich Ratzel*   298

    4. Mobility and the Movement of Peoples. *Ellen C. Semple*.   301

C. Primary and Secondary Contacts

    1. Village Life in America (from the *Diary of a Young Girl*). *Caroline C. Richards*   305

    2. Secondary Contacts and City Life. *Robert E. Park* .   311

    3. Publicity as a Form of Secondary Contact. *Robert E. Park*   315

    4. From Sentimental to Rational Attitudes. *Werner Sombart*   317

    5. The Sociological Significance of the "Stranger." *Georg Simmel*.   322

III. Investigations and Problems

    1. Physical Contacts   327

    2. Touch and the Primary Contacts of Intimacy . .   329

    3. Primary Contacts of Acquaintanceship   330

    4. Secondary Contacts   331

Bibliography: Materials for the Study of Social Contacts . . .   332

Topics for Written Themes   336

Questions for Discussion   336

CHAPTER VI. SOCIAL INTERACTION

I. Introduction

    1. The Concept of Interaction.   339

    2. Classification of the Materials   341

II. Materials

A. Society as Interaction

    1. The Mechanistic Interpretation of Society. *Ludwig Gumplowicz*   346

    2. Social Interaction as the Definition of the Group in Time and Space. *Georg Simmel*   348

PAGE

B. The Natural Forms of Communication
　　1. Sociology of the Senses: Visual Interaction. *Georg Simmel* 356
　　2. The Expression of the Emotions. *Charles Darwin* . 361
　　3. Blushing. *Charles Darwin* 365
　　4. Laughing. *L. Dugas* 370

C. Language and the Communication of Ideas
　　1. Intercommunication in the Lower Animals. *C. Lloyd Morgan* 375
　　2. The Concept as the Medium of Human Communication. *F. Max Müller* 379
　　3. Writing as a Form of Communication. *Charles H. Judd* 381
　　4. The Extension of Communication by Human Invention. *Carl Bücher* 385

D. Imitation
　　1. Definition of Imitation. *Charles H. Judd* . . . 390
　　2. Attention, Interest, and Imitation. *G. F. Stout* . 391
　　3. The Three Levels of Sympathy. *Th. Ribot* . . . 394
　　4. Rational Sympathy. *Adam Smith* 397
　　5. Art, Imitation, and Appreciation. *Yrjö Hirn* . . 401

E. Suggestion
　　1. A Sociological Definition of Suggestion. *W. v. Bechterew* 408
　　2. The Subtler Forms of Suggestion. *Albert Moll*. . 412
　　3. Social Suggestion and Mass or "Corporate" Action. *W. v. Bechterew* 415

III. Investigations and Problems
　　1. The Process of Interaction 420
　　2. Communication 421
　　3. Imitation 423
　　4. Suggestion 424
　　5. Invention 424
　Selected Bibliography 426
　Topics for Written Themes 431
　Questions for Discussion 432

CHAPTER VII. SOCIAL FORCES

I. Introduction
　　1. Sources of the Notion of Social Forces 435
　　2. History of the Concept of Social Forces 436
　　3. Classification of the Materials 437

PAGE

II. Materials

  A. Trends, Tendencies, and Public Opinion
     1. Social Forces in American History. *A. M. Simons* . 443
     2. Social Tendencies as Social Forces. *Richard T. Ely* 444
     3. Public Opinion and Legislation in England. *A. V.*
       Dicey 445

  B. Interests, Sentiments, and Attitudes
     1. Social Forces and Interaction. *Albion W. Small* . 451
     2. Interests. *Albion W. Small* 454
     3. Social Pressures. *Arthur F. Bentley* 458
     4. Idea-Forces. *Alfred Fouillée* 461
     5. Sentiments. *William McDougall* 464
     6. Social Attitudes. *Robert E. Park* 467

  C. The Four Wishes: A Classification of Social Forces
     1. The Wish, the Social Atom. *Edwin B. Holt*. . 478
     2. The Freudian Wish. *John B. Watson* . . . 482
     3. The Person and His Wishes. *W. I. Thomas*. . 488

III. Investigations and Problems
     1. Popular Notions of Social Forces 491
     2. Social Forces and History 493
     3. Interests, Sentiments, and Attitudes as Social Forces 494
     4. Wishes and Social Forces 497

  Selected Bibliography 498
  Topics for Written Themes 501
  Questions for Discussion 502

CHAPTER VIII. COMPETITION

I. Introduction
     1. Popular Conceptions of Competition 504
     2. Competition a Process of Interaction 506
     3. Classification of the Materials 510

II. Materials

  A. The Struggle for Existence
     1. Different Forms of the Struggle for Existence.
       J. Arthur Thomson 512
     2. Competition and Natural Selection. *Charles Darwin* 514
     3. Competition, Specialization, and Organization.
       Charles Darwin 518
     4. Man: An Adaptive Mechanism. *George W. Crile* . 521

B. Competition and Segregation

    1. Plant Migration, Competition, and Segregation. *F. E. Clements* 525

    2. Migration and Segregation. *Carl Bücher* . . . 528

    3. Demographic Segregation and Social Selection. *William Z. Ripley* 533

    4. Inter-racial Competition and Race Suicide. *Francis A. Walker* 538

    5. Competition, Commercial Organization, and the Metropolitan Economy. *N. S. B. Gras* 543

C. Economic Competition

    1. Changing Forms of Economic Competition. *John B. Clark* 545

    2. Competition and the Natural Harmony of Individual Interests. *Adam Smith*. 551

    3. Competition and Freedom. *Frédéric Bastiat* . . 552

    4. Money and Freedom. *Georg Simmel* 553

III. Investigations and Problems

    1. Biological Competition 554

    2. Economic Competition 555

    3. Competition and Human Ecology 559

    4. Competition and the "Inner Enemies": the Defectives, the Dependents, and the Delinquents . . . 560

Selected Bibliography 564

Topics for Written Themes 570

Questions for Discussion 571

CHAPTER IX. CONFLICT

I. Introduction

    1. The Concept of Conflict 574

    2. Classification of the Materials 576

II. Materials

A. Conflict as Conscious Competition

    1. The Natural History of Conflict. *W. I. Thomas* . 579

    2. Conflict as a Type of Social Interaction. *Georg Simmel* 582

    3. Types of Conflict Situations. *Georg Simmel* . . 586

B. War, Instincts, and Ideals

    1. War and Human Nature. *William A. White* . . 594

    2. War as a Form of Relaxation. *G. T. W. Patrick* . 598

    3. The Fighting Animal and the Great Society. *Henry Rutgers Marshall* 600

PAGE

C. Rivalry, Cultural Conflicts, and Social Organization

    1. Animal Rivalry. *William H. Hudson* 604

    2. The Rivalry of Social Groups. *George E. Vincent* . 605

    3. The Gang and Political Organization 610

    4. Cultural Conflicts and the Organization of Sects.
       Franklin H. Giddings 613

D. Racial Conflicts

    1. Social Contacts and Race Conflict. *Robert E. Park* . 619

    2. Conflict and Race Consciousness. *Robert E. Park* . 626

    3. Conflict and Accommodation. *Alfred H. Stone* . . 634

III. Investigations and Problems

    1. The Psychology and Sociology of Conflict, Conscious
       Competition, and Rivalry 641

    2. Types of Conflict 642

    3. The Literature of War 644

    4. Race Conflict 545

    5. Conflict Groups 646

Selected Bibliography 648

Topics for Written Themes 661

Questions for Discussion 661

CHAPTER X. ACCOMMODATION

I. Introduction

    1. Adaptation and Accommodation 663

    2. Classification of the Materials 666

II. Materials

A. Forms of Accommodation

    1. Acclimatization. *Daniel G. Brinton* 671

    2. Slavery Defined. *H. J. Nieboer* 674

    3. Excerpts from the Journal of a West India Slave
       Owner. *Matthew G. Lewis* 677

    4. The Origin of Caste in India. *John C. Nesfield* . 681

    5. Caste and the Sentiments of Caste Reflected in
       Popular Speech. *Herbert Risley* 684

B. Subordination and Superordination

    1. The Psychology of Subordination and Superordina-
       tion. *Hugo Münsterberg* 688

    2. Social Attitudes in Subordination: Memories of an
       Old Servant. *An Old Servant* 692

PAGE

3. The Reciprocal Character of Subordination and Superordination. *Georg Simmel* 695
4. Three Types of Subordination and Superordination. *Georg Simmel* 697

C. Conflict and Accommodation

1. War and Peace as Types of Conflict and Accommodation. *Georg Simmel* 703
2. Compromise and Accommodation. *Georg Simmel* . 706

D. Competition, Status, and Social Solidarity

1. Personal Competition, Social Selection, and Status. *Charles H. Cooley* 708
2. Personal Competition and the Evolution of Individual Types. *Robert E. Park* 712
3. Division of Labor and Social Solidarity. *Émile Durkheim* 714

III. Investigations and Problems

1. Forms of Accommodation 718
2. Subordination and Superordination 721
3. Accommodation Groups. 721
4. Social Organization 723

Selected Bibliography 725
Topics for Written Themes 732
Questions for Discussion 732

CHAPTER XI. ASSIMILATION

I. Introduction

1. Popular Conceptions of Assimilation 734
2. The Sociology of Assimilation 735
3. Classification of the Materials 737

II. Materials

A. Biological Aspects of Assimilation

1. Assimilation and Amalgamation. *Sarah E. Simons* 740
2. The Instinctive Basis of Assimilation. *W. Trotter* . 742

B. The Conflict and Fusion of Cultures

1. The Analysis of Blended Cultures. *W. H. R. Rivers* 746
2. The Extension of Roman Culture in Gaul. *John H. Cornyn.* 751
3. The Competition of the Cultural Languages. *E. H. Babbitt.* 754
4. The Assimilation of Races. *Robert E. Park* . . . 756

PAGE

C. Americanization as a Problem in Assimilation

    1. Americanization as Assimilation 762
    2. Language as a Means and a Product of Participation 763
    3. Assimilation and the Mediation of Individual
        Differences 766

III. Investigations and Problems

    1. Assimilation and Amalgamation 769
    2. The Conflict and Fusion of Cultures 771
    3. Immigration and Americanization 772

Selected Bibliography 775
Topics for Written Themes 782
Questions for Discussion 783

CHAPTER XII. SOCIAL CONTROL

I. Introduction

    1. Social Control Defined 785
    2. Classification of the Materials 787

II. Materials

A. Elementary Forms of Social Control

    1. Control in the Crowd and the Public. *Lieut. J. S.
        Smith* 800
    2. Ceremonial Control. *Herbert Spencer* 805
    3. Prestige. *Lewis Leopold* 807
    4. Prestige and Status in South East Africa. *Maurice
        S. Evans* 811
    5. Taboo. *W. Robertson Smith* 812

B. Public Opinion

    1. The Myth. *Georges Sorel* 816
    2. The Growth of a Legend. *Fernand van Langenhove* 819
    3. Ritual, Myth, and Dogma. *W. Robertson Smith* . 822
    4. The Nature of Public Opinion. *A. Lawrence Lowell* 826
    5. Public Opinion and the Mores. *Robert E. Park*. . 829
    6. News and Social Control. *Walter Lippmann* . . 834
    7. The Psychology of Propaganda. *Raymond Dodge* . 837

C. Institutions

    1. Institutions and the Mores. *W. G. Sumner* . . . 841
    2. Common Law and Statute Law. *Frederic J. Stimson* 843
    3. Religion and Social Control. *Charles A. Ellwood* . 846

PAGE

III. Investigations and Problems

    1. Social Control and Human Nature 848
    2. Elementary Forms of Social Control 849
    3. Public Opinion and Social Control 850
    4. Legal Institutions and Law. 851

Selected Bibliography 854
Topics for Written Themes 862
Questions for Discussion 862

CHAPTER XIII. COLLECTIVE BEHAVIOR

I. Introduction

    1. Collective Behavior Defined 865
    2. Social Unrest and Collective Behavior 866
    3. The Crowd and the Public 867
    4. Crowds and Sects 870
    5. Sects and Institutions 872
    6. Classification of the Materials 874

II. Materials

  A. Social Contagion

    1. An Incident in a Lancashire Cotton Mill . . . 878
    2. The Dancing Mania of the Middle Ages. *J. F. C.*
      Hecker 879

  B. The Crowd

    1. The "Animal" Crowd 881
      a) The Flock. *Mary Austin* 881
      b) The Herd. *W. H. Hudson* 883
      c) The Pack. *Ernest Thompson Seton* 886
    2. The Psychological Crowd. *Gustave Le Bon* . . . 887
    3. The Crowd Defined. *Robert E. Park* 893

  C. Types of Mass Movements

    1. Crowd Excitements and Mass Movements: The
      Klondike Rush. *T. C. Down* 895
    2. Mass Movements and the Mores: The Woman's
      Temperance Crusade. *Mrs. Annie Wittenmyer* . . 898
    3. Mass Movements and Revolution
      a) The French Revolution. *Gustave Le Bon*. . . 905
      b) Bolshevism. *John Spargo* 909
    4. Mass Movements and Institutions: Methodism.
      William E. H. Lecky. 915

PAGE

III. Investigations and Problems

    1. Social Unrest 924
    2. Psychic Epidemics 926
    3. Mass Movements 927
    4. Revivals, Religious and Linguistic. 929
    5. Fashion, Reform, and Revolution 933

Selected Bibliography 934
Topics for Written Themes 951
Questions for Discussion 951

CHAPTER XIV.   PROGRESS

I. Introduction

    1. Popular Conceptions of Progress 953
    2. The Problem of Progress 956
    3. History of the Concept of Progress 958
    4. Classification of the Materials 962

II. Materials

  A. The Concept of Progress

    1. The Earliest Conception of Progress.   *F. S. Marvin* 965
    2. Progress and Organization.   *Herbert Spencer* . . 966
    3. The Stages of Progress.   *Auguste Comte* 968
    4. Progress and the Historical Process.   *Leonard T. Hobhouse* 969

  B. Progress and Science

    1. Progress and Happiness.   *Lester F. Ward* . . . 973
    2. Progress and Prevision.   *John Dewey* 975
    3. Progress and the Limits of Scientific Prevision.   *Arthur J. Balfour* 977
    4. Eugenics as a Science of Progress.   *Francis Galton* . 979

  C. Progress and Human Nature

    1. The Nature of Man.   *George Santayana* 983
    2. Progress and the Mores.   *W. G. Sumner* . . . 983
    3. War and Progress.   *James Bryce* 984
    4. Progress and the Cosmic Urge
      a) The *Élan Vitale.*   *Henri Bergson* 989
      b) The *Dunkler Drang.*   *Arthur Schopenhauer* . . 994

III. Investigations and Problems

    1. Progress and Social Research 1000
    2. Indices of Progress 1002

Selected Bibliography 1004
Topics for Written Themes 1009
Questions for Discussion 1010

                                                              PAGE
Index of Names   1013
General Index   1025

.

CHAPTER I

SOCIOLOGY AND THE SOCIAL SCIENCES[1]

I. SOCIOLOGY AND "SCIENTIFIC" HISTORY

Sociology first gained recognition as an independent science with the publication, between 1830 and 1842, of Auguste Comte's *Cours de philosophie positive*. Comte did not, to be sure, create sociology. He did give it a name, a program, and a place among the sciences.

Comte's program for the new science proposed an extension to politics and to history of the positive methods of the natural sciences. Its practical aim was to establish government on the secure foundation of an exact science and give to the predictions of history something of the precision of mathematical formulae.

We have to contemplate social phenomena as susceptible of prevision, like all other classes, within the limits of exactness compatible with their higher complexity. Comprehending the three characteristics of political science which we have been examining, prevision of social phenomena supposes, first, that we have abandoned the region of metaphysical idealities, to assume the ground of observed realities by a systematic subordination of imagination to observation; secondly, that political conceptions have ceased to be absolute, and have become relative to the variable state of civilization, so that theories, following the natural course of facts, may admit of our foreseeing them; and, thirdly, that permanent political action is limited by determinate laws, since, if social events were always exposed to disturbance by the accidental intervention of the legislator, human or divine, no scientific prevision of them would be possible. Thus, we may concentrate the conditions of the spirit of positive social philosophy on this one great attribute of scientific prevision.[2]

Comte proposed, in short, to make government a technical science and politics a profession. He looked forward to a time when legislation, based on a scientific study of human nature, would

---

[1] From Robert E. Park, "Sociology and the Social Sciences," *American Journal of Sociology*, XXVI (1920–21), 401–24; XXVII (1921–22), 1–21; 169–83.

[2] Harriet Martineau, *The Positive Philosophy of Auguste Comte*, freely translated and condensed (London, 1893), II, 61.

assume the character of natural law. The earlier and more elementary sciences, particularly physics and chemistry, had given man control over external nature; the last science, sociology, was to give man control over himself.

Men were long in learning that Man's power of modifying phenomena can result only from his knowledge of their natural laws; and in the infancy of each science, they believed themselves able to exert an unbounded influence over the phenomena of that science. . . . . Social phenomena are, of course, from their extreme complexity, the last to be freed from this pretension: but it is therefore only the more necessary to remember that the pretension existed with regard to all the rest, in their earliest stage, and to anticipate therefore that social science will, in its turn, be emancipated from the delusion. . . . . It [the existing social science] represents the social action of Man to be indefinite and arbitrary, as was once thought in regard to biological, chemical, physical, and even astronomical phenomena, in the earlier stages of their respective sciences. . . . . The human race finds itself delivered over, without logical protection, to the ill-regulated experimentation of the various political schools, each one of which strives to set up, for all future time, its own immutable type of government. We have seen what are the chaotic results of such a strife; and we shall find that there is no chance of order and agreement but in subjecting social phenomena, like all others, to invariable natural laws, which shall, as a whole, prescribe for each period, with entire certainty, the limits and character of political action: in other words, introducing into the study of social phenomena the same positive spirit which has regenerated every other branch of human speculation.[1]

In the present anarchy of political opinion and parties, changes in the existing social order inevitably assume, he urged, the character, at the best, of a mere groping empiricism; at the worst, of a social convulsion like that of the French Revolution. Under the direction of a positive, in place of a speculative or, as Comte would have said, metaphysical science of society, progress must assume the character of an orderly march.

It was to be expected, with the extension of exact methods of investigation to other fields of knowledge, that the study of man and of society would become, or seek to become, scientific in the sense in which that word is used in the natural sciences. It is interesting, in this connection, that Comte's first name for sociology

[1] Harriet Martineau, *op. cit.*, II, 59–61.

was *social physics*. It was not until he had reached the fourth volume of his *Positive Philosophy* that the word sociological is used for the first time.

Comte, if he was foremost, was not first in the search for a positive science of society, which would give man that control over men that he had over external nature. Montesquieu, in his *The Spirit of Laws*, first published in 1747, had distinguished in the organization of society, between form, "the particular structure," and forces, "the human passions which set it in motion." In his preface to this first epoch-making essay in what Freeman calls "comparative politics," Montesquieu suggests that the uniformities, which he discovered beneath the wide variety of positive law, were contributions not merely to a science of law, but to a science of mankind.

I have first of all considered mankind; and the result of my thoughts has been, that amidst such an infinite diversity of laws and manners, they are not solely conducted by the caprice of fancy.[1]

Hume, likewise, put politics among the natural sciences.[2] Condorcet wanted to make history positive.[3] But there were, in the period between 1815 and 1840 in France, conditions which made the need of a new science of politics peculiarly urgent. The Revolution had failed and the political philosophy, which had directed and justified it, was bankrupt. France, between 1789 and 1815, had adopted, tried, and rejected no less than ten different constitutions. But during this period, as Saint-Simon noted, society, and the human beings who compose society, had not changed. It was evident that government was not, in any such sense as the philosophers had assumed, a mere artefact and legislative construction. Civilization, as Saint-Simon conceived it, was a part of nature. Social change was part of the whole cosmic process. He proposed, therefore, to make politics a science as positive as physics. The subject-matter of political science, as he conceived it, was not so

[1] Montesquieu, Baron M. de Secondat, *The Spirit of Laws*, translated by Thomas Nugent (Cincinnati, 1873), I, xxxi.

[2] David Hume, *Inquiry Concerning Human Understanding*, Part II, sec. 7.

[3] Condorcet, *Esquisse d'un tableau historique des progrès de l'esprit humain* (1795), 292. See Paul Barth, *Die Philosophie der Geschichte als Sociologie* (Leipzig, 1897), Part I, pp. 21–23.

much political forms as social conditions. History had been literature. It was destined to become a science.[1]

Comte called himself Saint-Simon's pupil. It is perhaps more
correct to say Saint-Simon formulated the problem for which Comte,
in his *Positive Philosophy*, sought a solution. It was Comte's notion
that with the arrival of sociology the distinction which had so long
existed, and still exists, between philosophy, in which men define
their wishes, and natural science, in which they describe the existing
order of nature, would disappear. In that case ideals would be defined
in terms of reality, and the tragic difference between what men want
and what is possible would be effaced. Comte's error was to mistake
a theory of progress for progress itself. It is certainly true that as
men learn what is, they will adjust their ideals to what is possible.
But knowledge grows slowly.

Man's knowledge of mankind has increased greatly since 1842.
Sociology, "the positive science of humanity," has moved steadily
forward in the direction that Comte's program indicated, but it has
not yet replaced history. Historians are still looking for methods of
investigation which will make history "scientific."

No one who has watched the course of history during the last generation
can have felt doubt of its tendency. Those of us who read Buckle's first
volume when it appeared in 1857, and almost immediately afterwards, in
1859, read the *Origin of Species* and felt the violent impulse which Darwin
gave to the study of natural laws, never doubted that historians would follow
until they had exhausted every possible hypothesis to create a science of
history. Year after year passed, and little progress has been made. Perhaps
the mass of students are more skeptical now than they were thirty years ago
of the possibility that such a science can be created. Yet almost every successful historian has been busy with it, adding here a new analysis, a new
generalization there; a clear and definite connection where before the rupture
of idea was absolute; and, above all, extending the field of study until it
shall include all races, all countries, and all times. Like other branches of
science, history is now encumbered and hampered by its own mass, but its
tendency is always the same, and cannot be other than what it is. That
the effort to make history a science may fail is possible, and perhaps probable; but that it should cease, unless for reasons that would cause all science
to cease, is not within the range of experience. Historians will not, and

---

[1] *Œuvres de Saint-Simon et d'Enfantin* (Paris, 1865–78), XVII, 228. Paul
Barth, *op. cit.*, Part I, p. 23.

even if they would they can not, abandon the attempt. Science itself would admit its own failure if it admitted that man, the most important of all its subjects, could not be brought within its range.[1]

Since Comte gave the new science of humanity a name and a point of view, the area of historical investigation has vastly widened and a number of new social sciences have come into existence—ethnology, archaeology, folklore, the comparative studies of cultural materials, i.e., language, mythology, religion, and law, and in connection with and closely related with these, folk-psychology, social psychology, and the psychology of crowds, which latter is, perhaps, the forerunner of a wider and more elaborate political psychology. The historians have been very much concerned with these new bodies of materials and with the new points of view which they have introduced into the study of man and of society. Under the influences of these sciences, history itself, as James Harvey Robinson has pointed out, has had a history. But with the innovations which the new history has introduced or attempted to introduce, it does not appear that there have been any fundamental changes in method or ideology in the science itself.

Fifty years have elapsed since Buckle's book appeared, and I know of no historian who would venture to maintain that we had made any considerable advance toward the goal he set for himself. A systematic prosecution of the various branches of social science, especially political economy, sociology, anthropology, and psychology, is succeeding in explaining many things; but history must always remain, from the standpoint of the astronomer, physicist, or chemist, a highly inexact and fragmentary body of knowledge. . . . . History can no doubt be pursued in a strictly scientific spirit, but the data we possess in regard to the past of mankind are not of a nature to lend themselves to organization into an exact science, although, as we shall see, they may yield truths of vital importance.[2]

History has not become, as Comte believed it must, an exact science, and sociology has not taken the place of History in the social sciences. It is important, however, for understanding the mutations which have taken place in sociology since Comte to

[1] Henry Adams, *The Degradation of the Democratic Dogma* (New York, 1919), p. 126.

[2] James Harvey Robinson, *The New History, Essays Illustrating the Modern Historical Outlook* (New York, 1912), pp. 54–55.

remember that it had its origin in an effort to make history exact. This, with, to be sure, considerable modifications, is still, as we shall see, an ambition of the science.

II.   HISTORICAL AND SOCIOLOGICAL FACTS

Sociology, as Comte conceived it, was not, as it has been characterized, "a highly important point of view," but a fundamental science, i.e., a method of investigation and "a body of discoveries about mankind."[1] In the hierarchy of the sciences, sociology, the last in time, was first in importance. The order was as follows: mathematics, astronomy, physics, chemistry, biology including psychology, sociology. This order represented a progression from the more elementary to the more complex. It was because history and politics were concerned with the most complex of natural phenomena that they were the last to achieve what Comte called the positive character. They did this in sociology.

Many attempts have been made before and since Comte to find a satisfactory classification of the sciences. The order and relation of the sciences is still, in fact, one of the cardinal problems of philosophy. In recent years the notion has gained recognition that the difference between history and the natural sciences is not one of degree, but of kind; not of subject-matter merely, but of method. This difference in method is, however, fundamental. It is a difference not merely in the interpretation but in the *logical character* of facts.

Every historical fact, it is pointed out, is concerned with a unique event. History never repeats itself. If nothing else, the mere circumstance that every event has a *date* and *location* would give historical facts an individuality that facts of the abstract sciences do not possess. Because historical facts always are located and dated, and cannot therefore be repeated, they are not subject to experiment and verification. On the other hand, a fact not subject to verification is not a fact for natural science. History, as distinguished from natural history, deals with individuals, i.e., individual events, persons, institutions. Natural science is concerned, not with individuals, but with classes, types, species. All the assertions that are valid for natural science concern classes. An illustration will make this distinction clear.

[1] James Harvey Robinson, *op. cit.*, p. 83.

Sometime in October, 1838, Charles Darwin happened to pick up and read Malthus' book on *Population*. The facts of "the struggle for existence," so strikingly presented in that now celebrated volume, suggested an explanation of a problem which had long interested and puzzled him, namely, the origin of species.

This is a statement of a historical fact, and the point is that it is not subject to empirical verification. It cannot be stated, in other words, in the form of a hypothesis, which further observation of other men of the same type will either verify or discredit.

On the other hand, in his *Descent of Man*, Darwin, discussing the rôle of sexual selection in evolution of the species, makes this observation: "Naturalists are much divided with respect to the object of the singing of birds. Few more careful observers ever lived than Montagu, and he maintained that the 'males of song-birds and of many others do not in general search for the female, but, on the contrary, their business in spring is to perch on some conspicuous spot, breathing out their full and amorous notes, which, by instinct, the female knows and repairs to the spot to choose her mate.' "

This is a typical statement of a fact of natural history. It is not, however, the rather vague generality of the statement that makes it scientific. It is its representative character, the character which makes it possible of verification by further observation which makes it a scientific fact.

It is from facts of this kind, collected, compared, and classified, irrespective of time or place, that the more general conclusions are drawn, upon which Darwin based his theory of the "descent of man." This theory, as Darwin conceived it, was not an *interpretation* of the facts but an *explanation*.

The relation between history and sociology, as well as the manner in which the more abstract social sciences have risen out of the more concrete, may be illustrated by a comparison between history and geography. Geography as a science is concerned with the visible world, the earth, its location in space, the distribution of the land masses, and of the plants, animals, and peoples upon its surface. The order, at least the fundamental order, which it seeks and finds among the objects it investigates is *spatial*. As soon as the geographer begins to compare and classify the plants, the animals, and the peoples with which he comes in contact, geography passes over into the special sciences, i.e., botany, zoölogy, and anthropology.

History, on the other hand, is concerned with a world of events. Not everything that happened, to be sure, is history, but every event that ever was or ever will be significant is history.

Geography attempts to reproduce for us the visible world as it exists in space; history, on the contrary, seeks to re-create for us in the present the significance of the past. As soon as historians seek to take events out of their historical setting, that is to say, out of their time·and space relations, in order to compare them and classify them; as soon as historians begin to emphasize the typical and representative rather than the unique character of events, history ceases to be history and becomes sociology.

The differences here indicated between history and sociology are based upon a more fundamental distinction between the historical and the natural sciences first clearly defined by Windelband, the historian of philosophy, in an address to the faculty of the University of Strassburg in 1894.

The distinction between natural science and history begins at the point where we seek to convert facts into knowledge. Here again we observe that the one (natural science) seeks to formulate laws, the other (history) to portray events. In the one case thought proceeds from the description of particulars to the general relations. In the other case it clings to a genial depiction of the individual object or event. For the natural scientist the object of investigation which cannot be repeated never has, as such, scientific value. It serves his purpose only so far as it may be regarded as a type or as a special instance of a class from which the type may be deduced. The natural scientist considers the single case only so far as he can see in it the features which serve to throw light upon a general law. For the historian the problem is to revive and call up into the present, in all its particularity, an event in the past. His aim is to do for an actual event precisely what the artist seeks to do for the object of his imagination. It is just here that we discern the kinship between history and art, between the historian and the writer of literature. It is for this reason that natural science emphasized he abstract; the historian, on the other hand, is interested mainly in the concrete.

The fact that natural science emphasizes the abstract and history the concrete will become clearer if we compare the results of the researches of the two sciences. However finespun the conceptions may be which the historical critic uses in working over his materials, the final goal of such study is always to create out of the mass of events a vivid portrait of the past. And what history offers us is pictures of men and of human life, with all the wealth of their individuality, reproduced in all their characteristic vivacity. Thus do the peoples and languages of the past, their forms and beliefs, their struggles for power and freedom, speak to us through the mouth of history.

How different it is with the world which the natural sciences have created for us! However concrete the materials with which they started, the goal of these sciences is theories, eventually mathematical formulations of laws of change. Treating the individual, sensuous, changing objects as mere unsubstantial appearances (phenomena), scientific investigation becomes a search for the universal laws which rule the timeless changes of events. Out of this colorful world of the senses, science creates a system of abstract concepts, in which the true nature of things is conceived to exist—a world of colorless and soundless atoms, despoiled of all their earthly sensuous qualities. Such is the triumph of thought over perception. Indifferent to change, science casts her anchor in the eternal and unchangeable. Not the change as such but the unchanging form of change is what she seeks.

This raises the question: What is the more valuable for the purposes of knowledge in general, a knowledge of law or a knowledge of events? As far as that is concerned, both scientific procedures may be equally justified. The knowledge of the universal laws has everywhere a practical value in so far as they make possible man's purposeful intervention in the natural processes. That is quite as true of the movements of the inner as of the outer world. In the latter case knowledge of nature's laws has made it possible to create those tools through which the control of mankind over external nature is steadily being extended.

Not less for the purposes of the common life are we dependent upon the results of historical knowledge. Man is, to change the ancient form of the expression, the animal who has a history. His cultural life rests on the transmission from generation to generation of a constantly increasing body of historical memories. Whoever proposes to take an active part in this cultural process must have an understanding of history. Wherever the thread is once broken—as history itself proves—it must be painfully gathered up and knitted again into the historical fabric.

It is, to be sure, true that it is an economy for human understanding to be able to reduce to a formula or a general concept the common characteristics of individuals. But the more man seeks to reduce facts to concepts and laws, the more he is obliged to sacrifice and neglect the individual. Men have, to be sure, sought, in characteristic modern fashion, "to make of history a natural science." This was the case with the so-called philosophy

of history of positivism.   What has been the net result of the laws of history
which it has given us?   A few trivial generalities which justify themselves
only by the most careful consideration of their numerous exceptions.

On, the other hand it is certain that all interest and values of life
are concerned with what is unique in men and events.   Consider how
quickly our appreciation is deadened as some object is multiplied or is
regarded as one case in a thousand.   "She is not the first" is one of the cruel
passages in *Faust*.   It is in the individuality and the uniqueness of an object
that all our sense of value has its roots.   It is upon this fact that Spinoza's
doctrine of the conquest of the passions by knowledge rests, since for him
knowledge is the submergence of the individual in the universal, the "once
for all" into the eternal.

The fact that all our livelier appreciations rest upon the unique character
of the object is illustrated above all in our relations to persons.   Is it not an
unendurable thought, that a loved object, an adored person, should have
existed at some other time in just the form in which it now exists for us?
Is it not horrible and unthinkable that one of us, with just this same
individuality should actually have existed in a second edition?

What is true of the individual man is quite as true of the whole historical
process: it has value only when it is unique.   This is the principle which the
Christian doctrine successfully maintained, as over against Hellenism in the
Patristic philosophy.   The middle point of their conception of the world was
the fall and the salvation of mankind as a unique event.   That was the first
and great perception of the inalienable metaphysical right of the historian to
preserve for the memory of mankind, in all their uniqueness and individuality, the actual events of life.[1]

Like every other species of animal, man has a natural history.
Anthropology is the science of man considered as one of the animal
species, *Homo sapiens*.   History and sociology, on the other hand,
are concerned with man as a person, as a "political animal," participating with his fellows in a common fund of social traditions and
cultural ideals.   Freeman, the English historian, said that history
was "past politics" and politics "present history."   Freeman uses

[1] Wilhelm Windelband, *Geschichte und Naturwissenschaft, Rede zum Antritt des
Rectorats der Kaiser-Wilhelms Universität Strassburg* (Strassburg, 1900). The logical
principle outlined by Windelband has been further elaborated by Heinrich Rickert
in *Die Grenzen der naturwissenschaftlichen Begriffsbildung, eine logische Einleitung in
die historischen Wissenschaften* (Tübingen u. Leipzig, 1902). See also Georg Simmel,
Die Probleme der Geschichtsphilosophie. eine erkenntnistheoretische Studie (2d ed.,
Leipzig, 1915), and Benedetto Croce, *History*. Its theory and practice (New
York, 1921).

the word politics in the large and liberal sense in which it was first used by Aristotle. In that broad sense of the word, the political process, by which men are controlled and states governed, and the cultural process, by which man has been domesticated and human nature formed, are not, as we ordinarily assume, different, but identical, procedures.

All this suggests the intimate relations which exist between history, politics, and sociology. The important thing, however, is not the identities but the distinctions. For, however much the various disciplines may, in practice, overlap, it is necessary for the sake of clear thinking to have their limits defined. As far as sociology and history are concerned the differences may be summed up in a word. Both history and sociology are concerned with the life of man as man. History, however, seeks to reproduce and interpret concrete events as they actually occurred in time and space. Sociology, on the other hand, seeks to arrive at natural laws and generalizations in regard to human nature and society, irrespective of time and of place.

In other words, history seeks to find out what actually happened and how it all came about. Sociology, on the other hand, seeks to explain, on the basis of a study of other instances, the nature of the process involved.

By nature we mean just that aspect and character of things in regard to which it is possible to make general statements and formulate laws. If we say, in explanation of the peculiar behavior of some individual, that it is natural or that it is after all "simply human nature," we are simply saying that this behavior is what we have learned to expect of this individual or of human beings in general. It is, in other words, a law.

Natural law, as the term is used here, is any statement which describes the behavior of a class of objects or the character of a class of acts. For example, the classic illustration of the so-called "universal proposition" familiar to students of formal logic, "all men are mortal," is an assertion in regard to a class of objects we call men. This is, of course, simply a more formal way of saying that "men die." Such general statements and "laws" get meaning only when they are applied to particular cases, or, to speak again in the terms of formal logic, when they find a place in a syllogism, thus: "Men are mortal. This is a man." But such syllogisms may always be stated in the form of a hypothesis. If this is a man, he is mortal. If a is b, a is also c. The statement, "Human nature is a product of social contact," is a general assertion familiar to students of sociology. This law or, more correctly, hypothesis, applied to an individual case explains the so-called feral man. Wild men, in the proper sense of the word, are not the so-called savages, but the men who have never been domesticated, of which an individual example is now and then discovered.

To state a law in the form of a hypothesis serves to emphasize the fact that laws—what we have called natural laws at any rate—are subject to verification and restatement. Under the circumstances the exceptional instance, which compels a restatement of the hypothesis, is more important for the purposes of science than other instances which merely confirm it.

Any science which operates with hypotheses and seeks to state facts in such a way that they can be compared and verified by further observation and experiment is, so far as method is concerned, a natural science.

III. HUMAN NATURE AND LAW

One thing that makes the conception of natural history and natural law important to the student of sociology is that in the field of the social sciences the distinction between natural and moral law has from the first been confused. Comte and the social philosophers in France after the Revolution set out with the deliberate purpose of superseding legislative enactments by laws of human nature, laws which were to be positive and "scientific." As a matter of fact, sociology, in becoming positive, so far from effacing, has rather emphasized the distinctions that Comte sought to abolish. Natural law may be distinguished from all other forms of law by the fact that it aims at nothing more than a description of the behavior of certain types or classes of objects. A description of the way in which a class, i.e., men, plants, animals, or physical objects, may be expected under ordinary circumstances to behave, tells us what we may in a general way expect of any individual member of that class. If natural science seeks to predict, it is able to do so simply because it operates with concepts or class names instead, as is the case with history, with concrete facts and, to use a logical phrase, "existential propositions."

That the chief end of science is descriptive formulation has probably been clear to keen analytic minds since the time of Galileo, especially to the great discoverers in astromony, mechanics, and dynamics. But as a definitely stated conception, corrective of misunderstandings, the view of science as essentially descriptive began to make itself felt about the beginning of the last quarter of the nineteenth century, and may be associated with the names of Kirchhoff and Mach. It was in 1876 that Kirchhoff defined the task of mechanics as that of "describing completely and in the simplest manner the motions which take place in nature." Widening this a little, we may say that the aim of science is to describe natural phenomena and occurrences as exactly as possible, as simply as possible, as completely as possible, as consistently as possible, and always in terms which are communicable and verifiable. This is a very different rôle from that of solving the riddles of the universe, and it is well expressed in what Newton said in regard to the law of gravitation: "So far I have accounted for the phenomena presented to us by the heavens and the sea by means of the force of gravity, but I have as yet assigned no cause to this gravity. . . . . I have not been able to deduce from phenomena the *raison d'être* of the properties of gravity and I have not set up hypotheses." (Newton, *Philosophiae naturalis principia Mathematica*, 1687.)

"We must confess," said Prof. J. H. Poynting (1900, p. 616), "that physical laws have greatly fallen off in dignity. No long time ago they were quite commonly described as the Fixed Laws of Nature, and were supposed sufficient in themselves to govern the universe. Now we can only assign to them the humble rank of mere descriptions, often erroneous, of similarities which we believe we have observed. . . . . A law of nature explains nothing, it has no governing power, it is but a descriptive formula which the careless have sometimes personified." It used to be said that "the laws of Nature are the thoughts of God"; now we say that they are the investigator's formulae summing up regularities of recurrence.[1]

If natural law aims at prediction it tells us what we can do. Moral laws, on the other hand, tell us, not what we can, but what we ought to do.[2] The civil or municipal law, finally, tells us not what we can, nor what we ought, but what we must do. It is very evident that these three types of law may be very intimately related.

[1] J. Arthur Thomson, *The System of Animate Nature* (New York, 1920), pp. 8–9. See also Karl Pearson, *The Grammar of Science* (2d ed.; London, 1900), chap. iii.

[2] See Max Weber, *Gesammelte Aufsätze zur Wissenschaftslehre.* "Die 'Objektivität' sozialwissenschaftlicher und sozialpolitischer Erkenntnis," pp. 146–214. Tübingen, 1922.

We do not know what we ought to do until we know what we can do; and we certainly should consider what men can do before we pass laws prescribing what they must do. There is, moreover, no likelihood that these distinctions will ever be completely abolished. As long as the words "can," "ought," and "must" continue to have any meaning for us the distinctions that they represent will persist in science as well as in common sense.

The immense prestige which the methods of the natural sciences have gained, particularly in their application to the phenomena of the physical universe, has undoubtedly led scientific men to overestimate the importance of mere conceptual and abstract knowledge. It has led them to assume that history also must eventually become "scientific" in the sense of the natural sciences. In the meantime the vast collections of historical facts which the industry of historical students has accumulated are regarded, sometimes even by historians themselves, as a sort of raw material, the value of which can only be realized after it has been worked over into some sort of historical generalization which has the general character of scientific and ultimately, mathematical formula.

"History," says Karl Pearson, "can never become science, can never be anything but a catalogue of facts rehearsed in a more. or less pleasing language until these facts are seen to fall into sequences which can be briefly resumed in scientific formulae."[1] And Henry Adams, in a letter to the American Historical Association already referred to, confesses that history has thus far been a fruitless quest for "the secret which would transform these odds and ends of philosophy into one self-evident, harmonious, and complete system."

You may be sure that four out of five serious students of history who are living today have, in the course of their work, felt that they stood on the brink of a great generalization that would reduce all history under a law as clear as the laws which govern the material world. As the great writers of our time have touched one by one the separate fragments of admitted law by which society betrays its character as a subject for science, not one of them can have failed to feel an instant's hope that he might find the secret which would transform these odds and ends of philosophy into one self-evident, harmonious, and complete system. He has seemed to have it, as the Spanish say, in his inkstand. Scores of times he must have dropped his pen to think how one short step, one sudden inspiration, would show all human knowledge; how, in these thickset forests of history, one corner

[1] Karl Pearson, *op. cit.*, p. 359.

turned, one faint trail struck, would bring him on the highroad of science. Every professor who has tried to teach the doubtful facts which we now call history must have felt that sooner or later he or another would put order in the chaos and bring light into darkness. Not so much genius or favor was needed as patience and good luck. The law was certainly there, and as certainly was in places actually visible, to be touched and handled, as though it were a law of chemistry or physics. No teacher with a spark of imagination or with an idea of scientific method can have helped dreaming of the immortality that would be achieved by the man who should successfully apply Darwin's method to the facts of human history.[1]

The truth is, however, that the concrete facts, in which history and geography have sought to preserve the visible, tangible, and, generally speaking, the experiential aspects of human life and the visible universe, have a value irrespective of any generalization or ideal constructions which may be inferred from or built up out of them. Just as none of the investigations or generalizations of individual psychology are ever likely to take the place of biography and autobiography, so none of the conceptions of an abstract sociology, no scientific descriptions of the social and cultural processes, and no laws of progress are likely, in the near future at any rate, to supersede the more concrete facts of history in which are preserved those records of those unique and never fully comprehended aspects of life which we call *events*.

It has been the dream of philosophers that theoretical and abstract science could and some day perhaps would succeed in putting into formulae and into general terms all that was significant in the concrete facts of life. It has been the tragic mistake of the so-called intellectuals, who have gained their knowledge from textbooks rather than from observation and research, to assume that science had already realized its dream. But there is no indication that science has begun to exhaust the sources or significance of concrete experience. The infinite variety of external nature and the inexhaustible wealth of personal experience have thus far defied, and no doubt will continue to defy, the industry of scientific classification, while, on the other hand, the discoveries of science are constantly making accessible to us new and larger areas of experience.

What has been said simply serves to emphasize the instrumental character of the abstract sciences. History and geography, all of

[1] Henry Adams, *op. cit.*, p. 127.

the concrete sciences, can and do measurably enlarge our experience of life. Their very purpose is to arouse new interests and create new sympathies; to give mankind, in short, an environment so vast and varied as will call out and activate all his instincts and capacities.

The more abstract sciences, just to the extent that they are abstract and exact, like mathematics and logic, are merely methods and tools for converting experience into knowledge and applying the knowledge so gained to practical uses.

IV. HISTORY, NATURAL HISTORY, AND SOCIOLOGY

Although it is possible to draw clear distinctions in theory between the purpose and methods of history and sociology, in practice the two forms of knowledge pass over into one another by almost imperceptible gradations.

The sociological point of view makes its appearance in historical investigation as soon as the historian turns from the study of "periods" to the study of institutions. The history of institutions, that is to say, the family, the church, economic institutions, political institutions, etc., leads inevitably to comparison, classification, the formation of class names or concepts, and eventually to the formulation of law. In the process, history becomes natural history, and natural history passes over into natural science. In short, history becomes sociology.

Westermarck's *History of Human Marriage* is one of the earliest attempts to write the natural history of a social institution. It is based upon a comparison and classification of marriage customs of widely scattered peoples, living under varied physical and social conditions. What one gets from a survey of this kind is not so much history as a study of human behavior. The history of marriage, as of any other institution, is, in other words, not so much an account of what certain individuals or groups of individuals did at certain times and certain places, as it is a description of the responses of a few fundamental human instincts to a variety of social situations. Westermarck calls this kind of history sociology.[1]

[1] Professor Robertson Smith (*Nature*, XLIV, 270), criticizing Westermarck's *History of Human Marriage*, complains that the author has confused history with natural history. "The history of an institution," he writes, "which is controlled by public opinion and regulated by law is not natural history. The true history of

It is in the firm conviction that the history of human civilization should be made an object of as scientific a treatment as the history of organic nature that I write this book. Like the phenomena of physical and psychical life those of social life should be classified into certain groups and each group investigated with regard to its origin and development. Only when treated in this way can history lay claim to the rank and honour of a science in the highest sense of the term, as forming an important part of Sociology, the youngest of the principal branches of learning.

Descriptive historiography has no higher object than that of offering materials to this science.[1]

Westermarck refers to the facts which he has collected in his history of marriage as phenomena. For the explanation of these phenomena, however, he looks to the more abstract sciences.

The causes on which social phenomena are dependent fall within the domain of different sciences—Biology, Psychology, or Sociology. The reader will find that I put particular stress upon the psychological causes, which have often been deplorably overlooked, or only imperfectly touched upon. And more especially do I believe that the mere instincts have played a very important part in the origin of social institutions and rules.[2]

Westermarck derived most of his materials for the study of marriage from ethnological materials. Ethnologists, students of folklore (German *Völkerkunde*), and archaeology are less certain than the historians of institutions whether their investigations are historical or sociological.

Jane Harrison, although she disclaims the title of sociologist, bases her conception of the origin of Greek religion on a sociological theory, the theory namely that "among primitive peoples religion reflects collective feeling and collective thinking." Dionysius, the

---

marriage begins where the natural history of pairing ends. . . . . To treat these topics (polyandry, kinship through the female only, infanticide, exogamy) as essentially a part of the natural history of pairing involves a tacit assumption that the laws of society are at bottom mere formulated instincts, and this assumption really underlies all our author's theories. His fundamental position compels him, if he will be consistent with himself, to hold that every institution connected with marriage that has universal validity, or forms an integral part of the main line of development, is rooted in instinct, and that institutions which are not based on instinct are necessarily exceptional and unimportant for scientific history."

[1] Edward Westermarck, *The History of Human Marriage* (London, 1901), p. 1.
[2] *Ibid.*, p. 5.

god of the Greek mysteries, is according to her interpretation a product of the group consciousness.

The mystery-god arises out of those instincts, emotions, desires which attend and express life; but these emotions, desires, instincts, in so far as they are religious, are at the outset rather of a group than of individual consciousness. . . . . It is a necessary and most important corollary to this doctrine, that the form taken by the divinity reflects the social structure of the group to which the divinity belongs. Dionysius is the Son of his Mother because he issues from a matrilinear group.[1]

This whole study is, in fact, merely an application of Durkheim's conception of "collective representations."

Robert H. Lowie, in his recent volume, *Primitive Society*, refers to "ethnologists and other historians," but at the same time asks: "What kind of an historian shall the ethnologist be?"

He answers the question by saying that, "If there are laws of social evolution, he [the ethnologist] must assuredly discover them," but at any rate, and first of all, "his duty is to ascertain the course civilization has *actually* followed. . . . . To strive for the ideals of another branch of knowledge may be positively pernicious, for it can easily lead to that factitious simplification which means falsification."

In other words, ethnology, like history, seeks to tell what actually happened. It is bound to avoid abstraction, "over-simplification," and formulae, and these are the ideals of another kind of scientific procedure. As a matter of fact, however, ethnology, even when it has attempted nothing more than a description of the existing cultures of primitive peoples, their present distribution and the order of their succession, has not freed itself wholly from the influence of abstract considerations. Theoretical problems inevitably arise for the solution of which it is necessary to go to psychology and sociology. One of the questions that has arisen in the study, particularly the comparative study, of cultures is: how far any existing cultural trait is borrowed and how far it is to be regarded as of independent origin.

In the historical reconstruction of culture the phenomena of distribution play, indeed, an extraordinary part. If a trait occurs everywhere, it might veritably be the product of some universally operative social law. If it is

[1] Jane Ellen Harrison, *Themis, A Study of the Social Origins of Greek Religion* (Cambridge, 1912), p. ix.

found in a restricted number of cases, it may still have evolved through some such instrumentality acting under specific conditions that would then remain to be determined by analysis of the cultures in which the feature is embedded. . . . . Finally, the sharers of a cultural trait may be of distinct lineage but through contact and borrowing have come to hold in common a portion of their cultures. . . . .

Since, as a matter of fact, cultural resemblances abound between peoples of diverse stock, their interpretation commonly narrows to a choice between two alternatives. Either they are due to like causes, whether these can be determined or not; or they are the result of borrowing. A predilection for one or the other explanation has lain at the bottom of much ethnological discussion in the past; and at present influential schools both in England and in continental Europe clamorously insist that all cultural parallels are due to diffusion from a single center. It is inevitable to envisage this moot-problem at the start, since uncompromising championship of either alternative has far-reaching practical consequences. For if every parallel is due to borrowing, then sociological laws, which can be inferred only from independently developing likenesses, are barred. Then the history of religion or social life or technology consists exclusively in a statement of the place of origin of beliefs, customs and implements, and a recital of their travels to different parts of the globe. On the other hand, if borrowing covers only part of the observed parallels, an explanation from like causes becomes at least the ideal goal in an investigation of the remainder.[1]

An illustration will exhibit the manner in which problems originally historical become psychological and sociological. Tylor in his *Early History of Mankind* has pointed out that the bellows used by the negro blacksmiths of continental Africa are of a quite different type from those used by natives of Madagascar. The bellows used by the Madagascar blacksmiths, on the other hand, are exactly like those in use by the Malays of Sumatra and in other parts of the Malay Archipelago. This indication that the natives of Madagascar are of Malay origin is in accordance with other anthropological and ethnological data in regard to these peoples, which prove the fact, now well established, that they are not of African origin.

Similarly Boas' study of the Raven cycle of American Indian mythology indicated that these stories originated in the northern part of British Columbia and traveled southward along the coast.

[1] Robert H. Lowie, *Primitive Society* (New York, 1920), pp. 7–8.

One of the evidences of the direction of this progress is the gradual diminution of complexity in the stories as they traveled into regions farther removed from the point of origin.

All this, in so far as it seeks to determine the point of origin, direction, speed, and character of changes that take place in cul-' tural materials in the process of diffusion, is clearly history and ethnology.

Other questions, however, force themselves inevitably upon the attention of the inquiring student. Why is it that certain cultural materials are more widely and more rapidly diffused than others? Under what conditions does this diffusion take place and why does it take place at all? Finally, what is the ultimate source of customs, beliefs, languages, religious practices, and all the varied technical devices which compose the cultures of different peoples? What are the circumstances and what are the processes by which cultural traits are independently created? Under what conditions do cultural fusions take place and what is the nature of this process?

These are all fundamentally problems of human nature, and as human nature itself is now regarded as a product of social intercourse, they are problems of sociology.

The cultural processes by which languages, myth, and religion have come into existence among primitive peoples have given rise in Germany to a special science. Folk-psychology (*Völkerpsychologie*) had its origin in an attempt to answer in psychological terms the problems to which a comparative study of cultural materials has given rise.

From two different directions ideas of folk-psychology have found their way into modern science. First of all there was a demand from the different social sciences [*Geisteswissenschaften*] for a psychological explanation of the phenomena of social life and history, so far as they were products of social [*geistiger*] interaction. In the second place, psychology itself required, in order to escape the uncertainties and ambiguities of pure introspection, a body of objective materials.

Among the social sciences the need for psychological interpretation first manifested itself in the studies of language and mythology. Both of these had already found outside the circle of the philological studies independent fields of investigation. As soon as they assumed the character of comparative sciences it was inevitable that they should be driven to recognize that in addition to the historical conditions, which everywhere determines the concrete form of these phenomena, there had been certain fundamental psychical forces at work in the development of language and myth.[1]

The aim of folk-psychology has been, on the whole, to explain the genesis and development of certain cultural forms, i.e., language, myth, and religion. The whole matter may, however, be regarded from a quite different point of view. Gabriel Tarde, for example, has sought to explain, not the genesis, but the transmission and diffusion of these same cultural forms. For Tarde, communication (transmission of cultural forms and traits) is the one central and significant fact of social life. "Social" is just what can be transmitted by imitation. Social groups are merely the centers from which new ideas and inventions are transmitted. Imitation is the social process.

There is not a word that you say, which is not the reproduction, now unconscious, but formerly conscious and voluntary, of verbal articulations reaching back to the most distant past, with some special accent due to your immediate surroundings. There is not a religious rite that you fulfil, such as praying, kissing the icon, or making the sign of the cross, which does not reproduce certain traditional gestures and expressions, established through imitation of your ancestors. There is not a military or civil requirement that you obey, nor an act that you perform in your business, which has not been taught you, and which you have not copied from some living model. There is not a stroke of the brush that you make, if you are a painter, nor a verse that you write, if you are a poet, which does not conform to the customs or the prosody of your school, and even your very originality itself is made up of accumulated commonplaces, and aspires to become commonplace in its turn.

Thus, the unvarying characteristic of every social fact whatsoever is that it is imitative. And this characteristic belongs exclusively to social facts.[2]

Tarde's theory of transmission by imitation may be regarded, in some sense, as complementary, if not supplementary, to Wundt's

[1] Wilhelm Wundt, *Völkerpsychologie, eine Untersuchung der Entwicklungsgesetze von Sprache, Mythus und Sitte.* Erster Band, *Die Sprache,* Erster Theil (Leipzig, 1900), p. 13. The name folk-psychology was first used by Lazarus and Steinthal, *Zeitschrift für Völkerpsychologie und Sprachwissenschaft,* I, 1860. Wundt's folk-psychology is a continuation of the tradition of these earlier writers.

[2] G. Tarde, *Social Laws, An Outline of Sociology,* translated from the French by Howard C. Warren (New York, 1899), pp. 40–41.

theory of origins, since he puts the emphasis on the fact of transmission rather than upon genesis. In a paper, "Tendencies in
Comparative Philology," read at the Congress of Arts and Sciences
at the St. Louis Exposition in 1904, Professor Hanns Oertel, of
Yale University, refers to Tarde's theory of imitation as an alternative explanation to that offered by Wundt for "the striking
uniformity of sound changes" which students of language have discovered in the course of their investigation of phonetic changes in
widely different forms of speech.

It seems hard to maintain that the change in a syntactical construction
or in the meaning of a word owes its universality to a simultaneous and independent primary change in all the members of a speech-community. By
adopting the theory of imitative spread, all linguistic changes may be viewed
as one homogeneous whole. In the second place, the latter view seems to
bring linguistic changes into line with the other social changes, such as modifications in institutions, beliefs, and customs. For is it not an essential characteristic of a social group that its members are not co-operative in the sense
that each member actively participates in the production of every single element which goes to make up either language, or belief, or customs? Distinguishing thus between *primary* and *secondary* changes and between the *origin*
of a change and its *spread*, it behooves us to examine carefully into the causes
which make the members of a social unit, either consciously or unconsciously,
willing to accept the innovation. What is it that determines acceptance or
rejection of a particular change? What limits one change to a small area,
while it extends the area of another? Before a final decision can be reached
in favor of the second theory of imitative spread it will be necessary to follow
out in minute detail the mechanism of this process in a number of concrete
instances; in other words to fill out the picture of which Tarde (*Les lois de
l'imitation*) sketched the bare outlines. If his assumptions prove true, then
we should have here a uniformity resting upon other causes than the physical
uniformity that appears in the objects with which the natural sciences deal.
It would enable us to establish a second group of uniform phenomena which
is psycho-physical in its character and rests upon the basis of social suggestion. The uniformities in speech, belief, and institutions would belong to
this second group.[1]

What is true of the comparative study of languages is true in
every other field in which a comparative study of cultural materials

[1] Hanns Oertel, "Some Present Problems and Tendencies in Comparative Philology," *Congress of Arts and Science, Universal Exposition, St. Louis, 1904*
(Boston, 1906), III, 59.

has been made. As soon as these materials are studied from the point of view of their similarities rather than from the point of view of their historical connections, problems arise which can only be explained by the more abstract sciences of psychology or sociology. Freeman begins his lectures on *Comparative Politics* with the statement that "the comparative method of study has been the greatest intellectual achievement of our time. It has carried light and order into whole branches of human knowledge which before were shrouded in darkness and confusion. It has brought a line of argument which reaches moral certainty into a region which before was given over to random guess-work. Into matters which are for the most part incapable of strictly external proof it has brought a form of strictly internal proof which is more convincing, more unerring."

Wherever the historian supplements *external* by *internal* proof, he is in a way to substitute a sociological explanation for historical interpretation. It is the very essence of the sociological method to be comparative. When, therefore, Freeman uses, in speaking of comparative politics, the following language he is speaking in sociological rather than historical terms:

For the purposes then of the study of Comparative Politics, a political constitution is a specimen to be studied, classified, and labelled, as a building or an animal is studied, classified, and labelled by those to whom buildings or animals are objects of study. We have to note the likenesses, striking and unexpected as those likenesses often are, between the political constitutions of remote times and places; and we have, as far as we can, to classify our specimens according to the probable causes of those likenesses.[1]

Historically sociology has had its origin in history. It owes its existence as a science to the attempt to apply exact methods to the explanation of historical facts. In the attempt to achieve this, however, it has become something quite different from history. It has become like psychology with which it is most intimately related, a natural and relatively abstract science, and auxiliary to the study of history, but not a substitute for it. The whole matter may be summed up in this general statement: history interprets, natural science explains. It is upon the interpretation of the facts of experience that we formulate our creeds and found our faiths. Our

---

[1] Edward A. Freeman, *Comparative Politics* (London, 1873), p. 23.

explanations of phenomena, on the other hand, are the basis for technique and practical devices for controlling nature and human nature, man and the physical world.

V. THE SOCIAL ORGANISM: HUMANITY OR LEVIATHAN?

After Comte the first great name in the history of sociology is Spencer. It is evident in comparing the writings of these two men that, in crossing the English Channel, sociology has suffered a sea change. In spite of certain similarities in their points of view there are profound and interesting differences. These differences exhibit themselves in the different ways in which they use the term "social organism."

Comte calls society a "collective organism" and insists, as Spencer does, upon the difference between an organism like a family, which is made up of independent individuals, and an organism like a plant or an animal, which is a physiological unit in which the different organs are neither free nor conscious. But Spencer, if he points out the differences between the social and the biological organisms, is interested in the analogy. Comte, on the other hand, while he recognizes the analogy, feels it important to emphasize the distinctions.

Society for Comte is not, as Lévy-Bruhl puts it, "a polyp." It has not even the characteristics of an animal colony in which the individuals are physically bound together, though physiologically independent. On the contrary, "this 'immense organism' is especially distinguished from other beings in that it is made up of separable elements of which each one can feel its own co-operation, can will it, or even withhold it, so long as it remains a direct one."[1]

On the other hand, Comte, although he characterized the social *consensus* and solidarity as "collective," nevertheless thought of the relations existing between human beings in society—in the family, for example, which he regards as the unit and model of all social relations—as closer and more intimate than those which exist between the organs of a plant or an animal. The individual, as Comte expressed it, is an abstraction. Man exists as man only by participation in the life of humanity, and "although the individual

[1] L. Lévy-Bruhl, *The Philosophy of Auguste Comte*, authorized translation; an Introduction by Frederic Harrison (New York, 1903), p. 337.

elements of society appear to be more separable than those of a living being, the social *consensus* is still closer than the vital."[1]

Thus the individual man was, in spite of his freedom and independence, in a very real sense "an organ of the Great Being" and the great being was humanity. Under the title of humanity Comte included not merely all living human beings, i.e., the human race, but he included all that body of tradition, knowledge, custom, cultural ideas and ideals, which make up the social inheritance of the race, an inheritance into which each of us is born, to which we contribute, and which we inevitably hand on through the processes of education and tradition to succeeding generations. This is what Comte meant by the social organism.

If Comte thought of the social organism, the great being, somewhat mystically as itself an individual and a person, Herbert Spencer, on the other hand, thought of it realistically as a great animal, a leviathan, as Hobbes called it, and a very low-order leviathan at that.[2]

Spencer's manner of looking at the social organism may be illustrated in what he says about growth in "social aggregates."

When we say that growth is common to social aggregates and organic aggregates, we do not thus entirely exclude community with inorganic aggregates. Some of these, as crystals, grow in a visible manner; and all of them on the hypothesis of evolution, have arisen by integration at some time or other. Nevertheless, compared with things we call inanimate, living bodies and societies so conspicuously exhibit augmentation of mass, that we may fairly regard this as characterizing them both. Many organisms grow throughout their lives; and the rest grow throughout considerable

---

[1] *Ibid.*, p. 234.

[2] Hobbes's statement is as follows: "For by art is created that great *Leviathan* called a *Commonwealth*, or *State*, in Latin *Civitas*, which is but an artificial man; though of greater stature and strength than the natural, for whose protection and defence it was intended; and in which the *sovereignty* is an artificial *soul*, as giving life and motion to the whole body; the *magistrates*, and other *officers* of judicature, artificial *joints; reward* and *punishment*, by which fastened to the seat of the sovereignty every joint and member is moved to perform his duty, are the *nerves*, that do the same in the body natural." Spencer criticizes this conception of Hobbes as representing society as a "factitious" and artificial rather than a "natural" product. Herbert Spencer, *The Principles of Sociology* (London, 1893), I, 437, 579–80. See also chap. iii, "Social Growth," pp. 453–58.

parts of their lives. Social growth usually continues either up to times when the societies divide, or up to times when they are overwhelmed.

Here, then, is the first trait by which societies ally themselves with the organic world and substantially distinguish themselves from the inorganic world.[1]

In this same way, comparing the characteristic general features of "social" and "living bodies," noting likeness and differences, particularly with reference to complexity of structure, differentiation of function, division of labor, etc., Spencer gives a perfectly naturalistic account of the characteristic identities and differences between societies and animals, between sociological and biological organizations. It is in respect to the division of labor that the analogy between societies and animals goes farthest and is most significant.

This division of labour, first dwelt upon by political economists as a social phenomenon, and thereupon recognized by biologists as a phenomenon of living bodies, which they called the "physiological division of labour," is that which in the society, as in the animal, makes it a living whole. Scarcely can I emphasize enough the truth that in respect of this fundamental trait, a social organism and an individual organism are entirely alike.[2]

The "social aggregate," although it is "discrete" instead of "concrete"—that is to say, composed of spatially separated units— is nevertheless, because of the mutual dependence of these units upon one another as exhibited in the division of labor, to be regarded as a living whole. It is "a living whole" in much the same way that the plant and animal communities, of which the ecologists are now writing so interestingly, are a living whole; not because of any intrinsic relations between the individuals who compose them, but because each individual member of the community, finds in the community as a whole, a suitable milieu, an environment adapted to his needs and one to which he is able to adapt himself.

Of such a society as this it may indeed be said, that it "exists for the benefit of its members, not its members for the benefit of society. It has ever to be remembered that great as may be the efforts made for the prosperity of the body politic, yet the claims of the body politic are nothing in themselves, and become something

[1] Herbert Spencer, op. cit., I, 437.

[2] Ibid., p. 440.

only in so far as they embody the claims of its component indi‧ viduals."[1]

In other words, the social organism, as Spencer sees it, exists not for itself but for the benefit of the separate organs of which it is composed, whereas, in the case of biological organism the situation is reversed. There the parts manifestly exist for the whole and not the whole for the parts.

Spencer explains this paradoxical conclusion by the reflection that in social organisms sentience is not localized as it is in biological organisms. This is, in fact, the cardinal difference between the two. There is no *social sensorium*.

In the one (the individual), consciousness is concentrated in a small part of the aggregate. In the other (society), it is diffused throughout the aggregate: all the units possess the capacities for happiness and misery, if not in equal degrees, still in degrees that approximate. As then, there is no social sensorium, the welfare of the aggregate, considered apart from that of the units, is not an end to be sought. The society exists for the benefit of its members; not its members for the benefit of the society.[2]

The point is that society, *as distinct from the individuals* who compose it, has no apparatus for feeling pain or pleasure. There are no *social* sensations. Perceptions and mental imagery are individual and not social phenomena. Society lives, so to speak, only in its separate organs or members, and each of these organs has its own brain and organ of control which gives it, among other things, the power of independent locomotion. This is what is meant when society is described as a collectivity.

VI. SOCIAL CONTROL AND SCHOOLS OF THOUGHT

The fundamental problem which Spencer's paradox raises is that of social control. How does a mere collection of individuals succeed in acting in a corporate and consistent way? How in the case of specific types of social group, for example an animal herd, a boys' gang, or a political party, does the group control its individual members; the whole dominate the parts? What are the specific *sociological* differences between plant and animal communities and human society? What kind of differences are *sociological differences*,

[1] *Ibid.*, p. 450.   [2] *Ibid.*, pp. 449–50.

and what do we mean in general by the expression "sociological" anyway?

Since Spencer's essay on the social organism was published in 1860,[1] this problem and these questions, in one form or another, have largely absorbed the theoretical interest of students of society. The attempts to answer them may be said to have created the existing schools into which sociologists are divided.

A certain school of writers, among them Paul Lilienfeld, Albert Schaeffle, and René Worms, have sought to maintain, to extend, or modify the biological analogy first advanced by Spencer. In doing so they have succeeded sometimes in restating the problem but have not solved it. René Worms has been particularly ingenious in discovering identities and carrying out the parallelism between the social and the biological organizations. As a result he has reached the conclusion that, as between a social and a biological organism, there is no difference of kind but only one of degree. Spencer, who could not find a "social sensorium," said that society was conscious only in the individuals who composed it. Worms, on the other hand, declares that we must assume the existence of a social consciousness, even without a sensorium, because we see everywhere the evidence of its existence.

Force manifests itself by its effects. If there are certain phenomena that we can only make intelligible, provided we regard them as the products of collective social consciousness, then we are bound to assume the existence of such a consciousness. There are many illustrations . . . . the attitude for example, of a crowd in the presence of a crime. Here the sentiment of indignation is unanimous. A murderer, if taken in the act, will get summary justice from the ordinary crowd. That method of rendering justice, "lynch law," is deplorable, but it illustrates the intensity of the sentiment which, at the moment, takes possession of the social consciousness.

Thus, always in the presence of great and common danger the collective consciousness of society is awakened; for example France of the Valois after the Treaty of Troyes, or modern France before the invasion of 1791 and before the German invasion in 1870; or Germany, herself, after the victories of Napoleon I. This sentiment of national unity, born of resistance to the stranger. goes so far that a large proportion of the members of society do not hesitate to give their lives for the safety and glory of the state; at such a moment the individual comprehends that he is only a small part of

[1] *Westminster Review*, January, 1860.

a large whole and that he belongs to the collectivity of which he is a member. The proof that he is entirely penetrated by the social consciousness is the fact that in order to maintain its existence he is willing to sacrifice his own.[1]

There is no question that the facts of crowd excitement, of class, caste, race, and national consciousness, do show the way in which the individual members of a group are, or seem to be, dominated, at certain moments and under certain circumstances, by the group as a whole. Worms gives to this fact, and the phenomena which accompany it, the title "collective consciousness." This gives the problem a name, to be sure, but not a solution. What the purpose of sociology requires is a description and an explanation. Under what conditions, precisely, does this phenomenon of collective consciousness arise? What are the mechanisms—physical, physiological, and social—by which the group imposes its control, or what seems to be control, upon the individual members of the group?

This question had arisen and been answered by political philosophers, in terms of political philosophy, long before sociology attempted to give an objective account of the matter. Two classic phrases, Aristotle's "Man is a political animal" and Hobbes's "War of each against all," *omnes bellum omnium*, measure the range and divergence of the schools upon this topic.

According to Hobbes, the existing moral and political order— that is to say the organization of control—is in any community a mere artefact, a control resting on consent, supported by a prudent calculation of consequences, and enforced by an external power. Aristotle, on the other hand, taught that man was made for life in society just as the bee is made for life in the hive. The relations between the sexes, as well as those between mother and child, are manifestly predetermined in the physiological organization of the individual man and woman. Furthermore, man is, by his instincts and his inherited dispositions, predestined to a social existence beyond the intimate family circle. Society must be conceived, therefore, as a part of nature, like a beaver's dam or the nests of birds.

As a matter of fact, man and society present themselves in a double aspect. They are at the same time products of nature and

[1] René Worms, *Organisme et Société*, "Bibliothèque Sociologique Internationale" (Paris, 1896), pp. 210–13.

of human artifice. Just as a stone hammer in the hand of a savage may be regarded as an artificial extension of the natural man, so tools, machinery, technical and administrative devices, including the formal organization of government and the informal "political machine," may be regarded as more or less artificial extensions of the natural social group.

So far as this is true, the conflict between Hobbes and Aristotle is not absolute. Society is a product both of nature and of design, of instinct and of reason. If, in its formal aspect, society is therefore an artefact, it is one which connects up with and has its roots in nature and in human nature.

This does not explain social control but simplifies the problem of corporate action. It makes clear, at any rate, that as members of society, men act as they do elsewhere from motives they do not fully comprehend, in order to fulfil aims of which they are but dimly or not at all conscious. Men are activated, in short, not merely by interests, in which they are conscious of the end they seek, but also by instincts and sentiments, the source and meaning of which they do not clearly comprehend. Men work for wages, but they will die to preserve their status in society, or commit murder to resent an insult. When men act thus instinctively, or under the influence of the mores, they are usually quite unconscious of the sources of the impulses that animate them or of the ends which are realized through their acts. Under the influence of the mores men act typically, and so representatively, not as individuals but as members of a group.

The simplest type of social group in which we may observe "social control" is in a herd or a flock. The behavior of a herd of cattle is, to be sure, not so uniform nor so simple a matter as it seems to the casual observer, but it may be very properly taken as an illustration of the sort of follow-the-leader uniformity that is more or less characteristic of all social groups. We call the disposition to live in the herd and to move in masses, gregariousness, and this gregariousness is ordinarily regarded as an instinct and undoubtedly is pretty regally determined in the original nature of gregarious animals.

There is a school of thought which seeks in the so-called gregarious instincts an explanation of all that is characteristically social in the behavior of human beings.

The cardinal quality of the herd is homogeneity. It is clear that the great advantage of the social habit is to enable large numbers to act as one, whereby in the case of the hunting gregarious animal strength in pursuit and attack is at once increased to beyond that of the creatures preyed upon, and in protective socialism the sensitiveness of the new unit to alarms is greatly in excess of that of the individual member of the flock.

To secure these advantages of homogeneity, it is evident that the members of the herd must possess sensitiveness to the behaviour of their fellows. The individual isolated will be of no meaning, the individual as a part of the herd will be capable of transmitting the most potent impulses. Each member of the flock tending to follow its neighbour and in turn to be followed, each is in some sense capable of leadership; but no lead will be followed that departs widely from normal behaviour. A lead will be followed only from its resemblance to the normal. If the leader go so far ahead as definitely to cease to be in the herd, he will necessarily be ignored.

The original in conduct, that is to say, resistiveness to the voice of the herd, will be suppressed by natural selection; the wolf which does not follow the impulses of the herd will be starved; the sheep which does not respond to the flock will be eaten.

Again, not only will the individual be responsive to impulses coming from the herd, but he will treat the herd as his normal environment. The impulse to be in and always to remain with the herd will have the strongest instinctive weight. Anything which tends to separate him from his fellows, as soon as it becomes perceptible as such, will be strongly resisted.[1]

According to sociologists of his school, public opinion, conscience, and authority in the state rest upon the natural disposition of the animal in the herd to conform to "the decrees of the herd."

Conscience, then, and the feelings of guilt and of duty are the peculiar possessions of the gregarious animal. A dog and a cat caught in the commission of an offence will both recognize that punishment is coming; but the dog, moreover, knows that he has done *wrong*, and he will come to be punished, unwillingly it is true, and as if dragged along by some power outside him, while the cat's sole impulse is to escape. The rational recognition of the sequence of act and punishment is equally clear to the gregarious and to the solitary animal, but it is the former only who understands that he has committed a *crime*, who has, in fact, the *sense of sin*.[2]

[1] W. Trotter, *Instincts of the Herd in Peace and War* (New York, 1916), pp. 29–30.

[2] *Ibid.*, pp. 40–41.

The concept upon which this explanation of society rests is *homogeneity*. If animals or human beings act under all circumstances in the same way, they will act or seem to act, as if they had a common purpose. If everybody follows the crowd, if everyone wears the same clothes, utters the same trite remarks, rallies to the same battles cries and is everywhere dominated, even in his most characteristically individual behavior, by an instinctive and passionate desire to conform to an external model and to the wishes of the herd, then we have an explanation of everything characteristic of society—except the variants, the nonconformists, the idealists, and the rebels. The herd instinct may be an explanation of conformity but it does not explain variation. Variation is an important fact in society as it is in nature generally.

Homogeneity and like-mindedness are, as explanations of the social behavior of men and animals, very closely related concepts. In "like response to like stimulus," we may discern the beginning of "concerted action" and this, it is urged, is the fundamental social fact. This is the "like-mindedness" theory of society which has been given wide popularity in the United States through the writings of Professor Franklin Henry Giddings. He describes it as a "developed form of the instinct theory, dating back to Aristotle's aphorism that man is a political animal."

Any given stimulus may happen to be felt by more than one organism, at the same or at different times. Two or more organisms may respond to the same given stimulus simultaneously or at different times. They may respond to the same given stimulus in like or in unlike ways; in the same or in different degrees; with like or with unlike promptitude; with equal or with unequal persistence. I have attempted to show that in like response to the same given stimulus we have the beginning, the absolute origin, of all concerted activity—the inception of every conceivable form of co-operation; while in unlike response, and in unequal response, we have the beginning of all those processes of individuation, of differentiation, of competition, which in their endlessly varied relations to combination, to co-operation, bring about the infinite complexity of organized social life.[1]

Closely related, logically if not historically, to Giddings' conception of "like-mindedness" is Gabriel Tarde's conception of

[1] Franklin Henry Giddings, *The Concepts and Methods of Sociology*, Congress of Arts and Science, Universal Exposition (St. Louis, 1904), pp. 789–90.

"imitation." If for Giddings "like response to like stimulus" is the fundamental social fact, for Tarde "imitation" is the process through which alone society exists. Society, said Tarde, exists in imitation. As a matter of fact, Tarde's doctrine may be regarded as a corollary to Giddings'. Imitation is the process by which that like-mindedness, by which Giddings explains corporate action, is effected. Men are not born like-minded, they are made so by imitation.

This minute inter-agreement of minds and wills, which forms the basis of the social life, even in troublous times—this presence of so many common ideas, ends, and means, in the minds and wills of all members of the same society at any given moment—is not due, I maintain, to organic heredity, which insures the birth of men quite similar to one another, nor to mere identity of geographical environment, which offers very similar resources to talents that are nearly equal; it is rather the effect of that suggestion-imitation process which, starting from one primitive creature possessed of a single idea or act, passed this copy on to one of its neighbors, then to another, and so on. Organic needs and spiritual tendencies exist in us only as potentialities which are realizable under the most diverse forms, in spite of their primitive similarity; and, among all these possible realizations, the indications furnished by some first initiator who is imitated determine which one is actually chosen.[1]

In contrast with these schools, which interpret action in terms of the herd and the flock—i.e., men act together because they act alike—is the theory of Émile Durkheim who insists that the social group has real corporate existence and that, in human societies at least, men act together not because they have like purposes but a *common purpose*. This common purpose imposes itself upon the individual members of a society at the same time as an ideal, a wish and an obligation. Conscience, the sense of obligation which members of a group feel only when there is conflict between the wishes of the individual and the will of the group, is a manifestation, *in* the individual consciousness, of the collective mind and the group will. The mere fact that in a panic or a stampede, human beings will sometimes, like the Gadarene swine, rush down a steep place into the sea, is a very positive indication of like-mindedness but not an evidence of a common purpose. The difference between an animal herd and a human crowd is that the crowd, what Le Bon calls the "organized crowd," the crowd "in being" to use a nautical term, is dominated by

[1] G. Tarde, *op. cit.*, pp. 38–39.

an impulse to achieve a purpose that is common to every member of the group. Men in a state of panic, on the other hand, although equally under the influence of the mass excitement, act not corporately but individually, each individual wildly seeking to save his own skin. Men in a state of panic have like purposes but no common purpose. If the "organized crowd," "the psychological crowd," is a society "in being," the panic and the stampede is a society "in dissolution."

Durkheim does not use these illustrations nor does he express himself in these terms. The conception of the "organized" or "psychological" crowd is not his, but Le Bon's. The fact is that Durkheim does not think of a society as a mere sum of particulars. Neither does he think of the sentiments nor the opinions which dominate the social group as private and subjective. When individuals come together *under certain circumstances*, the opinions and sentiments which they held as individuals are modified and changed under the influence of the new contacts. Out of the fermentation which association breeds, a new something (*autre chose*) is produced, an opinion and sentiment, in other words, that is not the sum of, and not like, the sentiments and opinions of the individuals from which it is derived. This new sentiment and opinion is public, and social, and the evidence of this is the fact that it imposes itself upon the individuals concerned as something more or less external to them. They feel it either as an inspiration, a sense of personal release and expansion, or as an obligation, a pressure and an inhibition. The characteristic social phenomenon is just this control by the group as a whole of the individuals that compose it. This fact of control, then, is the fundamental social fact.

Now society also gives the sensation of a perpetual dependence. Since it has a nature which is peculiar to itself and different from our individual nature, it pursues ends which are likewise special to it; but, as it cannot attain them except through our intermediacy, it imperiously demands our aid. It requires that, forgetful of our own interests, we make ourselves its servitors, and it submits us to every sort of inconvenience, privation and sacrifice, without which social life would be impossible. It is because of this that at every instant we are obliged to submit ourselves to rules of conduct and of thought which we have neither made nor desired, and which are sometimes even contrary to our most fundamental inclinations and instincts.

Even if society were unable to maintain these concessions and sacrifices from us except by a material constraint, it might awaken in us only the idea of a physical force to which we must give way of necessity, instead of that of a moral power such as religions adore.   But as a matter of fact, the empire which it holds over consciences is due much less to the physical supremacy of which it has the privilege than to the moral authority with which it is invested.   If we yield to its orders, it is not merely because it is strong enough to triumph over our resistance; it is primarily because it is the object of a venerable respect.

Now the ways of action to which society is strongly enough attached to impose them upon its members, are, by that very fact, marked with a distinctive sign provocative of respect.   Since they are elaborated in common, the vigour with which they have been thought of by each particular mind is retained in all the other minds, and reciprocally.   The representations which express them within each of us have an intensity which no purely private states of consciousness could ever attain; for they have the strength of the innumerable individual representations which have served to form each of them.   It is society who speaks through the mouths of those who affirm them in our presence; it is society whom we hear in hearing them; and the voice of all has an accent which that of one alone could never have.   The very violence with which society reacts, by way of blame or material suppression, against every attempted dissidence, contributes to strengthening its empire by manifesting the common conviction through this burst of ardour.   In a word, when something is the object of such a state of opinion, the representation which each individual has of it gains a power of action from its origins and the conditions in which it was born, which even those feel who do not submit themselves to it.   It tends to repel the representations which contradict it, and it keeps them at a distance; on the other hand it commands those acts which will realize it, and it does so, not by a material coercion or by the perspective of something of this sort, but by the simple radiation of the mental energy which it contains.[1]

But the same social forces, which are found organized in public opinion, in religious symbols, in social convention, in fashion, and in science—for "if a people did not have faith in science all the scientific demonstrations in the world would be without any influence whatsoever over their minds"—are constantly re-creating the old order, making new heroes, overthrowing old gods, creating new myths, and imposing new ideals.   And this is the nature of the cultural process of which sociology is a description and an explanation.

[1] Émile Durkheim, *Elementary Forms of Religious Life* (New York, 1915), pp. 206–8.

VII.   SOCIAL CONTROL AND THE COLLECTIVE MIND

Durkheim is sometimes referred to, in comparison with other contemporary sociologists, as a realist. This is a reference to the controversy of the medieval philosophers in regard to the nature of concepts. Those who thought a concept a mere class-name applied to a group of objects because of some common characteristics were called nominalists. Those who thought the concept was *real*, and not the name of a mere collection of individuals, were realists. In this sense Tarde and Giddings and all those writers who think of society as a collection of actually or potentially *like-minded* persons would be nominalists, while other writers like Simmel, Ratzenhofer, and Small, who think of society in terms of interaction and social process may be called realists. They are realist, at any rate, in so far as they think of the members of a society as bound together in a system of mutual influences which has sufficient character to be described as a process.

Naturally this process cannot be conceived of in terms of space or physical proximity alone. Social contacts and social forces are of a subtler sort but not less real than physical. We know, for example, that vocations are largely determined by personal competition; that the solidarity of what Sumner calls the "in" or "we" group is largely determined by its conflict with the "out" or "other" groups. We know, also, that the status and social position of any individual inside any social group is determined by his relation to all other members of that group and eventually of all other groups. These are illustrations of what is meant concretely by social interaction and social process and it is considerations of this kind which seem to justify certain writers in thinking of individual persons as "parts" and of society as a "whole" in some other sense than that in which a dust heap is a whole of which the individual particles are parts.

Society not only continues to exist *by* transmission, *by* communication, but it may fairly be said to exist *in* transmission, *in* communication. There is more than a verbal tie between the words common, community, and communication.[1]

Communication, if not identical with, is at least a form of, what has been referred to here as social interaction. But communication

[1] John Dewey, *Democracy and Education* (New York, 1916), p. 5.

as Dewey has defined the term, is something more and different than what Tarde calls "inter-stimulation." Communication is a process by which we "transmit" an experience from an individual to another but it is also a process by which these same individuals get a common experience.

Try the experiment of communicating, with fullness and accuracy, some experience to another, especially if it be somewhat complicated, and you will find your own attitude toward your experience changing; otherwise you resort to expletives and ejaculations. Except in dealing with commonplaces and catch phrases one has to assimilate, imaginatively, something of another's experience in order to tell him intelligently of one's own experience. All communication is like art.[1]

Not only does communication involve the creation, out of experiences that are individual and private, of an experience that is common and public but such a common experience becomes the basis for a common and public existence in which every individual, to greater or less extent, participates and is himself a part. Furthermore, as a part of this common life, there grows up a body of custom, convention, tradition, ceremonial, language, social ritual, public opinion, in short all that Sumner includes under the term "mores" and all that ethnologists include under the term "culture."

The thing that characterizes Durkheim and his followers is their insistence upon the fact that all cultural materials, and expressions, including language, science, religion, public opinion, and law, since they are the products of social intercourse and social interaction, are bound to have an objective, public, and social character such as no product of an individual mind either has or can have. Durkheim speaks of these mental products, individual and social, as representations. The characteristic product of the individual mind is the percept, or, as Durkheim describes it, the "individual representation." The percept is, and remains, a private and an individual matter. No one can reproduce, or communicate to another, subjective impressions or the mental imagery in the concrete form in which they come to the individual himself. My neighbor may be able to read my "thoughts" and understand the motives that impel me to action better than I understand myself, but he cannot reproduce the images, with just the fringes of sense and feeling with which they come to my mind.

[1] *Ibid.*, pp. 6–7.

The characteristic product of a group of individuals, in their efforts to communicate is, on the other hand, something objective and understood, that is, a gesture, a sign, a symbol, a word, or a concept in which an experience or purpose that was private becomes public. This gesture, sign, symbol, concept, or representation in which a common object is not merely indicated, but in a sense created, Durkheim calls a "collective representation."

Dewey's description of what takes place in communication may be taken as a description of the process by which these collective representations come into existence. "To formulate an experience," as Dewey says, "requires getting outside of it, seeing it as another would see it, considering what points of contact it has with the life of another so that it may be gotten into such form that he can appreciate its meaning." The result of such a conscious effort to communicate an experience is to transform it. The experience, after it has been communicated, is not the same for either party to the communication. To publish or to give publicity o an event is to make of that event something other than it was before publication. Furthermore, the event as published is still something different from the event as reflected in the minds of the individuals to whom the publication is addressed.

It will be evident upon reflection that public opinion is not the opinion of all, nor even of a majority of the persons who compose a public. As a matter of fact, what we ordinarily mean by public opinion is never the opinion of anyone in particular. It is composite opinion, representing a general tendency of the public as a whole. On the other hand, we recognize that public opinion exists, even when we do not know of any individual person, among those who compose the public, whose private and personal opinion exactly coincides with that of the public of which he or she is a part.

Nevertheless, the private and personal opinion of an individual who participates in making public opinion is influenced by the opinions of those around him, and by public opinion. In this sense every opinion is public opinion.

Public opinion, in respect to the manner in which it is formed and the manner in which it exists—that is to say relatively independent of the individuals who co-operate to form it—has the characteristics of collective representation in general. Collective representations are objective, in just the sense that public opinion is objective, and they impose themselves upon the individual as public opinion does, as relatively but not wholly external forces—stabilizing, standardizing, conventionalizing, as well as stimulating, extending, and generalizing individual representations, percepts.

The collective representations are exterior to the individual consciousness because they are not derived from the individuals taken in isolation but from their convergence and union (concours). . . . . Doubtless, in the elaboration of the common result, each (individual) bears his due share; but the private sentiments do not become social except by combining under the action of the forces *sui generis* which association develops. As a result of these combinations, and of the mutual alterations which result therefrom, they (the private sentiments) become something else (*autre chose*). A chemical synthesis results, which concentrates, unifies, the elements synthetized, and by that very process transforms them. . . . . The resultant derived therefrom extends then beyond (*deborde*) the individual mind as the whole is greater than the part. To know really what it is, one must take the aggregate in its totality. It is this that thinks, that feels, that wills, although it may not be able to will, feel, or act save by the intermediation of individual consciousnesses.[1]

This, then, after nearly a century of criticism, is what remains of Comte's conception of the social organism. If society is, as the realists insist, anything more than a collection of like-minded individuals, it is so because of the existence (1) of a social process and (2) of a body of tradition and opinion—the products of this process—which has a relatively objective character and imposes itself upon the individual as a form of control, social control. This process and its product are the social consciousness. The social consciousness, in its double aspect as process and product, is the social organism. The controversy between the realists and the nominalists reduces itself apparently to this question of the objectivity of social tradition and of public opinion. For the present we may let it rest there.

Meanwhile the conceptions of the social consciousness and the social mind have been adopted by writers on social topics who are not at all concerned with their philosophical implications or legitimacy.

---

[1] Émile Durkheim, "Représentations individuelles et représentations collectives," *Revue métaphysique*, VI (1898), 295. Quoted and translated by Charles Elmer Gehlke, "Émile Durkheim's Contributions to Sociological Theory," *Studies in History, Economics, and Public Law*, LXIII, 29–30.

We are just now seeing the first manifestations of two new types of sociology which call themselves, the one rural and the other urban sociology. Writers belonging to these two schools are making studies of what they call the "rural" and the "urban" minds. In using these terms they are not always quite certain whether the mind of which they are thinking is a collective mind, in Durkheim's realistic sense of the word, or whether it is the mind of the typical inhabitant of a rural or an urban community, an instance of "like-mindedness," in the sense of Giddings and the nominalists.

A similar usage of the word "mind," "the American mind," for example, is common in describing characteristic differences in the attitudes of different nations and their "nationals."

The origin of the phrase, "the American mind," was political. Shortly after the middle of the eighteenth century, there began to be a distinctly American way of regarding the debatable question of British Imperial control. During the period of the Stamp Act agitation our colonial-bred politicians and statesmen made the discovery that there was a mode of thinking and feeling which was native—or had by that time become a second nature—to all the colonists. Jefferson, for example, employs those resonant and useful words "the American mind" to indicate that throughout the American colonies an essential unity of opinion had been developed as regards the chief political question of the day.[1]

Here again, it is not quite clear, whether the American mind is a name for a characteristic uniformity in the minds of individual Americans; whether the phrase refers rather to an "essential unity of opinion," or whether, finally, it is intended to cover both the uniformity and the unity characteristic of American opinion.

Students of labor problems and of the so-called class struggle, on the other hand, use the term "psychology" in much the same way that the students of rural and urban sociology use the term "mind." They speak of the "psychology" of the laboring class, the "psychology" of the capitalistic class, in cases where psychology seems to refer indifferently either to the social attitudes of the members of a class, or to attitude and morale of the class as a whole.

The terms "class-conscious" and "class-consciousness," "national" and "racial" consciousness are now familiar terms to students although they seem to have been used, first of all, by the so-called

[1] Bliss Perry, *The American Mind* (Boston, 1912), p. 47.

"intelligentsia", who have been the leaders in the various types of mass movement to which these terms apply. "Consciousnr is," in the sense in which it is here used, has a similar, though somewhat different, connotation than the word "mind" when applied to a group. It is a name not merely for the attitudes characteristic of certain races or classes, but for these attitudes when they are in the focus of attention of the group, in the "fore-consciousness" to use a Freudian term. In this sense "conscious" suggests not merely the submergence of the individual and the consequent solidarity of the group, but it signifies a mental mobilization and preparedness of the individual and of the group for collective or corporate action. To be class-conscious is to be prepared to act in the sense of that class.

There is implicit in this rather ambiguous popular usage of the terms "social mind" and "social consciousness" a recognition of the dual aspect of society and of social groups. Society may be regarded at the same time from an individualistic and a collectivistic point of view. Looking at it from the point of view of the individual, we regard as social just that character of the individual which has been imparted to, and impressed upon, him as a result of his participation in the life of the group. Social psychology, from Baldwin's first studies of the development of personality in the child to Ellwood's studies of the society in its "psychological aspects" has been mainly concerned with the investigation of the effects upon the individual of his contacts with other individuals.[1]

On the other hand, we have had, in the description of the crowd and the public by Le Bon, Tarde, Sighele, and their successors, the beginnings of a study of collective behavior and "corporate action." In these two points of view we seem to have again the contrast and the opposition, already referred to, between the nominalistic and realistic conceptions of society. Nominalism represented by social psychology emphasizes, or seems to emphasize, the independence of the individual. Realism, represented by collective psychology, emphasizes the control of the group over the individual, of the whole over the part.

[1] James Mark Baldwin, *Mental Development in the Child and the Race* (New York and London, 1895); Charles A. Ellwood, *Sociology in Its Psychological Aspects* (New York and London, 1912).

While it is true that society has this double aspect, the individual and the collective, it is the assumption of this volume that the touchstone of society, the thing that distinguishes a mere collection of individuals from a society is not like-mindedness, but corporate action. We may apply the term social to any group of individuals which is capable of consistent action, that is to say, action, consciously or unconsciously, directed to a common end. This existence of a common end is perhaps all that can be legitimately included in the conception "organic" as applied to society.

From this point of view social control is the central fact and the central problem of society. Just as psychology may be regarded as an account of the manner in which the individual organism, as a whole, exercises control over its parts or rather of the manner in which the parts co-operate together to carry on the corporate existence of the whole, so sociology, speaking strictly, is a point of view and a method for investigating the processes by which individuals are inducted into and induced to co-operate in some sort of permanent corporate existence which we call society.

To put this emphasis on corporate action is not to overlook the fact that through this corporate action the individual member of society is largely formed, not to say created. It is recognized, however, that if corporate action tends to make of the individual an instrument, as well as an organic part, of the social group, it does not do this by making him "like" merely; it may do so by making him "different." The division of labor, in making possible an ever larger and wider co-operation among men, has indirectly multiplied individual diversities. What like-mindedness must eventually mean, if it is to mean anything, is the existence of so much of a consensus among the individuals of a group as will permit the group to act. This, then, is what is meant here by society, the social organism and the social group.

Sociology, so far as it can be regarded as a fundamental science and not mere congeries of social-welfare programs and practices, may be described as the science of collective behavior. With this definition it is possible to indicate in a general and schematic way its relation to the other social sciences.

Historically, sociology has had its origin in history. History has been and is the great mother science of all the social sciences. Of history it may be said nothing human is foreign to it. Anthropology, ethnology, folklore, and archaeology have grown up largely, if not wholly, to complete the task which history began and answer the questions which historical investigation first raised. In history and the sciences associated with it, i.e., ethnology, folklore, and archaeology, we have the concrete records of that human nature and experience which sociology has sought to explain. In the same sense that history is the concrete, sociology is the abstract, science of human experience and human nature.

On the other hand, the technical (applied) social sciences, that is, politics, education, social service, and economics—so far as economics may be regarded as the science of business—are related to

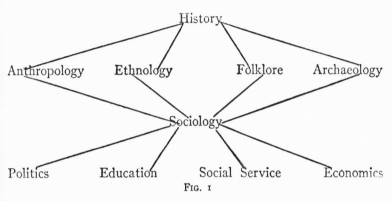

FIG. 1

sociology in a different way. They are, to a greater or lesser extent, applications of principles which it is the business of sociology and of psychology to deal with explicitly. In so far as this is true, sociology may be regarded as fundamental to the other social sciences.

VIII. SOCIOLOGY AND SOCIAL RESEARCH

Among the schools which, since Comte and Spencer, have divided sociological thinking between them the realists have, on the whole, maintained the tradition of Comte; the nominalists, on the other hand, have preserved the style and manner, if not the substance, of Spencer's thought. Later writers, however, realist as well as nominalist, have directed their attention less to society than to societies, i.e., social groups; they have been less interested in social progress than in social process; more concerned with social problems than with social philosophy.

This change marks the transformation of sociology from a philosophy of history to a science of society. The steps in this transition are periods in the history of the science, that is:

1. The period of Comte and Spencer; sociology, conceived in the grand style, is a philosophy of history, a "science" of progress (evolution).

2. The period of the "schools"; sociological thought, dispersed among the various schools, is absorbed in an effort to define its point of view and to describe the kinds of facts that sociology must look for to answer the questions that sociology asks.

3. The period of investigation and research, the period into which sociology is just now entering.

Sociological research is at present (1921) in about the situation in which psychology was before the introduction of laboratory methods, in which medicine was before Pasteur and the germ theory of disease. A great deal of social information has been collected merely for the purpose of determining what to do in a given case. Facts have not been collected to check social theories. Social problems have been defined in terms of common sense, and facts have been collected, for the most part, to support this or that doctrine, not to test it. In very few instances have investigations been made, disinterestedly, to determine the validity of a hypothesis.

Charles Booth's studies of poverty in London, which extended over eighteen years and were finally embodied in seventeen volumes, is an example of such a disinterested investigation. It is an attempt to put to the test of fact the popular conception of the relation between wages and welfare. He says:

My object has been to attempt to show the numerical relation which poverty, misery, and depravity bear to regular earnings and comparative comfort, and to describe the general conditions under which each class lives.

If the facts thus stated are of use in helping social reformers to find remedies for the evils which exist, or do anything to prevent the adoption of false remedies, my purpose is answered. It was not my intention to bring forward any suggestions of my own, and if I have ventured here and there, and especially in the concluding chapters, to go beyond my programme, it has been with much hesitation.

With regard to the disadvantages under which the poor labour, and the evils of poverty, there is a great sense of helplessness: the wage earners are helpless to regulate their work and cannot obtain a fair equivalent for the labour they are willing to give; the manufacturer or dealer can only work within the limits of competition; the rich are helpless to relieve want without stimulating its sources. To relieve this helplessness a better stating of the problems involved is the first step. . . . . In this direction must be sought the utility of my attempt to analyze the population of a part of London.[1]

This vast study did, indeed, throw great light, not only upon poverty in London, but upon human nature in general. On the other hand, it raised more questions than it settled and, if it demonstrated anything, it was the necessity, as Booth suggests, for a restatement of the problem.

Sociology seems now, however, in a way to become, in some fashion or other, an experimental science. It will become so as soon as it can state existing problems in such a way that the results in one case will demonstrate what can and should be done in another. Experiments are going on in every field of social life, in industry, in politics, and in religion. In all these fields men are guided by some implicit or explicit theory of the situation, but this theory is not often stated in the form of a hypothesis and subjected to a test of the negative instances. We have, if it is permitted to make a distinction between them, investigation rather than research.

What, then, in the sense in which the expression is here used, is social research? A classification of problems will be a sort of first aid in the search for an answer.

1. *Classification of social problems.*—Every society and every social group, *capable of consistent action*, may be regarded as an organization of the wishes of its members. This means that society rests on, and embodies, the appetites and natural desires of the individual man; but it implies, also, that wishes, in becoming *organized*, are necessarily disciplined and controlled in the interest of the group as a whole.

Every such society or social group, even the most ephemeral, will ordinarily have (a) some relatively formal method of defining its aim and formulating its policies, making them explicit, and (b) some machinery, functionary, or other arrangement for realizing its aim

[1] *Labour and Life of the People* (London, 1889), I, pp. 6-7.

and carrying its policies into effect. Even in the family there is government, and this involves something that corresponds to legislation, adjudication, and administration.

Social groups, however, maintain their organizations, agencies, and all formal methods of behavior on a basis and in a setting of instinct, of habit, and of tradition which we call human nature. Every social group has, or tends to have, its own culture, what Sumner calls "folkways," and this culture, imposing its patterns upon the natural man, gives him that particular individuality which characterizes the members of groups. Not races merely but nationalities and classes have marks, manners, and patterns of life by which we infallibly recognize and classify them.

Social problems may be conveniently classified with reference to these three aspects of group life, that is to say, problems of (a) organization and administration, (b) policy and polity (legislation), and (c) human nature (culture).

a) Administrative problems are mainly practical and technical. Most problems of government, of business and social welfare, are technical. The investigations, i.e., social surveys, made in different parts of the country by the Bureau of Municipal Research of New York City, are studies of local administration made primarily for the purpose of improving the efficiency of an existing administrative machine and its personnel rather than of changing the policy or purpose of the administration itself.

b) Problems of policy, in the sense in which that term is used here, are political and legislative. Most social investigations in recent years have been made in the interest of some legislative program or for the purpose of creating a more intelligent public opinion in regard to certain local problems. The social surveys conducted by the Sage Foundation, as distinguished from those carried out by the New York Bureau of Municipal Research, have been concerned with problems of policy, i.e., with changing the character and policy of social institutions rather than improving their efficiency. This distinction between administration and policy is not always clear, but it is always important. Attempts at reform usually begin with an effort to correct administrative abuses, but eventually it turns out that reforms must go deeper and change the character of the institutions themselves.

c) Problems of human nature are naturally fundamental to all other social problems. Human nature, as we have begun to conceive it in recent years, is largely a product of social intercourse; it is, therefore, quite as much as society itself, a subject for sociological investigation. Until recent years, what we are now calling the human factor has been notoriously neglected in most social experiments. We have been seeking to reform human nature while at the same time we refused to reckon with it. It has been assumed that we could bring about social changes by merely formulating our wishes, that is, by "arousing" public opinion and formulating legislation. This is the "democratic" method of effecting reforms. The older "autocratic" method merely decreed social changes upon the authority of the monarch or the ruling class. What reconciled men to it was that, like Christian Science, it frequently worked.

The oldest but most persistent form of social technique is that of "ordering-and-forbidding"—that is, meeting a crisis by an arbitrary act of will decreeing the disappearance of the undesirable or the appearance of the desirable phenomena, and the using arbitrary physical action to enforce the decree. This method corresponds exactly to the magical phase of natural technique. In both, the essential means of bringing a determined effect is more or less consciously thought to reside in the act of will itself by which the effect is decreed as desirable and of which the action is merely an indispensable vehicle or instrument; in both, the process by which the cause (act of will and physical action) is supposed to bring its effect to realization remains out of reach of investigation; in both, finally, if the result is not attained, some new act of will with new material accessories is introduced, instead of trying to find and remove the perturbing causes. A good instance of this in the social field is the typical legislative procedure of today.[1]

2. *Types of social group.*—The varied interests, fields of investigation, and practical programs which find at present a place within the limits of the sociological discipline are united in having one common object of reference, namely, *the concept of the social group.* All social problems turn out finally to be problems of group life, although each group and each type of group has its own distinctive

[1] Thomas and Znaniecki, *The Polish Peasant in Europe and America* (Boston, 1918), I, 3.

problems. Illustrations may be gathered from the most widely separated fields to emphasize the truth of this assertion.[1]

Religious conversion may be interpreted from one point of view as a change from one social group to another. To use the language of religious sentiment, the convert "comes out of a life of sin and enters into a life of grace." To be sure, this change involves profound disturbances of the personality, but permanence of the change in the individual is assured by the breaking up of the old and the establishment of new associations. So the process by which the immigrant makes the transition from the old country to the new involves profound changes in thought and habit. In his case the change is likely to take place slowly, but it is not less radical on that account.

The following paragraph from a recent social survey illustrates, from a quite different point of view, the manner in which the group is involved in changes in community life.

In short, the greatest problem for the next few years in Stillwater is the development of a *community consciousness*. We must stop thinking in terms of city of Stillwater, and country outside of Stillwater, and think in terms of *Stillwater Community*. We must stop thinking in terms of small groups and think in terms of the entire community, no matter whether it is industry, health, education, recreation or religion. Anything which is good will benefit the entire community. Any weakness will be harmful to all. Community co-operation in all lines indicated in this report will make this, indeed, the Queen of the St. Croix.[2]

In this case the solution of the community problem was the creation of "community consciousness." In the case of the professional criminal the character of the problem is determined, if we accept the description of a writer in the *Atlantic Monthly*, by the existence among professional criminals of a primary group consciousness:

The professional criminal is peculiar in the sense that he lives a very intense emotional life. He is isolated in the community. He is in it, but not of it. His social life—for all men are social—is narrow; but just because it is narrow, it is extremely tense. He lives a life of warfare and has

[1] Walter B. Bodenhafer, "The Comparative Rôle of the Group Concept in Ward's Dynamic Sociology and Contemporary American Sociology," *American Journal of Sociology*, XXVI (1920–21), 273–314; 425–74; 588–600; 716–43.

[2] *Stillwater, the Queen of the St. Croix*, a report of a social survey, published by The Community Service of Stillwater, Minnesota, 1920, p. 71.

the psychology of the warrior. He is at war with the whole community. Except his very few friends in crime he trusts no one and fears everyone. Suspicion, fear, hatred, danger, desperation and passion are present in a more tense form in his life than in that of the average individual. He is restless, ill-humored, easily roused and suspicious. He lives on the brink of a deep precipice. This helps to explain his passionate hatred, his brutality, his fear, and gives poignant significance to the adage that dead men tell no tales. He holds on to his few friends with a strength and passion rare among people who live a more normal existence. His friends stand between him and discovery. They are his hold upon life, his basis of security.

Loyalty to one's group is the basic law in the underworld. Disloyalty is treason and punishable by death; for disloyalty may mean the destruction of one's friends; it may mean the hurling of the criminal over the precipice on which his whole life is built.

To the community the criminal is aggressive. To the criminal his life is one of defense primarily. The greater part of his energy, of his hopes, and of his successes, centres around escapes, around successful flight, around proper covering-up of his tracks, and around having good, loyal, and trustworthy friends to participate in his activities, who will tell no tales and keep the rest of the community outside. The criminal is thus, from his own point of view—and I am speaking of professional criminals—living a life of defensive warfare with the community; and the odds are heavy against him. He therefore builds up a defensive psychology against it—a psychology of boldness, bravado, and self-justification. The good criminal— which means the successful one, he who has most successfully carried through a series of depradations against the enemy, the common enemy, the public—is a hero. He is recognized as such, toasted and feasted, trusted and obeyed. But always by a little group. They live in a world of their own, a life of their own, with ideals, habits, outlook, beliefs, and associations which are peculiarly fitted to maintain the morale of the group. Loyalty, fearlessness, generosity, willingness to sacrifice one's self, perseverance in the face of prosecution, hatred of the common enemy—these are the elements that maintain the morale, but all of them are pointed against the community as a whole.[1]

The manner in which the principle of the primary group was applied at Sing Sing in dealing with the criminal within the prison walls is a still more interesting illustration of the fact that social problems are group problems.[2]

[1] Frank Tannenbaum, "Prison Democracy," *Atlantic Monthly*, October, 1920, pp. 438–39. (Psychology of the criminal group.)

[2] *Ibid.*, pp. 443–46.

Assuming, then, that every social group may be presumed to have its own (a) administrative, (b) legislative, and (c) human-nature problems, these problems may be still further classified with reference to the type of social group. Most social groups fall naturally into one or the other of the following classes:

a) The family.

b) Language (racial) groups.

c) Local and territorial communities: (i) neighborhoods, (ii) rural communities, (iii) urban communities.

d) Conflict groups: (i) nationalities, (ii) parties, (iii) sects, (iv) labor organizations, (v) gangs, etc.

e) Accommodation groups: (i) classes, (ii) castes, (iii) vocational, (iv) denominational groups.

The foregoing classification is not quite adequate nor wholly logical. The first three classes are more closely related to one another than they are to the last two, i.e., the so-called "accommodation" and "conflict" groups. The distinction is far-reaching, but its general character is indicated by the fact that the family, language, and local groups are, or were originally, what are known as primary groups, that is, groups organized on intimate, face-to-face relations. The conflict and accommodation groups represent divisions which may, to be sure, have arisen within the primary group, but which have usually arisen historically by the imposition of one primary group upon another.

Every state in history was or is a *state of classes*, a polity of superior and inferior social groups, based upon distinctions either of rank or of property. This phenomenon must, then, be called the "State."[1]

It is the existence at any rate of conflict and accommodation within the limits of a larger group which distinguishes it from groups based on primary relations, and gives it eventually the character described as "secondary."

When a language group becomes militant and self-conscious, it assumes the character of a nationality. It is perhaps true, also, that the family which is large enough and independent enough to be self-conscious, by that fact assumes the character of a clan. Important in this connection is the fact that a group in becoming

[1] Franz Oppenheimer, *The State* (Indianapolis, 1914), p. 5.

group-conscious changes its character. External conflict has invariably reacted powerfully upon the internal organization of social groups.

Group self-consciousness seems to be a common characteristic of conflict and accommodation groups and distinguishes them from the more elementary forms of society represented by the family and the local community.

3. *Organization and structure of social groups.*—Having a general scheme for the classification of social groups, it is in order to discover methods of analysis that are applicable to the study of all types of groups, from the family to the sect. Such a scheme of analysis should reveal not only the organization and structure of typical groups, but it should indicate the relation of this organization and structure to those social problems that are actual and generally recognized. The sort of facts which are now generally recognized as important in the study, not merely of society, but the problems of society are:

a) Statistics: numbers, local distribution, mobility, incidence of births, deaths, disease, and crime.

b) Institutions: local distribution, classification (i.e., (i) industrial, (ii) religious, (iii) political, (iv) educational, (v) welfare and mutual aid), communal organization.

c) Heritages: the customs and traditions transmitted by the group, particularly in relation to religion, recreation and leisure time, and social control (politics).

d) Organization of public opinion: parties, sects, cliques, and the press.

4. *Social process and social progress.*—Social process is the name for all changes which can be regarded as changes in the life of the group. A group may be said to have a life when it has a history. Among social processes we may distinguish (*a*) the historical, (*b*) the cultural, (*c*) the political, and (*d*) the economic.

a) We describe as historical the processes by which the fund of social tradition, which is the heritage of every permanent social group, is accumulated and transmitted from one generation to another.

History plays the rôle in the group of memory in the individual. Without history social groups would, no doubt, rise and decline, but they would neither grow old nor make progress.

Immigrants, crossing the ocean, leave behind them much of their local traditions. The result is that they lose, particularly in the second generation, that control which the family and group tradition formerly exercised over them; but they are, for that very reason, all the more open to the influence of the traditions and customs of their adopted country.

b) If it is the function of the historical process to accumulate and conserve the common fund of social experience, it is the function of the cultural process to shape and define the social forms and the social patterns which each preceding generation imposes upon its successors.

The individual living in society has to fit into a pre-existing social world, to take part in the hedonistic, economic, political, religious, moral, aesthetic, intellectual activities of the group. For these activities the group has objective *systems*, more or less complex sets of schemes, organized either by traditional association or with a conscious regard to the greatest possible efficiency of the result, but with only a secondary, or even with no interest in the particular desires, abilities and experiences of the individuals who have to perform these activities.

There is no pre-existing harmony whatever between the individual and the social factors of personal evolution, and the fundamental tendencies of the individual are always in some disaccordance with the fundamental tendencies of social control. Personal evolution is always a struggle between the individual and society—a struggle for self-expression on the part of the individual, for his subjection on the part of society—and it is in the total course of this struggle that the personality—not as a static "essence" but as a dynamic, continually evolving set of activities—manifests and constructs itself.[1]

c) In general, standards of behavior that are in the mores are not the subject of discussion, except so far as discussion is necessary to determine whether this or that act falls under one or the other of the accepted social sanctions. The political as distinguished from the cultural process is concerned with just those matters in regard to which there is division and difference. Politics is concerned with issues.

The Negro, particularly in the southern states, is a constant theme of popular discussion. Every time a Negro finds himself in a new situation, or one in which the white population is unaccustomed to see him, the thing provokes comment in both races. On the other hand, when a southerner asks the question: "Would you want your

[1] Thomas and Znaniecki, *op. cit.*, III, 34–36.

daughter to marry a Negro?" it is time for discussion to cease. Any questions of relations between the races can always be immediately disposed of as soon as it is seen to come, directly or indirectly, under the intolerable formula. Political questions are matters of compromise and expediency. Miscegenation, on the other hand, is contrary to the mores. As such the rule against it is absolute.

The political process, by which a society or social group formulates its wishes and enforces them, goes on within the limits of the mores and is carried on by public discussion, legislation, and the adjudication of the courts.

d) The economic process, so far as it can be distinguished from the production and distribution of goods, is the process by which prices are made and an exchange of values is effected. Most values, i.e., my present social status, my hopes of the future, and memory of the past, are personal and not values that can be exchanged. The economic process is concerned with values that can be treated as commodities.

All these processes may, and do, arise within most but not every society or social group. Commerce presupposes the freedom of the individual to pursue his own profit, and commerce can take place only to the extent and degree that this freedom is permitted. Freedom of commerce is, however, limited on the one hand by the mores and on the other by formal law, so that the economic process takes place ordinarily within limitations that are defined by the cultural and the political processes. It is only where there is neither a cultural nor a political order that commerce is absolutely free.

The areas of (1) the cultural, (2) the political, (3) the economic processes and their relations to one another may be represented by concentric circles.

In this representation the area of widest cultural influences is coterminous with the area of commerce, because commerce in its widest extension is invariably carried on under some restraints of custom and customary law. Otherwise it is not commerce at all, but something predacious outside the law. But if the area of the economic process is almost invariably coterminous with the widest areas of cultural influence, it does not extend to the smaller social groups. As a rule trade does not invade the family. Family interests are always personal even when they are carried on under the forms of commerce. Primitive society, within the limits of the village, is usually communistic. All values are personal, and the relations of individuals to one another, economic or otherwise, are preordained by custom and law.

The impersonal values, values for exchange, seem to be in any given society or social group in inverse relation to the personal values.

The attempt to describe in this large way the historical, cultural, political, and economic processes, is justified in so far as it enables us to recognize that the aspects of social life, which are the subject-matter of the special social sciences, i.e., history, political science, and economics, are involved in specific forms of change that can

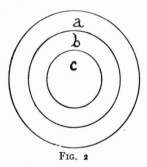

FIG. 2

a = area of most extended cultural influences and of commerce; b = area of formal political control; c = area of purely personal relationships, communism.

be viewed abstractly, formulated, compared, and related. The attempt to view them in their interrelations is at the same time an effort to distinguish and to see them as parts of one whole.

In contrast with the types of social change referred to there are other changes which are unilateral and progressive; changes which are described popularly as "movements," mass movements. These are changes which eventuate in new social organizations and institutions.

All more marked forms of social change are associated with certain social manifestations that we call social unrest. Social unrest issues, under ordinary conditions, as an incident of new social contacts, and is an indication of a more lively tempo in the process of communication and interaction.

All social changes are preceded by a certain degree of social and individual disorganization. This will be followed ordinarily under normal conditions by a movement of reorganization. All progress implies a certain amount of disorganization. In studying social changes, therefore, that, if not progressive, are at least unilateral, we are interested in:

(1) Disorganization: accelerated mobility, unrest, disease, and crime as manifestations and measures of social disorganization.

(2) Social movements (reorganization) include: (*a*) crowd movements (i.e., mobs, strikes, etc.); (*b*) cultural revivals, religious and linguistic; (*c*) fashion (changes in dress, convention, and social ritual); (*d*) reform (changes in social policy and administration); (*e*) revolutions (changes in institutions and the mores).

5. *The individual and the person.*—The person is an individual who has status. We come into the world as individuals. We acquire status, and become persons. Status means position in society. The individual inevitably has some status in every social group of which he is a member. In a given group the status of every member is determined by his relation to every other member of that group. Every smaller group, likewise, has a status in some larger group of which it is a part and this is determined by its relation to all the other members of the larger group.

The individual's self-consciousness—his conception of his rôle in society, his "self," in short—while not identical with his personality is an essential element in it. The individual's conception of himself, however, is based on his status in the social group or groups of which he is a member. The individual whose conception of himself does not conform to his status is an isolated individual. The completely isolated individual, whose conception of himself is in no sense an adequate reflection of his status, is probably insane.

It follows from what is said that an individual may have many "selves" according to the groups to which he belongs and the extent to which each of these groups is isolated from the others. It is true, also, that the individual is influenced in differing degrees and in a specific manner, by the different types of group of which he is a member. This indicates the manner in which the personality of the individual may be studied sociologically.

Every individual comes into the world in possession of certain characteristic and relatively fixed behavior patterns which we call instincts. This is his racial inheritance which he shares with all members of the species. He comes into the world, also, endowed with certain undefined capacities for learning other forms of behavior, capacities which vary greatly in different individuals. These individual differences and the instincts are what is called original nature.[1]

Sociology is interested in "original nature" in so far as it supplies the raw materials out of which individual personalities and the social order are created. Both society and the persons who compose society are the products of social processes working in and through the materials which each new generation of men contributes to it.

Charles Cooley, who was the first to make the important distinction between primary and secondary groups, has pointed out that the intimate, face-to-face associations of primary groups, i.e., the family, the neighborhood, and the village community, are fundamental in forming the social nature and ideals of the individual.[2]

There is, however, an area of life in which the associations are more intimate than those of the primary group as that group is ordinarily conceived. Such are the relations between mother and child, particularly in the period of infancy, and the relations between men and women under the influence of the sexual instinct. These are the associations in which the most lasting affections and the most violent antipathies are formed. We may describe it as the area of touch relationships.

Finally, there is the area of secondary contacts, in which relationships are relatively impersonal, formal, and conventional. It is in this region of social life that the individual gains, at the same time, a personal freedom and an opportunity for distinction that is denied him in the primary group.

As a matter of fact, many, if not most, of our present social problems have their source and origin in the transition of great masses of the population—the immigrants, for example—out of a society

[1] Original nature in its relation to social welfare and human progress has been made the subject-matter of a special science, eugenics. For a criticism of the claims of eugenics as a social science see Leonard T. Hobhouse, *Social Evolution and Political Theory* (Columbia University Press, 1917).

[2] Charles H. Cooley, *Social Organization*, p. 28.

based on primary group relationships into the looser, freer, and less controlled existence of life in great cities.

The "moral unrest" so deeply penetrating all western societies, the growing vagueness and indecision of personalities, the almost complete disappearance of the "strong and steady character" of old times, in short, the rapid and general increase of Bohemianism and Bolshevism in all societies, is an effect of the fact that not only the early primary group controlling all interests of its members on the general social basis, not only the occupational group of the mediaeval type controlling most of the interests of its members on a professional basis, but even the special modern group dividing with many others the task of organizing permanently the attitudes of each of its members, is more and more losing ground. The pace of social evolution has become so rapid that special groups are ceasing to be permanent and stable enough to organize and maintain organized complexes of attitudes of their members which correspond to their common pursuits. In other words, society is gradually losing all its old machinery for the determination and stabilization of individual characters.[1]

Every social group tends to create, from the individuals that compose it, its own type of character, and the characters thus formed become component parts of the social structure in which they are incorporated. All the problems of social life are thus problems of the individual; and all problems of the individual are at the same time problems of the group. This point of view is already recognized in preventive medicine, and to some extent in psychiatry. It is not yet adequately recognized in the technique of social case work.

Further advance in the application of social principles to social practice awaits a more thoroughgoing study of the problems, systematic social research, and an experimental social science.

REPRESENTATIVE WORKS IN SYSTEMATIC SOCIOLOGY
AND METHODS OF SOCIOLOGICAL RESEARCH

I. THE SCIENCE OF PROGRESS

(1) Comte, Auguste. *Cours de philosophie positive*, 5th ed. 6 vols. Paris, 1892.
(2) ———. *Positive Philosophy*. Translated by Harriet Martineau, 3d ed. London, 1893.
(3) Spencer, Herbert. *Principles of Sociology*, 3d ed. 3 vols. New York, 1906.

[1] Thomas and Znaniecki, *op. cit.*, III, 63–64.

(4) Schaeffle, Albert. *Bau und Leben des socialen Körpers.* 2d ed., 2 vols. Tuebingen, 1896.
(5) Lilienfeld, Paul von. *Gedanken über die Socialwissenschaft der Zukunft.* 5 vols. Mitau, 1873–81.
(6) Ward, Lester F. *Dynamic Sociology.* 2 vols. New York, 1883.
(7) De Greef, Guillaume. *Introduction à la sociologie.* 3 vols. Paris, 1886.
(8) Worms, René. *Organisme et société.* Paris, 1896.

II. THE SCHOOLS

A. *Realists*

(1) Ratzenhofer, Gustav. *Die sociologische Erkenntnis.* Leipzig, 1898.
(2) Small, Albion W. *General Sociology.* Chicago, 1905.
(3) Durkheim, Émile. *De la Division du travail social.* Paris, 1893.
(4) Simmel, Georg. *Soziologie.* Untersuchungen über die Formen der Vergesellschaftung. Leipzig, 1908.
(5) Spykman, N. J. *The Social Theory of Georg Simmel.* Chicago, 1925.
(6) Cooley, Charles Horton. *Social Organization.* A study of the larger mind. New York, 1909.
(7) Ellwood, Charles A. *Sociology in Its Psychological Aspects.* New York and London, 1912.

B. *Nominalists*

(1) Tarde, Gabriel. *Les Lois de l'imitation.* Paris, 1895.
(2) Giddings, Franklin H. *The Principles of Sociology.* New York, 1896.
(3) Ross, Edward Alsworth. *The Principles of Sociology.* New York, 1920.

C. *Collective Behavior*

(1) Le Bon, Gustave. *The Crowd.* A study of the popular mind. New York, 1903.
(2) Sighele, Scipio. *Psychologie des sectes.* Paris, 1898.
(3) Tarde, Gabriel. *L'Opinion et la foule.* Paris, 1901.
(4) McDougall, William. *The Group Mind.* Cambridge, 1920.
(5) Vincent, George E. *The Social Mind and Education.* New York, 1897.

III. METHODS OF SOCIOLOGICAL INVESTIGATION

A. *Critical Observation on Methods of Research*

(1) Small, Albion W. *The Meaning of Social Science.* Chicago, 1910.
(2) Bridges, J. H. *Illustrations of Positivism.* "Methods of Research," pp. 92–104. Chicago, 1915.
(3) Durkheim, Émile. *Les Régles de la méthode sociologique.* Paris, 1904.
(4) Thomas, W. I., and Znaniecki, F. *The Polish Peasant in Europe and America.* "Methodological Note," I, 1–86. 5 vols. Boston, 1918–20.

B. *Studies of Communities*

(1) Booth, Charles. *Labour and Life of the People: London.* 2 vols. London, 1891.
(2) Booth, Charles. *Life and Labour of the People in London.* 9 vols. London, 1892–97. 8 additional vols. London, 1902.

(3) *The Pittsburgh Survey.* Edited by Paul U. Kellogg. 6 vols. Russell Sage Foundation. New York, 1909–14.

(4) *The Springfield Survey.* Edited by Shelby M. Harrison. 3 vols. Russell Sage Foundation. New York, 1918–20.

(5) *Criminal Justice in Cleveland.* Reports of the Cleveland Foundation survey of the administration of criminal justice in Cleveland, Ohio. Directed by Roscoe Pound and Felix Frankfurter. Cleveland, 1922.

(6) Geddes, Patrick. *Cities in Evolution.* An introduction to the town-planning movement and to the study of civics. London, 1915.

C. *Studies of the Individual*

(1) Healy, William. *The Individual Delinquent.* Boston, 1915.

(2) Thomas, W. I., and Znaniecki, F. *The Polish Peasant in Europe and America.* "Life Record of an Immigrant," Vol. III. Boston, 1919.

(3) Thomas, W. I. *The Unadjusted Girl.* With cases and standpoint for behavior analysis. Especially chap. vi, "The Measurement of Social Influence," pp. 222–57. Boston, 1923.

(4) Healy, William, and Bronner, Augusta F. *Judge Baker Foundation Case Studies*, Series I. Boston, 1922–23.

(5) *The Equipment of the Workers.* An enquiry into the adequacy of the adult manual workers of Sheffield for the discharge of their responsibilities as heads of households, producers, and citizens. London, 1919.

D. *Studies of Public Opinion*

(1) *Americanization Studies.* Allen T. Burns, director. 10 vols. New York, 1920–23.

(2) *The Negro in Chicago.* A study of race relations and a race riot. By the Chicago Commission on Race Relations. Chicago, 1922.

E. *Field Studies*

(1) Chapin, F. Stuart. *Field Work and Social Research.* New York, 1920.

(2) Richmond, Mary. *Social Diagnosis.* Russell Sage Foundation. New York, 1917.

(3) Vignes, J.-B.-Maurice. *La Science Sociale.* D'après les principes de Le Play et de ses continuateurs. Paris, 1897.

(4) Rowntree, B. Seebohm. *Poverty.* A study of town life. London, 1901.

(5) Webb, Sidney and Beatrice. *Industrial Democracy.* Preface, pp. xxiii–xxxii. [London, 1920. "A brief account of the methods of investigation."]

(6) Webb, Sidney and Beatrice. *Problems of Modern Industry.* Chap. i, "The Diary of an Investigator," pp. 1–19. London, 1898.

(7) Wissler, Clark. *Man and Culture.* Chap. iv, "The Content of Culture," pp. 47–72; chap. v. "The Universal Pattern," pp. 73–98. [Defines "culture trait, complex, type, area, center, trait-complexes."] New York, 1923.

(8) Lindeman, Eduard C. *Social Discovery.* An approach to the study of functional groups. New York, 1924.

IV. PERIODICALS

(1) *American Journal of Sociology.* Chicago, University of Chicago Press, 1896-.
(2) *American Sociological Society, Papers and Proceedings.* Chicago, University of Chicago Press, 1907-.
(3) *Annales de l'institut international de sociologie.* Paris, M. Giard et Cie., 1895-.
(4) *L'Année sociologique.* Paris, F. Alcan, 1898-1912.
(5) *Chinese Journal of Sociology.* Peking, University of Peking, 1921-.
(6) *Indian Sociological Review.* Lucknow, Lucknow University Sociological Association, 1923-.
(7) *Journal of Applied Sociology.* Los Angeles, (Southern California Sociological Society and) University of Southern California, 1916-.
(8) *Journal of Social Forces.* Chapel Hill, University of North Carolina Press, 1922-.
(9) *Kölner Vierteljahrshefte für Soziologie.* Leipzig and München, Duncker und Humblot, 1921-.
(10) *Revue de l'institut de sociologie.* Bruxelles, l'Institut de Sociologie, 1920-. [Successor to *Bulletin de l'institut de sociologie Solvay.* Bruxelles, 1910-14.]
(11) *Rivista italiana di sociologia.* Roma, Fratelli Bocca, 1897-.
(12) *Revue internationale de sociologie.* Paris, M. Giard et Cie., 1893-.
(13) *Schmollers Jahrbuch für Gesetzgebung, Verwaltung und Volkswirtschaft im deutschen Reiche.* Leipzig, Duncker und Humblot, 1877-.
(14) *The Sociological Review.* Manchester, Sherratt and Hughes, 1908-. [Preceded by Sociological Papers, Sociological Society, London, 1905-7.]
(15) *Zeitschrift für Sozialwissenschaft.* Berlin, G. Reimer, 1898-.

TOPICS FOR WRITTEN THEMES

1. Comte's Conception of Humanity
2. Herbert Spencer on the Social Organism
3. The Social Process as Defined by Small
4. Imitation and Like-mindedness as Fundamental Social Facts
5. Social Control as a Sociological Problem
6. Group Consciousness and the Group Mind
7. Investigation and Research as Illustrated by the Pittsburgh Survey and the Carnegie Americanization Studies
8. The Concept of the Group in Sociology
9. The Person, Personality, and Status
10. Sociology in Its Relation to Economics and to Politics

QUESTIONS FOR DISCUSSION

1. What do you understand was Comte's purpose in demanding for sociology a place among the sciences?

2. Are social phenomena susceptible to scientific prevision? Compare with physical phenomena.

3. What is Comte's order of the sciences? What is your explanation for the late appearance of sociology in the series?

4. What do you understand by the term "positive" when applied to the social sciences?

5. Can sociology become positive without becoming experimental?

6. "Natural science emphasizes the abstract, the historian is interested in the concrete." Discuss.

7. How do you distinguish between the historical method and the method of natural science in dealing with the following phenomena: (a) electricity, (b) plants, (c) cattle, (d) cities?

8. Distinguish between history, natural history, and natural science.

9. Is Westermark's *Origin and Development of the Moral Ideas* history, natural history, or sociology? Why?

10. "History is past politics, politics is present history." Do you agree? Elaborate your position.

11. What is the value of history to the person?

12. Classify the following formulas of behavior under either (a) natural law (social law in the scientific sense), and (b) moral law (customary sanction, ethical principles), (c) civil law: "birds of a feather flock together"; "thou shalt not kill"; an ordinance against speeding; "honesty is the best policy"; monogamy; imitation tends to spread in geometric ratio; "women first"; the Golden Rule; "walk in the trodden paths"; the federal child-labor statute.

13. Give an illustration of a sociological hypothesis.

14. Of the following statements of fact, which are historical and which sociological?

Auguste Comte suffered from myopia.

"Man is born free, and everywhere he is in chains."

"Science works not at all for nationality or its spirit. It makes entirely for cosmopolitanism."

15. How would you verify each of the foregoing statements? Distinguish between the sociological and historical methods of verification.

16. Is the use of the comparative method that of history or that of natural science?

17. "The social organism: humanity or Leviathan?" What is your reaction to this alternative? Why?

18. What was the difference in the conception of the social organism held by Comte and that held by Spencer?

19. "How does a mere collection of individuals succeed in acting in a corporate and consistent way?" What was the answer to this question given by Hobbes, Aristotle, Worms?

20. "Man and society are at the same time products of nature and of human artifice." Explain.

21. What are the values and limitations of the following explanations of the control of the group over the behavior of its members: (a) homogeneity, (b) like-mindedness, (c) imitation, (d) common purpose?

22. What bearing have the facts of a panic or a stampede upon the theories of like-mindedness, imitation, and common purpose as explanations of group behavior?

23. "The characteristic social phenomenon is just this control by the group as a whole of the individuals which compose it. This fact of control is the fundamental social fact." Give an illustration of the control of the group over its members.

24. What is the difference between group mind and group consciousness as indicated in current usage in the phrases "urban mind," "rural mind," "public mind," "race consciousness," "national consciousness," "class consciousness"?

25. What do you understand by "a group in being"? Compare with the nautical expression "a fleet in being." Is "a fleet in being" a social organism? Has it a "social mind" and "social consciousness" in the sense that we speak of "race consciousness", for example, or "group consciousness"?

26. In what sense is public opinion objective? Analyze a selected case where the opinion of the group as a whole is different from the opinion of its members as individuals.

27. For what reason was the fact of "social control" interpreted in terms of "the collective mind"?

28. Which is the social reality (a) that society is a collection of like-minded persons, or (b) that society is a process and a product of interaction? What is the bearing upon this point of the quotation from Dewey: "Society may fairly be said to exist in transmission"?

29. What three steps were taken in the transformation of sociology from a philosophy of history to a science of society?

30. What value do you perceive in a classification of social problems?

31. Classify the following studies under (a) administrative problems or (l) problems of policy or (c) problems of human nature: a survey to determine the feasibility of health insurance to meet the problem of sickness; an investigation of the police force; a study of attitudes toward war; a survey of the contacts of racial groups; an investigation for the purpose of improving the technique of workers in a social agency; a study of the experiments in self-government among prisoners in penal institutions.

32. Is the description of great cities as "social laboratories" metaphor or fact?

33. What do you understand by the statement: Sociology will become an experimental science as soon as it can state its problems in such a way that the results in one instance show what can be done in another?

34. What would be the effect upon political life if sociology were able to predict with some precision the effects of political action, for example, the effect of prohibition?

35. Would you favor turning over the government to control of experts as soon as sociology became a positive science? Explain.

36. How far may the politician who makes a profession of controlling elections be regarded as a practicing sociologist?

37. What is the distinction between sociology as an art and as a science?

38. Distinguish between research and investigation as the terms are used in the text.

39. What illustrations in American society occur to you of the (a) autocratic and (b) democratic methods of social change?

40. "All social problems turn out finally to be problems of group life." Are there any exceptions?

41. Select twelve groups at random and enter under the heads in the classification of social groups. What groups are difficult to classify?

42. Study the organization and structure of one of the foregoing groups in terms of (a) statistical facts about it; (b) its institutional aspect; (c) its heritages; and (d) its collective opinion.

43. "All progress implies a certain amount of disorganization." Explain.

44. What do you understand to be the differences between the various social processes: (a) historical, (b) cultural, (c) economic, (d) political?

45. What is the significance of the relative diameters of the areas of the cultural, political, and economic processes?

46. "The person is an individual who has status." Does an animal have status?

47. "In a given group the status of every member is determined by his relation to every other member of that group." Give an illustration.

48. Why are the problems of the person, problems of the group as well?

49. What does the organization of the bibliography and the sequence of the volumes referred to suggest in regard to the development of sociological science?

50. How far does it seem to you that the emphasis upon process rather than progress accounts for the changes which have taken place in the sociological theory and point of view?

CHAPTER II

HUMAN NATURE

I. INTRODUCTION

1. Human Interest in Human Nature

The human interest in human nature is proverbial. It is an original tendency of man to be attentive to the behavior of other human beings. Experience heightens this interest because of the dependence of the individual upon other persons, not only for physical existence, but for social life.

The literature of every people is to a large extent but the crystallization of this persistent interest. Old saws and proverbs of every people transmit from generation to generation shrewd generalizations upon human behavior. In joke and in epigram, in caricature and in burlesque, in farce and in comedy, men of all races and times have enjoyed with keen relish the humor of the contrast between the conventional and the natural motives in behavior. In Greek mythology, individual traits of human nature are abstracted, idealized, and personified into gods. The heroes of Norse sagas and Teutonic legends are the gigantic symbols of primary emotions and sentiments. Historical characters live in the social memory not alone because they are identified with political, religious, or national movements but also because they have come to typify human relationships. The loyalty of Damon and Pythias, the grief of Rachel weeping for her children, the cynical cruelty of the egocentric Nero, the perfidy of Benedict Arnold, the comprehending sympathy of Abraham Lincoln, are proverbial, and as such have become part of the common language of all the peoples who participate in our occidental culture.

Poetry, drama, and the plastic arts are interesting and significant only so far as they reveal in new and ever changing circumstances the unchanging characteristics of a fundamental human nature. Illustrations of this naïve and unreflecting interest in the study of mankind are familiar enough in the experience and observation

64

of any of us. Intellectual interest in, and the scientific observation of, human traits and human behavior have their origin in this natural interest and unreflective observation by man of his fellows. History, ethnology, folklore, all the comparative studies of single cultural traits, i.e., of language, of religion, and of law, are but the more systematic pursuit of this universal interest of mankind in man.

2. Definition of Human Nature

The natural history of the expression "human nature" is interesting. Usage has given it various shades of meaning. In defining the term more precisely there is a tendency either unwarrantedly to narrow or unduly to extend and overemphasize some one or another of the different senses of the term. A survey of these varied uses reveals the common and fundamental meaning of the phrase.

The use which common sense makes of the term human nature is significant. It is used in varied contexts with the most divergent implications but always by way of explanation of behavior that is characteristically human. The phrase is sometimes employed with cynical deprecation as, "Oh, that's human nature." Or as often, perhaps, as an expression of approbation, "He's so human."

The weight of evidence as expressed in popular sayings is distinctly in depreciation of man's nature.

> It's human natur', p'raps,—if so,
> Oh, isn't human natur' low,

are two lines from Gilbert's musical comedy "Babette's Love." "To err is human, to forgive divine" reminds us of a familiar contrast. "Human nature is like a bad clock; it might go right now and then, or be made to strike the hour, but its inward frame is to go wrong," is a simile that emphasizes the popular notion that man's behavior tends to the perverse. An English divine settles the question with the statement, "Human nature is a rogue and a scoundrel, or why would it perpetually stand in need of laws and religion?"

Even those who see good in the natural man admit his native tendency to err. Sir Thomas Browne asserts that "human nature knows naturally what is good but naturally pursues what is evil." The Earl of Clarendon gives the equivocal explanation that "if we did not take great pains to corrupt our nature, our nature would never corrupt us." Addison, from the detached position of an observer and critic of manners and men, concludes that "as man is a creature made up of different extremes, he has something in him very great and very mean."

The most commonly recognized distinction between man and the lower animals lies in his possession of reason. Yet familiar sayings tend to exclude the intellectual from the human attributes. Lord Bacon shrewdly remarks that "there is in human nature, generally, more of the fool than of the wise." The phrase "he is a child of nature" means that behavior in social relations is impulsive, simple, and direct rather than reflective, sophisticated, or consistent. Wordsworth depicts this human type in his poem "She Was a Phantom of Delight":

> A creature not too bright or good
> For human nature's daily food;
> For transient sorrows, simple wiles,
> Praise, blame, love, kisses, tears and smiles.

The inconsistency between the rational professions and the impulsive behavior of men is a matter of common observation. "That's not the logic, reason, or philosophy of it, but it's the human nature of it." It is now generally recognized that the older English conception of the "economic man" and the "rational man," motivated by enlightened self-interest, was far removed from the "natural man" impelled by impulse, prejudice, and sentiment, in short, by human nature. Popular criticism has been frequently directed against the reformer in politics, the efficiency expert in industry, the formalist in religion and morals on the ground that they overlook or neglect the so-called "human factor" in the situation. Sir Arthur Helps says:

No doubt hard work is a great police-agent; if everybody were worked from morning till night, and then carefully locked up, the register of crimes might be greatly diminished. But what would become of human nature? Where would be the room for growth in such a system of things? It is through sorrow and mirth, plenty and need, a variety of passions, circumstances, and temptations, even through sin and misery, that men's natures are developed.

Certain sayings already quoted imply that the nature of man is a fact to be reckoned with in controlling his behavior. "There are limits to human nature" which cannot lightly be overstepped.

"Human nature," according to Periander, "is hard to overcome." Yet we also recognize with Swift that "it is the talent of human nature to run from one extreme to another." Finally, nothing is more trite and familiar than the statement that "human nature is the same all over the world." This fundamental likeness of human nature, despite artificial and superficial cultural differences, has found a classic expression in Kipling's line: "The Colonel's Lady an' Judy O'Grady are sisters under their skins!"

Human nature, then, as distinct from the formal wishes of the individual and the conventional order of society, is an aspect of human life that must be reckoned with. Common sense has long recognized this, but until recently no systematic attempt has been made to *isolate*, describe, and explain the distinctively human factors in the life either of the individual or of society.

Of all that has been written on this subject the most adequate statement is that of Cooley. He has worked out with unusual penetration and peculiar insight an interpretation of human nature as a product of group life.

By human nature we may understand those sentiments and impulses that are human in being superior to those of lower animals, and also in the sense that they belong to mankind at large, and not to any particular race or time. It means, particularly, sympathy and the innumerable sentiments into which sympathy enters, such as love, resentment, ambition, vanity, hero-worship, and the feeling of social right and wrong.

Human nature in this sense is justly regarded as a comparatively permanent element in society. Always and everywhere men seek honor and dread ridicule, defer to public opinion, cherish their goods and their children, and admire courage, generosity, and success. It is always safe to assume that people are and have been human.

Human nature is not something existing separately in the individual, but a *group nature or primary phase of society*, a relatively simple and general condition of the social mind. It is something more, on the one hand, than the mere instinct that is born in us—though that enters into it—and something less, on the other, than the more elaborate development of ideas and sentiments that makes up institutions. It is the nature which is developed and expressed in those simple, face-to-face groups that are somewhat alike in all societies; groups of the family, the playground, and the neighborhood. In the essential similarity of these is to be found the basis, in experience, for similar ideas and sentiments in the human mind.

In these, everywhere, human nature comes into existence. Man does not have it at birth; he cannot acquire it except through fellowship, and it decays in isolation.[1]

3. Classification of the Materials

With the tacit acceptance by biologists, psychologists, and sociologists of human behavior as a natural phenomenon, materials upon human nature have rapidly accumulated. The wealth and variety of these materials are all the greater because of the diversity of the points of view from which workers in this field have attacked the problem. The value of the results of these investigations is enhanced when they are brought together, classified, and compared.

The materials fall naturally into two divisions: (a) "The Original Nature of Man" and (b) "Human Nature and Social Life." This division is based upon a distinction between traits that are inborn and characters socially acquired; a distinction found necessary by students in this field. Selections under the third heading, "Personality and the Social Self" indicate the manner in which the individual develops under the social influences, from the raw material of "instinct" into the social product "the person." Materials in the fourth division, "Biological and Social Inheritance," contrast the method of the transmission of original tendencies through the germ plasm with the communication of the social heritage through education.

a) *The original nature of man.*—No one has stated more clearly than Thorndike that human nature is a product of two factors, (a) tendencies to response rooted in original nature and (b) the accumulated effects of the stimuli of the external and social environment. At birth man is a bundle of random tendencies to respond. Through experience, and by means of the mechanisms of habit and character, control is secured over instinctive reactions. In other words, the original nature of man is, as Comte said, an abstraction. It exists only in the psychic vacuum of antenatal life, or perhaps only in the potentiality of the germ plasm. The fact of observation is that the structure of the response is irrevocably changed in the process of reaction to the stimulus. The *Biography of a Baby* gives a concrete picture of the development of the plastic infant in the environment of the social group.

[1] Charles H. Cooley, *Social Organization*, pp. 28–30.

The three papers on differences between sexes, races, and individuals serve as an introduction into the problem of differentiating the aspects of behavior which are in *original nature* from those that are *acquired* through social experience. Are the apparent differences between men and women, white and colored, John and James, those which arise from differences in the germ plasm or from differences in education and in cultural contacts? The selections must not be taken as giving the final word upon the subject. At best they represent merely the conclusions reached by three investigators. Attempts to arrive at positive differences in favor either of original nature or of education are frequently made in the interest of preconceived opinion. The problem, as far as science is concerned, is to discover what limitations original nature places upon response to social copies, and the ways in which the inborn potentialities find expression or repression in differing types of social environment.

b) Human nature and social life.—Original nature is represented in human responses in so far as they are determined by the *innate structure of the individual organism.* The materials assembled under this head treat of inborn reactions as influenced, modified, and reconstructed by the *structure of the social organization.*

The actual reorganization of human nature takes place in response to the folkways and mores, the traditions and conventions, of the group. So potentially fitted for social life is the natural man, however, so manifold are the expressions that the plastic original tendencies may take, that instinct is replaced by habit, precedent, personal taboo, and good form. This remade structure of human nature, this objective mind, as Hegel called it, is fixed and transmitted in the folkways and mores, social ritual, i.e., *Sittlichkeit*, to use the German word, and convention.

c) Personality and the social self.—The selections upon "Personality and the Social Self" bring together and compare the different definitions of the term. These definitions fall under three heads:

(1) *The organism as personality:* This is a biological statement, satisfactory as a definition only as preparatory to further analysis.

(2) *Personality as a complex:* Personality defined in terms of the unity of mental life is a conception that has grown up in the recent "individual psychology," so called. Personality includes, in this case, not only the memories of the individual and his stream of

consciousness, but also the characteristic organization of mental complexes and trends which may be thought of as a supercomplex. The phenomena of double and multiple personalities occur when this unity becomes disorganized. Disorganization in releasing groups of complexes from control may even permit the formation of independent organizations. Morton Prince's book *The Dissociation of a Personality* is a classic case study of multiple personality. The selections upon "The Natural Person versus the Social and Conventional Person" and "The Divided Self and the Moral Consciousness" indicate the more usual and less extreme conflicts of opposing sentiments and interests within the organization of personality.

(3) *Personality as the rôle of the individual in the group:* The word personality is derived from the Latin *persona*, a mask used by actors. The etymology of the term suggests that its meaning is to be found in the rôle of the individual in the social group. By usage, personality carries the implication of the social expression of behavior. Personality may then be defined as the sum and organization of those traits which determine the rôle of the individual in the group. The following is a classification of the characteristics of the person which affect his social status and efficiency:

(a) physical traits, as physique, physiognomy, etc.;

(b) temperament;

(c) character;

(d) social expression, as by facial expression, gesture, manner, speech, writing, etc.;

(e) prestige, as by birth, past success, status, etc.;

(f) the individual's conception of his rôle.

The significance of these traits consists in the way in which they enter into the rôle of the individual in his social milieu. Chief among these may be considered the individual's conception of the part which he plays among his fellows. Cooley's discriminating description of "the looking-glass self" offers a picture of the process by which the person conceives himself in terms of the attitudes of others toward him.

The reflected or looking-glass self seems to have three principal elements: the imagination of our appearance to the other person; the imagination of his judgment of that appearance; and some sort of self-feeling, such as pride or mortification. The comparison with a looking-glass self hardly suggests the second element, the imagined judgment which is quite essential. The thing that moves us to pride or shame is not the mere mechanical reflection of ourselves, but an imputed sentiment, the imagined effect of this reflection upon another's mind. This is evident from the fact that the character and weight of that other, in whose mind we see ourselves, makes all the difference with our feeling.[1]

Veblen has made a subtle analysis of the way in which conduct is controlled by the individual's conception of his social rôle in his analysis of "invidious comparison" and "conspicuous expenditure."[2]

d) *Biological and social inheritance.*—The distinction between biological and social inheritance is sharply made by the noted biologist, J. Arthur Thomson, in the selection entitled "Nature and Nurture." The so-called "acquired characters" or modifications of original nature through experience, he points out, are transmitted not through the germ plasm but through communication.

Thorndike's "Inventory of Original Tendencies" offers a detailed classification of the traits transmitted biologically. Since there exists no corresponding specific analysis of acquired traits, the following brief inventory of types of social heritages is offered.

TYPES OF SOCIAL HERITAGES

(a) means of communication, as language, gesture, etc.;
(b) social attitudes, habits, wishes, etc.;
(c) character;
(d) social patterns, as folkways, mores, conventions, ideals, etc.;
(e) technique;
(f) culture (as distinguished from technique, formal organization, and machinery);
(g) social organization (primary group life, institutions, sects, secondary groups, etc.).

On the basis of the work of Mendel, biologists have made marked progress in determining the inheritance of specific traits of original nature. The selection from a foremost American student of heredity and eugenics, C. B. Davenport, entitled "Inheritance of Original Nature" indicates the precision and accuracy with which the prediction of the inheritance of individual innate traits is made.

[1] Charles H. Cooley, *Human Nature and the Social Order*, pp. 152–53.

[2] *The Theory of the Leisure Class* (New York, 1899).

The mechanism of the transmission of social heritages, while more open to observation than biological inheritance, has not been subjected to as intensive study. The transmission of the social heritage takes place by communication, as Keller points out, through the medium of the various senses. The various types of the social heritages are transmitted in two ways: (a) by tradition, as from generation to generation, and (b) by acculturation, as from group to group.

In the communication of the social heritages, either by tradition or by acculturation, two aspects of the process may be distinguished: (a) Because of temperament, interest, and run of attention of the members of the group, the heritage, whether a word, an act of skill, or a social attitude, may be selected, appropriated, and incorporated into its culture. This is communication by *imitation*. (b) On the other hand, the heritage may be imposed upon the members of the group through authority and routine, by tabu and repression. This is communication by *inculcation*. In any concrete situation the transmission of a social heritage may combine varying elements of both processes. Education, as the etymology of the term suggests, denotes culture of original tendencies; yet the routine of a school system is frequently organized about formal discipline rather than around interest, aptitude, and attention.

Historically, the scientific interest in the question of biological and social inheritance has concerned itself with the rather sterile problem of the weight to be attached on the one hand to physical heredity and on the other to social heritage. The selection,"Temperament, Tradition, and Nationality" suggests that a more important inquiry is to determine how the behavior patterns and the culture of a racial group or a social class are determined by the interaction of original nature and the social tradition. According to this conception, racial temperament is an active selective agency, determining interest and the direction of attention. The group heritages on the other hand represent a detached external social environment, a complex of stimuli, effective only in so far as they call forth responses. The culture of a group is the sum total and organization of the social heritages which have acquired a social meaning because of racial temperament and of the historical life of the group.

II. MATERIALS

A. THE ORIGINAL NATURE OF MAN

1. Original Nature Defined[1]

A man's nature and the changes that take place in it may be described in terms of the responses—of thought, feeling, action, and attitude—which he makes, and of the bonds by which these are connected with the situations which life offers. Any fact of intellect, character, or skill means a tendency to respond in a certain way to a certain situation—involves a *situation* or state of affairs influencing the man, a *response* or state of affairs in the man, and a *connection* or bond whereby the latter is the result of the former.

Any man possesses at the very start of his life—that is, at the moment when the ovum and spermatozoön which are to produce him have united—numerous well-defined tendencies to future behavior. Between the situations which he will meet and the responses which he will make to them, pre-formed bonds exist. It is already determined by the constitution of these two germs that under certain circumstances he will see and hear and feel and act in certain ways. His intellect and morals, as well as his bodily organs and movements, are in part the consequence of the nature of the embryo in the first moment of its life. What a man is and does throughout life is a result of whatever constitution he has at the start and of the forces that act upon it before and after birth. I shall use the term "original nature" for the former and "environment" for the latter. His original nature is thus a name for the nature of the combined germ-cells from which he springs, and his environment is a name for the rest of the universe, so far as it may, directly or indirectly, influence him.

Three terms, reflexes, instincts, and inborn capacities, divide the work of naming these unlearned tendencies. When the tendency concerns a very definite and uniform response to a very simple sensory situation, and when the connection between the situation and the response is very hard to modify and is also very strong so that it is almost inevitable, the connection or response to which it leads is called a reflex. Thus the knee-jerk is a very definite and uniform response to the simple sense-stimulus of sudden hard pressure against a certain spot.

[1] From Edward L. Thorndike, *The Original Nature of Man*, pp. 1–7. (Teachers College, Columbia University, 1913. Author's copyright.)

When the response is more indefinite, the situation more complex, and the connection more modifiable, instinct becomes the customary term. Thus one's misery at being scorned is too indefinite a response to too complex a situation and is too easily modifiable to be called a reflex. When the tendency is to an extremely indefinite response or set of responses to a very complex situation, as when the connection's final degree of strength is commonly due to very large contributions from training, it has seemed more appropriate to replace reflex and instinct by some term like capacity, or tendency, or potentiality. Thus an original tendency to respond to the circumstances of school education by achievement in learning the arts and sciences is called the capacity for scholarship.

There is, of course, no gap between reflexes and instincts, or between instincts and the still less easily describable original tendencies. The fact is that original tendencies range with respect to the nature of the responses from such as are single, simple, definite, uniform within the individual and only slightly variable amongst individuals, to responses that are highly compound, complex, vague, and variable within one individual's life and amongst individuals.

A typical reflex, or instinct, or capacity, as a whole, includes the ability to be sensitive to a certain situation, the ability to make a certain response, and the existence of a bond or connection whereby that response is made to that situation. For instance, the young chick is sensitive to the absence of other members of his species, is able to peep, and is so organized that the absence of other members of the species makes him peep. But the tendency to be sensitive to a certain situation may exist without the existence of a connection therewith of any further exclusive response, and the tendency to make a certain response may exist without the existence of a connection limiting that response exclusively to any single situation. The three-year-old child is by inborn nature markedly sensitive to the presence and acts of other human beings, but the exact nature of his response varies. The original tendency to cry is very strong, but there is no one situation to which it is exclusively bound. Original nature seems to decide that the individual will respond somehow to certain situations more often than it decides just what he will do, and to decide that he will make certain responses more often than it decides just when he will make them. So, for convenience in thinking about man's unlearned equipment, this appearance of *multiple response* to one same situation and *multiple causation* of one same response may be taken roughly as the fact.

2. No Separate Instincts[1]

It will be asserted that there are definite, independent, original instincts which manifest themselves in specific acts in a one-to-one correspondence. Fear, it will be said, is a reality, and so is anger, and rivalry, and love of mastery of others, and self-abasement, maternal love, sexual desire, gregariousness and envy, and each has its own appropriate deed as a result. Of course they are realities. So are suction, rusting of metals, thunder and lightning and lighter-than-air flying machines. But science and invention did not get on as long as men indulged in the notion of special forces to account for such phenomena. Men tried that road, and it only led them into learned ignorance. They spoke of nature's abhorrence of a vacuum; of a force of combustion; of intrinsic nisus toward this and that; of heaviness and levity as forces. It turned out that these "forces" were only the phenomena over again, translated from a specific and concrete form (in which they were at least actual) into a generalized form in which they were verbal. They converted a problem into a solution which afforded a simulated satisfaction.

Advance in insight and control came only when the mind turned squarely around. After it had dawned upon inquirers that their alleged causal forces were only names which condensed into a duplicate form a variety of complex occurrences, they set about breaking up phenomena into minute detail and searching for correlations, that is, for elements in other gross phenomena which also varied. Correspondence of variations of elements took the place of large and imposing forces. The psychology of behavior is only beginning to undergo similar treatment. But as yet we tend to regard sex, hunger, fear, and even much more complex active interests as if they were lump forces, like the combustion or gravity of old-fashioned physical science.

It is not hard to see how the notion of a single and separate tendency grew up in the case of simpler acts like hunger and sex. The paths of motor outlet or discharge are comparatively few and are

[1] Adapted from John Dewey, *Human Nature and Conduct*, pp. 149–57. (Henry Holt & Co., 1922.)

fairly well defined.   Specific bodily organs are conspicuously involved. Hence there is suggested the notion of a correspondingly separate psychic force or impulse.   There are two fallacies in this assumption. The first consists in ignoring the fact that no activity (even one that is limited by routine habit) is confined to the channel which is most flagrantly involved in its execution.   The whole organism is concerned in every act to some extent and in some fashion, internal organs as well as muscular, those of circulation, secretion, etc.   Since the total state of the organism is never exactly twice alike, in so far the phenomena of hunger and sex are never twice the same in fact.   The difference may be negligible for some purposes, and yet give the key for the purposes of a psychological analysis which shall terminate in a correct judgment of value.   Even physiologically the context of organic changes accompanying an act of hunger or sex makes the difference between a normal and a morbid phenomenon.

In the second place, the environment in which the act takes place is never twice alike.   Even when the overt organic discharge is substantially the same, the acts impinge upon a different environment and thus have different consequences.   It is impossible to regard these differences of objective result as indifferent to the quality of the acts.   They are immediately sensed if not clearly perceived; and they are the only *components of the meaning* of the act.   When feelings, dwelling antecedently in the soul, were supposed to be the causes of acts, it was natural to suppose that each psychic element had its own inherent quality which might be directly read off by introspection. But when we surrender this notion, it becomes evident that the only way of telling what an organic act is like is by the sensed or perceptible changes which it occasions.   Some of these will be intra-organic, and (as just indicated) they will vary with every act.   Others will be external to the organism, and these consequences are more important than the intra-organic ones for determining the quality of the act. For they are consequences in which others are concerned and which evoke reactions of favor and disfavor as well as co-operative and resisting activities of a more indirect sort.

A child gives way to what, grossly speaking, we call anger.   Its felt or appreciated quality depends in the first place upon the condition of his organism at the time, and this is never twice alike.   In the second place, the act is at once modified by the environment upon which it impinges so that different consequences are immediately reflected back to the doer. In one case, anger is directed say at older and stronger playmates who immediately avenge themselves upon the offender, perhaps cruelly. In another case, it takes effect upon weaker and impotent children, and the reflected appreciated consequence is one of achievement, victory, power and a knowledge of the means of having one's own way. The notion that anger still remains a single force is a lazy mythology. Even in the cases of hunger and sex, where the channels of action are fairly demarcated by antecedent conditions (or "nature"), the actual content and feel of hunger and sex are indefinitely varied according to their social contexts. Only when a man is starving, is hunger an unqualified natural impulse; as it approaches this limit, it tends to lose, moreover, its psychological distinctiveness and to become a raven of the entire organism.

The treatment of sex by psycho-analysts is most instructive, for it flagrantly exhibits both the consequences of artificial simplification and the transformation of social results into psychic causes. Writers, usually male, hold forth on the psychology of woman, as if they were dealing with a Platonic universal entity, although they habitually treat men as individuals, varying with structure and environment. They treat phenomena which are peculiarly symptoms of the civilization of the West at the present time as if they were the necessary effects of fixed native impulses of human nature. Romantic love as it exists today, with all the varying perturbations it occasions, is as definitely a sign of specific historic conditions as are big battle ships with turbines, internal-combustion engines, and electrically driven machines. It would be as sensible to treat the latter as effects of a single psychic cause as to attribute the phenomena of disturbance and conflict which accompany present sexual relations as manifestations of an original single psychic force or *Libido*. Upon this point at least a Marxian simplification is nearer the truth than that of Jung.

Again it is customary to suppose that there is a single instinct of fear, or at most a few well-defined sub-species of it. In reality, when one is afraid the whole being reacts, and this entire responding organism is never twice the same. In fact, also, every reaction takes place in a different environment, and its meaning is never twice alike, since the difference in environment makes a difference in consequences. There is no such thing as an environment in general; there are specific changing objects and events. Hence the kind of evasion or running away or shrinking up which takes place is directly correlated with specific surrounding conditions. There is no one fear having diverse manifestations; there are as many qualitatively different fears as there are objects responded to and different consequences sensed and observed.

Fear of the dark is different from fear of publicity, fear of the dentist from fear of ghosts, fear of conspicuous success from fear of humiliation, fear of a bat from fear of a bear. Cowardice, embarassment, caution and reverence may all be regarded as forms of fear. They all have certain physical organic acts in common—those of organic shrinkage, gestures of hesitation and retreat. But each is qualitatively unique. Each is what it is in virtue of its total interactions or correlations with other acts and with the environing medium, with consequences. High explosives and the aeroplane have brought into being something new in conduct. There is no error in calling it fear. But there is error, even from a limited clinical standpoint, in permitting the classifying name to blot from view the difference between fear of bombs dropped from the sky and the fears which previously existed. The new fear is just as much and just as little original and native as a child's fear of a stranger.

For any activity is original when it first occurs. As conditions are continually changing, new and *primitive* activities are continually occurring. The traditional psychology of instincts obscures recognition of this fact. It sets up a hard-and-fast preordained class under which specific acts are subsumed, so that their own quality and originality are lost from view. This is why the novelist and dramatist are so much more illuminating as well as more interesting commentators on conduct than is the schematizing psychologist.

The artist makes perceptible individual responses and thus displays a new phase of human nature evoked in new situations. In putting the case visibly and dramatically he reveals vital actualities. The scientific systematizer treats each art as merely another example of some old principle, or as a mechanical combination of elements drawn from a ready-made inventory.

When we recognize the diversity of native activities and the varied ways in which they are modified through interactions with one another in response to different conditions, we are able to understand moral phenomena otherwise baffling. In the career of any impulse activity there are speaking generally three possibilities. It may find a surging, explosive discharge—blind, unintelligent. It may be sublimated—that is, become a factor co-ordinated intelligently with others in a continuing course of action. Thus a gust of anger may, because of its dynamic incorporation into disposition, be converted into an abiding conviction of social injustice to be remedied, and furnish the dynamic to carry the conviction into execution. Or an excitation of sexual attraction may reappear in art or in tranquil domestic attachments and services. Such an outcome represents the normal or desirable functioning of impulse; in which, to use our previous language, the impulse operates as a pivot, or reorganization of habit. Or again a released impulsive activity may be neither immediately expressed in isolated spasmodic action, nor indirectly employed in an enduring interest. It may be "suppressed."

Suppression is not annihilation. "Psychic" energy is no more capable of being abolished than the forms we recognize as physical. If it is neither exploded nor converted, it is turned inwards, to lead a surreptitious, subterranean life. An isolated or spasmodic manifestation is a sign of immaturity, crudity, savagery; a suppressed activity is the cause of all kinds of intellectual and moral pathology. One form of the resulting pathology constitutes "reaction" in the sense in which the historian speaks of reactions. A conventionally familiar instance is Stuart license after Puritan restraint. A striking modern instance is the orgy of extravagance following upon the enforced economies and hardships of war, the moral let-down after its highstrung exalted idealisms, the deliberate carelessness after an attention too intense and too narrow. Outward manifestation of many normal activities had been suppressed. But activities were not suppressed. They were merely dammed up awaiting their chance.

3. Man Not Born Human[1]

Man is not born human. It is only slowly and laboriously, in fruitful contact, co-operation, and conflict with his fellows, that he attains the distinctive qualities of human nature. In the course of his prenatal life he has already passed roughly through, or, as the

[1] From Robert E. Park, *Principles of Human Behavior*, pp. 9–16. (The Zalaz Corporation, 1915.)

biologists say, "recapitulated," the whole history of his animal ancestors. He brings with him at birth a multitude of instincts and tendencies, many of which persist during life and many of which are only what G. Stanley Hall calls "vestigial traces" of his brute ancestry, as is shown by the fact that they are no longer useful and soon disappear.

These non-volitional movements of earliest infancy and of later childhood (such as licking things, clicking with the tongue, grinding the teeth, biting the nails, shrugging corrugations, pulling buttons, or twisting garments, strings, etc., twirling pencils, etc.) are relics of past forms of utilities now essentially obsolete. Ancient modes of locomotion, prehension, balancing, defense, attack, sensuality, etc., are all rehearsed, some quite fully and some only by the faintest mimetic suggestion, flitting spasmodic tensions, gestures, or facial expressions.

Human nature may therefore be regarded on the whole as a superstructure founded on instincts, dispositions, and tendencies, inherited from a long line of human and animal ancestors. It consists mainly in a higher organization of forces, a more subtle distillation of potencies latent in what Thorndike calls "the original nature of man."

The original nature of man is roughly what is common to all men minus all adaptations to tools, houses, clothes, furniture, words, beliefs, religions, laws, science, the arts, and to whatever in other men's behavior is due to adaptations to them. From human nature as we find it, take away, first, all that is in the European but not in the Chinaman, all that is in the Fiji Islander but not in the Esquimaux, all that is local or temporary. Then take away also the effects of all products of human art. What is left of human intellect and character is largely original—not wholly, for all those elements of knowledge which we call ideas and judgments must be subtracted from his responses. Man originally possesses only capacities which, after a given amount of education, will produce ideas and judgments.

Such, in general, is the nature of human beings before that nature has been modified by experience and formed by the education and the discipline of contact and intercourse with their fellows.

Several writers, among them William James, have attempted to make a rough inventory of the special instinctive tendencies with which human beings are equipped at birth. First of all there are the simpler reflexes such as "crying, sneezing, snoring, coughing, sighing, sobbing, gagging, vomiting, hiccuping, starting, moving the limb in response to its being tickled, touched or blown upon, spreading the toes in response to its being touched, tickled, or stroked on the sole of the foot, extending and raising the arms at any sudden sensory stimulus, or the quick pulsation of the eyelid."

Then there are the more complex original tendencies such as sucking, chewing, sitting up, and gurgling. Among the more general unlearned responses of children are fear, anger, pugnacity, envy, jealousy, curiosity, constructiveness, love of festivities, ceremonies and ordeals, sociability and shyness, secretiveness, etc. Thorndike, who quotes this list at length, has sought to give definiteness to its descriptions by clearly defining and distinguishing the character of the situation to which the behavior cited is a response. For example, to the situation, "strange man or animal, to solitude, black things, dark places, holes and corners, a human corpse," the native and unlearned response is fear. The original response of man to being alone is an experience of discomfort, to perceiving a crowd, "a tendency to join them and do what they are doing and an unwillingness to leave off and go home." It is part of man's original nature when he is in love to conceal his love affairs, and so forth.

It is evident from this list that what is meant by original nature is not confined to the behavior which manifests itself at birth, but includes man's spontaneous and unlearned responses to situations as they arise in the experience of the individual.

The widespread interest in the study of children has inspired in recent years a considerable literature bearing upon the original and inherited tendencies of human nature. The difficulty of distinguishing between what is original and what is acquired among the forms of behavior reported upon, and the further difficulty of obtaining accurate descriptions of the situations to which the behavior described was a response, has made much of this literature of doubtful value for scientific purposes. These studies have, nevertheless, contributed to a radical change in our conceptions of human nature. They have shown that the distinction between the mind of man and that of the lower animals is not so wide nor so profound as was once supposed. They have emphasized the fact that human nature rests on animal nature, and the transition from one to the other, in spite of the contrast in their separate achievements, has been made by imperceptible gradations. In the same way they have revealed, beneath differences in culture and individual achievement, the outlines of a pervasive and relatively unchanging human nature in which all races and individuals have a common share.

The study of human nature begins with description, but it goes on from that point to explanation. If the descriptions which we have thus far had of human nature are imperfect and lacking in precision, it is equally true that the explanations thus far invented have, on the whole, been inadequate. One reason for this has been the difficulty of the task. The mechanisms which control human behavior are, as might be expected, tremendously complicated, and the problem of analyzing them into their elementary forms and reducing their varied manifestations to precise and lucid formulas is both intricate and perplexing.

The foundation for the explanation of human nature has been laid, however, by the studies of behavior in animals and the comparative study of the physiology of the nervous system. Progress has been made, on the one hand, by seeking for the precise psychochemical process involved in the nervous reactions, and on the other, by reducing all higher mental processes to elementary forms represented by the tropisms and reflex actions.

In this, science has made a considerable advance upon common sense in its interpretations of human behavior, but has introduced no new principle; it has simply made its statements more detailed and exact. For example, common sense has observed that "the burnt child shuns the fire," that "the moth seeks the flame." These are both statements of truths of undoubted generality. In order to give them the validity of scientific truth, however, we need to know what there is in the nature of the processes involved that makes it inevitable that the child should shun the fire and the moth should seek the flame. It is not sufficient to say that the action in one case is instinctive and in the other intelligent, unless we are able to give precise and definite meanings to those terms; unless, in short, we are able to point out the precise mechanisms through which these reactions are carried out. The following illustration from Loeb's volume on the comparative physiology of the brain will illustrate the distinction between the common sense and the more precise scientific explanation of the behavior in man and the lower animals.

It is a well-known fact that if an ant be removed from a nest and afterward put back it will not be attacked, while almost invariably an ant belonging to another nest will be attacked. It has been customary to use the words memory, enmity, friendship, in describing this fact. Now Bethe made the following experiment: an ant was placed in the liquids (blood and lymph) squeezed out from the bodies of nest companions and was then put back into its nest; it was not attacked. It was then put in the juice taken from the inmates of a "hostile" nest and was at once attacked and killed. Bethe was able to prove by special experiments that these reactions of ants are not learned by experience, but are inherited. The "knowing" of "friend and foe" among ants is thus reduced to different reactions, depending upon the nature of the chemical stimulus and in no way depending upon memory.

Here, again, there is no essential difference between the common sense and the scientific explanation of the behavior of the ant except so far as the scientific explanation is more accurate, defining the precise mechanisms by which the recognition of "friend and foe" is effected, and the limitations to which it is subject.

Another result of the study of the comparative behavior of man and the lower animals has been to convince students that there is no fundamental difference between what was formerly called intelligent and instinctive behavior; that they may rather be reduced, as has been said, to the elementary form of reaction represented by the simple reflex in animals and the tropism in plants. Thus Loeb says:

A prominent psychologist has maintained that reflexes are to be considered as the mechanical effects of acts of volition of past generations. The ganglion-cell seems the only place where such mechanical effects could be stored up. It has therefore been considered the most essential element of the reflex mechanism, the nerve-fibers being regarded, and probably correctly, merely as conductors.

Both the authors who emphasize the purposefulness of the reflex act, and those who see in it only a physical process, have invariably looked upon the ganglion-cell as the principal bearer of the structures for the complex co-ordinated movements in reflex action.

I should have been as little inclined as any other physiologist to doubt the correctness of this conception had not the establishment of the identity of the reactions of animals and plants to light proved the untenability of this view and at the same time offered a different conception of reflexes.

The flight of the moth into the flame is a typical reflex process. The light stimulates the peripheral sense organs, the stimulus passes to the central nervous system, and from there to the muscles of the wings, and the moth is caused to fly into the flame. This reflex process agrees in every point with the heliotropic effects of light on plant organs. Since plants possess no nerves, this identity of animal with plant heliotropism can offer but one inference—these heliotropic effects must depend upon conditions which are common to both animals and plants.

On the other hand, Watson, in his *Introduction to Comparative Psychology*, defines the reflex as "a unit of analysis of instinct," and this means that instinctive actions in man and in animals may be regarded as combinations of simple reflex actions, that is to say of "fairly definite and generally predictable but unlearned responses of lower and higher organisms to stimuli." Many of these reflex responses are not fixed, as they were formerly supposed to be, but "highly unstable and indefinite." This fact makes possible the formation of habits, by combination and fixation of these inherited responses.

These views in the radical form in which they are expressed by Loeb and Watson have naturally enough been the subject of considerable controversy, both on scientific and sentimental grounds. They seem to reduce human behavior to a system of chemical and physical reactions, and rob life of all its spiritual values. On the other hand, it must be remembered that human beings, like other forms of nature, have this mechanical aspect and it is precisely the business of natural science to discover and lay them bare. It is only thus that we are able to gain control over ourselves and of others. It is a matter of common experience that we do form habits and that education and social control are largely dependent upon our ability to establish habits in ourselves and in others. Habit is, in fact, a characteristic example of just what is meant by "mechanism," in the sense in which it is here used. It is through the fixation of habit that we gain that control over our "original nature," which lifts us above the brutes and gives human nature its distinctive character as human. Character is nothing more than the sum and co-ordination of those mechanisms which we call habit and which are formed on the basis of the inherited and instinctive tendencies and dispositions which we share in so large a measure with the lower animals.

4. The Natural Man[1]

"Its first act is a cry, not of wrath, as Kant said, nor a shout of joy, as Schwartz thought, but a snuffling, and then a long, thin, tearless á-á, with the timbre of a Scotch bagpipe, purely automatic, but of discomfort. With this monotonous and dismal cry, with its red, shriveled, parboiled skin (for the child commonly loses weight the first few days), squinting, cross-eyed, pot-bellied, and bow-legged, it is not strange that, if the mother has not followed Froebel's exhortations and come to love her child before birth, there is a brief interval occasionally dangerous to the child before the maternal instinct is fully aroused."

The most curious of all the monkey traits shown by the new-born baby is the one investigated by Dr. Louis Robinson. It was suggested by *The Luck of Roaring Camp*. The question was raised in conversation whether a limp and molluscous baby, unable so much as to hold up its head on its helpless little neck, could do anything so positive as to "rastle with" Kentuck's finger; and the more knowing persons present insisted that a young baby does, as a matter of fact, have a good firm hand-clasp. It occurred to Dr. Robinson that if this was true it was a beautiful Darwinian point, for clinging and swinging by the arms would naturally have been a specialty with our ancestors if they ever lived a monkey-like life in the trees. The baby that could cling best to its mother as she used hands, feet, and tail to flee in the best time over the trees, or to get at the more inaccessible fruits and eggs in time of scarcity, would be the baby that lived to bequeath his traits to his descendants; so that to this day our housed and cradled human babies would keep in their clinging powers a reminiscence of our wild treetop days.

There is another class of movements, often confused with the reflex—that is, instinctive movements. Real grasping (as distinguished from reflex grasping), biting, standing, walking, are examples of this class. They are race movements, the habits of the species to which the animal belongs, and every normal member of the species is bound to come to them; yet they are not so fixed in the bodily mechanism as the reflex movements.

[1] Adapted from Milicent W. Shinn, *The Biography of a Baby*, pp. 20-77. (Houghton Mifflin Co., 1900. Author's copyright.'

The one instinct the human baby always brings into the world already developed is half a mere reflex act—that of sucking. It is started as a reflex would be, by the touch of some object—pencil, finger, or nipple, it may be—between the lips; but it does not act like a reflex after that. It continues and ceases without reference to this external stimulus, and a little later often begins without it, or fails to begin when the stimulus is given. If it has originally a reflex character, that character fades out and leaves it a pure instinct.

My little niece evidently felt a difference between light and darkness from the first hour, for she stopped crying when her face was exposed to gentle light. Two or three report also a turning of the head toward the light within the first week. The nurse, who was intelligent and exact, thought she saw this in the case of my niece. I did not, but I saw instead a constant turning of the eyes toward a person coming near her—that is, toward a large dark mass that interrupted the light. No other sign of vision appeared in the little one during the first fortnight. The eyes were directed to nothing, fixed on nothing. They did not wink if one made a pass at them. There was no change of focus for near or distant seeing.

The baby showed no sign of hearing anything until the third day, when she started violently at the sound of tearing paper, some eight feet from her. After that, occasional harsh or sudden sounds—oftener the rustling of paper than anything else—could make her start or cry. It is well established by the careful tests of several physiologists that babies are deaf for a period lasting from several hours to several days after birth.

Taste and smell were senses that the baby gave no sign of owning till much later. The satisfaction of hunger was quite enough to account for the contentment she showed in nursing; and when she was not hungry she would suck the most tasteless object as cheerfully as any other.

Our baby showed from the first that she was aware when she was touched. She stopped crying when she was cuddled or patted. She showed comfort in the bath, which may have been in part due to freedom from the contact of clothes, and to liking for the soft touches of the water. She responded with sucking motions to the first touch of the nipple on her lips.

Our baby showed temperament—luckily of the easy-going and cheerful kind—from her first day, though we could hardly see this except by looking backward. On the twenty-fifth day, toward evening, when the baby was lying on her grandmother's knee by the fire, in a condition of high well-being and content, gazing at her grandmother's face with an expression of attention, I came and sat down close by, leaning over the baby, so that my face must have come within the indirect range of her vision. At that she turned her eyes to my face and gazed at it with the same appearance of attention, and even of some effort, shown by the slight tension of brows and lips, then turned her eyes back to her grandmother's face, and again to mine, and so several times. The last time she seemed to catch sight of my shoulder, on which a high light struck from the lamp, and not only moved her eyes but threw her head far back to see it better, and gazed for some time with a new expression on her face—"a sort of dim and rudimentary eagerness," says my note. She no longer stared, but really looked.

The baby's increased interest in seeing centered especially on the faces about her, at which she gazed with rapt interest. Even during the period of mere staring, faces had oftenest held her eyes, probably because they were oftener brought within the range of her clearest seeing than other light surfaces. The large, light, moving patch of the human face (as Preyer has pointed out) coming and going in the field of vision, and oftener chancing to hover at the point of clearest seeing than any other object, embellished with a play of high lights on cheeks, teeth, and eyes, is calculated to excite the highest degree of attention a baby is capable of at a month old. So from the very first—before the baby has yet really seen his mother—her face and that of his other nearest friends become the most active agents in his development and the most interesting things in his experience.

Our baby was at this time in a way aware of the difference between companionship and solitude. In the latter days of the first month she would lie contentedly in the room with people near by, but would fret if left alone. But by the end of the month she was apt to fret when she was laid down on a chair or lounge, and to become content only when taken into the lap. This was not yet distinct memory and desire, but it showed that associations of pleasure had been formed with the lap, and that she felt a vague discomfort in the absence of these.

Nature has provided an educational appliance almost ideally adapted to the child's sense condition, in the mother's face, hovering close above him, smiling, laughing, nodding, with all manner of delightful changes in the high lights; in the thousand little meaningless caressing sounds, the singing, talking, calling, that proceed from it; the patting, cuddling, lifting, and all the ministrations that the baby feels while gazing at it, and associates with it, till finally they group together and round out into the idea of his mother as a whole.

Our baby's mother rather resented the idea of being to her baby only a collection of detached phenomena, instead of a mamma; but the more you think of it, the more flattering it is to be thus, as it were, dissolved into your elements and incorporated item by item into the very foundations of your baby's mental life. Herein is hinted much of the philosophy of personality; and Professor Baldwin has written a solid book, mainly to show from the development of babies and little children that all other people are part of each of us, and each of us is part of all other people, and so there is really no separate personality, but we are all one spirit, if we did but know it.

5. Sex Differences[1]

As children become physically differentiated in respect of sex, so also does a mental differentiation ensue. Differences are observed in the matter of occupation, of games, of movements, and numerous other details. Since man is to play the active part in life, boys rejoice especially in rough outdoor games. Girls, on the other hand, prefer such games as correspond to their future occupations. Hence their inclination to mother smaller children, and to play with dolls. Watch how a little girl takes care of her doll, washes it, dresses and undresses it. When only six or seven years of age she is often an excellent nurse. Her need to occupy herself in such activities is often so great that she pretends that her doll is ill.

In all kinds of ways, we see the little girl occupying herself in the activities and inclinations of her future existence. She practices house work; she has a little kitchen, in which she cooks for herself

[1] From Albert Moll, *Sexual Life of the Child*, pp. 38–49. Translated from the German by Dr. Eden Paul. (Published by The Macmillan Co., 1902. Reprinted by permission.)

and her doll. She is fond of needlework. The care of her own person, and more especially its adornment, is not forgotten. I remember seeing a girl of three who kept on interrupting her elders' conversation by crying out, "New clothes!" and would not keep quiet until these latter had been duly admired. The love of self-adornment is almost peculiar to female children; boys, on the other hand, prefer rough outdoor games, in which their muscles are actively employed, robber-games, soldier-games, and the like. And whereas, in early childhood, both sexes are fond of very noisy games, the fondness for these disappears earlier in girls than in boys.

Differences between the sexes have been established also by means of experimental psychology, based upon the examination of a very large number of instances. Berthold Hartmann has studied the childish circle of thought, by means of a series of experiments. Schoolboys to the number of 660 and schoolgirls to the number of 652, at ages between five and three-fourths and six and three-fourths years, were subjected to examination. It was very remarkable to see how, in respect to certain ideas, such as those of the triangle, cube, and circle, the girls greatly excelled the boys; whereas in respect of animals, minerals, and social ideas, the boys were better informed than the girls. Characteristic of the differences between the sexes, according to Meumann, from whom I take these details and some of those that follow, is the fact that the idea of "marriage" was known to only 70 boys as compared to 227 girls; whilst the idea of "infant baptism" was known to 180 boys as compared to 220 girls. The idea of "pleasure" was also much better understood by girls than by boys. Examination of the memory has also established the existence of differences between the sexes in childhood. In boys the memory for objects appears to be at first the best developed; to this succeeds the memory for words with a visual content; in the case of girls, the reverse of this was observed. In respect of numerous details, however, the authorities conflict. Very striking is the fact, one upon which a very large number of investigators are agreed, that girls have a superior knowledge of colors.

There are additional psychological data relating to the differences between the sexes in childhood. I may recall Stern's investigations concerning the psychology of evidence, which showed that girls were much more inaccurate than boys.

It has been widely assumed that these psychical differences between the sexes result from education, and are not inborn. Others, however, assume that the psychical characteristics by which the sexes are differentiated result solely from individual differences in education. Stern believes that in the case of one differential character, at least, he can prove that for many centuries there has been no difference between the sexes in the matter of education; this character is the capacity for drawing. Kerschensteiner has studied the development of this gift, and considers that his results have established beyond dispute that girls are greatly inferior in this respect to boys of like age. Stern points out that there can be no question here of cultivation leading to a sexual differentiation of faculty, since there is no attempt at a general and systematic teaching of draughtsmanship to the members of one sex to the exclusion of members of the other.

I believe that we are justified in asserting that at the present time the sexual differentiation manifested in respect of quite a number of psychical qualities is the result of direct inheritance. It would be quite wrong to assume that all these differences arise in each individual in consequence of education. It does, indeed, appear to me to be true that inherited tendencies may be increased or diminished by individual education; and further, that when the inherited tendency is not a very powerful one, it may in this way even be suppressed.

We must not forget the frequent intimate association between structure and function. Rough outdoor games and wrestling thus correspond to the physical constitution of the boy. So, also, it is by no means improbable that the little girl, whose pelvis and hips have already begun to indicate by their development their adaption for the supreme functions of the sexually mature woman, should experience obscurely a certain impulse toward her predestined maternal occupation, and that her inclinations and amusements should in this way be determined. Many, indeed, and above all the extreme advocates of women's rights, prefer to maintain that such sexually differentiated inclinations result solely from differences in individual education: if the boy has no enduring taste for dolls and cooking, this is because his mother and others have told him, perhaps with mockery, that such amusements are unsuited to a boy; whilst in a similar way the girl is dissuaded from the rough sports of boyhood. Such an assumption is the expression of that general psychological and educational tendency, which ascribes to the activity of the will an overwhelmingly powerful influence upon the development of the organs subserving the intellect, and secondarily also upon that of the other organs of the body. We cannot dispute the fact that in such a way the activity of the will may, within certain limits, be effective, especially in cases in which the inherited tendency thus counteracted is comparatively weak; but only within certain limits. Thus we can understand how it is that in some cases, by means of education, a child is impressed with characteristics normally foreign to its sex; qualities and tendencies are thus developed which ordinarily appear only in a child of the opposite sex. But even though we must admit that the activity of the individual may operate in this way, none the less we are compelled to assume that certain tendencies are inborn. The failure of innumerable attempts to counteract such inborn tendencies by means of education throws a strong light upon the limitations of the activity of the individual will; and the same must be said of a large number of other experiences.

Criminological experiences appear also to confirm the notion of an inherited sexual differentiation, in children as well as in adults. According to various statistics, embracing not only the period of childhood, but including as well the period of youth, we learn that girls constitute one-fifth only of the total number of youthful criminals. A number of different explanations have been offered to account for this disproportion. Thus, for instance, attention has been drawn to the fact that a girl's physical weakness renders her incapable of attempting violent assaults upon the person, and this would suffice to explain why it is that girls so rarely commit such crimes. In the case of offenses for which bodily strength is less requisite, such as fraud, theft, etc., the number of youthful female offenders is proportionately larger, although here also they are less numerous than males of corresponding age charged with the like offenses. It has been asserted that in the law courts girls find more sympathy than boys, and that for this reason the former receive milder sentences than the latter; hence it results that in appearance merely the criminality of girls is less than that of boys. Others, again, refer the differences in respect of criminality between the youthful members of the two sexes to the influences of education and general environ-ment. Morrison, however, maintains that all these influences com-bined are yet insufficient to account for the great disproportion between the sexes, and insists that there exists in youth as well as in adult life a specific sexual differentiation, based, for the most part, upon biological differences of a mental and physical character.

Such a marked differentiation as there is between the adult man and the adult woman certainly does not exist in childhood. Similarly in respect of many other qualities, alike bodily and mental, in respect of many inclinations and numerous activities, we find that in child-hood sexual differentiation is less marked than it is in adult life. None the less, a number of sexual differences can be shown to exist even in childhood; and as regards many other differences, though they are not yet apparent, we are nevertheless compelled to assume that they already exist potentially in the organs of the child.

6. Racial Differences[1]

The results of the Cambridge expedition to the Torres Straits have shown that in acuteness of vision, hearing, smell, etc., these peoples are not noticeably different from our own. We conclude that the remarkable tales adduced to the contrary by various travelers are to be explained, not by the acuteness of sensation, but by the acuteness of interpretation of primitive peoples. Take the savage into the streets of a busy city and see what a number of sights and sounds he will neglect because of their meaninglessness to him. Take the sailor whose powers of discerning a ship on the horizon appear to the landsman so extraordinary, and set him to detect micro-organisms in the field of a microscope. Is it then surprising that primitive man should be able to draw inferences which to the stranger appear mar-velous, from the merest specks in the far distance or from the faintest sounds, odors, or tracks in the jungle? Such behavior serves only to attest the extraordinary powers of observation in primitive man with respect to things which are of use and hence of interest to him. The same powers are shown in the vast number of words he will coin to denote the same object, say a certain tree at different stages of its growth.

[1] From C. S. Myers, "On the Permanence of Racial Differences," in *Papers on Inter-racial Problems*, edited by G. Spiller, pp. 74–76. (P. S. King & Son, 1911.)

We concluded, then, that no fundamental difference in powers of sensory acuity, nor, indeed, in sensory discrimination, exists between primitive and civilized communities. Further, there is no proof of any difference in memory between them, save, perhaps, in a greater tendency for primitive folk to use and to excel in mere mechanical learning, in preference to rational learning. But this surely is also the characteristic of the European peasant. He will never commit things to memory by thinking of their meaning, if he can learn them by rote.

In temperament we meet with just the same variations in primitive as in civilized communities. In every primitive society is to be found the flighty, the staid, the energetic, the indolent, the cheerful, the morose, the even-, the hot-tempered, the unthinking, the philosophical individual. At the same time, the average differences between different primitive peoples are as striking as those between the average German and the average Italian.

It is a common but manifest error to suppose that primitive man is distinguished from the civilized peasant in that he is freer and that his conduct is less under control. On the contrary, the savage is probably far more hidebound than we are by social regulations. His life is one round of adherence to the demands of custom. For instance, he may be compelled even to hand over his own children at their birth to others; he may be prohibited from speaking to certain of his relatives; his choice of a wife may be very strictly limited by traditional laws; at every turn there are ceremonies to be performed and presents to be made by him so that misfortune may be safely averted. As to the control which primitive folk exercise over their conduct, this varies enormously among different peoples; but if desired, I could bring many instances of self-control before you which would put to shame the members even of our most civilized communities.

Now since in all these various mental characters no appreciable difference exists between primitive and advanced communities, the question arises, what is the most important difference between them? I shall be told, in the capacity for logical and abstract thought. But by how much logical and abstract thought is the European peasant superior to his primitive brother? Study our country folklore, study the actual practices in regard to healing and religion which prevail in every European peasant community today, and what essential differences are discoverable? Of course, it will be urged that these practices are continued unthinkingly, that they are merely vestiges of a period when once they were believed and were full of meaning. But this, I am convinced, is far from being generally true, and it also certainly applies to many of the ceremonies and customs of primitive peoples.

It will be said that although the European peasant may not in the main think more logically and abstractly, he has, nevertheless, the potentiality for such thought, should only the conditions for its manifestations—education and the like—ever be given. From such as he have been produced the geniuses of Europe—the long line of artists and inventors who have risen from the lowest ranks.

I will consider this objection later. At present it is sufficient for my purpose to have secured the admission that the peasants of Europe do not as a whole use their mental powers in a much more logical or abstract manner than do primitive people. I maintain that such superiority as they have is due to differences (1) of environment and (2) of variability.

We must remember that the European peasant grows up in a (more or less) civilized environment; he learns a (more or less) well-developed and written language, which serves as an easier instrument and a stronger inducement for abstract thought; he is born into a (more or less) advanced religion. All these advantages and the advantage of a more complex education the European peasant owes to his superiors in ability and civilization. Rob the peasant of these opportunities, plunge him into the social environment of present primitive man, and what difference in thinking power will be left between them?

The answer to this question brings me to the second point of difference which I have mentioned—the difference in variability. I have already alluded to the divergencies in temperament to be found among the members of every primitive community. But well marked as are these and other individual differences, I suspect that they are less prominent among primitive than among more advanced peoples. This difference in variability, if really existent, is probably the outcome of more frequent racial admixture and more complex social environment in civilized communities. In another sense, the variability of the savage is indicated by the comparative data afforded by certain psychological investigations. A civilized community may not differ much from a primitive one in the mean or average of a given character, but the extreme deviations which it shows from that mean will be more numerous and more pronounced. This kind of variability has probably another source. The members of a primitive community behave toward the applied test in the simplest manner, by the use of a mental process which we will call A, whereas those of a more advanced civilization employ other mental processes, in addition to A, say B, C, D, or E, each individual using them in different degrees for the performance of one and the same test. Finally, there is in all likelihood a third kind of variability, whose origin is ultimately environmental, which is manifested by extremes of nervous instability. Probably the exceptionally defective and the exceptional genius are more common among civilized than among primitive peoples.

Similar features undoubtedly meet us in the study of sexual differences. The average results of various tests of mental ability applied to men and women are not, on the whole, very different for the two sexes, but the men always show considerably greater individual variation than the women. And here, at all events, the relation between the frequency of mental deficiency and genius in the two sexes is unquestionable. Our asylums contain a considerably greater number of males than of females, as a compensation for which genius is decidedly less frequent in females than in males.

7. Individual Differences[1]

The life of a man is a double series—a series of effects produced in him by the rest of the world, and a series of effects produced in that world by him. A man's make-up or nature equals his tendencies to be influenced in certain ways by the world and to react in certain ways to it.

If we could thus adequately describe each of a million human beings—if, for each one, we could prophesy just what the response would be to every possible situation of life—the million men would be found to differ widely. Probably no two out of the million would

[1] From Edward L. Thorndike, *Individuality*, pp. 1–8. (By permission of and special arrangement with Houghton Mifflin Co., 1911.)

be so alike in mental nature as to be indistinguishable by one who knew their entire natures. Each has an individuality which marks him off from other men. We may study a human being in respect to his common humanity, or in respect to his individuality. In other words, we may study the features of intellect and character which are common to all men, to man as a species; or we may study the differences in intellect and character which distinguish individual men.

Individuals are commonly considered as differing in respect to such traits either quantitatively or qualitatively, either in degree or in kind. A quantitative difference exists when the individuals have different amounts of the same trait. Thus, "John is more attentive to his teacher than James is"; "Mary loves dolls less than Lucy does"; "A had greater devotion to his country than B had"; are reports of quantitative differences, of differences in the amount of what is assumed to be the same kind of thing. A qualitative difference exists when some quality or trait possessed by one individual is lacking in the other. Thus, "Tom knows German, Dick does not"; "A is artistic, B is scientific"; "C is a man of thought, D is a man of action"; are reports of the fact that Tom has some positive amount or degree of the trait "knowledge of German" while Dick has none of it; that A has some positive amount of ability and interest in art while B has zero; whereas B has a positive amount of ability in science, of which A has none; and so on.

A qualitative difference in intellect or character is thus really a quantitative difference wherein one term is zero, or a compound of two or more quantitative differences. All intelligible differences are ultimately quantitative. The difference between any two individuals, if describable at all, is described by comparing the amounts which A possesses of various traits with the amounts which B possesses of the same traits. In intellect and character, differences of kind between one individual and another turn out to be definable, if defined at all, as compound differences of degree.

If we could list all the traits, each representing some one characteristic of human nature, and measure the amount of each of them possessed by a man, we could represent his nature—read his character—in a great equation. John Smith would equal so many units of this, plus so many units of that, and so on. Such a mental inventory would express his individuality conceivably in its entirety and with great exactitude. No such list has been made for any man, much less have the exact amounts of each trait possessed by him been measured. But in certain of the traits, many individuals have been measured; and certain individuals have been measured, each in a large number of traits.

It is useless to recount the traits in which men have been found to differ. For there is no trait in which they do not differ. Of course, if the scale by which individuals are measured is very coarsely divided, their differences may be hidden. If, for example, ability to learn is measured on a scale with only two divisions, (1) "ability to learn less than the average kitten can" and (2) "ability to learn more than the average kitten can," all men may be put in class two, just as if their heights were measured on a scale of one yard, two yards, or three yards, nearly all men would alike be called two yards high. But whenever the scale of measurement is made fine enough, differences at once appear. Their existence is indubitable to any impartial observer. The early psychologists neglected or failed to see them precisely because the early psychology was partial. It believed in a typical or pattern mind, after the manner of which all minds were created, and from whom they differed only by rare accidents. It studied "the mind," and neglected individual minds. It studied "the will" of "man," neglecting the interests, impulses, and habits of actual men.

The differences exist at birth and commonly increase with progress toward maturity. Individuality is already clearly manifest in children of school age. The same situation evokes widely differing responses; the same task is done at differing speeds and with different degrees of success; the same treatment produces differing results. There can be little doubt that of a thousand ten-year-olds taken at random, some will be four times as energetic, industrious, quick, courageous, or honest as others, or will possess four times as much refinement, knowledge of arithmetic, power of self-control, sympathy, or the like. It has been found that among children of the same age and, in essential respects, of the same home training and school advantages, some do in the same time six times as much, or do the same amount with only one-tenth as many errors.

B.   HUMAN NATURE AND SOCIAL LIFE

1.   Human Nature and Its Remaking[1]

Human beings as we find them are artificial products; and for better or for worse they must always be such. Nature has made us: social action and our own efforts must continually remake us. Any attempt to reject art for "nature" can only result in an artificial naturalness which is far less genuine and less pleasing than the natural work of art.

Further, as self-consciousness varies, the amount or degree of this remaking activity will vary. Among the extremely few respects in which human history shows unquestionable growth we must include the degree and range of self-consciousness. The gradual development of psychology as a science and the persistent advance of the subjective or introspective element in literature and in all fine art are tokens of this change. And as a further indication and result, the art of human reshaping has taken definite character, has left its incidental beginnings far behind, has become an institution, a group of institutions.

Wherever a language exists, as a magazine of established meanings, there will be found a repertoire of epithets of praise and blame, at once results and implements of this social process. The simple existence of such a vocabulary acts as a persistent force; but the effect of current ideals is redoubled when a coherent agency, such as public religion, assumes protection of the most searching social maxims and lends to them the weight of all time, all space, all wonder, and all fear. For many centuries religion held within itself the ripening self-knowledge and self-discipline of the human mind. Now, beside this original agency we have its offshoots, politics, education, legislation, the penal art. And the philosophical sciences, including psychology and ethics, are the especial servants of these arts.

As to structure, human nature is undoubtedly the most plastic part of the living world, the most adaptable, the most educable. Of all animals, it is man in whom heredity counts for least, and conscious building forces for most. Consider that his infancy is longest, his instincts least fixed, his brain most unfinished at birth, his powers of habit-making and habit-changing most marked, his susceptibility

[1] From W. E. Hocking, *Human Nature and Its Remaking*, pp. 2–12. (Yale University Press, 1918.)

to social impressions keenest; and it becomes clear that in every way nature, as a prescriptive power, has provided in him for her own displacement. His major instincts and passions first appear on the scene, not as controlling forces, but as elements of *play*, in a prolonged life of play. Other creatures nature could largely finish: the human creature must finish himself.

And as to history, it cannot be said that the results of man's attempts at self-modeling appear to belie the liberty thus promised in his constitution. If he has retired his natural integument in favor of a device called clothing, capable of expressing endless nuances, not alone of status and wealth, but of temper and taste as well— conservatism or venturesomeness, solemnity, gaiety, profusion, color, dignity, carelessness or whim, he has not failed to fashion his inner self into equally various modes of character and custom. That is a hazardous refutation of socialism which consists in pointing out that its success would require a change in human nature. Under the spell of particular ideas monastic communities have flourished, in comparison with whose demands upon human nature the change required by socialism—so far as it calls for purer altruism and not pure economic folly—is trivial. To any one who asserts as a dogma that "human nature never changes," it is fair to reply, "It is human nature to change itself."

When one reflects to what extent racial and national traits are manners of the mind, fixed by social rather than by physical heredity, while the bodily characters themselves may be due in no small measure to sexual choices at first experimental, then imitative, then habitual, one is not disposed to think lightly of the human capacity for self-modification. But it is still possible to be skeptical as to the depth and permanence of any changes which are genuinely voluntary. There are few maxims of conduct, and few laws so contrary to nature that they could not be put into momentary effect by individuals or by communities. Plato's Republic has never been fairly tried; but fragments of this and other Utopias have been common enough in history. No one presumes to limit what men can *attempt;* one only inquires what the silent forces are which determine what can *last.*

What, to be explicit, is the possible future of measures dealing with divorce, with war, with political corruption, with prostitution, with superstition? Enthusiastic idealism is too precious an energy to be wasted if we can spare it false efforts by recognizing those permanent ingredients of our being indicated by the words pugnacity, greed, sex, fear. Machiavelli was not inclined to make little of what an unhampered ruler could do with his subjects; yet he saw in such passions as these a fixed limit to the power of the Prince. "It makes him hated above all things to be rapacious, and to be violator of the property and women of his subjects, from both of which he must abstain." And if Machiavelli's despotism meets its master in the undercurrents of human instinct, governments of less determined stripe, whether of states or of persons, would hardly do well to treat these ultimate data with less respect.

2. Human Nature, Folkways, and the Mores[1]

It is generally taken for granted that men inherited some guiding instincts from their beast ancestry, and it may be true, although it has never been proved. If there were such inheritances, they controlled and aided the first efforts to satisfy needs. Analogy makes it easy to assume that the ways of beasts had produced channels of habit and predisposition along which dexterities and other psychophysical activities would run easily. Experiments with new born animals show that in the absence of any experience of the relation of means to ends, efforts to satisfy needs are clumsy and blundering. The method is that of trial and failure, which produces repeated pain, loss, and disappointments. Nevertheless, it is the method of rude experiment and selection. The earliest efforts of men were of this kind. Need was the impelling force. Pleasure and pain, on the one side and the other, were the rude constraints which defined the line on which efforts must proceed. The ability to distinguish between pleasure and pain is the only psychical power which is to be assumed. Thus ways of doing things were selected which were expedient. They answered the purpose better than other ways, or with less toil and pain. Along the course on which efforts were compelled to go, habit, routine, and skill were developed. The struggle to maintain existence was carried on, not individually, but in groups. Each profited by the other's experience; hence there was concurrence toward that which proved to be most expedient.

[1] From William G. Sumner, *Folkways*, pp. 2–8. (Ginn & Co., 1906.)

All at last adopted the same way for the same purpose; hence the ways turned into customs and became mass phenomena. Instincts were developed in connection with them. In this way folkways arise. The young learn them by tradition, imitation, and authority. The folkways, at a time, provide for all the needs of life then and there. They are uniform, universal in the group, imperative, and invariable.

The operation by which folkways are produced consists in the frequent repetition of petty acts, often by great numbers acting in concert or, at least, acting in the same way when face to face with the same need. The immediate motive is interest. It produces habit in the individual and custom in the group. It is, therefore, in the highest degree original and primitive. Out of the unconscious experiment which every repetition of the ways includes, there issues pleasure or pain, and then, so far as the men are capable of reflection, convictions that the ways are conducive to social welfare. When this conviction as to the relation to welfare is added to the folkways, they are converted into mores, and, by virtue of the philosophical and ethical element added to them, they win utility and importance and become the source of the science and the art of living.

It is of the first importance to notice that, from the first acts by which men try to satisfy needs, each act stands by itself, and looks no further than immediate satisfaction. From recurrent needs arise habits for the individual and customs for the group, but these results are consequences which were never conscious and never foreseen or intended. They are not noticed until they have long existed, and it is still longer before they are appreciated. Another long time must pass, and a higher stage of mental development must be reached, before they can be used as a basis from which to deduce rules for meeting, in the future, problems whose pressure can be foreseen. The folkways, therefore, are not creations of human purpose and wit. They are like products of natural forces which men unconsciously set in operation, or they are like the instinctive ways of animals, which are developed out of experience, which reach a final form of maximum adaptation to an interest, which are handed down by tradition and admit of no exception or variation, yet change to meet new conditions, still within the same limited methods, and without rational reflection or purpose. From this it results that all the life of human beings, in all ages and stages of culture, is primarily controlled by a vast mass of folkways handed down from the earliest existence of the race, having the nature of the ways of other animals, only the topmost layers of which are subject to change and control, and have been somewhat modified by human philosophy, ethics, and religion, or by other acts of intelligent reflection. We are told of savages that "it is difficult to exhaust the customs and small ceremonial usages of a savage people. Custom regulates the whole of a man's actions— his bathing, washing, cutting his hair, eating, drinking, and fasting. From his cradle to his grave he is the slave of ancient usage. In his life there is nothing free, nothing original, nothing spontaneous, no progress toward a higher and better life, and no attempt to improve his condition, mentally, morally, or spiritually." All men act in this way, with only a little wider margin of voluntary variation.

The folkways are, therefore: (1) subject to a strain of improvement toward better adaptation of means to ends, as long as the adaptation is so imperfect that pain is produced. They are also (2) subject to a strain of consistency with each other, because they all answer their several purposes with less friction and antagonism when they co-operate and support each other. The forms of industry, the forms of the family, the notions of property, the constructions of rights, and the types of religion show the strain of consistency with each other through the whole history of civilization. The two great cultural divisions of the human race are the oriental and occidental. Each is consistent throughout; each has its own philosophy and spirit; they are separated from top to bottom by different mores, different standpoints, different ways, and different notions of what societal arrangements are advantageous. In their contrast they keep before our minds the possible range of divergence in the solution of the great problems of human life, and in the views of earthly existence by which life-policy may be controlled. If two planets were joined in one, their inhabitants could not differ more widely as to what things are best worth seeking, or what ways are most expedient for well-living.

Custom is the product of concurrent action through time. We find it existent and in control at the extreme reach of our investigations. Whence does it begin, and how does it come to be? How can it give guidance "at the outset"? All mass actions seem to begin because the mass wants to act together. The less they know what it is right and best to do, the more open they are to suggestion from an incident in nature, or from a chance act of one, or from the current doctrines of ghost fear. A concurrent drift begins which is subject to later correction. That being so, it is evident that instinctive action, under the guidance of traditional folkways, is an operation of the first importance in all societal matters. Since the custom never can be antecedent to all action, what we should desire most is to see it arise out of the first actions, but, inasmuch as that is impossible, the course of the action after it is started is our field of study. The origin of primitive customs is always lost in mystery, because when the action begins the men are never conscious of historical action or of the historical importance of what they are doing. When they become conscious of the historical importance of their acts, the origin is already far behind.

3. Habit and Custom, the Individual and the General Will[1]

The term *Sitte* (mores) is a synonym of habit and of usage, of convention and tradition, but also of fashion, propriety, practise, and the like. Those words which characterize the habitual are usually regarded as having essentially unequivocal meanings. The truth is that language, careless of the more fundamental distinctions, confuses widely different connotations. For example, I find that custom—to return to this most common expression—has a threefold significance, namely:

1. *The meaning of a simple objective matter of fact.*—In this sense we speak of the man with the habit of early rising, or of walking at a particular time, or of taking an afternoon nap. By this we mean merely that he is accustomed to do so, he does it regularly, it is a part of his manner of life. It is easily understood how this meaning passes over into the next:

2. *The meaning of a rule, of a norm which the man sets up for himself.*—For example, we say he has made this or that a custom, and in a like meaning, he has made it a rule, or even a law; and we mean that this habit works like a law or a precept. By it a person governs himself and regards habit as an imperative command. a structure of subjective kind, that, however, has objective form and recognition.

[1] Translated and adapted from Ferdinand Tönnies, *Die Sitte*, pp. 7–14. (Literarische Anstalt, Rütten und Loening, 1909.)

The precept will be formulated, the original will be copied. A rule may be presented as enjoined, insisted upon, imposed as a command which brings up the third meaning of habit:

3. *An expression for a thing willed, or a will.*—This third meaning, which is generally given the least consideration, is the most significant. If, in truth, habit is the will of man, then this alone can be his real will. In this sense the proverb is significant that habit is called a second nature, and that man is a creature of habit. Habit is, in fact, a psychic disposition, which drives and urges to a specific act, and this is the will in its most outstanding form, as decision, or as "fixed" purpose.

Imperceptibly, the habitual passes over into the instinctive and the impulsive. What we are accustomed to do, that we do "automatically." Likewise we automatically make gestures, movements of welcome and aversion which we have never learned but which we do "naturally." They have their springs of action in the instinct of self-preservation and in the feelings connected with it. But what we are accustomed to do, we must first have learned and practiced. It is just that practice, the frequent repetition, that brings about the performance of the act "of itself," like a reflex, rapidly and easily. The rope dancer is able to walk the rope, because he is accustomed to it. Habit and practice are also the reasons not only why a man can perform something but also why he performs it with relatively less effort and attention. Habit is the basis not only for our knowing something but also for our actually doing it. Habit operates as a kind of stimulus, and, as may be said, as necessity. The "power of habit" has often been described and often condemned.

As a rule, opinions (mental attitudes) are dependent upon habit, by which they are conditioned and circumscribed. Yet, of course, opinions can also detach themselves from habit, and rise above it, and this is done successfully when they become general opinions, principles, convictions. As such they gain strength which may even break down and overcome habit. Faith, taken in the conventional religious sense of assurance of things hoped for, is a primitive form of will. While in general habit and opinion on the whole agree, there is nevertheless in their relations the seeds of conflict and struggle. Thought continually tends to become the dominating element of the mind, and man thereby becomes the more human.

The same meaning that the will, in the usual individual sense, has for individual man, the social will has for any community or society, whether there be a mere loose relationship, or a formal union and permanent association. And what is this meaning? I have pointed this out in my discussion of habit, and present here the more general statement: The social will is the general volition which serves for the government and regulation of individual wills. Every general volition can be conceived as corresponding to a "thou shalt," and in so far as an individual or an association of individuals directs this "thou shalt" to itself, we recognize the autonomy and freedom of this individual or of this association. The necessary consequence of this is that the individual against all opposing inclinations and opinions, the association against opposing individuals, wherever their opposition manifests itself, attempt, at least, to carry through their will so that they work as a constraint and exert pressure. And this is essentially independent of the means which are used to that end. These pressures extend, at least in the social sense, from measures of persuasion, which appeal to a sense of honor and of shame, to actual coercion and punishment which may take the form of physical compulsion. *Sitte* develops into the most unbending, overpowering force.

4. The Law, Conscience, and the General Will[1]

In the English language we have no name for it (*Sittlichkeit*), and this is unfortunate, for the lack of a distinctive name has occasioned confusion both of thought and of expression. *Sittlichkeit* is the system of habitual or customary conduct, ethical rather than legal, which embraces all those obligations of the citizen which it is "bad form" or "not the thing" to disregard. Indeed, regard for these obligations is frequently enjoined merely by the social penalty of being "cut" or looked on askance. And yet the system is so generally accepted and is held in so high regard, that no one can venture to disregard it without in some way suffering at the hands of his neighbors for so doing. If a man maltreats his wife and children, or habitually jostles his fellow-citizens in the street, or does things flagrantly selfish or in bad taste, he is pretty sure to find himself in a

[1] From Viscount Haldane, "Higher Nationality," in *International Conciliation*, November, 1913, No. 72, pp. 4-12.

minority and the worse off in the end. But not only does it not pay to do these things, but the decent man does not wish to do them. A feeling analogous to what arises from the dictates of his more private and individual conscience restrains him. He finds himself so restrained in the ordinary affairs of daily life. But he is guided in his conduct by no mere inward feeling, as in the case of conscience. Conscience and, for that matter, law, overlap parts of the sphere of social obligation about which I am speaking. A rule of conduct may, indeed, appear in more than one sphere, and may consequently have a twofold sanction. But the guide to which the citizen mostly looks is just the standard recognized by the community, a community made up mainly of those fellow-citizens whose good opinion he respects and desires to have. He has everywhere round him an object-lesson in the conduct of decent people toward each other and toward the community to which they belong. Without such conduct and the restraints which it imposes there could be no tolerable social life, and real freedom from interference would not be enjoyed. It is the instinctive sense of what to do and what not to do in daily life and behavior that is the source of liberty and ease. And it is this instinctive sense of obligation that is the chief foundation of society. Its reality takes objective shape and displays itself in family life and in our other civic and social institutions. It is not limited to any one form, and it is capable of manifesting itself in new forms and of developing and changing old forms. Indeed, the civic community is more than a political fabric. It includes all the social institutions in and by which the individual life is influenced—such as are the family, the school, the church, the legislature, and the executive. None of these can subsist in isolation from the rest; together they and other institutions of the kind form a single organic whole, the whole which is known as the nation. The spirit and habit of life which this organic entirety inspires and compels are what, for my present purpose, I mean by *Sittlichkeit.*

Sitte is the German for custom, and *Sittlichkeit* implies custom and a habit of mind and action. It also implies a little more. Fichte defines it in words which are worth quoting, and which I will put into English:

What, to begin with, does *Sitte* signify, and in what sense do we use the word? It means for us, and means in every accurate reference we make of it, those principles of conduct which regulate people in their relations to each other, and which have become matter of habit and second nature at the stage of culture reached, and of which, therefore, we are not explicitly conscious. Principles, we call them, because we do not refer to the sort of conduct that is casual or is determined on casual grounds, but to the hidden and uniform ground of action which we assume to be present in the man whose action is not deflected and from which we can pretty certainly predict what he will do. Principles, we say, which have become a second nature and of which we are not explicitly conscious. We thus exclude all impulses and motives based on free individual choice, the inward aspect of *Sittlichkeit*, that is to say, morality, and also the outward side, or law, alike. For what a man has first to reflect over and then freely to resolve is not for him a habit in conduct; and in so far as habit in conduct is associated with a particular age, it is regarded as the unconscious instrument of the Time Spirit.

The system of ethical habit in a community is of a dominating character, for the decision and influence of the whole community is embodied in that social habit. Because such conduct is systematic and covers the whole of the field of society, the individual will is closely related by it to the will and the spirit of the community. And out of this relation arises the power of adequately controlling the conduct of the individual. If this power fails or becomes weak, the community degenerates and may fall to pieces. Different nations excel in their *Sittlichkeit* in different fashions. The spirit of the community and its ideals may vary greatly. There may be a low level of *Sittlichkeit;* and we have the spectacle of nations which have even degenerated in this respect. It may possibly conflict with law and morality, as in the case of the duel. But when its level is high in a nation we admire the system, for we see it not only guiding a people and binding them together for national effort, but affording the greatest freedom of thought and action for those who in daily life habitually act in harmony with the General Will.

Thus we have in the case of a community, be it the city or be it the state, an illustration of a sanction which is sufficient to compel observance of a rule without any question of the application of force. This kind of sanction may be of a highly compelling quality, and it often extends so far as to make the individual prefer the good of the community to his own. The development of many of our social institutions, of our hospitals, of our universities, and of other establishments of the kind, shows the extent to which it reaches and is powerful.   But it has yet higher forms in which it approaches very nearly to the level of the obligation of conscience, although it is distinct from that form of obligation.   I will try to make clear what I mean by illustrations.   A man may be impelled to action of a high order by his sense of unity with the society to which he belongs, action of which, from the civic standpoint, all approve.   What he does in such a case is natural to him, and is done without thought of reward or punishment; but it has reference to standards of conduct set up by society and accepted just because society has set them up. There is a poem by the late Sir Alfred Lyall which exemplifies the high level that may be reached in such conduct.   The poem is called *Theology in Extremis*, and it describes the feelings of an Englishman who had been taken prisoner by Mahometan rebels in the Indian Mutiny.   He is face to face with a cruel death.   They offer him his life if he will repeat something from the Koran.   If he complies, no one is likely ever to hear of it, and he will be free to return to England and to the woman he loves.   Moreover, and here is the real point, he is not a believer in Christianity, so that it is no question of denying his Savior.   What ought he to do?   Deliverance is easy, and the relief and advantage would be unspeakably great.   But he does not really hesitate, and every shadow of doubt disappears when he hears his fellow-prisoner, a half-caste, pattering eagerly the words demanded.

I will take another example, this time from the literature of ancient Greece.   In one of the shortest but not least impressive of his *Dialogues*, the "Crito," Plato tells us of the character of Socrates, not as a philosopher, but as a good citizen.   He has been unjustly condemned by the Athenians as an enemy to the good of the state. Crito comes to him in prison to persuade him to escape.   He urges on him many arguments, his duty to his children included.   But Socrates refuses.   He chooses to follow, not what anyone in the crowd might do, but the example which the ideal citizen should set. It would be a breach of his duty to fly from the judgment duly passed in the Athens to which he belongs, even though he thinks the decree should have been different.   For it is the decree of the established justice of his city state.   He will not "play truant."   He hears the words, "Listen, Socrates, to us who have brought you up";

and in reply he refuses to go away, in these final sentences: "This is the voice which I seem to hear murmuring in my ears, like the sound of the flute in the ears of the mystic; that voice, I say, is murmuring in my ears, and prevents me from hearing any other. And I know that anything more which you may say will be vain."

Why do men of this stamp act so, it may be when leading the battle line, it may be at critical moments of quite other kinds? It is, I think, because they are more than mere individuals. Individual they are, but completely real, even as individual, only in their relation to organic and social wholes in which they are members, such as the family, the city, the state. There is in every truly organized community a Common Will which is willed by those who compose that community, and who in so willing are more than isolated men and women. It is not, indeed, as unrelated atoms that they have lived. They have grown, from the receptive days of childhood up to maturity, in an atmosphere of example and general custom, and their lives have widened out from one little world to other and higher worlds, so that, through occupying successive stations in life, they more and more come to make their own the life of the social whole in which they move and have their being. They cannot mark off or define their own individualities without reference to the individualities of others. And so they unconsciously find themselves as in truth pulse-beats of the whole system, and themselves the whole system. It is real in them and they in it. They are real only because they are social. The notion that the individual is the highest form of reality, and that the relationship of individuals is one of mere contract, the notion of Hobbes and of Bentham and of Austin, turns out to be quite inadequate. Even of an every-day contract, that of marriage, it has been well said that it is a contract to pass out of the sphere of contract, and that it is possible only because the contracting parties are already beyond and above that sphere. As a modern writer, F. H. Bradley of Oxford, to whose investigations in these regions we owe much, has finely said: "The moral organism is not a mere animal organism. In the latter the member is not aware of itself as such, while in the former it knows itself, and therefore knows the whole in itself. The narrow external function of the man is not the whole man. He has a life which we cannot see with our eyes, and there is no duty so mean that it is not the realization of this, and knowable as such. What counts is not the visible outer work so much as the spirit in which it is done. The breadth of my life is not measured by the multitude of my pursuits, nor the space I take up amongst other men; but by the fulness of the whole life which I know as mine. It is true that less now depends on each of us as this or that man; it is not true that our individuality is therefore lessened; that therefore we have less in us."

There is, according to this view, a General Will with which the will of the good citizen is in accord. He feels that he would despise himself were his private will not in harmony with it. The notion of the reality of such a will is no new one. It is as old as the Greeks, for whom the moral order and the city state were closely related; and we find it in modern books in which we do not look for it. Jean Jacques Rousseau is probably best known to the world by the famous words in which he begins the first chapter of the *Social Contract:* "Man is born free, and everywhere he is in chains. Those who think themselves to be the masters of others cease not to be greater slaves than the people they govern." He goes on in the next paragraph to tell us that if he were only to consider force and the effects of it, he would say that if a nation was constrained to obey and did obey, it did well, but that whenever it could throw off its yoke and did throw it off, it acted better. His words, written in 1762, became a text for the pioneers of the French Revolution. But they would have done well to read further into the book. As Rousseau goes on, we find a different conception. He passes from considering the fiction of a social contract to a discussion of the power over the individual of the General Will, by virtue of which a people becomes a people. This General Will, the *Volonté Générale*, he distinguishes from the *Volonté de Tous*, which is a mere numerical sum of individual wills. These particular wills do not rise above themselves. The General Will, on the other hand, represents what is greater than the individual volition of those who compose the society of which it is the will. On occasions, this higher will is more apparent than at other times. But it may, if there is social slackness, be difficult to distinguish from a mere aggregate of voices, from the will of a mob. What is interesting is that Rousseau, so often associated with doctrine of quite another kind, should finally recognize the bond of a General Will as what really holds the community together. For him, as for those who have had a yet clearer grasp of the principle, in willing the General Will we not only realize our true selves but we may rise above our ordinary habit of mind. We may reach heights which we could not reach, or which at all events most of us could not reach, in isolation. There are few observers who have not been impressed with the wonderful unity and concentration of purpose which an entire nation may display—above all, in a period of crisis. We see it in time of war, when a nation is fighting for its life or for a great cause. We have marvelled at the illustrations with which history abounds of the General Will rising to heights of which but few of the individual citizens in whom it is embodied have ever before been conscious even in their dreams.

By leadership a common ideal can be made to penetrate the soul of a people and to take complete possession of it. The ideal may be very high, or it may be of so ordinary a kind that we are not conscious of it without the effort of reflection. But when it is there it influences and guides daily conduct. Such idealism passes beyond the sphere of law, which provides only what is necessary for mutual protection and liberty of just action. It falls short, on the other hand, in quality of the dictates of what Kant called the Categorical Imperative that rules the private and individual conscience, but that alone, an Imperative which therefore gives insufficient guidance for ordinary and daily social life. Yet the ideal of which I speak is not the less binding; and it is recognized as so binding that the conduct of all good men conforms to it.

C. PERSONALITY AND THE SOCIAL SELF

1. The Organism as Personality[1]

The organism and the brain, as its highest representation, constitute the real personality, containing in itself all that we have been, and the possibility of all that we shall be. The complete individual character is inscribed there with all its active and passive aptitudes, sympathies, and antipathies; its genius, talents, or stupidity; its virtues, vices, torpor, or activity. Of all these, what emerges and actually reaches consciousness is only a small item com-

---

[1] From Th. Ribot, *The Diseases of Personality*, pp. 156–57. Translated from the French. (The Open Court Publishing Co., 1891.)

pared with what remains buried below, albeit still active. Conscious personality is always but a feeble portion of physical personality.

The unity of the ego, consequently, is not that of the one-entity of spiritualists which is dispersed into multiple phenomena, but the co-ordination of a certain number of incessantly renascent states, having for their support the vague sense of our bodies. This unity does not pass from above to below, but from below to above; the unity of the ego is not an initial, but a terminal point.

Does there really exist a perfect unity? Evidently not in the strict, mathematical sense. In a relative sense it is met with, rarely and incidentally. In a clever marksman in the act of taking aim, or in a skilled surgeon performing a difficult operation all is found to converge, both physically and mentally. Still, let us take note of the result: in these conditions the awareness of real personality disappears; the conscious individual is reduced to an idea; whence it would follow that perfect unity of consciousness and the awareness of personality exclude each other. By a different course we again reach the same conclusion; the ego is a co-ordination. It oscillates between two extreme points at which it ceases to exist: viz., perfect unity and absolute inco-ordination. All the intermediate degrees are met with, in fact, and without any line of demarcation between the healthy and the morbid; the one encroaches upon the other.

Even in the normal state the co-ordination is often sufficiently loose to allow several series to co-exist separately. We can walk or perform manual work with a vague and intermittent consciousness of the movements, at the same time singing, musing; but if the activity of thought increases, the singing will cease. With many people it is a kind of substitute for intellectual activity, an intermediate state between thinking and not-thinking.

The unity of the ego, in a psychological sense, is, therefore, the cohesion, during a given time, of a certain number of clear states of consciousness, accompanied by others less clear, and by a multitude of physiological states which, without being accompanied by consciousness like the others, yet operate as much as, and even more than, the former. Unity, in fact, means co-ordination. The conclusion to be drawn from the above remarks is namely this, that the consensus of consciousness being subordinate to the consensus of the organism, the problem of the unity of the ego is, in its ultimate form, a biological problem. To biology pertains the task of explaining, if it can, the genesis of organisms and the solidarity of their component parts. Psychological interpretation can only follow in its wake.

2. Personality as a Complex[1]

Ideas, after being experienced in consciousness, become dormant (conserved as physiological dispositions) and may or may not afterward be reawakened in consciousness as memories. Many such ideas, under conditions with some of which we are all familiar, tend to form part of our voluntary or involuntary memories and many do not. But when such is the case, the memories do not ordinarily include the whole of a given mental experience, but only excerpts or abstracts of it. Hence one reason for the fallibility of human memory and consequent testimony.

Now under special conditions, the ideas making up an experience at any given moment tend to become organized into a system or complex, so that when we later think of the experience or recall any of the ideas belonging to it, the complex as a whole is revived. This is one of the principles underlying the mechanism of memory. Thus it happens that memory may, to a large extent, be made up of complexes. These complexes may be very loosely organized in that the elementary ideas are weakly bound together, in which case, when we try to recall the original experience, only a part of it is recalled. Or a complex may be very strongly organized, owing to the conditions under which it is formed, and then a large part of the experience can be recalled. In this case, any idea associated with some element in the complex may, by the law of association, revive the whole original complex. If, for instance, we have gone through a railroad accident involving exciting incidents, loss of life, etc., the words "railroad," "accident," "death," or a sudden crashing sound, or the sight of blood, or even riding in a railroad train may recall the experience from beginning to end, or at least the prominent features in it, i.e., so much as was organized. The memory of the greater part of this experience is well organized, while the earlier events and those succeeding the accident may have passed out of all possibility of voluntary recall.

[1] From Morton Prince, "The Unconscious," in the *Journal of Abnormal Psychology*, III (1908–9), 277–96, 426.

To take an instance commonplace enough but which happens to have just come within my observation: A fireman was injured severely by being thrown from a hose wagon rushing to a fire against a telegraph pole with which the wagon collided. He narrowly escaped death. Although three years have passed he still cannot ride on a wagon to a fire without the memory of the whole accident rising in his mind. When he does so he again lives through the accident, including the thoughts just previous to the actual collision when, realizing his situation, he was overcome with terror, and he again manifests all the organic physical expressions of fear, viz.: perspiration, tremor, and muscular weakness. Here is a well-organized and fairly limited complex.

Among the loosely organized complexes in many individuals, and possibly in all of us, there are certain dispositions toward views of life which represent natural inclinations, desires, and modes of activity which, for one reason or another, we tend to suppress or are unable to give full play to. Many individuals, for example, are compelled by the exactions of their duties and responsibilities to lead serious lives, to devote themselves to pursuits which demand all their energies and thought and which, therefore, do not permit of indulgence in the lighter enjoyments of life, and yet there may be a natural inclination to partake of the pleasures which innately appeal to all mankind and which many pursue. The longing for these recurs from time to time. The mind dwells on them, the imagination is excited and weaves a fabric of pictures, thoughts, and emotions which thus become associated into a complex. There may be a rebellion and "kicking against the pricks" and thereby a liberation of the emotional force that impresses a stronger organization on the whole process. The recurrence of such a complex is one form of what we call a "mood," which has a distinctly emotional tone of its own. The revival of this feeling tone tends to revive the associated ideas and vice versa. Such a feeling-idea complex is often spoken of as "a side to one's character," to which a person may from time to time give play. Or the converse of this may hold, and a person who devotes his life to the lighter enjoyments may have aspirations and longings for more serious pursuits, and in this respect the imagination may similarly build up a complex which may express itself in a mood. Thus a person is often said to have "many sides to his character," and exhibits certain alternations of personality which may be regarded as normal prototypes of those which occur as abnormal states.

Most of what has been said about the formation of complexes is a statement of commonplace facts, and I would not repeat it here were it not that, in certain abnormal conditions, disposition, subject, and other complexes, though loosely organized, often play an important part. This is not the place to enter into an explanation of dissociated personality, but in such conditions we sometimes find that disposition complexes, for instance, come to the surface and displace or substitute themselves for the other complexes which make up a personality. A complex which is only a mood or a "side of the character" of a normal individual may, in conditions of dissociation, become the main, perhaps sole, complex and chief characteristic of the new personality. In Miss Beauchamp, for instance, the personality known as BI was made up almost entirely of the religious and ethical ideas which formed one side of the original self. In the personality known as Sally we had for the most part the complex which represented the enjoyment of youthful pleasures and sports, the freedom from conventionalities and artificial restraints generally imposed by duties and responsibilities. In BIV the complex represented the ambitions and activities of practical life. In Miss Beauchamp as a whole, normal, without disintegration, it was easy to recognize all three dispositions as "sides of her character," though each was kept ordinarily within proper bounds by the correcting influence of the others. It was only necessary to put her in an environment which encouraged one or the other side, to associate her with people who strongly suggested one or the other of her own characteristics, whether religious, social, pleasure loving, or intellectual, to see the characteristics of BI, Sally, or BIV stand out in relief as the predominant personality. Then we had the alternating play of these different sides of her character.

In fact, the total of our complexes, which, regarded as a whole and in view of their reaction to the environment, their behavior under the various conditions of social life, their aptitudes, feeling-tones, "habits," and faculties, we term character and personality, are in large part predetermined by the mental experiences of the past and the vestiges of memory which have been left as residual from these experiences. We are the offspring of our past.

The great mass of our ideas involve associations of the origin of which we are unaware because the memories of the original experience have become split and a large portion thus has become forgotten even if ever fully appreciated.   We all have our prejudices, our likes and dislikes, our tastes and aversions; it would tax our ingenuity to give a sufficient psychological account of their origin.   They were born long ago in educational, social, personal, and other experiences, the details of which we have this many a year forgotten.   It is the residua of these experiences that have persisted and become associated into complexes which are retained as traits of our personality.

3.   The Self as the Individual's Conception of His Rôle[1]

Suggestion may have its end and aim in the creation of a new personality.   The experimenter then chooses the sort of personality he wishes to induce and obliges the subject to realize it.   Experiments of this kind succeeding in a great many somnambulists, and usually producing very curious results, have long been known and have been repeated, one might say, almost to satiety within the last few years.

When we are awake and in full possession of all our faculties we can imagine sensations different from those which we ordinarily experience.   For example, when I am sitting quietly at my table engaged in writing this book, I can conceive the sensations that a soldier, a woman, an artist, or an Englishman would experience in such and such a situation.   But, however fantastic the conceptions may be that we form, we do not cease to be conscious withal of our own personal existence.   Imagination has taken flight fairly in space, but the memory of ourselves always remains behind.   Each of us knows that he is himself and not another, that he did this yesterday, that he has just written a letter, that he must write another such letter tomorrow, that he was out of Paris for a week, etc.   It is this memory of passed facts—a memory always present to the mind—that constitutes the consciousness of our normal personality.

It is entirely different in the case of the two women, A—— and B——, that M. Richet studied.

Put to sleep and subjected to certain influences, A—— and B—— forget their identity; their age, their clothing, their sex, their social position, their nationality, the place and the time of their life—all this has entirely

[1] From Alfred Binet, *Alterations of Personality*, pp. 248–57. (D. Appleton & Co., 1896.)

disappeared. Only a single idea remains—a single consciousness—it is the consciousness of the idea and of the new being that dawns upon their imagination.

They have lost the idea of their late existence. They live, talk, and think exactly like the type that is suggested to them. With what tremendous intensity of life these types are realized, only those who have been present at these experiments can know. Description can only give a weak and imperfect idea of it.

Instead of imagining a character simply, they realize it, objectify it. It is not like a hallucination, of which one witnesses the images unfolding before him, as a spectator would. He is rather like an actor who is seized with passion, imagines that the drama he plays is a reality, not a fiction, and that he has been transformed, body and soul, into the personality that he sets himself to play.

In order to have this transformation of personality work it is sufficient to pronounce a word with some authority. I say to A——, "You are an old woman," she considers herself changed into an old woman, and her countenance, her bearing, her feelings, become those of an old woman. I say to B——, "You are a little girl," and she immediately assumes the language, games, and tastes of a little girl.

Although the account of these scenes is quite dull and colorless compared with the sight of the astonishing and sudden transformations themselves, I shall attempt, nevertheless, to describe some of them. I quote some of M——'s *objectivations:*

As a peasant.—She rubs her eyes and stretches herself. "What time is it? Four o'clock in the morning!" She walks as if she were dragging sabots. "Now, then, I must get up. Let us go to the stable. Come up, red one! come up, get about!" She seems to be milking a cow. "Let me alone, Gros-Jean, let me alone, I tell you. When I am through my work. You know well enough that I have not finished my work. Oh! yes, yes, later."

As an actress.—Her face took a smiling aspect instead of the dull and listless manner which she had just had. "You see my skirt? Well, my manager makes me wear it so long. These managers are too tiresome. As for me, the shorter the skirt the better I like it. There is always too much of it. A simple fig leaf! Mon Dieu, that is enough! You agree with me, don't you, my dear, that it is not necessary to have more than a fig leaf? Look then at this great dowdy Lucie—where are her legs, eh?"

As a priest.—She imagines that she is the Archbishop of Paris. Her face becomes very grave. Her voice is mildly sweet and drawling, which forms a great contrast with the harsh, blunt tone she had as a general.

(Aside.) "But I must accomplish my charge." She leans her head on her hand and reflects. (Aloud.) "Ah! it is you, Monsieur Grand Vicar; what is your business with me? I do not wish to be disturbed. Yes, today is the first of January, and I must go to the cathedral. This throng of people is very respectful, don't you think so, monsieur? There is a great deal of religion in the people, whatever one does. Ah! a child! let him come to me to be blessed. There, my child." She holds out to him her imaginary bishop's ring to kiss. During this whole scene she is making gestures of benediction with her right hand on all sides. "Now I have a duty to perform. I must go and pay my respects to the president of the Republic. Ah! Mr. President, I come to offer you my allegiance. It is the wish of the church that you may have many years of life. She knows that she has nothing to fear, notwithstanding cruel attacks, while such an honorable man is at the head of the Republic." She is silent and seems to listen attentively. (Aside.) "Yes, fair promises. Now let us pray!" She kneels down.

As a religious sister.—She immediately kneels down and begins to say her prayers, making a great many signs of the cross; then she arises. "Now to the hospital. There is a wounded man in this ward. Well, my friend, you are a little better this morning, aren't you? Now, then, let me take off your bandage." She gestures as if she were unrolling a bandage. "I shall do it very gently; doesn't that relieve you? There! my poor friend, be as courageous before pain as you were before the enemy."

I might cite other objectivations from A——'s case, in the character of old woman, little girl, young man, gay woman, etc. But the examples given seem sufficient to give some idea of the entire transformation of the personality into this or that imaginary type. It is not a simple dream, it is a *living dream.*

The complete transformation of feelings is not the least curious phenomenon of these objectivations. A—— is timid, but she becomes very daring when she thinks herself a bold person. B—— is silent, she becomes talkative when she represents a talkative person. The disposition is thus completely changed. Old tastes disappear and give place to the new tastes that the new character represented is supposed to have.

In a more recent paper, prepared with the co-operation of M. Ferrari and M. Hericourt, M. Richet has added a curious detail to the preceding experiments. He has shown that the subject on whom a change of personality is imposed not only adapts his speech, gestures, and attitudes to the new personality, but that even his handwriting is modified and brought into relation with the new ideas that absorb his consciousness. This modification of handwriting is an especially interesting discovery, since handwriting, according to current theories, is nothing more than a sort of imitation. I cite some examples borrowed from these authors.

It is suggested in succession to a young student that he is a sly and crafty peasant, then a miser, and finally a very old man. While the subject's features and behavior generally are modified and brought into harmony with the idea of the personality suggested, we may observe also that his handwriting undergoes similar modifications which are not less marked. It has a special character peculiar to each of the new states of personality. In short, the graphic movements change like the gestures generally.

In a note on the handwriting of hysterical patients, I have shown that under the influence of suggested emotions, or under the influence of sensorial stimulations, the handwriting of a hysterical patient may be modified. It gets larger, for example, in cases of dynamogenic excitation.

The characteristic of the suggestion that we have just studied is that it does not bear exclusively on perception or movement— that is to say, on a limited psychic element; but there are comprehensive suggestions. They impose a topic on the subject that he is obliged to develop with all the resources of his intellect and imagination, and if the observations be carefully examined, it will also be seen that in these suggestions the faculties of perception are affected and perverted by the same standard as that of ideation. Thus the subject, under the influence of his assumed personality, ceases to perceive the external world as it exists. He has hallucinations in connection with his new psychological personality. When a bishop, he thinks he is in Notre Dame, and sees a host of the faithful. When a general, he thinks he is surrounded by troops, etc. Things that harmonize with the suggestion are conjured up. This systematic development of states of consciousness belongs to all kinds of suggestions, but is perhaps nowhere else so marked as in these transformations of personality.

On the other hand, everything that is inconsistent with the suggestion gets inhibited and leaves the subject's consciousness. As has been said, alterations of personality imply phenomena of amnesia. In order that the subject may assume the fictitious personality he must begin by forgetting his true personality. The infinite number of memories that represent his past experience and constitute the basis of his normal ego are for the time being effaced, because these memories are inconsistent with the ideal of the suggestion.

4. The Natural Person versus the Social and Conventional Self[1]

Somewhat after the order of Dr. Jekyll and Mr. Hyde I seem to possess two distinct personalities, being both at the same time but presenting no such striking contrast as the Jekyll-Hyde combination. They are about equally virtuous. Their main difference seems to be one of age, one being a decade or so in advance of the other.

At times they work harmoniously together and again at cross-purposes. I do not seem to have developed equally. Part of me sits humbly at the feet of the other part of me and receives advice and instruction. Part of me feels constrained to confess to the other part of me when it has done wrong and meekly receives rebuke. Part of me tries to shock the other part of me and to force the more dignified part to misbehave and giggle and do things not considered correct in polite society.

My younger part delights to tease the older, to doubt her motives, to interrupt her meditations. It wants to play, while my older self is more seriously inclined. My younger self is only twelve years old. This is my real self. To my own mind I am still a little girl with short dresses and a bunch of curls. For some reason my idea of self has never advanced beyond this point. The long dress and the hair piled high will never seem natural. Sometimes I enjoy this duality and again I do not. Sometimes the two parts mingle delightfully together, again they wrangle atrociously, while I (there seems to be a third part of me) sit off and watch the outcome.

The older part gets tired before the younger. The younger, still fresh and in a good humor, undertakes to furnish amusement for the older. I have often thrown myself on the bed wearied and exhausted and been made to shake with laughter at the capers of the younger part of me. They are capers indeed. On these occasions she will carry on conversations with friends—real friends—fairly bristling with witticisms, and although taking both parts herself, the parry and thrust is delightful.

[1] From L. G. Winston, "Myself and I," in the *American Journal of Psychology*, XIX (1908), 562–63.

Sometimes, however, the younger part of me seems to get up all awry. She will carry on quarrels—heated quarrels—from morning to night, taking both sides herself, with persons whom I (the combination) dearly love, and against whom I have no grievance whatever. These are a great distress to my older self.

On other days she seems to take the greatest delight in torturing me with imaginary horrors. She cuts my throat, pulls my eyes out of their sockets, removes tumors, and amputates limbs until I wonder that there is anything left of me. She does it all without administering anæsthetics and seems to enjoy my horror and disgust.

Again, some little jingle or tune will take her fancy and she will repeat it to herself until I am almost driven to madness. Sometimes it is only a word, but it seems to have a fascination for her and she rolls it as a sweet morsel under her tongue until sleep puts an end to it.

Again, if I (the combination) fall ill, one part of me, I have never discovered which, invariably hints that I am not ill at all but merely pretending. So much so that it has become with me a recognized symptom of incipient illness.

Moreover, the younger and older are never on the same side of any question. One leans to wisdom, the other to fun. I am a house divided against itself. The younger longs to dance, to go to the theater and to play cards, all of which the older disapproves. The younger mocks the older, calls her a hypocrite and the like until the older well-nigh believes it herself and almost yields to her pleadings. The older listens sedately to the sermon, while the younger plans her Easter suit or makes fun of the preacher.

The older declares she will never marry, while the younger scouts the idea of being an old maid. But even if she could gain the consent of the older, it were but little better, they differ so as to their ideals.

In society the difference is more marked. I seem to be a combination chaperone and protégée. The older appears at ease, the younger shy and awkward—she has never made her début. If one addresses a remark to her she is thrown into utter confusion until the older rushes to the rescue. My sympathy is with the younger, however, for even to this day I, the combination, can scarce resist the temptation to say nothing when there is nothing to say.

There is something tragic to me in this Siamese-twins arrangement of two so uncongenial. I am at one and the same time pupil and teacher, offender and judge, performer and critic, chaperone and protégée, a prim, precise, old maid and a rollicking schoolgirl, a tomboy and a prude, a saint and sinner. What can result from such a combination? That we get on tolerably is a wonder. Some days, however, we get on admirably together, part of me paying compliments to the other part of me—whole days being given to this—until each of us has such a good opinion of herself and the other that we feel on equal terms and are at our happiest.

But how dreadful are the days when we turn against each other! There are not words enough to express the contempt which we feel for ourselves. We seem to set each other in the corner and the combination as a whole is utterly miserable.

I can but wonder and enjoy and wait to see what Myself and I will make of Me.

5. The Divided Self and Moral Consciousness[1]

Two ways of looking at life are characteristic respectively of what we call the healthy-minded, who need to be born only once, and of the sick souls, who must be twice-born in order to be happy. The result is two different conceptions of the universe of our experience. In the religion of the once-born the world is a sort of rectilineal or one-storied affair, whose accounts are kept in one denomination, whose parts have just the values which naturally they appear to have, and of which a simple algebraic sum of pluses and minuses will give the total worth. Happiness and religious peace consist in living on the plus side of the account. In the religion of the twice-born, on the other hand, the world is a double-storied mystery. Peace cannot be reached by the simple addition of pluses and elimination of minuses from life. Natural good is not simply insufficient in amount and transient; there lurks a falsity in its very being. Cancelled as it all is by death, if not by earlier enemies, it gives no final balance, and can never be the thing intended for our lasting worship. It keeps us from our real good, rather; and renunciation and despair of it are our first step in the direction of the truth. There are two

[1] From William James, *The Varieties of Religious Experience*, pp. 166–73. (Longmans, Green & Co., 1902.)

lives, the natural and the spiritual, and we must lose the one before we can participate in the other.

In their extreme forms, of pure naturalism and pure salvationism, the two types are violently contrasted; though here, as in most other current classifications, the radical extremes are somewhat ideal abstractions, and the concrete human beings whom we oftenest meet are intermediate varieties and mixtures. Practically, however, you all recognize the difference: you understand, for example, the disdain of the Methodist convert for the mere sky-blue healthy-minded moralist; and you likewise enter into the aversion of the latter to what seems to him the diseased subjectivism of the Methodist, dying to live, as he calls it, and making of paradox and the inversion of natural appearances the essence of God's truth.

The psychological basis of the twice-born character seems to be a certain discordancy or heterogeneity in the native temperament of the subject, an incompletely unified moral and intellectual constitution.

"Homo duplex, homo duplex!" writes Alphonse Daudet. "The first time that I perceived that I was two was at the death of my brother Henri, when my father cried out so dramatically, 'He is dead, he is dead!' While my first self wept, my second self thought, 'How truly given was that cry, how fine it would be at the theater.' I was then fourteen years old. This horrible duality has often given me matter for reflection. Oh, this terrible second me, always seated whilst the other is on foot, acting, living, suffering, bestirring itself. This second me that I have never been able to intoxicate, to make shed tears, or put to sleep. And how it sees into things, and how it mocks!"

Some persons are born with an inner constitution which is harmonious and well balanced from the outset. Their impulses are consistent with one another, their will follows without trouble the guidance of their intellect, their passions are not excessive, and their lives are little haunted by regrets. Others are oppositely constituted; and are so in degrees which may vary from something so slight as to result in a merely odd or whimsical inconsistency, to a discordancy of which the consequences may be inconvenient in the extreme. Of the more innocent kinds of heterogeneity I find a good example in Mrs. Annie Besant's autobiography.

I have ever been the queerest mixture of weakness and strength, and have paid heavily for the weakness. As a child I used to suffer tortures of shyness, and if my shoe-lace was untied would feel shamefacedly that every eye was fixed on the unlucky string; as a girl I would shrink away from strangers and think myself unwanted and unliked, so that I was full of eager gratitude to anyone who noticed me kindly; as the young mistress of a house I was afraid of my servants, and would let careless work pass rather than bear the pain of reproving the ill-doer; when I have been lecturing and debating with no lack of spirit on the platform, I have preferred to go without what I wanted at the hotel rather than to ring and make the waiter fetch it. Combative on the platform in defense of any cause I cared for, I shrink from quarrel or disapproval in the house, and am a coward at heart in private while a good fighter in public. How often have I passed unhappy quarters of an hour screwing up my courage to find fault with some subordinate whom my duty compelled me to reprove, and how often have I jeered at myself for a fraud as the doughty platform combatant, when shrinking from blaming some lad or lass for doing their work badly. An unkind look or word has availed to make me shrink myself as a snail into its shell, while, on the platform, opposition makes me speak my best.

This amount of inconsistency will only count as amiable weakness; but a stronger degree of heterogeneity may make havoc of the subject's life. There are persons whose existence is little more than a series of zigzags, as now one tendency and now another gets the upper hand. Their spirit wars with their flesh, they wish for incompatibles, wayward impulses interrupt their most deliberate plans, and their lives are one long drama of repentance and of effort to repair misdemeanors and mistakes.

Whatever the cause of heterogeneous personality may be, we find the extreme examples of it in the psychopathic temperament. All writers about that temperament make the inner heterogeneity prominent in their descriptions. Frequently, indeed, it is only this trait that leads us to ascribe that temperament to a man at all. A *dégénéré supérieur* is simply a man of sensibility in many directions, who finds more difficulty than is common in keeping his spiritual house in order and running his furrow straight, because his feelings and impulses are too keen and too discrepant mutually. In the haunting and insistent ideas, in the irrational impulses, the morbid scruples, dreads, and inhibitions which beset the psychopathic temperament when it is thoroughly pronounced, we have exquisite examples of heterogeneous personality. Bunyan had an obsession of the words, "Sell Christ for this, sell him for that, sell him, sell him!" which would run through his mind a hundred times together, until one day out of breath with retorting, "I will not, I will not," he impulsively said, "Let him go if he will," and this loss of the battle kept him in despair for over a year. The lives of the saints are full of such blasphemous obsessions, ascribed invariably to the direct agency of Satan.

St. Augustine's case is a classic example of discordant personality. You all remember his half-pagan, half-Christian bringing up at Carthage, his emigration to Rome and Milan, his adoption of Manicheism and subsequent skepticism, and his restless search for truth and purity of life; and finally how, distracted by the struggle between the two souls in his breast, and ashamed of his own weakness of will when so many others whom he knew and knew of had thrown off the shackles of sensuality and dedicated themselves to chastity and the higher life, he heard a voice in the garden say, "Sume, lege" (take and read), and opening the Bible at random, saw the text, "not in chambering and wantonness," etc., which seemed directly sent to his address, and laid the inner storm to rest forever. Augustine's psychological genius has given an account of the trouble of having a divided self which has never been surpassed.

The new will which I began to have was not yet strong enough to overcome that other will, strengthened by long indulgence. So these two wills, one old, one new, one carnal, the other spiritual, contended with each other and disturbed my soul. I understood by my own experience what I had read, "Flesh lusteth against spirit, and spirit against flesh." It was myself indeed in both the wills, yet more myself in that which I approved in myself than in that which I disapproved in myself. Yet it was through myself that habit had obtained so fierce a mastery over me, because I had willingly come whither I willed not. Still bound to earth, I refused, O God, to fight on thy side, as much afraid to be freed from all bonds as I ought to have feared being trammeled by them.

Thus the thoughts by which I meditated upon thee were like the efforts of one who would awake, but being overpowered with sleepiness is soon asleep again. Often does a man when heavy sleepiness is on his limbs defer to shake it off, and though not approving it, encourage it; even so I was sure it was better to surrender to thy love than to yield to my own lusts, yet, though the former course convinced me, the latter pleased and held me bound. There was naught in me to answer thy call, "Awake, thou sleeper," but only drawling, drowsy words, "Presently; yes, presently; wait a little while." But the "presently" had no "present," and the "little while" grew long. For I was afraid thou wouldst hear me too soon, and heal me at once of my disease of lust, which I wished to satiate rather than to see extinguished. With what lashes of words did I not scourge my own soul. Yet it shrank back; it refused, though it had no excuse to offer. I said within myself: "Come, let it be done now," and as I said it, I was on the point of the resolve. I all but did it, yet I did not do it. And I made another effort, and almost succeeded, yet I did not reach it, and did not grasp it, hesitating to die to death, and live to life; and the evil to which I was so wonted held me more than the better life I had not tried.

There could be no more perfect description of the divided will, when the higher wishes lack just that last acuteness, that touch of explosive intensity, of dynamogenic quality (to use the slang of the psychologists), that enables them to burst their shell, and make irruption efficaciously into life and quell the lower tendencies forever.

6. Personality of Individuals and of Peoples[1]

In my opinion personality is not merely a unifying and directing principle which controls thought and action, but one which, at the same time, defines the relation of individuals to their fellows. The concept of personality includes, in addition to inner unity and co-ordination of the impulses, a definite attitude directed toward the outer world which is determined by the manner in which the individual organizes his external stimulations.

In this definition the objective aspect of personality is emphasized as over against the subjective. We should not in psychological matters be satisfied with subjective definitions. The mental life is not only a sum of subjective experiences but manifests itself invariably also in a definite series of objective expressions. These objective expressions are the contributions which the personality makes to its external social environment. More than that, only these objective expressions of personality are accessible to external observation and they alone have objective value.

[1] Translated from W. v. Bechterew (V. M. Bekhterev), *Die Persönlichkeit und die Bedingungen ihrer Entwicklung und Gesundheit*, pp. 3-5. (J. F. Bergmann, 1906.)

According to Ribot, the real personality is an organism which is represented at its highest in the brain. The brain embraces all our past and the possibilities of our future. The individual character with all its active and passive peculiarities, with all its antipathies, genius, talents, stupidities, virtues, and vices, its inertia and its energy is predetermined in the brain.

Personality, from the objective point of view, is the psychic individual with all his original characters, an individual in free association with his social *milieu*. Neither innate mental ability, nor creative energy, nor what we call will, in and of themselves, constitutes personality. Nothing less than the totality of psychical manifestations, all these including idiosyncrasies which distinguish one man from another and determine his positive individuality, may be said to characterize, from the objective point of view, the human personality.

The intellectual horizon of persons on different cultural levels varies, but no one, for that reason (because of intellectual inferiority), loses the right to recognition as a person, provided that he maintains, over against his environment, his integrity as an individual and remains a self-determining person. It is the loss of this self-determined individuality alone that renders man completely impersonal. When individual spontaneity is feebly manifested, we speak of an ill-defined or a "passive" personality. Personality is, in short, from the objective point of view, a self-determining individual with a unique nature and a definite status in the social world around him.

If now, on the basis of the preceding definition, we seek to define the significance of personality in social and public life, it appears that personality is the basis upon which all social institutions, movements, and conditions, in short all the phenomena of social life, rest. The people of our time are no more, as in the Golden Age, inarticulate masses. They are a totality of more or less active personalities connected by common interests, in part by racial origin, and by a certain similarity of fundamental psychic traits. A people is a kind of collective personality possessing particular ethnic and psychological characteristics, animated by common political aspirations and political traditions. The progress of peoples, their civilization, and their culture naturally are determined by the advancement of the personalities which compose them. Since the emancipation of mankind from a condition of subjection, the life of peoples and of societies has rested upon the active participation of each member of society in the common welfare which represents the aim of all. The personality, considered as a psychic self-determining individual, asserts itself the more energetically in the general march of historical events, the farther a people is removed from the condition of subjection in which the rights of personality are denied.

In every field of activity, the more advanced personality "blazes a new trail." The passive personality, born in subjection, is disposed merely to imitate and to repeat. The sheer existence of modern states depends less on the crude physical force and its personified agencies, than on the moral cohesion of the personalities who constitute the nation.

Since the beginning of time, it is only the moral values that have endured. Force can support the state only temporarily. When a nation disregards the moral forces and seeks its salvation in the rude clash of arms, it bears within itself the seeds of its own destruction. No army in the world is strong enough to maintain a state, the moral basis of which is shaken, for the strength of the army rests upon its morale.

The importance of personality in the historic life of peoples is manifest in periods when social conditions accelerate the movement of social life. Personality, like every other force, reaches its maximum when it encounters resistance, in conflict and in rivalry—when it fights—hence its great value in friendly rivalry of nations in industry and culture, and especially in periods of natural calamities or of enemies from without. Since the fruits of individual development contribute to the common fund of social values, it is clear that societies and peoples which, other things being equal, possess the most advanced and active personalities contribute most to the enrichment of civilization. It does not seem necessary to demonstrate that the pacific competition of nations and their success depends on the development of the personalities which compose them. A nation weak in the development of individualities, of social units which compose it, could not defend itself against the exploitation of nations composed of personalities with a superior development.

D. BIOLOGICAL AND SOCIAL HEREDITY

1. Nature and Nurture[1]

We have seen that the scientific position in regard to the transmissibility of modifications should be one of active scepticism, that there seems to be no convincing evidence in support of the affirmative position, and that there is strong presumption in favor of the negative.

A modification is a definite change in the individual body, due to some change in "nurture." There is no secure evidence that any such individual gain or loss can be transmitted as such, or in any representative degree. How does this affect our estimate of the value of "nurture"? How should the sceptical or negative answer, which we believe to be the scientific one, affect our practice in regard to education, physical culture, amelioration of function, improvement of environment, and so on? Let us give a practical point to what we have already said.

a) Every inheritance requires an appropriate nurture if it is to realize itself in development. Nurture supplies the liberating stimuli necessary for the full expression of the inheritance. A man's character as well as his physique is a function of "nature" and of "nurture." In the language of the old parable of the talents, what is given must be traded with. A boy may be truly enough a chip of the old block, but how far he shows himself such depends on "nurture." The conditions of nurture determine whether the expression of the inheritance is to be full or partial. It need hardly be said that the strength of an (inherited) individuality may be such that it expresses itself almost in the face of inappropriate nurture. History abounds in instances. As Goethe said, "Man is always achieving the impossible." Corot was the son of a successful milliner and prosperous tradesman, and he was thirty before he left the draper's shop to study nature.

b) Although modifications do not seem to be transmitted as such, or in any representative degree, there is no doubt that they or their secondary results may in some cases affect the offspring. This is especially the case in typical mammals, where there is before birth a prolonged (placental) connection between the mother and the unborn young. In such cases the offspring is for a time almost

[1] From J. Arthur Thomson, *Heredity*, pp. 244–49. (G. P. Putnam's Sons, 1908.)

part of the maternal body, and liable to be affected by modifications thereof, e.g., by good or bad nutritive conditions. In other cases, also, it may be that deeply saturating parental modifications, such as the results of alcoholic and other poisoning, affect the germ cells, and thus the offspring. A disease may saturate the body with toxins and waste products, and these may provoke prejudicial germinal variations.

c) Though modifications due to changed "nurture" do not seem to be transmissible, they may be re-impressed on each generation. Thus "nurture" becomes not less, but more, important in our eyes.

"Is my grandfather's environment not my heredity?" asks an American author quaintly and pathetically. Well, if not, let us secure for ourselves and for our children those factors in the "grandfather's environment" that made for progressive evolution, and eschew those that tended elsewhere.

Are modifications due to changed nurture not, as such, entailed on offspring? Perhaps it is just as well, for we are novices at nurturing even yet! Moreover, the non-transmissibility cuts both ways: if individual modificational gains are not handed on, neither are the losses.

Is the "nature"—the germinal constitution, to wit—all that passes from generation to generation, the capital sum without the results of individual usury; then we are freed, at least, from undue pessimism at the thought of the many harmful functions and environments that disfigure our civilization. Many detrimental acquired characters are to be seen all around us, but if they are not transmissible, they need not last.

In the development of "character," much depends upon early nurture, education, and surrounding influences generally, but how the individual reacts to these must largely depend on his inheritance. Truly the individual himself makes his own character, but he does so by his habitual adjustment of his (hereditarily determined) constitution to surrounding influences. Nurture supplies the stimulus for the expression of the moral inheritance, and how far the inheritance can express itself is limited by the nurture-stimuli available just as surely as the result of nurture is conditioned by the hereditarily determined nature on which it operates. It may be urged that character, being a product of habitual modes of feeling, thinking, and acting, cannot be spoken of as *inherited*, but bodily character is also a product dependent upon vital experience. It seems to us as idle to deny that some children are "born good" or "born bad," as it is to deny that some children are born strong and others weak, some energetic and others "tired" or "old." It may be difficult to tell how far the apparently hereditary goodness or badness of disposition is due to the nutritive influences of the mother, both before and after birth, and we must leave it to the reader's experience and observation to decide whether we are right or wrong in our opinion that quite apart from maternal nutritive influence there is a genuine inheritance of kindly disposition, strong sympathy, good humor, and good will. The further difficulty that the really organic character may be half-concealed by nurture-effects, or inhibited by the external heritage of custom and tradition, seems less serious, for the selfishness of an acquired altruism is as familiar as honor among thieves.

It is entirely useless to boggle over the difficulty that we are unable to conceive how dispositions for good or ill lie implicit within the protoplasmic unit in which the individual life begins. The fact is undoubted that the initiatives of moral character are in some degree transmissible, though from the nature of the case the influences of education, example, environment, and the like are here more potent than in regard to structural features. We cannot make a silk purse out of a sow's ear, though the plasticity of character under nurture is a fact which gives us all hope. Explain it we cannot, but the transmission of the raw material of character is a fact, and we must still say with Sir Thomas Browne: "Bless not thyself that thou wert born in Athens; but, among thy multiplied acknowledgments, lift up one hand to heaven that thou wert born of honest parents, that modesty, humility, and veracity *lay in the same egg*, and came into the world with thee."

2. Inheritance of Original Nature[1]

The principles of heredity (may be recapitulated as follows):

First of all, we find useful the principle of the unit-character. According to this principle, characters are, for the most part, inherited

---

[1] Adapted from C. B. Davenport, "The Inheritance of Physical and Mental Traits of Man and Their Application to Eugenics," in Castle, Coulter, Davenport, East, and Tower, *Heredity and Eugenics*, pp. 269–87. (The University of Chicago Press, 1912.)

independently of each other, and each trait is inherited as a unit or may be broken up into characters that are so inherited.

Next, it must be recognized that characters, as such, are not inherited. Strictly, my son has not my nose, because I still have it; what was transmitted was something that determined the shape of his nose, and that is called in brief a "determiner." So the second principle is that unit-characters are inherited through determiners in the germ cells.

And finally, it is recognized that there really is no inheritance from parent to child, but that parent and child resemble each other because they are derived from the same germ plasm, they are chips from the same old block; and the son is the half-brother to his father, by another mother.

These three principles are the three corner stones of heredity as we know it today, the principles of the independent unit-characters each derived from a determiner in the germ plasm.

How far are the known facts of heredity in man in accord with these principles? No doubt all human traits are inherited in accordance with these principles; but knowledge proceeds slowly in this field.

As a first illustration I may take the case of human eye color. The iris is made up of a trestle-work of fibers, in which are suspended particles that give the blue color. In addition, in many eyes much brown pigment is formed which may be small in amount and gathered around the pupil or so extensive as to suffuse the entire iris and make it all brown. It is seen, then, that the brown iris is formed by something additional to the blue. And brown iris may be spoken of as a *positive* character, depending on a determiner for brown pigment; and blue as a *negative* character, depending on the absence of the determiner for brown.

Now when both parents have brown eyes and come from an ancestry with brown eyes, it is probable that all of their germ cells contain the determiner for brown iris pigmentation. So when these germ cells, both carrying the determiner, unite, all of the progeny will receive the determiner from both sides of the house; consequently the determiners are double in their bodies and the resulting iris pigmentation may be said to be *duplex*. When a character is duplex in an individual, that means that when the germ cells ripen in the body of that individual each contains a determiner. So that individual is capable, so far as he is concerned, of transmitting his trait in undiminished intensity.

If a parent has pure blue eyes, that is evidence that in neither of the united germ cells from which he arose was there a determiner for iris pigmentation; consequently in respect to brown iris pigmentation such a person may be said to be *nulliplex*. If, now, such a person marry an individual duplex in eye color, in whom all of the germ cells contain the determiner, each child will receive the determiner for iris pigmentation from one side of the house only. This determiner will, of course, induce pigmentation, but the pigmentation is simplex, being induced by one determiner only. Consequently, the pigmentation is apt to be weak. When a person whose pigment determiners have come from one side of the house forms germ cells, half will have and half will lack the determiner. If such a person marry a consort all of whose germ cells contain the determiner for iris pigmentation, all of the children will, of course, receive the iris pigmentation, but in half it will be duplex and in the other half it will be simplex. If the two parents both be simplex, so that, in each, half of the germ cells possess and half lack the determiner in the union of germ cells, there are four events that are equally apt to occur: (1) an egg *with* the determiner unites with a sperm *with* the determiner; (2) an egg *with* the determiner unites with a sperm *without* the determiner; (3) an egg *without* the determiner unites with a sperm *with* the determiner; (4) an egg *without* the determiner unites with a sperm *without* the determiner. Thus the character is duplex in one case, simplex in two cases, and nulliplex in one case; that is, one in four will have no brown pigment, or will be blue eyed. If one parent be simplex, so that the germ cells are equally with and without the determiner, while the other be nulliplex, then half of the children will be simplex and half nulliplex in eye pigment. Finally, if both parents be nulliplex in eye pigmentation (that is, blue eyed), then none of their germ cells will have the determiner, and all children will be nulliplex, or blue eyed. The inheritance of eye color serves as a paradigm of the method of inheritance of any unit-character.

Let us now consider some of the physical traits of man that follow the same law as brown eye color, traits that are clearly positive, and due to a definite determiner in the germ plasm.

Hair color is due either to a golden-brown pigment that looks black in masses, or else to a red pigment. The lighter tints differ from the darker by the absence of some pigment granules. If neither parent has the capacity of producing a large quantity of pigment granules in the hair, the children cannot have that capacity, that is, two flaxen-haired parents have only flaxen-haired children. But a dark-haired parent may be either simplex or duplex; and so two such parents *may* produce children with light hair; but not more than one out of four. In general, the hair color of the children tends not to be darker than that of the darker parent. Skin pigment follows a similar rule. It is really one of the surprises of modern studies that skin pigment should be found to follow the ordinary law of heredity; it was commonly thought to blend. The inheritance of skin color is not dependent on race; two blonds never have brunette offspring, but brunettes may have blondes. The extreme case is that of albinos with no pigment in skin, hair, and iris. Two albinos have only albino children, but albinos may come from two pigmented parents.

Similarly, straight-haired parents lack curliness, and two such have only straight-haired children. Also two tall parents have only tall children. *Shortness* is the trait: tallness is a negative character. Also when both parents lack stoutness (are slender), all children tend to lack it.

We may now consider briefly the inheritance of certain pathological or abnormal states, to see in how far the foregoing principles hold for them also. Sometimes the abnormal condition is positive, due to a new trait; but sometimes, on the contrary, the normal condition is the positive one and the trait is due to a defect.

Deaf-mutism is due to a defect; but the nature of the defect is different in different cases. Deaf-mutism is so varied that frequently two unrelated deaf mutes may have hearing children. But if the deaf-mute parents are cousins, the chances that the deafness is due to the *same* unit defect are increased and all of the children will probably be deaf.

From the studies of Dr. Goddard and others, it appears that when both parents are feeble-minded all of the children will be so likewise; this conclusion has been tested again and again. But if *one* of the parents be normal and of normal ancestry, all of the children may be normal; whereas, if the normal person have defective germ cells, half of his progeny by a feeble-minded woman will be defective.

Many criminals, especially those who offend against the person, are feeble-minded, as is shown by the way they occur in fraternities with feeble-mindedness, or have feeble-minded parents. The test of the mental condition of relatives is one that may well be applied by judges in deciding upon the responsibility of an aggressor.

Not only the condition of imperfect mental development, but also that of inability to withstand stress upon the nervous system, may be inherited. From the studies of Dr. Rosanoff and his collaborators, it appears that if both parents be subject to manic depressive insanity or to dementia precox, all children will be neuropathic also; that if one parent be affected and come from a weak strain, half of the children are liable to go insane; and that nervous breakdowns of these types never occur if both parents be of sound stock.

Finally, a study of families with special abilities reveals a method of inheritance quite like that of nervous defect. If both parents be color artists or have a high grade of vocal ability or are littérateurs of high grade, then all of their children tend to be of high grade also. If one parent has high ability, while the other has low ability but has ancestry with high ability, part of the children will have high ability and part low. It seems like an extraordinary conclusion that high ability is inherited as though due to the absence of a determiner in the same way as feeble-mindedness and insanity are inherited. We are reminded of the poet: "Great wits to madness sure are near allied." Evidence for the relationship is given by pedigrees of men of genius that often show the combination of ability and insanity. May it not be that just that lack of control that permits "flights of the imagination" is related to the flightiness characteristic of those with mental weakness or defect?

These studies of inheritance of mental defect inevitably raise the question how to eliminate the mentally defective. This is a matter of great importance because, on the one hand, it is now coming to be recognized that mental defect is at the bottom of most of our social problems. Extreme alcoholism is usually a consequence of a mental make-up in which self-control of the appetite for liquor is lacking. Pauperism is a consequence of mental defects that make the pauper incapable of holding his own in the world's competition. Sex immorality in either sex is commonly due to a certain inability to appreciate consequences, to visualize the inevitableness of cause and effect, combined sometimes with a sex-hyperesthesia and lack of self-control. Criminality in its worst forms is similarly due to a lack of appreciation of or receptivity to moral ideas.

If we seek to know what is the origin of these defects, we must admit that it is very ancient. They are probably derived from our ape-like ancestors, in which they were *normal* traits. There occurs in man a strain that has not yet acquired those traits of inhibition that characterized the more highly developed civilized persons. The evidence for this is that, as far back as we go, we still trace back the black thread of defective heredity.

We have now to answer the question as to the eugenical application of the laws of inheritance of defects. First, it may be pointed out that traits due to the absence of a determiner are characterized by their usual sparseness in the pedigree, especially when the parents are normal; by the fact that they frequently appear where cousin marriages abound, because cousins tend to carry the same defects in their germ plasm, though normal themselves; by the fact that two affected parents have exclusively normal children, while two normal parents who belong to the same strain, or who both belong to strains containing the same defect, have some (about 25 per cent) defective children. But a defective married to a pure normal will have no defective offspring.

The clear eugenical rule is then this: Let abnormals marry normals without trace of the defect, and let their normal offspring marry in turn into strong strains; thus the defect may never appear again. Normals from the defective strain may marry normals of normal ancestry, but must particularly avoid consanguineous marriages.

The sociological conclusion is: Prevent the feeble-minded, drunkards, paupers, sex-offenders, and criminalistic from marrying their like or cousins or any person belonging to a neuropathic strain. Practically it might be well to segregate such persons during the reproductive period for one generation. Then the crop of defectives will be reduced to practically nothing.

3. Inheritance of Acquired Nature: Tradition[1]

The factor in societal evolution corresponding to heredity in organic evolution is tradition; and the agency of transmission is the nervous system by way of its various "senses" rather than the germ-plasm. The organs of transmission are the eye, ear, tongue, etc., and not those of sex. The term tradition, like variation and selection, is taken in the broad sense. Variation in nature causes the offspring to differ from the parents and from one another; variation in the folkways causes those of one period (or place) to differ from their predecessors and to some extent among themselves. It is the vital fact at the bottom of change. Heredity in nature causes the offspring to resemble or repeat the present type; tradition in societal evolution causes the mores of one period to repeat those of the preceding period. Each is a stringent conservator. Variation means diversity; heredity and tradition mean the preservation of type. If there were no force of heredity or tradition, there could be no system or classification of natural or of societal forms; the creation hypothesis would be the only tenable one, for there could be no basis for a theory of descent. If there were no variation, all of nature and all human institutions would show a monotony as of the desert sand. Heredity and tradition allow respectively of the accumulation of organic or societal variations through repeated selection, extending over generations, in this or that direction. In short, what one can say of the general effects of heredity in the organic realm he can say of tradition in the field of the folkways. That the transmission is in the one case by way of the sex organs and the germ-plasm, and in the other through the action of the vocal cords, the auditory nerves, etc., would seem to be of small moment in comparison with the essential identity in the functions discharged.

Tradition is, in a sense and if such a comparison were profitable, more conservative than heredity. There is in the content of tradition an invariability which could not exist if it were a dual composite, as is the constitution of the germ-plasm. Here we must recall certain essential qualities of the mores which we have hitherto viewed from another angle. Tradition always looks to the folkways as constituting the matter to be transmitted. But the folkways, after the

[1] From Albert G. Keller, *Societal Evolution*, pp. 212–15. (Published by The Macmillan Co., 1915. Reprinted by permission.)

concurrence in their practice has been established, come to include a judgment that they conduce to societal and, indeed, individual welfare. This is where they come to be properly called mores. They become the prosperity-policy of the group, and the young are reared up under their sway, looking to the older as the repositories of precedent and convention. But presently the older die, and in conformity with the ideas of the time, they become beings of a higher power toward whom the living owe duty, and whose will they do not wish to cross. The sanction of ghost-fear is thus extended to the mores, which, as the prosperity-policy of the group, have already taken on a stereotyped character. They thus become in an even higher degree "uniform, universal in a group, imperative, invariable. As time goes on, they become more and more arbitrary, positive, and imperative. If asked why they act in a certain way in certain cases, primitive people always answer that it is because they and their ancestors always have done so." Thus the transmission of the mores comes to be a process embodying the greatest conservatism and the least likelihood of change. This situation represents an adaption of society to life-conditions; it would seem that because of the rapidity of succession of variations there is need of an intensely conserving force (like ethnocentrism or religion) to preserve a certain balance and poise in the evolutionary movement.

Transmission of the mores takes place through the agency of imitation or of inculcation; through one or the other according as the initiative is taken by the receiving or the giving party respectively. Inculcation includes education in its broadest sense; but since that term implies in general usage a certain, let us say protective, attitude taken by the educator (as toward the young), the broader and more colorless designation is chosen. Acculturation is the process by which one group or people learns from another, whether the culture or civilization be gotten by imitation or by inculcation. As there must be contact, acculturation is sometimes ascribed to "contagion."

4. Temperament, Tradition, and Nationality[1]

The temperament of the Negro, as I conceive it, consists in a few elementary but distinctive characteristics, determined by physical

[1] From Robert E. Park, "Education in Its Relation to the Conflict and Fusion of Cultures," in the *Publications of the American Sociological Society*, XIII (1918), 58–63.

organizations and transmitted biologically. These characteristics manifest themselves in a genial, sunny, and social disposition, in an interest and attachment to external, physical things rather than to subjective states and objects of introspection, in a disposition for expression rather than enterprise and action.

The changes which have taken place in the manifestations of this temperament have been actuated by an inherent and natural impulse, characteristic of all living beings, to persist and maintain itself in a changed environment. Such changes have occurred as are likely to take place in any organism in its struggle to live and to use its environment to further and complete its own existence.

The result has been that this racial temperament has selected out of the mass of cultural materials to which it had access, such technical, mechanical, and intellectual devices as met its needs at a particular period of its existence. It has clothed and enriched itself with such new customs, habits, and cultural forms as it was able, or permitted to use. It has put into these relatively external things, moreover, such concrete meanings as its changing experience and its unchanging racial individuality demanded. Everywhere and always it has been interested rather in expression than in action; interested in life itself rather than in its reconstruction or reformation. The Negro is, by natural disposition, neither an intellectual nor an idealist, like the Jew; nor a brooding introspective, like the East Indian; nor a pioneer and frontiersman, like the Anglo-Saxon. He is primarily an artist, loving life for its own sake. His *metier* is expression rather than action. He is, so to speak, the lady among the races.

In reviewing the fortunes of the Negro's temperament as it is manifested in the external events of the Negro's life in America, our analysis suggests that this racial character of the Negro has exhibited itself everywhere in something like the rôle of the *wish* in the Freudian analysis of dream-life. The external cultural forms which he found here, like the memories of the individual, have furnished the materials in which the racial wish, i.e., the Negro temperament, has clothed itself. The inner meaning, the sentiment, the emphasis, the emotional color, which these forms assumed as the result of their transference from the white man to the Negro, these have been the Negro's own. They have represented his temperament—his temperament modified, however, by his experience and the tradition which he has accumulated in this country. The temperament is African, but the tradition is American.

If it is true that the Jew just because of his intellectuality is a natural-born idealist, internationalist, doctrinaire, and revolutionist, while the Negro, because of his natural attachment to known familiar objects, places, and persons, is pre-adapted to conservatism and to local and personal loyalties—if these things are true, we shall eventually have to take account of them practically. It is certain that the Negro has uniformly shown a disposition to loyalty during slavery to his master and during freedom to the South and the country as a whole. He has maintained this attitude of loyalty, too, under very discouraging circumstances. I once heard Kelly Miller, the most philosophical of the leaders and teachers of his race, say in a public speech that one of the greatest hardships the Negro suffered in this country was due to the fact that he was not permitted to be patriotic.

Of course all these alleged racial characteristics have a positive as well as a negative significance. Every race, like every individual, has the vices of its virtues. The question remains still to what extent so-called racial characteristics are actually racial, i.e., biological, and to what extent they are the effect of environmental conditions. The thesis of this paper, to state it again, is: (1) that fundamental temperamental qualities, which are the basis of interest and attention, act as selective agencies and as such determine what elements in the cultural environment each race will select; in what region it will seek and find its vocation in the larger social organization; (2) that, on the other hand, technique, science, machinery, tools, habits, discipline, and all the intellectual and mechanical devices with which the civilized man lives and works remain relatively external to the inner core of significant attitudes and values which constitute what we may call the will of the group. This racial will is, to be sure, largely social, that is, modified by social experience, but it rests ultimately upon a complex of inherited characteristics, which are racial.

The individual man is the bearer of a double inheritance. As a member of a race, he transmits by interbreeding a biological inheritance. As a member of society or a social group, on the other hand, he transmits by communication a social inheritance. The particular complex of inheritable characters which characterizes the individuals of a racial group constitutes the racial temperament. The particular group of habits, accommodations, sentiments, attitudes, and ideals transmitted by communication and education constitutes a social tradition. Between this temperament and this tradition there is, as has been generally recognized, a very intimate relationship. My assumption is that temperament is the basis of the interests; that as such it determines in the long run the general run of attention, and this, eventually, determines the selection in the case of an individual of his vocation, in the case of the racial group of its culture. That is to say, temperament determines what things the individual and the group will be interested in; what elements of the general culture, to which they have access, they will assimilate; what, to state it pedagogically, they will learn.

It will be evident at once that where individuals of the same race and hence the same temperament are associated, the temperamental interests will tend to reinforce one another, and the attention of members of the group will be more completely focused upon the specific objects and values that correspond to the racial temperament. In this way racial qualities become the basis for nationalities, a nationalistic group being merely a cultural and, eventually, a political society founded on the basis of racial inheritances.

On the other hand, when racial segregation is broken up and members of a racial group are dispersed, the opposite effect will take place. This explains the phenomena which have frequently been the subject of comment and observation, that the racial characteristics manifest themselves in an extraordinary way in large homogeneous gatherings. The contrast between a mass meeting of one race and a similar meeting of another is particularly striking. Under such circumstances characteristic racial and temperamental differences appear that would otherwise pass entirely unnoticed.

When the physical unity of a group is perpetuated by the succession of parents and children, the racial temperament, including fundamental attitudes and values which rest in it, is preserved intact. When, however, society grows and is perpetuated by immigration and adaptation, there ensues, as a result of miscegenation, a breaking up of the complex of the biologically inherited qualities which constitute the temperament of the race. This again initiates changes in the mores, traditions, and eventually in the institutions of the community. The changes which proceed from modification in the racial temperament will, however, modify but slightly the external forms of the social traditions, but they will be likely to change profoundly their content and meaning. Of course other factors, individual competition, the formation of classes, and especially the increase of communication, all co-operate to complicate the whole situation and to modify the effects which would be produced by racial factors working in isolation.

III. INVESTIGATIONS AND PROBLEMS

1. Conceptions of Human Nature Implicit in Religious and Political Doctrines

Although the systematic study of it is recent, there has always been a certain amount of observation and a great deal of assumption in regard to human nature. The earliest systematic treatises in jurisprudence, history, theology, and politics necessarily proceeded from certain more or less naïve assumptions in regard to the nature of man. In the extension of Roman law over subject peoples the distinction was made between *jus gentium* and *jus naturae*, i.e., the laws peculiar to a particular nation as contrasted with customs and laws common to all nations and derived from the nature of mankind. Macaulay writes of the "principles of human nature" from which it is possible to deduce a theory of government. Theologians, in devising a logical system of thought concerning the ways of God to man, proceeded on the basis of certain notions of human nature. The doctrines of original sin, the innate depravity of man, the war of the natural man and the spiritual man had a setting in the dogmas of the fall of man, redemption through faith, and the probationary character of life on earth. In striking contrast with the pessimistic attitude of theologians toward human nature, social revolutionists like Rousseau have condemned social institutions as inherently vicious and optimistically placed reliance upon human nature as innately good.

In all these treatises the assumptions about human nature are either preconceptions or rationalizations from experience incidental to the legal, moral, religious, or political system of thought. There is in these treatises consequently little or no analysis or detailed description of the traits attributed to men. Certainly, there is no evidence of an effort to arrive at an understanding of human behavior from an objective study of its nature.

Historic assumptions in regard to human nature, no matter how fantastic or unscientific, have exerted, nevertheless, a far-reaching influence upon group action. Periods of social revolution are ushered in by theorists who perceive only the evil in institutions and the good in human nature. On the other hand, the "guardians of society," distrustful of the impulses of human nature, place their reliance upon conventions and upon existing forms of social organization. Communistic societies have been organized upon certain ideas of human nature and have survived as long as these beliefs which inspired them controlled the behavior of members of the group.

Philosophers from the time of Socrates have invariably sought to justify their moral and political theories upon a conception, if not a definition, of the nature of man. Aristotle, in his *Politics* and Hobbes in his *Leviathan*, to refer to two classics, offer widely divergent interpretations of human nature. Aristotle emphasized man's altruistic traits, Hobbes stressed his egoistic disposition. These opposite conceptions of human behavior are explicit and in each case presented with a display of evidence. Yet students soon realize that neither philosopher, in fashioning his conception, is entirely without animus or ulterior motive. When these definitions are considered in the context in which they occur, they seem less an outgrowth of an analysis of human nature, than formulas devised in the interest of a political theory. Aristotle was describing the ideal state; Hobbes was interested in the security of an existing social order.

Still, the contribution made by social and political philosophers has been real. Their descriptions of human behavior, if inadequate and unscientific, at least recognized that an understanding of human nature was a precondition to social reorganization. The fact that philosophical conceptions and ideal constructions are themselves social forces and as such frequently represent vested interests, has been an obstacle to social as well as physical science.

Comte's notion that every scientific discipline must pass through a theological and metaphysical stage before it assumed the character of a positive science seems to be true as far as sociology is concerned. Machiavelli shocked the moral sense of his time, if not the moralists of all time, when he proposed to accept human nature as it is as a basis for political science. Herbert Spencer insisted upon the futility of expecting "golden conduct from leaden instincts." To the utopian social reformers of his day he pointed out a series of welfare measures in England in which the outcome was the direct opposite of the results desired.

This negative criticism of preconceived notions and speculations about human nature prepared the way for disinterested observation and comparison. Certain modern tendencies and movements gave an impetus to the detached study of human behavior. The ethnologists collected objective descriptions of the behavior of primitive people. In psychology interest developed in the study of the child and in the comparative study of human and animal behavior. The psychiatrist, in dealing with certain types of abnormal behavior like hysteria and multiple personality, was forced to study human behavior objectively. All this has prepared the way for a science of human nature and of society based upon objective and disinterested observation.

2. Literature and the Science of Human Nature

The poets were the first to recognize that "the proper study of mankind is man" as they were also the first to interpret it objectively. The description and appreciation of human nature and personality by the poet and artist preceded systematic and reflective analysis by the psychologist and the sociologist. In recent years, moreover, there has been a very conscious effort to make literature, as well as history, "scientific." Georg Brandes in his *Main Currents in Nineteenth Century Literature* set himself the task to "trace first and foremost the connection between literature and life." Taine's *History of English Literature* attempts to delineate British temperament and character as mirrored in literary masterpieces.

The novel which emphasizes "*milieu*" and "*character*," as contrasted with the novel which emphasizes "action" and "plot," is a literary device for the analysis of human nature and society. Émile Zola in an essay *The Experimental Novel* has presented with characteristic audacity the case for works of fiction as instruments for the scientific dissection and explanation of human behavior.

The novelist is equally an observer and an experimentalist. The observer in him gives the facts as he has observed them, suggests the points of departure, displays the solid earth on which his characters are to tread and the phenomena develop. Then the experimentalist appears and introduces an experiment, that is to say, sets his characters going in a certain story so as to show that the succession of facts will be such as the requirements of the determinism of the phenomena under examination call for. The novelist starts out in search of a truth. I will take as an example the character of the "Baron Hulot," in *Cousine Bette*, by Balzac. The general fact observed by Balzac is the ravages that the amorous temperament of a man makes in his home, in his family, and in society. As soon as he has chosen his subject he starts from known facts, then he makes his experiment and exposes Hulot to a series of trials, placing him among certain surroundings in order to exhibit how the complicated machinery of his passions works. It is then evident that there is not only observation there, but that there is also experiment, as Balzac does not remain satisfied with photographing the facts collected by him, but interferes in a direct way to place his characters in certain conditions, and of these he remains the master. The problem is to know what such a passion, acting in such surroundings and under such circumstances, would produce from the point of view of an individual and of society; and an experimental novel, *Cousine Bette*, for example, is simply the report of the experiment that the novelist conducts before the eyes of the public. In fact, the whole operation consists of taking facts in nature, then in studying the mechanism of these facts, acting upon them, by the modification of circumstances and surroundings, without deviating from the laws of nature. Finally, you possess knowledge of the man, scientific knowledge of him, in both his individual and social relations.[1]

After all that may be said for the experimental novel, however, its primary aim, like that of history, is appreciation and understanding, not generalization and abstract formulas. Insight and sympathy, the mystical sense of human solidarity, expressed in the saying "to comprehend all is to forgive all," this fiction has to give. And these are materials which the sociologist cannot neglect. As yet there is no autobiography or biography of an egocentric personality so convincing as George Meredith's *The Egoist*. The miser is a social type; but there are no case studies as sympathetic and discerning as George Eliot's *Silas Marner*. Nowhere in social science has the technique of case study developed farther than in criminology; yet Dostoévsky's delineation of the self-analysis of the murderer in *Crime and Punishment* dwarfs all comparison outside of similar studies in fiction.

[1] Émile Zola, *The Experimental Novel* (New York, 1893), pp. 8–9. Translated from the French by Belle M. Sherman.

The function of the so-called psychological or sociological novel stops, however, with its presentation of the individual incident or case; it is satisfied by the test of its appeal to the experience of the reader. The scientific study of human nature proceeds a step farther; it seeks generalizations. From the case studies of history and of literature it abstracts the laws and principles of human behavior.

3. Research in the Field of Original Nature

Valuable materials for the study of human nature have been accumulated in archaeology, ethnology, and folklore. William G. Sumner, in his book *Folkways*, worked through the ethnological data and made it available for sociological use. By classification and comparison of the customs of primi ive peoples he showed that cultural differences were based on variations in folkways and mores in adaptation to the environment, rather than upon fundamental differences in human nature.

The interests of research have resulted in a division of labor between the fields of original and acquired nature in man. The examination of original tendencies has been quite properly connected with the study of inheritance. For the history of research in this field, the student is referred to treatises upon genetics and evolution and to the works of Lamarck, Darwin, DeVries, Weismann, and Mendel. Recent discoveries in regard to the mechanism of biological inheritance have led to the organization of a new applied science, "eugenics." The new science proposes a social program for the improvement of the racial traits based upon the investigations of breeding and physical inheritance. Research in eugenics has been fostered by the Galton Laboratory in England, and by the Eugenics Record Office at Cold Spring Harbor in the United States. Interest has centered in the study of the inheritance of feeble-mindedness. Studies of feeble-minded families and groups, as *The Kallikak Family* by Goddard, *The Jukes* by Dugdale, and *The Tribe of Ishmael* by M'Culloch, have shown how mental defect enters as a factor into industrial inefficiency, poverty, prostitution, and crime.

4 The Investigation of Human Personality

The trend of research in human nature has been toward the study of personality. Scientific inquiry into the problems of personality was stimulated by the observation of abnormal behavior such as hysteria, loss of memory, etc., where the cause was not organic and, therefore, presumably psychic. A school of French psychiatrists and psychologists represented by Charcot, Janet, and Ribot have made signal contributions to an understanding of the maladies of personality. Investigation in this field, invaluable for an understanding of the person, has been made in the study of dual and multiple personality. The work of Freud, Jung, Adler, and others in psychoanalysis has thrown light upon the rôle of mental conflict, repression, and the wishes in the growth of personality.

In sociology, personality is studied, not only from the subjective standpoint of its organization, but even more in its objective aspects and with reference to the rôle of the person in the group. One of the earliest classifications of "kinds of conduct" has been ascribed by tradition to a disciple of Aristotle, Theophrastus, who styled himself "a student of human nature." *The Characters of Theophrastus* is composed of sketches—humorous and acute, if superficial—of types such as "the flatterer," "the boor," "the coward," "the garrulous man." They are as true to modern life as to the age of Alexander. Chief among the modern imitators of Theophrastus is La Bruyère, who published in 1688 *Les caractères, ou les mœurs de ce siècle*, a series of essays on the manners of his time, illustrated by portraits of his contemporaries.

Autobiography and biography provide source material for the study both of the subjective life and of the social rôle of the person. Three great autobiographies which have inspired the writing of personal narratives are themselves representative of the different types: Caesar's *Commentaries*, with his detached impersonal description of his great exploits; the *Confessions of St. Augustine*, with his intimate self-analysis and intense self-reproach, and the less well-known *De Vita Propria Liber* by Cardan. This latter is a serious attempt at scientific self-examination. Recently, attention has been directed to the accumulation of autobiographical and biographical materials which are interpreted from the point of view of psychiatry and psychoanalysis. The study *Der Fall Otto Weininger* by Dr. Ferdinand Probst is a representative monograph of this type. The outstanding example of this method and its use for sociological interpretation is "Life Record of an Immigrant" contained in the third volume of Thomas and Znaniecki, *The Polish Peasant*. In connection with the *Recreation Survey* of the Cleveland Foundation and the *Americanization Studies* of the Carnegie Corporation, the life-history has been developed as part of the technique of investigation.

5. The Measurement of Individual Differences

With the growing sense of the importance of individual differences in human nature, attempts at their measurement have been essayed. Tests for physical and mental traits have now reached a stage of accuracy and precision. The study of temperamental and social characteristics is still in the preliminary stage.

The field of the measurement of physical traits is dignified by the name "anthropometry." In the nineteenth century high hopes were widely held of the significance of measurements of the cranium and of physiognomy for an understanding of the mental and moral nature of the person. The lead into phrenology sponsored by Gall and Spursheim proved to be a blind trail. The so-called "scientific school of criminology" founded by Cesare Lombroso upon the identification of the criminal type by certain abnormalities of physiognomy and physique was undermined by the controlled study made by Charles Goring. At the present time the consensus of expert opinion is that only for a small group may gross abnormalities of physical development be associated with abnormal mental and emotional reactions.

In 1905–11 Binet and Simon devised a series of tests for determining the mental age of French school children. The purpose of the mental measurements was to gauge innate mental capacity. Therefore the tests excluded material which had to do with special social experience. With their introduction into the United States certain revisions and modifications, such as the Goddard Revision, the Terman Revision, the Yerkes-Bridges Point Scale, were made in the interests of standardization. The application of mental measurements to different races and social classes raised the question of the extent to which individual groups varied because of differences in social experience. While it is not possible absolutely to separate original tendencies from their expression in experience, it is practicable to devise tests which will take account of divergent social environments.

The study of volitional traits and of temperament is still in its infancy. Many recent attempts at classification of temperaments rest upon as impressionistic a basis as the popular fourfold division into sanguine, melancholic, choleric, and phlegmatic. Two of the efforts to define temperamental differences rest, however, upon first-hand study of cases. Dr. June E. Downey has devised a series of tests based upon handwriting material for measuring will traits. In her pamphlet *The Will Profile* she presents an analysis of twelve volitional traits: revision, perseverance, co-ordination of impulses, care for detail, motor inhibition, resistance, assurance, motor impulsion, speed of decision, flexibility, freedom from inertia, and speed of movement. From a study of several hundred cases she defined certain will patterns which apparently characterize types of individuals. In her experience she has found the rating of the subject by the will test to have a distinct value in supplementing the test for mentality.

Kraepelin, on the basis of his examination of abnormal mental states, offers a classification of types of psychopathic personalities. He distinguishes six groups: the excitable, the unstable, the psychopathic trend, the eccentric, the anti-social, and the contentious. In psychoanalysis a simpler twofold division is frequently made between the *introverts*, or the "introspective" and the *extroverts*, or the "objective" types of individual.

The study of social types is as yet an unworked field. Literature and life surround us with increasing specializations in personalities, but attempts at classification are still in the impressionistic stage. The division suggested by Thomas into the Philistine, Bohemian, and Creative types, while suggestive, is obviously too simple for an adequate description of the rich and complex variety of personalities.

This survey indicates the present status of attempts to define and measure differences in original and human nature. A knowledge of individual differences is important in every field of social control. It is significant that these tests have been devised to meet problems of policies and of administration in medicine, in industry, in education, and in penal and reformatory institutions. Job analysis, personnel administration, ungraded rooms, classes for exceptional children, vocational guidance, indicate fields made possible by the development of tests for measuring individual differences.

SELECTED BIBLIOGRAPHY

I. ORIGINAL NATURE

A. *Racial Inheritance*

(1) Thomson, J. Arthur. *Heredity.* London and New York, 1908.
(2) Washburn, Margaret F. *The Animal Mind.* New York, 1908.
(3) Morgan, C. Lloyd. *Habit and Instinct.* London and New York. 1896.
(4) ———. *Instinct and Experience.* New York, 1912.
(5) Loeb, Jacques. *Comparative Physiology of the Brain and Comparative Psychology.* New York, 1900.
(6) ———. *Forced Movements.* Philadelphia and London, 1918.
(7) Jennings, H. S. *Behavior of the Lower Organisms.* New York, 1906.
(8) Watson, John. *Behavior: an Introduction to Comparative Psychology.* New York, 1914.
(9) Thorndike, E. L. *The Original Nature of Man.* Vol. I of "Educational Psychology." New York, 1913.
(10) Paton, Stewart. *Human Behavior.* In relation to the study of educational, social, and ethical problems. New York, 1921.
(11) Faris, Ellsworth, "Are Instincts Data or Hypotheses?" *American Journal of Sociology*, XXVII (Sept., 1921), 184–96.

B. *Heredity and Eugenics*

1. Systematic Treatises:

(1) Castle, W. E., Coulter, J. M., Davenport, C. B., East, E. M., and Tower, W. L. *Heredity and Eugenics.* Chicago, 1912.
(2) Davenport, C. B. *Heredity in Relation to Eugenics.* New York, 1911.
(3) Goddard, Henry H. *Feeble-mindedness.* New York, 1914.

2. Inherited Inferiority of Families and Communities:

(1) Dugdale, Richard L. *The Jukes.* New York, 1877.
(2) M'Culloch, O. C. *The Tribe of Ishmael.* A study in social degradation. National Conference of Charities and Correction, 1888, 154–59; 1889, 265; 1890, 435–37.
(3) Goddard, Henry H. *The Kallikak Family.* New York, 1912.
(4) Winship, A. E. *Jukes-Edwards.* A study in education and heredity. Harrisburg, Pa., 1900.
(5) Estabrook, A. H., and Davenport, C. B. *The Nam Family.* A study in cacogenics. Cold Spring Harbor, N.Y., 1912.
(6) Danielson, F. H., and Davenport, C. B. *The Hill Folk.* Report on a rural community of hereditary defectives. Cold Spring Harbor, N.Y., 1912.
(7) Kite, Elizabeth S. "The Pineys," *Survey*, XXXI (October 4, 1913), 7–13, 38–40.
(8) Gesell, A. L. "The Village of a Thousand Souls," *American Magazine*, LXXVI (October, 1913), 11–13.
(9) Kostir, Mary S. *The Family of Sam Sixty.* Columbus. 1916.
(10) Finlayson, Anna W. *The Dack Family.* A study on hereditary lack of emotional control. Cold Spring Harbor, N.Y., 1916.

II. HUMAN NATURE

A. *Human Traits*

(1) Cooley, Charles H. *Human Nature and the Social Order.* New York, 1902.

(2) Shaler. N. S. *The Individual.* New York, 1900.

(3) Hocking, W. E. *Human Nature and Its Remaking.* New Haven, 1918.

(4) James, William. *Selected Papers on Philosophy.* New York, 1917. [Includes essays on "Energies of Men," "Habit," "The Will," "The Will to Believe."]

(5) Dewey, John. *Human Nature and Conduct.* An introduction to social psychology. New York, 1922.

(6) Edman, Irwin. *Human Traits and Their Social Significance.* Boston, 1919.

(7) Wallas, Graham. *Human Nature in Politics.* London, 1908.

(8) Baillie, J. B. *Studies in Human Nature.* London, 1921.

(9) Lippmann, Walter. *A Preface to Politics.* New York and London, 1913. [A criticism of present politics from the point of view of human-nature studies.]

(10) James, William. *The Varieties of Religious Experience.* A study in human nature. London and New York, 1902.

(11) Ellis, Havelock. *Studies in the Psychology of Sex.* 6 vols. Philadelphia, 1900-1905.

(12) Thomas. W. I. *Source Book for Social Origins.* Chicago, 1909. [Contains extensive bibliographies.]

[See bibliographies, "Intimate Social Contacts and the Sociology of the Senses," p. 332, and "Psychology and Sociology of War," p. 650.]

B. *The Mores*

1. Comparative Studies of Cultural Traits:

(1) Tylor E. B. *Primitive Culture.* Researches into the development of mythology, philosophy, religion, language, art, and custom. 4th ed. 2 vols. London, 1903.

(2) Sumner, W. G. *Folkways.* A study of the sociological importance of usages, manners, customs, mores, and morals. Boston, 1906.

(3) Westermarck, E. A. *The Origin and Development of the Moral Ideas.* London and New York, 1908.

(4) Lévy-Bruhl, Lucien. *Primitive Mentality.* New York, 1923.

(5) Ratzel, F. *History of Mankind.* Translated by A. J. Butler. London and New York, 1898.

(6) Vierkandt, A. *Naturvölker und Kulturvölker.* Leipzig, 1896.

(7) Lippert, Julius. *Kulturgeschichte der Menschheit in ihrem organischem Aufbau.* Stuttgart, 1886-87.

(8) Frazer, J. G. *The Golden Bough.* A study in magic and religion. 3d ed., 12 vols. (Volume XII is a bibliography of the preceding volumes.) London and New York, 1907-15.

(9) Goldenweiser, A. A. *Early Civilization.* An introduction to anthropology. New York, 1922.

(10) Dewey, John, and Tufts, James H. *Ethics.* New York, 1908.
(11) Thorndike, Lynn. *A History of Magic and Experimental Science.* During the first thirteen centuries of our era. New York, 1923.

2. Studies of Traits of Individual Peoples:

(1) Fouillée, A. *Psychologie du peuple français.* Paris, 1898.
(2) Demolins, Edmond. *Anglo-Saxon Superiority.* To what it is due. Translated from the French by L. B. Lavigne. 2d English ed. London, 1898.
(3) Rhŷs, J., and Brynmor-Jones, D. *The Welsh People.* London, 1900.
(4) Fishberg, M. *The Jews.* A study of race and environment. London and New York, 1911.
(5) Zollschan, Ignaz. *Das Rassenproblem.* Unter besonderer Berücksichtigung der theoretischen Grundlagen der jüdischen Rassenfrage. 3d ed. Wien, 1912.
(6) Odum, Howard W. *Social and Mental Traits of the Negro.* Research into the conditions of the Negro race in southern towns. A study in race traits, tendencies, and prospects. New York, 1910.
(7) Burton, Richard F. *The Jew, the Gypsy and El Islam.* "The Gypsy," pp. 136–285. London, 1898.
(8) Strausz, A. *Die Bulgaren.* Ethnographische Studien. Leipzig, 1898.
(9) Stern, B. *Geschichte der öffentlichen Sittlichkeit in Russland.* Kultur, Aberglaube, Sitten, und Gebräuche. Zwei Bände. Berlin, 1907–8.
(10) Krauss, F. S. *Sitte und Brauch der Südslaven.* Wien, 1885.
(11) Kidd, D. *The Essential Kafir.* London, 1904.
(12) Spencer, B., and Gillen, F. J. *The Native Tribes of Central Australia.* London and New York, 1899.

C. *Human Nature and Industry*

(1) Taylor, F. W. *The Principles of Scientific Management.* New York, 1911.
(2) Tead, O., and Metcalf, H. C. *Personnel Administration.* Its principles and practice. New York, 1920.
(3) Tead, O. *Instincts in Industry.* A study of working-class psychology. Boston, 1918.
(4) Parker, C. H. *The Casual Laborer and Other Essays.* New York, 1920.
(5) Walker, Charles R. *Steel.* The diary of a furnace worker. Boston, 1922.
(6) Lang, R., and Hellpach, W. *Gruppenfabrikation.* Berlin, 1922.

III. PERSONALITY

A. *The Genesis of Personality*

(1) Baldwin, J. M. *Mental Development in the Child and the Race: Methods and Processes.* 3d rev. ed. New York and London, 1906.

(2) Baldwin, J. M. *Social and Ethical Interpretations in Mental Developments* Chap. ii, "The Social Person," pp. 66–98. 3d ed., rev. and enl. New York and London, 1902.

(3) Sully, J. *Studies of Childhood*. rev. ed. New York, 1903.

(4) King, I. *The Psychology of Child Development*. Chicago, 1903.

(5) Thorndike, E. L. *Notes on Child Study*. New York, 1903.

(6) Hall, G. S. *Adolescence*. Its psychology and its relations to physiology, anthropology, sociology, sex, crime, religion, and education. 2 vols. New York, 1904.

(7) Shinn, Milicent W. *Notes on the Development of a Child*. University of California Studies. Nos. 1–4. 1893–99.

(8) Kirkpatrick, E. A. *The Individual in the Making*. Boston and New York, 1911.

B. *Psychology and Sociology of the Person*

(1) James, William. *The Principles of Psychology*. Chap. x, "Consciousness of Self," I, 291–401. New York, 1890.

(2) Bekhterev, V. M. (Bechterew, W. v.) *Die Persönlichkeit und die Bedingungen ihrer Entwicklung und Gesundheit*. "Grenzfragen des Nerven- und Seelenlebens," No. 45. Wiesbaden, 1906.

(3) Bekhterev, V. M. (Bechterew, W. v.) *Obshchie Osnovi Reflexologiyi Chelovyeka*. [General Principles of Human Reflexology. Guide to the objective-biological study of the individual.] Moscow, 1923.

(4) Binet, A. *Alterations of Personality*. Translated by H. G. Baldwin. New York, 1896.

(5) Ribot, T. A. *Diseases of Personality*. Authorized translation, 2d rev. ed. Chicago, 1895.

(6) Adler, A. *The Neurotic Constitution*. New York, 1917.

(7) Prince, M. *The Dissociation of a Personality*. A biographical study in abnormal psychology. 2d ed. New York, 1913.

(8) ———. *The Unconscious*. The fundamentals of human personality, normal and abnormal. 2d rev. ed. New York, 1921.

(9) Coblenz, Felix. *Ueber das betende Ich in den Psalmen*. Ein Beitrag zur Erklaerung des Psalters. Frankfort, 1897.

(10) Royce, J. *Studies of Good and Evil*. A series of essays upon problems of philosophy and life. Chap. viii, "Some Observations on the Anomalies of Self-consciousness," pp. 169–97. A paper read before the Medico-Psychological Association of Boston, March 21, 1894. New York, 1898.

(11) Stern, B. *Werden und Wesen der Persönlichkeit*. Biologische und historische Untersuchungen über menschliche Individualität. Wien und Leipzig, 1913.

(12) Spranger, Eduard. *Lebensformen*. Geisteswissenschaftliche Psychologie und Ethik der Persönlichkeit. Halle, 1922.

(13) Shand, A. F. *The Foundations of Character*. Being a study of the tendencies of the emotions and sentiments. London, 1914.

(14) White, A. K., and Macbeath, A. *The Moral Self*. Its nature and development. London, 1923.

C. *Materials for the Study of the Person*

(1) Theophrastus. *The Characters of Theophrastus.* Translated from the Greek by R. C. Jebb. London, 1870.

(2) La Bruyère, Jean de. *Les caractères, ou les mœurs de ce siècle.* Paris, 1916. *The "Characters" of Jean de La Bruyère.* Translated from the French by Henri Van Laun. London, 1885.

(3) Augustinus, Aurelius. *The Confessions of St. Augustine.* Translated from the Latin by E. B. Pusly. London, 1907.

(4) Wesley, John. *The Journal of the Rev. John Wesley.* New York and London, 1907.

(5) Amiel, H. *Journal intime.* Translated by Mrs. Ward. London and New York, 1885.

(6) Cellini, Benvenuto. *Memoirs of Benvenuto Cellini.* Translated from the Italian by J. A. Symonds. New York, 1898.

(7) Woolman, John. *Journal of the Life, Gospel Labors, and Christian Experiences of That Faithful Minister of Jesus Christ, John Woolman.* Dublin, 1794.

(8) Tolstoy, Count Leon. *My Confession.* Translated from the Russian. Paris and New York, 1887. *My Religion.* Translated from the French. New York, 1885.

(9) Riley, I. W. *The Founder of Mormonism.* A psychological study of Joseph Smith, Jr. New York, 1902.

(10) Wilde, Oscar. *De Profundis.* New York and London, 1905.

(11) Keller, Helen. *The Story of My Life.* New York, 1903.

(12) Simmel, Georg. *Goethe.* Leipzig, 1913.

(13) Thomas, W. I., and Znaniecki, F. *The Polish Peasant in Europe and America.* "Life-Record of an Immigrant," III, 89–400. Boston, 1919.

(14) Probst, Ferdinand. *Der Fall Otto Weininger.* "Grenzfragen des Nerven- und Seelenlebens," No. 31. Wiesbaden, 1904.

(15) Anthony, Katherine. *Margaret Fuller.* A psychological biography. New York, 1920.

(16) Willard, Josiah Flynt. *My Life.* New York, 1908.

(17) ———. *Tramping with Tramps.* New York, 1899.

(18) Cummings, B. F. *The Journal of Disappointed Man,* by Barbellion, W. N. P. [*pseud.*]. Introduction by H. G. Wells. New York, 1919.

(19) Audoux, Marguerite. *Marie Claire.* Introduction by Octave Mirabeau. Translated from the French by J. N. Raphael. London and New York, 1911.

(20) *A Young Girl's Diary.* Prefaced with a letter by Sigmund Freud. Translated from the German by Eden and Cedar Paul. New York, 1921.

(21) Björkman, Edwin A. *The Soul of a Child.* New York, 1922.

(22) Clemens, Samuel L. *The Adventures of Tom Sawyer,* by Mark Twain [*pseud.*]. New York, 1903.

(23) Hapgood, Hutchins. *The Autobiography of a Thief.* New York, 1903.

(24) Johnson, James W. *The Autobiography of an ex-Colored Man.* Published anonymously. Boston, 1912.

(25) Washington, Booker T. *Up from Slavery.* An autobiography. New York, 1901.
(26) Du Bois, W. E. B. *The Souls of Black Folk.* Chicago, 1903.
(27) Beers, C. W. *A Mind That Found Itself.* An autobiography. 4th rev. ed. New York, 1917.

IV. INDIVIDUAL DIFFERENCES

A. *The Nature of Individual Differences*

(1) Thorndike, E. L. *Individuality.* Boston, 1911.
(2) ———. "Individual Differences and Their Causes," *Educational Psychology,* III, 141–388. New York, 1913–14.
(3) Stern, W. *Ueber Psychologie der individuellen Differenzen.* Leipzig, 1900.
(4) Hollingworth, Leta S. *The Psychology of Subnormal Children.* Chap. i. "Individual Differences." New York, 1920.

B. *Mental Differences*

(1) Goddard, H. H. *Feeble-mindedness.* Its causes and consequences. New York, 1914.
(2) Tredgold, A. F. *Mental Deficiency.* 2d ed. New York, 1916.
(3) Bronner, Augusta F. *The Psychology of Special Abilities and Disabilities.* Boston, 1917.
(4) Healy, William. *Case Studies of Mentally and Morally Abnormal Types.* Cambridge, Mass., 1912.
(5) Pintner, Rudolf. *Intelligence Testing.* Methods and results. New York, 1923. [See bibliographies at end of chapters.]

C. *Temperamental Differences*

1. Systematic Treatises:

(1) Fouillée, A. *Tempérament et caractère selon les individus, les sexes et les races.* Paris, 1895.
(2) Hirt, Eduard. *Die Temperamente, ihr Wesen, ihre Bedeutung für das seelische Erleben und ihre besonderen Gestaltungen.* "Grenzfragen des Nerven- und Seelenlebens," No. 40. Wiesbaden, 1905.
(3) Hoch, A., and Amsden, G. S. "A Guide to the Descriptive Study of Personality," *Review of Neurology and Psychiatry,* (1913), 577–87.
(4) Kraepelin, E. *Psychiatrie.* Ein Lehrbuch für Studierende und Ärzte. Vol. IV, chap. xvi, pp. 1973–2116. 8th ed. 4 vols. Leipzig, 1909–15.
(5) Loewenfeld, L. *Ueber die geniale Geistesthätigkeit mit besonderer Berücksichtigung des Genie's für bildende Kunst.* "Grenzfragen des Nerven- und Seelenlebens," No. 21. Wiesbaden, 1903.

2. Temperamental Types:

(1) Lombroso, C. *The Man of Genius.* Translated from the Italian. London and New York, 1891.
(2) ———. *L'uomo delinquente in rapporto all'antropologia, alla giurisprudenza ed alle discipline carcerarie.* 3 vols. 5th ed. Torino, 1896–97.

(3) Goring, Charles. *The English Convict*. A statistical study London, 1913.

(4) Wilmanns, Karl. *Psychopathologie des Landstreichers*. Leipzig 1906.

(5) Downey, June E. *The Will-Temperament and Its Testing* New York, 1923.

(6) Pagnier, A. *Le vagabond*. Paris, 1910.

(7) Kowalewski, A. *Studien zur Psychologie des Pessimismus* "Grenzfragen des Nerven- und Seelenlebens." No. 24. Wies baden, 1904.

D. *Sex Differences*

(1) Ellis, H. H. *Man and Woman*. A study of human secondary sexual characters. 5th rev. ed. London and New York, 1914.

(2) Geddes, P., and Thomson, J. A. *The Evolution of Sex*. London 1889.

(3) Thompson, Helen B. *The Mental Traits of Sex*. An experimental investigation of the normal mind in men and women. Chicago, 1903.

(4) Montague, Helen, and Hollingworth, Leta S. "The Comparative Variability of the Sexes at Birth," *American Journal of Sociology*, XX (1914-15), 335-70.

(5) Thomas. W. I. *Sex and Society*. Chicago, 1907.

(6) Weidensall, C. J. *The Mentality of the Criminal Woman*. A comparative study of the criminal woman, the working girl, and the efficient working woman, in a series of mental and physical tests. Baltimore, 1916.

(7) Hollingworth, Leta S. "Variability as Related to Sex Differences in Achievement," *American Journal of Sociology*, XIX (1913-14), 510-30. [Bibliography.]

E. *Racial Differences*

(1) Boas, F. *The Mind of Primitive Man*. New York, 1911.

(2) *Cambridge Anthropological Expedition to Torres Straits*. 5 vols. Cambridge, 1901-8.

(3) Le Bon, G. *The Psychology of Peoples*. Its influence on their evolution. New York and London, 1898. [Translation.]

(4) Bruner, F. G. "Hearing of Primitive Peoples," *Archives of Psychology*, No. 11. New York, 1908.

(5) Woodworth, R. S. "Racial Differences in Mental Traits," *Science*, new series, XXI (1910), 171-86.

(6) Morse, Josiah. "A Comparison of White and Colored Children Measured by the Binet-Simon Scale of Intelligence," *Popular Science Monthly*, LXXXIV (1914), 75-79.

(7) Ferguson, G. O., Jr. "The Psychology of the Negro, an Experimental Study," *Archives of Psychology*, No. 36. New York, 1916. [Bibliography.]

(8) Peterson, Joseph. *The Comparative Abilities of White and Negro Children*. Baltimore, 1923. [Bibliography.]

See Bibliography, "Assimilation and Amalgamation," p. 776.]

TOPICS FOR WRITTEN THEMES

1. Cooley's Conception of Human Nature
2. Human Nature and the Instincts
3. Human Nature and the Mores
4. Studies in the Evolution of the Mores; Prohibition, Birth Control, the Social Status of Children
5. Labor Management as a Problem in Human Nature
6. Human Nature in Politics
7. Personality and the Self
8. Personality as a Sociological Concept
9. Temperament, Milieu, and Social Types; the Politician, Labor Leader, Minister, Actor, Lawyer, Taxi Driver, Chorus Girl, etc.
10. Bohemian, Philistine, and Genius
11. The Beggar, Vagabond, and Hobo
12. Literature as Source Material for the Study of Character
13. Outstanding Personalities in a Selected Community
14. Autobiography as Source Material for the Study of Human Nature
15. Individual and Racial Differences Compared
16. The Man of Genius as a Biological and a Sociological Product
17. The Jukes and Kindred Studies of Inferior Groups
18. History of the Binet-Simon Tests
19. Mental Measurements and Vocational Guidance
20. Psychiatry and Juvenile Delinquency
21. Recent Studies of the Adolescent Girl
22. Mental Inferiority and Crime

QUESTIONS FOR DISCUSSION

1. Is human nature that which is fundamental and alike in all individuals or is it those qualities which we recognize and appreciate as human when we meet them in individuals?
2. What is the relation between original nature and the environment?
3. What is the basis for the distinction made by Thorndike between reflexes, instincts, and inborn capacities?
4. What is the point of Dewey's article "No Separate Instincts"? What is the difference between the explosive discharge, the suppression, or the sublimation of an impulsive activity?
5. What do you understand by Park's statement that man is not born human?
6. "Human nature is a superstructure." What value has this metaphor? What are its limitations? Suggest a metaphor which more adequately illustrates the relation of original nature to acquired nature.
7. In what sense can it be said that habit is a means of controlling original nature?

8. What, according to Park. is the relation of character to instinct and habit? Do you agree with him?

9. What do you understand by the statement that "original nature is blind?"

10. What relation has an ideal to (a) instinct and (b) group life?

11. In what sense may we speak of the infant as the "natural man"?

12. To what extent are racial differences (a) those of original nature, (b) those acquired from experience?

13. What evidence is there for the position that sex differences in mental traits are acquired rather than inborn?

14. How do you distinguish between mentality and temperament?

15. How do you account for the great differences in achievement between the sexes?

16. What evidence is there of temperamental differences between the sexes? between races?

17. In the future will women equal men in achievement?

18. What, in your judgment. is the range of individual differences? Is it less or greater than that of racial and sex differences?

19. What do you understand is the distinction between racial inheritance as represented by the instincts. and innate individual differences? Do you think that both should be regarded as part of original nature?

20. What is the effect of education and the division of labor (a) upon instincts and (b) upon individual differences?

21. Are individual differences or likenesses more important for society?

22. What do you understand to be the significance of individual differences (a) for social life; (b) for education; (c) for industry?

23. What do you understand by the remaking of human nature? What is the importance of this principle for politics, industry, and social progress?

24. Explain the proverbs: "Habit is ten times nature," "Habit is second nature."

25. What is Cooley's definition of human nature? Do you agree or disagree with him? Elaborate your position.

26. To what extent does human nature differ with race and geographic environment?

27. How would you reinterpret Aristotle's and Hobbes's conception of human nature in the light of this definition?

28. What illustrations of the difference between folkways and mores would you suggest?

29. Classify the following forms of behavior under (a) folkways or (b) mores: tipping the hat, saluting an officer, monogamy, attending church, Sabbath observance, prohibition, immersion as a form of

baptism, the afternoon tea of the Englishman. the double standard of morals, the Ten Commandments, the Golden Rule, the Constitution of the United States.

30. What do you understand to be the relation of the mores to human nature?

31. In what way is (a) habit related to will? (b) custom related to the general will?

32. How do you distinguish the general will (a) from law, (b) from custom?

33. Does any one of the following terms embody your conception of what is expressed by *Sittlichkeit*: good form, decency, self-respect, propriety, good breeding, convention?

34. Describe and analyze several concrete social situations where *Sittlichkeit* rather than conscience or law controlled the behavior of the person or of the group.

35. What do you understand by convention? What is the relation of convention to instinct? Is convention a part of human nature to the same extent as loyalty, honor, etc.?

36. What is meant by the saying that mores, ritual, and convention are in the words of Hegel "objective mind"?

37. "The organism and the brain, as its highest representation, constitute the real personality." What characteristics of personality are stressed in this definition?

38. Is there any significance to the fact that personality is derived from the Latin word *persona* (mask worn by actors)?

39. Is the conventional self a product of habit, or of *Sittlichkeit*, or of law, or of conscience?

40. What is the importance of other people to the development of self-consciousness?

41. Under what conditions does self-consciousness arise?

42. What do you understand by personality as a complex? As a total of mental complexes?

43. What is the relation of memory to personality as illustrated in the case of dual personality and of moods?

44. What do you understand Cooley to mean by the looking-glass self?

45. What illustration would you suggest to indicate that an individual's sense of his personality depends upon his status in the group?

46. "All the world's a stage, and all the men and women merely players." Is personality adequately defined in terms of a person's conception of his rôle?

47. What is the sociological significance of the saying, "If you would have a virtue, feign it"?

48. What, according to Bechterew, is the relation of personality to the social *milieu*?

49. What do you understand by the personality of peoples? What is the relation of the personality of peoples and the personalities of individuals who constitute the peoples?

50. What do you understand by the difference between nature and nurture?

51. What are acquired characters? How are they transmitted?

52. What do you understand by the Mendelian principles of inheritance: (*a*) the hypothesis of unit characters; (*b*) the law of dominance; and (*c*) the law of segregation?

53. What illustrations of the differences between instinct and tradition would you suggest?

54. What is the difference between the blue eye as a defect in pigmentation, and of feeble-mindedness as a defective characteristic?

55. Should it be the policy of society to eliminate all members below a certain mental level either by segregation or by more drastic measures?

56. What principles of treatment of practical value to parents and teachers would you draw from the fact that feeble inhibition of temper is a trait transmitted by biological inheritance?

57. Why is an understanding of the principles of biological inheritance of importance to sociology?

58. In what two ways, according to Keller, are acquired characters transmitted by tradition?

CHAPTER III

SOCIETY AND THE GROUP

I. INTRODUCTION

1. Society, the Community, and the Group

Human nature and the person are products of society. This is the sum and substance of the readings in the preceding chapter. But what, then, is society—this web in which the lives of individuals are so inextricably interwoven, and which seems at the same time so external and in a sense alien to them? From the point of view of common sense, "society" is sometimes conceived as the sum total of social institutions. The family, the church, industry, the state, all taken together, constitute society. In this use of the word, society is identified with social structure, something more or less external to individuals.

In accordance with another customary use of the term, "society" denotes a collection of persons. This is a vaguer notion but it at least identifies society with individuals instead of setting it apart from them. But this definition is manifestly superficial. Society is not a collection of persons in the sense that a brick pile is a collection of bricks. However we may conceive the relation of the parts of society to the whole, society is not a mere physical aggregation and not a mere mathematical or statistical unit.

Various explanations that strike deeper than surface observation have been proposed as solutions for this cardinal problem of the social one and the social many; of the relation of society to the individual. Society has been described as a tool, an instrument, as it were, an extension of the individual organism. The argument runs something like this: The human hand, though indeed a part of the physical organism, may be regarded as an instrument of the body as a whole. If as by accident it be lost, it is conceivable that a mechanical hand might be substituted for it, which, though not a part of the body, would function for all practical purposes as a hand of flesh and blood. A hoe may be regarded as a highly specialized hand, so also logically, if less figuratively, a plow. So the hand of another person if it does your bidding may be regarded as your instrument, your hand. Language is witness to the fact that employers speak of "the hands" which they "work." Social institutions may likewise be thought of as tools of individuals for accomplishing their purposes. Logically, therefore, society, either as a sum of institutions or as a collection of persons, may be conceived of as a sum total of instrumentalities, extensions of the functions of the human organism which enable individuals to carry on life-activities. From this standpoint society is an immense co-operative concern of mutual services.

This latter is an aspect of society which economists have sought to isolate and study. From this point of view the relations of individuals are conceived as purely external to one another, like that of the plants in a plant community. Co-operation, so far as it exists, is competitive and "free."

In contrast with the view of society which regards social institutions and the community itself as the mere instruments and tools of the individuals who compose it, is that which conceives society as resting upon biological adaptations, that is to say upon instincts, gregariousness, for example, imitation, or like-mindedness. The classic examples of societies based on instinct are the social insects, the well-known bee and the celebrated ant. In human society the family, with its characteristic differences and interdependences of the sexes and the age groups, husband and wife, children and parents, most nearly realizes this description of society. In so far as the organization of society is predetermined by inherited or constitutional differences, as is the case pre-eminently in the so-called animal societies, competition ceases and the relations of its component individuals become, so to speak, internal, and a permanent part of the structure of the group.

The social organization of human beings, on the other hand, the various types of social groups, and the changes which take place in them at different times under varying circumstances, are determined not merely by instincts and by competition but by custom, tradition, public opinion, and contract. In animal societies as herds, flocks, and packs, collective behavior seems obviously to be explained in terms of instinct and emotion. In the case of man, however, instincts are changed into habits; emotions, into sentiments. Furthermore, all these forms of behavior tend to become conventionalized and thus become relatively independent of individuals and of instincts. The behavior of the person is thus eventually controlled by the formal standards which, implicit in the mores, are explicit in the laws. Society now may be defined as the social heritage of *habit and sentiment, folkways and mores, technique and culture,* all of which are incident or necessary to collective human behavior.

Human society, then, unlike animal society, is mainly a social heritage, created in and transmitted by communication. The continuity and life of a society depend upon its success in transmitting from one generation to the next its folkways, mores, technique, and ideals. From the standpoint of collective behavior these cultural traits may all be reduced to the one term "consensus." Society viewed abstractly is an organization of individuals; considered concretely it is a complex of organized habits, sentiments, and social attitudes—in short, consensus.

The terms society, community, and social group are now used by students with a certain difference of emphasis but with very little difference in meaning. Society is the more abstract and inclusive term, and society is made up of social groups, each possessing its own specific type of organization but having at the same time all the general characteristics of society in the abstract. Community is the term which is applied to societies and social groups where they are considered from the point of view of the geographical distribution of the individuals and institutions of which they are composed. It follows that every community is a society, but not every society is a community. An individual may belong to many social groups but he will not ordinarily belong to more than one community, except in so far as a smaller community of which he is a member is included in a larger of which he is also a member. However, an individual is not, at least from a sociological point of view, a member of a community because he lives in it but rather because, and to the extent that, he participates in the common life of the community.

The term social group has come into use with the attempts of students to classify societies. Societies may be classified with reference to the rôle which they play in the organization and life of larger social groups or societies. The internal organization of any given social group will be determined by its external relation to other groups in the society of which it is a part as well as by the relations of individuals within the group to one another.   A boys' gang, a girls' clique, a college class, or a neighborhood conforms to this definition quite as much as a labor union, a business enterprise, a political party, or a nation.   One advantage of the term "group" lies in the fact that it may be applied to the smallest as well as to the largest forms of human association.

2.   Classification of the Materials

Society, in the most inclusive sense of that term, the Great Society, as Graham Wallas described it, turns out upon analysis to be a constellation of other smaller societies, that is to say races, peoples, parties, factions, cliques, clubs, etc.   The community, the world-community, on the other hand, which is merely the Great Society viewed from the standpoint of the territorial distribution of its members, presents a different series of social groupings and the Great Society in this aspect exhibits a totally different pattern.   From the point of view of the territorial distribution of the individuals that constitute it, the world-community is composed of nations, colonies, spheres of influence, cities, towns, local communities, neighborhoods, and families.

These represent in a rough way the subject-matter of sociological science.   Their organization, interrelation, constituent elements, and the characteristic changes (social processes) which take place in them are the phenomena of sociological science.

Human beings as we meet them are mobile entities, variously distributed through geographical space.   What is the nature of the connection between individuals which permits them at the same time to preserve their distances and act corporately and consentiently— with a common purpose, in short?   These distances which separate individuals are not merely spatial, they are psychical.   Society exists where these distances have been *relatively* overcome.   Society exists, in short, not merely where there are people but where there is communication.

The materials in this chapter are intended to show (1) the fundamental character of the relations which have been established between individuals through communication; (2) the gradual evolution of these relations in animal and human societies.   On the basis of the principle thus established it is possible to work out a rational classification of social groups.

Espinas defines society in terms of corporate action.   Wherever separate individuals act together as a unit, where they co-operate as though they were parts of the same organism, there he finds society. Society from this standpoint is not confined to members of one species, but may be composed of different members of species where there is permanent joint activity.   In the study of symbiosis among animals, it is significant to note the presence of structural adaptations in one or both species.   In the taming and domestication of animals by man the effects of symbiosis are manifest.   Domestication, by the selection in breeding of traits desired by man, changes the original nature of the animal.   Taming is achieved by control of habits in transferring to man the filial and gregarious responses of the young naturally given to its parents and members of its kind.   Man may be thought of as domesticated through natural social selection.   Eugenics is a conscious program of further domestication by the elimination of defective physical and mental racial traits and by the improvement of the racial stock through the social selection of superior traits. Taming has always been a function of human society, but it is dignified by such denominations as "education," "social control," "punishment," and "reformation."

The plant community offers the simplest and least qualified example of the community.   Plant life, in fact, offers an illustration of a *community* which is *not a society*.   It is not a society because it is an organization of individuals whose relations, if not wholly external, are, at any rate, "unsocial" in so far as there is no consensus.   The plant community is interesting, moreover, because it exhibits in the barest abstraction, the character of *competitive co-operation*, the aspect of social life which constitutes part of the special subject-matter of economic science.

This struggle for existence, in some form or other, is in fact essential to the existence of society.   Competition, segregation, and accommodation serve to maintain the social distances, to fix the status, and preserve the independence of the individual in the social relation.   A society in which all distances, physical as well as psychical, had been abolished, in which there was neither taboo, prejudice, nor reserve of any sort; a society in which the intimacies were absolute, would be a society in which there were neither persons nor freedom. The processes of competition, segregation, and accommodation brought out in the description of the plant community are quite comparable with the same processes in animal and human communities. A village, town, city, or nation may be studied from the standpoint of the adaptation, struggle for existence, and survival of its individual members in the environment created by the community as a whole.

Society, as Dewey points out, if based on instinct is an effect of communication. *Consensus* even more than *co-operation* or *corporate action* is the distinctive mark of human society. Dewey, however, seems to restrict the use of consensus to group decisions in which all the members consciously and rationally participate. Tradition and sentiment are, however, forms of consensus quite as much as constitutions, rules, and elections.

Le Bon's classification of social groups into heterogeneous and homogeneous crowds, while interesting and suggestive, is clearly inadequate. Many groups familiar to all of us, as the family, the play-group, the neighborhood, the public, find no place in his system.[1]

Concrete descriptions of group behavior indicate three aspects in the consensus of the members of the group. The first is the characteristic state of group feeling called *esprit de corps*. The enthusiasm of the two sides in a football contest, the ecstasy of religious ceremonial, the fellowship of members of a fraternity, the brotherhood of a monastic band are all different manifestations of group spirit.

The second aspect of consensus has become familiar through the term "morale." Morale may be defined as the collective will. Like the will of the individual it represents an organization of behavior tendencies. The discipline of the individual, his subordination to the group, lies in his participation and reglementation in social activities.

The third aspect of consensus which makes for unified behavior of the members of the group has been analyzed by Durkheim under the term "collective representations." Collective representations are the concepts which embody the objectives of group activity.

[1] See *supra*, chap. i, pp. 50–51.

The totem of primitive man, the flag of a nation, a religious creed, the number system, and Darwin's theory of the descent of man—all these are collective representations. Every society and every social group has, or tends to have, its own symbols and its own language. The language and other symbolic devices by which a society carries on its collective existence are collective representations. Animals do not possess them.

II. MATERIALS

A. SOCIETY AND SYMBIOSIS

1. Definition of Society[1]

The idea of society is that of a permanent co-operation in which separate living beings undertake to accomplish an identical act. These beings may find themselves brought by their conditions to a point where their co-operation forces them to group themselves in space in some definite form, but it is by no means necessary that they should be in juxtaposition for them to act together and thus to form a society. A customary reciprocation of services among more or less independent individualities is the characteristic feature of the social life, a feature that contact or remoteness does not essentially modify, nor the apparent disorder nor the regular disposition of the parties in space.

Two beings may then form what is to the eyes a single mass, and may live, not only in contact with each other, but even in a state of mutual penetration without constituting a society. It is enough in such a case that one looks at them as entirely distinct, that their activities tend to opposite or merely different ends. If their functions, instead of co-operating, diverge; if the good of one is the evil of the other, whatever the intimacy of their contact may be, no social bond unites them.

But the nature of the functions and the form of the organs are inseparable. If two beings are endowed with functions that necessarily combine, they are also endowed with organs, if not similar, at least corresponding. And these beings with like or corresponding organs are either of the same species or of very nearly the same species.

[1] Translated from Alfred Espinas, *Des sociétés animales* (1878), pp. 157–60.

However, circumstances may be met where two beings with quite different organs and belonging even to widely remote species may be accidentally and at a single point useful to each other. A habitual relation may be established between their activities, but only on this one point, and in the time limits in which the usefulness exists. Such a case gives the occasion, if not for a society, at least for an association; that is to say, a union less necessary, less strict, less durable, may find its origin in such a meeting. In other words, beside the normal societies formed of elements specifically alike, which cannot exist without each other, there will be room for more accidental groupings, formed of elements more or less specifically unlike, which convenience unites and not necessity. We will commence with a study of the latter.

To society the most alien relations of two living beings which can be produced are those of the predator and his prey. In general, the predator is bulkier than his prey, since he overcomes him and devours him. Yet smaller ones sometimes attack larger creatures, consuming them, however, by instalments, and letting them live that they themselves may live on them as long as possible. In such a case they are forced to remain for a longer or a shorter time attached to the body of their victim, carried about by it wherever the vicissitudes of its life lead them. Such animals have received the name of parasites. Parasitism forms the line inside of which our subject begins; for if one can imagine that the parasite, instead of feeding on the animal from whom he draws his subsistence, is content to live on the remains of the other's meals, one will find himself in the presence, not yet of an actual society, but of half the conditions of a society; that is to say, a relation between two beings such that, all antagonism ceasing, one of the two is useful to the other. Such is commensalism. However, this association does not yet offer the essential element of all society, co-operation. There is co-operation when the commensal is not less useful to his host than the latter is to the commensal himself, when the two are concerned in living in a reciprocal relation and in developing their double activity in corresponding ways toward a single and an identical goal. One has given to this mode of activity the name of mutualism. Domestication is only one form of it. Parasitism, commensalism, mutualism, exist with animals among the different species.

2. Symbiosis (literally "living together")[1]

In gaining their wide and intimate acquaintance with the vegetable world the ants have also become acquainted with a large number of insects that obtain their nutriment directly from plants, either by sucking up their juices or by feeding on their foliage. To the former group belong the phytophthorous Homoptera, the plant lice, scale insects, or mealy bugs, tree-hoppers, lantern flies, and jumping plant lice; to the latter belong the caterpillars of the lycaenid butterflies, the "blues," or "azures," as they are popularly called. All of these creatures excrete liquids which are eagerly sought by the ants and constitute the whole, or, at any rate, an important part of the food of certain species. In return the Homoptera and caterpillars receive certain services from the ants, so that the relations thus established between these widely different insects may be regarded as a kind of symbiosis. These relations are most apparent in the case of the aphids, and these insects have been more often and more closely studied in Europe and America.

The consociation of the ants with the aphids is greatly facilitated by the gregarious and rather sedentary habits of the latter, especially in their younger, wingless stages, for the ants are thus enabled to obtain a large amount of food without losing time and energy in ranging far afield from their nests. Then, too, the ants may establish their nests in the immediate vicinity of the aphid droves or actually keep them in their nests or in "sheds" carefully constructed for the purpose.

Some ants obtain the honey-dew merely by licking the surface of the leaves and stems on which it has fallen, but many species have learned to stroke the aphids and induce them to void the liquid gradually so that it can be imbibed directly. A drove of plant lice, especially when it is stationed on young and succulent leaves or twigs, may produce enough honey-dew to feed a whole colony of ants for a considerable period.

As the relations between ants and the various Homoptera have been regarded as mutualistic, it may be well to marshal the facts which seem to warrant this interpretation. The term "mutualism" as applied to these cases means, of course, that the aphids, coccids,

[1] Adapted from William M. Wheeler, *Ants, Their Structure, Development, Behavior*, pp. 339–424. (Columbia University Press, 1910.)

and membracids are of service to the ants and in turn profit by the companionship of these more active and aggressive insects. Among the modifications in structure and behavior which may be regarded as indicating on the part of aphids unmistakable evidence of adaptation to living with ants, the following may be cited:

1. The aphids do not attempt to escape from the ants or to defend themselves with their siphons, but accept the presence of these attendants as a matter of course.

2. The aphids respond to the solicitations of the ants by extruding the droplets of honey-dew gradually and not by throwing them off to a distance with a sudden jerk, as they do in the absence of ants.

3. Many species of Aphididae that live habitually with ants have developed a perianal circlet of stiff hairs which support the drop of honey-dew till it can be imbibed by the ants. This circlet is lacking in aphids that are rarely or never visited by ants.

4. Certain observations go to show that aphids, when visited by ants, extract more of the plant juices than when unattended.

The adaptations on the part of the ants are, with a single doubtful exception, all modifications in behavior and not in structure.

1. Ants do not seize and kill aphids as they do when they encounter other sedentary defenseless insects.

2. The ants stroke the aphids in a particular manner in order to make them excrete the honey-dew, and know exactly where to expect the evacuated liquid.

3. The ants protect the aphids. Several observers have seen the ants driving away predatory insects.

4. Many aphidicolous ants, when disturbed, at once seize and carry their charges in their mandibles to a place of safety, showing very plainly their sense of ownership and interest in these helpless creatures.

5. This is also exhibited by all ants that harbor root-aphids and root-coccids in their nests. Not only are these insects kept in confinement by the ants, but they are placed by them on the roots. In order to do this the ants remove the earth from the surfaces of the roots and construct galleries and chambers around them so that the Homoptera may have easy access to their food and even move about at will.

6. Many ants construct, often at some distance from their nests, little closed pavilions or sheds of earth, carton, or silk, as a protection for their cattle and for themselves. The singular habit may be merely a more recent development from the older and more general habit of excavating tunnels and chambers about roots and subterranean stems.

7. The solicitude of the ants not only envelops the adult aphids and coccids, but extends also to their eggs and young. Numerous observers have observed ants in the autumn collecting and storing aphid eggs in the chambers of their nests, caring for them through the winter and in the spring placing the recently hatched plant lice on the stems and roots of the plants.

In the foregoing I have discussed the ethological relations of ants to a variety of other organisms. This, however, did not include an account of some of the most interesting symbiotic relations, namely, those of the ants to other species of their own taxonomic group and to termites. This living together of colonies of different species may be properly designated as social symbiosis, to distinguish it from the simple symbiosis that obtains between individual organisms of different species and the intermediate form of symbiosis exhibited by individual organisms that live in ant or termite colonies.

The researches of the past forty years have brought to light a remarkable array of instances of social symbiosis, varying so much in intimacy and complexity that it is possible to construct a series ranging from mere simultaneous occupancy of a very narrow ethological station, or mere contiguity of domicile, to an actual fusion, involving the vital dependence or parasitism of a colony of one species on that of another. Such a series is, of course, purely conceptual and does not represent the actual course of development in nature, where, as in the animal and vegetable kingdoms in general, development has not followed a simple linear course, but has branched out repeatedly and terminated in the varied types at the present time.

It is convenient to follow the European writers, von Hagens, Forel, Wasmann, and others, in grouping all the cases of social symbiosis under two heads, the compound nests and the mixed colonies. Different species of ants or of ants and termites are said to form compound nests when their galleries are merely contiguous or actually interpenetrate and open into one another, although the colonies which inhabit them bring up their respective offspring in different apartments. In mixed colonies, on the other hand, which, in a state of nature, can be formed only by species of ants of close taxonomic affinities, the insects live together in a single nest and bring up their young in common. Although each of these categories comprises a number of dissimilar types of social symbiosis, and although it is possible, under certain circumstances, as will be shown in the sequel, to convert a compound nest into a mixed colony, the distinction is nevertheless fundamental. It must be admitted, however, that both types depend in last analysis on the dependent, adoption-seeking instincts of the queen ant and on the remarkable plasticity which enables allied species and genera to live in very close proximity to one another. By a strange paradox these peculiarities have been produced in the struggle for existence, although this struggle is severer among different species of ants than between ants and other organisms. As Forel says: "The greatest enemies of ants are other ants, just as the greatest enemies of men are other men."

3. The Taming and the Domestication of Animals[1]

Primitive man was a hunter almost before he had the intelligence to use weapons, and from the earliest times he must have learned something about the habits of the wild animals he pursued for food or for pleasure, or from which he had to escape. It was probably as a hunter that he first came to adopt young animals which he found in the woods or the plains, and made the surprising discovery that these were willing to remain under his protection and were pleasing and useful. He passed gradually from being a hunter to becoming a keeper of flocks and herds. From these early days to the present time, the human race has taken an interest in the lower animals, and yet extremely few have been really domesticated. The living world would seem to offer an almost unlimited range of creatures which might be turned to our profit and as domesticated animals minister to our comfort or convenience. And yet it seems as if there were some obstacle rooted in the nature of animals or in the powers of man, for the date of the adoption by man of the few domesticated species lies in remote, prehistoric antiquity. The surface of the earth has been explored, the physiology of breeding and feeding

[1] Adapted from P. Chalmers Mitchell, *The Childhood of Animals*, pp. 204–21. (Frederick A. Stokes & Co., 1912.)

has been studied, our knowledge of the animal kingdom has been vastly increased, and yet there is hardly a beast bred in the farmyard today with which the men who made stone weapons were not acquainted and which they had not tamed. Most of the domestic animals of Europe, America, and Asia came originally from Central Asia, and have spread thence in charge of their masters, the primitive hunters who captured them.

No monkeys have been domesticated. Of the carnivores only the cat and the dog are truly domesticated. Of the ungulates there are horses and asses, pigs, cattle, sheep, goats, and reindeer. Among rodents there are rabbits and guinea-pigs, and possibly some of the fancy breeds of rats and mice should be included. Among birds there are pigeons, fowls, peacocks, and guinea-fowl, and aquatic birds such as swans, geese, and ducks, whilst the only really domesticated passerine bird is the canary. Goldfish are domesticated, and the invertebrate bees and silk-moths must not be forgotten. It is not very easy to draw a line between domesticated animals and animals that are often bred in partial or complete captivity. Such antelopes as elands, fallow-deer, roe-deer, and the ostriches of ostrich farms are on the border-line of being domesticated.

It is also difficult to be quite certain as to what is meant by a tame animal. Cockroaches usually scuttle away when they are disturbed and seem to have learnt that human beings have a just grievance against them. But many people have no horror of them. A pretty girl, clean and dainty in her ways, and devoted to all kinds of animals, used to like sitting in a kitchen that was infested with these repulsive creatures, and told me that when she was alone they would run over her dress and were not in the least startled when she took them up. I have heard of a butterfly which used to come and sip sugar from the hand of a lady; and those who have kept spiders and ants declare that these intelligent creatures learn to distinguish their friends. So also fish, like the great carp in the garden of the palace of Fontainebleau, and many fishes in aquaria and private ponds, learn to come to be fed. I do not think, however, that these ought to be called tame animals. Most of the wild animals in menageries very quickly learn to distinguish one person from another, to obey the call of their keeper and to come to be fed, although certainly they would be dangerous even to the keeper if he were to enter their cages. To my mind, tameness is something more than merely coming to be fed, and, in fact, many tame animals are least tame when they are feeding. Young carnivores, for instance, which can be handled freely and are affectionate, very seldom can be touched whilst they are feeding. The real quality of tameness is that the tame animal is not merely tolerant of the presence of man, not merely has learned to associate him with food, but takes some kind of pleasure in human company and shows some kind of affection.

On the other hand, we must not take our idea of tameness merely from the domesticated animals. These have been bred for many generations, and those that were most wild and that showed any resistance to man were killed or allowed to escape. Dogs are always taken as the supreme example of tameness, and sentimentalists have almost exhausted the resources of language in praising them. Like most people, I am very fond of dogs, but it is an affection without respect. Dogs breed freely in captivity, and in the enormous period of time that has elapsed since the first hunters adopted wild puppies there has been a constant selection by man, and every dog that showed any independence of spirit has been killed off. Man has tried to produce a purely subservient creature, and has succeeded in his task. No doubt a dog is faithful and affectionate, but he would be shot or drowned or ordered to be destroyed by the local magistrate if he were otherwise. A small vestige of the original spirit has been left in him, merely from the ambition of his owners to possess an animal that will not bite them, but will bite anyone else. And even this watch-dog trait is mechanical, for the guardian of the house will worry the harmless, necessary postman, and welcome the bold burglar with fawning delight. The dog is a slave, and the crowning evidence of his docility, that he will fawn on the person who has beaten him, is the result of his character having been bred out of him. The dog is an engaging companion, an animated toy more diverting than the cleverest piece of clockwork, but it is only our colossal vanity that makes us take credit for the affection and faithfulness of our own particular animal. The poor beast cannot help it; all else has been bred out of him generations ago.

When wild animals become tame, they are really extending or transferring to human beings the confidence and affection they naturally give their mothers, and this view will be found to explain more facts about tameness than any other. Every creature that would naturally enjoy maternal, or it would be better to say parental, care, as the father sometimes shares in or takes upon himself the duty of guarding the young, is ready to transfer its devotion to other animals or to human beings, if the way be made easy for it, and if it be treated without too great violation of its natural instincts. The capacity to be tamed is greatest in those animals that remain longest with their parents and that are most intimately associated with them. The capacity to learn new habits is greatest in those animals which naturally learn most from their parents, and in which the period of youth is not merely a period of growing, a period of the awakening of instincts, but a time in which a real education takes place. These capacities of being tamed and of learning new habits are greater in the higher mammals than in the lower mammals, in mammals than in birds, and in birds than in reptiles. They are very much greater in very young animals, where dependence on the parents is greatest, than in older animals, and they gradually fade away as the animal grows up, and are least of all in fully grown and independent creatures of high intelligence.

Young animals born in captivity are no more easy to tame than those which have been taken from the mother in her native haunts. If they remain with the mother, they very often grow up even shyer and more intolerant of man than the mothers themselves. There is no inherited docility or tameness, and a general survey of the facts fully bears out my belief that the process of taming is almost entirely a transference to human beings of the confidence and affection that a young animal would naturally give its mother. The process of domestication is different, and requires breeding a race of animals in captivity for many generations and gradually weeding out those in which youthful tameness is replaced by the wild instinct of adult life, and so creating a strain with new and abnormal instincts.

B.   PLANT COMMUNITIES AND ANIMAL SOCIETIES
1.   Plant Communities[1]

Certain species group themselves into natural associations, that is to say, into communities which we meet with more or less frequently

[1] Adapted from Eugenius Warming, *Oecology of Plants*, pp. 12-13, 91-95. (Oxford University Press, 1909.)

and which exhibit the same combination of growth-forms and the same facies. As examples in northern Europe may be cited a meadow with its grasses and perennial herbs, or a beech forest with its beech trees and all the species usually accompanying these. Species that form a community must either practice the same economy, making approximately the same demands on its environment (as regards nourishment, light, moisture, and so forth), or one species present must be dependent for its existence upon another species, sometimes to such an extent that the latter provides it with what is necessary or even best suited to it (Oxalis Acetosella and saprophytes which profit from the shade of the beech and from its humus soil); a kind of symbiosis seems to prevail between such species. In fact, one often finds, as in beech forests, that the plants growing under the shade and protection of other species, and belonging to the most diverse families, assume growth-forms that are very similar to one another, but essentially different from those of the forest trees, which, in their turn, often agree with one another.

The ecological analysis of a plant-community leads to the recognition of the growth-forms composing it as its ultimate units. From what has just been said in regard to growth-forms it follows that species of very diverse physiognomy can very easily occur together in the same natural community. But beyond this, as already indicated, species differing widely, not only in physiognomy but also in their whole economy, may be associated. We may therefore expect to find both great variety of form and complexity of interrelations among the species composing a natural community; as an example we may cite the richest of all types of communities—the tropical rain-forest. It may also be noted that the physiognomy of a community is not necessarily the same at all times of the year, the distinction sometimes being caused by a rotation of species.

The different communities, it need hardly be stated, are scarcely ever sharply marked off from one another. Just as soil, moisture, and other external conditions are connected by the most gradual transitions, so likewise are the plant-communities, especially in cultivated lands. In addition, the same species often occur in several widely different communities; for example, Linnaea borealis grows not only in coniferous forests, but also in birch woods, and even high above the tree limit on the mountains of Norway and on the fell-fields of Greenland. It appears that different combinations of external factors can replace one another and bring into existence approximately the same community, or at least can satisfy equally well one and the same species, and that, for instance, a moist climate often completely replaces the forest shade of dry climates.

The term "community" implies a diversity but at the same time a certain organized uniformity in the units. The units are the many individual plants that occur in every community, whether this be a beech forest, a meadow, or a heath. Uniformity is established when certain atmospheric, terrestrial, and other factors are co-operative, and appears either because a certain defined economy makes its impress on the community as a whole, or because a number of different growth-forms are combined to form a single aggregate which has a definite and constant guise.

The analysis of a plant-community usually reveals one or more of the kinds of symbiosis as illustrated by parasites, saprophytes, epiphytes, and the like. There is scarce a forest or a bushland where examples of these forms of symbiosis are lacking; if, for instance, we investigate the tropical rain-forest we are certain to find in it all conceivable kinds of symbiosis. But the majority of individuals of a plant-community are linked by bonds other than those mentioned— bonds that are best described as *commensal*. The term *commensalism* is due to Van Beneden, who wrote, "Le commensal est simplement un compagnon de table"; but we employ it in a somewhat different sense to denote the relationship subsisting between species which share with one another the supply of food-material contained in soil and air, and thus feed at the same table.

More detailed analysis of the plant-community reveals very considerable distinctions among commensals. Some relationships are considered in the succeeding paragraphs.

Like commensals.—When a plant-community consists solely of individuals belonging to one species—for example, solely of beech, ling, or Aira flexuosa—then we have the purest example of like commensals. These all make the same demands as regards nutriment, soil, light, and other like conditions; as each species requires a certain amount of space and as there is scarcely ever sufficient nutriment for all the offspring, a struggle for food arises among the plants so soon as the space is occupied by the definite numbers of individuals which, according to the species, can develop thereon.   The individuals lodged in unfavorable places and the weaklings are vanquished and exterminated.   This competitive struggle takes place in all plant-communities, with perhaps the sole exceptions of sub-glacial communities and in deserts.   In these *open communities* the soil is very often or always so open and so irregularly clothed that there is space for many more individuals than are actually present; the cause for this is obviously to be sought in the climatically unfavorable conditions of life, which either prevent plants from producing seed and other propagative bodies in sufficient numbers to clothe the ground or prevent the development of seedlings.   On such soil one can scarcely speak of a competitive struggle for existence; in this case a struggle takes place between the plant and inanimate nature, but to little or no extent between plant and plant.

That a congregation of individuals belonging to one species into one community may be profitable to the species is evident; it may obviously in several ways aid in maintaining the existence of the species, for instance, by facilitating abundant and certain fertilization (especially in anemophilous plants) and maturation of seeds; in addition, the social mode of existence may confer other less-known advantages.   But, on the other hand, it brings with it greater danger of serious damage and devastation wrought by parasites.

The bonds that hold like individuals to a like habitat are, as already indicated, identical demands as regards existence, and these demands are satisfied in their precise habitat to such an extent that the species can maintain itself here against rivals.   Natural unmixed associations of forest trees are the result of struggles with other species.   But there are differences as regards the ease with which a community can arise and establish itself.   Some species are more social than others, that is to say, better fitted to form communities. The causes for this are biological, in that some species, like Phragmites, Scirpus lacustris, Psamma (Ammophila) arenaria, Tussilago, Farfara, and Asperula odorata, multiply very readily by means of stolons; or others, such as Cirsium arvense, and Sonchus arvensis, produce buds from their roots; or yet others produce numerous seeds which are easily dispersed and may remain for a long time capable of germinating, as is the case with Calluna, Picea excelsa, and Pinus; or still other species, such as beech and spruce, have the power of enduring shade or even suppressing other species by the shade they cast. A number of species, such as Pteris aquilina, Acorus Calamus, Lemna minor, and Hypnum Schreberi, which are social, and likewise very widely distributed, multiply nearly exclusively by vegetative means, rarely or never producing fruit. On the contrary, certain species, for example, many orchids and Umbelliferae, nearly always grow singly.

In the case of many species certain geological conditions have favored their grouping together into pure communities. The forests of northern Europe are composed of few species, and are not mixed in the same sense as are those in the tropics, or even those in Austria and other southern parts of Europe: the cause for this may be that the soil is geologically very recent, inasmuch as the time that has elapsed since the glacial epoch swept it clear has been too short to permit the immigration of many competitive species.

Unlike commensals.—The case of a community consisting of individuals belonging to one species is, strictly speaking, scarcely ever met with; but the dominant individuals of a community may belong to a single species, as in the case of a beech forest, spruce forest, or ling heath—and only thus far does the case proceed. In general, many species grow side by side, and many different growth-forms and types of symbiosis, in the extended sense, are found collected in a community. For even when one species occupies an area as completely as the nature of the soil will permit, other species can find room and can grow between its individuals; in fact, if the soil is to be completely covered the vegetation must necessarily always be heterogeneous. The greatest aggregate of existence arises where the greatest diversity prevails. The kind of communal life resulting will depend upon the nature of the demands made by the species in regard to conditions of life. As in human communities, so in this case, the *struggle between the like* is the *most severe*, that is, between the species making more or less the same demands and wanting the same dishes from the common table. In a tropical mixed forest there are hundreds of species of trees growing together in such profuse variety that the eye can scarce see at one time two individuals of the same species, yet all of them undoubtedly represent tolerable uniformity in the demands they make as regards conditions of life, and in so far they are alike. And among them a severe competition for food must be taking place. In those cases in which certain species readily grow in each other's company—and cases of this kind are familiar to florists—when, for instance, Isoetes, Lobelia Dortmanna, and Litorella lacustris occur together—the common demands made as regards external conditions obviously form the bond that unites them. Between such species a competitive struggle must take place. Which of the species shall be represented by the greatest number of individuals certainly often depends upon casual conditions, a slight change in one direction or the other doubtless often playing a decisive rôle; but apart from this it appears that morphological and biological features, for example, development at a different season, may change the nature of the competition.

Yet there are in every plant-community numerous species which *differ widely* in the demands they make for light, heat, nutriment, and so on. Between such species there is less competition, the greater the disparity in their wants; the case is quite conceivable in which the *one species should require exactly what the other would avoid;* the two species would then be complementary to one another in their occupation and utilization of the same soil.

There are also obvious cases in which different species are of service to each other. The carpet of moss in a pine forest, for example, protects the soil from desiccation and is thus useful to the pine; yet, on the other hand, it profits from the shade cast by the latter.

As a rule, limited numbers of definite species are the most potent, and, like absolute monarchs, can hold sway over the whole area; while other species, though possibly present in far greater numbers than these, are subordinate or even dependent on them. This is the case where subordinate species only flourish in the shade or among the fallen fragments of dominant species. Such is obviously the relationship between trees and many plants growing on the ground of high forest, such as mosses, fungi, and other saprophytes, ferns, Oxalis Acetosella, and their associates. In this case, then, there is a commensalism in which individuals feed at the same table but on different fare. An additional factor steps in when species do not absorb their nutriment at the same season of the year. Many spring plants—for instance, Galanthus nivalis, Corydalis solida, and C. cava—have withered before the summer plants commence properly to develop. Certain species of animals are likewise confined to certain plant-communities. But one and the same tall plant may, in different places or soils, have different species of lowly plants as companions; the companion plants of high beech forests depend, for instance, upon climate and upon the nature of the forest soil; Pinus nigra, according to von Beck, can maintain under it in the different parts of Europe a Pontic, a central European, or a Baltic vegetation.

There are certain points of resemblance between communities of plants and those of human beings or animals; one of these is the competition for food which takes place between similar individuals and causes the weaker to be more or less suppressed. But far greater are the distinctions. The plant-community is the lowest form; it is merely a congregation of units, among which there is no co-operation for the common weal, but rather a ceaseless struggle of all against all. Only in a loose sense can we speak of certain individuals protecting others, as for example, when the outermost and most exposed individuals of scrub serve to shelter from the wind others, which consequently become taller and finer; for they do not afford protection from any special motive, such as is met with in some animal communities, nor are they in any way specially adapted to act as guardians against a common foe. In the plant-community egoism reigns supreme. The plant-community has no higher units or personages in the sense employed in connection with human communities, which have their own organizations and their members co-operating, as prescribed by law, for the common good. In plant-communities there is, it is true, often (or always) a certain natural dependence or reciprocal influence of many species upon one another; they give rise to definite organized units of a higher order; but there is no thorough or organized division of labor such as is met with in human and animal communities, where certain individuals or groups of individuals work as organs, in the wide sense of the term, for the benefit of the whole community.

Woodhead has suggested the term *complementary association* to denote a community of species that live together in harmony, because their rhizomes occupy different depths in the soil; for example, he described an "association" in which Holcus mollis is the "surface plant," Pteris aquilina has deeper-seated rhizomes, and Scilla festalis buries its bulbs at the greatest depth. The photophilous parts of

these plants are "seasonably complementary." The opposite
extreme is provided by *competitive associations,* composed of species
that are battling with each other.

2. Ant Society[1]

There is certainly a striking parallelism between the development
of human and ant societies. Some anthropologists, like Topinard,
distinguish in the development of human societies six different types
or stages, designated as the hunting, pastoral, agricultural, commercial, industrial, and intellectual. The ants show stages corresponding
to the first three of these, as Lubbock has remarked.

Some species, such as *Formica fusca,* live principally on the produce of
the chase; for though they feed partially on the honey-dew of aphids, they
have not domesticated these insects. These ants probably retain the
habits once common to all ants. They resemble the lower races of men,
who subsist mainly by hunting. Like them they frequent woods and
wilds, live in comparatively small communities, as the instincts of collective action are but little developed among them. They hunt singly, and
their battles are single combats, like those of Homeric heroes. Such
species as *Lasius flavus* represent a distinctly higher type of social life;
they show more skill in architecture, may literally be said to have domesticated certain species of aphids, and may be compared to the pastoral stage
of human progress—to the races which live on the products of their flocks
and herds. Their communities are more numerous; they act much more
in concert; their battles are not mere single combats, but they know how
to act in combination. I am disposed to hazard the conjecture that they
will gradually exterminate the mere hunting species, just as savages disappear before more advanced races. Lastly, the agricultural nations may
be compared with the harvesting ants.

Granting the resemblances above mentioned between ant and
human societies, there are nevertheless three far-reaching differences
between insect and human organization and development to be constantly borne in mind:

a) Ant societies are societies of females. The males really take
no part in the colonial activities, and in most species are present in
the nest only for the brief period requisite to secure the impregnation

[1] Adapted from William M. Wheeler, *Ants, Their Structure, Development, and
Behavior,* pp. 5–7. (Columbia University Press, 1910.)

of the young queens. The males take no part in building, provisioning, or guarding the nest or in feeding the workers or the brood. They are in every sense the *sexus sequior*. Hence the ants resemble certain mythical human societies like the Amazons, but unlike these, all their activities center in the multiplication and care of the coming generations.

b) In human society, apart from the functions depending on sexual dimorphism, and barring individual differences and deficiencies which can be partially or wholly suppressed, equalized, or augmented by an elaborate system of education, all individuals have the same natural endowment. Each normal individual retains its various physiological and psychological needs and powers intact, not necessarily sacrificing any of them for the good of the community. In ants, however, the female individuals, of which the society properly consists, are not all alike but often very different, both in their structure (polymorphism) and in their activities (physiological division of labor). Each member is *visibly* predestined to certain social activities to the exclusion of others, not as a man through the education of some endowment common to all the members of the society, but through the exigencies of structure, fixed at the time of hatching, i.e., the moment the individual enters on its life as an active member of the community.

c) Owing to this pre-established structure and the specialized functions which it implies, ants are able to live in a condition of anarchistic socialism, each individual instinctively fulfilling the demands of social life without "guide, overseer, or ruler," as Solomon correctly observed, but not without the imitation and suggestion involved in an appreciation of the activities of its fellows.

An ant society, therefore, may be regarded as little more than an expanded family, the members of which co-operate for the purpose of still further expanding the family and detaching portions of itself to found other families of the same kind. There is thus a striking analogy, which has not escaped the philosophical biologist, between the ant colony and the cell colony which constitutes the body of a Metazoan animal; and many of the laws that control the cellular origin, development, growth, reproduction, and decay of the individual Metazoan, are seen to hold good also of the ant society regarded as an individual of a higher order. As in the case of the individual animal, no further purpose of the colony can be detected than that of maintaining itself in the face of a constantly changing environment till it is able to reproduce other colonies of a like constitution. The queen-mother of the ant colony displays the generalized potentialities of all the individuals, just as the Metazoan egg contains *in potentia* all the other cells of the body. And, continuing the analogy, we may say that since the different castes of the ant colony are morphologically specialized for the performance of different functions, they are truly comparable with the differentiated tissues of the Metazoan body.

C. HUMAN SOCIETY

1. Social Life[1]

The most notable distinction between living and inanimate beings is that the former maintain themselves by renewal. A stone when struck resists. If its resistance is greater than the force of the blow struck, it remains outwardly unchanged. Otherwise, it is shattered into smaller bits. Never does the stone attempt to react in such a way that it may maintain itself against the blow, much less so as to render the blow a contributing factor to its own continued action. While the living thing may easily be crushed by superior force, it none the less tries to turn the energies which act upon it into means of its own further existence. If it cannot do so, it does not just split into smaller pieces (at least in the higher forms of life), but loses its identity as a living thing.

As long as it endures, it struggles to use surrounding energies in its own behalf. It uses light, air, moisture, and the material of soil. To say that it uses them is to say that it turns them into means of its own conservation. As long as it is growing, the energy it expends in thus turning the environment to account is more than compensated for by the return it gets: it grows. Understanding the word "control" in this sense, it may be said that a living being is one that subjugates and controls for its own continued activity the energies that would otherwise use it up. Life is a self-renewing process through action upon the environment. Continuity of life means continual readaptation of the environment to the needs of living organisms.

[1] From John Dewey, *Democracy and Education*, pp. 1-7. (Published by The Macmillan Co., 1916. Reprinted by permission.)

We have been speaking of life in its lowest terms—as a physical thing. But we use the word "life" to denote the whole range of experience, individual and racial. When we see a book called the *Life of Lincoln* we do not expect to find within its covers a treatise on physiology. We look for an account of social antecedents; a description of early surroundings, of the conditions and occupation of the family; of the chief episodes in the development of character; of signal struggles and achievements; of the individual's hopes, tastes, joys, and sufferings. In precisely similar fashion we speak of the life of a savage tribe, of the Athenian people, of the American nation. "Life" covers customs, institutions, beliefs, victories and defeats, recreations and occupations.

We employ the word "experience" in the same pregnant sense. And to it, as well as to life in the bare physiological sense, the principle of continuity through renewal applies. With the renewal of physical existence goes, in the case of human beings, the re-creation of beliefs, ideals, hopes, happiness, misery, and practices. The continuity of any experience, through renewing of the social group, is a literal fact. Education, in its broadest sense, is the means of this social continuity of life. Every one of the constituent elements of a social group, in a modern city as in a savage tribe, is born immature, helpless, without language, beliefs, ideas, or social standards. Each individual, each unit who is the carrier of the life-experience of his group, in time passes away. Yet the life of the group goes on.

Society exists through a process of transmission, quite as much as biological life. This transmission occurs by means of communication of habits of doing, thinking, and feeling from the older to the younger. Without this communication of ideals, hopes, expectations, standards, opinions from those members of society who are passing out of the group life to those who are coming into it, social life could not survive.

Society not only continues to exist *by* transmission, *by* communication, but it may fairly be said to exist *in* transmission, *in* communication. There is more than a verbal tie between the words common, community, and communication. Men live in a community in virtue of the things which they have in common; and communication is the way in which they come to possess things in common. What they must have in common in order to form a community or society are aims, beliefs, aspirations, knowledge—a common understanding—like-mindedness, as the sociologists say. Such things cannot be passed physically from one to another, like bricks; they cannot be shared as persons would share a pie by dividing it into physical pieces. The communication which insures participation in a common under-standing is one which secures similar emotional and intellectual dis-positions—like ways of responding to expectations and requirements.

Persons do not become a society by living in physical proximity any more than a man ceases to be socially influenced by being so many feet or miles removed from others. A book or a letter may institute a more intimate association between human beings separated thousands of miles from each other than exists between dwellers under the same roof. Individuals do not even compose a social group because they all work for a common end. The parts of a machine work with a maximum of co-operativeness for a common result, but they do not form a community. If, however, they were all cognizant of the common end and all interested in it so that they regulated their specific activity in view of it, then they would form a community. But this would involve communication. Each would have to know what the other was about and would have to have some way of keeping the other informed as to his own purpose and progress. Consensus demands communications.

We are thus compelled to recognize that within even the most social group there are many relations which are not as yet social. A large number of human relationships in any social group are still upon the machine-like plane. Individuals use one another so as to get desired results, without reference to the emotional and intellectual disposition and consent of those used. Such uses express physical superiority, or superiority of position, skill, technical ability, and command of tools, mechanical or fiscal. So far as the relations of parent and child, teacher and pupil, employer and employee, gover-nor and governed, remain upon this level, they form no true social group, no matter how closely their respective activities touch one another. Giving and taking of orders modifies action and results, but does not of itself effect a sharing of purposes, a communication of interests.

Not only is social life identical with communication, but all communication (and hence all genuine social life) is educative. To be a recipient of a communication is to have an enlarged and changed experience. One shares in what another has thought and felt, and in so far, meagerly or amply, has his own attitude modified. Nor is the one who communicates left unaffected. Try the experiment of communicating, with fulness and accuracy, some experience to another, especially if it be somewhat complicated, and you will find your own attitude toward your experience changing; otherwise you resort to expletives and ejaculations. The experience has to be formulated in order to be communicated. To formulate requires getting outside of it, seeing it as another would see it, considering what points of contact it has with the life of another so that it may be got into such form that he can appreciate its meaning. Except in dealing with commonplaces and catch phrases one has to assimilate, imaginatively, something of another's experience in order to tell him intelligently of one's own experience. All communication is like art. It may fairly be said, therefore, that any social arrangement that remains vitally social, or vitally shared, is educative to those who participate in it. Only when it becomes cast in a mold and runs in a routine way does it lose its educative power.

In final account, then, not only does social life demand teaching and learning for its own permanence, but the very process of living together educates. It enlarges and enlightens experience; it stimulates and enriches imagination; it creates responsibility for accuracy and vividness of statement and thought. A man really living alone (alone mentally as well as physically) would have little or no occasion to reflect upon his past experience to extract its net meaning. The inequality of achievement between the mature and the immature not only necessitates teaching the young, but the necessity of this teaching gives an immense stimulus to reducing experience to that order and form which will render it most easily communicable and hence most usable.

2. Behavior and Conduct[1]

The word "behavior" is commonly used in an interesting variety of ways. We speak of the behavior of ships at sea, of soldiers in battle, and of little boys in Sunday school.

[1] From Robert E. Park, *Principles of Human Behavior*, pp. 1–9. (The Zalaz Corporation, 1915.)

"The geologist," as Lloyd Morgan remarks, "tells us that a glacier behaves in many respects like a river, and discusses how the crust of the earth behaves under the stresses to which it is subjected. Weatherwise people comment on the behavior of the mercury in the barometer as a storm approaches. When Mary, the nurse maid, returns with the little Miss Smiths from Master Brown's birthday party, she is narrowly questioned as to their behavior."

In short, the word is familiar both to science and to common sense, and is applied with equal propriety to the actions of physical objects and to the manners of men. The abstract sciences, quite as much as the concrete and descriptive, are equally concerned with behavior. "The chemist and the physicist often speak of the behavior of the atoms and the molecules, or of that of gas under changing conditions of temperature and pressure." The fact is that every science is everywhere seeking to describe and explain the movements, changes, and reactions, that is to say the behavior, of some portion of the world about us. Indeed, wherever we consciously set ourselves to observe and reflect upon the changes going on about us, it is always behavior that we are interested in. Science is simply a little more persistent in its curiosity and a little nicer and more exact in its observation than common sense. And this disposition to observe, to take a disinterested view of things, is, by the way, one of the characteristics of human nature which distinguishes it from the nature of all other animals.

Since every science has to do with some form of behavior, the first question that arises is this: What do we mean by behavior in human beings as distinguished from that in other animals? What is there distinctive about the actions of human beings that marks them off and distinguishes them from the actions of animals and plants with which human beings have so much in common?

The problem is the more difficult because, in some one or other of its aspects, human behavior involves processes which are characteristic of almost every form of nature. We sometimes speak, for example, of the human machine. Indeed, from one point of view human beings may be regarded as psycho-physical mechanisms for carrying on the vital processes of nutrition, reproduction, and movement. The human body is, in fact, an immensely complicated machine, whose operations involve an enormous number of chemical and physical reactions, all of which may be regarded as forms of human behavior.

Human beings are, however, not wholly or merely machines; they are living organisms and as such share with the plants and the lower animals certain forms of behavior which it has not thus far, at any rate, been possible to reduce to the exact and lucid formulas of either chemistry or physics.

Human beings are, however, not merely organisms: they are the home and the habitat of minuter organisms. The human body is, in a certain sense, an organization—a sort of social organization—of the minute and simple organisms of which it is composed, namely, the cells, each of which has its own characteristic mode of behavior. In fact, the life of human beings, just as the life of all other creatures above the simple unicellular organisms, may be said to consist of the corporate life of the smaller organisms of which it is composed. In human beings, as in some great city, the division of labor among the minuter organisms has been carried further, the interdependence of the individual parts is more complete, and the corporate life of the whole more complex.

It is not strange, therefore, that Lloyd Morgan begins his studies of animal behavior by a description of the behavior of the cells and Thorndike in his volume, *The Original Nature of Man*, is led to the conclusion that the original tendencies of man have their basis in the neurones, or nerve cells, and in the changes which these cells and their ancestors have undergone, as a result of the necessity of carrying on common and corporate existences as integral parts of the human organism. All acquired characteristics of men, everything that they learn, is due to mutual stimulations and associations of the neurones, just as sociologists are now disposed to explain civilization and progress as phenomena due to the interaction and association of human beings, rather than to any fundamental changes in human nature itself. In other words, the difference between a savage and a civilized man is not due to any fundamental differences in their brain cells but to the connections and mutual stimulations which are established by experience and education between those cells. In the savage those possibilities are not absent but latent. In the same way the difference between the civilization of Central Africa and that of Western Europe is due, not to the difference in native abilities of the individuals and the peoples who have created them, but rather to the form which the association and interaction between those individuals and groups of individuals has taken. We sometimes attribute the difference in culture which we meet among races to the climate and physical conditions generally, but, in the long run, the difference is determined by the way in which climate and physical condition determine the contacts and communications of individuals.

So, too, in the corporate life of the individual man it is the association of the nerve cells, their lines of connection and communication, that is responsible for the most of the differences between the ignorant and the educated, the savage and civilized man. The neurone, however, is a little unicellular animal, like the amoeba or the paramecium. Its life consists of: (1) eating, (2) excreting waste products, (3) growing, (4) being sensitive, and (5) movement, and, as Thorndike expresses it: "The safest provisional hypothesis about the action of the neurones singly is that they retain the modes of behavior common to unicellular animals, so far as consistent with the special conditions of their life as an element of man's nervous system."

In the widest sense of the term, behavior may be said to include all the chemical and physical changes that go on inside the organism, as well as every response to stimulus either from within or from without the organism. In recent studies of animal behavior, however, the word has acquired a special and technical meaning in which it is applied exclusively to those actions that have been, or may be, modified by conscious experience. What the animal does in its efforts to find food is behavior, but the processes of digestion are relegated to another field of observation, namely, physiology.

In all the forms of behavior thus far referred to, human and animal nature are not fundamentally distinguished. There are, however, ways of acting that are peculiar to human nature, forms of behavior that man does not share with the lower animals. One thing which seems to distinguish man from the brute is self-consciousness. One of the consequences of intercourse, as it exists among human beings, is that they are led to reflect upon their own impulses and motives for action, to set up standards by which they seek to govern themselves. The clock is such a standard. We all know from experience that time moves more slowly on dull days, when there is nothing doing, than in moments of excitement. On the other hand, when life is active and stirring, time flies. The clock standardizes our subjective tempos and we control ourselves by the clock. An animal never looks at the clock and this is typical of the different ways in which human beings and animals behave.

Human beings, so far as we have yet been able to learn, are the only creatures who habitually pass judgment upon their own actions, or who think of them as right or wrong. When these thoughts about our actions or the actions of others get themselves formulated and expressed they react back upon and control us. That is one reason we hang mottoes on the wall. That is why one sees on the desk of a busy man the legend "Do it now!" The brutes do not know these devices. They do not need them perhaps. They have no aim in life. They do not work.

What distinguishes the action of men from animals may best be expressed in the word "conduct." Conduct as it is ordinarily used is applied to actions which may be regarded as right or wrong, moral or immoral. As such it is hardly a descriptive term since there does not seem to be any distinctive mark about the actions which men have at different times and places called moral or immoral. I have used it here to distinguish the sort of behavior which may be regarded as distinctively and exclusively human, namely, that which is self-conscious and personal. In this sense blushing may be regarded as a form of conduct, quite as much as the manufacture of tools, trade and barter, conversation or prayer.

No doubt all these activities have their beginnings in, and are founded upon, forms of behavior of which we may find the rudiments in the lower animals. But there is in all distinctively human activities a conventional, one might almost say a contractual, element which is absent in action of other animals. Human actions are more often than not controlled by a sense or understanding of what they look like or appear to be to others. This sense and understanding gets itself embodied in some custom or ceremonial observance. In this form it is transmitted from generation to generation, becomes an object of sentimental respect, gets itself embodied in definite formulas, is an object not only of respect and reverence but of reflection and speculation as well. As such it constitutes the mores, or moral customs, of a group and is no longer to be regarded as an individual possession

3. Instinct and Character[1]

In no part of the world, and at no period of time, do we find the behavior of men left to unchartered freedom. Everywhere human life is in a measure organized and directed by customs, laws, beliefs, ideals, which shape its ends and guide its activities. As this guidance of life by rule is universal in human society, so upon the whole it is peculiar to humanity. There is no reason to think that any animal except man can enunciate or apply general rules of conduct. Nevertheless, there is not wanting something that we can call an organization of life in the animal world. How much of intelligence underlies the social life of the higher animals is indeed extremely hard to determine. In the aid which they often render to one another, in their combined hunting, in their play, in the use of warning cries, and the employment of "sentinels," which is so frequent among birds and mammals, it would appear at first sight that a considerable measure of *mutual understanding* is implied, that we find at least an analogue to human custom, to the assignment of functions, the division of labor, which mutual reliance renders possible. How far the analogy may be pressed, and whether terms like "custom" and "mutual understanding," drawn from human experience, are rightly applicable to animal societies, are questions on which we shall touch presently. Let us observe first that as we descend the animal scale the sphere of *intelligent activity* is gradually narrowed down, and yet behavior is still regulated. The lowest organisms have their definite methods of action under given conditions. The amoeba shrinks into itself at a touch, withdraws the pseudopodium that is roughly handled, or makes its way round the small object which will serve it as food. Given the conditions, it acts in the way best suited to avoid danger or to secure nourishment. We are a long way from the intelligent regulation of conduct by a general principle, but we still find action adapted to the requirements of organic life.

When we come to human society we find the basis for a social organization of life already laid in the animal nature of man. Like others of the higher animals, man is a gregarious beast. His interests lie in his relations to his fellows, in his love for wife and children, in his companionship, possibly in his rivalry and striving with his fellow-

[1] Adapted from L. T. Hobhouse, *Morals in Evolution*, pp. 1-2, 10-12. (Henry Holt & Co., 1915.)

men. His loves and hates, his joys and sorrows, his pride, his wrath, his gentleness, his boldness, his timidity—all these permanent qualities, which run through humanity and vary only in degree, belong to his inherited structure. Broadly speaking, they are of the nature of instincts, but instincts which have become highly plastic in their mode of operation and which need the stimulus of experience to call them forth and give them definite shape.

The mechanical methods of reaction which are so prominent low down in the animal scale fill quite a minor place in human life. The ordinary operations of the body, indeed, go upon their way mechanically enough. In walking or in running, in saving ourselves from a fall, in coughing, sneezing, or swallowing, we react as mechanically as do the lower animals; but in the distinctly human modes of behavior, the place taken by the inherited structure is very different. Hunger and thirst no doubt are of the nature of instincts, but the methods of satisfying hunger and thirst are acquired by experience or by teaching. Love and the whole family life have an instinctive basis, that is to say, they rest upon tendencies inherited with the brain and nerve structure; but everything that has to do with the satisfaction of these impulses is determined by the experience of the individual, the laws and customs of the society in which he lives, the woman whom he meets, the accidents of their intercourse, and so forth. Instinct, already plastic and modifiable in the higher animals, becomes in man a basis of character which determines how he will take his experience, but without experience is a mere blank form upon which nothing is yet written.

For example, it is an ingrained tendency of average human nature to be moved by the opinion of our neighbors. This is a powerful motive in conduct, but the kind of conduct to which it will incite clearly depends on the kind of thing that our neighbors approve. In some parts of the world ambition for renown will prompt a man to lie in wait for a woman or child in order to add a fresh skull to his collection. In other parts he may be urged by similar motives to pursue a science or paint a picture. In all these cases the same hereditary or instinctive element is at work, that quality of character which makes a man respond sensitively to the feelings which others manifest toward him. But the kind of conduct which this sensitiveness may dictate depends wholly on the social environment in which

the man finds himself. Similarly it is, as the ordinary phrase quite
justly puts it, "in human nature" to stand up for one's rights. A
man will strive, that is, to secure that which he has counted on as
his due. But as to what he counts upon, as to the actual treatment
which he expects under given circumstances, his views are determined
by the "custom of the country," by what he sees others insisting on
and obtaining, by what has been promised him, and so forth. Even
such an emotion as sexual jealousy, which seems deeply rooted in
the animal nature, is largely limited in its exercise and determined
in the form it takes by custom. A hospitable savage, who will lend
his wife to a guest, would kill her for acting in the same way on her
own motion. In the one case he exercises his rights of proprietorship;
in the other, she transgresses them. It is the maintenance of a claim
which jealousy concerns itself with, and the standard determining
the claim is the custom of the country.

In human society, then, the conditions regulating conduct are
from the first greatly modified. Instinct, becoming vague and more
general, has evolved into "character," while the intelligence finds
itself confronted with customs to which it has to accommodate conduct. But how does custom arise? Let us first consider what
custom is. It is not merely a habit of action; but it implies also a
judgment upon action, and a judgment stated in general and impersonal terms. It would seem to imply a bystander or third party.
If A hits B, B probably hits back. It is his "habit" so to do. But
if C, looking on, pronounces that it was or was not a fair blow, he will
probably appeal to the "custom" of the country—the traditional
rules of fighting, for instance—as the ground of his judgment. That
is, he will lay down a rule which is general in the sense that it would
apply to other individuals under similar conditions, and by it he
will, as an impartial third person, appraise the conduct of the contending parties. The formation of such rules, resting as it does on
the power of framing and applying general conceptions, is the prime
differentia of human morality from animal behavior. The fact
that they arise and are handed on from generation to generation
makes social tradition at once the dominating factor in the regulation
of human conduct. Without such rules we can scarcely conceive
society to exist, since it is only through the general conformity to
custom that men can understand each other, that each can know

how the other will act under given circumstances, and without this amount of understanding the reciprocity, which is the vital principle of society, disappears.

4. Collective Representation and Intellectual Life[1]

Logical thought is made up of concepts. Seeking how society can have played a rôle in the genesis of logical thought thus reduces itself to seeking how it can have taken a part in the formation of concepts.

The concept is opposed to sensual representations of every order —sensations, perceptions, or images—by the following properties.

Sensual representations are in a perpetual flux; they come after each other like the waves of a river, and even during the time that they last they do not remain the same thing. Each of them is an integral part of the precise instant when it takes place. We are never sure of again finding a perception such as we experienced it the first time; for if the thing perceived has not changed, it is we who are no longer the same. On the contrary, the concept is, as it were, outside of time and change; it is in the depths below all this agitation; it might be said that it is in a different portion of the mind, which is serener and calmer. It does not move of itself, by an internal and spontaneous evolution, but, on the contrary, it resists change. It is a manner of thinking that, at every moment of time, is fixed and crystallized. In so far as it is what it ought to be, it is immutable. If it changes, it is not because it is its nature to do so, but because we have discovered some imperfection in it; it is because it had to be rectified. The system of concepts with which we think in everyday life is that expressed by the vocabulary of our mother-tongue; for every word translates a concept. Now language is something fixed; it changes but very slowly, and consequently it is the same with the conceptual system which it expresses. The scholar finds himself in the same situation in regard to the special terminology employed by the science to which he has consecrated himself, and hence in regard to the special scheme of concepts to which this terminology corresponds. It is true that he can make innovations, but these are always a sort of violence done to the established ways of thinking.

[1] Adapted from Émile Durkheim, *The Elementary Forms of Religious Life*, pp. 432–37. (Allen & Unwin, 1915.)

And at the same time that it is relatively immutable, the concept is universal, or at least capable of becoming so. A concept is not my concept; I hold it in common with other men, or, in any case, can communicate it to them. It is impossible for me to make a sensation pass from my consciousness into that of another; it holds closely to my organism and personality and cannot be detached from them. All that I can do is to invite others to place themselves before the same object as myself and to leave themselves to its action. On the other hand, conversation and all intellectual communication between men is an exchange of concepts. The concept is an essentially impersonal representation; it is through it that human intelligences communicate.

The nature of the concept, thus defined, bespeaks its origin. If it is common to all, it is the work of the community. Since it bears the mark of no particular mind, it is clear that it was elaborated by a unique intelligence, where all others meet each other, and after a fashion, come to nourish themselves. If it has more stability than sensations or images, it is because the collective representations are more stable than the individual ones; for while an individual is conscious even of the slight changes which take place in his environment, only events of a greater gravity can succeed in affecting the mental status of a society. Every time that we are in the presence of a *type* of thought or action which is imposed uniformly upon particular wills or intelligences, this pressure exercised over the individual betrays the intervention of the group. Also, as we have already said, the concepts with which we ordinarily think are those of our vocabulary. Now it is unquestionable that language, and consequently the system of concepts which it translates, is the product of collective elaboration. What it expresses is the manner in which society as a whole represents the facts of experience. The ideas which correspond to the diverse elements of language are thus collective representations.

Even their contents bear witness to the same fact. In fact, there are scarcely any words among those which we usually employ whose meaning does not pass, to a greater or less extent, the limits of our personal experience. Very frequently a term expresses things which we have never perceived or experiences which we have never had or of which we have never been the witnesses. Even when we know some of the objects which it concerns, it is only as particular examples that they serve to illustrate the idea which they would never have been able to form by themselves. Thus there is a great deal of knowledge condensed in the word which I never collected, and which is not individual; it even surpasses me to such an extent that I cannot even completely appropriate all its results. Which of us knows all the words of the language he speaks and the entire signification of each?

This remark enables us to determine the sense in which we mean to say that concepts are collective representations. If they belong to a whole social group, it is not because they represent the average of the corresponding individual representations; for in that case they would be poorer than the latter in intellectual content, while, as a matter of fact, they contain much that surpasses the knowledge of the average individual. They are not abstractions which have a reality only in particular consciousnesses, but they are as concrete representations as an individual could form of his own personal environment; they correspond to the way in which this very special being, society, considers the things of its own proper experience. If, as a matter of fact, the concepts are nearly always general ideas, and if they express categories and classes rather than particular objects, it is because the unique and variable characteristics of things interest society but rarely; because of its very extent, it can scarcely be affected by more than their general and permanent qualities. Therefore it is to this aspect of affairs that it gives its attention: it is a part of its nature to see things in large and under the aspect which they ordinarily have. But this generality is not necessary for them, and, in any case, even when these representations have the generic character which they ordinarily have, they are the work of society and are enriched by its experience.

The collective consciousness is the highest form of the psychic life, since it is the consciousness of the consciousnesses. Being placed outside of and above individual and local contingencies, it sees things only in their permanent and essential aspects, which it crystallizes into communicable ideas. At the same time that it sees from above, it sees farther; at every moment of time, it embraces all known reality; that is why it alone can furnish the mind with the molds which are applicable to the totality of things and which make it possible to think of them. It does not create these molds artificially; it finds them within itself; it does nothing but become conscious of them. They translate the ways of being which are found in all the stages of reality but which appear in their full clarity only at the summit, because the extreme complexity of the psychic life which passes there necessitates a greater development of consciousness. Collective representations also contain subjective elements, and these must be progressively rooted out if we are to approach reality more closely. But howsoever crude these may have been at the beginning, the fact remains that with them the germ of a new mentality was given, to which the individual could never have raised himself by his own efforts; by them the way was opened to a stable, impersonal and organized thought which then had nothing to do except to develop its nature.

D.   THE SOCIAL GROUP

1. Definition of the Group[1]

The term "group" serves as a convenient sociological designation for any number of people, larger or smaller, between whom such relations are discovered that they must be thought of together. The "group" is the most general and colorless term used in sociology for combinations of persons. A family, a mob, a picnic party, a trade union, a city precinct, a corporation, a state, a nation, the civilized or the uncivilized population of the world, may be treated as a group. Thus a "group" for sociology is a number of persons whose relations to each other are sufficiently impressive to demand attention. The term is merely a commonplace tool. It contains no mystery. It is only a handle with which to grasp the innumerable varieties of arrangements into which people are drawn by their variations of interest. The universal condition of association may be expressed in the same commonplace way: people always live in groups, and the same persons are likely to be members of many groups.

Individuals nowhere live in utter isolation. There is no such thing as a social vacuum. The few Robinson Crusoes are not exceptions to the rule. If they are, they are like the Irishman's horse. The

[1] From Albion W. Small, *General Sociology*, pp. 495-97. (The University of Chicago Press, 1905.)

moment they begin to get adjusted to the exceptional condition, they die. Actual persons always live and move and have their being in groups. These groups are more or less complex, more or less continuous, more or less rigid in character. The destinies of human beings are always bound up with the fate of the groups of which they are members. While the individuals are the real existences, and the groups are only relationships of individuals, yet to all intents and purposes the groups which people form are just as distinct and efficient molders of the lives of individuals as though they were entities that had existence entirely independent of the individuals.

The college fraternity or the college class, for instance, would be only a name, and presently not even that, if each of its members should withdraw. It is the members themselves, and not something outside of themselves. Yet to A, B, or C the fraternity or the class might as well be a river or a mountain by the side of which he stands, and which he is helpless to remove. He may modify it somewhat. He is surely modified by it somewhat; and the same is true of all the other groups in which A, B, or C belong. To a very considerable extent the question, Why does A, B, or C do so and so? is equivalent to the question, What are the peculiarities of the group to which A, B, or C belongs? It would never occur to A, B, or C to skulk from shadow to shadow of a night, with paint-pot and brush in hand, and to smear Arabic numerals of bill-poster size on sidewalk or buildings, if "class spirit" did not add stimulus to individual bent. Neither A, B, nor C would go out of his way to flatter and cajole a Freshman, if membership in a fraternity did not make a student something different from an individual. These are merely familiar cases which follow a universal law.

In effect, the groups to which we belong might be as separate and independent of us as the streets and buildings of a city are from the population. If the inhabitants should migrate in a body, the streets and buildings would remain. This is not true of human groups, but their reaction upon the persons who compose them is no less real and evident. We are in large part what our social set, our church, our political party, our business and professional circles are. This has always been the case from the beginning of the world, and will always be the case. To understand what society is, either in its larger or its smaller parts, and why it is so, and how far it is possible to make it different, we must invariably explain groups on the one hand, no less than individuals on the other. There is a striking illustration in Chicago at present (summer, 1905). Within a short time a certain man has made a complete change in his group-relations. He was one of the most influential trade-union leaders in the city. He has now become the executive officer of an association of employers. In the elements that are not determined by his group-relationships he is the same man that he was before. Those are precisely the elements, however, that may be canceled out of the social problem. All the elements in his personal equation that give him a distinct meaning in the life of the city are given to him by his membership in the one group or the other. Till yesterday he gave all his strength to organizing labor against capital. Now he gives all his strength to the service of capital against labor.

Whatever social problem we confront, whatever persons come into our field of view, the first questions involved will always be: To what groups do these persons belong? What are the interests of these groups? What sort of means do the groups use to promote their interests? How strong are these groups, as compared with groups that have conflicting interests? These questions go to one tap root of all social interpretation, whether in the case of historical events far in the past, or of the most practical problems of our own neighborhood.

2. The Unity of the Social Group[1]

It has long been a cardinal problem in sociology to determine just how to conceive in objective terms so very real and palpable a thing as the continuity and persistence of social groups. Looked at as a physical object society appears to be made up of mobile and independent units. The problem is to understand the nature of the bonds that bind these independent units together and how these connections are maintained and transmitted.

Conceived of in its lowest terms the unity of the social group may be compared to that of the plant communities. In these com-

[1] From R. E. Park, "Education in Its Relation to the Conflict and Fusion of Cultures," in the *Publications of the American Sociological Society*, VIII (1918), 38–40.

munities, the relation between the individual species which compose them seems at first wholly fortuitous and external. Co-operation and community, so far as it exists, consists merely in the fact that within a given geographical area, certain species come together merely because each happens to provide by its presence an environment in which the life of the other is easier, more secure, than if they lived in isolation. It seems to be a fact, however, that this communal life of the associated plants fulfils, as in other forms of life, a typical series of changes which correspond to growth, decay and death. The plant community comes into existence, matures, grows old, and eventually dies. In doing this, however, it provides by its own death an environment in which another form of community finds its natural habitat. Each community thus precedes and prepares the way for its successor. Under such circumstances the succession of the individual communities itself assumes the character of a life-process.

In the case of the animal and human societies we have all these conditions and forces and something more. The individuals associated in an animal community not only provide, each for the other, a physical environment in which all may live, but the members of the community are organically pre-adapted to one another in ways which are not characteristic of the members of a plant community. As a consequence, the relations between the members of the animal community assume a much more organic character. It is, in fact, a characteristic of animal society that the members of a social group are organically adapted to one another and therefore the organization of animal society is almost wholly transmitted by physical inheritance.

In the case of human societies we discover not merely organically inherited adaptation, which characterizes animal societies, but, in addition, a great body of habits and accommodations which are transmitted in the form of social inheritance. Something that corresponds to social tradition exists, to be sure, in animal societies. Animals learn by imitation from one another, and there is evidence that this social tradition varies with changes in environment. In man, however, association is based on something more than habits or instinct. In human society, largely as a result of language, there exists a conscious community of purpose. We have not merely folkways, which by an extension of that term might be attributed to animals, but we have mores and formal standards of conduct.

In a recent notable volume on education, John Dewey has formulated a definition of the educational process which he identifies with the process by which the social tradition of human society is transmitted. Education, he says in effect, is a self-renewing process, a process in which and through which the social organism lives.

With the renewal of physical existence goes, in the case of human beings, the re-creation of beliefs, ideals, hopes, happiness, misery and practices. The continuity of experience, through renewal of the social group, is a literal fact. Education, in its broadest sense, is the means of this social continuity of life.

Under ordinary circumstances the transmission of the social tradition is from the parents to the children. Children are born into the society and take over its customs, habits, and standards of life simply, naturally, and without conflict. But it will at once occur to anyone that the physical life of society is not always continued and maintained in this natural way, i.e., by the succession of parents and children. New societies are formed by conquest and by the imposition of one people upon another. In such cases there arises a conflict of cultures, and as a result the process of fusion takes place slowly and is frequently not complete. New societies are frequently formed by colonization, in which case new cultures are grafted on to older ones. The work of missionary societies is essentially one of colonization in this sense. Finally we have societies growing up, as in the United States, by immigration. These immigrants, coming as they do from all parts of the world, bring with them fragments of divergent cultures. Here again the process of assimilation is slow, often painful, not always complete.

3. Types of Social Groups [1]

Between the two extreme poles—the crowd and the state (nation) —between these extreme links of the chain of human association, what are the other intermediate groups, and what are their distinctive characteristics?

Gustave Le Bon thus classifies the different types of crowds (aggregations):

    A. Heterogeneous crowds
        1. Anonymous (street crowds, for example)
        2. Not anonymous (parliamentary assemblies, for example)

[1] Translated from S. Sighele, *Psychologie des Sectes*, pp. 42–51. (M. Giard et Cie., 1898.)

B. Homogeneous crowds
  1. Sects (political, religious, etc.)
  2. Castes (military, sacerdotal, etc.)
  3. Classes (bourgeois, working-men, etc.)

This classification is open to criticism. First of all, it is inaccurate to give the name of crowd indiscriminately to every human group. Literally (from the etymological standpoint) this objection seems to me unanswerable. Tarde more exactly distinguishes between crowds, associations, and corporations.

But we retain the generic term of "crowd" because it indicates the first stage of the social group which is the source of all the others, and because with these successive distinctions it does not lend itself to equivocal meaning.

In the second place, it is difficult to understand why Le Bon terms the sect a *homogeneous* crowd, while he classifies parliamentary assemblies among the *heterogeneous* crowds. The members of a sect are usually far more different from one another in birth, education, profession, social status, than are generally the members of a political assembly.

Turning from this criticism to note without analyzing heterogeneous crowds, let us then proceed to determine the principal characteristics of the three large types of homogeneous crowds, the classes, the castes, the sects.

The heterogeneous crowd is composed of *tout le monde*, of people like you, like me, like the first passer-by. *Chance* unites these individuals physically, the *occasion* unites them psychologically; they do not know each other, and after the moment when they find themselves together, they may never see each other again. To use a metaphor, it is a psychological meteor, of the most unforeseen, ephemeral, and transitory kind.

On this accidental and fortuitous foundation are formed here and there other crowds, always heterogeneous, but with a certain character of stability or, at least, of periodicity. The audience at a theater, the members of a club, of a literary or social gathering, constitute also a crowd but a different crowd from that of the street. The members of these groups know each other a little; they have, if not a common aim, at least a common custom. They are nevertheless "anonymous crowds," as Le Bon calls them, because they do not have within themselves the nucleus of organization.

Proceeding further, we find crowds still heterogeneous, but not so anonymous—juries, for example, and assemblies. These small crowds experience a new sentiment, unknown to anonymous crowds, that of responsibility which may at times give to their actions a different orientation. Then the parliamentary crowds are to be distinguished from the others because, as Tarde observes with his habitual penetration, they are double crowds: they represent a majority in conflict with one or more minorities, which safeguards them in most cases from unanimity, the most menacing danger which faces crowds.

We come now to homogeneous crowds, of which the first type is the sect. Here are found again individuals differing in birth, in education, in profession, in social status, but united and, indeed, voluntarily cemented by an extremely strong bond, a common faith and ideal. Faith, religious, scientific, or political, rapidly creates a communion of sentiments capable of giving to those who possess it a high degree of homogeneity and power. History records the deeds of the barbarians under the influence of Christianity, and the Arabs transformed into a sect by Mahomet. Because of their sectarian organization, a prediction may be made of what the future holds in store for the socialists.

The sect is a crowd, picked out and permanent; the crowd is a transitory sect which has not chosen its members. The sect is a chronic kind of crowd; the crowd is an acute kind of sect. The crowd is composed of a multitude of grains of sand without cohesion; the sect is a block of marble which resists every effort. When a sentiment or an idea, having in itself a reason for existence, slips into the crowd, its members soon crystallize and form a sect. The sect is then the first crystallization of every doctrine. From the confused and amorphous state in which it manifests itself to the crowd, every idea is predestined to define itself in the more specific form of the sect, to become later a party, a school, or a church—scientific, political, or religious.

Any faith, whether it be Islamism, Buddhism, Christianity, patriotism, socialism, anarchy, cannot but pass through this sectarian phase. It is the first step, the point where the human group in leaving the twilight zone of the anonymous and mobile crowd raises itself to a definition and to an integration which then may lead up to the highest and most perfect human group, the nation.

If the sect is composed of individuals united by a common idea and aim, in spite of diversity of birth, education, and social status, the caste unites, on the contrary, those who could have—and who have sometimes—diverse ideas and aspirations, but who are brought together through identity of profession. The sect corresponds to the community of faith, the caste to the community of professional ideas. The sect is a *spontaneous* association; the caste is, in many ways, a *forced* association. After having chosen a profession—let it be priest, soldier, magistrate—a man belongs necessarily to a caste. A person, on the contrary, does not necessarily belong to a sect. And when one belongs to a caste—be he the most independent man in the world—he is more or less under the influence of that which is called *esprit de corps*.

The caste represents the highest degree of organization to which the homogeneous crowd is susceptible. It is composed of individuals who by their tastes, their education, birth, and social status, resemble each other in the fundamental types of conduct and mores. There are even certain castes, the military and sacerdotal, for example, in which the members at last so resemble one another in appearance and bearing that no disguise can conceal the nature of their profession.

The caste offers to its members ideas already molded, rules of conduct already approved; it relieves them, in short, of the fatigue of thinking with their own brains. When the caste to which an individual belongs is known, all that is necessary is to press a button of his mental mechanism to release a series of opinions and of phrases already made which are identical in every individual of the same caste.

This harmonious collectivity, powerful and eminently conservative, is the most salient analogy which the nations of the Occident present to that of India. In India the caste is determined by birth, and it is distinguished by a characteristic trait: the persons of one caste can live with, eat with, and marry only individuals of the same caste.

In Europe it is not only birth, but circumstances and education which determine the entrance of an individual into a caste; to marry, to frequent, to invite to the same table only people of the same caste, exists practically in Europe as in India.   In Europe the above-mentioned prescriptions are founded on convention, but they are none the less observed.   We all live in a confined circle, where we find our friends, our guests, our sons- and daughters-in-law.

Misalliances are assuredly possible in Europe; they are impossible in India.   But if there religion prohibits them, with us public opinion and convention render them very rare.   And at bottom the analogy is complete.

The class is superior to the caste in extent.   If the psychological bond of the sect is community of faith, and that of the caste community of profession, the psychological bond of the class is community of interests.

Less precise in its limits, more diffuse and less compact than the caste or the sect, the class represents today the veritable crowd in a dynamic state, which can in a moment's time descend from that place and become statically a crowd.   And it is from the sociological standpoint the most terrible kind of crowd; it is that which today has taken a bellicose attitude, and which by its attitude and precepts prepares the brutal blows of mobs.

We speak of the "conflict of the classes," and from the theoretical point of view and in the normal and peaceful life that signifies only a contest of ideas by legal means.   Always depending upon the occasion, the audacity of one or many men, the character of the situation, the conflict of the classes is transformed into something more material and more violent—into revolt or into revolution.

Finally we arrive at the state (nation).   Tocqueville said that the classes which compose society form so many distinct nations. They are the greatest collectivities before coming to the nation, the state.

This is the most perfect type of organization of the crowd, and the final and supreme type, if there is not another collectivity superior in number and extension, the collectivity formed by race.

The bond which unites all the citizens of a state is language and nationality.   Above the state there are only the crowds determined by race, which comprise many states.   And these are, like the states and like the classes, human aggregates which in a moment could be transformed into violent crowds.   But then, and justly, because their evolution and their organization are more developed, their mobs are called armies, and their violences are called wars, and they have the seal of legitimacy unknown in other crowds. In this order of ideas war could be defined as the supreme form of collective crimes.

4. *Esprit de Corps,* Morale, and Collective Representations of Social Groups[1]

War is no doubt the least human of human relationships. It can begin only when persuasion ends, when arguments fitted to move minds are replaced by the blasting-powder fitted to move rocks and hills. It means that one at least of the national wills concerned has deliberately set aside its human quality—as only a human will can do—and has made of itself just such a material obstruction or menace. Hence war seems, and is often called, a contest of brute forces. Certainly it is the extremest physical effort men make, every resource of vast populations bent to increase the sum of power at the front, where the two lines writhe like wrestlers laboring for the final fall.

Yet it is seldom physical force that decides a long war. For war summons skill against skill, head against head, staying-power against staying-power, as well as numbers and machines against machines and numbers. When an engine "exerts itself" it spends more power, eats more fuel, but uses no nerve; when a man exerts himself, he must bend his will to it. The extremer the physical effort, the greater the strain on the inner or moral powers. Hence the paradox of war: just because it calls for the maximum material performance, it calls out a maximum of moral resource. As long as guns and bayonets have men behind them, the quality of the men, the quality of their minds and wills, must be counted with the power of the weapons.

And as long as men fight in nations and armies, that subtle but mighty influence that passes from man to man, the temper and spirit of the group, must be counted with the quality of the individual citizen and soldier. But how much does this intangible, psychological factor count? Napoleon in his day reckoned it high: "In war, the moral is to the physical as three to one."

[1] Adapted from William E. Hocking, *Morale and Its Enemies*, pp. 3–37. (Yale University Press. 1918.)

For war, completely seen, is no mere collision of physical forces; it is a collision of will against will. It is, after all, the mind and will of a nation—a thing intangible and invisible—that assembles the materials of war, the fighting forces, the ordnance, the whole physical array. It is this invisible thing that wages the war; it is this same invisible thing that on one side or the other must admit the finish and so end it. As things are now, it is the element of "morale" that controls the outcome.

I say, as things are now; for it is certainly not true as a rule of history that will-power is enough to win a war, even when supported by high fighting spirit, brains, and a good conscience: Belgium had all this, and yet was bound to fall before Germany had she stood alone. Her spirit worked miracles at Liége, delayed by ten days the marching program of the German armies, and thereby saved— perhaps Paris, perhaps Europe. But the day was saved because the issue raised in Serbia and in Belgium drew to their side material support until their forces could compare with the physical advantages of the enemy. Morale wins, not by itself, but by turning scales; it has a value like the power of a minority or of a mobile reserve. It adds to one side or the other the last ounce of force which is to its opponent the last straw that breaks its back.

Perhaps the simplest way of explaining the meaning of morale is to say that what "condition" is to the athlete's body, morale is to the mind. Morale is condition; good morale is good condition of the inner man: it is the state of will in which you can get most from the machinery, deliver blows with the greatest effect, take blows with the least depression, and hold out for the longest time. It is both fighting-power and staying-power and strength to resist the mental infections which fear, discouragement, and fatigue bring with them, such as eagerness for any kind of peace if only it gives momentary relief, or the irritability that sees large the defects in one's own side until they seem more important than the need of defeating the enemy. And it is the perpetual ability to come back.

From this it follows that good morale is not the same as good spirits or enthusiasm. It is anything but the cheerful optimism of early morning, or the tendency to be jubilant at every victory. It has nothing in common with the emotionalism dwelt on by psychologists of the "crowd." It is hardly to be discovered in the early stages of war. Its most searching test is found in the question, How does war-weariness affect you?

No one going from America to Europe in the last year could fail to notice the wide difference between the mind of nations long at war and that of a nation just entering. Over there, "crowd psychology" had spent itself. There was little flag-waving; the common purveyors of music were not everywhere playing (or allowed to play) the national airs. If in some Parisian cinema the Marseillaise was given, nobody stood or sang. The reports of atrocities roused little visible anger or even talk—they were taken for granted. In short, the simpler emotions had been worn out, or rather had resolved themselves into clear connections between knowledge and action. The people had found the mental gait that can be held indefinitely. Even a great advance finds them on their guard against too much joy. As the news from the second victory of the Marne begins to come in, we find this despatch: "Paris refrains from exultation."

And in the trenches the same is true in even greater degree. All the bravado and illusion of war are gone, also all the nervous revulsion; and in their places a grimly reliable resource of energy held in instant, almost mechanical, readiness to do what is necessary. The hazards which it is useless to speculate about, the miseries, delays, tediums, casualties, have lost their exclamatory value and have fallen into the sullen routine of the day's work. Here it is that morale begins to show in its more vital dimensions. Here the substantial differences between man and man, and between side and side, begin to appear as they can never appear in training camp.

Fitness and readiness to act, the positive element in morale, is a matter not of good and bad alone, but of degree. Persistence, courage, energy, initiative, may vary from zero upward without limit. Perhaps the most important dividing line—one that has already shown itself—at various critical points—is that between the willingness to defend and the willingness to attack, between the defensive and the aggressive mentality. It is the difference between docility and enterprise, between a faith at second hand dependent on neighbor or leader, and a faith at first hand capable of assuming for itself the position of leadership.

III. INVESTIGATIONS AND PROBLEMS

1. The Scientific Study of Societies

Interest in the study of "society as it is" has had its source in two different motives. Travelers' tales have always fascinated mankind. The ethnologists began their investigations by criticising and systematizing the novel and interesting observations of travelers in regard to customs, cultures, and behavior of people of different races and nationalities. Their later more systematic investigations were, on the whole, inspired by intellectual curiosity divorced from any overwhelming desire to change the manner of life and social organizations of the societies studied.

The second motive for the systematic observation of actual society came from persons who wanted social reforms but who were forced to realize the futility of utopian projects. The science of sociology as conceived by Auguste Comte was to substitute fact for doctrines about society. But his attempt to interpret social evolution resulted in a philosophy of history, not a natural science of society.

Herbert Spencer appreciated the fact that the new science of sociology required an extensive body of materials as a basis for its generalizations. Through the work of assistants he set himself the monumental task of compiling historical and cultural materials not only upon primitive and barbarous peoples but also upon the Hebrews, the Phoenicians, the French and the English. These data were classified and published in eight large volumes under the title *Descriptive Sociology*.

The study of human societies was too great to be satisfactorily compassed by the work of one man. Besides that, Spencer, like most English sociologists, was more interested in the progress of civilization than in its processes. Spencer's *Sociology* is still a philosophy of history rather than a science of society. The philosophy of history took for its unit of investigation and interpretation the evolution of human society as a whole. The present trend in sociology is toward the study of *societies* rather than *society*. Sociological research has been directed less to a study of the stages of evolution than to the diagnosis and control of social problems.

Modern sociology's chief inheritance from Comte and Spencer was a problem in logic: What is a society?

Manifestly if the relations between individuals in society are not merely formal, and if society is something more than the sum of its parts, then these relations must be defined in terms of interaction, that is to say, in terms of process. What then is *the social process;* what are the social processes? How are social processes to be distinguished from physical, chemical, or biological processes? What is, in general, the nature of the relations that need to be established in order to make of individuals in society, members of society? These questions are fundamental since they define the point of view of sociology and describe the sort of facts with which the science seeks to deal. Upon these questions the schools have divided and up to the present time there is no very general consensus among sociologists in regard to them. The introductory chapter to this volume is at once a review of the points of view and an attempt to find answers. In the literature to which reference is made at the close of chapter iii the logical questions involved are discussed in a more thoroughgoing way than has been possible to do in this volume.

Fortunately science does not wait to define its points of view nor solve its theoretical problems before undertaking to analyze and collect the facts. The contrary is nearer the truth. Science collects facts and answers the theoretical questions afterward. In fact, it is just its success in analyzing and collecting facts which throw light upon human problems that in the end justifies the theories of science.

2. Surveys of Communities

The historian and the philosopher introduced the sociologist to the study of society. But it was the reformer, the social worker, and the business man who compelled him to study the community.

The study of the community is still in its beginnings. Nevertheless, there is already a rapidly growing literature on this topic. Ethnologists have presented us with vivid and detailed pictures of primitive communities as in McGee's *The Seri Indians*, Jenks's *The Bontoc Igorot*, Rivers' *The Todas*. Studies of the village communities of India, of Russia, and of early England have thrown new light upon the territorial factor in the organization of societies.

More recently the impact of social problems has led to the intensive study of modern communities. The monumental work of

Charles Booth, *Life and Labour of the People in London,* is a comprehensive description of conditions of social life in terms of the community. In the United States, interest in community study is chiefly represented by the social-survey movement which received impetus from the Pittsburgh Survey of 1907. For sociological research of greater promise than the survey are the several monographs which seek to make a social analysis of the community, as Williams, *An American Town,* or Galpin, *The Social Anatomy of an Agricultural Community.* With due recognition of these auspicious beginnings, it must be confessed that there is no volume upon human communities comparable with several works upon plant and animal communities.

3. The Group as a Unit of Investigation

The study of societies is concerned primarily with types of social organization and with attitudes and cultural elements embodied in them. The survey of communities deals essentially with social situations and the problems connected with them.

The study of social groups was a natural outgrowth of the study of the individual. In order to understand the person it is necessary to consider the group. Attention first turned to social institutions, then to conflict groups, and finally to crowds and crowd influences.

Social institutions were naturally the first groups to be studied with some degree of detachment. The work of ethnologists stimulated an interest in social origins. Evolution, though at first a purely biological conception, provoked inquiry into the historical development of social structure. Differences in institutions in contemporary societies led to comparative study. Critics of institutions, both iconoclasts without and reformers within, forced a consideration of their more fundamental aspects.

The first written accounts of conflict groups were quite naturally of the propagandist type both by their defenders and by their opponents. Histories of nationalities, for example, originated in the patriotic motive of national glorification. With the acceptance of objective standards of historical criticism the ground was prepared for the sociological study of nationalities as conflict groups. A school of European sociologists represented by Gumplowicz, Ratzenhofer, and Novicow stressed conflict as the characteristic behavior of social groups. Beginnings, as indicated in the bibliography, have been made of the study of various conflict groups as gangs, labor unions, parties, and sects.

The interest in the mechanism of the control of the individual by the group has been focused upon the study of the crowd. Tarde and Le Bon in France, Sighele in Italy, and Ross in the United States were the pioneers in the description and interpretation of the behavior of mobs and crowds. The crowd phenomena of the Great War have stimulated the production of several books upon crowds and crowd influences which are, in the main, but superficial and popular elaborations of the interpretations of Tarde and Le Bon. Concrete material upon group behavior has rapidly accumulated, but little or no progress has been made in its sociological explanation.

At present there are many signs of an increasing interest in the study of group behavior. Contemporary literature is featuring realistic descriptions. Sinclair Lewis in *Main Street* describes concretely the routine of town life with its outward monotony and its inner zest. Newspapers and magazines are making surveys of the buying habits of their readers as a basis for advertising. The federal department of agriculture in co-operation with schools of agriculture is making intensive studies of rural communities. Social workers are conscious that a more fundamental understanding of social groups is a necessary basis for case work and community organization. Surveys of institutions and communities are now being made under many auspices and from varied points of view. All this is having a fruitful reaction upon the sociological theory.

4. The Study of the Family

The family is the earliest, the most elementary, and the most permanent of social groups. It has been more completely studied, in all its various aspects, than other forms of human association. Methods of investigation of family life are typical of methods that may be employed in the description of other forms of society. For that reason more attention is given here to studies of family life than it is possible or desirable to give to other and more transient types of social groups.

The descriptions of travelers, of ethnologists and of historians made the first contributions to our knowledge of marriage, ceremonials, and family organization among primitive and historical peoples. Early students of, these data devised theories of stages in the evolution of the family. An anthology might be made of the conceptions that students have formulated of the original form of the family, for example, the theory of the matriarchate by Bachofen, of group marriage growing out of earlier promiscuous relations by Morgan, of the polygynous family by Darwin, of pair marriage by Westermarck. An example of the ingenious, but discarded method of arranging all types of families observed in a series representing stages of the evolution is to be found in Morgan's *Ancient Society*. A survey of families among primitive peoples by Hobhouse, Ginsberg, and Wheeler makes the point that even family life is most varied upon the lower levels of culture, and that the historical development of the family with any people must be studied in relation to the physical and social environment.

The evolutionary theory of the family has, however, furnished a somewhat detached point of view for the criticism of the modern family. Social reformers have used the evolutionary theory as a formula to justify attacks upon the family as an institution and to support the most varied proposals for its reconstruction. Books like Ellen Key's *Love and Marriage* and Meisel-Hess, *The Sexual Crisis* are not scientific studies of the family but rather social political philippics directed against marriage and the family.

The interest stimulated by ethnological observation, historical study, and propagandist essays has, however, turned the attention of certain students to serious study of the family and its problems. Howard's *History of Matrimonial Institutions* is a scholarly and comprehensive treatise upon the evolution of the legal status of the family. Annual statistics of marriage and divorce are now compiled and published by all the important countries except the United States government. In the United States, however, three studies of marriages and divorces have been made; one in 1887–88, by the Department of Labor, covering the twenty years from 1867–86 inclusive; another in 1906–7, by the Bureau of the Census, for the twenty years 1887–1906; and the last, also by the Bureau of the Census, for the year 1916.

The changes in family life resulting from the transition from home industry to the factory system have created new social problems. Problems of woman and child labor, unemployment, and poverty are a product of the machine industry. Attempts to relieve the distress under conditions of city life resulted in the formation of charity organization societies and other philanthropic institutions, and in attempts to control the behavior of the individuals and families assisted. The increasing body of experience gained by social agencies has gradually been incorporated in the technique of the workers. Mary Richmond in *Social Diagnosis* has analyzed and standardized the procedure of the social case worker.

Less direct but more fundamental studies of family life have been made by other investigators. Le Play, a French social economist, who lived with the families which he observed, introduced the method of the monographic study of the economic organization of family life. Ernst Engel, from his study of the expenditure of Saxon working-class families, formulated so-called "laws" of the relation between family income and family outlay. Recent studies of family incomes and budgets by Chapin, Ogburn, and others have thrown additional light upon the relationship between wages and the standard of living. Interest in the economics of the family is manifested by an increasing number of studies in dietetics, household administration and domestic science.

Westermarck in his *History of Human Marriage* attempted to write a sociology of the family. Particularly interesting is his attempt to compare the animal family with that of man. The effect of this was to emphasize instinctive and biological aspects of the family rather than its institutional character. The basis for a psychology of family life was first laid in the *Studies in the Psychology of Sex* by Havelock Ellis. The case studies of individuals by psychoanalysts often lead into family complexes and illuminate the structure of family attitudes and wishes.

The sociological study of the family as a natural and a cultural group is only now in its beginnings. An excellent theoretical study of the family as a unity of interacting members is presented in Bosanquet, *The Family*. The family as defined in the mores has been described and interpreted, as for example, by Thomas in his analysis of the organization of the large peasant family group in the first two volumes of the *Polish Peasant*. Materials upon the family in the United States have been brought together by Calhoun in his *Social History of the American Family*.

While the family is listed by Cooley among primary groups, the notion is gaining ground that it is primary in a unique sense which sets it apart from all other social groups. The biological interdependence and co-operation of the members of the family, intimacies of closest and most enduring contacts have no parallel among other human groups. The interplay of the attractions, tensions, and accommodations of personalities in the intimate bonds of family life have up to the present found no concrete description or adequate analysis in sociological inquiry.

The best case studies of family life at present are in fiction, not in the case records of social agencies, nor yet in sociological literature. Arnold Bennett's trilogy, *Clayhanger*, *Hilda Lessways*, and *These Twain*, suggests a pattern not unworthy of consideration by social workers and sociologists. *The Pastor's Wife*, by the author of *Elizabeth and Her German Garden*, is a delightful contrast of English and German mores in their effect upon the intimate relations of family life.

In the absence of case studies of the family as a natural and cultural group the following tentative outline for sociological study is offered:

1. *Location and extent in time and space.*—Genealogical tree as retained in the family memory; geographical distribution and movement of members of small family group and of large family group; stability or mobility of family; its rural or urban location.

2. *Family traditions and ceremonials.*—Family romance; family skeleton; family ritual, as demonstration of affection, family events, etc.

3. *Family economics.*—Family communism; division of labor between members of the family; effect of occupation of its members.

4. *Family organization and control.*—Conflicts and accommodation; superordination and subordination; typical forms of control—patriarchy, matriarchy, consensus, etc.; family *esprit de corps*, family morale, family objectives; status in community.

5. *Family behavior.*—Family life from the standpoint of the four wishes (security, response, recognition, and new experience); family crises; the family and the community; familism versus individualism; family life and the development of personality.

SELECTED BIBLIOGRAPHY

I. THE DEFINITION OF SOCIETY

(1) Kistiakowski, Dr. Th. *Gesellschaft und Einzelwesen; eine methodologische Studie.* Berlin, 1899. [A review and criticism of the principal conceptions of society with reference to their value for a natural science of society.]

(2) Weber, Max. *Gesammelte Aufsätze zur Wissenschaftslehre.* Tübingen. 1922. [Review of a series of essays upon the methodology of the historical, economic, and sociological sciences.]

(3) Bosanquet, Bernard. *The Philosophical Theory of the State.* Chap. ii, "Sociological compared with Philosophical Theory," pp. 17–52. London, 1899.

(4) Barth, Paul. *Die Philosophie der Geschichte als Sociologie.* Leipzig, 1897. [A comparison of the different schools and an attempt to interpret them as essays in the philosophy of history.]

(5) Espinas, Alfred. *Des sociétés animales.* Paris, 1877. [A definition of society based upon a comparative study of animal associations, communities, and societies.]

(6) Spencer, Herbert. "The Social Organism," *Essays, Scientific, Political and Speculative,* I, 265–307. New York, 1892. [First published in *The Westminster Review* for January, 1860.]

(7) Lazarus, M., and Steinthal, H. "Einleitende Gedanken zur Völkerpsychologie als Einladung zu einer Zeitschrift für Völkerpsychologie und Sprachwissenschaft," *Zeitschrift für Völkerpsychologie und Sprachwissenschaft,* I (1860), 1–73. [This is the most important early attempt to interpret social phenomena from a social psychological point of view. See p. 35 for definition of *Volk* "the people."]

(8) Knapp, G. Friedrich. "Quételet als Theoretiker," *Jahrbücher für Nationalökonomie und Statistik,* XVIII (1872), 89–124.

(9) Lazarus, M. *Das Leben der Seele in Monographieen über seine Erscheinungen und Gesetze.* Berlin, 1876.

(10) Durkheim, Émile. "Représentations individuelles et représentations collectives," *Revue de métaphysique et de morale,* VI (1898), 273–302.

(11) Simmel, Georg. *Über sociale Differenzierung.* Sociologische und psychologische Untersuchungen. Leipzig, 1890.

(12) Weber, Max. *Grundriss der Sozialökonomik.* III. Abteilung. Wirtschaft und Gesellschaft. Tübingen, 1922. [An attempt to define society as a control organization within the limits of an economic community.]

[See also in Bibliography, chap. i, volumes listed under Systematic Treatises.]

II. PLANT COMMUNITIES AND ANIMAL SOCIETIES

(1) Clements, Frederic E. *Plant Succession.* An analysis of the development of vegetation. Carnegie Institution of Washington, 1916.

(2) Wheeler, W. M. "The Ant-Colony as an Organism," *Journal of Morphology,* XXII (1911), 307–25.

(3) ———. *Social Life among the Insects.* New York, 1923.

(4) Parmelee, Maurice. *The Science of Human Behavior.* Biological and Psychological Foundations. New York, 1913. [Bibliography.]

(5) Massart, J., and Vandervelde, É. *Parasitism, Organic and Social.* 2d ed. Translated by W. Macdonald. Revised by J. Arthur Thomson. London, 1907.
(6) Warming, Eug. *Oecology of Plants.* An introduction to the study of plant communities. Oxford, 1909. [Bibliography.]
(7) Adams, Charles C. *Guide to the Study of Animal Ecology.* New York, 1913. [Bibliography.]
(7) Waxweiler, E. "Esquisse d'une sociologie," *Travaux de l'Institut de Sociologie (Solvay), Notes et mémoires,* Fasc. 2. Bruxelles, 1906.
(9) Reinheimer, H. *Symbiosis.* A socio-physiological study of evolution. London, 1920.

III. THE CLASSIFICATION OF SOCIAL GROUPS

A. *Types of Social Groups*

1. Non-territorial Groups:
   (1) Le Bon, Gustave. *The Crowd.* A study of the popular mind. London, 1897.
   (2) Sighele, S. *Psychologie des sectes.* Paris, 1898.
   (3) Tarde, G. *L'opinion et la foule.* Paris, 1901.
   (4) Fahlbeck, Pontus. *Klasserna och Samhallet.* Stockholm, 1920. [Book review in *American Journal of Sociology,* XXVI (1920–21), 633–34.]
   (5) Nesfield, John C. *Brief View of the Caste System of the Northwestern Provinces and Oudh.* Allahabad, 1885.

2. Territorial Groups:
   (1) McKenzie, R. D. "The Ecological Approach to the Study of the Human Community," *American Journal of Sociology,* XIX, November, 1924.
   (2) Hassert, Kurt. *Die Städte geographisch betrachtet.* Leipzig, 1907.
   (3) Cornish, Vaughan. *The Great Capitals. An Historical Geography.* New York, 1922.
   (4) Aurousseau, M. "Recent Contributions to Urban Geography: a Review," *Geographical Review,* XIV (1924), 444–55. [Bibliographical survey.]
   (5) Simmel, Georg. "Die Grossstädte und das Geistesleben," *Die Grossstadt,* Vorträge und Aufsätze zur Städteausstellung, von K. Bücher, F. Ratzel, G. v. Mayr, H. Waentig, G. Simmel, Th. Peterman, und D. Schäfer. Dresden, 1903.
   (6) Galpin, C. J. *The Social Anatomy of an Agricultural Community.* Madison, Wis., 1915. (Agricultural experiment station of the University of Wisconsin. Research Bulletin 34.) [See also *Rural Life,* New York, 1918.]
   (7) Aronovici, Carol. *The Social Survey.* Philadelphia, 1916.
   (8) McKenzie, R. D. *The Neighborhood.* A study of local life in Columbus, Ohio. Chicago, 1923.
   (9) Park, Robert E. "The City. Suggestions for the Investigation of Human Behavior in the City Environment," *American Journal of Sociology,* XX (1914–15), 577–612.
   (10) Sims, Newell L. *The Rural Community, Ancient and Modern.* New York, 1920.

B. *Studies of Individual Communities*

    (1) Maine, Sir Henry. *Village-Communities in the East and West.* London, 1871.

    (2) Baden-Powell, H. *The Indian Village Community.* Examined with reference to the physical, ethnographic, and historical conditions of the provinces. London, 1896.

    (3) Seebohm, Frederic. *The English Village Community.* Examined in its relations to the manorial and tribal systems and to the common or open field system of husbandry. An essay in economic history. London, 1883.

    (4) McGee, W J. "The Seri Indians," *Bureau of American Ethnology 17th Annual Report 1895–96.* Washington, 1898.

    (5) Rivers, W. H. R. *The Todas.* London and New York, 1906.

    (6) Jenks, Albert. *The Bontoc Igorot.* Manila, 1905.

    (7) Stow, John. *A Survey of London.* Reprinted from the text of 1603 with introduction and notes by C. L. Kingsford. Oxford, 1908.

    (8) Gamble, Sidney D., and Burgess, John S. *Peking.* A social survey. New York, 1921.

    (9) Booth, Charles. *Life and Labour of the People in London.* 9 vols. London and New York, 1892–97. 8 additional volumes, 1902.

    (10) Kellogg, P. U., ed. *The Pittsburgh Survey.* Findings in 6 vols. Russell Sage Foundation, New York, 1909–14.

    (11) Woods, Robert. *The City Wilderness.* A settlement study, south end of Boston. Boston, 1898.

    ———. *Americans in Process.* A settlement study, north and west ends of Boston. Boston, 1902.

    (12) Kenngott, G. F. *The Record of a City.* A social survey of Lowell, Massachusetts,. New York, 1912.

    (13) Harrison, Shelby M., ed. *The Springfield Survey.* A study of social conditions in an American city. Findings in 3 vols. Russell Sage Foundation. New York, 1918.

    (14) Roberts, Peter. *Anthracite Coal Communities.* A study of the demography, the social, educational, and moral life of the anthracite regions. New York and London, 1904.

    (15) Williams, J. M. *An American Town.* A sociological study. New York, 1906.

    (16) Wilson, Warren H. *Quaker Hill.* A sociological study. New York, 1907.

    (17) Taylor, Graham R. *Satellite Cities.* A study of industrial suburbs. New York and London, 1915.

    (18) Lewis, Sinclair. *Main Street.* New York, 1920.

    (19) Kobrin, Leon. *A Lithuanian Village.* Translated from the Yiddish by Isaac Goldberg. New York, 1920.

IV. THE STUDY OF THE FAMILY

A. *The Primitive Family*

    1. The Natural History of Marriage:

        (1) Bachofen, J. J. *Das Mutterrecht.* Eine Untersuchung über die Gynaikokratie der alten Welt nach ihrer religiösen und rechtlichen Natur. Stuttgart, 1861.

(2) Westermarck, E. *The History of Human Marriage.* 5th ed. 3 vols. New York, 1922.

(3) McLennan, J. F. *Primitive Marriage.* An inquiry into the origin of the form of capture in marriage ceremonies. Edinburgh, 1865.

(4) Tylor, E. B. "The Matriarchal Family System," *Nineteenth Century.* XL (1896), 81–96.

(5) Dargun, L. von. *Mutterrecht und Vaterrecht.* Leipzig, 1892.

(6) Maine, Sir Henry. *Dissertations on Early Law and Custom.* Chap. vii. London, 1883.

(7) Letourneau, C. *The Evolution of Marriage and of the Family.* (Trans.) New York, 1891.

(8) Kovalevsky, M. *Tableau des origines et de l'evolution de la famille et de la propriété.* Stockholm, 1890.

(9) Lowie, Robert H. *Primitive Society.* New York, 1920.

(10) Starcke, C. N. *The Primitive Family in Its Origin and Development.* New York, 1889.

(11) Hobhouse, L. T., Wheeler, G. C., and Ginsberg, M. *The Material Culture and Social Institutions of the Simpler Peoples.* London, 1915.

(12) Parsons, Elsie Clews. *The Family.* An ethnographical and historical outline. New York and London, 1906.

(13) Todd, Arthur J. *The Primitive Family as an Educational Agency.* New York, 1913.

(14) Rivers, W. H. R. Kinship and Social Organization. London, 1914.

2. Studies of Family Life in Different Cultural Areas:

(1) Spencer, B., and Gillen, F. J. *The Native Tribes of Central Australia.* Chap. iii, "Certain Ceremonies Concerned with Marriage," pp. 92–111. London and New York, 1899.

(2) Rivers, W. H. R. *Kinship and Social Organization.* "Studies in Economics and Political Science," No. 36. In the series of monographs by writers connected with the London School of Economics and Political Science. London, 1914.

(3) ———. "Kinship," *Cambridge Anthropological Expedition to Torres Straits, Report,* V, 129–47; VI, 92–125; Cambridge, 1904–8.

(4) Kovalevsky, M. "La famille matriarcale au Caucase," *L'Anthropologie,* IV (1893), 259–78.

(5) Thomas, N. W. *Kinship Organizations and Group Marriage in Australia.* Cambridge, 1906.

(6) Malinowski, Bronislaw. *The Family among the Australian Aborigines.* A sociological study. London, 1913.

B. *Materials for the Study of Familial Attitudes and Sentiments*

(1) Frazer, J. G. *Totemism and Exogamy.* A treatise on certain early forms of superstition and society. London, 1910.

(2) Durkheim, É. "La prohibition de l'inceste et ses origines," *L'année sociologique,* I (1896–97), 1–70.

(3) Ploss, H. *Das Weib in der Natur- und Völkerkunde.* Leipzig, 1902.

(4) Lasch, R. "Der Selbstmord aus erotischen Motiven bei den primitiven Völkern." *Zeitschrift für Socialwissenschaft* II (1899) 578–85

(5) Jacobowski, L. "Das Weib in der Poesie der Hottentotten," *Globus*, LXX (1896), 173–76.

(6) Stoll, O. *Das Geschlechtsleben in der Völkerpsychologie.* Leipzig 1908.

(7) Crawley, A. E. "Sexual Taboo: A Study in the Relations of the Sexes," *The Journal of the Anthropological Institute*, XXIV (1894–95), 116–25; 219–35; 430–46.

(8) Simmel. G. "Zur Psychologie der Frauen," *Zeitschrift für Völkerpsychologie und Sprachwissenschaft*, XX, 6–46.

(9) Finck, Henry T. *Romantic Love and Personal Beauty.* Their development, causal relations. historic and national peculiarities. London and New York, 1887.

(10) ———. *Primitive Love and Love Stories.* New York, 1899.

(11) Kline, L. W. "The Migratory Impulse versus Love of Home," *American Journal of Psychology*, X (1898–99). 1–81.

(12) Key, Ellen. *Love and Marriage.* Translated from the Swedish by A. G. Chater; with a critical and biographical introduction by Havelock Ellis. New York and London, 1912.

(13) Meisel-Hess, Grete. *The Sexual Crisis.* A critique of our sex life. Translated from the German by E. and C. Paul. New York, 1917.

(14) Bloch, Iwan. *The Sexual Life of Our Time in Its Relation to Modern Civilization.* Translated from the 6th German ed. by M. Eden Paul. Chap. viii, "The Individualization of Love," pp. 159–76. London, 1908.

C. *Economics of the Family*

(1) Grosse, Ernst. *Die Formen der Familie und die Formen der Wirtschaft.* Freiburg, 1896.

(2) Le Play, P. G. Frédéric. *Les ouvriers européens.* Études sur les travaux, la vie domestique, et la condition morale des populations ouvrières de l'Europe. Précédées d'un exposé de la méthode d'observation. Paris, 1855. [Comprises a series of 36 monographs on the budgets of typical families selected from the most diverse industries.]

(3) Le Play, P. G. Frédéric. *L'organisation de la famille.* Selon le vrai modèle signalé par l'histoire de toutes les races et de tous les temps. Paris, 1871.

(4) Engel, Ernst. *Die Lebenskosten belgischer Arbeiter-Familien früher und jetzt.* Ermittelt aus Familien-Haushaltrechnungen und vergleichend zusammengestellt. Dresden, 1895.

(5) Chapin, Robert C. *The Standard of Living among Workingmen's Families in New York City.* Russell Sage Foundation. New York, 1909.

(6) Talbot, Marion, and Breckinridge, Sophonisba P. *The Modern Household.* Rev. ed. Boston, 1919. [Bibliography at the end of each chapter.]

(7) Nesbitt, Florence. *Household Management.* Preface by Mary E. Richmond. Russell Sage Foundation. New York, 1918.

D. *The Sociology of the Family*

1. Studies in Family Organization:

   (1) Bosanquet, Helen. *The Family.* London and New York. 1906.
   (2) Durkheim, É. "Introduction à la sociologie de la famille." *Annales de la faculté des lettres de Bordeaux* (1888), pp. 257–81.
   (3) Durkheim, É. "La famille conjugale," *Revue philosophique,* XLI (1921), 1–14.
   (4) Flügel, John Carl. *The Psycho-analytic Study of the Family.* London, 1921.
   (5) Howard, G. E. *A History of Matrimonial Institutions Chiefly in England and the United States.* With an introductory analysis of the literature and theories of primitive marriage and the family. 3 vols. Chicago. 1904.
   (6) Thwing, Charles F. and Carrie F. B. *The Family.* A historical and social study. Boston, 1887.
   (7) Goodsell, Willystine. *A History of the Family as a Social and Educational Institution.* New York, 1915.
   (8) Dealey, J. Q. *The Family in Its Sociological Aspects.* Boston. 1912.
   (9) Calhoun, Arthur W. *A Social History of the American Family from Colonial Times to the Present.* 3 vols. Cleveland, 1917–19. [Bibliography.]
   (10) Thomas, W. I., and Znaniecki, F. *The Polish Peasant in Europe and America.* "Primary-Group Organization," I, 87–524, II. Boston, 1918. [A study based on correspondence between members of the family in America and Poland.]
   (11) Du Bois, W. E. B. *The Negro American Family.* Atlanta, 1908. [Bibliography.]
   (12) Su, S. G. *The Chinese Family System.* New York, 1922. [Bibliography.]
   (13) Williams, James M. "Outline of a Theory of Social Motives," *American Journal of Sociology,* XV (1909–10), 741–80. [Theory of motives based upon observation of rural and urban families.]

2. Materials for the Study of Family Disorganization:

   (1) Willcox, Walter F. *The Divorce Problem.* A study in statistics. ("Columbia University Studies in History, Economics and Public Law," Vol. I. New York, 1891.)
   (2) Lichtenberger, J. P. *Divorce.* A study in social causation. New York, 1909.
   (3) United States Bureau of the Census. *Marriage and Divorce,* 1867–1906. 2 vols. Washington, 1908–9. [Results of two federal investigations.]
   (4) ————. *Marriage and Divorce, 1916.* Washington, 1919.
   (5) Eubank, Earle E. *A Study in Family Desertion.* Department of Public Welfare. Chicago, 1916. [Bibliography.]
   (6) Breckinridge, Sophonisba P., and Abbott, Edith. *The Delinquent Child and the Home.* A study of the delinquent wards of the Juvenile Court of Chicago. Russell Sage Foundation. New York, 1912.

(7) Colcord, Joanna. *Broken Homes*. A study of family desertion and its social treatment. Russell Sage Foundation. New York. 1919.

(8) Kammerer, Percy G. *The Unmarried Mother*. A study of five hundred cases. Boston, 1918.

(9) Ellis, Havelock. *The Task of Social Hygiene*. Boston, 1912.

(10) Myerson, Abraham. "Psychiatric Family Studies," *American Journal of Insanity*, LXXIV (April, 1918), 497–555.

(11) Morrow, Prince A. *Social Diseases and Marriage*. Social prophylaxis. New York, 1904.

(12) Periodicals on Social Hygiene:
Zeitschrift für Sexualwissenschaft, Bd. 1, April, 1914–, Bonn [1915–].
Social Hygiene, Vol. I, December, 1914–, New York [1915].
Die Neue Generation, Bd. 1, 1908–, Berlin [1908–]. Preceded by *Mutterschutz*, Vols. I–III.

TOPICS FOR WRITTEN THEMES

1. Society and the Individual: The Cardinal Problem of Sociology
2. Historic Conceptions of Society: Aristotle, Hobbes, Rousseau, etc.
3. Plant Communities
4. Animal Societies: The Ant Colony, the Bee Hive
5. Animal Communities, or Studies in Animal Ecology
6. Human Communities, Human Ecology, and Economics
7. The Natural Areas of the City
8. Studies in Group Consciousness: National, Sectional, State, Civic
9. Co-operation versus Consensus
10. Taming as a Form of Social Control
11. Domestication among Plants, Animals, and Man
12. Group Unity and the Different Forms of Consensus: *Esprit de corps*, Morale, Collective Representations
13. The Social Nature of Concepts
14. Conduct and Behavior

QUESTIONS FOR DISCUSSION

1. What, in your opinion, are the essential elements in Espinas' definition of society?
2. In what sense does society differ from association?
3. According to Espinas' definition, which of the following social relations would constitute society: robber and robbed; beggar and almsgiver, charity organization and recipients of relief; master and slave; employer and employee?
4. What illustrations of symbiosis in human society occur to you?

5. Are changes resulting from human symbiosis changes (*a*) of structure, or (*b*) of function?

6. What are the likenesses and the differences between social symbiosis in human and in ant society?

7. What is the difference between taming and domestication?

8. What is the relation of domestication to society?

9. Is man a *tamed* or a *domesticated* animal?

10. What are the likenesses between a plant and a human community? What are the differences?

11. What is the fundamental difference between a plant community and an ant society?

12. What are the differences between human and animal societies?

13. Does the ant have customs? ceremonies?

14. Do you think that there is anything akin to public sentiment in ant society?

15. What is the relation of education to social heredity?

16. In what way do you differentiate between the characteristic behavior of machines and human beings?

17. "Society not only continues to exist *by* transmission, *by* communication, but it may fairly be said to exist *in* transmission, *in* communication." Interpret.

18. How does Dewey's definition of society differ from that of Espinas? Which do you prefer? Why?

19. Is consensus synonymous with co-operation?

20. Under what conditions would Dewey characterize the following social relations as society: master and slave; employer and employee; parent and child; teacher and student?

21. In what sense does the communication of an experience to another person change the experience itself?

22. In what sense are concepts *social* in contrast with sensations which are *individual*? Would it be possible to have concepts outside of group life?

23. How does Park distinguish between behavior and conduct?

24. In what ways is human society in its origin and continuity based on conduct?

25. To what extent does "the animal nature of man" (Hobhouse) provide a basis for the social organization of life?

26. What, according to Hobhouse, are the *differentia* of human morality from animal behavior?

27. What do you understand by a collective representation?

28. How do you distinguish between the terms society, social community and group? Can you name a society that could not be considered as a community? Can you name a community that is not a society?

29. In what. fundamentally, does the unity of the group consist?
30. What groups are omitted in Le Bon's classification of social groups? Make a list of all the groups, formal and informal, of which you are a member. Arrange these groups under the classification given in the General Introduction (p. 50). Compare this classification with that made by Le Bon.
31. How do you distinguish between *esprit de corps*, morale, and collective representation as forms of consensus?
32. Classify under *esprit de corps*, morale, or collective representation the following aspects of group behavior: rooting at a football game; army discipline; the flag; college spirit; the so-called "war psychosis"; the fourteen points of President Wilson; "the English never know when they are beaten"; slogans; "Paris refrains from exultation"; crowd enthusiasm; the Golden Rule; "where there's a will there's a way"; Grant's determination, "I'll fight it out this way if it takes all summer"; ideals.
33. "The human mind has a large capacity for adopting beliefs that fit the trends of its habits and feelings" Give concrete illustrations outside of army life.
34. What is the importance of the study of the family as a social group?

CHAPTER IV

ISOLATION

I. INTRODUCTION

1. Geographical and Biological Conceptions of Isolation

Relations of persons with persons, and of groups with groups, may be either those of isolation or those of contact. The emphasis in this chapter is placed upon *isolation*, in the next chapter upon *contact* in a comparison of their effects upon personal conduct and group behavior.

Absolute isolation of the person from the members of his group is unthinkable. Even biologically, two individuals of the higher animal species are the precondition to a new individual existence. In man, postnatal care by the parent for five or six years is necessary even for the physiological survival of the offspring. Not only biologically but sociologically complete isolation is a contradiction in terms. Sociologists following Aristotle have agreed with him that human nature develops within and decays outside of social relations. Isolation, then, in the social as well as the biological sense is *relative*, not *absolute*.

The term "isolation" was first employed in anthropogeography, the study of the relation of man to his physical environment. To natural barriers, as mountains, oceans, and deserts, was attributed an influence upon the location of races and the movements of peoples and the kind and the degree of cultural contact. The nature and the extent of separation of persons and groups was considered by geographers as a reflex of the physical environment.

In biology, isolation as a factor in the evolution and the life of the species, is studied from the standpoint of the animal group more than from that of the environment. Consequently, the separation of species from each other is regarded as the outcome not only of a sheer physical impossibility of contact, but even more of other factors as differences in physical structure, in habits of life, and in the instincts of the animal groups.   J. Arthur Thomson in his work on "Heredity" presents the following compact and illuminating statement of isolation as a factor in inheritance.

The only other directive evolution-factor that biologists are at all agreed about, besides selection, is isolation—a general term for all the varied ways in which the radius of possible intercrossing is narrowed. As expounded by Wagner, Weismann, Romanes, Gulick, and others, isolation takes many forms—spatial, structural, habitudinal, and psychical—and it has various results.

It tends to the segregation of species into sub-species, it makes it easier for new variations to establish themselves, it promotes prepotency, or what the breeders call "transmitting power," it fixes characters. One of the most successful breeds of cattle (Polled Angus) seems to have had its source in one farmsteading; its early history is one of close inbreeding, its prepotency is remarkable, its success from our point of view has been great. It is difficult to get secure data as to the results of isolation in nature, but Gulick's recent volume on the subject abounds in concrete illustrations, and we seem warranted in believing that conditions of isolation have been and are of frequent occurrence.

Reibmayr has collected from human history a wealth of illustrations of various forms of isolation, and there seems much to be said for his thesis that the establishment of a successful race or stock requires the alternation of periods of inbreeding (endogamy) in which characters are fixed, and periods of outbreeding (exogamy) in which, by the introduction of fresh blood, new variations are promoted. Perhaps the Jews may serve to illustrate the influence of isolation in promoting stability of type and prepotency; perhaps the Americans may serve to illustrate the variability which a mixture of different stocks tends to bring about. In historical inquiry into the difficult problem of the origin of distinct races, it seems legitimate to think of periods of "mutation"—of discontinuous sporting— which led to numerous offshoots from the main stock, of the migration of these variants into new environments where in relative isolation they became prepotent and stable.[1]

The biological use of the term "isolation" introduces a new emphasis. Separation may be spatial, but its effects are increasingly structural and functional. Indeed, spatial isolation was a factor in the origin of species because of specialized organic adaptation to varied geographic conditions. In other words, the structure of

[1] J Arthur Thomson, *Heredity*, pp. 536–37.   (G. P. Putnam's Sons, 1908.)

the species, its habits of life, and its original and acquired responses, tend to isolate it from other species.

Man as an animal species in his historical development has attempted with fair success to destroy the barriers separating him from other animals. Through domestication and taming he has changed the original nature and habits of life of many animals. The dog, the companion of man, is the summit of human achievement in association with animals. Nevertheless, the barriers that separate the dog and his master are insurmountable. Even if "a candidate for humanity," the dog is forever debarred from any share in human tradition and culture.

2.   Isolation and Segregation

In geography, isolation denotes separation in space. In sociology, the essential characteristic of isolation is found in exclusion from communication.

Geographical forms of isolation are sociologically significant in so far as they prevent communication. The isolation of the mountain whites in the southern states, even if based on spatial separation, consisted in the absence of contacts and competition, participation in the progressive currents of civilization.

Biological differences, whether physical or mental, between the different races are sociologically important to the extent to which they affect communication. Of themselves, differences in skin color between races would not prevent intercommunication of ideas. But the physical marks of racial differences have invariably become the symbols of racial solidarity and racial exclusiveness. The problems of humanity are altogether different from what they would have been were all races of one complexion as they are of one blood.

Certain physical and mental defects and differences in and of themselves tend to separate the individual from his group. The deafmute and the blind are deprived of normal avenues to communication. "My deafness," wrote Beethoven, "forces me to live in exile." The physically handicapped are frequently unable to participate in certain human activities on equal terms with their fellows. Minor physical defects and marked physical variations from the normal tend to become the basis of social discrimination.

Mental differences frequently offer still greater obstacles to social contacts. The idiot and the imbecile are obviously debarred from normal communication with their intelligent associates. The "dunce" was isolated by village ridicule and contempt long before the term "moron" was coined, or the feeble-minded segregated in institutions and colonies. The individual with the highest native endowments, the genius, and the talented enjoy or suffer from a more subtle type of isolation from their fellows, that is, the isolation of eminence. "The reason of isolation," says Thoreau, a lover of solitude, "is not that we love to be alone, but that we love to soar; and when we soar, the company grows thinner and thinner until there is none left."

So far, isolation as a tool of social analysis has been treated as an effect of geographical separation or of structural differentiation resulting in limitation of communication. Social distances are frequently based on other subtler forms of isolation.

The study of cultural differences between groups has revealed barriers quite as real and as effective as those of physical space and structure. Variations in language, folkways, mores, conventions, and ideals separate individuals and peoples from each other as widely as oceans and deserts. Communication between England and Australia is far closer and freer than between Germany and France.

Conflict groups, like sects and parties, and accommodation groups like castes and classes depend for survival upon isolation. Free intercourse of opposing parties is always a menace to their morale. Fraternization between soldiers of contending armies, or between ministers of rival denominations is fraught with peril to the fighting efficiency of the organizations they represent. The solidarity of the group, like the integrity of the individual, implies a measure at least of isolation from other groups and persons as a necessary condition of its existence.

The life-history of any group when analyzed is found to incorporate within it elements of isolation as well as of social contact. Membership in a group makes for increasing contacts within the circle of participants, but decreasing contacts with persons without. Isolation is for this reason a factor in the preservation of individuality and unity. The *esprit de corps* and morale of the group is in large part maintained by the fixation of attention upon certain collective

representations to the exclusion of others. The memories and sentiments of the members have their source in common experiences of
the past from which non-members are isolated. This natural tendency toward exclusive experiences is often reinforced by conscious
emphasis upon secrecy. Primitive and modern secret societies,
sororities, and fraternities have been organized around the principle
of isolation. Secrecy in a society, like reserve in an individual, protects it from a disintegrating publicity. The family has its "skeleton
in the closet," social groups avoid the public "washing of dirty linen";
the community banishes from consciousness, if it can, its slums, and
parades its parks and boulevards. Every individual who has any
personality at all maintains some region of privacy.

A morphological survey of group formation in any society discloses the fact that there are lateral as well as vertical divisions in
the social structure. Groups are arranged in strata of relative
superiority and inferiority. In a stratified society the separation
into castes is rigid and quite unalterable. In a free society competition tends to destroy classes and castes. New devices come into
use to keep aspiring and insurgent individuals and groups at the
proper social level. If "familiarity breeds contempt" respect may
be secured by reserve. In the army the prestige of the officer is
largely a matter of "distance." The "divinity that doth hedge the
king" is due in large part to the hedge of ceremonial separating him
from his subjects. Condescension and pity, while they denote external contact, involve an assumption of spiritual eminence not to
be found in consensus and sympathy. As protection against the
penetration of the inner precincts of personality and the group individuality, there are the defenses of suspicion and aversion, of
reticence and reserve, designed to insure the proper social distance.

3. Classification of the Materials

The materials in the present chapter are intended to illustrate
the fact that individuality of the person and of the group is both an
effect of and a cause of isolation.

The first selections under the heading "Isolation and Personal
Individuality" bring out the point that the function of isolation in
personal development lies not so much in sheer physical separation
from other persons as in freedom from the control of external social

contacts. Thus Rousseau constructs an ideal society in the solitude of his forest retreat. The lonely child enjoys the companionship of his imaginary comrade. George Eliot aspires to join the choir invisible. The mystic seeks communion with divinity.

This form of isolation within the realm of social contacts is known as privacy. Indeed privacy may be defined as withdrawal from the group, with, at the same time, ready access to it. It is in solitude that the creative mind organizes the materials appropriated from the group in order to make novel and fruitful innovations. Privacy affords opportunity for the individual to reflect, to anticipate, to recast, and to originate. Practical recognition of the human demand for privacy has been realized in the study of the minister, the office of the business man, and the den of the boy. Monasteries and universities are institutions providing leisure and withdrawal from the world as the basis for personal development and preparation for life's work. Other values of privacy are related to the growth of self-consciousness, self-respect, and personal ideals of conduct.

Many forms of isolation, unlike privacy, prevent access to stimulating social contact. Selections under the heading "Isolation and Retardation" indicate conditions responsible for the arrest of mental and personal growth.

The cases of feral men, in the absence of contradictory evidence, seem adequate in support of Aristotle's point that social contacts are indispensable for human development. The story by Helen Keller, the talented and celebrated blind deaf-mute, of her emergence from the imprisonment of sense deprivation into the free life of communication is a most significant sociological document. With all of us the change from the animal-like isolation of the child at birth to personal participation in the fullest human life is gradual. In Helen Keller's case the transformation of months was telescoped into minutes. The "miracle" of communication when sociologically analyzed seems to consist in the transition from the experience of *sensations* and *sense perceptions* which man shares in common with animals to the development of *ideas* and *self-consciousness* which are the unique attributes of human beings.

The remaining selections upon isolation and retardation illustrate the different types of situations in which isolation makes for retardation and retardation in turn emphasizes the isolation. The reversion of a man of scientific training in the solitudes of Patagonia to the animal level of mentality suggests that the low intelligence of the savage, the peasant, and the backward races is probably due more to the absence of stimulating contacts than to original mental inferiority. So the individuality and conservatism of the farmer, his failure to keep pace with the inhabitant of the town and city, Galpin assigns to deficiency in social contacts. Then, too, the subtler forms of handicap in personal development and achievement result from social types of isolation, as race prejudice, the sheltered life of woman, exclusiveness of social classes, and make for increased isolation.

Up to this point, isolation has been treated statically as a cause. Under the heading, "Isolation and Segregation" it is conceived as an effect, an effect of competition, and the consequent selection and segregation.

The first effect of the introduction of competition in any society is to break up all types of isolation and provincialism based upon lack of communication and contact. But as competition continues, natural and social selection comes into play. Successful types emerge in the process of competitive struggle while variant individuals who fail to maintain the pace or conform to standard withdraw or are ejected from the group. Exiled variants from several groups under auspicious circumstances may in turn form a community where the process of selection will be directly opposite to that in their native groups. In the new community the process of selection naturally accentuates and perfects the traits originally responsible for exclusion. The outcome of segregation is the creation of specialized social types with the maximum of isolation. The circle of isolation is then complete.

This circular effect of the processes of competition, selection, and segregation, from isolation to isolation, may be found everywhere in modern western society. Individual variants with criminalistic tendencies exiled from villages and towns through the process of selection form a segregated group in city areas popularly called "breeding places of crime." The tribe of Pineys Tin Town, The Village of a Thousand Souls, are communities made up by adverse selection of feeble-minded individuals, outcasts of the competitive struggle of intelligent, "high-minded" communities. The result is the formation of a criminal type and of a feeble-minded caste. These slums and outcast groups are in turn isolated from full and free communication with the progressive outside world.

National individuality in the past, as indicated in the selections upon "Isolation and National Individuality," has been in large degree the result of a cultural process based upon isolation. The historical nations of Europe, biologically hybrid, are united by common language, folkways, and mores. This unity of mother tongue and culture is the product of historical and cultural processes circumscribed, as Shaler points out, by separated geographical areas.

A closer examination of the cultural process in the life of progressive historical peoples reveals the interplay of isolation and social contacts. Grote gives a penetrating analysis of Grecian achievement in terms of the individuality based on small isolated land areas and the contacts resulting from maritime communication. The world-hegemony of English-speaking peoples today rests not only upon naval supremacy and material resources but even more upon the combination of individual development in diversified areas with large freedom in international contacts.

II. MATERIALS

A. ISOLATION AND PERSONAL INDIVIDUALITY

1. Society and Solitude[1]

It had been hard for him that spake it to have put more truth and untruth together in few words than in that speech: "Whosoever is delighted in solitude is either a wild beast or a god." For it is most true that a natural and secret hatred and aversation towards society in any man hath somewhat of the savage beast; but it is most untrue that it should have any character at all of the divine nature except it proceed, not out of a pleasure in solitude, but out of a love and desire to sequester a man's self for a higher conversation, such as is found to have been falsely and feignedly in some of the heathen, as Epimenides the Candian, Numa the Roman, Empedocles the Sicilian, and Apollonius of Tyana; and truly and really in divers of the ancient hermits and Holy Fathers of the Church. But little do men perceive what solitude is, and how far it extendeth. For a crowd is not company, and faces are but a gallery of pictures, and

[1] From Francis Bacon, *Essays*, "Of Friendship."

talk but a tinkling cymbal, where there is no love.   The Latin adage meeteth with it a little: *Magna civitas magna solitudo* ("A great town is a great solitude"), because in a great town friends are scattered, so that there is not that fellowship, for the most part, which is in less neighborhoods.   But we may go further, and affirm most truly that it is a mere and miserable solitude to want true friends, without which the world is but a wilderness; and, even in this sense also of solitude, whosoever in the frame of his nature and affections is unfit for friendship, he taketh it of the beast and not from humanity.

2.   Society in Solitude[1]

What period do you think, sir, I recall most frequently and most willingly in my dreams?   Not the pleasures of my youth: they were too rare, too much mingled with bitterness, and are now too distant. I recall the period of my seclusion, of my solitary walks, of the fleeting but delicious days that I have passed entirely by myself, with my good and simple housekeeper, with my beloved dog, my old cat, with the birds of the field, the hinds of the forest, with all nature, and her inconceivable Author.

But what, then, did I enjoy when I was alone?   Myself; the entire universe; all that is; all that can be; all that is beautiful in the world of sense; all that is imaginable in the world of intellect. I gathered around me all that could delight my heart;   my desires were the limit of my pleasures.   No, never have the voluptuous known such enjoyments; and I have derived a hundred times more happiness from my chimeras than they from their realities.

The wild spot of the forest [selected by Rousseau for his solitary walks and meditations] could not long remain a desert to my imagination.   I soon peopled it with beings after my own heart, and, dismissing opinion, prejudice, and all factitious passions, I brought to these sanctuaries of nature men worthy of inhabiting them.   I formed with these a charming society, of which I did not feel myself unworthy. I made a golden age according to my fancy, and, filling up these bright days with all the scenes of my life that had left the tenderest recollections, and with all that my heart still longed for, I affected myself to tears over the true pleasures of humanity—pleasure so

[1] Adapted from Jean Jacques Rousseau, *Letter to the President de Malesherbes, 1762.*

delicious, so pure, and yet so far from men! Oh, if in these moments any ideas of Paris, of the age, and of my little author vanity, disturbed my reveries, with what contempt I drove them instantly away, to give myself up entirely to the exquisite sentiments with which my soul was filled. Yet, in the midst of all this, I confess the nothingness of my chimeras would sometimes appear, and sadden me in a moment.

3. Prayer as a Form of Isolation[1]

He who prays begins his prayer with some idea of God, generally one that he has received from instruction or from current traditions. He commonly retires to a quiet place, or to a place having mental associations of religious cast, in order to "shut out the world." This beginning of concentration is followed by closing the eyes, which excludes a mass of irrelevant impressions. The body bows, kneels, or assumes some other posture that requires little muscular tension and that may favor extensive relaxation. Memory now provides the language of prayer or of hallowed scripture, or makes vivid some earlier experiences of one's own. The worshiper represents to himself his needs, or the interests (some of them happy ones) that seem most important, and he brings them into relation to God by thinking how God regards them. The presupposition of the whole procedure is that God's way of looking at the matters in question is the true and important one. Around God, then, the interests of the individual are now freshly organized. Certain ones that looked large before the prayer began, now look small because of their relation to the organizing idea upon which attention has focused. On the other hand, interests that express this organizing idea gain emotional quality by this release from competing, inhibiting considerations. To say that the will now becomes organized toward unity and that it acquires fresh power thereby is simply to name another aspect of the one movement. This movement is ideational, emotional, and volitional concentration, all in one, achieved by fixation of attention upon the idea of God.

Persons who have been troubled with insomnia, or wakefulness or disturbing dreams, have been enabled to secure sound sleep by

[1] Adapted from George Albert Coe, *The Psychology of Religion*, pp. 311-18. (The University of Chicago Press, 1917.)

merely relaxing the muscles and repeating mechanically, without effort at anything more, some formula descriptive of what is desired. The main point is that attention should fix upon the appropriate organizing idea. When this happens in a revival meeting one may find one's self unexpectedly converted. When it happens in prayer one may be surprised to find one's whole mood changed from discouragement to courage, from liking something to hating it (as in the case of alcoholic drinks, or tobacco), or from loneliness to the feeling of companionship with God.

This analysis of the structure of prayer has already touched upon some of its functions. It is a way of getting one's self together, of mobilizing and concentrating one's dispersed capacities, of begetting the confidence that tends toward victory over difficulties. It produces in a distracted mind the repose that is power. It freshens a mind deadened by routine. It reveals new truth, because the mind is made more elastic and more capable of sustained attention. Thus does it remove mountains in the individual, and, through him, in the world beyond.

The values of prayer in sickness, distress, and doubt are by no means measurable by the degree to which the primary causes thereof are made to disappear. There is a real conquest of trouble, even while trouble remains. It is sometimes a great source of strength, also, merely to realize that one is fully understood. The value of having some friend or helper from whom I reserve no secrets has been rendered more impressive than ever by the Freud-Jung methods of relieving mental disorders through (in part) a sort of mental house-cleaning, or bringing into the open the patient's hidden distresses and even his most intimate and reticent desires. Into the psychology of the healings that are brought about by this psychoanalysis we need not go, except to note that one constant factor appears to be the turning of a private possession into a social possession, and particularly the consciousness that another understands. I surmise that we shall not be far from the truth here if we hold that, as normal experience has the *ego-alter* form, so the continuing possession of one's self in one's developing experience requires development of this relation. We may, perhaps, go as far as to believe that the bottling up of any experience as merely private is morbid. But, however this may be, there are plenty of occasions when the road to poise, freedom, and joy is that of social sharing. Hence the prayer of confession, not only because it helps us to see ourselves as we are, but also because it shares our secrets with another, has great value for organizing the self. In this way we get relief from the misjudgments of others, also, and from the mystery that we are to ourselves, for we lay our case, as it were, before a judge who does not err. Thus prayer has value in that it develops the essentially social form of personal self-realization.

To complete this functional view of prayer we must not fail to secure the evolutionary perspective. If we glance at the remote beginnings, and then at the hither end, of the evolution of prayer we discover that an immense change has taken place. It is a correlate of the transformed character of the gods, and of the parallel disciplining of men's valuations. In the words of Fosdick, prayer may be considered as dominant desire. But it is also a way of securing domination over desire. It is indeed self-assertion; sometimes it is the making of one's supreme claim, as when life reaches its most tragic crisis; yet it is, even in the same act, submission to an overself. Here, then, is our greater problem as to the function of prayer. It starts as the assertion of any desire; it ends as *the organization of one's own desires into a system of desires recognized as superior and then made one's own.*

4. Isolation, Originality, and Erudition[1]

The question as to how far the world's leaders in thought and action were great readers is not quite an easy one to answer, partly because the sources of information are sometimes scanty, and partly because books themselves have been few in number. If we could prove that since the days of Caxton the world's total of original thought declined in proportion to the increase of published works, we should stand on firm ground, and might give orders for a holocaust such as that which Hawthorne once imagined. But no such proof is either possible or probable. We can only be impressed by the fact that the finest intellectual epoch of history was marked by a comparative absence of the manuscripts which were books to the Greeks, and if a further analysis of the lives of men of light and leading in all

[1] From T. Sharper Knowlson, *Originality*, pp. 173–75. (T. Werner Laurie, 1918.)

ages should show that their devotion to the books of the period was slight, it will only accentuate the suspicion that even today we are still minus the right perspective between the printed volume and the thinking mind.

Buddha, Christ, St. Paul, Mohammed—these are names of men who changed the course of history. But do they suggest vast scholarship, or a profound acquaintance with books in any sense whatever? They were great originators, even though they built on other men's foundations, but their originality was not inspired by libraries. Can we imagine Mohammed poring over ancient manuscripts in order to obtain the required knowledge and impetus for his new religion? With Buddha was it not 1 per cent papyrus roll and 99 per cent meditation? When St. Paul was struck down on the way to Damascus, he did not repair to the nearest Jewish seminary to read up prophecy. He says: "I went into Arabia." The desert solitude was the only place in which to find a rationale of his new experience. And was it not in a similar life of solitude that Jesus—Essene-like—came to self-realization? Deane's *Pseudepigrapha: Books that Influenced our Lord and His Apostles* does not suggest that the Messiah obtained his ideas from the literature of the Rabbis, much less from Greek or other sources; indeed, the New Testament suggests that in the earliest years he showed a genius for divine things.

It will be urged that to restrict this inquiry to great names in religion would be unfair because such leaders are confessedly independent of literature; indeed, they are often the creators of it. True; but that fact alone is suggestive. If great literature can come from meditation alone, are we not compelled to ask: "Where shall wisdom be found and where is the place of understanding?" Is enlightenment to be found only in the printed wisdom of the past? We know it is not, but we also know it is useless to set one source of truth over against another, as if they were enemies. The soul has its place and so has the book; but need it be said that the soul has done more wonderful things than the book? Language is merely the symbol; the soul is the reality.

But let us take other names with different associations—e.g., Plato, Charlemagne, Caesar, Shakespeare, Napoleon, Bismarck. Can it be said of any one of these that he owed one-third of his distinction to what he learned from manuscripts or books? We do know, indeed, that Bismarck was a wide reader, but it was on the selective principle as a student of history and affairs. His library grew under the influence of the controlling purpose of his life—i.e., the unification of Germany, so that there was no vague distribution of energy. Of Shakespeare's reading we know less, but there is no evidence that he was a collector of books or that he was a student after the manner of the men of letters of his day. The best way to estimate him as a reader is to judge him by the references in his plays, and these do not show an acquaintance with literature so extensive as it is intensive. The impression he made on Ben Jonson, an all-round scholar, was not one of learning—quite otherwise. The qualities that impressed the author of *Timber, or Discoveries upon Men and Matter*, were Shakespeare's "open and free nature," his "excellent fancy, brave notions, and gentle expressions wherein he flowed with that facility that sometimes it was necessary he should be stopped." And, true to himself, Ben Jonson immediately adds: "*Sufflaminandus erat*, as Augustus said of Haterius." Shakespeare, when in the company of kindred spirits, showed precisely the kind of talk we should expect—not Latin and Greek or French and Italian quotations, not a commentary on books past or present, but a stream of conversation marked by brilliant fancy, startling comparison, unique contrast, and searching pathos, wherein life, not literature, was the chief subject.

B.   ISOLATION AND RETARDATION

1.   Feral Men[1]

What would the results be if children born with a normal organism and given food and light sufficient to sustain life were deprived of the usual advantage of human intercourse? What psychic growth would be possible?

Perhaps no character ever aroused greater interest than Caspar Hauser. More than a thousand articles of varying merit have been written concerning him. In the theaters of England, France, Germany, Hungary, and Austria, plays were founded on his strange story and many able men have figured in the history of his case.

[1] From Maurice H. Small, "On Some Psychical Relations of Society and Solitude," in the *Pedagogical Seminary*, VII, No. 2 (1900), 32–36.

According to a letter which he bore when found at Nürnberg one afternoon in 1828, he was born in 1812, left on the doorstep of a Hungarian peasant's hut, adopted by him, and reared in strict seclusion.

At the time of his appearance in Nürnberg, he could walk only with difficulty. He knew no German, understood but little that was said to him, paid no heed to what went on about him, and was ignorant of social customs. When taken to a stable, he at once fell asleep on a heap of straw. In time it was learned that he had been kept in a low dark cell on the ground; that he had never seen the face of the man who brought him food, that sometimes he went to sleep after the man gave him a drink; that on awakening he found his nails cut and clean clothing on his body; and that his only playthings had been two wooden horses with red ribbons.

When first found, he suffered much pain from the light, but he could see well at night. He could distinguish fruit from leaves on a tree, and read the name on a doorplate where others could see nothing in the darkness. He had no visual idea of distance and would grasp at remote objects as though they were near. He called both men and women *Bua* and all animals *Rosz*. His memory span for names was marvelous. Drawing upon the pages of Von Kolb and Stanhope, a writer in *The Living Age* says that he burned his hand in the first flame that he saw and that he had no fear of being struck with swords, but that the noise of a drum threw him into convulsions. He thought that pictures and statuary were alive, as were plants and trees, bits of paper, and anything that chanced to be in motion. He delighted in whistles and glittering objects, but disliked the odor of paint, fabrics, and most flowers. His hearing was acute and his touch sensitive at first, but after interest in him had lessened, all his senses showed evidence of rapid deterioration. He seemed to be wanting in sex instinct and to be unable to understand the meaning of religious ceremonies. Merker, who observed him secretly during the early days which he spent in jail, declared that he was "in all respects like a child." Meyer, of the school at Ansbach, found him "idle, stupid, and vain." Dr. Osterhausen found a deviation from the normal in the shape of his legs, which made walking difficult, but Caspar never wearied of riding on horseback.

His autopsy revealed a small brain without abnormalities. It simply gave evidence of a lack of development.

To speak of children who have made the struggle for life with only animals for nurses and instructors is to recall the rearing of Cyrus in a kennel and the fabulous story of the founding of Rome. Yet Rauber has collected many cases of wild men and some of them taken as they are from municipal chronicles and guaranteed by trustworthy writers, must be accepted as authentic.

a) The Hessian Boy. Was discovered by hunters in 1341, running on all fours with wolves; was captured and turned over to the landgrave. Was always restless, could not adapt himself to civilized life, and died untamed. The case is recorded in the Hessian chronicles by Wilhelm Dilich. Rousseau refers to it in his *Discours sur l'origine et les fondements de l'inégalité parmi les hommes.*

b) The Irish Boy. Studied and described by Dr. Tulp, curator of the gymnasium at Amsterdam; features animal, body covered with hair; lived with sheep and bleated like them; stolid, unconscious of self; did not notice people; fierce, untamable, and indocible; skin thick, sense of touch blunted so that thorns and stones were unnoticed. Age about sixteen. (Rauber.)

c) The Lithuanian Boys. Three are described. The first was found with bears in 1657; face not repulsive nor beastlike; hair thick and white; skin dry and insensitive; voice a growl; great physical strength. He was carefully instructed and learned to obey his trainer to some degree but always kept the bear habit; ate vegetable food, raw flesh, and anything not containing oils; had a habit of rolling up in secluded places and taking long naps. The second, said to have been captured in 1669, is not so well described as the third, which Dr. Connor, in the *History of Poland*, says was found in 1694. This one learned to walk erect with difficulty, but was always leaping restlessly about; he learned to eat from a table, but mastered only a few words, which he spoke in a voice harsh and inhuman. He showed great sagacity in wood life.

d) The Girl of Cranenburg. Born in 1700; lost when sixteen months old; skin dark, rough, hard; understood but little that was said to her; spoke little and stammeringly; food—roots, leaves, and milk. (Rauber.)

e) Clemens of Overdyke. This boy was brought to Count von der Ricke's Asylum after the German struggle with Napoleon. He knew little and said little. After careful training it was gathered that his parents were dead and that a peasant had adopted him and set him to herd pigs. Little food was given him, and he learned to suck a cow and eat grass with the pigs. At Overdyke he would get down on his hands and knees and pull up vegetables with his teeth. He was of low intelligence, subject to fits of passion, and fonder of pigs than of men.[1]

f) Jean de Liége. Lost at five; lived in the woods for sixteen years; food—roots, plants, and wild fruit; sense of smell extraordinarily keen; could distinguish people by odor as a dog would recognize his master; restless in manner, and always trying to escape. (Rauber.)

g) The Savage of Aveyron. After capture, was given into the care of Dr. Itard by Abbé Sicard. Dermal sense duller than in animals; gaze wandering; language wanting and ideas few; food— raw potatoes, acorns, and fruit; would eagerly tear open a bird and eat it raw; indolent, secretive; would hide in the garden until hunger drove him to the kitchen; rolled in new snow like an animal; paid no heed to the firing of a gun, but became alert at the cracking of a nut; sometimes grew wildly angry; all his powers were then enlarged; was delighted with hills and woods, and always tried to escape after being taken to them; when angry would gnaw clothing and hurl furniture about; feared to look from a height, and Itard cured him of spasms of rage by holding his head out of a window; met all efforts to teach him with apathy, and learned but little of language.[2]

h) The Wolf Children of India. The two cases described by a writer in *Chambers' Journal* and by Rauber were boys of about ten years. Both ate raw food but refused cooked food; one never spoke, smiled, or laughed; both shunned human beings of both sexes, but would permit a dog to eat with them; they pined in captivity, and lived but a short time.[3]

i) Peter of Hanover. Found in the woods of Hanover; food— buds, barks, roots, frogs, eggs of birds, and anything else that he could get out of doors; had a habit of wandering away in the spring; always went to bed as soon as he had his supper; was unable to walk in shoes at first, and it was long before he would tolerate a

---

[1] *Anthropological Review*, I (London, 1863), 21 ff.

[2] *All the Year*, XVIII, 302 ff.   [3] *Chambers' Journal*, LIX, 579 ff.

covering for his head. Although Queen Caroline furnished him a teacher, he could never learn to speak; he became docile, but remained stoical in manner; he learned to do farm work willingly unless he was compelled to do it; his sense of hearing and of smell was acute, and before changes in the weather he was sullen and irritable; he lived to be nearly seventy years old.[1]

j) The Savage of Kronstadt. Of middle size, wild-eyed, deep-jawed, and thick-throated; elbows and knees thick; cuticle insensitive; unable to understand words or gestures perfectly; generally indifferent; found 1784.[2]

k) The Girl of Songi. According to Rauber, this is one of the most frequently quoted of feral cases. The girl came out of the forest near Chalons in 1731. She was thought to be nine years old. She carried a club in her hand, with which she killed a dog that attacked her. She climbed trees easily, and made niches on walls and roofs, over which she ran like a squirrel. She caught fish and ate them raw; a cry served for speech. She showed an instinct for decorating herself with leaves and flowers. She found it difficult to adapt herself to the customs of civilized life and suffered many fits of sickness. In 1747 she was put into a convent at Chalons. She learned something of the French language, of domestic science, and embroidery. She readily understood what was pointed out to her but always had certain sounds which were not understood. She claimed to have first begun to reflect after the beginning of her education. In her wild life she thought only of her own needs. She believed that the earth and the trees produced her, and her earliest memory of shelter was of holes in the ground.[3]

2. From Solitude to Society[4]

The most important day I remember in all my life is the one on which my teacher, Anne Mansfield Sullivan, came to me. I am

[1] *The Penny Magazine*, II, 113.

[2] Wagner, *Beiträge zur philosophischen Anthropologie:* Rauber, pp. 49–55.

[3] "Histoire d'une jeune fille sauvage trouvée dans les bois à l'âge de dix ans," *Magazin der Natur, Kunst, und Wissenschaft*, Leipzig, 1756, pp. 219–72; *Mercure de France*, December, 1731; Rudolphi, *Grundriss der Physiologie*, I, 25; Blumenbach, *Bei ge zur Naturgeschichte*, II, 38.

[4] Adapted from Helen Keller, *The Story of My Life*, pp. 22–24. (Doubleday, Page & Co., 1917.)

filled with wonder when I consider the immeasurable contrast between the two lives which it connects. It was the third of March, 1887, three months before I was seven years old.

The morning after my teacher came she led me into her room and gave me a doll. The little blind children at the Perkins Institution had sent it and Laura Bridgman had dressed it; but I did not know this until afterward. When I had played with it a little while, Miss Sullivan slowly spelled into my hand the word "d-o-l-l." I was at once interested in this finger play and tried to imitate it. When I finally succeeded in making the letters correctly I was flushed with childish pleasure and pride. Running downstairs to my mother I held up my hand and made the letters for doll. I did not know that I was spelling a word or even that words existed; I was simply making my fingers go in monkey-like imitation. In the days that followed I learned to spell in this uncomprehending way a great many words, among them *pin*, *hat*, *cup* and a few verbs like *sit*, *stand*, and *walk*. But my teacher had been with me several weeks before I understood that everything has a name.

One day, while I was playing with my new doll, Miss Sullivan put my big rag doll into my lap also, spelled "d-o-l-l" and tried to make me understand that "d-o-l-l" applied to both. Earlier in the day we had had a tussle over the words "m-u-g" and "w-a-t-e-r." Miss Sullivan had tried to impress it upon me that "m-u-g" is *mug* and that "w-a-t-e-r" is *water*, but I persisted in confounding the two. In despair she had dropped the subject for the time, only to renew it at the first opportunity. I became impatient at her repeated attempts and, seizing the new doll, I dashed it upon the floor. I was keenly delighted when I felt the fragments of the broken doll at my feet. Neither sorrow nor regret followed my passionate outburst. I had not loved the doll. In the still, dark world in which I lived there was no strong sentiment or tenderness. I felt my teacher sweep the fragments to one side of the hearth, and I had a sense of satisfaction that the cause of my discomfort was removed. She brought me my hat, and I knew I was going out into the warm sunshine. This thought, if a wordless sensation may be called a thought, made me hop and skip with pleasure.

We walked down the path to the well-house, attracted by the fragrance of the honeysuckle with which it was covered. Some one was drawing water and my teacher placed my hand under the spout. As the cool stream gushed over one hand she spelled into the other the word *water*, first slowly, then rapidly. I stood still, my whole attention fixed upon the motions of her fingers. Suddenly I felt a misty consciousness as of something forgotten—a thrill of returning thought; and somehow the mystery of language was revealed to me. I knew then that "w-a-t-e-r" meant the wonderful cool something that was flowing over my hand. That living word awakened my soul, gave it light, hope, joy, set it free! There were barriers still, it is true, but barriers that could in time be swept away.

I left the well-house eager to learn. Everything had a name, and each name gave birth to a new thought. As we returned to the house every object which I touched seemed to quiver with life. That was because I saw everything with the strange, new sight that had come to me. On entering the door I remembered the doll I had broken. I felt my way to the hearth and picked up the pieces. I tried vainly to put them together. Then my eyes filled with tears; for I realized what I had done, and for the first time I felt repentance and sorrow.

I learned a great many new words that day. I do not remember what they all were; but I do know that *mother, father, sister, teacher*, were among them—words that were to make the world blossom for me, "like Aaron's rod, with flowers." It would have been difficult to find a happier child than I was as I lay in my crib at the close of that eventful day and lived over the joys it had brought me, and for the first time longed for a new day to come.

3. Mental Effects of Solitude[1]

I spent the greater part of one winter at a point on the Rio Negro, seventy or eighty miles from the sea. It was my custom to go out every morning on horseback with my gun, and, followed by one dog, to ride away from the valley; and no sooner would I climb the terrace and plunge into the gray universal thicket, than I would find myself as completely alone as if five hundred instead of only five miles separated me from the valley and river. So wild and solitary and remote seemed that gray waste, stretching away into infinitude, a waste

[1] Adapted from W. H. Hudson, "The Plains of Patagonia," *Universal Review*, VII (1890), 551-57.

untrodden by man, and where the wild animals are so few that they have made no discoverable path in the wilderness of thorns.

Not once nor twice nor thrice, but day after day I returned to this solitude, going to it in the morning as if to attend a festival, and leaving it only when hunger and thirst and the westering sun compelled me. And yet I had no object in going—no motive which could be put into words; for, although I carried a gun, there was nothing to shoot—the shooting was all left behind in the valley. Sometimes I would pass an entire day without seeing one mammal and perhaps not more than a dozen birds of any size. The weather at that time was cheerless, generally with a gray film of cloud spread over the sky, and a bleak wind, often cold enough to make my bridle hand quite numb. At a slow pace, which would have seemed intolerable in other circumstances, I would ride about for hours at a stretch. On arriving at a hill, I would slowly ride to its summit, and stand there to survey the prospect. On every side it stretched away in great undulations, wild and irregular. How gray it all was! Hardly less so near at hand than on the haze-wrapped horizon, where the hills were dim and the outline blurred by distance. Descending from my outlook, I would take up my aimless wanderings again, and visit other elevations to gaze on the same landscape from another point; and so on for hours; and at noon I would dismount and sit or lie on my folded poncho for an hour or longer. One day, in these rambles, I discovered a small grove composed of twenty or thirty trees, growing at a convenient distance apart, that had evidently been resorted to by a herd of deer or other wild animals. This grove was on a hill differing in shape from other hills in its neighborhood; and after a time I made a point of finding and using it as a resting-place every day at noon. I did not ask myself why I made choice of that one spot, sometimes going miles out of my way to sit there, instead of sitting down under any one of the millions of trees and bushes on any other hillside. I thought nothing at all about it, but acted unconsciously. Only afterward it seemed to me that, after having rested there once, each time I wished to rest again the wish came associated with the image of that particular clump of trees, with polished stems and clean bed of sand beneath; and in a short time I formed a habit of returning, animal-like, to repose at that same spot.

It was perhaps a mistake to say that I would sit down and rest, since I was never tired: and yet, without being tired, that noonday pause, during which I sat for an hour without moving, was strangely grateful. All day there would be no sound, not even the rustle of a leaf. One day while *listening* to the silence, it occurred to my mind to wonder what the effect would be if I were to shout aloud. This seemed at the time a horrible suggestion, which almost made me shudder; but during those solitary days it was a rare thing for any thought to cross my mind. In the state of mind I was in, thought had become impossible. My state was one of *suspense* and *watchfulness;* yet I had no expectation of meeting with an adventure, and felt as free from apprehension as I feel now when sitting in a room in London. The state seemed familiar rather than strange, and accompanied by a strong feeling of elation; and I did not know that something had come between me and my intellect until I returned to my former self—to thinking, and the old insipid existence.

I had undoubtedly *gone back;* and that state of intense watchfulness, or alertness rather, with suspension of the higher intellectual faculties, represented the mental state of the pure savage. He thinks little, reasons little, having a surer guide in his instincts; he is in perfect harmony with nature, and is nearly on a level, mentally, with the wild animals he preys on, and which in their turn sometimes prey on him.

4. Isolation and the Rural Mind[1]

As an occupation farming has dealt largely, if not exclusively, with the growth and care of plant and animal life. Broadly speaking, the farmer has been engaged in a struggle with nature to produce certain staple traditional raw foods and human comfort materials in bulk. He has been excused, on the whole, from the delicate situations arising from the demands of an infinite variety of human wishes, whims, and fashions, perhaps because the primary grains, fruits, vegetables, fibers, animals, and animal products, have afforded small opportunity for manipulation to satisfy the varying forms of human taste and caprice. This exemption of the farmer in the greater part of his activity from direct work upon and with persons and from

[1] Adapted from C. J. Galpin, *Rural Social Centers in Wisconsin,* pp. 1-3. (Wisconsin Experiment Station, Bulletin 234, 1913.)

strenuous attempts to please persons, will doubtless account very largely, perhaps more largely than mere isolation on the land, for the strong individualism of the country man.

In striking contrast, the villager and city worker have always been occupied in making things or parts of things out of such impressionable materials as iron, wood, clay, cloth, leather, gold, and the like, to fit, suit, and satisfy a various and increasingly complex set of human desires; or they have been dealing direct with a kaleidoscopic human mind, either in regard to things or in regard to troubles and ideals of the mind itself. This constant dealing with persons in business will account even more than mere congestion of population for the complex organization of city life. The highly organized social institutions of the city, moreover, have reinforced the already keen-edged insight of the city man of business, so that he is doubly equipped to win his struggles. The city worker knows men, the farmer knows nature. Each has reward for his deeper knowledge, and each suffers some penalty for his circle of ignorance.

Modern conditions underlying successful farm practice and profit-making require of the farmer a wider and more frequent contact with men than at any time in the past. His materials, too, have become more plastic, subject to rapid change by selection and breeding.

The social problem of the farmer seems to be how to overcome the inevitable handicap of a social deficiency in the very nature of his occupation, so as to extend his acquaintance with men; and secondly, how to erect social institutions on the land adequate to reinforce his individual personality so as to enable him to cope with his perplexities.

Occasions must be created, plans must be made, to bring people together in a wholesale manner so as to facilitate this interchange of community acquaintance. Especially is it necessary for rural children to know many more children. The one-room district school has proved its value in making the children of the neighborhood acquainted with one another. One of the large reasons for the consolidated and centralized school is the increased size of territorial unit, with more children to know one another and mingle together. Intervisiting of district schools—one school, teachers and pupils, playing host to a half-dozen other schools, with some regularity, using plays and games, children's readiest means of getting acquainted—is a successful means of extending acquaintance under good auspices.

If large-scale acquaintance—men with men, women with women, children with children—in a rural community once becomes a fact, the initial step will have been taken for assuring the rise of appropriate social institutions on the land of that community.

5. The Subtler Effects of Isolation[1]

The mechanics of modern culture is complicated. The individual has access to materials outside his group, from the world at large. His consciousness is built up not only by word of mouth but by the printed page. He may live as much in German books as in fireside conversation. Much more mail is handled every day in the New York post-office than was sent out by all the thirteen states in a year at the close of the eighteenth century. But by reason of poverty, geographical isolation, caste feeling, or "pathos," individuals, communities, and races may be excluded from some of the stimulations and copies which enter into a high grade of mind. The savage, the Negro, the peasant, the slum dwellers, and the white woman are notable sufferers by exclusion.

Easy communication of ideas favors differentiation of a rational and functional sort, as distinguished from the random variations fostered by isolation. And it must be remembered that any sort is rational and functional that really commends itself to the human spirit. Even revolt from an ascendant type is easier now than formerly because the rebel can fortify himself with the triumphant records of the non-conformers of the past.

The peasant [at the middle of the nineteenth century], limited in a cultural respect to his village life, thinks, feels, and acts solely in the bounds of his native village; his thought never goes beyond his farm and his neighbor; toward the political, economic, or national events taking place outside of his village, be they of his own or of a foreign country, he is completely indifferent, and even if he has learned something of them, this is described by him in a fantastic, mythological way, and only in this adopted form is it added to his cultural condition and transmitted to his descendants. Every peasant farm produced almost exclusively for itself, only to the most limited extent for exchange; every village formed an economic unit, which stood in only a loose economic connection with the outer world. Outwardly complete isolation of the village settlements and their inhabitants from

[1] Adapted from W. I. Thomas, "Race Psychology," in the *American Journal of Sociology*, XVII (1911-12), 744-47.

each other and from the rest of the country and other classes of society; inwardly complete homogeneity, one and the same economic, social, and cultural equality of the peasant mass, no possibility of advance for the more gifted and capable individuals, everyone pressed down to a flat level. The peasant of one village holds himself, if not directly hostile, at least as a rule not cordial to the peasants of another village. The nobles living in the same village territory even wanted to force upon the peasants an entirely different origin, in that with the assistance of the Biblical legend they wished to trace him from the accursed Ham (from this the curse and insult *Ty chamie*, "Thou Ham"), but themselves from Japhet, of better repute in the Bible, while they attributed to the Jews, Shem as an ancestor.

The pathetic effect of isolation on the state of knowledge is recorded in many of the stories of runaway slaves:

With two more boys, I started for the free states. We did not know where they were, but went to try to find them. We crossed the Potomac and hunted round and round and round. Some one showed us the way to Washington; but we missed it, and wandered all night; then we found ourselves where we set out.

For our purposes race prejudice may be regarded as a form of isolation. And in the case of the American Negro this situation is aggravated by the fact that the white man has developed a determination to keep him in isolation—"in his place." Now, when the isolation is willed and has at the same time the emotional nature of a tabu, the handicap is very grave indeed. It is a fact that the most intelligent Negroes are usually half or more than half white, but it is still a subject for investigation whether this is due to mixed blood or to the fact that they have been more successful in violating the tabu.

The humblest white employee knows that the better he does his work, the more chance there is for him to rise in the business. The black employee knows that the better he does his work, the longer he may do it; he cannot often hope for promotion.

All these careers are at the very outset closed to the Negro on account of his color; what lawyer would give even a minor case to a Negro assistant? Or what university would appoint a promising young Negro as tutor? Thus the white young man starts in life knowing that within some limits and barring accidents, talent and application will tell. The young Negro starts knowing that on all sides his advance is made doubly difficult, if not wholly shut off, by his color.

In all walks of life the Negro is liable to meet some objection to his presence or some discourteous treatment. If an invitation is issued to the public for any occasion, the Negro can never know whether he would be welcomed or not; if he goes he is liable to have his feelings hurt and get into unpleasant altercation; if he stays away, he is blamed for indifference. If he meet a lifelong white friend on the street, he is in a dilemma; if he does not greet the friend he is put down as boorish and impolite; if he does greet the friend he is liable to be flatly snubbed. If by chance he is introduced to a white woman or man, he expects to be ignored on the next meeting, and usually is. White friends may call on him, but he is scarcely expected to call on them, save for strictly business matters. If he gain the affections of a white woman and marry her he may invariably expect that slurs will be thrown on her reputation and on his, and that both his and her race will shun their company. When he dies he cannot be buried beside white corpses.

Kelly Miller, himself a full-blooded black (for which the Negroes have expressed their gratitude), refers to the backwardness of the negro in the following terms:

To expect the Negroes of Georgia to produce a great general like Napoleon when they are not even allowed to carry arms, or to deride them for not producing scholars like those of the Renaissance when a few years ago they were forbidden the use of letters, verges closely upon the outer rim of absurdity. Do you look for great Negro statesmen in states where black men are not allowed to vote? Above all, for southern white men to berate the Negro for failing to gain the highest rounds of distinction reaches the climax of cruel inconsistency. One is reminded of the barbarous Teutons in *Titus Andronicus*, who, after cutting out the tongue and hacking off the hands of the lovely Lavinia, ghoulishly chided her for not calling for sweet water with which to wash her delicate hands.

It is not too much to say that no Negro and no mulatto, in America at least, has ever been fully in the white man's world. But we must recognize that their backwardness is not wholly due to prejudice. A race with an adequate technique can live in the midst of prejudice and even receive some stimulation from it. But the Negro has lost many of the occupations which were particularly his own, and is outclassed in others—not through prejudice but through the faster pace of his competitors.

Obviously obstacles which discourage one race may stimulate another. Even the extreme measures in Russia and Roumania against the Jew have not isolated him. He has resources and traditions and technique of his own, and we have even been borrowers from him.

C. ISOLATION AND SEGREGATION

1. Segregation as a Process[1]

Within the limitations prescribed, however, the inevitable processes of human nature proceed to give these regions and these buildings a character which it is less easy to control. Under our system of individual ownership, for instance, it is not possible to determine in advance the extent of concentration of population in any given area. The city cannot fix land values, and we leave to private enterprise, for the most part, the task of determining the city's limits and the location of its residential and industrial districts. Personal tastes and convenience, vocational and economic interests, infallibly tend to segregate and thus to classify the populations of great cities. In this way the city acquires an organization which is neither designed nor controlled.

Physical geography, natural advantages, and the means of transportation determine in advance the general outlines of the urban plan. As the city increases in population, the subtler influences of sympathy, rivalry, and economic necessity tend to control the distribution of population. Business and manufacturing seek advantageous locations and draw around them a certain portion of the population. There spring up fashionable residence quarters from which the poorer classes are excluded because of the increased value of the land. Then there grow up slums which are inhabited by great numbers of the poorer classes who are unable to defend themselves from association with the derelict and vicious. In the course of time every section and quarter of the city takes on something of the character and qualities of its inhabitants. Each separate part of the city is inevitably stained with the peculiar sentiments of its population. The effect of this is to convert what was at first a mere geographical expression into a neighborhood, that is to say, a locality with sentiments, traditions, and a history of its own. Within this

[1] Adapted from Robert E. Park, "The City: Suggestions for the Investigation of Behavior in the City Environment," in the *American Journal of Sociology*, XX (1915), 579–83.

neighborhood the continuity of the historical processes is somehow maintained. The past imposes itself upon the present and the life of every locality moves on with a certain momentum of its own, more or less independent of the larger circle of life and interests about it.

In the city environment the neighborhood tends to lose much of the significance which it possessed in simpler and more primitive forms of society. The easy means of communication and of transportation, which enables individuals to distribute their attention and to live at the same time in several different worlds, tends to destroy the permanency and intimacy of the neighborhood. Further than that, where individuals of the same race or of the same vocation live together in segregated groups, neighborhood sentiment tends to fuse together with racial antagonisms and class interests.

In this way physical and sentimental distances reinforce each other, and the influences of local distribution of the population participate with the influences of class and race in the evolution of the social organization. Every great city has its racial colonies, like the Chinatowns of San Francisco and New York, the Little Sicily of Chicago, and various other less pronounced types. In addition to these, most cities have their segregated vice districts, like that which until recently existed in Chicago, and their rendezvous for criminals of various sorts. Every large city has its occupational suburbs like the Stockyards in Chicago, and its residence suburbs like Brookline in Boston, each of which has the size and the character of a complete separate town, village, or city, except that its population is a selected one. Undoubtedly the most remarkable of these cities within cities, of which the most interesting characteristic is that they are composed of persons of the same race, or of persons of different races but of the same social class, is East London, with a population of 2,000,000 laborers.

The people of the original East London have now overflowed and crossed the Lea, and spread themselves over the marshes and meadows beyond. This population has created new towns which were formerly rural villages, West Ham, with a population of nearly 300,000; East Ham, with 90,000; Stratford, with its "daughters," 150,000; and other "hamlets" similarly overgrown. Including these new populations we have an aggregate of nearly two millions of people. The population is greater than that of Berlin or Vienna, or St. Petersburg, or Philadelphia.

It is a city full of churches and places of worship, yet there are no cathedrals, either Anglican or Roman; it has a sufficient supply of elementary schools, but it has no public or high school, and it has no colleges for the higher education, and no university; the people all read newspapers, yet there is no East London paper except of the smaller and local kind. . . . . In the streets there are never seen any private carriages; there is no fashionable quarter . . . . one meets no ladies in the principal thoroughfares. People, shops, houses, conveyances—all together are stamped with the unmistakable seal of the working class.

Perhaps the strangest thing of all is this: in a city of two millions of people there are no hotels! That means, of course, that there are no visitors.

In the older cities of Europe, where the processes of segregation have gone farther, neighborhood distinctions are likely to be more marked than they are in America. East London is a city of a single class, but within the limits of that city the population is segregated again and again by racial and vocational interests. Neighborhood sentiment, deeply rooted in local tradition and in local custom, exercises a decisive selective influence upon city population and shows itself ultimately in a marked way in the characteristics of the inhabitants.

2. Isolation as a Result of Segregation[1]

There is the observed tendency of mental defectives to congregate in localized centers, with resulting inbreeding. Feeble-mindedness is a social level and the members of this level, like those in other levels, are affected by social and biological tendencies, such as the congregation of like personalities and the natural selection in matings of persons of similar mental capacities. These are general tendencies and not subject to invariable laws. The feeble-minded are primarily quantitatively different from normals in mental and social qualities, and do not constitute a separate species. The borderline types of high-grade feeble-minded and low-grade normals may therefore prove exceptions to the general rule. But such studies as Davenport and Danielson's "Hill Folk," Davenport and Estabrook's "Nams," Dugdale's "Jukes," Kostir's "Sam Sixty," Goddard's "Kallikaks," Key's "Vennams" and "Fale-Anwals," Kite's "Pineys," and many others emphatically prove that mental defectives show a tendency

---

[1] Adapted from L. W. Crafts and E. A. Doll, "The Proportion of Mental Defectives among Juvenile Delinquents," in the *Journal of Delinquency*, II (1917), 123-37.

to drift together, intermarry, and isolate themselves from the rest of the community, just as the rich live in exclusive suburbs. Consequently they preponderate in certain localities, counties, and cities. In a large measure this segregation is not so much an expression of voluntary desire as it is a situation forced upon mental defectives through those natural intellectual and social deficiencies which restrict them to environments economically and otherwise less desirable to normal people. This phenomenon is most conspicuous in rural communities where such migratory movements as the modern city-drift have exercised a certain natural selection, but it is also plainly evident in the slums and poorer sections of the cities, both large and small, as any field worker will testify. Closely related to this factor of isolation are the varying percentages of mental defectives found in different states anu in different sections of the same state, city or community. It is therefore likely that the percentages of mental defectives among different groups of juvenile delinquents will vary according to the particular ward, city, county, or state, whence the delinquents come. For this reason it is essential to any study of the number of mental defectives in a group of juvenile delinquents coming from a particular locality, that some idea should be available as to the probable or approximate number of mental defectives in that community. If more mental defectives are found among the population in the slum quarter of a city than in the residential quarter, it is to be expected that there will be more mental defectives in groups of juvenile delinquents from the slum quarter, because, in the first place, they constitute a larger proportion of the population, and because, secondly, of their greater proneness to social offenses. Moreover, the prevalence of the feeble-minded in certain localities may affect the attitude of the law-enforcing machinery toward the children of that community.

A further result of the innate characteristics and tendencies of the feeble-minded is to be found in the effect upon them of the biological law of natural selection, resulting from the universal struggle for existence and the survival of the fittest. We need not discuss here its profound influences, economic and otherwise, upon the lives of the mentally defective in general, but it will be profitable to review briefly the effect of natural selection upon the juvenile delinquent group.

Any group of delinquents is subject to this selection from the times of offenses to final commitment. It undergoes a constant sifting

process whose operation is mainly determined by the natural consequences of the group members; a large proportion of the "lucky,"
the intelligent, or the socially favored individuals escape from the
group, so that the remaining members of the group are the least fit
socially and intellectually. The mentally defective delinquents constitute an undue proportion of this unfit residue, for although they
may receive as many favors of chance as do their intellectually normal
fellow-delinquents, they cannot, like them, by reason of intelligence
or social status, escape the consequences of their delinquent acts.
Furthermore, the feeble-minded offender is caught oftener than are
his more clever and energetic companions of normal endowments,
and after apprehension he is less likely to receive the benefits of police
and court prejudices, or the advantages of family wealth and social
influence. If placed on probation he is more likely to fail, because
of his own weaknesses and his unfavorable environment. Hence
the feeble-minded delinquent is much more likely to come before
the court and also to be committed to a reformatory, jail, or industrial
school than is his companion of normal mind. Therefore practically
every group of juvenile delinquents which ultimately reaches commitment will have a very different aspect with regard to its proportion
of mental defectives from that larger group of offenders, apprehended
or non-apprehended, of which it was once a part. In fact, it is doubtful if any group of apprehended, detained, or probationed offenders
can be said to be representative, or at least to be exactly representative, of the true proportion of mental defectives among all
delinquents. Except where specific types of legal procedure bring
about the elimination of the defectives, it seems as if it must inevitably
result that the operation of natural selection will continually increase
the proportion of mental defectives above that existing in the original
group.

This factor of natural selection has not to our knowledge been
given adequate consideration in any published investigation on
delinquency. But if our estimate of its effects is at all justified,
then most examinations of juvenile delinquents, especially in reform
and industrial schools, have disclosed proportions of mental defectives distinctly in excess of the original proportion previously existent
among the entire mass of all offenders. The reports of these examinations have given rise to quite erroneous impressions concerning the

extent of criminality among the feeble-minded and its relation to the whole volume of crime, and have consequently led to inaccurate deductions. The feeble-minded are undoubtedly more prone to commit crime than are the average normals; but through disregard of the influences of this factor of natural selection, as well as of others, both the proportion of crime committed by mental defectives and the true proportion of mental defectives among delinquents and criminals have very often been exaggerated.

D. ISOLATION AND NATIONAL INDIVIDUALITY

1. Historical Races as Products of Isolation[1]

The continent of Europe differs from the other great land-masses in the fact that it is a singular aggregation of peninsulas and islands, originating in separate centers of mountain growth, and of enclosed valleys walled about from the outer world by elevated summits. Other continents are somewhat peninsulated; Asia approaches Europe in that respect; North America has a few great dependencies in its larger islands and considerable promontories; but Africa, South America, and Australia are singularly united lands.

The highly divided state of Europe has greatly favored the development within its area of isolated fields, each fitted for the growth of a separate state, adapted even in this day for local life although commerce in our time binds lands together in a way which it did not of old. These separated areas were marvelously suited to be the cradles of peoples; and if we look over the map of Europe we readily note the geographic insulations which that remarkably varied land affords.

Beginning with the eastern Mediterranean, we have the peninsula on which Constantinople stands—a region only partly protected from assault by its geographic peculiarities; and yet it owes to its partial separation from the mainlands on either side a large measure of local historic development. Next, we have Greece and its associated islands, which—a safe stronghold for centuries—permitted the nurture of the most marvelous life the world has ever known. Farther to the west the Italian peninsula, where during three thousand years

[1] Adapted from N. S. Shaler, *Nature and Man in America*, pp. 151–66. (Charles Scribner's Sons, 1900.)

the protecting envelope of the sea and the walls of Alps and Apennines have enabled a score of states to attain a development; where the Roman nation, absorbing, with its singular power of taking in other life, a number of primitive centers of civilization, grew to power which made it dominant in the ancient world. Sicily, Sardinia, Corsica, have each profited by their isolation, and have bred diverse qualities in man and contributed motives which have interacted in the earth's history. Again, in Spain we have a region well fitted to be the cradle of a great people; to its geographic position it owed the fact that it became the seat of the most cultivated Mahometanism the world has ever known. To the Pyrenees, the mountain wall of the north, we owe in good part the limitation of that Mussulman invasion and the protection of central Europe from its forward movement, until luxury and half-faith had sapped its energies. Going northward, we find in the region of Normandy the place of growth of that fierce but strong folk, the ancient Scandinavians, who, transplanted there, held their ground, and grew until they were strong enough to conquer Britain and give it a large share of the quality which belongs to our own state.

To a trifling geographic accident we owe the isolation of Great Britain from the European continent; and all the marvelous history of the English folk, as we all know, hangs upon the existence of that narrow strip of sea between the Devon coast and the kindred lowlands of northern France.

East of Britain lie two peninsulas which have been the cradle of very important peoples. That of Sweden and Norway is the result of mountain development; that of Denmark appears to be in the main the product of glacial and marine erosion, differing in its non-mountainous origin from all the other peninsulas and islands of the European border. Thus on the periphery of Europe we have at least a dozen geographical isolated areas, sufficiently large and well separated from the rest of the world to make them the seats of independent social life. The interior of the country has several similarly, though less perfectly, detached areas. Of these the most important lie fenced within the highlands of the Alps. In that extensive system of mountain disturbances we have the geographical conditions which most favor the development of peculiar divisions of men, and which guard such cradled peoples from the destruction which so often awaits them on the plains. Thus, while the folk of the European lowlands have been overrun by the successive tides of invasion, their qualities confused, and their succession of social life interrupted, Switzerland has to a great extent, by its mountain walls, protected its people from the troubles to which their lowland neighbors have been subjected. The result is that within an area not twice as large as Massachusetts we find a marvelous diversity of folk, as is shown by the variety in physical aspect, moral quality, language, and creed in the several important valleys and other divisions of that complicated topography.

After a race has been formed and bred to certain qualities within a limited field, after it has come to possess a certain body of characteristics which gives it its particular stamp, the importance of the original cradle passes away. There is something very curious in the permanence of race conditions after they have been fixed for a thousand years or so in a people. When the assemblage of physical and mental motives are combined in a body of country folk, they may endure under circumstances in which they could not have originated; thus, even in our domesticated animals and plants, we find that varieties created under favorable conditions, obtaining their inheritances in suitable conditions, may then flourish in many conditions of environment in which they could not by any chance have originated. The barnyard creatures of Europe, with their established qualities, may be taken to Australia, and there retain their nature for many generations; even where the form falls away from the parent stock, the decline is generally slow and may not for a great time become apparent.

This fixity of race characteristics has enabled the several national varieties of men to go forth from their nurseries, carrying the qualities bred in their earlier conditions through centuries of life in other climes. The Gothic blood of Italy and of Spain still keeps much of its parent strength; the Aryan's of India, though a world apart in its conditions from those which gave it character in its cradle, is still, in many of its qualities, distinctly akin to that of the home people. Moor, Hun and Turk—all the numerous folk we find in the present condition of the world so far from their cradle-lands—are still to a great extent what their primitive nurture made them. On this rigidity which comes to mature races in the lower life as well as in man, depends the vigor with which they do their appointed work.

2. Geographical Isolation and Maritime Contact[1]

Greece, considering its limited total extent, offers but little motive, and still less of convenient means, for internal communication among its various inhabitants. Each village or township occupying its plain with the inclosing mountains, supplied its own main wants, whilst the transport of commodities by land was sufficiently difficult to discourage greatly any regular commerce with neighbors. In so far as the face of the interior country was concerned, it seemed as if nature had been disposed from the beginning to keep the population of Greece socially and politically disunited by providing so many hedges of separation and so many boundaries, generally hard, sometimes impossible, to overleap. One special motive to intercourse, however, arose out of this very geographical constitution of the country, and its endless alternation of mountain and valley. The difference of climate and temperature between the high and low grounds is very great; the harvest is secured in one place before it is ripe in another, and the cattle find during the heat of summer shelter and pasture on the hills, at a time when the plains are burnt up. The practice of transferring them from the mountains to the plain according to the change of season, which subsists still as it did in ancient times, is intimately connected with the structure of the country, and must from the earliest period have brought about communication among the otherwise disunited villages.

Such difficulties, however, in the internal transit by land were to a great extent counteracted by the large proportion of coast and the accessibility of the country by sea. The prominences and indentations in the line of Grecian coast are hardly less remarkable than the multiplicity of elevations and depressions which everywhere mark the surface. There was no part of Greece proper which could be considered as out of reach of the sea, while most parts of it were convenient and easy of access. As the only communication between them was maritime, so the sea, important even if we look to Greece proper exclusively, was the sole channel for transmitting ideas and improvements, as well as for maintaining sympathies—social, political, religious, and literary—throughout these outlying members of the Hellenic aggregate.

[1] Adapted from George Grote, *History of Greece*, II, 149-57. (John Murray, 1888.)

The ancient philosophers and legislators were deeply impressed with the contrast between an inland and a maritime city: in the former, simplicity and uniformity of life, tenacity of ancient habits and dislike of what is new or foreign, great force of exclusive sympathy and narrow range both of objects and ideas; in the latter, variety and novelty of sensations, expansive imagination, toleration, and occasional preference for extraneous customs, greater activity of the individual and corresponding mutability of the state. This distinction stands prominent in the many comparisons instituted between the Athens of Periclês and the Athens of the earlier times down to. Solon. Both Plato and Aristotle dwell upon it emphatically—and the former especially, whose genius conceived the comprehensive scheme of prescribing beforehand and insuring in practice the whole course of individual thought and feeling in his imaginary community, treats maritime communication, if pushed beyond the narrowest limits, as fatal to the success and permanence of any wise scheme of education. Certain it is that a great difference of character existed between those Greeks who mingled much in maritime affairs and those who did not. The Arcadian may stand as a type of the pure Grecian landsman, with his rustic and illiterate habits—his diet of sweet chestnuts, barley cakes, and pork (as contrasted with the fish which formed the chief seasoning for the bread of an Athenian)—his superior courage and endurance—his reverence for Lacedaemonian headship as an old and customary influence—his sterility of intellect and imagination as well as his slackness in enterprise—his unchangeable rudeness of relations with the gods, which led him to scourge and prick Pan if he came back empty-handed from the chase; while the inhabitant of Phokaea or Miletus exemplifies the Grecian mariner, eager in search of gain—active, skilful, and daring at sea, but inferior in steadfast bravery on land—more excitable in imagination as well as more mutable in character—full of pomp and expense in religious manifestations toward the Ephesian Artemis or the Apollo of Branchidae: with a mind more open to the varieties of Grecian energy and to the refining influences of Grecian civilization.

The configuration of the Grecian territory, so like in many respects to that of Switzerland, produced two effects of great moment upon the character and history of the people. In the first place, it materially strengthened their powers of defense: it shut up the country against those invasions from the interior which successively subjugated all their continental colonies; and it at the same time rendered each fraction more difficult to be attacked by the rest, so as to exercise a certain conservative influence in assuring the tenure of actual possessors: for the pass of Thermopylae between Thessaly and Phokis, that of Kithaeron between Boeotia and Attica, or the mountainous range of Oneion and Geraneia along the Isthmus of Corinth, were positions which an inferior number of brave men could hold against a much greater force of assailants. But, in the next place, while it tended to protect each section of Greeks from being conquered, it also kept them politically disunited and perpetuated their separate autonomy. It fostered that powerful principle of repulsion, which disposed even the smallest township to constitute itself a political unit apart from the rest, and to resist all idea of coalescence with others, either amicable or compulsory. To a modern reader, accustomed to large political aggregations, and securities for good government through the representative system, it requires a certain mental effort to transport himself back to a time when even the smallest town clung so tenaciously to its right of self-legislation. Nevertheless, such was the general habit and feeling of the ancient world, throughout Italy, Sicily, Spain, and Gaul. Among the Hellens it stands out more conspicuously, for several reasons—first, because they seem to have pushed the multiplication of autonomous units to an extreme point, seeing that even islands not larger than Peparethos and Amorgos had two or three separate city communities; secondly, because they produced, for the first time in the history of mankind, acute systematic thinkers on matters of government, amongst all of whom the idea of the autonomous city was accepted as the indispensable basis of political speculation; thirdly, because this incurable subdivision proved finally the cause of their ruin, in spite of pronounced intellectual superiority over their conquerors; and lastly, because incapacity of political coalescence did not preclude a powerful and extensive sympathy between the inhabitants of all the separate cities, with a constant tendency to fraternize for numerous purposes, social, religious, recreative, intellectual, and aesthetical. For these reasons, the indefinite multiplication of self-governing towns, though in truth a phenomenon common to ancient Europe as contrasted with the large monarchies of Asia, appears more marked among the ancient Greeks than elsewhere; and there cannot be any doubt that they owe it, in a considerable degree, to the multitude of insulating boundaries which the configuration of their country presented.

Nor is it rash to suppose that the same causes may have tended to promote that unborrowed intellectual development for which they stand so conspicuous. General propositions respecting the working of climate and physical agencies upon character are indeed treacherous; for our knowledge of the globe is now sufficient to teach us that heat and cold, mountain and plain, sea and land, moist and dry atmosphere, are all consistent with the greatest diversities of resident men: moreover, the contrast between the population of Greece itself, for the seven centuries preceding the Christian era, and the Greeks of more modern times, is alone enough to inculcate reserve in such speculations. Nevertheless we may venture to note certain improving influences, connected with their geographical position, at a time when they had no books to study, and no more advanced predecessors to imitate.

We may remark, first, that their position made them at once mountaineers and mariners, thus supplying them with great variety of objects, sensations, and adventures; next, that each petty community, nestled apart amidst its own rocks, was sufficiently severed from the rest to possess an individual life and attributes of its own, yet not so far as to subtract it from the sympathies of the remainder; so that an observant Greek, commercing with a great diversity of half-countrymen, whose language he understood, and whose idiosyncrasies he could appreciate, had access to a larger mass of social and political experience than any other man in so unadvanced an age could personally obtain. The Phœnician, superior to the Greek on shipboard, traversed wider distances and saw a greater number of strangers, but had not the same means of intimate communion with a multiplicity of fellows in blood and language. His relations, confined to purchase and sale, did not comprise that mutuality of action and reaction which pervaded the crowd at a Grecian festival. The scene which here presented itself was a mixture of uniformity and variety highly stimulating to the observant faculties of a man of genius—who at the same time, if he sought to communicate his own impressions, or to act upon this mingled and diverse audience, was forced to shake off what was peculiar to his own town or community, and to put forth matter in harmony with the feelings of all. It is thus that we may explain, in part, that penetrating apprehension of human life and character, and that power of touching sympathies common to all ages and nations, which surprises us so much in the unlettered authors of the old epic. Such periodical intercommunion of brethren habitually isolated from each other was the only means then open of procuring for the bard a diversified range of experience and a many-colored audience; and it was to a great degree the result of geographical causes. Perhaps among other nations such facilitating causes might have been found, yet without producing any results comparable to the Iliad and Odyssey. But Homer was nevertheless dependent upon the conditions of his age, and we can at least point out those peculiarities in early Grecian society without which Homeric excellence would never have existed—the geographical position is one, the language another.

3. Isolation as an Explanation of National Differences

To decide between race and environment as the efficient cause of any social phenomenon is a matter of singular interest at this time. A school of sociological writers, dazzled by the recent brilliant discoveries in European ethnology, show a decided inclination to sink the racial explanation up to the handle in every possible phase of social life in Europe. It must be confessed that there is provocation for it. So persistent have the physical characteristics of the people shown themselves that it is not surprising to find theories of a corresponding inheritance of mental attributes in great favor.

This racial school of social philosophers derives much of its data from French sources. For this reason, and also because our anthropological knowledge of that country is more complete than for any other part of Europe, we shall confine our attention primarily to France. In the unattractive upland areas of isolation is the Alpine broad-headed race common to central Europe. At the north, extending down in a broad belt diagonally as far as Limoges and along the coast of Brittany, there is intermixture with the blond, long-headed Teutonic race; while along the southern coast, penetrating up the Rhone Valley, is found the extension of the equally long-headed but brunet

---

[1] From William Z. Ripley, *The Races of Europe*, pp. 515-30. (D. Appleton & Co., 1899.)

Mediterranean stock. These ethnic facts correspond to physical ones; three areas of geographical isolation are distinct centers of distribution of the Alpine race.

The organization of the family is the surest criterion of the stage of social evolution attained by a people. No other phase of human association is so many-sided, so fundamental, so pregnant for the future. For this reason we may properly begin our study by an examination of a phenomenon which directly concerns the stability of the domestic institution—viz., divorce. What are the facts as to its distribution in France? Marked variations between different districts occur. Paris is at one extreme; Corsica, as always, at the other. Of singular interest to us is the parallel which at once appears between this distribution of divorce and that of head form. The areas of isolation peopled by the Alpine race are characterized by almost complete absence of legal severance of domestic relations between husband and wife.

Do the facts instanced above have any ethnic significance? Do they mean that the Alpine type, as a race, holds more tenaciousiy than does the Teuton to its family traditions, resenting thereby the interference of the state in its domestic institutions? A foremost statistical authority, Jacques Bertillon, has devoted considerable space to proving that some relation between the two exists. Confronted by the preceding facts, his explanation is this: that the people of the southern departments, inconstant perhaps and fickle, nevertheless are quickly pacified after a passionate outbreak of any kind. Husband and wife may quarrel, but the estrangement is dissipated before recourse to the law can take place. On the other hand, the Norman peasant, Teutonic by race, cold and reserved, nurses his grievances for a long time; they abide with him, smoldering but persistent. "Words and even blows terminate quarrels quickly in the south; in the north they are settled by the judge." From similar comparisons in other European countries, M. Bertillon draws the final conclusion that the Teutonic race betrays a singular preference for this remedy for domestic ills. It becomes for him an ethnic trait.

Another social phenomenon has been laid at the door of the Teutonic race of northern Europe; one which even more than divorce is directlv the concomitant of modern intellectual and economic progress. We refer to suicide. Morselli devotes a chapter of his interesting treatise upon this subject to proving that "the purer the German race—that is to say, the stronger the Germanism (e.g., Teutonism) of a country—the more it reveals in its psychical character an extraordinary propensity to self-destruction."

Consider for a moment the relative frequency of suicide with reference to the ethnic composition of France. The parallel between the two is almost exact in every detail. There are again our three areas of Alpine racial occupation—Savoy, Auvergne, and Brittany— in which suicide falls annually below seventy-five per million inhabitants. There, again, is the Rhone Valley and the broad diagonal strip from Paris to Bordeaux, characterized alike by strong infusion of Teutonic traits and relative frequency of the same social phenomenon.

Divorce and suicide will serve as examples of the mode of proof adopted for tracing a number of other social phenomena to an ethnic origin. Thus Lapouge attributes the notorious depopulation of large areas in France to the sterility incident upon intermixture between the several racial types of which the population is constituted. This he seeks to prove from the occurrence of a decreasing birth-rate in all the open, fertile districts where the Teutonic element has intermingled with the native population. Because wealth happens to be concentrated in the fertile areas of Teutonic occupation, it is again assumed that this coincidence demonstrates either a peculiar acquisitive aptitude in this race or else a superior measure of frugality.

By this time our suspicions are aroused. The argument is too simple. Its conclusions are too far-reaching. By this we do not mean to deny the facts of geographical distribution in the least. It is only the validity of the ethnic explanation which we deny. We can do better for our races than even its best friends along such lines of proof. With the data at our disposition there is no end to the racial attributes which we might saddle upon our ethnic types. Thus, it would appear that the Alpine type in its sterile areas of isolation was the land-hungry one described by Zola in his powerful novels. For, roughly speaking, individual land-holdings are larger in them on the average than among the Teutonic populations. Peasant proprietorship is more common also; there are fewer tenant farmers. Crime in the two areas assumes a different aspect. We find that among populations of Alpine type, in the isolated uplands, offenses against the person predominate in the criminal calendar. In the Seine basin, along the Rhone Valley, wherever the Teuton is in evidence, on the other hand, there is less respect for property; so that offenses against the person, such as assault, murder, and rape, give place to embezzlements, burglary, and arson. It might just as well be argued that the Teuton shows a predilection for offenses against property; the native Celt an equal propensity for crimes against the person.

Appeal to the social geography of other countries, wherein the ethnic balance of power is differently distributed, may be directed against almost any of the phenomena we have instanced in France as seemingly of racial derivation. In the case either of suicide or divorce, if we turn from France to Italy or Germany, we instantly perceive all sorts of contradictions. The ethnic type, which is so immune from propensity to self-destruction or domestic disruption in France, becomes in Italy most prone to either mode of escape from temporary earthly ills. For each phenomenon culminates in frequency in the northern half of the latter country, stronghold of the Alpine race. Nor is there an appreciable infusion of Teutonism, physically speaking, herein, to account for the change of heart. Of course, it might be urged that this merely shows that the Mediterranean race of southern Italy is as much less inclined to the phenomenon than the Alpine race in these respects, as it in turn lags behind the Teuton. For it must be confessed that even in Italy neither divorce nor suicide is so frequent anywhere as in Teutonic northern France. Well, then, turn to Germany. Compare its two halves in these respects again. The northern half of the empire is most purely Teutonic by race; the southern is not distinguishable ethnically, as we have sought to prove, from central France. Bavaria, Baden, and Würtemberg are scarcely more Teutonic by race than Auvergne. Do we find differences in suicide, for example, following racial boundaries here? Far from it; for Saxony is its culminating center; and Saxony, as we know, is really half-Slavic at heart. as is also eastern Prussia. Suicide should be most frequent in Schleswig-Holstein and Hanover, if racial causes were appreciably operative. The argument, in fact, falls to pieces of its own weight, as Durkheim has shown. His conclusion is thus stated:

"If the Germans are more addicted to suicide, it is not because of the blood in their veins, but of the civilization in which they have been raised."

A summary view of the class of social phenomena seemingly characteristic of the distinct races in France, if we extend our field of vision to cover all Europe, suggests an explanation for the curious coincidences and parallelisms noted above, which is the exact opposite of the racial one.

Our theory, then, is this: that most of the social phenomena we have noted as peculiar to the areas occupied by the Alpine type are the necessary outcome, not of racial proclivities but rather of the geographical and social isolation characteristic of the habitat of this race. The ethnic type is still pure for the very same reason that social phenomena are primitive. Wooden ploughs pointed with stone, blood revenge, an undiminished birth-rate, and relative purity of physical type are all alike derivatives from a common cause, isolation, directly physical and coincidently social. We discover, primarily, an influence of environment where others perceive phenomena of ethnic inheritance.

4. Natural versus Vicinal Location in National Development[1]

In contradistinction to continental and intercontinental location, anthropogeography recognizes two other narrower meanings of the term. The innate mobility of the human race, due primarily to the eternal food-quest and increase of numbers, leads a people to spread out over a territory till they reach the barriers which nature has set up, or meet the frontiers of other tribes and nations. Their habitat or their specific geographic location is thus defined by natural features of mountain, desert, and sea, or by the neighbors whom they are unable to displace, or more often by both.

A people has, therefore, a twofold location, an immediate one, based upon their actual territory, and a mediate or vicinal one, growing out of its relations to the countries nearest them. The first is a question of the land under their feet; the other, of the neighbors about them. The first or natural location embodies the complex of local geographic conditions which furnish the basis for their tribal or national existence. This basis may be a peninsula, island, archi-

[1] Adapted from Ellen C. Semple, *Influences of Geographic Environment*, pp. 132-33. (Henry Holt & Co., 1911.)

pelago, an oasis, an arid steppe, a mountain system, or a fertile lowland. The stronger the vicinal location, the more dependent is the people upon the neighboring states, but the more potent the influence which it can, under certain circumstances, exert upon them. Witness Germany in relation to Holland, France, Austria, and Poland. The stronger the natural location, on the other hand, the more independent is the people and the more strongly marked is the national character. This is exemplified in the people of mountain lands like Switzerland, Abyssinia, and Nepal; of peninsulas like Korea, Spain, and Scandinavia; and of islands like England and Japan. Today we stand amazed at that strong primordial brand of the Japanese character which nothing can blur or erase.

Clearly defined natural locations, in which barriers of mountains and sea draw the boundaries and guarantee some degree of isolation, tend to hold their people in a calm embrace, to guard them against outside interference and infusion of foreign blood, and thus to make them develop the national genius in such direction as the local geographic conditions permit. In the unceasing movements which have made up most of the historic and prehistoric life of the human race, in their migrations and counter-migrations, their incursions, retreats, and expansions over the face of the earth, vast unfenced areas, like the open lowlands of Russia and the grasslands of Africa, present the picture of a great thoroughfare swept by pressing throngs. Other regions, more secluded, appear as quiet nooks, made for a temporary halt or a permanent rest. Here some part of the passing human flow is caught as in a vessel and held till it crystallizes into a nation. These are the conspicuous areas of race characterization. The development of the various ethnic and political offspring of the Roman Empire in the naturally defined areas of Italy, the Iberian Peninsula, and France illustrates the process of national differentiation which goes on in such secluded locations.

III. INVESTIGATIONS AND PROBLEMS

1. Isolation in Anthropogeography and Biology

A systematic treatise upon isolation as a sociological concept remains to be written. The idea of isolation as a tool of investigation has been fashioned with more precision in geography and in biology than in sociology.

Research in human geography has as its object the study of man in his relations to the earth. Students of civilization, like Montesquieu and Buckle, sought to explain the culture and behavior of peoples as the direct result of the physical environment. Friedrich Ratzel with his "thorough training as a naturalist, broad reading, and travel" and above all, his comprehensive knowledge of ethnology, recognized the importance of direct effects, such as cultural isolation. Jean Brunhes, by the selection of small natural units, his so-called "islands," has made intensive studies of isolated groups in the oases of the deserts of the Sub and of the Mzab, and in the high mountains of the central Andes.

Biology indicates isolation as one of the factors in the origin of the species. Anthropology derives the great races of mankind—the Caucasian, the Ethiopian, the Malay, the Mongolian, and the Indian—from geographical separation following an assumed prehistoric dispersion. A German scholar, Dr. Georg Gerland, has prepared an atlas which plots differences in physical traits, such as skin color and hair texture, as indicating the geographical distribution of races.

2. Isolation and Social Groups

Anthropogeographical and biological investigations have proceeded upon the assumption, implicit or explicit, that the geographic environment, and the physical and mental traits of races and individuals, *determine* individual and collective behavior. What investigations in human geography and heredity actually demonstrate is that the geographic environment and the original nature of man *condition* the culture and conduct of groups and of persons. The explanations of isolation, so far as it affects social life, which have gained currency in the writings of anthropologists and geographers, are therefore too simple. Sociologists are able to take into account forms of isolation not considered by the students of the physical environment and of racial inheritance. Studies of folkways, mores, culture, nationality, the products of a historical or cultural process, disclose types of social contact which transcend the barriers of geographical or racial separation, and reveal social forms of isolation which prevent communication where there is close geographical contact or common racial bonds.

The literature upon isolated peoples ranges from investigations of arrest of cultural development as, for example, the natives of

Australia, the Mountain Whites of the southern states, or the inhabitants of Pitcairn Island to studies of hermit nations, of caste systems as in India, or of outcast groups such as feeble-minded "tribes" or hamlets, fraternities of criminals, and the underworld of commercialized prostitution. Special research in dialects, in folklore, and in provincialism shows how spatial isolation fixes differences in speech, attitudes, folkways, and mores which, in turn, enforce isolation even when geographic separation has disappeared.

The most significant contribution to the study of isolation from the sociological standpoint has undoubtedly been made by Fishberg in a work entitled *The Jews, a Study of Race and Environment.* The author points out that the isolation of the Jew has been the result of neither physical environment nor of race, but of social barriers. "Judaism has been preserved throughout the long years of Israel's dispersion by two factors: its separative ritualism, which prevented close and intimate contact with non-Jews, and the iron laws of the Christian theocracies of Europe which encouraged and enforced 'isolation.' "[1]

3. Isolation and Personality

Philosophers, mystics, and religious enthusiasts have invariably stressed privacy for meditation, retirement for ecstatic communion with God, and withdrawal from the contamination of the world. In 1784–86 Zimmermann wrote an elaborate essay in which he dilates upon "the question whether it is easier to live virtuously in society or in solitude," considering in Part I "the influence of occasional retirement upon the mind and the heart" and in Part II "the pernicious influence of a total exclusion from society upon the mind and the heart."

Actual research upon the effect of isolation upon personal development has more of future promise than of present accomplishment. The literature upon cases of feral men is practically all of the anecdotal type with observations by persons untrained in the modern scientific method. One case, however, "the savage of Aveyron" was studied intensively by Itard, the French philosopher and otologist who cherished high hopes of his mental and social development. After five years spent in a patient and varied but futile attempt at education, he confessed his bitter disappointment. "Since my pains are lost

[1] Fishberg, *op. cit.*, p. 555.

and efforts fruitless, take yourself back to your forest and primitive tastes; or if your new wants make you dependent on society, suffer the penalty of being useless, and go to Bicêtre, there to die in wretchedness."

Only second in importance to the cases of feral men are the investigations which have been made of the results of solitary confinement. Morselli, in his well-known work on *Suicide*, presented statistics showing that self-destruction was many times as frequent among convicts under the system of absolute isolation as compared with that of association during imprisonment. Studies of Auburn prison in New York, of Mountjoy in England, and penal institutions on the continent show the effects of solitary incarceration in the increase of cases of suicides, insanity, invalidism, and death.

Beginnings have been made in child study, psychiatry, and psychoanalysis of the effects of different types of isolation upon personal development. Some attention has been given to the study of effects upon mentality and personality of physical defects such as deaf-mutism and blindness. Students of the so-called "morally defective child," that is the child who appears deficient in emotional and sympathetic responses, suggest as a partial explanation the absence in infancy and early childhood of intimate and sympathetic contacts with the mother. An investigation not yet made but of decisive bearing upon this point will be a comparative study of children brought up in families with those reared in institutions.

Psychiatry and psychoanalysis in probing mental life and personality have related certain mental and social abnormalities to isolation from social contact. Studies of paranoia and of egocentric personalities have resulted in the discovery of the only or favorite child complex. The exclusion of the boy or girl in the one-child family from the give and take of democratic relations with brothers and sisters results, according to the theory advanced, in a psychopathic personality of the self-centered type. A contributing cause of homosexuality, it is said by psychoanalysts, is the isolation during childhood from usual association with individuals of the same sex. Research in dementia praecox discloses a symptom and probably a cause of this mental malady to be the withdrawal of the individual from normal social contacts and the substitution of an imaginary for a real world of persons and events. Dementia praecox has been related by one psychoanalyst to the "shut-in" type of personality.

The literature on the subject of privacy in its relation to personal development is fragmentary but highly promising for future research. The study of the introspective type of personality suggests that self-analysis is the counterpart of the inhibition of immediate and impulsive self-expression in social relations. Materials for an understanding of the relation of retirement and privacy to the aesthetic, moral, and creative life of the person may be found in the lives of hermits, inventors, and religious leaders; in the studies of seclusion, prayer, and meditation; and in research upon taboo, prestige, and attitudes of superiority and inferiority.

BIBLIOGRAPHY: MATERIALS FOR THE STUDY OF ISOLATION

I. CHARACTERISTIC SENTIMENTS AND ATTITUDES OF THE
ISOLATED PERSON

(1) Zimmermann, Johann G. *Solitude*. Or the effects of occasional retirement on the mind, the heart, general society. Translated from the German. London, 1827.
(2) Canat, René. *Une forme du mal du siècle*. Du sentiment de la solitude morale chez les romantiques et les parnassiens. Paris, 1904.
(3) Goltz, E. von der. *Das Gebet in der aeltesten Christenheit*. Leipzig, 1901.
(4) Strong, Anna L. *A Consideration of Prayer from the Standpoint of Social Psychology*. Chicago, 1908.
(5) Hoch, A. "On Some of the Mental Mechanisms in Dementia Praecox," *Journal of Abnormal Psychology*, V (1910), 255–73. [A study of the isolated person.]
(6) Bohannon, E. W. "Only Child," *Pedagogical Seminary*, V (1897–98), 475–96.
(7) Brill, A. A. *Psychanalysis*. Its theories and practical application. "The Only or Favorite Child in Adult Life," pp. 253–65. 2d rev. ed Philadelphia and London, 1914.
(8) Neter, Eugen. *Das einzige Kind und seine Erziehung*. Ein ernstes Mahnwort an Eltern und Erzieher. München, 1914.
(9) Whiteley, Opal S. *The Story of Opal*. Boston, 1920.
(10) Delbrück, A. *Die pathologische Lüge und die psychisch abnormen Schwindler*. Stuttgart, 1891.
(11) Healy, Wm. *Pathological Lying*. Boston, 1915.
(12) Dostoévsky, F. *The House of the Dead; or, Prison Life in Siberia*. Translated from the Russian by Constance Garnett. New York, 1915.
(13) Griffiths, Arthur. *Secrets of the Prison House, or Gaol Studies and Sketches*, I, 262–80. London, 1894.
(14) Kingsley, Charles. *The Hermits*. London and New York, 1871.
(15) Baring-Gould, S. *Lives of Saints*. 16 vols. Rev. ed. Edinburgh, 1916. [See references in index to hermits.]
(16) Varendonck, J. *The Psychology of Day-dreams*. London, 1921.

II. TYPES OF ISOLATION AND TYPES OF SOCIAL GROUPS

(1) Fishberg, Maurice. *The Jews.* A study of race and environment. London and New York, 1911.
(2) Gummere, Amelia M. *The Quaker.* A study in costume. Philadelphia, 1901.
(3) Webster, Hutton. *Primitive Secret Societies.* A study in early politics and religion. New York, 1908.
(4) Heckethorn, C. W. *The Secret Societies of all Ages and Countries.* A comprehensive account of upwards of one hundred and sixty secret organizations—religious, political, and social—from the most remote ages down to the present time. 2 vols. New ed., rev. and enl. London, 1897.
(5) Fosbroke, Thomas D. *British Monachism, or Manners and Customs of the Monks and Nuns of England.* London, 1817.
(6) Wishart, Alfred W. *A Short History of Monks and Monasteries.* Trenton, N.J., 1900. [Chap. i, pp. 17–70, gives an account of the monk as a type of human nature.]

III. GEOGRAPHICAL ISOLATION AND CULTURAL AREAS

(1) Ratzel, Friedrich. *Politische Geographie; oder, Die Geographie der Staaten, des Verkehres und des Krieges.* 2d ed. München, 1903.
(2) Semple, Ellen. *Influences of Geographic Environment, on the Basis of Ratzel's System of Anthropogeography.* Chap. xiii, "Island Peoples," pp. 409–72. New York, 1911. [Bibliography.]
(3) Brunhes, Jean. *Human Geography.* An attempt at a positive classification, principles, and examples. 2d ed. Translated from the French by T. C. LeCompte. Chicago, 1920. [See especially chaps. vi, vii, and viii, pp. 415–569.]
(4) Vallaux, Camille. *La Mer.* (Géographie Sociale.) Populations maritimes, migrations, pêches, commerce, domination de la mer. Chap. iii, "Les isles et l'insularité." Paris, 1908.
(5) Gerland, Georg. *Atlas der Völkerkunde.* Gotha, 1892. [Indicates the geographical distribution of differences in skin color, hair form, clothing, customs, languages, etc.]
(6) Ripley, William Z. *The Races of Europe.* A sociological study. New York, 1899.
(7) Campbell, John C. *The Southern Highlander and His Homeland.* New York, Russell Sage Foundation, 1921. [Bibliography.]
(8) Barrow, Sir John. *A Description of Pitcairn's Island and Its Inhabitants.* With an authentic account of the mutiny of the ship "Bounty and of the subsequent fortunes of the mutineers. New York, 1832.
(9) Routledge, Mrs. Scoresby. *The Mystery of Easter Island.* The story of an expedition. Chap. xx, "Pitcairn Island." London, 1919.
(10) Galpin, Charles J. *Rural Life.* New York, 1918.

IV. LANGUAGE FRONTIERS AND NATIONALITY

(1) Dominian, Leon. *The Frontiers of Language and Nationality in Europe.* New York, 1917. [Bibliography, pp. 348–56.]
(2) Auerbach, Bertrand. *Les Races et les nationalités en Autriche-Hongrie.* 2d rev. ed. Paris, 1917.

(3) Bernhard, L. *Das polnische Gemeinwesen im preussischen Staat.* Die Polenfrage. Leipzig, 1910.
(4) Bourgoing, P. de. *Les guerres d'idiome et de nationalité.* Tableaux, esquisses, et souvenirs d'histoire contemporaine. Paris, 1849.
(5) *Cambridge Modern History,* Vol. XI, "The Growth of Nationalities." Cambridge, 1909.
(6) Meillet, A. "Les Langues et les Nationalités," *Scientia,* XVIII (Sept., 1915), 192–201.
(7) Pfister, Ch. "La limite de la langue française et de la langue allemande en Alsace-Lorraine," Considérations historiques. *Bull. Soc. Géogr. de l'Est,* Vol. XII, 1890.
(8) This, G. "Die deutsch-französische Sprachgrenze in Lothringen," *Beiträge zur Landes- und Volkskunde von Elsass-Lothringen,* Vol. I, Strassburg, 1887.
(9) ———. "Die deutsch-französische Sprachgrenze in Elsass," *ibid.,* 1888.

V. DIALECTS AS A FACTOR IN ISOLATION

(1) Babbitt, Eugene H. "College Words and Phrases," *Dialect Notes,* II (1900–1904), 3–70.
(2) ———. "The English of the Lower Classes in New York City and Vicinity," *Dialect Notes,* Vol. I, Part ix, 1896.
(3) ———. "The Geography of the Great Languages," *World's Work,* Feb. 15 (1907–8), 9903–7.
(4) Churchill, William. *Beach-la-mar: the Jargon or Trade Speech of the Western Pacific.* Washington, 1911.
(5) Dana, Richard H., Jr. *A Dictionary of Sea Terms.* London, 1841.
(6) Elliott, A. M. "Speech-Mixture in French Canada: English and French," *American Journal of Philology,* X (1889), 133.
(7) Flaten, Nils. "Notes on American-Norwegian with a Vocabulary," *Dialect Notes,* II (1900–1904), 115–26.
(8) Harrison, James A. "Negro-English," *Transactions and Proceedings American Philological Association,* XVI (1885), Appendix, pp. xxxi–xxxiii.
(9) Hempl, George. "Language-Rivalry and Speech-Differentiation in the Case of Race-Mixture," *Transactions and Proceedings of the American Philological Association,* XXIX (1898), 31–47.
(10) Knortz, Karl. *Amerikanische Redensarten und Volksgebräuche.* Leipzig, 1907.
(11) Letzner, Karl. *Wörterbuch der englischen Volkssprache Australiens und der englischen Mischsprachen.* Halle, 1891.
(12) Pettman, Charles. *Africanderisms.* A glossary of South African colloquial words and phrases and of place and other names. London and New York, 1913.
(13) Ralph, Julian. "The Language of the Tenement-Folk," *Harper's Weekly,* XLI (Jan. 23, 1897), 90.
(14) Skeat, Walter W. *English Dialects from the Eighth Century to the Present Day.* Cambridge, 1911.
(15) Yule, Henry, and Burnell, A. C. *Hobson-Jobson.* A glossary of colloquial Anglo-Indian words and phrases, and of kindred terms,

etymological, historical, geographical, and discursive: new ed. by Wm. Crooke, London, 1903.

[See bibliography, "Slang, Argot, and Universes of Discourse," pp. 428–29.]

VI. PHYSICAL DEFECT AS A FORM OF ISOLATION

(1) Bell, Alexander G. "Memoir upon the Formation of a Deaf Variety of the Human Race." *National Academy of Sciences, Memoirs*, II, 177–262. Washington, D.C., 1884.
(2) Fay, Edward A. *Marriages of the Deaf in America*. An inquiry concerning the results of marriages of the deaf in America. Washington, D.C., 1893.
(3) Desagher, Maurice. "La timidité chez les aveugles," *Revue philosophique*, LXXVI (1913), 269–74.
(4) Best, Harry. *The Deaf*. Their position in society and the provision for their education in the United States. New York, 1914.
(5) ———. *The Blind*. Their condition and the work being done for them in the United States. New York, 1919.

VII. FERAL MEN

(1) Rauber, August. *Homo Sapiens Ferus;* oder, Die Zustände der Verwilderten und ihre Bedeutung für Wissenschaft, Politik, und Schule. Leipzig, 1885.
(2) Seguin, Edward. *Idiocy and Its Treatment by the Physiological Method*, pp. 14–23. New York, 1866.
(3) Bonnaterre, J. P. *Notice historique sur le sauvage de l'Aveyron, et sur quelques autres individus qu'on a trouvés dans les forêts à différentes époques*. Paris, 1800.
(4) Itard, Jean E. M. G. *De l'éducation d'un homme sauvage, et des premiers developpements physiques et moraux du jeune sauvage de l'Aveyron*, pp. 45–46. Paris, 1801.
(5) Feuerbach, Paul J. A. von. *Caspar Hauser*. An account of an individual kept in a dungeon from early childhood, to about the age of seventeen. Translated from the German by H. G. Linberg. London, 1834.
(6) Stanhope, Philip Henry [4th Earl]. *Tracts relating to Caspar Hauser*. Translated from the original German. London, 1836.
(7) Lang, Andrew. *Historical Mysteries*. London, 1904.
(8) Tredgold, A. F. *Mental Deficiency*. "Isolation Amentia," pp. 297–305. 3d rev. ed. New York, 1920.

[See bibliography, "The Industrially Handicapped," pp. 568–69.]

TOPICS FOR WRITTEN THEMES

1. Isolation as a Condition of Originality
2. The Relation of Social Contact and of Isolation to Historic Inventions and Discoveries, as the Law of Gravitation, Mendelian Inheritance, the Electric Light, etc.

3. Isolated Types: the Hermit, the Mystic, the Prophet, the Stranger, and the Saint
4. Isolation, Segregation, and the Physically Defective: as the Blind, the Deaf-Mute, the Physically Handicapped
5. Isolated Areas and Cultural Retardation: the Southern Mountaineer, Pitcairn Islanders, the Australian Aborigines
6. "Moral" Areas, Isolation, and Segregation: City Slums, Vice Districts, "Breeding-places of Crime"
7. The Controlled versus the Natural process of Segregation of the Feeble-minded
8. Isolation and Insanity
9. Privacy in the Home
10. Isolation and Prestige
11. Isolation as a Defence against the Invasion of Personality
12. Nationalism as a Form of Isolation
13. Biological and Social Immunity: or Biological Immunity from Infection, Personal or Group Immunity against Social Contagion
14. The Only Child
15. The Pathological Liar Considered from the Point of View of Isolation

QUESTIONS FOR DISCUSSION

1. Is the distinction between isolation and social contact relative or absolute?
2. What illustrations of the various forms of isolation, spatial, structural, habitudinal, and psychical, occur to you?
3. By what process does isolation cause racial differentiation?
4. What is the relation of endogamy and exogamy (a) to isolation, and (b) to the establishment of a successful stock or race?
5. In what ways do the Jews and the Americans as racial types illustrate the effects of isolation and of contact?
6. What do you understand to be Bacon's definition of solitude?
7. What is the point in the saying "A great town is a great solitude"?
8. What is the sociology of the creation by a solitary person of imaginary companions?
9. Under what conditions does an individual prefer solitude to society? Give illustrations.
10. What are the devices used in prayer to secure isolation?
11. "Prayer has value in that it develops the essentially social form of personal self-realization." Explain.
12. What are the interrelations of social contact and of privacy in the development of the ideal self?
13. What do you understand by the relation of erudition to originality?

14. In what ways does isolation (a) promote, (b) impede originality? What other factors beside isolation are involved in originality?

15. What is the value of privacy?

16. What was the value of the monasteries?

17. What conclusions do you derive from the study of the cases of feral men? Do these cases bear out the theory of Aristotle in regard to the effect of isolation upon the individual?

18. What is the significance of Helen Keller's account of how she broke through the barriers of isolation?

19. What were the mental effects of solitude described by Hudson? How do you explain the difference between the descriptions of the effect of solitude in the accounts given by Rousseau and by Hudson?

20. How does Galpin explain the relation of isolation to the development of the "rural mind"?

21. What are the effects of isolation upon the young man or young woman reared in the country?

22. Was Lincoln the product of isolation or of social contact?

23. To what extent are rural problems the result of isolation?

24. What do you understand by Thomas' statement, "The savage, the Negro, the peasant, the slum dwellers, and the white woman are notable sufferers by exclusion"?

25. What other of the subtler forms of isolation occur to you?

26. Is isolation to be regarded as always a disadvantage?

27. What do you understand by segregation as a process?

28. Give illustrations of groups other than those mentioned which have become segregated as a result of isolation.

29. How would you describe the process by which isolation leads to the segregation of the feeble-minded?

30. Why does a segregated group, like the feeble-minded, become an isolated group?

31. What are other illustrations of isolation resulting from segregation?

32. How would you compare Europe with the other continents with reference to number and distribution of isolated areas?

33. What do you understand to be the nature of the influence of the cradle land upon "the historical race"?

34. What illustrations from the Great War would you give of the effects (a) of central location; (b) of peripheral location?

35. How do you explain the contrast between the characteristics of the inhabitants of the Grecian inland and maritime cities?

36. To what extent may (a) the rise of the Greek city state, (b) Grecian intellectual development, and (c) the history of Greece, be interpreted in terms of geographic isolation?

37. To what extent can you explain the cultural retardation of Africa, as compared with European progress, by isolation?
38. Does race or isolation explain more adequately the following cultural differences for the several areas of France—divorce, intensity of suicide, distribution of awards, relative frequency of men of letters?
39. What is the relation of village and city emigration and immigration to isolation?
40. What is the difference between a natural and a vicinal location?
41. In what ways does isolation affect national development?
42. What is the relation of geographical position in area to literature?

CHAPTER V

SOCIAL CONTACTS

I. INTRODUCTION

1. Preliminary Notions of Social Contact

The fundamental social process is that of interaction. This interaction is (a) of persons with persons, and (b) of groups with groups. The simplest aspect of interaction, or its primary phase, is contact. Contact may be considered as the initial stage of interaction, and preparatory to the later stages. The phenomena of social contact require analysis before proceeding to the more difficult study of the mechanism of social interaction.

"With whom am I in contact?" Common sense has in stock ready answers to this question.

There is, first of all, the immediate circle of contact through the senses. Touch is the most intimate kind of contact. Face-to-face relations include, in addition to touch, visual and auditory sensations. Speech and hearing by their very nature establish a bond of contact between persons.

Even in common usage, the expression "social contact" is employed beyond the limits fixed by the immediate responses of touch, sight, and hearing. Its area has expanded to include connection through all the forms of communication, i.e., language, letters, and the printed page; connection through the medium of the telephone, telegraph, radio, moving picture, etc. The evolution of the devices for communication has taken place in the fields of two senses alone, those of hearing and seeing. Touch remains limited to the field of primary association. But the newspaper with its elaborate mechanism of communication gives publicity to events in London, Moscow, and Tokio, and the motion picture unreels to our gaze scenes from distant lands and foreign peoples with all the illusion of reality.

The frontiers of social contact are farther extended to the widest horizons, by commerce. The economists, for example, include in their conception of society the intricate and complex maze of relations created by the competition and co-operation of individuals and societies within the limits of a world-wide economy. This inclusion of unconscious as well as conscious reciprocal influences in the concept of social relations brings into "contact" the members of a village missionary society with the savages of the equatorial regions of Africa; or the pale-faced drug addict, with the dark-skinned Hindu laborers upon the opium fields of Benares; or the man gulping down coffee at the breakfast table, with the Java planter; the crew of the Pacific freighter and its cargo of spices with the American whole-saler and retailer in food products. In short, everyone is in a real, though concealed and devious, way in contact with every other person in the world. Contacts of this type, remote from the familiar experiences of everyday life, have reality to the intellectual and the mystic and are appreciated by the masses only when co-operation breaks down, or competition becomes conscious and passes into conflict.

These three popular meanings of contacts emphasize (1) the intimacy of sensory responses, (2) the extension of contact through devices of communication based upon sight and hearing, and (3) the solidarity and interdependence created and maintained by the fabric of social life, woven as it is from the intricate and invisible strands of human interests in the process of a world-wide competition and co-operation.

2. The Sociological Concept of Contact

The use of the term "contact" in sociology is not a departure from, but a development of, its customary significance. In the preceding chapter the point was made that the distinction between isolation and contact is not absolute but relative. Members of a society spatially separate, but socially in contact through sense perception and through communication of ideas, may be thereby mobilized to collective behavior. Sociological interest in this situation lies in the fact that the various kinds of social contacts between persons and groups determine behavior. The student of problems of American society, for example, realizes the necessity of understanding the mutual reactions involved in the contacts of the foreign and the native-born, of the white and the negro, and of employers and employees. In other words, contact, as the first stage of social interaction, conditions and controls the later stages of the process.

It is convenient, for certain purposes, to conceive of contact in terms of space. The contacts of persons and of groups may then be plotted in units of *social distance.* This permits graphic representation of relations of sequence and of coexistence in terms both of units of separation and of contact. This spatial conception may now be applied to the explanation of the readings in social contacts.

3. Classification of the Materials

In sociological literature there have grown up certain distinctions between types of social contacts. Physical contacts are distinguished from social contacts; relations within the "in-group" are perceived to be different from relations with the "out-group"; contacts of historical continuity are compared with contacts of mobility; primary contacts are set off from secondary contacts. How far and with what advantage may these distinctions be stated in spatial terms?

a) *Land as a basis for social contacts.*—The position of persons and peoples on the earth gives us a literal picture of the spatial conception of social contact. The cluster of homes in the Italian agricultural community suggests the difference in social life in comparison with the isolated homesteads of rural America. A gigantic spot map of the United States upon which every family would be indicated by a dot would represent schematically certain different conditions influencing group behavior in arid areas, the open country, hamlets, villages, towns, and cities. The movements of persons charted with detail sufficient to bring out variations in the daily, weekly, monthly, and yearly routine, would undoubtedly reveal interesting identities and differences in the intimacy and intensity of social contacts. It would be possible and profitable to classify people with reference to the routine of their daily lives.

b) *Touch as the physiological basis of social contact.*—According to the spatial conception the closest contacts possible are those of touch. The physical proximity involved in tactile sensations is, however, but the symbol of the intensity of the reactions to contact. Desire and aversion for contacts, as Crawley shows in his selection, arise in the most intimate relations of human life. Love and hate, longing and disgust, sympathy and hostility increase in intensity with intimacy of association. It is a current sociological fallacy that closeness of contact results only in the growth of good will. The fact is, that with increasing contact either attraction or repulsion may be the outcome, depending upon the situation and upon factors not yet fully analyzed. Peculiar conditions of contact, as its prolonged duration, its frequent repetition, just as in the case of isolation from normal association, may lead to the inversion of the original impulses and sentiments of affection and antipathy.[1]

c) *Contacts with the "in-group" and with the "out-group."*—The conception of the we-group in terms of distance is that of a group in which the solidarity of units is so complete that the movements and sentiments of all are completely regulated with reference to their interests and behavior as a group. This control by the in-group over its members makes for solidity and impenetrability in its relations with the out-group. Sumner in his *Folkways* indicates how internal sympathetic contacts and group egotism result in double standards of behavior: good-will and co-operation within the members of the in-group, hostility and suspicion toward the out-group and its members. The essential point is perhaps best brought out by Shaler in his distinction between sympathetic and categoric contacts. He describes the transition from contacts of the out-group to those of the in-group, or from remote to intimate relations. From a distance, a person has the characteristics of his group, upon close acquaintance he reveals his individuality.

d) *Historical continuity and mobility.*—Historical continuity, which maintains the identity of the present with the past, implies the existence of a body of tradition which is transmitted from the older to the younger generations. Through the medium of tradition, including in that term all the learning, science, literature, and practical arts, not to speak of the great body of oral tradition which is after all a larger part of life than we imagine, the historical and

---

[1] Alexander Pope, in smooth lines, and with apt phrases, has concretely described this process of perversion:

> "Vice is a monster of so frightful mien,
> As to be hated needs but to be seen;
> Yet seen too oft, familiar with her face,
> We first endure, then pity, then embrace."

cultural life is maintained. This is the meaning of the long period of childhood in man during which the younger generation is living under the care and protection of the older. When, for any reason, this contact of the younger with the older generation is interrupted—as is true in the case of immigrants—a very definite cultural deterioration frequently ensues.

Contacts of mobility are those of a changing present, and measure the number and variety of the stimulations which the social life and movements—the discovery of the hour, the book of the moment, the passing fads and fashions—afford. Contacts of mobility give us novelty and news. It is through contacts of this sort that change takes place.

Mobility, accordingly, measures not merely the social contacts that one gains from travel and exploration, but the stimulation and suggestions that come to us through the medium of communication, by which sentiments and ideas are put in social circulation. Through the newspaper, the common man of today participates in the social movements of his time. His illiterate forbear of yesterday, on the other hand, lived unmoved by the current of world-events outside his hamlet. The *tempo* of modern societies may be measured comparatively by the relative perfection of devices of communication and the rapidity of the circulation of sentiments, opinions, and facts. Indeed, the efficiency of any society or of any group is to be measured not alone in terms of numbers or of material resources, but also in terms of mobility and access through communication and publicity to the common fund of tradition and culture.

e) Primary and secondary contacts.—Primary contacts are those of "intimate face-to-face association"; secondary contacts are those of externality and greater distance. A study of primary association indicates that this sphere of contact falls into two areas: one of intimacy and the other of acquaintance. In the diagram which follows, the field of primary contacts has been subdivided so that it includes (*x*) a circle of greater intimacy, (*y*) a wider circle of acquaintanceship. The completed chart would appear as shown on page 285.

Primary contacts of the greatest intimacy are (*a*) those represented by the affections that ordinarily spring up within the family, particularly between parents and children, husband and wife; and (*b*) those of fellowship and affection outside the family as between lovers,

bosom friends, and boon companions. These relations are all manifestations of a craving for response. These personal relationships
are the nursery for the development of human nature and personality.
John Watson, who studied several hundred new-born infants in the
psychological laboratory, concludes that "the first few years are the
all-important ones, for shaping the emotional life of the child."[1]
The primary virtues and ideals of which Cooley writes so sympathetically are, for the most part, projections from family life. Certainly
in these most intimate relations of life in the contacts of the family
circle, in the closest friendships, personality is most severely tried,
realizes its most characteristic expressions, or is most completely
disorganized.

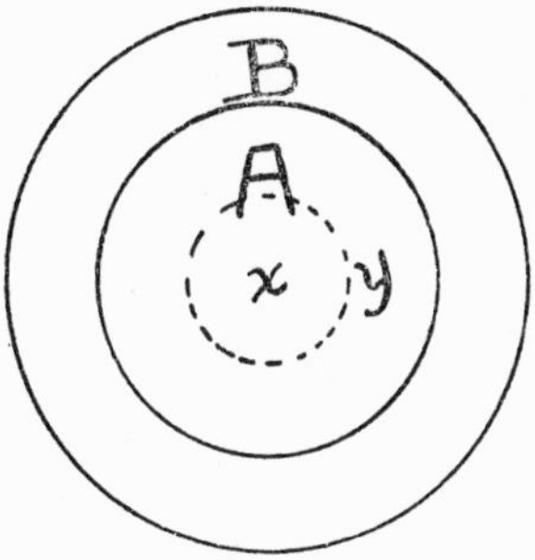

FIG. 3

A, primary contacts; *x*, greater intimacy; *y*, acquaintanceship;
B, secondary contacts

Just as the life of the family represents the contacts of touch and
response, the neighborhood or the village is the natural area of primary
contacts and the city the social environment of secondary contacts.
In primary association individuals are in contact with each other
at practically all points of their lives. In the village "everyone
knows everything about everyone else." Canons of conduct are
absolute, social control is omnipotent, the status of the family and
the individual is fixed. In secondary association individuals are in
contact with each other at only one or two points in their lives. In
the city, the individual becomes anonymous; at best he is generally
known in only one or two aspects of his life. Standards of behavior

[1] H. S. Jennings, John B. Watson, Adolph Meyer, and W. I. Thomas, "Practical and Theoretical Problems in Instinct and Habit," *Suggestions of Modern
Science Concerning Education*, p. 174.

are relative; the old primary controls have disappeared; the new secondary instruments of discipline, necessarily formal, are for the most part crude and inefficient; the standing of the family and of the individual is uncertain and subject to abrupt changes upward or downward in the social scale.

Simmel has made a brilliant contribution in his analysis of the sociological significance of "the stranger." "The stranger" in the sociological sense is the individual who unites in his social relations primary and secondary contacts. Simmel himself employs the conception of social distance in his statement of the stranger as the combination of the near and the far. It is interesting and significant to determine the different types of the union of intimacy and externality in the relations of teacher and student, physician and patient, minister and layman, lawyer and client, social worker and applicant for relief.

A complete analysis of the bearing upon personal and cultural life of changes from a society based upon contacts of continuity and of primary relations to a society of increasing mobility organized around secondary contacts cannot be given here. Certain of the most obvious contrasts of the transition may, however, be stated. Increasing mobility of persons in society almost inevitably leads to change and therefore to loss of continuity. In primary groups, where social life moves slowly, there is a greater sense of continuity than in secondary groups where it moves rapidly.

There is a further contrast if not conflict between direct and intimate contacts and contacts based upon communication of ideas. All sense of values, as Windelband has pointed out,[1] rests upon concrete experience, that is to say upon sense contacts. Society, to the extent that it is organized about secondary contacts, is based upon abstractions, upon science and technique. Secondary contacts of this type have only secondary values because they represent means rather than ends. Just as all behavior arises in sense impressions it must also terminate in sense impressions to realize its ends and attain its values. The effect of life in a society based on secondary contacts is to build up between the impulse and its end a world of means, to project values into the future, and to direct life toward the realization of distant hopes.

[1] See Introduction, pp. 8–10.

The ultimate effect upon the individual as he becomes accommodated to secondary society is to find a substitute expression for his primary response in the artificial physical environment of the city. The detachment of the person from intimate, direct, and spontaneous contacts with social reality is in large measure responsible for the intricate maze of problems of urban life.

The change from concrete and personal to abstract and impersonal relations in economic and social life began with the Industrial Revolution. The machine is the symbol of the monotonous routine of impersonal, unskilled, large-scale production just as the hand tool is the token of the interesting activity of personal, skilled, handicraft work. The so-called "instinct of workmanship" no longer finds expression in the anonymous standardized production of modern industry.[1]

It is not in industry alone that the natural impulses of the person for response, recognition, and self-expression are balked. In social work, politics, religion, art, and sport the individual is represented now by proxies where formerly he participated in person. All the forms of communal activity in which all persons formerly shared have been taken over by professionals. The great mass of men in most of the social activities of modern life are no longer actors, but spectators. The average man of the present time has been relegated by the influence of the professional politician to the rôle of taxpayer. In social work organized charity has come between the giver and the needy.

In these and other manifold ways the artificial conditions of city life have deprived the person of most of the natural outlets for the expression of his interests and his energies. To this fact is to be attributed in large part the restlessness, the thirst for novelty and excitement so characteristic of modern life. This emotional unrest has been capitalized by the newspapers, commercialized recreations, fashion, and agitation in their appeal to the sensations, the emotions, and the instincts loosened from the satisfying fixations of primary-group life. The *raison d'être* of social work, as well as the fundamental problem of all social institutions in city life must be understood in its relation to this background.

[1] Thorstein Veblen, *The Instinct of Workmanship, and the State of the Industrial Arts.* (New York, 1914.)

II. MATERIALS

A. PHYSICAL CONTACT AND SOCIAL CONTACT

1. The Frontiers of Social Contact[1]

Sociology deals especially with the phenomena of *contact*. The reactions which result from voluntary or involuntary contact of human beings with other human beings are the phenomena peculiarly "social," as distinguished from the phenomena that belong properly to biology and psychology.

In the first place, we want to indicate, not the essence of the social, but the location, the sphere, the extent, of the social. If we can agree where it is, we may then proceed to discover what it is. The social, then, is the term next beyond the individual. Assuming, for the sake of analysis, that our optical illusion, "the individual," is an isolated and self-sufficient fact, there are many sorts of scientific problems that do not need to go beyond this fact to satisfy their particular terms. Whether the individual can ever be abstracted from his conditions and remain himself is not a question that we need here discuss. At all events, the individual known to our experience is not isolated. He is connected in various ways with one or more individuals. The different ways in which individuals are connected with each other are indicated by the inclusive term "contact." Starting, then, from the individual, to measure him in all his dimensions and to represent him in all his phases, we find that each person is what he is by virtue of the existence of other persons, and by virtue of an alternating current of influence between each person and all the other persons previously or at the same time in existence. The last native of Central Africa around whom we throw the dragnet of civilization, and whom we inoculate with a desire for whiskey, adds an increment to the demand for our distillery products, and affects the internal revenue of the United States, and so the life-conditions of every member of our population. This is what we mean by "contact." So long as that African tribe is unknown to the outside world, and the world to it, so far as the European world is concerned, the tribe might as well not exist. The moment the tribe comes within touch of the rest of the world, the aggregate of the world's contacts is by so much enlarged; the social world is by so much

[1] From Albion W. Small, *General Sociology*, pp. 486–89. (The University of Chicago Press, 1905.)

extended. In other words, the realm of the social is the realm of circuits of reciprocal influence between individuals and the groups which individuals compose. The general term "contact" is proposed to stand for this realm, because it is a colorless word that may mark boundaries without prejudging contents. Wherever there is physical or spiritual contact between persons, there is inevitably a circuit of exchange of influence. The realm of the social is the realm constituted by such exchange. It extends from the producing of the baby by the mother, and the simultaneous producing of the mother by the baby, to the producing of merchant and soldier by the world-powers, and the producing of the world-powers by merchant and soldier.

The most general and inclusive way in which to designate all the phenomena that sociology proper considers, without importing into the term premature hypotheses by way of explanation, is to assert that they are the phenomena of "contact" between persons.

In accordance with what was said about the division of labor between psychology and sociology, it seems best to leave to the psychologist all that goes on inside the individual and to say that the work of the sociologist begins with the things that take place between individuals. This principle of division is not one that can be maintained absolutely, any more than we can hold absolutely to any other abstract classification of real actions. It serves, however, certain rough uses. Our work as students of society begins in earnest when the individual has become equipped with his individuality. This stage of human growth is both cause and effect of the life of human beings side by side in greater or lesser numbers. Under those circumstances individuals are produced; they act as individuals; by their action as individuals they produce a certain type of society; that type reacts on the individuals and helps to transform them into different types of individuals, who in turn produce a modified type of society; and so the rhythm goes on forever. Now the medium through which all this occurs is the fact of contacts, either physical or spiritual. In either case, contacts are collisions of interests in the individuals.

2. The Land and the People[1]

Every clan, tribe, state, or nation includes two ideas, a people and its land, the first unthinkable without the other. History,

[1] From Ellen C. Semple, *Influences of Geographic Environment*, pp. 51–53. (Henry Holt & Co., 1911.)

sociology, ethnology, touch only the inhabited areas of the earth. These areas gain their final significance because of the people who occupy them; their local conditions of climate, soil, natural resources, physical features, and geographic situation are important primarily as factors in the development of actual or possible inhabitants. A land is fully comprehended only when studied in the light of its influence upon its people, and a people cannot be understood apart from the field of its activities. More than this, human activities are fully intelligible only in relation to the various geographic conditions which have stimulated them in different parts of the world. The principles of the evolution of navigation, of agriculture, of trade, as also the theory of population, can never reach their correct and final statement, unless the data for the conclusions are drawn from every part of the world and each fact interpreted in the light of the local conditions whence it sprang. Therefore anthropology, sociology, and history should be permeated by geography.

Most systems of sociology treat man as if he were in some way detached from the earth's surface; they ignore the land basis of society. The anthropogeographer recognizes the various social forces, economic and psychologic, which sociologists regard as the cement of societies; but he has something to add. He sees in the land occupied by a primitive tribe or a highly organized state the underlying material bond holding society together, the ultimate basis of their fundamental social activities, which are therefore derivatives from the land. He sees the common territory exercising an integrating force—weak in primitive communities where the group has established only a few slight and temporary relations with its soil, so that this low social complex breaks up readily like its organic counterpart, the low animal organism found in an amœba; he sees it growing stronger with every advance in civilization involving more complex relations to the land—with settled habitations, with increased density of population, with a discriminating and highly differentiated use of the soil, with the exploitation of mineral resources, and, finally, with that far-reaching exchange of commodities and ideas which means the establishment of varied extra-territorial relations. Finally, the modern society or state has grown into every foot of its own soil, exploited its every geographic advantage, utilized its geographic location to enrich itself by international trade, and, when possible, to absorb outlying territories by means of colonies. The broader this geographic base, the richer, more varied, its resources, and the more favorable its climate to their exploitation, the more numerous and complex are the connections which the members of a social group can establish with it, and through it with each other; or, in other words, the greater may be its ultimate historical significance.

3. Touch and Social Contact[1]

General ideas concerning human relations are the medium through which sexual taboo works, and these must now be examined. If we compare the facts of social taboo generally, or of its subdivision, sexual taboo, we find that the ultimate test of human relations, in both *genus* and *species*, is *contact*. An investigation of primitive ideas concerning the relations of man with man, when guided by this clue, will lay bare the principles which underlie the theory and practice of sexual taboo. Arising, as we have seen, from sexual differentiation, and forced into permanence by difference of occupation and sexual solidarity, this segregation receives the continuous support of religious conceptions as to human relations. These conceptions center upon contact, and ideas of contact are at the root of all conceptions of human relations at any stage of culture; contact is the one universal test, as it is the most elementary form, of mutual relations. Psychology bears this out, and the point is psychological rather than ethnological.

As I have pointed out before and shall have occasion to do so again, a comparative examination, assisted by psychology, of the emotions and ideas of average modern humanity is a most valuable aid to ethnological inquiry. In this connection, we find that desire or willingness for physical contact is an animal emotion, more or less subconscious, which is characteristic of similarity, harmony, friendship, or love. Throughout the world, the greeting of a friend is expressed by contact, whether it be nose-rubbing, or the kiss, the embrace, or the clasp of hands; so the ordinary expression of friendship by a boy, that eternal savage, is contact of arm and shoulder. More interesting still for our purpose is the universal expression by

[1] From Ernest Crawley, *The Mystic Rose*, pp. 76–79. (Published by The Macmillan Co., 1902. Reprinted by permission.)

contact of the emotion of love. To touch his mistress is the ever-present desire of the lover, and in this impulse, even if we do not trace it back, as we may without being fanciful, to polar or sexual attraction inherent in the atoms, the φιλία of Empedocles, yet we may place the beginning and ending of love. When analyzed, the emotion always comes back to contact.

Further, mere willingness for contact is found universally when the person to be touched is healthy, if not clean, or where he is of the same age or class or caste, and, we may add, for ordinary humanity the same sex.

On the other hand, the avoidance of contact, whether consciously or subconsciously presented, is no less the universal characteristic of human relations where similarity, harmony, friendship, or love is absent. This appears in the attitude of men to the sick, to strangers, distant acquaintances, enemies, and in cases of difference of age, position, sympathies or aims, and even of sex. Popular language is full of phrases which illustrate this feeling.

Again, the pathology of the emotions supplies many curious cases where the whole being seems concentrated upon the sense of touch, with abnormal desire or disgust for contact; and in the evolution of the emotions from physiological pleasure and pain, contact plays an important part in connection with functional satisfaction or dissatisfaction with the environment.

In the next place, there are the facts, first, that an element of thought inheres in all sensation, while sensation conditions thought; and secondly, that there is a close connection of all the senses, both in origin—each of them being a modification of the one primary sense of touch—and in subsequent development, where the specialized organs are still co-ordinated through tactile sensation, in the sensitive surface of organism. Again, and here we see the genesis of ideas of contact, it is by means of the tactile sensibility of the skin and membranes of sense-organs, forming a sensitized as well as a protecting surface, that the nervous system conveys to the brain information about the external world, and this information is in its original aspect the response to impact. Primitive physics, no less than modern, recognizes that contact is a modified form of a blow. These considerations show that contact not only plays an important part in the life of the soul but must have had a profound influence on the development of ideas, and it may now be assumed that ideas of contact have been a universal and original constant factor in human relations and that they are so still. The latter assumption is to be stressed, because we find that the ideas which lie beneath primitive taboo are still a vital part of human nature, though mostly emptied of their religious content; and also because, as I hold, ceremonies and etiquette, such as still obtain, could not possess such vitality as they do unless there were a living psychological force behind them, such as we find in elementary ideas which come straight from functional processes.

These ideas of contact are *primitive* in each sense of the word, at whatever stage of culture they appear. They seem to go back in origin and in character to that highly developed sensibility of all animal and even organized life, which forms at once a biological monitor and a safeguard for the whole organism in relation to its environment. From this sensibility there arise subjective ideas concerning the safety or danger of the environment, and in man we may suppose these subjective ideas as to his environment, and especially as to his fellow-men, to be the origin of his various expressions of avoidance or desire for contact.

Lastly, it is to be observed that avoidance of contact is the most conspicuous phenomenon attaching to cases of taboo when its dangerous character is prominent. In taboo the connotation of "not to be touched" is the salient point all over the world, even in cases of permanent taboo such as belongs to Samoan and Maori chiefs, with whom no one dared come in contact; and so we may infer the same aversion to be potential in all such relations.

B. SOCIAL CONTACT IN RELATION TO SOLIDARITY AND TO MOBILITY

1. The In-Group and the Out-Group[1]

The conception of "primitive society" which we ought to form is that of small groups scattered over a territory. The size of the groups is determined by the conditions of the struggle for existence. The internal organization of each group corresponds to its size. A group of groups may have some relation to each other (kin, neighborhood, alliance, connubium, and commercium) which draws them

[1] From W. G. Sumner, *Folkways*, pp. 12–13. (Ginn & Co., 1906.)

together and differentiates them from others.   Thus a differentiation arises between ourselves, the we-group, or in-group, and everybody else, or the others-groups, out-groups.   The insiders in a we-group are in a relation of peace, order, law, government, and industry, to each other.   Their relation to all outsiders, or others-groups, is one of war and plunder, except so far as agreements have modified it. If a group is exogamic, the women in it were born abroad somewhere. Other foreigners who might be found in it are adopted persons, guest-friends, and slaves.

The relation of comradeship and peace in the we-group and that of hostility and war toward others-groups are correlative to each other.   The exigencies of war with outsiders are what make peace inside, lest internal discord should weaken the we-group for war. These exigencies also make government and law in the in-group, in order to prevent quarrels and enforce discipline.   Thus war and peace have reacted on each other and developed each other, one within the group, the other in the intergroup relation.   The closer the neighbors, and the stronger they are, the intenser is the warfare, and then the intenser is the internal organization and discipline of each.   Sentiments are produced to correspond.   Loyalty to the group, sacrifice for it, hatred and contempt for outsiders, brother-hood within, warlikeness without—all grow together, common prod-ucts of the same situation.

Ethnocentrism is the technical name for this view of things in which one's own group is the center of everything and all others are scaled and rated with reference to it.   Folkways correspond to it to cover both the inner and the outer relation.   Each group nourishes its own pride and vanity, boasts itself superior, exalts its own divini-ties, and looks with contempt on outsiders.   Each group thinks its own folkways the only right ones, and if it observes that other groups have other folkways, these excite its scorn.   Opprobrious epithets are derived from these differences.   "Pig-eater," "cow-eater," "uncir-cumcised," "jabberers," are epithets of contempt and abomination.

2.   Sympathetic Contacts versus Categoric Contacts[1]

Let us now consider what takes place when two men, mere strangers to one another, come together.   The motive of classification,

[1] Adapted from N. S. Shaler, *The Neighbor*, pp. 207-27. (Houghton Mifflin Co., 1904.)

which I have considered in another chapter, leads each of them at once to recognize the approaching object first as living, then as human. The shape and dress carry the categorizing process yet farther, so that they are placed in groups, as of this or that tribe or social class, and as these determinations are made they arouse the appropriate sympathies or hatreds such as by experience have become associated with the several categories. Be it observed that these judgments are spontaneous, instinctive, and unnoticed. They are made so by immemorial education in the art of contact which man has inherited from the life of the ancestral beasts and men; they have most likely been in some measure affirmed by selection, for these determinations as to the nature of the neighbor were in the lower stages of existence in brute and man of critical importance, the creatures lived or died according as they determined well or ill, swiftly or slowly. If we observe what takes place in our own minds at such meetings we will see that the action in its immediateness is like that of the eyelids when the eye is threatened. As we say, it is done before we know it.

With this view as to the conditions of human contact, particularly of what occurs when men first meet one another, let us glance at what takes place in near intercourse. We have seen that at the beginning of any acquaintance the fellow-being is inevitably dealt with in the categoric way. He is taken as a member of a group, which group is denoted to us by a few convenient signs; as our acquaintance with a particular person advances, this category tends to become qualified. Its bounds are pushed this way and that until they break down. It is to be noted in this process that the category fights for itself, or we for it, so that the result of the battle between the immediate truth and the prejudice is always doubtful. It is here that knowledge, especially that gained by individual experience, is most helpful. The uninformed man, who begins to find, on the nearer view of an Israelite, that the fellow is like himself, holds by his category in the primitive way. The creature *is* a Jew, therefore the evidence of kinship must not count. He who is better informed is, or should be, accustomed to amend his categories. He may, indeed, remember that he is dealing with a neighbor of the race which gave us not only Christ, but all the accepted prophets who have shaped our own course, and his understanding helps to cast down the barriers of instinctive prejudice.

At the stage of advancing acquaintance where friendship is attained, the category begins to disappear from our minds. We may, indeed, measure the advance in this relation by the extent to which it has been broken down. Looking attentively at our mental situation as regards those whom we know pretty well, we see that most of them are still, though rather faintly, classified into groups. While a few of the nearer stand forth by themselves, all of the nearest to our hearts are absolutely individualized, so that our judgments of them are made on the basis of our own motives and what we of ourselves discern. We may use categoric terms concerning our lovers, spouses, or children, but they have no real meaning; these persons are to us purely individual, all trace of the inclusive category has disappeared; they are, in the full sense of the word, our neighbors, being so near that when we look upon them we see nothing else, not even ourselves.

Summing up these considerations concerning human contact, it may be said that the world works by a system of individualities rising in scale as we advance from the inorganic through the organic series until we find the summit in man. The condition of all these individuals is that of isolation; each is necessarily parted from all the others in the realm, each receiving influences, and, in turn, sending forth its peculiar tide of influences to those of its own and other kinds. This isolation in the case of man is singularly great for the reason that he is the only creature we know in the realm who is so far endowed with consciousness that he can appreciate his position and know the measure of his solitude. In the case of all individuals the discernible is only a small part of what exists. In man the measure of this presentation is, even to himself, very small, and that which he can readily make evident to his neighbor is an exceedingly limited part of the real whole. Yet it is on this slender basis that we must rest our relations with the fellow man if we are to found them upon knowledge. The imperfection of this method of ascertaining the fellow-man is well shown by the trifling contents of the category discriminations we apply to him. While, as has been suggested, much can be done by those who have gained in knowledge of our kind by importing understandings into our relations with men, the only effective way to the betterment of those relations is through the sympathies.

What can be done by knowledge in helping us to a comprehension of the fellow-man is at best merely explanatory of his place in the phenomenal world; of itself it has only scientific value. The advantage of the sympathetic way of approach is that in this method the neighbor is accounted for on the supposition that he is ourself in another form, so we feel for and with him on the instinctive hypothesis that he is essentially ourself. There can be no question that this method of looking upon other individualities is likely to lead to many errors. We see examples of these blunders in all the many grades of the personifying process, from the savage's worship of a tree or stone to the civilized man's conception of a human-like god. We see them also in the attribution to the lower animals of thoughts and feelings which are necessarily limited to our own kind, but in the case of man the conception of identity gives a minimum of error and a maximum of truth. It, indeed, gives a truer result than could possibly be attained by any scientific inquiries that we could make, or could conceive of being effectively made, and this for the following reasons.

When, as in the sympathetic state, we feel that the neighbor of our species is essentially ourself, the tacit assumption is that his needs and feelings are as like our own as our own states of mind at diverse times are like one another, so that we might exchange motives with him without experiencing any great sense of strangeness. What we have in mind is not the measure of instruction or education, not the class or station or other adventitious circumstances, but the essential traits of his being. Now this supposition is entirely valid. All we know of mankind justifies the statement that, as regards all the qualities and motives with which the primal sympathies deal, men are remarkably alike. Their loves, hates, fears, and sorrows are alike in their essentials; so that the postulate of sympathy that the other man is essentially like one's self is no idle fancy but an established truth. It not only embodies the judgment of all men in thought and action but has its warrant from all the science we can apply to it.

It is easy to see how by means of sympathy we can at once pass the gulf which separates man from man. All the devices of the ages in the way of dumb or spoken language fail to win across the void, and leave the two beings apart; but with a step the sympathetic spirit passes the gulf. In this strange feature we have the completion of the series of differences between the inorganic and the organic groups of individualities. In the lower or non-living isolations there is no reason why the units should do more than mechanically interact. All their service in the realm can be best effected by their remaining forever completely apart. But when we come to the organic series, the units begin to have need of understanding their neighbors, in order that they may form those beginnings of the moral order which we find developing among the members even of the lowliest species. Out of this sympathetic accord arises the community, which we see in its simple beginnings in the earlier stages of life; it grows with the advance in the scale of being, and has its supreme success in man. Human society, the largest of all organic associations, requires that its units be knit together in certain common purposes and understandings, and the union can only be made effective by the ways of sympathy—by the instinctive conviction of essential kinship.

3. Historical Continuity and Civilization[1]

In matters connected with political and economical institutions we notice among the natural races very great differences in the sum of their civilization. Accordingly we have to look among them, not only for the beginnings of civilization, but for a very great part of its evolution, and it is equally certain that these differences are to be referred less to variations in endowment than to great differences in the conditions of their development. Exchange has also played its part, and unprejudiced observers have often been more struck in the presence of facts by agreement than by difference. "It is astonishing," exclaims Chapman, when considering the customs of the Damaras, "what a similarity there is in the manners and practices of the human family throughout the world. Even here, the two different classes of Damaras practice rites in common with the New Zealanders, such as that of chipping out the front teeth and cutting off the little finger." It is less astonishing if, as the same traveler remarks, their agreement with the Bechuanas goes even farther. Now since the essence of civilization lies first in the amassing of experiences, then in the fixity with which these are retained, and lastly in the capacity to carry them farther or to increase them, our first question must be, how is it possible to realize the first funda-

---

[1] From Friedrich Ratzel, *The History of Mankind*, I, 21–25. (Published by The Macmillan Co., 1896. Reprinted by permission.)

mental condition of civilization, namely, the amassing a stock of culture in the form of handiness, knowledge, power, capital? It has long been agreed that the first step thereto is the transition from complete dependence upon what Nature freely offers to a conscious exploitation through man's own labor, especially in agriculture or cattle-breeding, of such of her fruits as are most important to him. This transition opens at one stroke all the most remote possibilities of Nature, but we must always remember at the same time that it is still a long way from the first step to the height which has now been attained.

The intellect of man and also the intellect of whole races shows a wide discrepancy in regard to differences of endowment as well as in regard to the different effects which external circumstances produce upon it. Especially are there variations in the degree of inward coherence and therewith of the fixity or duration of the stock of intellect. The want of coherence, the breaking up of this stock, characterizes the lower stages of civilization no less than its coherence, its inalienability, and its power of growth do the higher. We find in low stages a poverty of tradition which allows these races neither to maintain a consciousness of their earlier fortunes for any appreciable period nor to fortify and increase their stock of intelligence either through the acquisitions of individual prominent minds or through the adoption and fostering of any stimulus. Here, if we are not entirely mistaken, is the basis of the deepest-seated differences between races. The opposition of historic and non-historic races seems to border closely upon it.

There is a distinction between the quickly ripening immaturity of the child and the limited maturity of the adult who has come to a stop in many respects. What we mean by "natural" races is something much more like the latter than the former. We call them races deficient in civilization, because internal and external conditions have hindered them from attaining to such permanent developments in the domain of culture as form the mark of the true civilized races and the guaranties of progress. Yet we should not venture to call any of them cultureless, so long as none of them is devoid of the primitive means by which the ascent to higher stages can be made— language, religion, fire, weapons, implements; while the very possession of these means, and many others, such as domestic animals and cultivated plants, testifies to varied and numerous dealings with those races which are completely civilized.

The reasons why they do not make use of these gifts are of many kinds. Lower intellectual endowment is often placed in the first rank. That is a convenient but not quite fair explanation. Among the savage races of today we find great differences in endowments. We need not dispute that in the course of development races of even slightly higher endowments have got possession of more and more means of culture, and gained steadiness and security for their progress, while the less endowed remained behind. But external conditions, in respect to their furthering or hindering effects, can be more clearly recognized and estimated; and it is juster and more logical to name them first. We can conceive why the habitations of the savage races are principally to be found on the extreme borders of the inhabited world, in the cold and hot regions, in remote islands, in secluded mountains, in deserts. We understand their backward condition in parts of the earth which offer so few facilities for agriculture and cattle-breeding as Australia, the Arctic regions, or the extreme north and south of America. In the insecurity of incompletely developed resources we can see the chain which hangs heavily on their feet and confines their movements within a narrow space. As a consequence their numbers are small, and from this again results the small total amount of intellectual and physical accomplishment, the rarity of eminent men, the absence of the salutary pressure exercised by surrounding masses on the activity and forethought of the individual, which operates in the division of society into classes, and the promotion of a wholesome division of labor. A partial consequence of this insecurity of resources is the instability of natural races. A nomadic strain runs through them all, rendering easier to them the utter incompleteness of their unstable political and economical institutions, even when an indolent agriculture seems to tie them to the soil. Thus it often comes about that, in spite of abundantly provided and well-tended means of culture, their life is desultory, wasteful of power, unfruitful. This life has no inward consistency, no secure growth; it is not the life in which the germs of civilization first grew up to the grandeur in which we frequently find them at the beginnings of what we call history. It is full rather of fallings-away from civilization and dim memories from civilized spheres which in many cases must have existed long before the commencement of history as we have it.

By the word "civilization" or "culture" we denote usually the sum of all the acquirements at a given time of the human intelligence. When we speak of stages, of higher and lower, of semi-civilization, of civilized and "natural" races, we apply to the various civilizations of the earth a standard which we take from the degree that we have ourselves attained. Civilization means *our* civilization.

The confinement, in space as in time, which isolates huts, villages, races, no less than successive generations, involves the negation of culture; in its opposite, the intercourse of contemporaries and the interdependence of ancestors and successors, lies the possibility of development. The union of contemporaries secures the retention of culture, the linking of generations its unfolding. The development of civilization is a process of hoarding. The hoards grow of themselves so soon as a retaining power watches over them. In all domains of human creation and operation we shall see the basis of all higher development in intercourse. Only through co-operation and mutual help, whether between contemporaries, whether from one generation to another, has mankind succeeded in climbing to the stage of civilization on which its highest members now stand. On the nature and extent of this intercourse the growth depends. Thus the numerous small assemblages of equal importance, formed by the family stocks, in which the individual had no freedom, were less favorable to it than the larger communities and states of the modern world, with their encouragement to individual competition.

4. Mobility and the Movement of Peoples[1]

Every country whose history we examine proves the recipient of successive streams of humanity. Even sea-girt England has received various intruding peoples, from the Roman occupation to the recent influx of Russian Jews. In prehistoric times it combined several elements in its population, as the discovery of the "long barrow" men and "round barrow" men by archaeologists and the identification of a surviving Iberian or Mediterranean strain by ethnologists go to prove. Egypt, Mesopotamia, and India tell the same story,

[1]Adapted from Ellen C. Semple, *Influences of Geographic Environment*, pp. 75–84, 186–87. (Henry Holt & Co., 1911.)

whether in their recorded or unrecorded history. Tropical Africa lacks a history; but all that has been pieced together by ethnologists and anthropologists, in an effort to reconstruct its past, shows incessant movement—growth, expansion, and short-lived conquest, followed by shrinkage, expulsion, or absorption by another invader. To this constant shifting of races and peoples the name of historical movement has been given, because it underlies most of written history and constitutes the major part of unwritten history, especially that of savage and nomadic tribes.

Among primitive peoples this movement is simple and monotonous. It involves all members of the tribe, either in pursuit of game or following the herd over the tribal territory, or in migrations seeking more and better land. Among civilized peoples it assumes various forms and especially is differentiated for different members of the social group. The civilized state develops specialized frontiers—men, armies, explorers, maritime traders, colonists, and missionaries, who keep a part of the people constantly moving and directing external expansion, while the mass of the population converts the force once expended in the migrant food-quest into internal activity. Here we come upon a paradox. The nation as a whole, with the development of sedentary life, increases its population and therewith its need for external movements; it widens its national area and its circle of contact with other lands, enlarges its geographical horizon, and improves its internal communication over a growing territory; it evolves a greater mobility within and without, which attaches, however, to certain classes of society, not to the entire social group. This mobility becomes the outward expression of a whole complex of economic wants, intellectual needs, and political ambitions. It is embodied in the conquests which build up empires, in the colonization which develops new lands, in the world-wide exchange of commodities and ideas which lifts the level of civilization till this movement of peoples becomes a fundamental fact of history.

Otis Mason finds that the life of a social group involves a variety of movements characterized by different ranges or scopes: (1) The daily round from bed to bed. (2) The annual round from year to year, like that of the Tunguse Orochon of Siberia who, in pursuit of various fish and game, change their residence within their territory from month to month, or the pastoral nomads who move with the

seasons from pasture to pasture. (3) Less systematic outside movements covering the tribal sphere of influence, such as journeys or
voyages to remote hunting or fishing grounds, forays or piratical
descents upon neighboring lands, eventuating usually in conquest,
expansion into border regions for occasional occupation, or colonization. (4) Participation in streams of barter or commerce. (5) And,
at a higher stage, in the great currents of human intercourse, experience, and ideas, which finally compass the world. In all this series
the narrower movement prepares for the broader, of which it constitutes at once an impulse and a part.

Civilized man is at once more and less mobile than his primitive
brother. Every advance in civilization multiplies and tightens the
bonds uniting him with his soil, makes him a sedentary instead of a
migratory being. On the other hand, every advance in civilization
is attended by the rapid clearing of the forests, by the construction
of bridges and interlacing roads, the invention of more effective
vehicles for transportation whereby intercourse increases, and the
improvement of navigation to the same end. Civilized man progressively modifies the land which he occupies, removes or reduces
obstacles to intercourse, and thereby approximates it to the open
plain. Thus far he facilitates movements. But while doing this he
also places upon the land a dense population, closely attached to the
soil, strong to resist incursion, and for economic reasons inhospitable
to any marked accession of population from without. Herein lies
the great difference between migration in empty or sparsely inhabited
regions, such as predominated when the world was young, and in the
densely populated countries of our era. As the earth grew old and
humanity multiplied, peoples themselves became the greatest barriers
to any massive migrations, till in certain countries of Europe and
Asia the historical movement has been reduced to a continual pressure, resulting in compression of population here, repression there.
Hence, though political boundaries may shift, ethnic boundaries
scarcely budge. The greatest wars of modern Europe have hardly
left a trace upon the distribution of its peoples. Only in the
Balkan Peninsula, as the frontiers of the Turkish Empire have
been forced back from the Danube, the alien Turks have with-
drawn to the shrinking territory of the Sultan and especially to
Asia Minor.

Where a population too great to be dislodged occupies the land, conquest results in the eventual absorption of the victors and their civilization by the native folk, as happened to the Lombards in Italy, the Vandals in Africa, and the Normans in England. Where the invaders are markedly superior in culture, though numerically weak, conquest results in the gradual permeation of the conquered with the religion, economic methods, language, and customs of the new-comers. The latter process, too, is always attended by some inter-mixture of blood, where no race repulsion exists, but this is small in comparison to the diffusion of civilization. This was the method by which Greek traders and colonists Hellenized the countries about the eastern Mediterranean and spread their culture far back from the shores which their settlements had appropriated. In this way Saracen armies, soon after the death of Mohammed, Arabized the whole eastern and southern sides of the Mediterranean from Syria to Spain, and Arab merchants set the stamp of their language and religion on the coasts of East Africa as far as Mozambique. The handful of Spanish adventurers who came upon the relatively dense populations of Mexico and Peru left among them a civilization essentially European, but only a thin strain of Castilian blood. Thus the immigration of small bands of people sufficed to influence the culture of that big territory known as Latin America.

Throughout the life of any people, from its fetal period in some small locality to its well-rounded adult era marked by the occupation and organization of a wide national territory, gradations in area mark gradations of development. And this is true, whether we consider the compass of their commercial exchanges, the scope of their mari-time ventures, the extent of their linguistic area, the measure of their territorial ambitions, or the range of their intellectual interests and human sympathies. From land to ethics, the rule holds good. Peoples in the lower stages of civilization have contracted spatial ideas, desire and need at a given time only a limited territory, though they may change that territory often; they think in small linear terms, have a small horizon, a small circle of contact with others, a small range of influence, only tribal sympathies; they have an exaggerated conception of their own size and importance, because their basis of comparison is fatally limited. With a mature, wide-spread people like the English or French, all this is different; they have made the earth their own, so far as possible.

Just because of this universal tendency toward the occupation of ever larger areas and the formation of vaster political aggregates, in making a sociological or political estimate of different peoples, we should never lose sight of the fact that all racial and national characteristics which operate toward the absorption of more land and impel to political expansion are of fundamental value. A ship of state manned by such a crew has its sails set to catch the winds of the world.

Territorial expansion is always preceded by an extension of the circle of influence which a people exerts through its traders, its deep-sea fishermen, its picturesque marauders and more respectable missionaries, and earlier still by a widening of its mere geographical horizon through fortuitous or systematic exploration.

C. PRIMARY AND SECONDARY CONTACTS

1. Village Life in America (from the Diary of a Young Girl)[1]

November 21, 1852.—I am ten years old to-day, and I think I will write a journal and tell who I am and what I am doing. I have lived with my Grandfather and Grandmother Beals ever since I was seven years old, and Anna, too, since she was four. Our brothers, James and John, came too, but they are at East Bloomfield at Mr. Stephen Clark's Academy. Miss Laura Clark of Naples is their teacher.

Anna and I go to school at District No. 11. Mr. James C. Cross is our teacher, and some of the scholars say he is cross by name and cross by nature, but I like him. He gave me a book by the name of *Noble Deeds of American Women*, for reward of merit, in my reading class.

Friday.—Grandmother says I will have a great deal to answer for, because Anna looks up to me so and tries to do everything that I do and thinks whatever I say is "gospel truth." The other day the girls at school were disputing with her about something and she said, "It is so, if it ain't so, for Calline said so." I shall have to "toe the mark," as Grandfather says, if she keeps watch of me all the time and walks in my footsteps.

---

[1] Adapted from Caroline C. Richards, *Village Life in America*, pp. 21–138. (Henry Holt & Co., 1912.)

April 1, 1853.—Before I go to school every morning I read three chapters in the Bible. I read three every day and five on Sunday and that takes me through the Bible in a year. Those I read this morning were the first, second, and third chapters of Job. The first was about Eliphaz reproveth Job; second, benefit of God's correction; third, Job justifieth his complaint. I then learned a text to say at school. I went to school at quarter to nine and recited my text and we had prayers and then proceeded with the business of the day. Just before school was out, we recited in *Science of Things Familiar*, and in Dictionary, and then we had calisthenics.

July.—Hiram Goodrich, who lives at Mr. Myron H. Clark's, and George and Wirt Wheeler ran away on Sunday to seek their fortunes. When they did not come back everyone was frightened and started out to find them. They set out right after Sunday school, taking their pennies which had been given them for the contribution, and were gone several days. They were finally found at Palmyra. When asked why they had run away, one replied that he thought it was about time they saw something of the world. We heard that Mr. Clark had a few moments' private conversation with Hiram in the barn and Mr. Wheeler the same with his boys and we do not think they will go traveling on their own hook again right off. Miss Upham lives right across the street from them and she was telling little Morris Bates that he must fight the good fight of faith and he asked her if that was the fight that Wirt Wheeler fit. She probably had to make her instructions plainer after that.

1854, Sunday.—Mr. Daggett's text this morning was the twenty-second chapter of Revelation, sixteenth verse, "I am the root and offspring of David and the bright and morning star." Mrs. Judge Taylor taught our Sunday-school class today and she said we ought not to read our Sunday-school books on Sunday. I always do. Mine today was entitled, *Cheap Repository Tracts by Hannah More*, and it did not seem unreligious at all.

Tuesday.—Mrs. Judge Taylor sent for me to come over to see her today. I didn't know what she wanted, but when I got there she said she wanted to talk and pray with me on the subject of religion. She took me into one of the wings. I never had been in there before and was frightened at first, but it was nice after I got used to it. After she prayed, she asked me to, but I couldn't think of anything but "Now I lay me down to sleep," and I was afraid she would not like that, so I didn't say anything. When I got home and told Anna, she said, "Caroline, I presume probably Mrs. Taylor wants you to be a missionary, but I shan't let you go." I told her she needn't worry for I would have to stay at home and look after her. After school tonight I went out into Abbie Clark's garden with her and she taught me how to play "mumble te peg." It is fun, but rather dangerous. I am afraid Grandmother won't give me a knife to play with. Abbie Clark has beautiful pansies in her garden and gave me some roots.

Sunday.—I almost forgot that it was Sunday this morning and talked and laughed just as I do week days. Grandmother told me to write down this verse before I went to church so I would remember it: "Keep thy foot when thou goest to the house of God, and be more ready to hear than to offer the sacrifice of fools." I will remember it now, sure. My feet are all right anyway with my new patten leather shoes on, but I shall have to look out for my head. Mr. Thomas Howell read a sermon today as Mr. Daggett is out of town. Grandmother always comes upstairs to get the candle and tuck us in before she goes to bed herself, and some nights we are sound asleep and do not hear her, but last night we only pretended to be asleep. She kneeled down by the bed and prayed aloud for us, that we might be good children and that she might have strength given her from on high to guide us in the straight and narrow path which leads to life eternal. Those were her very words. After she had gone downstairs we sat up in bed and talked about it and promised each other to be good, and crossed our hearts and "hoped to die," if we broke our promise. Then Anna was afraid we would die, but I told her I didn't believe we would be as good as that, so we kissed each other and went to sleep.

Sunday.—Rev. Mr. Tousley preached today to the children and told us how many steps it took to be bad. I think he said lying was first, then disobedience to parents, breaking the Sabbath, swearing, stealing, drunkenness. I don't remember just the order they came. It was very interesting, for he told lots of stories and we sang a great many times. I should think Eddy Tousley would be an awful good boy with his father in the house with him all the while, but probably he has to be away part of the time preaching to other children.

December 20, 1855.—Susan B. Anthony is in town and spoke in Bemis Hall this afternoon. She made a special request that all the seminary girls should come to hear her as well as all the women and girls in town. She had a large audience and she talked very plainly about our rights and how we ought to stand up for them, and said the world would never go right until the women had just as much right to vote and rule as the men. She asked us all to come up and sign our names who would promise to do all in our power to bring about that glad day when equal rights would be the law of the land. A whole lot of us went up and signed the paper. When I told Grandmother about it she said she guessed Susan B. Anthony had forgotten that St. Paul said the women should keep silence. I told her no, she didn't, for she spoke particularly about St. Paul and said if he had lived in these times, instead of eighteen hundred years ago, he would have been as anxious to have the women at the head of the government as she was. I could not make Grandmother agree with her at all and she said we might better all of us stayed at home. We went to prayer meeting this evening and a woman got up and talked. Her name was Mrs. Sands. We hurried home and told Grandmother and she said she probably meant all right and she hoped we did not laugh.

February 21, 1856.—We had a very nice time at Fannie Gaylord's party and a splendid supper. Lucilla Field laughed herself almost to pieces when she found on going home that she had worn her leggins all the evening. We had a pleasant walk home but did not stay till it was out. Someone asked me if I danced every set and I told them no, I set every dance. I told Grandmother and she was very much pleased. Some one told us that Grandfather and Grandmother first met at a ball in the early settlement of Canandaigua. I asked her if it was so and she said she never danced since she became a professing Christian and that was more than fifty years ago.

May, 1856.—We were invited to Bessie Seymour's party last night and Grandmother said we could go. The girls all told us at school that they were going to wear low neck and short sleeves. We have caps on the sleeves of our best dresses and we tried to get the sleeves out, so we could go bare arms, but we couldn't get them out. We had a very nice time, though, at the party. Some of the Academy boys were there and they asked us to dance but of course we couldn't do that. We promenaded around the rooms and went out to supper with them. Eugene Stone and Tom Eddy asked to go home with us but Grandmother sent our two girls for us, Bridget Flynn and Hannah White, so they couldn't. We were quite disappointed, but perhaps she won't send for us next time.

Thursday, 1857.—We have four sperm candles in four silver candlesticks and when we have company we light them. Johnnie Thompson, son of the minister, Rev. M. L. R. P., has come to the academy to school and he is very full of fun and got acquainted with all the girls very quick. He told us this afternoon to have "the other candle lit" for he was coming down to see us this evening. Will Schley heard him say it and he said he was coming too. *Later.*—The boys came and we had a very pleasant evening but when the 9 o'clock bell rang we heard Grandfather winding up the clock and scraping up the ashes on the hearth to cover the fire so it would last till morning and we all understood the signal and they bade us good night. "We won't go home till morning" is a song that will never be sung in this house.

September, 1857.—Grandmother let Anna have six little girls here to supper to-night: Louisa Field, Hattie Paddock, Helen Coy, Martha Densmore, Emma Wheeler, and Alice Jewett. We had a splendid supper and then we played cards. I do not mean regular cards, mercy no! Grandfather thinks those kinds are contageous or outrageous or something dreadful and never keeps them in the house. Grandmother said they found a pack once, when the hired man's room was cleaned, and they went into the fire pretty quick. The kind we played was just "Dr. Busby," and another "The Old Soldier and His Dog." There are counters with them, and if you don't have the card called for you have to pay one into the pool. It is real fun. They all said they had a very nice time, indeed, when they bade Grandmother good night, and said: "Mrs. Beals, you must let Carrie and Anna come and see us some time," and she said she would. I think it is nice to have company.

August 30, 1858.—Some one told us that when Bob and Henry Antes were small boys they thought they would like to try, just for once, to see how it would seem to be bad, so in spite of all of Mr. Tousley's sermons they went out behind the barn one day and in a whisper Bob said, "I swear," and Henry said, "So do I." Then they came into the house looking guilty and quite surprised, I suppose, that they were not struck dead just as Ananias and Sapphira were for lying.

February, 1859.—Mary Wheeler came over and pierced my ears today, so I can wear my new earrings that Uncle Edward sent me. She pinched my ear until it was numb and then pulled a needle through, threaded with silk. Anna would not stay in the room. She wants hers done but does not dare. It is all the fashion for girls to cut off their hair and friz it. Anna and I have cut off ours and Bessie Seymour got me to cut off her lovely long hair today. It won't be very comfortable for us to sleep with curl papers all over our heads, but we must do it now. I wanted my new dress waist which Miss Rosewarne is making to hook up in front, but Grandmother said I would have to wear it that way all the rest of my life so I had better be content to hook it in the back a little longer. She said when Aunt Glorianna was married, in 1848, it was the fashion for grown-up women to have their waists fastened in the back, so the bride had hers made that way but she thought it was a very foolish and inconvenient fashion. It is nice, though, to dress in style and look like other people. I have a Garibaldi waist and a Zouave jacket and a balmoral skirt.

1860, Sunday.—Frankie Richardson asked me to go with her to teach a class in the colored Sunday School on Chapel Street this afternoon. I asked Grandmother if I could go and she said she never noticed that I was particularly interested in the colored race and she said she thought I only wanted an excuse to get out for a walk Sunday afternoon. However, she said I could go just this once. When we got up as far as the Academy, Mr. Noah T. Clarke's brother, who is one of the teachers, came out and Frank said he led the singing at the Sunday school and she said she would give me an introduction to him, so he walked up with us and home again. Grandmother said that when she saw him opening the gate for me, she understood my zeal in missionary work. "The dear little lady," as we often call her, has always been noted for her keen discernment and wonderful sagacity and loses none of it as she advances in years. Some one asked Anna the other day if her Grandmother retained all her faculties and Anna said, "Yes, indeed, to an alarming degree." Grandmother knows that we think she is a perfect angel even if she does seem rather strict sometimes. Whether we are seven or seventeen we are children to her just the same, and the Bible says, "Children obey your parents in the Lord for this is right." We are glad that we never will seem old to her. I had the same company home from church in the evening. His home is in Naples.

Christmas, 1860.—I asked Grandmother if Mr. Clarke could take Sunday night supper with us and she said she was afraid he did not know the catechism. I asked him Friday night and he said he would learn it on Saturday so that he could answer every third question anyway. So he did and got along very well. I think he deserves a pretty good supper.

2. Secondary Contacts and City Life[1]

Modern methods of urban transportation and communication— the electric railway, the automobile, and the telephone—have silently and rapidly changed in recent years the social and industrial organization of the modern city. They have been the means of concentrating traffic in the business districts; have changed the whole character of retail trade, multiplying the residence suburbs and making the department store possible. These changes in the industrial organization and in the distribution of population have been accompanied by corresponding changes in the habits, sentiments, and character of the urban population.

The general nature of these changes is indicated by the fact that the growth of cities has been accompanied by the substitution of indirect, "secondary," for direct, face-to-face, "primary" relations in the associations of individuals in the community.

By primary groups I mean those characterized by intimate face-to-face association and co-operation. They are primary in several senses, but chiefly in that they are fundamental in forming the social nature and ideals of the individual. The result of intimate association, psychologically, is a certain fusion of individualities in a common whole, so that one's very self, for many purposes at least, is the common life and purpose of the group. Perhaps the simplest way of describing this wholeness is by saying that it is a "we"; it involves the sort of sympathy and mutual identification for which "we" is the natural expression. One lives in the feeling of the whole and finds the chief aims of his will in that feeling.

[1] From Robert E. Park, "The City," in the *American Journal of Sociology*, XX (1914–15), 593–609.

Touch and sight, physical contact, are the basis for the first and most elementary human relationships. Mother and child, husband and wife, father and son, master and servant, kinsman and neighbor, minister, physician, and teacher—these are the most intimate and real relationships of life and in the small community they are practically inclusive.

The interactions which take place among the members of a community so constituted are immediate and unreflecting. Intercourse is carried on largely within the region of instinct and feeling. Social control arises, for the most part spontaneously, in direct response to personal influences and public sentiment. It is the result of a personal accommodation rather than the formulation of a rational and abstract principle.

In a great city, where the population is unstable, where parents and children are employed out of the house and often in distant parts of the city, where thousands of people live side by side for years without so much as a bowing acquaintance, these intimate relationships of the primary group are weakened and the moral order which rested upon them is gradually dissolved.

Under the disintegrating influences of city life most of our traditional institutions, the church, the school, and the family, have been greatly modified. The school, for example, has taken over some of the functions of the family. It is around the public school and its solicitude for the moral and physical welfare of the children that something like a new neighborhood and community spirit tends to get itself organized.

The church, on the other hand, which has lost much of its influence since the printed page has so largely taken the place of the pulpit in the interpretation of life, seems at present to be in process of readjustment to the new conditions.

It is probably the breaking down of local attachments and the weakening of the restraints and inhibitions of the primary group, under the influence of the urban environment, which are largely responsible for the increase of vice and crime in great cities. It would be interesting in this connection to determine by investigation how far the increase in crime keeps pace with the increasing mobility of the population. It is from this point of view that we should seek to interpret all those statistics which register the disintegration of the moral order, for example, the statistics of divorce, of truancy, and of crime.

Great cities have always been the melting-pots of races and of cultures. Out of the vivid and subtle interactions of which they have been the centers, there have come the newer breeds and the newer social types. The great cities of the United States, for example, have drawn from the isolation of their native villages great masses of the rural populations of Europe and America. Under the shock of the new contacts the latent energies of these primitive peoples have been released, and the subtler processes of interaction have brought into existence not merely vocational but temperamental types.

Transportation and communication have effected, among many other silent but far-reaching changes, what I have called the "mobilization of the individual man." They have multiplied the opportunities of the individual man for contact and for association with his fellows, but they have made these contacts and associations more transitory and less stable. A very large part of the populations of great cities, including those who make their homes in tenements and apartment houses, live much as people do in some great hotel, meeting but not knowing one another. The effect of this is to substitute fortuitous and casual relationship for the more intimate and permanent associations of the smaller community.

Under these circumstances the individual's status is determined to a considerable degree by conventional signs—by fashion and "front"—and the art of life is largely reduced to skating on thin surfaces and a scrupulous study of style and manners.

Not only transportation and communication, but the segregation of the urban population, tends to facilitate the mobility of the individual man. The processes of segregation establish moral distances which make the city a mosaic of little worlds which touch but do not interpenetrate. This makes it possible for individuals to pass quickly and easily from one moral milieu to another and encourages the fascinating but dangerous experiment of living at the same time in several different contiguous, perhaps, but widely separated worlds. All this tends to give to city life a superficial and adventitious character; it tends to complicate social relationships and to produce new and divergent individual types. It introduces, at the same time, an element of chance and adventure, which adds to the stimulus of city life and gives it for young and fresh nerves a peculiar attractiveness. The lure of great cities is perhaps a consequence of stimulations which act directly upon the reflexes.   As a type of human behavior it may be explained, like the attraction of the flame for the moth, as a sort of tropism.

The attraction of the metropolis is due in part, however, to the fact that in the long run every individual finds somewhere among the varied manifestations of city life the sort of environment in which he expands and feels at ease; finds, in short, the moral climate in which his peculiar nature obtains the stimulations that bring his innate qualities to full and free expression.   It is, I suspect, motives of this kind which have their basis, not in interest nor even in sentiment, but in something more fundamental and primitive which draw many, if not most, of the young men and young women from the security of their homes in the country into the big, booming confusion and excitement of city life.   In a small community it is the normal man, the man without eccentricity or genius, who seems most likely to succeed.   The small community often tolerates eccentricity.   The city, on the contrary, rewards it.   Neither the criminal, the defective, nor the genius has the same opportunity to develop his innate disposition in a small town that he invariably finds in a great city.

Fifty years ago every village had one or two eccentric characters who were treated ordinarily with a benevolent toleration, but who were regarded meanwhile as impracticable and queer.   These exceptional individuals lived an isolated existence, cut off by their very eccentricities, whether of genius or of defect, from genuinely intimate intercourse with their fellows.   If they had the making of criminals, the restraints and inhibitions of the small community rendered them harmless.   If they had the stuff of genius in them, they remained sterile for lack of appreciation or opportunity.   Mark Twain's story of *Pudd'n Head Wilson* is a description of one such obscure and unappreciated genius.   It is not so true as it was that—

> Full many a flower is born to blush unseen
> And waste its fragrance on the desert air.

Gray wrote the "Elegy in a Country Churchyard" before the existence of the modern city.

In the city many of these divergent types now find a milieu in which for good or for ill their dispositions and talents parturiate and bear fruit.

3. Publicity as a Form of Secondary Contact[1]

In contrast with the political machine, which has founded its organized action on the local, personal, and immediate interests represented by the different neighborhoods and localities, the good-government organizations, the bureaus of municipal research, and the like have sought to represent the interests of the city as a whole and have appealed to a sentiment and opinion neither local nor personal. These agencies have sought to secure efficiency and good government by the education of the voter, that is to say, by investigating and publishing the facts regarding the government.

In this way publicity has come to be a recognized form of social control, and advertising—"social advertising"—has become a profession with an elaborate technique supported by a body of special knowledge.

It is one of the characteristic phenomena of city life and of society founded on secondary relationships that advertising should have come to occupy so important a place in its economy.

In recent years every individual and organization which has had to deal with the public, that is to say, the public outside the smaller and more intimate communities of the village and small town, has come to have its press agent, who is often less an advertising man than a diplomatic man accredited to the newspapers, and through them to the world at large. Institutions like the Russell Sage Foundation, and to a less extent the General Education Board, have sought to influence public opinion directly through the medium of publicity. The Carnegie Report upon Medical Education, the Pittsburgh Survey, the Russell Sage Foundation Report on Comparative Costs of Public-School Education in the Several States, are something more than scientific reports. They are rather a high form of journalism, dealing with existing conditions critically, and seeking through the agency of publicity to bring about radical reforms. The work of the Bureau of Municipal Research in New York has had a similar

[1] From Robert E. Park, "The City," in the *American Journal of Sociology,* XX (1914–15), 604–7.

practical purpose. To these must be added the work accomplished by the child-welfare exhibits, by the social surveys undertaken in different parts of the country, and by similar propaganda in favor of public health.

As a source of social control public opinion becomes important in societies founded on secondary relationships of which great cities are a type.   In the city every social group tends to create its own milieu, and, as these conditions become fixed, the mores tend to accommodate themselves to the conditions thus created.   In secondary groups and in the city, fashion tends to take the place of custom, and public opinion rather than the mores becomes the dominant force in social control.

In any attempt to understand the nature of public opinion and its relation to social control, it is important to investigate, first of all, the agencies and devices which have come into practical use in the effort to control, enlighten, and exploit it.

The first and the most important of these is the press, that is, the daily newspaper and other forms of current literature, including books classed as current.

After the newspaper, the bureaus of research which are now springing up in all the large cities are the most interesting and the most promising devices for using publicity as a means of control.

The fruits of these investigations do not reach the public directly, but are disseminated through the medium of the press, the pulpit and other sources of popular enlightenment.

In addition to these, there are the educational campaigns in the interest of better health conditions, the child-welfare exhibits, and the numerous "social advertising" devices which are now employed, sometimes upon the initiative of private societies, sometimes upon that of popular magazines or newspapers, in order to educate the public and enlist the masses of the people in the movement for the improvement of conditions of community life.

The newspaper is the great medium of communication within the city, and it is on the basis of the information which it supplies that public opinion rests.   The first function which a newspaper supplies is that which was formerly performed by the village gossip.

In spite, however, of the industry with which newspapers pursue facts of personal intelligence and human interest, they cannot compete with the village gossips as a means of social control. For one thing, the newspaper maintains some reservations not recognized by gossip, in the matters of personal intelligence. For example, until they run for office or commit some other overt act that brings them before the public conspicuously, the private life of individual men or women is a subject that is for the newspaper taboo. It is not so with gossip, partly because in a small community no individual is so obscure that his private affairs escape observation and discussion; partly because the field is smaller. In small communities there is a perfectly amazing amount of personal information afloat among the individuals who compose them.

The absence of this in the city is what, in large part, makes the city what it is.

4. From Sentimental to Rational Attitudes[1]

I can imagine it to be of exceeding great interest to write the history of mankind from the point of view of the stranger and his influence on the trend of events. From the earliest dawn of history we may observe how communities developed in special directions, no less in important than in insignificant things, because of influences from without. Be it religion or technical inventions, good form in conduct or fashions in dress, political revolutions or stock-exchange machinery, the impetus always—or, at least, in many cases—came from strangers. It is not surprising, therefore, that in the history of the intellectual and religious growth of the bourgeois the stranger should play no small part. Throughout the whole of the Middle Ages in Europe, and to a large extent in the centuries that followed, families left their homes to set up their hearths anew in other lands. The wanderers were in the majority of cases economic agents with a strongly marked tendency toward capitalism, and they originated capitalist methods and cultivated them. Accordingly, it will be helpful to trace the interaction of migrations and the history of the capitalist spirit.

First, as to the facts themselves. Two sorts of migrations may be distinguished—those of single individuals and those of groups. In the first category must be placed the removal, of their own free will,

[1] Adapted from Werner Sombart, *The Quintessence of Capitalism*, pp. 292–307. (T. F. Unwin, Ltd., 1915.)

of a family, or it may even be of a few families, from one district or country to another. Such cases were universal. But we are chiefly concerned with those instances in which the capitalist spirit manifested itself, as we must assume it did where the immigrants were acquainted with a more complex economic system or were the founders of new industries. Take as an instance the Lombards and other Italian merchants, who in the early Middle Ages carried on business in England, France, and elsewhere. Or recall how in the Middle Ages many an industry, more especially silk weaving, that was established in any district was introduced by foreigners, and very often on a capitalist basis. "A new phase in the development of the Venetian silk industry began with the arrival of traders and silkworkers from Lucca, whereby the industry reached its zenith. The commercial element came more and more to the fore; the merchants became the organizers of production, providing the master craftsman with raw materials which he worked up." So we read in Broglio d'Ajano. We are told a similar tale about the silk industry in Genoa, which received an enormous impetus when the Berolerii began to employ craftsmen from Lucca. In 1341 what was probably the first factory for silk manufacture was erected by one Bolognino di Barghesano, of Lucca. Even in Lyons tradition asserts that Italians introduced the making of silk, and, when in the sixteenth century the industry was placed on a capitalist basis, the initiative thereto came once more from aliens. It was the same in Switzerland, where the silk industry was introduced by the Pelligari in 1685. In Austria likewise we hear the same tale.

Silk-making in these instances is but one example; there were very many others. Here one industry was introduced, there another; here it was by Frenchmen or Germans, there by Italians or Dutchmen. And always the new establishments came at the moment when the industries in question were about to become capitalistic in their organization.

Individual migrations, then, were not without influence on the economic development of society. But much more powerful was the effect of the wanderings of large groups from one land to another. From the sixteenth century onward migrations of this sort may be distinguished under three heads: (1) Jewish migrations; (2) the migration of persecuted Christians, more especially of Protestants;

and (3) the colonizing movement, particularly the settlement in America.

We come, then, to the general question, Is it not a fact that the "stranger," the immigrant, was possessed of a specially developed capitalist spirit, and this quite apart from his environment, and, to a lesser degree, his religion or his nationality? We see it in the old states of Europe no less than in the new settlements beyond; in Jews and Gentiles alike; in Protestants and Catholics (the French in Louisiana were, by the middle of the nineteenth century, not a whit behind the Anglo-Saxons of the New England states in this respect). The assumption therefore forces itself upon us that this particular social condition—migration or change of habitat—was responsible for the unfolding of the capitalist spirit. Let us attempt to show how.

If we are content to find it in a single cause, it would be the breach with all old ways of life and all old social relationships. Indeed, the psychology of the stranger in a new land may easily be explained by reference to this one supreme fact. His clan, his country, his people, his state, no matter how deeply he was rooted in them, have now ceased to be realities for him. His first aim is to make profit. How could it be otherwise? There is nothing else open to him. In the old country he was excluded from playing his part in public life; in the colony of his choice there is no public life to speak of. Neither can he devote himself to a life of comfortable, slothful ease; the new lands have little comfort. Nor is the newcomer moved by sentiment. His environment means nothing to him. At best he regards it as a means to an end—to make a living. All this must surely be of great consequence for the rise of a mental outlook that cares only for gain; and who will deny that colonial activity generates it? "Our rivulets and streams turn mill wheels and bring rafts into the valleys, as they do in Scotland. But not one ballad, not a single song, reminds us that on their banks men and women live who experience the happiness of love and the pangs of separation; that under each roof in the valleys life's joys and sorrows come and go." This plaint of an American of the old days expresses my meaning; it has been noted again and again, particularly by those who visited America at the beginning of the nineteenth century. The only relationship between the Yankee and his environment is one of practical usefulness. The soil, as one of them says, is not regarded as "the mother of men, the hearth of the gods, the abiding resting-place of the past generations, but only as a means to get rich." There is nothing of "the poetry of the place" anywhere to check commercial devastations. The spire of his village is for the American like any other spire; in his eyes the newest and most gaudily painted is the most beautiful. A waterfall for him merely represents so much motive power. "What a mighty volume of water!" is, as we are assured, the usual cry of an American on seeing Niagara for the first time, and his highest praise of it is that it surpasses all other waterfalls in the world in its horsepower.

Nor has the immigrant or colonial settler a sense of the present or the past. He has only a future. Before long the possession of money becomes his one aim and ambition, for it is clear to him that by its means alone will he be able to shape that future. But how can he amass money? Surely by enterprise. His being where he is proves that he has capacities, that he can take risks; is it remarkable, then, that sooner or later his unbridled acquisitiveness will turn him into a restless capitalist undertaker? Here again we have cause and effect. He undervalues the present; he overvalues the future. Hence his activities are such as they are. Is it too much to say that even today American civilization has something of the unfinished about it, something that seems as yet to be in the making, something that turns from the present to the future?

Another characteristic of the newcomer everywhere is that there are no bounds to his enterprise. He is not held in check by personal considerations; in all his dealings he comes into contact only with strangers like himself. As we have already had occasion to point out, the first profitable trade was carried on with strangers; your own kith and kin received assistance from you. You lent out money at interest only to the stranger, as Antonio remarked to Shylock, for from the stranger you could demand more than you lent.

Nor is the stranger held in check by considerations other than personal ones. He has no traditions to respect; he is not bound by the policy of an old business. He begins with a clean slate; he has no local connections that bind him to any one spot. Is not every locality in a new country as good as every other? You therefore decide upon the one that promises most profit. As Poscher says, a man who has risked his all and left his home to cross the ocean in search of his fortune will not be likely to shrink from a small speculation if this means a change of abode. A little traveling more or less can make no difference.

So it comes about that the feverish searching after novelties manifested itself in the American character quite early. "If to live means constant movement and the coming and going of thoughts and feelings in quick succession, then the people here live a hundred lives. All is circulation, movement, and vibrating life. If one attempt fails, another follows on its heels, and before every one undertaking has been completed, the next has already been entered upon" (Chevalier). The enterprising impulse leads to speculation; and here again early observers have noticed the national trait. "Everybody speculates and no commodity escapes from the speculating rage. It is not tulip speculation this time, but speculations in cottons, real estate, banks, and railways."

One characteristic of the stranger's activity, be he a settler in a new or an old land, follows of necessity. I refer to the determination to apply the utmost rational effort in the field of economic and technical activity. The stranger must carry through plans with success because of necessity or because he cannot withstand the desire to secure his future. On the other hand, he is able to do it more easily than other folk because he is not hampered by tradition. This explains clearly enough why alien immigrants, as we have seen, furthered commercial and industrial progress wherever they came. Similarly we may thus account for the well-known fact that nowhere are technical inventions so plentiful as in America, that railway construction and the making of machinery proceed much more rapidly there than anywhere else in the world. It all comes from the peculiar conditions of the problem, conditions that have been termed colonial— great distances, dear labor, and the will to progress. The state of mind that will have, nay, must have, progress is that of the stranger, untrammeled by the past and gazing toward the future.

Yet results such as these are not achieved by strangers merely because they happen to be strangers. Place a negro in a new environment; will he build railways and invent labor-saving machines? Hardly. There must be a certain fitness; it must be in the blood. In short, other forces beside that of being merely a stranger in a strange land are bound to co-operate before the total result can be fully accounted for. There must be a process of selection, making the best types available, and the ethical and moral factor, too, counts for much. Nevertheless, the migrations themselves were a very powerful element in the growth of capitalism.

5. The Sociological Significance of the "Stranger"[1]

If wandering, considered as the liberation from every given point in space, is the conceptual opposite to fixation at such a point, then surely the sociological form of "the stranger" presents the union of both of these specifications. It discloses, indeed, the fact that relations to space are only, on the one hand, the condition, and, on the other hand, the symbol, of relations to men. The stranger is not taken here, therefore, in the sense frequently employed, of the wanderer who comes today and goes tomorrow, but rather of the man who comes today and stays tomorrow, the potential wanderer, so to speak, who, although he has gone no further, has not quite got over the freedom of coming and going. He is fixed within a certain spatial circle, but his position within it is peculiarly determined by the fact that he does not belong in it from the first, that he brings qualities into it that are not, and cannot be, native to it.

The union of nearness and remoteness, which every relation between men comprehends, has here produced a system of relations or a constellation which may, in the fewest words, be thus formulated: The distance within the relation signifies that the Near is far; the very fact of being alien, however, that the Far is near. For the state of being a stranger is naturally a quite positive relation, a particular form of interaction. The inhabitants of Sirius are not exactly strangers to us, at least not in the sociological sense of the word as we are considering it. In that sense they do not exist for us at all. They are beyond being far and near. The stranger is an element of the group itself, not otherwise than the Poor and the various "inner enemies," an element whose inherent position and membership involve both an exterior and an opposite. The manner, now, in which mutually repulsive and opposing elements here compose a form of a joint and interacting unity may now be briefly analyzed.

In the whole history of economics the stranger makes his appearance everywhere as the trader, the trader his as the stranger. As

[1] Translated from Georg Simmel, *Soziologie*, pp. 685–91. (Leipzig: Duncker und Humblot, 1908.)

long as production for one's own needs is the general rule, or products are exchanged within a relatively narrow circle, there is no need of any middleman within the group. A trader is only required with those products which are produced entirely outside of the group. Unless there are people who wander out into foreign lands to buy these necessities, in which case they are themselves "strange" merchants in this other region, the trader must be a stranger. No other has a chance for existence.

This position of the stranger is intensified in our consciousness if, instead of leaving the place of his activity, he fixes himself in it. This will be possible for him only if he can live by trade in the rôle of a middleman. Any closed economic group in which the division of the land and of the crafts which satisfy the local demands has been achieved will still grant an existence to the trader. For trade alone makes possible unlimited combinations, in which intelligence finds ever wider extensions and ever newer accessions, a thing rarely possible in the case of the primitive producer with his lesser mobility and his restriction to a circle of customers which could only very gradually be increased. Trade can always absorb more men than primary production, and it is therefore the most favorable province for the stranger, who thrusts himself, so to speak, as a supernumerary into a group in which all the economic positions are already possessed. History offers as the classic illustration the European Jew. The stranger is by his very nature no landowner—in saying which, land is taken not merely in a physical sense but also in a metaphorical one of a permanent and a substantial existence, which is fixed, if not in space, then at least in an ideal position within the social order. The special sociological characteristics of the stranger may now be presented.

a) Mobility.—In the more intimate relations of man to man, the stranger may disclose all possible attractions and significant characters, but just as long as he is regarded as a stranger, he is in so far no landowner. Now restriction to trade, and frequently to pure finance, as if by a sublimation from the former, gives the stranger the specific character of mobility. With this mobility, when it occurs within a limited group, there occurs that synthesis of nearness and remoteness which constitutes the formal position of the stranger; for the merely mobile comes incidentally into contact with every single element but is not bound up organically, through the established ties of kinship, locality, or profession, with any single one.

b) *Objectivity.*—Another expression for this relation lies in the objectivity of the stranger. Because he is not rooted in the peculiar attitudes and biased tendencies of the group, he stands apart from all these with the peculiar attitude of the "objective," which does not indicate simply a separation and disinterestedness but is a peculiar composition of nearness and remoteness, concern and indifference. I call attention to the domineering positions of the stranger to the group, as whose archtype appeared that practice of Italian cities of calling their judges from without, because no native was free from the prejudices of family interests and factions.

c) *Confidant.*—With the objectivity of the stranger is connected the phenomenon which indeed belongs chiefly, but not indeed exclusively, to the mobile man: namely, that often the most surprising disclosures and confessions, even to the character of the confessional disclosure, are brought to him, secrets such as one carefully conceals from every intimate. Objectivity is by no means lack of sympathy, for that is something quite outside and beyond either subjective or objective relations. It is rather a positive and particular manner of sympathy. So the objectivity of a theoretical observation certainly does not mean that the spirit is a *tabula rasa* on which things inscribe their qualities, but it means the full activity of a spirit working according to its own laws, under conditions in which accidental dislocations and accentuations have been excluded, the individual and subjective peculiarities of which would give quite different pictures of the same object.

d) *Freedom from convention.*—One can define objectivity also as freedom. The objective man is bound by no sort of proprieties which can prejudice for him his apprehension, his understanding, his judgment of the given. This freedom which permits the stranger to experience and deal with the relation of nearness as though from a bird's-eye view, contains indeed all sorts of dangerous possibilities. From the beginnings of things, in revolutions of all sorts, the attacked party has claimed that there has been incitement from without, through foreign emissaries and agitators. As far as that is concerned, it is simply an exaggeration of the specific rôle of the stranger; he is the freer man, practically and theoretically; he examines the relations with less prejudice; he submits them to more general, more objective, standards, and is not confined in his action by custom, piety, or precedents.

e) Abstract relations.—Finally, the proportion of nearness and remoteness which gives the stranger the character of objectivity gets another practical expression in the more abstract nature of the relation to him. This is seen in the fact that one has certain more general qualities only in common with the stranger, whereas the relation with those organically allied is based on the similarity of just those specific differences by which the members of an intimate group are distinguished from those who do not share that intimacy. All personal relations whatsoever are determined according to this scheme, however varied the form which they assume. What is decisive is not the fact that certain common characteristics exist side by side with individual differences which may or may not affect them but rather that the influence of this common possession itself upon the personal relation of the individuals involved is determined by certain conditions: Does it exist in and for these individuals and for these only? Does it represent qualities that are general in the group, to be sure, but peculiar to it? Or is it merely felt by the members of the group as something peculiar to individuals themselves whereas, in fact, it is a common possession of a group, or a type, or mankind? In the last case an attenuation of the effect of the common possession enters in, proportional to the size of the group. Common characteristics function, it is true, as a basis for union among the elements, but it does not specifically refer these elements to each other. A similarity so widely shared might serve as a common basis of each with every possible other. This too is evidently one way in which a relation may at the same moment comprehend both nearness and remoteness. To the extent to which the similarities become general, the warmth of the connection which they effect will have an element of coolness, a feeling in it of the adventitiousness of this very connection. The powers which united have lost their specific, centripetal character.

This constellation (in which similarities are shared by large numbers) acquires, it seems to me, an extraordinary and fundamental preponderance—as against the individual and personal elements we have been discussing—in defining our relation to the stranger. The stranger is near to us in so far as we feel between him and ourselves similarities of nationality or social position, of profession or of general human nature. He is far from us in so far as these similarities reach out over him and us, and only ally us both because in fact they ally a great many.

In this sense a trait of this strangeness easily comes into even the most intimate relations. Erotic relations show a very decided aversion, in the stage of first passion, to any disposition to think of them in general terms. A love such as this (so the lover feels) has never existed before, nor is there anything to be compared with our passion for the beloved person. An estrangement is wont, whether as cause or as result it is difficult to decide, to set in at that moment in which the sentiment of uniqueness disappears from the connection. A scepticism of its value in itself and for us fastens itself to the very thought that after all one has only drawn the lot of general humanity, one has experienced a thousand times re-enacted adventure, and that, if one had not accidentally encountered this precise person, any other one would have acquired the same meaning for us. And something of this cannot fail to be present in any relation, be it ever so intimate, because that which is common to the two is perhaps never common only to them but belongs to a general conception, which includes much else, many possibilities of similarities. As little actuality as they may have, often as we may forget them, yet here and there they crowd in like shadows between men, like a mist gliding before every word's meaning, which must actually congeal into solid corporeality in order to be called rivalry. Perhaps this is in many cases a more general, at least more insurmountable, strangeness than that afforded by differences and incomprehensibilities. There is a feeling, indeed, that these are actually not the peculiar property of just that relation but of a more general one that potentially refers to us and to an uncertain number of others, and therefore the relation experienced has no inner and final necessity.

On the other hand, there is a sort of strangeness, in which this very connection on the basis of a general quality embracing the parties is precluded. The relation of the Greeks to the Barbarians is a typical example; so are all the cases in which the general characteristics which one takes as peculiarly and merely human are disallowed to the other. But here the expression "the stranger" has no longer any positive meaning. The relation with him is a non-relation. He is not a member of the group itself. As such he is much more to be considered as near and far at the same moment, seeing that the foundation of the relation is now laid simply on a general human similarity. Between these two elements there occurs, however, a peculiar tension, since the consciousness of having only the absolutely general in common has exactly the effect of bringing into particular emphasis that which is not common. In the case of strangers according to country, city, or race, the individual characteristics of the person are not perceived; but attention is directed to his alien extraction which he has in common with all the members of his group. Therefore the strangers are perceived, not indeed as individuals, but chiefly as strangers of a certain type. Their remoteness is no less general than their nearness.

With all his inorganic adjacency, the stranger is yet an organic member of the group, whose uniform life is limited by the peculiar dependence upon this element. Only we do not know how to designate the characteristic unity of this position otherwise than by saying that it is put together of certain amounts of nearness and of remoteness, which, characterizing in some measure any sort of relation, determine in a certain proportion and with characteristic mutual tension the specific, formal relation of "the stranger."

III. INVESTIGATIONS AND PROBLEMS

1. Physical Contacts

The literature of the research upon social contacts falls naturally under four heads: physical contacts, sensory contacts, primary contacts, and secondary contacts.

The reaction of the person to contacts with things as contrasted with his contacts with persons is an interesting chapter in social psychology. Observation upon children shows that the individual tends to respond to inanimate objects, particularly if they are unfamiliar, as if they were living and social. The study of animism among primitive peoples indicates that their attitude toward certain animals whom they regarded as superior social beings is a specialization of this response. A survey of the poetry of all times and races discloses that nature to the poet as well as to the mystic is personal.

Homesickness and nostalgia are an indication of the personal and intimate nature of the relation of man to the physical world.

It seems to be part of man's original nature to take the world socially and personally. It is only as things become familiar and controllable that he gains the concept of mechanism. It is natural science and machinery that has made so large a part of the world impersonal for most of us.

The scientific study of the actual reaction of persons and groups to their physical environment is still in the pioneer stage. The anthropogeographers have made many brilliant suggestions and a few careful and critical studies of the direct and indirect effects of the physical environment not merely upon man's social and political organization but upon his temperament and conduct. Huntington's suggestive observations upon the effect of climate upon manners and efficiency have opened a wide field for investigation.[1]

Interest is growing in the psychology and sociology of the responses of individuals and groups to the physical conditions of their environment. Communities, large and small in this country, as they become civic conscious, have devised city plans. New York has made an elaborate report on the zoning of the city into business, industrial, and residential areas. A host of housing surveys present realistic pictures of actual conditions of physical existence from the standpoint of the hygienic and social effects of low standards of dwelling, overcrowding, the problem of the roomer. Even historic accounts and impressionistic observations of art and ornament, decoration and dress, indicate the relation of these material trappings to the self-consciousness of the individual in his social milieu.

The reservation must be made that studies of zoning, city planning, and housing have taken account of economic, aesthetic, and hygienic factors rather than those of contacts. Implicit, however, in certain aspects of these studies, certainly present often as an unconscious motive, has been an appreciation of the effects of the urban, artificial physical environment upon the responses and the very nature of plastic human beings, creatures more than creators of the modern leviathan, the Great City.

Glimpses into the nature and process of these subtle effects appear only infrequently in formal research. Occasionally such a book as *The*

[1] Ellsworth Huntington, *Climate and Civilization.* (New Haven, 1915.)

Spirit of Youth and the City Streets by Jane Addams throws a flood of light upon the contrasts between the warmth, the sincerity, and the wholesomeness of primary human responses and the sophistication, the coldness, and the moral dangers of the secondary organization of urban life.

A sociological study of the effect of the artificial physical and social environment of the city upon the person will take conscious account of these social factors. The lack of attachment to home in the city tenant as compared with the sentiments and status of home-ownership in the village, the mobility of the urban dweller in his necessary routine of work and his restless quest for pleasure, the sophistication, the front, the self-seeking of the individual emancipated from the controls of the primary group—all these present problems for research.

There are occasional references in literature to what may be called the inversion of the natural attitudes of the city child. His attention, his responses, even his images become fixed by the stimuli of the city streets.[1] To those interested in child welfare and human values this is the supreme tragedy of the city.

2. Touch and the Primary Contacts of Intimacy

The study of the senses in their relations to personal and social behavior had its origins in psychology, in psychoanalysis, in ethnology, and in the study of races and nationalities with reference to the conflict and fusion of cultures. Darwin's theory of the origin of the species increased interest in the instincts and it was the study of the instincts that led psychologists finally to define all forms of behavior in terms of stimulus and response. A "contact" is simply a stimulation that has significance for the understanding of group behavior.

In psychoanalysis, a rapidly growing literature is accessible to sociologists upon the nature and the effects of the intimate contacts of sex and family life. Indeed, the Freudian concept of the *libido* may be translated for sociological purposes into the desire for response.

---

[1] The following is one of the typical illustrations of this point. An art teacher conducted a group of children from a settlement, in a squalid city area, to the country. She asked the children to draw any object they wished. On examination of the drawings she was astonished to find not rural scenes but pictures of the city streets, as lamp-posts and smokestacks.

The intensity of the sentiments of love and hate that cement and disrupt the family is indicated in the analyses of the so-called "family romance." Life histories reveal the natural tendencies toward reciprocal affection of mother and son or father and daughter, and the mutual antagonism of father and son or mother and daughter.

In ethnology, attention was early directed to the phenomena of taboo with its injunction against contamination by contacts. The literature of primitive communities is replete with the facts of avoidance of contact, as between the sexes, between mother-in-law and son-in-law, with persons "with the evil eye," etc. Frazer's volume on "Taboo and the Perils of the Soul" in his series entitled *The Golden Bough*, and Crawley, in his book, *The Mystic Rose*, to mention two outstanding examples, have assembled, classified, and interpreted many types of taboo. In the literature of taboo is found also the ritualistic distinction between "the clean" and "the unclean" and the development of reverence and awe toward "the sacred" and "the holy."

Recent studies of the conflict of races and nationalities, generally considered as exclusively economic or political in nature, bring out the significance of disgusts and fears based fundamentally upon characteristic racial odors, marked variations in skin color and in physiognomy as well as upon differences in food habits, personal conduct, folkways, mores, and culture.

3. Primary Contacts of Acquaintanceship

Two of the best sociological statements of primary contacts are to be found in Professor Cooley's analysis of primary groups in his book *Social Organization* and in Shaler's exposition of the sympathetic way of approach in his volume *The Neighbor*. A mass of descriptive material for the further study of the primary contacts is available from many sources. Studies of primitive peoples indicate that early social organizations were based upon ties of kinship and primary group contacts. Village life in all ages and with all races exhibits absolute standards and stringent primary controls of behavior. The Blue Laws of Connecticut are little else than primary-group attitudes written into law. Common law, the traditional code of legal conduct sanctioned by the experience of primary groups, may be compared with statute law, which is an abstract prescription for social life in secondary societies. Here also should be included the consideration of programs and projects for community organization upon the basis of primary contacts, as for example, Ward's *The Social Center*.

4. Secondary Contacts

The transition from feudal societies of villages and towns to our modern world-society of great cosmopolitan cities has received more attention from economics and politics than from sociology. Studies of the industrial basis of city life have given us the external pattern of the city: its topographical conditions, the concentration of population as an outcome of large-scale production, division of labor, and specialization of effort. Research in municipal government has proceeded from the muck-raking period, indicated by Lincoln Steffens' *The Shame of the Cities*, to surveys of public utilities and city administration of the type of those made by the New York Bureau of Municipal Research.

Social interest in the city was first stimulated by the polemics against the political and social disorders of urban life. There were those who would destroy the city in order to remedy its evils and restore the simple life of the country. Sociology sought a surer basis for the solution of the problems from a study of the facts of city life. Statistics of population by governmental departments provide figures upon conditions and tendencies. Community surveys have translated into understandable form a mass of information about the formal aspects of city life.

Naturally enough, sympathetic and arresting pictures of city life have come from residents of settlements as in Jane Addam's *Twenty Years at Hull House*, Robert Woods's *The City Wilderness*, Lillian Wald's *The House on Henry Street* and Mrs. Simkhovitch's *The City Worker's World*. Georg Simmel has made the one outstanding contribution to a sociology or, perhaps better, a social philosophy of the city in his paper "The Great City and Cultural Life."

BIBLIOGRAPHY: MATERIALS FOR THE STUDY OF SOCIAL CONTACTS

I.   THE NATURE AND IMPORTANCE OF SOCIAL CONTACTS

(1) Small, Albion W. *General Sociology.* An exposition of the main development in sociological theory from Spencer to Ratzenhofer, pp. 486–91. Chicago, 1905.

(2) Tarde, Gabriel. *The Laws of Imitation.* Translated from the French by Elsie Clews Parsons. Chap. iii, "What Is a Society?" New York, 1903.

(3) Thomas, W. I. "Race Psychology: Standpoint and Questionnaire, with Particular Reference to the Immigrant and the Negro," *American Journal of Sociology,* XVII (May, 1912), 725–75.

(4) Boas, Franz. *The Mind of Primitive Man.* New York, 1911.

(5) Weber, Max. *Gesammelte Aufsätze zur Wissenschaftslehre.* "Ueber einige Kategorien der verstehenden Soziologie," pp. 403–50. Tübingen, 1922.

(6) Bullough, Edward. " 'Psychical Distance' as a Factor in Art and an Aesthetic Principle," *The British Journal of Psychology,* V (1912–13), 87–118.

II.   INTIMATE SOCIAL CONTACTS AND THE SOCIOLOGY OF THE SENSES

(1) Simmel, Georg. *Soziologie.* Untersuchungen über die Formen der Vergesellschaftung. Exkurs über die Soziologie der Sinne, pp. 646–65. Leipzig, 1908.

(2) Crawley, E. *The Mystic Rose.* A study of primitive marriage. London and New York, 1902.

(3) Sully, James. *Sensation and Intuition.* Studies in psychology and aesthetics. Chap. iv, "Belief: Its Varieties and Its Conditions." London, 1874.

(4) Hudson, William H. *A Hind in Richmond Park.* (Chaps. vi–viii, pp. 72–117, discuss the sociological significance of smell.) New York, 1923.

(5) Moll, Albert. *Der Rapport in der Hypnose.* Leipzig, 1892.

(6) Elworthy, F. T. *The Evil Eye.* An account of this ancient and widespread superstition. London, 1895.

(7) Lévy-Bruhl, L. *Les fonctions mentales dans les sociétés inférieures.* Paris, 1910.

(8) Starbuck, Edwin D. "The Intimate Senses as Sources of Wisdom," *The Journal of Religion,* I (March, 1921), 129–45.

(9) Paulhan, Fr. *Les transformations sociales des sentiments.* Paris, 1920.

(10) Stoll, O. *Suggestion und Hypnotismus in der Völkerpsychologie.* Chap. ix, pp. 225–29. Leipzig, 1904.

(11) Hooper, Charles E. *Common Sense.* An analysis and interpretation. Being a discussion of its general character, its distinction from discursive reasoning, its origin in mental imagery, its speculative outlook, its value for practical life and social well-being, its relation to scientific knowledge, and its bearings on the problems of natural and rational causation. London, 1913.

(12) Weigall, A. "The Influence of the Kinematograph upon National Life," *Nineteenth Century and After*, LXXXIX (April, 1921), 661–72.

III. MATERIALS FOR THE STUDY OF MOBILITY

(1) Vallaux, Camille. "Le sol et l'état," *Geographie sociale*. Paris, 1911.

(2) Demolins, Edmond. *Comment la route crée le type social*. Les grandes routes des peuples: essai de géographie social. 2 vols. Paris, 1901.

(3) Vandervelde, É. *L'exode rural et le retour aux champs*. Chap. iv, "Les conséquences de l'exode rural." (Sec. 3 discusses the political and intellectual, the physical and moral consequences of the rural exodus, pp. 202–13.) Paris, 1903.

(4) Bury, J. B. *A History of Freedom of Thought*. London and New York, 1913.

(5) Bloch, Iwan. *Die Prostitution*. Handbuch der gesamten Sexualwissenschaft in Einzeldarstellungen. Berlin, 1912.

(6) Pagnier, Armand. *Du vagabondage et des vagabonds*. Étude psychologique, sociologique et médico-légale. Lyon, 1906.

(7) Laubach, Frank C. *Why There Are Vagrants*. A study based upon an examination of one hundred men. New York, 1916.

(8) Ribton-Turner, Charles J. *A History of Vagrants and Vagrancy and Beggars and Begging*. London, 1887.

(9) Florian, Eugenio. *I vagabondi*. Studio sociologicogiuridico. Parte prima, "L'Evoluzione del vagabondaggio," pp. 1–124. Torino, 1897–1900.

(10) Devine, Edward T. "The Shiftless and Floating City Population," *Annals of the American Academy of Political and Social Science*, X (September, 1897), 149–164.

(11) Anderson, Nels. *The Hobo*. The sociology of the homeless man. Chicago, 1923.

IV. SOCIAL CONTACTS IN PRIMARY GROUPS

(1) Sumner, Wm. G. *Folkways*. A study of the sociological importance of usages, manners, customs, mores, and morals. "The In-Group and the Out-Group," pp. 12–16. Boston, 1906.

(2) Crothers, Samuel M. *The Book of Friendship*. New York, 1922.

(3) Vierkandt, Alfred. *Naturvölker und Kulturvölker*. Ein Beitrag zur Socialpsychologie. Leipzig, 1896.

(4) Pandian, T. B. *Indian Village Folk*. Their works and ways. London, 1897.

(5) Dobschütz, Ernst von. *Die urchristlichen Gemeinden*. Sittengeschichtliche Bilder. Leipzig, 1902.

(6) Kautsky, Karl. *Communism in Central Europe in the Time of the Reformation*. Translated by J. L. and E. G. Mulliken. London, 1897.

(7) Hupka, S. von. *Entwicklung der westgalizischen Dorfzustände in der 2. Hälfte des 19. Jahrhunderts, verfolgt in einem Dörferkomplex*. Zürich, 1910.

(8) Wallace, D. Mackenzie. *Russia*. Chaps. vi, vii, viii, and ix. New York, 1905.

(9) Ditchfield, P. H. *Old Village Life, or, Glimpses of Village Life through All Ages*. New York, 1920.

(10) Smith, Arthur H. *Village Life in China*. A study in sociology. New York, 1899.

(11) Hammond, John L., and Hammond, Barbara. *The Village Labourer, 1760–1832*. A study in the government of England before the reform bill. London, 1911.

(12) *The Blue Laws of Connecticut*. A collection of the earliest statutes and judicial proceedings of that colony, being an exhibition of the rigorous morals and legislation of the Puritans. Edited with an introduction by Samuel M. Schmucker. Philadelphia, 1861.

(13) Nordhoff, C. *The Communistic Societies of the United States*. From personal visit and observation. Including detailed accounts of the Economists, Zoarites, Shakers, the Amana, Oneida, Bethel, Aurora, Icarian, and other existing societies, their religious creeds, social practices, numbers, industries, and present condition. New York, 1875.

(14) Hinds, William A. *American Communities and Co-operative Colonies*. 2d rev. ed. Chicago, 1908. [Contains notices of 144 communities in the United States.]

(15) L'Houet, A. *Zur Psychologie des Bauerntums*. Ein Beitrag. Tübingen, 1905.

(16) Pennington, Patience. *A Woman Rice-Planter*. New York, 1913.

(17) Smedes, Susan D. *A Southern Planter*. London, 1889.

(18) Sims, Newell L. *The Rural Community, Ancient and Modern*. Chap. iv, "The Disintegration of the Village Community." New York, 1920.

(19) Anderson, Wilbert L. *The Country Town*. A study of rural evolution. New York, 1906.

(20) Zola, Émile. *La Terre*. Paris, 1907. [Romance.]

V. SOCIAL CONTACTS IN SECONDARY GROUPS

(1) Weber, Adna Ferrin. *The Growth of Cities in the Nineteenth Century*. A study in statistics. New York, 1899.

(2) Preuss, Hugo. *Die Entwicklung des deutschen Städtewesens*. I Band. Leipzig, 1906.

(3) Burgess, Ernest W. "The Growth of the City; an Introduction to a Research Project," *Publications of the American Sociological Society*, XVIII (1923), 85–97.

(4) Green, Alice S. A. (Mrs. J. R.). *Town Life in the Fifteenth Century*. London and New York, 1894.

(5) Toynbee, Arnold. *Lectures on the Industrial Revolution of the Eighteenth Century in England*. London, 1890.

(6) Hammond, J. L., and Hammond, Barbara. *The Town Labourer, 1760–1832*. The new civilization. London, 1917.

(7) ———. *The Skilled Labourer, 1760–1832*. London, 1919. [Presents the detailed history of particular bodies of skilled workers during the great change of the Industrial Revolution.]

(8) Jastrow, J. "Die Stadtgemeinschaft in ihren kulturellen Beziehungen." (Indicates the institutions which have come into existence under conditions of urban community life.) *Zeitschrift für Socialwissenschaft*, X (1907), 42–51, 92–101. [Bibliography.]

(9) Sombart, Werner. *The Jews and Modern Capitalism.* Translated from the German by M. Epstein. London, 1913.

(10) ———. *The Quintessence of Capitalism.* A study of the history and psychology of the modern business man. Translated from the German by M. Epstein. New York, 1915.

(11) Pound, Arthur. *The Iron Man in Industry.* An outline of the social significance of automatic machinery. Boston, 1922.

(12) Spengler, Oswald. *Der Untergang des Abendlandes.* Umrisse einer Morphologie der Weltgeschichte. Vol. II, chap. ii, "Städte und Völker," pp. 100–224. München, 1922.

(13) Wallas, Graham. *The. Great Society.* A psychological analysis. New York, 1914.

(14) Booth, Charles. *Life and Labour of the People in London.* V, East London, chap. ii, "The Docks." III, chap. iv, "Influx of Population." London, 1892.

(15) Marpillero, G. "Saggio di psicologia dell'urbanismo," *Rivista italiana di sociologia*, XII (1908), 599–626.

(16) Besant, Walter. *East London.* London and New York, 1901.

(17) *The Pittsburgh Survey—the Pittsburgh District.* Robert A. Woods, "Pittsburgh, an Interpretation." Allen T. Burns, "Coalition of Pittsburgh Coal Fields." New York, 1914.

(18) *Hull House Maps and Papers.* A presentation of nationalities and wages in a congested district of Chicago, together with comments and essays on problems growing out of the social conditions. New York, 1895.

(19) Addams, Jane. *Twenty Years at Hull House.* With autobiographical notes. New York, 1910.

(20) ———. *The Spirit of Youth and the City Streets.* New York, 1909.

(21) Simkhovitch, Mary K. *The City Worker's World in America.* New York, 1917.

(22) Park, R. E., and Miller, H. A. *Old World Traits Transplanted.* New York, 1921.

(23) Park, Robert E. *The Immigrant Press and Its Control.* New York, 1922.

(24) Steiner, J. F. *The Japanese Invasion.* A study in the psychology of inter-racial contacts. Chicago, 1917.

(25) Thomas, W. I., and Znaniecki, F. *The Polish Peasant in Europe and America.* Monograph of an immigrant group. Vol. IV. Boston, 1918.

(26) Park, Robert E. "Magic, Mentality, and City Life," *Publications of the American Sociological Society*, XVIII (1923), 102–15.

[See also bibliography, "Personal Documents," pp. 781–82.]

TOPICS FOR WRITTEN THEMES

1. The Land as the Basis for Social Contacts
2. Density of Population, Social Contacts and Social Organization
3. Mobility and Social Types, as the Gypsy, the Nomad, the Hobo, the Pioneer, the Commercial Traveler, the Missionary, the Globe-Trotter, the Wandering Jew
4. Stability and Social Types, as the Farmer, the Home-Owner, the Business Man
5. Sensory Experience and Human Behavior. Nostalgia (Homesickness)
6. Race Prejudice and Primary Contacts
7. Taboo and Social Contact
8. Social Contacts in a Primary Group, as the Family, the Play Group, the Neighborhood, the Village
9. Social Control in Primary Groups
10. The Substitution of Secondary for Primary Contacts as the Cause of Social Problems, as Poverty, Crime, Prostitution, etc.
11. Control of Problems through Secondary Contacts, as Charity Organization Society, Social Service Registration Bureau, Police Department, Morals Court, Publicity through the Press, etc.
12. The Industrial Revolution and the Great Society
13. Attempts to Revive Primary Groups in the City, as the Social Center, the Settlement, the Social Unit Experiment, etc.
14. Attempts to Restore Primary Contacts between Employer and Employee
15. The Anonymity of the Newspaper
16. Standardization and Impersonality of the Great Society
17. The Sociology of the Stranger; a Study of the Revivalist, the Expert, the Genius, the Trader

QUESTIONS FOR DISCUSSION

1. What do you understand by the term contact?
2. What are the ways in which geographic conditions influence social contacts?
3. What are the differences in contact with the land between primitive and modern peoples?
4. In what ways do increasing social contacts affect contacts with the soil? Give concrete illustrations.
5. What is the social significance of touch as compared with that of the other senses?
6. In what sense is touch a social contact?
7. By what principle do you explain desire or aversion for contact?

8. Give illustrations indicating the significance of touch in various fields of social life.

9. How do you explain the impulse to touch objects which attract attention?

10. What are the differences in contacts within and without the group in primitive society?

11. In what way do external relations affect the contacts within the group?

12. Give illustrations of group egotism or ethnocentrism.

13. To what extent does the dependence of the solidarity of the in-group upon its relations with the out-groups have a bearing upon present international relations?

14. To what extent is the social control of the immigrant dependent upon the maintenance of the solidarity of the immigrant group?

15. What are our reactions upon meeting a person? a friend? a stranger?

16. What do you understand Shaler to mean by the statement that "at the beginning of any acquaintance the fellow-being is evidently dealt with in the categoric way"?

17. How far is "the sympathetic way of approach" practical in human relations?

18. What is the difference in the basis of continuity between animal and human society?

19. What types of social contacts make for historical continuity?

20. What are the differences of social contacts in the movements of primitive and civilized peoples?

21. To what extent is civilization dependent upon increasing contacts and intimacy of contacts?

22. Does mobility always mean increasing contacts?

23. Under what conditions does mobility contribute to the increase of experience?

24. Does the hobo get more experience than the schoolboy?

25. Contrast the advantages and limitations of historical continuity and of mobility.

26. What do you understand by a primary group?

27. Are primary contacts limited to members of face-to-face groups?

28. What attitudes and relations characterize village life?

29. Interpret sociologically the control by the group of the behavior of the individual in a rural community.

30. Why has the growth of the city resulted in the substitution of secondary for primary social contacts?

31. What problems grow out of the breakdown of primary relations? What problems are solved by the breakdown of primary relations?

32. Do the contacts of city life make for the development of individuality? personality? social types?

33. In what ways does publicity function as a form of secondary contact in American life?

34. Why does the European peasant first become a reader of newspapers after his immigration to the United States?

35. Why does the shift from country to city involve a change (a) from concrete to abstract relations; (b) from absolute to relative standards of life; (c) from personal to impersonal relations; and (d) from sentimental to rational attitudes?

36. How far is social solidarity based upon concrete and sentimental rather than upon abstract and rational relations?

37. Why does immigration make for change from sentimental to rational attitudes toward life?

38. In what way is capitalism associated with the growth of secondary contacts?

39. How does "the stranger" include externality and intimacy?

40. In what ways would you illustrate the relation described by Simmel that combines "the near" and "the far"?

41. Why is it that "the stranger" is associated with revolutions and destructive forces in the group?

42. Why does "the stranger" have prestige?

43. In what sense is the attitude of the academic man that of "the stranger" as compared with the attitude of the practical man?

44. To what extent does the professional man have the characteristics of "the stranger"?

45. Why does the feeling of a relation as unique give it value that it loses when thought of as shared by others?

46. What would be the effect upon the problem of the relation of the whites and negroes in the United States of the recognition that this relation is of the same kind as that which exists between other races in similar situations?

CHAPTER VI

SOCIAL INTERACTION

I. INTRODUCTION

1. The Concept of Interaction

The idea of interaction is not a notion of common sense. It represents the culmination of long-continued reflection by human beings in their ceaseless effort to resolve the ancient paradox of unity in diversity, the "one" and the "many," to find law and order in the apparent chaos of physical changes and social events; and thus to find explanations for the behavior of the universe, of society, and of man.

The disposition to be curious and reflective about the physical and social universe is human enough. For men, in distinction from animals, live in a world of ideas as well as in a realm of immediate reality. This world of ideas is something more than the mirror that sense-perception offers us; something less than that ultimate reality to which it seems to be a prologue and invitation. Man, in his ambition to be master of himself and of nature, looks behind the mirror, to analyze phenomena and seek causes, in order to gain control. Science, natural science, is a research for causes, that is to say, for mechanisms, which in turn find application in technical devices, organization, and machinery, in which mankind asserts its control over physical nature and eventually over man himself. Education, in its technical aspects at least, is a device of social control, just as the printing press is an instrument that may be used for the same purpose.

Sociology, like other natural sciences, aims at prediction and control based on an investigation of the nature of man and society, and nature means here, as elsewhere in science, just those aspects of life that are determined and predictable. In order to describe man and society in terms which will reveal their nature, sociology is compelled to reduce the complexity and richness of life to the simplest terms, i.e., elements and forces. Once the concepts "elements" or "forces" have been accepted, the notion of interaction is an inevitable, logical development. In astronomy, for example, these elements are (*a*) the masses of the heavenly bodies, (*b*) their position, (*c*) the direction of their movement, and (*d*) their velocity. In sociology, these forces are institutions, tendencies, human beings, ideas, anything that embodies and expresses motives and wishes. In *principle*, and with reference to their logical character, the "forces" and "elements" in sociology may be compared with the forces and elements in any other natural science.

Ormond, in his *Foundations of Knowledge*,[1] gives an illuminating analysis of interaction as a concept which may be applied equally to the behavior of physical objects and persons.

The notion of interaction is not simple but very complex. The notion involves not simply the idea of bare collision and rebound, but something much more profound, namely, the internal modifiability of the colliding agents. Take for example the simplest possible case, that of one billiard ball striking against another. We say that the impact of one ball against another communicates motion, so that the stricken ball passes from a state of rest to one of motion, while the striking ball has experienced a change of an opposite character. But nothing is explained by this account, for if nothing happens but the communication of motion, why does it not pass through the stricken ball and leave its state unchanged? The phenomenon cannot be of this simple character, but there must be a point somewhere at which the recipient of the impulse gathers itself up, so to speak, into a knot and becomes the subject of the impulse which is thus translated into movement. We have thus movement, impact, impulse, which is translated again into activity, and outwardly the billiard ball changing from a state of rest to one of motion; or in the case of the impelling ball, from a state of motion to one of rest. Now the case of the billiard balls is one of the simpler examples of interaction. We have seen that the problem it supplies is not simple but very complex. The situation is not thinkable at all if we do not suppose the internal modifiability of the agents, and this means that these agents are able somehow to receive internally and to re-act upon impulses which are communicated externally in the form of motion or activity. The simplest form of interaction involves the supposition, therefore, of internal subject-points or their analogues from which impulsions are received and responded to.

[1] Pp. 70 and 72.

Simmel, among sociological writers, although he nowhere expressly defines the term, has employed the conception of interaction with a clear sense of its logical significance. Gumplowicz, on the other hand, has sought to define social interaction as a principle fundamental to all natural sciences, that is to say, sciences that seek to describe change in terms of a process, i.e., physics, chemistry, biology, psychology. The logical principle is the same in all these sciences; the *processes* and the *elements* are different.

2. Classification of the Materials

The material in this chapter will be considered here under three main heads: (*a*) society as interaction, (*b*) communication as the medium of interaction, and (*c*) imitation and suggestion as mechanisms of interaction.

a) Society as interaction.—Society stated in mechanistic terms reduces to interaction. A person is a member of society so long as he responds to social forces; when interaction ends, he is isolated and detached; he ceases to be a person and becomes a "lost soul." This is the reason that the limits of society are coterminous with the limits of interaction, that is, of the participation of persons in the life of society. One way of measuring the wholesome or the normal life of a person is by the sheer external fact of his membership in the social groups of the community in which his lot is cast.

Simmel has illustrated in a wide survey of concrete detail how interaction defines the group in time and space. Through contacts of historical continuity, the life of society extends backward to prehistoric eras. More potent over group behavior than contemporary discovery and invention is the control exerted by the "dead hand of the past" through the inertia of folkways and mores, through the revival of memories and sentiments and through the persistence of tradition and culture. Contacts of mobility, on the other hand, define the area of the interaction of the members of the group in space. The degree of departure from accepted ideas and modes of behavior and the extent of sympathetic approach to the strange and the novel largely depend upon the rate, the number, and the intensity of the contacts of mobility.

b) Communication as the medium of social interaction.—Each science postulates its own medium of interaction. Astronomy and physics assume a hypothetical substance, the ether. Physics has its principles of molar action and reaction; chemistry studies molecular interaction. Biology and medicine direct their research to the physiological interaction of organisms. Psychology is concerned with the behavior of the individual organism in terms of the inter- action of stimuli and responses. Sociology, as collective psychology, deals with communication. Sociologists have referred to this process as intermental stimulation and response.

The readings on communication are so arranged as to make clear the three natural levels of interaction: (x) that of the senses; (y) that of the emotions; and (z) that of sentiments and ideas.

Interaction through sense-perceptions and emotional responses may be termed the natural forms of communication since they are common to man and to animals. Simmel's interpretation of inter- action through the senses is suggestive of the subtle, unconscious, yet profound, way in which personal attitudes are formed. Not alone vision, but hearing, smell and touch exhibit in varying degrees the emotional responses of the type of appreciation. This means understanding other persons or objects on the perceptual basis.

The selections from Darwin and from Morgan upon emotional expression in animals indicate how natural expressive signs become a vehicle for communication. A prepossession for speech and ideas blinds man to the important rôle in human conduct still exerted by emotional communication, facial expression, and gesture. Blushing and laughter are peculiarly significant, because these forms of emo- tional response are distinctively human. To say that a person blushes when he is self-conscious, that he laughs when he is detached from, and superior to, and yet interested in, an occurrence means that blushing and laughter represent contrasted attitudes to a social situation. The relation of blushing and laughter to social control, as an evidence of the emotional dependence of the person upon the group, is at its apogee in adolescence.

Interaction through sensory impressions and emotional expres- sion is restricted to the communication of attitudes and feelings. The selections under the heading "Language and the Communication of Ideas" bring out the uniquely human character of speech. Con- cepts, as Max Müller insists, are the common symbols wrought out in social experience. They are more or less conventionalized, objective, and intelligible symbols that have been defined in terms of a common experience or, as the logicians say, of a universe of discourse. Every group has its own universe of discourse. In short, to use Durkheim's phrase, concepts are "collective representations."

History has been variously conceived in terms of great events, epoch-making personalities, social movements, and cultural changes. From the point of view of sociology social evolution might profitably be studied in its relation to the development and perfection of the means and technique of communication. How revolutionary was the transition from word of mouth and memory to written records! The beginnings of ancient civilization with its five independent centers in Egypt, the Euphrates River Valley, China, Mexico, and Peru appear to be inextricably bound up with the change from pictographs to writing, that is to say from symbols representing words to symbols representing sounds. The modern period began with the invention of printing and the printing press. As books became the possession of the common man the foundation was laid for experiments in democracy. From the sociological standpoint the book is an organized objective mind whose thoughts are accessible to all. The rôle of the book in social life has long been recognized but not fully appreciated. The Christian church, to be sure, regards the Bible as the word of God. The army does not question the infallibility of the Manual of Arms. Our written Constitution has been termed "the ark of the covenant." The orthodox Socialist appeals in unquestioning faith to the ponderous tomes of Marx.

World-society of today, which depends upon the almost instantaneous communication of events and opinion around the world, rests upon the invention of telegraphy and the laying of the great ocean cables. Wireless telegraphy and radio have only perfected these earlier means and render impossible a monopoly or a censorship of inter-communication between peoples. The traditional cultures, the social inheritances of ages of isolation, are now in a world-process of interaction and modification as a result of the rapidity and the impact of these modern means of the circulation of ideas and sentiments. At the present time it is so popular to malign the newspaper that few recognize the extent to which news has freed mankind from the control of political parties, social institutions, and, it may be added, from the "tyranny" of books.

c) Imitation and suggestion the mechanistic forms of interaction.—
In all forms of communication behavior changes occur, but in two
cases the processes have been analyzed, defined, and reduced to
simple terms, viz., in imitation and in suggestion.

Imitation, as the etymology of the term implies, is a process of
copying or learning. But imitation is learning only so far as it has
the character of an experiment, or trial and error. It is also obvious
that so-called "instinctive" imitation is not learning at all. Since
the results of experimental psychology have limited the field of
instinctive imitation to a few simple activities, as the tendencies to
run when others run, to laugh when others laugh, its place in human
life becomes of slight importance as compared with imitation which
involves persistent effort at reproducing standard patterns of behavior.

This human tendency, under social influences, to reproduce the
copy Stout has explained in psychological terms of attention and
interest. The interests determine the run of attention, and the
direction of attention fixes the copies to be imitated. Without in
any way discounting the psychological validity of this explanation,
or its practical value in educational application, social factors controlling interest and attention should not be disregarded. In a
primary group, social control narrowly restricts the selection of
patterns and behavior. In an isolated group the individual may
have no choice whatsoever. Then, again, attention may be determined, not by interests arising from individual capacity or aptitude,
but rather from *rapport*, that is, from interest in the prestige or in
the personal traits of the individual presenting the copy.

The relation of the somewhat complex process of imitation to the
simple method of trial and error is of significance. Learning by
imitation implies at once both identification of the person with the
individual presenting the copy and yet differentiation from him.
Through imitation we appreciate the other person. We are in
sympathy or *en rapport* with him, while at the same time we appropriate his sentiment and his technique. Ribot and Adam Smith
analyze this relation of imitation to sympathy and Hirn points out
that in art this process of internal imitation is indispensable for
aesthetic appreciation.

In this process of appreciation and learning the primitive method
of trial and error comes into the service of imitation. In a real sense

imitation is mechanical and conservative; it provides a basis for originality, but its function is to transmit, not to originate the new. On the other hand, the simple process of trial and error, a common possession of man and the animals, results in discovery and invention.

The most scientifically controlled situation for the play of suggestion is in hypnosis. An analysis of the observed facts of hypnotism will be helpful in arriving at an understanding of the mechanism of suggestion in everyday life. The essential facts of hypnotism may be briefly summarized as follows: (a) The establishment of a relation of *rapport* between the experimenter and the subject of such a nature that the latter carries out suggestions presented by the former. (b) The successful response by the subject to the suggestion is conditional upon its relation to his past experience. (c) The subject responds to his own idea of the suggestion, and not to the idea as conceived by the experimenter. A consideration of cases is sufficient to convince the student of a complete parallel between suggestion in social life with suggestion in hypnosis, so far, at least, as concerns the last two points. Wherever rapport develops between persons, as in the love of mother and son, the affection of lovers, the comradeship of intimate friends, there also arises the mechanism of the reciprocal influence of suggestion. But in normal social situations, unlike hypnotism, there may be the effect of suggestion where no rapport exists.

Herein lies the significance of the differentiation made by Bechterew between active perception and passive perception. In passive perception ideas and sentiments evading the "ego" enter the "subconscious mind" and, uncontrolled by the active perception, form organizations or complexes of "lost" memories. It thus comes about that in social situations, where no rapport exists between two persons, a suggestion may be made which, by striking the right chord of memory or by resurrecting a forgotten sentiment, may transform the life of the other, as in conversion. The area of suggestion in social life is indicated in a second paper selected from Bechterew. In later chapters upon "Social Control" and "Collective Behavior" the mechanism of suggestion in the determination of group behavior will be further considered.

Imitation and suggestion are both mechanisms of social interaction in which an individual or group is controlled by another individual or group.   The distinction between the two processes is now clear.   The characteristic mark of imitation is the tendency, under the influence of copies socially presented, to build up mechanisms of habits, sentiments, ideals, and patterns of life.   The process of suggestion, as differentiated from imitation in social interaction, is to release under the appropriate social stimuli mechanisms already organized, whether instincts, habits, or sentiments.   The other differences between imitation and suggestion grow out of this fundamental distinction.   In imitation attention is alert, now on the copy and now on the response.   In suggestion the attention is either absorbed in, or distracted from, the stimulus.   In imitation the individual is self conscious; the subject in suggestion is unconscious of his behavior.   In imitation the activity tends to reproduce the copy; in suggestion the response may be like or unlike the copy.

II.   MATERIALS

A.   SOCIETY AS INTERACTION

1.   The Mechanistic Interpretation of Society[1]

In every natural process we may observe the two essential factors which constitute it, namely, heterogeneous elements and their reciprocal interaction which we ascribe to certain natural forces.   We observe these factors in the natural process of the stars, by which the different heavenly bodies exert certain influences over each other, which we ascribe either to the force of attraction or to gravity.

"No material bond unites the planets to the sun.   The direct activity of an elementary force, the general force of attraction, holds both in an invisible connection by the elasticity of its influence."

In the chemical natural process we observe the most varied elements related to each other in the most various ways.   They attract or repulse each other.   They enter into combinations or they withdraw from them.   These are nothing but actions and interactions which we ascribe to certain forces inherent in these elements.

The vegetable and animal natural process begins, at any rate, with the contact of heterogeneous elements which we characterize as sexual cells (gametes).   They exert upon each other a reciprocal influence which sets into activity the vegetable and animal process.

[1] Translated and adapted from Ludwig Gumplowicz, *Der Rassenkampf*, pp. 158–61.   (Innsbruck: Wagnerische Univ. Buchhandlung, 1883.)

The extent to which science is permeated by the hypothesis that heterogeneous elements reacting upon each other are necessary to a natural process is best indicated by the atomic theory.

Obviously, it is conceded that the origins of all natural processes cannot better be explained than by the assumption of the existence in bodies of invisible particles, each of which has some sort of separate existence and reacts upon the others.

The entire hypothesis is only the consequence of the concept of a natural process which the observation of nature has produced in the human mind.

Even though we conceive the social process as characteristic and different from the four types of natural processes mentioned above, still there must be identified in it the two essential factors which constitute the generic conception of the natural process. And this is, in fact, what we find. The numberless human groups, which we assume as the earliest beginnings of human existence, constitute the great variety of heterogeneous ethnic elements. These have decreased with the decrease in the number of hordes and tribes. From the foregoing explanation we are bound to assume as certain that in this field we are concerned with ethnically different and heterogeneous elements.

The question now remains as to the second constitutive element of a natural process, namely, the definite interaction of these elements, and especially as to those interactions which are characterized by regularity and permanency. Of course, we must avoid analogy with the reciprocal interaction of heterogeneous elements in the domain of other natural processes. In strict conformity with the scientific method we take into consideration merely such interactions as the facts of common knowledge and actual experience offer us. Thus will we be able, happily, to formulate a principle of the reciprocal interaction of heterogeneous ethnic, or, if you will, social elements, the mathematical certainty and universality of which cannot be denied irrefutably, since it manifests itself ever and everywhere in the field of history and the living present.

This principle may be very simply stated: Every stronger ethnic or social group strives to subjugate and make serviceable to its purposes every weaker element which exists or may come within the field of its influence. This thesis of the relation of heterogeneous ethnic and social elements to each other, with all the consequences proceeding from it, contains within it the key to the solution of the entire riddle of the natural process of human history. We shall see this thesis illustrated ever and everywhere in the past and the present in the interrelations of heterogeneous ethnic and social elements and become convinced of its universal validity. In this latter relation it does not correspond at all to such natural laws, as, for example, attraction and gravitation or chemical affinity, or to the laws of vegetable and animal life. In order better to conceive of this social natural law in its general validity, we must study it in its different consequences and in the various forms which it assumes according to circumstances and conditions.

2. Social Interaction as the Definition of the Group in Time and Space[1]

Society exists wherever several individuals are in reciprocal relationship. This reciprocity arises always from specific impulses or by virtue of specific purposes. Erotic, religious, or merely associative impulses, purposes of defense or of attack, of play as well as of gain, of aid and instruction, and countless others bring it to pass that men enter into group relationships of acting for, with, against, one another; that is, men exercise an influence upon these conditions of association and are influenced by them. These reactions signify that out of the individual bearers of those occasioning impulses and purposes a unity, that is, a "society," comes into being.

An organic body is a unity because its organs are in a relationship of more intimate interchange of their energies than with any external being. A *state* is *one* because between its citizens the corresponding relationship of reciprocal influences exists. We could, indeed, not call the world *one* if each of its parts did not somehow influence every other, if anywhere the reciprocity of the influences, however mediated, were cut off. That unity, or socialization, may, according to the kind and degree of reciprocity, have very different gradations, from the ephemeral combination for a promenade to the family; from all relationships "at will" to membership in a state; from the temporary aggregation of the guests in a hotel to the intimate bond of a medieval guild.

[1] Translated from Georg Simmel, *Soziologie*, by Albion W. Small, *American Journal of Sociology*, XV (1909), 296–98; III (1898), 667–83.

Everything now which is present in the individuals—the immediate concrete locations of all historical actuality—in the nature of impulse, interest, purpose, inclination, psychical adaptability, and movement of such sort that thereupon or therefrom occurs influence upon others, or the reception of influence from them—all this I designate as the content or the material of socialization. In and of themselves, these materials with which life is filled, these motivations which impel it, are not social in their nature. Neither hunger nor love, neither labor nor religiosity, neither the technique nor the functions and results of intelligence, as they are given immediately and in their strict sense, signify socialization. On the contrary, they constitute it only when they shape the isolated side-by-sideness of the individuals into definite forms of with-and-for-one-another, which belong under the general concept of reciprocity. Socialization is thus the *form*, actualizing itself in countless various types, in which the individuals—on the basis of those interests, sensuous or ideal, momentary or permanent, conscious or unconscious, casually driving or purposefully leading—grow together into a unity, and within which these interests come to realization.

That which constitutes "society" is evidently types of reciprocal influencing. Any collection of human beings whatsoever becomes "society," not by virtue of the fact that in each of the number there is a life-content which actuates the individual as such, but only when the vitality of these contents attains the form of reciprocal influencing. Only when an influence is exerted, whether immediately or through a third party, from one upon another has society come into existence in place of a mere spatial juxtaposition or temporal contemporaneousness or succession of individuals. If, therefore, there is to be a science, the object of which is to be "society" and nothing else, it can investigate only these reciprocal influences, these kinds and forms of socialization. For everything else found within "society" and realized by means of it is not "society" itself, but merely a content which builds or is built by this form of coexistence, and which indeed only together with "society" brings into existence the real structure, "society," in the wider and usual sense.

The persistence of the group presents itself in the fact that, in spite of the departure and the change of members, the group remains identical. We say that it is the same state, the same association, the same army, which now exists that existed so and so many decades or centuries ago;

this, although no single member of the original organization remains. Here is one of the cases in which the temporal order of events presents a marked analogy with the spatial order. Out of individuals existing side by side, that is, apart from each other, a social unity is formed. The inevitable sepaiation which space places between men is nevertheless overcome by the spiritual bond between them, so that there arises an appearance of unified interexistence. In like manner the temporal separation of individuals and of generations presents their union in our conceptions as a coherent, uninterrupted whole. In the case of persons spatially separated, this unity is effected by the reciprocity maintained between them across the dividing distance. The unity of complex being means nothing else than the cohesion of elements which is produced by the reciprocal exercise of forces. In the case of temporally separated persons, however, unity cannot be effected in this manner, because reciprocity is lacking. The earlier may influence the later, but the later cannot influence the earlier. Hence the persistence of the social unity in spite of shifting membership presents a peculiar problem which is not solved by explaining how the group came to exist at a given moment.

a) Continuity by continuance of locality.—The first and most obvious element of the continuity of group unity is the continuance of the locality, of the place and soil on which the group lives. The state, still more the city, and also countless other associations, owe their unity first of all to the territory which constitutes the abiding substratum for all change of their contents. To be sure, the continuance of the locality does not of itself alone mean the continuance of the social unity, since, for instance, if the whole population of a state is driven out or enslaved by a conquering group, we speak of a changed civic group in spite of the continuance of the territory. Moreover, the unity of whose character we are speaking is psychical, and it is this psychical factor itself which makes the territorial substratum a unity. After this has once taken place, however, the locality constitutes an essential point of attachment for the further persistence of the group. But it is only one such element, for there are groups that get along without a local substratum. On the one hand, there are the very small groups, like the family, which continue precisely the same after the residence is changed. On the other hand, there are the very large groups, like that ideal community of the "republic of letters," or the other international associations in the interest of culture, or the groups conducting international commerce.

Their peculiar character comes from entire independence of all attachment to a definite locality.

b) *Continuity through blood relationship.*—In contrast with this more formal condition for the maintenance of the group is the physiological connection of the generations. Community of stock is not always enough to insure unity of coherence for a long time. In many cases the local unity must be added. The social unity of the Jews has been weakened to a marked degree since the dispersion, in spite of their physiological and confessional unity. It has become more compact in cases where a group of Jews have lived for a time in the same territory, and the efforts of the modern "Zionism" to restore Jewish unity on a larger scale calculate upon concentration in one locality. On the other hand, when other bonds of union fail, the physiological is the last recourse to which the self-maintenance of the group resorts. The more the German guilds declined, the weaker their inherent power of cohesion became, the more energetically did each guild attempt to make itself exclusive, that is, it insisted that no persons should be admitted as guildmasters except sons or sons-in-law of masters or the husbands of masters' widows.

The physiological coherence of successive generations is of incomparable significance for the maintenance of the unitary self of the group, for the special reason that the displacement of one generation by the following *does not take place all at once.* By virtue of this fact it comes about that a continuity is maintained which conducts the vast majority of the individuals who live in a given moment into the life of the next moment. The change, the disappearance and entrance of persons, affects in two contiguous moments a number relatively small compared with the number of those who remain constant. Another element of influence in this connection is the fact that human beings are not bound to a definite mating season, but that children are begotten at any time. It can never properly be asserted of a group, therefore, that at any given moment a new generation begins. The departure of the older and the entrance of the younger elements proceed so gradually and continuously that the group seems as much like a unified self as an organic body in spite of the change of its atoms.

If the change were instantaneous, it is doubtful if we should be justified in calling the group "the same" after the critical moment as before. The circumstance alone that the transition affected in a given moment only a minimum of the total life of the group makes it possible for the group to retain its selfhood through the change. We may express this schematically as follows: If the totality of individuals or other conditions of the life of the group be represented by *a, b, c, d, e;* in a later moment by *m, n, o, p, q;* we may nevertheless speak of the persistence of identical selfhood if the development takes the following course: *a, b, c, d, e—m, b, c, d, e—m, n, c, d, e— m, n, o, d, e—m, n, o, p, e—m, n, o, p, q.* In this case each stage is differentiated from the contiguous stage by only one member, and at each moment it shares the same chief elements with its neighboring moments.

c) Continuity through membership in the group.—This continuity in change of the individuals who are the vehicles of the group unity is most immediately and thoroughly visible when it rests upon procreation. The same form is found, however, in cases where this physical agency is excluded, as, for example, within the Catholic clerus. Here the continuity is secured by provision that enough persons always remain in office to initiate the neophytes. This is an extremely important sociological fact. It makes bureaucracies tenacious, and causes their character and spirit to endure in spite of all shifting of individuals. The physiological basis of self-maintenance here gives place to a psychological one. To speak exactly, the preservation of group identity in this case depends, of course, upon the amount of invariability in the vehicles of this unity, but, at all events, the whole body of members belonging in the group at any given moment only separate from the group after they have been associated with their successors long enough to assimilate the latter fully to themselves, i.e., to the spirit, the form, the tendency of the group. The immortality of the group depends upon the fact that the change is sufficiently slow and gradual.

The fact referred to by the phrase "immortality of the group" is of the greatest importance. The preservation of the identical selfhood of the group through a practically unlimited period gives to the group a significance which, *ceteris paribus*, is far superior to that of the individual. The life of the individual, with its purposes, its valuations, its force, is destined to terminate within a limited time, and to a certain extent each individual must start at the beginning. Since the life of the group has no such a priori fixed time limit, and its forms are really arranged as though they were to last forever, the group accomplishes a summation of the achievements, powers, experiences, through which it makes itself far superior to the fragmentary individual lives. Since the early Middle Ages this has been the source of the power of municipal corporations in England. Each had from the beginning the right, as Stubbs expresses it, "of perpetuating its existence by filling up vacancies as they occur." The ancient privileges were given expressly only to the burghers and their heirs. As a matter of fact, they were exercised as a right to add new members so that, whatever fate befell the members and their physical descendants, the corporation, as such, was held intact. This had to be paid for, to be sure, by the disappearance of the individual importance of the units behind their rôle as vehicles of the maintenance of the group, for the group security must suffer, the closer it is bound up with the perishable individuality of the units. On the other hand, the more anonymous and unpersonal the unit is, the more fit is he to step into the place of another, and so to insure to the group uninterrupted self-maintenance. This was the enormous advantage through which during the Wars of the Roses the Commons repulsed the previously superior power of the upper house. A battle that destroyed half the nobility of the country took also from the House of Lords one-half its force, because this is attached to the personalities. The House of Commons is in principle assured against such weakening. That estate at last got predominance which, through the equalizing of its members, demonstrated the most persistent power of group existence. This circumstance gives every group an advantage in competition with an individual.

d) Continuity through leadership.—On this account special arrangements are necessary so soon as the life of the group is intimately bound up with that of a leading, commanding individual. What dangers to the integrity of the group are concealed in this sociological form may be learned from the history of all interregnums—dangers which, of course, increase in the same ratio in which the ruler actually forms the central point of the functions through which the group preserves its unity, or, more correctly, at each moment creates its unity anew. Consequently a break between rulers may be a matter of indifference where the prince only exercises a nominal sway—"reigns, but does not govern"—while, on the other hand, we observe even in the swarm of bees that anarchy results so soon as the queen is removed. Although it is entirely false to explain this latter phenomenon by analogy of a human ruler, since the queen bee gives no orders, yet the queen occupies the middle point of the activity of the hive. By means of her antennae she is in constant communication with the workers, and so all the signals coursing through the hive pass through her. By virtue of this very fact the hive feels itself a unity, and this unity dissolves with the disappearance of the functional center.

e) Continuity through the hereditary principle.—In political groups the attempt is made to guard against all the dangers of personality, particularly those of possible intervals between the important persons, by the principle: "The king never dies." While in the early Middle Ages the tradition prevailed that when the king dies his peace dies with him, this newer principle contains provision for the self-preservation of the group. It involves an extraordinarily significant sociological conception, viz., the king is no longer king as a person, but the reverse is the case, that is, his person is only the in itself irrelevant vehicle of the abstract kingship, which is as unalterable as the group itself, of which the kingship is the apex. The group reflects its immortality upon the kingship, and the sovereign in return brings that immortality to visible expression in his own person, and by so doing reciprocally strengthens the vitality of the group. That mighty factor of social coherence which consists of loyalty of sentiment toward the reigning power might appear in very small groups in the relation of fidelity toward the person of the ruler. For large groups the definition that Stubbs once gave must certainly apply, viz.: "Loyalty is a habit of strong and faithful attachment to a person, not so much by reason of his personal character as of his official position." By becoming objectified in the deathless office, the princely principle gains a new psychological power for concentration and cohesion within the group, while the old princely principle that rested on the mere personality of the prince necessarily lost power as the size of the group increased.

f) Continuity through a material symbol.—The objectification of the coherence of the group may also do away with the personal form to such an extent that it attaches itself to a material symbol. Thus in the German lands in the Middle Ages the imperial jewels were looked upon as the visible realization of the idea of the realm and of its continuity, so that the possession of them gave to a pretender a decided advantage over all other aspirants, and this was one of the influences which evidently assisted the heir of the body of the deceased emperor in securing the succession.

In view of the destructibility of a material object, since too this disadvantage cannot be offset, as in the case of a person, by the continuity of heredity, it is very dangerous for the group to seek such a support for its self-preservation. Many a regiment has lost its coherence with the loss of its standard. Many kinds of associations have dissolved after their palladium, their storehouse, their grail, was destroyed. When, however, the social coherence is lost in this way, it is safe to say that it must have suffered serious internal disorder before, and that in this case the loss of the external symbol representing the unity of the group is itself only the symbol that the social elements have lost their coherence. When this last is not the case, the loss of the group symbol not only has no disintegrating effect but it exerts a direct integrating influence. While the symbol loses its corporeal reality, it may, as mere thought, longing, ideal, work much more powerfully, profoundly, indestructibly. We may get a good view of these two opposite influences of the forms of destruction of the group symbol upon the solidity of the group by reference to the consequences of the destruction of the Jewish temple by Titus. The hierarchal Jewish state was a thorn in the flesh of the Roman statecraft that aimed at the unity of the empire. The purpose of dissolving this state was accomplished, so far as a certain number of the Jews were concerned, by the destruction of the temple. Such was the effect with those who cared little, anyway, about this centralization. Thus the alienation of the Pauline Christians from Judaism was powerfully promoted by this event. For the Palestinian Jews, on the other hand, the breach between Judaism and the rest of the world was deepened. By this destruction of its symbol their national religious exclusiveness was heightened to desperation.

g) Continuity through group honor.—The sociological significance of honor as a form of cohesion is extraordinarily great. Through the appeal to honor, society secures from its members the kind of conduct conducive to its own preservation, particularly within the spheres of conduct intermediate between the purview of the criminal code, on the one hand, and the field of purely personal morality, on the other. By the demands upon its members contained in the group standard of honor the group preserves its unified character and its distinctness from the other groups within the same inclusive association. The essential thing is the specific idea of honor in narrow groups—family honor, officers' honor, mercantile honor, yes, even the "honor among thieves." Since the individual belongs to various groups, the individual may, at the same time, be under the demands of several sorts of honor which are independent of each other. One may preserve his mercantile honor, or his scientific honor as an investigator, who has forfeited his family honor, and vice versa; the robber may strictly observe the requirements of thieves' honor after he has violated every other; a woman may have lost her womanly honor and in every other respect be most honorable, etc. Thus honor consists in the relation of the individual to a particular circle, which in this respect manifests its separateness, its sociological distinctness, from other groups.

h) Continuity through specialized organs.—From such recourse of social self-preservation to individual persons, to a material substance, to an ideal conception, we pass now to the cases in which social persistence takes advantage of an organ composed of a number of persons. Thus a religious community embodies its coherence and its life principle in its priesthood; a political community its inner principle of union in its administrative organization, its union against foreign power in its military system; this latter in its corps of officers; every permanent union in its official head; transitory associations in their committees; political parties in their parliamentary representatives.

B.   THE NATURAL FORMS OF COMMUNICATION

1.   Sociology of the Senses: Visual Interaction[1]

It is through the medium of the senses that we perceive our fellow-men. This fact has two aspects of fundamental sociological significance: (*a*) that of appreciation, and (*b*) that of comprehension.

a) Appreciation.—Sense-impressions may induce in us affective responses of pleasure or pain, of excitement or calm, of tension or

[1] Translated and adapted from Georg Simmel, *Soziologie*, pp. 646–51. (Leipzig: Duncker und Humblot, 1908.)

relaxation, produced by the features of a person, or by the tone of his voice, or by his mere physical presence in the same room. These affective responses, however, do not enable us to understand or to define the other person. Our emotional response to the sense-image of the other leaves his real self outside.

b) Comprehension.—The sense-impression of the other person may develop in the opposite direction when it becomes the medium for understanding the other. What I see, hear, feel of him is only the bridge over which I reach his real self. The sound of the voice and its meaning, perhaps, present the clearest illustration. The speech, quite as much as the appearance, of a person, may be immediately either attractive or repulsive. On the other hand, what he says enables us to understand not only his momentary thoughts but also his inner self. The same principle applies to all sense-impressions.

The sense-impressions of any object produce in us not only emotional and aesthetic attitudes toward it but also an understanding of it. In the case of reaction to non-human objects, these two responses are, in general, widely separated. We may appreciate the emotional value of any sense-impression of an object. The fragrance of a rose, the charm of a tone, the grace of a bough swaying in the wind, is experienced as a joy engendered within the soul. On the other hand, we may desire to understand and to comprehend the rose, or the tone, or the bough. In the latter case we respond in an entirely different way, often with conscious endeavor. These two diverse reactions which are independent of each other are with human beings generally integrated into a unified response. Theoretically, our sense-impressions of a person may be directed on the one hand to an appreciation of his emotional value, or on the other to an impulsive or deliberate understanding of him. Actually, these two reactions are coexistent and inextricably interwoven as the basis of our relation to him. Of course, appreciation and comprehension develop in quite different degrees. These two diverse responses—to the tone of voice and to the meaning of the utterance; to the appearance of a person and to his individuality; to the attraction or repulsion of his personality and to the impulsive judgment upon his character as well as many times upon his grade of culture—are present in any perception in very different degrees and combinations.

Of the special sense-organs, the eye has a uniquely sociological function. The union and interaction of individuals is based upon mutual glances. This is perhaps the most direct and purest reciprocity which exists anywhere. This highest psychic reaction, however, in which the glances of eye to eye unite men, crystallizes into no objective structure; the unity which momentarily arises between two persons is present in the occasion and is dissolved in the function. So tenacious and subtle is this union that it can only be maintained by the shortest and straightest line between the eyes, and the smallest deviation from it, the slightest glance aside, completely destroys the unique character of this union. No objective trace of this relationship is left behind, as is universally found, directly or indirectly, in all other types of associations between men, as, for example, in interchange of words. The interaction of eye and eye dies in the moment in which the directness of the function is lost. But the totality of social relations of human beings, their self-assertion and self-abnegation, their intimacies and estrangements, would be changed in unpredictable ways if there occurred no glance of eye to eye. This mutual glance between persons, in distinction from the simple sight or observation of the other, signifies a wholly new and unique union between them.

The limits of this relation are to be determined by the significant fact that the glance by which the one seeks to perceive the other is itself expressive. By the glance which reveals the other, one discloses himself. By the same act in which the observer seeks to know the observed, he surrenders himself to be understood by the observer. The eye cannot take unless at the same time it gives. The eye of a person discloses his own soul when he seeks to uncover that of another. What occurs in this direct mutual glance represents the most perfect reciprocity in the entire field of human relationships.

Shame causes a person to look at the ground to avoid the glance of the other. The reason for this is certainly not only because he is thus spared the visible evidence of the way in which the other regards his painful situation, but the deeper reason is that the lowering of his glance to a certain degree prevents the other from comprehending the extent of his confusion. The glance in the eye of the other serves not only for me to know the other but also enables him to know me. Upon the line which unites the two eyes, it conveys to the other the real personality, the real attitude, and the real impulse. The "ostrich policy" has in this explanation a real justification: who does not see the other actually conceals himself in part from the observer. A person is not at all completely present to another, when the latter sees him, but only when he also sees the other.

The sociological significance of the eye has special reference to the expression of the face as the first object of vision between man and man. It is seldom clearly understood to what an extent even our practical relations depend upon mutual recognition, not only in the sense of all external characteristics, as the momentary appearance and attitude of the other, but what we know or intuitively perceive of his life, of his inner nature, of the immutability of his being, all of which colors unavoidably both our transient and our permanent relations with him. The face is the geometric chart of all these experiences. It is the symbol of all that which the individual has brought with him as the pre-condition of his life. In the face is deposited what has been precipitated from past experience as the substratum of his life, which has become crystallized into the permanent features of his face. To the extent to which we thus perceive the face of a person, there enters into social relations, in so far as it serves practical purposes, a super-practical element. It follows that a man is first known by his countenance, not by his acts. The face as a medium of expression is entirely a theoretical organ; it does not act, as the hand, the foot, the whole body; it transacts none of the internal or practical relations of the man, it only tells about him. The peculiar and important sociological art of "knowing" transmitted by the eye is determined by the fact that the countenance is the essential object of the inter-individual sight. This knowing is still somewhat different from understanding. To a certain extent, and in a highly variable degree, we know at first glance with whom we have to do. Our unconsciousness of this knowledge and its fundamental significance lies in the fact that we direct our attention from this self-evident intuition to an understanding of special features which determine our practical relations to a particular individual. But if we become conscious of this self-evident fact, then we are amazed how much we know about a person in the first glance at him. We do not obtain meaning from his expression, susceptible to analysis into individual traits. We cannot unqualifiedly say whether he is clever or stupid, good- or ill-natured, temperamental or phlegmatic. All these traits are general characteristics which he shares with unnumbered others. But what this first glance at him transmits to us cannot be analyzed or appraised into any such conceptual and expressive elements. Yet our initial impression remains ever the keynote of all later knowledge of him; it is the direct perception of his individuality which his appearance, and especially his face, discloses to our glance.

The sociological attitude of the blind is entirely different from that of the deaf-mute. For the blind, the other person is actually present only in the alternating periods of his utterance. The expression of the anxiety and unrest, the traces of all past events, exposed to view in the faces of men, escape the blind, and that may be the reason for the peaceful and calm disposition, and the unconcern toward their surroundings, which is so often observed in the blind. Indeed, the majority of the stimuli which the face presents are often puzzling; in general, what we see of a man will be interpreted by what we hear from him, while the opposite is more unusual. Therefore the one who sees, without hearing, is much more perplexed, puzzled, and worried, than the one who hears without seeing. This principle is of great importance in understanding the sociology of the modern city.

Social life in the large city as compared with the towns shows a great preponderance of occasions to *see* rather than to *hear* people. One explanation lies in the fact that the person in the town is acquainted with nearly all the people he meets. With these he exchanges a word or a glance, and their countenance represents to him not merely the visible but indeed the entire personality. Another reason of especial significance is the development of public means of transportation. Before the appearance of omnibuses, railroads, and street cars in the nineteenth century, men were not in a situation where for periods of minutes or hours they could or must look at each other without talking to one another. Modern social life increases in ever growing degree the rôle of mere visual impression which always characterizes the preponderant part of all sense relationship between man and man, and must place social attitudes and feelings upon an entirely changed basis. The greater perplexity which characterizes the person who only sees, as contrasted with the one who only hears, brings us to the problems of the emotions of modern life: the lack of orientation in the collective life, the sense of utter lonesomeness, and the feeling that the individual is surrounded on all sides by closed doors.

2. The Expression of the Emotions[1]

Actions of all kinds, if regularly accompanying any state of the mind, are at once recognized as expressive. These may consist of movements of any part of the body, as the wagging of a dog's tail, the shrugging of a man's shoulders, the erection of the hair, the exudation of perspiration, the state of the capillary circulation, labored breathing, and the use of the vocal or other sound-producing instruments. Even insects express anger, terror, jealousy, and love by their stridulation. With man the respiratory organs are of especial importance in expression, not only in a direct, but to a still higher degree in an indirect, manner.

Few points are more interesting in our present subject than the extraordinarily complex chain of events which lead to certain expressive movements. Take, for instance, the oblique eyebrows of a man suffering from grief or anxiety. When infants scream loudly from hunger or pain, the circulation is affected, and the eyes tend to become gorged with blood; consequently the muscles surrounding the eyes are strongly contracted as a protection. This action, in the course of many generations, has become firmly fixed and inherited; but when, with advancing years and culture, the habit of screaming is partially repressed, the muscles round the eyes still tend to contract, whenever even slight distress is felt. Of these muscles, the pyramidals of the nose are less under the control of the will than are the others, and their contraction can be checked only by that of the central fasciae of the frontal muscle; these latter fasciae draw up the inner ends of the eyebrows and wrinkle the forehead in a peculiar manner, which we instantly recognize as the expression of grief or anxiety. Slight movements, such as these just described, or the scarcely perceptible drawing down of the corners of the mouth, are the last remnants or rudiments of strongly marked and intelligible movements. They are as full of significance to us in regard to

[1] Adapted from Charles Darwin, *The Expression of the Emotions*, pp. 350–67. (John Murray, 1873.)

expression as are ordinary rudiments to the naturalist in the classification and genealogy of organic beings.

That the chief expressive actions exhibited by man and by the lower animals are now innate or inherited—that is, have not been learned by the individual—is admitted by everyone. So little has learning or imitation to do with several of them that they are from the earliest days and throughout life quite beyond our control; for instance, the relaxation of the arteries of the skin in blushing, and the increased action of the heart in anger. We may see children only two or three years old, and even those born blind, blushing from shame; and the naked scalp of a very young infant reddens from passion. Infants scream from pain directly after birth, and all their features then assume the same form as during subsequent years. These facts alone suffice to show that many of our most important expressions have not been learned; but it is remarkable that some, which are certainly innate, require practice in the individual before they are performed in a full and perfect manner; for instance, weeping and laughing. The inheritance of most of our expressive actions explains the fact that those born blind display them, as I hear from the Rev. R. H. Blair, equally well with those gifted with eyesight. We can thus also understand the fact that the young and the old of widely different races, both with man and animals, express the same state of mind by the same movement.

We are so familiar with the fact of young and old animals displaying their feelings in the same manner that we hardly perceive how remarkable it is that a young puppy should wag its tail when pleased, depress its ears and uncover its canine teeth when pretending to be savage, just like an old dog; or that a kitten should arch its little back and erect its hair when frightened and angry, like an old cat. When, however, we turn to less common gestures in ourselves, which we are accustomed to look at as artificial or conventional— such as shrugging the shoulders as a sign of impotence, or the raising the arms with open hands and extended fingers as a sign of wonder— we feel perhaps too much surprise at finding that they are innate. That these and some other gestures are inherited we may infer from their being performed by very young children, by those born blind, and by the most widely distinct races of man. We should also bear in mind that new and highly peculiar tricks, in association with certain states of the mind, are known to have arisen in certain individuals and to have been afterward transmitted to their offspring, in some cases for more than one generation.

Certain other gestures, which seem to us so natural that we might easily imagine that they were innate, apparently have been learned like the words of a language. This seems to be the case with the joining of the uplifted hands and the turning up of the eyes in prayer. So it is with kissing as a mark of affection; but this is innate, in so far as it depends on the pleasure derived from contact with a beloved person. The evidence with respect to the inheritance of nodding and shaking the head as signs of affirmation and negation is doubtful, for they are not universal, yet seem too general to have been independently acquired by all the individuals of so many races.

We will now consider how far the will and consciousness have come into play in the development of the various movements of expression. As far as we can judge, only a few expressive movements, such as those just referred to, are learned by each individual; that is, were consciously and voluntarily performed during the early years of life for some definite object, or in imitation of others, and then became habitual. The far greater number of the movements of expression, and all the more important ones, are, as we have seen, innate or inherited; and such cannot be said to depend on the will of the individual. Nevertheless, all those included under our first principle were at first voluntarily performed for a definite object, namely, to escape some danger, to relieve some distress, or to gratify some desire. For instance, there can hardly be a doubt that the animals which fight with their teeth have acquired the habit of drawing back their ears closely to their heads when feeling savage from their progenitors having voluntarily acted in this manner in order to protect their ears from being torn by their antagonists; for those animals which do not fight with their teeth do not thus express a savage state of mind. We may infer as highly probable that we ourselves have acquired the habit of contracting the muscles round the eyes whilst crying gently, that is, without the utterance of any loud sound, from our progenitors, especially during infancy, having experienced during the act of screaming an uncomfortable sensation in their eyeballs. Again, some highly expressive movements result from the endeavor to check or prevent other expressive movements;

thus the obliquity of the eyebrows and the drawing down of the corners of the mouth follow from the endeavor to prevent a screaming-fit from coming on or to check it after it has come on. Here it is obvious that the consciousness and will must at first have come into play; not that we are conscious in these or in other such cases what muscles are brought into action, any more than when we perform the most ordinary voluntary movements.

The power of communication between the members of the same tribe by means of language has been of paramount importance in the development of man; and the force of language is much aided by the expressive movements of the face and body. We perceive this at once when we converse on an important subject with any person whose face is concealed. Nevertheless there are no grounds, as far as I can discover, for believing that any muscle has been developed or even modified exclusively for the sake of expression. The vocal and other sound-producing organs by which various expressive noises are produced seem to form a partial exception; but I have elsewhere attempted to show that these organs were first developed for sexual purposes, in order that one sex might call or charm the other. Nor can I discover grounds for believing that any inherited movement which now serves as a means of expression was at first voluntarily and consciously performed for this special purpose—like some of the gestures and the finger-language used by the deaf and dumb. On the contrary, every true or inherited movement of expression seems to have had some natural and independent origin. But when once acquired, such movements may be voluntarily and consciously employed as a means of communication. Even infants, if carefully attended to, find out at a very early age that their screaming brings relief, and they soon voluntarily practice it. We may frequently see a person voluntarily raising his eyebrows to express surprise, or smiling to express pretended satisfaction and acquiescence. A man often wishes to make certain gestures conspicuous or demonstrative, and will raise his extended arms with widely opened fingers above his head to show astonishment or lift his shoulders to his ears to show that he cannot or will not do something.

We have seen that the study of the theory of expression confirms to a certain limited extent the conclusion that man is derived from some lower animal form, and supports the belief of the specific or subspecific unity of the several races; but as far as my judgment serves, such confirmation was hardly needed. We have also seen that expression in itself, or the language of the emotions, as it has sometimes been called, is certainly of importance for the welfare of mankind. To understand, as far as is possible, the source or origin of the various expressions which may be hourly seen on the faces of the men around us, not to mention our domesticated animals, ought to possess much interest for us. From these several causes we may conclude that the philosophy of our subject has well deserved that attention which it has already received from several excellent observers, and that it deserves still further attention, especially from any able physiologist.

3. Blushing[1]

Blushing is the most peculiar and the most human of all expressions. Monkeys redden from passion, but it would require an overwhelming amount of evidence to make us believe that any animal could blush. The reddening of the face from a blush is due to the relaxation of the muscular coats of the small arteries, by which the capillaries become filled with blood; and this depends on the proper vasomotor center being affected. No doubt if there be at the same time much mental agitation, the general circulation will be affected; but it is not due to the action of the heart that the network of minute vessels covering the face becomes under a sense of shame gorged with blood. We can cause laughing by tickling the skin, weeping or frowning by a blow, trembling from the fear of pain, and so forth; but we cannot cause a blush by any physical means— that is, by any action on the body. It is the mind which must be affected. Blushing is not only involuntary, but the wish to restrain it, by leading to self-attention, actually increases the tendency.

The young blush much more freely than the old, but not during infancy, which is remarkable, as we know that infants at a very early age redden from passion. I have received authentic accounts of two little girls blushing at the ages of between two and three years; and of another sensitive child, a year older, blushing when reproved for a fault. Many children at a somewhat more advanced

[1] Adapted from Charles Darwin, *The Expression of the Emotions*, pp. 310-37. (John Murray, 1873.)

age blush in a strongly marked manner. It appears that the mental powers of infants are not as yet sufficiently developed to allow of their blushing. Hence, also, it is that idiots rarely blush. Dr. Crichton Browne observed for me those under his care, but never saw a genuine blush, though he has seen their faces flush, apparently from joy, when food was placed before them, and from anger. Nevertheless some, if not utterly degraded, are capable of blushing. A microcephalous idiot, for instance, thirteen years old, whose eyes brightened a little when he was pleased or amused, has been described by Dr. Behn as blushing and turning to one side when undressed for medical examination.

Women blush much more than men. It is rare to see an old man, but not nearly so rare to see an old woman, blushing. The blind do not escape. Laura Bridgman, born in this condition, as well as completely deaf, blushes. The Rev. R. H. Blair, principal of the Worcester College, informs me that three children born blind, out of seven or eight then in the asylum, are great blushers. The blind are not at first conscious that they are observed, and it is a most important part of their education, as Mr. Blair informs me, to impress this knowledge on their minds; and the impression thus gained would greatly strengthen the tendency to blush, by increasing the habit of self-attention.

The tendency to blush is inherited. Dr. Burgess gives the case of a family consisting of a father, mother, and ten children, all of whom, without exception, were prone to blush to a most painful degree. The children were grown up; "and some of them were sent to travel in order to wear away this diseased sensibility, but nothing was of the slightest avail." Even peculiarities in blushing seem to be inherited. Sir James Paget, whilst examining the spine of a girl, was struck at her singular manner of blushing; a big splash of red appeared first on one cheek, and then other splashes, variously scattered over the face and neck. He subsequently asked the mother whether her daughter always blushed in this peculiar manner and was answered, "Yes, she takes after me." Sir J. Paget then perceived that by asking this question he had caused the mother to blush and she exhibited the same peculiarity as her daughter.

In most cases the face, ears, and neck are the sole parts which redden; but many persons, whilst blushing intensely, feel that their whole bodies grow hot and tingle; and this shows that the entire surface must be in some manner affected. Blushes are said sometimes to commence on the forehead, but more commonly on the cheeks, afterward spreading to the ears and neck. In two albinos examined by Dr. Burgess, the blushes commenced by a small circumscribed spot on the cheeks, over the parotidean plexus of nerves, and then increased into a circle; between this blushing circle and the blush on the neck there was an evident line of demarcation, although both arose simultaneously. The retina, which is naturally red in the albino, invariably increased at the same time in redness. Every one must have noticed how easily after one blush fresh blushes chase each other over the face. Blushing is preceded by a peculiar sensation in the skin. According to Dr. Burgess the reddening of the skin is generally succeeded by a slight pallor, which shows that the capillary vessels contract after dilating. In some rare cases paleness instead of redness is caused under conditions which would naturally induce a blush. For instance, a young lady told me that in a large and crowded party she caught her hair so firmly on the button of a passing servant that it took some time before she could be extricated; from her sensation she imagined that she had blushed crimson but was assured by a friend that she had turned extremely pale.

The mental states which induce blushing consist of shyness, shame, and modesty, the essential element in all being self-attention. Many reasons can be assigned for believing that originally self-attention directed to personal appearance, in relation to the opinion of others, was the exciting cause, the same effect being subsequently produced, through the force of association, by self-attention in relation to moral conduct. It is not the simple act of reflecting on our own appearance, but the thinking what others think of us, which excites a blush. In absolute solitude the most sensitive person would be quite indifferent about his appearance. We feel blame or disapprobation more acutely than approbation; and consequently depreciatory remarks or ridicule, whether of our appearance or conduct, cause us to blush much more readily than does praise. But undoubtedly praise and admiration are highly efficient: a pretty girl blushes when a man gazes intently at her, though she may know perfectly well that he is not depreciating her. Many children, as well as old and sensitive persons, blush when they are much praised. Hereafter the question will be discussed how it has arisen that the consciousness that others are attending to our personal appearance should have led to the capillaries, especially those of the face, instantly becoming filled with blood.

My reasons for believing that attention directed to personal appearance, and not to moral conduct, has been the fundamental element in the acquirement of the habit of blushing will now be given. They are separately light, but combined possess, as it appears to me, considerable weight. It is notorious that nothing makes a shy person blush so much as any remark, however slight, on his personal appearance. One cannot notice even the dress of a woman much given to blushing without causing her face to crimson. It is sufficient to stare hard at some persons to make them, as Coleridge remarks, blush—"account for that he who can."

With the two albinos observed by Dr. Burgess, "the slightest attempt to examine their peculiarities" invariably caused them to blush deeply. Women are much more sensitive about their personal appearance than men are, especially elderly women in comparison with elderly men, and they blush much more freely. The young of both sexes are much more sensitive on this same head than the old, and they also blush much more freely than the old. Children at a very early age do not blush; nor do they show those other signs of self-consciousness which generally accompany blushing; and it is one of their chief charms that they think nothing about what others think of them. At this early age they will stare at a stranger with a fixed gaze and unblinking eyes, as on an inanimate object, in a manner which we elders cannot imitate.

It is plain to everyone that young men and women are highly sensitive to the opinion of each other with reference to their personal appearance; and they blush incomparably more in the presence of the opposite sex than in that of their own. A young man, not very liable to blush, will blush intensely at any slight ridicule of his appearance from a girl whose judgment on any important subject he would disregard. No happy pair of young lovers, valuing each other's admiration and love more than anything else in the world, probably ever courted each other without many a blush. Even the barbarians of Tierra del Fuego, according to Mr. Bridges, blush "chiefly in regard to women, but certainly also at their own personal appearance."

Of all parts of the body, the face is most considered and regarded, as is natural from its being the chief seat of expression and the source of the voice. It is also the chief seat of beauty and of ugliness, and throughout the world is the most ornamented. The face, therefore, will have been subjected during many generations to much closer and more earnest self-attention than any other part of the body; and in accordance with the principle here advanced we can understand why it should be the most liable to blush. Although exposure to alternations of temperature, etc., has probably much increased the power of dilatation and contraction in the capillaries of the face and adjoining parts, yet this by itself will hardly account for these parts blushing much more than the rest of the body; for it does not explain the fact of the hands rarely blushing. With Europeans the whole body tingles slightly when the face blushes intensely; and with the races of men who habitually go nearly naked, the blushes extend over a much larger surface than with us. These facts are, to a certain extent, intelligible, as the self-attention of primeval man, as well as of the existing races which still go naked, will not have been so exclusively confined to their faces, as is the case with the people who now go clothed.

We have seen that in all parts of the world persons who feel shame for some moral delinquency are apt to avert, bend down, or hide their faces, independently of any thought about their personal appearance. The object can hardly be to conceal their blushes, for the face is thus averted or hidden under circumstances which exclude any desire to conceal shame, as when guilt is fully confessed and repented of. It is, however, probable that primeval man before he had acquired much moral sensitiveness would have been highly sensitive about his personal appearance, at least in reference to the other sex, and he would consequently have felt distress at any depreciatory remarks about his appearance; and this is one form shame. And as the face is the part of the body which is regarded, it is intelligible that any one ashamed of his personal ance would desire to conceal this part of his body. T having been thus acquired, would naturally be carried on from strictly moral causes was felt; and it is not eas see why under these circumstances there should be the face more than any other part of the body

The habit, so general with everyone who feels ashamed, of turning away or lowering his eyes, or restlessly moving them from side to side, probably follows from each glance directed toward those present, bringing home the conviction that he is intently regarded; and he endeavors, by not looking at those present, and especially not at their eyes, momentarily to escape from this painful conviction.

4. Laughing[1]

Sympathy, when it is not the direct cause, is conditional to the existence of laughter. Sometimes it provokes it; always it spreads it, sustains and strengthens it.

First of all, it is so much the nature of laughter to communicate itself that when it no longer communicates itself it ceases to exist. One might say that outbursts of merriment need to be encouraged, that they are not self-sufficient. Not to share them is to blow upon them and extinguish them. When, in an animated and mirthful group, some one remains cold or gloomy, the laughter immediately stops or is checked. Yet those whom the common people call, in their picturesque language, wet blankets, spoil-sports, or kill-joys, are not necessarily hostile to the gaiety of the rest. They may only have, and, in fact, very often do have, nothing but the one fault of being out of tune with this gaiety. But even their calm appears an offense to the warmth and the high spirits of the others and kills by itself alone this merriment.

Not only is laughter maintained by sympathy but it is even ⁿ of sympathy. The world is composed of two kinds of people: who make one laugh and those who are made to laugh, these eing infinitely more numerous. How many there are, indeed, ⸱ no sense of humor, and who, of themselves, would not ughing at things at which they do nevertheless laugh ˙se they see others laugh. As for those who have a ready of the comic, do they not enjoy the success of their from not more, than their jokes themselves? Their t least, grows with the joy of spreading it. Very many good humorists are temperamentally far t their jokes only on the rebound, echoing

[1] Tra (Félix Alca

from L. Dugas, *Psychologie du rire*, pp. 32–153.

the laughter which they provoke. To laugh, then, is to share the gaiety of others, whether this gaiety is communicated from them to us or from us to them. It seems that we can be moved to laughter only by the merriment of others, that we possess ours only indirectly when others send it to us. Human solidarity never appears more clearly than in the case of laughter.

Yet can one say that sympathy actually produces laughter? Is it not enough to say that it increases it, that it strengthens its effects? All our sentiments are without doubt in a sense revealed to us by others. How many, as Rochefoucald says, would be ignorant of love if they had never read novels! How many in the same way would never have discovered by themselves the laughable side of people and things. Yet even the feelings which one experiences by contagion one can experience only of one's own accord, in one's own way, and according to one's disposition. This fact alone of their contagion proves that from one's birth one carries the germ in himself. Sympathy would explain, then, contagion, but not the birth, of laughter. The fact is that our feelings exist for ourselves only when they acquire a communicative or social value; they have to be diffused in order to manifest themselves. Sympathy does not create them but it gives them their place in the world. It gives them just that access of intensity without which their nature cannot develop or even appear: thus it is that our laughter would be for us as if it did not exist, if it did not find outside itself an echo which increases it.

From the fact that sympathy is the law of laughter, does it follow that it is the cause? Not at all. It would be even contradictory to maintain this. A laugh being given, others are born out of sympathy. But the first laugh or one originally given, where does it get its origin? Communicated laughter implies spontaneous laughter as the echo implies a sound. If sympathy explains one, it is, it would seem, an antipathy or the absence of sympathy which produces the other. "The thing at which we laugh," says Aristotle, "is a defect or ugliness which is not great enough to cause suffering or injury. Thus, for example, a ridiculous face is an ugly or misshapen face, but one on which suffering has not marked." Bain says likewise, "The laughable is the deformed or ugly thing which is not pushed to the point where it is painful or injurious. An occasion for laughter is the degradation of a person of dignity in circumstances which do not arouse a strong emotion," like indignation, anger, or pity. Descartes puts still more limits upon laughter. Speaking of malice he says that laughter cannot be provoked except by misfortunes not only *light* but also *unforseen* and *deserved.* "Derision or mockery," he says, "is a kind of joy mixed with hate, which comes from one's perceiving some *little misfortune* in a person *who one thinks deserves it.* We hate this misfortune but are happy at seeing it in some one who merits it, and, *when this happens unexpectedly, surprise causes us to burst out laughing.* But this misfortune must be small, for if it is great we cannot believe that he who meets it deserves it, unless one has a very malicious or hateful nature."

This fact can be established directly by analyzing the most cruel laughter. If we enter into the feelings of the one who laughs and set aside the disagreeable sentiments, irritation, anger, and disgust, which at times they produce upon us, we come to understand even the savage sneer which appears to us as an insult to suffering; the laugh of the savage, trampling his conquered enemy under foot, or that of the child torturing unfortunate animals. This laugh is, in fact, inoffensive in its way, it is cruel in fact but not in intention. What it expresses is not a perverse, satanic joy but a *heartlessness,* as is so properly said. In the child and the savage sympathy has not been born, that is to say, the absence of imagination for the sufferings of others is complete. As a result we have a negative cruelty, a sort of altruistic or social anaesthesia.

When such an anaesthesia is not complete, when the altruistic sensibility of one who laughs is only dull, his egotism being very keen, his laughter might appear still less hatefully cruel. It would express then not properly the joy of seeing others suffer but that of not having to undergo their suffering and the power of seeing it only as a spectacle.

Analogous facts may be cited closer to us, easier to verify. Those who enjoy robust health often laugh at invalids: their imagination does not comprehend physical suffering, they are incapable of sympathizing with those who experience it. Likewise those who possess calm and even dispositions cannot witness without laughing an excess of mad anger or of impotent rage. In general we do not take seriously those feelings to which we ourselves are strangers; we consider them extravagant and amusing. "How can one be a

Persian?" To laugh is to detach one's self from others, to separate one's self and to take pleasure in this separation, to amuse one's self by contrasting the feelings, character, and temperament of others and one's own feelings, character, and temperament. *Insensibility* has been justly noted by M. Bergson as an essential characteristic of him who laughs. But this *insensibility*, this heartlessness, gives very much the effect of a positive and real ill nature, and M. Bergson had thus simply repeated and expressed in a new way, more precise and correct, the opinion of Aristotle: the cause of laughter is malice mitigated by insensibility or the absence of sympathy.

Thus defined, malice is after all essentially relative, and when one says that the object of our laughter is the misfortune of someone else, *known by us* to be endurable and slight, it must be understood that this misfortune may be *in itself* very serious as well as undeserved, and in this way laughter is often really cruel.

The coarser men are, the more destitute they are of sympathetic imagination, and the more they laugh at one another with an offensive and brutal laugh. There are those who are not even touched by contact with physical suffering; such ones have the heart to laugh at the shufflings of a bandy-legged man, at the ugliness of a hunchback, or the repulsive hideousness of an idiot. Others there are who are moved by physical suffering but who are not at all affected by moral suffering. These laugh at a self-love touched to the quick, at a wounded pride, at the tortured self-consciousness of one abashed or humiliated. These are, in their eyes, harmless, and slight pricks which they themselves, by a coarseness of nature, or a fine moral health, would endure perhaps with equanimity, which at any rate they do not feel in behalf of others, with whom they do not suffer in sympathy.

Castigat ridendo mores. According to M. A. Michiels, the author of a book upon the *World of Humor and of Laughter*, this maxim must be understood in its broadest sense. "Everything that is contrary to the absolute ideal of human perfection," in whatever order it be, whether physical, intellectual, moral, or social, arouses laughter. The fear of ridicule is the most dominant of our feelings, that which controls us in most things and with the most strength. Because of this fear one does "what one would not do for the sake of justice, scrupulousness, honor, or good will;" one submits to an infinite number

of obligations which morality would not dare to prescribe and which
are not included in the laws. "Conscience and the written laws,"
says A. Michiels, "form two lines of ramparts against evil, the ludicrous
is the third line of defense, it stops, brands, and condemns the little
misdeeds which the guards have allowed to pass."

Laughter is thus the great censor of vices, it spares none, it does
not even grant indulgence to the slightest imperfections, of whatever
nature they be. This mission, which M. Michiels attributes to
laughter, granting that it is fulfilled, instead of taking its place in
the natural or providential order of things, does it not answer simply
to those demands, whether well founded or not, which society makes
upon each of us? M. Bergson admits this, justly enough, it appears,
when he defines laughter as a social bromide. But then it is
no longer mere imperfection in general, it is not even immorality, properly speaking; it is merely unsociability, well or badly
understood, which laughter corrects. More precisely, it is a special
unsociability, one which escapes all other penalties, which it is the
function of laughter to reach. What can this unsociability be? It
is the self-love of each one of us in so far as it has anything disagreeable to others in it, an abstraction of every injurious or hateful element. It is the harmless self-love, slight, powerless, which one does
not fear but one scorns, yet for all that does not pardon but on the
contrary pitilessly pursues, wounds, and galls. Self-love thus defined
is vanity, and what is called the moral correction administered by
laughter is the wound to self-love. "The specific remedy for vanity,"
says M. Bergson, "is laughter, and the essentially ridiculous is vanity."

One sees in what sense laughter is a "correction." Whether one
considers the jests uttered, the feelings of the jester, or of him at
whom one jests, laughter appears from the point of view of morality
as a correction most often undeserved, unjust—or at least dispro-
portionate to the fault—pitiless, and cruel.

In fact, the self-love at which one laughs is, as we have said,
harmless. Besides it is often a natural failing, a weakness, not
a vice. Even if it were a vice, the jester would not be justified in
laughing at it, for it does not appear that he himself is exempt. On
the contrary, his vanity is magnified when that of others is upon
the rack. Finally the humiliation caused by laughter is not a
chastisement which one accepts but a torture to which one submits;

it is a feeling of resentment, of bitterness, not a wholesome sense of shame, nor one from which anyone is likely to profit. Laughter may then have a social use; but it is not an act of justice. It is a quick and summary police measure which will not stand too close a scrutiny but which it would be imprudent either to condemn or to approve without reserve. Society is established and organized according to natural laws which seem to be modeled on those of reason, but self-loves discipline themselves, they enter into conflict and hold each other in check.

C. LANGUAGE AND THE COMMUNICATION OF IDEAS

1. Intercommunication in the Lower Animals[1]

The foundations of intercommunication, like those of imitation, are laid in certain instinctive modes of response, which are stimulated by the acts of other animals of the same social group.

Some account has already been given of the sounds made by young birds, which seem to be instinctive and to afford an index of the emotional state at the time of utterance. That in many cases they serve to evoke a like emotional state and correlated expressive behavior in other birds of the same brood cannot be questioned. The alarm note of a chick will place its companions on the alert; and the harsh "krek" of a young moor-hen, uttered in a peculiar crouching attitude, will often throw others into this attitude, though the maker of the warning sound may be invisible. That the cries of her brood influence the conduct of the hen is a matter of familiar observation; and that her danger signal causes them at once to crouch or run to her for protection is not less familar. No one who has watched a cat with her kittens, or a sheep with her lambs, can doubt that such "dumb animals" are influenced in their behavior by suggestive sounds. The important questions are, how they originate, what is their value, and how far such intercommunication—if such we may call it—extends.

There can be but little question that in all cases of animals under natural conditions such behavior has an instinctive basis. Though the effect may be to establish a means of communication, such is not

[1] Adapted from C. Lloyd Morgan, *Animal Behaviour*, pp. 193–205. (Edward Arnold, 1908.)

their conscious purpose at the outset. They are presumably congenital and hereditary modes of emotional expression which serve to evoke responsive behavior in another animal—the reciprocal action being generally in its primary origin between mate and mate, between parent and offspring, or between members of the same family group. *And it is this reciprocal action which constitutes it a factor in social evolution.* Its chief interest in connection with the subject of behavior lies in the fact that it shows the instinctive foundations on which intelligent and eventually rational modes of intercommunication are built up. For instinctive as the sounds are at the outset, by entering into the conscious situation and taking their part in the association-complex of experience, they become factors in the social life as modified and directed by intelligence. To their original instinctive value as the outcome of stimuli, and as themselves affording stimuli to responsive behavior, is added a value for consciousness in so far as they enter into those guiding situations by which intelligent behavior is determined. And if they also serve to evoke, in the reciprocating members of the social group, similar or allied emotional states, there is thus added a further social bond, inasmuch as there are thus laid the foundations of sympathy.

"What makes the old sow grunt and the piggies sing and whine?" said a little girl to a portly, substantial farmer. "I suppose they does it for company, my dear," was the simple and cautious reply. So far as appearances went, that farmer looked as guiltless of theories as man could be. And yet he gave terse expression to what may perhaps be regarded as the most satisfactory hypothesis as to the primary purpose of animal sounds. They are a means by which each indicates to others the fact of his comforting presence; and they still, to a large extent, retain their primary function. The chirping of grasshoppers, the song of the cicada, the piping of frogs in the pool, the bleating of lambs at the hour of dusk, the lowing of contented cattle, the call-notes of the migrating host of birds—all these, whatever else they may be, are the reassuring social links of sound, the grateful signs of kindred presence. Arising thus in close relation to the primitive feelings of social sympathy, they would naturally be called into play with special force and suggestiveness at times of strong emotional excitement, and the earliest differentiations would, we may well believe, be determined along lines of emotional expression.

Thus would originate mating cries, male and female after their kind; and parental cries more or less differentiated into those of mother and offspring, the deeper note of the ewe differing little save in pitch and timbre from the bleating of her lamb, while the cluck of the hen differs widely from the peeping note of the chick in down. Thus, too, would arise the notes of anger and combat, of fear and distress, of alarm and warning. If we call these the instinctive language of emotional expression, we must remember that such "language" differs markedly from the "language" of which the sentence is the recognized unit.

It is, however, not improbable that, through association in the conscious situation, sounds, having their origin in emotional expression and evoking in others like emotional states, may acquire a new value in suggesting, for example, the presence of particular enemies. An example will best serve to indicate my meaning. The following is from H. B. Medlicott:

In the early dawn of a grey morning I was geologizing along the base of the Muhair Hills in South Behar, when all of a sudden there was a stampede of many pigs from the fringe of the jungle, with porcine shrieks of *sauve qui peut* significance. After a short run in the open they took to the jungle again, and in a few minutes there was another uproar, but different in sound and in action; there was a rush, presumably of the fighting members, to the spot where the row began, and after some seconds a large leopard sprang from the midst of the scuffle. In a few bounds he was in the open, and stood looking back, licking his chops. The pigs did not break cover, but continued on their way. They were returning to their lair after a night's feeding on the plain, several families having combined for mutual protection; while the beasts of prey were evidently waiting for the occasion. I was alone, and, though armed, I did not care to beat up the ground to see if in either case a kill had been effected. The numerous herd covered a considerable space, and the scrub was thick. The prompt concerted action must in each case have been started by the special cry. I imagine that the first assailant was a tiger, and the case was at once known to be hopeless, the cry prompting instant flight, while in the second case the cry was for defense. It can scarcely be doubted that in the first case each adult pig had a vision of a tiger, and in the second of a leopard or some minor foe.

If we accept Mr. Medlicott's interpretation as in the main correct, we have in this case: (1) common action in social behavior, (2) community of emotional state, and (3) the suggestion of natural enemies not unfamiliar in the experience of the herd. It is a not improbable hypothesis, therefore, that in the course of evolution the initial value of uttered sounds is emotional; but that on this may be grafted in further development the indication of particular enemies. If, for example, the cry which prompts instant flight among the pigs is called forth by a tiger, it is reasonable to suppose that this cry would give rise to a representative generic image of that animal having its influence on the conscious situation. But if the second cry, for defense, was prompted sometimes by a leopard and sometimes by some other minor foe, then this cry would not give rise to a representative image of the same definiteness. Whether animals have the power of intentionally differentiating the sounds they make to indicate different objects is extremely doubtful. Can a dog bark in different tones to indicate "cat" or "rat," as the case may be? Probably not. It may, however, be asked why, if a pig may squeak differently, and thus, perhaps, incidentally indicate on the one hand "tiger" and on the other hand "leopard," should not a dog bark differently and thus indicate appropriately "cat" or "rat"? Because it is assumed that the two different cries in the pig are the instinctive expression of two different emotional states, and Mr. Medlicott could distinguish them; whereas, in the case of the dog, we can distinguish no difference between his barking in the one case and the other, nor do the emotional states appear to be differentiated. Of course there may be differences which we have failed to detect. What may be regarded, however, as improbable is the *intentional* differentiation of sounds by barking in different tones with the *purpose* of indicating "cat" or "rat."

Such powers of intercommunication as animals possess are based on direct association and refer to the here and the now. A dog may be able to suggest to his companion the fact that he has descried a worriable cat; but can a dog tell his neighbor of the delightful worry he enjoyed the day before yesterday in the garden where the man with the biscuit tin lives? Probably not, bark he never so expressively.

From the many anecdotes of dogs calling others to their assistance or bringing others to those who feed them or treat them kindly, we may indeed infer the existence of a social tendency and of the suggestive effects of behavior, but we cannot derive conclusive evidence of anything like descriptive communication.

Such intentional communication as is to be found in animals, if indeed we may properly so call it, seems to arise by an association of the performance of some act in a conscious situation involving further behavior for its complete development. Thus the cat which touches the handle of the door when it wishes to leave the room has had experience in which the performance of this act has coalesced with a specific development of the conscious situation. The case is similar when your dog drops a ball or stick at your feet, wishing you to throw it for him to fetch. Still, it is clear that such an act would be the perceptual precursor of the deliberate conduct of the rational being by whom the sign is definitely realized as a sign, the intentional meaning of which is distinctly present to thought. This involves a judgment concerning the sign as an object of thought; and this is probably beyond the capacity of the dog. For, as Romanes himself says, "It is because the human mind is able, so to speak, to stand outside of itself and thus to constitute its own ideas the subject-matter of its own thought that it is capable of judgment, whether in the act of conception or in that of predication. We have no evidence to show that any animal is capable of objectifying its own ideas; and therefore we have no evidence that any animal is capable of judgment."

2. The Concept as the Medium of Human Communication[1]

There is a petrified philosophy in language, and if we examine the most ancient word for "name," we find it is *nâman* in Sanskrit, *nomen* in Latin, *namô* in Gothic. This *nâman* stands for *gnâman*, and is derived from the root *gnâ*, to know, and meant originally that by which we know a thing.

And how do we know things?

The first step toward the real knowledge, a step which, however small in appearance, separates man forever from all other animals, is *the naming of a thing*, or the making a thing knowable. All naming is classification, bringing the individual under the general; and

[1] Adapted from F. Max Müller, *The Science of Language*, I, 520–27. (Longmans, Green & Co., 1891.)

whatever we know, whether empirically or scientifically, we know it by means of our general ideas.

At the very point where man parts company with the brute world, at the first flash of reason as the manifestation of the light within us, there we see the true genesis of language. Analyze any word you like and you will find that it expresses a general idea peculiar to the individual to whom the name belongs. What is the meaning of moon? The measurer. What is the meaning of sun? The begetter. What is the meaning of earth? The ploughed.

If the serpent is called in Sankrit *sarpa*, it is because it was conceived under the general idea of creeping, an idea expressed by the root *srip*.

An ancient word for man was the Sanskrit *marta*, the Greek *brotos*, the Latin *mortalis*. *Marta* means "he who dies," and it is remarkable that, where everything else was changing, fading, and dying, this should have been chosen as the distinguishing name for man.

There were many more names for man, as there were many names for all things in ancient languages. Any feature that struck the observing mind as peculiarly characteristic could be made to furnish a new name. In common Sanskrit dictionaries we find 5 words for hand, 11 for light, 15 for cloud, 20 for moon, 26 for snake, 33 for slaughter, 35 for fire, 37 for sun. The sun might be called the bright, the warm, the golden, the preserver, the destroyer, the wolf, the lion, the heavenly eye, the father of light and life. Hence that superabundance of synonyms in ancient dialects, and hence that struggle for life carried on among these words, which led to the destruction of the less strong, the less fertile, the less happy words, and ended in the triumph of *one* as the recognized and proper name for every object in every language. On a very small scale this process of natural selection, or, as it would better be called, elimination, may still be watched even in modern languages, that is to say, even in languages so old and stricken in years as English and French. What it was at the first burst of dialects we can only gather from such isolated cases as when von Hammer counts 5,744 words all relating to the camel.

The fact that every word is originally a predicate—that names, though signs of individual conceptions, are all, without exception, derived from general ideas—is one of the most important discoveries in the science of language. It was known before that language is the distinguishing characteristic of man; it was known also that the having of general ideas is that which puts a perfect distinction betwixt man and brutes; but that these two were only different expressions of the same fact was not known till the theory of roots had been established as preferable to the theories both of onomatopoieia and of interjections. But, though our modern philosophy did not know it, the ancient poets and framers of language must have known it. For in Greek, language is *logos*, but *logos* means also reason, and *alogon* was chosen as the name and the most proper name, for brute. No animal, so far as we know, thinks and speaks except man. Language and thought are inseparable. Words without thought are dead sounds; thoughts without words are nothing. To think is to speak low; to speak is to think aloud. The word is the thought incarnate.

What are the two problems left unsettled at the end of the *Science of Language:* "How do mere cries become phonetic types?" and "How can sensations be changed into concepts?" What are these two, if taken together, but the highest problem of all philosophy, viz., "What is the origin of reason?"

3. Writing as a Form of Communication[1]

The earliest stages of writing were those in which pictographic forms were used; that is, a direct picture was drawn upon the writing surface, reproducing as nearly as possible the kind of impression made upon the observer by the object itself. To be sure, the drawing used to represent the object was not an exact reproduction or full copy of the object, but it was a fairly direct image. The visual memory image was thus aroused by a direct perceptual appeal to the eye. Anyone could read a document written in this pictograph form, if he had ever seen the objects to which the pictures referred. There was no special relation between the pictures or visual forms at this stage of development and the sounds used in articulate language. Concrete examples of such writing are seen in early monuments, where the moon is represented by the crescent, a king by the drawing of a man wearing a crown.

[1] Adapted from Charles H. Judd, *Psychology*, pp. 219–24. (Ginn & Co., 1917.)

The next stage of development in writing began when the picto-graphic forms were reduced in complexity to the simplest possible lines. The reduction of the picture to a few sketchy lines depended upon the growing ability of the reader to contribute the necessary interpretation. All that was needed in the figure was something which would suggest the full picture to the mind. Indeed, it is prob-ably true that the full picture was not needed, even in the reader's consciousness. Memory images are usually much simplified repro-ductions of the perceptual facts. In writing we have a concrete expression of this tendency of memory to lose its full reproductive form and to become reduced to the point of the most meager contents for conscious thought. The simplification of the written forms is attained very early, and is seen even in the figures which are used by savage tribes. Thus, to represent the number of an enemy's army, it is not necessary to draw full figures of the forms of the enemy; it is enough if single straight lines are drawn with some brief indica-tion, perhaps at the beginning of the series of lines, to show that these stand each for an individual enemy. This simplification of the drawing leaves the written symbol with very much larger pos-sibilities of entering into new relations in the mind of the reader. Instead, now, of being a specific drawing related to a specific object, it invites by its simple character a number of different interpretations. A straight line, for example, can represent not only the number of an enemy's army but it can represent also the number of sheep in a flock, or the number of tents in a village, or anything else which is capable of enumeration. The use of a straight line for these various purposes stimulates new mental developments. This is shown by the fact that the development of the idea of the number relation, as distinguished from the mass of possible relations in which an object may stand, is greatly facilitated by this general written symbol for numbers. The intimate relation between the development of ideas on the one hand and the development of language on the other is here very strikingly illustrated. The drawing becomes more useful be-cause it is associated with more elaborate ideas, while the ideas develop because they find in the drawing a definite content which helps to mark and give separate character to the idea.

As soon as the drawing began to lose its significance as a direct perceptual reproduction of the object and took on new and broader meanings through the associations which attached to it, the written form became a symbol, rather than a direct appeal to visual memory. As a symbol it stood for something which, in itself, it was not. The way was thus opened for the written symbol to enter into relation with oral speech, which is also a form of symbolism. Articulate sounds are simplified forms of experience capable through association with ideas of expressing meanings not directly related to the sounds themselves. When the written symbol began to be related to the sound symbol, there was at first a loose and irregular relation between them. The Egyptians seem to have established such relations to some extent. They wrote at times with pictures standing for sounds, as we now write in rebus puzzles. In such puzzles the picture of an object is intended to call up in the mind of the reader, not the special group of ideas appropriate to the object represented in the picture, but rather the sound which serves as the name of this object. When the sound is once suggested to the reader, he is supposed to attend to that and to connect with it certain other associations appropriate to the sound. To take a modern illustration, we may, for example, use the picture of the eye to stand for the first personal pronoun. The relationship between the picture and the idea for which it is used is in this case through the sound of the name of the object depicted. That the early alphabets are of this type of rebus pictures appears in their names. The first three letters of the Hebrew alphabet, for example, are named, respectively, *aleph* which means ox, *beth* which means house, and *gimmel* which means camel.

The complete development of a sound alphabet from this type of rebus writing required, doubtless, much experimentation on the part of the nations which succeeded in establishing the association. The Phoenicians have generally been credited with the invention of the forms and relations which we now use. Their contribution to civilization cannot be overestimated. It consisted, not in the presentation of new material or content to conscious experience, but rather in the bringing together by association of groups of contents which, in their new relation, transformed the whole process of thought and expression. They associated visual and auditory content and gave to the visual factors a meaning through association which was of such unique importance as to justify us in describing the association as a new invention.

There are certain systems of writing which indicate that the type of relationship which we use is not the only possible type of relationship. The Chinese, for example, have continued to use simple symbols which are related to complex sounds, not to elementary sounds, as are our own letters. In Chinese writing the various symbols, though much corrupted in form, stand each for an object. It is true that the forms of Chinese writing have long since lost their direct relationship to the pictures in which they originated. The present forms are simplified and symbolical. So free has the symbolism become that the form has been arbitrarily modified to make it possible for the writer to use freely the crude tools with which the Chinaman does his writing. These practical considerations could not have become operative, if the direct pictographic character of the symbols had not long since given place to a symbolical character which renders the figure important, not because of what it shows in itself, but rather because of what it suggests to the mind of the reader. The relation of the symbol to elementary sounds has, however, never been established. This lack of association with elementary sounds keeps the Chinese writing at a level much lower and nearer to primitive pictographic forms than is our writing.

Whether we have a highly elaborated symbolical system, such as that which appears in Chinese writing, or a form of writing which is related to sound, the chief fact regarding writing, as regarding all language, is that it depends for its value very much more upon the ideational relations into which the symbols are brought in the individual's mind than upon the impressions which they arouse.

The ideational associations which appear in developed language could never have reached the elaborate form which they have at present if there had not been social co-operation. The tendency of the individual when left to himself is to drop back into the direct adjustments which are appropriate to his own life. He might possibly develop articulation to a certain extent for his own sake, but the chief impulse to the development of language comes through intercourse with others. As we have seen, the development of the simplest forms of communication, as in animals, is a matter of social imitation. Writing is also an outgrowth of social relations. It is extremely doubtful whether even the child of civilized parents would ever have any sufficient motive for the development of writing, if it were not for the social encouragement he receives.

4. The Extension of Communication by Human Invention[1]

No one who is asked to name the agencies that weave the great web of intellectual and material influences and counter-influences by which modern humanity is combined into the unity of society will need much reflection to give first rank to the newspaper, along with the post, railroad, and telegraph.

In fact, the newspaper forms a link in the chain of modern commercial machinery; it is one of those contrivances by which in society the exchange of intellectual and material goods is facilitated. Yet it is not an instrument of commercial intercourse in the sense of the post or the railway, both of which have to do with the transport of persons, goods, and news, but rather in the sense of the letter and circular. These make the news capable of transport only because they are enabled by the help of writing and printing to cut it adrift, as it were, from its originator and give it corporeal independence.

However great the difference between letter, circular, and newspaper may appear today, a little reflection shows that all three are essentially similar products, originating in the necessity of communicating news and in the employment of writing in its satisfaction. The sole difference consists in the letter being addressed to individuals, the circular to several specified persons, the newspaper to many unspecified persons. Or, in other words, while letter and circular are instruments for the private communication of news, the newspaper is an instrument for its publication.

Today we are, of course, accustomed to the regular printing of the newspaper and its periodical appearance at brief intervals. But neither of these is an essential characteristic of the newspaper as a means of news publication. On the contrary, it will become apparent directly that the primitive paper from which this mighty instrument of commercial intercourse is sprung appeared neither in printed form nor periodically, but that it closely resembled the letter from which, indeed, it can scarcely be distinguished. To be sure, repeated appearance at brief intervals is involved in the very nature of news publication. For news has value only so long as it is fresh; and to preserve for it the charm of novelty its publication must follow in the footsteps of the events. We shall, however, soon see that the

[1] Adapted from Carl Bücher, *Industrial Evolution*. Translated by S. Morley Wickett, pp. 216–43. (Henry Holt & Co., 1907.)

periodicity of these intervals, as far as it can be noticed in the infancy of journalism, depended upon the regular recurrence of opportunities to transport the news, and was in no way connected with the essential nature of the newspaper.

The regular collection and despatch of news presupposes a widespread interest in public affairs, or an extensive area of trade exhibiting numerous commercial connections and combinations of interest, or both at once. Such interest is not realized until people are united by some more or less extensive political organization into a certain community of life-interest. The city republics of ancient times required no newspaper; all their needs of publication could be met by the herald and by inscriptions, as occasion demanded. Only when Roman supremacy had embraced or subjected to its influence all the countries of the Mediterranean was there need of some means by which those members of the ruling class who had gone to the provinces as officials, tax-farmers, and in other occupations, might receive the current news of the capital. It is significant that Caesar, the creator of the military monarchy and of the administrative centralization of Rome, is regarded as the founder of the first contrivance resembling a newspaper.

Indeed, long before Caesar's consulate it had become customary for Romans in the provinces to keep one or more correspondents at the capital to send them written reports on the course of political movement and on other events of the day. Such a correspondent was generally an intelligent slave or freedman intimately acquainted with affairs at the capital, who, moreover, often made a business of reporting for several. He was thus a species of primitive reporter, differing from those of today only in writing, not for a newspaper, but directly for readers. On recommendation of their employers, these reporters enjoyed at times admission even to the senate discussions. Antony kept such a man, whose duty it was to report to him not merely on the senate's resolutions but also on the speeches and votes of the senators. Cicero, when proconsul, received through his friend, M. Caelius, the reports of a certain Chrestus, but seems not to have been particularly well satisfied with the latter's accounts of gladiatorial sports, law-court proceedings, and the various pieces of city gossip. As in this case, such correspondence never extended beyond a rude relation of facts that required supplementing through letters from party friends of the absent person. These friends, as we know from Cicero, supplied the real report on political feeling.

The innovation made by Caesar consisted in instituting the publication of a brief record of the transactions and resolutions of the senate, and in his causing to be published the transactions of the assemblies of the plebs, as well as other important matters of public concern.

The Germanic peoples who, after the Romans, assumed the lead in the history of Europe were neither in civilization nor in political organization fitted to maintain a similar constitution of the news service; nor did they require it. All through the Middle Ages the political and social life of men was bounded by a narrow horizon; culture retired to the cloisters and for centuries affected only the people of prominence. There were no trade interests beyond the narrow walls of their own town or manor to draw men together. It is only in the later centuries of the Middle Ages that extensive social combinations once more appear. It is first the church, embracing with her hierarchy all the countries of Germanic and Latin civilization, next the burgher class with its city confederacies and common trade interests, and, finally, as a counter-influence to these, the secular territorial powers, who succeed in gradually realizing some form of union. In the twelfth and thirteenth centuries we notice the first traces of an organized service for transmission of news and letters in the messengers of monasteries, the universities, and the various spiritual dignitaries; in the fourteenth and fifteenth centuries we have advanced to a comprehensive, almost postlike, organization of local messenger bureaus for the epistolary intercourse of traders and of municipal authorities. And now, for the first time, we meet with the word *Zeitung*, or newspaper. The word meant originally that which was happening at the time (*Zeit*="time"), a present occurrence; then information on such an event, a message, a report, news.

Venice was long regarded as the birthplace of the newspaper in the modern acceptation of the word. As the channel of trade between the East and the West, as the seat of a government that first organized the political news service and the consular system in the modern sense, the old city of lagoons formed a natural collecting center for important news items from all lands of the known world. Even early in the fifteenth century, as has been shown by the investigations of Valentinelli, the librarian of St. Mark's Library, collections of news had been made at the instance of the council of Venice regarding events that had either occurred within the republic or been reported by ambassadors, consuls, and officials, by ships' captains, merchants, and the like. These were sent as circular despatches to the Venetian representatives abroad to keep them posted on international affairs. Such collections of news were called *fogli d'avvisi.*

The further development of news publication in the field that it has occupied since the more general adoption of the printing-press has been peculiar. At the outset the publisher of a periodical printed newspaper differed in no wise from the publisher of any other printed work—for instance, of a pamphlet or a book. He was but the multiplier and seller of a literary product, over whose content he had no control. The newspaper publisher marketed the regular post-news in its printed form just as another publisher offered the public a herbal or an edition of an old writer.

But this soon changed. It was readily perceived that the contents of a newspaper number did not form an entity in the same sense as the contents of a book or pamphlet. The news items there brought together, taken from different sources, were of varying reliability. They needed to be used judicially and critically: in this a political or religious bias could find ready expression. In a still higher degree was this the case when men began to discuss contemporary political questions in the newspapers and to employ them as a medium for disseminating party opinions.

This took place first in England during the Long Parliament and the Revolution of 1640. The Netherlands and a part of the imperial free towns of Germany followed later. In France the change was not consummated before the era of the great Revolution: in most other countries it occurred in the nineteenth century. The newspaper, from being a mere vehicle for the publication of news, became an instrument for supporting and shaping public opinion and a weapon of party politics.

The effect of this upon the internal organization of the newspaper undertaking was to introduce a third department, the *editorship*, between news collecting and news publication. For the newspaper publisher, however, it signified that from a mere seller of news he had become a dealer in public opinion as well.

At first this meant nothing more than that the publisher was placed in a position to shift a portion of the risk of his undertaking upon a party organization, a circle of interested persons, or a government. If the leanings of the paper were distasteful to the readers, they ceased to buy the paper. Their wishes thus remained, in the final analysis, the determining factor for the contents of the newspapers.

The gradually expanding circulation of the printed newspapers nevertheless soon led to their employment by the authorities for making public announcements. With this came, in the first quarter of the last century, the extension of private announcements, which have now attained, through the so-called advertising bureaus, some such organization as political news-collecting possesses in the correspondence bureaus.

The modern newspaper is a capitalistic enterprise, a sort of news-factory in which a great number of people (correspondents, editors, typesetters, correctors, machine-tenders, collectors of advertisements, office clerks, messengers, etc.) are employed on wage, under a single administration, at very specialized work. This paper produces wares for an unknown circle of readers, from whom it is, furthermore, frequently separated by intermediaries, such as delivery agencies and postal institutions. The simple needs of the reader or of the circle of patrons no longer determine the quality of these wares; it is now the very complicated conditions of competition in the publication market. In this market, however, as generally in wholesale markets, the consumers of the goods, the newspaper readers, take no direct part; the determining factors are the wholesale dealers and the speculators in news: the governments, the telegraph bureaus dependent upon their special correspondents, the political parties, artistic and scientific cliques, men on 'change, and, last but not least, the advertising agencies and large individual advertisers.

Each number of a great journal which appears today is a marvel of economic division of labor, capitalistic organization, and mechanical technique; it is an instrument of intellectual and economic intercourse, in which the potencies of all other instruments of commerce—the railway, the post, the telegraph, and the telephone— are united as in a focus.

D.   IMITATION

1.   Definition of Imitation[1]

The term "imitation" is used in ordinary language to designate any repetition of any act or thought which has been noted by an observer.   Thus one imitates the facial expression of another, or his mode of speech.   The term has been brought into prominence in scientific discussions through the work of Gabriel Tarde, who in his *Les lois de l'imitation* points out that imitation is a fundamental fact underlying all social development.   The customs of society are imitated from generation to generation.   The fashions of the day are imitated by large groups of people without any consciousness of the social solidarity which is derived from this common mode of behavior.   There is developed through these various forms of imitation a body of experiences which is common to all of the members of a given social group.   In complex society the various imitations which tend to set themselves up are frequently found to be in conflict; thus the tendency toward elaborate fashions in dress is constantly limited by the counter-tendency toward simpler fashions.   The conflict of tendencies leads to individual variations from the example offered at any given time, and, as a result, there are new examples to be followed.   Complex social examples are thus products of conflict.

This general doctrine of Tarde has been elaborated by a number of recent writers.   Royce calls attention to the fundamental importance of imitation as a means of social inheritance.   The same doctrine is taken up by Baldwin in his *Mental Development in the Child and Race*, and in *Social and Ethical Interpretations*.   With these later writers, imitation takes on a significance which is somewhat technical and broader than the significance which it has either with Tarde or in the ordinary use of the term.   Baldwin uses the term to cover that case in which an individual repeats an act because he has himself gone through the act.   In such a case one imitates himself and sets up what Baldwin terms a circular reaction.   The principle of imitation is thus introduced into individual psychology as well as into general social psychology, and the relation between the individual's

[1] From Charles H. Judd, "Imitation," in *Monroe's Cyclopedia of Education*, III, 388–89. (Published by The Macmillan Co., 1912. Reprinted by permission.)

acts and his own imagery is brought under the same general principle as the individual's responses to his social environment. The term "imitation" in this broader sense is closely related to the processes of sympathy.

The term "social heredity" has very frequently been used in connection with all of the processes here under discussion. Society tends to perpetuate itself in the new individual in a fashion analogous to that in which the physical characteristics of the earlier generation tend to perpetuate themselves in the physical characteristics of the new generation. Since modes of behavior, such as acts of courtesy, cannot be transmitted through physical structure, they would tend to lapse if they were not maintained through imitation from generation to generation. Thus imitation gives uniformity to social practices and consequently is to be treated as a form of supplementary inheritance extending beyond physical inheritance and making effective the established forms of social practice.

2. Attention, Interest, and Imitation[1]

Imitation is a process of very great importance for the development of mental life in both men and animals. In its more complex forms it presupposes trains of ideas; but in its essential features it is present and operative at the perceptual level. It is largely through imitation that the results of the experience of one generation are transmitted to the next, so as to form the basis for further development. Where trains of ideas play a relatively unimportant part, as in the case of animals, imitation may be said to be the sole form of social tradition. In the case of human beings, the thought of past generations is embodied in language, institutions, machinery, and the like. This distinctively human tradition presupposes trains of ideas in past generations, which so mold the environment of a new generation that in apprehending and adapting itself to this environment it must re-think the old trains of thought. Tradition of this kind is not found in animal life, because the animal mind does not proceed by way of trains of ideas. None the less, the more intelligent animals depend largely on tradition. This tradition consists essentially in imitation by the young of the actions of their parents, or

[1] Adapted from G. F. Stout, *A Manual of Psychology*, pp. 390-91. (The University Tutorial Press, 1913.)

of other members of the community in which they are born. The same directly imitative process, though it is very far from forming the whole of social tradition in human beings, forms a very important part of it.

a) The imitative impulse.—We must distinguish between ability to imitate and impulse to imitate. We may be already fully able to perform an action, and the sight of it as performed by another may merely prompt us to reproduce it. But the sight of an act performed by another may also have an educational influence; it may not only stimulate us to do what we are already able to do without its aid; it may also enable us to do what we could not do without having an example to follow. When the cough of one man sets another coughing, it is evident that imitation here consists only in the impulse to follow suit. The second man does not learn how to cough from the example of the first. He is simply prompted to do on this particular occasion what he is otherwise quite capable of doing. But if I am learning billiards and someone shows me by his own example how to make a particular stroke, the case is different. It is not his example which in the first instance prompts me to the action. He merely shows the way to do what I already desire to do.

We have then first to discuss the nature of the imitative impulse — the impulse to perform an action which arises from the perception of it as performed by another.

This impulse is an affair of attentive consciousness. The perception of an action prompts us to reproduce it when and so far as it excites interest or is at least intimately connected with what does excite interest. Further, the interest must be of such a nature that it is more fully gratified by partially or wholly repeating the interesting action. Thus imitation is a special development of attention. Attention is always striving after a more vivid, more definite, and more complete apprehension of its object. Imitation is a way in which this endeavor may gratify itself when the interest in the object is of a certain kind. It is obvious that we do not try to imitate all manner of actions, without distinction, merely because they take place under our eyes. What is familiar and commonplace or what for any other reason is unexciting or insipid fails to stir us to re-enact it. It is otherwise with what is strikingly novel or in any way impressive, so that our attention dwells on it with relish or fascination. It is, of course, not true that whatever act fixes attention prompts to imitation. This is only the case where imitation helps attention, where it is, in fact, a special development of attention. This is so when interest is directly concentrated on the activity itself for its own sake rather than for the sake of its possible consequences and the like ulterior motives. But it is not necessary that the act in itself should be interesting; in a most important class of cases the interest centers, not directly in the external act imitated, but in something else with which this act is so intimately connected as virtually to form a part of it. Thus there is a tendency to imitate not only interesting acts but also the acts of interesting persons. Men are apt to imitate the gestures and modes of speech of those who excite their admiration or affection or some other personal interest. Children imitate their parents or their leaders in the playground. Even the mannerisms and tricks of a great man are often unconsciously copied by those who regard him as a hero. In such instances the primary interest is in the whole personality of the model; but this is more vividly and distinctly brought before consciousness by reproducing his external peculiarities. Our result, then, is that interest in an action prompts to imitation in proportion to its intensity, provided the interest is of a kind which will be gratified or sustained by imitative activity.

b) Learning by imitation.—Let us now turn to the other side of the question. Let us consider the case in which the power of performing an action is acquired in and by the process of imitation itself. Here there is a general rule which is obvious when once it is pointed out. It is part of the still more general rule that "to him that hath shall be given." Our power of imitating the activity of another is strictly proportioned to our pre-existing power of performing the same general kind of action independently. For instance, one devoid of musical faculty has practically no power of imitating the violin playing of Joachim. Imitation may develop and improve a power which already exists, but it cannot create it. Consider the child beginning for the first time to write in a copybook. He learns by imitation; but it is only because he has already some rudimentary ability to make such simple figures as pothooks that the imitative process can get a start. At the outset, his pothooks are very unlike the model set before him. Gradually he improves; increased power of independent production gives step by step increased power of imitation, until he approaches too closely the limits of his capacity in this direction to make any further progress of an appreciable kind.

But this is an incomplete account of the matter. The power of learning by imitation is part of the general power of learning by experience; it involves mental plasticity. An animal which starts life with congenital tendencies and aptitudes of a fixed and stereotyped kind, so that they admit of but little modification in the course of individual development, has correspondingly little power of learning by imitation.

At higher levels of mental development the imitative impulse is far less conspicuous because impulsive activity in general is checked and overruled by activity organized in a unified system. Civilized men imitate not so much because of immediate interest in the action imitated as with a view to the attainment of desirable results.

3. The Three Levels of Sympathy[1]

Sympathy is not an instinct or a tendency, i.e., a group of co-ordinated movements adapted to a particular end, and showing itself in consciousness as an emotion, such as fear, anger, sex attraction; it is, on the contrary, a highly generalized psycho-physiological property. To the specialized character of each emotion it opposes a character of almost unlimited plasticity. We have not to consider it under all its aspects but as one of the most important manifestations of emotional life, as the basis of the tender emotions, and one of the foundations of social and moral existence.

a) The first phase.—In its primitive form sympathy is reflex, automatic, unconscious, or very slightly conscious; it is, according to Bain, the tendency to produce in ourselves an attitude, a state, a bodily movement which we perceive in another person. This is imitation in its most rudimentary form. Between sympathy and imitation, at any rate in this primitive period, I see only one difference of aspect: sympathy everywhere marks the passive, receptive side of the phenomenon; imitation, its active and motor side.

It manifests itself in animals forming aggregates (not societies), such as a flock of sheep, or a pack of dogs who run, stop, bark all at

[1] Adapted from Th. Ribot, *The Psychology of the Emotions*, pp. 230-34. (Charles Scribner's Sons, 1898.)

the same time, through a purely physical impulse of imitation; in man, infectious laughter or yawning, walking in step, imitating the movements of a rope-walker while watching him, feeling a shock in one's legs when one sees a man falling, and a hundred other occurrences of this kind are cases of physiological sympathy. It plays a great part in the psychology of crowds, with their rapid attacks and sudden panics. In nervous diseases, there is a superfluity of examples: epidemics of hysteric fits, convulsive barking, hiccup, etc. I omit the mental maladies (epidemics of suicide, double or triple madness) since we are only considering the purely physiological stage.

To sum up, sympathy is originally a property of living matter: as there is an organic memory and an organic sensitiveness, being those of the tissues and ultimate elements which compose them, there is an organic sympathy, made up of receptivity and imitative movements.

b) The second phase.—The next phase is that of sympathy in the psychological sense, necessarily accompanied by consciousness; it creates in two or more individuals analogous emotional states. Such are the cases in which we say that fear, indignation, joy, or sorrow are communicated. It consists in feeling an emotion existing in another, and is revealed to us by its physiological expression. This phase consists of two stages.

(1) The first might be defined as psychological unison. If, during this period of unison, we could read the minds of those who sympathize, we should see a single emotional fact reflected in the consciousness of several individuals. L. Noiré, in his book, *Ursprung der Sprache*, has proposed the theory that language originated in community of action among the earliest human beings. When working, marching, dancing, rowing, they uttered (according to this writer) sounds which became the appellatives of these different actions, or of various objects; and these sounds, being uttered by all, must have been understood by all. Whether this theory be correct or not (it has been accepted as such by Max Müller), it will serve as an illustration. But this state of sympathy does not by itself constitute a tie of affection or tenderness between those who feel it; it only prepares the way for such an emotion. It may be the basis of a certain social solidarity, because the same internal states excite the same acts of a mechanical, exterior, non-moral solidarity.

(2) The second stage is that of sympathy, in the restricted and popular sense of the word. This consists of psychological unison, *plus* a new element: there is added another emotional manifestation, tender emotion (benevolence, sympathy, pity, etc.). It is no longer sympathy pure and simple, it is a binary compound. The common habit of considering phenomena only under their higher and complete forms often misleads us as to their origin and constitution. Moreover, in order to understand that this is a case of duality—the fusion of two distinct elements—and that our analysis is not a factitious one, it is sufficient to point out that sympathy (in the etymological sense) may exist without any tender emotion—nay, that it may exclude instead of excite it. According to Lubbock, while ants carry away their wounded, bees—though forming a society—are indifferent toward each other. It is well known that gregarious animals nearly always shun and desert a wounded member of the herd. Among men, how many there are who, when they see suffering, hasten to withdraw themselves from the spectacle, in order to escape the pain which it sympathetically awakens in them. This impulse may go to the length of aversion, as typified by Dives in the Gospel. It is therefore a complete psychological error to consider sympathy as capable, unaided, of delivering men from egoism; it only takes the first step, and not always that.

c) *The third phase.*—Under its intellectual form, sympathy is an agreement in feelings and actions, founded on unity of representation. The law of development is summed up in Spencer's formula, "The degree and range of sympathy depend on the clearness and extent of representation." I should, however, add: on condition of being based on an emotional temperament. This last is the source *par excellence* of sympathy, because it vibrates like an echo; the active temperament lends itself less to such impulses, because it has so much to do in manifesting its own individuality that it can scarcely manifest those of others; finally, the phlegmatic temperament does so least of all, because it presents a minimum of emotional life; like Leibnitz' monads, it has no windows.

In passing from the emotional to the intellectual phase, sympathy gains in extent and stability. In fact, emotional sympathy requires some analogy in temperament or nature; it can scarcely be established between the timid and the daring, between the cheerful and the melancholic; it may be extended to all human beings and to the animals nearest us, but not beyond them. On the contrary, it is the special attribute of intelligence to seek resemblances or analogies everywhere, to unify; it embraces the whole of nature. By the law of transfer (which we have already studied) sympathy follows this invading march and comprehends even inanimate objects, as in the case of the poet, who feels himself in communion with the sea, the woods, the lakes, or the mountains. Besides, intellectual sympathy participates in the relative fixity of representation; we find a simple instance of this in animal societies, such as those of the bees, where unity or sympathy among the members is only maintained by the perception or representation of the queen.

4. Rational Sympathy[1]

As we have no immediate experience of what other men feel, we can form no idea of the manner in which they are affected but by conceiving what we ourselves should feel in the like situation. Though our brother is upon the rack, as long as we ourselves are at our ease our senses will never inform us of what he suffers. They never did, and never can, carry us beyond our own person, and it is by the imagination only that we can form any conception of what are his sensations. Neither can that faculty help us to this any other way than by representing to us what would be our own, if we were in his case. It is the impressions of our own senses only, not those of his, which our imaginations copy. By the imagination we place ourselves in his situation, we conceive ourselves enduring all the same torments, we enter as it were into his body and become in some measure the same person with him, and thence form some idea of his sensations, and even feel something which, though weaker in degree, is not altogether unlike them. His agonies, when they are thus brought home to ourselves, when we have thus adopted and made them our own, begin at last to affect us, and we then tremble and shudder at the thought of what he feels. For, as to be in pain or distress of any kind excites the most excessive sorrow, so to conceive or to imagine that we are in it excites some degree of the same emotion, in proportion to the vivacity or dulness of the conception.

[1] Adapted from Adam Smith, *The Theory of Moral Sentiments*, pp. 3-10. (G. Bell & Sons, 1893.)

That this is the source of our fellow-feeling for the misery of others, that it is by changing places in fancy with the sufferer that we come either to conceive or to be affected by what he feels, may be demonstrated by many obvious observations, if it should not be thought sufficiently evident of itself. When we see a stroke aimed, and just ready to fall upon the leg or arm of another person, we naturally shrink and draw back our own leg or our own arm; and when it does fall, we feel it in some measure and are hurt by it as well as the sufferer. The mob, when they are gazing at a dancer on the slack rope, naturally writhe and twist and balance their own bodies as they see him do, and as they feel that they themselves must do if in his situation. Persons of delicate fibers and a weak constitution of body complain that in looking on the sores and ulcers which are exposed by beggars in the streets they are apt to feel an itching or uneasy sensation in the corresponding part of their own bodies. The horror which they conceive at the misery of those wretches affects that particular part in themselves more than any other because that horror arises from conceiving what they themselves would suffer if they really were the wretches whom they are looking upon, and if that particular part in themselves was actually affected in the same miserable manner. The very force of this conception is sufficient, in their feeble frames, to produce that itching or uneasy sensation complained of. Men of the most robust make observe that in looking upon sore eyes they often feel a very sensible soreness in their own, which proceeds from the same reason; that organ, being in the strongest man more delicate than any other part of the body, is the weakest.

Upon some occasions sympathy may seem to arise merely from the view of a certain emotion in another person. The passions upon some occasions may seem to be transfused from one man to another instantaneously and antecedent to any knowledge of what excited them in the person principally concerned. Grief and joy, for example, strongly expressed in the look and gestures of any person at once affect the spectator with some degree of a like painful or agreeable emotion. A smiling face is, to everybody that sees it, a cheerful object, as a sorrowful countenance, on the other hand, is a melancholy one.

This, however, does not hold universally, or with regard to every passion. There are some passions of which the expressions excite no sort of sympathy, but, before we are acquainted with what gave occasion to them, serve rather to disgust and provoke us against them. The furious behavior of an angry man is more likely to exasperate us against himself than against his enemies. As we are unacquainted with his provocation, we cannot bring his case home to ourselves, nor conceive anything like the passions which it excites. But we plainly see what is the situation of those with whom he is angry, and to what violence they may be exposed from so enraged an adversary. We readily, therefore, sympathize with their fear or resentment, and are immediately disposed to take part against the man from whom they appear to be in danger.

If the very appearances of grief and joy inspire us with some degree of the like emotions, it is because they suggest to us the general idea of some good or bad fortune that has befallen the person in whom we observe them: and in these passions this is sufficient to have some little influence upon us. The effects of grief and joy terminate in the person who feels these emotions, of which the expressions do not, like those of resentment, suggest to us the idea of any other person for whom we are concerned and whose interests are opposite to his. The general idea of good or bad fortune, therefore, creates some concern for the person who has met with it; but the general idea of provocation excites no sympathy with the anger of the man who has received it. Nature, it seems, teaches us to be more averse to enter into this passion, and, till informed of its cause, to be disposed rather to take part against it.

Even our sympathy with the grief or joy of another, before we are informed of the cause of either, is always extremely imperfect. General lamentations, which express nothing but the anguish of the sufferer, create rather a curiosity to inquire into his situation, along with some disposition to sympathize with him, than any actual sympathy that is very sensible. The first question which we ask is, What has befallen you? Till this be answered, though we are uneasy both from the vague idea of his misfortune and still more from torturing ourselves with conjectures about what it may be, yet our fellow-feeling is not very considerable.

Sympathy, therefore, does not arise so much from the view of the passion as from that of the situation which excites it. We sometimes feel for another a passion of which he himself seems to be altogether incapable, because when we put ourselves in his case, that passion arises in our breast from the imagination, though it does not in his from the reality.   We blush for the impudence and rudeness of another, though he himself appears to have no sense of the impropriety of his own behavior, because we cannot help feeling with what confusion we ourselves should be covered, had we behaved in so absurd a manner.

Of all the calamities to which the condition of mortality exposes mankind, the loss of reason appears, to those who have the least spark of humanity, by far the most dreadful; and they behold that last stage of human wretchedness with deeper commiseration than any other.   But the poor wretch who is in it laughs and sings, perhaps, and is altogether insensible to his own misery.   The anguish which humanity feels, therefore, at the sight of such an object cannot be the reflection of any sentiment of the sufferer.   The compassion of the spectator must arise altogether from the consideration of what he himself would feel if he was reduced to the same unhappy situation, and, what perhaps is impossible, was at the same time able to regard it with his present reason and judgment.

What are the pangs of a mother when she hears the moanings of her infant, that, during the agony of disease, cannot express what it feels?   In her idea of what it suffers, she joins to its real helplessness her own consciousness of that helplessness and her own terrors for the unknown consequences of its disorder; and, out of all these, forms for her own sorrow the most complete image of misery and distress.   The infant, however, feels only the uneasiness of the present instant, which can never be great.   With regard to the future it is perfectly secure in its thoughtlessness and want of anxiety, the great tormentors of the human breast, from which reason and philosophy will in vain attempt to defend it when it grows up to a man.

But whatever may be the cause of sympathy, or however it may be excited, nothing pleases us more than to observe in other men a fellow-feeling with all the emotions of our own breast; nor are we ever so much shocked as by the appearance of the contrary.   Those who are fond of deducing all our sentiments from certain refinements of self-love think themselves at no loss to account, according to their own principles, both for this pleasure and for this pain.   Man, say they, conscious of his own weakness and of the need which he has for the assistance of others, rejoices whenever he observes that they adopt his own passions because he is then assured of that assistance and grieves whenever he observes the contrary, because he is then assured of their opposition. But both the pleasure and the pain are always felt so instantaneously, and often upon such frivolous occasions, that it seems evident that neither of them can be derived from any such self-interested consideration. A man is mortified when, after having endeavored to divert the company, he looks round and sees that nobody laughs at his jests but himself. On the contrary, the mirth of the company is highly agreeable to him and he regards this correspondence of their sentiments with his own as the greatest applause.

5. Art, Imitation, and Appreciation[1]

The investigation into the psychology of masses, as well as the experiments on suggestive therapeutics, have proved to how great an extent mental states may be transmitted from individual to individual by unconscious imitation of the accompanying movements. The doctrine of universal sympathy, a clear statement of which was given long ago in the ethical theory of Adam Smith, has thus acquired a psychological justification in the modern theories of imitative movement. Contemporary science has at last learned to appreciate the fundamental importance of imitation for the development of human culture. And some authors have even gone so far as to endeavor to deduce all sociological laws from this one principle. At the same time natural history has begun to pay more and more attention to the indispensability of imitation for the full development of instincts, as well as for training in those activities which are the most necessary in life.

It is fortunate for the theory of art that the importance of the imitative functions has thus been simultaneously acknowledged in various departments of science. Whatever one may think of the somewhat audacious generalizations which have been made in the recent application of this new principle, it is incontestable that the aesthetic activities can be understood and explained only by reference to the universal tendency to imitate. It is also significant that writers on aesthetic had felt themselves compelled to set up a theory

[1] From Yrjö Hirn, *The Origins of Art*, pp. 74–85. (Published by The Macmillan Co., 1900. Reprinted by permission.)

of imitation long before experimental psychologists had begun to turn their attention in this direction. In Germany the enjoyment of form and form-relations has, since Vischer's time, been interpreted as the result of the movements by which, not only our eye, but also our whole body follows the outlines of external things. In France Jouffroy stated the condition for the receiving of aesthetic impressions to be a "power of internally imitating the states which are externally manifested in living nature." In England, finally, Vernon Lee and Anstruther Thompson have founded a theory of beauty and ugliness upon this same psychical impulse to copy in our own unconscious movements the forms of objects. And in the writings of, for instance, Home, Hogarth, Dugald Stewart, and Spencer, there can be found a multitude of isolated remarks on the influence which is in a direct way exercised on our mental life by the perception of lines and forms.

In most of these theories and observations, however, the imitative activity has been noticed only in so far as it contributes to the aesthetic delight which may be derived from sensual impressions. But its importance is by no means so restricted as this; on the contrary, we believe it to be a fundamental condition for the existence of intuition itself. Without all these imperceptible tracing movements with which our body accompanies the adaptation of the eye-muscles to the outlines of external objects, our notions of depth, height, and distance, and so on, would certainly be far less distinct than they are. On the other hand, the habit of executing such movements has, so to say, brought the external world within the sphere of the internal. The world has been measured with man as a standard, and objects have been translated into the language of mental experience. The impressions have hereby gained, not only in emotional tone, but also in intellectual comprehensibility.

Greater still is the importance of imitation for our intuition of moving objects. And a difficult movement itself is fully understood only when it has been imitated, either internally or in actual outward activity. The idea of a movement, therefore, is generally associated with an arrested impulse to perform it. Closer introspection will show everyone to how great a part our knowledge, even of persons, is built up of motor elements. By unconscious and imperceptible copying in our own body the external behavior of a man, we may learn to understand him with benevolent or malevolent sympathy.

And it will, no doubt, be admitted by most readers that the reason why they know their friends and foes better than they know anyone else is that they carry the remembrance of them not only in their eyes, but in their whole body. When in idle moments we find the memory of an absent friend surging up in our minds with no apparent reason, we may often note, to our astonishment, that we have just been unconsciously adopting one of his characteristic attitudes, or imitating his peculiar gestures or gait.

It may, however, be objected that the above-mentioned instances refer only to a particular class of individuals. In other minds, it will be said, the world-picture is entirely built up of visual and acoustic elements. It is also impossible to deny that the classification of minds in different types, which modern psychology has introduced, is as legitimate as it is advantageous for the purposes of research. But we can hardly believe that such divisions have in view anything more than a relative predominance of the several psychical elements. It is easily understood that a man in whose store of memory visual or acoustic images occupy the foremost place may be inclined to deny that motor sensations of unconscious copying enter to any extent into his psychical experience. But an exclusively visual world-image, if such a thing is possible, must evidently be not only emotionally poorer, but also intellectually less distinct and less complete, than an intuition, in which such motor elements are included.

The importance of motor sensations in the psychology of knowledge is by itself of no aesthetic interest. The question has been touched upon in this connection only because of the illustration which it gives to the imitation theory. If, as we believe is the case, it is really necessary, for the purpose of acquiring a complete comprehension of things and events, to "experience" them—that is to say, to pursue and seize upon them, not only with that particular organ of sense to which they appeal, but also by tracing movements of the whole body—then there is no need to wonder at the universality of the imitative impulse. Imitation does not only, according to this view, facilitate our training in useful activities, and aid us in deriving an aesthetic delight from our sensations; it serves also, and perhaps primarily, as an expedient for the accommodating of ourselves to the external world, and for the explaining of things by reference to ourselves. It is therefore natural that imitative movements should occupy so great a place among the activities of children and primitive men. And we can also understand why this fundamental impulse, which has played so important a part in racial as well as in individual education, may become so great as to be a disease and dominate the whole of conscious life. As children we all imitated before we comprehended, and we have learned to comprehend by imitating. It is only when we have grown familiar by imitation with the most important data of perception that we become capable of appropriating knowledge in a more rational way. Although no adult has any need to resort to external imitation in order to comprehend new impressions, it is still only natural that in a pathological condition he should relapse into the primitive imitative reaction. And it is equally natural that an internal, i.e., arrested, imitation should take place in all our perceptions. After this explanation of the universality of this phenomenon we have no further need to occupy ourselves with the general psychology of imitation. We have here only to take notice of its importance for the communication of feeling.

As is well known, it is only in cases of abnormally increased sensibility—for instance, in some of the stages of hypnotism and thought transmission—that the motor counterpart of a mental state can be imitated with such faithfulness and completeness that the imitator is thereby enabled to partake of all the *intellectual* elements of the state existing in another. The hedonic qualities, on the other hand, which are physiologically conditioned by much simpler motor counterparts, may of course be transmitted with far greater perfection: it is easier to suggest a pleasure than a thought. It is also evident that it is the most general hedonic and volitional elements which have been considered by the German authors on aesthetic in their theories on internal imitation ("Die innere Nachahmung"). They seem to have thought that the adoption of the attitudes and the performance of the movements which usually accompany a given emotional state will also succeed to some extent in producing a similar emotional state. This assumption is perfectly legitimate, even if the connection between feeling and movement be interpreted in the associative way. And it needs no justification when the motor changes are considered as the physiological correlate of the feeling itself.

Everyday experience affords many examples of the way in which feelings are called into existence by the imitation of their expressive movements. A child repeats the smiles and the laughter of its parents, and can thus partake of their joy long before it is able to understand its cause. Adult life naturally does not give us many opportunities of observing this pure form of direct and almost automatic transmission. But even in adult life we may often meet with an exchange of feeling which seems almost independent of any intellectual communication. Lovers know it, and intimate friends like the brothers Goncourt, to say nothing of people who stand in so close a rapport with each other as a hypnotiser and his subject. And even where there is no previous sympathetic relation, a state of joy or sadness may often, if it is only distinctly expressed, pass over, so to say, from the individual who has been under the influence of its objective cause, to another who, as it were, borrows the feeling, but remains unconscious of its cause. We experience this phenomenon almost daily in the influence exerted upon us by social intercourse, and even by those aspects of nature—for instance, blue open sky or overhanging mountains—which naturally call up in us the physical manifestation of emotional states. The coercive force with which our surroundings—animate or inanimate—compel us to adopt the feelings which are suggested by their attitudes, forms, or movements, is perhaps as a rule too weak to be noticed by a self-controlled, unemotional man. But if we want an example of this influence at its strongest, we need but remember how difficult it is for an individual to resist the contagion of collective feeling. On public occasions the common mood, whether of joy or sorrow, is often communicated even to those who were originally possessed by the opposite feeling. So powerful is the infection of great excitement that—according to M. Féré—even a perfectly sober man who takes part in a drinking bout may often be tempted to join in the antics of his drunken comrades in a sort of second-hand intoxication, "drunkenness by induction." In the great mental epidemics of the Middle Ages this kind of contagion operated with more fatal results than ever before or afterward. But even in modern times a popular street riot may often show us something of the same phenomenon. The great tumult in London in 1886 afforded, it is said, a good opportunity of observing how people who had originally maintained an indifferent attitude were gradually carried away by the general excitement, even to the extent of joining in the outrages. In this instance the contagious effect of expressional movements was undoubtedly facilitated by their connection with so primary an impulse as that of rapine and destruction. But the case is the same with all the activities which appear as the outward manifestations of our strongest feeling-states. They all consist of instinctive actions with which everyone is well familiar from his own experience. It is therefore natural that anger, hate, or love may be communicated almost automatically from an individual to masses, and from masses to individuals.

Now that the principle of the interindividual diffusion of feeling has been stated and explained, we may return to our main line of research and examine its bearings on the expressional impulse. We have seen that in the social surroundings of the individual there is enacted a process resembling that which takes place within his own organism. Just as functional modifications spread from organ to organ, just as wider and wider zones of the system are brought into participation in the primary enhancement or inhibition, so a feeling is diffused from an individual to a circle of sympathisers who repeat its expressional movements. And just as all the widened "somatic resonances" contribute to the primary feeling-tone increased strength and increased definiteness, so must the emotional state of an individual be enhanced by retroactive stimulation from the expressions by which the state has, so to say, been continued in others. By the reciprocal action of primary movements and borrowed movements, which mutually imitate each other, the social expression operates in the same way as the individual expression. And we are entitled to consider it as a secondary result of the general expressional impulse, that when mastered by an overpowering feeling we seek enhancement or relief by retroaction from sympathisers, who reproduce and in their expression represent the mental state by which we are dominated.

In point of fact, we can observe in the manifestations of all strong feelings which have not found a satisfactory relief in individual expression, a pursuit of social resonance. A happy man wants to see glad faces around him, in order that from their expression he may derive further nourishment and increase for his own feeling. Hence the benevolent attitude of mind which as a rule accompanies all strong and pure joy. Hence also the widespread tendency to express joy by gifts or hospitality. In moods of depression we similarly desire a response to our feeling from our surroundings. In the depth of despair we may long for a universal cataclysm to extend, as it were, our own pain. As joy naturally makes men good, so pain often makes them hard and cruel. That this is not always the case is a result of the increased power of sympathy which we gain by every experienced pain. Moreover, we have need of sympathetic rapport for our motor reactions against pain. All the active manifestations of sorrow, despair, or anger which are not wholly painful in themselves are facilitated by the reciprocal influence of collective excitement. Thus all strong feelings, whether pleasurable or painful, act as socialising factors. This socialising action may be observed at all stages of development. Even the animals seek their fellows in order to stimulate themselves and each other by the common expression of an overpowering feeling. As has been remarked by Espinas, the flocking together of the male birds during the pairing season is perhaps as much due to this craving for mutual stimulation as to the desire to compete for the favor of the hen. The howling choirs of the macaws and the drum concerts of the chimpanzees are still better and unmistakable instances of collective emotional expression. In man we find the results of the same craving for social expression in the gatherings for rejoicing or mourning which are to be met with in all tribes, of all degrees of development. And as a still higher development of the same fundamental impulse, there appears in man the artistic activity.

The more conscious our craving for retroaction from sympathisers, the more there must also be developed in us a conscious endeavor to cause the feeling to be appropriated by as many as possible and as completely as possible. The expressional impulse is not satisfied by the resonance which an occasional public, however sympathetic, is able to afford. Its natural aim is to bring more and more sentient beings under the influence of the same emotional state. It seeks to vanquish the refractory and arouse the indifferent. An echo, a true and powerful echo—that is what it desires with all the energy of an unsatisfied longing. As a result of this craving the expressional activities lead to artistic production. The work of art presents itself as the most effective means by which the individual is enabled to convey to wider and wider circles of sympathisers an emotional state similar to that by which he is himself dominated.

E. SUGGESTION

I. A Sociological Definition of Suggestion[1]

The nature of suggestion manifestly consists not in any external peculiarities whatever. It is based upon the peculiar kind of relation of the person making the suggestion to the "ego" of the subject during the reception and realization of the suggestion.

Suggestion is, in general, one of many means of influence of man on man that is exercised with or without intention on persons, who respond either consciously or unconsciously.

For a closer acquaintance with what we call "suggestion," it may be observed that our perceptive activities are divided into (a) active, and (b) passive.

a) *Active perception.*—In the first case the "ego" of the subject necessarily takes a part, and according to the trend of our thinking or to the environmental circumstances directs the attention to these or those external impressions. These, since they enter the mind through the participation of attention and will and through reflection and judgment, are assimilated and permanently incorporated in the personal consciousness or in our "ego." This type of perception leads to an enrichment of our personal consciousness and lies at the bottom of our points of view and convictions. The organization of more or less definite convictions is the product of the process of reflection instituted by active perception. These convictions, before they become the possession of our personal consciousness, may conceal themselves awhile in the so-called subconsciousness. They are capable of being aroused at any moment at the desire of the "ego" whenever certain experienced representations are reproduced.

b) *Passive perception.*—In contrast to active perception we perceive much from the environment in a passive manner without that participation of the "ego." This occurs when our attention is diverted in any particular direction or concentrated on a certain thought, and when its continuity for one or another reason is broken up, which, for instance, occurs in cases of so-called distraction. In these cases the object of the perception does not enter into the personal consciousness, but it makes its way into other spheres of

[1] Translated and adapted from the German, *Die Bedeutung der Suggestion im Sozialen Leben*, pp. 10–15, from the original Russian of W. v. Bechterew. (J. F. Bergmann, Wiesbaden, 1905.)

our mind, which we call the general consciousness. The general consciousness is to a certain degree independent of the personal consciousness. For this reason everything that enters into the general consciousness cannot be introduced at will into the personal consciousness. Nevertheless products of the general consciousness make their way into the sphere of the personal consciousness, without awareness by it of their original derivation.

In passive perception, without any participation of attention, a whole series of varied impressions flow in upon us and press in past our "ego" directly to the general consciousness. These impressions are the sources of those influences from the outer world so unintelligible even to ourselves, which determine our emotional attitudes and those obscure motives and impulses which often possess us in certain situations.

The general consciousness, in this way, plays a permanent rôle in the spiritual life of the individual. Now and then an impression passively received in the train of an accidental chain of ideas makes its way into the sphere of the personal consciousness as a mental image, whose novelty astounds us. In specific cases this image or illusion takes the form of a peculiar voice, a vision, or even a hallucination, whose origin undoubtedly lies in the general consciousness. When the personal consciousness is in abeyance, as in sleep or in profound hypnosis, the activity of the general consciousness comes into the foreground. The activity of the general consciousness is limited neither by our ways of viewing things nor by the conditions under which the personal consciousness operates. On this account, in a dream and in profound hypnosis acts appear feasible and possible which with our full personal consciousness we would not dare to contemplate.

This division of our mind into a personal and a general consciousness affords a basis for a clear understanding of the principles of suggestion. The personal consciousness, the so-called "ego," aided by the will and attention, largely controls the reception of external impressions, influences the trend of our ideas, and determines the execution of our voluntary behavior. Every impression that the personal consciousness transmits to the mind is usually subject to a definite criticism and remodeling which results in the development of our points of view and of our convictions.

This mode of influence from the outer world upon our mind is that of "logical conviction." As the final result of that inner reconstruction of impressions appears always the conviction: "This is true, that useful, inevitable, etc." We can say this inwardly when any reconstruction of the impressions has been effected in us through the activity of the personal consciousness. Many impressions get into our mind without our remarking them. In case of distraction, when our voluntary attention is in abeyance, the impression from without evades our personal consciousness and enters the mind without coming into contact with the "ego." Not through the front door, but—so to speak—up the back steps, it gets, in this case, directly into the inner rooms of the soul.

Suggestion may now be defined as the direct infection of one person by another of certain mental states. In other words, suggestion is the penetration or inoculation of a strange idea into the consciousness, without direct immediate participation of the "ego" of the subject. Moreover, the personal consciousness in general appears quite incapable of rejecting the suggestion, even when the "ego" detects its irrationality. Since the suggestion enters the mind without the active aid of the "ego," it remains outside the borders of the personal consciousness. All further effects of the suggestion, therefore, take place without the control of the "ego."

By the term suggestion we do not usually understand the effect upon the mind of the totality of external stimuli, but the influence of person upon person which takes place through passive perception and is therefore independent of the activity of the personal consciousness. Suggestion is, moreover, to be distinguished from the other type of influences operating through mental processes of attention and the participation of the personal consciousness, which result in logical convictions and the development of definite points of view.

Loewenfeld emphasized a distinction between the actual process of "suggesting" and its result, which one simply calls "suggestion." It is self-evident that these are two different processes, which should not be mistaken for each other. A more adequate definition might be accepted, which embraces at once the characteristic manner of the "suggesting," and the result of its activity.

Therefore for suggestion it is not alone the process itself that is characteristic, or the kind of psychic influence, but also the result of this reaction. For that reason I do not understand under "suggesting" alone a definite sort and manner of influence upon man but at the same time the eventual result of it; and under "suggestion" not only a definite psychical result but to a certain degree also the manner in which this result was obtained.

An essential element of the concept of suggestion is, first of all, a pronounced directness of action. Whether a suggestion takes place through words or through attitudes, impressions, or acts, whether it is a case of a verbal or of a concrete suggestion, makes no difference here so long as its effect is never obtained through logical conviction. On the other hand, the suggestion is always immediately directed to the mind by evading the personal consciousness, or at least without previous recasting by the "ego" of the subject. This process represents a real infection of ideas, feelings, emotions, or other psychophysical states.

In the same manner there arise somewhat similar mental states known as autosuggestion. These do not require an external influence for their appearance but originate immediately in the mind itself. Such is the case, for instance, when any sort of an image forces itself into the consciousness as something complete, whether it is in the form of an idea that suddenly emerges and dominates consciousness, or a vision, a premonition, or the like.

In all these cases psychic influences which have arisen without external stimulus have directly inoculated the mind, thereby evading the criticism of the "ego" or of personal consciousness.

"Suggesting" signifies, therefore, to inoculate the mind of a person more or less directly with ideas, feelings, emotions, and other psychical states, in order that no opportunity is left for criticism and consideration. Under "suggestion," on the other hand, is to be understood that sort of direct inoculation of the mind of an individual with ideas, feelings, emotions, and other psychophysical states which evade his "ego," his personal self-consciousness, and his critical attitude.

Now and then, especially in the French writers, one will find besides "suggestion" the term "psychic contagion," under which, however, nothing further than involuntary imitation is to be understood (compare A. Vigouroux and P. Juquelier, *La contagion mentale*, Paris, 1905). If one takes up the conception of suggestion in a wider sense, and considers by it the possibility of involuntary suggestion in the way of example and imitation, one will find that the conceptions of suggestion and of psychic contagion depend upon each other most intimately, and to a great extent are not definitely to be distinguished from each other. In any case, it is to be maintained that a strict boundary between psychic contagion and suggestion does not always exist, a fact which Vigouroux and Juquelier in their paper have rightly emphasized.

2.   The Subtler Forms of Suggestion[1]

In one very particular respect hypnotism has given us a lesson of the greatest importance to psychology: it has proved that special precautionary measures must be taken in planning psychological experiments. The training of hypnotics has thrown light on this source of error. A hypnotizer may, often without knowing it, by the tone of his voice or by some slight movement cause the hypnotic to exhibit phenomena that at first could only be produced by explicit verbal suggestion, and that altogether the signs used by the hypnotizer to cause suggestions may go on increasing in delicacy. A dangerous source of error is provided by the hypnotic's endeavor to divine and obey the experimenter's intentions. This observation has also proved useful in non-hypnotic experiments. We certainly knew before the days of hypnotism that the signs by which A betrays his thoughts to B may gradually become more delicate. We see this, for example, in the case of the schoolboy, who gradually learns how to detect from the slightest movement made by his master whether the answer he gave was right or not. We find the same sort of thing in the training of animals—the horse, for instance, in which the rough methods at first employed are gradually toned down until in the end an extremely slight movement made by the trainer produces the same effect that the rougher movements did originally. But even if this lessening in the intensity of the signals exists independently of hypnosis, it is the latter that has shown us how easily neglect of this factor may lead to erroneous conclusions being drawn. The suggestibility of the hypnotic makes these infinitesimal signals specially dangerous in his case. But when once this danger was recognized, greater attention was paid to this source of error in

[1] Adapted from Albert Moll, *Hypnotism*, pp. 453-57. The Contemporary Science Series. (Walter Scott, 1909.)

non-hypnotic cases than before. It is certain that many psychological experiments are vitiated by the fact that the subject knows what the experimenter wishes. Results are thus brought about that can only be looked upon as the effects of suggestion; they do not depend on the external conditions of the experiment but on what is passing in the mind of the subject.

An event which at the time of its occurrence created a considerable commotion (I refer to the case of Clever Hans), will show how far we may be led by neglecting the above lesson taught us by hypnotism. If the Berlin psychologist Stumpf, the scientific director of the committee of investigation, had but taken into consideration the teachings of hypnotism, he would never have made the fiasco of admitting that the horse, Clever Hans, had been educated like a boy, not trained like an animal.

Clever Hans answered questions by tapping his hoof on the stage; and the observers, more particularly the committee presided over by Stumpf, believed that answers tapped out were the result of due deliberation on the part of the horse, exactly as spiritists believe that the spirits hold intelligent intercourse with them by means of "raps." One tap denoted a, two taps b, three taps c, etc.; or, where numbers were concerned, one tap signified 1, two taps 2, etc. In this way the animal answered the most complicated questions. For instance, it apparently not only solved such problems as 3 times 4 by tapping 12 times, and 6 times 3 by tapping 18 times, but even extracted square roots, distinguished between concords and discords, also between ten different colors, and was able to recognize the photographs of people; altogether, Clever Hans was supposed to be at that time about upon a level with fifth-form boys (the fifth form is the lowest form but one in a German gymnasium). After investigating the matter, Stumpf and the members of his committee drew up the following conjoint report, according to which only one of two things was possible—either the horse could think and calculate independently, or else he was under telepathic, perhaps occult, influence:

The undersigned met together to decide whether there was any trickery in the performance given by Herr v. Osten with his horse, i.e., whether the latter was helped or influenced intentionally. As the result of the exhaustive tests employed, they have come to the unanimous conclusion that, apart from the personal character of Herr v. Osten, with which most of them were well acquainted, the precautions taken during the investigation altogether precluded any such assumption. Notwithstanding the most careful observation, they were well unable to detect any gestures, movements, or other intimations that might serve as signs to the horse. To exclude the possible influence of involuntary movements on the part of spectators, a series of experiments was carried out solely in the presence of Herr Busch, councilor of commissions. In some of these experiments, tricks of the kind usually employed by trainers were, in his judgment as an expert, excluded. Another series of experiments was so arranged that Herr v. Osten himself could not know the answer to the question he was putting to the horse. From previous personal observations, moreover, the majority of the undersigned knew of numerous individual cases in which other persons had received correct answers in the momentary absence of Herr v. Osten and Herr Schillings. These cases also included some in which the questioner was either ignorant of the solution or only had an erroneous notion of what it should be. Finally, some of the undersigned have a personal knowledge of Herr v. Osten's method, which is essentially different from ordinary "training" and is copied from the system of instruction employed in primary schools. In the opinion of the undersigned, the collective results of these observations show that even unintentional signs of the kind at present known were excluded. It is their unanimous opinion that we have here to deal with a case that differs in principle from all former and apparently similar cases; that it has nothing to do with "training" in the accepted sense of the word, and that it is consequently deserving of earnest and searching scientific investigation. Berlin, September 12, 1904. [Here follow the signatures, among which is that of Privy Councilor Dr. C. Stumpf, university professor, director of the Psychological Institute, member of the Berlin Academy of Sciences.]

Anyone who has done critical work in the domain of hypnotism after the manner insisted on by the Nancy school cannot help considering Stumpf's method of investigation erroneous from the very outset. A first source of error that had to be considered was that someone present—it might have been Herr v. Osten or it might have been anyone else—unintentionally had given the horse a sign when to stop tapping. It cannot be considered sufficient, as stated in Stumpf's report, that Herr v. Osten did not know the answer; no one should be present who knows it. This is the first condition to be fulfilled when making such experiments. Anybody who has been engaged in training hypnotized subjects knows that these insignificant signs constitute one of the chief sources of error. Some of the leading modern investigators in the domain of hypnotism—Charcot and Heidenhain, for instance—were misled by them at the time they thought they had discovered new physical reflexes in hypnosis. But in 1904, by which time suggestion had been sufficiently investigated to prevent such an occurrence, a psychologist should not have fallen into an error that had been sufficiently made more than twenty years previously. But the main point is this: signs that are imperceptible to others are nevertheless perceived by a subject trained to do so, no matter whether that subject be a human being or an animal.

3. Social Suggestion and Mass or "Corporate" Action[1]

In most cases the crowd naturally is under leaders, who, with an instinctive consciousness of the importance and strength of the crowd, seek to direct it much more through the power of suggestion than by sound conviction.

It is conceivable, therefore, that anyone who understands how to arrest the attention of the crowd, may always influence it to do great deeds, as history, indeed, sufficiently witnesses. One may recall from the history of Russia Minin, who with a slogan saved his native land from the gravest danger. His "Pawn your wife and child, and free your fatherland" necessarily acted as a powerful suggestion on the already intense crowd. How the crowd and its sentiments may be controlled is indicated in the following account by Boris Sidis:

On the 11th of August, 1895, there took place in the open air a meeting at Old Orchard, Maine. The business at hand was a collection for missionary purposes. The preacher resorted to the following suggestions: "The most remarkable remembrance which I have of foreign lands is that of multitudes, the waves of lost humanity who ceaselessly are shattered on the shores of eternity. How despairing are they, how poor in love--their religion knows no joy, no pleasure, nor song. Once I heard a Chinaman say why he was a Christian. It seemed to him that he lay in a deep abyss, out of which he could not escape. Have you ever wept for the sake of the lost world, as did Jesus Christ? If not, then woe to you. Your religion is then only a dream and a blind. We see Christ test his disciples. Will he take them with him? My beloved, today he will test you. [Indirect

---

[1] Translated and adapted from the German, *Die Bedeutung der Suggestion im Sozialen Leben*, pp. 134-42, from the original Russian of W. v. Bechterew. (Wiesbaden: J. F. Bergmann, 1905.)

suggestion.] He could convert a thousand millionaires, but he gives you an opportunity to be saved. [More direct suggestion.] Are you strong enough in faith? [Here follows a discussion about questions of faith.] Without faith God can do no great things. I believe that Jesus will appear to them who believe firmly in him. My dear ones, if only you give for the sake of God, you have become participants in the faith. [Still more direct suggestion.] The youth with the five loaves and the two little fishes [the story follows]. When everything was ended, he did not lose his loaves; there were twelve baskets left over. O my dear ones, how will that return! Sometime the King of Kings will call to you and give you an empire of glory, and simply because you have had a little faith in him. It is a day of much import to you. Sometime God will show us how much better he has guarded our treasure than we ourselves." The suggestion had the desired effect. Money streamed from all sides; hundreds became thousands, tens of thousands. The crowd gave seventy thousand dollars.

Of analogous importance are the factors of suggestions in wars, where the armies go to brilliant victories. Discipline and the sense of duty unite the troops into a single mighty giant's body. To develop its full strength, however, this body needs some inspiration through a suggested idea, which finds an active echo in the hearts of the soldiers. Maintenance of the warlike spirit in decisive moments is one of the most important problems for the ingenious general.

Even when the last ray of hope for victory seems to have disappeared, the call of an honored war chief, like a suggestive spark, may fire the hosts to self-sacrifice and heroism. A trumpet signal, a cry "hurrah," the melody of the national hymn, can here at the decisive moment have incalculable effects. There is no need to recall the rôle of the "Marsellaise" in the days of the French Revolution. The agencies of suggestion in such cases make possible, provided that they are only able to remove the feeling of hopelessness, results which a moment before are neither to be anticipated nor expected. Where will and the sense of duty alone seem powerless, the mechanisms of suggestion may develop surprising effects.

Excited masses are, it is well known, capable of the most inhuman behavior, and indeed for the very reason that, instead of sound logic, automatism and impulsiveness have entered in as direct results of suggestion. The modern barbarities of the Americans in the shape of lynch law for criminals or those who are only under a suspicion of a crime redound to the shame of the land of freedom, but find their full explanation in that impulsiveness of the crowd which knows no mercy.

The multitude can, therefore, ever be led according to the content of the ideas suggested to it, as well to sublime and noble deeds as, on the other hand, to expressions of the lower and barbaric instincts. That is the art of manipulating the masses.

It is a mistake to regard popular assemblies who have adopted a certain uniform idea simply as a sum of single elements, as is now and then attempted. For one is dealing in such cases, not with accidental, but with actual psychical, processes of fusion, which reciprocal suggestion is to a high degree effective in establishing and maintaining. The aggressiveness of the single elements of the mass arrives in this at their high point at one and the same time, and with complete spiritual unanimity the mass can now act as *one* man; it moves, then, like one enormous social body, which unites in itself the thoughts and feelings of all by the very fact that there is a temper of mind common to all. Easily, however, as the crowd is excited to the highest degrees of activity, as quickly—indeed, much more quickly—does it allow itself, as we have already seen, to be dispersed by a panic. Here too the panic rests entirely on suggestion, contrasuggestion, and the instinct of imitation, not on logic and conviction. Automatism, not intelligence, is the moving factor therein.

Other, but quite generally favorable, conditions for suggestions are universally at hand in the human society, whose individual members in contrast to the crowd are physically separated from each other but stand in a spiritual alliance to each other. Here obviously those preliminary conditions for the dissemination of psychical infections are lacking as they exist in the crowd, and the instruments of the voice, of mimicry, of gestures, which often fire the passions with lightning rapidity, are not allowed to assert themselves. There exists much rather a certain spiritual cohesion on the ground perhaps of common impressions (theatrical representations), a similar direction of thoughts (articles in periodicals, etc.). These conditions are quite sufficient to prepare the foundation on which similar feelings propagate themselves from individual to individual by the method of suggestion and autosuggestion, and similar decisions for many are matured.

Things occur here more slowly, more peacefully, without those passionate outbreaks to which the crowd is subjected; but this slow infection establishes itself all the more surely in the feelings, while the infection of the crowd often only continues for a time until the latter is broken up.

Moreover, such contagious examples in the public do not usually lead to such unexpected movements as they easily induce in the crowd. But here, too, the infection frequently acts in defiance of a man's sound intelligence; complete points of view are accepted upon trust and faith, without further discussion, and frequently immature resolutions are formed. On the boards representing the stage of the world there are ever moving idols, who after the first storm of admiration which they call out, sink back into oblivion. The fame of the people's leaders maintains itself in quite the same way by means of psychical infection through the similar national interest of a unified group. It has often happened that their brightness was extinguished with the first opposition which the masses saw setting its face against their wishes and ideals. What we, however, see in close popular masses recurs to a certain degree in every social milieu, in every larger society.

Between the single elements of such social spheres there occur uninterrupted psychical infections and contra-infections. Ever according to the nature of the material of the infection that has been received, the individual feels himself attracted to the sublime and the noble, or to the lower and bestial. Is, then, the intercourse between teacher and pupil, between friends, between lovers, uninfluenced by reciprocal suggestion? Suicide pacts and other mutual acts present a certain participation of interacting suggestion. Yet more. Hardly a single deed whatever occurs that stands out over the everyday, hardly a crime is committed, without the concurrence of third persons, direct or indirect, not unseldom bearing a likeness to the effects of suggestion.

We must here admit that Tarde was right when he said that it is less difficult to find crimes of the crowd than to discover crimes which were not such and which would indicate no sort of promotion or participation of the environment. That is true to such a degree that one may ask whether there are any individual crimes at all, as the question is also conceivable whether there are any works of genius which do not have a collective character.

Many believe that crimes are always pondered. A closer insight into the behavior of criminals testifies, however, in many cases that even when there is a long period of indecision, a single encouraging word from the environment, an example with a suggestive effect, is quite sufficient to scatter all considerations and to bring the criminal intention to the deed. In organized societies, too, a mere nod from the chief may often lead with magic power to a crime.

The ideas, efforts, and behavior of the individual may by no means be looked on as something sharply distinct, individually peculiar, since from the form and manner of these ideas, efforts, and behavior, there shines forth ever, more or less, the influence of the milieu.

In close connection with this fact there stands also the so-called astringent effect of the milieu upon the individuals who are incapable of rising out of their environment, of stepping out of it. In society that bacillus for which one has found the name "suggestion" appears certainly as a leveling element, and, accordingly, whether the individual stands higher or lower than his environment, whether he becomes worse or better under its influence, he always loses or gains something from the contact with others. This is the basis of the great importance of suggestion as a factor in imposing a social uniformity upon individuals.

The power of suggestion and contra-suggestion, however, extends yet further. It enhances sentiments and aims and enkindles the activity of the masses to an unusual degree.

Many historical personages who knew how to embody in themselves the emotions and the desires of the masses—we may think of Jeanne d'Arc, Mahomet, Peter the Great, Napoleon I—were surrounded with a nimbus by the more or less blind belief of the people in their genius; this frequently acted with suggestive power upon the surrounding company which it carried away with a magic force to its leaders, and supported and aided the mission historically vested in the latter by means of their spiritual superiority. A nod from a beloved leader of any army is sufficient to enkindle anew the courage of the regiment and to lead them irresistibly into sure death.

Many, it is well known, are still inclined to deny the individual personality any influence upon the course of historic events. The individual is to them only an expression of the views of the mass, an embodiment of the epoch, something, therefore, that cannot actively strike at the course of history; he is much rather himself heaved up out of the mass by historic events, which, unaffected by the individual, proceed in the courses they have themselves chosen.

We forget in such a theory the influences of the suggestive factors which, independently of endowments and of energy, appear as a mighty lever in the hands of the fortunately situated nature and of those created to be the rulers of the masses. That the individual reflects his environment and his time, that the events of world-history only take their course upon an appropriately prepared basis and under appropriately favorable circumstances, no one will deny. There rests, however, in the masters of speech and writing, in the demagogues and the favorites of the people, in the great generals and statesmen, an inner power which welds together the masses for battle for an ideal, sweeps them away to heroism, and fires them to do deeds which leave enduring impressions in the history of humanity.

I believe, therefore, that suggestion as an active agent should be the object of the most attentive study for the historians and the sociologists. Where this factor is not reckoned with, a whole series of historical and social phenomena is threatened with the danger of incomplete, insufficient, and perhaps even incorrect elucidation.

III. INVESTIGATIONS AND PROBLEMS

1. The Process of Interaction

The concept of universal interaction was first formulated in philosophy. Kant listed community or reciprocity among his dynamic categories. In the Herbartian theory of a world of coexisting individuals, the notion of reciprocal action was central. The distinctive contribution of Lotze was his recognition that interaction of the parts implies the unity of the whole since external action implies internal changes in the interacting objects. Ormond in his book *The Foundations of Knowledge* completes this philosophical conception by embodying in it a conclusion based on social psychology. Just as society is constituted by interacting persons whose innermost nature, as a result of interaction, is internal to each, so the universe is constituted by the totality of interacting units internally predisposed to interaction as elements and products of the process.

In sociology, Gumplowicz arrived at the notions of a "natural social process" and of "reciprocal action of heterogeneous elements" in his study of the conflict of races.   Ratzenhofer, Simmel, and Small place the social process and socialization central in their systems of sociology.   Cooley's recent book *The Social Process* is an intimate and sympathetic exposition of "interaction" and the "social process." "Society is a complex of forms or processes each of which is living and growing by interaction with the others, the whole being so unified that what takes place in one part affects all the rest.   It is a vast tissue of reciprocal activity, differentiated into innumerable systems, some of them quite distinct, others not readily traceable, and all interwoven to such a degree that you see different systems according to the point of view you take."[1]

This brief résumé of the general literature upon the social process and social interaction is introductory to an examination of the more concrete material upon communication, imitation, and suggestion.

2.   Communication

"Many works have been written on Expression, but a greater number on Physiognomy" wrote Charles Darwin in 1872.   Physiognomy, or the interpretation of character through the observation of the features, has long been relegated by the scientific world to the limbo occupied by astrology, alchemy, phrenology, and the practice of charlatans.

While positive contributions to an appreciation of human expression were made before Darwin, as by Sir Charles Bell, Pierre Gratiolet, and Dr. Piderit, his volume on *The Expression of the Emotions in Man and Animals* marked an epoch in the thinking upon the subject. Although his three principles of utility, antithesis, and direct nervous discharge to explain the signs of emotions may be open to question, as the physiological psychologist, Wilhelm Wundt, asserts, the great value of his contribution is generally conceded.   His convincing demonstration of the universal similarity of emotional expression in the various human races, a similarity based on a common human inheritance, prepared the way for further study.

Darwin assumed that the emotion was a mental state which preceded and caused its expression.   According to the findings of later observation, popularly known as the James-Lange Theory, the

[1] *The Social Process*, p. 28.

emotion is the mental sign of a behavior change whose external aspects constitute the so-called "expression." The important point brought out by this new view of the emotion was an emphasis upon the nature of physiological changes involved in emotional response. Certain stimuli affect visceral processes and thereby modify the perception of external objects.

The impetus to research upon this subject given by Darwin was first manifest in the reports of observation upon the expression of different emotions. Fear, anger, joy, were made the subjects of individual monographs. Several brilliant essays, as those by Sully, Dugas, and Bergson, appeared in one field alone, that of laughter. In the last decade there has been a distinct tendency toward the experimental study of the physiological and chemical changes which constitute the inner aspect of emotional responses, as for example, the report of Cannon upon his studies in his book *Bodily Changes in Pain, Hunger, Fear, and Rage.*

Simultaneous with this study of the physiological aspect of the emotional responses went further observation of its expression, the manifestation of the emotion. The research upon the communication of emotions and ideas proceeded from natural signs to gesture and finally to language. Genetic psychologists pointed out that the natural gesture is an abbreviated act. Mallery's investigation upon "Sign Language among North American Indians Compared with that among Other Peoples and Deaf Mutes" disclosed the high development of communication by gestures among Indian tribes. Wilhelm Wundt in his study of the origin of speech indicated the intimate relation between language and gesture in his conclusion that speech is vocal gesture. Similarly research in the origin of writing derives it, as indicated earlier in this chapter, through the intermediate form of pictographs from pictures.

The significance for social life of the extension of communication through inventions has impressed ethnologists, historians, and sociologists. The ethnologist determines the beginnings of ancient civilization by the invention of writing. Historians have noted and emphasized the relation of the printing press to the transition from medieval to modern society. Graham Wallas in his *Great Society* interprets modern society as a creation of the machine and of the artificial means of communication.

Sociological interest in language and writing is turning from studies of origins to investigations of their function in group life. Material is now available which indicates the extent to which the group may be studied through its language. Accordingly the point of view for the study of orthodox speech, or "correct" English, is that of the continuity of society; just as the standpoint for the study of heterodox language, or "slang," is that of the life of the group at the moment. The significance of the fact that "every group has its own language" is being recognized in its bearings upon research. Studies of dialects of isolated groups, of the argot of social classes, of the technical terms of occupational groups, of the precise terminology of scientific groups suggest the wide range of concrete materials. The expression "different universes of discourse" indicates how communication separates as well as unites persons and groups.

3. Imitation

Bagehot's *Physics and Politics* published in 1872, with its chapter on "Imitation," was the first serious account of the nature of the rôle of imitation in social life. Gabriel Tarde, a French magistrate, becoming interested in imitation as an explanation of the behavior of criminals, undertook an extensive observation of its effects in the entire field of human activities. In his book *Laws of Imitation*, published in 1890, he made imitation synonymous with all intermental activity. "I have always given it (imitation) a very precise and characteristic meaning, that of the action at a distance of one mind upon another. . . . . By imitation I mean every impression of inter-psychical photography, so to speak, willed or not willed, passive or active."[1] "The unvarying characteristic of every social fact whatsoever is that it is imitative, and this characteristic belongs exclusively to social facts."[2]

In this unwarranted extension of the concept of imitation Tarde undeniably had committed the unpardonable sin of science, i.e., he substituted for the careful study and patient observation of imitative behavior, easy and glittering generalizations upon uniformities in society. Contributions to an understanding of the actual process of imitation came from psychologists. Baldwin brought forward the concept of circular reaction to explain the interrelation of stimulus

[1] P, xiv.　　　　　[2] P. 41.

and response in imitation. He also indicated the place of imitation in personal development in his description of the dialectic of personal growth where the self develops in a process of give-and-take with other selves. Dewey, Stout, Mead, Henderson, and others, emphasizing the futility of the mystical explanation of imitation by imitation, have pointed out the influence of interest and attention upon imitation as a learning process. Mead, with keen analysis of the social situation, interprets imitation as the process by which the person practices rôles in social life. The studies of Thorndike may be mentioned as representative of the important experimental research upon this subject.

4. Suggestion

The reflective study of imitation originated in attempts at the explanation of uniformities in the behavior of individuals. Research in suggestion began in the narrow but mysterious field of the occult. In 1765 Mesmer secured widespread attention by advancing the theory that heavenly bodies influence human beings by means of a subtle fluid which he called "animal magnetism." Abbé Faria, who came to Paris from India in 1814–15, demonstrated by experiments that the cause of the hypnotic sleep was subjective. With the experiments in 1841 of Dr. James Braid, the originator of the term "hypnotism," the scientific phase of the development of hypnotism began. The acceptance of the facts of hypnotism by the scientific world was the result of the work of Charcot and his students of the so-called Nancy School of Psychology.

From the study of hypnotism to observation upon the rôle of suggestion in social life was a short step. Binet, Sidis, Münsterberg have formulated psychological definitions of suggestion and indicated its significance for an understanding of so-called crowd phenomena in human behavior. Bechterew in his monograph *Die Bedeutung der Suggestion im Sozialen Leben* has presented an interpretation of distinct value for sociological research. At the present time there are many promising developments in the study of suggestion in special fields, such as advertising, crowd psychology, leadership, politics, religion.

5. Invention

It has been said that it is impossible to will to do anything new. What one wants is something that one has already had or known.

It is in the effort to realize an old value in a new situation that men make discoveries and inventions. The statement rests, as do most other general statements of the sort, upon a definition. What do we mean by "new"; what is an invention?

Darwin, in describing the process of biological evolution, assumed the existence of variations. Individual organisms exhibit variations from type. No two individuals are exactly alike. The process of natural selection determines which of these individuals shall survive and be transmitted. In this way new types are gradually evolved.

In the same way it may be assumed that society in "the struggle for existence," that is to say, in the effort to realize, in a new environment and under changed conditions, recognized and accepted values, selects and accumulates, and so creates new values.

This leaves unanswered the question: How do variations occur? For the student of society the question assumes, finally, a somewhat different form, namely: Under what conditions do inventions arise?

Under the title of "Suggestion and Imitation" psychologists have sought to describe the processes by which recognized values, and the devices by which these values may be realized, are communicated. The literature listed under invention[1] is intended to indicate the manner in which biologists, psychologists, and sociologists have sought to formulate and investigate the problem of invention. But, as yet, no adequate sociological study of invention has been made.

In general it may, perhaps, be said that inventions arise in the effort of individuals and society to act. Invention, in the sense of an idea, social program, device, or conscious construction to meet some conscious and recognized need of individuals or society, is dependent finally upon the existing organization of social life and the ability of man to predict and control his own future. Social changes are always and everywhere taking place, and society, by processes that are only partly conscious and controlled, is steadily selecting and appropriating them. But invention, in the narrower and stricter use of that term, may be said to take place only so far as man can foresee and predict his future in terms of his past and present.[2]

[1] See p. 431.

[2] See chap. xiv, "Progress," especially pp. 955–56 and 1001–2.

SELECTED BIBLIOGRAPHY

I. INTERACTION AND SOCIAL INTERACTION

(1) Lotze, Hermann. *Metaphysic.* Vol. I, chap. vi, "The Unity of Things." Oxford, 1887.

(2) Ormond, Alexander T. *Foundations of Knowledge.* Chap. vii, "Community or Interaction." London and New York, 1900.

(3) Gumplowicz, L. *Der Rassenkampf.* Sociologische Untersuchungen. Pp. 158–75. Innsbruck, 1883.

(4) Simmel, Georg. "Über sociale Differenzierung, sociologische und psychologische Untersuchungen." *Staats- und Socialwissenschaftliche Forschungen,* edited by G. Schmoller. Vol. X. Leipzig, 1891.

(5) Royce, J. *The World and the Individual.* 2d ser. "Nature, Man, and the Moral Order," Lecture IV. "Physical and Social Reality." London and New York, 1901.

(6) Boodin, J. E. "Social Systems," *American Journal of Sociology,* XXIII (May, 1918), 705–34.

(7) Tosti, Gustavo. "Social Psychology and Sociology," *The Psychological Review,* V (July, 1898), 348–61.

(8) Small, Albion W. *General Sociology.* Chicago, 1905.

(9) Cooley, Charles H. *The Social Process.* New York, 1918.

II. SOCIAL INTERACTION AND SOCIAL CONSCIOUSNESS

(1) Marshall, Henry R. *Consciousness.* Chap. vii, "Of Consciousnesses More Complex than Human Consciousness." New York and London, 1909.

(2) Baldwin, James Mark. *Social and Ethical Interpretations in Mental Development.* A study in social psychology. New York and London, 1906.

(3) Royce, Josiah. "Self-Consciousness, Social Consciousness and Nature," *Philosophical Review,* IV (1895), 465–85; 577–602.

(4) ———. "The External World and the Social Consciousness," *Philosophical Review,* III (1894), 513–45.

(5) Worms, René. *Organisme et Société.* Chap. x, "Fonctions de Relation." Paris, 1896.

(6) Mead, G. H. "Social Consciousness and the Consciousness of Meaning," *Psychological Bulletin,* VII (Dec. 15, 1910), 397–405.

(7) ———. "Psychology of Social Consciousness Implied in Instruction," *Science,* N.S., XXI (1910), 688–93.

(8) Novicow, J. *Conscience et volonté sociales.* Paris, 1897.

(9) McDougall, W. *The Group Mind.* A sketch of the principles of collective psychology with some attempt to apply them to the interpretation of national life and character. New York and London, 1920.

(10) Perry, Ralph Barton. "Is There a Social Mind?" *American Journal of Sociology,* XXVII (1922), 561–72, 721–36.

(11) Ames, Edward S. "Religion in Terms of Social Consciousness," *Journal of Religion,* I (1921), 264–70.

(12) Burgess, E. W. *The Function of Socialization in Social Evolution.* Chicago, 1916.

(13) Maciver, R. M. *Community.* A sociological study, an attempt to set out the nature and fundamental laws of social life. London, 1917.

III. COMMUNICATION AND INTERACTION

A. *The Emotions and Emotional Expression*

(1) James, William. *The Principles of Psychology.* Vol. II, chap. xxv. New York, 1896.
(2) Dewey, John. "The Theory of Emotion," *Psychological Review,* I (1894), 553–69; II (1895), 13–32.
(3) Wundt, Wilhelm. *Grundzüge der physiologischen Psychologie.* 3 vols. 6th ed. Leipzig, 1908–11.
(4) Ribot, T. *The Psychology of the Emotions.* London and New York, 1898.
(5) Darwin, Charles. *The Expression of the Emotions in Man and Animals.* London and New York, 1873.
(6) Rudolph, Heinrich. *Der Ausdruck der Gemütsbewegungen des Menschen dargestellt und erklärt auf Grund der Urformen und der Gesetze des Ausdrucks und der Erregungen.* Dresden, 1903.
(7) Piderit, T. *Mimik und Physiognomik.* Rev. ed. Detmold, 1886.
(8) Hirn, Yrjö. *The Origins of Art.* A psychological and sociological inquiry. London and New York, 1900.
(9) Cannon, Walter B. *Bodily Changes in Pain, Hunger, Fear, and Rage.* An account of recent researches into the function of emotional excitement. New York and London, 1915.
(10) Hall, G. Stanley. "A Study of Fears," *American Journal of Psychology,* VIII (1896–97), 147–249.
(11) Saunders, F. H., and Hall, G. Stanley. "Pity," *American Journal of Psychology* XI (1899–1900), 534–91.
(12) Stanley, H. M. "The Psychology of Pity," *Science,* N.S., XII (1900), 487–88.
(13) Bergson, H. *Le Rire.* Essai sur la signification du comique. Paris, 1900.
(14) Sully, James. *An Essay on Laughter.* Its forms, its causes, its development, and its value. London and New York, 1902.
(15) Dugas, L. *Psychologie du rire.* Paris, 1902.
(16) Greig, J. Y. T. *The Psychology of Laughter and Comedy.* New York, 1923.
(17) Groos, Karl. *The Play of Man.* Translated from the German by Elizabeth L. Baldwin. New York, 1901.
(18) ———. *The Play of Animals.* Translated from the German by Elizabeth L. Baldwin. New York, 1898.
(19) Royce, J. *The Spirit of Modern Philosophy.* An essay in the form of lectures. Chap. xii, "Physical Law and Freedom: The World of Description and the World of Appreciation." Boston, 1892.
(20) Bücher, Karl. *Arbeit und Rhythmus.* Leipzig, 1902.
(21) Mallery, Garrick. "Sign Language among North American Indians compared with That among Other Peoples and Deaf Mutes." *United States Bureau of American Ethnology. First Annual Report.* Washington, 1881.
(22) Ogden, C. K., and Richards, I. A. *The Meaning of Meaning.* A study of the influence of language upon thought and of the science of symbolism. London, 1923.

B. *Language and the Printing Press*

(1) Schmoller. Gustav. *Grundriss der allgemeinen Volkswirtschaftslehre.* Chap. ii, 2, "Die psychophysischen Mittel menschlicher Verständigung: Sprache und Schrift." Leipzig, 1900.

(2) Jespersen, Otto. *Language.* Its nature, development, and origin. London, 1922.

(3) Vendryes, J. *Le Langage.* Introduction linguistique a l'histoire. Paris, 1921.

(4) Lazarus, Moritz. "Das Leben der Seele," *Geist und Sprache,* Vol. II. Berlin, 1878.

(5) Wundt, Wilhelm. "Völkerpsychologie." Eine Untersuchung der Entwicklungsgesetze von Sprache, Mythus, und Sitte. *Die Sprache,* Vol. I. Part 1. Leipzig, 1900.

(6) Wuttke, Heinrich. *Die deutschen Zeitschriften und die Entstehung der öffentlichen Meinung.* Ein Beitrag zur Geschichte des Zeitungswesens. Leipzig, 1875.

(7) Mason, William A. *A History of the Art of Writing.* New York, 1920.

(8) Bücher, Carl. *Industrial Evolution.* Translated from the German by S. M. Wickett. Chap. vi, "The Genesis of Journalism." New York, 1901.

(9) Dibblee, G. Binney. *The Newspaper.* New York and London, 1913.

(10) Payne, George Henry. *History of Journalism in the United States.* New York and London, 1920.

(11) Kawabé, Kisaburō. *The Press and Politics in Japan.* A study of the relation between the newspaper and the political development of modern Japan. Chicago, 1921.

(12) Münsterberg, Hugo. *The Photoplay.* A psychological study. New York, 1916.

(13) Kingsbury, J. E. *The Telephone and Telephone Exchanges.* Their invention and development. London and New York, 1915.

(14) Borght, R. van der. *Das Verkehrswesen.* Leipzig, 1894.

(15) Mason, O. T. *Primitive Travel and Transportation.* New York, 1897.

[See bibliographies, "The Newspaper as an Organ of Public Opinion," pp. 858–59, and "Language Revivals and Nationalism," pp. 945–46.]

C. *Slang, Argot, and Universes of Discourse*

(1) Farmer, John S. *Slang and Its Analogues Past and Present.* A dictionary, historical and comparative, of the heterodox speech of all classes of society for more than three hundred years. With synonyms in English, French, German, Italian, etc. London. 1890–1904.

(2) Lisch, R. *Sondersprachen und ihre Entstehung.* Wien, 1907.

(3) Sechrist, Frank K. *The Psychology of Unconventional Language.* Worcester, Mass., 1913.

(4) Ware, J. Redding. *Passing English of the Victorian Era.* A dictionary of heterodox English, slang and phrase. New York, 1909.

(5) Hotten, John C. *A Dictionary of Modern Slang, Cant, and Vulgar Words.* Used at the present day in the streets of London; the universities of Oxford and Cambridge; the houses of Parliament; the dens of St. Giles; and the palaces of St. James. Preceded by a history of cant and vulgar language; with glossaries of two secret languages, spoken by the wandering tribes of London, the costermongers, and the patterers. London, 1859.

(6) ———. *The Slang Dictionary.* Etymological, historical, and anecdotal. New York, 1898.

(7) Farmer, John S. *The Public School Word-Book.* A contribution to a historical glossary of words, phrases, and turns of expression, obsolete and in present use, peculiar to our great public schools, together with some that have been or are modish at the universities. London, 1900.

(8) *A New Dictionary of the Terms Ancient and Modern of the Canting Crew.* In its several tribes of gypsies, beggars, thieves, cheats, etc., with an addition of some proverbs, phrases, and figurative speeches, etc. London, 1690. Reprinted, 19–.

(9) Kluge, F. *Rotwelsch.* Quellen und Wortschatz der Gaunersprache und der verwandten Geheimsprachen. Strassburg, 1901.

(10) Barrère, Albert, and Leland, C. G., editors. *A Dictionary of Slang, Jargon, and Cant.* Embracing English, American, and Anglo-Indian slang, pidgin English, gypsies' jargon, and other irregular phraseology. 2 vols. London, 1897.

(11) Villatte, Césaire. *Parisismen.* Alphabetisch geordnete Sammlung der eigenartigen Ausdrucksweisen des Pariser Argot. Ein Supplement zu allen französisch-deutschen Wörterbüchern. Berlin, 1899.

(12) Delesalle, Georges. *Dictionnaire argot-français et français-argot.* Nouvelle édition. Paris, 1899.

(13) Villon, François. *Le jargon et jobelin de François Villon, suivi du jargon au théâtre.* Paris, 1888.

(14) Săineanu, Lazar. *L'Argot ancien (1455–1850).* Ses éléments constitutifs, ses rapports avec les langues secrètes de l'Europe méridionale et l'argot moderne, avec un appendice sur l'argot juge par Victor Hugo et Balzac; par Lazare Sainéan, pseud. Paris, 1907.

(15) Klenz, Heinrich. *Die deutsche Druckersprache.* Strassburg, 1900.

(16) Dauzat, Albert. *Les argots des métiers franco-provençaux.* Paris, 1917.

(17) Leland, Charles G. *The English Gypsies and Their Languages.* 4th ed. New York, 1893.

(18) *Dictionnaire des termes militaires et de l'argot poilu.* Paris, 1916.

(19) Empey, Arthur Guy. *Over the Top.* By an American soldier who went, Arthur Guy Empey, machine gunner, serving in France; together with Tommy's dictionary of the trenches. New York and London, 1917.

(20) Smith, L. N. *Lingo of No Man's Land; or, War Time Lexicon.* Compiled by Sergt. Lorenzo N. Smith. Chicago, 1918.

(21) Săineanu, Lazar. *L'Argot des tranchées.* D'après les lettres des poilus et les journaux du front. Paris, 1915.

(22) Horn, Paul. *Die deutsche Soldatensprache.* Giessen, 1905.

[See bibliography, "Dialects as a Factor in Isolation," pp. 275–76.]

IV. IMITATION, SUGGESTION, AND INVENTION

A. *Imitation*

(1) Bagehot, Walter. *Physics and Politics; or, Thoughts on the Application of the Principles of "Natural Selection" and "Inheritance" to Political Society.* New York, 1873.

(2) Tarde, Gabriel. *The Laws of Imitation.* Translated from the 2d French ed. by Elsie Clews Parsons. New York, 1903.

(3) Baldwin, James M. *Mental Development in the Child and the Race.* Methods and processes. 3d rev. ed. New York, 1906.

(4) ———. *Social and Ethical Interpretations in Mental Development.* A study in social psychology. 4th ed. New York, 1906.

(5) Royce, Josiah. *Outlines of Psychology.* An elementary treatise with some practical applications. New York, 1903.

(6) Henderson, Ernest N. *A Text-Book in the Principles of Education.* Chap. xi, "Imitation." New York, 1910.

(7) Thorndike, E. L. *Educational Psychology.* Vol. I, The Original Nature of Man. Chap. viii, pp. 108–22. New York, 1913.

(8) Hughes, Henry. *Die Mimik des Menschen auf Grund voluntarischer Psychologie.* Frankfurt a. M., 1900.

(9) Park, Robert E. *Masse und Publikum.* Eine methodologische und soziologische Untersuchung. Chap. ii, "Der soziologische Prozess," describes the historical development of the conception of imitation in its relation to sympathy and mimicry in the writings of Hume, Butler, and Dugald Stewart. Bern, 1904.

(10) Smith, Adam. *The Theory of Moral Sentiments.* To which is added a dissertation on the origin of languages. London, 1892.

(11) Ribot, T. *The Psychology of the Emotions.* Part II, chap. iv, "Sympathy and the Tender Emotions," pp. 230–38. Translated from the French. 2d ed. London, 1911.

(12) Dewey, John. "Imitation in Education," *Cyclopedia of Education,* III, 389–90.

(13) Hirn, Yrjö. *The Origins of Art.* A psychological and sociological inquiry. Chap. vi, "Social Expression." London and New York, 1900.

B. *Suggestion*

(1) Moll, Albert. *Hypnotism.* Including a study of the chief points of psychotherapeutics and occultism. Translated from the 4th enl. ed. by A. F. Hopkirk. London and New York, 1909.

(2) Binet, A., and Féré, Ch. *Animal Magnetism.* New York, 1892.

(3) Janet, Pierre. *L'Automisme psychologique.* Essai de psychologie expérimentale sur les formes inférieures de l'activité humaine. Paris, 1889.

(4) Bernheim, H. *Hypnotisme, Suggestion, Psychothérapie.* Paris, 1891.

(5) Richet, Ch. *Experimentelle Studien auf dem Gebiete der Gedankenübertragung und des sogenannten Hellsehens.* Deutsch von Frhrn. von Schrenck-Notzing. Stuttgart, 1891.

(6) Pfungst, Oskar. *Clever Hans (The Horse of Mr. von Osten).* A contribution to experimental animal and human psychology. New York, 1911. [Bibliography.]

(7) Hansen, F. C. C., and Lehmann, A. *Über unwillkürliches Flüstern.* Philosophische Studien, Leipzig, XI (1895), 471–530.

(8) Féré, Ch. *Sensation et mouvement.* Chap. xix, pp. 120–24. Paris, 1887.

(9) Sidis, Boris. *The Psychology of Suggestion.* A research into the subconscious nature of man and society. New York, 1898.

(10) Bechterew, W. v. *Die Bedeutung der Suggestion im Sozialen Leben.* Grenzfragen des Nerven- und Seelenlebens. Wiesbaden, 1905.

(11) Stoll, Otto. *Suggestion und Hypnotismus in der Völkerpsychologie.* Leipzig, 1904.

(12) Binet, Alfred. *La Suggestibilité.* Paris, 1900.

(13) Münsterberg, Hugo. *Psychotherapy.* Chap. v, "Suggestion and Hypnotism," pp. 85–124. New York, 1909.

(14) Cooley, Charles. *Human Nature and the Social Order.* Chap. ii. New York, 1902.

(15) Gulick, Sidney. *The American Japanese Problem.* A study of the racial relations of the East and the West. Pp. 118–68. New York, 1914.

(16) Fishberg, Maurice. *The Jews.* A study of race and environment. London and New York, 1911. [Attempts to explain certain so-called "racial traits" as a result of imitation and suggestion.]

C. *Invention*

(1) Baldwin, J. M. *Social and Ethical Interpretations in Mental Development.* Part II, "The Inventive Person," pp. 57–184. New York, 1897.

(2) Morgan, C. L. *Emergent Evolution.* London, 1923.

(3) Ribot, Th. *Essay on the Creative Imagination.* Translated from the French by Albert H. N. Baron. Chicago, 1906.

(4) Royce, Josiah. "Psychology of Invention," *Psychological Review,* V (1898).

(5) Mason, O. T. *Origins of Invention.* A study of industry among primitive peoples. London, 1895.

(6) Cooley, Charles H. "Genius, Fame, and the Comparison of Races," *Annals of the American Academy,* IX (1897), 317–58.

(7) Tanner, Amy E. "Certain Social Aspects of Invention," *American Journal of Psychology,* XXVI (1915), 388–416. [Bibliography.]

TOPICS FOR WRITTEN THEMES

1. A History of the Concept of Social Interaction
2. Interaction and the Atomic Theory
3. Interaction and Social Consciousness
4. Interaction and Self-Consciousness
5. Religion and Social Consciousness
6. Publicity and Social Consciousness
7. Interaction and the Limits of the Group
8. The Senses and Communication: a Comparative Study of the Rôle of Touch, Smell, Sight, and Hearing in Social Intercourse

9. Facial Expression as a Form of Communication
10. Laughter and Blushing and Self-Consciousness
11. The Sociology of Gesture
12. The Subtler Forms of Interaction; "Mind-Reading," "Thought Transference"
13. Rapport, A Study of Mutual Influence in Intimate Associations
14. A History of Imitation as a Sociological Theory
15. Suggestion as an Explanation of Collective Behavior
16. Adam Smith's Theory of the Relation of Sympathy and Moral Judgment
17. Interest, Attention, and Imitation
18. Imitation and Appreciation
19. The History of Printing and of the Press
20. Modern Extensions of Communication: the Telephone, the Telegraph, Radio, the Motion Picture, Popular Music
21. An Explanation of Secondary Society in Terms of Secondary Devices of Communication
22. Graham Wallas' Conception of the Problem of Social Heritages in Secondary Society

QUESTIONS FOR DISCUSSION

1. What do you understand Gumplowicz to mean by a "natural process"?
2. Do you think that the idea of a "natural process" is applicable to society?
3. Is Gumplowicz' principle of the interaction of social elements valid?
4. What do you understand Simmel to mean by society? by socialization?
5. Do you agree with Simmel when he says, "In and of themselves, these materials with which life is filled, these motivations which impel it, are not social in their nature"?
6. In what ways, according to Simmel, does interaction maintain the mechanism of the group in time?
7. What do you understand to be the distinction which Simmel makes between attitudes of appreciation and comprehension?
8. "The interaction of individuals based upon mutual glances is perhaps the most direct and purest reciprocity which exists." Explain.
9. Explain the sociology of the act of looking down to avoid the glance of the other.
10. In what way does Simmel's distinction between the reactions to other persons of the blind and the deaf-mute afford an explanation of the difference between the social life of the village and of the large city?

11. In what sense are emotions expressive? To whom are they expressive?

12. What is the relation of emotional expression to communication?

13. Why would you say Darwin states that "blushing is the most peculiar and the most human of all expressions"?

14. Does a person ever blush in isolation?

15. What in your opinion is the bearing of the phenomenon of blushing upon interaction and communication?

16. What is the difference between the function of blushing and of laughing in social life?

17. In what sense is sympathy the "law of laughter"?

18. What determines the object of laughter?

19. What is the sociological explanation of the rôle of laughter and ridicule in social control?

20. What are the likenesses and differences between intercommunication among animals and language among men?

21. What is the criterion of the difference between man and the animal, according to Max Müller?

22. In your opinion, was the situation in which language arose one of unanimity or diversity of attitude?

23. "Language and ideational processes developed together and are necessary to each other." Explain.

24. What is the relation of the evolution of writing as a form of communication (a) to the development of ideas, and (b) to social life?

25. What difference in function, if any, is there between communication carried on (a) merely through expressive signs, (b) language, (c) writing, (d) printing?

26. How does the evolution of publicity exhibit the extension of communication by human invention?

27. In what ways is the extension of communication related to primary and secondary contacts?

28. Does the growth of communication make for or against the development of individuality?

29. How do you define imitation?

30. What is the relation of attention and interest to the mechanism of imitation?

31. What is the relation of imitation to learning?

32. What is the relation of imitation to the three phases of sympathy differentiated by Ribot?

33. What do you understand by Smith's definition of sympathy? How does it differ from that of Ribot?

34. Under what conditions is the sentiment aroused in the observer likely to resemble that of the observed? When is it likely to be different?

35. In what sense is sympathy the basis for passing a moral judgment upon a person or an act?
36. What do you understand by "internal imitation"?
37. What is the significance of imitation for artistic appreciation?
38. What do you understand by the term "appreciation"? Distinguish between "appreciation" and "comprehension." (Compare Hirn's distinction with that made by Simmel.)
39. Upon what is the nature of suggestion based? How do you define suggestion?
40. What do you understand by Bechterew's distinction between active perception and passive perception?
41. Why can we speak of suggestion as a mental automatism?
42. How real is the analogy of suggestion to an infection or an inoculation?
43. What do you understand by the distinction between personal consciousness and general consciousness?
44. What is the significance of attention in determining the character of suggestion?
45. What is the relation of rapport to suggestion?
46. How would you distinguish suggestion from other forms of stimulus and response?
47. Is suggestion a term of individual or of social psychology?
48. What is the significance of the case of Clever Hans for the interpretation of so-called telepathy? of muscle reading?
49. How extensive, would you say, are the subtler forms of suggestion in normal life? What illustrations would you give?
50. What is the rôle of social contagion in mass action?
51. What do you understand Bechterew to mean by "the psychological processes of fusion"? "spiritual cohesion," etc.?
52. What does it mean to say that historical personages "embody in themselves the emotions and the desires of the masses"?
53. What, in your judgment, are the differentiating criteria of suggestion and imitation?
54. What do you understand is meant by speaking of imitation and suggestion as mechanisms of interaction?

CHAPTER VII

SOCIAL FORCES

I. INTRODUCTION

1. Sources of the Notion of Social Forces

The concept of interaction is an abstraction so remote from ordinary experience that it seems to have occurred only to scientists and philosophers. The idea of forces behind the manifestations of physical nature and of society is a notion which arises naturally out of the experience of the ordinary man. Historians, social reformers, and students of community life have used the term in the language of common sense to describe factors in social situations which they recognized but did not attempt to describe or define. Movements for social reform have usually met with unexpected obstacles. Public welfare programs have not infrequently been received with popular antagonism instead of popular support. Lack of success has led to the search for causes, and investigation has revealed the obstacles, as well as the aids, to reform embodied in influential persons, "political bosses," "union leaders," "the local magnate," and in powerful groups such as party organizations, unions, associations of commerce, etc. Social control, it appears, is resident, not in individuals as individuals, but as members of communities and social groups. Candid recognition of the rôle of these persons and groups led popular writers on social, political, and economic topics to give them the impersonal designation "social forces."

A student made the following crude and yet illuminating analysis of the social forces in a small community where he had lived: the community club, "the Davidson clique," and the "Jones clique" (these two large family groups are intensely hostile and divide village life); the community Methodist church; the Presbyterian church group (no church); the library; two soft-drink parlors where all kinds of beverages are sold; the daily train; the motion-picture show; the dance hall; a gambling clique; sex attraction; gossip; the "sporting" impulse; the impulse to be "decent."

"The result," he states, "is a disgrace to our modern civilization. It is one of the worst communities I ever saw."

The most significant type of community study has been the social survey, with a history which antedates its recent developments. Yet the survey movement from the *Domesday Survey*, initiated in 1085 by William the Conqueror, to the recent *Study of Methods of Americanization* by the Carnegie Corporation, has been based upon an implicit or explicit recognition of the interrelations of the community and its constituent groups. The *Domesday Survey*, although undertaken for financial and political purposes, gives a picture of the English nation as an organization of isolated local units, which the Norman Conquest first of all forced into closer unity. The surveys of the Russell Sage Foundation have laid insistent emphasis upon the study of social problems and of social institutions in their context within the life of the community. The central theme of the different divisions of the Carnegie *Study of Methods of Americanization* is the nature and the degree of the participation of the immigrant in our national and cultural life. In short, the survey, wittingly or unwittingly, has tended to penetrate beneath surface observations to discover the interrelations of social groups and institutions and has revealed community life as a *constellation of social forces*.

2. History of the Concept of Social Forces

The concept of social forces has had a history different from that of interaction. It was in the writings of the historians rather than of the sociologists that the term first gained currency. The historians, in their description and interpretation of persons and events, discerned definite motives or tendencies, which served to give to the mere temporal sequence of the events a significance which they did not otherwise possess. These tendencies historians called "social forces."

From the point of view and for the purposes of reformers social forces were conceived as embodied in institutions. For the purposes of the historian they are merely tendencies which combine to define the general trend of historical change. The logical motive, which has everywhere guided science in formulating its conceptions, is here revealed in its most naïve and elementary form. Natural science invariably seeks to describe change in terms of process, that is to say, in terms of interaction of tendencies. These tendencies are what science calls forces.

For the purposes of an adequate description, however, it is necessary not merely to conceive change in terms of the interplay of forces, but to think of these forces as somehow objectively embodied, as social forces are conceived to be embodied in institutions, organizations, and persons. These objects in which the forces are, or seem to be, resident are not forces in any real or metaphysical sense, as the physicists tell us. They are mere points of reference which enable us to visualize the direction and measure the intensity of change.

Institutions and social organizations may, in any given situation, be regarded as social forces, but they are not ultimate nor elementary forces. One has but to carry the analysis of the community a little farther to discover the fact that institutions and organizations may be further resolved into factors of smaller and smaller denominations until we have arrived at individual men and women. For common sense the individual is quite evidently the ultimate factor in every community or social organization.

Sociologists have carried the analysis a step farther. They have sought to meet the problem raised by two facts: (1) the same individual may be a member of different societies, communities, and social groups at the same time; (2) under certain circumstances his interests as a member of one group may conflict with his interests as a member of another group, so that the conflict between different social groups will be reflected in the mental and moral conflicts of the individual himself. Furthermore, it is evident that the individual is, as we frequently say, "not the same person" at different times and places. The phenomena of moods and of dual personality have sociological significance in just this connection.

From all this it is quite evident that the individual is not elementary in a sociological sense. It is for this reason that sociologists have invariably sought the sociological element, not in the individual but in his appetites, desires, wishes—the human motives which move him to action.

3. Classification of the Materials

The readings in this chapter are arranged in the natural order of the development of the notion of social forces. They were first thought of by historians as tendencies and trends. Then in the popular sociology social forces were identified with significant social objects in which the factors of the situations under consideration were embodied. This was a step in the direction of a definition of the elementary social forces. Later the terms interests, sentiments, and attitudes made their appearance in the literature of economics, social psychology, and sociology. Finally the concept of the wishes, first vaguely apprehended by sociologists under the name "desires," having gained a more adequate description and definition in the use made of it by psychoanalysis, has been reintroduced into sociology by W. I. Thomas under the title of the "four wishes." This brief statement is sufficient to indicate the motives determining the order of the materials included under "Social Forces."

In the list of social forces just enumerated, attitudes are, for the purposes of sociology, elementary. They are elementary because, being tendencies to act, they are expressive and communicable. They present us human motives in the only form in which we can know them objectively, namely, as behavior. Human motives become social forces only so far as they are communicable, only when they are communicated. Because attitudes have for the purposes of sociology this elementary character, it is desirable to define the term "attitude" before attempting to define its relation to the wishes and sentiments.

a) The social element defined.—What is an attitude? Attitudes are not instincts, nor appetites, nor habits, for these refer to specific tendencies to act that condition attitudes but do not define them. Attitudes are not the same as emotions or sentiments although attitudes always are emotionally toned and frequently supported by sentiments. Opinions are not attitudes. An opinion is rather a statement made to justify and make intelligible an existing attitude or bias. A wish is an inherited tendency or instinct which has been fixed by attention directed to objects, persons, or patterns of behavior, all of which then assume the character of values. An attitude is the tendency of the person to react positively or negatively to the total situation. Accordingly, attitudes may be defined as the mobilization of the will of the person.

Attitudes are as many and as varied as the situations to which they are a response. It is, of course, not to be gainsaid that instincts, appetites, habits, emotions, sentiments, opinions, and wishes are involved in and with the attitudes. Attitudes are mobilizations and organizations of the wishes with reference to definite situations. My wishes may be very positive and definite in a given situation, but my attitude may be wavering and undetermined. On the other hand, my attitude may be clearly defined in situations where my wishes are not greatly involved. It is characteristic of the so-called academic, as distinguished from the "practical" and emotional, attitude that, under its influence, the individual seeks to emphasize all the factors in the situation and thus qualifies and often weakens the will to act. The wishes enter into attitudes as components. How many, varied, ill-defined, and conflicting may be and have been the wishes that have determined at different times the attitudes and the sentiments of individuals and nations toward the issues of war and peace? The fundamental wishes, we may assume, are the same in all situations. The attitudes and sentiments, however, in which the wishes of the individual find expression are determined not merely by these wishes, but by other factors in the situation, the wishes of other individuals, for example. The desire for recognition is a permanent and universal trait of human nature, but in the case of an egocentric personality, this wish may take the form of an excessive humility or a pretentious boasting. The wish is the same but the attitudes in which it finds expression are different.

The attitudes which are elementary for *sociological analysis* may be resolved by *psychological analysis* into smaller factors so that we may think, if we choose, of attitudes as representing constellations of smaller components which we call wishes. In fact it has been one of the great contributions of psychoanalysis to our knowledge of human behavior that it has been able to show that attitudes may be analyzed into still more elementary components and that these components, like the attitudes, are involved in a process of interaction among themselves. In other words there is organization, tension, and change in the constituent elements of the attitudes. This accounts, in part, for their mutability.

b) Attitudes as behavior patterns.—If the attitude may be said to play the rôle in sociological analysis that the elementary substances play in chemical analysis, then the rôle of the wishes may be compared to that of the electrons.

The clearest way to think of attitudes is as behavior patterns or units of behavior. The two most elementary behavior patterns are the tendency to approach and the tendency to withdraw. Translated into terms of the individual organism these are tendencies to expand and to contract. As the self expands to include other selves, as in sympathy and in fellowship, there is an extension of self-feeling to the whole group. Self-consciousness passes over, in the rapport thus established, into group consciousness. In the expansive movements characteristic of individuals under the influence of crowd excitements the individual is submerged in the mass.

On the other hand, in movements of withdrawal or of recoil from other persons, characteristic of fear and embarrassment, there is a heightening of self-consciousness. The tendency to identify one's self with other selves, to lose one's self in the ecstasy of psychic union with others, is essentially a movement toward contact; while the inclination to differentiate one's self, to lead a self-sufficient existence, apart from others, is as distinctly a movement resulting in isolation.

The simplest and most fundamental types of behavior of individuals and of groups are represented in these contrasting tendencies to approach an object or to withdraw from it. If instead of thinking of these two tendencies as unrelated, they are thought of as conflicting responses to the same situation, where the tendency to approach is modified and complicated by a tendency to withdraw, we get the phenomenon of *social distance*. There is the tendency to approach, but not too near. There is a feeling of interest and sympathy of A for B, but only when B remains at a certain distance. Thus the Negro in the southern states is "all right in his place." The northern philanthropist is interested in the advancement of the Negro but wants him to remain in the South. At least he does not want him for a neighbor. The southern white man likes the Negro as an individual, but he is not willing to treat him as an equal. The northern white man is willing to treat the Negro as an equal but he does not want him too near. The wishes are in both cases essentially the same but the attitudes are different.

The accommodations between conflicting tendencies, so flagrantly displayed in the facts of race prejudice, are not confined to the relation of white men and black. The same mechanisms are involved in all the subordinations, exclusions, privacies, social distances, and reserves which we seek everywhere, by the subtle devices of taboo and social ritual, to maintain and defend. Where the situation calls forth rival or conflicting tendencies, the resulting attitude is likely to be an accommodation, in which what has been described as distance is the determining factor. When an accommodation takes the form of the domination of A and the submission of B, the original tendencies of approach and withdrawal are transformed into attitudes of super-ordination and subordination. If primary attitudes of expansion and of contraction are thought of in terms of lateral distance, then attitudes of superiority and inferiority may be charted in the vertical plane as illustrated by the following diagram:

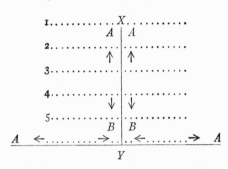

FIG. 4.—A = tendency to approach; B = tendency to withdraw; 1, 2, 3, 4, 5 = distance defining levels of accommodation; X = superordination; Y = subordination.

This polar conception of attitudes, in which they are conceived in terms of movements of expansion and contraction, of approach and withdrawal, of attraction and repulsion, of domination and submission, may be applied in an analysis of the sentiments.

A sentiment, as defined by McDougall, is "an organized system of emotional dispositions centered about the idea of some object." The polarity of the sentiments is, however, one of its evident and striking characteristics. Love and hate, affection and dislike, attachment and aversion, self-esteem and humility have this character of polarity because each pair of sentiments and attitudes represents a different constellation of the same component wishes.

A significant feature of sentiments and attitudes is inner tension and consequent tendency to mutation. Love changes into hate, or dislike is transformed into affection, or humility is replaced by self-assertion. This mutability is explained by the fact, just mentioned, that the sentiment-attitude is a complex of wishes and desires organized around a person or object. In this complex one motive—love, for example—is for a moment the dominant component.   In this case components which tend to excite repulsion, hostility, and disgust are for the moment suppressed.   With a change in the situation, as in the distance, these suppressed components are released and, gaining control, convert the system into the opposite sentiment, as hate.

c) *Attitudes and wishes.*—The wishes, as popularly conceived, are as numerous as the objects or values toward which they are directed. As there are positive and negative values, so there are positive and negative wishes.   Fears are negative wishes.   The speculations of the Freudian school of psychology have attempted to reduce all wishes to one, the *libido*.   In that case, the wishes, as we know them and as they present themselves to us in consciousness, are to be regarded as offshoots or, perhaps better, specifications of the *one wish*.   As the one wish is directed to this or that object, it makes of that object a value and the object gives its name to the wish.   In this way the one wish becomes many wishes.

Science demands, however, not a theory of the origin of the wishes but a classification based on fundamental natural differences; differences which it is necessary to take account of in explaining human behavior.   Thomas' fourfold classification fulfils this purpose.   The wish for security, the wish for new experience, the wish for response, and the wish for recognition are the permanent and fundamental unconscious motives of the person which find expression in the many and changing concrete and conscious wishes.   As wishes find expression in characteristic forms of behavior they may also be thought of in spatial terms as tendencies to move toward or away from their specific objects.   The wish for security may be represented by position, mere immobility; the wish for new experience by the greatest possible freedom of movement and constant change of position; the wish for response, by the number and closeness of points of contact; the wish for recognition, by the level desired or reached in the vertical plane of superordination and subordination.

The fundamental value for social research of the classification inheres in the fact that the wishes in one class cannot be substituted for wishes in another.   The desire for response and affection cannot be satisfied by fame and recognition or only partially so.   The wholesome individual is he who in some form or other realizes all the four fundamental wishes.   The security and permanence of any society or association depends upon the extent to which it permits the individuals who compose it to realize their fundamental wishes. The restless individual is the individual whose wishes are not realized even in dreams.

This suggests the significance of the classification for the purposes of social science. Human nature, and personality as we know it, requires for its healthy growth security, new experience, response, and recognition. In all races and in all times these fundamental longings of human nature have manifested themselves; the particular patterns in which the wish finds expression and becomes fixed depends upon some special experience of the person, is influenced by individual differences in original nature, and is circumscribed by the folkways, the mores, the conventions, and the culture of his group.

II. MATERIALS

A. TRENDS, TENDENCIES, AND PUBLIC OPINION

1. Social Forces in American History[1]

That political struggles are based upon economic interests is today disputed by few students of society. The attempt has been made in this work to trace the various interests that have arisen and struggled in each social stage and to determine the influence exercised by these contending interests in the creation of social institutions.

Back of every political party there has always stood a group or class which expected to profit by the activity and the success of that party. When any party has attained to power, it has been because it has tried to establish institutions or to modify existing ones in accord with its interests.

Changes in the industrial basis of society—inventions, new processes, and combinations and methods of producing and distributing goods—create new interests with new social classes to represent them. These improvements in the technique of production are the dynamic element that brings about what we call progress in society.

In this work I have sought to begin at the origin of each line of social progress. I have first endeavored to describe the steps in

[1] Adapted from A. M. Simons, in the Preface to *Social Forces in American History*, pp. vii–viii. (Published by The Macmillan Co., 1912. Reprinted by permission.)

mechanical progress, then the social classes brought into prominence by the mechanical changes, then the struggle by which these new classes sought to gain social power, and, finally, the institutions which were created or the alterations made in existing institutions as a consequence of the struggle or as a result of the victory of a new class.

It has seemed to me that these underlying social forces are of more importance than the individuals that were forced to the front in the process of these struggles, or even than the laws that were established to record the results of the conflict. In short, I have tried to describe the dynamics of history rather than to record the accomplished facts, to answer the question, "Why did it happen?" as well as, "What happened?"

An inquiry into causes is manifestly a greater task than the recording of accomplished facts. To determine causes it is necessary to spend much time in the study of "original documents"—the newspapers, magazines, and pamphlet literature of each period. In these, rather than in the "musty documents" of state, do we find history in the making. Here we can see the clash of contending interests before they are crystallized into laws and institutions.

2. Social Tendencies as Social Forces[1]

The philosophy of the eighteenth century viewed external nature as the principal thing to be considered in a study of society, and not society itself. The great force in society was extraneous to society. But according to the philosophy of our times, the chief forces working in society are truly social forces, that is to say, they are immanent in society itself.

Let us briefly examine the social forces which are at work, either concentrating or diffusing the ownership of wealth. If it is true that, necessarily, there is going forward a concentration of property, that the rich are necessarily becoming richer, that wealth is passing into fewer and fewer hands, this gives a strong reason for believing that those are right who hold to the fact that every field of production must soon be controlled by monopoly. If, on the other hand, we find that the forces which make for diffusion are dominant, we may believe that it is quite possible for society to control the forces of production.

[1] Adapted from Richard T. Ely, *Evolution of Industrial Society*, pp. 456–84. (Published by The Macmillan Co., 1903. Reprinted by permission.)

a) Forces operating in the direction of concentration of wealth: (1) The unearned increment of land, especially in cities, is no doubt a real force. (2) The trust movement is operating in its earlier phases, at least, in the direction of concentration. (3) In the third place, war, whenever it comes, carries with it forces which bring wealth to the few rather than to the many. (4) Arrangements of one kind and another may be mentioned by means of various trust devices to secure the ends of primogeniture and entail. (5) Another force operating to concentrate the ownership of wealth may be called economic inertia. According to the principle of inertia, forces continue to operate until they are checked by other forces coming into contact with them.

b) Forces which operate to diffuse wealth: (1) Education, broadly considered, should be mentioned first of all. (2) Next, mention must be made of the public control of corporations. (3) Changes in taxation are the third item in this enumeration of forces. (4) The development of the idea of property as a trust is next mentioned. (5) Profit-sharing and co-operation. (6) Sound currency is next mentioned. (7) Public ownership of public utilities is a further force. (8) Labor organizations. (9) Institutions, especially in the interest of the wage-earning and economically weaker elements in the community. (10) Savings institutions and insurance.

3. Public Opinion: School of Thought and Legislation in England[1]

Public legislative opinion, as it has existed in England during the nineteenth century, presents several noteworthy aspects or characteristics. They may conveniently be considered under five heads: the existence at any given period of a predominant public opinion; the origin of such opinion; the development and continuity thereof; the checks imposed on such opinion by the existence of counter-currents and cross-currents of opinion; the action of laws themselves as the creators of legislative opinion.

First, there exists at any given time a body of beliefs, convictions, sentiments, accepted principles, or firmly rooted prejudices, which, taken together, make up the public opinion of a particular era, or what we may call the reigning or predominant current of opinion,

[1] Adapted from A. V. Dicey, *Law and Public Opinion in England*, pp. 19–41. (Published by The Macmillan Co., 1905. Reprinted by permission.)

and, as regards at any rate the last three or four centuries, and especially the nineteenth century, the influence of this dominant current of opinion has, in England, if we look at the matter broadly, determined, directly or indirectly, the course of legislation.

Second, the opinion which affects the development of the law has, in modern England at least, often originated with some single thinker or school of thinkers. No doubt it is at times allowable to talk of a prevalent belief or opinion as "being in the air," by which expression is meant that a particular way of looking at things has become the common possession of all the world. But though a belief, when it prevails, may at last be adopted by the whole of a generation, it rarely happens that a widespread conviction has grown up spontaneously among the multitude. "The initiation," it has been said, "of all wise or noble things comes, and must come, from individuals; generally at first from some one individual," to which it ought surely to be added that the origination of a new folly or of a new form of baseness comes, and must in general come, at first from individuals or from some one individual. The peculiarity of individuals, as contrasted with the crowd, lies neither in virtue nor in wickedness but in originality. It is idle to credit minorities with all the good without ascribing to them most, at least, of the evils due to that rarest of all human qualities—inventiveness.

The course of events in England may often, at least, be thus described: A new and, let us assume, a true idea presents itself to some one man of originality or genius; the discoverer of the new conception, or some follower who has embraced it with enthusiasm, preaches it to his friends or disciples, they in their turn become impressed with its importance and its truth, and gradually a whole school accepts the new creed. These apostles of a new faith are either persons endowed with special ability or, what is quite as likely, they are persons who, owing to their peculiar position, are freed from a bias, whether moral or intellectual, in favor of prevalent errors. At last the preachers of truth make an impression, either directly upon the general public or upon some person of eminence, say a leading statesman, who stands in a position to impress ordinary people and thus to win the support of the nation. Success, however, in converting mankind to a new faith, whether religious or economical or political, depends but slightly on the strength of the reasoning by which the faith can be defended, or even on the enthusiasm of its adherents. A change of belief arises, in the main, from the occurrence of circumstances which incline the majority of the world to hear with favor theories which, at one time, men of common sense derided as absurdities or distrusted as paradoxes. The doctrine of free trade, for instance, has in England for about half a century held the field as an unassailable dogma of economic policy, but a historian would stand convicted of ignorance or folly who should imagine that the fallacies of protection were discovered by the intuitive good sense of the people, even if the existence of such a quality as the good sense of the people be more than a political fiction. The principle of free trade may, as far as Englishmen are concerned, be treated as the doctrine of Adam Smith. The reasons in its favor never have been, nor will, from the nature of things, be mastered by the majority of any people. The apology for freedom of commerce will always present, from one point of view, an air of paradox. Every man feels or thinks that protection would benefit his own business, and it is difficult to realize that what may be a benefit for any man taken alone may be of no benefit to a body of men looked at collectively. The obvious objections to free trade may, as free traders conceive, be met; but then the reasoning by which these objections are met is often elaborate and subtle and does not carry conviction to the crowd. It is idle to suppose that belief in freedom of trade—or indeed in any other creed—ever won its way among the majority of converts by the mere force of reasoning. The course of events was very different. The theory of free trade won by degrees the approval of statesmen of special insight, and adherents to the new economic religion were one by one gained among persons of intelligence. Cobden and Bright finally became potent advocates of truths of which they were in no sense the discoverers. This assertion in no way detracts from the credit due to these eminent men. They performed to admiration the proper function of popular leaders; by prodigies of energy and by seizing a favorable opportunity, of which they made the very most use that was possible, they gained the acceptance by the English people of truths which have rarely, in any country but England, acquired popularity. Much was due to the opportuneness of the time. Protection wears its most offensive guise when it can be identified with a tax on bread, and therefore can, without patent injustice, be described as the parent of famine and starvation. The unpopularity, moreover, inherent in a tax on corn is all but fatal to a protective tariff when the class which protection enriches is comparatively small, whilst the class which would suffer keenly from dearness of bread and would obtain benefit from free trade is large, and, having already acquired much, is certain soon to acquire more political power. Add to all this that the Irish famine made the suspension of the corn laws a patent necessity. It is easy, then, to see how great in England was the part played by external circumstances—one might almost say by accidental conditions—in determining the overthrow of protection. A student should further remark that after free trade became an established principle of English policy, the majority of the English people accepted it mainly on authority. Men who were neither land-owners nor farmers perceived with ease the obtrusive evils of a tax on corn, but they and their leaders were far less influenced by arguments against protection generally than by the immediate and almost visible advantage of cheapening the bread of artisans and laborers. What, however, weighed with most Englishmen, above every other consideration, was the harmony of the doctrine that commerce ought to be free, with that disbelief in the benefits of state intervention which in 1846 had been gaining ground for more than a generation.

It is impossible, indeed, to insist too strongly upon the consideration that whilst opinion controls legislation, public opinion is itself far less the result of reasoning or of argument than of the circumstances in which men are placed. Between 1783 and 1861 negro slavery was abolished—one might almost say ceased of itself to exist—in the northern states of the American Republic; in the South, on the other hand, the maintenance of slavery developed into a fixed policy, and before the War of Secession the "peculiar institution" had become the foundation stone of the social system. But the religious beliefs and, except as regards the existence of slavery, the political institutions prevalent throughout the whole of the United States were the same. The condemnation of slavery in the North, and the apologies for slavery in the South, must therefore be referred to difference of circumstances. Slave labor was obviously out of place in Massachusetts, Vermont, or New York; it appeared to be, even if in reality it was not, economically profitable in South Carolina. An institution, again, which was utterly incompatible with the social condition of the northern states harmonized, or appeared to harmonize, with the social conditions of the southern states. The arguments against the peculiar institution were in themselves equally strong in whatever part of the Union they were uttered, but they carried conviction to the white citizens of Massachusetts, whilst, even when heard or read, they did not carry conviction to the citizens of South Carolina. Belief, and, to speak fairly, honest belief, was to a great extent the result, not of argument, nor even of direct self-interest, but of circumstances. What was true in this instance holds good in others. There is no reason to suppose that in 1830 the squires of England were less patriotic than the manufacturers, or less capable of mastering the arguments in favor of or against the reform of Parliament. But everyone knows that, as a rule, the country gentlemen were Tories and anti-reformers, whilst the manufacturers were Radicals and reformers. Circumstances are the creators of most men's opinions.

Third, the development of public opinion generally, and therefore of legislative opinion, has been in England at once gradual, or slow, and continuous. The qualities of slowness and continuity may conveniently be considered together, and are closely interconnected, but they are distinguishable and essentially different.

Legislative public opinion generally changes in England with unexpected slowness. Adam Smith's *Wealth of Nations* was published in 1776; the policy of free exchange was not completely accepted by England till 1846. All the strongest reasons in favor of Catholic emancipation were laid before the English world by Burke between 1760 and 1797; the Roman Catholic Relief Act was not carried till 1829.

The opinion which changes the law is in one sense the opinion of the time when the law is actually altered; in another sense it has often been in England the opinion prevalent some twenty or thirty years before that time; it has been as often as not in reality the opinion, not of today, but of yesterday.

Legislative opinion must be the opinion of the day, because, when laws are altered, the alteration is of necessity carried into effect by legislators who act under the belief that the change is an amendment; but this law-making opinion is also the opinion of yesterday, because the beliefs which have at last gained such hold on the legislature as to produce an alteration in the law have generally been created by thinkers or writers who exerted their influence long before the change in the law took place. Thus it may well happen that an innovation is carried through at a time when the teachers who supplied the arguments in its favor are in their graves, or even—and this is well worth noting—when in the world of speculation a movement has already set in against ideas which are exerting their full effect in the world of action and of legislation.

Law-making in England is the work of men well advanced in life; the politicians who guide the House of Commons, to say nothing of the peers who lead the House of Lords, are few of them below thirty, and most of them are above forty, years of age. They have formed or picked up their convictions, and, what is of more consequence, their prepossessions, in early manhood, which is the one period of life when men are easily impressed with new ideas. Hence English legislators retain the prejudices or modes of thinking which they acquired in their youth; and when, late in life, they take a share in actual legislation, they legislate in accordance with the doctrines which were current, either generally or in the society to which the law-givers belonged, in the days of their early manhood. The lawmakers, therefore, of 1850 may give effect to the opinions of 1830, whilst the legislators of 1880 are likely enough to impress upon the statute book the beliefs of 1860, or rather the ideas which in the one case attracted the young men of 1830 and in the other the youth of 1860. We need not therefore be surprised to find that a current of opinion may exert its greatest legislative influence just when its force is beginning to decline. The tide turns when at its height; a school of thought or feeling which still governs law-makers has begun to lose its authority among men of a younger generation who are not yet able to influence legislation.

Fourth, the reigning legislative opinion of the day has never, at any rate during the nineteenth century, exerted absolute or despotic authority. Its power has always been diminished by the existence of counter-currents or cross-currents of opinion which were not in harmony with the prevalent opinion of the time.

A counter-current here means a body of opinion, belief, or sentiment more or less directly opposed to the dominant opinion of a particular era. Counter-currents of this kind have generally been supplied by the survival of ideas or convictions which are gradually

losing their hold upon a given generation, and particularly the youthful part thereof. This kind of "conservatism" which prompts men
to retain convictions which are losing their hold upon the mass of the
world is found, it should be remarked, as much among the adherents
of one religious or political creed as of another. Any Frenchman
who clung to Protestantism during the reign of Louis the Fourteenth;
any north-country squire who in the England of the eighteenth century adhered to the Roman Catholicism of his fathers; Samuel
Johnson, standing forth as a Tory and a High Churchman amongst
Whigs and Free Thinkers; the Abbé Gregoire, retaining in 1830 the
attitude and the beliefs of a bishop of that constitutional church of
France whereof the claims have been repudiated at once by the Church
and by the State; James Mill, who, though the leader in 1832 of
philosophic Radicals, the pioneers as they deemed themselves of
democratic progress, was in truth the last "of the eighteenth century"
—these are each and all of them examples of that intellectual and
moral conservatism which everywhere, and especially in England,
has always been a strong force. The past controls the present.

Counter-currents, again, may be supplied by new ideals which
are beginning to influence the young. The hopes or dreams of the
generation just coming into the field of public life undermine the
energy of a dominant creed.

Counter-currents of opinion, whatever their source, have one
certain and one possible effect. The certain effect is that a check is
imposed upon the action of the dominant faith.

Fifth, laws foster or create law-making opinion. This assertion
may sound, to one who has learned that laws are the outcome of
public opinion, like a paradox; when properly understood, it is nothing
but an undeniable, though sometimes neglected, truth.

B.   INTERESTS, SENTIMENTS, AND ATTITUDES

1.   Social Forces and Interaction[1]

We must guard at the outset against an illusion that has exerted
a confusing influence. There are no social forces which are not at
the same time forces lodged in individuals, deriving their energy from
individuals and operating in and through individuals. There are no

[1] Adapted from Albion W. Small, *General Sociology*, pp. 532–36. (The University of Chicago Press, 1905.)

social forces that lurk in the containing ether, and affect persons without the agency of other persons.   There are, to be sure, all the physical conditions that affect persons just as they affect all other forms of matter.   So far, these are not social forces at all.   They do not get to be social forces until they get into persons, and in these persons they take the form of feelings which impel them to react upon other persons.   Persons are thus transmuters of physical forces into social forces; but all properly designated social forces are essentially personal.   They are within some persons, and stimulate them to act upon other persons; or they are in other persons, and exert themselves as external stimuli upon otherwise inert persons.   In either case social forces are personal influences passing from person to person and producing activities that give content to the association.

The conception of social forces was never challenged so long as it was merely an everyday commonplace.   When it passed into technical forms of expression, doubts began to be urged.   If anyone in the United States had questioned the existence of Mrs. Grundy fifty years ago, he would have been pitied and ignored as a harmless "natural."   Social forces in the form of gossip, and personified in Mrs. Grundy, were real to everybody.   But the particular species of social forces which Mrs. Grundy represented were neither more nor less real than the other social forces which had no name in folklore.   Persons incessantly influence persons.   The modes of this influence are indescribably varied.   They are conscious and unconscious, accidental and momentary, or deliberate and persistent; they are conventional and continuous, the result of individual habit, or of customs crystallized into national or racial institutions.

The simple fact which the concept "social forces" stands for is that every individual acts and is acted upon in countless ways by the other persons with whom he associates.   These modes of action and reaction between persons may be classified, and the more obvious and recurrent among them may be enumerated.   More than this, the action of these social forces may be observed, and the results of observation may be organized into social laws.   Indeed, there would be only two alternatives, if we did not discover the presence and action of social forces.   On the one hand, social science would at most be a subdivision of natural science; on the other hand, the remaining alternative would be the impossibility of social science altogether.

But social forces are just as distinctly discernible as chemical forces. The fact that we are not familiar with them no more makes against their existence and their importance than general ignorance of the pressure of the atmosphere takes that phenomenon out of the physical world. They are not only the atmosphere but they are a very large part of the moral world in general. If we could compose a complete account of the social forces, we should at the same time have completed, from one point of attention at least, a science of everything involved in human society.

"All beings which can be said to perform actions do so in obedience to those mental states which are denominated desires." But we have gone back a step beyond the desires and have found it necessary to assume the existence of underlying interests. These have to desires very nearly the relation of substance to attribute, or, in a different figure, of genus to species. Our interests may be beyond or beneath our ken; our desires are strong and clear. I may not be conscious of my health interests in any deep sense, but the desires that my appetites assert are specific and concrete and real. The implicit interests, of which we may be very imperfectly aware, move us to desires which may correspond well or ill with the real content of the interests. At all events, it is these desires which make up the active social forces, whether they are more or less harmonious with the interests from which they spring. The desires that the persons associating actually feel are practically the elemental forces with which we have to reckon. They are just as real as the properties of matter. They have their ratios of energy, just as certainly as though they were physical forces. They have their peculiar modes of action, which may be formulated as distinctly as the various modes of chemical action.

Every desire that any man harbors is a force making or marring, strengthening or weakening, the structure and functions of the society of which he is a part. What the human desires are, what their relations are to each other, what their peculiar modifications are under different circumstances—these are questions of detail which must be answered in general by social psychology, and in particular by specific analysis of each social situation. The one consideration to be urged at this point is that the concept "social forces" has a real content. It represents reality. There are social forces. They are the desires of persons. They range in energy from the vagrant whim that makes the individual a temporary discomfort to his group, to the inbred feelings that whole races share. It is with these subtle forces that social arrangements and the theories of social arrangements have to deal.

2. Interests[1]

During the past generation, the conception of the "atom" has been of enormous use in physical discovery. Although no one has ever seen an atom, the supposition that there are ultimate particles of matter in which the "promise and potency" of all physical properties and actions reside has served as a means of investigation during the most intensive period of research in the history of thought. Without the hypothesis of the atom, physics and chemistry, and in a secondary sense biology, would have lacked chart and compass upon their voyages of exploration. Although the notion of the atom is rapidly changing, and the tendency of physical science is to construe physical facts in terms of motion rather than of the traditional atom, it is probably as needless as it is useless for us to concern ourselves as laymen with this refinement. Although we cannot avoid speaking of the smallest parts into which matter can be divided, and although we cannot imagine, on the other hand, how any portions of matter can exist and not be divisible into parts, we are probably quite as incapable of saving ourselves from paradox by resort to the vortex hypothesis in any form. That is, these subtleties are too wonderful for most minds. Without pushing analysis too far, and without resting any theory upon analogy with the atom of physical theory, it is necessary to find some starting-place from which to trace up the composition of sentient beings, just as the physicists assumed that they found their starting-place in the atom. The notion of interests is accordingly serving the same purpose in sociology which the notion of atoms has served in physical science. Interests are the stuff that men are made of. More accurately expressed, the last elements to which we can reduce the actions of human beings are units which we may conveniently name "interests." It is merely inverting the form of expression to say: *Interests are the simplest modes of motion which we can trace in the conduct of human beings.*

[1] Adapted from Albion W. Small, *General Sociology*, pp. 425-36. (The University of Chicago Press, 1905.)

To the psychologist the individual is interesting primarily as a center of knowing, feeling, and willing. To the sociologist the individual begins to be interesting when he is thought as knowing, feeling, and willing *something*. In so far as a mere trick of emphasis may serve to distinguish problems, this ictus indicates the sociological starting-point. The individual given in experience is thought to the point at which he is available for sociological assumption, when he is recognized as a center of activities which make for something outside of the psychical series in which volition is a term. These activities must be referred primarily to desires, but the desires themselves may be further referred to certain universal interests. In this character the individual becomes one of the known or assumed terms of sociology. The individual as a center of active interests may be thought both as the lowest term in the social equation and as a composite term whose factors must be understood. These factors are either the more evident desires, or the more remote interests which the individual's desires in some way represent. At the same time, we must repeat the admission that these assumed interests are like the atom of physics. They are the metaphysical recourse of our minds in accounting for concrete facts. We have never seen or touched them. They are the hypothetical substratum of those regularities of conduct which the activities of individuals display.

We may start with the familiar popular expressions, "the farming interest," "the railroad interest," "the packing interest," "the milling interest," etc., etc. Everyone knows what the expressions mean. Our use of the term "interest" is not co-ordinate with these, but it may be approached by means of them. All the "interests" that are struggling for recognition in business and in politics are highly composite. The owner of a flour mill, for example, is a man before he is a miller. He becomes a miller at last because he is a man; i.e., because he has interests—in a deeper sense than that of the popular expressions—which impel him to act in order to gain satisfactions. The clue to all social activity is in this fact of individual interests. Every act that every man performs is to be traced back to an interest. We eat because there is a desire for food; but the desire is set in motion by a bodily interest in replacing exhausted force. We sleep because we are tired; but the weariness is a function of the bodily interest in rebuilding used-up tissue. We play because there is a bodily interest in use of the muscles. We study because there is a mental interest in satisfying curiosity. We mingle with our fellow-men because there is a mental interest in matching our personality against that of others. We go to market to supply an economic interest, and to war because of some social interest of whatever mixed or simple form.

With this introduction, we may venture an extremely abstract definition of our concept "interest." In general, *an interest is an unsatisfied capacity, corresponding to an unrealized condition, and it is predisposition to such rearrangement as would tend to realize the indicated condition.* Human needs and human wants are incidents in the series of events between the latent existence of human interest and the achievement of partial satisfaction. Human interests, then, are the ultimate terms of calculation in sociology. *The whole life-process, so far as we know it, whether viewed in its individual or in its social phase, is at last the process of developing, adjusting, and satisfying interests.*

No single term is of more constant use in recent sociology than this term "interests." We use it in the plural partly for the sake of distinguishing it from the same term in the sense which has become so familiar in modern pedagogy. The two uses of the term are closely related, but they are not precisely identical. The pedagogical emphasis is rather on the voluntary attitude toward a possible object of attention. The sociological emphasis is on attributes of persons which may be compared to the chemical affinities of different elements.

To distinguish the pedagogical from the sociological use of the term "interest," we may say pedagogically of a supposed case: "The boy has no *interest* in physical culture, or in shopwork, or in companionship with other boys, or in learning, or in art, or in morality." That is, attention and choice are essential elements of interest in the pedagogical sense. On the other hand, we may say of the same boy, in the sociological sense: "He has not discovered his health, wealth, sociability, knowledge, beauty, and rightness *interests*." We thus imply that interests, in the sociological sense, are not necessarily matters of attention and choice. They are affinities, latent in persons, pressing for satisfaction, whether the persons are conscious of them either generally or specifically, or not; they are indicated spheres of activity which persons enter into and occupy in the course of realizing their personality.

Accordingly, we have virtually said that interests are merely specifications in the makeup of the personal units. We have several times named the most general classes of interests which we find serviceable in sociology, viz.: *health, wealth, sociability, knowledge, beauty,* and *rightness.*

We need to emphasize, in addition, several considerations about these interests which are the motors of all individual and social action. First, there is a subjective and an objective aspect of them all. It would be easy to use terms of these interests in speculative arguments in such a way as to shift the sense fallaciously from the one aspect to the other; e.g., moral conduct, as an actual adjustment of the person in question with other persons, is that person's "interest," in the objective sense. On the other hand, we are obliged to think of something in the person himself impelling him, however unconsciously, toward that moral conduct, i.e., interest as "unsatisfied capacity" in the subjective sense. So with each of the other interests. The fact that these two senses of the term are always concerned must never be ignored; but, until we reach refinements of analysis which demand use for these discriminations, they may be left out of sight. Second, human interests pass more and more from the latent, subjective, unconscious state to the active, objective, conscious form. That is, before the baby is self-conscious, the baby's essential interest in bodily well-being is operating in performance of the organic functions. A little later the baby is old enough to understand that certain regulation of his diet, certain kinds of work or play, will help to make and keep him well and strong. Henceforth there is in him a co-operation of interest in the fundamental sense, and interest in the derived, secondary sense, involving attention and choice. If we could agree upon the use of terms, we might employ the word "desire" for this development of interest; i.e., physiological performance of function is, strictly speaking, the health interest; the desires which men actually pursue within the realm of bodily function may be normal or perverted, in an infinite scale of variety. So with each of the other interests. Third, with these qualifications provided for, resolution of human activities into pursuit of differentiated interests becomes the first clue to the combination that unlocks the mysteries of society.

For our purposes in this argument we need not trouble ourselves very much about nice metaphysical distinctions between the aspects of interest, because we have mainly to do with interests in the same sense in which the man of affairs uses the term. The practical politician looks over the lobby at Washington and he classifies the elements that compose it. He says: "Here is the railroad interest, the sugar interest, the labor interest, the army interest, the canal interest, the Cuban interest, etc." He uses the term "interest" essentially in the sociological sense but in a relatively concrete form, and he has in mind little more than variations of the wealth interest. He would explain the legislation of a given session as the final balance between these conflicting pecuniary interests. He is right, in the main; and every social action is, in the same way, an accommodation of the various interests which are represented in the society concerned.

3. Social Pressures[1]

The phenomena of government are from start to finish phenomena of force. But force is an objectionable word. I prefer to use the word pressure instead of force, since it keeps the attention closely directed upon the groups themselves, instead of upon any mystical "realities" assumed to be underneath and supporting them, and since its connotation is not limited to the narrowly "physical." We frequently talk of "bringing pressure to bear" upon someone, and we can use the word here with but slight extension beyond this common meaning.

Pressure, as we shall use it, is always a group phenomenon. It indicates the push and resistance between groups. The balance of the group pressures *is* the existing state of society. Pressure is broad enough to include all forms of the group influence upon group, from battle and riot to abstract reasoning and sensitive morality. It takes up into itself "moral energy" and the finest discriminations of conscience as easily as bloodthirsty lust of power. It allows for humanitarian movements as easily as for political corruption. The tendencies to activity are pressures, as well as the more visible activities.

[1] Adapted from Arthur F. Bentley, *The Process of Government*, pp. 258–381. (The University of Chicago Press, 1908.)

All phenomena of government are phenomena of groups pressing one another, forming one another, and pushing out new groups and group representatives (the organs or agencies of government) to mediate the adjustments. It is only as we isolate these group activities, determine their representative values, and get the whole process stated in terms of them that we approach to a satisfactory knowledge of government.

When we take such an agency of government as a despotic ruler, we cannot possibly advance to an understanding of him except in terms of the group activities of his society which are most directly represented through him, along with those which almost seem not to be represented through him at all, or to be represented to a different degree or in a different manner. And it is the same with democracies, even in their "purest" and simplest forms, as well as in their most complicated forms. We cannot fairly talk of despotisms or of democracies as though they were absolutely distinct types of government to be contrasted offhand with each other or with other types. All depends for each despotism and each democracy and each other form of government on the given interests, their relations, and their methods of interaction. The interest groups create the government and work through it; the government, as activity, works "for" the groups; the government, from the viewpoint of certain of the groups, may at times be their private tool; the government, from the viewpoint of others of the groups, seems at times their deadly enemy; but the process is all one, and the joint participation is always present, however it may be phrased in public opinion or clamor.

It is convenient most of the time in studying government to talk of these groups as interests. But I have already indicated with sufficient clearness that the interest is nothing other than the group activity itself. The words by which we name the interests often give the best expression to the value of the group activities in terms of other group activities: if I may be permitted that form of phrasing, they are more qualitative than quantitative in their implications. But that is sometimes a great evil as well as sometimes an advantage. We must always remember that there is nothing in the interests purely because of themselves and that we can depend on them only as they stand for groups which are acting or tending toward activity or pressing themselves along in their activity with other groups.

When we get the group activities on the lower planes worked out and show them as represented in various forms of higher groups, culminating in the political groups, then we make progress in our interpretations. Always and everywhere our study must be a study of the interests that work through government; otherwise we have not got down to facts. Nor will it suffice to take a single interest group and base our interpretation upon it, not even for a special time and a special place. No interest group has meaning except with reference to other interest groups; and those other interest groups are pressures; they count in the government process. The lowest of despised castes, deprived of rights to the protection of property and even life, will still be found to be a factor in the government, if only we can sweep the whole field and measure the caste in its true degree of power, direct or represented, in its potentiality of harm to the higher castes, and in its identification with them for some important purposes, however deeply hidden from ordinary view. No slaves, not the worst abused of all, but help to form the government. They are an interest group within it.

Tested by the interest groups that function through them, legislatures are of two general types. First are those which represent one class or set of classes in the government as opposed to some other class, which is usually represented in a monarch. Second are those which are not the exclusive stronghold of one class or set of classes, but are instead the channel for the functioning of all groupings of the population. The borders between the two types are of course indistinct, but they approximate closely to the borders between a society with class organization and one with classes broken down into freer and more changeable group interests.

Neither the number of chambers in the legislative body nor the constitutional relations of the legislature to the executive can serve to define the two types. The several chambers may represent several classes, or again the double-chamber system may be in fact merely a technical division, with the same interests present in both chambers. The executive may be a class representative, or merely a co-ordinate organ, dividing with the legislature the labor of providing channels through which the same lot of manifold interest groups can work.

It lies almost on the surface that a legislature which is a class agency will produce results in accordance with the class pressure behind it. Its existence has been established by struggle, and its life is a continual struggle against the representatives of the opposite class. Of course there will be an immense deal of argument to be heard on both sides, and the argument will involve the setting forth of "reasons" in limitless number. It is indeed because of the advantages (in group terms, of course) of such argument as a technical means of adjustment that the legislative bodies survive. Argument under certain conditions is a greater labor-saver than blows, and in it the group interests more fully unfold themselves. But beneath all the argument lies the strength. The arguments go no farther than the strength goes. What the new Russian duma will get, if it survives, will be what the people it solidly represents are strong enough to make it get, and no more and no less, with bombs and finances, famine and corruption funds alike in the scale.

But the farther we advance among legislatures of the second type, and the farther we get away from the direct appeal to muscle and weapon, the more difficult becomes the analysis of the group components, the greater is the prominence that falls to the process of argumentation, the more adroitly do the group forces mask themselves in morals, ideals, and phrases, the more plausible becomes the interpretation of the legislature's work as a matter of reason, not of pressure, and the more common it is to hear condemnations of those portions of the process at which violence shows through the reasoning as though they were per se perverted, degenerate, and the bearers of ruin. There is, of course, a strong, genuine group opposition to the technique of violence, which is an important social fact; but a statement of the whole legislative process in terms of the discussion forms used by that anti-violence interest group is wholly inadequate.

4. Idea-Forces[1]

The principle that I assume at the outset is that every idea tends to act itself out. If it is an isolated idea, or if it is not counterbalanced by a stronger force, its realization must take place. Thus the principle of the struggle for existence and of selection, taking the latter word in its broadest sense, is in my opinion as applicable to ideas as to individuals and living species; a selection takes place

[1] Adapted from Alfred Fouillée, *Education from a National Standpoint*, pp. 10-16. (D. Appleton & Co., 1897.)

in the brain to the advantage of the strongest and most exclusive idea, which is thus able to control the whole organism. In particular, the child's brain is an arena of conflict for ideas and the impulses they include; in the brain the new idea is a new force which encounters the ideas already installed, and the impulses already developed therein. Assume a mind, as yet a blank, and suddenly introduce into it the representation of any movement, the idea of any action—such as raising the arm. This idea being isolated and unopposed, the wave of disturbance arising in the brain will take the direction of the arm, because the nerves terminating in the arm are disturbed by the representation of the arm. The arm will therefore be lifted. Before a movement begins, we must think of this; now no movement that has taken place is lost; it is necessarily communicated from the brain to the organs if unchecked by any other representation or impulse. The transmission of the idea to the limbs is inevitable as long as the idea is isolated or unopposed. This I have called the law of idea-forces, and I think I have satisfactorily explained the curious facts in connection with the impulsive actions of the idea.

The well-known experiments of Chevreul on the "pendule explora-teur," and on the divining rod, show that if we represent to ourselves a movement in a certain direction, the hand will finally execute this movement without our consciousness, and so will transmit it to the instrument. Table-turning is the realization of the expected movement by means of the unconscious motion of the hands. Thought-reading is the interpretation of imperceptible movements, in which the thought of the subject betrays itself, even without his being conscious of it. In the process that goes on when we are fascinated or on the point of fainting, a process more obvious in children than in adults, there is an inchoate movement which the paralysis of the will fails to check. When I was a lad, I was once running over a plank across the weir of a river, it never entering my head that I ran any risk of falling; suddenly this idea came into play like a force obliquely compounded with the straight course of thought which had up to that moment been guiding my footsteps. I felt as if an invisible arm had seized me and was dragging me down. I shrieked and stood trembling above the foaming water until assistance came. Here the mere idea of vertigo produced vertigo. A plank on the ground may be crossed without arousing any idea of falling; but if it is above a precipice, and we think of the distance below, the impulse to fall is very strong. Even when we are in perfect safety we may feel what is known as the "fascination" of a precipice. The sight of the gulf below, becoming a fixed idea, produces a resultant inhibition on all other ideas. Temptation, which is always besetting a child because everything is new to it, is nothing but the power of an idea and its motor impulse.

The power of an idea is the greater, the more prominently it is singled out from the general content of consciousness. This selection of an idea, which becomes so exclusive that the whole consciousness is absorbed in it, is called *monoïdeism*. This state is precisely that of a person who has been hypnotized. What is called hypnotic suggestion is nothing but the artificial selection of one idea to the exclusion of all others, so that it passes into action. Natural somnambulism similarly exhibits the force of ideas; whatever idea is conceived by the somnambulist, he carries into action. The kind of dream in which children often live is not without analogy to somnambulism. The fixed idea is another instance of the same phenomenon, which is produced in the waking state, and which, when exaggerated, becomes monomania, a kind of morbid monoïdeism; children, having very few ideas, would very soon acquire fixed ideas, if it were not for the mobility of attention which the ceaseless variation of the surrounding world produces in them. Thus all the facts grouped nowadays under the name of auto-suggestion may, in my opinion, be explained. Here we shall generalize the law in this form: every idea conceived by the mind is an auto-suggestion, the selective effect of which is only counterbalanced by other ideas producing a different auto-suggestion. This is especially noticeable in the young, who so rapidly carry into action what is passing through their minds.

The philosophers of the seventeenth century, with Descartes and Pascal, considered sentiments and passions as indistinct thoughts, as "thoughts, as it were, in process of precipitation." This is true. Beneath all our sentiments lies a totality of imperfectly analyzed ideas, a swelling stream of crowded and indistinct reasons by the momentum of which we are carried away and swept along. Inversely, sentiments underlie all our ideas; they smoulder in the dying embers of abstractions. Even language has a power because it arouses all the sentiments which it condenses in a formula; the mere names "honor" and "duty" arouse infinite echoes in the consciousness. At the name of "honor" alone, a legion of images is on the point of surging up; vaguely, as with eyes open in the dark, we see all the possible witnesses of our acts, from father and mother to friends and fellow-countrymen; further, if our imagination is vivid enough, we can see those great ancestors who did not hesitate under similar circumstances. "We must; forward!" We feel that we are enrolled in an army of gallant men; the whole race, in its most heroic representatives, is urging us on. There is a social and even a historical element beneath moral ideas. Besides, language, a social product, is also a social force. The pious mind goes farther still; duty is personified as a being—the living Good whose voice we hear.

Some speak of lifeless formulas; of these there are very few. A word, an idea, is a formula of possible action and of sentiments ready to pass into acts; they are "verbs." Now, every sentiment, every impulse which becomes formulated with, as it were, a *fiat*, acquires by this alone a new and quasi-creative force; it is not merely rendered visible by its own light to itself but it is defined, specified, and selected from the rest, and *ipso facto* directed in its course. That is why formulas relative to action are so powerful for good or evil; a child feels a vague temptation, a tendency for which it cannot account. Pronounce in its hearing the formula, change the blind impulse into the luminous idea, and this will be a new suggestion which may, perhaps, cause it to fall in the direction to which it was already inclined. On the other hand, some formulas of generous sentiments will carry away a vast audience immediately they are uttered. The genius is often the man who translates the aspirations of his age into ideas; at the sound of his voice a whole nation is moved. Great moral, religious, and social revolutions ensue when the sentiments, long restrained and scarcely conscious of their own existence, become formulated into ideas and words; the way is then opened, the means and the goal are visible alike, selection takes place, all the volitions are simultaneously guided in the same direction, like a torrent which has found the weakest point in the dam.

5. Sentiments[1]

We seldom experience the primary emotions in the pure or unmixed forms in which they are commonly manifested by the animals. Our

[1] Adapted from William McDougall, *An Introduction to Social Psychology*, pp. 121–64. (John W. Luce & Co., 1916.)

emotional states commonly arise from the simultaneous excitement of two or more of the instinctive dispositions; and the majority of the names currently used to denote our various emotions are the names of such mixed, secondary, or complex emotions. That the great variety of our emotional states may be properly regarded as the result of the compounding of a relatively small number of primary or simple emotions is no new discovery. Descartes, for example, recognized only six primary emotions, or passions as he termed them, namely—admiration, love, hatred, desire, joy, and sadness, and he wrote, "All the others are composed of some out of these six and derived from them." He does not seem to have formulated any principles for the determination of the primaries and the distinction of them from the secondaries.

The compounding of the primary emotions is largely, though not wholly, due to the existence of sentiments, and some of the complex emotional processes can only be generated from sentiments. Before going on to discuss the complex emotions, we must therefore try to understand as clearly as possible the nature of a sentiment.

The word "sentiment" is still used in several different senses. M. Ribot and other French authors use its French equivalent as covering all the feelings and emotions, as the most general name for the affective aspect of mental processes. We owe to Mr. A. F. Shand the recognition of features of our mental constitution of a most important kind that have been strangely overlooked by other psychologists, and the application of the word "sentiments" to denote features of this kind. Mr. Shand points out that our emotions, or, more strictly speaking, our emotional dispositions, tend to become organized in systems about the various objects and classes of objects that excite them. Such an organized system of emotional tendencies is not a fact or mode of experience, but is a feature of the complexly organized structure of the mind that underlies all our mental activity. To such an organized system of emotional tendencies centered about some object Mr. Shand proposes to apply the name "sentiment." This application of the word is in fair accordance with its usage in popular speech, and there can be little doubt that it will rapidly be adopted by psychologists.

The organization of the sentiments in the developing mind is determined by the course of experience; that is to say, the sentiment is a growth in the structure of the mind that is not natively given in the inherited constitution. This is certainly true in the main, though the maternal sentiment might almost seem to be innate; but we have to remember that in the human mother this sentiment may, and generally does, begin to grow up about the idea of its object, before the child is born.

The growth of the sentiments is of the utmost importance for the character and conduct of individuals and of societies; it is the organization of the affective and conative life. In the absence of sentiments our emotional life would be a mere chaos, without order, consistency, or continuity of any kind; and all our social relations and conduct, being based on the emotions and their impulses, would be correspondingly chaotic, unpredictable, and unstable. It is only through the systematic organization of the emotional dispositions in sentiments that the volitional control of the immediate promptings of the emotions is rendered possible. Again, our judgments of value and of merit are rooted in our sentiments; and our moral principles have the same source, for they are formed by our judgments of moral value.

The sentiments may be classified according to the nature of their objects; they then fall into three main classes: the concrete particular, the concrete general, and the abstract sentiments—e.g., the sentiment of love for a child, of love for children in general, of love for justice or virtue. Their development in the individual follows this order, the concrete particular sentiments being, of course, the earliest and most easily acquired. The number of sentiments a man may acquire, reckoned according to the number of objects in which they are centered, may, of course, be very large; but almost every man has a small number of sentiments—perhaps one only—that greatly surpass all the rest in strength and as regards the proportion of his conduct that springs from them.

Each sentiment has a life-history, like every other vital organization. It is gradually built up, increasing in complexity and strength and may continue to grow indefinitely, or may enter upon a period of decline, and may decay slowly or rapidly, partially or completely.

When any one of the emotions is strongly or repeatedly excited by a particular object, there is formed the rudiment of a sentiment. Suppose that a child is thrown into the company of some person given to frequent outbursts of violent anger, say, a violent-tempered father who is otherwise indifferent to the child and takes no further notice of him than to threaten, scold, and, perhaps, beat him. At first the child experiences fear at each exhibition of violence, but repetition of these incidents very soon creates the habit of fear, and in the presence of his father, even in his mildest moods, the child is timorous; that is to say, the mere presence of the father throws the child's fear-disposition into a condition of sub-excitement, which increases on the slightest occasion until it produces all the subjective and objective manifestations of fear. As a further stage, the mere idea of the father becomes capable of producing the same effects as his presence; this idea has become associated with the emotion; or, in stricter language, the psychophysical disposition whose excitement involves the rise to consciousness of this idea, has become associated or intimately connected with the psychophysical disposition whose excitement produces the bodily and mental symptoms of fear. Such an association constitutes a rudimentary sentiment that we can only call a sentiment of fear.

In a similar way, a single act of kindness done by A to B may evoke in B the emotion of gratitude; and if A repeats his kindly acts, conferring benefits on B, the gratitude of B may become habitual, may become an enduring emotional attitude of B towards A—a sentiment of gratitude. Or, in either case, a single act—one evoking very intense fear or gratitude—may suffice to render the association more or less durable and the attitude of fear, or gratitude, of B toward A more or less permanent.

6. Social Attitudes[1]

"Consciousness," says Jacques Loeb, "is only a metaphysical term for phenomena which are determined by associative memory. By associative memory I mean that mechanism by which a stimulus brings about not only the effects which its nature and the specific structure of the irritable organ call for, but by which it brings about also the effects of other stimuli which formerly acted upon the organism almost or quite simultaneously with the stimulus in question. If an animal can be trained, if it can learn, it possesses associative memory." In short, because we have memories we are able to profit by experiences.

[1] From Robert E. Park, *Principles of Human Behavior*, pp. 18–34. (The Zalaz Corporation, 1915.)

It is the memories that determine, on the whole, what objects shall mean to us, and how we shall behave toward them. We cannot say, however, that a perception or an object is ever wholly without meaning to us. The flame to which the child stretches out its hand means, even before he has any experience of it, "something to be reached for, something to be handled." After the first experience of touching it, however, it means "something naturally attractive but still to be avoided." Each new experience, so far as it is preserved in memory, adds new meanings to the objects with which it is associated.

Our perceptions and our ideas embody our experiences of objects and so serve as signs of what we may expect of them. They are the means by which we are enabled to control our behavior toward them. On the other hand, if we lose our memories, either temporarily or permanently, we lose at the same time our control over our actions and are still able to respond to objects, but only in accordance with our inborn tendencies. After all our memories are gone, we still have our original nature to fall back upon.

There is a remarkable case reported by Sidis and Goodhart which illustrates the rôle that memory plays in giving us control over our inherited tendencies. It is that of Rev. Thomas C. Hanna, who, while attempting to alight from a carriage, lost his footing, fell to the ground and was picked up unconscious. When he awoke it was found that he had not only lost the faculty of speech but he had lost all voluntary control of his limbs. He had forgotten how to walk. He had not lost his senses. He could feel and see, but he was not able to distinguish objects. He had no sense of distance. He was in a state of complete "mental blindness." At first he did not distinguish between his own movements and those of other objects. "He was as much interested in the movements of his own limbs as in that of external things." He had no conception of time. "Seconds, minutes, and hours were alike to him." He felt hunger but he did not know how to interpret the feeling and had no notion of how to satisfy it. When food was offered him he did not know what to do with it. In order to get him to swallow food it had to be placed far back in his throat, in order to provoke reflex swallowing movements. In their report of the case the authors say:

Like an infant, he did not know the meaning of the simplest words, nor did he understand the use of language. Imitation was the factor in his first education. He learned the meaning of words by imitating definite articulate sounds made in connection with certain objects and activities. The pronunciation of words and their combination into whole phrases he acquired in the same imitative way. At first he simply repeated any word and sentence heard, thinking that this meant something to others. This manner of blind repetition and unintelligent imitation was, however, soon given up, and he began systematically to learn the meaning of words in connection with the objective content they signified. As in the case of children who, in their early developmental stage, use one word to indicate many objects different in their nature, but having some common point of superficial resemblance, so was it in the case of Mr. Hanna: the first word he acquired was used by him to indicate all the objects he wanted.

The first word he learned was "apple" and for a time apple was the only word he knew. At first he learned only the names of particular objects. He did not seem able to learn words with an abstract or general significance. But although he was reduced to a state of mental infancy, his "intelligence" remained, and he learned with astonishing rapidity. "His faculty of judgment, his power of reasoning, were as sound and vigorous as ever," continues the report. "The content of knowledge seemed to have been lost, but the form of knowledge remained as active as before the accident and was perhaps even more precise and definite."

One reason why man is superior to the brutes is probably that he has a better natural memory. Another reason is that there are more things that he can do, and so he has an opportunity to gain a wider and more varied experience. Consider what a man can do with his hands! To this he has added tools and machinery, which are an extension of the hand and have multiplied its powers enormously. It is now pretty well agreed, however, that the chief advantage which mankind has over the brutes is in the possession of speech by which he can communicate his ideas. In comparatively recent times he has supplemented this means of communication by the invention of the printing press, the telegraph, and the telephone. In this way he has been able not only to communicate his experiences but to fund and transmit them from one generation to another.

As soon as man began to point out objects and associate them with vocal sounds, he had obtained possession of a symbol by which he was able to deliberately communicate his desires and his intentions to other men in a more precise and definite way than he had been able to do through the medium of spontaneous emotional expression.

The first words, we may suppose, were onomatopoetic, that is to say, vocal imitations of the objects to which they referred. At any rate they arose spontaneously in connection with the situation that inspired them. They were then imitated by others and thus became the common and permanent possession of the group. Language thus assumed for the group the rôle of perception in the individual. It became the sign and symbol of those meanings which were the common possession of the group.

As the number of such symbols was relatively small in comparison to the number of ideas, words inevitably came to have different meanings in different contexts. In the long run the effect of this was to detach the words from the particular contexts in which they arose and loosen their connections with the particular sentiments and attitudes with which they were associated. They came to have thus a more distinctively symbolic and formal character. It was thus possible to give them more precise definitions, to make of them abstractions and mental toys, which the individual could play with freely and disinterestedly. Like the child who builds houses with blocks, he was able to arrange them in orders and systems, create ideal structures, like the constructions of mathematics, which he was then able to employ as means of ordering and systematizing his more concrete experiences.

All this served to give the individual a more complete control over his own experience and that of the group. It made it possible to analyze and classify his own experiences and compare them with those of his fellows and so, eventually, to erect the vast structure of formal and scientific knowledge on the basis of which men are able to live and work together in co-operation upon the structure of a common civilization.

The point is that the breadth of the experience over which man has control and the disinterestedness with which he is able to view it is the basis of the intellectual attainment of the individual, as of the race.

If human beings were thoroughly rational creatures, we may presume that they would act, at every instant, on the basis of all their experience and all the knowledge that they were able to obtain from the experience of others. The truth is, however, that we are never able, at any one time, to mobilize, control, and use all the experience and all the knowledge that we now possess and which, if we were less human than we are, might serve to guide and control our actions. It is precisely the function of science to collect, organize, and make available for our practical uses the fund of experience and of knowledge we do possess.

Not only do we already have more knowledge than we can use, but much of our personal and individual experience drops out and is lost in the course of a lifetime. Meanwhile, later experiences are constantly adding themselves to the earlier ones. In this way the meaning of the world is constantly changing for us, much as the surface of the earth is constantly under the influence of the weather.

The actual constellation of our memories and ideas is determined at any given moment not merely by processes of association but also by processes of dissociation. Practical interests, sentiments, and emotional outbursts—love, fear, and anger—are constantly interrupting the logical and constructive processes of the mind. These forces tend to dissolve established connections between ideas and disintegrate our memories so that they rarely function as a whole or as a unit, but rather as more or less dissociated systems.

The mere act of attention, for example, so far as it focuses the activities upon a single object, tends to narrow the range of associations, check deliberation, and, by isolating one idea or system of ideas, prepares us to act in accordance with them without regard to the demands of other ideas in the wider but now suppressed context of our experience. The isolation of one group of ideas implies the suppression of other groups which are inconsistent with them or hinder the indicated action.

When the fundamental instinct-emotions are aroused, they invariably have the effect of isolating the ideas with which they are associated and of inhibiting the contrary emotions. This is the explanation of war. When the fighting instincts are stirred, men lose the fear of death and the horror of killing.

When an idea, particularly one that is associated with some original tendency of human nature, is thus isolated in consciousness, the tendency is to respond to it automatically, just as one would respond to a simple reflex. This explains the phenomena of suggestion. A state of suggestibility is always a pre-condition of suggestion, and suggestibility means just such an isolation and dissociation of the suggested idea as has been described. Hypnotic trance may be defined as a condition of abnormal suggestibility, in which the subject tends to carry out automatically the commands of the experimenter, "as if," as the familiar phrase puts it, "he had no will of his own," or rather, as if the will of the experimenter had been substituted for that of the subject. In fact the phenomena of auto-suggestion, in which one obeys his own suggestion, seems to differ from other forms of the same phenomena only in the fact that the subject obeys his own commands instead of those of the experimenter. Not only suggestion and auto-suggestion, but imitation, which is nothing more than another form of suggestion, are made possible by the existence of mental mechanisms created by dissociation.

Hypnotism represents an extreme but temporary form of dissociation of the memories, artificially produced. Fascination and abstraction (absent-mindedness) are milder forms of the same phenomena with this difference, that they occur "in nature" and without artificial stimulation.

A more permanent dissociation is represented in moods. The memories which connect themselves with moods are invariably such as will support the dominant emotion. At the same time memories which tend in any way to modify the prevailing tone of the mood are spontaneously suppressed.

It is a familiar fact that persons whose occupations or whose mode of life brings them habitually into different worlds, so that the experiences in one have little or nothing in common with those of the other, inevitably develop something akin to a dual personality. The business man, for example, is one person in the city and another at his home in the suburbs.

The most striking and instructive instances of dissociation, however, are the cases of dual or multiple personality in which the same individual lives successively or simultaneously two separate lives, each of which is wholly oblivious of the other. The classic instance of this kind is the case of the Rev. Ansel Bourne reported by William James in his *Principles of Psychology*. Ansel Bourne was an itinerant preacher living at Greene, Rhode Island. On January 19, 1887, he drew $551.00 from a bank in Providence and entered a Pawtucket horse car and disappeared. He was advertised as missing, foul play being suspected.

On the morning of March 24, at Norristown, Pennsylvania, a man calling himself A. J. Brown awoke in a fright and called on the people of the house to tell him who he was. Later he said he was Ansel Bourne. Nothing was known of him in Norristown except that six weeks before he had rented a small shop, stocked it with stationery, confectionery, and other small articles, and was carrying on a quiet trade "without seeming to anyone unnatural or eccentric." At first it was thought he was insane, but his story was confirmed and he was returned to his home. It was then deemed that he had lost all memory of the period which had elapsed since he boarded the Pawtucket car. What he had done or where he had been between the time he left Providence and arrived in Norristown, no one had the slightest information.

In 1890 he was induced by William James to submit to hypnotism in order to see whether in his trance state his "Brown" memories would come back. The experiment was so successful that, as James remarks, "it proved quite impossible to make him, while in hypnosis, remember any of the facts of his normal life." The report continues:

He had heard of Ansel Bourne, but "didn't know as he had ever met the man." When confronted with Mrs. Bourne he said that he had "never seen the woman before," etc. On the other hand, he told of his peregrinations during the lost fortnight, and gave all sorts of details about the Norristown episode. The whole thing was prosaic enough; and the Brown-personality seems to be nothing but a rather shrunken, dejected, and amnesic extract of Mr. Bourne himself. He gave no motive for the wandering except that there was "trouble back there" and he "wanted rest." During the trance he looks old, the corners of his mouth are drawn down, his voice is slow and weak, and he sits screening his eyes and trying vainly to remember what lay before and after the two months of the Brown experience. "I'm all hedged in," he says, "I can't get out at either end. I don't know what set me down in that Pawtucket horse-car, and I don't know how I ever left that store or what became of it." His eyes are practically normal, and all his sensibilities (save for tardier response) about the same in hypnosis as in waking. I had hoped by suggestion to run the two personalities into one, and make the memories continuous, but no artifice would avail to accomplish this, and Mr. Bourne's skull today still covers two distinct personal selves.

An interesting circumstance with respect to this case and others is that the different personalities, although they inhabit the same body and divide between them the experiences of a single individual, not only regard themselves as distinct and independent persons but they exhibit marked differences in character, temperament, and tastes, and frequently profess for one another a decided antipathy. The contrasts in temperament and character displayed by these split-off personalities are illustrated in the case of Miss Beauchamp, to whose strange and fantastic history Morton Prince has devoted a volume of nearly six hundred pages.

In this case, the source of whose morbidity was investigated by means of hypnotism, not less than three distinct personalities in addition to that of the original and real Miss Beauchamp were evolved. Each one of these was distinctly different and decidedly antipathetic to the others.

Pierre Janet's patient, Madam B, however, is the classic illustration of this dissociated personality. From the time she was sixteen years of age, Léonie, as she was called, had been so frequently hypnotized and subjected to so much clinical experimentation that a well-organized secondary personality was elaborated, which was designated as Léontine. Léonie was a poor peasant woman, serious, timid, and melancholy. Léontine was gay, noisy, restless, and ironical. Léontine did not recognize that she had any relationship with Léonie, whom she referred to as "that good woman," "the other," who "is not I, she is too stupid." Eventually a third personality, known as Léonore, appeared who did not wish to be mistaken for either that "good but stupid woman" Léonie, nor for the "foolish babbler" Léontine.

Of these personalities Léonie possessed only her own memories, Léontine possessed the memories of Léonie and her own, while the memories of Léonore, who was superior to them both, included Madam B's whole life.

What is particularly interesting in connection with this phenomenon of multiple personality is the fact that it reveals in a striking way the relation of the subconscious to the conscious. The term subconscious, as it occurs in the literature of psychology, is a word of various meanings. In general, however, we mean by subconscious a region of consciousness in which the dissociated memories, the "suppressed complexes," as they are called, maintain some sort of conscious existence and exercise an indirect though very positive influence upon the ideas in the focus of consciousness, and so upon the behavior of the individual. The subconscious, in short, is the region of the suppressed memories. They are suppressed because they have come into conflict with the dominant complex in consciousness which represents the personality of the individual.

"Emotional conflicts" have long been the theme of literary analysis and discussion. In recent years they have become the subject of scientific investigation. In fact a new school of medical psychology with a vast literature has grown up around and out of the investigations of the effects of the suppression of a single instinct— the sexual impulse. A whole class of nervous disorders, what are known as psychoneuroses, are directly attributed by Dr. Sigmund Freud and the psychoanalytic school, as it is called, to these suppressions, many of which consist of memories that go back to the period of early childhood before the sexual instinct had attained the form that it has in adults.

The theory of Freud, stated briefly, amounts to this: As a result of emotional conflicts considerable portions of the memories of certain individuals, with the motor impulses connected with them, are thrust into the background of the mind, that is to say, the subconscious. Such suppressed memories, with the connected motor dispositions, he first named "suppressed complexes." Now it is found that these suppressed complexes, which no longer respond to stimulations as they would under normal conditions, may still exercise an indirect influence upon the ideas which are in the focus of consciousness. Under certain conditions they may not get into consciousness at all but manifest themselves, for example, in the form of hysterical tics, twitchings, and muscular convulsions.

Under other circumstances the ideas associated with the suppressed complexes tend to have a dominating and controlling place in the life of the individual. All our ideas that have a sentimental setting are of this character. We are all of us a little wild and insane upon certain subjects or in regard to certain persons or objects. In such cases a very trivial remark or even a gesture will fire one of these loaded ideas. The result is an emotional explosion, a sudden burst of weeping, a gust of violent, angry, and irrelevant emotion, or, in case the feelings are more under control, merely a bitter remark or a chilling and ironical laugh. It is an interesting fact that a jest may serve as well to give expression to the "feelings" as an expletive or any other emotional expression. All forms of fanaticism, fixed ideas, phobias, ideals, and cherished illusions may be explained as the effects of mental mechanisms created by the suppressed complexes.

From what has been said we are not to assume that there is any necessary and inevitable conflict among ideas. In our dreams and day-dreams, as in fairyland, our memories come and go in the most disorderly and fantastic way, so that we may seem to be in two places at the same time, or we may even be two persons, ourselves and some-one else. Everything trips lightly along, in a fantastic pageant without rhyme or reason. We discover something of the same free-dom when we sit down to speculate about any subject. All sorts of ideas present themselves; we entertain them for a moment, then dismiss them and turn our attention to some other mental picture which suits our purpose better. At such times we do not observe any particular conflict between one set of ideas and another. The lion and the lamb lie down peacefully together, and even if the lamb happens to be inside we are not particularly disturbed.

Conflict arises between memories when our personal interests are affected, when our sentiments are touched, when some favorite opinion is challenged. Conflict arises between our memories when they are connected with some of our motor dispositions, that is to say, when we begin to act. Memories which are suppressed as a result of emotional conflicts, memories associated with established motor dispositions, inevitably tend to find some sort of direct or sym-bolic expression. In this way they give rise to the symptoms which we meet in hysteria and psychasthenia—fears, phobias, obsessions, and tics, like stammering.

The suppressed complexes do not manifest themselves in the pathological forms only, but neither do the activities of the normal complexes give any clear and unequivocal evidence of themselves in ordinary consciousness. We are invariably moved to act by motives of which we are only partially conscious or wholly unaware. Not only is this true, but the accounts we give to ourselves and others of the motives upon which we acted are often wholly fictitious, although they may be given in perfect good faith.

A simple illustration will serve, however, to indicate how this can be effected. In what is called post-hypnotic suggestion we have an illustration of the manner in which the waking mind may be influenced by impulses of whose origin and significance the subject is wholly unaware. In a state of hypnotic slumber the suggestion is given that after awaking the subject will, upon a certain signal, rise and open the window or turn out the light. He is accordingly awakened and, at the signal agreed upon while he was in the hypnotic slumber but of which he is now wholly unconscious, he will immediately carry out the command as previously given. If the subject is then asked why he opened the window or turned out the light, he will, in evident good faith, make some ordinary explanation, as that "it seemed too hot in the room," or that he "thought the light in the room was disagreeable." In some cases, when the command given seems too absurd, the subject may not carry it out, but he will then show signs of restlessness and discomfort, just for instance as one feels when he is conscious that he has left something undone which he intended to do, although he can no longer recall what it was. Sometimes when the subject is not disposed to carry out the command actually given, he will perform some other related act as a substitute, just as persons who have an uneasy conscience, while still unwilling to make restitution or right the wrong which they have committed, will perform some other act by way of expiation.

Our moral sentiments and social attitudes are very largely fixed and determined by our past experiences of which we are only vaguely conscious.

"This same principle," as Morton Prince suggests, "underlies what is called the 'social conscience,' the 'civic' and 'national conscience,' 'patriotism,' 'public opinion,' what the Germans call 'Sittlichkeit,' the war attitude of mind, etc. All these mental attitudes may be reduced to common habits of thought and conduct derived from mental experiences common to a given community and conserved as complexes in the unconscious of the several individuals of the community."

Sentiments were first defined and distinguished from the emotions by Shand, who conceived of them as organizations of the emotions about some particular object or type of object. Maternal love, for example, includes the emotions of fear, anger, joy, or sorrow, all organized about the child. This maternal love is made up of innate tendencies but is not itself a part of original nature. It is the mother's fostering care of the child which develops her sentiments toward it, and the sentiment attaches to any object that is bound up with the life of the child. The cradle is dear to the mother because it is connected with her occupation in caring for the child. The material fears for its welfare, her joy in its achievements, her anger with those who injure or even disparage it, are all part of the maternal sentiment.

The mother's sentiment determines her attitude toward her child, toward other children, and toward children in general. Just as back of every sensation, perception, or idea there is some sort of motor disposition, so our attitudes are supported by our sentiments. Back of every political opinion there is a political sentiment and it is the sentiment which gives force and meaning to the opinion.

Thus we may think of opinions merely as representative of a psycho-physical mechanism, which we may call the sentiment-attitude. These sentiment-attitudes are to be regarded in turn as organizations of the original tendencies, the instinct-emotions, about some memory, idea, or object which is, or once was, the focus and the end for which the original tendencies thus organized exist. In this way opinions turn out, in the long run, to rest on original nature, albeit original nature modified by experience and tradition.

C. THE FOUR WISHES: A CLASSIFICATION OF SOCIAL FORCES

1. The Wish, the Social Atom[1]

The Freudian psychology is based on the doctrine of the "wish," just as physical science is based, today, on the concept of function. Both of these are what may be called dynamic concepts, rather than static; they envisage natural phenomena not as things but as processes and largely to this fact is due their pre-eminent explanatory value. Through the "wish" the "thing" aspect of mental phenomena, the more substantive "content of consciousness," becomes somewhat modified and reinterpreted. This "wish," which as a concept Freud does not analyze, includes all that would commonly be so classed, and also whatever would be called impulse, tendency, desire, purpose,

---

[1] Adapted from Edwin B. Holt, *The Freudian Wish and Its Place in Ethics*, pp. 3–56. (Henry Holt & Co., 1915.)

attitude, and the like, not including, however, any emotional components thereof. Freud also acknowledges the existence of what he calls "negative wishes," and these are not fears but negative purposes. An exact definition of the "wish" is that it is *a course of action* which some mechanism of the body is *set* to carry out, whether it actually does so or does not. All emotions, as well as the feelings of pleasure and displeasure, are separable from the "wishes," and this precludes any thought of a merely hedonistic psychology. The wish is any purpose or project for *a course of action*, whether it is being merely entertained by the mind or is being actually executed—a distinction which is really of little importance. We shall do well if we consider this to be, as in fact it is, dependent on a *motor attitude* of the physical body, which goes over into overt action and *conduct* when the wish is carried into execution.

It is this "wish" which transforms the principal doctrines of psychology and recasts the science, much as the "atomic theory" and later the "ionic theory" have reshaped earlier conceptions of chemistry. This so-called "wish" becomes the unit of psychology, replacing the older unit commonly called "sensation," which latter, it is to be noted, was a *content* of consciousness unit, whereas the "wish" is a more dynamic affair.

Unquestionably the mind is somehow "embodied" in the body. But how? Well, if the unit of mind and character is a "wish," it is easy enough to perceive how it is incorporated. It is, this "wish," something which the body as a piece of mechanism can do—a course of action with regard to the environment which the machinery of the body is capable of carrying out. This capacity resides clearly in the parts of which the body consists and in the way in which these are put together, not so much in the matter of which the body is composed, as in the forms which this matter assumes when organized.

In order to look at this more closely we must go a bit down the evolutionary series to the fields of biology and physiology. Here we find much talk of nerves and muscles, sense-organs, reflex arcs, stimulation, and muscular response, and we feel that somehow these things do not reach the core of the matter, and that they never can; that spirit is not nerve or muscle; and that intelligent conduct, to say nothing of conscious thought, can never be reduced to reflex arcs and the like—just as a printing press is not merely wheels and rollers, and still less is it chunks of iron. The biologist has only himself to thank if he has overlooked a thing which lay directly under his nose. He has overlooked the *form of organization* of these his reflex arcs, has left out of account that step which assembles wheels and rollers into a printing press, and that which organizes reflex arcs, as we shall presently see, into an intelligent, conscious creature. Evolution took this important little step of organization ages ago, and thereby produced the rudimentary "wish."

Now in the reflex arc a sense-organ is stimulated and the energy of stimulation is transformed into nervous energy, which then passes along an afferent nerve to the central nervous system, passes through this and out by an efferent or motor nerve to a muscle, where the energy is again transformed and the muscle contracts. Stimulation at one point of the animal organism produces contraction at another. The principles of irritability and of motility are involved, but all further study of *this* process will lead us only to the physics and chemistry of the energy transformations—will lead us, that is, in the direction of *analysis*. If, however, we inquire in what way such reflexes are combined or "integrated" into more complicated processes, we shall be led in exactly the opposite direction, that of *synthesis*, and here we soon come, as is not surprising, to a synthetic novelty. This is *specific response* or *behavior*.

In this single reflex something is done to a sense-organ and the process within the organ is comparable to the process in any unstable substance when foreign energy strikes it; it is strictly a chemical process, and so for the conducting nerve, likewise for the contracting muscle. It happens, as a physiological fact, that in this process stored energy is released so that a reflex contraction is literally comparable to the firing of a pistol. But the reflex arc is not "aware" of anything, and indeed there is nothing more to say about the process unless we should begin to analyze it. But even two such processes going on together in one organism are a very different matter. Two such processes require two sense-organs, two conduction paths, and two muscles; and since we are considering the result of the two in combination, the relative anatomical location of these six members is of importance. For simplicity I will take a hypothetical but strictly possible case. A small water animal has an eyespot located on each side of its anterior end; each spot is connected by a nerve with a vibratory silium or fin on the side of the posterior end; the thrust exerted by each fin is toward the rear. If, now, light strikes one eye, say the right, the left fin is set in motion and the animal's body is set rotating toward the right like a rowboat with one oar. This is all that one such reflex arc could do for the animal. Since, however, there are now two, when the animal comes to be turned far enough toward the right so that some of the light strikes the second eyespot (as will happen when the animal comes around facing the light), the second fin, on the right side, is set in motion, and the two together propel the animal forward in a straight line. The direction of this line will be that in which the animal lies when its two eyes receive equal amounts of light. In other words, by the combined operation of two reflexes the animal swims *toward the light*, while either reflex alone would only have set it spinning like a top. It now responds specifically in the direction of the light, whereas before it merely spun when lashed.

Suppose, now, that it possess a *third* reflex arc—a "heat spot" so connected with the same or other fins that when stimulated by a certain intensity of heat it initiates a nervous impulse which stops the forward propulsion. The animal is still "lashed," but nevertheless no light can force it to swim "blindly to its death" by scalding. It has the rudiments of "intelligence." But so it had before. For as soon as two reflex arcs capacitate it mechanically to swim *toward light*, it was no longer exactly like a pinwheel; it could respond specifically toward at least one thing in its environment.

It is this objective reference of a process of release that is significant. The mere reflex does not refer to anything beyond itself; if it drives an organism in a certain direction, it is only as a rocket ignited at random shoots off in some direction, depending on how it happened to lie. But specific response is not merely in some random direction, it is *toward an object*, and if this object is moved, the responding organism changes its direction and still moves after it. And the objective reference is that the organism is *moving with reference to some object or fact of the environment*. For the organism, while a very interesting mechanism in itself, is one whose movements turn on objects outside of itself, much as the orbit of the earth turns upon the sun; and these external, and sometimes very distant, objects are as much *constituents* of the behavior process as is the organism which does the turning.   It is this *pivotal outer object*, the object of specific response, which seems to me to have been overneglected.

It is not surprising, then, that in animals as highly organized reflexly as are many of the invertebrates, even though they should possess no other principle of action than that of specific response, the various life-activities should present an appearance of considerable intelligence.   And I believe that in fact this intelligence is solely the product of accumulated specific responses.   Our present point is that the specific response and the "wish" as Freud uses the term, are one and the same thing.

2.   The Freudian Wish[1]

"If wishes were horses, beggars would ride" is a nursery saw which, in the light of recent developments in psychology, has come to have a much more universal application than it was formerly supposed to have.   If the followers of the Freudian school of psychologists can be believed—and there are many reasons for believing them—all of us, no matter how apparently contented we are and how well we are supplied with the good things of the earth, are "beggars," because at one time or another and in one way or another we are daily betraying the presence of unfulfilled wishes.   Many of these wishes are of such a character that we ourselves cannot put them into words.   Indeed, if they were put into words for us, we should straightway deny that such a wish is or was ever harbored by us in our waking moments.   But the stretch of time indicated by "waking moments" is only a minor part of the twenty-four hours.   Even during the time we are not asleep we are often abstracted, day-dreaming, letting moments go by in reverie.   Only during a limited part of our waking moments are we keenly and alertly "all there" in the possession of our faculties.   There are thus, even apart from sleep, many unguarded moments when these so-called "repressed wishes" may show themselves.

In waking moments we wish only for the conventional things which will not run counter to our social traditions or code of living.   But these open and above-board wishes are not very interesting to the psychologist.   Since they are harmless and call for the kinds of things that everybody in our circle wishes for, we do not mind admit-

[1] Adapted from John B. Watson, "The Psychology of Wish Fulfillment," in the *Scientific Monthly*, III (1916), 479–86.

ting them and talking about them. Open and uncensored wishes are best seen in children (though children at an early age begin to show repressions). Only tonight I heard a little girl of nine say: "I wish I were a boy and were sixteen years old—I'd marry Ann" (her nine-year old companion). And recently I heard a boy of eight say to his father: "I wish you would go away forever; then I could marry mother." The spontaneous and uncensored wishes of children gradually disappear as the children take on the speech conventions of the adult. But even though the crassness of the form of expression of the wish disappears with age, there is no reason to suppose that the human organism ever gets to the point where wishes just as unconventional as the above do not rise to trouble it. Such wishes, though, are immediately repressed; we never harbor them nor do we express them clearly to ourselves in our waking moments.

The steps by which repression takes place in the simpler cases are not especially difficult to understand. When the child wants something it ought not to have, its mother hands it something else and moves the object about until the child reaches out for it. When the adult strives for something which society denies him, his environment offers him, if he is normal, something which is "almost as good," although it may not wholly take the place of the thing he originally strove for. This in general is the process of substitution or sublimation. It is never complete from the first moment of childhood. Consequently it is natural to suppose that many of the things which have been denied us should at times beckon to us. But since they are banned they must beckon in devious ways. These sometime grim specters both of the present and of the past cannot break through the barriers of our staid and sober waking moments, so they exhibit themselves, at least to the initiated, in shadowy form in reverie, and in more substantial form in the slips we make in conversation and in writing, and in the things we laugh at; but clearest of all in dreams. I say the meaning is clear to the initiated because it does require special training and experience to analyze these seemingly nonsensical slips of tongue and pen, these highly elaborated and apparently meaningless dreams, into the wishes (instinct and habit impulses) which gave them birth. It is fortunate for us that we are protected in this way from having to face openly many of our own wishes and the wishes of our friends.

We get our clue to the dream as being a wish fulfilment by taking the dreams of children. Their dreams are as uncensored as is their conversation. Before Christmas my own children dreamed nightly that they had received the things they wanted for Christmas. The dreams were clear, logical, and open wishes. Why should the dreams of adults be less logical and less open unless they are to act as concealers of the wish? If the dream processes in the child run in an orderly and logical way, would it indeed not be curious to find the dream processes of the adult less logical and full of meaning?

This argument gives us good a priori grounds for supposing that the dreams of adults too are full of meaning and are logical; that there is a wish in every dream and that the wish is fulfilled in the dream. The reason dreams appear illogical is due to the fact that if the wish were to be expressed in its logical form it would not square with our everyday habits of thought and action. We should be disinclined to admit even to ourselves that we have such dreams. Immediately upon waking only so much of the dream is remembered, that is, put into ordinary speech, as will square with our life at the time. The dream is "censored," in other words.

The question immediately arises, who is the censor or what part of us does the censoring? The Freudians have made more or less of a "metaphysical entity" out of the censor. They suppose that when wishes are repressed, they are repressed into the "unconscious," and that this mysterious censor stands at the trapdoor lying between the conscious and the unconscious. Many of us do not believe in a world of the unconscious (a few of us even have grave doubts about the usefulness of the term consciousness), hence we try to explain censorship along ordinary biological lines. We believe that one group of habits can "down" another group of habits—or instincts. In this case our ordinary system of habits—those which we call expressive of our "real selves"—inhibit or quench (keep inactive or partially inactive) those habits and instinctive tendencies which belong largely in the past.

This conception of the dream as having both censored and uncensored features has led us to divide the dream into its specious or manifest content (face value, which is usually nonsensical) and its latent or logical content. We should say that while the manifest content of the dream is nonsensical, its true or latent content is usually logical and expressive of some wish that has been suppressed in the waking state.

On examination the manifest content of dreams is found to be full of symbols. As long as the dream does not have to be put into customary language, it is allowed to stand as it is dreamed—the symbolic features are uncensored. Symbolism is much more common than is ordinarily supposed. All early language was symbolic. The language of children and of savages abounds in symbolism. Symbolic modes of expression both in art and in literature are among the earliest forms of treating difficult situations in delicate and inoffensive ways. In other words, symbols in art are a necessity and serve the same purpose as does the censor in the dreams. Even those of us who have not an artistic education, however, have become familiar with the commoner forms of symbolism through our acquaintance with literature. In the dream, when the more finely controlled physiological processes are in abeyance, there is a tendency to revert to the symbolic modes of expression. This has its use, because on awaking the dream does not shock us, since we make no attempt to analyze or trace back in the dream the symbol's original meaning. Hence we find that the manifest content is often filled with symbols which occasionally give us the clue to the dream analysis.

The dream then brings surcease from our maladjustments: If we are denied power, influence, or love by society or by individuals, we can obtain these desiderata in our dreams. We can possess in dreams the things which we cannot have by day. In sleep the poor man becomes a Midas, the ugly woman handsome, the childless woman surrounded by children, and those who in daily life live upon a crust in their dreams dine like princes (after living upon canned goods for two months in the Dry Tortugas, the burden of my every dream was food). Where the wished-for things are compatible with our daily code, they are remembered on awaking as they were dreamed. Society, however, will not allow the unmarried woman to have children, however keen her desire for them. Hence her dreams in which the wish is gratified are remembered in meaningless words and symbols.

Long before the time Freud's doctrine saw the light of day, William James gave the key to what I believed to be the true explanation of the wish. Thirty years ago he wrote:

> I am often confronted by the necessity of standing by one of my selves and relinquishing the rest. Not that I would not, if I could, be both handsome and fat and well dressed, and a great athlete, and make a million a year, be a wit, a *bon vivant*, and a lady-killer, as well as a philospher. a philanthropist, a statesman, a warrior, and African explorer, as well as a "tone-poet" and a saint. But the thing is simply impossible. The millionaire's work would run counter to the saint's; the *bon vivant* and the philanthropist would trip each other up; the philosopher and the lady-killer could not well keep house in the same tenement of clay. Such different characters may conceivably at the outset of life be alike possible to a man. But to make any one of them actual, the rest must more or less be suppressed.

What James is particularly emphasizing here is that the human organism is instinctively capable of developing along many different lines, but that due to the stress of civilization some of these instinctive capacities must be thwarted. In addition to these impulses which are instinctive, and therefore hereditary, there are many habit impulses which are equally strong and which for similar reasons must be given up. The systems of habits we form (i.e., the acts we learn to perform) at four years of age will not serve us when we are twelve, and those formed at the age of twelve will not serve us when we become adults. As we pass from childhood to man's estate, we are constantly having to give up thousands of activities which our nervous and muscular systems have a tendency to perform. Some of these instinctive tendencies born with use are poor heritages; some of the habits we early develop are equally poor possessions. But, whether they are "good" or "bad," they must give way as we put on the habits required of adults. Some of them yield with difficulty and we often get badly twisted in attempting to put them away, as every psychiatric clinic can testify. It is among these frustrated impulses that I would find the biological basis of the unfulfilled wish. Such "wishes" need never have been "conscious" and *need never have been suppressed into Freud's realm of the unconscious.* It may be inferred from this that there is no particular reason for applying the term "wish" to such tendencies. What we discover then in dreams and in conversational slips and other lapses are really at heart "reaction tendencies"—tendencies which we need never have faced nor put into words at any time. On Freud's theory these "wishes" have at one time been faced and put into words by the individual, and when faced they were recognized as not squaring with his ethical code. They were then immediately "repressed into the unconscious."

A few illustrations may help in understanding how thwarted tendencies may lay the basis for the so-called unfulfilled wish which later appears in the dream. One individual becomes a psychologist in spite of his strong interest in becoming a medical man, because at the time it was easier for him to get the training along psychological lines. Another pursues a business career, when, if he had had his choice, he would have become a writer of plays. Sometimes on account of the care of a mother or of younger brothers and sisters, a young man cannot marry, even though the mating instinct is normal; such a course of action necessarily leaves unfulfilled wishes and frustrated impulses in its train. Again a young man will marry and settle down when mature consideration would show that his career would advance much more rapidly if he were not burdened with a family. Again, an individual marries and without even admitting to himself that his marriage is a failure he gradually shuts himself off from any emotional expression—protects himself from the married state by sublimating his natural domestic ties, usually in some kind of engrossing work, but often in questionable ways—by hobbies, speed manias, and excesses of various kinds. In connection with this it is interesting to note that the automobile, quite apart from its utilitarian value, is coming to be a widely used means of repression or wish sublimation. I have been struck by the enormously increasing number of women drivers. Women in the present state of society have not the same access to absorbing kinds of works that men have (which will shortly come to be realized as a crime far worse than that of the Inquisition). Hence their chances of normal sublimation are limited. For this reason women seek an outlet by rushing to the war as nurses, in becoming social workers, pursuing aviation, etc. Now if I am right in this analysis these unexercised tendencies to do things other than we are doing are never quite got rid of. We cannot get rid of them unless we could build ourselves over again so that our organic machinery would work only along certain lines and only for certain occupations. Since we cannot completely live these tendencies down, we are all more or less "unadjusted" and ill adapted. These maladjustments are exhibited whenever the brakes are off, that is, whenever our higher and well-developed habits of speech and action are dormant, as in sleep, in emotional disturbances, etc.

Many but not all of these "wishes" can be traced to early childhood or to adolescence, which is a time of stress and strain and a period of great excitement. In childhood the boy often puts himself in his father's place; he wishes that he were grown like his father and could take his father's place, for then his mother would notice him more and he would not have to feel the weight of authority. The girl likewise often becomes closely attached to her father and wishes her mother would die (which in childhood means to disappear or go away) so that she could be all in all to her father. These wishes, from the standpoint of popular morality, are perfectly innocent; but as the children grow older they are told that such wishes are wrong and that they should not speak in such a "dreadful" way. Such wishes are, then, gradually suppressed—replaced by some other mode of expression. But the replacement is often imperfect. The apostle's saying, "When we become men we put away childish things" was written before the days of psychoanalysis.

3. The Person and His Wishes[1]

The human being has a great variety of "wishes," ranging from the desire to have food to the wish to serve humanity.

Anything capable of being appreciated (wished for) is a "value." Food, money, a poem, a political doctrine, a religious creed, a member of the other sex, etc., are values.

There are also negative values—things which exist but which the individual does not want, which he may even despise. Liquor or the Yiddish language may be a positive value for one person and a negative value for another.

---

[1] A restatement from a paper by William I. Thomas, "The Persistence of Primary-Group Norms in Present-Day Society," in Jennings, Watson, Meyer, and Thomas, *Suggestions of Modern Science Concerning Education*. (Published by The Macmillan Co., 1917.)

The state of mind of the individual toward a value is an "attitude." Love of money, desire for fame, appreciation of a given poem, reverence for God, hatred of the Jew, are attitudes.

We divide wishes into four classes: (1) the desire for new experience; (2) the desire for security; (3) the desire for recognition; (4) the desire for response.

1. The desire for new experience is seen in simple forms in the prowling and meddling activities of the child, and the love of adventure and travel in the boy and the man. It ranges in moral quality from the pursuit of game and the pursuit of pleasure to the pursuit of knowledge and the pursuit of ideals. It is found equally in the vagabond and the scientific explorer. Novels, theaters, motion pictures, etc., are means of satisfying this desire vicariously, and their popularity is a sign of the elemental force of this desire.

In its pure form the desire for new experience implies motion, change, danger, instability, social irresponsibility. The individual dominated by it shows a tendency to disregard prevailing standards and group interests. He may be a complete failure, on account of his instability; or a conspicuous success, if he converts his experiences into social values—puts them in the form of a poem, makes of them a contribution to science, etc.

2. The desire for security is opposed to the desire for new experience. It implies avoidance of danger and death, caution, conservatism. Incorporation in an organization (family, community, state) provides the greatest security. In certain animal societies (e.g., the ants) the organization and co-operation are very rigid. Similarly among the peasants of Europe, represented by our immigrant groups, all lines of behavior are predetermined for the individual by tradition. In such a group the individual is secure as long as the group organization is secure, but evidently he shows little originality or creativeness.

3. The desire for recognition expresses itself in devices for securing distinction in the eyes of the public. A list of the different modes of seeking recognition would be very long. It would include courageous behavior, showing off through ornament and dress, the pomp of kings, the display of opinions and knowledge, the possession of special attainments—in the arts, for example. It is expressed alike in arrogance and in humility, even in martyrdom. Certain modes of

seeking recognition we define as "vanity," others as "ambition." The "will to power" belongs here. Perhaps there has been no spur to human activity so keen and no motive so naïvely avowed as the desire for "undying fame," and it would be difficult to estimate the rôle the desire for recognition has played in the creation of social values.

4. The desire for response is a craving, not for the recognition of the public at large, but for the more intimate appreciation of individuals. It is exemplified in mother-love (touch plays an important rôle in this connection), in romantic love, family affection, and other personal attachments. Homesickness and loneliness are expressions of it. Many of the devices for securing recognition are used also in securing response.

Apparently these four classes comprehend all the positive wishes. Such attitudes as anger, fear, hate, and prejudice are attitudes toward those objects which may frustrate a wish.

Our hopes, fears, inspirations, joys, sorrows are bound up with these wishes and issue from them. There is, of course, a kaleidoscopic mingling of wishes throughout life, and a single given act may contain a plurality of them. Thus when a peasant emigrates to America he may expect to have a good time and learn many things (new experience), to make a fortune (greater security), to have a higher social standing on his return (recognition), and to induce a certain person to marry him (response).

The "character" of the individual is determined by the nature of the organization of his wishes. The dominance of any one of the four types of wishes is the basis of our ordinary judgment of his character. Our appreciation (positive or negative) of the character of the individual is based on his display of certain wishes as against others, and on his modes of seeking their realization.

The individual's attitude toward the totality of his attitudes constitutes his conscious "personality." The conscious personality represents the conception of self, the individual's appreciation of his own character.

III. INVESTIGATIONS AND PROBLEMS

Literature on the concept of social forces falls under four heads: (1) popular notions of social forces; (2) social forces and history; (3) interests, sentiments, and attitudes as social forces; and (4) wishes as social forces.

1. Popular Notions of Social Forces

The term "social forces" first gained currency in America with the rise of the "reformers," so called, and with the growth of popular interest in the problems of city life; that is, labor and capital, municipal reform and social welfare, problems of social politics.

In the rural community the individual had counted; in the city he is likely to be lost. It was this declining weight of the individual in the life of great cities, as compared with that of impersonal social organizations, the parties, the unions, and the clubs, that first suggested, perhaps, the propriety of the term social forces. In 1897 Washington Gladden published a volume entitled *Social Facts and Forces: the Factory, the Labor Union, the Corporation, the Railway, the City, the Church.* The term soon gained wide currency and general acceptance.

At the twenty-eighth annual National Conference of Charities and Correction, at Washington, D.C., Mary E. Richmond read a paper upon "Charitable Co-operation" in which she presented a diagram and a classification of the social forces of the community from the point of view of the social worker,[1] given on page 492.

Beginning in October, 1906, there appeared for several years in the journal of social workers, *Charities and Commons,* now *The Survey,* editorial essays upon social, industrial, and civic questions under the heading "Social Forces." In the first article E. T. Devine made the following statement: "In this column the editor intends to have his say from month to month about the persons, books, and events which have significance as social forces. . . . . Not all the social forces are obviously forces of good, although they are all under the ultimate control of a power which makes for righteousness."

Ten years later a group of members in the National Conference of Social Work formed a division under the title "The Organization

[1] *Proceedings of the National Conference of Charities and Correction,* 1901, p. 300.

DIAGRAM OF FORCES WITH WHICH THE CHARITY WORKER
MAY CO-OPERATE

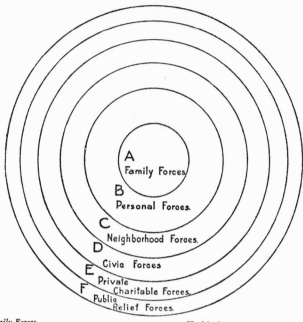

A.—*Family Forces.*
    Capacity of each member for
        Affection
        Training
        Endeavor
        Social development.

B.—*Personal Forces.*
    Kindred.
    Friends.

C.—*Neighborhood Forces.*
    Neighbors, landlords, tradesmen.
    Former and present employers.
    Clergymen, Sunday-school teachers, fellow church members.
    Doctors.
    Trade-unions, fraternal and benefit societies, social clubs, fellow-workmen.
    Libraries, educational clubs, classes, settlements, etc.
    Thrift agencies, savings-banks, stamp-savings, building and loan associations.

D.—*Civic Forces.*
    School-teachers, truant officers.
    Police, police magistrates, probation officers, reformatories.

Health department, sanitary inspectors, factory inspectors.
Postmen.
Parks, baths, etc.

E.—*Private Charitable Forces.*
    Charity organization society.
    Church of denomination to which family belongs.
    Benevolent individuals.
    National, special, and general relief societies.
    Charitable employment agencies and work-rooms.
    Fresh-air society, children's aid society, society for protection of children, children's homes, etc.
    District nurses, sick-diet kitchens, dispensaries, hospitals, etc.
    Society for suppression of vice, prisoner's aid society, etc.

F.—*Public Relief Forces.*
    Almshouses.
    Outdoor poor department.
    Public hospitals and dispensaries.

of the Social Forces of the Community." The term community, in connection with that of social forces, suggests that every community may be conceived as a definite constellation of social forces. In this form the notion has been fruitful in suggesting a more abstract, intelligible, and, at the same time, sounder conception of the community life.

Most of the social surveys made in recent years are based upon this conception of the community as a complex of social forces embodied in institutions and organizations. It is the specific task of every community survey to reveal the community in its separated and often isolated organs. The references to the literature on the community surveys at the conclusion of chapter iii, "Society and the Group,"[1] will be of service in a further study of the application of the concept of social forces to the study of the community.

2. Social Forces and History

Historians, particularly in recent years, have frequently used the expression "social forces" although they have nowhere defined it. Kuno Francke, in the Preface of his book entitled *A History of German Literature as Determined by Social Forces*, states that it "is an honest attempt to analyze the social, religious, and moral forces which determined the growth of German literature as a whole." Taine in the Preface to *The Ancient Régime* says: "Without taking any side, curiosity becomes scientific and centres on the secret forces which direct the wonderful process. These forces consist of the situations, the passions, the ideas, and the wills of each group of actors, and which can be defined and almost measured."[2]

It is in the writings of historians, like Taine in France, Buckle in England, and Karl Lamprecht in Germany, who started out with the deliberate intention of writing history as if it were natural history, that we find the first serious attempts to use the concept of social forces in historical analysis. Writers of this school are quite as much interested in the historical process as they are in historical fact, and there is a constant striving to treat the individual as representative of the class, and to define historical tendencies in general and abstract terms.

[1] See p. 219.

[2] H. A. Taine, *The Ancient Régime*, Preface, p. viii. (New York, 1891.)

But history conceived in those terms tends to become sociology. "History," says Lamprecht, "is *a socio-psychological science*. In the conflict between the old and the new tendencies in historical investigation, the main question has to do with social-psychic, as compared and contrasted with individual-psychic factors; or to speak somewhat generally, the understanding on the one hand of conditions, on the other of heroes, as the motive powers in the course of history."[1] It was Carlyle—whose conception of history is farthest removed from that of Lamprecht—who said, "Universal history is at bottom the history of great men."

The criticism of history by historians and the attempts, never quite successful, to make history positive furnish further interesting comment on this topic.[2]

3. Interest, Sentiments, and Attitudes as Social Forces

More had been written, first and last, about human motives than any other aspect of human life. Only in very recent years, however, have psychologists and social psychologists had either a point of view or methods of investigation which enabled them to analyze and explain the facts. The tendency of the older introspective psychology was to refer in general terms to the motor tendencies and the will, but in the analysis of sensation and the intellectual processes, will disappeared.

The literature on this subject covers all that has been written by the students of animal behavior and instinct, Lloyd Morgan, Thorndike, Watson, and Loeb. It includes the interesting studies of human behavior by Bechterew, Pavlow, and the so-called objective school of psychology in Russia. It should include likewise writers like Graham Wallas in England, Carleton Parker and Ordway Tead in America, who are seeking to apply the new science of human nature to the problems of society.[3]

Every social science has been based upon some theory, implicit or explicit, of human motives. Economics, political science, and ethics, before any systematic attempt had been made to study the matter empirically, had formulated theories of human nature to justify their presuppositions and procedures.

[1] Karl Lamprecht, *What Is History?* p. 3. (New York, 1905.)

[2] See chap. i, "Sociology and the Social Sciences," pp. 6–12.

[3] See references, chap. ii, "Human Nature," p. 149.

In classical political economy the single motive of human action was embodied in the abstraction "the economic man." The utilitarian school of ethics reduced all human motives to self-interest. Disinterested conduct was explained as enlightened self-interest. This theory was criticized as reducing the person to "an intellectual calculating machine." The theory of evolution suggested to Herbert Spencer a new interpretation of human motives which reasserted their individualistic origin, but explained altruistic sentiments as the slowly accumulated products of evolution. Altruism to Spencer was the enlightened self-interest of the race.

It was the English economists of the eighteenth century who gave us the first systematic account of modern society in deterministic terms. The conception of society implicit in Adam Smith's *Wealth of Nations* reflects at once the temper of the English people and of the age in which he lived.[1] The eighteenth century was the age of individualism, laissez faire and freedom. Everything was in process of emancipation except woman.

The attention of economists at this time was directed to that region of social life in which the behavior of the individual is most individualistic and least controlled, namely, the market place. The economic man, as the classical economists conceived him, is more completely embodied in the trader in the auction pit, than in any other figure in any other situation in society. And the trader in that position performs a very important social function.[2]

[1] For a discussion of the philosophical background of Adam Smith's political philosophy see Wilhelm Hasbach, *Untersuchungen über Adam Smith.* (Leipzig, 1891.)

[2] "The science of Political Economy as we have it in England may be defined as the science of business, such as business is in large productive and trading communities. It is an analysis of that world so familiar to many Englishmen—the 'great commerce' by which England has become rich. It assumes the principal facts which make that commerce possible, and as is the way of an abstract science it isolates and simplifies them: it detaches them from the confusion with which they are mixed in fact. And it deals too with the men who carry on that commerce, and who make it possible. It assumes a sort of human nature such as we see everywhere around us, and again it simplifies that human nature; it looks at one part of it only. Dealing with matters of 'business,' it assumes that man is actuated only by motives of business. It assumes that every man who makes anything, makes it for money, that he always makes that which brings him in most at least cost, and that he will make it in the way that will produce most and

There are, however, other social situations which have created other social types, and the sociologists have, from the very first, directed their attention to a very different aspect of social life, namely, its unity and solidarity. Comte conceived humanity in terms of the family, and most sociologists have been disposed to take the family as representative of the type of relations they are willing to call social. Not the auction pit but the family has been the basis of the sociological conception of society. Not competition but control has been the central fact and problem of sociology.

Socialization, when that word is used as a term of appreciation rather than of description, sets up as the goal of social effort a world in which conflict, competition, and the externality of individuals, if they do not disappear altogether, will be so diminished that all men may live together as members of one family. This, also, is the goal of progress according to our present major prophet, H. G. Wells.[1]

It is intelligible, therefore, that sociologists should conceive of social forces in other terms than self-interest. If there had been no other human motives than those attributed to the economic man there would have been economics but no sociology, at least in the sense in which we conceive it today.

In the writings of Ratzenhofer and Small human interests are postulated as both the unconscious motives and the conscious ends of behavior. Small's classification of interests—health, wealth, sociability, knowledge, beauty, rightness—has secured general acceptance.

"Sentiment" was used by French writers, Ribot, Binet, and others, as a general term for the entire field of affective life. A. F. Shand in two articles in *Mind*, "Character and the Emotions" and "Ribot's Theory of the Passions," has made a distinct contribution by distinguishing the sentiments from the emotions. Shand pointed out that the sentiment, as a product of social experience, is an organization of emotions around the idea of an object. McDougall in his

---

spend least; it assumes that every man who buys, buys with his whole heart, and that he who sells, sells with his whole heart, each wanting to gain all possible advantage. Of course we know that this is not so, that men are not like this; but we assume it for simplicity's sake, as an hypothesis."—Walter Bagehot, *The Postulates of English Political Economy*. (New York and London, 1885.)

[1] H. G. Wells, *The Outline of History*, Vol. II, pp. 579–95. (New York, 1920.)

Social Psychology adopted Shand's definition and described the organization of typical sentiments, as love and hate.

Thomas was the first to make fruitful use of the term attitude, which he defined as a "tendency to act." Incidentally he points out that attitudes are social, that is, the product of interaction.

4. Wishes and Social Forces

Ward had stated that "The social forces are wants seeking satisfaction through efforts, and are thus social motives or motors inspiring activities which either create social structures through social synergy or modify the structures already created through innovation and conation."[1] Elsewhere Ward says that "desire is the only motive to action."[2]

The psychoanalytic school of psychiatrists have attempted to reduce all motives to one—the wish, or *libido*. Freud conceived that sex appetite and memories connected with it were the unconscious sources of some if not all of the significant forms of human behavior. Freud's interpretation of sex, however, seemed to include the whole field of desires that have their origin in touch stimulations. To Jung the *libido* is vital energy motivating the life-adjustments of the person. Adler from his study of organic inferiority interpreted the *libido* as the wish for completeness or perfection. Curiously enough, these critics of Freud, while not accepting his interpretation of the unconscious wish, still seek to reduce all motives to a single unit. To explain all behavior by one formula, however, is to explain nothing.

On the other hand, interpretation by a multitude of unrelated conscious desires in the fashion of the older sociological literature is no great advance beyond the findings of common sense. The distinctive value of the definition, and classification, of Thomas lies in the fact that it reduces the multitude of desires to four. These four wishes, however, determine the simplest as well as the most complex behavior of persons. The use made of this method in his study of the Polish peasant indicated its possibilities for the analysis of the organization of the life of persons and of social groups.

[1] *Pure Sociology*, p. 261. (New York, 1903.)
[2] *Dynamic Sociology*, II, 90. (New York, 1883.)

SELECTED BIBLIOGRAPHY

I. CURRENT NOTIONS OF SOCIAL FORCES

(1) Patten, Simon N. *The Theory of Social Forces.* Philadelphia, 1896.

(2) Gladden, Washington. *Social Facts and Forces.* The factory, the labor union, the corporation, the railway, the city, the church. New York, 1897.

(3) Richmond, Mary. "Charitable Co-operation," *Proceedings of the National Conference of Charities and Correction,* 1901, pp. 298–313. (See "Diagram of Forces with which Charity Worker may Co-operate.")

(4) Devine, Edward T. *Social Forces.* From the editor's page of *The Survey.* New York, 1910.

(5) Edie, Lionel D., Editor. *Current Social and Industrial Forces.* Introduction by James Harvey Robinson. New York, 1920.

(6) Burns, Allen T. "Organization of Community Forces for the Promotion of Social Programs," *Proceedings of the National Conference of Charities and Correction,* 1916, pp. 62–78.

(7) *Social Forces.* A topical outline with bibliography. Wisconsin Woman's Suffrage Association, Educational Committee. Madison, Wis., 1915.

(8) Wells, H. G. *Social Forces in England and America.* London, 1914.

(9) Willey, Malcolm M., and Rice, Stuart A. "William J. Bryan as a Social Force," *Journal of Social Forces,* II (1923–24), 338–44.

(10) Ogburn, William F. "Business Fluctuations as Social Forces," *Journal of Social Forces,* I (1922–23), 73–78.

(11) McKenzie, R. D. "Community Forces, a Study in Non-partisan Politics," *Journal of Social Forces,* II (1924), 266–75, 415–21, 560–68.

(12) Giddings, Franklin H. "The Measurement of Social Forces," *Journal of Social Forces,* I, 1921–22.

II. HISTORICAL TENDENCIES AS SOCIAL FORCES

(1) Lamprecht, Karl. *What Is History?* Five lectures on the modern science of history. Translated from the German by E. A. Andrews. London and New York, 1905.

(2) Loria, A. *The Economic Foundations of Society.* Translated from the 2d French ed. by L. M. Keasbey. London and New York, 1899.

(3) Beard, Charles A. *An Economic Interpretation of the Constitution of the United States.* New York, 1913.

(4) Brandes, Georg. *Main Currents in Nineteenth-Century Literature.* 6 vols. London, 1906.

(5) Taine, H. A. *The Ancient Régime.* Translated from the French by John Durand. New York, 1891.

(6) Buckle, Henry Thomas. *History of Civilization in England.* 2 vols. New York, 1892.

(7) Lacombe, Paul. *De l'histoire considérée comme science.* Paris, 1894.

(8) Francke, Kuno. *Social Forces in German Literature.* A study in the history of civilization. New York, 1896.

(9) Hart, A. B. *Social and Economic Forces in American History.* From *The American Nation, A History.* London and New York, 1904.

(10) Turner, Frederick J. "Social Forces in American History," *The American Historical Review,* XVI (1910–11), 217–33.

(11) Woods, F. A. *The Influence of Monarchs.* Steps in a new science of history. New York, 1913.
(12) Cheyney, Edward P. "Law in History," *American Historical Review,* XXIX (1924), 231–48.

III. INTERESTS AND WANTS

A. *Interests, Desires, and Wants as Defined by the Sociologist*

(1) Ward, Lester F. *Dynamic Sociology, or Applied Social Science.* As based upon statical sociology and the less complex sciences. "The Social Forces," I, 468–699. New York, 1883.
(2) ———. *Pure Sociology.* A treatise on the origin and spontaneous development of society. Chap. xii, "Classification of the Social Forces," pp. 256–65. New York, 1903.
(3) ———. *The Psychic Factors of Civilization.* Chap. ix, "The Philosophy of Desire," pp. 50–58; chap. xviii, "The Social Forces," pp. 116–24. Boston, 1901.
(4) Small, Albion W. *General Sociology.* Chaps. xxvii and xxxi, pp. 372–94; 425–42. Chicago, 1905.
(5) Ross, Edward A. *The Principles of Sociology.* Part II, "Social Forces," pp. 41–73. New York, 1920.
(6) Blackmar, F. W., and Gillin, J. L. *Outlines of Sociology.* Part III, chap. ii, "Social Forces," pp. 283–315. New York, 1915.
(7) Hayes, Edward C. "The 'Social Forces' Error," *American Journal of Sociology,* XVI (1910–11), 613–25; 636–44.
(8) Fouillée, Alfred. *Education from a National Standpoint.* Translated from the French by W. J. Greenstreet. Chap. i. New York, 1892.
(9) ———. *Morale des idées-forces.* 2d ed. Paris, 1908. [Book II, Part II, chap. iii, pp. 290–311, describes opinion, custom, law, education from the point of view of "Idea-Forces."]

B. *Interests and Wants as Defined by the Economist*

(1) Hermann, F. B. W. v. *Staatswirthschaftliche Untersuchungen.* Chap. ii. München, 1870. [First of the modern attempts to classify wants.]
(2) Walker, F. A. *Political Economy.* 3d ed. New York, 1888. [See discussion of competition, pp. 91–111.]
(3) Marshall, Alfred. *Principles of Economics.* An introductory volume. Chap. ii, "Wants in Relation to Activities," pp. 86–91. 6th ed. London, 1910.
(4) ———. "Some Aspects of Competition," *Journal of the Royal Statistical Society.* Sec. VII, "Modern Analysis of the Motives of Business Competition," LIII (1890), 634–37. [See also Sec. VIII, "Growing Importance of Public Opinion as an Economic Force," pp. 637–41.]
(5) Menger, Karl. *Grundsätze der Volkswirthschaftslehre.* Chap. ii, Wien, 1871.
(6) ———. *Untersuchungen über die Methode der Socialwissenschaften und der politischen Ökonomie insbesondere.* Chap. vii, "Über das Dogma," etc. Leipzig, 1883.

(7) Jevons, W. S. *The Theory of Political Economy.* Chap. ii, "Theory of Pleasure and Pain," pp. 28–36; "The Laws of Human Wants," pp. 39–43. 4th ed. London, 1911.

(8) Bentham, Jeremy. "A Table of the Springs of Action." Showing the several species of pleasures and pains of which man's nature is susceptible; together with the several species of *interests, desires,* and *motives* respectively corresponding to them; and the several sets of appellatives, *neutral, eulogistic,* and *dyslogistic,* by which each species of *motive* is wont to be designated. [First published in 1817.] *The Works of Jeremy Bentham,* I, 195–219. London, 1843.

(9) Dickinson, Z. C. *Economic Motives.* A study in the psychological foundations of economic theory, with reference to other social sciences. Cambridge, Mass., 1922.

C. *Wants and Values*

(1) Kreibig, Josef K. *Psychologische Grundlegung eines Systems der Wert-Theorie.* Wien, 1902.

(2) Simmel, Georg. *Einleitung in die Moralwissenschaft.* Eine Kritik der ethischen Grundbegriffe. Vol. I, chap. iv, "Die Glückseligkeit." 2 vols. Berlin, 1904–5.

(3) Meinong, Alexius. *Psychologische-ethische Untersuchungen zur Wert-Theorie.* Graz, 1894.

(4) Ehrenfels, Chrn. v. *System der Wert-Theorie.* 2 vols. Leipzig, 1897–98.

(5) Brentano, Franz. *Psychologie vom empirischen Standpunkte.* Chaps. vi–ix, pp. 256–350. Leipzig, 1874.

(6) Urban, Wilbur Marshall. *Valuation, Its Nature and Laws.* Being an introduction to the general theory of value. London, 1909.

(7) Cooley, Charles H. *Social Process.* Part VI, "Valuation," pp. 283–348. New York, 1918.

IV. SENTIMENTS, ATTITUDES, AND WISHES

(1) White, W. A. *Mechanisms of Character Formation.* An introduction to psychoanalysis. New York, 1916.

(2) Pfister, Oskar. *The Psychoanalytic Method.* Translated from the German by Dr. C. R. Payne. New York, 1917.

(3) Jung, Carl G. *Analytical Psychology.* Translated from the German by Dr. Constance E. Long. New York, 1916.

(4) Adler, Alfred. *The Neurotic Constitution.* Outlines of a comparative individualistic psychology and psychotherapy. Translated from the German by Bernard Glueck. New York, 1917.

(5) Freud, Sigmund. *General Introduction to Psychoanalysis.* New York, 1920.

(6) Tridon, André. *Psychoanalysis and Behavior.* New York, 1920.

(7) Holt, Edwin B. *The Freudian Wish and Its Place in Ethics.* New York, 1915.

(8) Mercier, C. A. *Conduct and Its Disorders Biologically Considered.* London, 1911.

(9) Bechterew, W. v. *La psychologie objective.* Translated from the Russian. Paris, 1913.

(10) Kostyleff, N. *Le mécanisme cérébral de la pensée.* Paris, 1914.

(11) Bentley, A. F. *The Process of Government.* A study of social pressures. Chicago, 1908.

(12) Veblen, T. *The Theory of the Leisure Class.* An economic study in the evolution of institutions. New York, 1899. [Discusses the wish for recognition.]

(13) ———. *The Instinct of Workmanship, and the State of the Industrial Arts.* New York, 1914. (Discusses the wish for recognition.]

(14) McDougall, William. *An Introduction to Social Psychology.* Chaps. v–vi, pp. 121–73. 13th ed. Boston, 1918.

(15) Shand, A. F. "Character and the Emotions," *Mind.*, n. s., V (1896), 203–26.

(16) ———. "M. Ribot's Theory of the Passions," *Mind.*, n. s., XVI (1907), 477–505.

(17) ———. *The Foundations of Character.* Being a study of the tendencies of the emotions and sentiments. Chaps. iv–v, "The Systems of the Sentiments," pp. 35–63. London, 1914.

(18) Thomas, W. I., and Znaniecki, F. *The Polish Peasant in Europe and America*, III, 5–81. Boston, 1919.

(19) Eliot, Thomas D. "A Psychoanalytic Interpretation of Group Formation and Behavior," *American Journal of Sociology*, XXVI (1920–21), 333–52.

TOPICS FOR WRITTEN THEMES

1. The Concept of Forces in the Natural Sciences
2. Historical Interpretation and Social Forces
3. The Concept of Social Forces in Recent Studies of the Local Community
4. Institutions as Social Forces: The Church, the Press, the School, etc.
5. Institutions as Organizations of Social Forces: Analysis of a Typical Institution, Its Organization, Dominant Personalities, etc.
6. Persons as Social Forces: Analysis of the Motives determining the Behavior of a Dominant Personality in a Typical Social Group
7. Group Opinion as a Social Force
8. Tendencies, Trends, and the Spirit of the Age
9. History of the Concepts of Attitudes, Sentiments, and Wishes as Defined in Psychology, Psychoanalysis, and Sociology
10. Attitudes as the Organizations of Wishes
11. The Freudian Wish
12. Personal and Social Disorganization from the Standpoint of the Four Wishes
13. The Law of the Four Wishes: All the Wishes Must Be Realized. A Wish of One Type, Recognition, Is Not a Substitute for a Wish of Another Type, Response
14. The Dominant Wish: Its Rôle in the Organization of the Person and of the Group

15. Typical Attitudes: Familism, Individualism, "Oppressed Nationality Psychosis," Race Prejudice
16. The Mutability of the Sentiment-Attitude: Love and Hate, Self-esteem and Humility, etc.

QUESTIONS FOR DISCUSSION

1. Make a list of the outstanding social forces affecting social life in a community which you know. What is the value of such an analysis?
2. How does Simons use the term "social forces" in analyzing the course of events in American history?
3. In what sense do you understand Ely to use the term "social forces"?
4. Would there be, in your opinion, a social tendency without conflict with other tendencies?
5. How far is it correct to predict from present tendencies what the future will be?
6. What do you understand by *Zeitgeist*, "trend of the times," "spirit of the age"?
7. What do you understand by public opinion? How does it originate?
8. Is legislation in the United States always a result of public opinion?
9. Does the trend of public opinion determine corporate action?
10. Is public opinion the same as the sum of the opinion of the members of the group?
11. What is the relation of social forces to interaction?
12. Is it possible to study trends, tendencies, and public opinion as integrations of interests, sentiments, and attitudes?
13. Are desires the fundamental "social elements"?
14. What do you understand Small to mean when he says, "The last elements to which we can reduce the actions of human beings are units which we may conveniently name 'interests'"?
15. What is Small's classification of interests? Do you regard it as satisfactory?
16. What do you think is the difference between an impulse and an interest?
17. Do people behave according to their interests or their impulses?
18. Make a chart showing the difference in interests of six persons with whom you are acquainted.
19. Make a chart indicating the variations in interests of six selected groups.
20. What difference is there, in your opinion, between interests and social pressures?
21. Do you consider the following statement of Bentley's correct: "No slaves, not the worst abused of all, but help to form the government"?

22. Does the group exert social pressure upon its members? Give illustrations.
23. What do you understand to be the differences between an idea and an idea-force?
24. Give illustrations of idea-forces.
25. Are there any ideas that are not idea-forces?
26. What do you understand by a sentiment?
27. What is the difference between an interest and a sentiment? Give an illustration of each.
28. Are sentiments or interests more powerful in influencing the behavior of a person or of a group?
29. What do you understand by a social attitude?
30. What is a mental conflict?
31. To what extent does unconsciousness rather than consciousness determine the behavior of a person? Give an illustration where the behavior of a person was inconsistent with his rational determination.
32. What do you understand by mental complexes?
33. What is the relation of memory to mental complexes?
34. What do you understand by personality? What is its relation to mental complexes?
35. What is meant by common sense?
36. How does Holt define the Freudian wish?
37. What distinction does he make between the wish and the motor attitude?
38. How would you illustrate the difference between an attitude and a wish as defined in the introduction?
39. How far would you say that the attitude may be described as an organization of the wishes?
40. How far is the analogy between the wish as the social atom and the attitude as the social element justified?
41. What is the "psychic censor"?
42. What is the Freudian theory of repression? Is repression conscious or unconscious?
43. What is the relation of wishes to occupational selection?
44. Give illustrations of the "four wishes."
45. Describe a person in terms of the type of expression of these four wishes.
46. What social problems arise because of the repression of certain wishes?
47. "Wishes in one class cannot be substituted for wishes in another." Do you agree? Elaborate your position.
48. Analyze the organization of a group from the standpoint of the four wishes.

CHAPTER VIII

COMPETITION

I. INTRODUCTION

1. Popular Conception of Competition

Competition, as a universal phenomenon, was first clearly conceived and adequately described by the biologists. As defined in the evolutionary formula "the struggle for existence" the notion captured the popular imagination and became a commonplace of familiar discourse. Prior to that time competition had been regarded as an economic rather than a biological phenomenon.

It was in the eighteenth century and in England that we first find any general recognition of the new rôle that commerce and the middleman were to play in the modern world. "Competition is the life of trade" is a trader's maxim, and the sort of qualified approval that it gives to the conception of competition contains the germ of the whole philosophy of modern industrial society as that doctrine was formulated by Adam Smith and the physiocrats.

The economists of the eighteenth century were the first to attempt to rationalize and justify the social order that is based on competition and individual freedom. They taught that there was a natural harmony in the interests of men, which once liberated would inevitably bring about, in the best of all possible worlds, the greatest good to the greatest number.

The individual man, in seeking his own profit, will necessarily seek to produce and sell that which has most value for the community, and so "he is in this, as in many other cases," as Adam Smith puts it, "led by an invisible hand to promote an end which was no part of his intention."

The conception has been stated with even greater unction by the French writer, Frédéric Bastiat.

Since goods which seem at first to be the exclusive property of individuals become by the estimable decrees of a wise providence [competition] the common possession of all; since the natural advantages of situation, the fertility, temperature, mineral richness of the soil and even industrial skill do not accrue to the producers, because of competition among themselves, but contribute so much the more to the profit of the consumer; it follows that there is no country that is not interested in the advancement of all the others.[1]

The freedom which commerce sought and gained upon the principle of laissez faire has enormously extended the area of competition and in doing so has created a world-economy where previously there were only local markets. It has created at the same time a division of labor that includes all the nations and races of men and incidentally has raised the despised middleman to a position of affluence and power undreamed of by superior classes of any earlier age. And now there is a new demand for the control of competition in the interest, not merely of those who have not shared in the general prosperity, but in the interest of competition itself.

"Unfair competition" is an expression that is heard at the present time with increasing frequency. This suggests that there are rules governing competition by which, in its own interest, it can and should be controlled. The same notion has found expression in the demand for "freedom of competition" from those who would safeguard competition by controlling it. Other voices have been raised in denunciation of competition because "competition creates monopoly." In other words, competition, if carried to its logical conclusion, ends in the annihilation of competition. In this destruction of competition by competition we seem to have a loss of freedom by freedom, or, to state it in more general terms, unlimited liberty, without social control, ends in the negation of freedom and the slavery of the individual. But the limitation of competition by competition, it needs to be said, means simply that the process of competition tends invariably to establish an equilibrium.

The more fundamental objection is that in giving freedom to economic competition society has sacrificed other fundamental interests that are not directly involved in the economic process. In any case economic freedom exists in an order that has been created and maintained by society. Economic competition, as we know it, pre-

[1] Bastiat, Frédéric, *Œuvres complètes*, tome VI, "Harmonies économiques," 9e édition, p. 381. (Paris, 1884.)

supposes the existence of the right of private property, which is a creation of the state. It is upon this premise that the more radical social doctrines, communism and socialism, seek to abolish competition altogether.

2. Competition a Process of Interaction

Of the four great types of interaction—competition, conflict, accommodation, and assimilation—competition is the elementary, universal and fundamental form. Social contact, as we have seen, initiates interaction. But competition, strictly speaking, is *interaction without social contact.* If this seems, in view of what has already been said, something of a paradox, it is because in human society competition is always complicated with other processes, that is to say, with conflict, assimilation, and accommodation.

It is only in the plant community that we can observe the process of competition in isolation, uncomplicated with other social processes. The members of a plant community live together in a relation of mutual interdependence which we call social probably because, while it is close and vital, it is not biological. It is not biological because the relation is a merely external one and the plants that compose it are not even of the same species. They do not interbreed. The members of a plant community adapt themselves to one another as all living things adapt themselves to their environment, but there is no conflict between them because they are not conscious. Competition takes the form of conflict or rivalry only when it becomes conscious, when competitors identify one another as rivals or as enemies.

This suggests what is meant by the statement that competition is interaction *without social contact.* It is only when minds meet, only when the meaning that is in one mind is communicated to another mind so that these minds mutually influence one another, that social contact, properly speaking, may be said to exist.

On the other hand, social contacts are not limited to contacts of touch or sense or speech, and they are likely to be more intimate and more pervasive than we imagine. Some years ago the Japanese, who are brown, defeated the Russians, who are white. In the course of the next few months the news of this remarkable event penetrated, as we afterward learned, uttermost ends of the earth. It sent a thrill through all Asia and it was known in the darkest corners of Central Africa. Everywhere it awakened strange and fantastic dreams. This is what is meant by social contact.

a) Competition and competitive co-operation.—Social contact, which inevitably initiates conflict, accommodation, or assimilation, invariably creates also sympathies, prejudices, personal and moral relations which modify, complicate, and control competition. On the other hand, within the limits which the cultural process creates, and custom, law, and tradition impose, competition invariably tends to create an impersonal social order in which each individual, being free to pursue his own profit, and, in a sense, compelled to do so, makes every other individual a means to that end. In doing so, however, he inevitably contributes through the mutual exchange of services so established to the common welfare. It is just the nature of the trading transaction to isolate the motive of profit and make it the basis of business organization, and so far as this motive becomes dominant and exclusive, business relations inevitably assume the impersonal character so generally ascribed to them.

"Competition," says Walker, "is opposed to sentiment. Whenever any economic agent does or forbears anything under the influence of any sentiment other than the desire of giving the least and gaining the most he can in exchange, be that sentiment patriotism, or gratitude, or charity, or vanity, leading him to do otherwise than as self interest would prompt, in that case also, the rule of competition is departed from. Another rule is for the time substituted."[1]

This is the significance of the familiar sayings to the effect that one "must not mix business with sentiment," that "business is business," "corporations are heartless," etc. It is just because corporations are "heartless," that is to say impersonal, that they represent the most advanced, efficient, and responsible form of business organization. But it is for this same reason that they can and need to be regulated in behalf of those interests of the community that cannot be translated immediately into terms of profit and loss to the individual.

The plant community is the best illustration of the type of social organization that is created by competitive co-operation because in the plant community competition is unrestricted.

[1] Walker, Francis A., *Political Economy*, p. 92. (New York, 1887.)

b) Competition and freedom.—The economic organization of society, so far as it is an effect of free competition, is an ecological organization. There is a human as well as a plant and an animal ecology.

If we are to assume that the economic order is fundamentally ecological, that is, created by the struggle for existence, an organization like that of the plant community in which the relations between individuals are conceivably at least wholly external, the question may be very properly raised why the competition and the organization it has created should be regarded as social at all. As a matter of fact sociologists have generally identified the social with the moral order, and Dewey, in his *Democracy and Education*, makes statements which suggest that the purely economic order, in which man becomes a means rather than an end to other men, is unsocial, if not antisocial.

The fact is, however, that this character of *externality* in human relations is a fundamental aspect of society and social life. It is merely another manifestation of what has been referred to as the distributive aspect of society. Society is made up of individuals spatially separated, territorially distributed, and capable of independent locomotion. This capacity of independent. locomotion is the basis and the symbol of every other form of independence. Freedom is fundamentally freedom to move and individuality is inconceivable without the capacity and the opportunity to gain an individual experience as a result of independent action.

On the other hand, it is quite as true that society may be said to exist only so far as this independent activity of the individual is *controlled* in the interest of the group as a whole. That is the reason why the problem of control, using that term in its evident significance, inevitably becomes the central problem of sociology.

c) Competition and control.—Conflict, assimilation and accommodation as distinguished from competition are all intimately related to control. Competition is the process through which the distributive and ecological organization of society is created. Competition determines the distribution of population territorially and vocationally. The division of labor and all the vast organized economic interdependence of individuals and groups of individuals characteristic of modern life are a product of competition. On the other hand, the moral and political order, which imposes itself upon this competitive organization, is a product of conflict, accommodation and assimilation.

Competition is universal in the world of living things. Under ordinary circumstances it goes on unobserved even by the individuals who are most concerned. It is only in periods of crisis, when men are making new and conscious efforts to control the conditions of their common life, that the forces with which they are competing get identified with persons, and competition is converted into conflict. It is in what has been described as the *political process* that society consciously deals with its crises.[1] War is the political process par excellence. It is in war that the great decisions are made. Political organizations exist for the purpose of dealing with conflict situations. Parties, parliaments and courts, public discussion and voting are to be considered simply as substitutes for war.

d) *Accommodation, assimilation, and competition.*—Accommodation, on the other hand, is the process by which the individuals and groups make the necessary internal adjustments to social situations which have been created by competition and conflict. War and elections change situations. When changes thus effected are decisive and are accepted, conflict subsides and the tensions it created are resolved in the process of accommodation into profound modifications of the competing units, i.e., individuals and groups. A man once thoroughly defeated is, as has often been noted, "never the same again." Conquest, subjugation, and defeat are psychological as well as social processes. They establish a new order by changing, not merely the status, but the attitudes of the parties involved. Eventually the new order gets itself fixed in habit and custom and is then transmitted as part of the established social order to succeeding generations. Neither the physical nor the social world is made to satisfy at once all the wishes of the natural man. The rights of property, vested interests of every sort, the family organization, slavery, caste and class, the whole social organization, in fact, represent accommodations, that is to say, limitations of the natural wishes of the individual. These socially inherited accommodations have presumably grown up in the pains and struggles of previous generations, but they have been transmitted to and accepted by succeeding generations as part of the natural, inevitable social order. All of these are forms of control in which competition is limited by status.

[1] See chap. i, pp. 51–54.

Conflict is then to be identified with the political order and with conscious control. Accommodation, on the other hand, is associated with the social order that is fixed and established in custom and the mores.

Assimilation, as distinguished from accommodation, implies a more thoroughgoing transformation of the personality—a transformation which takes place gradually under the influence of social. contacts of the most concrete and intimate sort.

Accommodation may be regarded, like religious conversion, as a kind of mutation. The wishes are the same but their organization is different. Assimilation takes place not so much as a result of changes in the organization as in the content, i.e., the memories, of the personality. The individual units, as a result of intimate association, interpenetrate, so to speak, and come in this way into possession of a common experience and a common tradition. The permanence and solidarity of the group rest finally upon this body of common experience and tradition. It is the rôle of history to preserve this body of common experience and tradition, to criticise and reinterpret it in the light of new experience and changing conditions, and in this way to preserve the continuity of the social and political life.

The relation of social structures to the processes of competition, conflict, accommodation, and assimilation may be represented schematically as follows:

SOCIAL PROCESS	SOCIAL ORDER
Competition	The economic equilibrium
Conflict	The political order
Accommodation	Social organization
Assimilation	Personality and the cultural heritage

3. Classification of the Materials

The materials in this chapter have been selected to exhibit (1) the rôle which competition plays in social life and all life, and (2) the types of organization that competition has everywhere created as a result of the division of labor it has everywhere enforced. These materials fall naturally under the following heads: (a) the struggle for existence; (b) competition and segregation; and (c) economic competition.

This order of the materials serves the purpose of indicating the stages in the growth and extension of man's control over nature and over man himself. The evolution of society has been the progressive extension of control over nature and the substitution of a moral for the natural order.

Competition has its setting in the struggle for existence. This struggle is ordinarily represented as a chaos of contending individuals in which the unfit perish in order that the fit may survive. This conception of the natural order as one of anarchy, "the war of each against all," familiar since Hobbes to the students of society, is recent in biology. Before Darwin, students of plant and animal life saw in nature, not disorder, but order; not selection, but design. The difference between the older and the newer interpretation is not so much a difference of fact as of point of view. Looking at the plant and animal species with reference to their classification they present a series of relatively fixed and stable types. The same thing may be said of the plant and animal communities. Under ordinary circumstances the adjustment between the members of the plant and animal communities and the environment is so complete that the observer interprets it as an order of co-operation rather than a condition of competitive anarchy.

Upon investigation it turns out, however, that the plant and animal communities are in a state of unstable equilibrium, such that any change in the environment may destroy them. Communities of this type are not organized to resist or adapt themselves as communities to changes in the environment. The plant community, for example, is a mere product of segregation, an aggregate without nerves or means of communication that would permit the individuals to be controlled in the interest of the community as a whole.[1]

The situation is different in the so-called animal societies. Animals are adapted in part to the situation of competition, but in part also to the situation of co-operation. With the animal, maternal instinct, gregariousness, sex attraction restrict competition to a greater or less extent among individuals of the same family, herd, or

[1] The introduction of the rabbit into Australia, where predatory competitors are absent, has resulted in so great a multiplication of the members of this species that their numbers have become an economic menace. The appearance of the boll weevil, an insect which attacks the cotton boll, has materially changed the character of agriculture in areas of cotton culture in the South. Scientists are now looking for some insect enemy of the boll weevil that will restore the equilibrium.

species. In the case of the ant community competition is at a minimum and co-operation at a maximum.

With man the free play of competition is restrained by sentiment, custom, and moral standards, not to speak of the more conscious control through law.

It is a characteristic of competition, when unrestricted, that it is invariably more severe among organisms of the same than of different species. Man's greatest competitor is man. On the other hand, man's control over the plant and animal world is now well-nigh complete, so that, generally speaking, only such plants and animals are permitted to exist as serve man's purpose.

Competition among men, on the other hand, has been very largely converted into rivalry and conflict. The effect of conflict has been to extend progressively the area of control and to modify and limit the struggle for existence within these areas. The effect of war has been, on the whole, to extend the area over which there is peace. Competition has been restricted by custom, tradition, and law, and the struggle for existence has assumed the form of struggle for a livelihood and for status.

Absolute free play of competition is neither desirable nor even possible. On the other hand, from the standpoint of the individual, competition means mobility, freedom, and, from the point of view of society, pragmatic or experimental change. Restriction of competition is synonymous with limitation of movement, aquiescence in control, and telesis, Ward's term for changes ordained by society in distinction from the natural process of change.

The political problem of every society is the practical one: how to secure the maximum values of competition, that is, personal freedom, initiative, and originality, and at the same time to control the energies which competition has released in the interest of the community.

II. MATERIALS

A. THE STRUGGLE FOR EXISTENCE

1. Different Forms of the Struggle for Existence[1]

The formula "struggle for existence," familiar in human affairs, was used by Darwin in his interpretation of organic life, and he

[1] Adapted from J. Arthur Thomson, *Darwinism and Human Life*, pp. 72-75. (Henry Holt & Co., 1910.)

showed that we gain clearness in our outlook on animate nature if we recognize there, in continual process, a struggle for existence not merely analogous to, but fundamantally the same as, that which goes on in human life. He projected on organic life a sociological idea, and showed that it fitted. But while he thus vindicated the relevancy and utility of the sociological idea within the biological realm, he declared explicitly that the phrase "struggle for existence" was meant to be a shorthand formula, summing up a vast variety of strife and endeavor, of thrust and parry, of action and reaction.

Some of Darwin's successors have taken pains to distinguish a great many different forms of the struggle for existence, and this kind of analysis is useful in keeping us aware of the complexities of the process. Darwin himself does not seem to have cared much for this logical mapping out and defining; it was enough for him to insist that the phrase was used "in a large and metaphorical sense," and to give full illustrations of its various modes. For our present purpose it is enough for us to follow his example.

a) Struggle between fellows.—When the locusts of a huge swarm have eaten up every green thing, they sometimes turn on one another. This cannibalism among fellows of the same species—illustrated, for instance, among many fishes—is the most intense form of the struggle for existence. The struggle does not need to be direct to be real; the essential point is that the competitors seek after the same desiderata, of which there is a limited supply.

As an instance of keen struggle between nearly related species, Darwin referred to the combats of rats. The black rat was in possession of many European towns before the brown rat crossed the Volga in 1727; whenever the brown rat arrived, the black rat had to go to the wall. Thus at the present day there are practically no black rats in Great Britain. Here the struggle for existence is again directly competitive. It is difficult to separate the struggle for food and foothold from the struggle for mates, and it seems clearest to include here the battles of the stags and the capercailzies, or the extraordinary lek of the blackcock, showing off their beauty at sunrise on the hills.

b) Struggle between foes.—In the locust swarm and in the rats' combats there is competition between fellows of the same or nearly related species, but the struggle for existence includes much wider antipathies. We see it between foes of entirely different nature, between carnivores and herbivores, between birds of prey and small mammals. In both these cases there may be a stand-up fight, for instance between wolf and stag, or between hawk and ermine; but neither the logic nor the biology of the process is different when all the fight is on one side. As the lemmings, which have overpopulated the Scandinavian valleys, go on the march they are followed by birds and beasts of prey, which thin their ranks. Moreover, the competition between species need not be direct; it will come to the same result if both types seek after the same things. The victory will be with the more effective and the more prolific.

c) *Struggle with fate.*—Our sweep widens still further, and we pass beyond the idea of competition altogether to cases where the struggle for existence is between the living organism and the inanimate conditions of its life—for instance, between birds and the winter's cold, between aquatic animals and changes in the water, between plants and drought, between plants and frost—in a wide sense, between Life and Fate.

We cannot here pursue the suggestive idea that, besides struggle between individuals, there is struggle between groups of individuals—the latter most noticeably developed in mankind. Similarly, working in the other direction, there is struggle between parts or tissues in the body, between cells in the body, between equivalent germ-cells, and, perhaps, as Weismann pictures, between the various multiplicate items that make up our inheritance.

2. Competition and Natural Selection[1]

The term "struggle for existence" is used in a large and metaphorical sense, including dependence of one being on another, and including (which is more important) not only the life of the individual but success in leaving progeny. Two canine animals in a time of dearth may be truly said to struggle with each other which shall get food and live. But a plant on the edge of a desert is said to struggle for life against the drought, though more properly it should be said

[1] Adapted from Charles Darwin, *The Origin of Species*, pp. 50–61. (D. Appleton & Co., 1878.)

to be dependent on the moisture. A plant which annually produces a thousand seeds, of which only one of an average comes to maturity, may be more truly said to struggle with the plants of the same and other kinds which already clothe the ground. The mistletoe is dependent on the apple and a few other trees, but can only in a far-fetched sense be said to struggle with these trees, for, if too many of these parasites grow on the same tree, it languishes and dies. But several seedling mistletoes growing close together on the same branch may more truly be said to struggle with each other. As the mistletoe is disseminated by birds, its existence depends on them; and it may metaphorically be said to struggle with other fruit-bearing plants in tempting the birds to devour and thus disseminate its seeds. In these several senses which pass into each other, I use for convenience' sake the general term of "struggle for existence."

A struggle for existence inevitably follows from the high rate at which all organic beings tend to increase. Every being which during its natural lifetime produces several eggs or seeds must suffer destruction during some period of its life, and during some season or occasional year, otherwise, on the principle of geometrical increase, its numbers would quickly become so inordinately great that no country could support the product. Hence, as more individuals are produced than can possibly survive, there must in every case be a struggle for existence, either one individual with another of the same species, or with the individuals of distinct species, or with the physical conditions of life. It is the doctrine of Malthus applied with manifold force to the whole animal and vegetable kingdoms; for in this case there can be no artificial increase of food, and no prudential restraint from marriage. Although some species may be now increasing more or less rapidly in numbers, all cannot do so, for the world would not hold them.

There is no exception to the rule that every organic being naturally increases at so high a rate that, if not destroyed, the earth would soon be covered by the progeny of a single pair. Even slow-breeding man has doubled in twenty-five years, and at this rate in less than a thousand years there would literally not be standing-room for his progeny. Linnaeus has calculated that if an annual plant produced only two seeds—and there is no plant so unproductive as this—and their seedlings next year produced two, and so on, then in twenty years there would be a million plants.   The elephant is reckoned the slowest breeder of all known animals, and I have taken some pains to estimate its probable minimum rate of natural increase; it will be safest to assume that it begins breeding when thirty years old and goes on breeding till ninety years old, bringing forth six young in the interval and surviving till one hundred years old; if this be so, after a period of from 740 to 750 years there would be nearly nineteen million elephants alive, descended from the first pair.

The struggle for life is most severe between individuals and varieties of the same species.   As the species of the same genus usually have, though by no means invariably, much similarity in habits and constitution, and always similarity in structure, the struggle will generally be more severe between them if they come into competition with each other than between the species of distinct genera.   We see this in the recent extension over parts of the United States of one species of swallow having caused the decrease of another species. The recent increase of the missel-thrush in parts of Scotland has caused the decrease of the song-thrush.   How frequently we hear of one species of rat taking the place of another species under the most different climates!   In Russia the small Asiatic cockroach has everywhere driven before it its great congener.   In Australia the imported hive-bee is rapidly exterminating the small, stingless native bee. We can dimly see why the competition should be most severe between allied forms which fill nearly the same place in the economy of nature; but probably in no one case could we precisely say why one species has been victorious over another in the great battle of life.

A corollary of the highest importance may be deduced from the foregoing remarks, namely, that the structure of every organic being is related, in the most essential yet often hidden manner, to that of all the other organic beings with which it comes into competition for food or residence or from which it has to escape or on which it preys.   This is obvious in the structure of the teeth and talons of the tiger; and in that of the legs and claws of the parasite which clings to the hair on the tiger's body.   But in the beautifully plumed seed of the dandelion, and in the flattened and fringed legs of the water-beetle, the relation seems at first confined to the elements of air and water.   Yet the advantage of plumed seeds no doubt stands in the closest relations to the land being already thickly clothed with other plants; so that the seeds may be widely distributed and fall on unoccupied ground. In the water beetle, the structure of its legs, so well adapted for diving, allows it to compete with other aquatic insects, to hunt for its own prey, and to escape serving as prey to other animals.

The store of nutriment laid up within the seeds of many plants seems at first sight to have no sort of relation to other plants. But from the strong growth of young plants produced from such seeds, as peas and beans, when sown in the midst of long grass, it may be suspected that the chief use of the nutriment in the seed is to favor the growth of seedlings whilst struggling with other plants growing vigorously all around.

Look at a plant in the midst of its range; why does it not double or quadruple its numbers? We know that it can perfectly well withstand a little more heat or cold, dampness or dryness, for elsewhere it ranges into slightly hotter or colder, damper or drier, districts. In this case we can clearly see that if we wish in imagination to give the plant the power of increasing in number, we should have to give it some advantage over its competitors, or over the animals which prey upon it. On the confines of its geographical range, a change of constitution with respect to climate would clearly be an advantage to our plant; but we have reason to believe that only a few plants or animals range so far, that they are destroyed exclusively by the rigor of the climate. Not until we reach the extreme confines of life, in the Arctic regions or on the borders of an utter desert, will competition cease. The land may be extremely cold or dry, yet there will be competition between some few species, or between the individuals of the same species, for the warmest or dampest spots.

Hence we can see that when a plant or an animal is placed in a new country amongst new competitors, the conditions of its life will generally be changed in an essential manner, although the climate may be exactly the same as in its former home. If its average numbers are to increase in its new home, we should have to modify it in a different way to what we should have had to do in its native country; for we should have to give it some advantage over a different set of competitors or enemies.

It is good thus to try in imagination to give to any one species an advantage over another. Probably in no single instance should we know what to do.   This ought to convince us of our ignorance on the mutual relations of all organic beings, a conviction as necessary as it is difficult to acquire.   All that we can do is to keep steadily in mind that each organic being is striving to increase in a geometrical ratio; that each at some period of its life, during some season of the year, during each generation or at intervals, has to struggle for life and to suffer great destruction.   When we reflect on this struggle, we may console ourselves with the full belief that the war of nature is not incessant, that no fear is felt, that death is generally prompt, and that the vigorous, the healthy, and the happy survive and multiply.

3.   Competition, Specialization, and Organization[1]

Natural selection acts exclusively by the preservation and accumulation of variations, which are beneficial under the organic and inorganic conditions to which each creature is exposed at all periods of life.   The ultimate result is that each creature tends to become more and more improved in relation to its conditions.   This improvement inevitably leads to the gradual advancement of the organization of the greater number of living beings throughout the world.

But here we enter on a very intricate subject, for naturalists have not defined to each other's satisfaction what is meant by an advance in organization.   Amongst the vertebrata the degree of intellect and an approach in structure to man clearly come into play.   It might be thought that the amount of change which the various parts and organs pass through in their development from the embryo to maturity would suffice as a standard of comparison; but there are cases, as with certain parasitic crustaceans, in which several parts of the structure become less perfect, so that the mature animal cannot be called higher than its larva.   Von Baer's standard seems the most widely applicable and the best, namely, the amount of differentiation of the parts of the same organic being, in the adult state, as I should be inclined to add, and their specialization for different functions; or, as Milne Edwards would express it, the completeness of the division of physiological labor.   But we shall see how obscure this subject is if we look, for instance, to fishes, amongst which some naturalists rank those as highest which, like the sharks, approach nearest to

[1] Adapted from Charles Darwin, *The Origin of Species*, pp. 97–100. (D. Appleton & Co., 1878.)

amphibians; whilst other naturalists rank the common bony or teleostean fishes as the highest, inasmuch as they are most strictly fishlike and differ most from the other vertebrate classes. We see still more plainly the obscurity of the subject by turning to plants, amongst which the standard of intellect is, of course, quite excluded; and here some botanists rank those plants as highest which have every organ, as sepals, petals, stamens, and pistils, fully developed in each flower; whereas other botanists, probably with more truth, look at the plants which have their several organs much modified and reduced in number as the highest.

If we take as the standard of high organization the amount of differentiation and specialization of the several organs in each being when adult (and this will include the advancement of the brain for intellectual purposes), natural selection clearly leads toward this standard; for all physiologists admit that the specialization of organs, inasmuch as in this state they perform their functions better, is an advantage to each being; and hence the accumulation of variations tending toward specialization is within the scope of natural selection. On the other hand, we can see, bearing in mind that all organic beings are striving to increase at a high ratio and to seize on every unoccupied or less well-occupied place in the economy of nature, that it is quite possible for natural selection gradually to fit a being to a situation in which several organs would be superfluous or useless: in such cases there would be retrogression in the scale of organization.

But it may be objected that if all organic beings thus tend to rise in the scale, how is it that throughout the world a multitude of the lowest forms still exist; and how is it that in each great class some forms are far more highly developed than others? Why have not the more highly developed forms everywhere supplanted and exterminated the lower? On our theory the continued existence of lowly organisms offers no difficulty for natural selection, or the survival of the fittest does not necessarily include progressive development—it only takes advantage of such variations as arise and are beneficial to each creature under its complex relations of life. And it may be asked what advantage, as far as we can see, would it be to an infusorian animalcule—to an intestinal worm, or even to an earthworm—to be highly organized. If it were no advantage, these forms would be left, by natural selection, unimproved or but little improved, and might remain for indefinite ages in their present lowly condition. And geology tells us that some of the lowest forms, as the infusoria and rhizopods, have remained for an enormous period in nearly their present state. But to suppose that most of the many low forms now existing have not in the least advanced since the first dawn of life would be extremely rash; for every naturalist who has dissected some of the beings now ranked as very low in the scale must have been struck with their really wondrous and beautiful organization.

Nearly the same remarks are applicable if we look to the different grades of organization within the same great group; for instance, in the vertebrata to the coexistence of mammals and fish; amongst mammalia to the coexistence of man and the ornithorhynchus; amongst fishes to the coexistence of the shark and the lancelet (Amphioxus), which later fish in the extreme simplicity of its structure approaches the invertebrate classes. But mammals and fish hardly come into competition with each other; the advancement of the whole class of mammals, or of certain members in this class, to the highest grade would not lead to their taking the place of fishes. Physiologists believe that the brain must be bathed by warm blood to be highly active, and this requires aerial respiration; so that warm-blooded mammals when inhabiting the water lie under a disadvantage in having to come continually to the surface to breathe. With fishes, members of the shark family would not tend to supplant the lancelet; for the lancelet, as I hear from Fritz Müller, has as sole companion and competitor on the barren sandy shore of South Brazil an anomalous annelid. The three lowest orders of mammals, namely, marsupials, edentata, and rodents, coexist in South America in the same region with numerous monkeys, and probably interfere little with each other.

Although organization, on the whole, may have advanced and may be still advancing throughout the world, yet the scale will always present many degrees of perfection; for the high advancement of certain whole classes, or of certain members of each class, does not at all necessarily lead to the extinction of those groups with which they do not enter into close competition. In some cases, lowly organized forms appear to have been preserved to the present day from inhabiting confined or peculiar stations, where they have been subjected to less severe competition and where their scanty numbers have retarded the chance of favorable variations arising.

Finally, I believe that many lowly organized forms now exist throughout the world from various causes. In some cases variations or individual differences of a favorable nature may never have arisen for natural selection to act on and accumulate. In no case, probably, has time sufficed for the utmost possible amount of development. In some few cases there has been what we must call retrogression of organization. But the main cause lies in the fact that under very simple conditions of life a high organization would be of no service— possibly would be of actual disservice, as being of a more delicate nature and more liable to be put out of order and injured.

4. Man: An Adaptive Mechanism[1]

Everything in nature, living or not living, exists and develops at the expense of some other thing, living or not living. The plant borrows from the soil; the soil from the rocks and the atmosphere; men and animals take from the plants and from each other the elements which they in death return to the soil, the atmosphere, and the plants. Year after year, century after century, eon after eon, the mighty, immeasurable, ceaseless round of elements goes on, in the stupendous process of chemical change, which marks the eternal life of matter.

To the superficial observer, nature in all her parts seems imbued with a spirit of profound peace and harmony; to the scientist it is obvious that every infinitesimal particle of the immense concourse is in a state of desperate and ceaseless struggle to obtain such share of the available supply of matter and energy as will suffice to maintain its present ephemeral form in a state of equilibrium with its surroundings. Not only is this struggle manifest among living forms, among birds and beasts and insects in their competition for food and habitat, but—if we may believe the revelations of the science of radio-activity—a process of transmutation, of disintegration of the atoms of one element with simultaneous formation of another element, is taking place in every fragment of inanimate matter, a process which parallels in character the more transitory processes

[1] Adapted from George W. Crile, *Man: An Adaptive Mechanism*, pp. 17-39. (Published by The Macmillan Co.. 1916. Reprinted by permission.)

of life and death in organisms and is probably a representation of the primary steps in that great process of evolution by which all terrestrial forms, organic and inorganic, have been evolved from the original ether by an action inconceivably slow, continuous, and admitting of no break in the series from inanimate to animate forms.

From colloidal slime to man is a long road, the conception of which taxes our imaginations to the utmost, but it is an ascent which is now fairly well demonstrated. Indeed, the problems of the missing links are not so difficult as is the problem of the origin of the organs and functions which man has acquired as products of adaptation. For whether we look upon the component parts of our present bodies as useful or useless mechanisms, we must regard them as the result of age-long conflicts between environmental forces and organisms.

Everywhere something is pursuing and something is escaping another creature. It is a constant drama of getting food and of seeking to escape being made food, evolving in the conflict structures fitted to accomplish both reactions. Everywhere the strong prey upon the weak, the swift upon the slow, the clever upon the stupid; and the weak, the slow, the stupid, retaliate by evolving mechanisms of defense, which more or less adequately repel or render futile the oppressor's attack. For each must live, and those already living have proved their right to existence by a more or less complete adaptation to their environment. The result of this twofold conflict between living beings is to evolve the manifold structures and functions— teeth, claws, skin, color, fur, feathers, horns, tusks, wily instincts, strength, stealth, deceit, and humility—which make up character in the animal world. According to the nature and number of each being's enemies has its own special mechanism been evolved, distinguishing it from its fellows and enabling it to get a living in its particular environment.

In every case the fate of each creature seems to have been staked upon one mechanism. The tiger by its teeth and claws, the elephant and the rhinoceros by their strength, the bird by its wings, the deer by its fleetness, the turtle by its carapace—all are enabled to counter the attacks of enemies and to procreate. Where there is a negative defense, such as a shell or quills, there is little need and no evidence of intelligence; where a rank odor, no need and no presence of claws or carapace; where sting or venom, no need and no possession of odor, claws, shell, extraordinary strength, or sagacity. Where the struggle is most bitter, there exist the most complex and most numerous contrivances for living.

Throughout its whole course the process of evolution, where it is visible in the struggle of organisms, has been marked by a progressive victory of brain over brawn. And this, in turn, may be regarded as but a manifestation of the process of survival by *lability* rather than by *stability*. Everywhere the organism that exhibits the qualities of quick response, of extreme sensibility to stimuli, of capacity to change, is the individual that survives, "conquers," "advances." The quality most useful in nature, from the point of view of the domination of a wider environment, is the quality of *changeableness, plasticity, mobility*, or *versatility*. Man's particular means of adaptation to his environment is this quality of versatility. By means of this quality expressed through the manifold reactions of his highly organized central nervous system, man has been able to dominate the beasts and to maintain himself in an environment many times more extensive than theirs. Like the defensive mechanisms of shells, poisons, and odors, man's particular defensive mechanism—his versatility of nervous response (mind)—was acquired automatically as a result of a particular combination of circumstances in his environment.

In the Tertiary era—some twenty millions of years ago—the earth, basking in the warmth of a tropical climate, had produced a luxuriant vegetation and a swarming progeny of gigantic small-brained animals for which the exuberant vegetation provided abundant and easily acquired sustenance. They were a breed of huge, clumsy, and grotesque monsters, vast in bulk and strength, but of little intelligence, that wandered heavily on the land and gorged lazily on the abundant food at hand. With the advance of the carnivora, the primitive forerunners of our tigers, wolves, hyenas, and foxes, came a period of stress, comparable to a seven years of famine following a seven years of plenty, which subjected the stolid herbivorous monsters to a severe selective struggle.

Before the active onslaught of lighter, lither, more intelligent foes, the clumsy, inelastic types succumbed, those only surviving which, through the fortunate possession of more varied reactions, were able to evolve modes of defense equal to the modes of attack possessed by their enemies.   Many, unable to evolve the acute senses and the fleet limbs necessary for the combat on the ground, shrank from the fray and acquired more negative and passive means of defense.   Some, like the bat, escaped into the air.   Others, such as the squirrel and the ape, took refuge in the trees.

It was in this concourse of weak creatures which fled to the trees because they lacked adequate means of offense, defense, or escape on the ground that the lineaments of man's ancient ancestor might have been discerned.   One can imagine what must have been the pressure from the carnivora that forced a selective transformation of the feet of the progenitor of the anthropoids into grasping hands. Coincidentally with the tree life, man's special line of adaptation— *versatility*—was undoubtedly rapidly evolved.   Increased versatility and the evolution of hands enabled man to come down from the trees millions of years thereafter, to conquer the world by the further evolution and exercise of his organ of strategy—the brain.   Thus we may suppose have arisen the intricate reactions we now call mind, reason, foresight, invention, etc.

Man's claim to a superior place among animals depends less upon *different* reactions than upon a *greater number* of reactions as compared with the reactions of "lower" animals.   Ability to respond adaptively to more elements in the environment gives a larger dominion, that is all.

The same measure applies within the human species—the number of nervous reactions of the artist, the financier, the statesman, the scientist, being invariably greater than the reactions of the stolid savage.   That man alone of all animals should have achieved the degree of versatility sufficient for such advance is no more remarkable than that the elephant should have evolved a larger trunk and tusks than the boar; that the legs of the deer should be fleeter than those of the ox; that the wings of the swallow should outfly those of the bat.   Each organism, in evolving the combination of characters commensurate with safety in its particular environment, has touched the limit of both its necessity and its power to "advance."   There exists abundant and reliable evidence of the fact that wherever man has been subjected to the stunting influences of an unchanging environment fairly favorable to life, he has shown no more disposition to progress than the most stolid animals.   Indeed, he has usually retrograded. The need to fight for food and home has been the spur that has ever driven man forward to establish the manifold forms of physical and mental life which make up human existence today. Like the simple adaptive mechanisms of the plant by which it gets air, and of the animal by which it overcomes its rivals in battle, the supremely differentiated functions of thought and human relations are the outcome of the necessity of the organism to become adapted to entities in its environment.

B. COMPETITION AND SEGREGATION

1. Plant Migration, Competition, and Segregation[1]

Invasion is the complete or complex process of which migration, ecesis (the adjustment of a plant to a new home), and competition are the essential parts. It embraces the whole movement of a plant or group of plants from one area into another and their colonization in the latter. From the very nature of migration, invasion is going on at all times and in all directions.

Effective invasion is predominantly local. It operates in mass only between bare areas and adjacent communities which contain species capable of pioneering, or between contiguous communities which offer somewhat similar conditions or contain species of wide range of adjustment. Invasion into a remote region rarely has any successional effect (effect tending to transform the character of a plant community), as the invaders are too few to make headway against the plants in possession or against those much nearer a new area. Invasion into a new area or a plant community begins with migration when this is followed by ecesis. In new areas, ecesis produces reaction (the effect which a plant or a community exerts upon its habitat) at once, and this is followed by aggregation and competition, with increasing reaction. In an area already occupied by plants, ecesis and competition are concomitant and quickly produce reactions. Throughout the development migrants are entering and leaving, and the interactions of the various processes come to be complex in the highest degree.

[1] Adapted from F. E. Clements, *Plant Succession*. An analysis of the development of vegetation, pp. 75-79. (Carnegie Institution of Washington, 1916.)

Local invasion in force is essentially *continuous* or *recurrent*. Between contiguous communities it is *mutual*, unless they are too dissimilar. The result is a transition area or ecotone which epitomizes the next stage in development. By far the greater amount of invasion into existing vegetation is of this sort. The movement into a bare area is likewise continuous, though it is necessarily not mutual, and hence there is no ecotone during the earlier stages. The significant feature of continuous invasion is that an outpost may be repeatedly reinforced, permitting rapid aggregation and ecesis, and the production of new centers from which the species may be extended over a wide area. Contrasted with continuous invasion is intermittent or periodic movement into distant regions, but this is rarely concerned in succession. When the movement of invaders into a community is so great that the original occupants are driven out, the invasion is *complete*.

A topographic feature or a physical or a biological agency that restricts or prevents invasions is a barrier. Topographic features are usually permanent and produce permanent barriers. Biological ones are often temporary and exist for a few years or even a single season. Temporary barriers are often recurrent, however. Barriers are complete or incomplete with respect to the thoroughness of their action. They may affect invasion either by limiting migration or by preventing ecesis.

Biological barriers comprise plant communities, man and animals, and parasitic plants. The limiting effect of a plant community is exhibited in two ways. In the first place, an association acts as a barrier to the ecesis of species invading it from associations of another type, on account of the physical differences of the habitats. Whether such a barrier be complete or partial will depend upon the relative unlikeness of the two areas. Shade plants are unable to invade a prairie, though the species of open thickets or woodland may do so to a certain degree. Closed communities (one in which all the soil is occupied) likewise exert a marked influence in decreasing invasion by reason of the intense and successful competition which all invaders must meet. Closed associations usually act as complete barriers, while more open ones restrict invasion in direct proportion to the degree of occupation. To this fact may be traced the fundamental law of succession (the law by which one type of community or formation is succeeded by another) that the number of stages is determined largely by the increasing difficulty of invasion as the area becomes stabilized. Man and animals affect invasion by the destruction of germules. Both in bare areas and in seral stages the action of rodents and birds is often decisive to the extent of altering the whole course of development. Man and animals operate as marked barriers to ecesis wherever they alter conditions unfavorably to invaders or where they turn the scale in competition by cultivating, grazing, camping, parasitism, etc. The absence of pollinating insects is sometimes a curious barrier to the complete ecesis of species far out of their usual habitat or region. Parasitic fungi decrease migration in so far as they affect seed production. They restrict or prevent ecesis either by the destruction of invaders or by placing them at a disadvantage with respect to the occupants.

By the term *reaction* is understood the effect which a plant or a community exerts upon its habitat. In connection with succession, the term is restricted to this special sense alone. It is entirely distinct from the response of the plant or group, i.e., its adjustment and adaptation to the habitat. In short, the habitat causes the plant to function and grow, and the plant then reacts upon the habitat, changing one or more of its factors in decisive or appreciable degree. The two processes are mutually complementary and often interact in most complex fashion.

The reaction of a community is usually more than the sum of the reactions of the component species and individuals. It is the individual plant which produces the reaction, though the latter usually becomes recognizable through the combined action of the group. In most cases the action of the group accumulates or emphasizes an effect which would otherwise be insignificant or temporary. A community of trees casts less shade than the same number of isolated individuals, but the shade is constant and continuous, and hence controlling. The significance of the community reaction is especially well shown in the case of leaf mold and duff. The leaf litter is again only the total of the fallen leaves of all the individuals but its formation is completely dependent upon the community. The reaction of plants upon wind-borne sand and silt-laden waters illustrates the same fact.

2. Migration and Segregation[1]

All prehistoric investigation, as far as it relates to the phenomena of the animate world, necessarily rests upon the hypothesis of migration. The distribution of plants, of the lower animals, and of men over the surface of the earth; the relationships existing between the different languages, religious conceptions, myths and legends, customs and social institutions—all these seem in this one assumption to find their common explanation.

Each fresh advance in culture commences, so to speak, with a new period of wandering. The most primitive agriculture is nomadic, with a yearly abandonment of the cultivated area; the earliest trade is migratory trade; the first industries that free themselves from the household husbandry and become the special occupations of separate individuals are carried on itinerantly. The great founders of religion, the earliest poets and philosophers, the musicians and actors of past epochs, are all great wanderers. Even today, do not the inventor, the preacher of a new doctrine, and the virtuoso travel from place to place in search of adherents and admirers—notwithstanding the immense recent development in the means of communicating information?

As civilization grows older, settlement becomes more permanent. The Greek was more settled than the Phoenician, the Roman than the Greek, because one was always the inheritor of the culture of the other. Conditions have not changed. The German is more migratory than the Latin, the Slav than the German. The Frenchman cleaves to his native soil; the Russian leaves it with a light heart to seek in other parts of his broad fatherland more favorable conditions of living. Even the factory workman is but a periodically wandering peasant.

To all that can be adduced from experience in support of the statement that in the course of history mankind has been ever growing more settled, there comes a general consideration of a twofold nature. In the first place, the extent of fixed capital grows with advancing culture; the producer becomes stationary with his means of production.

[1] Adapted from Carl Bücher, *Industrial Evolution*, pp. 345–69. (Henry Holt & Co., 1907.)

The itinerant smith of the southern Slav countries and the West-phalian iron works, the pack-horses of the Middle Ages and the great warehouses of our cities, the Thespian carts and the resident theater mark the starting and the terminal points of this evolution. In the second place, the modern machinery of transportation has in a far higher degree facilitated the transport of goods than of persons. The distribution of labor determined by locality thereby attains greater importance than the natural distribution of the means of production; the latter in many cases draws the former after it, where previously the reverse occurred.

The migrations occurring at the opening of the history of European peoples are migrations of whole tribes, a pushing and pressing of collective units from east to west, which lasted for centuries. The migrations of the Middle Ages ever affect individual classes alone; the knights in the crusades, the merchants, the wage-craftsmen, the journeymen hand-workers, the jugglers and minstrels, the villeins seeking protection within the walls of a town. Modern migrations, on the contrary, are generally a matter of private concern, the individuals being led by the most varied motives. They are almost invariably without organization. The process repeating itself daily a thousand times is united only through the one characteristic, that it is everywhere a question of change of locality by persons seeking more favorable conditions of life.

Among all the phenomena of masses in social life suited to statistical treatment, there is without doubt scarcely one that appears to fall of itself so completely under the general law of causality as migrations; and likewise hardly one concerning whose real cause such misty conceptions prevail.

The whole department of migrations has never yet undergone systematic statistical observation; exclusive attention has hitherto been centered upon remarkable individual occurrences of such phenomena. Even a rational classification of migrations in accord with the demand of social science is at the present moment lacking.

Such a classification would have to take as its starting-point the result of migrations from the point of view of population. On this basis they would fall into these groups: (1) migrations with continuous change of locality; (2) migrations with temporary change of settlement; (3) migrations with permanent settlement.

To the *first* group belong gypsy life, peddling, the carrying on of itinerant trades, tramp life; to the *second*, the wandering of journeymen craftsmen, domestic servants, tradesmen seeking the most favorable spots for temporary undertakings, officials to whom a definite office is for a time entrusted, scholars attending foreign institutions of learning; to the *third*, migration from place to place within the same country or province and to foreign parts, especially across the ocean.

An intermediate stage between the first and second group is found in the *periodical migrations*. To this stage belong the migrations of farm laborers at harvest-time, of the sugar laborers at the time of the *campagne*, of the masons of Upper Italy and the Ticino district, common day-laborers, potters, chimney-sweeps, chestnut-roasters, etc., which occur at definite seasons.

In this division the influence of the natural and political insulation of the different countries is, it is true, neglected. It must not, however, be overlooked that in the era of nationalism and protection of national labor political allegiance has a certain importance in connection with the objective point of the migrations. It .would, therefore, in our opinion, be more just to make another division, taking as a basis the politico-geographical extent of the migrations. From this point of view migrations would fall into *internal* and *foreign* types.

Internal migrations are those whose points of departure and destination lie within the same national limits; foreign, those extending beyond these. The foreign may again be divided into *continental* and *extra-European* (generally transmaritime) emigration. One can, however, in a larger sense designate all migrations that do not leave the limits of the Continent as internal, and contrast with them real emigration, or transfer of domicile to other parts of the globe.

Of all these manifold kinds of migration, the transmaritime alone has regularly been the subject of official statistics; and even it has been but imperfectly treated, as every student of this subject knows. The periodic emigrations of labor and the peddling trade have occasionally been also subjected to statistical investigation—mostly with the secondary aim of legislative restriction. Yet these migrations from place to place within the same country are vastly more numerous and in their consequences vastly more important than all other kinds of migration put together.

Of the total population of the kingdom of Belgium there were, according to the results of the census of December 31, 1880, not less than 32.8 per cent who were born outside the municipality in which they had their temporary domicile; of the population of Austria (1890), 34.8 per cent. In Prussia, of 27,279,111 persons, 11,552,033, or 42.4 per cent, were born outside the municipality where they were domiciled. More than two-fifths of the population had changed their municipality at least once.

If we call the total population born in a given place and domiciled anywhere within the borders of the country that locality's *native* population, then according to the conditions of interchange of population just presented the native population of the country places is greater than their actual population; that of the cities, smaller.

A balancing of the account of the internal migrations in the grand duchy of Oldenburg gives the cities a surplus, and country municipalities a deficit, of 15,162 persons. In the economy of population one is the complement of the other, just as in the case of two brothers of different temperament, one of whom regularly spends what the other has laboriously saved. To this extent, then, we are quite justified from the point of view of population in designating the cities man-consuming and the country municipalities man-producing social organisms.

There is a very natural explanation for this condition of affairs in the country. Where the peasant, on account of the small population of his place of residence, is much restricted in his local choice of help, adjoining communities must supplement one another. In like manner the inhabitants of small places will intermarry more frequently than the inhabitants of larger places where there is a greater choice among the native population. Here we have the occasion for very numerous migrations to places not far removed. Such migrations, however, only mean a local exchange of socially allied elements.

This absorption of the surplus of emigration over immigration is the characteristic of modern cities. If in our consideration of this problem we pay particular attention to this urban characteristic and to a like feature of the factory districts—where the conditions as to internal migrations are almost similar—we shall be amply repaid by the discovery that in such settlements the result of internal shiftings of population receives its clearest expression. Here, where the immigrant elements are most numerous, there develops between them and the native population a social struggle—a struggle for the best conditions of earning a livelihood or, if you will, for existence, which ends with the adaptation of one part to the other, or perhaps with the final subjugation of the one by the other. Thus, according to Schliemann, the city of Smyrna had in the year 1846 a population of 80,000 Turks and 8,000 Greeks; in the year 1881, on the contrary, there were 23,000 Turks and 76,000 Greeks. The Turkish portion of the population had thus in thirty-five years decreased by 71 per cent, while the Greeks had increased ninefold.

Not everywhere, to be sure, do those struggles take the form of such a general process of displacement; but in individual cases it will occur with endless frequency within a country that the stronger and better-equipped element will overcome the weaker and less well-equipped.

Thus we have here a case similar to that occurring so frequently in nature: on the same terrain where a more highly organized plant or animal has no longer room for subsistence, others less exacting in their demands take up their position and flourish. The coming of the new is in fact not infrequently the cause of the disappearance of those already there and of their withdrawal to more favorable surroundings.

If these considerations show that by no means the majority of internal migrations find their objective point in the cities, they at the same time prove that the trend toward the great centers of population can in itself be looked upon as having an extensive social and economic importance. It produces an alteration in the distribution of population throughout the state; and at its originating and objective points it gives rise to difficulties which legislative and executive authority has hitherto labored, usually with but very moderate success, to overcome. It transfers large numbers of persons almost directly from a sphere of life where barter predominates into one where money and credit exchange prevail, thereby affecting the social conditions of life and the social customs of the manual laboring classes in a manner to fill the philanthropist with grave anxiety.

3. Demographic Segregation and Social Selection[1]

There are two ways in which demographic crystallization may have taken place. A people may have become rigid horizontally, divided into castes, or social strata; or it may be geographically segregated into localized communities, varying in size all the way from the isolated hamlet to the highly individualized nation. Both of these forms of crystallization are breaking down today under the pressure of modern industrialism and democracy, in Europe as well as in America.

The sudden growth of great cities is the first result of the phenomenon of migration which we have to note. We think of this as essentially an American problem. We comfort ourselves in our failures of municipal administration with that thought. This is a grievous deception. Most of the European cities have increased in population more rapidly than in America. This is particularly true of great German urban centers. Berlin has outgrown our own metropolis, New York, in less than a generation, having in twenty-five years added as many actual new residents as Chicago, and twice as many as Philadelphia. Hamburg has gained twice as many in population since 1875 as Boston; Leipzig has distanced St. Louis. The same demographic outburst has occurred in the smaller German cities as well. Beyond the confines of the German Empire, from Norway to Italy, the same is true.

Contemporaneously with this marvellous growth of urban centers we observe a progressive depopulation of the rural districts. What is going on in our New England states, especially in Massachusetts, is entirely characteristic of large areas in Europe. Take France, for example. The towns are absorbing even more than the natural increment of country population; they are drawing off the middle-aged as well as the young. Thus great areas are being actually depopulated.

A process of selection is at work on a grand scale. The great majority today who are pouring into the cities are those who, like the emigrants to the United States in the old days of natural migration, come because they have the physical equipment and the mental

[1] From William Z. Ripley, *The Races of Europe*, pp. 537–59. (D. Appleton & Co., 1899.)

disposition to seek a betterment of their fortunes away from home. Of course, an appreciable contingent of such migrant types is composed of the merely discontented, of the restless, and the adventurous; but, in the main, the best blood of the land it is which feeds into the arteries of city life.

Another more certain mode of proof is possible for demonstrating that the population of cities is largely made up either of direct immigrants from the country or of their immediate descendants. In German cities, Hansen found that nearly one-half their residents were of direct country descent. In London it has been shown that over one-third of its population are immigrants; and in Paris the same is true. For thirty of the principal cities of Europe it has been calculated that only about one-fifth of their increase is from the loins of their own people, the overwhelming majority being of country birth.

The first physical characteristic of urban populations, as compared with those of country districts, which we have to note, is their tendency toward that shape of head characteristic of two of our racial types, Teutonic and Mediterranean respectively. It seems as if for some reason the broad-headed Alpine race was a distinctly rural type. Thirty years ago an observer in the ethnically Alpine district of south central France noted an appreciable difference between town and country in the head form of the people. In a half-dozen of the smaller cities his observations pointed to a greater prevalence of the long-headed type than in the country roundabout. Dr. Ammon of Carlsruhe, working upon measurements of thousands of conscripts of the Grand Duchy of Baden, discovered radical differences here between the head form in city and country, and between the upper and lower classes in the larger towns. Several explanations for this were possible. The direct influence of urban life might conceivably have brought it about, acting through superior education, habits of life, and the like. There was no psychological basis for this assumption. Another tenable hypothesis was that in these cities, situated, as we have endeavored to show, in a land where two racial types of population were existing side by side, the city for some reason exerted superior powers of attraction upon the long-headed race. If this were true, then by a combined process of social and racial selection, the towns would be continually drawing unto themselves that tall and blond Teutonic type of population which, as history teaches us, has dominated social and political affairs in Europe for centuries. This suggested itself as the probable solution of the question; and investigations all over Europe during the last five years have been directed to the further analysis of the matter.

Is this phenomenon, the segregation of a long-headed physical type in city populations, merely the manifestation of a restless tendency on the part of the Teutonic race to reassert itself in the new phases of nineteenth-century competition? All through history this type has been characteristic of the dominant classes, especially in military and political, perhaps rather than purely intellectual, affairs. All the leading dynasties of Europe have long been recruited from its ranks. The contrast of this type, whose energy has carried it all over Europe, with the persistently sedentary Alpine race is very marked. A certain passivity, or patience, is characteristic of the Alpine peasantry. As a rule, not characterized by the domineering spirit of the Teuton, this Alpine type makes a comfortable and contented neighbor, a resigned and peaceful subject. Whether this rather negative character of the Alpine race is entirely innate, or whether it is in part, like many of its social phenomena, merely a reflection from the almost invariably inhospitable habitat in which it has long been isolated, we may not pretend to decide.

Let us now for a moment take up the consideration of a second physical characteristic of city populations—viz., stature. If there be a law at all in respect of average statures, it demonstrates rather the depressing effects of city life than the reverse. For example, Hamburg is far below the average for Germany. All over Britain there are indications of this law, that town populations are, on the average, comparatively short of stature. Dr. Beddoe, the great authority upon this subject, concludes his investigation of the population of Great Britain thus: "It may therefore be taken as *proved* that the stature of men in the large towns of Britain is lowered considerably below the standard of the nation, and as *probable* that such degradation is hereditary and progressive."

A most important point in this connection is the great variability of city populations in size. All observers comment upon this. It is of profound significance. The people of the west and east ends in each city differ widely. The population of the aristocratic quarters is often found to exceed in stature the people of the tenement districts. We should expect this, of course, as a direct result of the depressing influence of unfavorable environment. Yet there is apparently another factor underlying that—viz., social selection. While cities contain so large a proportion of degenerate physical types as on the average to fall below the surrounding country in stature, nevertheless they also are found to include an inordinately large number of very tall and well-developed individuals. In other words, compared with the rural districts, where all men are subject to the same conditions of life, we discover in the city that the population has differentiated into the very tall and the very short.

The explanation for this phenomenon is simple. Yet it is not direct, as in Topinard's suggestion that it is a matter of race or that a change of environment operates to stimulate growth. Rather does it appear that it is the growth which suggests the change. The tall men are in the main those vigorous, mettlesome, presumably healthy individuals who have themselves, or in the person of their fathers, come to the city in search of the prizes which urban life has to offer to the successful. On the other hand, the degenerate, the stunted, those who entirely outnumber the others so far as to drag the average for the city as a whole below the normal, are the grist turned out by the city mill. They are the product of the tenement, the sweat shop, vice, and crime. Of course, normally developed men, as ever, constitute the main bulk of the population, but these two widely divergent classes attain a very considerable representation.

We have seen thus far that evidence seems to point to an aggregation of the Teutonic long-headed population in the urban centers of Europe. Perhaps a part of the tall stature in some cities may be due to such racial causes. A curious anomaly now remains, however, to be noted. City populations appear to manifest a distinct tendency toward brunetness—that is to say, they seem to comprise an abnormal proportion of brunet traits, as compared with the neighboring rural districts. This tendency was strikingly shown to characterize the entire German Empire when its six million school children were examined under Virchow's direction. In twenty-five out of thirty-three of the larger cities were the brunet traits more frequent than in the country.

Austria offers confirmation of the same tendency toward brunetness in twenty-four out of its thirty-three principal cities. Farther south, in Italy, it was noted much earlier that cities contained fewer blonds than were common in the rural districts roundabout. In conclusion let us add, not as additional testimony, for the data are too defective, that among five hundred American students at the Institute of Technology in Boston, roughly classified, there were 9 per cent of pure brunet type among those of country birth and training, while among those of urban birth and parentage the percentage of such brunet type rose as high as 15.

It is not improbable that there is in brunetness, in the dark hair and eye, some indication of vital superiority. If this were so, it would serve as a partial explanation for the social phenomena which we have been at so much pains to describe. If in the same community there were a slight vital advantage in brunetness, we should expect to find that type slowly aggregating in the cities; for it requires energy and courage, physical as well as mental, not only to break the ties of home and migrate, but also to maintain one's self afterward under the stress of urban life.

From the preceding formidable array of testimony it appears that the tendency of urban populations is certainly not toward the pure blond, long-headed, and tall Teutonic type. The phenomenon of urban selection is something more complex than a mere migration of a single racial element in the population toward the cities. The physical characteristics of townsmen are too contradictory for ethnic explanations alone. To be sure, the tendencies are slight; we are not even certain of their universal existence at all. We are merely watching for their verification or disproof. There is, however, nothing improbable in the phenomena we have noted. Naturalists have always turned to the environment for the final solution of many of the great problems of nature. In this case we have to do with one of the most sudden and radical changes of environment known to man. Every condition of city life, mental as well as physical, is at the polar extreme from those which prevail in the country. To deny that great modifications in human structure and functions may be effected by a change from one to the other is to gainsay all the facts of natural history.

4. Inter-racial Competition and Race Suicide[1]

I have thus far spoken of the foreign arrivals at our ports, as estimated. Beginning with 1820, however, we have custom-house statistics of the numbers of persons annually landing upon our shores. Some of these, indeed, did not remain here; yet, rudely speaking, we may call them all immigrants. Between 1820 and 1830, population grew to 12,866,020. The number of foreigners arriving in the ten years was 151,000. Here, then, we have for forty years an increase, substantially all out of the loins of the four millions of our own people living in 1790, amounting to almost nine millions, or 227 per cent. Such a rate of increase was never known before or since, among any considerable population over any extensive region.

About this time, however, we reach a turning-point in the history of our population. In the decade 1830–40 the number of foreign arrivals greatly increased. Immigration had not, indeed, reached the enormous dimensions of these later days. Yet, during the decade in question, the foreigners coming to the United States were almost exactly fourfold those coming in the decade preceding, or 599,000. The question now of vital importance is this: Was the population of the country correspondingly increased? I answer, No! The population of 1840 was almost exactly what, by computation, it would have been had no increase in foreign arrivals taken place. Again, between 1840 and 1850, a still further access of foreigners occurred, this time of enormous dimensions, the arrivals of the decade amounting to not less than 1,713,000. Of this gigantic total, 1,048,000 were from the British Isles, the Irish famine of 1846–47 having driven hundreds of thousands of miserable peasants to seek food upon our shores. Again we ask, Did this excess constitute a net gain to the population of the country? Again the answer is, No! Population showed no increase over the proportions established before immigration set in like a flood. In other words, as the foreigners began to come in larger numbers, the native population more and more withheld their own increase.

Now this correspondence might be accounted for in three different ways: (1) It might be said that it was a mere coincidence, no relation

[1] Adapted from Francis A. Walker, *Economics and Statistics*, II, 421–26. (Henry Holt & Co., 1899.)

of cause and effect existing between the two phenomena. (2) It might he said that the foreigners came because the native population was relatively declining, that is, failing to keep up its pristine rate of increase. (3) It might be said that the growth of the native population was checked by the incoming of the foreign elements in such large numbers.

The view that the correspondence referred to was a mere coincidence, purely accidental in origin, is perhaps that most commonly taken. If this be the true explanation, the coincidence is a most remarkable one. In the June number of this magazine, I cited the predictions as to the future population of the country made by Elkanah Watson, on the basis of the censuses of 1790, 1800, and 1810, while immigration still remained at a minimum. Now let us place together the actual census figures for 1840 and 1850, Watson's estimates for those years, and the foreign arrivals during the preceding decade:

	1840	1850
The census	17,069,453	23,191,876
Watson's estimates	17,116,526	23,185,368
The difference	−47,073	+6,508
Foreign arrivals during the preceding decade	599,000	1,713,000

Here we see that, in spite of the arrival of 500,000 foreigners during the period 1830–40, four times as many as had arrived during any preceding decade, the figures of the census coincided closely with the estimate of Watson, based on the growth of population in the pre-immigration era, falling short of it by only 47,073 in a total of 17,000,000; while in 1850 the actual population, in spite of the arrival of 1,713,000 more immigrants, exceeded Watson's estimates by only 6,508 in a total of 23,000,000. Surely, if this correspondence between the increase of the foreign element and the relative decline of the native element is a mere coincidence, it is one of the most astonishing in human history. The actuarial degree of improbability as to a coincidence so close, over a range so vast, I will not undertake to compute.

If, on the other hand, it be alleged that the relation of cause and effect existed between the two phenomena, this might be put in two widely different ways: either that the foreigners came in increasing numbers because the native element was relatively declining, or that the native element failed to maintain its previous rate of increase because the foreigners came in such swarms. What shall we say of the former of these explanations? Does anything more need to be said than that it is too fine to be the real explanation of a big human fact like this we are considering? To assume that at such a distance in space, in the then state of news-communication and ocean-transportation, and in spite of the ignorance and extreme poverty of the peasantries of Europe from which the immigrants were then generally drawn, there was so exact a degree of knowledge not only of the fact that the native element here was not keeping up its rate of increase but also of the precise ratio of that decline as to enable those peasantries, with or without a mutual understanding, to supply just the numbers necessary to bring our population up to its due proportions, would be little less than laughable. Today, with quick passages, cheap freights, and ocean transportation there is not a single wholesale trade in the world carried on with this degree of knowledge, or attaining anything like this point of precision in results.

The true explanation of the remarkable fact we are considering I believe to be the last of the three suggested. The access of foreigners, at the time and under the circumstances, constituted a shock to the principle of population among the native element. That principle is always acutely sensitive alike to sentimental and to economic conditions. And it is to be noted, in passing, that not only did the decline in the native element, as a whole, take place in singular correspondence with the excess of foreign arrivals, but it occurred chiefly in just those regions to which the newcomers most freely resorted.

But what possible reason can be suggested why the incoming of the foreigner should have checked the disposition of the native toward the increase of population at the traditional rate? I answer that the best of good reasons can be assigned. Throughout the northeastern and northern middle states, into which, during the period under consideration, the newcomers poured in such numbers, the standard of material living, of general intelligence, of social decency, had been singularly high. Life, even at its hardest, had always had its luxuries; the babe had been a thing of beauty, to be delicately nurtured and proudly exhibited; the growing child had been decently dressed, at least for school and church; the house had been kept in order, at whatever cost, the gate hung, the shutters in place, while the front yard had been made to bloom with simple flowers; the village church, the public schoolhouse, had been the best which the community, with great exertions and sacrifices, could erect and maintain. Then came the foreigner, making his way into the little village, bringing—small blame to him!—not only a vastly lower standard of living, but too often an actual present incapacity even to understand the refinements of life and thought in the community in which he sought a home. Our people had to look upon houses that were mere shells for human habitations, the gate unhung, the shutters flapping or falling, green pools in the yard, babes and young children rolling about half naked or worse, neglected, dirty, unkempt. Was there not in this a sentimental reason strong enough to give a shock to the principle of population? But there was, besides, an economic reason for a check to the native increase. The American shrank from the industrial competition thus thrust upon him. He was unwilling himself to engage in the lowest kind of day labor with these new elements of the population; he was even more unwilling to bring sons and daughters into the world to enter into that competition. For the first time in our history, the people of the free states became divided into classes. Those classes were natives and foreigners. Politically, the distinction had only a certain force, which yielded more or less readily under partisan pressure; but socially and industrially that distinction has been a tremendous power, and its chief effects have been wrought upon population. Neither the social companionship nor the industrial competition of the foreigner has, broadly speaking, been welcome to the native.

It hardly needs to be said that the foregoing descriptions are not intended to apply to all of the vast body of immigrants during this period. Thousands came over from good homes; many had all the advantages of education and culture; some possessed the highest qualities of manhood and citizenship.

But let us proceed with the census. By 1860 the causes operating to reduce the growth of the native element—to which had then manifestly been added the force of important changes in the manner of living, the introduction of more luxurious habits, the influence of city life, and the custom of "boarding"—had reached such a height as, in spite of a still-increasing immigration, to leave the population of the country 310,503 below the estimate. The fearful losses of the Civil War and the rapid extension of habits unfavorable to increase of numbers make any further use of Watson's computations uninstructive; yet still the great fact protrudes through all the subsequent history of our population that the more rapidly foreigners came into the United States, the smaller was the rate of increase, not merely among the native population separately, but throughout the population of the country, as a whole, including the foreigners. The climax of this movement was reached when, during the decade 1880–90, the foreign arrivals rose to the monstrous total of five and a quarter millions (twice what had ever before been known), while the population, even including this enormous re-enforcement, increased more slowly than in any other period of our history except, possibly, that of the great Civil War.

If the foregoing views are true, or contain any considerable degree of truth, foreign immigration into this country has, from the time it first assumed large proportions, amounted, not to a reinforcement of our population, but to a replacement of native by foreign stock. That if the foreigners had not come the native element would long have filled the places the foreigners usurped, I entertain not a doubt. The competency of the American stock to do this it would be absurd to question, in the face of such a record as that for 1790 to 1830. During the period from 1830 to 1860 the material conditions of existence in this country were continually becoming more and more favorable to the increase of population from domestic sources. The old man-slaughtering medicine was being driven out of civilized communities; houses were becoming larger; the food and clothing of the people were becoming ampler and better. Nor was the cause which, about 1840 or 1850, began to retard the growth of population here to be found in the climate which Mr. Clibborn stigmatizes so severely. The climate of the United States has been benign enough to enable us to take the English shorthorn and greatly to improve it, as the re-exportation of that animal to England at monstrous prices abundantly proves; to take the English race-horse and to improve him to a degree of which the startling victories of Parole, Iroquois, and Foxhall afford but a suggestion; to take the Englishman and to improve him, too, adding agility to his strength, making his eye keener and his hand steadier, so that in rowing, in riding, in shooting, and in boxing, the American of pure English stock is today the better animal. No! Whatever were the causes which checked the growth of the native population, they were neither physiological nor climatic. They were mainly social and economic; and chief among them was the access of vast hordes of foreign immigrants, bringing with them a standard of living at which our own people revolted.

5. Competition, Commercial Organization, and the Metropolitan Economy[1]

If we cast our thought no farther back than the permanent settlement of clans and tribes, we see that there are three general stages which sum up much of the economic life of the times: village economy, town economy, and metropolitan economy. Each is a unit of production. Each has a center of trade, though the importance of trade is, of course, not so great at first as later. . . . . In the progression from one stage to another we see not only a greater specialization, but a greater general division of labor, a larger surplus and store of goods, and more immunity from distress and famine.

Just as the tribal and later the feudal state reflected the village, as the early national state reflected the town, so does the state today reflect the metropolis. The village mobilized labor, the town mobilized skill in trade and manufacture, and now the metropolis mobilizes capital and management in support of the state.

By metropolitan economy is meant the concentration of the trade of a wide area in one great city. While the radius of the area dominated commercially by the medieval town had rarely been more than a score of miles, the radius of the area dominated by a metropolis is roughly a hundred miles or more in length.

The structure of the metropolitan economic unit is made up, firstly, of the metropolis itself with its merchants, bankers, warehousemen, transport officials, and other specialized men of business; and secondly, of the district or hinterland with its towns and villages, its countryside of farms, forests, streams, and mines. The metropolis

[1] From N. S. B. Gras, "The Development of Metropolitan Economy in Europe and America," *American Historical Review*, XXVII (1921–22), 698–705.

and its hinterland are integral parts of the metropolitan unit, but they are not constant in the areas which they occupy. While the metropolis itself widens its confines with general economic development, the hinterland decreases in size. The area occupied by greater London increases year by year, while the hinterland diminishes as Manchester-Liverpool grows in strength and influence. Greater Chicago grows while its hinterland is being nibbled away by Cleveland, St. Louis, Kansas City, and the Twin Cities.

The essential part of the metropolitan economy is not size or structure but function. The metropolis concentrates the trade of a wide district. It is the gathering-place for the products of that district. It is also the place from which wares already concentrated from many lands and sections radiate to the whole hinterland. Moreover, it is the point through which the hinterland normally trades with other metropolitan units. It is more economical for a few dealers in a metropolis to specialize in the inter-metropolitan trade, which is usually wholesale, than for traders located in small towns in the hinterland to maintain connections and credits with distant parts. If we wish to visualize the whole metropolitan mechanism we have only to think of a web with the master spider in the center. The concentration and radiation of such a pattern are in marked contrast to the duplication and parallelism of the alternative checkerboard. The saving in materials, labor, and management is enormous; otherwise the spider would not have so constructed its net. Metropolitan economy likewise exists because of its efficiency as a unit in production. Public policy, national administration, even socialism would hardly long continue an attempt to alter so economical an organization.

If we wish to visualize metropolitan growth we have only to examine the metropolis itself. The retail section may represent the old town economy. The wholesale district is the prosaic memorial of the first phase of metropolitan economy. The industrial suburb contains most of what is left of metropolitan manufacture after the period of decentralization. The wharves and the railroad terminals show where extended and hinterland trade meet within the metropolis. And the financial district with its mint, stock exchange, banks, insurance offices, and brokers constitutes the most sensitive spot in the metropolitan nerve-center.

Such is the fully developed metropolitan organization in the sense that it has a constitution, or that there is an agreement whereby transactions are made. It is just a unit of public economy that has grown up gradually to perform cheaply and efficiently the business of managing production. Goods enter the metropolis and leave it. The metropolis performs one set of tasks, the hinterland another. Both are industrial, financial, and commercial, but the metropolis is pre-eminently commercial and financial.

C. ECONOMIC COMPETITION

1. Changing Forms of Economic Competition[1]

There is a sense in which much of the orthodox system of political economy is eternally true. Conclusions reached by valid reasoning are always as true as the hypotheses from which they are deduced. It will remain forever true that if unlimited competition existed, most of the traditional laws would be realized in the practical world. It will also be true that in those corners of the industrial field which still show an approximation to Ricardian competition there will be seen as much of correspondence between theory and fact as candid reasoners claim. If political economy will but content itself with this kind of truth, it need never be disturbed by industrial revolutions. The science need not trouble itself to progress.

This hypothetical truth, or science of what would take place if society were fashioned after an ideal pattern, is not what Ricardo believed that he had discovered. His system was positive; actual life suggested it by developing tendencies for which the scientific formulas which at that time were traditional could not account. It was a new industrial world which called for a modernized system of economic doctrine. Ricardo was the first to understand the situation, to trace the new tendencies to their consummation, and to create a scientific system by insight and foresight. He outran history in the process, and mentally created a world more relentlessly competitive than any which has existed; and yet it was fact and not imagination that lay at the basis of the whole system. Steam had been utilized, machines were supplanting hand labor, workmen were migrating

[1] Adapted from John B. Clark, "The Limits of Competition," in Clark and Giddings, *The Modern Distributive Process*, pp. 2–8. (Ginn & Co., 1888.)

to new centers of production, guild regulations were giving way, and competition of a type unheard of before was beginning to prevail.

A struggle for existence had commenced between parties of unequal strength. In manufacturing industries the balance of power had been disturbed by steam, and the little shops of former times were disappearing. The science adapted to such conditions was an economic Darwinism; it embodied the laws of a struggle for existence between competitors of the new and predatory type and those of the peaceable type which formerly possessed the field. Though the process was savage, the outlook which it afforded was not wholly evil. The survival of crude strength was, in the long run, desirable. Machines and factories meant, to every social class, cheapened goods and more comfortable living. Efficient working establishments were developing; the social organism was perfecting itself for its contest with crude nature. It was a fuller and speedier dominion over the earth which was to result from the concentration of human energy now termed centralization.

The error unavoidable to the theorists of the time lay in basing a scientific system on the facts afforded by a state of revolution. This was attempting to derive permanent principles from transient phenomena. Some of these principles must become obsolete; and the work demanded of modern economists consists in separating the transient from the permanent in the Ricardian system. How much of the doctrine holds true when the struggle between unequal competitors is over, and when a few of the very strongest have possession of the field?

In most branches of manufacturing, and in other than local transportation, the contest between the strong and the weak is either settled or in process of rapid settlement. The survivors are becoming so few, so powerful, and so nearly equal that if the strife were to continue, it would bid fair to involve them all in a common ruin. What has actually developed is not such a battle of giants but a system of armed neutralities and federations of giants. The new era is distinctly one of consolidated forces; rival establishments are forming combinations, and the principle of union is extending itself to the labor and the capital in each of them. Laborers who once competed with each other are now making their bargains collectively with their employers.

Employers who under the old régime would have worked independently are merging their capital in corporations and allowing it to be managed as by a single hand.

Predatory competition between unequal parties was the basis of the Ricardian system. This process was vaguely conceived and never fully analyzed; what was prominent in the thought of men in connection with it was the single element of struggle. Mere effort to survive, the Darwinian feature of the process, was all that, in some uses, the term "competition" was made to designate. Yet the competitive action of an organized society is systematic; each part of it is limited to a specific field, and tends, within these limits, to self-annihilation.

An effort to attain a conception of competition that should remove some of the confusion was made by Professor Cairnes. His system of "non-competing groups" is a feature of his value theory, which is a noteworthy contribution to economic thought. Mr. Mill had followed Ricardo in teaching that the natural price of commodities is governed by the cost of producing them. Professor Cairnes accepts this statement, but attaches to it a meaning altogether new. He says, in effect:

Commodities do indeed exchange according to their cost of production; but cost is something quite different from what currently passes by that name. That is merely the outlay incurred by the capitalist-employer for raw materials, labor, etc. The real cost is the personal sacrifice made by the producing parties, workmen as well as employers. It is not a mercantile but a psychological phenomenon, a reaction upon the men themselves occasioned by the effort of the laborer and the abstinence of the capitalist. These personal sacrifices gauge the market value of commodities within the fields in which, in the terms of the theory, competition is free. The adjustment takes place through the spontaneous movement of capital and labor from employments that yield small returns to those that give larger ones. Capital migrates freely from place to place and from occupation to occupation. If one industry is abnormally profitable, capital seeks it, increases and cheapens its product, and reduces its profits to the prevailing level. Profits tend to a general uniformity.

Wages are said to tend to equality only within limits. The transfer of labor from one employment to another is checked by barriers.

What we find, in effect [continues Professor Cairnes], is not a whole population competing indiscriminately for all occupations, but a series of industrial layers, superimposed on one another, within each of which the various candidates for employment possess a real and effective power of selection, while those occupying the several strata are, for all purposes of effective competition, practically isolated from each other. We may perhaps venture to arrange them in some such order as this: first, at the bottom of the scale there would be the large group of unskilled or nearly unskilled laborers, comprising agricultural laborers, laborers engaged in miscellaneous occupations in towns, or acting in attendance on skilled labor. Secondly, there would be the artisan group, comprising skilled laborers of the secondary order—carpenters, joiners, smiths, masons, shoemakers, tailors, hatters, etc., etc.—with whom might be included the very large class of small retail dealers, whose means and position place them within the reach of the same industrial opportunities as the class of artisans. The third layer would contain producers and dealers of a higher order, whose work would demand qualifications only obtainable by persons of substantial means and fair educational opportunities; for example, civil and mechanical engineers, chemists, opticians, watchmakers, and others of the same industrial grade, in which might also find a place the superior class of retail tradesmen; while above these there would be a fourth, comprising persons still more favorably circumstanced, whose ampler means would give them a still wider choice. This last group would contain members of the learned professions, as well as persons engaged in the various careers of science and art, and in the higher branches of mercantile business.

It is essential to the theory that not only workmen but their children should be confined to a producing group. The equalizing process may take place even though men do not actually abandon one occupation and enter another; for there exists, in the generation of young men not yet committed to any occupation, a disposable fund of labor which will gravitate naturally to the occupations that pay the largest wages. It is not necessary that blacksmiths should ever become shoemakers, or vice versa, but only that the children of both classes of artisans should be free to enter the trade that is best rewarded.

Professor Cairnes does not claim that his classification is exhaustive, nor that the demarcation is absolute:

No doubt the various ranks and classes fade into each other by imperceptible gradations, and individuals from all classes are constantly passing up or dropping down; but while this is so, it is nevertheless true that the average workman, from whatever rank he be taken, finds his power of competition limited for practical purposes to a certain range of occupations, so that, however high the rates of remuneration in those which lie beyond may rise, he is excluded from sharing them. We are thus compelled to recognize the existence of non-competing industrial groups as a feature of our social economy.

It will be seen that the competition which is here under discussion is of an extraordinary kind; and the fact that the general term is applied to it without explanation is a proof of the vagueness of the conceptions of competition with which acute writers have contented themselves. Actual competition consists invariably in an effort to undersell a rival producer. A carpenter competes with a carpenter because he creates a similar utility and offers it in the market. In the theory of Professor Cairnes the carpenter is the competitor of the blacksmith, because his children may enter the blacksmith's calling. In the actual practice of his own trade, the one artisan in no wise affects the other. It is potential competition rather than actual that is here under discussion; and even this depends for its effectiveness on the action of the rising generation.

Modern methods of production have obliterated Professor Cairnes's dividing lines. Potential competition extends to every part of the industrial field in which men work in organized companies. Throwing out of account the professions, a few trades of the highest sort, and the class of labor which is performed by employers themselves and their salaried assistants, it is practically true that labor is in a universal ebb and flow; it passes freely to occupations which are, for the time being, highly paid, and reduces their rewards to the general level.

This objection to the proposed grouping is not theoretical. The question is one of fact; it is the development of actual industry that has invalidated the theory which, in the seventies, expressed an important truth concerning economic relations in England. Moreover, the author of the theory anticipated one change which would somewhat lessen its applicability to future conditions. He recorded his belief that education would prove a leveler, and that it would merge to some extent the strata of industrial society. The children of hod-carriers might become machinists, accountants, or lawyers when they could acquire the needed education. He admitted also that new countries afford conditions in which the lines of demarcation are faint. He was not in a position to appreciate the chief leveling agency, namely, the machine method of production as now extended and perfected. Education makes the laborer capable of things relatively difficult, and machines render the processes which he needs to master relatively easy. The so-called unskilled workmen stand on a higher personal level than those of former times; and the new methods of manufacturing are reducing class after class to that level. Mechanical labor is resolving itself into processes so simple that anyone may learn them. An old-time shoemaker could not become a watchmaker, and even his children would have found difficulties in their way had they attempted to master the higher trade; but a laster in a Lynn shoe factory can, if he will, learn one of the minute trades that are involved in the making of a Waltham watch. His children may do so without difficulty; and this is all that is necessary for maintaining the normal balance between the trades.

The largest surviving differences between workmen are moral. Bodily strength still counts for something, and mental strength for more; but the consideration which chiefly determines the value of a workman to the employer who intrusts to him costly materials and a delicate machine is the question of fidelity. Character is not monopolized by any social class; it is of universal growth, and tends by the prominent part which it plays in modern industry, to reduce to their lowest terms the class differences of the former era.

The rewards of professional life are gauged primarily by character and native endowment, and are, to this extent, open to the children of workmen. New barriers, however, arise here in the ampler education which, as time advances, is demanded of persons in these pursuits; and these barriers give to a part of the fourth and highest class in the scheme that we are criticising a permanent basis of existence. Another variety of labor retains a pre-eminence based on native adaptations and special opportunities. It is the work of the employer himself. It is an organizing and directing function, and in large industries is performed only in part by the owners. A portion of this work is committed to hired assistants. Strictly speaking, the entrepreneur, or employer, of a great establishment is not one man, but many, who work in a collective capacity, and who receive a reward that, taken in the aggregate, constitutes the "wages of superintendence." To some members of this administrative body the returns come in the form of salaries, while to others they come partly in the form of dividends; but if we regard their work in its entirety, and consider their wages in a single sum, we must class it with entrepreneur's profits rather than with ordinary wages. It is a different part of the product from the sum distributed among day laborers; and this fact separates the administrative group from the class considered in our present inquiry. Positions of the higher sort are usually gained either through the possession of capital or through relations to persons who possess it. Though clerkships of the lower grade demand no attainments which the children of workmen cannot gain, and though promotion to the higher grades is still open, the tendency of the time is to make the transition from the ranks of labor to those of administration more and more difficult. The true laboring class is merging its subdivisions, while it is separating more sharply from the class whose interests, in test questions, place them on the side of capital.

2. Competition and the Natural Harmony of Individual Interests[1]

The general industry of the society never can exceed what the capital of the society can employ. As the number of workmen that can be kept in employment by any particular person must bear a certain proportion to his capital, so the number of those that can be continually employed by all the members of a great society must bear a certain proportion to the whole capital of that society and never can exceed that proportion. No regulation of commerce can increase the quantity of industry in any society beyond what its capital can maintain. It can only divert a part of it into a direction into which it might not otherwise have gone; and it is by no means certain that this artificial direction is likely to be more advantageous to the society than that into which it would have gone of its own accord.

Every individual is continually exerting himself to find out the most advantageous employment for whatever capital he can command. It is his own advantage, indeed, and not that of the society,

[1] Adapted from Adam Smith, *An Inquiry into the Nature and Causes of the Wealth of Nations*, I (1904), 419, 421. (By kind permission of Messrs. Methuen & Co.. Ltd.)

which he has in view.   But the study of his own advantage naturally, or rather necessarily, leads him to prefer that employment which is most advantageous to the society.

As every individual, therefore, endeavors as much as he can both to employ his capital in the support of domestic industry and so to direct that industry that its product may be of the greatest value; every individual necessarily labors to render the annual revenue of the society as great as he can.   He generally, indeed, neither intends to promote the public interest nor knows how much he is promoting it. By preferring the support of domestic to that of foreign industry, he intends only his own security;   and by directing that industry in such a manner that its product may be of the greatest value, he intends only his own gain, and he is in this, as in many other cases, led by an invisible hand to promote an end which was no part of his intention.   Nor is it always worse for the society that it was no part of it.   By pursuing his own interest he frequently promotes that of the society more effectually than when he really intends to promote it.   I have never known much good done by those who affected to trade for the public good.   It is an affectation, indeed, not very common among merchants, and very few words need be employed in dissuading them from it.

What is the species of domestic industry which his capital can employ, and of which the product is likely to be of the greatest value, every individual, it is evident, can, in his local situation, judge much better than any statesman or lawgiver can do for him.   The statesman who should attempt to direct private people in what manner they ought to employ their capitals would not only load himself with a most unnecessary attention but assume an authority which could safely be trusted, not only to no single person, but to no council or senate whatever, and which would nowhere be so dangerous as in the hands of a man who had folly and presumption enough to fancy himself fit to exercise it.

3.   Competition and Freedom[1]

What, after all, is competition?   Is it something that exists and acts of itself, like the cholera?   No, competition is simply the absence of oppression.   In reference to the matters that interest me, I *prefer*

[1] Translated from Frédéric Bastiat, *Œuvres complètes*, tome VI, "Harmonies économiques," 9° édition, p. 350.   (Paris, 1884.)

to choose for myself and I do not want anyone else to choose for me against my will; that's all. And if anyone undertakes to substitute his judgment for mine in matters that concern me I shall demand the privilege of substituting my wishes for his in matters which concern him. What guaranty is there that this arrangement will improve matters? It is evident that competition is liberty. To destroy liberty of action is to destroy the possibility and consequently the faculty of choosing, judging, comparing; it is to kill intelligence, to kill thought, to kill man himself. Whatever the point of departure, there is where modern reforms always end; in order to improve society it is necessary to annihilate the individual, upon the assumption that the individual is the source of all evil, and as if the individual was not likewise the source of all good.

4. Money and Freedom[1]

Money not only makes the relation of individuals to the group a more independent one, but the content of the special forms of associations and the relations of the participants to these associations is subject to an entirely new process of differentiation.

The medieval corporations included in themselves all the human interests. A guild of cloth-makers was not an association of individuals which cultivated the interests of cloth-making exclusively. It was a community in a vocational, personal, religious, political sense and in many other respects. And however technical the interests that might be grouped together in such an association, they had an immediate and lively interest for all members. Members were wholly bound up in the association.

In contrast to this form of organization the capitalistic system has made possible innumerable associations which either require from their members merely money contributions or are directed toward mere money interests. In the case of the business corporation, especially, the basis of organization of members is exclusively an interest in the dividends, so exclusively that it is a matter of entire indifference to the individual what the society (enterprise) actually produces.

The independence of the person of the concrete objects, in which he has a mere money interest, is reflected, likewise, in his independence,

[1] Translated from Georg Simmel, *Philosophie des Geldes*, pp. 351–52. (Duncker und Humblot, 1900.)

in his personal relations, of the other individuals with whom he is connected by an exclusive money interest. This has produced one of the most effective cultural formations—one which makes it possible for individuals to take part in an association whose objective aim it will promote, use, and enjoy without this association bringing with it any further personal connection or imposing any further obligation. Money has brought it about that one individual may unite himself with others without being compelled to surrender any of his personal freedom or reserve. That is the fundamental and unspeakably significant difference between the medieval form of organization which made no difference between the association of men as men and the association of men as members of an organization. The medieval form or organization united equally in one circle the entire business, religious, political, and friendly interests of the individuals who composed it.

III. INVESTIGATIONS AND PROBLEMS

1. Biological Competition

The conception of competition has had a twofold origin: in the notions (a) of the struggle for existence and (b) of the struggle for livelihood. Naturally, then, the concept of competition has had a parallel development in biology and in economics. The growth of the notion in these two fields of thought, although parallel, is not independent. Indeed, the fruitful process of interaction between the differing formulations of the concept in biology and economics is a significant illustration of the cross-fertilization of the sciences. Although Malthus was a political economist, his principle of population is essentially biological rather than economic. He is concerned with the struggle for existence rather than for livelihood. Reacting against the theories of Condorcet and of Godwin concerning the natural equality, perfectibility, and inevitable progress of man, Malthus in 1798 stated the dismal law that population tends to increase in geometrical progression and subsistence in arithmetica progression. In the preface to the second edition of his *Essay on the Principle of Population* Malthus acknowledged his indebtedness to "Hume, Wallace, Dr. Adam Smith and Dr. Price." Adam Smith no doubt anticipated and perhaps suggested to Malthus his thesis in such passages in the *Wealth of Nations* as, "Every species of animals

naturally multiplies in proportion to the means of their subsistence,"
"The demand for men necessarily regulates the production of men."
These statements of the relation of population to food supply, however, are incidental to Smith's general theories of economics; the
contribution of Malthus lay in taking this principle out of its limited
context, giving it the character of scientific generalization, and applying it to current theories and programs of social reform.

The debt of biology to Malthus is acknowledged both by Darwin
and by Wallace. Fifteen months after Darwin had commenced his
inquiry a chance reading of Malthus' *Essay on the Principle of
Population* gave him the clue to the explanation of the origin of species
through the struggle for existence. During an attack of intermittent
fever Wallace recalled Malthus' theory which he had read twelve
years before and in it found the solution of the problem of biological
evolution.

Although the phrase "the struggle for existence" was actually
used by Malthus: Darwin, Wallace, and their followers first gave it
a general application to all forms of life. Darwin in his *The Origin
of Species*, published in 1859, analyzed with a wealth of detail the
struggle for existence, the nature and forms of competition, natural
selection, the survival of the fittest, the segregation and consequent
specialization of species.

Biological research in recent years has directed attention away
from the theory of evolution to field study of plant and animal
communities. Warming, Adams, Wheeler, and others have described,
in their plant and animal ecologies, the processes of competition and
segregation by which communities are formed. Clements in two
studies, *Plant Succession* and *Plant Indicators*, has described in detail
the life-histories of some of these communities. His analysis of the
succession of plant communities within the same geographical area
and of the relations of competitive co-operation of the different
species of which these communities are composed might well serve
as a model for similar studies in human ecology.

2. Economic Competition

Research upon competition in economics falls under two heads:
(*a*) the natural history of competition, and (*b*) the history of theories
of competition.

a) Competition on the economic level, i.e., of struggle for live-lihood, had its origins in the market place. Sir Henry Maine, on the basis of his study of village communities, states in effect that the beginnings of economic behavior are first to be seen in neutral meeting places of strangers and foes.

In order to understand what a market originally was, you must try to picture to yourselves a territory occupied by village-communities, self-acting and as yet autonomous, each cultivating its arable land in the middle of its waste, and each, I fear I must add, at perpetual war with its neighbour. But at several points, points probably where the domains of two or three villages converged, there appear to have been spaces of what we should now call neutral ground. These were the Markets. They were probably the only places at which the members of the different primitive groups met for any purpose except warfare, and the persons who came to them were doubtless at first persons especially empowered to exchange the pro-duce and manufactures of one little village-community for those of another. But, besides the notion of neutrality, another idea was anciently associated with markets. This was the idea of sharp practice and hard bargaining.

What is the real origin of the feeling that it is not creditable to drive a hard bargain with a near relative or friend? It can hardly be that there is any rule of morality to forbid it. The feeling seems to me to bear the traces of the old notion that men united in natural groups do not deal with one another on principles of trade. The only natural group in which men are now joined is the family; and the only bond of union resembling that of the family is that which men create for themselves by friendship.

The general proposition which is the basis of Political Economy, made its first approach to truth under the only circumstances which admitted of men meeting at arm's length, not as members of the same group, but as strangers. Gradually the assumption of the right to get the best price has penetrated into the interior of these groups, but it is never completely received so long as the bond of connection between man and man is assumed to be that of family or clan connection. The rule only triumphs when the primitive community is in ruins. What are the causes which have general-ized a Rule of the Market until it has been supposed to express an original and fundamental tendency of human nature, it is impossible to state fully, so multifarious have they been. Everything which has helped to convert a society into a collection of individuals from being an assemblage of families has helped to add to the truth of the assertion made of human nature by the Political Economists.[1]

[1] Henry S. Maine, *Village-Communities in the East and West*, pp. 192-97. (New York, 1889.)

The extension of the relations of the market place to practically all aspects of life having to do with livelihood has been the outcome of the industrial revolution and the growth of Great Society. Standardization of commodities, of prices, and of wages, the impersonal nature of business relations, the "cash-nexus" and the credit basis of all human relations have greatly extended the external competitive forms of interaction. Money, with its abstract standards of value, is not only a medium of exchange, but at the same time symbol par excellence of the economic nature of modern competitive society.

The literature describing change from the familial communism, typical of primitive society, to the competitive economy of modern capitalistic society is indicated in the bibliography.

b) The history of competition as a concept in political economy goes back to the Physiocrats. This French school of economists, laying stress upon the food supply as the basis and the measure of the wealth of the nation, demanded the abolition of restrictions upon agricultural production and commerce. The Physiocrats based their theories upon the natural rights of individuals to liberty.

The miserable state of the nation seemed to demand a *volte face*. Taxes were many and indirect. Let them be single and direct. Liberty of enterprise was shackled. Let it be free. State-regulation was excessive. *Laissez-faire!* Their economic plea for liberty is buttressed by an appeal to Nature, greater than kings or ministers, and by an assertion of the natural, inherent rights of man to be unimpeded in his freedom except so far as he infringes upon that of others.[1]

While the Physiocrats emphasized the beneficent effects of freedom in industry to which the individual has a natural right, Adam Smith, in his book *The Wealth of Nations*, emphasized the advantages of competition. To him competition was a protection against monopoly. "It [competition] can never hurt either the consumer or the producer; on the contrary it must tend to make the retailers both sell cheaper and buy dearer than if the whole trade was monopolized by one or two persons."[2] It was at the same time of benefit to both producer and consumer. "Monopoly is a great enemy to good management which can never be universally established but in con-

---

[1] Henry Higgs, *The Physiocrats*, p. 142. (London, 1897.)

[2] Adam Smith, *Wealth of Nations* (Cannan's edition), I, 342. London, 1904.

sequence of that free and universal competition which forces everybody to have recourse to it for the sake of self-defence."[1]

Before Darwin, competition had been conceived in terms of freedom and of the natural harmony of interests. His use of the term introduced into competition the notion of struggle for existence and the survival of the fittest. This new conception, in which competition appears as a fundamental process in all life, has been a powerful prop to the laissez faire policy and has led to its continuance regardless of the misery and destitution which, if it did not create, it certainly did not remedy. The works of Herbert Spencer, the greatest expounder of the doctrine of evolution, contain a powerful massing of evidence in favor of laissez faire as a conclusion to be drawn from a scientific study of human behavior. "Nothing but the slow modifications of human nature by the discipline of social life," he said, "can produce permanently advantageous changes. A fundamental error pervading the thinking of nearly all parties, political and social, is that evils admit of immediate and radical remedies."[2]

With the growth of large-scale production with the tendency to the formation of combinations and monopolies, as a result of freedom of competition, works began to appear on the subject of unrestricted competition. The expressions "unfair" and "cut-throat" competition, which occur frequently in recent literature, suggest the new point of view. Another euphemism under which other and more far-reaching proposals for the limitation of competition and laissez faire have been proposed is "social justice." In the meantime the trend of legislation in England for a hundred years, as Mr. A. V. Dicey[3] has pointed out, has been, in spite of Herbert Spencer, away from the individualistic and in the direction of a collectivistic social order. This means more legislation, more control, and less individual liberty.

The full meaning of this change in law and opinion can only be fully understood, however, when it is considered in connection with the growth of communication, economic organization, and cities, all

[1] *Ibid.* I, 148.

[2] Thomas Mackay, *A Plea for Liberty.* An argument against socialism and socialistic legislation, consisting of an introduction by Herbert Spencer and essays by various writers, p. 24. (New York, 1891.)

[3] *Lectures on the Relation between Law and Opinion in England, during the Nineteenth Century.* 2d ed. (London, 1914).

of which have so increased the mutual interdependence of all members of society as to render illusory and unreal the old freedoms and liberties which the system of laissez faire was supposed to guarantee.

3. Competition and Human Ecology

The ecological conception of society is that of a society created by competitive co-operation. Adam Smith's *Wealth of Nations* was a description of society in so far as it is a product of economic competition. David Ricardo, in his *Principles of Political Economy*, defined the process of competition more abstractly and states its consequences with more ruthless precision and consistency. "His theory," says Kolthamer in his introduction, "seems to be an everlasting justification of the *status quo*. As such at least it was used."

But Ricardo's doctrines were both "a prop and a menace to the middle classes," and the errors which they canonized have been the presuppositions of most of the radical and revolutionary programs since that time.

The socialists, adopting his theories of value and wages, interpreted Ricardo's crude expressions to their own advantage. To alter the Ricardian conclusions, they said, alter the social conditions upon which they depend: to improve upon subsistence wage, deprive capital of what it steals from labour—the value which labour creates. The land-taxers similarly used the Ricardian theory of rent: rent is a surplus for the existence of which no single individual is responsible—take it therefore for the benefit of all, whose presence creates it.[1]

The anarchistic, socialistic, and communistic doctrines, to which reference is made in the bibliography, are to be regarded as themselves sociological phenomena, without reference to their value as programs. They are based on ecological and economic conceptions of society in which competition is the fundamental fact and, from the point of view of these doctrines, the fundamental evil of society. What is sociologically important in these doctrines is the wishes that they express. They exhibit among other things, at any rate, the character which the hopes and the wishes of men take in this vast, new, restless world, the Great Society, in which men find themselves but in which they are not yet, and perhaps never will be, at home.

[1] *The Principles of Taxation.* Everyman's Library. Preface by F. W. Kolthamer, p. xii.

4. Competition and the "Inner Enemies": the Defectives, the Dependents, and the Delinquents

Georg Simmel, referring, in his essay on "The Stranger," to the poor and the criminal, bestowed upon them the suggestive title of "The Inner Enemies." The criminal has at all times been regarded as a rebel against society, but only recently has the existence of the dependent and the defective been recognized as inimical to the social order.[1]

Modern society, so far as it is free, has been organized on the basis of competition. Since the status of the poor, the criminal, and the dependent, has been largely determined by their ability or willingness to compete, the literature upon defectiveness, dependency, and delinquency may be surveyed in its relation to the process of competition. For the purposes of this survey the dependent may be defined as one who is unable to compete; the defective as the person who is, if not unable, at least handicapped, in his efforts to compete. The criminal, on the other hand, is one who is perhaps unable, but at any rate refuses, to compete according to the rules which society lays down.

Malthus' *Essay on the Principle of Population* first called attention to the pathological effects of the struggle for existence in modern society and emphasized the necessity of control, not merely in the interest of the defeated and rejected members of society, but in the interest of society itself. Malthus sought a mitigation, if not a remedy, for the evils of overpopulation by what he called "moral restraint," that is, "a restraint from marriage, from prudential motives, with a conduct strictly moral during the period of restraint." The alternatives were war, famine, and pestilence. These latter have, in fact, been up to very recent times the effective means through which the problem of overpopulation has been solved.

The Neo-Malthusian movement, under the leadership of Francis Place, Richard Carlile, and Robert Dale Owen in the decade of 1820–30 and of Charles Bradlaugh and Annie Besant in the decade of 1870–80, advocated the artificial restriction of the family. The differential decline in the birth-rate, that is, the greater decrease in the number of children in the well-to-do and educated classes as

[1] *Soziologie*, p. 686. (Leipzig, 1908.)

compared with the poor and uneducated masses, was disclosed through investigations by the Galton Eugenics Laboratory in England and characterized as a national menace. In the words of David Heron, a study of districts in London showed that "one-fourth of the married population was producing one-half of the next generation." In United States less exhaustive investigation showed the same tendency at work and the alarm which the facts created found a popular expression in the term "race-sucide."

It is under these circumstances and as a result of investigations and agitations of the eugenists, that the poor, the defective, and the delinquent have come to be regarded as "inner enemies" in a sense that would scarcely have been understood a hundred years ago.

Poverty and dependency in modern society have a totally different significance from that which they have had in societies in the past. The literature descriptive of primitive communities indicated that in the economic communism of a society based on kinship, famines were frequent but poverty was unknown. In ancient and medieval societies the dependency, where it was not professional, as in the case of the mendicant religious orders, was intimate and personal. In this respect it differed widely from the organized, official, and supervised philanthropy of our modern cities.

With the abolition of serfdom, the break-up of the medieval guilds, and the inauguration of a period of individual freedom and relatively unrestricted competition (laissez faire) which ushered in the modern industrial order, the struggle for existence ceased to be communal, and became individual. The new order based on individual freedom, as contrasted with the old order based on control, has been described as a system in which every individual was permitted to "go to hell in his own individual way." "The only purpose for which power can be rightfully exercised over any member of a civilized community, against his will," said Mill, "is to prevent harm to others. His own good either physical or moral is not a sufficient warranty." Only when the individual became a criminal or a pauper did the state or organized society attempt to control or assist him in the competitive struggle for existence.[1]

Since competitive industry has its beginnings in England, the study of the English poor laws is instructive. Under the influence

[1] John Stuart Mill, *On Liberty*. (London, 1859.)

of Malthus and of the classical economists the early writers upon poverty regarded it as an inevitable and natural consequence of the operation of the "iron laws" of political economy. For example, when Harriet Martineau was forced to admit, by the evidence collected by the Factory Commissioners in 1833, that "the case of these wretched factory children seems desperate," she goes on to add "the only hope seems to be that the race will die out in two or three generations."

Karl Marx, accepting the Ricardian economics, emphasized the misery and destitution resulting from the competitive process, and demanded the abolition of competition and the substitution therefor of the absolute control of a socialistic state.

Recent studies treat poverty and dependency as a disease and look to its prevention and cure. Trade unions, trade associations, and social insurance are movements designed to safeguard industry and the worker against the now generally recognized consequences of unlimited competition. The conceptions of industrial democracy and citizenship in industry have led to interesting and promising experiments.

In this connection, the efforts of employers to protect themselves as well as the community from accidents and occupational diseases may be properly considered. During and since the Great War efforts have been made on a grand scale to rehabilitate, re-educate, and restore to usefulness the war's wounded soldiers. This interest in the former soldiers and the success of the efforts already made have led to an increased interest in all classes of the industrially handicapped. A number of surveys have been made, in different parts of the country, of the crippled, and efforts are in progress to discover occupations and professions in which the deaf, the blind, and otherwise industrially handicapped can be employed and thus restored to usefulness and relative independence.

The wide extension of the police power in recent times in the interest of public health, sanitation, and general public welfare represents the effort of the government, in an individualistic society in which the older sanctions and securities no longer exist, to protect the individual as well as the community from the effects of unrestricted competition.

The literature of criminology has sought an answer to the enigma of the criminal. The writings of the European criminologists run the gamut of explanation from Lombroso, who explained crime as an inborn tendency of the criminal, to Tarde, who defines the criminal as a purely social product.

W. A. Bonger,[1] a socialist, has sought to show that criminality is a direct product of the modern economic system. Without accepting either the evidence or the conclusions of Bonger, it cannot be gainsaid that the modern offender must be studied from the standpoint of his failure to participate in a wholesome and normal way in our competitive, secondary society which rests upon the institution of private property and individual competition.

The failure of the delinquent to conform to the social code may be studied from two standpoints: (a) that of the individual as an organization of original mental and temperamental traits, and (b) that of a person with a status and a rôle in the social group. The book *The Individual Delinquent*, by William Healy, placed the study of the offender as an individual upon a sound scientific basis. That the person can and should be regarded as part and parcel of his social milieu has been strikingly illustrated by T. M. Osborne in two books, *Within Prison Walls* and *Society and Prisons*. *The Judge Baker Foundation Case Studies*, by William Healy and Augusta F. Bronner, *The Three Problem Children*, by the Joint-Committee on Methods of Preventing Delinquency, and *The Unadjusted Girl*, by William I. Thomas, all published within the year 1923–24, evince the present trend to a study of the delinquent as a person, that is, from the standpoint of his wishes and of his rôles in the family, the play group, and the community.

The fact seems to be that the problem of crime is essentially like that of the other major problems of our social order, and its solution involves three elements, namely: (a) the analysis of the aptitudes of the individual and the wishes of the person; (b) the analysis of the activities of our society with its specialization and division of labor; and (c) the accommodation or adjustment of the individual to the social and economic environment. The older notions that dependency, deficiency, and delinquency were to be treated as due either to biological defects or to the inequalities in economic conditions arising out of competition are now being sharply challenged. Poverty, physical and mental defects, and crime are coming to be conceived in the larger

[1] *Criminality and Economic Conditions.* (Boston, 1916.)

setting of human nature, social interaction, and social forces. Family case work, physical rehabilitation, vocational training, and the social treatment of delinquents are more and more concerned with problems of personality, that is, with attitudes, sentiments, and wishes which immediately determine behavior.

SELECTED BIBLIOGRAPHY

I. BIOLOGICAL COMPETITION

(1) Crile, George W. *Man an Adaptive Mechanism.* New York, 1901.
(2) Darwin, Charles. *The Origin of Species.* London, 1859.
(3) Wallace, Alfred Russel. *Studies Scientic and Social.* 2 vols. New York, 1900.
(4) ———. *Darwinism.* An exposition of the theory of natural selection with some of its applications. Chap. iv, "The Struggle for Existence," pp. 14–40; chap. v, "Natural Selection by Variation and Survival of the Fittest," pp. 102–25. 3d ed. London, 1901.
(5) Weismann, August. *On Germinal Selection as a Source of Definite Variation.* Translated from the German. Chicago, 1896.
(6) Malthus, T. R. *An Essay on the Principle of Population.* Or a view of its past and present effects on human happiness, with an inquiry into our prospects respecting the future removal or mitigation of the evils which it occasions. 2d ed. London, 1803. [1st ed., 1798.]
(7) Carr-Saunders, A. M. *The Population Problem.* A study in human evolution. Oxford, 1922. [Bibliography.]
(8) Knapp, G. F. "Darwin und Socialwissenschaften," *Jahrbücher für Nationalökonomie und Statistik.* Erste Folge, XVIII (1872), 233–47.
(9) Thomson, J. Arthur. *Darwinism and Human Life.* New York, 1918.

II. ECONOMIC COMPETITION

(1) Wagner, Adolf. *Grundlegung der politischen Ökonomie.* Pp. 794–828. [The modern private industrial system of free competition.] Pp. 71–137. [The industrial nature of men.] Leipzig, 1892–94.
(2) Effertz, Otto. *Arbeit und Boden.* System der politischen Ökonomie. Vol. II, chaps. xix, xx, xxi, xxiii, xxiv, pp. 237–320. Berlin, 1897.
(3) Marshall, Alfred. *Principles of Economics.* Appendix A, "The Growth of Free Industry and Enterprise," pp. 723–54. London, 1910.
(4) Seligman, E. R. A. *Principles of Economics.* Chap. x, pp. 139–53. New York, 1905.
(5) Schatz, Albert. *L'Individualisme économique et social, ses origines, son évolution, ses formes contemporaines.* Paris, 1907.
(6) Cunningham, William. *An Essay on Western Civilization in Its Economic Aspects.* Medieval and modern times. Cambridge, 1913.

III. FREEDOM AND LAISSEZ FAIRE

(1) Simmel, Georg. *Philosophie des Geldes.* Chap. iv, "Die individuelle Freiheit," pp. 279–364. Leipzig, 1900.
(2) Bagehot, Walter. *Postulates of English Political Economics.* With a preface by Alfred Marshall. New York and London, 1885.

(3) Oncken, August. *Die Maxime Laissez Faire et Laissez Passer, ihr Ursprung, ihr Werden.* Bern, 1886.
(4) Bastiat, Frédéric. *Harmonies économiques.* 9th ed. Paris, 1884.
(5) Cunningham, William. *The Growth of English Industry and Commerce in Modern Times.* Vol. III, "Laissez Faire." 3 vols. 3d ed. Cambridge, 1903.
(6) Ingram, John K. *A History of Political Economy.* Chap. v, "Third Modern Phase; System of Natural Liberty." 2d ed. New York, 1908.
(7) Hall, W. P. "Certain Early Reactions against Laissez Faire," *Annual Report of the American Historical Association for the Year 1913.* I, 127-38. Washington, 1915.
(8) Adams, Henry C. "Relation of the State to Industrial Action," *Publications of the American Economic Association,* I (1887), 471-549.

IV. THE MARKETS

(1) Walker, Francis A. *Political Economy.* Chap. ii, pp. 97-102. 3d ed. New York, 1887. [Market defined.]
(2) Grierson, P. J. H. *The Silent Trade.* A contribution to the early history of human intercourse. Edinburgh, 1903. [Bibliography.]
(3) Maine, Henry S. *Village Communities in the East and West.* Lecture VI, "The Early History of Price and Rent," pp. 175-203. New York, 1885.
(4) Walford, Cornelius. *Fairs, Past and Present.* A chapter in the history of commerce. London, 1883.
(5) Bourne, H. R. F. *English Merchants.* Memoirs in illustration of the progress of British commerce. New ed. London, 1898.
(6) Webb, Sidney and Beatrice. *Industrial Democracy.* Part III, chap. ii, "The Higgling of the Market," pp. 654-702. New ed. London, 1902.
(7) Bagehot, Walter. *Lombard Street.* A description of the money market. New York, 1876.

V. COMPETITION AND INDUSTRIAL ORGANIZATION

(1) Gras, N. S. B. *An Introduction to Economic History.* New York, 1922. [Describes the stages in the historical development of the world-wide economic community.]
(2) Knowles, L. C. A. *The Industrial and Commercial Revolutions in Great Britain during the Nineteenth Century.* London, 1921.
(3) Tawney, Richard H. *The Acquisitive Society.* New York, 1920.
(4) Crowell, John F. *Trusts and Competition.* Chicago, 1915. [Bibliography.]
(5) Macrosty, Henry W. *Trusts and the State.* A sketch of competition. London, 1901.
(6) Carter, George R. *The Tendency toward Industrial Combination.* A study of the modern movement toward industrial combination in some spheres of British industry; its forms and developments, their causes, and their determinant circumstances. London, 1913.
(7) Levy, Hermann. *Monopoly and Competition.* A study in English industrial organization. London, 1911.

(8) Haney, Lewis H. *Business Organization and Combination*. An analysis of the evolution and nature of business organization in the United States and a tentative solution of the corporation and trust problems. New York, 1914.

(9) Van Hise, Charles R. *Concentration and Control*. A solution of the trust problem in the United States. New York, 1912.

(10) Kohler, Josef. *Der unlautere Wettbewerb*. Darstellung des Wettbewerbsrechts. Berlin und Leipzig, 1914.

(11) Nims, Harry D. *The Law of Unfair Business Competition*. Including chapters on trade secrets and confidential business relations; unfair interference with contracts; libel and slander of articles of merchandise, trade names and business credit and reputation. New York, 1909.

(12) Stevens, W. H. S. *Unfair Competition*. A study of certain practices with some reference to the trust problem in the United States of America. Chicago, 1917.

(13) Eddy, Arthur J. *The New Competition*. An examination of the conditions underlying the radical change that is taking place in the commercial and industrial world; the change from a competitive to a co-operative basis. New York, 1912.

(14) Kropotkin, P. *Mutual Aid*. A factor of evolution. London, 1902.

(15) Willoughby, W. W. *Social Justice*. A critical essay. Chap. ix, "The Ethics of the Competitive Process," pp. 269–315. New York, 1900.

(16) Rogers, Edward S. *Good Will, Trade-Marks and Unfair Trading*. Chicago, 1914.

VI. SOCIALISM AND ANARCHISM

(1) Stirner, Max. (Kaspar Schmidt). *The Ego and His Own*. Translated from the German by S. T. Byington. New York, 1918.

(2) Godwin, William. *An Enquiry Concerning Political Justice and Its Influence on General Virtue and Happiness*. Book V, chap. xxiv. London, 1793.

(3) Proudhon, Pierre Joseph. *What Is Property?* An inquiry into the principle of right and of government. Translated from the French by B. R. Tucker. New York, 189–?

(4) Zenker, E. V. *Anarchism*. A criticism and history of the anarchist theory. Translated from the German. New York, 1897. [With bibliographical references.]

(5) Bailie, William. *Josiah Warren, the First American Anarchist*. A sociological study. Boston, 1906.

(6) Russell, B. A. W. *Proposed Roads to Freedom*. Socialism, anarchism, and syndicalism. New York, 1919.

(7) Mackay, Thomas, editor. *A Plea for Liberty*. An argument against socialism and socialistic legislation. New York, 1891.

(8) Spencer, Herbert. "The Man *versus* the State," Appendix to *Social Statics*. New York, 1897.

(9) Marx, Karl, and Engels, Frederick. *Manifesto of the Communist Party*. Authorized English translation edited and annotated by Frederick Engels. London, 1888.

(10) Stein, L. *Der Socialismus und Communismus des heutigen Frankreichs*. Ein Beitrag zur Zeitgeschichte. Leipzig, 1848.

(11) Guyot, Édouard. *Le Socialisme et l'évolution de l'Angleterre contemporaine* (1880–1911). Paris, 1913.
(12) Flint, Robert. *Socialism*. 2d ed. London, 1908.
(13) Beer, M. *A History of British Socialism*. Vol. I, "From the ·Days of the Schoolmen to the Birth of Chartism." Vol. II, "From Chartism to 1920." London, 1919–21.
(14) Levine, Louis. *Syndicalism in France*. 2d ed. New York, 1914.
(15) Brissenden, Paul F. *The I.W.W.* A study of American syndicalism. New York, 1919. [Bibliography.]
(16) Brooks, John Graham. *American Syndicalism*. New York, 1913.
(17) ———. *Labor's Challenge to the Social Order*. Democracy its own critic and educator. New York, 1920.

[See bibliography, "Utopias," p. 1008.]

VII. COMPETITION AND "THE INNER ENEMIES"

A. *The Struggle for Existence and Its Social Consequences*

(1) Henderson, Charles R. *Introduction to the Study of the Dependent, Defective, and Delinquent Classes, and of Their Social Treatment.* 2d ed. Boston, 1908.
(2) Grotjahn, Alfred. *Soziale Pathologie.* Versuch einer Lehre von den sozialen Beziehungen der menschlichen Krankheiten als Grundlage der sozialen Medizin und der sozialen Hygiene. Berlin, 1912
(3) Lilienfeld, Paul de. *La Pathologie sociale.* Avec une préface de René Worms. Paris, 1896.
(4) Elster, Alexander. *Sozialbiologie.* Bevölkerungswissenschaft und Gesellschaftshygiene. Berlin, 1923.
(5) Thompson, Warren S. *Population.* A study in Malthusianism. New York, 1915.
(6) Reuter, E. B. *Population Problems.* Philadelphia, 1923.
(7) Field, James A. "The Early Propagandist Movement in English Population Theory," *American Economic Association Bulletin*, 4th Ser., I (1911), 207–36.
(8) Heron, David. *On the Relation of Fertility in Man to Social Status.* And on the changes in this relation that have taken place during the last fifty years. London, 1906.
(9) Elderton, Ethel M. "Report on the English Birthrate." University of London, Francis Galton Laboratory for National Eugenics. *Eugenics Laboratory Memoirs*, XIX–XX. London, 1914.
(10) D'Ambrosio, Manlio A. *Passività Economica.* Primi principi di una teoria sociologica della popolazione economicamente passiva. Napoli, 1909.
(11) Ellwood, Charles A. *Sociology and Modern Social Problems.* Rev. ed. New York, 1913.

B. *Poverty, Labor, and the Proletariat*

(1) Woods, Robert A., Elsing, W. T., and others. *The Poor in Great Cities.* Their problems and what is being done to solve them. New York, 1895.
(2) Rowntree, B. Seebohm. *Poverty, a Study of Town Life.* London, 1901.

(3) Devine, Edward T. *Misery and Its Causes.* New York, 1909.

(4) Marx, Karl. *Capital.* A critical analysis of capitalist production. Chap. xv, "Machinery and Modern Industry." Translated from the third German edition by Samuel Moore and Edward Aveling, and edited by Frederick Engels. London, 1908.

(5) Hobson, John A. *Problems of Poverty.* An inquiry into the industrial condition of the poor. London, 1891.

(6) Kydd, Samuel [Alfred, pseud.] *The History of the Factory Movement.* From the year 1802 to the enactment of the ten hours' bill in 1847. 2 vols. London, 1857.

(7) Rowntree, B. S., and Lasker, Bruno. *Unemployment, a Social Study.* London, 1911.

(8) Beveridge, William Henry. *Unemployment.* A problem of industry. 3d ed. London, 1912.

(9) Parmelee, Maurice. *Poverty and Social Progress.* New York, 1916.

(10) Gillin, John L. *Poverty and Dependency.* Their relief and prevention. New York, 1921.

(11) Sombart, Werner. *Das Proletariat; Bilder und Studien.* Frankfurt am Main, 1906.

(12) Riis, Jacob A. *How the Other Half Lives.* Studies among the tenements of New York. New York, 1890.

(13) Nevinson, Margaret W. *Workhouse Characters and Other Sketches of the Life of the Poor.* London, 1918.

(14) Sims, George R. *How the Poor Live; and Horrible London.* London, 1898.

C. *The Industrially Handicapped*

(1) Best, Harry. *The Deaf.* Their position in society and the provision for their education in the United States. New York, 1914.

(2) ———. *The Blind.* Their condition and the work being done for them in the United States. New York, 1919.

(3) United States Bureau of the Census. *The Blind and the Deaf, 1900.* Washington, 1906.

(4) ———. *Deaf-Mutes in the United States.* Analysis of the census of 1910 with summary of state laws relating to the deaf as of January 1, 1918. Washington, 1918.

(5) ———. *The Blind in the United States 1910.* Washington, 1917.

(6) Niceforo, Alfredo. *Les Classes pauvres.* Recherches anthropologiques et sociales. Paris, 1905.

(7) Goddard, Henry H. *Feeble-mindedness, Its Causes and Consequences.* Chap. i, "Social Problems," pp. 1–20. New York, 1914.

(8) Popenoe, Paul B., and Johnson, Roswell H. *Applied Eugenics.* Chap. ix, "The Dysgenic Classes," pp. 176–83. New York, 1918.

(9) Pintner, Rudolf, and Toops, Herbert A. "Mental Test of Unemployed Men," *Journal of Applied Psychology,* I (1917), 325–41; II (1918), 15–25.

(10) Oliver, Thomas. *Dangerous Trades.* The historical, social, and legal aspects of industrial occupations affecting health, by a number of experts. New York, 1902.

(11) Jarrett, Mary C. "The Psychopathic Employee: a Problem of Industry," *Bulletin of the Massachusetts Commission on Mental Diseases*, I (1917-18), Nos. 3-4, 223-38. Boston, 1918.

(12) Thompson, W. Gilman. *The Occupational Diseases.* Their causation, treatment, and prevention. New York, 1914.

(13) Kober, George M., and Hanson, William C., editors. *Diseases of Occupation and Vocational Hygiene.* Philadelphia, 1916.

(14) Great Britain Ministry of Munitions. *Health of Munition Workers Committee.* Hours, fatigue, and health in British munition factories. Reprints of the memoranda of the British Health of Munition Workers Committee, April, 1917. Washington, 1917.

(15) Great Britain Home Department. *Report of the Committee on Compensation for Industrial Diseases.* London, 1907.

(16) McMurtrie, Douglas C. *The Disabled Soldier.* With an introduction by Jeremiah Milbank. New York, 1919.

(17) Rubinow, I. M. "A Statistical Consideration of the Number of Men Crippled in War and Disabled in Industry," *Publication of Red Cross Institute for Crippled and Disabled Men.* Series I, No. 4, Feb. 14, 1918.

(18) Love, Albert G., and Davenport, C. B. *Defects Found in Drafted Men.* Statistical information compiled from the draft records showing the physical condition of the men registered and examined in pursuance of the requirements of the selective-service act. War Department, U.S. Surgeon General's Office, Washington, 1920.

D. *Alcoholism and Drug Addiction*

(1) Partridge, George E. *Studies in the Psychology of Intemperance.* New York, 1912.

(2) Kelynack, T. N. *The Drink Problem of Today in Its Medico-sociological Aspects.* New York, 1916.

(3) Kerr, Norman S. *Inebriety or Narcomania.* Its etiology, pathology, treatment, and jurisprudence. 3d ed. London, 1894.

(4) Elderton, Ethel M. "A First Study of the Influence of Parental Alcoholism on the Physique and Ability of the Offspring." *Eugenics Laboratory Memoirs,* University of London, Francis Galton Laboratory for National Eugenics. London, 1910.

(5) Koren, John. *Economic Aspects of the Liquor Problem.* An investigation made for the Committee of Fifty under the direction of Henry W. Farnam. Boston, 1899.

(6) Towns, Charles B. *Habits that Handicap.* The menace of opium, alcohol, and tobacco, and the remedy. New York, 1916.

(7) Wilbert, Martin I. "The Number and Kind of Drug Addicts," *U.S. Public Health Reprint,* No. 294. Washington, 1915.

(8) Rowntree, B. Seebohm. *Land and Labour: Lessons from Belgium.* Chap. xxvi, "The Drink Problem." London, 1910.

(9) McIver, J., and Price, G. F. "Drug Addiction," *Journal of the American Medical Association,* LXVI (1915), 476-80. [A study of 147 cases.]

(10) Stanley, L. L. "Drug Addictions," *Journal of the American Institute of Criminal Law and Criminology,* X (1919), 62-70. [Four case studies.]

E. *Crime and Competition*

(1) Parmelee, Maurice. *Criminology.* Chap. vi, pp. 67–91. New York, 1918.

(2) Bonger, William A. *Criminality and Economic Conditions.* Translated from the French by H. P. Horton, with editorial preface by Edward Lindsey and with an introduction by Frank H. Norcross. Boston, 1916.

(3) Tarde, G. "La Criminalité et les phénomènes économiques," *Archives d'anthropologie criminelle,* XVI (1901), 565–75.

(4) Kan, J. Van. *Les Causes économiques de la criminalité.* Étude historique et critique d'étiologie criminelle. Lyon, 1903.

(5) Fornasari di Verce, E. *La Criminalità e le vicende economiche d'Italia, dal 1873 al 1890, con prefazione di Ces. Lombroso.* Torino, 1894.

(6) Devon, J. *The Criminal and the Community.* London and New York, 1912.

(7) Breckinridge, Sophonisba, and Abbott, Edith. *The Delinquent Child and the Home.* Chap. iv, "The Poor Child: The Problem of Poverty," pp. 70–89. New York, 1912.

(8) Flexner, Abraham. *Prostitution in Europe.* New York, 1914.

(9) Kneeland, George J. *Commercialized Prostitution in New York City.* With a supplementary chapter by Katharine Bement Davis. Rev. ed. New York, 1917.

(10) Woolston, Howard B. *Prostitution in the United States.* New York, 1923.

(11) Donovan, Frances. *The Woman Who Waits.* Boston, 1920.

(12) Fernald, Mabel R., Hayes, Mary H. S., and Dawley, Almena. *A Study of Women Delinquents in New York State.* With statistical chapter by Beardsley Ruml; preface by Katharine Bement Davis. Chap. xi, "Occupational History and Economic Efficiency," pp. 304–79. New York, 1920.

(13) Miner, Maude. *The Slavery of Prostitution.* A plea for emancipation. Chap. iii, "Social Factors Leading to Prostitution," pp. 53–88. New York, 1916.

(14) Ryckère, Raymond de. *La Servante criminelle.* Étude de criminologie professionelle. Paris, 1908.

TOPICS FOR WRITTEN THEMES

1. The Struggle for Existence and the Survival of the Fittest
2. Economic Competition and the Economic Equilibrium
3. "Unfair" Competition and Social Control
4. Competition versus Sentiment
5. The History of the Market, the Exchange, the Board of Trade
6. The Natural History of the Laissez-Faire Theory in Economics and Politics
7. Competition, Money, and Freedom
8. Biological Competition and the Geographical Distribution of Races and Nationalities
9. Competition and Segregation in Industry and in Society

10. The Distribution and Segregation of Economic and Occupational Classes in the Community
11. Family Budgets and Changes in the Standard of Living
12. The Neo-Malthusian Movement and Race Suicide
13. The Economic Order of Competition and "the Inner Enemies"
14. Physical and Mental Deficiency and the Program of Eugenics
15. The History of the English Poor Law
16. Unemployment and Poverty in a Competitive, Secondary Society
17. Modern Economy and the Psychology of Intemperance
18. Modern Industry, the Physically Handicapped and Programs of Rehabilitation
19. Crime in Relation to Economic Conditions
20. Methods of Social Amelioration: Philanthropy, Welfare Work in Industry, Social Insurance, etc.
21. Experiments in the Limitation of Competition: Collective Bargaining, Trade Associations, Trade Boards, etc.
22. The Process of Competition in Relation to the Theories of Socialism and Anarchism

QUESTIONS FOR DISCUSSION

1. In what fields did the popular conceptions of competition originate?
2. In what way does competition as a form of interaction differ from conflict, accommodation, and assimilation?
3. What do you understand to be the difference between struggle, conflict, competition, and rivalry?
4. What are the different forms of the struggle for existence?
5. In what different meanings do you understand Darwin to use the term "the struggle for existence"? How many of these are applicable to human society?
6. What do you understand Darwin to mean when he says: "The structure of every organic being is related, in the most essential yet often hidden manner, to that of all the other organic beings with which it comes into competition for food or residence, or from which it has to escape, or on which it preys"? Does his principle, in your opinion, also apply to the structure of social groups?
7. What examples of competition occur to you in human or social relations? In what respects are they (a) alike, (b) different, from competition in plant communities?
8. To what extent is biological competition present in modern human society?
9. Does competition always lead to increased specialization and higher organization?

10. What evidences are there in society of the effect of competition upon specialization and organization?

11. What do you understand Crile to mean by the sentence: "In every case the fate of each creature seems to have been staked upon one mechanism"? What is this mechanism with man?

12. Do you think that Crile has given an adequate explanation of the evolution of mind?

13. Is there a difference in the character of the struggle for existence of animals and of man?

14. What is the difference in competition within a community based on likenesses and one based on diversities?

15. Compare the ecological concept "reaction" with the sociological conception "control."

16. What do you understand by the expression "the reaction of a community is usually more than the sum of the reaction of the component species and individuals"? Explain.

17. How far can the terms migration, ecesis, and competition, as used by Clements in his analysis of the invasion of one plant community by another, be used in the analysis of the process by which immigrants "invade" this country, i.e., migrate, settle, and are assimilated, "Americanized"?

18. What are the social forces involved in (a) internal, (b) foreign, migrations?

19. What do you understand by the term segregation? To what extent are the social forces making for segregation (a) economic, (b) sentimental? Illustrate.

20. In what ways has immigration to the United States resulted in segregation?

21. Does the segregation of the immigrant in our American cities make for or against (a) competition, (b) conflict, (c) social control, (d) accommodation, and (e) assimilation?

22. What are the factors producing internal migration in the United States?

23. In what sense is the drift to the cities a result of competition?

24. What is Ripley's conclusion in regard to urban selection and the ethnic composition of cities?

25. What are the outstanding results of demographic segregation and social selection in the United States?

26. What, in your judgment, are the chief characteristics of inter-racial competition?

27. To what extent do you agree with Walker's analysis of the social forces involved in race suicide in the United States?

28. In what specific ways is competition now a factor in race suicide?

29. What will be the future effects of inter-racial competition upon the ethnic stock of the American people?

30. Compare the essential features of village economy, town economy, and metropolitan economy.

31. What is the relation of the hinterland to the metropolis?

32. What are the social consequences of metropolitan growth?

33. "There is a sense in which much of the orthodox system of political economy is eternally true." Explain.

34. To what extent and in what sense is economic competition unconscious?

35. What differences other than innate mental ability enter into competition between different social groups and different persons?

36. Who are your competitors?

37. Of the existence (as identified persons) of what proportion of these competitors are you unconscious?

38. What is meant by competitive co-operation? Illustrate. (See pp. 508, 558.)

39. What do you understand by the term "economic equilibrium"?

40. Is "economic equilibrium" identical with "social solidarity"? What is the relation, if any, between the two concepts?

41. To what extent does competition make for a natural harmony of individual interests?

42. What did Adam Smith mean by "an invisible hand"?

43. "Civilization is the resultant not of conscious co-operation but of the unconscious competition of individuals." Do you agree or disagree with this statement?

44. "By pursuing his own interest he frequently promotes that of the society more effectually than when he really intends to promote it." What is the argument for and against this position?

45. Why has the laissez-faire theory in economics been largely abandoned?

46. What do you understand by the term "freedom"? How far may freedom be identified with freedom of competition?

47. Do you accept the conception of Bastiat that "competition is liberty"?

48. How does money make for freedom? Does it make for or against co-operation? Are co-operation and competition antagonistic terms?

49. What do you understand by the statement that anarchism, socialism, and communism are based upon the ecological conceptions of society?

50. From what point of view may the dependent, the delinquent, and the defective be regarded as "inner enemies"?

CHAPTER IX

CONFLICT

I. INTRODUCTION

1. The Concept of Conflict

The distinction between competition and conflict has already been indicated. Both are forms of interaction, but competition is a struggle between individuals, or groups of individuals, who are not necessarily in contact and communication; while conflict is a contest in which contact is an indispensable condition. Competition, unqualified and uncontrolled as with plants, and in the great impersonal life-struggle of man with his kind and with all animate nature, is unconscious. Conflict is always conscious, indeed, it evokes the deepest emotions and strongest passions and enlists the greatest concentration of attention and of effort. Both competition and conflict are forms of struggle. Competition, however, is continuous and impersonal, conflict is intermittent and personal.

Competition is a struggle for position in an economic order. The distribution of populations in the world-economy, the industrial organization in the national economy, and the vocation of the individual in the division of labor—all these are determined, in the long run, by competition. The status of the individual, or a group of individuals, in the social order, on the other hand, is determined by rivalry, by war, or by subtler forms of conflict.

"Two is company, three is a crowd" suggests how easily the social equilibrium is disturbed by the entrance of a new factor in a social situation. The delicate nuances and grades of attention given to different individuals moving in the same social circle are the superficial reflections of rivalries and conflicts beneath the smooth and decorous surfaces of polite society.

In general, we may say that competition determines the position of the individual in the community; conflict fixes his place in society. Location, position, ecological interdependence—these are the characteristics of the community. Status, subordination and super-ordination, control—these are the distinctive marks of a society.

The notion of conflict, like the fact, has its roots deep in human interest. Mars has always held a high rank in the hierarchy of the gods. Whenever and wherever struggle has taken the form of conflict, whether of races, of nations, or of individual men, it has invariably captured and held the attention of spectators. And these spectators, when they did not take part in the fight, always took sides. It was this conflict of the non-combatants that made public opinion, and public opinion has always played an important rôle in the struggles of men. It is this that has raised war from a mere play of physical forces and given it the tragic significance of a moral struggle, a conflict of good and evil.

The result is that war tends to assume the character of litigation, a judicial procedure, in which custom determines the method of procedure, and the issue of the struggle is accepted as a judgment in the case.

The duello, as distinguished from the wager of battle, although it never had the character of a judicial procedure, developed a strict code which made it morally binding upon the individual to seek redress for wrongs, and determined in advance the methods of procedure by which such redress could and should be obtained. The penalty was a loss of status in the particular group of which the individual was a member.

It was the presence of the public, the ceremonial character of the proceedings, and the conviction that the invisible powers were on the side of truth and justice that gave the trial by ordeal and the trial by battle a significance that neither the duello nor any other form of private vengeance ever had.

It is interesting in this connection, also, that political and judicial forms of procedure are conducted on a conflict pattern. An election is a contest in which we count noses when we do not break heads. A trial by jury is a contest in which the parties are represented by champions, as in the judicial duels of an earlier time.

In general, then, one may say competition becomes conscious and personal in conflict. In the process of transition competitors are transformed into rivals and enemies. In its higher forms, however, conflict becomes impersonal—a struggle to establish and maintain rules of justice and a moral order. In this case the welfare not merely of individual men but of the community is involved. Such are the struggles of political parties and religious sects. Here the issues are not determined by the force and weight of the contestants immediately involved, but to a greater or less extent, by the force and weight of public opinion of the community, and eventually by the judgment of mankind.

2. Classification of the Materials

The materials on conflict have been organized in the readings under four heads: (a) conflict as conscious competition; (b) war, instincts, and ideals; (c) rivalry, cultural conflicts, and social organization; and (d) race conflicts.

a) *Conscious competition.*—Self-consciousness in the individual arises in the contacts and conflicts of the person with other persons. It manifests itself variously in pride and in humility, vanity and self-respect, modesty and arrogance, pity and disdain, as well as in race prejudice, chauvinism, class and caste distinctions, and in every other social device by which the social distances are maintained.

It is in these various responses called forth by social contacts and intercourse that the personality of the individual is developed and his status defined. It is in the effort to maintain this status or improve it; to defend this personality, enlarge its possessions, extend its privileges, and maintain its prestige that conflicts arise. This applies to all conflicts, whether they are personal and party squabbles, sectarian differences, or national and patriotic wars, for the personality of the individual is invariably so bound up with the interests and order of his group and clan, that, in a struggle, he makes the group cause his own.

Much has been said and written about the economic causes of war, but whatever may be the ultimate sources of our sentiments, it is probably true that men never go to war for economic reasons merely. It is because wealth and possessions are bound up with prestige, honor, and position in the world, that men and nations fight about them.

b) *War, instincts, and ideals.*—War is the outstanding and the typical example of conflict. In war, where hostility prevails over every interest of sentiment or utility which would otherwise unite the contending parties or groups, the motives and the rôle of conflict in social life present themselves in their clearest outline. There is, moreover, a practical reason for fixing upon war as an illustration of conflict. The tremendous interest in all times manifested in war, the amazing energies and resources released in peoples organized for military aggression or defense, the colossal losses and sacrifices endured for the glory, the honor, or the security of the fatherland have made wars memorable. Of no other of the larger aspects of collective life have we such adequate records.

The problem of the relation of war to human instincts, on the one hand, and to human ideals, on the other, is the issue about which most recent observation and discussion has centered. It seems idle to assert that hostility has no roots in man's original nature. The concrete materials given in this chapter show beyond question how readily the wishes and the instincts of the person may take the form of the fighting pattern. On the other hand, the notion that tradition, culture, and collective representations have no part in determining the attitudes of nations toward war seems equally untenable. The significant sociological inquiry is to determine just in what ways a conjunction of the tendencies in original nature, the forces of tradition and culture, and the exigencies of the situation determine the organization of the fighting pattern. We have historical examples of war-like peoples becoming peaceful and of pacific nations militaristic. An understanding of the mechanism of the process is a first condition to any exercise of control.

c) Rivalry, cultural conflicts, and social organization.—Rivalry is a sublimated form of conflict where the struggle of individuals is subordinated to the welfare of the group. In the rivalry of groups, likewise, conflict or competition is subordinated to the interests of an inclusive group. Rivalry may then be defined as conflict controlled by the group in its interest. A survey of the phenomena of rivalry brings out its rôle as an organizing force in group life.

In the study of conflict groups it is not always easy to apply with certainty the distinction between rivalry and conflict made here. The sect is a conflict group. In its struggle for survival and success with other groups, its aim is the highest welfare of the inclusive society. Actually, however, sectarian warfare may be against the moral, social, and religious interests of the community. The denomination, which is an accommodation group, strives through rivalry and competition, not only to promote the welfare of the inclusive society, but also of its other component groups.

In cultural and political conflict the function of conflict in social life becomes understandable and reasonable. The rôle of mental conflicts in the life of the individual is for the purpose of making adjustments to changing situations and of assimilating new experiences. It is through this process of conflict of divergent impulses to act that the individual arrives at decisions—as we say, "makes up his mind." Only where there is conflict is behavior conscious and self-conscious; only here are the conditions for rational conduct.

d) Race conflicts.—Nowhere do social contacts so readily provoke conflicts as in the relations between the races, particularly when racial differences are re-enforced, not merely by differences of culture, but of color. Nowhere, it might be added, are the responses to social contact so obvious and, at the same time, so difficult to analyze and define.

Race prejudice, as we call the sentiments that support the racial taboos, is not, in America at least, an obscure phenomenon. But no one has yet succeeded in making it wholly intelligible. It is evident that there is in race prejudice, as distinguished from class and caste prejudice, an instinctive factor based on the fear of the unfamiliar and the uncomprehended. Color, or any other racial mark that emphasizes physical differences, becomes the symbol of moral divergences which perhaps do not exist. We at once fear and are fascinated by the stranger, and an individual of a different race always seems more of a stranger to us than one of our own. This naïve prejudice, unless it is re-enforced by other factors, is easily modified, as the intimate relations of the Negroes and white man in slavery show.

A more positive factor in racial antagonism is the conflict of cultures: the unwillingness of one race to enter into personal competition with a race of a different or inferior culture. This turns out, in the long run, to be the unwillingness of a people or a class occupying a superior status to compete on equal terms with a people of a lower status. Race conflicts like wars are fundamentally the struggles of racial groups for status. In this sense and from this point of view the struggles of the European nationalities and the so-called "subject peoples" for independence and self-determination are actually struggles for status in the family of nations.

Under the conditions of this struggle, racial or national consciousness as it manifests itself, for example, in Irish nationalism, Jewish Zionism, and Negro race consciousness, is the natural and obvious response to a conflict situation. The nationalistic movements in Europe, in India, and in Egypt are, like war, rivalry and more personal forms of conflict, mainly struggles for recognition— that is, honor, glory, and prestige.

II. MATERIALS

A. CONFLICT AS CONSCIOUS COMPETITION

1. The Natural History of Conflict[1]

All classes of society, and the two sexes to about the same degree, are deeply interested in all forms of contest involving skill and chance, especially where the danger or risk is great. Everybody will stop to watch a street fight, and the same persons would show an equal interest in a prize fight or a bull fight, if certain scruples did not stand in the way of their looking on. Our socially developed sympathy and pity may recoil from witnessing a scene where physical hurt is the object of the game, but the depth of our interest in the conflict type of activity is attested by the fascination which such a game as football has for the masses, where our instinctive emotional reaction to a conflict situation is gratified to an intense degree by a scene of the conflict pattern.

If we examine, in fact, our pleasures and pains, our moments of elation and depression, we find that they go back for the most part to instincts developed in the struggle for food and rivalry for mates. The structure of the organism has been built up gradually through the survival of the most efficient structures. Corresponding with a structure mechanically adapted to successful movements, there is developed on the psychic side an interest in the conflict situation as complete and perfect as is the structure itself. The emotional states are, indeed, organic preparations for action, corresponding broadly with

[1] Adapted from William I. Thomas, "The Gaming Instinct," in the *American Journal of Sociology*, VI (1900–1901), 750–63.

a tendency to advance or retreat; and a connection has even been made out between pleasurable states and the extensor muscles, and painful states and the flexor muscles. We can have no adequate idea of the time consumed and the experiments made in nature before the development of these types of structure and interest of the conflict pattern, but we know from the geological records that the time and experiments were long and many, and the competition so sharp that finally, not in man alone, but in all the higher classes of animals, body and mind, structure and interest, were working perfectly in motor actions of the violent type involved in a life of conflict, competition, and rivalry. There could not have been developed an organism depending on offensive and defensive movements for food and life without an interest in what we call a dangerous or precarious situation. A type without this interest would have been defective, and would have dropped out in the course of development.

The fact that our interests and enthusiasms are called out in situations of the conflict type is shown by a glance at the situations which arouse them most readily. War is simply an organized form of fight, and as such is most attractive, or, to say the least, arouses the interests powerfully. With the accumulation of property and the growth of sensibility and intelligence it becomes apparent that war is a wasteful and unsafe process, and public and personal interests lead us to avoid it as much as possible. But, however genuinely war may be deprecated, it is certainly an exciting game. The Rough Riders in this country recently, and more recently the young men of the aristocracy of England, went to war from motives of patriotism, no doubt, but there are unmistakable evidences that they also regarded it as the greatest sport they were likely to have a chance at in a lifetime. And there is evidence in plenty that the emotional attitude of women toward war is no less intense. Grey relates that half a dozen old women among the Australians will drive the men to war with a neighboring tribe over a fancied injury. The Jewish maidens went out with music and dancing and sang that Saul had slain his thousands, but David his ten thousands. The young women of Havana are alleged, during the late Spanish War, to have sent pieces of their wardrobe to young men of their acquaintance who hesitated to join the rebellion, with the suggestion that they wear these until they went to the war.

The feud is another mode of reaction of the violent, instinctive, and attractive type. The feud was originally of defensive value to the individual and to the tribe, since in the absence of criminal law the feeling that retaliation would follow was a deterrent from acts of aggression. But it was an expensive method of obtaining order in early society, since response to stimulus reinstated the stimulus, and every death called for another death; so, finally, after many experiments and devices, the state has forbidden the individual to take justice into his own hands. In out-of-the-way places, however, where governmental control is weak, men still settle their disputes personally, and one who is familiar with the course of a feud cannot avoid the conclusion that this practice is kept up, not because there is no law to resort to, but because the older mode is more immediate and fascinating. I mean simply that the emotional possibilities and actual emotional reactions in the feud are far more powerful than in due legal process.

Gladiatorial shows, bear baiting, bull fighting, dog and cock fighting, and prize fighting afford an opportunity to gratify the interest in conflict. The spectator has by suggestion emotional reactions analogous to those of the combatant, but without personal danger; and vicarious contests between slaves, captives, and animals, whose blood and life are cheap, are a pleasure which the race allowed itself until a higher stage of morality was reached. Pugilism is the modification of the fight in a slightly different way. The combatants are members of society, not slaves or captives, but the conflict is so qualified as to safeguard their lives, though injury is possible and is actually planned. The intention to do hurt is the point to which society and the law object. But the prize fight is a fight as far as it goes, and the difficulties which men will surmount to "pull off" and to witness these contests are sufficient proof of their fascination. A football game is also a fight, with the additional qualification that no injury is planned, and with an advantage over the prize fight in the fact that it is not a single-handed conflict, but an organized mêlée—a battle where the action is more massive and complex and the strategic opportunities are multiplied. It is a fact of interest in this connection that, unless appearances are deceptive, altogether the larger number of visitors to a university during the year are visitors to the football field. It is the only phase of university life which appeals directly and powerfully to the instincts, and it is consequently the only phase of university life which appeals equally to the man of culture, the artist, the business man, the man about town, the all-round sport, and, in fact, to all the world.

The instincts of man are congenital; the arts and industries are acquired by the race and must be learned by the individual after birth. We have seen why the instinctive activities are pleasurable and the acquired habits irksome. The gambler represents a class of men who have not been weaned from their instincts. There are in every species biological "sports" and reversions, and there are individuals of this kind among sporting men who are not reached by ordinary social suggestion and stimuli. But granting that what we may call the instinctive interests are disproportionately strong in the sporting class, as compared with, say, the merchant class, yet these instincts are also strongly marked in what may roughly be called the artist class and in spite of a marked psychic disposition for stimuli of the emotional type; and precisely because of this disposition, the artist class has a very high social value. Art products are, indeed, perhaps more highly esteemed than any other products whatever. The artist class is not, therefore, socially unmanageable because of its instinctive interest, though perhaps we may say that some of its members are saved from social vagabondage only because their emotional predisposition has found an expression in emotional activities to which some social value can be attached.

2. Conflict as a Type of Social Interaction[1]

That conflict has sociological significance inasmuch as it either produces or modifies communities of interest, unifications, organizations, is in principle never contested. On the other hand, it must appear paradoxical to the ordinary mode of thinking to ask whether conflict itself, without reference to its consequences or its accompaniments, is not a form of socialization. This seems, at first glance, to be merely a verbal question. If every reaction among men is a socialization, of course conflict must count as such, since it is one of the most intense reactions and is logically impossible if restricted to a

[1] Adapted from a translation of Georg Simmel, *Soziologie*, by Albion W. Small, "The Sociology of Conflict," in the *American Journal of Sociology*, IX (1903–4), 490–501.

single element. The actually dissociating elements are the causes of the conflict—hatred and envy, want and desire. If, however, from these impulses conflict has once broken out, it is in reality the way to remove the dualism and to arrive at some form of unity, even if through annihilation of one of the parties. The case is, in a way, illustrated by the most violent symptoms of disease. They frequently represent the efforts of the organism to free itself from disorders and injuries. This is by no means equivalent merely to the triviality, *si vis pacem para bellum*, but it is the wide generalization of which that special case is a particular. Conflict itself is the resolution of the tension between the contraries. That it eventuates in peace is only a single, specially obvious and evident, expression of the fact that it is a conjunction of elements.

As the individual achieves the unity of his personality, not in such fashion that its contents invariably harmonize according to logical or material, religious or ethical, standards, but rather as contradiction and strife not merely precede that unity but are operative in it at every moment of life; so it is hardly to be expected that there should be any social unity in which the converging tendencies of the elements are not incessantly shot through with elements of divergence. A group which was entirely centripetal and harmonious—that is, "unification" merely—is not only impossible empirically, but it would also display no essential life-process and no stable structure. As the cosmos requires *Liebe und Hass*, attraction and repulsion, in order to have a form, society likewise requires some quantitative relation of harmony and disharmony, association and dissociation, liking and disliking, in order to attain to a definite formation. Society, as it is given in fact, is the result of both categories of reactions, and in so far both act in a completely positive way. The misconception that the one factor tears down what the other builds up, and that what at last remains is the result of subtracting the one from the other (while in reality it is much rather to be regarded as the addition of one to the other), doubtless springs from the equivocal sense of the concept of unity.

We describe as unity the agreement and the conjunction of social elements in contrast with their disjunctions, separations, disharmonies. We also use the term unity, however, for the total synthesis of the persons, energies, and forms in a group, in which the final wholeness is made up, not merely of those factors which are unifying in the narrower sense, but also of those which are, in the narrower sense, dualistic. We associate a corresponding double meaning with disunity or opposition. Since the latter displays its nullifying or destructive sense *between the individual elements*, the conclusion is hastily drawn that it must work in the same manner upon the *total relationship*. In reality, however, it by no means follows that the factor which is something negative and diminutive in its action between individuals, considered in a given direction and separately, has the same working throughout the totality of its relationships. In this larger circle of relationships the perspective may be quite different. That which was negative and dualistic may, after deduction of its destructive action in particular relationships, on the whole, play an entirely positive rôle. This visibly appears especially in those instances where the social structure is characterized by exactness and carefully conserved purity of social divisions and gradations.

The social system of India rests not only upon the hierarchy of the castes but also directly upon the reciprocal repulsion. Enmities not merely prevent gradual disappearance of the boundaries within the society—and for this reason these enmities may be consciously promoted, as guaranty of the existing social constitution—but more than this, the enmities are directly productive sociologically. They give classes and personalities their position toward each other, which they would not have found if these objective causes of hostility had been present and effective in precisely the same way but had not been accompanied by the feeling of enmity. It is by no means certain that a secure and complete community life would always result if these energies should disappear which, looked at in detail, seem repulsive and destructive, just as a qualitatively unchanged and richer property results when unproductive elements disappear; but there would ensue rather a condition as changed, and often as unrealizable, as after the elimination of the forces of co-operation—sympathy, assistance, harmony of interests.

The opposition of one individual element to another in the same association is by no means merely a negative social factor, but it is in many ways the only means through which coexistence with individuals intolerable in themselves could be possible. If we had not power and right to oppose tyranny and obstinacy, caprice and tactlessness, we could not endure relations with people who betray such characteristics. We should be driven to deeds of desperation which would put the relationships to an end. This follows not alone for the self-evident reason—which, however, is not here essential—that such disagreeable circumstances tend to become intensified if they are endured quietly and without protest; but, more than this, opposition affords us a subjective satisfaction, diversion, relief, just as under other psychological conditions, whose variations need not here be discussed, the same results are brought about by humility and patience. Our opposition gives us the feeling that we are not completely crushed in the relationship. It permits us to preserve a consciousness of energy, and thus lends a vitality and a reciprocity to relationships from which, without this corrective, we should have extricated ourselves at any price. In case the relationships are purely external, and consequently do not reach deeply into the practical, the latent form of conflict discharges this service, i.e., aversion, the feeling of reciprocal alienation and repulsion, which in the moment of a more intimate contact of any sort is at once transformed into positive hatred and conflict. Without this aversion life in a great city, which daily brings each into contact with countless others, would have no thinkable form. The activity of our minds responds to almost every impression received from other people in some sort of a definite feeling, all the unconsciousness, transience, and variability of which seem to remain only in the form of a certain indifference. In fact, this latter would be as unnatural for us as it would be intolerable to be swamped under a multitude of suggestions among which we have no choice. Antipathy protects us against these two typical dangers of the great city. It is the initial stage of practical antagonism. It produces the distances and the buffers without which this kind of life could not be led at all. The mass and the mixtures of this life, the forms in which it is carried on, the rhythm of its rise and fall—these unite with the unifying motives, in the narrower sense, to give to a great city the character of an indissoluble whole. Whatever in this whole seems to be an element of division is thus in reality only one of its elementary forms of socialization.

A struggle for struggle's sake seems to have its natural basis in a certain formal impulse of hostility, which forces itself sometimes upon psychological observation, and in various forms. In the first place, it appears as that natural enmity between man and man which is often emphasized by skeptical moralists. The argument is: Since there is something not wholly displeasing to us in the misfortune of our best friends, and, since the presupposition excludes, in this instance, conflict of material interests, the phenomenon must be traced back to an a priori hostility, to that *homo homini lupus*, as the frequently veiled, but perhaps never inoperative, basis of all our relationships.

3. Types of Conflict Situations[1]

a) War.—The reciprocal relationship of primitive groups is notoriously, and for reasons frequently discussed almost invariably, one of hostility. The decisive illustration is furnished perhaps by the American Indians, among whom every tribe on general principles was supposed to be on a war footing toward every other tribe with which it had no express treaty of peace. It is, however, not to be forgotten that in early stages of culture war constitutes almost the only form in which contact with an alien group occurs. So long as inter-territorial trade was undeveloped, individual tourneys unknown, and intellectual community did not extend beyond the group boundaries, there was, outside of war, no sociological relationship whatever between the various groups. In this case the relationship of the elements of the group to each other and that of the primitive groups to each other present completely contrasted forms. Within the closed circle hostility signifies, as a rule, the severing of relationships, voluntary isolation, and the avoidance of contact. Along with these negative phenomena there will also appear the phenomena of the passionate reaction of open struggle. On the other hand, the group as a whole remains indifferently side by side with similar groups so long as peace exists. The consequence is that these groups become significant for each other only when war breaks out. That the attitude of hostility, considered likewise from this point of view, may arise independently in the soul is the less to be doubted since it represents here, as in many another easily observable situation, the

[1] Adapted from a translation of Georg Simmel, *Soziologie*, by Albion W. Small, "The Sociology of Conflict," in the *American Journal of Sociology*, IX (1903–4), 505–8.

embodiment of an impulse which is in the first place quite general, but which also occurs in quite peculiar forms, namely, *the impulse to act in relationships with others.*

In spite of this spontaneity and independence, which we may thus attribute to the antagonistic impulse, there still remains the question whether it suffices to account for the total phenomena of hostility. This question must be answered in the negative. In the first place, the spontaneous impulse does not exercise itself upon every object but only upon those that are in some way promising. Hunger, for example, springs from the subject. It does not have its origin in the object. Nevertheless, it will not attempt to satisfy itself with wood or stone but it will select only edible objects. In the same way, love and hatred, however little their impulses may depend upon external stimuli, will yet need some sort of opposing object, and only with such co-operation will the complete phenomena appear. On the other hand, it seems to me probable that the hostile impulse, on account of its formal character, in general intervenes, only as a reinforcement of conflicts stimulated by material interest, and at the same time furnishes a foundation for the conflict. And where a struggle springs up from sheer formal love of fighting, which is also entirely impersonal and indifferent both to the material at issue and to the personal opponent, hatred and fury against the opponent as a person unavoidably increase in the course of the conflict, and probably also the interest in the stake at issue, because these affections stimulate and feed the psychical energy of the struggle. It is advantageous to hate the opponent with whom one is for any reason struggling, as it is useful to love him with whom one's lot is united and with whom one must co-operate. The reciprocal attitude of men is often intelligible only on the basis of the perception that actual adaptation to a situation teaches us those feelings which are appropriate to it; feelings which are the most appropriate to the employment or the overcoming of the circumstances of the situation; feelings which bring us, through psychical association, the energies necessary for discharging the momentary task and for defeating the opposing impulses.

Accordingly, no serious struggle can long continue without being supported by a complex of psychic impulses. These may, to be sure, gradually develop into effectiveness in the course of the struggle.

The purity of conflict merely for conflict's sake, accordingly, under-goes adulteration, partly through the admixture of objective interests, partly by the introduction of impulses which may be satisfied other-wise than by struggle, and which, in practice, form a bridge between struggle and other forms of reciprocal relationship. I know in fact only a single case in which the stimulus of struggle and of victory in itself constitutes the exclusive motive, namely, the war game, and only in the case that no further gain is to arise than is included in the outcome of the game itself. In this case the pure sociological attrac-tion of self-assertion and predominance over another in a struggle of skill is combined with purely individual pleasure in the exercise of purposeful and successful activity, together with the excitement of taking risks with the hazard of fortune which stimulates us with a sense of mystic harmony of relationship to powers beyond the indi-vidual, as well as the social occurrences. At all events, the war game, *in its sociological motivation*, contains absolutely nothing but struggle itself. The worthless markers, for the sake of which men often play with the same earnestness with which they play for gold pieces, indicate the formalism of this impulse which, even in the play for gold pieces, often far outweighs the material interest. The thing to be noticed, however, is that, in order that the foregoing situations may occur, certain sociological forms—in the narrower sense, uni-fications—are presupposed. There must be agreement in order to struggle, and the struggle occurs under reciprocal recognition of norms and rules. In the motivation of the whole procedure these unifications, as said above, do not appear, but the whole transaction shapes itself under the forms which these explicit or implicit agree-ments furnish. They create the technique. Without this, such a conflict, excluding all heterogeneous or objective factors, would not be possible. Indeed, the conduct of the war game is often so rigorous, so impersonal, and observed on both sides with such nice sense of honor that unities of a corporate order can seldom in these respects compare with it.

b) Feud and faction.—The occasion for separate discussion of the feud is that here, instead of the consciousness of difference, an entirely new motive emerges—the peculiar phenomenon of social hatred, that is, of hatred toward a member of a group, not from personal motives, but because he threatens the existence of the group.

In so far as such a danger threatens through feud within the group, the one party hates the other, not alone on the material ground which instigated the quarrel, but also on the sociological ground, namely, that we hate the enemy of the group as such; that is, the one from whom danger to its unity threatens. Inasmuch as this is a reciprocal matter, and each attributes the fault of endangering the whole to the other, the antagonism acquires a severity which does not occur when membership in a group-unity is not a factor in the situation. Most characteristic in this connection are the cases in which an actual dismemberment of the group has not yet occurred. If this dismemberment has already taken place, it signifies a certain termination of the conflict. The individual difference has found its sociological termination, and the stimulus to constantly renewed friction is removed. To this result the tension between antagonism and still persisting unity must directly work. As it is fearful to be at enmity with a person to whom one is nevertheless bound, from whom one cannot be freed, whether externally or subjectively, even if one will, so there is increased bitterness if one will not detach himself from the community because he is not willing to give up the value of membership in the containing unity, or because he feels this unity as an objective good, the threatening of which deserves conflict and hatred. From such a correlation as this springs the embittering with which, for example, quarrels are fought out within a political faction or a trade union or a family.

The individual soul offers an analogy. The feeling that a conflict between sensuous and ascetic feelings, or selfish and moral impulses, or practical and intellectual ambitions, within us not merely lowers the claims of one or both parties and permits neither to come to quite free self-realization but also threatens the unity, the equilibrium, and the total energy of the soul as a whole—this feeling may in many cases repress conflict from the beginning. In case the feeling cannot avail to that extent, it, on the contrary, impresses upon the conflict a character of bitterness and desperation, an emphasis as though a struggle were really taking place for something much more essential than the immediate issue of the controversy. The energy with which each of these tendencies seeks to subdue the others is nourished not only by their egoistic interest but by the interest which goes much farther than that and attaches itself to the unity of the ego, for which this struggle means dismemberment and destruction if it does not end with a victory for unity. Accordingly, struggle within a closely integrated group often enough grows beyond the measure which its object and its immediate interest for the parties could justify. The feeling accumulates that this struggle is an affair not merely of the party but of the group as a whole; that each party must hate in its opponent, not an opponent merely, but at the same time the enemy of its higher sociological unity.

c) *Litigation.*—Moreover, what we are accustomed to call the joy and passion of conflict in the case of a legal process is probably, in most cases, something quite different, namely, the energetic sense of justice, the impossibility of tolerating an actual or supposed invasion of the sphere of right with which the ego feels a sense of solidarity. The whole obstinacy and uncompromising persistence with which parties in such struggles often maintain the controversy to their own hurt has, even in the case of the aggressive party, scarcely the character of an attack in the proper sense, but rather of a defense in a deeper significance. The point at issue is the self-preservation of the personality which so identifies itself with its possessions and its rights that any invasion of them seems to be a destruction of the personality; and the struggle to protect them at the risk of the whole existence is thoroughly consistent. This individualistic impulse, and not the sociological motive of struggle, will consequently characterize such cases.

With respect to the form of the struggle itself, however, judicial conflict is, to be sure, of an absolute sort; that is, the reciprocal claims are asserted with a relentless objectivity and with employment of all available means, without being diverted or modified by personal or other extraneous considerations. The judicial conflict is, therefore, absolute conflict in so far as nothing enters the whole action which does not properly belong in the conflict and which does not serve the ends of conflict; whereas, otherwise, even in the most savage struggles, something subjective, some pure freak of fortune, some sort of interposition from a third side, is at least possible. In the legal struggle everything of the kind is excluded by the matter-of-factness with which the contention, and absolutely nothing outside the contention, is kept in view. This exclusion from the judicial controversy of everything which is not material to the conflict may to be sure, lead to a formalism of the struggle which may come to have an independent character in contrast with the content itself. This occurs, on the one hand, when real elements are not weighed against each other at all. but only quite abstract notions maintain controversy with each other. On the other hand, the controversy is often shifted to elements which have no relation whatever to the subject which is to be decided by the struggle. Where legal controversies, accordingly, in higher civilizations are fought out by attorneys, the device serves to abstract the controversy from all personal associations which are essentially irrelevant. If, on the other hand, Otto the Great ordains that a legal controversy shall be settled by judicial duel between professional fighters, there remains of the whole struggle of interests only the bare form, namely, that there shall be struggle and victory.

This latter case portrays, in the exaggeration of caricature, the reduction of the judicial conflict to the mere struggle element. But precisely through its pure objectivity because it stands quite beyond the subjective antitheses of pity and cruelty, this unpitying type of struggle, as a whole, rests on the presupposition of a unity and a community of the parties never elsewhere so severely and constantly maintained. The common subordination to the law, the reciprocal recognition that the decision can be made only according to the objective weight of the evidence, the observance of forms which are held to be inviolable by both parties, the consciousness throughout the whole procedure of being encompassed by a social power and order which are the means of giving to the procedure its significance and security—all this makes the legal controversy rest upon a broad basis of community and consensus between the opponents. It is really a unity of a lesser degree which is constituted by the parties to a compact or to a commercial transaction, a presupposition of which is the recognition, along with the antithesis of interests, that they are subject to certain common, constraining, and obligatory rules. The common presuppositions, which exclude everything that is merely personal from the legal controversy, have that character of pure objectivity to which, on its side, the sharpness, the inexorableness, and the absoluteness of the species of struggle correspond. The reciprocity between the dualism and the unity of the sociological relationship is accordingly shown by the judicial struggle not less than by the war game. Precisely the most extreme and unlimited phases of struggle occur in both cases, since the struggle is surrounded and maintained by the severe unity of common norms and limitations.

d) The conflict of impersonal ideals.—Finally, there is the situation in which the parties are moved by an objective interest; that is, where the interest of the struggle, and consequently the struggle itself, is differentiated from the personality. The consciousness of being merely the representative of superindividual claims—that is, of fighting not for self but only for the thing itself—may lend to the struggle a radicalism and mercilessness which have their analogy in the total conduct of many very unselfish and high-minded men. Because they grant themselves no consideration, they likewise have none for others and hold themselves entirely justified in sacrificing everybody else to the idea to which they are themselves a sacrifice. Such a struggle, into which all the powers of the person are thrown, while victory accrues only to the cause, carries the character of respectability, for the reputable man is the wholly personal, who, however, understands how to hold his personality entirely in check. Hence objectivity operates as *noblesse*. When, however, this differentiation is accomplished, and struggle is objectified, it is not subjected to a further reserve, which would be quite inconsistent; indeed, that would be a sin against the content of the interest itself upon which the struggle had been localized. On the basis of this common element between the parties—namely, that each defends merely the issue and its right, and excludes from consideration everything selfishly personal—the struggle is fought out without the sharpness, but also without the mollifyings, which come from intermingling of the personal element. Merely the immanent logic of the situation is obeyed with absolute precision. This form of antithesis between unity and antagonism intensifies conflict perhaps most perceptibly in cases where both parties actually pursue one and the same purpose; for example, in the case of scientific controversies, in which the issue is the establishment of the truth. In such a case, every concession, every polite consent to stop short of exposing the errors of the opponent in the most unpitying fashion, every conclusion of peace previous to decisive victory, would be treason against that reality for the sake of which the personal element is excluded from the conflict.

With endless varieties otherwise, the social struggles since Marx have developed themselves in the above form. Since it is recognized that the situation of laborers is determined by the objective organization and formulas of the productive system, independent of the will and power of individual persons, the personal embitterment incident to the struggle in general and to local conflicts exemplifying the general conflict necessarily diminishes. The entrepreneur is no longer, as such, a blood-sucker and damnable egotist; the laborer is no longer universally assumed to act from sinful greed; both parties begin, at least, to abandon the program of charging the other with demands and tactics inspired by personal malevolence. This literalizing of the conflict has come about in Germany rather along the lines of theory; in England, through the operation of the trade unions, in the course of which the individually personal element of the antagonism has been overcome. In Germany this was effected largely through the more abstract generalization of the historical and class movement. In England it came about through the severe superindividual unity in the actions of the unions and of the combinations of employers. The intensity of the struggle, however, has not on that account diminished. On the contrary, it has become much more conscious of its purpose, more concentrated, and at the same time more aggressive, through the consciousness of the individual that he is struggling not merely, and often not at all, for himself but rather for a vast superpersonal end.

A most interesting symptom of this correlation was presented by the boycotting of the Berlin breweries by the labor body in the year 1894. This was one of the most intense local struggles of the last decade. It was carried on by both sides with extraordinary energy, yet without any personal offensiveness on either side toward the other, although the stimulus was close at hand. Indeed, two of the party leaders, in the midst of the struggle, published their opinions about it in the same journal. They agreed in their formulation of the objective facts, and disagreed in a partisan spirit only in the practical conclusions drawn from the facts. Inasmuch as the struggle eliminated everything irrelevantly personal, and thereby restricted antagonism quantitatively, facilitating an understanding about everything personal, producing a recognition of being impelled on both sides by historical necessities, this common basis did not reduce but rather increased, the intensity, the irreconcilability, and the obstinate consistency of the struggle.

B.   WAR, INSTINCTS, AND IDEALS

1.   War and Human Nature[1]

What can be said of the causes of war—not its political and economic causes, nor yet the causes that are put forth by the nations engaged in the conflict, but its psychological causes?

The fact that war to no small extent removes cultural repressions and allows the instincts to come to expression in full force is undoubtedly a considerable factor.   In his unconscious man really takes pleasure in throwing aside restraints and permitting himself the luxury of the untrammeled expression of his primitive animal tendencies.   The social conventions, the customs, the forms, and institutions which he has built up in the path of his cultural progress represent so much energy in the service of repression. Repression represents continuous effort, while a state of war permits a relaxation of this effort and therefore relief.

We are familiar, in other fields, with the phenomena of the unconscious, instinctive tendencies breaking through the bounds imposed upon them by repression.   The phenomena of crime and of so-called "insanity" represent such examples, while drunkenness is one instance familiar to all.   *In vino veritas* expresses the state of the drunken man when his real, that is, his primitive, self frees itself from restraint and runs riot.   The psychology of the crowd shows this mechanism at work, particularly in such sinister instances as lynching, while every crowd of college students marching yelling and howling down the main street of the town after a successful cane rush exhibits the joy of unbottling the emotions in ways that no individual would for a moment think of availing himself.

In addition to these active demonstrations of the unconscious there are those of a more passive sort.   Not a few men are only too glad to step aside from the burden of responsibilities which they are forced to carry and seek refuge in a situation in which they no longer have to take the initiative but must only do as they are directed by a superior authority.   The government in some of its agencies takes

[1] Adapted from William A. White, *Thoughts of a Psychiatrist on the War and After*, pp. 75–87.   (Paul B. Hoeber, 1919.)

over certain of their obligations, such as the support of wife and children, and they clear out, free from the whole sordid problem of poverty, into a situation filled with dramatic interest. Then, too, if anything goes wrong at home they are not to blame, they have done their best, and what they have done meets with public approval. Is it any wonder that an inhabitant of the slums should be glad to exchange poverty and dirt, a sick wife and half-starved children, for glorious freedom, especially when he is urged by every sort of appeal to patriotism and duty to do so?

But all these are individual factors that enter into the causes of war. They represent some of the reasons why men like to fight, for it is difficult not to believe that if no one wanted to fight war would be possible at all. They too represent the darker side of the picture. War as already indicated offers, on the positive side, the greatest opportunities for the altruistic tendencies; it offers the most glorious occasion for service and returns for such acts the greatest possible premium in social esteem. But it seems to me that the causes of war lie much deeper, that they involve primarily the problems of the herd rather than the individual, and I think there are good biological analogies which make this highly probable.

The mechanism of integration explains how the development of the group was dependent upon the subordination of the parts to the whole. This process of integration tends to solve more and more effectively the problems of adjustment, particularly in some aspects, in the direction of ever-increasing stability. It is the process of the structuralization of function. This increase in stability, however, while it has the advantage of greater certainty of reaction, has the disadvantage of a lessened capacity for variation, and so is dependent for its efficiency upon a stable environment. As long as nothing unusual is asked of such a mechanism it works admirably, but as soon as the unusual arises it tends to break down completely. Life, however, is not stable; it is fluid, in a continuous state of flux, so, while the development of structure to meet certain demands of adaptation is highly desirable and necessary, it of necessity has limits which must sooner or later be reached in every instance. The most typical example of this is the process of growing old. The child is highly adjustable and for that reason not to be depended upon; the adult is more dependable but less adjustable; the old man has become stereotyped in his reactions. Nature's solution of this *impasse* is death. Death insures the continual removal of the no longer adjustable, and the places of those who die are filled by new material capable of the new demands. But it is the means that nature takes to secure the renewal of material still capable of adjustment that is of significance. From each adult sometime during the course of his life nature provides that a small bit shall be detached which, in the higher animals, in union with a similar detached bit of another individual will develop into a child and ultimately be ready to replace the adult when he becomes senile and dies. Life is thus maintained by a continuous stream of germ plasm and is not periodically interrupted in its course, as it seems to be, by death.

The characteristics of this detached bit of germ plasm are interesting. It does not manifest any of that complicated structure which we meet with in the other parts of the body. The several parts of the body are highly differentiated, each for a specific function. Gland cells are developed to secrete, muscle cells to contract, bone cells to withstand mechanical stresses, etc. Manifestly development along any one of these lines would not produce an individual possessing, in its several parts, all of these qualities. Development has to go back of the point of origin of these several variations in order to include them all. In other words, regeneration has to start with relatively undifferentiated material. This is excellently illustrated by many of the lower, particularly the unicellular, animals, in which reproduction is not yet sexual, but by the simple method of division. A cell comes to rest, divides into two, and each half then leads an independent existence. Before such a division and while the cell is quiescent—in the resting stage, as it is called—the differentiations of structure which it had acquired in its lifetime disappear; it becomes undifferentiated, relatively simple in structure. This process has been called dedifferentiation. When all the differentiations which had been acquired have been eliminated, then division—rejuvenescence—takes place.

From this point of view we may see in war the preliminary process of rejuvenescence. International adjustments and compromises are made until they can be made no longer; a condition is brought about which in Europe has been termed the balance of power, until the situation becomes so complicated that each new adjustment has such wide ramifications that it threatens the whole structure. Finally, as the result of the accumulated structure of diplomatic relations and precedents, a situation arises to which adjustment, with the machinery that has been developed, is impossible and the whole house of cards collapses. The collapse is a process of dedifferentiation during which the old structures are destroyed, precedents are disavowed, new situations occur with bewildering rapidity, for dealing with which there is no recognized machinery available. Society reverts from a state in which a high grade of individual initiative and development was possible to a relatively communistic and paternalistic state, the slate is wiped clear, and a start can be made anew along lines of progress mapped out by the new conditions—rejuvenescence is possible.

War, from this point of view, is a precondition for development along new lines of necessity, and the dedifferentiation is the first stage of a constructive process. Old institutions have to be torn down before the bricks with which they were built can be made available for new structures. This accounts for the periodicity of war, which thus is the outward and evident aspect of the progress of the life-force which in human societies, as elsewhere, advances in cycles. It is only by such means that an *impasse* can be overcome.

War is an example of ambivalency on the grandest scale. That is, it is at once potent for the greatest good and the greatest evil: in the very midst of death it calls for the most intense living; in the face of the greatest renunciation it offers the greatest premium; for the maximum of freedom it demands the utmost giving of one's self; in order to live at one's best it demands the giving of life itself. "No man has reached his ethical majority who would not die if the real interests of the community could thus be furthered. What would the world be without the values that have been bought at the price of death?" In this sense the great creative force, love, and the supreme negation, death, become one. That the larger life of the race should go forward to greater things, the smaller life of the individual must perish. In order that man shall be born again, he must first die.

Does all this necessarily mean that war, from time to time, in the process of readjustment, is essential? I think no one can doubt that it has been necessary in the past. Whether it will be in the future depends upon whether some sublimated form of procedure can adequately be substituted. We have succeeded to a large extent in dealing with our combative instincts by developing sports and the competition of business, and we have largely sublimated our hate instinct in dealing with various forms of anti-social conduct as exhibited in the so-called "criminal." It remains to be seen whether nations can unite to a similar end and perhaps, by the establishment of an international court, and by other means, deal in a similar way with infractions of international law.

2. War as a Form of Relaxation[1]

The fact is that it does not take a very careful reader of the human mind to see that all the utopias and all the socialistic schemes are based on a mistaken notion of the nature of this mind.

It is by no means sure that what man wants is peace and quiet and tranquillity. That is too close to ennui, which is his greatest dread. What man wants is not peace but a battle. He must pit his force against someone or something. Every language is most rich in synonyms for battle, war, contest, conflict, quarrel, combat, fight. German children play all day long with their toy soldiers. Our sports take the form of contests in football, baseball, and hundreds of others. Prize fights, dog fights, cock fights, have pleased in all ages. When Rome for a season was not engaged in real war, Claudius staged a sea fight for the delectation of an immense concourse, in which 19,000 gladiators were compelled to take a tragic part, so that the ships were broken to pieces and the waters of the lake were red with blood.

You may perhaps recall Professor James's astonishing picture of his visit to a Chautauqua. Here he found modern culture at its best, no poverty, no drunkenness, no zymotic diseases, no crime, no police, only polite and refined and harmless people. Here was a middle-class paradise, kindergarten and model schools, lectures and classes and music, bicycling and swimming, and culture and kindness

[1] From G. T. W. Patrick, "The Psychology of War," in the *Popular Science Monthly*, LXXXVII (1915), 166–68.

and elysian peace. But at the end of a week he came out into the real world, and he said:

Ouf! What a relief! Now for something primordial and savage, even though it were as bad as an Armenian massacre, to set the balance straight again. This order is too tame, this culture too second-rate, this goodness too uninspiring. This human drama, without a villain or a pang; this community so refined that ice-cream soda-water is the utmost offering it can make to the brute animal in man; this city simmering in the tepid lakeside sun; this atrocious harmlessness of all things—I cannot abide with them.

What men want, he says, is something more precipitous, something with more zest in it, with more adventure. Nearly all the utopias paint the life of the future as a kind of giant Chautauqua, in which every man and woman is at work, all are well fed, satisfied, and cultivated. But as man is now constituted he would probably find such a life flat, stale, and unprofitable.

Man is not originally a working animal. Civilization has imposed work upon man, and if you work him too hard he will quit work and go to war. Nietzsche says man wants two things—danger and play. War represents danger.

It follows that all our social utopias are wrongly conceived. They are all based on a theory of pleasure economy. But history and evolution show that man has come up from the lower animals through a pain economy. He has struggled up—fought his way up through never-ceasing pain and effort and struggle and battle. The utopias picture a society in which man has ceased to struggle. He works his eight hours a day—everybody works—and he sleeps and enjoys himself the other hours. But man is not a working animal, he is a fighting animal. The utopias are ideal—but they are not psychological. The citizens for such an ideal social order are lacking. Human beings will not serve.

Our present society tends more and more in its outward form in time of peace toward the Chautauqua plan, but meanwhile striving and passion burn in the brain of the human units, till the time comes when they find this insipid life unendurable. They resort to amusement crazes, to narcotic drugs. to political strife, to epidemics of crime, and finally to war. The alcohol question well illustrates the tendencies we are pointing out. Science and hygiene have at last shown beyond all question that alcohol, whether in large or smaller doses, exerts a damaging effect upon both mind and body. It lessens physical and mental efficiency, shortens life, and encourages social disorder. In spite of this fact and, what is still more amazing, in spite of the colossal effort now being put forth to suppress by legislative means the traffic in liquor, the per capita consumption of alcoholic drinks in the United States increases from year to year. From a per capita consumption of four gallons in 1850, it has steadily risen to nearly twenty-five gallons in 1913.

Narcotic drugs, such as alcohol and tobacco, relieve in an artificial way the tension upon the brain by slightly paralyzing temporarily the higher and more recently developed brain centers. The increase in the use of these drugs is therefore both an index of the tension of modern life and at the same time a means of relieving it to some extent. Were the use of these drugs suddenly checked, no student of psychology or of history could doubt that there would be an immediate increase of social irritability, tending to social instability and social upheavals.

Psychology, therefore, forces upon us this conclusion. Neither war nor alcohol can be banished from the world by summary means nor direct suppressions. The mind of man must be made over. As the mind of man is constituted, he will never be content to be a mere laborer, a producer and a consumer. He loves adventure, self-sacrifice, heroism, relaxation.

These things must somehow be provided. And then there must be a system of education of our young differing widely from our present system. The new education will not look to efficiency merely and ever more efficiency, but to the production of a harmonized and balanced personality. We must cease our worship of American efficiency and German *Streberthum* and go back to Aristotle and his teaching of "the mean."

3. The Fighting Animal and the Great Society[1]

We must agree that man as he has existed, so far as we can read the story of his development, has been, and as he exists today still is, a fighting animal—that is to say that he has in the past answered,

[1] Adapted from Henry Rutgers Marshall, *War and the Ideal of Peace*, pp. 96–110. (Duffield & Co., 1915.)

and still answers, certain stimuli by the immediate reactions which constitute fighting.

We find evidence of the existence of this fighting instinct in the ordinary men around us. Remove but for a moment the restraints given in our civilized lands and this tendency is likely to become prominent upon the slightest stimulation. We see this exemplified in the lives of the pioneer and adventurer the world over: in that of the cowboy of the far West, in that of the rubber collector on the Amazon, in that of the ivory trader on the Congo.

Then, too, the prize fighter is still a prominent person in our community, taken as a whole, and even in our sports, as engaged in by "gentlemen amateurs," we find it necessary to make rigid rules to prevent the friendly contest from developing into a fierce struggle for individual physical dominance.

But man gained his pre-eminent position among the animals mainly through his ability to form co-operative groups working to common ends; and long before the times of which anthropological research give us any clear knowledge, man had turned his individualistic fighting instincts to the service of his group or clan. That is to say, he had become a warrior, giving his best strength to co-operative aggression in behalf of satisfactions that could not be won by him as an individual acting for himself.

Our earlier studies have taught us also that if man's instinctive tendencies could in any manner be inhibited or modified, so that he came to display other characteristics than those observed in the present expression of these inborn instincts, then the law of his nature would in that very fact be changed. We are thus led to ask whether the biologist finds evidence that an animal's instincts can be thus changed in mode of expression.

The biologist speaks to us somewhat as follows. Although new racial characteristics have very rarely, if ever, been gained by the obliteration of instincts, changes in racial characteristics have not infrequently occurred as the result of the control, rather than the loss, of these inherited instincts.

This control may become effective in either one of two ways: first, by the thwarting or inhibition of the expression of the instincts; or secondly, by the turning of its expression to other uses than that which originally resulted in its fixation.

As an example of the thwarting of the expression of an instinct we may take the functioning of the sexual instinct, which, as we see it in animals in general, has been inhibited in the human animal by the habits acquired by man as he has risen in the scale.

This mode of change—that of the mere chaining of the instinctive tendency—is subject to one great difficulty. The chain may by chance be broken; the inhibition may be removed; then the natural instinctive tendency at once shows itself. Remove the restraints of civilized society but a little, and manifestations of the sexual instinct of our race appear in forms that are not far removed from those observed in the animal. Place a man under conditions of starvation and he shows himself as greedy as the dog.

The second mode of change—that of the transference of functioning of the instincts into new channels—meets this special difficulty, for it does not depend upon the chaining of the instinct. It actually makes use of the instinct. And the more important to the race the newer reference of the instinct's functioning turns out to be, the more certain is it to replace the original reference. If the new mode of functioning brings marked advantage that is lost by reversion to the earlier manifestation of the instinct, so that such a reversion to this earlier manifestation is a detriment to the race, then the change is likely to become a permanent one.

No better example of this second mode of change of an instinct's functioning can be found than in the very existence of war itself. The basic instinct is one that led the savage man to fight to protect himself or to gain something for himself by aggressive attack. War has come into being as the result of a transfer of the functioning of this instinct, which at first had only an individualistic reference, so that it has come to have a clan or national reference. The early man found he could not have success as an individual unless he joined with his fellow-men in defense and aggression; and that meant war.

And note that this transfer of reference of the expression of this fighting instinct soon became so important to the race that reversion to its primal individualistic reference had to be inhibited. Aggressive attack by an individual upon another of his own clan or nation necessarily tended to weaken the social unit and to reduce its strength in its protective and aggressive wars; and thus such attacks by individuals came to be discountenanced and finally in large measure repressed.

Here, it will be observed, the fighting instinct of the individual has not been obliterated; it has not even been bound with chains; but its modes of expression have been altered to have racial significance, and to have so great a significance in this new relation that reversion to its primary form of expression has become a serious obstacle to racial advance.

So it appears after all that, although instincts can rarely if ever be obliterated, their manifestations may be so altered as to give the animal quite new characteristics. And this means that if the characteristics which we describe as the expressions of man's fighting instincts could be so changed that these expressions were inhibited or turned into quite new channels, the man would no longer be describable as a fighting animal.

The first indication in our conscious life of any tendency to inhibit or modify the functioning of any instinct or habit must appear in the form of a dislike of, a revulsion from, the resultants of this functioning; and in the creation of án ideal of functioning that shall avoid the discomforts attendant upon this revulsion. And when such an ideal has once been gained, it is possible, as we have seen, that the characteristics of nature may be changed by our creative efficiency through the devising of means looking to the realization of the ideal.

We have the clearest evidence that this process is developing in connection with these special instincts that make for war; for we men and women in these later times are repelled by the results of the functioning of these fighting instincts, and we have created the ideal of peace, the conception of a condition that is not now realized in nature, but which we think of as possible of realization.

But the very existence of an ideal is indicative of a tendency, on the part of the man who entertains it, to modify his characteristic activities. Thus it appears that we have in the very existence of this ideal of peace the evidence that we may look for a change in man's nature, the result of which will be that we shall no longer be warranted in describing him as a fighting animal.

C. RIVALRY, CULTURAL CONFLICTS, AND SOCIAL ORGANIZATION

1. Animal Rivalry[1]

Among mammals the instinct of one and all is to lord it over the others, with the result that the one more powerful or domineering gets the mastery, to keep it thereafter as long as he can. The lower animals are, in this respect, very much like us; and in all kinds that are at all fierce-tempered the mastery of one over all, and of a few under him over the others, is most salutary; indeed, it is inconceivable that they should be able to exist together under any other system.

On cattle-breeding establishments on the pampas, where it is usual to keep a large number of fierce-tempered dogs, I have observed these animals a great deal and presume they are much like feral dogs and wolves in their habits. Their quarrels are incessant; but when a fight begins, the head of the pack as a rule rushes to the spot, whereupon the fighters separate and march off in different directions or else cast themselves down and deprecate their tyrant's wrath with abject gestures and whines. If the combatants are both strong and have worked themselves into a mad rage before their head puts in an appearance, it may go hard with him; they know him no longer and all he can do is to join in the fray; then if the fighters turn on him he may be so injured that his power is gone and the next best dog in the pack takes his place. The hottest contests are always between dogs that are well matched; neither will give place to the other and so they fight it out; but from the foremost in power down to the weakest there is a gradation of authority; each one knows just how far he can go, which companion he can bully when he is in a bad temper or wishes to assert himself, and to which he must humbly yield in his turn. In such a state the weakest one must yield to all the others and cast himself down, seeming to call himself a slave and worshiper of any other member of the pack that chances to snarl at him or command him to give up his bone with good grace.

This masterful or domineering temper, so common among social mammals, is the cause of the persecution of the sick and weakly. When an animal begins to ail he can no longer hold his own; he ceases to resent the occasional ill-natured attacks made on him; his non-

[1] Adapted from William H. Hudson, "The Strange Instincts of Cattle," *Longman's Magazine*, XVIII (1891), 393–94.

combative condition is quickly discovered, and he at once drops down to a place below the lowest; it is common knowledge in the herd that he may be buffeted with impunity by all, even by those that have hitherto suffered buffets but have given none. But judging from my own observation, this persecution is not, as a rule, severe, and is seldom fatal.

2. The Rivalry of Social Groups[1]

Conflict, competition, and rivalry are the chief causes which force human beings into groups and largely determine what goes on within them. Conflicts, like wars, revolutions, riots, still persist, but possibly they may be thought of as gradually yielding to competitions which are chiefly economic. Many of these strivings seem almost wholly individual, but most of them on careful analysis turn out to be intimately related to group competition. A third form, rivalry, describes struggle for status, for social prestige, for the approval of inclusive publics which form the spectators for such contests. The nation is an arena of competition and rivalry.

Much of this emulation is of a concealed sort. Beneath the union services of churches there is an element, for the most part unconscious, of rivalry to secure the approval of a public which in these days demands brotherliness and good will rather than proselyting and polemics. Many public subscriptions for a common cause are based upon group rivalry or upon individual competition which is group-determined. The Rhodes scholarships are in one sense a means of furthering imperial interest. Christmas presents lavished upon children often have a bearing upon the ambition of the family to make an impression upon rival domestic groups. In the liberal policy of universities which by adding to the list of admission subjects desire to come into closer relations with the public schools, there is some trace of competition for students and popular applause. The interest which nations manifest in the Hague Tribunal is tinged with a desire to gain the good will of the international, peace-praising public. The professed eagerness of one or both parties in a labor dispute to have the differences settled by arbitration is a form of competition for the favor of the onlooking community. Thus in

[1] Adapted from George E. Vincent, "The Rivalry of Social Groups," in the *American Journal of Sociology*, XVI (1910-11), 471-84.

international relationships and in the life-process of each nation count-less groups are in conflict, competition, or rivalry.

This idea of the group seeking survival, mastery, aggrandizement, prestige, in its struggles with other groups is a valuable means of interpretation. Let us survey rapidly the conditions of success as a group carries on its life of strife and emulation. In order to survive or to succeed the group must organize, cozen, discipline, and stimulate its members. Fortunately it finds human nature in a great measure fashioned for control.

Collective pride or group egotism is an essential source of strength in conflict. Every efficient group cultivates this sense of honor, importance, superiority, by many devices of symbol, phrase, and legend, as well as by scorn and ridicule of rivals. The college fraternity's sublime self-esteem gives it strength in its competition for members and prestige. There is a chauvinism of "boom" towns and religious sects, as well as of nations. What pride and self-confidence are to the individual, ethnocentrism, patriotism, local loyalty are to social unities. Diffidence, humility, self-distrust, toler-ance, are as dangerous to militant groups as to fighting men.

Then too the group works out types of personality, hero types to be emulated, traitor types to be execrated. These personality types merge into abstract ideals and standards. "Booster" and "knocker" bring up pictures of a struggling community which must preserve its hopefulness and self-esteem at all hazards. "Statesman" and "dema-gogue" recall the problem of selection which every self-governing community must face. "Defender of the faith" and "heretic" are eloquent of the Church's dilemma between rigid orthodoxy and flexible accommodation to a changing order.

With a shifting in the conflict or rivalry crises, types change in value or emphasis, or new types are created in adjustment to the new needs. The United States at war with Spain sought martial heroes. The economic and political ideals of personality, the cap-tains of industry, the fascinating financiers, the party idols, were for the time retired to make way for generals and admirals, soldiers and sailors, the heroes of camp and battleship. The war once over, the displaced types reappeared along with others which are being created to meet new administrative, economic, and ethical problems. The competing church retires its militant and disputatious leaders in an age which gives its applause to apostles of concord, fraternal feeling, and co-operation. At a given time the heroes and traitors of a group reflect its competitions and rivalries with other groups.

Struggle forces upon the group the necessity of cozening, beguiling, managing its members. The vast majority of these fall into a broad zone of mediocrity which embodies group character and represents a general adjustment to life-conditions. From this medial area individuals vary, some in ways which aid the group in its competition, others in a fashion which imperils group success. It is the task of the group both to preserve the solidarity of the medial zone and to discriminate between the serviceable and the menacing variants. The latter must be coerced or suppressed, the former encouraged and given opportunity. In Plato's *Republic* the guardians did this work of selection which in modern groups is cared for by processes which seem only slightly conscious and purposeful.

The competing group in seeking to insure acquiescence and loyalty elaborates a protective philosophy by which it creates within its members the belief that their lot is much to be preferred to that of other comradeships and associations. Western Americans take satisfaction in living in a free, progressive, hospitable way in "God's country." They try not to be pharisaical about the narrowness of the East, but they achieve a sincere scorn for the hidebound conventions of an effete society. Easterners in turn count themselves fortunate in having a highly developed civilization, and they usually attain real pity for those who seem to live upon a psychic, if not a geographic, frontier. The middle class have a philosophy with which they protect themselves against the insidious suggestions that come from the life of the conspicuous rich. These, on the other hand, half suspecting that simplicity and domesticity may have some virtue, speak superciliously of middle-class smugness and the bourgeois "home." The less prosperous of the professional classes are prone to lay a good deal of stress upon their intellectual resources as compared with the presumptive spiritual poverty of the affluent. Country folk encourage themselves by asserting their fundamental value to society and by extolling their own simple straightforward virtues, which present so marked a contrast to the devious machinations of city-dwellers. Booker Washington's reiterated assertion that if he were to be born again he would choose to be a Negro because the Negro race is the only one which has a great problem contains a suggestion of this protective philosophy. This tendency of a group to fortify itself by a satisfying theory of its lot is obviously related to group egotism and is immediately connected with group rivalry.

The competing group derides many a dissenter into conformity. This derision may be spontaneous, or reflective and concerted. The loud guffaw which greets one who varies in dress or speech or idea may come instantly or there may be a planned and co-operative ridicule systematically applied to the recalcitrant. Derision is one of the most effective devices by which the group sifts and tests the variants.

Upon the small number of rebels who turn a deaf ear to epithets, ostracism is brought to bear. This may vary from the "cold shoulder" to the complete "boycott." Losing the friendship and approval of comrades, being cut off from social sympathy, is a familiar form of group pressure. Ridicule and derision are a kind of evanescent ostracism, a temporary exclusion from the comradeship. There are many degrees in the lowering of the social temperature: coolness, formality of intercourse, averted looks, "cutting dead," "sending to Coventry," form a progressive series. Economic pressure is more and more a resort of modern groups. Loss of employment, trade, or professional practice brings many a rebel to time. All coercion obviously increases as the group is hard pressed in its conflicts, competitions, and rivalries.

These crises and conflicts of a competing group present problems which must be solved—problems of organization, of inventions of many kinds, of new ideas and philosophies, of methods of adjustment. The conditions of competition or rivalry upset an equilibrium of habit and custom, and a process of problem-solving ensues. A typhoid epidemic forces the village to protect itself against the competition of a more healthful rival. The resourceful labor union facing a corporation which offers profit-sharing and retiring allowances must formulate a protective theory and practice. A society clique too closely imitated by a lower stratum must regain its distinction and supremacy. A nation must be constantly alert to adjust itself to the changing conditions of international trade and to the war equipment and training of its rivals.

The theory of group rivalry throws light upon the individual. The person has as many selves as there are groups to which he belongs. He is simple or complex as his groups are few and harmonious or many and conflicting. What skilful management is required to keep business and moral selves from looking each other in the eye, to prevent scientific and theological selves from falling into discussion! Most men of many groups learn, like tactful hosts, to invite at a given time only congenial companies of selves. A few brave souls resolve to set their house in order and to entertain only such selves as can live together with good will and mutual respect. With these earnest folk their groups have to reckon. The conflicts of conscience are group conflicts.

Tolerance is a sign that once vital issues within the group are losing their significance, or that the group feels secure, or that it is slowly, even unconsciously, merging into a wider grouping. Theological liberality affords a case in point. In the earlier days of sectarian struggle tolerance was a danger both to group loyalty and to the militant spirit. Cynicism for other reasons is also a menace. It means loss of faith in the collective ego, in the traditions, shibboleths, symbols, and destiny of the group. Fighting groups cannot be tolerant; nor can they harbor cynics. Tolerance and cynicism are at once causes and results of group decay. They portend dissolution or they foreshadow new groupings for struggle over other issues on another plane. Evangelical churches are drawing together with mutual tolerance to present a united front against modern skepticism and cynicism which are directed against the older faiths and moralities.

The subjective side of group rivalry offers an important study. The reflection of the process of control in personal consciousness is full of interest. The means by which the rebellious variant protects himself against the coercion of his comrades have been already suggested in the description of ridicule and epithet. These protective methods resolve themselves into setting one group against another in the mind of the derided or stigmatized individual.

A national group is to be thought of as an inclusive unity with a fundamental character, upon the basis of which a multitude of groups compete with and rival each other. It is the task of the nation to control and to utilize this group struggle, to keep it on as high a plane as possible, to turn it to the common account. Government gets its chief meaning from the rivalry of groups to grasp political power in their own interests. Aristocracy and democracy may be interpreted in terms of group antagonism, the specialized few versus the undifferentiated many. The ideal merges the two elements of efficiency and solidarity in one larger group within which mutual confidence and emulation take the place of conflict. Just as persons must be disciplined into serving their groups, groups must be subordinated to the welfare of the nation. It is in conflict or competition with other nations that a country becomes a vivid unity to the members of constituent groups. It is rivalry which brings out the sense of team work, the social consciousness.

3. The Gang and Political Organization[1]

The importance of the gang as a social factor which the politician manipulates has never been fully appreciated except by the politician. It is a sufficiently commonplace trait of human nature for people to associate themselves together in groups and cliques, according to the attractions of congeniality. This force, however, seems to work with great intensity in the tenement-house districts. Without pausing to inquire the reasons, I shall describe the structure of the gang, and later show its relation to ward politics.

The tendency begins among the children. Almost every boy in the tenement-house quarters of the district is member of a gang. The boy who does not belong to one is not only the exception, but the very rare exception. There are certain characteristics in the make-up and life of all gangs. To begin with, every gang has a "corner" where its members meet. This "hang out," as it is sometimes called, may be in the centre of a block, but still the gang speak of it as the "corner." The size of a gang varies: it may number five or forty. As a rule, all the boys composing it come from the immediate vicinity of the corner. . . . .

Nightly after supper the boys drift to their "corner," not by appointment, but naturally. Then ensue idle talk, "jawing matches," as one boy expressed it, rough jokes, and horse-play. No eccentric

[1] From "The Roots of Political Power" in *The City Wilderness, a Settlement Study* edited by Robert A. Woods, pp. 114–23. (Houghton, Mifflin & Company, Boston, 1898. Author's copyright.)

individual gets by the gang without insult. Nearly every gang has "talent": one or two members who can sing, perhaps a quartette; also a buck-dancer, one or two who can play on the jew's-harp, and a "funny man." I am referring now more particularly to boys over fourteen years old. As a rule, the boys stay around their corner, finding amusement in these ways. The songs are always new ones; old ones are scorned. Not infrequently the singing, the horse-play, or the dancing is interrupted by the roundsman. At the sight of the brass buttons, there is an excited call of "cheese it," and singing or talking, as it may be, is suddenly stopped; the gang disbands, dissolves, and the boys flee down alleyways, into doorsteps and curious hiding-places, and reappear only when the "cop" is well down the street.

It sometimes happens that members of the gang are arrested, for standing on the corners, for insulting passers-by, or for some other offense. As a rule, the other fellows raise the money to pay the fine To reimburse themselves or the one who loaned the money, a dance is "run" or a raffle is held. To show still further the *tenaciousness of gang life:* the influx of Jews has caused many of the Irish to move away from the South End to other parts of the city, but the boys on Sunday may be found with the gang at their corner. About thirty young men belonging to one of the gangs I know meet every Sunday afternoon at their corner. Of this number, fully half are fellows who live in the Highlands, at the edge of Roxbury. I know a boy in the High School—he will graduate next year—who moved to Dorchester, but comes regularly to the old corner on Sunday afternoon. No new friends can supplant the gang. It is little wonder. The life of the gang is exciting, melodramatic; the corner is full of associations, of jokes and songs and good times, of escapades planned and carried out. In comparison with this, the life of the suburb is tame.

It is interesting to know what becomes of these various gangs when the boys get to be seventeen or eighteen years old. The more respectable gangs, as a rule, club together and hire a room. The more vicious gangs prefer to use what little money they have in carousing. If by any chance they get a room, their rowdyism will cause their ejection either by the landlord or by the police. Consequently they have to fall back on the corner or some saloon, as their meeting-place. They nearly always seek a back street or the wharves, unfrequented by the police. . . . .

At this point, it is necessary to give some account of the *young men's clubs*, in order that the important part that these clubs play in ward politics may be seen; for all this network of social life is taken in hand by the politician. As I said before, the gangs which coalesce and form these clubs are the most respectable ones. They are led to do this partly through a desire to have a warm room, and partly because they are tired of standing on the corner and meeting the rebuffs of the policeman. Then such a club opens up the freedom of the district, socially, to them. . . . .

Nearly all of the clubs have a common programme. In the first place, *each club*, without any exception, *gives a ball* each winter in some large hall. The tickets invariably sell for fifty cents. These balls are important social functions in the district. As a rule, they are well managed financially, one club clearing $165 last winter. Then besides this annual ball, each club has a "social" once a week. This is a dance of a lower type than the balls, being interspersed with comic songs, humorous recitations, and buck-dancing. About the same class of girls attend all the socials; they go from one club to the other. Almost without exception they are factory girls, and nearly all of them are bold and vulgar. It is a curious fact that the members do not want their sisters to attend these dances; and their custom is to leave the girls with whom they have danced before they reach the street. . . . .

Another feature of these clubs is the smoke talks. They are always held on holidays, and sometimes on Sundays. Several barrels of beer are on tap; and tonic is ordered for abstainers, but they are few. The smoke talk usually begins in the afternoon, and lasts as long as the beer does. When the end comes, those who are sober are in the minority. For entertainment there are comic songs and buck-dances, but the principal feature is the story-telling. . . . .

The worst *dance halls* are very nearly allied to the clubs, for all the halls have their special clientage. This clientage, like the club, is made up, though not so distinctly, of gangs. Consequently at nearly all the halls, the dancers are known to one another, and have more or less loyalty for the hall. . . . .

In addition to these social groups which taken on a political character at election time, there are usually in the tenement-house sections several distinctly political clubs. Standing at the head of these clubs is the "*machine club.*" It is now quite the custom of those in control of the party, and known as the "machine," to have such an organization. All the men in the ward having good political jobs are members. In one local club it is estimated that the City employees belonging to it draw salaries to the amount of $30,000 per year; in another club, outside the district, $80,000. It is natural that all the men in these clubs are anxious to maintain the machine. It is a question of bread and butter with them. In addition to City employees the various machine workers are enrolled. The room of the club is ordinarily very pleasant. There are, of course, in these clubs the usual social attractions, among other things poker and drinking. At the head of the club stands the boss of the ward.

4. Cultural Conflicts and the Organization of Sects[1]

It is assumed, I suppose, that contradictions among ideas and beliefs are of various degrees and of various modes besides that specific one which we call logical incompatibility. A perception, for example, may be pictorially inconsistent or tonically discordant with another perception; a mere faith unsupported by objective evidence may be emotionally antagonistic to another mere faith, as truly as a judgment may be logically irreconcilable with another judgment. And this wide possibility of contradiction is particularly to be recognized when the differing ideas or beliefs have arisen not within the same individual mind but in different minds, and are therefore colored by personal or partisan interest and warped by idiosyncrasy of mental constitution. The contradictions of, or rather *among*, ideas and beliefs, with which we are now concerned, are more extensive and more varied than mere logical duels; they are also less definite, less precise. In reality they are culture conflicts in which the opposing forces, so far from being specific ideas only or pristine beliefs only, are in fact more or less bewildering complexes of ideas, beliefs, prejudices, sympathies, antipathies, and personal interests.

It is assumed also, I suppose, that any idea or group of ideas, any belief or group of beliefs, may happen to be or may become a common interest, shared by a small or a large number of individuals.

[1] Adapted from Franklin H. Giddings, "Are Contradictions of Ideas and Beliefs Likely to Play an Important Group-making Rôle in the Future?" in the *American Journal of Sociology*, XIII (1907-8), 784-91.

It may draw and hold them together in bonds of acquaintance, of association, even of co-operation. It thus may play a group-making rôle. Contradictory ideas or beliefs, therefore, may play a group-making rôle in a double sense. Each draws into association the individual minds that entertain it or find it attractive. Each also repels those minds to whom it is repugnant, and drives them toward the group which is being formed about the contradictory idea or belief. Contradictions among ideas and beliefs, then, it may be assumed, tend on the whole to sharpen the lines of demarcation between group and group.

These assumptions are, I suppose, so fully justified by the everyday observation of mankind and so confirmed by history that it is unnecessary now to discuss them or in any way to dwell upon them. The question before us therefore becomes specific: "Are contradictions among ideas and beliefs likely to play an *important* group-making rôle in the future?" I shall interpret the word important as connoting quality as well as quantity. I shall, in fact, attempt to answer the question set for me by translating it into this inquiry, namely: What kind or type of groups are the inevitable contradictions among ideas and beliefs most likely to create and to maintain within the progressive populations of the world from this time forth?

Somewhat more than three hundred years ago, Protestantism and geographical discovery had combined to create conditions extraordinarily favorable to the formation of groups or associations about various conflicting ideas and beliefs functioning as nuclei; and for nearly three hundred years the world has been observing a remarkable multiplication of culture groups of two fundamentally different types. One type is a sect, or denomination, having no restricted local habitation but winning adherents here and there in various communes, provinces, or nations, and having, therefore, a membership either locally concentrated or more or less widely dispersed; either regularly or most irregularly distributed. The culture group of the other type, or kind, is a self-sufficing community. It may be a village, a colony, a state, or a nation. Its membership is concentrated, its habitat is defined.

To a very great extent, as everybody knows, American colonization proceeded through the formation of religious communities. Such were the Pilgrim and the Puritan commonwealths. Such were the Quaker groups of Rhode Island and Pennsylvania. Such were the localized societies of the Dunkards, the Moravians, and the Mennonites.

As late as the middle of the nineteenth century the American people witnessed the birth and growth of one of the most remarkable religious communities known in history. The Mormon community of Utah, which, originating in 1830 as a band of relatives and acquaintances, clustered by an idea that quickly became a dogma, had become in fifty years a commonwealth *de facto*, defying the authority *de jure* of the United States.

We are not likely, however, again to witness a phenomenon of this kind in the civilized world. Recently we have seen the rise and the astonishingly rapid spread of another American religion, namely, the Christian Science faith. But it has created no community group. It has created only a dispersed sect. It is obvious to any intelligent observer, however untrained in sociological discrimination he may be, that the forces of Protestantism, still dividing and differentiating as they are, no longer to any great extent create new self-sufficing communities. They create only associations of irregular geographical dispersion, of more or less unstable or shifting membership. In a word, the conflicting-idea forces, which in our colonial days tended to create community groups as well as sects, tend now to create sectarian bodies only—mere denominational or partisan associations.

A similar contrast between an earlier and a later stage of culture group-making may be observed if we go back to centuries before the Protestant Reformation, there to survey a wider field and a longer series of historical periods.

It is a commonplace of historical knowledge that in all of the earliest civilizations there was an approximate identification of religion with ethnic consciousness and of political consciousness with both religious and race feeling. Each people had its own tribal or national gods, who were inventoried as national assets at valuations quite as high as those attached to tribal or national territory.

When, however, Roman imperial rule had been extended over the civilized world, the culture conflicts that then arose expended their group-creating force in simply bringing together like believers in sectarian association. Christianity, appealing to all bloods, in some measure to all economic classes, and spreading into all sections of the eastern Mediterranean region, did not to any great extent create communities. And what was true of Christianity was in like manner true of the Mithras cult, widely diffused in the second Christian century. Even Mohammedanism, a faith seemingly well calculated to create autonomous states, in contact with a world prepared by Roman organization could not completely identify itself with definite political boundaries.

The proximate causes of these contrasts are not obscure. We must suppose that a self-sufficing community might at one time, as well as at another, be drawn together by formative beliefs. But that it may take root somewhere and, by protecting itself against destructive external influences, succeed for a relatively long time in maintaining its integrity and its solidarity, it must enjoy a relative isolation. In a literal sense it must be beyond easy reach of those antagonistic forces which constitute for it the outer world of unbelief and darkness.

Such isolation is easily and often possible, however, only in the early stages of political integration. It is always difficult and unusual in those advanced stages wherein nations are combined in world-empires. It is becoming well-nigh impossible, now that all the continents have been brought under the sovereignty of the so-called civilized peoples, while these peoples themselves, freely communicating and intermingling, maintain with one another that good understanding which constitutes them, in a certain broad sense of the term, a world-society. The proximate effects also of the contrast that has been sketched are generally recognized.

So long as blood sympathy, religious faith, and political consciousness are approximately coterminous, the groups that they form, whether local communities or nations, must necessarily be rather sharply delimited. They must be characterized also by internal solidarity. Their membership is stable because to break the bond of blood is not only to make one's self an outcast but is also to be unfaithful to the ancestral gods; to change one's religion is not only to be impious but is also to commit treason; to expatriate one's self is not only to commit treason but is also to blaspheme against high heaven.

But when associations of believers or of persons holding in common any philosophy or doctrine whatsoever are no longer self-sufficing communities, and when nations composite in blood have become compound in structure, all social groups, clusters, or organizations, not only the cultural ones drawn together by formative ideas, but also the economic and the political ones, become in some degree plastic. Their membership then becomes to some extent shifting and renewable. Under these circumstances any given association of men, let it be a village, a religious group, a trade union, a corporation, or a political party, not only takes into itself new members from time to time; it also permits old members to depart. Men come and men go, yet the association or the group itself persists. As group or as organization it remains unimpaired.

The economic advantage secured by this plasticity and renewableness is beyond calculation enormous. It permits and facilitates the drafting of men at any moment from points where they are least needed, for concentration upon points where they are needed most. The spiritual or idealistic advantage is not less great. The concentration of attention and of enthusiasm upon strategic points gives ever-increasing impetus to progressive movements.

Let us turn now from these merely proximate causes and effects of group formation to take note of certain developmental processes which lie farther back in the evolutionary sequence and which also have significance for our inquiry, since, when we understand them, they may aid us in our attempt to answer the question, What kind of group-making is likely to be accomplished by cultural conflicts from this time forth?

The most readily perceived, because the most pictorial, of the conflicts arising between one belief and another are those that are waged between beliefs that have been localized and then through geographical expansion have come into competition throughout wide frontier areas. Of all such conflicts, that upon which the world has now fully entered between occidental and oriental ideas is not merely the most extensive; it is also by far the most interesting and picturesque.

Less picturesque but often more dramatic are the conflicts that arise within each geographical region, within each nation, between old beliefs and new—the conflicts of sequent, in distinction from coexistent, ideas; the conflicts in time, in distinction from the conflicts in space. A new knowledge is attained which compels us to question old dogmas. A new faith arises which would displace the ancient traditions. As the new waxes strong in some region favorable to it, it begins there, within local limits, to supersede the old. Only then, when the conflict between the old as old and the new as new is practically over, does the triumphant new begin to go forth spatially as a conquering influence from the home of its youth into regions outlying and remote.

Whatever the form, however, that the culture conflict assumes, whether serial and dramatic or geographical and picturesque, its antecedent psychological conditions are in certain great essentials the same. Men array themselves in hostile camps on questions of theory and belief, not merely because they are variously and conflictingly informed, but far more because they are mentally unlike, their minds having been prepared by structural differentiation to seize upon different views and to cherish opposing convictions. That is to say, some minds have become rational, critical, plastic, open, outlooking, above all, intuitive of objective facts and relations. Others in their fundamental constitution have remained dogmatic, intuitive only of personal attitudes or of subjective moods, temperamentally conservative and instinctive. Minds of the one kind welcome the new and wider knowledge; they go forth to embrace it. Minds of the other kind resist it.

In the segregation thus arising, there is usually discoverable a certain tendency toward grouping by sex.

Whether the mental and moral traits of women are inherent and therefore permanent, or whether they are but passing effects of circumscribed experience and therefore possibly destined to be modified, is immaterial for my present purpose. It is not certain that either the biologist or the psychologist is prepared to answer the question. It is certain that the sociologist is not. It is enough for the analysis that I am making now if we can say that, as a merely descriptive fact, women thus far in the history of the race have generally been more instinctive, more intuitive of subjective states, more emotional, more conservative than men; and that men, more generally than women, have been intuitive of objective relations, inclined therefore to break with instinct and to rely on the later-developed reasoning processes of the brain, and willing, consequently, to take chances, to experiment, and to innovate.

If so much be granted, we may perhaps say that it is because of these mental differences that in conflicts between new and old ideas, between new knowledge and old traditions, it usually happens that a large majority of all women are found in the camp of the old, and that the camp of the new is composed mainly of men.

In the camp of the new, however, are always to be found women of alert intelligence, who happen also to be temperamentally radical; women in whom the reasoning habit has asserted sway over instinct, and in whom intuition has become the true scientific power to discern objective relations. And in the camp of the old, together with a majority of all women, are to be found most of the men of conservative instinct, and most of those also whose intuitive and reasoning powers are unequal to the effort of thinking about the world or anything in it in terms of impersonal causation. Associated with all of these elements, both male and female, may usually be discovered, finally, a contingent of priestly personalities; not necessarily religious priests, but men who love to assert spiritual dominion, to wield authority, to be reverenced and obeyed, and who naturally look for a following among the non-skeptical and easily impressed.

Such, very broadly and rudely sketched, is the psychological background of culture conflict. It is, however, a background only, a certain persistent grouping of forces and conditions; it is not the cause from which culture conflicts proceed.

D. RACIAL CONFLICTS

1. Social Contacts and Race Conflict[1]

There is a conviction, widespread in America at the present time, that among the most fruitful sources of international wars are racial prejudice and national egotism. This conviction is the nerve of much present-day pacifism. It has been the inspiration of such unofficial diplomacy, for example, as that of the Federal Council of the Churches of Christ in its effort to bring about a better understanding between the Japanese and America. This book, *The Japanese Invasion*, by Jesse F. Steiner, is an attempt to study this phenomenon of race prejudice and national egotism, so far as it reveals itself in the relations of the Japanese and the Americans in this country, and to esti-

[1] From Robert E. Park, Introduction to Jesse F. Steiner, *The Japanese Invasion*. (A. C. McClurg & Co., 1917.)

mate the rôle it is likely to play in the future relations of the two countries.

So far as I know, an investigation of precisely this nature has not hitherto been made. One reason for this is, perhaps, that not until very recent times did the problem present itself in precisely this form. So long as the nations lived in practical isolation, carrying on their intercourse through the medium of professional diplomats, and knowing each other mainly through the products they exchanged, census reports, and the discreet observations of polite travelers, racial prejudice did not disturb international relations. With the extension of international commerce, the increase of immigration, and the interpenetration of peoples, the scene changes. The railway, the steamship, and the telegraph are rapidly mobilizing the peoples of the earth. The nations are coming out of their isolation, and distances which separated the different races are rapidly giving way before the extension of communication.

The same human motives which have led men to spread a network of trade-communication over the whole earth in order to bring about an exchange of commodities are now bringing about a new distribution of populations. When these populations become as mobile as the commodities of commerce, there will be practically no limits— except those artificial barriers, like the customs and immigration restrictions, maintained by individual states—to a world-wide economic and personal competition. Furthermore when the natural barriers are broken down, artificial barriers will be maintained with increasing difficulty.

Some conception of the extent of the changes which are taking place in the world under the influence of these forces may be gathered from the fact that in 1870 the cost of transporting a bushel of grain in Europe was so great as to prohibit its sale beyond a radius of two hundred miles from a primary market. By 1883 the importation of grains from the virgin soil of the western prairies in the United States had brought about an agricultural crisis in every country in western Europe.

One may illustrate, but it is scarcely possible to estimate, the economic changes which have been brought about by the enormous increase in ocean transportation. In 1840 the first Cunard liner, of 740 horse-power with a speed of 8.5 knots per hour, was launched.

In 1907, when the Lusitania was built, ocean-going vessels had attained a speed of 25 knots an hour and were drawn by engines of 70,000 horse-power.

It is difficult to estimate the economic changes which have been brought about by the changes in ocean transportation represented by these figures. It is still less possible to predict the political effects of the steadily increasing mobility of the peoples of the earth. At the present time this mobility has already reached a point at which it is often easier and cheaper to transport the world's population to the source of raw materials than to carry the world's manufactures to the established seats of population.

With the progressive rapidity, ease, and security of transportation, and the increase in communication, there follows an increasing detachment of the population from the soil and a concurrent concentration in great cities. These cities in time become the centers of vast numbers of uprooted individuals, casual and seasonal laborers, tenement and apartment-house dwellers, sophisticated and emancipated urbanites, who are bound together neither by local attachment nor by ties of family, clan, religion, or nationality. Under such conditions it is reasonable to expect that the same economic motive which leads every trader to sell in the highest market and to buy in the lowest will steadily increase and intensify the tendency, which has already reached enormous proportions of the population in overcrowded regions with diminished resources, to seek their fortunes, either permanently or temporarily, in the new countries of undeveloped resources.

Already the extension of commerce and the increase of immigration have brought about an international and inter-racial situation that has strained the inherited political order of the United States. It is this same expansive movement of population and of commerce, together with the racial and national rivalries that have sprung from them, which first destroyed the traditional balance of power in Europe and then broke up the scheme of international control which rested on it. Whatever may have been the immediate causes of the world-war, the more remote sources of the conflict must undoubtedly be sought in the great cosmic forces which have broken down the barriers which formerly separated the races and nationalities of the world, and forced them into new intimacies and new forms of competition, rivalry, and conflict.

Since 1870 the conditions which I have attempted to sketch have steadily forced upon America and the nations of Europe the problem of assimilating their heterogeneous populations. What we call the race problem is at once an incident of this process of assimilation and an evidence of its failure.

The present volume, *The Japanese Invasion: A Study in the Psychology of Inter-racial Contact*, touches but does not deal with the general situation which I have briefly sketched. It is, as its title suggests, a study in "racial contacts," and is an attempt to distinguish and trace to their sources the attitudes and the sentiments—that is to say, mutual prejudices—which have been and still are a source of mutual irritation and misunderstanding between the Japanese and American peoples.

Fundamentally, prejudice against the Japanese in the United States is merely the prejudice which attaches to every alien and immigrant people. The immigrant from Europe, like the immigrant from Asia, comes to this country because he finds here a freedom of individual action and an economic opportunity which he did not find at home. It is an instance of the general tendency of populations to move from an area of relatively closed, to one of relatively open, resources. The movement is as inevitable and, in the long run, as resistless as that which draws water from its mountain sources to the sea. It is one way of redressing the economic balance and bringing about an economic equilibrium.

The very circumstances under which this modern movement of population has arisen implies then that the standard of living, if not the cultural level, of the immigrant is lower than that of the native population. The consequence is that immigration brings with it a new and disturbing form of competition, the competition, namely, of peoples of a lower and of a higher standard of living. The effect of this competition, where it is free and unrestricted, is either to lower the living standards of the native population; to expel them from the vocations in which the immigrants are able or permitted to compete; or what may, perhaps, be regarded as a more sinister consequence, to induce such a restriction of the birth rate of the native population as to insure its ultimate extinction. The latter is, in fact, what seems to be happening in the New England manufacturing towns where the birth rate in the native population for some years past has fallen below the death rate, so that the native stock has long since ceased to reproduce itself. The foreign peoples, on the other hand, are rapidly replacing the native stocks, not merely by the influence of new immigration, but because of a relatively high excess of births over deaths.

It has been assumed that the prejudice which blinds the people of one race to the virtues of another and leads them to exaggerate that other's faults is in the nature of a misunderstanding which further knowledge will dispel. This is so far from true that it would be more exact to say that our racial misunderstandings are merely the expression of our racial antipathies. Behind these antipathies are deep-seated, vital, and instinctive impulses. Racial antipathies represent the collision of invisible forces, the clash of interests, dimly felt but not yet clearly perceived. They are present in every situation where the fundamental interests of races and peoples are not yet regulated by some law, custom, or any other *modus vivendi* which commands the assent and the mutual support of both parties. We hate people because we fear them, because our interests, as we understand them at any rate, run counter to theirs. On the other hand, good will is founded in the long run upon co-operation. The extension of our so-called altruistic sentiments is made possible only by the organization of our otherwise conflicting interests and by the extension of the machinery of co-operation and social control.

Race prejudice may be regarded as a spontaneous, more or less instinctive, defense-reaction, the practical effect of which is to restrict free competition between races. Its importance as a social function is due to the fact that free competition, particularly between people with different standards of living, seems to be, if not the original source, at least the stimulus to which race prejudice is the response.

From this point of view we may regard caste, or even slavery, as one of those accommodations through which the race problem found a natural solution. Caste, by relegating the subject race to an inferior status, gives to each race at any rate a monopoly of its own tasks. When this status is accepted by the subject people, as is the case where the caste or slavery systems become fully established, racial competition ceases and racial animosity tends to disappear. That is the explanation of the intimate and friendly relations which so often existed in slavery between master and servant. It is for this reason that we hear it said today that the Negro is all right in his place. In his place he is a convenience and not a competitor. Each race being in its place, no obstacle to racial co-operation exists.

The fact that race prejudice is due to, or is in some sense dependent upon, race competition is further manifest by a fact that Mr. Steiner has emphasized, namely, that prejudice against the Japanese is nowhere uniform throughout the United States. It is only where the Japanese are present in sufficient numbers to actually disturb the economic status of the white population that prejudice has manifested itself to such a degree as to demand serious consideration. It is an interesting fact also that prejudice against the Japanese is now more intense than it is against any other oriental people. The reason for this, as Mr. Steiner has pointed out, is that the Japanese are more aggressive, more disposed to test the sincerity of that statement of the Declaration of Independence which declares that all men are equally entitled to "life, liberty, and the pursuit of happiness"—a statement, by the way, which was merely a forensic assertion of the laissez faire doctrine of free and unrestricted competition as applied to the relations of individual men.

The Japanese, the Chinese, they too would be all right in their place, no doubt. That place, if they find it, will be one in which they do not greatly intensify and so embitter the struggle for existence of the white man. The difficulty is that the Japanese is still less disposed than the Negro or the Chinese to submit to the regulations of a caste system and to stay in his place. The Japanese are an organized and morally efficient nation. They have the national pride and the national egotism which rests on the consciousness of this efficiency. In fact, it is not too much to say that national egotism, if one pleases to call it such, is essential to national efficiency, just as a certain irascibility of temper seems to be essential to a good fighter.

Another difficulty is that caste and the limitation of free competition is economically unsound, even though it be politically desirable. A national policy of national efficiency demands that every individual have not merely the opportunity but the preparation necessary to perform that particular service for the community for which his natural disposition and aptitude fit him, irrespective of race or "previous condition."

Finally, caste and the limitation of economic opportunity is contrary, if not to our traditions, at least to our political principles. That means that there will always be an active minority opposed to any settlement based on the caste system as applied to either the black or the brown races, on grounds of political sentiment. This minority will be small in parts of the country immediately adversely affected by the competition of the invading race. It will be larger in regions which are not greatly affected. It will be increased if immigration is so rapid as to make the competition more acute. We must look to other measures for the solution of the Japanese problem, if it should prove true, as seems probable, that we are not able or, for various reasons, do not care permanently to hold back the rising tide of the oriental invasion.

I have said that fundamentally and in principle prejudice against the Japanese in America today was identical with the prejudice which attaches to any immigrant people. There is, as Mr. Steiner has pointed out, a difference. This is due to the existence in the human mind of a mechanism by which we inevitably and automatically classify every individual human being we meet. When a race bears an external mark by which every individual member of it can infallibly be identified, that race is by that fact set apart and segregated. Japanese, Chinese, and Negroes cannot move among us with the same freedom as the members of other races because they bear marks which identify them as members of their race. This fact isolates them. In the end the effect of this isolation, both in its effects upon the Japanese themselves and upon the human environment in which they live, is profound. Isolation is at once a cause and an effect of race prejudice. It is a vicious circle—isolation, prejudice; prejudice, isolation. Were there no other reasons which urge us to consider the case of the Japanese and the oriental peoples in a category different from that of the European immigrant, this fact, that they are bound to live in the American community a more or less isolated life, would impel us to do so.

In conclusion, I may perhaps say in a word what seems to me the practical bearing of Mr. Steiner's book. Race prejudice is a mechanism of the group mind which acts reflexly and automatically in response to its proper stimulus. That stimulus seems to be, in the cases where I have met it, unrestricted competition of peoples with different standards of living. Racial animosities and the so-called racial misunderstandings that grow out of them cannot be explained or argued away. They can only be affected when there has been a readjustment of relations and an organization of interests in such a way as to bring about a larger measure of co-operation and a lesser amount of friction and conflict. This demands something more than a diplomacy of kind words. It demands a national policy based on an unflinching examination of the facts.

2. Conflict and Race Consciousness[1]

The Civil War weakened but did not fully destroy the *modus vivendi* which slavery had established between the slave and his master. With emancipation the authority which had formerly been exercised by the master was transferred to the state, and Washington, D.C., began to assume in the mind of the freedman the position that formerly had been occupied by the "big house" on the plantation. The masses of the Negro people still maintained their habit of dependence, however, and after the first confusion of the change had passed, life went on, for most of them, much as it had before the war. As one old farmer explained, the only difference he could see was that in slavery he "was working for old Marster and now he was working for himself."

There was one difference between slavery and freedom, nevertheless, which was very real to the freedman. And this was the liberty to move. To move from one plantation to another in case he was discontented was one of the ways in which a freedman was able to realize his freedom and to make sure that he possessed it. This liberty to move meant a good deal more to the plantation Negro than one not acquainted with the situation in the South is likely to understand.

If there had been an abundance of labor in the South; if the situation had been such that the Negro laborer was seeking the opportunity to work, or such that the Negro tenant farmers were

[1] From Robert E. Park, "Racial Assimilation in Secondary Groups," in *Publications of the American Sociological Society*, VIII (1913), 75-82.

competing for the opportunity to get a place on the land, as is so frequently the case in Europe, the situation would have been fundamentally different from what it actually was. But the South was, and is today, what Nieboer called a country of "open," in contradistinction to a country of "closed" resources. In other words, there is more land in the South than there is labor to till it. Land owners are driven to competing for laborers and tenants to work their plantations.

Owing to his ignorance of business matters and to a long-established habit of submission, the Negro after emancipation was placed at a great disadvantage in his dealings with the white man. His right to move from one plantation to another became, therefore, the Negro tenant's method of enforcing consideration from the planter. He might not dispute the planter's accounts, because he was not capable of doing so, and it was unprofitable to attempt it, but if he felt aggrieved he could move.

This was the significance of the exodus in some of the southern states which took place about 1879, when 40,000 people left the plantations in the Black Belts of Louisiana and Mississippi and went to Kansas. The masses of the colored people were dissatisfied with the treatment they were receiving from the planters and made up their minds to move to "a free country," as they described it. At the same time it was the attempt of the planter to bind the Negro tenant who was in debt to him to his place on the plantation that gave rise to the system of peonage that still exists in a mitigated form in the South today.

When the Negro moved off the plantation upon which he was reared he severed the personal relations which bound him to his master's people. It was just at this point that the two races began to lose touch with each other. From this time on the relations of the black man and white, which in slavery had been direct and personal, became every year, as the old associations were broken, more and more indirect and secondary. There lingers still the disposition on the part of the white man to treat every Negro familiarly, and the disposition on the part of every Negro to treat every white man respectfully. But these are habits which are gradually disappearing. The breaking down of the instincts and habits of servitude and the acquisition by the masses of the Negro people of the instincts and habits of freedom have proceeded slowly but steadily. The reason the change seems to have gone on more rapidly in some cases than others is explained by the fact that at the time of emancipation 10 per cent of the Negroes in the United States were already free, and others, those who had worked in trades, many of whom had hired their own time from their masters, had become more or less adapted to the competitive conditions of free society.

One of the effects of the mobilization of the Negro has been to bring him into closer and more intimate contact with his own people. Common interests have drawn the blacks together, and caste sentiment has kept the black and white apart. The segregation of the races, which began as a spontaneous movement on the part of both, has been fostered by the policy of the dominant race. The agitation of the Reconstruction period made the division between the races in politics absolute. Segregation and separation in other matters have gone on steadily ever since. The Negro at the present time has separate churches, schools, libraries, hospitals, Y.M.C.A. associations, and even separate towns. There are, perhaps, a half-dozen communities in the United States, every inhabitant of which is a Negro. Most of these so-called Negro towns are suburban villages; two of them, at any rate, are the centers of a considerable Negro farming population. In general it may be said that where the Negro schools, churches, and Y.M.C.A. associations are not separate they do not exist.

It is hard to estimate the ultimate effect of this isolation of the black man. One of the most important effects has been to establish a common interest among all the different colors and classes of the race. This sense of solidarity has grown up gradually with the organization of the Negro people. It is stronger in the South, where segregation is more complete, than it is in the North where, twenty years ago, it would have been safe to say it did not exist. Gradually, imperceptibly, within the larger world of the white man, a smaller world, the world of the black man, is silently taking form and shape.

Every advance in education and intelligence puts the Negro in possession of the technique of communication and organization of the white man, and so contributes to the extension and consolidation of the Negro world within the white.

The motive for this increasing solidarity is furnished by the increasing pressure, or perhaps I should say by the increasing sensibility of Negroes to the pressure and the prejudice without. The sentiment of racial loyalty, which is a comparatively recent manifestation of the growing self-consciousness of the race, must be regarded as a response and "accommodation" to changing internal and external relations of the race. The sentiment which Negroes are beginning to call "race pride" does not exist to the same extent in the North as in the South, but an increasing disposition to enforce racial distinctions in the North, as in the South, is bringing it into existence.

One or two incidents in this connection are significant. A few years ago a man who is the head of the largest Negro publishing business in this country sent to Germany and had a number of Negro dolls manufactured according to specifications of his own. At the time this company was started, Negro children were in the habit of playing with white dolls. There were already Negro dolls on the market, but they were for white children and represented the white man's conception of the Negro and not the Negro's ideal of himself. The new Negro doll was a mulatto with regular features slightly modified in favor of the conventional Negro type. It was a neat, prim, well-dressed, well-behaved, self-respecting doll. Later on, as I understand, there were other dolls, equally tidy and respectable in appearance, but in darker shades, with Negro features a little more pronounced. The man who designed these dolls was perfectly clear in regard to the significance of the substitution that he was making. He said that he thought it was a good thing to let Negro girls become accustomed to dolls of their own color. He thought it important, as long as the races were to be segregated, that the dolls, which, like other forms of art, are patterns and represent ideals, should be segregated also.

This substitution of the Negro model for the white is a very interesting and a very significant fact. It means that the Negro has begun to fashion his own ideals and in his own image rather than in that of the white man. It is also interesting to know that the Negro doll company has been a success and that these dolls are now widely sold in every part of the United States. Nothing exhibits more clearly the extent to which the Negro had become assimilated in slavery or the extent to which he has broken with the past in recent years than this episode of the Negro doll.

The incident is typical. It is an indication of the nature of tendencies and of forces that are stirring in the background of the Negro's mind, although they have not succeeded in forcing themselves, except in special instances, into clear consciousness.

In this same category must be reckoned the poetry of Paul Lawrence Dunbar, in whom, as William Dean Howells has said, the Negro "attained civilization." Before Paul Lawrence Dunbar, Negro literature had been either apologetic or self-assertive, but Dunbar "studied the Negro objectively." He represented him as he found him, not only without apology, but with an affectionate understanding and sympathy which one can have only for what is one's own. In Dunbar, Negro literature attained an ethnocentric point of view. Through the medium of his verses the ordinary shapes and forms of the Negro's life have taken on the color of his affections and sentiments, and we see the black man, not as he looks, but as he feels and is.

It is a significant fact that a certain number of educated—or rather the so-called educated—Negroes were not at first disposed to accept at their full value either Dunbar's dialect verse or the familiar pictures of Negro life which are the symbols in which his poetry usually found expression. The explanation sometimes offered for the dialect poems was that "they were made to please white folk." The assumption seems to have been that if they had been written for Negroes it would have been impossible in his poetry to distinguish black people from white. This was a sentiment which was never shared by the masses of the people, who, upon the occasions when Dunbar recited to them, were fairly bowled over with amusement and delight because of the authenticity of the portraits he offered them. At the present time Dunbar is so far accepted as to have hundreds of imitators.

Literature and art have played a similar and perhaps more important rôle in the racial struggles of Europe than of America. One reason seems to be that racial conflicts, as they occur in secondary groups, are primarily sentimental and secondarily economic. Literature and art, when they are employed to give expression to racial sentiment and form to racial ideals, serve, along with other agencies, to mobilize the group and put the masses *en rapport* with their leaders and with each other. In such cases art and literature are like silent drummers which summon into action the latent instincts and energies of the race.

These struggles, I might add, in which a submerged people seek to rise and make for themselves a place in a world occupied by superior and privileged races, are not less vital or less important because they are bloodless. They serve to stimulate ambitions and inspire ideals which years, perhaps, of subjection and subordination have suppressed. In fact, it seems as if it were through conflicts of this kind, rather than through war, that the minor peoples were destined to gain the moral concentration and discipline that fit them to share, on anything like equal terms, in the conscious life of the civilized world.

Until the beginning of the last century the European peasant, like the Negro slave, bound as he was to the soil, lived in the little world of direct and personal relations, under what we may call a domestic régime. It was military necessity that first turned the attention of statesmen like Frederick the Great of Prussia to the welfare of the peasant. It was the overthrow of Prussia by Napoleon in 1807 that brought about his final emancipation in that country. In recent years it has been the international struggle for economic efficiency which has contributed most to mobilize the peasant and laboring classes in Europe.

As the peasant slowly emerged from serfdom he found himself a member of a depressed class, without education, political privileges, or capital. It was the struggle of this class for wider opportunity and better conditions of life that made most of the history of the previous century. Among the peoples in the racial borderland the effect of this struggle has been, on the whole, to substitute for a horizontal organization of society—in which the upper strata, that is to say, the wealthy or privileged class, was mainly of one race and the poorer and subject class was mainly of another—a vertical organization in which all classes of each racial group were united under the title of their respective nationalities. Thus organized, the nationalities represent, on the one hand, intractable minorities engaged in a ruthless partisan struggle for political privilege or economic advantage and, on the other, they represent cultural groups, each struggling to maintain a sentiment of loyalty to the distinctive traditions, language, and institutions of the race they represent.

This sketch of the racial situation in Europe is, of course, the barest abstraction and should not be accepted realistically. It is intended merely as an indication of similarities, in the broader outlines, of the motives that have produced nationalities in Europe and are making the Negro in America, as Booker Washington says, "a nation within a nation."

It may be said that there is one profound difference between the Negro and the European nationalities, namely, that the Negro has had his separateness and consequent race consciousness thrust upon him because of his exclusion and forcible isolation from white society. The Slavic nationalities, on the contrary, have segregated themselves in order to escape assimilation and escape racial extinction in the larger cosmopolitan states.

The difference is, however, not so great as it seems. With the exception of the Poles, nationalistic sentiment may be said hardly to have existed fifty years ago. Forty years ago when German was the language of the educated classes, educated Bohemians were a little ashamed to speak their own language in public. Now nationalist sentiment is so strong that, where the Czech nationality has gained control, it has sought to wipe out every vestige of the German language. It has changed the names of streets, buildings, and public places. In the city of Prag, for example, all that formerly held German associations now fairly reeks with the sentiment of Bohemian nationality.

On the other hand, the masses of the Polish people cherished very little nationalist sentiment until after the Franco-Prussian War. The fact is that nationalist sentiment among the Slavs, like racial sentiment among the Negroes, has sprung up as the result of a struggle against privilege and discrimination based upon racial distinctions. The movement is not so far advanced among Negroes; sentiment is not so intense, and for several reasons probably never will be.

From what has been said it seems fair to draw one conclusion, namely: under conditions of secondary contact, that is to say, conditions of individual liberty and individual competition, characteristic of modern civilization, depressed racial groups tend to assume the form of nationalities. A nationality, in this narrower sense, may be defined as the racial group which has attained self-consciousness, no matter whether it has at the same time gained political independence or not.

In societies organized along horizontal lines the disposition of individuals in the lower strata is to seek their models in the strata above them. Loyalty attaches to individuals, particularly to the upper classes, who furnish, in their persons and in their lives, the models for the masses of the people below them. Long after the nobility has lost every other social function connected with its vocation the ideals of the nobility have survived in our conception of the gentleman, genteel manners and bearing—gentility.

The sentiment of the Negro slave was, in a certain sense, not merely loyalty to his master but to the white race. Negroes of the older generations speak very frequently, with a sense of proprietorship, of "our white folks." This sentiment was not always confined to the ignorant masses. An educated colored man once explained to me "that we colored people always want our white folks to be superior." He was shocked when I showed no particular enthusiasm for that form of sentiment.

The fundamental significance of the nationalist movement must be sought in the effort of subject races, sometimes consciously, sometimes unconsciously, to substitute, for those supplied them by aliens, models based on their own racial individuality and embodying sentiments and ideals which spring naturally out of their own lives.

After a race has achieved in this way its moral independence, assimilation, in the sense of copying, will still continue. Nations and races borrow from those whom they fear as well as from those whom they admire. Materials taken over in this way, however, are inevitably stamped with the individuality of the nationalities that appropriate them. These materials will contribute to the dignity, to the prestige, and to the solidarity of the nationality which borrows them, but they will no longer inspire loyalty to the race from which they are borrowed. A race which has attained the character of a nationality may still retain its loyalty to the state of which it is a part, but only in so far as that state incorporates, as an integral part of its organization, the practical interests, the aspirations and ideals of that nationality.

The aim of the contending nationalities in Austria-Hungary at the present time seems to be a federation, like that of Switzerland, based upon the autonomy of the different races composing the empire. In the South, similarly, the races seem to be tending in the direction of a bi-racial organization of society, in which the Negro is gradually gaining a limited autonomy. What the ultimate outcome of this movement may be it is not safe to predict.

3.   Conflict and Accommodation[1]

In the first place, what is race friction? To answer this elementary question it is necessary to define the abstract mental quality upon which race friction finally rests. This is racial "antipathy," popularly spoken of as "race prejudice." Whereas prejudice means mere predilection, either for or against, antipathy means "natural contrariety," "incompatibility," or "repugnance of qualities." To quote the Century Dictionary, antipathy "expresses most of constitutional feeling and least of volition"; "it is a dislike that seems constitutional toward persons, things, conduct, etc.; hence it involves a dislike for which sometimes no good reason can be given." I would define racial antipathy, then, as a natural contrariety, repugnancy of qualities, or incompatibility between individuals or groups which are sufficiently differentiated to constitute what, for want of a more exact term, we call races. What is most important is that it involves an instinctive feeling of dislike, distaste, or repugnance, for which sometimes no good reason can be given. Friction is defined primarily as a "lack of harmony," or a "mutual irritation." In the case of races it is accentuated by antipathy. We do not have to depend on race riots or other acts of violence as a measure of the growth of race friction. Its existence may be manifested by a look or a gesture as well as by a word or an act.

A verbal cause of much useless and unnecessary controversy is found in the use of the word "race." When we speak of "race problems" or "racial antipathies," what do we mean by "race"? Clearly nothing scientifically definite, since ethnologists themselves are not agreed upon any classification of the human family along racial lines.

[1] Adapted from Alfred H. Stone, "Is Race Friction between Blacks and Whites in the United States Growing and Inevitable?" in the *American Journal of Sociology*, XIII (1907-8), 677-96.

Nor would this so-called race prejudice have the slightest regard for such classification, if one were agreed upon. It is something which is not bounded by the confines of a philological or ethnological definition. The British scientist may tell the British soldier in India that the native is in reality his brother, and that it is wholly absurd and illogical and unscientific for such a thing as "race prejudice" to exist between them. Tommy Atkins simply replies with a shrug that to him and his messmates the native is a "nigger"; and in so far as their attitude is concerned, that is the end of the matter. The same suggestion, regardless of the scientific accuracy of the parallel, if made to the American soldier in the Philippines, meets with the same reply. We have wasted an infinite amount of time in interminable controversies over the relative superiority and inferiority of different races. Such discussions have a certain value when conducted by scientific men in a purely scientific spirit. But for the purpose of explaining or establishing any fixed principle of race relations they are little better than worthless. The Japanese is doubtless quite well satisfied of the superiority of his people over the mushroom growths of western civilization, and finds no difficulty in borrowing from the latter whatever is worth reproducing, and improving on it in adapting it to his own racial needs. The Chinese do not waste their time in idle chatter over the relative status of their race as compared with the white barbarians who have intruded themselves upon them with their grotesque customs, their heathenish ideas, and their childishly new religion. The Hindu regards with veiled contempt the racial pretensions of his conqueror, and, while biding the time when the darker races of the earth shall once more come into their own, does not bother himself with such an idle question as whether his temporary overlord is his racial equal. Only the white man writes volumes to establish on paper the fact of a superiority which is either self-evident and not in need of demonstration, on the one hand, or is not a fact and is not demonstrable, on the other. The really important matter is one about which there need be little dispute—the fact of racial differences. It is the practical question of differences—the fundamental differences of physical appearance, of mental habit and thought, of social customs and religious beliefs, of the thousand and one things keenly and clearly appreciable, yet sometimes elusive and undefinable—these are the things which at once create and find expression in what we call race problems and race prejudices, for want of better terms. In just so far as these differences are fixed and permanently associated characteristics of two groups of people will the antipathies and problems between the two be permanent.

Probably the closest approach we shall ever make to a satisfactory classification of races as a basis of antipathy will be that of grouping men according to color, along certain broad lines, the color being accompanied by various and often widely different, but always fairly persistent, differentiating physical and mental characteristics. This would give us substantially the white—not Caucasian, the yellow—not Chinese or Japanese, and the dark—not Negro, races. The antipathies between these general groups and between certain of their subdivisions will be found to be essentially fundamental, but they will also be found to present almost endless differences of degrees of actual and potential acuteness. Here elementary psychology also plays its part. One of the subdivisions of the Negro race is composed of persons of mixed blood. In many instances these are more white than black, yet the association of ideas has through several generations identified them with the Negro—and in this country friction between this class and white people is on some lines even greater than between whites and blacks.

Race conflicts are merely the more pronounced concrete expressions of such friction. They are the visible phenomena of the abstract quality of racial antipathy—the tangible evidence of the existence of racial problems. The form of such expressions of antipathy varies with the nature of the racial contact in each instance. Their different and widely varying aspects are the confusing and often contradictory phenomena of race relations. They are dependent upon diverse conditions, and are no more susceptible of rigid and permanent classification than are the whims and moods of human nature. It is more than a truism to say that a condition precedent to race friction or race conflict is contact between sufficient numbers of two diverse racial groups. There is a definite and positive difference between contact between individuals and contact between masses. The association between two isolated individual members of two races may be wholly different from contact between masses of the same race groups. The factor of numbers embraces, indeed, the very crux of the problems arising from contact between different races.

A primary cause of race friction is the vague, rather intangible, but wholly real, feeling of "pressure" which comes to the white man almost instinctively in the presence of a mass of people of a different race. In a certain important sense all racial problems are distinctly problems of racial distribution. Certainly the definite action of the controlling race, particularly as expressed in laws, is determined by the factor of the numerical difference between its population and that of the inferior group. This fact stands out prominently in the history of our colonial legislation for the control of Negro slaves. These laws increased in severity up to a certain point as the slave population increased in numbers. The same condition is disclosed in the history of the ante-bellum legislation of the southern, eastern, New England, and middle western states for the control of the free Negro population. So today no state in the Union would have separate car laws where the Negro constituted only 10 or 15 per cent of its total population. No state would burden itself with the maintenance of two separate school systems with a negro element of less than 10 per cent. Means of local separation might be found but there would be no expression of law on the subject.

Just as a heavy increase of Negro population makes for an increase of friction, direct legislation, the protection of drastic social customs, and a general feeling of unrest or uneasiness on the part of the white population, so a decrease of such population, or a relatively small increase as compared with the whites, makes for less friction, greater racial tolerance, and a lessening of the feeling of necessity for severely discriminating laws or customs. And this quite aside from the fact of a difference of increase or decrease of actual points of contact, varying with differences of numbers. The statement will scarcely be questioned that the general attitude of the white race, as a whole, toward the Negro would become much less uncompromising if we were to discover that through two census periods the race had shown a positive decrease in numbers. Racial antipathy would not decrease, but the conditions which provoke its outward expression would undergo a change for the better. There is a direct relation between the mollified attitude of the people of the Pacific coast toward the Chinese population and the fact that the Chinese population decreased between 1890 and 1900. There would in time be a difference of feeling toward the Japanese now there if the immigration of more were prohibited by treaty stipulation. There is the same immediate relation between the tolerant attitude of whites toward the natives in the Hawaiian Islands and the feeling that the native is a decadent and dying race. Aside from the influence of the Indian's warlike qualities and of his refusal to submit to slavery, the attitude and disposition of the white race toward him have been influenced by considerations similar to those which today operate in Hawaii. And the same influence has been a factor in determining the attitude of the English toward the slowly dying Maoris of New Zealand.

At no time in the history of the English-speaking people and at no place of which we have any record where large numbers of them have been brought into contact with an approximately equal number of Negroes have the former granted to the latter absolute equality, either political, social, or economic. With the exception of five New England states, with a total Negro population of only 16,084 in 1860, every state in the Union discriminated against the Negro politically before the Civil War. The white people continued to do so— North as well as South—as long as they retained control of the suffrage regulations of their states. The determination to do so renders one whole section of the country practically a political unit to this day. In South Africa we see the same determination of the white man to rule, regardless of the numerical superiority of the black. The same determination made Jamaica surrender the right of self-government and renders her satisfied with a hybrid political arrangement today. The presence of practically 100,000 Negroes in the District of Columbia makes 200,000 white people content to live under an anomaly in a self-governing country. The proposition is too elementary for discussion that the white man when confronted with a sufficient number of Negroes to create in his mind a sense of political unrest or danger either alters his form of government in order to be rid of the incubus or destroys the political strength of the Negro by force, by evasion, or by direct action.

In the main, the millions in the South live at peace with their white neighbors. The masses, just one generation out of slavery and thousands of them still largely controlled by its influences, accept the superiority of the white race as a race, whatever may be their private opinion of some of its members. And, furthermore, they accept this relation of superior and inferior as a mere matter of course—as part of their lives—as something neither to be questioned, wondered at, or worried over. Despite apparent impressions to the contrary, the average southern white man gives no more thought to the matter than does the Negro. As I tried to make clear at the outset, the status of superior and inferior is simply an inherited part of his instinctive mental equipment—a concept which he does not have to reason out. The respective attitudes are complementary, and under the mutual acceptance and understanding there still exist unnumbered thousands of instances of kindly and affectionate relations—relations of which the outside world knows nothing and understands nothing. In the mass, the southern Negro has not bothered himself about the ballot for more than twenty years, not since his so-called political leaders let him alone; he is not disturbed over the matter of separate schools and cars, and he neither knows nor cares anything about "social equality."

But what of the other class? The "masses" is at best an unsatisfactory and indefinite term. It is very far from embracing even the southern Negro, and we need not forget that seven years ago there were 900,000 members of the race living outside of the South. What of the class, mainly urban and large in number, who have lost the typical habit and attitude of the Negro of the mass, and who, more and more, are becoming restless and chafing under existing conditions? There is an intimate and very natural relation between the social and intellectual advance of the so-called Negro and the matter of friction along social lines. It is, in fact, only as we touch the higher groups that we can appreciate the potential results of contact upon a different plane from that common to the masses in the South. There is a large and steadily increasing group of men, more or less related to the Negro by blood and wholly identified with him by American social usage, who refuse to accept quietly the white man's attitude toward the race. I appreciate the mistake of laying too great stress upon the utterances of any one man or group of men, but the mistakes in this case lie the other way. The American white man knows little or nothing about the thought and opinion of the colored men and women who today largely mold and direct Negro public opinion in this country. Even the white man who considers himself a student of "the race question" rarely exhibits anything more than profound ignorance of the Negro's side of the problem. He does not know what the other man is thinking and saying on the subject. This composite type which we poetically call "black," but which in reality is every shade from black to white, is slowly developing a consciousness of its own racial solidarity. It is finding its own distinctive voice, and through its own books and papers and magazines, and through its own social organizations, is at once giving utterance to its discontent and making known its demands.

And with this dawning consciousness of race there is likewise coming an appreciation of the limitations and restrictions which hem in its unfolding and development. One of the best indices to the possibilities of increased racial friction is the Negro's own recognition of the universality of the white man's racial antipathy toward him. This is the one clear note above the storm of protest against the things that are, that in his highest aspirations everywhere the white man's "prejudice" blocks the colored man's path. And the white man may with possible profit pause long enough to ask the deeper significance of the Negro's finding of himself. May it not be only part of a general awakening of the darker races of the earth? Captain H. A. Wilson, of the English army, says that through all Africa there has penetrated in some way a vague confused report that far off somewhere, in the unknown, outside world, a great war has been fought between a white and a yellow race, and won by the yellow man. And even before the Japanese-Russian conflict, "Ethiopianism" and the cry of "Africa for the Africans" had begun to disturb the English in South Africa. It is said time and again that the dissatisfaction and unrest in India are accentuated by the results of this same war. There can be no doubt in the mind of any man who carefully reads American Negro journals that their rejoicing over the Japanese victory sounded a very different note from that of the white American. It was far from being a mere expression of sympathy with a people fighting for national existence against a power which had made itself odious to the civilized world by its treatment of its subjects. It was, instead, a quite clear cry of exultation over the defeat of a white race by a dark one. The white man is no wiser than the ostrich if he refuses to see the truth that in the possibilities of race friction the Negro's increasing consciousness of race is to play a part scarcely less important than the white man's racial antipathies, prejudices, or whatever we may elect to call them.

III. INVESTIGATIONS AND PROBLEMS

1. The Psychology and Sociology of Conflict, Conscious Competition, and Rivalry

Consciousness has been described as an effect of conflict—conflict of motor tendencies in the individual, conflict of sentiments, attitudes, and cultures in the group. The individual, activated in a given situation by opposing tendencies, is compelled to redefine his attitude. Consciousness is an incident of this readjustment.

Frequently adjustment involves a suppression of one tendency in the interest of another, of one wish in favor of another. Where these suppressions are permanent, they frequently result in disorders of conduct and disorganization of the personality. The suppressed wish, when suppression results in disturbances of the conscious life, has been called by psychoanalysts a *complex*. Freud and his colleagues have isolated and described certain of these complexes. Most familiar of these are the Oedipus complex, which is explained as an effect of the unconscious conflict of father and son for the love of the mother; and the Electra complex, which similarly has as its source the unconscious struggle of mother and daughter for the affection of the father. Adler, in his description of the "inferiority" complex, explains it as an effect of the conflict growing out of the contrast between the ideal and the actual status of the person. Other mental conflicts described by the psychoanalysts are referred to the "adopted child" complex, the Narcissus complex, the sex shock, etc. These conflicts which disturb the mental life of the person are all the reflections of social relations and are to be explained in terms of status and the rôle of the individual in the group.

Emulation and rivalry represent conflict at higher social levels, where competition has been translated into forms that inure to the survival and success of the group. Research in this field, fragmentary as it is, confirms the current impression of the stimulation of effort in the person through conscious competition with his fellows. Adler's theory of "psychic compensation" is based on the observation that handicapped individuals frequently excel in the very fields in which they are apparently least qualified to compete. Demosthenes, for example, became a great orator in spite of the fact that he stuttered.

Ordahl presents the only comprehensive survey of the literature in this field.

Simmel has made the outstanding contribution to the sociological conception of conflict. Just as the attitudes of the individual person represent an organization of antagonistic elements, society, as he interprets it, is a unity of which the elements are conflicting tendencies. Society, he insists, would be quite other than it is, were it not for the aversions, antagonisms, differences, as well as the sympathies, affections, and similarities between individuals and groups of individuals. The unity of society includes these opposing forces, and, as a matter of fact, society is organized upon the basis of conflict.

Conflict is an organizing principle in society. Just as the individual, under the influences of contact and conflict with other individuals, acquires a status and develops a personality, so groups of individuals, in conflict with other groups, achieve unity, organization, group consciousness, and assume the forms characteristic of conflict groups—that is to say, they become parties, sects, nationalities, etc.

2.   Types of Conflict

Simmel, in his study of conflict, distinguished four types—namely, war, feud and faction, litigation, and discussion, i.e., the impersonal struggles of parties and causes. This classification, while discriminating, is certainly not complete. There are, for example, the varied forms of sport, in which conflict assumes the form of rivalry. These are nevertheless organized on a conflict pattern. Particularly interesting in this connection are games of chance, gambling and gambling devices which appeal to human traits so fundamental that no people is without example of them in its folkways.

Gambling is, according to Groos, "a fighting play," and the universal human interest in this sport is due to the fact that "no other form of play displays in so many-sided a fashion the combativeness of human nature."[1]

The history of the duel, either in the form of the judicial combat, the wager of battle of the Middle Ages, or as a form of private vengeance, offers interesting material for psychological or sociological

[1] Karl Groos, *The Play of Man*, p. 213. (New York, 1901.)

investigation. The transition from private vengeance to public prosecution, of which the passing of the duel is an example, has not been completed. In fact, new forms are in some cases gradually gaining social sanction. We still have our "unwritten laws" for certain offenses. It is proverbially difficult to secure the conviction, in certain parts of the country, Chicago, for example, of a woman who kills her husband or her lover. The practice of lynching Negroes in the southern states, for offenses against women, and for any other form of conduct that is construed as a challenge to the dominant race, is an illustration from a somewhat different field, not merely of the persistence, but the gradual development of the so-called unwritten law. The circumstances under which these and all other unwritten laws arise, in which custom controls in contravention of the formal written code, have not been investigated from the point of view of sociology and in their human-nature aspects.

Several studies of games and gambling, in some respects the most unique objectivations of human interest, have been made from the point of view of the fundamental human traits involved, notably Thomas' article on *The Gaming Instinct*, Groos's chapter on "Fighting Play," in his *Play of Man*, and G. T. W. Patrick's *Psychology of Relaxation*, in which the theory of catharsis, familiar since Aristotle, is employed to explain play, laughter, profanity, the drink habit, and war.

Original materials exist in abundance for the study of feud, litigation, and war. No attempt seems to have been made to study feud and litigation comparatively, as Westermark has studied marriage institutions. Something has indeed been done in this direction with the subject of war, notably by Letourneau in France and by Frobenius in Germany. Sumner's notable essay on *War* is likewise an important contribution to the subject. The literature upon war, however, is so voluminous and so important that it will be discussed later, separately, and in greater detail.

Quite as interesting and important as that of war is the natural history of discussion, including under that term political and religious controversy and social agitation, already referred to as impersonal or secondary conflict.

The history of discussion, however, is the history of freedom—freedom, at any rate, of thought and of speech. It is only when peace and freedom have been established that discussion is practicable or possible. A number of histories have been written in recent years describing the rise of rationalism, as it is called, and the rôle of discussion and agitation in social life. Draper's *History of the Intellectual Development of Europe* and Lecky's *History of the Rise and Influence of the Spirit of Rationalism in Europe* are among the earlier works in this field. Robertson's *History of Free Thought* is mainly a survey of religious skepticism but contains important and suggestive references to the natural processes by which abstract thought has arisen out of the cultural contacts and conflicts among peoples, which conquest and commerce have brought into the same universe of discourse. What we seem to have in these works are materials for the study of the communal processes through which thought is formulated. Once formulated it becomes a permanent factor in the life of the group. The rôle of discussion in the communal process will be considered later in connection with the newspaper, the press agent, propaganda, and the various factors and mechanisms determining the formation of public opinion.

3. The Literature of War

The emphasis upon the struggle for existence which followed the publication of Darwin's *The Origin of Species*, in 1859, seemed to many thinkers to give a biological basis for the necessity and the inevitability of war. No distinction was made by writers of this school of thought between competition and conflict. Both were supposed to be based on instinct. Nicolai's *The Biology of War* is an essay with the avowed design of refuting the biological justification of war.

Psychological studies of war have explained war either as an expression of instinct or as a reversion to a primordial animal-human type of behavior. Patrick, who is representative of this latter school, interprets war as a form of relaxation. G. W. Crile has offered a mechanistic interpretation of war and peace based on studies of the chemical changes which men undergo in warfare. Crile comes to the conclusion, however, that war is an action pattern, fixed in the social heredity of the national group, and not a type of behavior determined biologically.

The human nature of war and the motives which impel the person to the great adventure and the supreme risk of war have not been subjected to sociological study. A mass of material, however, consisting of personal documents of all types, letters, common-sense observation, and diaries is now available for such study.

Much of the literature of war has been concentrated on the problem of the abolition of war. There are the idealists and the conscientious objectors who look to good will, humanitarian sentiment, and pacificism to end war by the transformation of attitudes of men and the policies of nations. On the other hand, there are the hard-headed and practical thinkers and statesmen who believe, with Hobbes, that war will not end until there is established a power strong enough to overawe a recalcitrant state. Finally, there is a third group of social thinkers who emphasize the significance of the formation of a world public opinion. This "international mind" they regard of far greater significance for the future of humanity than the problem of war or peace, of national rivalries, or of future race conflicts.

4. Race Conflict

A European school of sociologists emphasizes conflict as the fundamental social process. Gumplowicz, in his book *Der Rassenkampf*, formulated a theory of social contacts and conflicts upon the conception of original ethnic groups in terms of whose interaction the history of humanity might be written. Novicow and Ratzenhofer maintain similar, though not so extreme, theories of social origins and historical developments.

With the tremendous extension of communication and growth of commerce, the world is today a great community in a sense that could not have been understood a century ago. But the world, if it is now one community, is not yet one society. Commerce has created an economic interdependence, but contact and communication have not resulted in either a political or a cultural solidarity. Indeed, the first evidences of the effects of social contacts appear to be disruptive rather than unifying. In every part of the world in which the white and colored races have come into intimate contact, race problems have presented the most intractable of all social problems.

Interest in this problem manifests itself in the enormous literature on the subject. Most of all that has been written, however, is superficial. Much is merely sentimental, interesting for the attitudes it exhibits, but otherwise adding nothing to our knowledge of the facts. The best account of the American situation is undoubtedly Ray Stannard Baker's *Following the Color Line*. The South African situation is interestingly and objectively described by Maurice Evans in *Black and White in South East Africa*. Steiner's book, *The Japanese Invasion*, is, perhaps, the best account of the Japanese-American situation.

The race problem merges into the problem of the nationalities and the so-called subject races. The struggles of the minor nationalities for self-determination is a phase of racial conflict; a phase, however, in which language rather than color is the basis of division and conflict.

5. Conflict Groups

In chapter i conflict groups were divided into gangs, labor organizations, sects, parties, and nationalities.[1] Common to these groups is an organization and orientation with reference to conflict with other groups of the same kind or with a more or less hostile social environment, as in the case of religious sects.

The spontaneous organizations of boys and youths called gangs attracted public attention in American communities because of the relation of these gangs to juvenile delinquency and adolescent crime. An interesting but superficial literature upon the gang has developed in recent years, represented typically by J. Adams Puffer *The Boy and his Gang*. The brief but picturesque descriptions of individual gangs seem to indicate that the play group tends to pass over into the gang when it comes into conflict with other groups of like type or with the community. The fully developed gang appears to possess a restricted membership, a natural leader, a name—usually that of a leader or a locality—a body of tradition, custom and a ritual, a rendezvous, a territorial area which it holds as a sort of possession and defends against invasion by other groups. Attention was early called, as by Mr. Brewster Adams in an article *The Street Gang as a Factor in Politics*, to the facility with which the gang graduates into a local political organization, representing thus the sources of political power of the typical American city.

[1] *Supra*, p. 50.

Although the conflict of economic groups is not a new nor even a modern phenomenon, no such permanent conflict groups as those represented by capital and labor existed until recent times. Veblen has made an acute observation upon this point. The American Federation of Labor, he states, "is not organized for production but for bargaining." It is, in effect, an organization for the strategic defeat of employers and rival organizations, by recourse to enforced unemployment and obstruction; not for the production of goods and services.[1]

Research in the labor problem by the Webbs in England and by Commons, Hoxie, and others in this country has been primarily concerned with the history and with the structure and functions of trade unions. At present there is a tendency to investigate the human-nature aspects of the causes of the industrial conflict. The current phrases "instincts in industry," "the human factor in economics," "the psychology of the labor movement," "industry, emotion, and unrest" indicate the change in attitude. The essential struggle is seen to lie not in the conflict of classes, intense and ruthless as it is, but more and more in the fundamental struggle between a mechanical and impersonal system, on the one hand, and the person with his wishes unsatisfied and insatiable on the other. All attempts to put the relations of capital and labor upon a moral basis have failed hitherto. The latest and most promising experiment in this direction is the so-called labor courts established by the Amalgamated Clothing Workers and their employers.

The literature upon sects and parties has been written for the most part with the purpose of justifying, to a critical and often hostile public, the sectarian and partisan aims and acts of their several organizations. In a few works such as Sighele's *Psychologie des sectes* and Michels' *Political Parties* an attempt has been made at objective description and analysis of the mechanisms of the behavior of the sect and of the party.

The natural history of the state from the tribe to the modern nation has been that of a political society based on conflict. Franz Oppenheimer maintains the thesis in his book *The State: Its History and Development Viewed Sociologically* that conquest has been the historical basis of the state. The state is, in other words, an organi-

[1] *The Dial,* LXVII (Oct. 4, 1919), 297.

zation of groups that have been in conflict, i.e., classes and castes; or of groups that are in conflict, i.e., political parties.

A nationality, as distinct from a nation, as for instance the Irish nationality, is a language and cultural group which has become group conscious through its struggle for status in the larger imperial or international group. Nationalism is, in other words, a phenomenon of internationalism.

The literature upon this subject is enormous. The most interesting recent works on the general topic are Dominian's *The Frontiers of Language and Nationality in Europe*, Pillsbury's *The Psychology of Nationality and Internationalism*, and Oakesmith's *Race and Nationality*.

SELECTED BIBLIOGRAPHY

I.   PSYCHOLOGY AND SOCIOLOGY OF CONFLICT

A. *Conflict and Social Process*

(1) Simmel, Georg. "The Sociology of Conflict." Translated from the German by Albion W. Small. *American Journal of Sociology*, IX (1903–4), 490–525; 672–89; 798–811.

(2) Gumplowicz, Ludwig. *Der Rassenkampf*. Sociologische Untersuchungen. Innsbruck, 1883.

(3) Novicow, J. *Les Luttes entre sociétés humaines et leurs phases successives*. Paris, 1893.

(4) Ratzenhofer, Gustav. *Wesen und Zweck der Politik*. Als Theil der Sociologie und Grundlage der Staatswissenschaften. 3 vols. Leipzig, 1893.

(5) ———. *Die sociologische Erkenntnis*. Positive Philosophie des Socialen Lebens. Leipzig, 1898.

(6) Sorel, Georges. *Reflections on Violence*. New York, 1914.

B. *Conflict and Mental Conflict*

(1) Healy, William. *Mental Conflicts and Misconduct*. Boston, 1917.

(2) Prince, Morton. *The Unconscious*. The fundamentals of personality, normal and abnormal. Chap. xv, ""Instincts, Sentiments, and Conflicts," pp. 446–87; chap. xvi, "General Phenomena Resulting from Emotional Conflicts," pp. 488–528. New York, 1914.

(3) Adler, Alfred. *The Neurotic Constitution*. Outlines of a comparative individualistic psychology and psychotherapy. Translated by Bernard Glueck and John E. Lind. New York, 1917.

(4) Southard, E. E., and Jarrett, Mary C. *The Kingdom of Evils*. Psychiatric social work presented in one hundred case histories, together with a classification of social divisions of evil. New York, 1922.

(5) Adler, Alfred. *A Study of Organ Inferiority and Its Psychical Compensation.* A contribution to clinical medicine. Translated by S. E. Jelliffe. "Nervous and Mental Disease Monograph Series," No. 24. New York, 1917.

(6) Lay, Wilfrid. *Man's Unconscious Conflict.* A popular exposition of psychoanalysis. New York, 1917.

(7) Blanchard, Phyllis. *The Adolescent Girl.* A study from the psychoanalytic viewpoint. Chap. iii, "The Adolescent Conflict," pp. 87–115. New York, 1920.

(8) Weeks, Arland D. *Social Antagonisms.* Chicago, 1918.

C. *Rivalry*

(1) Baldwin, J. Mark, editor. *Dictionary of Philosophy and Psychology.* Article on "Rivalry." Vol. II, pp. 476–78.

(2) Vincent, George E. "The Rivalry of Social Groups," *American Journal of Sociology,* XVI (1910–11), 469–84.

(3) Ordahl, G. "Rivalry: Its Genetic Development and Pedagogy," *The Pedagogical Seminary,* XV (1908), 492–549. [Bibliography.]

(4) Ely, Richard T. *Studies in the Evolution of Industrial Society.* Chap. ii, "Rivalry and Success in Economic Life," pp. 152–63. New York, 1903.

(5) Cooley, Charles H. *Personal Competition: Its Place in the Social Order and Effect upon Individuals; with Some Considerations on Success.* "Economic Studies," Vol. IV, No. 2. New York, 1899.

(6) Triplett, N. "The Dynamogenic Factors in Pacemaking and Competition," *American Journal of Psychology,* IX (1897–98), 507–33.

(7) Baldwin, J. Mark. "La Concurrence sociale et l'individualisme," *Revue internationale de sociologie,* XVIII (1910), 641–57.

(8) Groos, Karl. *The Play of Man.* Translated with author's co-operation by Elizabeth L. Baldwin with a preface by J. Mark Baldwin. New York, 1901.

D. *Discussion*

(1) Bagehot, Walter. *Physics and Politics.* Or thoughts on the application of the principles of "Natural Selection" and "Inheritance" to political society. Chap. v, "The Age of Discussion," pp. 156–204. New York, 1875.

(2) Robertson, John M. *A Short History of Free Thought, Ancient and Modern.* 2 vols. New York, 1906.

(3) Windelband, Wilhelm. *Geschichte der alten Philosophie.* "Die Sophistik und Sokrates," pp. 63–92. München, 1894.

(4) Mackay, R. W. *The Progress of the Intellect as Exemplified in the Religious Development of the Greeks and Hebrews.* London, 1850.

(5) Stephen, Sir Leslie. *History of English Thought in the Eighteenth Century.* 2d ed., 2 vols. London, 1881.

(6) Damiron, J. Ph. *Mémoires pour servir à l'histoire de la philosophie au 18 e siècle.* 3 vols. Paris, 1858–64.

(7) Draper, J. W. *History of the Intellectual Development of Europe.* Rev. ed., 2 vols. New York, 1904.

(8) ———. *History of the Conflict between Religion and Science.* New York, 1873.

(9) Lecky, W. E. H. *History of the Rise and Influence of the Spirit of Rationalism in Europe.* Rev. ed., 2 vols. New York, 1903.
(10) White, Andrew D. *History of the Warfare of Science with Theology.* An expansion of an earlier essay, "The Warfare of Science," 2d ed., 1877. 2 vols. New York, 1896.
(11) Haynes, E. S. P. *Religious Persecution.* A study in political psychology. London, 1904.
(12) Chafee, Zechariah, Jr. *Freedom of Speech.* New York, 1920.

II. TYPES OF CONFLICT

A. *War*

1. Psychology and Sociology of War:

(1) Darwin, Charles. *The Descent of Man.* Chaps. xvii and xviii. "Secondary Sexual Characters of Mammals," pp. 511–67. (Gives account of the fighting instinct in males and the methods of fighting of animals.) 2d rev. ed. New York, 1907.
(2) Bovet, Pierre. *The Fighting Instinct.* Translated from the French by J. Y. Greig. New York, 1923.
(3) Thorndike, Edward L. *The Original Nature of Man.* "Fighting," pp. 68–75. New York, 1913.
(4) Hall, G. Stanley. "A Study of Anger," *American Journal of Psychology*, X (1898–99), 516–91.
(5) Stratton, George M. *Anger.* Its religious and moral significance. New York, 1923.
(6) Patrick, G. T. W. *The Psychology of Social Reconstruction.* Boston, 1920.
(7) ———. *The Psychology of Relaxation.* Chap. vi, "The Psychology of War," pp. 219–52. Boston, 1916.
(8) Pillsbury, W. B. *The Psychology of Nationalism and Internationalism.* New York, 1919.
(9) Trotter, W. *Instincts of the Herd in Peace and War.* London, 1916.
(10) La Grasserie, R. de. "De l'intolérance comme phénomène social," *Revue Internationale de Sociologie*, XVIII (1910), 76–113.
(11) Percin, Alexandre. *Le Combat.* Paris, 1914.
(12) Huot, Louis, and Voivenel, Paul. *Le Courage.* Paris, 1917.
(13) Porter, W. T. *Shock at the Front.* Boston, 1918.
(14) Lord, Herbert G. *The Psychology of Courage.* Boston, 1918.
(15) Hall, G. Stanley. *Morale, the Supreme Standard of Life and Conduct.* New York, 1920.
(16) Roussy, G., and Lhermitte, J. *The Psychoneuroses of War.* Translated by W. B. Christopherson. London, 1918.
(17) Babinski, J. F., and Froment, J. *Hysteria or Pithiatism, and Reflex Nervous Disorders in the Neurology of the War.* Translated by J. D. Rolleston, with a preface by E. Farquhar Buzzard. London, 1918.

2. The Natural History of War:

(1) Sumner, William G. *War and Other Essays.* Edited with an introduction by Albert Galloway Keller. New Haven, 1911.
(2) Letourneau, Ch. *La Guerre dans les diverses races humaines.* Paris, 1895.

(3) Frobenius, Leo. *Weltgeschichte des Krieges.* Unter Mitwirkung von Oberstleutnant a.D. H. Frobenius u. Korvetten-Kapitän a.D. E. Kohlhauer. Hannover, 1903.

(4) Bakeless, John. *The Economic Causes of Modern Wars.* A study of the period 1878-1918. New York, 1921.

(5) Crosby, Oscar T. *International War, Its Causes and Its Cure.* London, 1919.

(6) Sombart, Werner. *Krieg und Kapitalismus.* Studien zur Entwicklungsgeschichte des modernen Kapitalismus. Vol. II, München, 1913.

(7) Lagorgette, Jean. *Le Rôle de la guerre.* Étude de sociologie générale. Préface de M. Anatole Leroy-Beaulieu. Paris, 1906.

(8) Steinmetz, S. R. *Der Krieg als sociologisches Problem.* Pp. 21 ff. Amsterdam, 1899.

(9) ———. *Die Philosophie des Krieges.* "Natur- und kulturphilosophische Bibliothek," Band VI. Leipzig, 1907.

(10) Constantin, A. *Le rôle sociologique de la guerre et le sentiment national.* Suivi de la guerre comme moyen de sélection collective, par S. R. Steinmetz. "Bibliothèque scientifique internationale," Tome CVIII. Paris, 1907.

(11) Keller, Albert G. *Through War to Peace.* New York, 1918.

(12) Worms, René, editor. "Les luttes sociales." *Annales de l'institut international de sociologie.* Tome XI. Paris, 1907.

(13) Fielding-Hall, H. *Nature of War and Its Causes.* London, 1917.

(14) Oliver, Frederick S. *Ordeal by Battle.* London, 1915.

3. War and Human Nature:

(1) Petit-Dutaillis, C. E. "L'Appel de guerre en Dauphiné Isére 2 août 1914," *Annales de l'Université de Grenoble,* XXVII (1915), 1-59. [Documents consisting of letters written by instructors and others describing the sentiments with which the declaration of war was received.]

(2) Wood, W., editor. *Soldiers' Stories of the War.* London, 1915.

(3) Buswell, Leslie. *Ambulance No. 10: Personal Letters from the Front.* Boston, 1916.

(4) Kilpatrick, James A. *Tommy Atkins at War as Told in His Own Letters.* New York, 1914.

(5) Fadl, Said Memun Abul. "Die Frauen des Islams und der Weltkrieg," *Nord und Süd,* CLV (Nov., 1915), 171-74. [Contains a letter from a Turkish mother to her son at the front.]

(6) Maublanc, René. "La guerre vue par des enfants (septembre, 1914)." (Récits par des enfants de campagne.) *Revue de Paris,* XXII (septembre-octobre, 1915), 396-418

(7) Daudet, Ernest, editor. "L'âme française et l'âme allemande." Lettres de soldats. *Documents pour l'histoire de la guerre.* Paris, 1915.

(8) "Heimatsbriefe an russische Soldaten." (Neue philologische Rundschau; hrsg. von dr. C. Wagener und dr. E. Ludwig in Bremen. Jahrg. 1886-1908.) *Die neue Rundschau.* II (1915), 1673-83.

(9) "The Attack at Loos," by a French Lieutenant. "Under Shell-Fire at Dunkirk," by an American Nurse. "The Winter's War," by a British Captain. "The Bitter Experience of Lorraine," by the Prefect of Meurthe-et-Moselle. *Atlantic Monthly*, CXVI (1915), 688–711.

(10) Böhme, Margarete. *Kriegsbriefe der Familie Wimmel.* (Personal experiences in the Great War). Dresden, 1915.

(11) Chevillon, André. "Lettres d'un soldat," *Revue de Paris*, XXII (juillet-août, 1915), 471–95.

(12) Boutroux, Pièrre. "Les soldats allemands en campagne, d'après leur correspondance," *Revue de Paris*, XXII (septembre-octobre, 1915), 323–43; 470–91.

(13) West, Arthur G. *The Diary of a Dead Officer.* London, 1918.

(14) Mayer, Émile. "Émotions des chefs en campagne," *Bibliothèque universelle et Revue Suisse*, LXIX (1913), 98–131.

(15) Wehrhan, K. "Volksdichtung über unsere gefallenen Helden," *Die Grenzboten*, LXXIV (No. 28, July 14, 1915), 58–64. [Calls attention to growth of a usage (anfangs, wagte sich der Brauch nur schüchtern, hier und da, hervor) of printing verses, some original, some quoted, in the death notices.]

(16) Naumann, Friedrich. "Der Kriegsglaube," *Die Hilfe*, XXI (No. 36, Sept. 9, 1915), 576. [Sketches the forces that have created a war creed, in which all confessions participate, immediately and without formalities.]

(17) Roepke, Dr. Fritz. "Der Religiöse Geist in deutschen Soldatenbriefen," *Die Grenzboten*, LXXIV (No. 30, July 28, 1915), 124–28. [An interesting analysis of letters which are not reproduced in full.]

(18) Wendland, Walter. "Krieg und Religion," *Die Grenzboten*, LXXIV (No. 33, Sept. 11, 1915), 212–19. [Reviews the literature of war and religion.]

(19) Bang, J. P. *Hurrah and Hallelujah.* The teaching of Germany's poets, prophets, professors, and preachers; a documentation. From the Danish by Jessie Bröchner. London and New York, 1917.

B. *Industrial Conflicts*

(1) Schwittau, G. *Die Formen des wirtschaftlichen Kampfes, Streik, Boykott, Aussperrung, usw.* Eine volkswirtschaftliche Untersuchung auf dem Gebiete der gegenwärtigen Arbeitspolitik. Berlin, 1912. [Bibliography.]

(2) Hall, Frederick S. *Sympathetic Strikes and Sympathetic Lockouts.* "Columbia University Studies in Political Science." Vol. X. New York, 1898. [Bibliography.]

(3) Bing, Alexander M. *War-time Strikes and Their Adjustment.* With an introduction by Felix Adler. New York, 1921.

(4) Egerton, Charles E., and Durand, E. Dana. *U. S. Industrial Commission Reports of the Industrial Commission on Labor Organizations.* "Labor Disputes and Arbitration." Washington, 1901.

(5) Janes, George M. *The Control of Strikes in American Trade Unions.* Baltimore, 1916.

(6) United States Strike Commission, 1895. *Report on the Chicago Strike of June–July, 1894, by the United States Strike Commission.* Washington, 1895.

(7) Warne, Frank J. "The Anthracite Coal Strike," *Annals of the American Academy,* XVII (1901), 15–52.

(8) Anthracite Coal Strike Commission, 1902–3. *Report to the President on the Anthracite Coal Strike of May–October, 1902, by the Anthracite Coal Strike Commission.* Washington, 1903.

(9) Hanford, Benjamin. *The Labor War in Colorado.* New York, 1904.

(10) Rastall, B. M. *The Labor History of the Cripple Creek District.* A study in industrial evolution. Madison, Wis., 1908.

(11) United States Bureau of Labor. *Report on Strike at Bethlehem Steel Works, South Bethlehem, Pennsylvania.* Prepared under the direction of Charles P. Neill, commissioner of labor. Washington, 1910.

(12) Wright, Arnold. *Disturbed Dublin.* The story of the great strike of 1913–14, with a description of the industries of the Irish Capital. London, 1914.

(13) Seattle General Strike Committee. *The Seattle General Strike.* An account of what happened in the Seattle labor movement, during the general strike, February 6–11, 1919. Seattle, 1919.

(14) Interchurch World Movement. *Report on the Steel Strike of 1919.* New York, 1920.

(15) U.S. Bureau of Labor Statistics. *Report in Regard to the Strike of Mine Workers in the Michigan Copper District.* Bulletin No. 139. February 7, 1914.

(16) ———. *Strikes and Lockouts, 1881–1905.* Twenty-first annual report, 1906.

(17) Foster, William Z. *The Great Steel Strike and Its Lessons.* New York, 1920.

(18) Wolman, Leo. "The Boycott in American Trade Unions," *Johns Hopkins University Studies in Historical and Political Science,* Vol. XXXIV. Baltimore, 1916.

(19) Laidler, Harry W. *Boycotts and the Labor Struggle.* Economic and legal aspects. With an introduction by Henry R. Seager. New York and London, 1914.

(20) Hunter, Robert. *Violence and the Labour Movement.* New York, 1914. [Bibliography.]

(21) Case, Clarence M. *Non-Violent Coercion.* A study in methods of social pressure. New York, 1923.

[See bibliography, "Social Unrest," pp. 935–36.]

C. *Race Conflict*

1. Race Relations in General:

(1) Bryce, James. *The Relations of the Advanced and the Backward Races of Mankind.* Oxford, 1903.

(2) Simpson, Bertram L. *The Conflict of Colour.* The threatened upheaval throughout the world, by Weale, B. L. P. [*pseud.*]. London, 1910.

(3) Steiner, Jesse F. *The Japanese Invasion.* A study in the psychology of inter-racial contacts. Chicago, 1917.
(4) Stoddard, T. Lothrop. *The Rising Tide of Color against White World-Supremacy.* New York, 1920.
(5) Blyden, Edward W. *Christianity, Islam, and the Negro Race.* London, 1888.
(6) Spiller, G., editor. *Papers on Inter-racial Problems.* Communicated to the First Universal Races Congress, London, 1911, pp. 463–77. Boston, 1911. [Bibliography on Race Problems.]
(7) Baker, Ray S. *Following the Color Line.* An account of Negro citizenship in the American democracy. New York, 1908.
(8) Miller, Kelly. *Race Adjustment.* Essays on the Negro in America. New York, 1908.
(9) Stephenson, Gilbert T. *Race Distinctions in American Law.* New York, 1910.
(10) Mecklin, John M. *Democracy and Race Friction.* A study in social ethics. New York, 1914.
(11) Evans, Maurice. *Black and White in South East Africa.* London, 1911.
(12) ———. *Black and White in the Southern States.* A study of the race problem in the United States from a South African point of view. London, 1915.
(13) Brailsford, H. N. *Macedonia: Its Races and Their Future.* London, 1906.
(14) Means, Philip A. *Racial Factors in Democracy.* Boston, 1918.

2. Race Friction and Race Prejudice:

(1) Crawley, Ernest. *The Mystic Rose.* A study of primitive marriage. Pp. 33–58; 76–235. London, 1902. [Taboo as a mechanism for regulating contacts.]
(2) Thomas, W. I. "The Psychology of Race-Prejudice," *American Journal of Sociology,* IX (1903–4), 593–611.
(3) Finot, Jean. *Race Prejudice.* Translated from the French by Florence Wade-Evans. London, 1906.
(4) Pillsbury, W. B. *The Psychology of Nationality and Internationalism.* Chap. iii, "Hate as a Social Force," pp. 63–89.
(5) Shaler, N. S. "Race Prejudices," *Atlantic Monthly,* LVIII (1886), 510–18.
(6) Stone, Alfred H. *Studies in the American Race Problem.* Chap. vi, "Race Friction," pp. 211–41. New York, 1908.
(7) Mecklin, John M. *Democracy and Race Friction.* A study in social ethics. Chap. v, "Race-Prejudice," pp. 123–56. New York, 1914.
(8) Belloc, Hilaire. *The Jews.* London, 1922.
(9) Heifetz, Elias. *The Slaughter of the Jews in the Ukraine in 1919.* New York, 1921.
(10) Bailey, T. P. *Race Orthodoxy in the South.* And other aspects of the negro question. New York, 1914.
(11) Parton, James. "Antipathy to the Negro," *North American Review,* CXXVII (1878), 476–91.

(12) Duncan, Sara Jeannette. "Eurasia," *Popular Science Monthly*, XLII (1892), 1–9.

(13) Morse, Josiah. "The Psychology of Prejudice," *International Journal of Ethics*, XVII (1906–7), 490–506.

(14) McDougall, William. *An Introduction to Social Psychology.* Chap. xi, "The Instinct of Pugnacity," pp. 279–95; "The Instinct of Pugnacity and the Emotion of Anger," pp. 49–61. 4th rev. ed. Boston, 1912.

(15) Royce, Josiah. *Race Questions, Provincialism, and Other American Problems.* Chap. i, "Race Questions and Prejudices," pp. 1–53. New York, 1908.

(16) Thomas, W. I. "Race Psychology: Standpoint and Questionnaire, with Particular Reference to the Immigrant and the Negro," *American Journal of Sociology*, XVII (1912–13), 725–75.

(17) Schoell, Franck L. *La question des noirs aux États-Unis.* Paris, 1923.

(18) Park, Robert E. "Negro Race Consciousness as Reflected in Race Literature," *American Review*, I, (1923), 505–17.

(19) Bryce, James. *Race Sentiment as a Factor in History.* London, 1915.

3. Lynch Law and Lynching:

(1) Walling, W. E. "The Race War in the North," *Independent*, LXV (July–Sept., 1908), 529–34.

(2) "The So-Called Race Riot at Springfield," by an Eye Witness. *Charities*, XX (1908), 709–11.

(3) Seligmann, H. J. "Race War?" *New Republic*, XX (1919), 48–50. [The Washington race riot.]

(4) Leonard, O. "The East St. Louis Pogrom," *Survey*, XXXIII (1917), 331–33.

(5) Sandburg, C. *The Chicago Race Riots, July, 1919.* New York, 1919.

(6) Chicago Commission on Race Relations. *The Negro in Chicago.* Chicago, 1922.

(7) Cutler, James E. *Lynch-Law.* An investigation into the history of lynching in the United States. New York, 1905.

(8) National Association for the Advancement of Colored People. *Thirty Years of Lynching in the United States, 1899–1918.* New York, 1919.

(9) ———. *Burning at Stake in the United States.* A record of the public burning by mobs of six men, during the first six months of 1919, in the states of Arkansas, Florida, Georgia, Mississippi, and Texas. New York, 1919.

D. *Feuds*

(1) Miklosich, Franz. *Die Blutrache bei den Slaven.* Wien, 1887.

(2) Johnston, C. "The Land of the Blood Feud," *Harper's Weekly*, LVII (Jan. 11, 1913), 42.

(3) Davis, H., and Smyth, C. "The Land of Feuds," *Munsey's*, XXX (1903–4), 161–72.

(4) "Avenging Her Father's Death," *Literary Digest*, XLV (November 9, 1912), 864–70.

(5) Campbell, John C. *The Southern Highlander and His Homeland*, pp. 110-13. New York, 1921.

(6) Wermert, Georg. *Die Insel Sicilien, in volkswirtschaftlicher, kultureller, and sozialer Beziehung.* Chap. xxvii, "Volkscharacter und Mafia." Berlin, 1901.

(7) Heijningen, Hendrik M. K. van. *Het Straf- en Wraakrecht in den Indischen Archipel.* Leiden, 1916.

(8) Steinmetz, S. R. *Ethnologische Studien zur ersten Entwicklung der Strafe, nebst einer psychologischen Abhandlung über Grausamkeit und Rachsucht.* 2 vols. Leiden, 1894.

(9) Wesnitsch, Milenko R. *Die Blutrache bei den Südslaven.* Ein Beitrag zur Geschichte des Strafrechts. Stuttgart, 1889.

(10) Bourde, Paul. *En Corse.* L'esprit de clan—les mœurs politiques —les vendettas—le banditisme. Correspondances adressées au "Temps." Cinquième édition. Paris, 1906.

(11) Dorsey, J. Owen. "Omaha Sociology," chap. xii, "The Law," sec. 310, "Murder," p. 369. In *Third Annual Report of the U.S. Bureau of American Ethnology, 1881-82.* Washington, 1884.

(12) Woods, A. "The Problem of the Black Hand," *McClure's,* XXXIII (1909), 40-47.

(13) Park, Robert E., and Miller, Herbert A. *Old World Traits Transplanted.* New York, 1921. [See pp. 241-58 for details of rise and decline of Black Hand in New York.]

(14) White, F. M. "The Passing of the Black Hand," *Century,* XCV, N.S. 73 (1917-18), 331-37.

(15) Cutrera, A. *La Mafia e i mafiosi.* Origini e manifestazioni. Studio di sociologia criminale, con una carta a colori su la densità della Mafia in Sicilia. Palermo, 1900.

E. *The Duel and the Ordeal of Battle*

(1) Millingen, J. G. *The History of Duelling.* Including narrative of the most remarkable personal encounters that have taken place from the earliest period to the present time. 2 vols. London, 1841.

(2) Steinmetz, Andrew. *The Romance of Duelling in All Times and Countries.* London, 1868.

(3) Sabine, Lorenzo. *Notes on Duels and Duelling.* Boston, 1855.

(4) Glotz, Gustave. "Les ordalies en Grèce," *Revue historique,* XC (1906), 1-17.

(5) Patetta, F. *Le Ordalie.* Studio di storia del diritto e scienza del diritto comparato. Turino, 1890.

(6) Lea, Henry C. *Superstition and Force.* Essays on the wager of law, the wager of battle, the ordeal, torture. 4th ed., rev. Philadelphia, 1892.

(7) Neilson, George. *Trial by Combat.* In Great Britain. Glasgow and London, 1890.

[See bibliography, "Ancient and Primitive Law," pp. 860-61.]

F. *Games and Gambling*

(1) Culin, Stewart. "Street Games of Boys in Brooklyn, N.Y.," *The Journal of American Folk-Lore,* IV (1891), 221-37.

(2) ———. *Korean Games.* With notes on the corresponding games of China and Japan. Philadelphia, 1895.

(3) ———. "Games of the North American Indians," *Twenty-fourth Annual Report of the Bureau of American Ethnology, 1902–3.* Washington, 1907.

(4) Steinmetz, Andrew. *The Gaming Table: Its Votaries and Victims, in All Times and Countries, Especially in England and in France.* London, 1870.

(5) Thomas, W. I. "The Gaming Instinct," *American Journal of Sociology,* VI (1900–1901), 750–63.

(6) O'Brien, Frederick. *White Shadows in the South Seas.* Chap. xxii, pp. 240–48. [Memorable Game for Matches in the Cocoanut Grove of Lano Kaioo.]

III. CONFLICT GROUPS

A. *Gangs*

(1) Johnson, John H. *Rudimentary Society Among Boys.* "Johns Hopkins University Studies in Historical and Political Science," 2d series, XI, 491–546. Baltimore, 1884.

(2) Puffer, J. Adams. *The Boy and His Gang.* Boston, 1912.

(3) Sheldon, H. D., "Institutional Activities of American Children," *American Journal of Psychology,* IX (1899), 425–48.

(4) Thurston, Henry W. *Delinquency and Spare Time.* A study of a few stories written into the court records of the city of Cleveland. Cleveland, Ohio, 1918.

(5) Woods, Robert A., editor. *The City Wilderness.* A settlement study by residents and associates of the South End House. Chap. vi, "The Roots of Political Power," pp. 114–47. Boston, 1898.

(6) Hoyt, F. C. "The Gang in Embryo," *Scribner's,* LXVIII (1920), 146–54. [Presiding justice of the Children's Court of the city of New York.]

(7) *Boyhood and Lawlessness.* Chap. iv, "His Gangs," pp. 39–54. Russell Sage Foundation, New York, 1914.

(8) Culin, Stewart. "Street Games of Boys in Brooklyn, N.Y.," *The Journal of American Folklore,* IV (1891), 221–37. [For observations on gangs see p. 235.]

(9) Adams, Brewster. "The Street Gang as a Factor in Politics," *Outlook,* LXXIV (1903), 985–88.

(10) Lane, W. D. "The Four Gunmen," *The Survey,* XXXII (1914), 13–16.

(11) Rhodes, J. F. "The Molly Maguires in the Anthracite Region of Pennsylvania," *American Historical Review,* XV (1909–10), 547–61.

(12) Train, Arthur. "Imported Crime: The Story of the Camorra in America," *McClure's,* XXXIX (1912), 82–94.

B. *Sects*

(1) Nordhoff, Charles. *The Communistic Societies of the United States from Personal Visit and Observation.* Including chapters on "The Amana Society," "The Separatists of Zoar," "The Shakers," "The Oneida and Wallingford Perfectionists," "The Aurora and Bethel Communes." New York, 1875.

(2) Gillin, John L. *The Dunkers: A Sociological Interpretation.* New York, 1906. [Columbia University dissertation, V, 2.]
(3) Milmine, Georgine. *The Life of Mary Baker G. Eddy and the History of Christian Science.* New York, 1909.
(4) Gehring, Johannes. *Die Sekten der russischen Kirche, 1003-1897.* Nach ihrem Ursprunge und inneren Zusammenhange dargestellt. Leipzig, 1898.
(5) Grass, K. K. *Die russischen Sekten.* I, "Die Gottesleute oder Chlüsten"; II, "Die weissen Tauben oder Skopzen." Leipzig, 1907-9.
(6) Lea, Henry Charles. *The Moriscos of Spain.* Their conversion and expulsion. Philadelphia, 1901.
(7) Friesen, P. M. *Geschichte der alt-evangelischen mennoniten Brüderschaft in Russland (1789-1910) im Rahmen der mennonitischen Gesamtgeschichte.* Halbstadt, 1911.
(8) Kalb, Ernst. *Kirchen und Sekten der Gegenwart.* Unter Mitarbeit verschiedener evangelischer Theologen. Stuttgart, 1905.
(9) Blanchard, R. H. "Notes on Egyptian Saints," *Harvard African Studies,* I (1917), 182-92.
(10) Mathiez, Albert. *Les origines des cultes révolutionnaires.* (1789-92.) Paris, 1904.
(11) Rossi, Pasquale. *Mistici e Settarii.* Studio di psicopatologia collettiva. Milan, 1900.
(12) Rohde, Erwin. *Psyche: Seelencult und Unsterblichkeitsglaube der Griechen.* Freiburg, 1890.

C. *Economic Conflict Groups*

(1) Webb, Sidney and Beatrice. *Industrial Democracy.* London, 1897.
(2) ———. *The History of Trade Unionism.* (Revised edition extended to 1920.) New York and London, 1920.
(3) Commons, John R., editor. *Trade Unionism and Labor Problems,* Boston, 1905.
(4) ———. *History of Labor in the United States.* 2 vols. New York, 1918.
(5) Groat, George G. *An Introduction to the Study of Organized Labor in America.* New York, 1916.
(6) Hoxie, R. F. *Trade Unionism in the United States.* New York, 1917.
(7) Marot, Helen. *American Labor Unions.* By a member. New York, 1914.
(8) Carlton, Frank T. *Organized Labor in American History.* New York, 1920.
(9) Levine, Louis. *Syndicalism in France.* 2d rev. ed. of *The Labor Movement in France.* New York and London, 1914.
(10) Brissenden, Paul Frederick. *The I.W.W., A Study of American Syndicalism.* New York, 1919. [Bibliography.]
(11) Brooks, John Graham. *American Syndicalism; the I.W.W.* New York, 1913.
(12) ———. *Labor's Challenge to the Social Order.* Democracy its own critic and educator. New York, 1920.
(13) Baker, Ray Stannard. *The New Industrial Unrest.* Reasons and remedies. New York, 1920.

(14) Commons, John R. *Industrial Democracy.* New York, 1921.
(15) Brentano, Lujo. *On the History and Development of Gilds and the Origin of Trade Unions.* London, 1870.

D. *Parties*

(1) Bluntschli, Johann K. *Charakter und Geist der politischen Parteien.* Nördlingen, 1869.
(2) Ostrogorskïi, Moisei. *Democracy and the Organization of Political Parties.* Translated from the French by F. Clarke with a preface by Right Hon. James Bryce. New York and London, 1902.
(3) Lowell, A. Lawrence. *Governments and Parties in Continental Europe.* 2 vols. Boston, 1896.
(4) Merriam, Charles E. *The American Party System.* An introduction to the study of political parties in the United States. New York, 1922.
(5) Haynes, F. E. *Third Party Movements since the Civil War, with Special Reference to Iowa.* A study in social politics. Iowa City, 1916.
(6) Ray, P. O. *An Introduction to Political Parties and Practical Politics.* New York, 1913.
(7) Bryce, James. *The American Commonwealth.* 2 vols. New rev. ed. New York, 1911.
(8) Hadley, Arthur T. *Undercurrents in American Politics.* Being the Ford Lectures, delivered at Oxford University, and the Barbour-Page Lectures, delivered at the University of Virginia in the spring of 1914. New Haven, 1915.
(9) Lowell, A. Lawrence. *Annual Report of the American Historical Association, 1901.* 2 vols. "The Influence of Party upon Legislation in England and America" (with four diagrams), I, 319–542. Washington, 1902.
(10) Beard, Charles A. *Economic Origins of Jeffersonian Democracy.* New York, 1915.
(11) Morgan, W. T. *English Political Parties and Leaders in the Reign of Queen Anne, 1702–1710.* New Haven, 1920.
(12) Michels, Robert. *Political Parties.* A sociological study of the oligarchical tendencies of modern democracy. Translated by Eden and Cedar Paul. New York, 1915.
(13) Haines, Lynn. *Your Congress.* An interpretation of the political and parliamentary influences that dominate law-making in America. Washington, D.C., 1915.
(14) Hichborn, Franklin. *Story of the Session of the California Legislature.* San Francisco, 1909, 1911, 1913, 1915.
(15) Myers, Gustavus. *The History of Tammany Hall.* 2d ed. rev. and enl. New York, 1917.
(16) Roosevelt, Theodore. *An Autobiography.* New York, 1913.
(17) Platt, Thomas C. *Autobiography.* Compiled and edited by Louis J. Lang. New York, 1910.
(18) Older, Fremont. *My Own Story.* San Francisco, 1919.
(19) Orth, Samuel P. *The Boss and the Machine.* A chronicle of the politicians and party organization. New Haven, 1919.

(20) Riordon, William L. *Plunkitt of Tammany Hall*. A series of very plain talks on very practical politics, delivered by ex-Senator George Washington Plunkitt, the Tammany philosopher, from his rostrum—the New York County Court House boot-black stand. New York, 1905.

(21) Gosnell, H. F. *Boss Platt and His New York Machine*. A study of the political leadership of Thomas C. Platt, Theodore Roosevelt, and others. With an introduction by C. E. Merriam, Chicago, 1924.

E. *Nationalities*

(1) Oakesmith, John. *Race and Nationality*. An inquiry into the origin and growth of patriotism. New York, 1919.

(2) Lillehei, Ingebrigt. "Landsmaal and the Language Movement in Norway," *Journal of English and Germanic Philology*, XIII (1914), 60–87.

(3) Morris, Lloyd R. *The Celtic Dawn*. A survey of the renascence in Ireland, 1889–1916. New York, 1917.

(4) Keith, Arthur. *Nationality and Race from an Anthropologist's Point of View*. London, 1919.

(5) Barnes, Harry E. "Nationality and Historiography" in the article "History, Its Rise and Development," *Encyclopedia Americana*, XIV, 234–43.

(6) Fisher, H. A. "French Nationalism," *Hibbert Journal*, XV (1916–17), 217–29.

(7) Ellis, H. "The Psychology of the English," *Edinburgh Review*, CCXXIII (April, 1916), 223–43.

(8) Bevan, Edwyn R. *Indian Nationalism*. An independent estimate. London, 1913.

(9) Le Bon, Gustave. *The Psychology of Peoples*. London, 1898.

(10) Francke, K. "The Study of National Culture," *Atlantic Monthly*, XCIX (1907), 409–16.

(11) Auerbach, Bertrand. *Les races et nationalités en Autriche-Hongrie*. Deuxième édition revisée. Paris, 1917.

(12) Butler, Ralph. *The New Eastern Europe*. London, 1919.

(13) Kerlin, Robert T. *The Voice of the Negro 1919*. New York, 1920. [A compilation from the colored press of America for the four months immediately succeeding the Washington riots.]

(14) Boas, F. "Nationalism," *Dial*, LXVI (March 8, 1919), 232–37.

(15) Buck, Carl D. "Language and the Sentiment of Nationality," *The American Political Science Review*, X (1916), 44–69.

(16) McLaren, A. D. "National Hate," *Hibbert Journal*, XV (1916–17), 407–18.

(17) Miller, Herbert A. "The Rising National Individualism," *Publications of the American Sociological Society*, VIII (1913), 49–65.

(18) Zimmern, Alfred E. *Nationality and Government*. With other wartime essays. London and New York, 1918.

(19) Small, Albion W. "Bonds of Nationality," *American Journal of Sociology*, XX (1915–16), 629–83.

(20) Faber, Geoffrey. "The War and Personality in Nations," *Fortnightly Review*, CIII (1915), 538–46. Also in *Living Age*, CCLXXXV (1915), 265–72.

TOPICS FOR WRITTEN THEMES

1. The History of Conflict as a Sociological Concept
2. Types of Conflict: War, the Duello, Litigation, Gambling, the Feud, Discussion, etc.
3. Conflict Groups: Gangs, Labor Organizations, Sects, Parties, Nationalities, etc.
4. Mental Conflicts and the Development of Personality
5. Sex Differences in Conflict
6. Subtler Forms of Conflict: Rivalry, Emulation, Jealousy, Aversion, etc.
7. Personal Rivalry in Polite Society
8. Conflict and Social Status
9. The Strike as an Expression of the Wish for Recognition
10. Popular Justice: the History of the Molly Maguires, of the Night Riders, etc.
11. The Sociology of Race Prejudice
12. Race Riots in the North and the South
13. War as an Action Pattern, Biological or Social?
14. War as a Form of Relaxation
15. The Great War Interpreted by Personal Documents
16. Conflict and Social Organization
17. Conflict and Social Progress

QUESTIONS FOR DISCUSSION

1. How do you differentiate between competition and conflict?
2. Is conflict always conscious?
3. How do you explain the emotional interest in conflict?
4. In your opinion, are the sexes in about the same degree interested in conflict?
5. In what way do you understand Simmel to relate conflict to the social process?
6. What are the interrelations of war and social contacts?
7. "Without aversion life in a great city would have no thinkable form." Explain.
8. "It is advantageous to hate the opponent with whom one is struggling." Explain.
9. Give illustrations of feuds not mentioned by Simmel.
10. How do you distinguish between feuds and litigation?
11. What examples occur to you of conflicts of impersonal ideals?
12. What are the psychological causes of war?
13. "We may see in war the preliminary process of rejuvenescence." Explain.
14. Has war been essential to the process of social adjustment? Is it still essential?

15. What do you understand by war as a form of relaxation?
16. How do you interpret Professor James's reaction to the Chautauqua?
17. What is the rôle of conflict in recreation?
18. Is it possible to provide psychic equivalents for war?
19. What application of the sociological theory of the relation of ideals to instinct would you make to war?
20. How do you distinguish rivalry from competition and conflict?
21. What bearing have the facts of animal rivalry upon an understanding of rivalry in human society?
22. What are the different devices by which the group achieves and maintains solidarity? How many of these were characteristic of the war-time situation?
23. What are the common characteristics of gangs?
24. By what process is the gang incorporated in the political organization?
25. What do you understand by Giddings' distinction between cultural conflicts and "logical duels"?
26. Have you reason for thinking that cultural conflicts will play a lesser rôle in the future than in the past?
27. To what extent was the world-war a cultural conflict?
28. Under what circumstances do social contacts make (a) for conflict, and (b) for co-operation?
29. What has been the effect of the extension of communication upon the relations of nations? Elaborate.
30. What do you understand by race prejudice as a "more or less instinctive defense-reaction"?
31. To what extent is race prejudice based upon race competition?
32. Do you believe that it is possible to remove the causes of race prejudice?
33. In what ways does race conflict make for race consciousness?
34. What are the different elements or forces in the interaction of races making for race conflict and race consciousness?
35. Is a heightening of race consciousness of value or of disadvantage to a racial group?
36. How do you explain the present tendency of the Negro to substitute the copying of colored models for the imitation of white models?
37. "In the South, the races seem to be tending in the direction of a bi-racial organization of society, in which the Negro is gradually gaining a limited autonomy." Interpret.
38. "All racial problems are distinctly problems of racial distribution." Explain with reference to relative proportion of Negroes, Chinese, and Japanese in certain sections of the United States.
39. Why have few or no race riots occurred in the South?
40. Under what circumstances have race riots occurred in the North?

CHAPTER X

ACCOMMODATION

I. INTRODUCTION

1. Adaptation and Accommodation

The term *adaptation* came into vogue with Darwin's theory of the origin of the species by natural selection. This theory was based upon the observation that no two members of a biological species or of a family are ever exactly alike. Everywhere there is variation and individuality. Darwin's theory assumed this variation and explained the species as the result of natural selection. The individuals best fitted to live under the conditions of life which the environment offered, survived and produced the existing species. The others perished and the species which they represented disappeared. The differences in the species were explained as the result of the accumulation and perpetuation of the individual variations which had "survival value." Adaptations were the variations which had been in this way selected and transmitted.

The term *accommodation* is a kindred concept with a slightly different meaning. The distinction is that adaptation is applied to organic modifications which are transmitted biologically; while accommodation is used with reference to changes in habit, which are transmitted, or may be transmitted, sociologically, that is, in the form of social tradition. The term first used in this sense by Baldwin is defined in the *Dictionary of Philosophy and Psychology*.

In view of modern biological theory and discussion, two modes of adaptation should be distinguished: (*a*) adaptation through variation [hereditary]; (*b*) adaptation through modification [acquired]. For the functional adjustment of the individual to its environment [(*b*) above] J. Mark Baldwin has suggested the term "accommodation," recommending that adaptation be confined to the structural adjustments which are congenital and heredity [(*a*) above]. The term "accommodation" applies to any acquired alteration of function resulting in better adjustment to environment and to the functional changes which are thus effected.[1]

The term accommodation, while it has a limited field of application in biology, has a wide and varied use in sociology. All the social heritages, traditions, sentiments, culture, technique, are accommodations—that is, acquired adjustments that are socially and not biologically transmitted. They are not a part of the racial inheritance of the individual, but are acquired by the person in social experience. The two conceptions are further distinguished in this, that adaptation is an effect of competition, while accommodation, or more properly social accommodation, is the result of conflict.

The outcome of the adaptations and accommodations, which the struggle for existence enforces, is a state of relative equilibrium among the competing species and individual members of these species. The equilibrium which is established by adaptation is biological, which means that, in so far as it is permanent and fixed in the race or the species, it will be transmitted by biological inheritance.

The equilibrium based on accommodation, however, is not biological; it is economic and social and is transmitted, if at all, by tradition. The nature of the economic equilibrium which results from competition has been fully described in chapter viii. The plant community is this equilibrium in its absolute form.

In animal and human societies the community has, so to speak, become incorporated in the individual members of the group. The individuals are adapted to a specific type of communal life, and these adaptations, in animal as distinguished from human societies, are represented in the division of labor between the sexes, in the instincts which secure the protection and welfare of the young, in the so-called gregarious instinct, and all these represent traits that are transmitted biologically. But human societies, although providing for the expression of original tendencies, are organized about tradition, mores, collective representations, in short, *consensus*. And consensus represents, not biological adaptations, but social accommodations.

Social organization, with the exception of the order based on competition and adaptation, is essentially an accommodation of differences through conflicts. This fact explains why diverse-mindedness rather than like-mindedness is characteristic of human as

[1] *Dictionary of Philosophy and Psychology*, I, 15, 8.

distinguished from animal society. Professor Cooley's statement of this point is clear:

The unity of the social mind consists not in agreement but in organization, in the fact of reciprocal influence or causation among its parts, by virtue of which everything that takes place in it is connected with everything else, and so is an outcome of the whole.[1]

The distinction between accommodation and adaptation is illustrated in the difference between domestication and taming. Through domestication and breeding man has modified the original inheritable traits of plants and animals. He has changed the character of the species. Through taming, individuals of species naturally in conflict with man have become accommodated to him. Eugenics may be regarded as a program of biological adaptation of the human race in conscious realization of social ideals. Education, on the other hand, represents a program of accommodation or an organization, modification, and culture of original traits.

Every society represents an organization of elements more or less antagonistic to each other but united for the moment, at least, by an arrangement which defines the reciprocal relations and respective spheres of action of each. This accommodation, this *modus vivendi*, may be relatively permanent as in a society constituted by castes, or quite transitory as in societies made up of open classes. In either case, the accommodation, while it is maintained, secures for the individual or for the group a recognized status.

Accommodation is the natural issue of conflicts. In an accommodation the antagonism of the hostile elements is, for the time being, regulated, and conflict disappears as overt action, although it remains latent as a potential force. With a change in the situation, the adjustment that had hitherto successfully held in control the antagonistic forces fails. There is confusion and unrest which may issue in open conflict. Conflict, whether a war or a strike or a mere exchange of polite innuendoes, invariably issues in a new accommodation or social order, which in general involves a changed status in the relations among the participants. It is only with assimilation that this antagonism, latent in the organization of individuals or groups, is likely to be wholly dissolved.

[1] *Social Organization*, p. 4.

2. Classification of the Materials

The selections on accommodation in the materials are organized under the following heads: (*a*) forms of accommodation; (*b*) subordination and superordination; (*c*) conflict and accommodation; and (*d*) competition, status, and social solidarity.

a) *Forms of accommodation.*—There are many forms of accommodation. One of the most subtle is that which in human geography is called acclimatization, "accommodation to new climatic conditions." Recent studies like those of Huntington in his "Climate and Civilization" have emphasized the effects of climate upon human behavior. The selection upon acclimatization by Brinton states the problems involved in the adjustment of racial groups to different climatic environments. The answers which he gives to the questions raised are not to be regarded as conclusive but only as representative of one school of investigators and as contested by other authorities in this field.

Naturalization, which in its original sense means the process by which a person is made "natural," that is, familiar and at home in a strange social milieu, is a term used in America to describe the legal process by which a foreigner acquires the rights of citizenship. Naturalization, as a social process, is naturally something more fundamental than the legal ceremony of naturalization. It includes accommodation to the folkways, the mores, the conventions, and the social ritual (*Sittlichkeit*). It assumes also participation, to a certain extent at least, in the memories, the tradition, and the culture of a new social group. The proverb "In Rome do as the Romans do" is a basic principle of naturalization. The cosmopolitan is the person who readily accommodates himself to the codes of conduct of new social milieus.[1]

[1] A teacher in the public schools of Chicago came in possession of the following letter written to a friend in Mississippi by a Negro boy who had come to the city from the South two months previously. It illustrates his rapid accommodation to the situation including the hostile Irish group (the Wentworth Avenue "Mickeys").

Dear leon I write to you—to let you hear from me—Boy you dont know the time we have with Sled. it Snow up here Regular. We Play foot Ball. But Now we have So much Snow we dont Play foot Ball any More. We Ride on Sled. Boy I have a Sled call The king of The hill and She king to. tell Mrs. Sara that Coln Roscoe Conklin Simon Spoke at St Mark the church we Belong to.

Gus I havnt got chance to Beat But to Boy. Sack we show Runs them Mickeys. Boy them scoundle is bad on Wentworth Avenue.

Add ₃123a Breton St Chi ill.

The difficulty of social accommodation to a new social milieu is not always fully appreciated. The literature on homesickness and nostalgia indicates the emotional dependence of the person upon familiar associations and upon early intimate personal relations. Leaving home for the first time, the intense lonesomeness of the rural lad in the crowds of the city, the perplexity of the immigrant in the confusing maze of strange, and to him inexplicable, customs are common enough instances of the personal and social barriers to naturalization. But the obstacles to most social adjustments for a person in a new social world are even more baffling because of their subtle and intangible nature.

Just as in biology balance represents "a state of relatively good adjustment due to structural adaptation of the organism as a whole" so accommodation, when applied to groups rather than individuals, signifies their satisfactory co-ordination from the standpoint of the inclusive social organization.

Historically, the organization of the more inclusive society— i.e., states, confederations, empires, social and political units composed of groups accommodated but not fully assimilated—presents four typical constellations of the component group. Primitive society was an organization of kinship groups. Ancient society was composed of masters and slaves, with some special form of accommodation for the freeman and the stranger, who was not a citizen, to be sure, but was not a slave either.

Medieval society rested upon a system of class, approaching castes in the distances it enforced. In all these different situations competition took place only between individuals of the same status.

In contrast with this, modern society is made up of economic and social classes with freedom of economic competition and freedom in passage, therefore, from one class to the other.

b) Subordination and superordination.—Accommodation, in the area of personal relations, tends to take the form of subordination and superordination. Even where accommodation has been imposed, as in the case of slavery, by force, the personal relations of master and slave are invariably supported by appropriate attitudes and sentiments. The selection "Excerpts from the Journal of a West India Slave Owner" is a convincing exhibit of the way in which attitudes of superordination and subordination may find expression in the sentiments of a conscientious and self-complacent paternalism on the part of the master and of an ingratiating and reverential loyalty on the part of the slave. In a like manner the selection from the "Memories of an Old Servant" indicates the natural way in which sentiments of subordination which have grown up in conformity with an accepted situation eventually become the basis of a life-philosophy of the person.

Slavery and caste are manifestly forms of accommodation. The facts of subordination are quite as real, though not as obvious, in other phases of social life. The peculiar intimacy which exists, for example, between lovers, between husband and wife, or between physician and patient, involves relations of subordination and superordination, though not recognized as such. The personal domination which a coach exercises over the members of a ball team, a minister over his congregation, the political leader over his party followers are instances of the same phenomena.

Simmel in his interesting discussion of the subject points out the fact that the relations of subordination and superordination are reciprocal. In order to impose his will upon his slaves it was necessary for the master to retain their respect. No one had a keener appreciation of the aristocracy nor a greater scorn for the "poor white" than the Negro slaves in the South before the war.

The leader of the gang, although he seems to have decisions absolutely in his hand, has a sense of the attitudes of his followers. So the successful political leader, who sometimes appears to be taking risks in his advocacy of new issues, keeps "his ear close to the grass roots of public opinion."

In the selection upon "The Psychology of Subordination and Superordination" Münsterberg interprets suggestion, imitation, and sympathy in terms of domination and submission. Personal influence, prestige, and authority, in whatever form they find expression, are based, to a greater or less extent, on the subtle influences of suggestion.

The natural affections are social bonds which not infrequently assume the form of bondage. Many a mother has been reduced to a condition of abject subjection through her affection for a son or a daughter. The same thing is notoriously true of the relations between the sexes. It is in social complexes of this sort, rather than in the formal procedures of governments, that we must look for the fundamental mechanism of social control.

The conflicts and accommodations of persons with persons and of groups with groups have their prototypes in the conflicts and accommodations of the wishes of the person. The conflicts and accommodations in the mental life of the person have received the name in psychoanalysis of *sublimation*. The sublimation of a wish means its expression in a form which represents an accommodation with another conflicting wish which had repressed the original response of the first wish. The progressive organization of personality depends upon the successful functioning of this process of sublimation. The wishes of the person at birth are inchoate; with mental development these wishes come into conflict with each other and with the enveloping social milieu. Adolescence is peculiarly the period of "storm and stress." Youth lives in a maze of mental conflicts, of insurgent and aspiring wishes. Conversion is the sudden mutation of life-attitudes through a reorganization or transformation of the wishes.

c) *Conflict and accommodation*—The intrinsic relation between conflict and accommodation is stated in the materials by Simmel in his analysis of war and peace and the problems of compromise. "The situations existing in time of peace are precisely the conditions out of which war emerges." War, on the other hand, brings about the adjustments in the relations of competing and conflict groups which make peace possible. The problem, therefore, must find a solution in some method by which the conflicts which are latent in, or develop out of, the conditions of peace may be adjusted without a resort to war. In so far as war is an effect of the mere inhibitions which the conditions of peace impose, substitutes for war must provide, as William James has suggested, for the expression of the expanding energies of individuals and nations in ways that will contribute to the welfare of the community and eventually of mankind as a whole. The intention is to make life more interesting and at the same time more secure.

The difficulty is that the devices which render life more secure frequently make it less interesting and harder to bear. Competition, the struggle for existence and for, what is often more important than mere existence, namely, status, may become so bitter that peace is unendurable.

More than that, under the condition of peace, peoples whose life-habits and traditions have been formed upon a basis of war frequently multiply under conditions of peace to such an extent as to make an ultimate war inevitable. The natives of South Africa, since the tribal wars have ceased, have so increased in numbers as to be an increasing menace to the white population. Any amelioration of the condition of mankind that tends to disturb the racial equilibrium is likely to disturb the peace of nations. When representatives of the Rockefeller Medical Foundation proposed to introduce a rational system of medicine in China, certain of the wise men of that country, it is reported, shook their heads dubiously over the consequences that were likely to follow any large decrease in the death-rate, seeing that China was already overpopulated.

In the same way education, which is now in a way to become a heritage of all mankind, rather than the privilege of so-called superior peoples, undoubtedly has had the effect of greatly increasing the mobility and restlessness of the world's population. In so far as this is true, it has made the problem of maintaining peace more difficult and dangerous.

On the other hand, education and the extension of intelligence undoubtedly increase the possibility of compromise and conciliation which, as Simmel points out, represent ways in which peace may be restored and maintained other than by complete victory and subjugation of the conquered people. It is considerations of this kind that have led men like von Moltke to say that "universal peace is a dream and not even a happy one," and have led other men like Carnegie to build peace palaces in which the nations of the world might settle their differences by compromise and according to law.

d) Competition, status, and social solidarity.—Under the title "Competition, Status, and Social Solidarity" selections are introduced in the materials which emphasize the relation of competition to accommodation. Up to this point in the materials only the relations of conflict to accommodation have been considered. Status has been described as an effect of conflict. But it is clear that economic competition frequently becomes conscious and so passes over into some of the milder forms of conflict. Aside from this it is evident that competition in so far as it determines the vocation of the individual, determines indirectly also his status, since it determines the class of which he is destined to be a member. In the same way competition is indirectly responsible for the organization of society in so far as it determines the character of the accommodations and understandings which are likely to exist between conflict groups. Social types as well as status are indirectly determined by competition, since most of them are vocational. The social types of the modern city, as indicated by the selection on "Personal Competition and the Evolution of Individual Types," are an outcome of the division of labor. Durkheim points out that the division of labor in multiplying the vocations has increased and not diminished the unity of society. The interdependence of differentiated individuals and groups has made possible a social solidarity that otherwise would not exist.

II. MATERIALS

A. FORMS OF ACCOMMODATION

1. Acclimatization[1]

The most important ethnic question in connection with climate is that of the possibility of a race adapting itself to climatic conditions widely different from those to which it has been accustomed. This is the question of acclimatization.

Its bearings on ethnic psychology can be made at once evident by posing a few practical inquiries: Can the English people flourish in India? Will the French colonize successfully the Sudan? Have the Europeans lost or gained in power by their migration to the United States? Can the white or any other race ultimately become the sole residents of the globe?

It will be seen that on the answers to such questions depends the destiny of races and the consequences to the species of the facilities of transportation offered by modern inventions. The subject has therefore received the careful study of medical geographers and statisticians.

I can give but a brief statement of their conclusions. They are to the effect, first, that when the migration takes place along approximately the same isothermal lines, the changes in the system are slight; but as the mean annual temperature rises, the body becomes increasingly unable to resist its deleterious action until a difference of 18° F. is reached, at which continued existence of the

[1] From Daniel G. Brinton, *The Basis of Social Relations*, pp. 194–99. (Courtesy of G. P. Putnam's Sons, New York and London, 1902.)

more northern races becomes impossible. They suffer from a chemical change in the condition of the blood cells, leading to anemia in the individual and to extinction of the lineage in the third generation.

This is the general law of the relation to race and climate. Like most laws it has its exceptions, depending on special conditions. A stock which has long been accustomed to change of climate adapts itself to any with greater facility. This explains the singular readiness of the Jews to settle and flourish in all zones. For a similar reason a people who at home are accustomed to a climate of wide and sudden changes, like that of the eastern United States, supports others with less loss of power than the average.

A locality may be extremely hot but unusually free from other malefic influences, being dry with regular and moderate winds, and well drained, such as certain areas between the Red Sea and the Nile, which are also quite salubrious.

Finally, certain individuals and certain families, owing to some fortunate power of resistance which we cannot explain, acclimate successfully where their companions perish. Most of the instances of alleged successful acclimatization of Europeans in the tropics are due to such exceptions, the far greater number of the victims being left out of the count.

If these alleged successful cases, or that of the Jews or Arabs, be closely examined, it will almost surely be discovered that another physiological element has been active in bringing about acclimatization, and that is the mingling of blood with the native race. In the American tropics the Spaniards have survived for four centuries; but how many of the *Ladinos* can truthfully claim an unmixed descent? In Guatemala, for example, says a close observer, *not any*. The Jews of the Malabar coast have actually become black, and so has also in Africa many an Arab claiming direct descent from the Prophet himself.

But along with this process of adaptation by amalgamation comes unquestionably a lowering of the mental vitality of the higher race. That is the price it has to pay for the privilege of survival under the new conditions. But, in conformity to the principles already laid down as accepted by all anthropologists, such a lowering must correspond to a degeneration in the highest grades of structure, the brain cells.

We are forced, therefore, to reach the decision that the human species attains its highest development only under moderate conditions of heat, such as prevail in the temperate zones (an annual mean of 8°–12° C.); and the more startling conclusion that the races now native to the polar and tropical areas are distinctly *pathological*, are types of degeneracy, having forfeited their highest physiological elements in order to purchase immunity from the unfavorable climatic conditions to which they are subject. We must agree with a French writer, that "man is not cosmopolitan," and if he insists on becoming a "citizen of the world" he is taxed heavily in his best estate for his presumption.

The inferences in racial psychology which follow this opinion are too evident to require detailed mention. Natural selection has fitted the Eskimo and the Sudanese for their respective abodes, but it has been by the process of regressive evolution; progressive evolution in man has confined itself to less extreme climatic areas.

The facts of acclimatization stand in close connection with another doctrine in anthropology which is interesting for my theme, that of "ethno-geographic provinces." Alexander von Humboldt seems to have been the first to give expression to this system of human grouping, and it has been diligently cultivated by his disciple, Professor Bastian. It rests upon the application to the human species of two general principles recognized as true in zoölogy and botany. The one is that every organism is directly dependent on its environment (the *milieu*), action and reaction going on constantly between them; the other is, that no two faunal or floral regions are of equal rank in their capacity for the development of a given type of organism.

The features which distinguish one ethno-geographic province from another are chiefly, according to Bastian, meteorological, and they permit, he claims, a much closer division of human groups than the general continental areas which give us an African, a European, and an American subspecies.

It is possible that more extended researches may enable ethnographers to map out, in this sense, the distribution of our species; but the secular alterations in meteorologic conditions, combined with the migratory habits of most early communities, must greatly interfere with a rigid application of these principles in ethnography.

The historic theory of "centres of civilisation" is allied to that of ethno-geographic provinces. The stock examples of such are familiar. The Babylonian plain, the valley of the Nile, in America the plateaus of Mexico and of Tiahuanuco are constantly quoted as such. The geographic advantages these situations offered—a fertile soil, protection from enemies, domesticable plants, and a moderate climate—are offered as reasons why an advanced culture rapidly developed in them, and from them extended over adjacent regions.

Without denying the advantages of such surroundings, the most recent researches in both hemispheres tend to reduce materially their influence. The cultures in question did not begin at one point and radiate from it, but arose simultaneously over wide areas, in different linguistic stocks, with slight connections; and only later, and secondarily, was it successfully concentrated by some one tribe—by the agency, it is now believed, of cognatic rather than geographic aids.

Assyriologists no longer believe that Sumerian culture originated in the delta of the Euphrates, and Egyptologists look for the sources of the civilization of the Nile Valley among the Libyans; while in the New World not one but seven stocks partook of the Aztec learning, and half a dozen contributed to that of the Incas. The prehistoric culture of Europe was not one of Carthaginians or Phoenicians, but was self-developed.

2. Slavery Defined[1]

In most branches of knowledge the phenomena the man of science has to deal with have their technical names, and, when using a scientific term, he need not have regard to the meaning this term conveys in ordinary language; he knows he will not be misunderstood by his fellow-scientists. For instance, the Germans call a whale *Wallfisch*, and the English speak of shellfish; but a zoölogist, using the word fish, need not fear that any competent person will think he means whales or shellfish.

In ethnology the state of things is quite different. There are a few scientific names bearing a definite meaning, such as the terms "animism" and "survival," happily introduced by Professor Tylor. But most phenomena belonging to our science have not yet been

[1] From Dr. H. J. Nieboer, *Slavery as an Industrial System*, pp. 1–7. (Martinus Nijhoff, The Hague, 1910.)

investigated, so it is no wonder that different writers (sometimes even the same writer on different pages) give different names to the same phenomenon, whereas, on the other hand, sometimes the same term (e.g., matriarchate) is applied to widely different phenomena. As for the subject we are about to treat of, we shall presently see that several writers have given a definition of slavery; but no one has taken the trouble to inquire whether his definition can be of any practical use in social science. Therefore, we shall try to give a good definition and justify it.

But we may not content ourselves with this; we must also pay attention to the meaning of the term "slavery" as commonly employed. There are two reasons for this. First, we must always rely upon the statements of ethnographers. If an ethnographer states that some savage tribe carries on slavery, without defining in what this "slavery" consists, we have to ask: What may our informant have meant? And as he is likely to have used the word in the sense generally attached to it, we have to inquire: What is the ordinary meaning of the term "slavery"?

The second reason is this. Several theoretical writers speak of slavery without defining what they mean by it; and we cannot avail ourselves of their remarks without knowing what meaning they attach to this term. And as they too may be supposed to have used it in the sense in which it is generally used, we have again to inquire: What is the meaning of the term "slavery" in ordinary language?

The general use of the word, as is so often the case, is rather inaccurate. Ingram says:

Careless or rhetorical writers use the words "slave" and "slavery" in a very lax way. Thus, when protesting against the so-called "Subjection of Women," they absurdly apply those terms to the condition of the wife in the modern society of the west—designations which are inappropriate even in the case of the inmate of Indian zenanas; and they speak of the modern worker as a "wage-slave," even though he is backed by a powerful trade-union. Passion has a language of its own, and poets and orators must doubtless be permitted to denote by the word "slavery" the position of subjects of a state who labor under civil disabilities or are excluded from the exercise of political power; but in sociological study things ought to have their right names, and those names should, as far as possible, be uniformly employed.

But this use of the word we may safely regard as a metaphor; nobody will assert that these laborers and women are really slaves. Whoever uses the term slavery in its ordinary sense attaches a fairly distinct idea to it. What is this idea? We can express it most generally thus: a slave is one who is not free. There are never slaves without there being freemen too; and nobody can be at the same time a slave and a freeman. We must, however, be careful to remember that, man being a "social animal," no man is literally free; all members of a community are restricted in their behavior toward each other by social rules and customs. But freemen at any rate are relatively free; so a slave must be one who does not share in the common amount of liberty, compatible with the social connection.

The condition of the slave as opposed to that of the freeman presents itself to us under the three following aspects:

First, every slave has his master to whom he is subjected. And this subjection is of a peculiar kind. Unlike the authority one freeman sometimes has over another, the master's power over his slave is unlimited, at least in principle; any restriction put upon the master's free exercise of his power is a mitigation of slavery, not belonging to its nature, just as in Roman law the proprietor may do with his property whatever he is not by special laws forbidden to do. The relation between master and slave is therefore properly expressed by the slave being called the master's "possession" or "property"— expressions we frequently meet with.

Secondly, slaves are in a lower condition as compared with freemen. The slave has no political rights; he does not choose his government, he does not attend the public councils. Socially he is despised.

In the third place, we always connect with slavery the idea of compulsory labor. The slave is compelled to work; the free laborer may leave off working if he likes, be it at the cost of starving. All compulsory labor, however, is not slave labor; the latter requires that peculiar kind of compulsion that is expressed by the word "possession" or "property" as has been said before.

Recapitulating, we may define a slave in the ordinary sense of the word as a man who is the property of another, politically and socially at a lower level than the mass of the people, and performing compulsory labor.

The great function of slavery can be no other than a *division of labor*. Division of labor is taken here in the widest sense, as including not only a qualitative division, by which one man does one kind of work and another a different kind, but also a quantitative one, by which one man's wants are provided for, not by his own work only, but by another's. A society without any division of labor would be one in which each man worked for his own wants, and nobody for another's; in any case but this there is a division of labor in this wider sense of the word. Now this division can be brought about by two means. "There are two ways" says Puchta "in which we can avail ourselves of the strength of other men which we are in need of. One is the way of free commerce, that does not interfere with the liberty of the person who serves us, the making of contracts by which we exchange the strength and skill of another, or their products, for other performances on our part: hire of services, purchase of manufactures, etc. The other way is the subjugation of such persons, which enables us to dispose of their strength in our behalf but at the same time injures the personality of the subjected. This subjection can be imagined as being restricted to certain purposes, for instance to the cultivation of the land, as with soil-tilling serfs, the result of which is that this subjection, for the very reason that it has a definite and limited aim, does not quite annul the liberty of the subjected. But the subjection can also be an unlimited one, as is the case when the subjected person, in the whole of his outward life, is treated as but a means to the purposes of the man of power, and so his personality is entirely absorbed. This is the institution of slavery."

3. Excerpts from the Journal of a West India Slave Owner[1]

Soon after nine o'clock we reached Savannah la Mar, where I found my trustee, and a whole cavalcade, waiting to conduct me to my own estate; for he had brought with him a curricle and pair for myself, a gig for my servant, two black boys upon mules, and a cart with eight oxen to convey my baggage. The road was excellent, and we had not above five miles to travel; and as soon as the carriage entered my gates, the uproar and confusion which ensued sets all description at defiance. The works were instantly all abandoned;

[1] From Matthew G. Lewis, *Journal of a West India Proprietor*, pp. 60-337. (John Murray, 1834.)

everything that had life came flocking to the house from all quarters; and not only the men, and the women, and the children, but, "by a bland assimilation," the hogs, and the dogs, and the geese, and the fowls, and the turkeys, all came hurrying along by instinct, to see what could possibly be the matter, and seemed to be afraid of arriving too late.   Whether the pleasure of the negroes was sincere may be doubted; but certainly it was the loudest that I ever witnessed: they all talked together, sang, danced, shouted, and, in the violence of their gesticulations, tumbled over each other, and rolled about upon the ground.   Twenty voices at once enquired after uncles, and aunts, and grandfathers, and great-grandmothers of mine, who had been buried long before I was in existence, and whom, I verily believe, most of them only knew by tradition.   One woman held up her little naked black child to me, grinning from ear to ear, "Look, Massa, look here! him nice lilly neger for Massa!"   Another complained, "So long since none come see we, Massa; good Massa, come at last." As for the old people, they were all in one and the same story: now they had lived once to see Massa, they were ready for dying tomorrow, "them no care."

The shouts, the gaiety, the wild laughter, their strange and sudden bursts of singing and dancing, and several old women, wrapped up in large cloaks, their heads bound round with different-colored hand-kerchiefs, leaning on a staff, and standing motionless in the middle of the hubbub, with their eyes fixed upon the portico which I occupied, formed an exact counterpart of the festivity of the witches in Macbeth. Nothing could be more odd or more novel than the whole scene; and yet there was something in it by which I could not help being affected; perhaps it was the consciousness that all these human beings were my *slaves;*—to be sure, I never saw people look more happy in my life; and I believe their condition to be much more comfortable than that of the laborers of Great Britain; and, after all, slavery, in *their* case, is but another name for servitude, now that no more negroes can be forcibly carried away from Africa and sub- jected to the horrors of the voyage and of the seasoning after their arrival; but still I had already experienced, in the morning, that Juliet was wrong in saying "What's in a name?"   For soon after my reaching the lodging-house at Savannah la Mar, a remarkably clean-looking negro lad presented himself with some water and a towel—I concluded him to belong to the inn—and, on my returning the towel, as he found that I took no notice of him, he at length ventured to introduce himself by saying, "Massa not know me; *me your slave!*—and really the sound made me feel a pang at the heart. The lad appeared all gaiety and good humor, and his whole countenance expressed anxiety to recommend himself to my notice, but the word "slave" seemed to imply that, although he did feel pleasure then in serving me, if he had detested me he must have served me still. I really felt quite humiliated at the moment, and was tempted to tell him, "Do not say that again; say that you are my negro, but do not call yourself my slave."

As I was returning this morning from Montego Bay, about a mile from my own estate, a figure presented itself before me, I really think the most picturesque that I ever beheld: it was a mulatto girl, born upon Cornwall, but whom the overseer of a neighboring estate had obtained my permission to exchange for another slave, as well as two little children, whom she had borne to him; but, as yet, he had been unable to procure a substitute, owing to the difficulty of purchasing single negroes, and Mary Wiggins is still my slave. However, as she is considered as being manumitted, she had not dared to present herself at Cornwall on my arrival, lest she should have been considered as an intruder; but she now threw herself in my way to tell me how glad she was to see me, for that she had always thought till now (which is the general complaint) that "*she had no massa;*" and also to obtain a regular invitation to my negro festival tomorrow. By this universal complaint, it appears that, while Mr. Wilberforce is lamenting their hard fate in being subject to a master, *their* greatest fear is the not having a master whom they know; and that to be told by the negroes of another estate that "they belong to no massa," is one of the most contemptuous reproaches that can be cast upon them. Poor creatures, when they happened to hear on Wednesday evening that my carriage was ordered for Montego Bay the next morning, they fancied that I was going away for good and all, and came up to the house in such a hubbub that my agent was obliged to speak to them, and pacify them with the assurance that I should come back on Friday without fail.

But to return to Mary Wiggins: she was much too pretty not to obtain her invitation to Cornwall; on the contrary, I *insisted* upon her coming, and bade her tell her *husband* that I admired his taste very much for having chosen her.   I really think that her form and features were the most *statue-like* that I ever met with; her complexion had no yellow in it and yet was not brown enough to be dark—it was more of an ash-dove color than anything else; her teeth were admirable, both for color and shape; her eyes equally mild and bright; and her face merely broad enough to give it all possible softness and grandness of contour: her air and countenance would have suited Yarico; but she reminded me most of Grassini in "La Vergine del Sole," only that Mary Wiggins was a thousand times more beautiful, and that, instead of a white robe, she wore a mixed dress of brown, white, and dead yellow, which harmonized excellently with her complexion; while one of her beautiful arms was thrown across her brow to shade her eyes, and a profusion of rings on her fingers glittered in the sunbeams.   Mary Wiggins and an old cotton tree are the most picturesque objects that I have seen for these twenty years.

I really believe that the negresses can produce children at pleasure, and where they are barren, it is just as hens will frequently not lay eggs on shipboard, because they do not like their situation.   Cubina's wife is in a family way, and I told him that if the child should live, I would christen it for him, if he wished it.   "Tank you, kind massa, me like it very much: much oblige if massa do that for *me*, too." So I promised to baptize the father and the baby on the same day, and said that I would be godfather to any children that might be born on the estate during my residence in Jamaica.   This was soon spread about, and, although I have not yet been here a week, two women are in the straw already, Jug Betty and Minerva: the first is wife to my head driver, The Duke of Sully, but my sense of propriety was much gratified at finding that Minerva's husband was called Captain.   I think nobody will be able to accuse me of neglecting the religious education of my negroes, for I have not only promised to baptize all the infants, but, meeting a little black boy this morning, who said that his name was Moses, I gave him a piece of silver, and told him that it was for the sake of Aaron; which, I flatter myself, was planting in his young mind the rudiments of Christianity.

On my former visit to Jamaica, I found on my estate a poor woman nearly one hundred years old, and stone blind.   She was too infirm to walk, but two young negroes brought her on their backs to the steps of my house, in order, as she said, that she might at least touch massa, although she could not see him. When she had kissed my hand, "that was enough," she said: "now me hab once kiss a massa's hand, me willing to die tomorrow, me no care." She had a woman appropriated to her service and was shown the greatest care and attention; however, she did not live many months after my departure. There was also a mulatto, about thirty years of age, named Bob, who had been almost deprived of the use of his limbs by the horrible cocoa-bay, and had never done the least work since he was fifteen. He was so gentle and humble and so fearful, from the consciousness of his total inability of soliciting my notice, that I could not help pitying the poor fellow; and whenever he came in my way I always sought to encourage him by little presents and other trifling marks of favor. His thus unexpectedly meeting with distinguishing kindness, where he expected to be treated as a worthless incumbrance, made a strong impression on his mind.

4. The Origin of Caste in India[1]

If it were possible to compress into a single paragraph a theory so complex as that which would explain the origin and nature of Indian caste, I should attempt to sum it up in some such words as the following: A caste is a marriage union, the constituents of which were drawn from various different tribes (or from various other castes similarly formed) in virtue of some industry, craft, or function, either secular or religious, which they possessed in common. The internal discipline, by which the conditions of membership in regard to connubial and convivial rights are defined and enforced, has been borrowed from the tribal period which preceded the period of castes by many centuries, and which was brought to a close by the amalgamation of tribes into a nation under a common scepter. The differentia of *caste* as a marriage union consist in some community of function; while the differentia of *tribe* as a marriage union consisted in a common ancestry, or a common worship, or a common totem, or in fact in any kind of common property except that of a common function.

---

[1] From "Modern Theories of Caste: Mr. Nesfield's Theory," Appendix V, in Sir Herbert Risley, *The People of India*, pp. 407-8. (W. Thacker & Co., 1915.)

Long before castes were formed on Indian soil, most of the industrial classes, to which they now correspond, had existed for centuries, and as a rule most of the industries which they practiced were hereditary on the male side of the parentage. These hereditary classes were and are simply the concrete embodiments of those successive stages of culture which have marked the industrial development of mankind in every part of the world. Everywhere (except at least in those countries where he is still a savage), man has advanced from the stage of hunting and fishing to that of nomadism and cattle-grazing, and from nomadism to agriculture proper. Everywhere has the age of metallurgy and of the arts and industries which are coeval with it been preceded by a ruder age, when only those arts were known or practiced which sufficed for the hunting, fishing, and nomad states. Everywhere has the class of ritualistic priests and lettered theosophists been preceded by a class of less-cultivated worshipers, who paid simple offerings of flesh and wine to the personified powers of the visible universe without the aid of a hereditary professional priesthood. Everywhere has the class of nobles and territorial chieftains been preceded by a humbler class of small peasant proprietors, who placed themselves under their protection and paid tribute or rent in return. Everywhere has this class of nobles and chieftains sought to ally itself with that of the priests or sacerdotal order; and everywhere has the priestly order sought to bring under its control those chiefs and rulers under whose protection it lives.

All these classes had been in existence for centuries before any such thing as caste was known on Indian soil; and the only thing that was needed to convert them into castes, such as they now are, was that the Brāhman, who possessed the highest of all functions— the priestly—should set the example. This he did by establishing for the first time the rule that no child, either male or female, could inherit the name and status of Brāhman, unless he or she was of Brāhman parentage on *both* sides. By the establishment of this rule the principle of marriage unionship was superadded to that of functional unionship; and it was only by the combination of these two principles that a caste in the strict sense of the term could or can be formed. The Brāhman, therefore, as the Hindu books inform us, was "the first-born of castes." When the example had thus been set by an arrogant and overbearing priesthood, whose pretensions it was impossible to put down, the other hereditary classes followed in regular order downward, partly in imitation and partly in self-defence. Immediately behind the Brāhman came the Kshatriya, the military chieftain or landlord. He therefore was the "second-born of castes." Then followed the bankers or upper trading classes (the Agārwal, Khattri, etc.); the scientific musician and singer (Kathak); the writing or literary class (Kāyasth); the bard or genealogist (Bhāt); and the class of inferior nobles (Taga and Bhuinhār) who paid no rent to the landed aristocracy. These, then, were the third-born of castes. Next in order came those artisan classes, who were coeval with the age and art of metallurgy; the metallurgic classes themselves; the middle trading classes; the middle agricultural classes, who placed themselves under the protection of the Kshatriya and paid him rent in return (Kurmi, Kāchhi, Māli, Tāmboli); and the middle serving classes, such as Napit and Baidya, who attended to the bodily wants of their equals and superiors. These, then, were the fourth-born of castes; and their rank in the social scale has been determined by the fact that their manners and notions are farther removed than those of the preceding castes from the Brāhmanical ideal. Next came the inferior artisan classes, those who preceded the age and art of metallurgy (Teli, Kumhār, Kalwār, etc.); the partly nomad and partly agricultural classes (Jāt, Gūjar, Ahir, etc.); the inferior serving classes, such as Kahār; and the inferior trading classes, such as Bhunja. These, then, were the fifth-born of castes, and their mode of life is still farther removed from the Brāhmanical ideal than that of the preceding. The last-born, and therefore the lowest, of all the classes are those semisavage communities, partly tribes and partly castes, whose function consists in hunting or fishing, or in acting as butcher for the general community, or in rearing swine and fowls, or in discharging the meanest domestic services, such as sweeping and washing, or in practicing the lowest of human arts, such as basket-making, hide-tanning, etc. Thus throughout the whole series of Indian castes a double test of social precedence has been in active force, the industrial and the Brāhmanical; and these two have kept pace together almost as evenly as a pair of horses harnessed to a single carriage. In proportion as the function practiced by any given caste stands high or low in the scale of industrial development, in the same proportion does the caste itself, impelled by the general tone of society by which it is surrounded, approximate more nearly or more remotely to the Brāhmanical idea of life. It is these two criteria combined which have determined the relative ranks of the various castes in the Hindu social scale.

5. Caste and the Sentiments of Caste Reflected in Popular Speech[1]

No one indeed can fail to be struck by the intensely popular character of Indian proverbial philosophy and by its freedom from the note of pedantry which is so conspicuous in Indian literature. These quaint sayings have dropped fresh from the lips of the Indian rustic; they convey a vivid impression of the anxieties, the troubles, the annoyances, and the humors of his daily life; and any sympathetic observer who has felt the fascination of an oriental village would have little difficulty in constructing from these materials a fairly accurate picture of rural society in India. The *mise en scène* is not altogether a cheerful one. It shows us the average peasant dependent upon the vicissitudes of the season and the vagaries of the monsoon, and watching from day to day to see what the year may bring forth. Should rain fall at the critical moment his wife will get golden earrings. but one short fortnight of drought may spell calamity when "God takes all at once." Then the forestalling Baniya flourishes by selling rotten grain, and the Jāt cultivator is ruined. First die the improvident Musalmān weavers, then the oil-pressers for whose wares there is no demand; the carts lie idle, for the bullocks are dead, and the bride goes to her husband without the accustomed rites. But be the season good or bad, the pious Hindu's life is ever overshadowed by the exactions of the Brāhman—"a thing with a string round its neck" (a profane hit at the sacred thread), a priest by appearance, a butcher at heart, the chief of a trio of tormentors gibbeted in the rhyming proverb:

> Blood-suckers three on earth there be,
> The bug, the Brāhman, and the flea.

Before the Brāhman starves the king's larder will be empty; cakes must be given to him while the children of the house may lick

[1] From Sir Herbert Risley, *The People of India*, pp. 130–39. (W. Thacker & Co., 1915.)

the grindstone for a meal; his stomach is a bottomless pit; he eats so immoderately that he dies from wind. He will beg with a lakh of rupees in his pocket, and a silver begging-bowl in his hand. In his greed for funeral fees he spies out corpses like a vulture, and rejoices in the misfortunes of his clients. A village with a Brāhman in it is like a tank full of crabs; to have him as a neighbor is worse than leprosy; if a snake has to be killed the Brāhman should be set to do it, for no one will miss him. If circumstances compel you to perjure yourself, why swear on the head of your son, when there is a Brāhman handy? Should he die (as is the popular belief) the world will be none the poorer. Like the devil in English proverbial philosophy, the Brāhman can cite scripture for his purpose; he demands worship himself but does not scruple to kick his low-caste brethren; he washes his sacred thread but does not cleanse his inner man; and so great is his avarice that a man of another caste is supposed to pray "O God, let me not be reborn as a Brāhman priest, who is always begging and is never satisfied." He defrauds even the gods; Vishnu gets the barren prayers while the Brāhman devours the offerings. So Pan complains in one of Lucian's dialogues that he is done out of the good things which men offer at his shrine.

The next most prominent figure in our gallery of popular portraits is that of the Baniya, money-lender, grain-dealer, and monopolist, who dominates the material world as the Brāhman does the spiritual. His heart, we are told, is no bigger than a coriander seed; he has the jaws of an alligator and a stomach of wax; he is less to be trusted than a tiger, a scorpion, or a snake; he goes in like a needle and comes out like a sword; as a neighbor he is as bad as a boil in the armpit. If a Baniya is on the other side of a river you should leave your bundle on this side, for fear he should steal it. When four Baniyas meet they rob the whole world. If a Baniya is drowning you should not give him a hand: he is sure to have some base motive for drifting down stream. He uses light weights and swears that the scales tip themselves; he keeps his accounts in a character that no one but God can read; if you borrow from him, your debt mounts up like a refuse heap or gallops like a horse; if he talks to a customer he "draws a line" and debits the conversation; when his own credit is shaky he writes up his transactions on the wall so that they can easily be rubbed out. He is so stingy that the dogs starve at his feast, and he scolds his wife if she spends a farthing on betel-nut. A Jain Baniya drinks dirty water and shrinks from killing ants and flies, but will not stick at murder in pursuit of gain. As a druggist the Baniya is in league with the doctor; he buys weeds at a nominal price and sells them very dear. Finally, he is always a shocking coward: eighty-four Khatris will run away from four thieves.

Nor does the clerical caste fare better at the hands of the popular epigrammatist. Where three Kāyasths are gathered together a thunderbolt is sure to fall; when honest men fall out the Kāyasth gets his chance. When a Kāyasth takes to money-lending he is a merciless creditor. He is a man of figures; he lives by the point of his pen; in his house even the cat learns two letters and a half. He is a versatile creature, and where there are no tigers he will become a shikāri; but he is no more to be trusted than a crow or a snake without a tail. One of the failings sometimes imputed to the educated Indian is attacked in the saying, "Drinking comes to a Kāyasth with his mother's milk."

Considering the enormous strength of the agricultural population of India, one would have expected to find more proverbs directed against the great cultivating castes. Possibly the reason may be that they made most of the proverbs, and people can hardly be expected to sharpen their wit on their own shortcomings. In two provinces, however, the rural Pasquin has let out very freely at the morals and manners of the Jāt, the typical peasant of the eastern Punjab and the western districts of the United Provinces. You may as well, we are told, look for good in a Jāt as for weevils in a stone. He is your friend only so long as you have a stick in your hand. If he cannot harm you he will leave a bad smell as he goes by. To be civil to him is like giving treacle to a donkey. If he runs amuck it takes God to hold him. A Jāt's laugh would break an ordinary man's ribs. When he learns manners, he blows his nose with a mat, and there is a great run on the garlic. His baby has a plowtail for a plaything. The Jāt stood on his own corn heap and called out to the King's elephant-drivers, "Hi there, what will you take for those little donkeys?" He is credited with practicing fraternal polyandry, like the Venetian nobility of the early eighteenth century, as a measure of domestic economy, and a whole family are said to have one wife between them.

The Doms, among whom we find scavengers, vermin-eaters, executioners, basket-makers, musicians, and professional burglars, probably represent the remnants of a Dravidian tribe crushed out of recognition by the invading Aryans and condemned to menial and degrading occupations. Sir G. Grierson has thrown out the picturesque suggestion that they are the ancestors of the European gypsies and that Rom or Romany is nothing more than a variant of Dom. In the ironical language of the proverbs the Dom figures as "the lord of death" because he provides the wood for the Hindu funeral pyre. He is ranked with Brāhmans and goats as a creature useless in time of need. A common and peculiarly offensive form of abuse is to tell a man that he has eaten a Dom's leavings. A series of proverbs represents him as making friends with members of various castes and faring ill or well in the process. Thus the Kanjar steals his dog, and the Gūjar loots his house; on the other hand, the barber shaves him for nothing, and the silly Jolāhā makes him a suit of clothes. His traditions associate him with donkeys, and it is said that if these animals could excrete sugar, Doms would no longer be beggars. "A Dom in a palanquin and a Brāhman on foot" is a type of society turned upside down. Nevertheless, outcast as he is, the Dom occupies a place of his own in the fabric of Indian society. At funerals he provides the wood and gets the corpse clothes as his perquisite; he makes the discordant music that accompanies a marriage procession; and baskets, winnowing-fans, and wicker articles in general are the work of his hands.

In the west of India, Mahārs and Dheds hold much the same place as the Dom. In the walled villages of the Marāthā country the Mahār is the scavenger, watchman, and gate-keeper. His presence pollutes; he is not allowed to live in the village; and his miserable shanty is huddled up against the wall outside. But he challenges the stranger who comes to the gate, and for this and other services he is allowed various perquisites, among them that of begging for broken victuals from house to house. He offers old blankets to his god, and his child's playthings are bones. The Dhed's status is equally low. If he looks at a water jar he pollutes its contents; if you run up against him by accident, you must go off and bathe. If you annoy a Dhed he sweeps up the dust in your face. When he dies, the world is so much the cleaner. If you go to the Dheds' quarter you find there nothing but a heap of bones.

This relegation of the low castes to a sort of ghetto is carried to great lengths in the south of India where the intolerance of the Brāhman is very conspicuous. In the typical Madras village the Pariahs—"dwellers in the quarter" (*pārā*) as this broken tribe is now called—live in an irregular cluster of conical hovels of palm leaves known as the *pārchery*, the squalor and untidiness of which present the sharpest contrasts to the trim street of tiled masonry houses where the Brāhmans congregate. "Every village," says the proverb, "has its Pariah hamlet"—a place of pollution the census of which is even now taken with difficulty owing to the reluctance of the high-caste enumerator to enter its unclean precincts. "A palm tree," says another, "casts no shade; a Pariah has no caste and rules." The popular estimate of the morals of the Pariah comes out in the saying, "He that breaks his word is a Pariah at heart"; while the note of irony predominates in the pious question, "If a Pariah offers boiled rice will not the god take it?" the implication being that the Brāhman priests who take the offerings to idols are too greedy to inquire by whom they are presented.

B. SUBORDINATION AND SUPERORDINATION

1. The Psychology of Subordination and Superordination[1]

The typical suggestion is given by words. But the impulse to act under the influence of another person arises no less when the action is proposed in the more direct form of showing the action itself. The submission then takes the form of imitation. This is the earliest type of subordination. It plays a fundamental rôle in the infant's life, long before the suggestion through words can begin its influence. The infant imitates involuntarily as soon as connections between the movement impulses and the movement impressions have been formed. At first automatic reflexes produce all kinds of motions, and each movement awakes kinesthetic and muscle sensations. Through association these impressions become bound up with the motor impulses. As soon as the movements of other persons arouse similar visual sensations the kinesthetic sensations are associated and realize the corresponding movement. Very soon the associative

[1] From Hugo Münsterberg, *Psychology, General and Applied*, pp. 259–64. (D. Appleton & Co., 1914.)

irradiation becomes more complex, and whole groups of emotional reactions are imitated. The child cries and laughs in imitation.

Most important is the imitation of the speech movement. The sound awakes the impulse to produce the same vocal sound long before the meaning of the word is understood. Imitation is thus the condition for the acquiring of speech, and later the condition for the learning of all other abilities. But while the imitation is at first simply automatic, it becomes more and more volitional. The child intends to imitate what the teacher shows as an example. This intentional imitation is certainly one of the most important vehicles of social organization. The desire to act like certain models becomes the most powerful social energy. But even the highest differentiation of society does not eliminate the constant working of the automatic, impulsive imitation.

The inner relation between imitation and suggestion shows itself in the similarity of conditions under which they are most effective. Every increase of suggestibility facilitates imitation. In any emotional excitement of a group every member submits to the suggestion of the others, but the suggestion is taken from the actual movements. A crowd in a panic or a mob in a riot shows an increased suggestibility by which each individual automatically repeats what his neighbors are doing. Even an army in battle may become, either through enthusiasm or through fear, a group in which all individuality is lost and everyone is forced by imitative impulses to fight or escape. The psychophysical experiment leaves no doubt that this imitative response releases the sources of strongest energy in the mental mechanism. If the arm lifts the weight of an ergograph until the will cannot overcome the fatigue, the mere seeing of the movement carried out by others whips the motor centers to new efficiency.

We saw that our feeling states are both causes and effects of our actions. We cannot experience the impulse to action without a new shading of our emotional setting. Imitative acting involves, therefore, an inner imitation of feelings too. The child who smiles in response to the smile of his mother shares her pleasant feeling. The adult who is witness of an accident in which someone is hurt imitates instinctively the cramping muscle contractions of the victim, and as a result he feels an intense dislike without having the pain sensations themselves. From such elementary experiences an imitative emotional life develops, controlled by a general sympathetic tendency. We share the pleasures and the displeasures of others through an inner imitation which remains automatic. In its richer forms this sympathy becomes an *altruistic sentiment;* it stirs the desire to remove the misery around us and unfolds to a general mental setting through which every action is directed toward the service to others. But from the faintest echoing of feelings in the infant to the highest self-sacrifice from altruistic impulse, we have the common element of submission. The individual is feeling, and accordingly acting, not in the realization of his individual impulses, but under the influence of other personalities.

This subordination to the feelings of others through sympathy and pity and common joy takes a new psychological form in the affection of tenderness and especially parental love. The relation of parents to children involves certainly an element of superordination, but the mentally strongest factor remains the subordination, the complete submission to the feelings of those who are dependent upon the parents' care. In its higher development the parental love will not yield to every momentary like or dislike of the child, but will adjust the educative influence to the lasting satisfactions and to the later sources of unhappiness. But the submission of the parents to the feeling tones in the child's life remains the fundamental principle of the family instinct. While the parents' love and tenderness mean that the stronger submits to the weaker, even up to the highest points of self-sacrifice, the loving child submits to his parents from feelings which are held together by a sense of dependence. This feeling of dependence as a motive of subordination enters into numberless human relations. Everywhere the weak lean on the strong, and choose their actions under the influence of those in whom they have confidence. The corresponding feelings show the manifold shades of modesty, admiration, gratitude, and hopefulness. Yet it is only another aspect of the social relation if the consciousness of dependence upon the more powerful is felt with fear and revolt, or with the nearly related emotion of envy.

The desire to assert oneself is no less powerful, in the social interplay, than the impulse to submission. Society needs the leaders as well as the followers. Self-assertion presupposes contact with other individuals. Man protects himself against the dangers of nature, and man masters nature; but he asserts himself against men who interfere with him or whom he wants to force to obedience. The most immediate reaction in the compass of self-assertion is indeed the *rejection of interference*. It is a form in which even the infant shows the opposite of submission. He repels any effort to disturb him in the realization of the instinctive impulses. From the simplest reaction of the infant disturbed in his play or his meal, a straight line of development leads to the fighting spirit of man, whose pugnaciousness and whose longing for vengeance force his will on his enemies. Every form of rivalry, jealousy, and intolerance finds in this feeling group its source of automatic response. The most complex intellectual processes may be made subservient to this self-asserting emotion.

But the effort to impose one's will on others certainly does not result only from conflict. An entirely different emotional center is given by the mere desire for *self-expression*. In every field of human activity the individual may show his inventiveness, his ability to be different from others, to be a model, to be imitated by his fellows. The normal man has a healthy, instinctive desire to claim recognition from the members of the social group. This interferes neither with the spirit of co-ordination nor with the subordination of modesty. In so far as the individual demands acknowledgement of his personal behavior and his personal achievement, he raises himself by that act above others. He wants his mental attitude to influence and control the social surroundings. In its fuller development this inner setting becomes the ambition for leadership in the affairs of practical life or in the sphere of cultural work.

The superficial counterpart is the desire for *self-display* with all its variations of vanity and boastfulness. From the most bashful submission to the most ostentatious self-assertion, from the self-sacrifice of motherly love to the pugnaciousness of despotic egotism, the social psychologist can trace the human impulses through all the intensities of the human energies which interfere with equality in the group. Each variation has its emotional background and its impulsive discharge. Within normal limits they are all equally useful for the biological existence of the group and through the usefulness for the group ultimately serviceable to its members. Only through superordination and subordination does the group receive the inner firmness which transforms the mere combination of men into working units. They give to human society that strong and yet flexible organization which is the necessary condition for its successful development.

2. Social Attitudes in Subordination: Memories of an Old Servant[1]

Work is a great blessing, and it has been wisely arranged by our divine Master that all his creatures should have a work to do of some kind. Some are weak and some are strong. Old and young, rich and poor, there is that work expected from us, and how much happier we are when we are at our work.

There are so many things to learn, so many different kinds of work that must be done to make the world go on right. And some work is easier than others; but all ought to be well done, and in a cheerful, contented manner. Some prefer working with hands and feet; they say it is easier than the head work; but surely both are heavy work, for it does depend on your ability.

Boys and girls do not leave school so early as they did fifty or sixty years ago. The boys went out quite happy and manly to do their herding at some farm, and would be very useful for some years till they preferred learning some trade, etc.; then a younger boy just filled his place; and by doing this they did learn farming a good bit, and this helped them on in after years if they wanted to go back to farming again. We regret to see that the page-boy is not wanted so much as he used to be; and what a help that used to be for a young boy. He learns a great deal by being first of all a while in the stable yard or garage before he goes into the gentleman's house, and he is neat and tidy at all times for messages. We have seen many of them in our young days; and even the waif has been picked up by a good master, and began in the stables and worked his way up to be a respected valet in the same household, and often and often told the story of his waif life in the servants' hall.

The old servant has seen many changes and in many cases prefers the good old ways; there may be some better arrangements made, we cannot doubt that, but we are surprised at good old practices that our late beloved employers had ignored by their own children

[1] Adapted from *Domestic Service*, by An Old Servant, pp. 10–110. (Houghton Mifflin Co., 1917.)

after they have so far grown up. Servants need the good example from their superiors, and when they hear the world speak well of them they do look for the good ways in the home life. We all like to hold up an employer's good name, surely we do if we are interested at all in our work, and if we feel that we cannot do our duty to them we ought to go elsewhere and not deceive them. We are trusted with a very great deal, and it is well for us if we are doing all we can as faithful servants, and in the end lay down our tools with the feeling that we have tried to do our best.

We must remember that each one is born in his station in life, wisely arranged by "One Who Knows and Who Is Our Supreme Ruler." No one can alter this nor say to him, "What Doest Thou?" so we must each and all keep our station and honor the rich man and the poor man who humbly tries to live a Christian life, and when their faults are seen by us may we at once turn to ourselves and look if we are not human, too, and may be as vile as they.

We have noticed some visitors very rude to the servants and so different to our own employers, and we set a mark on them, for we would not go to serve them. We remember once when our lady's brother was showing a visiting lady some old relics near the front door they came upon the head housemaid who was cleaning the church pew chairs (they were carried in while the church was being repaired), and she was near a very old grand piano. The lady asked in such a jeer, "And is this the housemaid's piano"? The gentleman looked very hard at the housemaid, for we were sure that he was very annoyed at her, but we did not hear his answer; but the housemaid had the good sense to keep quiet, but she could have told her to keep her jeers, for we were not her class of servant, neither was she our class of employer. We heard her character after, and never cared to see her. Some servants take great liberties, and then all are supposed to be alike; but we are glad that all ladies are not like this, for the world would be poor indeed; they would soon ruin all the girls—and no wonder her husband had left her. We heard of a gentleman who fancied his laundry-maid, so he called his servants together and told them that he was to marry her and bring her home as the lady of his house, and he hoped they would all stay where they were; but if they felt that they could not look upon her as their mistress and his wife, they were free to go away. And not one of them left, for they stayed on with them for years. This is a true story from one who knew them and could show us their London house. Now we have lived with superior servants, and we would much rather serve them even now in our old age than serve any lady who can never respect a servant.

Nothing brings master and servant closer together than the sudden sore bereavement, and very likely this book could not be written so sad were it not for the many sad days that have been spent in service, and now so very few of the employers are to be seen; and when they are with us we feel that we are still respected by them, for there is the usual welcome—for they would look back the same as we do on days that are gone by. In our young days the curtsy was fashionable; you would see every man's daughter bobbing whenever they met the lady or gentlemen or when they met their teacher. The custom is gone now, and we wonder why; but the days are changed, and some call it education that is so far doing this; it cannot be education, for we do look for more respect from the educated than from the class that we called the ignorant.

How well off the servants are in these years of war, for they have no rent to worry about and no anxiety about their coal bill, nor how food, etc., is to be got in and paid for, no taxes nor cares like so many poor working men; they are also sure of their wages when quarter day comes round. It is true she may have a widow mother who requires some help with rent, coals, or food, but there are many who ought to value a good situation, whether in the small comfortable house as general or in larger good situations where a few servants are, for we have seen them all and know what they have been like, and so we say that all as a rule ought to be very thankful that they are the domestic servant and so study to show gratitude by good deeds to all around, as there is work just now for everyone to do.

A great deal more could easily be written, and we hope some old servant may also speak out in favor of domestic service, and so let it be again what it has been, and when both will look on each other as they ought, for there has always been master and servant, and we have the number of servants, or near the number, given here by one who knows, 1,330,783 female domestic servants at the last census in 1911, and so the domestic service is the largest single industry that is; there are more people employed as domestic servants thar any other class of employment. Before closing this book the writer would ask that a kinder interest may be taken in girls who may have at one time been in disgrace; many of them have no homes and we might try to help them into situations. This appeal is from the old housekeeper and so from one who has had many a talk with young girls for their good; but they have often been led far astray. We ought to give them the chance again, by trying to get them situations, and if the lady is not her friend, nor the housekeeper, we pity her.

3. The Reciprocal Character of Subordination and Superordination[1]

Every social occurrence consists of an interaction between individuals. In other words, each individual is at the same time an active and a passive agent in a transaction. In case of superiority and inferiority, however, the relation assumes the appearance of a one-sided operation; the one party appears to exert, while the other seems merely to receive, an influence. Such, however, is not in fact the case. No one would give himself the trouble to gain or to maintain superiority if it afforded him no advantage or enjoyment. This return to the superior can be derived from the relation, however, only by virtue of the fact that there is a reciprocal action of the inferior upon the superior. The decisive characteristic of the relation at this point is this, that the effect which the inferior actually exerts upon the superior is determined by the latter. The superior causes the inferior to produce a given effect which the superior shall experience. In this operation, in case the subordination is really absolute, no sort of spontaneity is present on the part of the subordinate. The reciprocal influence is rather the same as that between a man and a lifeless external object with which the former performs an act for his own use. That is, the person acts upon the object in order that the latter may react upon himself. In this reaction of the object no spontaneity on the part of the object is to be observed, but merely the further operation of the spontaneity of the person. Such an extreme case of superiority and inferiority will scarcely occur among human beings. Rather will a certain measure of independence, a certain direction of the relation proceed also from the self-will and

[1] Adapted from a translation of Georg Simmel by Albion W. Small, "Superiority and Subordination," in the *American Journal of Sociology*, II (1896–97), 169–71.

the character of the subordinate. The different cases of superiority and inferiority will accordingly be characterized by differences in the relative amount of spontaneity which the subordinates and the superiors bring to bear upon the total relation. In exemplification of this reciprocal action of the inferior, through which superiority and inferiority manifests itself as proper socialization, I will mention only a few cases, in which the reciprocity is difficult to discern.

When in the case of an absolute despotism the ruler attaches to his edicts the threat of penalty or the promise of reward, the meaning is that the monarch himself will be bound by the regulation which he has ordained. The inferior shall have the right, on the other hand, to demand something from the lawgiver. Whether the latter subsequently grants the promised reward or protection is another question. The spirit of the relation as contemplated by the law is that the superior completely controls the inferior, to be sure, but that a certain claim is assured to the latter, which claim he may press or may allow to lapse, so that even this most definite form of the relation still contains an element of spontaneity on the part of the inferior.

Still farther; the concept "law" seems to connote that he who gives the law is in so far unqualifiedly superior. Apart from those cases in which the law is instituted by those who will be its subjects, there appears in lawgiving as such no sign of spontaneity on the part of the subject of the law. It is, nevertheless, very interesting to observe how the Roman conception of law makes prominent the reciprocity between the superior and the subordinate elements. Thus *lex* means originally "compact," in the sense, to be sure, that the terms of the same are fixed by the proponent, and the other party can accept or reject it only *en bloc*. The *lex publica populi Romani* meant originally that the king proposed and the people accepted the same. Thus even here, where the conception itself seems to express the complete one-sidedness of the superior, the nice social instinct of the Romans pointed in the verbal expression to the co-operation of the subordinate. In consequence of like feeling of the nature of socialization the later Roman jurists declared that the *societas leonina* is not to be regarded as a social compact. Where the one absolutely controls the other, that is, where all spontaneity of the subordinate is excluded, there is no longer any socialization.

Once more, the orator who confronts the assembly, or the teacher his class, seems to be the sole leader, the temporary superior. Nevertheless everyone who finds himself in that situation is conscious of the limiting and controlling reaction of the mass which is apparently merely passive and submissive to his guidance. This is the case not merely when the parties immediately confront each other. All leaders are also led, as in countless cases the master is the slave of his slaves. "I am your leader, therefore I must follow you," said one of the most eminent German parliamentarians, with reference to his party. Every journalist is influenced by the public upon which he seems to exert an influence entirely without reaction. The most characteristic case of actual reciprocal influence, in spite of what appears to be subordination without corresponding reaction, is that of hypnotic suggestion. An eminent hypnotist recently asserted that in every hypnosis there occurs an actual if not easily defined influence of the hypnotized upon the hypnotist, and that without this the effect would not be produced.

4. Three Types of Subordination and Superordination[1]

Three possible types of superiority present themselves. Superiority may be exercised (a) by an individual, (b) by a group, (c) by an objective principle higher than individuals.

a) *Subordination to an individual.*—The subordination of a group to a single person implies a very decided unification of the group. This is equally the case with both the characteristic forms of this subordination, viz.: (1) when the group with its head constitutes a real internal unity; when the superior is more a leader than a master and only represents in himself the power and the will of the group; (2) when the group is conscious of opposition between itself and its head, when a party opposed to the head is formed. In both cases the unity of the supreme head tends to bring about an inner unification of the group. The elements of the latter are conscious of themselves as belonging together, because their interests converge at one point. Moreover the opposition to this unified controlling power compels the group to collect itself, to condense itself into unity

[1] Adapted from a translation of Georg Simmel by Albion W. Small, "Superiority and Subordination," in the *American Journal of Sociology*, II (1896–97), 172–86.

This is true not alone of the political group. In the factory, the ecclesiastical community, a school class, and in associated bodies of every sort it is to be observed that the termination of the organization in a head, whether in case of harmony or of opposition, helps to effect unification of the group. This is most conspicuous to be sure in the political sphere. History has shown it to be the enormous advantage of monarchies that they unify the political interests of the popular mass. The totality has a common interest in holding the prerogatives of the crown within their boundaries, possibly in restricting them; or there is a common field of conflict between those whose interests are with the crown and those who are opposed. Thus there is a supreme point with reference to which the whole people constitutes either a single party or, at most, two. Upon the disappearance of its head, to which all are subordinate—with the end of this political pressure—all political unity often likewise ceases. There spring up a great number of party factions which previously, in view of that supreme political interest for or against the monarchy, found no room.

Wonder has often been felt over the irrationality of the condition in which a single person exercises lordship over a great mass of others. The contradiction will be modified when we reflect that the ruler and the individual subject in the controlled mass by no means enter into the relationship with an equal *quantum* of their personality. The mass is composed through the fact that many individuals unite fractions of their personality—one-sided purposes, interests and powers, while that which each personality as such actually is towers above this common level and does not at all enter into that "mass," i.e., into that which is really ruled by the single person. Hence it is also that frequently in very despotically ruled groups individuality may develop itself very freely, in those aspects particularly which are not in participation with the mass. Thus began the development of modern individuality in the despotisms of the Italian Renaissance. Here, as in other similar cases (for example, under Napoleon I and Napoleon III), it was for the direct interest of the despots to allow the largest freedom to all those aspects of personality which were not identified with the regulated mass, i.e., to those aspects most apart from politics. Thus subordination was more tolerable.

b) Subordination to a group.—In the second place the group may assume the form of a pyramid. In this case the subordinates stand over against the superior not in an equalized mass but in very nicely graded strata of power. These strata grow constantly smaller in extent but greater in significance. They lead up from the inferior mass to the head, the single ruler.

This form of the group may come into existence in two ways. It may emerge from the autocratic supremacy of an individual. The latter often loses the substance of his power and allows it to slip downward, while retaining its form and titles. In this case more of the power is retained by the orders nearest to the former autocrat than is acquired by those more distant. Since the power thus gradually percolates, a continuity and graduation of superiority and inferiority must develop itself. This is, in fact, the way in which in oriental states the social forms often arise. The power of the superior orders disintegrates, either because it is essentially incoherent and does not know how to attain the above-emphasized proportion between subordination and individual freedom; or because the persons comprising the administration are too indolent or too ignorant of governmental technique to preserve supreme power. For the power which is exercised over a large circle is never a constant possession. It must be constantly acquired and defended anew if anything more than its shadow and name is to remain.

The other way in which a scale of power is constructed up to a supreme head is the reverse of that just described. Starting with a relative equality of the social elements, certain elements gain greater significance; within the circle of influence thus constituted certain especially powerful individuals differentiate themselves until this development accommodates itself to one or to a few heads. The pyramid of superiority and inferiority is built in this case from below upward, while in the former case the development was from above downward. This second form of development is often found in economic relationships, where at first there exists a certain equality between the persons carrying on the work of a certain industrial society. Presently some of the number acquire wealth; others become poor; others fall into intermediate conditions which are as dependent upon an aristocracy of property as the lower orders are upon the middle strata; this aristocracy rises in manifold gradations to the magnates, of whom sometimes a single individual is appropriately designated as the "king" of a branch of industry. By a sort of combination of the two ways in which graded superiority and inferiority of the group come into being the feudalism of the Middle Ages arose. So long as the full citizen—either Greek, Roman, or Teutonic—knew no subordination under an individual, there existed for him on the one hand complete equality with those of his own order, but on the other hand rigid exclusiveness toward those of lower orders. Feudalism remodeled this characteristic social form into the equally characteristic arrangement which filled the gap between freedom and bondage with a scale of classes.

A peculiar form of subordination to a number of individuals is determination by vote of a majority. The presumption of majority rule is that there is a collection of elements originally possessing equal rights. In the process of voting the individual places himself in subordination to a power of which he is a part, but in this way, that it is left to his own volition whether he will belong to the superior or the inferior, i.e., the outvoted party. We are not now interested in cases of this complex problem in which the superiority is entirely formal, as, for example, in resolves of scientific congresses, but only with those in which the individual is constrained to an action by the will of the party outvoting him, that is, in which he must practically subordinate himself to the majority. This dominance of numbers through the fact that others, though only equal in right, have another opinion, is by no means the matter of course which it seems to us today in our time of determinations by masses. Ancient German law knew nothing of it. If one did not agree with the resolve of the community, he was not bound by it. As an application of this principle, unanimity was later necessary in the choice of king, evidently because it could not be expected or required that one who had not chosen the king would obey him. The English baron who had opposed authorizing a levy, or who had not been present, often refused to pay it. In the tribal council of the Iroquois, as in the Polish Parliament, decisions had to be unanimous. There was therefore no subordination of an individual to a majority, unless we consider the fact that a proposition was regarded as rejected if it did not receive unanimous approval, a subordination, an outvoting, of the person proposing the measure.

When, on the contrary, majority rule exists, two modes of subordination of the minority are possible, and discrimination between them is of the highest sociological significance. Control of the minority may, in the first place, arise from the fact that the many are more powerful than the few. Although, or rather because, the individuals participating in a vote are supposed to be equals, the majority have the physical power to coerce the minority. The taking of a vote and the subjection of the minority serves the purpose of avoiding such actual measurement of strength, but accomplishes practically the same result through the count of votes, since the minority is convinced of the futility of such resort to force. There exist in the group two parties in opposition as though they were two groups, between which relative strength, represented by the vote, is to decide.

Quite another principle is in force, however, in the second place, where the group as a unity predominates over all individuals and so proceeds that the passing of votes shall *merely give expression to the unitary group will*. In the transition from the former to this second principle the enormously important step is taken from a unity made up merely of the sum of the individuals to recognition and operation of an abstract objective group unity. Classic antiquity took this step much earlier—not only absolutely but relatively earlier—than the German peoples. Among the latter the oneness of the community did not exist over against the individuals who composed it but entirely in them. Consequently the group will was not only not enacted but it did not even exist so long as a single member dissented. The group was not complete unless all its members were united, since it was only in the sum of its members that the group consisted. In case the group, however, is a self-existent structure—whether consciously or merely in point of fact—in case the group organization effected by union of the individuals remains along with and in spite of the individual changes, this self-existent unity—state, community, association for a distinctive purpose—must surely will and act in a definite manner. Since, however, only one of two contradictory opinions can ultimately prevail, it is assumed as more probable that the majority knows or represents this will better than the minority. According to the presumptive principle involved the minority is, in this case, not excluded but included. The subordination of the minority is thus in this stage of sociological development quite different from that in case the majority simply represents the stronger power. In the case in hand the majority does not speak in its own name but in that of the ideal unity and totality. It is only to this unity, which speaks by the mouth of the majority, that the minority subordinates itself. This is the immanent principle of our parliamentary decisions.

c) *Subordination to an impersonal principle.*—To these must be joined, third, those formations in which subordination is neither to an individual nor yet to a majority, but to an impersonal objective principle. Here, where we seem to be estopped from speaking of a *reciprocal influence* between the superior and the subordinate, a sociological interest enters in but two cases: first, when this ideal superior principle is to be interpreted as the psychological consolidation of a real social power; second, when the principle establishes specific and characteristic relationships between those who are subject to it in common. The former case appears chiefly in connection with the moral imperatives. In the moral consciousness we feel ourselves subject to a decree which does not appear to be issued by any personal human power; we hear the voice of conscience only in ourselves, although with a force and definiteness, in contrast with all subjective egoism, which, as it seems, could have had its source only from an authority outside the subject. As is well known, the attempt has been made to resolve this contradiction by the assumption that we have derived the content of morality from social decrees. Whatever is serviceable to the species and to the group, whatever on that account is demanded of the members for the self-preservation of the group, is gradually bred into individuals as an instinct, so that it asserts itself as a peculiar autonomous impression by the side of the properly personal, and consequently often contradictory, impulses. Thus would be explained the double character of the moral command. On the one side it appears to us as an impersonal order to which we have simply to yield. On the other side, however, no visible external power but only our own most real and personal instinct enforces it upon us. Sociologically this is of interest as an example of a wholly peculiar form of reaction between the individual and his group. The social force is here completely grown into the individual himself.

We now turn to the second sociological question raised by the case of subordination to an impersonal ideal principle. How does this subordination affect the reciprocal relation of the persons thus subordinated in common? The development of the position of the *pater familias* among the Aryans exhibits this process clearly. The power of the *pater familias* was originally unlimited and entirely subjective; that is, his momentary desire, his personal advantage, was permitted to give the decision upon all regulations. But this arbitrary power gradually became limited by a feeling of responsibility. The unity of the domestic group, embodied in the *spiritus familiaris*, grew into the ideal power, in relation to which the lord of the whole came to regard himself as merely an obedient agent. Accordingly it follows that morals and custom, instead of subjective preference, determine his acts, his decisions, his judicial judgments; that he no longer behaves as though he were absolute lord of the family property, but rather the manager of it in the interest of the whole; that his position bears more the character of an official station than that of an unlimited right. Thus the relation between superiors and inferiors is placed upon an entirely new basis. The family is thought of as standing above all the individual members. The guiding patriarch himself is, like every other member, subordinate to the family idea. He may give directions to the other members of the family only in the name of the higher ideal unity.

C. CONFLICT AND ACCOMMODATION

1. War and Peace as Types of Conflict and Accommodation[1]

It is obvious that the transition from war to peace must present a more considerable problem than the reverse, i.e., the transition from peace to war. The latter really needs no particular scrutiny. For the situations existing in time of peace are precisely the conditions out of which war emerges and contain in themselves struggle in a diffused, unobserved, or latent form. For instance, if the economic advantage which the southern states of the American Union had over the northern states in the Civil War as a consequence of the slave system was also the reason for this war, still, so long as no antagonism arises from it, but is merely immanent in the existing conditions, this source of conflict did not become specifically a question of war and peace. At the moment, however, at which the antagonism began to assume a color which meant war, an accumulation of antagonisms,

[1] Adapted from a translation of Georg Simmel by Albion W. Small, "The Sociology of Conflict," in the *American Journal of Sociology*, IX (1903–4), 799–802

feelings of hatred, newspaper polemics, frictions between private persons, and on the borders reciprocal moral equivocations in matters outside of the central antithesis at once manifested themselves. The transition from peace to war is thus not distinguished by a special sociological situation. Rather out of relationships existing within a peaceful situation antagonism is developed immediately, in its most visible and energetic form. The case is different, however, if the matter is viewed from the opposite direction. Peace does not follow so immediately upon conflict. The termination of strife is a special undertaking which belongs neither in the one category nor in the other, like a bridge which is of a different nature from that of either bank which it unites. The sociology of struggle demands, therefore, at least as an appendix, an analysis of the forms in which conflict is terminated, and these exhibit certain special forms of reaction not to be observed in other circumstances.

The particular motive which in most cases corresponds with the transition from war to peace is the simple longing for peace. With the emergence of this factor there comes into being, as a matter of fact, peace itself, at first in the form of the wish immediately parallel with the struggle itself, and it may without any special transitional form displace struggle. We need not pause long to observe that the desire for peace may spring up both directly and indirectly; the former may occur either through the return to power of this peaceful character in the party which is essentially in favor of peace; or through the fact that, through the mere change of the formal stimulus of struggle and of peace which is peculiar to all natures, although in different rhythms, the latter comes to the surface and assumes a control which is sanctioned by its own nature alone. In the case of the indirect motive, however, we may distinguish, on the one hand, the exhaustion of resources which, without removal of the persistent contentiousness, may instal the demand for peace; and, on the other hand, the withdrawal of interest from struggle through a higher interest in some other object. The latter case begets all sorts of hypocrisies and self-deceptions. It is asserted and believed that peace is desired from ideal interest in peace itself and the suppression of antagonism, while in reality only the object fought for has lost its interest and the fighters would prefer to have their powers free for other kinds of activity.

The simplest and most radical sort of passage from war to peace is victory—a quite unique phenomenon in life, of which there are, to be sure, countless individual forms and measures, which, however, have no resemblance to any of the otherwise mentioned forms which may occur between persons. Victory is a mere watershed between war and peace; when considered absolutely, only an ideal structure which extends itself over no considerable time. For so long as struggle endures there is no definitive victor, and when peace exists a victory *has been* gained but the act of victory has ceased to exist. Of the many shadings of victory, through which it qualifies the following peace, I mention here merely as an illustration the one which is brought about, not exclusively by the preponderance of the one party, but, at least in part, through the resignation of the other. This confession of inferiority, this acknowledgment of defeat, or this consent that victory shall go to the other party without complete exhaustion of the resources and chances for struggle, is by no means always a simple phenomenon. A certain ascetic tendency may also enter in as a purely individual factor, the tendency to self-humiliation and to self-sacrifice, not strong enough to surrender one's self from the start without a struggle, but emerging so soon as the consciousness of being vanquished begins to take possession of the soul; or another variation may be that of finding its supreme charm in the contrast to the still vital and active disposition to struggle. Still further, there is impulse to the same conclusion in the feeling that it is worthier to yield rather than to trust to the last moment in the improbable chance of a fortunate turn of affairs. To throw away this chance and to elude at this price the final consequences that would be involved in utter defeat—this has something of the great and noble qualities of men who are sure, not merely of their strengths, but also of their weaknesses, without making it necessary for them in each case to make these perceptibly conscious. Finally, in this voluntariness of confessed defeat there is a last proof of power on the part of the agent; the latter has of himself been able to act. He has therewith virtually made a gift to the conqueror. Consequently, it is often to be observed in personal conflicts that the concession of the one party, before the other has actually been able to compel it, is regarded by the latter as a sort of insult, as though this latter party were really the weaker, to whom, however, for some reason or other, there is made a concession without its being really necessary. Behind the objective reasons for yielding "for the sake of sweet peace" a mixture of these subjective motives is not seldom concealed. The latter may not be entirely without visible consequences, however, for the further sociological attitude of the parties. In complete antithesis with the end of strife by victory is its ending by compromise. One of the most characteristic ways of subdividing struggles is on the basis of whether they are of a nature which admits of compromise or not.

2.   Compromise and Accommodation[1]

On the whole, compromise, especially of that type which is brought to pass through negotiation, however commonplace and matter of fact it has come to be in the processes of modern life, is one of the most important inventions for the uses of civilization. The impulse of uncivilized men, like that of children, is to seize upon every desirable object without further consideration, even though it be already in the possession of another. Robbery and gift are the most naïve forms of transfer of possession, and under primitive conditions change of possession seldom takes place without a struggle. It is the beginning of all civilized industry and commerce to find a way of avoiding this struggle through a process in which there is offered to the possessor of a desired object some other object from the possessions of the person desiring the exchange. Through this arrangement a reduction is made in the total expenditure of energy as compared with the process of continuing or beginning a struggle. All exchange is a compromise. We are told of certain social conditions in which it is accounted as knightly to rob and to fight for the sake of robbery; while exchange and purchase are regarded in the same society as undignified and vulgar. The psychological explanation of this situation is to be found partly in the fact of the element of compromise in exchange, the factors of withdrawal and renunciation which make exchange the opposite pole to all struggle and conquest. Every exchange presupposes that values and interest have assumed an objective character. The decisive element is accordingly no longer the mere subjective passion of desire, to which struggle alone corresponds, but the value of the object, which is recognized by both interested parties but which without essential modification may be

[1] Adapted from a translation of Georg Simmel by Albion W. Small, "The Sociology of Conflict," in the *American Journal of Sociology*, IX (1903–4), 804–6.

represented by various objects. Renunciation of the valued object in question, because one receives in another form the quantum of value contained in the same, is an admirable reason, wonderful also in its simplicity, whereby opposed interests are brought to accommodation without struggle. It certainly required a long historical development to make such means available, because it presupposes a psychological generalization of the universal valuation of the individual object, an abstraction, in other words, of the value for the objects with which it is at first identified; that is, it presupposes ability to rise above the prejudices of immediate desire. Compromise by representation, of which exchange is a special case, signifies in principle, although realized only in part, the possibility of avoiding struggle or of setting a limit to it before the mere force of the interested parties has decided the issue.

In distinction from the objective character of accommodation of struggle through compromise, we should notice that conciliation is a purely subjective method of avoiding struggle. I refer here not to that sort of conciliation which is the consequence of a compromise or of any other adjournment of struggle but rather to the reasons for this adjournment. The state of mind which makes conciliation possible is an elementary attitude which, entirely apart from objective grounds, seeks to end struggle, just as, on the other hand, a disposition to quarrel, even without any real occasion, promotes struggle. Probably both mental attitudes have been developed as matters of utility in connection with certain situations; at any rate, they have been developed psychologically to the extent of independent impulses, each of which is likely to make itself felt where the other would be more practically useful. We may even say that in the countless cases in which struggle is ended otherwise than in the pitiless consistency of the exercise of force, this quite elementary and unreasoned tendency to conciliation is a factor in the result—a factor quite distinct from weakness, or good fellowship; from social morality or fellow-feeling. This tendency to conciliation is, in fact, a quite specific sociological impulse which manifests itself exclusively as a pacificator, and is not even identical with the peaceful disposition in general. The latter avoids strife under all circumstances, or carries it on, if it is once undertaken, without going to extremes, and always with the undercurrents of longing for peace. The spirit of conciliation, however, manifests itself frequently in its full peculiarity precisely after complete surrender to the struggle, after the conflicting energies have exercised themselves to the full in the conflict.

Conciliation depends very definitely upon the external situation. It can occur both after the complete victory of the one party and after the progress of indecisive struggle, as well as after the arrangement of the compromise. Either of these situations may end the struggle without the added conciliation of the opponents. To bring about the latter it is not necessary that there shall be a supplementary repudiation or expression of regret with reference to the struggle. Moreover, conciliation is to be distinguished from the situation which may follow it. This may be either a relationship of attachment or alliance, and reciprocal respect, or a certain permanent distance which avoids all positive contacts. Conciliation is thus a removal of the roots of conflict, without reference to the fruits which these formerly bore, as well as to that which may later be planted in their place.

D.   COMPETITION, STATUS, AND SOCIAL SOLIDARITY

1.   Personal Competition, Social Selection, and Status[1]

The function of personal competition, considered as a part of the social system, is to assign to each individual his place in that system. If "all the world's a stage," this is a process that distributes the parts among the players. It may do it well or ill, but after some fashion it does it. Some may be cast in parts unsuited to them; good actors may be discharged altogether and worse ones retained; but nevertheless the thing is arranged in some way and the play goes on.

That such a process must exist can hardly, it seems to me, admit of question; in fact, I believe that those who speak of doing away with competition use the word in another sense than is here intended. Within the course of the longest human life there is necessarily a complete renewal of the persons whose communication and cooperation make up the life of society. The new members come into the world without any legible sign to indicate what they are fit for, a mystery to others from the first and to themselves as soon as they

[1] Adapted from Charles H. Cooley, "Personal Competition," in *Economic Studies*, IV (1899), No. 2, 78–86.

are capable of reflection: the young man does not know for what he is adapted, and no one else can tell him. The only possible way to get light upon the matter is to adopt the method of experiment. By trying one thing and another and by reflecting upon his experience, he begins to find out about himself, and the world begins to find out about him. His field of investigation is of course restricted, and his own judgment and that of others liable to error, but the tendency of it all can hardly be other than to guide his choice to that one of the available careers in which he is best adapted to hold his own. I may say this much, perhaps, without assuming anything regarding the efficiency or justice of competition as a distributor of social functions, a matter regarding which I shall offer some suggestions later. All I wish to say here is that the necessity of some selective process is inherent in the conditions of social life.

It will be apparent that, in the sense in which I use the term, competition is not necessarily a hostile contention, nor even something of which the competing individual is always conscious. From our infancy onward throughout life judgments are daily forming regarding us of which we are unaware, but which go to determine our careers. "The world is full of judgment days." A and B, for instance, are under consideration for some appointment; the experience and personal qualifications of each are duly weighed by those having the appointment to make, and A, we will say, is chosen. Neither of the two need know anything about the matter until the selection is made. It is eligibility to perform some social function that makes a man a competitor, and he may or may not be aware of it, or, if aware of it, he may or may not be consciously opposed to others. I trust that the reader will bear in mind that I always use the word competition in the sense here explained.

There is but one alternative to competition as a means of determining the place of the individual in the social system, and that is some form of status, some fixed, mechanical rule, usually a rule of inheritance, which decides the function of the individual without reference to his personal traits, and thus dispenses with any process of comparison. It is possible to conceive of a society organized entirely upon the basis of the inheritance of functions, and indeed societies exist which may be said to approach this condition. In India, for example, the prevalent idea regarding the social function of the individual is that it is unalterably determined by his parentage, and the village blacksmith, shoemaker, accountant, or priest has his place assigned to him by a rule of descent as rigid as that which governs the transmission of one of the crowns of Europe. If all functions were handed down in this way, if there were never any deficiency or surplus of children to take the place of their parents, if there were no progress or decay in the social system making necessary new activities or dispensing with old ones, then there would be no use for a selective process. But precisely in the measure that a society departs from this condition, that individual traits are recognized and made available, or social change of any sort comes to pass, in that measure must there be competition.

Status is not an active process, as competition is; it is simply a rule of conservation, a makeshift to avoid the inconveniences of continual readjustment in the social structure. Competition or selection is the only constructive principle, and everything worthy the name of organization had at some time or other a competitive origin. At the present day the eldest son of a peer may succeed to a seat in the House of Lords simply by right of birth; but his ancestor got the seat by competition, by some exercise of personal qualities that made him valued or loved or feared by a king or a minister.

Sir Henry Maine has pointed out that the increase of competition is a characteristic trait of modern life, and that the powerful ancient societies of the old world were for the most part non-competitive in their structure. While this is true, it would be a mistake to draw the inference that status is a peculiarly natural or primitive principle of organization and competition a comparatively recent discovery. On the contrary the spontaneous relations among men, as we see in the case of children, and as we may infer from the life of the lower animals, are highly competitive, personal prowess and ascendency being everything and little regard being paid to descent simply as such. The régime of inherited status, on the other hand, is a comparatively complex and artificial product, necessarily of later growth, whose very general prevalence among the successful societies of the old world is doubtless to be explained by the stability and consequently the power which it was calculated to give to the social system. It survived because under certain conditions it was the fittest. It was not and is not universally predominant among savages or barbarous peoples. With the American Indians, for example, the definiteness and authority of status were comparatively small, personal prowess and initiative being correspondingly important. The interesting monograph on Omaha sociology, by Dorsey, published by the United States Bureau of Ethnology, contains many facts showing that the life of this people was highly competitive. When the tribe was at war any brave could organize an expedition against the enemy, if he could induce enough others to join him, and this organizer usually assumed the command. In a similar way the managers of the hunt were chosen because of personal skill; and, in general, "any man can win a name and rank in the state by becoming 'wacuce' or brave, either in war or by the bestowal of gifts and the frequent giving of feasts."

Throughout history there has been a struggle between the principles of status and competition regarding the part that each should play in the social system. Generally speaking the advantage of status is in its power to give order and continuity. As Gibbon informs us, "The superior prerogative of birth, when it has obtained the sanction of time and popular opinion, is the plainest and least invidious of all distinctions among mankind," and he is doubtless right in ascribing the confusion of the later Roman Empire largely to the lack of an established rule for the transmission of imperial authority. The chief danger of status is that of suppressing personal development, and so of causing social enfeeblement, rigidity, and ultimate decay. On the other hand, competition develops the individual and gives flexibility and animation to the social order, its danger being chiefly that of disintegration in some form or other. The general tendency in modern times has been toward the relative increase of the free or competitive principle, owing to the fact that the rise of other means of securing stability has diminished the need for status. The latter persists, however, even in the freest countries, as the method by which wealth is transmitted, and also in social classes, which, so far as they exist at all, are based chiefly upon inherited wealth and the culture and opportunities that go with it. The ultimate reason for this persistence—without very serious opposition—in the face of the obvious inequalities and limitations upon liberty that it perpetuates is perhaps the fact that no other method of transmission has arisen that has shown itself capable of giving continuity and order to the control of wealth.

2. Personal Competition and the Evolution of Individual Types[1]

The ancient city was primarily a fortress, a place of refuge in time of war. The modern city, on the contrary, is primarily a convenience of commerce and owes its existence to the market place around which it sprang up. Industrial competition and the division of labor, which have probably done most to develop the latent powers of mankind, are possible only upon condition of the existence of markets, of money and other devices for the facilitation of trade and commerce.

The old adage which describes the city as the natural environment of the free man still holds so far as the individual man finds in the chances, the diversity of interests and tasks, and in the vast unconscious co-operation of city life, the opportunity to choose his own vocation and develop his peculiar individual talents. The city offers a market for the special talents of individual men. Personal competition tends to select for each special task the individual who is best suited to perform it.

The difference of natural talents in different men is, in reality, much less than we are aware of; and the very different genius which appears to distinguish men of different professions, when grown up to maturity, is not upon many occasions so much the cause, as the effect of the division of labour. The difference between the most dissimilar characters, between a philosopher and a common street porter, for example, seems to arise not so much from nature, as from habit, custom and education. When they came into the world, and for the first six or eight years of their existence, they were perhaps very much alike, and neither their parents nor playfellows could perceive any remarkable difference. About that age, or soon after, they come to be employed in different occupations. The difference of talents comes then to be taken notice of, and widens by degrees, till at last the vanity of the philosopher is willing to acknowledge scarce any resemblance. But without the disposition to truck, barter, and exchange, every man must have procured to himself every necessary and conveniency of life which he wanted. All must have had the same duties to perform, and the same work to do, and there could have been no such difference of

[1] From Robert E. Park, "The City," in the *American Journal of Sociology*, XX (1915), 584-86.

employment as could alone give occasion to any great difference of talent.

As it is the power of exchanging that gives occasion to the division of labour, so the extent of this division must always be limited by the extent of that power, or, in other words, by the extent of the market. . . . . There are some sorts of industry, even of the lowest kind, which can be carried on nowhere but in a great town.

Success, under conditions of personal competition, depends upon concentration upon some single task, and this concentration stimulates the demand for rational methods, technical devices, and exceptional skill. Exceptional skill, while based on natural talent, requires special preparation, and it has called into existence the trade and professional schools, and finally bureaus for vocational guidance. All of these, either directly or indirectly, serve at once to select and emphasize individual differences.

Every device which facilitates trade and industry prepares the way for a further division of labor and so tends further to specialize the tasks in which men find their vocations.

The outcome of this process is to break down or modify the older organization of society, which was based on family ties, on local associations, on culture, caste, and status, and to substitute for it an organization based on vocational interests.

In the city every vocation, even that of a beggar, tends to assume the character of a profession, and the discipline which success in any vocation imposes, together with the associations that it enforces, emphasizes this tendency.

The effect of the vocations and the division of labor is to produce, in the first instance, not social groups but vocational types—the actor, the plumber, and the lumber-jack. The organizations, like the trade and labor unions, which men of the same trade or profession form are based on common interests. In this respect they differ from forms of association like the neighborhood, which are based on contiguity, personal association, and the common ties of humanity. The different trades and professions seem disposed to group themselves in classes, that is to say, the artisan, business, and professional classes. But in the modern democratic state the classes have as yet attained no effective organization. Socialism, founded on an effort to create an organization based on "class consciousness," has never succeeded in creating more than a political party.

The effects of the division of labor as a discipline may therefore be best studied in the vocational types it has produced. Among the types which it would be interesting to study are: the shopgirl, the policeman, the peddler, the cabman, the night watchman, the clair-voyant, the vaudeville performer, the quack doctor, the bartender, the ward boss, the strike-breaker, the labor agitator, the school teacher, the reporter, the stockbroker, the pawnbroker; all of these are characteristic products of the conditions of city life; each with its special experience, insight, and point of view determines for each vocational group and for the city as a whole its individuality.

3. Division of Labor and Social Solidarity[1]

The most remarkable effect of the division of labor is not that it accentuates the distinction of functions already divided but that it makes them interdependent. Its rôle in every case is not simply to embellish or perfect existing societies but to make possible societies which, without it, would not exist. Should the division of labor between the sexes be diminished beyond a certain point, the family would cease to exist and only ephemeral sexual relations would remain. If the sexes had never been separated at all, no form of social life would ever have arisen. It is possible that the economic utility of the division of labor has been a factor in producing the existing form of conjugal society. Nevertheless, the society thus created is not limited to merely economic interests; it represents a unique social and moral order. Individuals are mutually bound together who otherwise would be independent. Instead of develop-ing separately, they concert their efforts; they are interdependent parts of a unity which is effective not only in the brief moments during which there is an interchange of services but afterward indefi-nitely. For example, does not conjugal solidarity of the type which exists today among the most cultivated people exert its influence constantly and in all the details of life? On the other hand, societies which are created by the division of labor inevitably bear the mark of their origin. Having this special origin, it is not possible that they should resemble those societies which have their origin in the attrac-tion of like for like; the latter are inevitably constituted in another

[1] Translated and adapted from Émile Durkheim, *La division du travail social*, pp. 24–209. (Félix Alcan, 1902.)

manner, repose on other foundations, and appeal to other sentiments.

The assumption that the social relations resulting from the
division of labor consist in an exchange of services merely is a misconception of what this exchange implies and of the effects it produces.
It assumes that two beings are mutually dependent the one on the
other, because they are both incomplete without the other. It
interprets this mutual dependence as a purely external relation.
Actually this is merely the superficial expression of an internal and
more profound state. Precisely because this state is constant, it
provokes a complex of mental images which function with a continuity independent of the series of external relations. The image
of that which completes us is inseparable from the image of ourselves,
not only because it is associated with us, but especially because it is
our natural complement. It becomes then a permanent and integral
part of self-consciousness to such an extent that we cannot do without it and seek by every possible means to emphasize and intensify
it. We like the society of the one whose image haunts us, because
the presence of the object reinforces the actual perception and gives
us comfort. We suffer, on the contrary, from every circumstance
which, like separation and death, is likely to prevent the return or
diminish the vivacity of the idea which has become identified with
our idea of ourselves.

Short as this analysis is, it suffices to show that this complex is
not identical with that which rests on sentiments of sympathy which
have their source in mere likeness. Unquestionably there can be
the sense of solidarity between others and ourselves only so far as
we conceive others united with ourselves. When the union results
from a perception of likeness, it is a cohesion. The two representations become consolidated because, being undistinguished totally or
in part, they are mingled and are no more than one, and are consolidated only in the measure in which they are mingled. On the
contrary, in the case of the division of labor, each is outside the other,
and they are united only because they are distinct. It is not possible
that sentiments should be the same in the two cases, nor the social
relations which are derived from them the same.

We are then led to ask ourselves if the division of labor does not play
the same rôle in more extended groups; if, in the contemporaneous

societies where it has had a development with which we are familiar, it does not function in such a way as to integrate the social body and to assure its unity. It is quite legitimate to assume that the facts which we have observed reproduce themselves there, but on a larger scale. The great political societies, like smaller ones, we may assume maintain themselves in equilibrium, thanks to the specialization of their tasks. The division of labor is here, again, if not the only, at least the principal, source of the social solidarity. Comte had already reached this point of view. Of all the sociologists, so far as we know, he is the first who has pointed out in the division of labor anything other than a purely economic phenomenon. He has seen there "the most essential condition of the social life," provided that one conceives it "in all its rational extent, that is to say, that one applies the conception to the ensemble of all our diverse operations whatsoever, instead of limiting it, as we so often do, to the simple material usages." Considered under this aspect, he says:

It immediately leads us to regard not only individuals and classes but also, in many respects, the different peoples as constantly participating, in their own characteristic ways and in their own proper degree, in an immense and common work whose inevitable development gradually unites the actual co-operators in a series with their predecessors and at the same time in a series with their successors. It is, then, the continuous redivison of our diverse human labors which mainly constitutes social solidarity and which becomes the elementary cause of the extension and increasing complexity of the social organism.

If this hypothesis is demonstrated, division of labor plays a rôle much more important than that which has ordinarily been attributed to it. It is not to be regarded as a mere luxury, desirable perhaps, but not indispensable to society; it is rather a condition of its very existence. It is this, or at least it is mainly this, that assures the solidarity of social groups; it determines the essential traits of their constitution. It follows—even though we are not yet prepared to give a final solution to the problem, we can nevertheless foresee from this point—that, if such is really the function of the division of labor, it may be expected to have a moral character, because the needs of order, of harmony, of social solidarity generally, are what we understand by moral needs.

Social life is derived from a double source: (*a*) from a similarity of minds, and (*b*) from the division of labor. The individual is socialized in the first case, because, not having his own individuality, he is confused, along with his fellows, in the bosom of the same collective type; in the second case, because, even though he possesses a physiognomy and a temperament which distinguish him from others, he is dependent upon these in the same measure in which he is distinguished from them. Society results from this union.

Like-mindedness gives birth to judicial regulations which, under the menace of measures of repression, impose upon everybody uniform beliefs and practices. The more pronounced this like-mindedness, the more completely the social is confused with the religious life, the more nearly economic institutions approach communism.

The division of labor, on the other hand, gives birth to regulations and laws which determine the nature and the relations of the divided functions, but the violation of which entails only punitive measures not of an expiatory character.

Every code of laws is accompanied by a body of regulations purely moral. Where the penal law is voluminous, moral consensus is very extended; that is to say, a multitude of collective activities is under the guardianship of public opinion. Where the right of reparation is well developed, there each profession maintains a code of professional ethics. In a group of workers there invariably exists a body of opinion, diffused throughout the limits of the group, which, although not fortified with legal sanctions, still enforces its decrees. There are manners and customs, recognized by all the members of a profession, which no one of them could infringe without incurring the blame of society. Certainly this code of morals is distinguished from the preceding by differences analogous to those which separate the two corresponding kinds of laws. It is, in fact, a code localized in a limited region of society. Furthermore, the repressive character of the sanctions which are attached to it is sensibly less accentuated. Professional faults arouse a much feebler response than offenses against the mores of the larger society.

Nevertheless, the customs and code of a profession are imperative. They oblige the individual to act in accordance with ends which to him are not his own, to make concessions, to consent to compromises, to take account of interests superior to his own. The consequence is that, even where the society rests most completely upon the division of labor, it does not disintegrate into a dust of atoms, between which there can exist only external and temporary contacts. Every function which one individual exercises is invariably dependent upon functions exercised by others and forms with them a system of interdependent parts. It follows that, from the nature of the task one chooses, corresponding duties follow. Because we fill this or that domestic or social function, we are imprisoned in a net of obligations from which we do not have the right to free ourselves. There is especially one organ toward which our state of dependencies is ever increasing—the state. The points at which we are in contact with it are multiplying. So are the occasions in which it takes upon itself to recall us to a sense of the common solidarity.

There are then two great currents in the social life, collectivism and individualism, corresponding to which we discover two types of structure not less different. Of these currents, that which has its origin in like-mindedness is at first alone and without rival. At this moment it is identified with the very life of the society; little by little it finds its separate channels and diminishes, whilst the second becomes ever larger. In the same way, the segmentary structure of society is more and more overlaid by the other, but without ever disappearing completely.

III. INVESTIGATIONS AND PROBLEMS

1. Forms of Accommodation

The literature upon accommodation will be surveyed under four heads; (a) forms of accommodation; (b) subordination and superordination; (c) accommodation groups; and (d) social organization.

The term accommodation, as has been noted, developed as a differentiation within the field of the biological concept of adaptation. Ward's dictum that "the environment transforms the animal, while man transforms the environment"[1] contained the distinction. Thomas similarly distinguished between the animal with its method of adaptation and man with his method of control. Bristol in his work on *Social Adaptation* is concerned, as the subtitle of the volume indicates, "with the development of the doctrine of adaptation as a

[1] *Pure Sociology*, p. 16.

theory of social progress." Of the several types of adaptation that he proposes, however, all but the first represent accommodations. Baldwin, though not the first to make the distinction, was the first student to use the separate term accommodation. "By accommodation old habits are broken up, and new co-ordinations are made which are more complex."[1]

Baldwin suggested a division of accommodation into the three fields: acclimatization, naturalization, and equilibrium. The term equilibrium accurately describes the type of organization established by competition between the different biological species and the environment, but not the more permanent organizations of individuals and groups which we find in human society. In human society equilibrium means organization. The research upon acclimatization is considerable, although there is far from unanimity of opinion in regard to its findings.

Closely related to acclimatization but in the field of social naturalization are the accommodations that take place in colonization and immigration. In colonization the adjustment is not only to climatic conditions but to the means of livelihood and habits of life required by the new situation. Historic colonial settlements have not infrequently been made in inhospitable areas, and that involved accommodations to primitive peoples of different and generally lower cultural level than the settlers. Professor Keller's work on *Colonization* surveys the differences in types of colonial ventures and describes the adjustments involved. It includes also a valuable bibliography of the literature of the subject.

In immigration the accommodation to the economic situation and to the folkways and mores of the native society are more important than in colonization. The voluminous literature upon immigration deals but slightly with the interesting accommodations of the newcomer to his new environment. One of the important factors in the process, as emphasized in the recent "Americanization Study" of the Carnegie Corporation, is the immigrant community which serves as a mediating agency between the familiar and the strange. The greater readiness of accommodation of recent immigrants as compared with that of an earlier period has been explained in terms of facilities

[1] *Mental Development in the Child and the Race*, p. 23.

of transportation, communication, and even more in the mobility of employment in large-scale modern industry with its minute subdivision of labor and its slight demand for skill and training on the part of the employees.

The more subtle forms of accommodation to new social situations have not been subjected to analysis, although there is a small but important number of studies upon homesickness. In fiction, to be sure, the difficulties of the tenderfoot in the frontier community, or the awkward rural lad in an urban environment and the *nouveaux riches* in their successful entrée among the social élite are often accurately and sympathetically described. The recent immigrant autobiographies contain materials which throw much new light on the situation of the immigrant in process of accommodation to the American environment.

The whole process of social organization is involved in the processes by which persons find their places in groups and groups are articulated into the life of the larger and more inclusive societies. The literature on the taming of animals, the education of juveniles and adults, and on social control belongs in this field. The writings on diplomacy, on statescraft, and upon adjudication of disputes are also to be considered here. The problem of the person whether in the narrow field of social work or the broader fields of human relations is fundamentally a problem of the adjustment of the person to his social milieu, to his family, to his primary social groups, to industry, and to cultural, civic, and religious institutions. The problems of community organization are for the most part problems of accommodation, of articulation of groups within the community and of the adjustment of the local community to the life of the wider community of which it is a part.

Adjustments of personal and social relations in the past have been made unreflectively and with a minimum of personal and social consciousness. The extant literature reveals rather an insistent demand for these accommodations than any systematic study of the processes by which the accommodations take place. Simmel's observation upon subordination and superordination is almost the only attempt that has been made to deal with the subject from the point of view of sociology.

2. Subordination and Superordination

Materials upon subordination and superordination may be found in the literature under widely different names. Thorndike, Mc-Dougall, and others have reported upon the original tendencies in the individual to domination and submission or to self-assertion and self-abasement. Veblen approaches nearer to a sociological explanation in his analysis of the self-conscious attitudes of invidious comparison and conspicuous waste in the leisure class.

The application of our knowledge of rapport, esprit de corps, and morale to an explanation of personal conduct and group behavior is one of the most promising fields for future research. In the family, rapport and consensus represent the most complete co-ordination of its members. The life of the family should be studied intensively in order to define more exactly the nature of the family consensus, the mechanism of family rapport, and minor accommodations made to minimize conflict and to avert tendencies to disintegration in the interest of this real unity.

Strachey's *Life of Queen Victoria* sketches an interesting case of subordination and superordination in which the queen is the subordinate, and her adroit but cynical minister, Disraeli, is the master.

Future research will provide a more adequate sociology of subordination and superordination. A survey of the present output of material upon the nature and the effects of personal contacts reinforces the need for such a fundamental study. The obsolete writings upon personal magnetism have been replaced by the so-called "psychology of salesmanship," "scientific methods of character reading," and "the psychology of leadership." The wide sale of these books indicates the popular interest, quite as much as the lack of any fundamental understanding of the technique of human relations.

3. Accommodation Groups

The field of investigation available for the study of accommodation groups and their relation to conflict groups may perhaps be best illustrated by the table on page 722.

The existence of conflict groups like parties, sects, nationalities, represents the area in any society of unstable equilibrium. Accommodation groups, classes, castes, and denominations on the other hand, represent in this same society the areas of stable equilibrium. A boys' club carries on contests, under recognized rules, with similar organizations. A denomination engages in fraternal rivalry with other denominations for the advancement of common interests of the church universal. A nation possesses status, rights, and responsibilities only in a commonwealth of nations of which it is a member.

The works upon accommodation groups are concerned almost exclusively with the principles, methods, and technique of organization. There are, indeed, one or two important descriptive works

Conflict Groups	Accommodation Group
1. Gangs	1. Clubs
2. Labor organizations, employers' associations, middle-class unions, tenant protective unions	2. Social classes, vocational groups
3. Races	3. Castes
4. Sects	4. Denominations
5. Nationalities	5. Nations

upon secret organizations in primitive and modern times. The books and articles, however, on organized boys' groups deal with the plan of organization of Boy Scouts, Boys' Brotherhood Republic, George Junior Republics, Knights of King Arthur, and many other clubs of these types. They are not studies of natural groups.

The comparative study of social classes and vocational groups is an unworked field. The differentiation of social types, especially in urban life, and the complexity and subtlety of the social distinctions separating social and vocational classes, opens a fruitful prospect for investigation. Scattered through a wide literature, ranging from official inquiries to works of fiction, there are, in occasional paragraphs, pages, and chapters, observations of value.

In the field of castes the work of research is well under way. The caste system of India has been the subject of careful examination and analysis. Sighele points out that the prohibition of intermarriage observed in its most rigid and absolute form is a fundamental distinction of the caste. If this be regarded as the fundamental criterion, the Negro race in the United States occupies the position of a caste. The prostitute, in America, until recently constituted a separate caste. With the systematic breaking up of the segregated vice districts in our great cities prostitution, as a caste, seems to have disappeared. The place of the prostitute seems to have been occupied by the demimondaine who lives on the outskirts of society but who is not by any means an outcast.

It is difficult to dissociate the materials upon nationalities from those upon nations. The studies, however, of the internal organization of the state, made to promote law and order, would come under the latter head. Here, also, would be included studies of the extension of the police power to promote the national welfare. In international relations studies of international law, of international courts of arbitration, of leagues or associations of nations manifest the increasing interest in the accommodations that would avert or postpone conflicts of militant nationalities.

In the United States there is a considerable literature upon church federation and the community church. This literature is one expression of the transition of the Protestant churches from sectarian bodies, engaged in warfare for the support of distinctive doctrines and dogmas, to co-operating denominations organized into the Federal Council of the Churches of Christ in America.

4. Social Organization

Until recently there has been more interest manifested in elaborating theories of the stages in the evolution of society than in analyzing the structure of different types of societies. Durkheim, however, in *De la division du travail social*, indicated how the division of labor and the social attitudes, or the mental accommodations to the life-situation, shape social organization. Cooley, on the other hand, in his work *Social Organization* conceived the structure of society to be "the larger mind," or an outgrowth of human nature and human ideals.

The increasing number of studies of individual primitive communities has furnished data for the comparative study of different kinds of social organization. Schurtz, Vierkandt, Rivers, Lowie, and others in the last twenty years have made important comparative studies in this field. The work of these scholars has led to the abandonment of the earlier notions of uniform evolutionary stages of culture in which all peoples, primitive, ancient, and modern alike, might be classified. New light has been thrown upon the actual accommodations in the small family, in the larger family group, the clan, gens or sib, in the secret society, and in the tribe which determined the patterns of life of primitive peoples under different geographical and historical conditions.

At the present time, the investigations of social organization of current and popular interest have to do with the problems of social work and of community life. "Community organization," "community action," "know your own community" are phrases which express the practical motives behind the attempts at community study. Such investigations as have been made, with a few shining exceptions, the Pittsburgh Survey and the community studies of the Russell Sage Foundation, have been superficial. All, perhaps, have been tentative and experimental. The community has not been studied from a fundamental standpoint. Indeed, there was not available, as a background of method and of orientation, any adequate analysis of social organization.

A penetrating analysis of the social structure of a community must quite naturally be based upon studies of human geography. Plant and animal geography has been studied, but slight attention has been given to human geography, that is, to the local distribution of persons who constitute a community and the accommodations that are made because of the consequent physical distances and social relationships.

Ethnological and historical studies of individual communities furnish valuable comparative materials for a treatise upon human ecology which would serve as a guidebook for studies in community organization. C. J. Galpin's *The Social Anatomy of an Agricultural Community* is an example of the recognition of ecological factors as basic in the study of social organization.

In the bibliography of this chapter is given a list of references to certain of the experiments in community organization. Students should study this literature in the light of the more fundamental studies of types of social groups and studies of individual communities listed in an earlier bibliography.[1] It is at once apparent that the rural community has been more carefully studied than has the urban community. Yet more experiments in community organization have been tried out in the city than in the country. Reports upon social-center activities, upon community councils, and other types of community organization have tended to be enthusiastic rather than factual and critical. The most notable experiment of community organization, the Social Unit Plan, tried out in Cincinnati, was what the

[1] *Supra*, pp. 218–19.

theatrical critics call a *succès d'estime*, but after the experiment had been tried it was abandoned. Control of conditions of community life is not likely to meet with success unless based on an appreciation and understanding of human nature on the one hand, and of the natural or ecological organization of community life on the other.

SELECTED BIBLIOGRAPHY

I. THE PSYCHOLOGY AND SOCIOLOGY OF ACCOMMODATION

A. *Accommodation Defined*

(1) Morgan, C. Lloyd, and Baldwin, J. Mark. Articles on "Accommodation and Adaptation," *Dictionary of Philosophy and Psychology*, I, 7–8, 14–15.

(2) Baldwin, J. Mark. *Mental Development in the Child and the Race.* Methods and processes. Chap. xvi, "Habit and Accommodation," pp. 476–88. New York, 1895.

(3) Simmel, Georg. *Soziologie.* Untersuchungen über die Formen der Vergesellschaftung. "Kompromiss und Versöhnung," pp. 330–36. Leipzig, 1908.

(4) Bristol, L. M. *Social Adaptation.* A study in the development of the doctrine of adaptation as a theory of social progress. Cambridge, Mass., 1915.

(5) Ross, E. A. *Principles of Sociology.* "Toleration," "Compromise," "Accommodation," pp. 225–34. New York, 1920.

(6) Ritchie, David G. *Natural Rights.* Chap. viii, "Toleration," pp. 157–209. London, 1895.

(7) Morley, John. *On Compromise.* London, 1874.

(8) Tardieu, É. "Le cynisme: étude psychologique," *Revue philosophique*, LVII (1904), 1–28.

(9) Jellinek, G. *Die Lehre von den Staatenverbindungen.* Berlin, 1882.

B. *Acclimatization and Colonization*

(1) Wallace, Alfred R. Article on "Acclimatization." *Encyclopaedia Britannica*, I, 114–19.

(2) Brinton, D. G. *The Basis of Social Relations.* A study in ethnic psychology. Part II, chap. iv, "The Influence of Geographic Environment," pp. 180–99. New York, 1902.

(3) Ripley, W. Z. *The Races of Europe.* A sociological study. Chap. xxi, "Acclimatization: the Geographical Future of the European Races," pp. 560–89. New York, 1899. [Bibliography.]

(4) Virchow, Rudolph. "Acclimatization," *Popular Science Monthly*, XXVIII (1886), 507–17.

(5) Boas, Franz. "Changes in Bodily Form of Descendants of Immigrants," *Report of Immigration Commission, 1907.* Washington, 1911.

(6) Keller, Albert G. *Colonization.* A study of the founding of new societies. Boston, 1908. [Bibliography.]

(7) ———. "The Value of the Study of Colonies for Sociology," *American Journal of Sociology*, XII (1906), 417–20.

(8) Roscher, W., and Jannasch, R. *Kolonien, Kolonialpolitik und Auswanderung.* 3d ed. Leipzig, 1885.

(9) Leroy-Beaulieu, P. *De la colonisation chez les peuples modernes.* 5th ed., 2 vols. Paris, 1902.

(10) Huntington, Ellsworth. *Civilization and Climate.* Chap. iii, "The White Man in the Tropics," pp. 35–48. New Haven, 1915.

(11) Ward, Robert De C. *Climate.* Considered especially in relation to man. Chap. viii, "The Life of Man in the Tropics," pp. 220–71. New York, 1908.

(12) Bryce, James. "British Experience in the Government of Colonies," *Century*, LVII (1898–99), 718–29.

C. *Superordination and Subordination*

(1) Simmel, Georg. "Superiority and Subordination as Subject Matter of Sociology," translated from the German by Albion W. Small, *American Journal of Sociology*, II (1896–97), 167–89, 392–415.

(2) Thorndike, E. L. *The Original Nature of Man.* "Mastering and Submissive Behavior," pp. 92–97. New York, 1913.

(3) McDougall, William. *An Introduction to Social Psychology.* "The Instincts of Self-Abasement (or Subjection) and of Self-Assertion (or Self-Display) and the Emotions of Subjection and Elation," pp. 62–66. 12th ed. Boston, 1917.

(4) Münsterberg, Hugo. *Psychology, General and Applied.* Chap. xviii, "Submission," pp. 254–64. New York, 1914.

(5) Galton, Francis. *Inquiries into Human Faculty and Its Development.* "Gregarious and Slavish Instincts," pp. 68–82. New York, 1883.

(6) Ellis, Havelock. *Studies in the Psychology of Sex.* Vol. III, "Analysis of the Sexual Impulse." "Sexual Subjection," pp. 60–71; 85–87. Philadelphia, 1914.

(7) Calhoun, Arthur W. *A Social History of the American Family.* From colonial times to the present. Vol. II, "From Independence through the Civil War." Chap. iv, "The Social Subordination of Woman," pp. 79–101. 3 vols. Cincinnati, 1918.

(8) Galton, Francis. "The First Steps toward the Domestication of Animals," *Transactions of the Ethnological Society of London*, III, 122–38.

(9) Shaler, Nathaniel S. *Domesticated Animals.* "The Problem of Domestication," pp. 218–64. New York, 1895.

D. *Conversion*

(1) Starbuck, Edwin D. *The Psychology of Religion.* London, 1899.

(2) James, William. *The Varieties of Religious Experience.* Lectures ix and x, "Conversion," pp. 189–258. London, 1902.

(3) Coe, George A. *The Psychology of Religion.* Chap. x, "Conversion," pp. 152–74. Chicago, 1916.

(4) Prince, Morton. "The Psychology of Sudden Religious Conversion," *Journal of Abnormal Psychology*, I (1906–7), 42–54.

(5) Tawney, G. A. "The Period of Conversion," *Psychological Review*, XI (1904), 210–16.

(6) Partridge, G. E. *Studies in the Psychology of Intemperance.* Pp. 152–63. New York, 1912. [Mental cures of alcoholism.]

(7) Begbie, Harold. *Twice-born Men.* A clinic in regeneration. A footnote in narrative to Professor William James's *The Varieties of Religious Experience.* New York, 1909.

(8) Burr, Anna R. *Religious Confessions and Confessants.* With a chapter on the history of introspection. Boston, 1914.

(9) Patterson, R. J. *Catch-My-Pal.* A story of Good Samaritanship. New York, 1913.

(10) Weber, John L. "A Modern Miracle, the Remarkable Conversion of Former Governor Patterson of Tennessee," *Congregationalist,* XCIX (1914), 6, 8. [See also "The Conversion of Governor Patterson," *Literary Digest,* XLVIII (1914), 111–12.]

II. FORMS OF ACCOMMODATION

A. *Slavery*

(1) Letourneau, Ch. *L'évolution de l'esclavage dans les diverses races humaines.* Paris, 1897.

(2) Nieboer, Dr. H. J. *Slavery as an Industrial System.* Ethnological researches. The Hague, 1900. [Bibliography.]

(3) Wallon, H. *Histoire de l'esclavage dans l'antiquité.* 2d ed., 3 vols. Paris, 1879.

(4) Sugenheim, S. *Geschichte der Aufhebung der Leibeigenschaft und Hörigkeit in Europa bis um die Mitte des neunzehnten Jahrhunderts.* St. Petersburg, 1861.

(5) Edwards, Bryan. *The History, Civil and Commercial, of the British Colonies in the West Indies.* 3 vols. London, 1793–1801.

(6) Helps, Arthur. *Life of Las Casas, "the Apostle of the Indies."* 5th ed. London, 1890.

(7) Phillips, Ulrich B. *American Negro Slavery.* A survey of the supply, employment, and control of Negro labor as determined by the plantation régime. New York, 1918.

(8) ——. *Plantation and Frontier, 1649–1863.* Documentary history of American industrial society. Vols. I–II. Cleveland, 1910–11.

(9) *A Professional Planter.* Practical rules for the management and medical treatment of Negro slaves in the Sugar Colonies. London, 1803. [Excerpt in Phillips, U. B., *Plantation and Frontier,* I, 129–30.]

(10) Russell, J. H. "Free Negro in Virginia, 1619–1865," *Johns Hopkins University Studies in Historical and Political Science.* Baltimore, 1913.

(11) Olmstead, F. L. *A Journey in the Seaboard Slave States.* With remarks on their economy. New York, 1856.

(12) Smedes, Susan D. *Memorials of a Southern Planter.* Baltimore, 1887.

(13) Sartorius von Walterhausen, August. *Die Arbeitsverfassung der englischen Kolonien in Nordamerika.* Strassburg, 1894.

(14) Ballagh, James C. "A History of Slavery in Virginia," *Johns Hopkins University Studies in Historical and Political Science.* Baltimore, 1902.

(15) McCormac, E. I. "White Servitude in Maryland, 1634–1820," *Johns Hopkins University Studies in Historical and Political Science.* Baltimore, 1904.

(16) Kemble, Frances A. *Journal of a Residence on a Georgian Plantation in 1838–1839.* New York, 1863.

B. *Caste*

(1) Risley, Herbert H. *The People of India.* London, 1915.
(2) ———. *India.* Ethnographic Appendices, being the data upon which the caste chapter of the report is based. Appendix IV. Typical Tribes and Castes. Calcutta, 1903.
(3) Bouglé, M. C. "Remarques générales sur le régime des castes," *L'Année sociologique,* IV (1899–1900), 1–64.
(4) Crooke, W. "The Stability of Caste and Tribal Groups in India," *Journal of the Anthropological Institute,* XLIV (1914), 270–81.
(5) Bhattacharya, Jogendra Nath. *Hindu Castes and Sects.* An exposition of the origin of the Hindu caste system and the bearing of the sects toward each other and toward other religious systems. Calcutta, 1896.
(6) Somló, F. *Der Güterverkehr in der Urgesellschaft.* "Zum Ursprung der Kastenbildung," pp. 157–59. Instituts Solvay: Travaux de l'Institut de Sociologie. Bruxelles, 1909.
(7) Ratzel, Friedrich. *Völkerkunde.* I, 81. 2d rev. ed. Leipzig and Wien, 1894. [The origin of caste in the difference of occupation.]
(8) Iyer, L. K. A. K. *The Cochin Tribes and Castes.* London, 1909.
(9) Bailey, Thomas P. *Race Orthodoxy in the South.* And other aspects of the Negro question. New York, 1914.

C. *Classes*

(1) Bücher, Carl. *Industrial Evolution.* Translated from the 3d German edition by S. Morley Wickett. Chap. ix, "Organization of Work and the Formation of Social Classes," pp. 315–44. New York, 1907.
(2) Hobhouse, L. T. *Morals in Evolution.* A study in comparative ethics. Part I, chap. vii, "Class Relations," pp. 270–317. New York, 1915.
(3) Schmoller, Gustav. *Grundriss der allgemeinen Volkswirtschaftslehre.* Vol. I, Book II, chap. vi, "Die gesellschaftliche Klassenbildung," pp. 391–411. 6. Aufl. Leipzig, 1901.
(4) Cooley, Charles H. *Social Organization.* Part IV, "Social Classes," pp. 209–309. New York, 1909.
(5) Bauer, Arthur. "Les classes sociales," *Revue internationale de sociologie,* XI (1903), 119–35; 243–58; 301–16; 398–413; 474–98; 576–87. [Includes discussions at successive meetings of the Société de Sociologie de Paris by G. Tarde, Ch. Limousin, H. Monin, René Worms, E. Delbet, L. Philippe, M. Coicou, H. Blondel, G. Pinet, P. Vavin, E. de Roberty, G. Lafargue, M. le Gouix, M. Kovalewsky, I. Loutschisky, E. Séménoff, Mme. de Mouromtzeff, R. de la Grasserie, E. Cheysson, D. Draghicesco.]
(6) Bouglé, C. *Les idées égalitaires.* Étude sociologique. Paris, 1899.
(7) Thomas, William I. *Source Book for Social Origins.* "The Relation of the Medicine Man to the Origin of the Professional Occupations," pp. 281–303. Chicago, 1909.

(8) Tarde, Gabriel. "L'hérédité des professions," *Revue internationale de sociologie*, VIII (1900), 50–59. [Discussion of the subject was continued under the title "L'hérédité et la continuité des professions," pp. 117–24, 196–207.]

(9) Knapp, Georg F. *Die Bauernbefreiung und der Ursprung der Landarbeiter in den älteren Theilen Preussens.* Leipzig, 1887.

(10) Zimmern, Alfred E. *The Greek Commonwealth.* Politics and economics in fifth-century Athens. Pp. 255–73, 323–47, 378–94. 2d rev. ed. Oxford, 1915.

(11) Mallock, W. H. *Aristocracy and Evolution.* A study of the rights, the origin, and the social functions of the wealthier classes. New York, 1898.

(12) Veblen, Thorstein. *The Theory of the Leisure Class.* An economic study in the evolution of institutions. New York, 1899.

(13) D'Aeth, F. G. "Present Tendencies of Class Differentiation," *Sociological Review*, III (1910), 267–76.

III. ACCOMMODATION AND ORGANIZATION

A. *Social Organization*

(1) Durkheim, É. *De la division du travail social.* 2d ed. Paris, 1902.

(2) Cooley, Charles H. *Social Organization.* A study of the larger mind. Part V, "Institutions," pp. 313–92. New York, 1909.

(3) Salz, Arthur. "Zur Geschichte der Berufsidee," *Archiv für Sozialwissenschaft*, XXXVII (1913), 380–423.

(4) Rivers, W. H. R. *Social Organization.* Preface by G. Elliot Smith. New York, 1924.

(5) Schurtz, Heinrich. *Altersklassen und Männerbünde.* Eine Darstellung der Grundformen der Gesellschaft. Berlin, 1902.

(6) Vierkandt, A. "Die politischen Verhältnisse der Naturvölker," *Zeitschrift für Sozialwissenschaft*, IV, 417–26, 497–510.

(7) Lowie, Robert H. *Primitive Society.* Chap. x, "Associations," chap. xi, "Theory of Associations," pp. 257–337. New York, 1920.

(8) Zimmern, Alfred E. *The Greek Commonwealth.* Politics and economics in fifth-century Athens. 2d rev. ed. Oxford, 1915.

(9) Thomas, William I. *Source Book for Social Origins.* Ethnological materials, psychological standpoint, classified and annotated bibliographies for the interpretation of savage society. Part VII, "Social Organization, Morals, the State," pp. 753–869. Chicago, 1909. [Bibliography.]

B. *Secret Societies*

(1) Simmel, Georg. "The Sociology of Secrecy and of Secret Societies," translated from the German by Albion W. Small, *American Journal of Sociology*, XI (1905–6), 441–98.

(2) Heckethorn, C. W. *The Secret Societies of All Ages and Countries.* A comprehensive account of upward of one hundred and sixty secret organizations—religious, political, and social—from the most remote ages down to the present time. New ed., rev. and enl., 2 vols. London, 1897.

(3) Webster, Hutton. *Primitive Secret Societies*. A study in early politics and religion. New York, 1908.

(4) Schuster, G. *Die geheimen Gesellschaften, Verbindungen und Orden.* 2 vols. Leipzig, 1906.

(5) Boas, Franz. "The Social Organization and the Secret Societies of the Kwakiutl Indians," *U.S. National Museum, Annual Report, 1895,* pp. 311–738. Washington, 1897.

(6) Frobenius, L. "Die Masken und Geheimbünde Afrikas," *Abhandlungen der Kaiserlichen Leopoldinisch-Carolinischen deutschen Akademie der Naturforscher*, LXXIV, 1–278.

(7) Pfleiderer, Otto. *Primitive Christianity, Its Writings and Teachings in Their Historical Connections.* Vol. III, chap. i, "The Therapeutae and the Essenes," pp. 1–22. Translated from the German by W. Montgomery. New York, 1910.

(8) Jennings, Hargrave. *The Rosicrucians, Their Rites and Mysteries.* 3d rev. and enl. ed., 2 vols. London, 1887.

(9) Stillson, Henry L., and Klein, Henri F. Article on "The Masonic Fraternity," *The Americana*, XVIII, 383–89. [Bibliography.]

(10) Johnston, R. M. *The Napoleonic Empire in Southern Italy and the Rise of the Secret Societies.* Part II, "The Rise of the Secret Societies," Vol. II, pp. 3–139, 153–55; especially chap. ii, "Origin and Rites of the Carbonari," Vol. II, pp. 19–44. London, 1904. [Bibliography.]

(11) Fleming, Walter L. *Documentary History of Reconstruction.* Vol. II, chap. xii, "The Ku Klux Movement," pp. 327–77. Cleveland, 1907.

(12) Lester, J. C., and Wilson, D. L. *The Ku Klux Klan.* Its origin, growth, and disbandment. With appendices containing the prescripts of the Ku Klux Klan, specimen orders and warnings. With introduction and notes by Walter L. Fleming. New York and Washington, 1905.

(13) Mecklin, John M. *The Ku Klux Klan.* A study of the American mind. New York, 1924.

(14) La Hodde, Lucien de. *The Cradle of Rebellions.* A history of the secret societies of France. Translated from the French by J. W. Phelps. New York, 1864.

(15) Spadoni, D. *Sètte, cospirazioni e cospiratori nello Stato Pontificio all'indomani della restaurazioni.* Torino, 1904.

(16) "Societies, Criminal," *The Americana*, XXV, 201–5.

(17) Clark, T. A. *The Fraternity and the College.* Being a series of papers dealing with fraternity problems. Menasha, Wis., 1915.

C. *Social Types*

(1) Thomas, W. I., and Znaniecki, F. *The Polish Peasant in Europe and America.* Monograph of an immigrant group. Vol. III, "Life Record of an Immigrant." Boston, 1919. ["Introduction." pp. 5–88, analyzes and interprets three social types: the philistine, the bohemian, and the creative.]

(2) Paulhan, Fr. *Les caractères.* Livre II, "Les types déterminés par les tendances sociales," pp. 143–89. Paris, 1902.

(3) Rousiers, Paul de. *L'élite dans la société moderne*. Paris, 1914.
(4) Bradford, Gamaliel, Jr. *Types of American Character*. New York, 1895.
(5) Kellogg, Walter G. *The Conscientious Objector*. Introduction by Newton D. Baker. New York, 1919.
(6) Hapgood, Hutchins. *Types from City Streets*. New York, 1910.
(7) Bab, Julius. *Die Berliner Bohème*. Berlin, 1905.
(8) Cory, H. E. *The Intellectuals and the Wage Workers*. A study in educational psychoanalysis. New York, 1919.
(9) Anderson, Nels. *The Hobo*. The sociology of the homeless man. Chicago, 1923.
(10) Buchanan, J. R. *The Story of a Labor Agitator*. New York, 1903.
(11) Taussig, F. W. *Inventors and Money-Makers*. New York, 1915.
(12) Stoker, Bram. *Famous Impostors*. London, 1910.

D. *Community Organization*

(1) Galpin, Charles J. "Rural Relations of the Village and Small City," *University of Wisconsin Bulletin No. 411*.
(2) ————. *Rural Life*. Chaps. vii–xi, pp. 153–314. New York, 1918.
(3) Hayes, A. W. *Rural Community Organization*. Chicago, 1921.
(4) Vogt, Paul. *An Introduction to Rural Sociology*. New York, 1917.
(5) Morgan, E. L. "Mobilizing a Rural Community," *Massachusetts Agricultural College, Extension Bulletin No. 23*. Amherst, 1918.
(6) "Rural Organization," *Proceedings of the Third National Country Life Conference, Springfield, Massachusetts, 1920*. Chicago, 1921.
(7) Hart, Joseph K. *Community Organization*. New York, 1920.
(8) Woods, Robert A., and Kennedy, Albert J. *Handbook of Settlements*. New York, 1911.
(9) *National Social Unit Organization, Bulletins 1, 2, 2a, 3, 4, 5*. Cincinnati, 1917–19.
(10) Devine, Edward T. "Social Unit in Cincinnati," *Survey*, XLIII (1919), 115–26.
(11) Hicks, Mary L., and Eastman, Rae S. "Block Workers as Developed under the Social Unit Experiment in Cincinnati," *Survey*, XLIV (1920), 671–74.
(12) Ward, E. J. *The Social Center*. New York, 1913. [Bibliography.]
(13) Collier, John. "Community Councils—Democracy Every Day," *Survey*, XL (1918), 604–6; 689–91; 709–11. [Describes community defense organizations formed in rural and urban districts during the war.]
(14) Weller, Charles F. "Democratic Community Organization," An after-the-war experiment in Chester, *Survey*, XLIV (1920), 77–79.
(15) Rainwater, Clarence E. *Community Organization*. Sociological Monograph No. 15, University of Southern California. Los Angeles, 1920. [Bibliography.]
(16) Lindeman, Eduard C. *The Community*. An introduction to the study of community leadership and organization. New York, 1921
(17) Steiner, Jesse F. "Community Organization," *Journal of Social Forces*, I (1922–23), 11–18, 102–7, 221–26.

TOPICS FOR WRITTEN THEMES

1. Biological Accommodation and Social Accommodation
2. Acclimatization as Accommodation
3. The Psychology of Accommodation
4. Conversion as a Form of Accommodation: A Study of Mutations of Attitudes in Religion, Politics, Morals, Personal Relation, etc.
5. The Psychology and Sociology of Homesickness and Nostalgia
6. Conflict and Accommodation: War and Peace, Enmity and Conciliation, Rivalry and Status
7. Compromise as a Form of Accommodation
8. The Subtler Forms of Accommodation: Flattery, "Front," Ceremony, etc.
9. The Organization of Attitudes in Accommodation; Prestige, Taboo, Rapport, Prejudice, Fear, etc.
10. Slavery, Caste, and Class as Forms of Accommodation
11. The Description and Analysis of Typical Examples of Accommodation: the Political "Boss" and the Voter, Physician and Patient, the Coach and the Members of the Team, the Town Magnate and His Fellow-Citizens, "The Four Hundred" and "Hoi Polloi," etc.
12. Social Solidarity as the Organization of Competing Groups
13. Division of Labor as a Form of Accommodation
14. A Survey of Historical Types of the Family in Terms of the Changes in Forms of Subordination and Superordination of Its Members
15. Social Types as Accommodations: the Quack Doctor, the Reporter, the Strike Breaker, the Schoolteacher, the Stockbroker, etc.

QUESTIONS FOR DISCUSSION

1. How do you distinguish between biological adaptation and social accommodation?
2. Is domestication biological adaptation or accommodation?
3. Give illustrations of acclimatization as a form of accommodation.
4. Discuss phenomena of colonization with reference to accommodation.
5. What is the relation of lonesomeness to accommodation?
6. Do you agree with Nieboer's definition of slavery?
   Is the slave a person? If so, to what extent?
   How would you compare the serf with the slave in respect to his status?
7. To what extent do slavery and caste as forms of accommodation rest upon (*a*) physical force, (*b*) mental attitudes?
8. What is the psychology of subordination and superordination?
9. What do you understand to be the relation of suggestion and rapport to subordination and superordination?

10. What is meant by a person "knowing his place"?

11. How do you explain the attitude of "the old servant" to society? Do you agree with her in lamenting the change in attitude of persons engaged in domestic service?

12. What types of the subtler forms of accommodation occur to you?

13. What arguments would you advance for the proposition that the relation of superiority and inferiority is reciprocal?

14. "All leaders are also led, as in countless cases the master is the slave of his slaves." Explain.

15. What illustrations, apart from the text, occur to you of reciprocal relations in superiority and subordination?

16. What do you understand to be the characteristic differences of the three types of superordination and subordination?

17. How would you classify the following groups according to these three types: the patriarchal family, the modern family, England from 1660 to 1830, manufacturing enterprise, labor union, army, boys' gang, boys' club, Christianity, humanitarian movement?

18. What do you think Simmel means by the term "accommodation"?

19. How is accommodation related to peace?

20. Does accommodation end struggle?

21. In what sense does commerce imply accommodation?

22. What type of interaction is involved in compromise? What illustrations would you suggest to bring out your point?

23. Does compromise make for progress?

24. Is a compromise better or worse than either or both of the proposals involved in it?

25. What, in your judgment, is the relation of personal competition to the division of labor?

26. What examples of division of labor outside the economic field would you suggest?

27. What do you understand to be the relation of personal competition and group competition?

28. In what different ways does status (a) grow out of, and (b) prevent, the processes of personal competition and group competition?

29. To what extent, at the present time, is success in life determined by personal competition, and social selection by status?

30. In what ways does the division of labor make for social solidarity?

31. What is the difference between social solidarity based upon like-mindedness and based upon diverse-mindedness?

CHAPTER XI

ASSIMILATION

I. INTRODUCTION

1. Popular Conceptions of Assimilation

The concept assimilation, so far as it has been defined in popular usage, gets its meaning from its relation to the problem of immigration. The more concrete and familiar terms are the abstract noun Americanization and the verbs Americanize, Anglicize, Germanize, and the like. All of these words are intended to describe the process by which the culture of a community or a country is transmitted to an adopted citizen. Negatively, assimilation is a process of denationalization and this is, in fact, the form it has taken in Europe.

The difference between Europe and America, in relation to the problem of cultures, is that in Europe difficulties have arisen from the forcible incorporation of minor cultural groups, i.e., nationalities, within the limits of a larger political unit, i.e., an empire. In America the problem has arisen from the voluntary migration to this country of peoples who have abandoned the political allegiances of the old country and are gradually acquiring the culture of the new. In both cases the problem has its source in an effort to establish and maintain a political order in a community that has no common culture. Fundamentally the problem of maintaining a democratic form of government in a southern village composed of whites and blacks, and the problem of maintaining an international order based on anything but force are the same. The ultimate basis of the existing moral and political order is still kinship and culture. Where neither exist, a political order, not based on caste or class, is at least problematic.

Assimilation, as popularly conceived in the United States, was expressed symbolically some years ago in Zangwill's dramatic parable of *The Melting Pot*. William Jennings Bryan has given oratorical expression to the faith in the beneficent outcome of the process: "Great has been the Greek, the Latin, the Slav, the Celt, the Teuton, and the Saxon; but greater than any of these is the American, who combines the virtues of them all."

Assimilation, as thus conceived, is a natural and unassisted process, and practice, if not policy, has been in accord with this laissez faire conception, which the outcome has apparently justified. In the United States, at any rate, the tempo of assimilation has been more rapid than elsewhere.

Closely akin to this "magic crucible" notion of assimilation is the theory of "like-mindedness." This idea was partly a product of Professor Giddings' theory of sociology, partly an outcome of the popular notion that similarities and homogeneity are identical with unity. The ideal of assimilation was conceived to be that of feeling, thinking, and acting alike. Assimilation and socialization have both been described in these terms by contemporary sociologists.

Another and a different notion of assimilation or Americanization is based on the conviction that the immigrant has contributed in the past and may be expected in the future to contribute something of his own in temperament, culture, and philosophy of life to the future American civilization. This conception had its origin among the immigrants themselves, and has been formulated and interpreted by persons who are, like residents in social settlements, in close contact with them. This recognition of the diversity in the elements entering into the cultural process is not, of course, inconsistent with the expectation of an ultimate homogeneity of the product. It has called attention, at any rate, to the fact that the process of assimilation is concerned with differences quite as much as with likenesses.

2. The Sociology of Assimilation

Accommodation has been described as a process of adjustment, that is, an organization of social relations and attitudes to prevent or to reduce conflict, to control competition, and to maintain a basis of security in the social order for persons and groups of divergent interests and types to carry on together their varied life-activities. Accommodation in the sense of the composition of conflict is invariably the goal of the political process.

Assimilation is a process of interpenetration and fusion in which persons and groups acquire the memories, sentiments, and attitudes of other persons or groups, and, by sharing their experience and history, are incorporated with them in a common cultural life. In so far as assimilation denotes this sharing of tradition, this intimate participation in common experiences, assimilation is central in the historical and cultural processes.

This distinction between accommodation and assimilation, with reference to their rôle in society, explains certain significant formal differences between the two processes. An accommodation of a conflict, or an accommodation to a new situation, may take place with rapidity. The more intimate and subtle changes involved in assimilation are more gradual. The changes that occur in accommodation are frequently not only sudden but revolutionary, as in the mutation of attitudes in conversion. The modifications of attitudes in the process of assimilation are not only gradual, but moderate, even if they appear considerable in their accumulation over a long period of time. If mutation is the symbol for accommodation, growth is the metaphor for assimilation. In accommodation the person or the group is generally, though not always, highly conscious of the occasion, as in the peace treaty that ends the war, in the arbitration of an industrial controversy, in the adjustment of the person to the formal requirements of life in a new social world. In assimilation the process is typically unconscious; the person is incorporated into the common life of the group before he is aware and with little conception of the course of events which brought this incorporation about.

James has described the way in which the attitude of the person changes toward certain subjects, woman's suffrage, for example, not as the result of conscious reflection, but as the outcome of the unreflective responses to a series of new experiences. The intimate associations of the family and of the play group, participation in the ceremonies of religious worship and in the celebrations of national holidays, all these activities transmit to the immigrant and to the alien a store of memories and sentiments common to the native-born, and these memories are the basis of all that is peculiar and sacred in our cultural life.

As social contact initiates interaction, assimilation is its final perfect product. The nature of the social contacts is decisive in the process. Assimilation naturally takes place most rapidly where contacts are primary, that is, where they are the most intimate and intense, as in the area of touch relationship, in the family circle and in intimate congenial groups. Secondary contacts facilitate accommodations, but do not greatly promote assimilation. The contacts here are external and too remote.

A common language is indispensable for the most intimate association of the members of the group; its absence is an insurmountable barrier to assimilation. The phenomenon "that every group has its own language," its peculiar "universe of discourse," and its cultural symbols is evidence of the interrelation between communication and assimilation.

Through the mechanisms of imitation and suggestion, communication effects a gradual and unconscious modification of the attitudes and sentiments of the members of the group. The unity thus achieved is not necessarily or even normally like-mindedness; it is rather a unity of experience and of orientation, out of which may develop a community of purpose and action.

3. Classification of the Materials

The selections in the materials on assimilation have been arranged under three heads: (a) biological aspects of assimilation; (b) the conflict and fusion of cultures; and (c) Americanization as a problem in assimilation. The readings proceed from an analysis of the nature of assimilation to a survey of its processes, as they have manifested themselves historically, and finally to a consideration of the problems of Americanization.

a) *Biological aspects of assimilation.*—Assimilation is to be distinguished from amalgamation, with which it is, however, closely related. Amalgamation is a biological process, the fusion of races by interbreeding and intermarriage. Assimilation, on the other hand, is limited to the fusion of cultures. Miscegenation, or the mingling of races, is a universal phenomenon among the historical races. There are no races, in other words, that do not interbreed. Acculturation, or the transmission of cultural elements from one social group to another, however, has invariably taken place on a larger scale and over a wider area than miscegenation.

Amalgamation, while it is limited to the crossing of racial traits through intermarriage, naturally promotes assimilation or the cross-fertilization of social heritages. The offspring of a "mixed" marriage not only biologically inherits physical and temperamental traits from both parents, but also acquires in the nurture of family life the attitudes, sentiments, and memories of both father and mother. Thus amalgamation of races insures the conditions of primary social contacts most favorable for assimilation.

b) The conflict and fusion of cultures.—The survey of the process of what the ethnologists call *acculturation*, as it is exhibited historically in the conflicts and fusions of cultures, indicates the wide range of the phenomena in this field.

(1) Social contact, even when slight or indirect, is sufficient for the transmission from one cultural group to another of the material elements of civilization. Stimulants and firearms spread rapidly upon the objective demonstration of their effects. The potato, a native of America, has preceded the white explorer in its penetration into many areas of Africa.

(2) The changes in languages in the course of the contacts, conflicts, and fusions of races and nationalities afford data for a more adequate description of the process of assimilation. Under what conditions does a ruling group impose its speech upon the masses, or finally capitulate to the vulgar tongue of the common people? In modern times the printing-press, the book, and the newspaper have tended to fix languages. The press has made feasible language revivals in connection with national movements on a scale impossible in earlier periods.

The emphasis placed upon language as a medium of cultural transmission rests upon a sound principle. For the idioms, particularly of a spoken language, probably reflect more accurately the historical experiences of a people than history itself. The basis of unity among most historical peoples is linguistic rather than racial. The Latin peoples are a convenient example of this fact. The experiment now in progress in the Philippine Islands is significant in this connection. To what extent will the national and cultural development of those islands be determined by native temperament, by Spanish speech and tradition, or by the English language and the American school system?

(3) Rivers in his study of Melanesian and Hawaiian cultures was impressed by the persistence of fundamental elements of the social structure. The basic patterns of family and social life remained practically unmodified despite profound transformations in technique,

in language, and in religion. Evidently many material devices and
formal expressions of an alien society can be adopted without significant changes in the native culture.

The question, however, may be raised whether or not the complete
adoption of occidental science and organization of industry would
not produce far-reaching changes in social organization. The trend
of economic, social, and cultural changes in Japan will throw light on
this question. Even if revolutionary social changes actually occur,
the point may well be made that they will be the outcome of the new
economic system, and therefore not effects of acculturation.

(4) The rapidity and completeness of assimilation depends
directly upon the intimacy of social contact. By a curious paradox,
slavery, and particularly household slavery, has probably been, aside
from intermarriage, the most efficient device for promoting assimilation.

Adoption and initiation among primitive peoples provided a
ceremonial method for inducting aliens and strangers into the group,
the significance of which can only be understood after a more adequate
study of ceremonial in general.

c) *Americanization as a problem of assimilation.*—Any consideration of policies, programs, and methods of Americanization gain
perspective when related to the sociology of assimilation. The "Study
of Methods of Americanization," of the Carnegie Corporation, defines
Americanization as "the participation of the immigrant in the life
of the community in which he lives." From this standpoint participation is both the medium and the goal of assimilation. Participation of the immigrant in American life in any area of life prepares
him for participation in every other. What the immigrant and the
alien need most is an opportunity for participation. Of first importance, of course, is the language. In addition he needs to know how
to use our institutions for his own benefit and protection. But
participation, to be real, must be spontaneous and intelligent, and
that means, in the long run, that the immigrant's life in America must
be related to the life he already knows. Not by the suppression of
old memories, but by their incorporation in his new life is assimilation
achieved. The failure of conscious, coercive policies of denationalization in Europe and the great success of the early, passive phase of
Americanization in this country afford in this connection an impressive

contrast. It follows that assimilation cannot be promoted directly, but only indirectly, that is, by supplying the conditions that make for participation.

There is no process but life itself that can effectually wipe out the immigrant's memory of his past. The inclusion of the immigrant in our common life may perhaps be best reached, therefore, in co-operation that looks not so much to the past as to the future. The second generation of the immigrant may share fully in our memories, but practically all that we can ask of the foreign-born is participation in our ideals, our wishes, and our common enterprises.

II. MATERIALS

A. BIOLOGICAL ASPECTS OF ASSIMILATION

1. Assimilation and Amalgamation[1]

Writers on historical and social science are just beginning to turn their attention to the large subject of social assimilation. That the subject has until recently received little attention is readily seen by a mere glance at the works of our leading sociologists and historians. The word itself rarely appears; and when the theme is touched upon, no clearly defined, stable idea seems to exist, even in the mind of the author. Thus Giddings at one time identifies assimilation with "reciprocal accommodation." In another place he defines it as "the process of growing alike," and once again he tells us it is the method by which foreigners in the United States society become Americans. Nor are M. Novicow's ideas on the subject perfectly lucid, for he considers assimilation sometimes as a *process*, at other times as an *art*, and again as a *result*. He makes the term "denationalization" coextensive with our "assimilation," and says that the ensemble of measures which a government takes for inducing a population to abandon one type of culture for another is denationalization. Dena-tionalization by the authority of the state carries with it a certain amount of coercion; it is always accompanied by a measure of violence. In the next sentence, however, we are told that the word "denationalization" may also be used for the non-coercive *process*

[1] Adapted from Sarah E. Simons, "Social Assimilation," in the *American Journal of Sociology*, VI (1901), 790–801.

by which one nationality is assimilated with another. M. Novicow further speaks of the *art* of assimilation, and he tells us that the *result* of the intellectual struggle between races living under the same government, whether free or forced, is in every case assimilation. Burgess also takes a narrow view of the subject, restricting the operation of assimilating forces to the present and considering assimilation a result of modern political union. He says: "In modern times the political union of different races under the leadership of the dominant race results in assimilation."

From one point of view assimilation is a process with its active and passive elements; from another it is a result. In this discussion, however, assimilation is considered as a process due to prolonged contact. It may, perhaps, be defined as that process of adjustment or accommodation which occurs between the members of two different races, if their contact is prolonged and if the necessary psychic conditions are present. The result is group homogeneity to a greater or less degree. Figuratively speaking, it is the process by which the aggregation of peoples is changed from a mere mechanical mixture into a chemical compound.

The process of assimilation is of a psychological rather than of a biological nature, and refers to the growing alike in character, thoughts, and institutions, rather than to the blood-mingling brought about by intermarriage. The intellectual results of the process of assimilation are far more lasting than the physiological. Thus in France today, though nineteen-twentieths of the blood is that of the aboriginal races, the language is directly derived from that imposed by the Romans in their conquest of Gaul. Intermarriage, the inevitable result to a greater or less extent of race contact, plays its part in the process of assimilation, but mere mixture of races will not cause assimilation. Moreover, assimilation is possible, partially at least, without intermarriage. Instances of this are furnished by the partial assimilation of the Negro and the Indian of the United States. Thinkers are beginning to doubt the great importance once attributed to intermarriage as a factor in civilization. Says Mayo-Smith, "It is not in unity of blood but in unity of institutions and social habits and ideals that we are to seek that which we call nationality," and nationality is the result of assimilation.

2. The Instinctive Basis of Assimilation[1]

It is a striking fact that among animals there are some whose conduct can be generalized very readily in the categories of self-preservation, nutrition, and sex, while there are others whose conduct cannot be thus summarized. The behavior of the tiger and the cat is simple and easily comprehensible, whereas that of the dog with his conscience, his humor, his terror of loneliness, his capacity for devotion to a brutal master, or that of the bee with her selfless devotion to the hive, furnishes phenomena which no sophistry can assimilate without the aid of a fourth instinct. But little examination will show that the animals whose conduct it is difficult to generalize under the three primitive instinctive categories are gregarious. If, then, it can be shown that gregariousness is of a biological significance approaching in importance that of the other instincts we may expect to find in it the source of these anomalies of conduct, and of the complexity of human behavior.

Gregariousness seems frequently to be regarded as a somewhat superficial character, scarcely deserving, as it were, the name of an instinct, advantageous, it is true, but not of fundamental importance or likely to be deeply ingrained in the inheritance of the species. This attitude may be due to the fact that among mammals, at any rate, the appearance of gregariousness has not been accompanied by any very gross physical changes which are obviously associated with it.

To whatever it may be due, this method of regarding the social habit is, in the opinion of the present writer, not justified by the facts, and prevents the attainment of conclusions of considerable fruitfulness.

A study of bees and ants shows at once how fundamental the importance of gregariousness may become. The individual in such communities is completely incapable, often physically, of existing apart from the community, and this fact at once gives rise to the suspicion that, even in communities less closely knit than those of the ant and the bee, the individual may in fact be more dependent on communal life than appears at first sight.

Another very striking piece of general evidence of the significance of gregariousness as no mere late acquirement is the remarkable coincidence of its occurrence with that of exceptional grades of intelli-

[1] Adapted from W. Trotter, "Herd Instinct," in the *Sociological Review*, I (1908), 231-42.

gence or the possibility of very complex reactions to environment. It can scarcely be regarded as an unmeaning accident that the dog, the horse, the ape, the elephant, and man are all social animals. The instances of the bee and the ant are perhaps the most amazing. Here the advantages of gregariousness seem actually to outweigh the most prodigious differences of structure, and we find a condition which is often thought of as a mere habit, capable of enabling the insect nervous system to compete in the complexity of its power of adaptation with that of the higher vertebrates.

From the biological standpoint the probability of gregariousness being a primitive and fundamental quality in man seems to be considerable. It would appear to have the effect of enlarging the advantages of variation. Varieties not immediately favorable, varieties departing widely from the standard, varieties even unfavorable to the individual, may be supposed to be given by it a chance of survival. Now the course of the development of man seems to present many features incompatible with its having proceeded among isolated individuals exposed to the unmodified action of natural selection. Changes so serious as the assumption of the upright posture, the reduction in the jaw and its musculature, the reduction in the acuity of smell and hearing, demand, if the species is to survive, either a delicacy of adjustment with the compensatingly developing intelligence so minute as to be almost inconceivable, or the existence of some kind of protective enclosure, however imperfect, in which the varying individuals may be sheltered from the direct influence of natural selection. The existence of such a mechanism would compensate losses of physical strength in the individual by the greatly increased strength of the larger unit, of the unit, that is to say, upon which natural selection still acts unmodified.

The cardinal quality of the herd is homogeneity. It is clear that the great advantage of the social habit is to enable large numbers to act as one, whereby in the case of the hunting gregarious animal strength in pursuit and attack is at once increased beyond that of the creatures preyed upon, and in protective socialism the sensitiveness of the new unit to alarms is greatly in excess of that of the individual member of the flock.

To secure these advantages of homogeneity, it is evident that the members of the herd must possess sensitiveness to the behavior of their fellows. The individual isolated will be of no meaning; the individual as part of the herd will be capable of transmitting the most potent impulses. Each member of the flock tending to follow his neighbor, and in turn to be followed, each is in some sense capable of leadership; but no lead will be followed that departs widely from normal behavior. A lead will only be followed from its resemblance to the normal. If the leader go so far ahead as definitely to cease to be in the herd, he will necessarily be ignored.

The original in conduct, that is to say, resistiveness to the voice of the herd, will be suppressed by natural selection; the wolf which does not follow the impulses of the herd will be starved; the sheep which does not respond to the flock will be eaten.

Again, not only will the individual be responsive to impulses coming from the herd but he will treat the herd as his normal environment. The impulse to be in and always to remain with the herd will have the strongest instinctive weight. Anything which tends to separate him from his fellows, as soon as it becomes perceptible as such, will be strongly resisted.

So far we have regarded the gregarious animal objectively. Let us now try to estimate the mental aspects of these impulses. Suppose a species in possession of precisely the instinctive endowments which we have been considering to be also self-conscious, and let us ask what will be the forms under which these phenomena will present themselves in its mind. In the first place, it is quite evident that impulses derived from herd feeling will enter the mind with the value of instincts— they will present themselves as "a priori syntheses of the most perfect sort needing no proof but their own evidence." They will not, however, it is important to remember, necessarily always give this quality to the same specific acts, but will show this great distinguishing characteristic that they may give to any opinion whatever the characters of instinctive belief, making it into an "a priori synthesis"; so that we shall expect to find acts which it would be absurd to look upon as the results of specific instincts carried out with all the enthusiasm of instinct and displaying all the marks of instinctive behavior.

In interpreting into mental terms the consequences of gregariousness we may conveniently begin with the simplest. The conscious individual will feel an unanalysable primary sense of comfort in the actual presence of his fellows and a similar sense of discomfort in their absence. It will be obvious truth to him that it is not good for man to be alone. Loneliness will be a real terror insurmountable by reason.

Again, certain conditions will become secondarily associated with presence with, or absence from, the herd. For example, take the sensations of heat and cold. The latter is prevented in gregarious animals by close crowding and experienced in the reverse condition; hence it comes to be connected in the mind with separation and so acquires altogether unreasonable associations of harmfulness. Similarly, the sensation of warmth is associated with feelings of the secure and salutary.

Slightly more complex manifestations of the same tendency to homogeneity are seen in the desire for identification with the herd in matters of opinion. Here we find the biological explanation of the ineradicable impulse mankind has always displayed toward segregation into classes. Each one of us in his opinions, and his conduct, in matters of dress, amusement, religion, and politics, is compelled to obtain the support of a class, of a herd within the herd. The most eccentric in opinion or conduct is, we may be sure, supported by the agreement of a class, the smallness of which accounts for his apparent eccentricity, and the preciousness of which accounts for his fortitude in defying general opinion. Again, anything which tends to emphasize difference from the herd is unpleasant. In the individual mind there will be an analysable dislike of the novel in action or thought. It will be "wrong," "wicked," "foolish," "undesirable," or, as we say, "bad form," according to varying circumstances which we can already to some extent define.

Manifestations relatively more simple are shown in the dislike of being conspicuous, in shyness, and in stage fright. It is, however, sensitiveness to the behavior of the herd which has the most important effects upon the structure of the mind of the gregarious animal. This sensitiveness is, as Sidis has clearly seen, closely associated with the suggestibility of the gregarious animal, and therefore with that of man. The effect of it will clearly be to make acceptable those suggestions which come from the herd, and those only. It is of especial importance to note that this suggestibility is not general, and that it is only herd suggestions which are rendered acceptable by the action of instinct.

B. THE CONFLICT AND FUSION OF CULTURES

1. The Analysis of Blended Cultures[1]

In the analysis of any culture, a difficulty which soon meets the investigator is that he has to determine what is due to mere contact and what is due to intimate intermixture, such intermixture, for instance, as is produced by the permanent blending of one people with another, either through warlike invasion or peaceful settlement. The fundamental weakness of most of the attempts hitherto made to analyze existing cultures is that they have had their starting-point in the study of material objects, and the reason for this is obvious. Owing to the fact that material objects can be collected by anyone and subjected at leisure to prolonged study by experts, our knowledge of the distribution of material objects and of the technique of their manufacture has very far outrun that of the less material elements. What I wish now to point out is that in distinguishing between the effects of mere contact and the intermixture of peoples, material objects are the least trustworthy of all the constituents of culture. Thus in Melanesia we have the clearest evidence that material objects and processes can spread by mere contact, without any true admixture of peoples and without influence on other features of the culture. While the distribution of material objects is of the utmost importance in suggesting at the outset community of culture, and while it is of equal importance in the final process of determining points of contact and in filling in the details of the mixture of cultures, it is the least satisfactory guide to the actual blending of peoples which must form the solid foundation of the ethnological analysis of culture.   The case for the value of magico-religious institutions is not much stronger. Here, again, in Melanesia there is little doubt that whole cults can pass from one people to another without any real intermixture of peoples.   I do not wish to imply that such religious institutions can pass from people to people with the ease of material objects, but to point out that there is evidence that they can and do so pass with very little, if any, admixture of peoples or of the deeper and more fundamental elements of the culture.   Much more important is language; and if you will think over the actual conditions when one

[1] From W. H. R. Rivers, "The Ethnological Analysis of Culture," in *Nature*, LXXXVII (1911), 358–60.

people either visit or settle among another, this greater importance will be obvious. Let us imagine a party of Melanesians visiting a Polynesian island, staying there for a few weeks, and then returning home (and here I am not taking a fictitious occurrence, but one which really happens). We can readily understand that the visitors may take with them their betel-mixture, and thereby introduce the custom of betel-chewing into a new home; we can readily understand that they may introduce an ornament to be worn in the nose and another to be worn on the chest; that tales which they tell will be remembered, and dances they perform will be imitated. A few Melanesian words may pass into the language of the Polynesian island, especially as names for the objects or processes which the strangers have introduced; but it is incredible that the strangers should thus in a short visit produce any extensive change in the vocabulary, and still more that they should modify the structure of the language. Such changes can never be the result of mere contact or transient settlement but must always indicate a far more deeply seated and fundamental process of blending of peoples and cultures.

Few will perhaps hesitate to accept this position; but I expect my next proposition to meet with more skepticism, and yet I believe it to be widely, though not universally, true. This proposition is that the social structure, the framework of society, is still more fundamentally important and still less easily changed except as the result of the intimate blending of peoples, and for that reason furnishes by far the firmest foundation on which to base the process of analysis of culture. I cannot hope to establish the truth of this proposition in the course of a brief address, and I propose to draw your attention to one line of evidence only.

At the present moment we have before our eyes an object-lesson in the spread of our own people over the earth's surface, and we are thus able to study how external influence affects different elements of culture. What we find is that mere contact is able to transmit much in the way of material culture. A passing vessel, which does not even anchor, may be able to transmit iron, while European weapons may be used by people who have never even seen a white man. Again, missionaries introduce the Christian religion among people who cannot speak a word of English or any language but their own or only use such European words as have been found necessary to express ideas or objects connected with the new religion.   There is evidence how readily language may be affected, and here again the present day suggests a mechanism by which such a change takes place.   English is now becoming the language of the Pacific and of other parts of the world through its use as a *lingua franca*, which enables natives who speak different languages to converse not only with Europeans but with one another, and I believe that this has often been the mechanism in the past; that, for instance, the introduction of what we now call the Melanesian structure of language was due to the fact that the language of an immigrant people who settled in a region of great linguistic diversity came to be used as a *lingua franca*, and thus gradually became the basis of the languages of the whole people.

But now let us turn to social structure.   We find in Oceania islands where Europeans have been settled as missionaries or traders perhaps for fifty or a hundred years; we find the people wearing European clothes and European ornaments, using European utensils and even European weapons when they fight; we find them holding the beliefs and practicing the ritual of a European religion; we find them speaking a European language, often even among themselves, and yet investigation shows that much of their social structure remains thoroughly native and uninfluenced, not only in its general form, but often even in its minute details.   The external influence has swept away the whole material culture, so that objects of native origin are manufactured only to sell to tourists; it has substituted a wholly new religion and destroyed every material, if not every moral, vestige of the old; it has caused great modification and degeneration of the old language; and yet it may have left the social structure in the main untouched.   And the reasons for this are clear.   Most of the essential social structure of a people lies so below the surface, it is so literally the foundation of the whole life of the people, that it is not seen; it is not obvious, but can only be reached by patient and laborious exploration.   I will give a few specific instances.   In several islands of the Pacific, some of which have had European settlers on them for more than a century, a most important position in the community is occupied by the father's sister.   If any native of these islands were asked who is the most important person in the determination of his life-history, he would answer, "My father's sister";

and yet the place of this relative in the social structure has remained absolutely unrecorded, and, I believe, absolutely unknown, to the European settlers in those islands. Again, Europeans have settled in Fiji for more than a century, and yet it is only during this summer that I have heard from Mr. A. M. Hocart, who is working there at present, that there is the clearest evidence of what is known as the dual organization of society as a working social institution at the present time. How unobtrusive such a fundamental fact of social structure may be comes home to me in this case very strongly, for it wholly eluded my own observation during a visit three years ago.

Lastly, the most striking example of the permanence of social structure which I have met is in the Hawaiian Islands. There the original native culture is reduced to the merest wreckage. So far as material objects are concerned, the people are like ourselves; the old religion has gone, though there probably still persists some of the ancient magic. The people themselves have so dwindled in number, and the political conditions are so altered, that the social structure has also necessarily been greatly modified, and yet I was able to ascertain that one of its elements, an element which I believe to form the deepest layer of the foundation, the very bedrock of social structure, the system of relationship, is still in use unchanged. I was able to obtain a full account of the system as actually used at the present time, and found it to be exactly the same as that recorded forty years ago by Morgan and Hyde, and I obtained evidence that the system is still deeply interwoven with the intimate mental life of the people.

If, then, social structure has this fundamental and deeply seated character, if it is the least easily changed, and only changed as the result either of actual blending of peoples or of the most profound political changes, the obvious inference is that it is with social structure that we must begin the attempt to analyze culture and to ascertain how far community of culture is due to the blending of peoples, how far to transmission through mere contact or transient settlement.

The considerations I have brought forward have, however, in my opinion an importance still more fundamental. If social institutions have this relatively great degree of permanence, if they are so deeply seated and so closely interwoven with the deepest instincts and sentiments of a people that they can only gradually suffer change, will not the study of this change give us our surest criterion of what is early and what is late in any given culture, and thereby furnish a guide for the analysis of culture? Such criteria of early and late are necessary if we are to arrange the cultural elements reached by our analysis in order of time, and it is very doubtful whether mere geographical distribution itself will ever furnish a sufficient basis for this purpose. I may remind you here that before the importance of the complexity of Melanesian culture had forced itself on my mind, I had already succeeded in tracing out a course for the development of the structure of Melanesian society, and after the complexity of the culture had been established, I did not find it necessary to alter anything of essential importance in this scheme. I suggest, therefore, that while the ethnological analysis of cultures must furnish a necessary preliminary to any general evolutionary speculations, there is one element of culture which has so relatively high a degree of permanence that its course of development may furnish a guide to the order in time of the different elements into which it is possible to analyze a given complex.

If the development of social structure is thus to be taken as a guide to assist the process of analysis, it is evident that there will be involved a logical process of considerable complexity in which there will be the danger of arguing in a circle. If, however, the analysis of culture is to be the primary task of the anthropologist, it is evident that the logical methods of the science will attain a complexity far exceeding those hitherto in vogue. I believe that the only logical process which will in general be found possible will be the formulation of hypothetical working schemes into which the facts can be fitted, and that the test of such schemes will be their capacity to fit in with themselves, or, as we generally express it, "explain" new facts as they come to our knowledge. This is the method of other sciences which deal with conditions as complex as those of human society. In many other sciences these new facts are discovered by experiment. In our science they must be found by exploration, not only of the cultures still existent in living form, but also of the buried cultures of past ages.

2. The Extension of Roman Culture in Gaul[1]

The Roman conquest of Gaul was partially a feat of arms; but it was much more a triumph of Roman diplomacy and a genius for colonial government. Roman power in Gaul was centered in the larger cities and in their strongly fortified camps. There the laws and decrees of Rome were promulgated and the tribute of the conquered tribes received. There, too, the law courts were held and justice administered. Rome bent her efforts to the Latinizing of her newly acquired possessions. Gradually she forced the inhabitants of the larger cities to use the Latin tongue. But this forcing was done in a diplomatic, though effective, manner. Even in the days of Caesar, Latin was made the only medium for the administration of the law, the promulgation of decrees, the exercise of the functions of government, the administration of justice, and the performing of the offices of religion. It was the only medium of commerce and trade with the Romans, of literature and art, of the theater and of social relations. Above all, it was the only road to office under the Roman government and to political preferment. The Roman officials in Gaul encouraged and rewarded the mastery of the Latin tongue and the acquirement of Roman culture, customs, and manners. Thanks to this well-defined policy of the Roman government, native Gauls were found in important offices even in Caesar's time. The number of these Gallo-Roman offices increased rapidly, and their influence was steadily exercised in favor of the acquirement, by the natives, of the Latin language. A greater inducement still was held out to the Gauls to acquire the ways and culture of their conquerors. This was the prospect of employment or political preference and honors in the imperial city of Rome itself. Under this pressure so diplomatically applied, the study of the Latin language, grammar, literature, and oratory became a passion throughout the cities of Gaul, which were full of Roman merchants, traders, teachers, philosophers, lawyers, artists, sculptors, and seekers for political and other offices. Latin was the symbol of success in every avenue of life. Native Gauls became noted merchant princes, lawyers, soldiers, local potentates at home, and favorites of powerful political personages in Rome and even in the colonies outside Gaul. Natives of

[1] From John H. Cornyn, "French Language," in the *Encyclopedia Americana*, XI (1919), 646–47.

Gaul, too, reached the highest offices in the land, becoming even members of the Senate; and later on a native Gaul became one of the most noted of the Roman emperors. The political policy of Rome made the imposition of the Latin language upon the cities of Gaul a comparatively easy matter, requiring only time to assure its accomplishment. Everywhere throughout the populous cities of Gaul there sprang up schools that rivaled, in their efficacy and reputation, the most famous institutions of Rome. Rich Romans sent their sons to these schools because of their excellence and the added advantage that they could acquire there a first-hand knowledge of the life and customs of the natives, whom they might be called upon in the future to govern or to have political or other relations with. Thus all urban Gaul traveled Rome-ward—"all roads led to Rome."

The influence of Roman culture extended itself much more slowly over the rural districts, the inhabitants of which, in addition to being much more conservative and passionately attached to their native institutions and language, lacked the incentive of ambition and of commercial and trade necessity. A powerful Druidical priesthood held the rural Celts together and set their faces against Roman culture and religion. But even in the rural districts Latin made its way slowly and in a mangled form, yet none the less surely. This was accomplished almost entirely through the natural pressure from without exercised by the growing power of the Latin tongue, which had greatly increased during the reign of the Emperor Claudius (41-54 A.D.). Claudius, who was born in Lyon and educated in Gaul, opened to the Gauls all the employments and dignities of the empire. On the construction of the many extensive public works he employed many inhabitants of Gaul in positions requiring faithfulness, honesty, and skill. These, in their turn, frequently drew laborers from the rural districts of Gaul. These latter, during their residence in Rome or other Italian cities, or in the populous centers of Gaul, acquired some knowledge of Latin. Thus, in time, through these and other agencies, a sort of *lingua franca* sprang up throughout the rural districts of Gaul and served as a medium of communication between the Celtic-speaking population and the inhabitants of the cities and towns. This consisted of a frame of Latin words stripped of most of their inflections and subjected to word-contractions and other modifications. Into this frame were fitted many native words which had already become the property of trade and commerce and the other activities of life in the city, town, and country. Thus, as the influence of Latin became stronger in the cities, it continued to exercise greater pressure on the rural districts. This pressure soon began to react upon the centers of Latin culture. The uneducated classes of Gaul everywhere, even in the cities, spoke very imperfect Latin, the genius of which is so different from that of the native tongues of Gaul. But while the cities afforded some correction for this universal tendency among the masses to corrupt the Latin language, the life of the rural districts, where the native tongues were still universally spoken, made the disintegration of the highly inflected Roman speech unavoidable. As the masses in the city and country became more Latinized, at the expense of their native tongues, the corrupted Latin spoken over immense districts of the country tended to pass current as the speech of the populace and to crowd out classical or school Latin. As this corrupted local Latin varied greatly in different parts of the country, due to linguistic and other influences, there resulted numerous Roman dialects throughout Gaul, many of which are still in existence.

The introduction of Christianity gave additional impulse to the study of Latin, which soon became the official language of the Christian church; and it was taught everywhere by the priests to the middle and upper classes, and they also encouraged the masses to learn it. It seemed as if this was destined to maintain the prestige of Latin as the official language of the country. But in reality it hastened its downfall by making it more and more the language of the illiterate masses. Soon the rural districts furnished priests who spoke their own Roman tongue; and the struggle to rehabilitate the literary Latin among the masses was abandoned. The numerous French dialects of Latin had already begun to assume shape when the decline of the Roman Empire brought the Germanic tribes down upon Gaul and introduced a new element into the Romanic speech, which had already worked its will upon the tongue of the Caesars. Under its influence the loose Latin construction disappeared; articles and prepositions took the place of the inflectional terminations brought to a high state of artificial perfection in Latin; and the wholesale suppression of unaccented syllables had so contracted the

Latin words that they were often scarcely recognizable. The modification of vowel sounds increased the efficacy of the disguise assumed by Latin words masquerading in the Romanic dialects throughout Gaul; and the Celtic and other native words in current use to designate the interests and occupations of the masses helped to differentiate the popular speech from the classical Latin. Already Celtic, as a spoken tongue, had almost entirely disappeared from the cities; and even in the rural districts it had fallen into a certain amount of neglect, as the *lingua franca* of the first centuries of Roman occupation, reaching out in every direction, became the ever-increasing popular speech.

3. The Competition of the Cultural Languages[1]

Some time ago a typewriter firm, in advertising a machine with Arabic characters, made the statement that the Arabic alphabet is used by more people than any other. A professor of Semitic languages was asked: "How big a lie is that?" He answered: "It is true."

In a certain sense, it is true; the total population of all the countries whose inhabitants use the Arabic alphabet (if they use any) is slightly larger than that of those who use the Latin alphabet and its slight variations, or the Chinese characters (which of course are not an alphabet), or the Russian alphabet. If, however, the question is how many people can actually use any alphabet or system of writing, the Arabic stands lowest of the four.

The question of the relative importance of a language as a literary medium is a question of how many people want to read it. There are two classes of these: those to whom it is vernacular, and those who learn it in addition to their own language. The latter class is of the greater importance in proportion to its numbers; a man who has education enough to acquire a foreign language is pretty sure to use it, while many of the former class, who can read, really do read very little. Those who count in this matter are those who can get information from a printed page as easily as by listening to someone talking. A fair index of the relative number of these in a country is the newspaper circulation there.

    [1] Adapted from E. H. Babbitt, "The Geography of the Great Languages," in *World's Work*, XV (1907–8), 9903–7.

A language must have a recognized literary standard and all the people in its territory must learn to use it as such before its influence goes far abroad. English, French, and German, and they alone, have reached this point. French and German have no new country, and practically the whole of their country is now literate; their relative share in the world's reading can only increase as their population increases. Spanish and Russian, on the other hand, have both new country and room for a much higher percentage of literacy.

It is probable that all the countries in temperate zones will have universal literacy by the end of the century. In this case, even if no one read English outside its vernacular countries, it would still hold its own as the leading literary language. German and French are bound to fall off relatively as vernaculars, and this implies a falling off of their importance as culture languages; but the importance of English in this respect is bound to grow. The first place among foreign languages has been given to it in the schools of many European and South American countries; Mexico and Japan make it compulsory in all schools of upper grades; and China is to follow Japan in this respect as soon as the work can be organized.

The number of people who can actually read, or will learn if now too young, for the various languages of the world appears to be as follows:

	Number in Millions	Per Cent
English	136	27.2
German	82	16.4
Chinese*	70	14.0
French	28	9.6
Russian	30	6.0
Arabic	25	5.0
Italian	18	4.6
Spanish	12	2.6
Scandinavian	11	2.2
Dutch and Flemish	9	1.9
Minor European†	34	6.8
Minor Asiatic†	16	3.2
Minor African and Polynesian†	2+	0.5
Total	473+	100.0

* Not a spoken language, but a system of writing.
† None representing as much as 1 per cent of total.

English, therefore, now leads all other languages in the number of its readers. Three-fourths of the world's mail matter is addressed in English. More than half of the world's newspapers are printed in English, and, as they have a larger circulation than those in other languages, probably three-fourths of the world's newspaper reading is done in English.

The languages next in importance, French and German, cannot maintain their relative positions because English has more than half of the new land in the temperate zone and they have none. The languages which have the rest of the new territory, Spanish and Russian, are not established as culture languages, as English is. No other language, not even French or German, has a vernacular so uniform and well established, and with so few variations from the literary language. English is spoken in the United States by more than fifty million people with so slight variations that no foreigner would ever notice them. No other language whatever can show more than a fraction of this number of persons who speak so nearly alike.

It is then probable that, within the century, English will be the vernacular of a quarter instead of a tenth of the people of the world, and be read by a half instead of a quarter of the people who can read.

4. The Assimilation of Races[1]

The race problem has sometimes been described as a problem in assimilation. It is not always clear, however, what assimilation means. Historically the word has had two distinct significations. According to earlier usage it meant "to compare" or "to make like." According to later usage it signifies "to take up and incorporate."

There is a process that goes on in society by which individuals spontaneously acquire one another's language, characteristic attitudes, habits, and modes of behavior. There is also a process by which individuals and groups of individuals are taken over and incorporated into larger groups. Both processes have been concerned in the formation of modern nationalities. The modern Italian, Frenchman, and German is a composite of the broken frag-

[1] From Robert E. Park, "Racial Assimilation in Secondary Groups," in the *Publications of the American Sociological Society*, VIII (1914), 66–72.

ments of several different racial groups. Interbreeding has broken up the ancient stocks, and interaction and imitation have created new national types which exhibit definite uniformities in language, manners, and formal behavior.

It has sometimes been assumed that the creation of a national type is the specific function of assimilation and that national solidarity is based upon national homogeneity and "like-mindedness." The extent and importance of the kind of homogeneity that individuals of the same nationality exhibit have been greatly exaggerated. Neither interbreeding nor interaction has created, in what the French term "nationals," a more than superficial likeness or like-mindedness. Racial differences have, to be sure, disappeared or been obscured, but individual differences remain. Individual differences, again, have been intensified by education, personal competition, and the division of labor, until individual members of cosmopolitan groups probably represent greater variations in disposition, temperament, and mental capacity than those which distinguished the more homogeneous races and peoples of an earlier civilization.

What then, precisely, is the nature of the homogeneity which characterizes cosmopolitan groups?

The growth of modern states exhibits the progressive merging of smaller, mutually exclusive, into larger and more inclusive, social groups. This result has been achieved in various ways, but it has usually been followed or accompanied by a more or less complete adoption by the members of the smaller groups of the language, technique, and mores of the larger and more inclusive ones. The immigrant readily takes over the language, manners, the social ritual, and outward forms of his adopted country. In America it has become proverbial that a Pole, Lithuanian, or Norwegian cannot be distinguished, in the second generation, from an American born of native parents.

There is no reason to assume that this assimilation of alien groups to native standards has modified to any great extent fundamental racial characteristics. It has, however, erased the external signs which formerly distinguished the members of one race from those of another.

On the other hand, the breaking up of the isolation of smaller groups has had the effect of emancipating the individual man, giving him room and freedom for the expansion and development of his individual aptitudes.

What one actually finds in cosmopolitan groups, then, is a superficial uniformity, a homogeneity in manners and fashion, associated with relatively profound differences in individual opinions, sentiments, and beliefs. This is just the reverse of what one meets among primitive peoples, where diversity in external forms, as between different groups, is accompanied by a monotonous sameness in the mental attitudes of individuals. There is a striking similarity in the sentiments and mental attitudes of peasant peoples in all parts of the world, although the external differences are often great. In the Black Forest, in Baden, Germany, almost every valley shows a different style of costume, a different type of architecture, although in each separate valley every house is like every other and the costume, as well as the religion, is for every member of each separate community absolutely after the same pattern. On the other hand, a German, Russian, or Negro peasant of the southern states, different as each is in some respects, are all very much alike in certain habitual attitudes and sentiments.

What, then, is the rôle of homogeneity and like-mindedness, such as we find them to be, in cosmopolitan states? So far as it makes each individual look like every other—no matter how different under the skin—homogeneity mobilizes the individual man. It removes the social taboo, permits the individual to move into strange groups, and thus facilitates new and adventurous contacts. In obliterating the external signs, which in secondary groups seem to be the sole basis of caste and class distinctions, it realizes, for the individual, the principle of *laissez faire, laissez aller*. Its ultimate economic effect is to substitute personal for racial competition, and to give free play to forces that tend to relegate every individual, irrespective of race or status, to the position he or she is best fitted to fill.

As a matter of fact, the ease and rapidity with which aliens, under existing conditions in the United States, have been able to assimilate themselves to the customs and manners of American life have enabled this country to swallow and digest every sort of normal human difference, except the purely external ones, like the color of the skin.

It is probably true, also, that like-mindedness of the kind that expresses itself in national types contributes indirectly by facilitating the intermingling of the different elements of the population to the national solidarity. This is due to the fact that the solidarity of modern states depends less on the homogeneity of population than, as James Bryce has suggested, upon the thorough-going mixture of heterogeneous elements. Like-mindedness, so far as that term signifies a standard grade of intelligence, contributes little or nothing to national solidarity. Likeness is, after all, a purely formal concept which of itself cannot hold anything together.

In the last analysis social solidarity is based on sentiment and habit. It is the sentiment of loyalty and the habit of what Sumner calls "concurrent action" that gives substance and insures unity to the state as to every other type of social group. This sentiment of loyalty has its basis in a *modus vivendi*, a working relation and mutual understanding of the members of the group. Social institutions are not founded in similarities any more than they are founded in differences, but in relations, and in the mutual interdependence of parts. When these relations have the sanction of custom and are fixed in individual habit, so that the activities of the group are running smoothly, personal attitudes and sentiments, which are the only forms in which individual minds collide and clash with one another, easily accommodate themselves to the existing situation.

It may, perhaps, be said that loyalty itself is a form of like-mindedness or that it is dependent in some way upon the like-mindedness of the individuals whom it binds together. This, however, cannot be true, for there is no greater loyalty than that which binds the dog to his master, and this is a sentiment which that faithful animal usually extends to other members of the household to which he belongs. A dog without a master is a dangerous animal, but the dog that has been domesticated is a member of society. He is not, of course, a citizen, although he is not entirely without rights. But he has got into some sort of practical working relations with the group to which he belongs.

It is this practical working arrangement, into which individuals with widely different mental capacities enter as co-ordinate parts, that gives the corporate character to social groups and insures their solidarity. It is the process of assimilation by which groups of individuals, originally indifferent or perhaps hostile, achieve this corporate character, rather than the process by which they acquire a formal like-mindedness, with which this paper is mainly concerned.

The difficulty with the conception of assimilation which one ordinarily meets in discussions of the race problem is that it is based on observations confined to individualistic groups where the characteristic relations are indirect and secondary. It takes no account of the kind of assimilation that takes place in primary groups where relations are direct and personal—in the tribe, for example, and in the family.

Thus Charles Francis Adams, referring to the race problem in an address at Richmond, Virginia, in November, 1908, said:

The American system, as we know, was founded on the assumed basis of a common humanity, that is, absence of absolutely fundamental racial characteristics was accepted as an established truth. Those of all races were welcomed to our shores. They came, aliens; they and their descendants would become citizens first, natives afterward. It was a process first of assimilation and then of absorption. On this all depended. There could be no permanent divisional lines. That theory is now plainly broken down. We are confronted by the obvious fact, as undeniable as it is hard, that the African will only partially assimilate and that he cannot be absorbed. He remains an alien element in the body politic. A foreign substance, he can neither be assimilated nor thrown out.

More recently an editorial in the *Outlook*, discussing the Japanese situation in California, made this statement:

The hundred millions of people now inhabiting the United States must be a united people, not merely a collection of groups of different peoples, different in racial cultures and ideals, agreeing to live together in peace and amity. These hundred millions must have common ideals, common aims, a common custom, a common culture, a common language, and common characteristics, if the nation is to endure.

All this is quite true and interesting, but it does not clearly recognize the fact that the chief obstacle to the assimilation of the Negro and the Oriental are not mental but physical traits. It is not because the Negro and the Japanese are so differently constituted that they do not assimilate. If they were given an opportunity, the Japanese are quite as capable as the Italians, the Armenians, or the Slavs of acquiring our culture and sharing our national ideals. The trouble is not with the Japanese mind but with the Japanese skin. The Jap is not the right color.

The fact that the Japanese bears in his features a distinctive racial hallmark, that he wears, so to speak, a racial uniform, classifies him. He cannot become a mere individual, indistinguishable in the cosmopolitan mass of the population, as is true, for example, of the Irish, and, to a lesser extent, of some of the other immigrant races. The Japanese, like the Negro, is condemned to remain among us an abstraction, a symbol—and a symbol not merely of his own race but of the Orient and of that vague, ill-defined menace we sometimes refer to as the "yellow peril." This not only determines to a very large extent the attitude of the white world toward the yellow man but it determines the attitude of the yellow man toward the white. It puts between the races the invisible but very real gulf of self-consciousness.

There is another consideration. Peoples we know intimately we respect and esteem. In our casual contact with aliens, however, it is the offensive rather than the pleasing traits that impress us. These impressions accumulate and reinforce natural prejudices. Where races are distinguished by certain external marks, these furnish a permanent physical substratum upon which and around which the irritations and animosities, incidental to all human intercourse, tend to accumulate and so gain strength and volume.

Assimilation, as the word is here used, brings with it a certain borrowed significance which it carried over from physiology, where it is employed to describe the process of nutrition. By a process of nutrition, somewhat similar to the physiological one, we may conceive alien peoples to be incorporated with, and made part of, the community or state. Ordinarily assimilation goes on silently and unconsciously, and only forces itself into popular conscience when there is some interruption or disturbance of the process.

At the outset it may be said, then, that assimilation rarely becomes a problem except in secondary groups. Admission to the primary group, that is to say, the group in which relationships are direct and personal, as, for example, in the family and in the tribe, makes assimilation comparatively easy and almost inevitable.

The most striking illustration of this is the fact of domestic slavery. Slavery has been, historically, the usual method by which peoples have been incorporated into alien groups. When a member of an alien race is adopted into the family as a servant or as a slave, and particularly when that status is made hereditary, as it was in the case of the Negro after his importation to America, assimilation followed rapidly and as a matter of course.

It is difficult to conceive two races farther removed from each other in temperament and tradition than the Anglo-Saxon and the Negro, and yet the Negro in the southern states, particularly where he was adopted into the household as a family servant, learned in a comparatively short time the manners and customs of his master's family. He very soon possessed himself of so much of the language, religion, and the technique of the civilization of his master as, in his station, he was fitted or permitted to acquire. Eventually, also, Negro slaves transferred their allegiance to the state of which they were only indirectly members, or at least to their masters' families, with whom they felt themselves in most things one in sentiment and interest.

The assimilation of the Negro field hand, where the contact of the slave with his master and his master's family was less intimate, was naturally less complete. On the large plantations, where an overseer stood between the master and the majority of his slaves, and especially on the sea island plantations off the coast of South Carolina, where the master and his family were likely to be merely winter visitors, this distance between master and slave was greatly increased. The consequence is that the Negroes in these regions are less touched today by the white man's influence and civilization than elsewhere in the southern states.

C. AMERICANIZATION AS A PROBLEM IN ASSIMILATION[1]

1. Americanization as Assimilation

The Americanization Study has assumed that the fundamental condition of what we call "Americanization" is the participation of the immigrant in the life of the community in which he lives. The point here emphasized is that patriotism, loyalty, and common sense

[1] The three selections under this heading are adapted from *Memorandum on Americanization*, prepared by the Division of Immigrant Heritages, of the Study of Methods of Americanization, of the Carnegie Corporation, New York City, 1919.

are neither created nor transmitted by purely intellectual processes. Men must live and work and fight together in order to create that community of interest and sentiment which will enable them to meet the crises of their common life with a common will.

It is evident, however, that the word "participation" as here employed has a wide application, and it becomes important for working purposes to give a more definite and concrete meaning to the term.

2. Language as a Means and a Product of Participation

Obviously any organized social activity whatever and any participation in this activity implies "communication." In human, as distinguished from animal, society common life is based on a common speech. To share a common speech does not guarantee participation in the community life but it is an instrument of participation, and its acquisition by the members of an immigrant group is rightly considered a sign and a rough index of Americanization.

It is, however, one of the ordinary experiences of social intercourse that words and things do not have the same meanings with different people, in different parts of the country, in different periods of time, and, in general, in different contexts. The same "thing" has a different meaning for the naïve person and the sophisticated person, for the child and the philosopher; the new experience derives its significance from the character and organization of the previous experiences. To the peasant a comet, a plague, and an epileptic person may mean a divine portent, a visitation of God, a possession by the devil; to the scientific man they mean something quite different. The word "slavery" had very different connotations in the ancient world and today. It has a very different significance today in the southern states and in the northern states. "Socialism" has a very different significance to the immigrant from the Russian pale living on the "East Side" of New York City, to the citizen on Riverside Drive, and to the native American in the hills of Georgia.

Psychologists explain this difference in the connotation of the same word among people using the same language in terms of difference in the "apperception mass" in different individuals and different groups of individuals. In their phraseology the "apperception mass" represents the body of memories and meanings deposited in the consciousness of the individual from the totality of his experiences. It is the body of material with which every new datum of experience comes into contact, to which it is related, and in connection with which it gets its meaning.

When persons interpret data on different grounds, when the apperception mass is radically different, we say popularly that they live in different worlds. The logician expresses this by saying that they occupy different "universes of discourse"—that is, they cannot talk in the same terms. The ecclesiastic, the artist, the mystic, the scientist, the Philistine, the Bohemian, represent more or less different "universes of discourse." Even social workers occupy universes of discourse not mutually intelligible.

Similarly, different races and nationalities as wholes represent different apperception masses and consequently different universes of discourse and are not mutually intelligible. Even our remote forefathers are with difficulty intelligible to us, though always more intelligible than the Eastern immigrant because of the continuity of our tradition. Still it is almost as difficult for us to comprehend *Elsie Dinsmore* or the *Westminster Catechism* as the Koran or the Talmud.

It is apparent, therefore, that in the wide extension and vast complexity of modern life, in which peoples of different races and cultures are now coming into intimate contact, the divergences in the meanings and values which individuals and groups attach to objects and forms of behavior are deeper than anything expressed by differences in language.

Actually common participation in common activities implies a common "definition of the situation." In fact, every single act, and eventually all moral life, is dependent upon the definition of the situation. A definition of the situation precedes and limits any possible action, and a redefinition of the situation changes the character of the action. An abusive person, for example, provokes anger and possibly violence, but if we realize that the man is insane this redefinition of the situation results in totally different behavior.

Every social group develops systematic and unsystematic means of defining the situation for its members. Among these means are the "don'ts" of the mother, the gossip of the community, epithets ("liar," "traitor," "scab"), the sneer, the shrug, the newspaper, the theater, the school, libraries, the law, and the gospel. Education in the widest sense—intellectual, moral, aesthetic—is the process of defining the situation. It is the process by which the definitions of an older generation are transmitted to a younger. In the case of the immigrant it is the process by which the definitions of one cultural group are transmitted to another.

Differences in meanings and values, referred to above in terms of the "apperception mass," grow out of the fact that different individuals and different peoples have defined the situation in different ways. When we speak of the different "heritages" or "traditions" which our different immigrant groups bring, it means that, owing to different historical circumstances, they have defined the situation differently. Certain prominent personalities, schools of thought, bodies of doctrine, historical events, have contributed in defining the situation and determining the attitudes and values of our various immigrant groups in characteristic ways in their home countries. To the Sicilian, for example, marital infidelity means the stiletto; to the American, the divorce court. And even when the immigrant thinks that he understands us, he nevertheless does not do this completely. At the best he interprets our cultural traditions in terms of his own. Actually the situation is progressively redefined by the consequences of the actions, provoked by the previous definitions, and a prison experience is designed to provide a datum toward the redefinition of the situation.

It is evidently important that the people who compose a community and share in the common life should have a sufficient body of common memories to understand one another. This is particularly true in a democracy, where it is intended that the public institutions should be responsive to public opinion. There can be no public opinion except in so far as the persons who compose the public are able to live in the same world and speak and think in the same universe of discourse. For that reason it seems desirable that the immigrants should not only speak the language of the country but should know something of the history of the people among whom they have chosen to dwell. For the same reason it is important that native Americans should know the history and social life of the countries from which the immigrants come.

It is important also that every individual should share as fully as possible a fund of knowledge, experience, sentiments, and ideals common to the whole community and himself contribute to this fund. It is for this reason that we maintain and seek to maintain freedom of speech and free schools. The function of literature, including poetry, romance, and the newspaper, is to enable all to share victoriously and imaginatively in the inner life of each. The function of science is to gather up, classify, digest, and preserve, in a form in which they may become available to the community as a whole, the ideas, inventions, and technical experience of the individuals composing it. Thus not merely the possession of a common language but the wide extension of the opportunities for education become conditions of Americanization.

The immigration problem is unique in the sense that the immigrant brings divergent definitions of the situation, and this renders his participation in our activities difficult. At the same time this problem is of the same general type as the one exemplified by "syndicalism," "bolshevism," "socialism," etc., where the definition of the situation does not agree with the traditional one. The modern "social unrest," like the immigrant problem, is a sign of the lack of participation and this is true to the degree that certain elements feel that violence is the only available means of participating.

3. Assimilation and the Mediation of Individual Differences

In general, a period of unrest represents the stage in which a new definition of the situation is being prepared. Emotion and unrest are connected with situations where there is loss of control. Control is secured on the basis of habits and habits are built up on the basis of the definition of the situation. Habit represents a situation where the definition is working. When control is lost it means that the habits are no longer adequate, that the situation has changed and demands a redefinition. This is the point at which we have unrest —a heightened emotional state, random movements, unregulated behavior—and this continues until the situation is redefined. The unrest is associated with conditions in which the individual or society feels unable to act. It represents energy, and the problem is to use it constructively.

The older societies tended to treat unrest by defining the situation in terms of the suppression or postponement of the wish; they tried to make the repudiation of the wish itself a wish. "Contentment," "conformity to the will of God," ultimate "salvation in a better world, are representative of this. The founders of America defined the situation in terms of participation, but this has actually taken too exclusively the form of "political participation." The present tendency is to define the situation in terms of social participation, including demand for the improvement of social conditions to a degree which will enable all to participate.

But, while it is important that the people who are members of the same community should have a body of common memories and a common apperception mass, so that they may talk intelligibly to one another, it is neither possible nor necessary that everything should have the same meaning for everyone. A perfectly homogeneous consciousness would mean a tendency to define all situations rigidly and sacredly and once and forever. Something like this did happen in the Slavic village communities and among all savage people, and it was the ideal of the medieval church, but it implies a low level of efficiency and a slow rate of progress.

Mankind is distinguished, in fact, from the animal world by being composed of persons of divergent types, of varied tastes and interests, of different vocations and functions. Civilization is the product of an association of widely different individuals, and with the progress of civilization the divergence in individual human types has been and must continue to be constantly multiplied. Our progress in the arts and sciences and in the creation of values in general has been dependent on specialists whose distinctive worth was precisely their divergence from other individuals. It is even evident that we have been able to use productively individuals who in a savage or peasant society would have been classed as insane—who perhaps were indeed insane.

The ability to participate productively implies thus a diversity of attitudes and values in the participants, but a diversity not so great as to lower the morals of the community and to prevent effective co-operation. It is important to have ready definitions for all immediate situations, but progress is dependent on the constant redefinitions for all immediate situations, and the ideal condition for this is the presence of individuals with divergent definitions, who contribute, in part consciously and in part unconsciously, through their individualism and labors to a common task and a common end.

It is only in this way that an intelligible world, in which each can participate according to his intelligence, comes into existence. For it is only through their consequences that words get their meanings or that situations become defined. It is through conflict and co-operation, or, to use a current phrase of economists, through "competitive co-operation," that a distinctively human type of society does anywhere exist. Privacy and publicity, "society" and solitude, public ends and private enterprises, are each and all distinctive factors in human society everywhere. They are particularly characteristic of historic American democracy.

In this whole connection it appears that the group consciousness and the individual himself are formed by communication and participation, and that the communication and participation are themselves dependent for their meaning on common interests.

But it would be an error to assume that participation always implies an intimate personal, face-to-face relation. Specialists participate notably and productively in our common life, but this is evidently not on the basis of personal association with their neighbors. Darwin was assisted by Lyell, Owen, and other contemporaries in working out a new definition of the situation, but these men were not his neighbors. When Mayer worked out his theory of the transmutation of energy, his neighbors in the village of Heilbronn were so far from participating that they twice confined him in insane asylums. A postage stamp may be a more efficient instrument of participation than a village meeting.

Defining the situation with reference to the participation of the immigrant is of course not solving the problem of immigration. This involves an analysis of the whole significance of the qualitative and quantitative character of a population, with reference to any given values—standards of living, individual level of efficiency, liberty and determinism, etc. We have, for instance, in America a certain level of culture, depending, let us say as a minimum, on the perpetuation of our public-school system. But, if by some conceivable *lusus naturae* the birth rate was multiplied a hundred fold, or by some conceivable cataclysm a hundred million African blacks were landed annually on our eastern coast and an equal number of Chinese coolies on our western coast, then we should have neither teachers enough nor buildings enough nor material resources enough to impart even the three R's to a fraction of the population, and the outlook of democracy, so far as it is dependent upon participation, would become very dismal. On the other hand, it is conceivable that certain immigrant populations in certain numbers, with their special temperaments, endowments, and social heritages, would contribute positively and increasingly to our stock of civilization. These are questions to be determined, but certainly if the immigrant is admitted on any basis whatever the condition of his Americanization is that he shall have the widest and freest opportunity to contribute in his own way to the common fund of knowledge, ideas, and ideals which makes up the culture of our common country. It is only in this way that the immigrant can "participate" in the fullest sense of the term.

III. INVESTIGATIONS AND PROBLEMS

1. Assimilation and Amalgamation

The literature upon assimilation falls naturally under three main heads: (1) assimilation and amalgamation; (2) the conflict and fusion of cultures; and (3) immigration and Americanization.

Literature on assimilation is very largely a by-product of the controversy in regard to the relative superiority and inferiority of races. This controversy owes its existence, in the present century, to the publication in 1854 of Gobineau's *The Inequality of Human Races*. This treatise appeared at a time when the dominant peoples of Europe were engaged in extending their benevolent protection over all the "unprotected" lesser breeds, and this book offered a justification, on biological grounds, of the domination of the "inferior" by the "superior" races.

Gobineau's theory, and that of the schools which have perpetuated and elaborated his doctrines, defined culture as an essentially racial trait. Other races might accommodate themselves to, but could not originate nor maintain a superior culture. This is the aristocratic theory of the inequalities of races and, as might be expected, was received with enthusiasm by the chauvinists of the "strong" nations.

The opposing school is disposed to treat the existing civilizations as largely the result of historical accident. The superior peoples are those who have had access to the accumulated cultural materials of the peoples that preceded them.   Modern Europe owes its civilization to the fact that it went to school to the ancients.   The inferior peoples are those who did not have this advantage.

Ratzel was one of the first to venture the theory that the natural and the cultural peoples were fundamentally alike and that the existing differences, great as they are, were due to geographical and cultural isolation of the less advanced races.   Boas' *Mind of Primitive Man* is the most systematic and critical statement of that view of the matter.

The discussion which these rival theories provoked has led students to closer studies of the effects of racial contacts and to a more penetrating analysis of the cultural process.

The contacts of races have invariably led to racial intermixture, and the mixed breed, as in the case of the mulatto, the result of the white-Negro cross, has tended to create a distinct cultural as well as a racial type.   E. B. Reuter's volume on *The Mulatto* is the first serious attempt to study the mixed blood as a cultural type and define his rôle in the conflict of races and cultures.

Historical cases of the assimilation of one group by another are frequent.   Kaindl's investigations of the German settlements in the Carpathian lands are particularly instructive.   The story of the manner in which the early German settlers in Cracow, Galicia, were Polonized mainly under the influence of the Polish nobility, is all the more interesting when it is contrasted with the German colonists in the Siebenbürgen, which have remained strongholds of the German language and culture in the midst of a population of Roumanian peasants for nearly eight hundred years.   Still more interesting are the recent attempts of the Prussians to Germanize the former province of Posen, now reunited to Poland.   Prussia's policy of colonization of German peasants in Posen failed for several reasons, but it failed finally because the German peasant, finding himself isolated in the midst of a Polish community, either gave up the land the government had acquired for him and returned to his native German province, or identified himself with the Polish community and was thus lost to the cause of German nationalism.   The whole interesting history of that episode is related in Bernhard's *Die Polenfrage*, which is at the same time an account of the organization of an autonomous Polish community within the limits of a German state.

The competition and survival of languages afford interesting material for the study of cultural contacts and the conditions that determine assimilation. Investigations of the racial origins of European peoples have discovered a great number of curious cultural anomalies. There are peoples like the Spreewälder who inhabit a little cultural island of about 240 miles square in the Province of Brandenburg, Prussia. Surviving remnants of a Slavic people, they still preserve their language and their tribal costumes, and, although but thirty thousand in number and surrounded by Germans, maintain a lively literary movement all their own. On the other hand, the most vigorous and powerful of the Germanic nationalities, the Prussian, bears the name of a conquered Slavic people whose language, "Old Prussian," not spoken since the seventeenth century, is preserved only in a few printed books, including a catechism and German-Prussian vocabulary, which the German philologists have rescued from oblivion.

2. The Conflict and Fusion of Cultures

The contacts and transmission of cultures have been investigated in different regions of social life under different titles. The ethnologists have investigated the process among primitive peoples under the title acculturation. Among historical peoples, on the other hand, acculturation has been called assimilation. The aim of missions has been, on the whole, to bring the world under the domination of a single moral order; but in seeking to accomplish this task they have contributed greatly to the fusion and cross-fertilization of racial and national cultures.

The problem of origin is the first and often the most perplexing problem which the study of primitive cultures presents.[1] Was a given cultural trait, i.e., a weapon, a tool, or a myth, borrowed or invented? For example, there are several independent centers of origin and propagation of the bow and arrow. Writing approached or reached perfection in at least five different, widely separated regions. Other problems of acculturation which have been studied include the following: the degree and order of transmissibility of different cultural traits; the persistence or the immunity against change of different traits; the modification of cultural traits in the

[1] See chap. i, pp. 16–24.

process of transmission; the character of social contacts between cultural groups; the distance that divides cultural levels; and the rôle of prestige in stimulating imitation and copying.

The development of a world-commerce, the era of European colonization and imperial expansion in America, Asia, and Africa and Australia, the forward drive of occidental science and the Western system of large-scale competitive industry have created racial contacts, cultural changes, conflicts, and fusions of unprecedented and unforeseen extent, intensity, and immediateness. The crash of a fallen social order in Russia reverberates throughout the world; reports of the capitalization of new enterprises indicate that India is copying the economic organization of Europe; the feminist movement has invaded Japan; representatives of close to fifty nations of the earth meet in conclave in the assembly of the League of Nations.

So complete has been in recent years the interpenetration of peoples and cultures that nations are now seeking to preserve their existence not alone from assault from without by force of arms, but they are equally concerned to protect themselves from the more insidious attacks of propaganda from within. Under these circumstances the ancient liberties of speech and press are being scrutinized and questioned. Particularly is this true when this freedom of speech and press is exercised by alien peoples, who criticize our institutions in a foreign tongue and claim the right to reform native institutions before they have become citizens and even before they are able to use the native language.

3. Immigration and Americanization

The presence of large groups of foreign-born in the United States was first conceived of as a problem of immigration. From the period of the large Irish immigration to this country in the decades following 1820 each new immigrant group called forth a popular literature of protest against the evils its presence threatened. After 1890 the increasing volume of immigration and the change in the source of the immigrants from northwestern Europe to southeastern Europe intensified the general concern. In 1907 the Congress of the United States created the Immigration Commission to make "full inquiry, examination, and investigation into the subject of immigration." The plan and scope of the work as outlined by the Commission "included a study of the sources of recent immigration in Europe, the general character of incoming immigrants, the methods employed here and abroad to prevent the immigration of persons classed as undesirable in the United States immigration law, and finally a thorough investigation into the general status of the more recent immigrants as residents of the United States, and the effect of such immigration upon the institutions, industries, and people of this country." In 1910 the Commission made a report of its investigations and findings together with its conclusions and recommendations which were published in forty-one volumes.

The European War focused the attention of the country upon the problem of Americanization. The public mind became conscious of the fact that "the stranger within our gates," whether naturalized or unnaturalized, tended to maintain his loyalty to the land of his origin, even when it seemed to conflict with loyalty to the country of his sojourn or his adoption. A large number of superficial investigations called "surveys" were made of immigrant colonies in the larger cities of the country. Americanization work of many varieties developed apace. A vast literature sprang up to meet the public demand for information and instruction on this topic. In view of this situation the Carnegie Corporation of New York City undertook in 1918 a "Study of the Methods of Americanization or Fusion of Native and Foreign Born." The point of view from which the study was made may be inferred from the following statement by its director, Allen T. Burns:

Americanization is the uniting of new with native born Americans in fuller common understanding and appreciation to secure by means of self-government the highest welfare of all. Such Americanization should produce no unchangeable political, domestic, and economic régime delivered once for all to the fathers, but a growing and broadening national life, inclusive of the best wherever found. With all our rich heritages, Americanism will develop through a mutual giving and taking of contributions from both newer and older Americans in the interest of the common weal. This study will follow such an understanding of Americanization.

The study, as originally planned, was divided into ten divisions, as follows: the schooling of the immigrant, the press and the theater, adjustment of homes and family life, legal protection and correction, health standards and care, naturalization and political life, industrial and economic amalgamation, treatment of immigrant heritages, neighborhood agencies, and rural developments. The findings of these different parts of the study are presented in separate volumes.

This is the most recent important survey-investigation of the immigrant, although there are many less imposing but significant studies in this field. Among these are the interesting analyses of the assimilation process in Julius Drachsler's *Democracy and Assimilation* and in A. M. Dushkin's study of *Jewish Education in New York City*.

The natural history of assimilation may be best studied in personal narratives and documents, such as letters and autobiographies, or in monographs upon urban and rural immigrant communities. In recent years a series of personal narrative and autobiographical sketches have revealed the intimate personal aspects of the assimilation process. The expectancy and disillusionment of the first experiences, the consequent nostalgia and homesickness, gradual accommodation to the new situation, the first participations in American life, the fixation of wishes in the opportunities of the American social environment, the ultimate identification of the person with the memories, sentiments, and future of his adopted country—all these steps in assimilation are portrayed in such interesting books as *The Far Journey* by Abraham Rihbany, *The Promised Land* by Mary Antin, *Out of the Shadow* by Rose Cohen, *An American in the Making* by M. E. Ravage, *My Mother and I* by E. G. Stern.

The most reflective use of personal documents for the study of the problems of the immigrant has been made by Thomas and Znaniecki in *The Polish Peasant in Europe and America*. In these studies letters and life-histories have been, for the first time, methodically employed to exhibit the processes of adjustment in the transition from a European peasant village to the immigrant colony of an American industrial community.

The work of Thomas and Znaniecki is in a real sense a study of the Polish community in Europe and America. Less ambitious studies have been made of individual immigrant communities. Several religious communities composed of isolated and unassimilated groups, such as the German Mennonites, have been intensively studied.

Materials valuable for the study of certain immigrant communities, assembled for quite other purposes, are contained in the almanacs, yearbooks, and local histories of the various immigrant communities. The most interesting of these are the *Jewish Communal Register* of New York and the studies made by the Norwegian Lutheran Church in America under the direction of O. M. Norlie.[1]

SELECTED BIBLIOGRAPHY

I. ASSIMILATION AND AMALGAMATION

A. *The Psychology and Sociology of Assimilation*

(1) Wundt, Wilhelm. "Bemerkungen zur Associationslehre," *Philosophische Studien*, VII (1892), 329–61. ["Complication und Assimilation," pp. 334–53.]

(2) ———. *Grundzüge der physiologischen Psychologie.* "Assimilationen," III, 528–35. 5th ed. Leipzig, 1903.

(3) Ward, James. "Association and Assimilation," *Mind*, N.S., II (1893), 347–62; III (1894), 509–32.

(4) Baldwin, J. Mark. *Mental Development in the Child and the Race.* Methods and processes. "Assimilation, Recognition," pp. 308–19. New York, 1895.

(5) Novicow, J. *Les Luttes entre sociétés humaines et leur phases successives.* Book II, chap. vii, "La Dénationalisation," pp. 125–53. Paris, 1893. [Definition of denationalization.]

(6) Ratzenhofer, Gustav. *Die sociologische Erkenntnis*, pp. 41–42. Leipzig, 1898.

(7) Park, Robert E. "Racial Assimilation in Secondary Groups with Particular Reference to the Negro," *American Journal of Sociology*, XIX (1913–14), 606–23.

(8) Simons, Sarah E. "Social Assimilation," *American Journal of Sociology*, VI (1900–1901), 790–822; VII (1901–2), 53–79, 234–48, 386–404, 539–56. [Bibliography.]

(9) Jenks, Albert E. "Assimilation in the Philippines as Interpreted in Terms of Assimilation in America," *Publications of the American Sociological Society*, VIII (1913), 140–58.

(10) McKenzie, F. A. "The Assimilation of the American Indian," *Publications of the American Sociological Society*, VIII (1913), 37–48. [Bibliography.]

(11) Ciszewski, S. *Künstliche Verwandschaft bei den Südslaven.* Leipzig, 1897.

(12) Windisch, H. *Taufe und Sünde im ältesten Christentum bis auf Origines.* Ein Beitrag zur altchristlichen Dogmengeschichte. Tübingen, 1908.

[1] See *Menighetskalenderen.* (Minneapolis, Minn.: Augsburg Publishing Co., 1917.)

B. *Assimilation and Amalgamation*

    (1) Gumplowicz, Ludwig. *Der Rassenkampf.* Sociologische Unter-
suchungen, sec. 38, "Wie die Amalgamirung vor sich geht,"
pp. 253–63. Innsbruck, 1883.

    (2) Commons, John R. *Races and Immigrants in America.* Chap.
ix, "Amalgamation and Assimilation," pp. 198–238. New ed.
New York, 1920. [See also pp. 17–21.]

    (3) Ripley, William Z. *The Races of Europe.* A sociological study.
Chap. ii, "Language, Nationality, and Race," pp. 15–36. Chap.
xviii, "European Origins: Race and Culture," pp. 486–512.
New York, 1899.

    (4) Fischer, Eugen. *Die Rehobother Bastards und das Bastardierungs-
problem beim Menschen.* Anthropologische und ethnographische
Studien am Rehobother Bastardvolk in Deutsch-Südwest Afrika.
Jena, 1913.

    (5) Mayo-Smith, Richmond. "Theories of Mixture of Races and
Nationalities," *Yale Review,* III (1894), 166–86.

    (6) Smith, G. Elliot. "The Influence of Racial Admixture in Egypt,"
Eugenics Review, VII (1915–16), 163–83.

    (7) Reuter, E. B. *The Mulatto in the United States.* Including a
study of the rôle of mixed races throughout the world. Boston,
1918.

    (8) Weatherly, Ulysses G. "The Racial Element in Social Assimi-
lation," *Publications of the American Sociological Society,* V (1910),
57–76.

    (9) ———. "Race and Marriage," *American Journal of Sociology,*
XV (1909–10), 433–53.

    (10) Roosevelt, Theodore. "Brazil and the Negro," *Outlook,* CVI
(1904), 409–11.

    (11) Drachsler, Julius. *Intermarriage in New York City.* A statistical
study of the amalgamation of European peoples. New York, 1921.

II. THE CONFLICT AND FUSION OF CULTURES

A. *Process of Acculturation*

    (1) Ratzel, Friedrich. *The History of Mankind.* Vol. I, Book I,
sec. 4, "Nature, Rise and Spread of Civilization," pp. 20–30.
Vol. II, sec. 31, "Origin and Development of the Old American
Civilization," pp. 160–70. Translated from the 2d German ed.
by A. J. Butler. 3 vols. London, 1896–98.

    (2) Rivers, W. H. R. "The Ethnological Analysis of Culture,"
*Report of the 81st Meeting of the British Association for the Advance-
ment of Science,* 1911, pp. 490–99.

    (3) Frobenius, L. *Der Ursprung der afrikanischen Kulturen.* Berlin,
1898.

    (4) Boas, Franz. *The Mind of Primitive Man.* Chap. vi, "The
Universality of Cultural Traits," pp. 155–73. Chap. vii, "The
Evolutionary Viewpoint," pp. 174–96. New York, 1911.

    (5) Vierkandt, A. *Die Stetigkeit im Kulturwandel.* Eine sociologische
Studie. Leipzig, 1908.

(6) McGee, W J. "Piratical Acculturation," *American Anthropologist*, XI (1898), 243–51.

(7) Crooke, W. "Method of Investigation and Folklore Origins," *Folklore*, XXIV (1913), 14–40.

(8) Graebner, F. "Die melanesische Bogenkultur und ihre Verwandten," *Anthropos*, IV (1909), 726–80, 998–1032.

(9) Lowie, Robert H. "On the Principle of Convergence in Ethnology," *Journal of American Folklore*, XXV (1912), 24–42.

(10) Goldenweiser, A. A. "The Principle of Limited Possibilities in the Development of Culture," *Journal of American Folklore*, XXVI (1913), 259–90.

(11) Dixon, R. B. "The Independence of the Culture of the American Indian," *Science*, N.S., XXXV (1912), 46–55.

(12) Johnson, W. *Folk-Memory*. Or the continuity of British archaeology. Oxford, 1908.

(13) Wundt, Wilhelm. *Völkerpsychologie*. Eine Untersuchung der Entwicklungsgesetze von Sprache, Mythus, und Sitte. Band I, "Die Sprache." 3 vols. Leipzig, 1900–1909.

(14) Tarde, Gabriel. *The Laws of Imitation*. Translated from the 2d French ed. by Clews Parsons. New York, 1903.

B. *Nationalization and Denationalization*

(1) Bauer, Otto. *Die Nationalitätenfrage und die Sozialdemokratie*. Chap. vi, sec. 30, "Der Sozialismus und das Nationalitätsprinzip," pp. 507–21. In: Adler, M., and Hildering, R. *Marx-Studien; Blätter zur Theorie und Politik des wissenschaftlichen Sozialismus*. Band II. Wien, 1907.

(2) Kerner, R. J. *Slavic Europe*. A selected bibliography in the western European languages, comprising history, languages, and literature. "The Slavs and Germanization," Nos. 2612–13, pp. 193–95. Cambridge, Mass., 1918.

(3) Delbrück, Hans. "Das Polenthum," *Preussische Jahrbücher*, LXXVI (April, 1894), 173–86.

(4) Warren, H. C. "Social Forces and International Ethics," *International Journal of Ethics*, XXVII (1917), 350–56.

(5) Prince, M. "A World Consciousness and Future Peace," *Journal of Abnormal Psychology*, XI (1917), 287–304.

(6) Reich, Emil. *General History of Western Nations, from 5000 B.C. to 1900 A.D.* "Europeanization of Humanity," pp. 33–65, 480–82. (Vols. I–II published.) London, 1908.

(7) Thomas, William I. "The Prussian-Polish Situation: an Experiment in Assimilation," *American Journal of Sociology*, XIX (1913–14), 624–39.

(8) Parkman, Francis. *Conspiracy of Pontiac and the Indian Wars after the Conquest of Canada*. 8th ed., 2 vols. Boston, 1877. [Discusses the cultural effects of the mingling of French and Indians in Canada.]

(9) Moore, William H. *The Clash*. A study in nationalities. New York, 1919. [French and English cultural contacts in Canada.]

(10) Mayo-Smith, Richmond. "Assimilation of Nationalities in the United States," *Political Science Quarterly*, IX (1894), 426–44, 649–70.

(11) Kelly, J. Liddell. "New Race in the Making; Many Nationalities in the Territory of Hawaii—Process of Fusion Proceeding—the Coming Pacific Race," *Westminster Review*, CLXXV (1911), 357–66.

(12) Kallen, H. M. *Structure of Lasting Peace.* An inquiry into the motives of war and peace. Boston, 1918.

(13) Westermarck, Edward. "Finland and the Czar," *Contemporary Review*, LXXV (1899), 652–59.

(14) Brandes, Georg. "Denmark and Germany," *Contemporary Review*, LXXVI (1899), 92–104.

(15) Marvin, Francis S. *The Unity of Western Civilization.* Essays. London and New York, 1915.

(16) Fishberg, Maurice. *The Jews: a Study in Race and Environment.* London and New York, 1911. [Chap. xxii deals with assimilation versus nationalism.]

(17) Bailey, W. F., and Bates, Jean V. "The Early German Settlers in Transylvania," *Fortnightly Review*, CVII (1917), 661–74.

(18) Auerbach, Bertrand. *Les Races et les nationalitiés en Autriche-Hongrie.* Paris, 1898.

(19) Cunningham, William. *Alien Immigrants to England.* London and New York, 1897.

(20) Kaindl, Raimund Friedrich. *Geschichte der Deutschen in den Karpathenländern.* Vol. I, "Geschichte der Deutschen in Galizien bis 1772." 3 vols. in 2. Gotha, 1907–11.

C. *Missions*

(1) Moore, Edward C. *The Spread of Christianity in the Modern World.* Chicago, 1919. [Bibliography.]

(2) World Missionary Conference. *Report of the World Missionary Conference, 1910.* 9 vols. Chicago, 1910.

(3) Faunce, W. H. P. *The Social Aspects of Foreign Missions.* New York, 1914.

(4) Robinson, Charles H. *History of Christian Missions.* New York, 1915.

(5) Speer, Robert E. *Missions and Modern History.* A study of the missionary aspects of some great movements of the nineteenth century. 2 vols. New York, 1904.

(6) Warneck, Gustav. *Outline of a History of Protestant Missions from the Reformation to the Present Time.* A contribution to modern church history. Translated from the German by George Robson. Chicago, 1901.

(7) Creighton, Louise. *Missions.* Their rise and development. New York, 1912. [Bibliography.]

(8) Pascoe, C. F. *Two Hundred Years of the Society for the Propagation of the Gospel, 1701–1900.* Based on a digest of the Society's records. London, 1901.

(9) Parkman, Francis. *The Jesuits in North America in the Seventeenth Century.* Part II. "France and England in North America." Boston, 1902.

(10) Bryce, James. *Impressions of South Africa.* Chap. xxii, "Missions," pp. 384–93. 3d ed. New York, 1900.
(11) Sumner, W. G. *Folkways.* "Missions and Antagonistic Mores," pp. 111–14, 629–31. New York, 1906.
(12) Price, Maurice T. *Christian Missions and Oriental Civilizations.* With an introduction by Robert E. Park. Shanghai, China, 1924.
(13) Coffin, Ernest W. "On the Education of Backward Races," *Pedagogical Seminary,* XV (1908), 1–62. [Bibliography.]
(14) Blackmar, Frank W. *Spanish Colonization in the South West.* "The Mission System," pp. 28–48. "Johns Hopkins University Studies in Historical and Political Science." Baltimore, 1890.
(15) Johnston, Harry H. *George Grenfell and the Congo.* A history and description of the Congo Independent State and adjoining districts of Congoland, together with some account of the native peoples and their languages, the fauna and flora, and similar notes on the Cameroons, and the Island of Fernando Pô, the whole founded on the diaries and researches of the late Rev. George Grenfell, B.M.S., F.R.S.G.; and on the records of the British Baptist Missionary society; and on additional information contributed by the author, by the Rev. Lawson Forfeitt, Mr. Emil Torday, and others. 2 vols. London, 1908.
(16) Kingsley, Mary H. *West African Studies.* Pp. 107–9, 272–75. 2d ed. London, 1901.
(17) Morel, E. D. *Affairs of West Africa.* Chaps. xxii–xxiii, "Islam in West Africa," pp. 208–37. London, 1902.
(18) Sapper, Karl. "Der Charakter der mittelamerikanischen Indianer," *Globus,* LXXXVII (1905), 128–31.
(19) Fleming, Daniel J. *Devolution in Mission Administration.* As exemplified by the legislative history of five American missionary societies in India. New York, 1916. [Bibliography.]

III. IMMIGRATION AND AMERICANIZATION

A. *Immigration and the Immigrant*

(1) United States Immigration Commission. *Reports of the Immigration Commission.* 41 vols. Washington, 1911.
(2) Lauck, William J., and Jenks, Jeremiah. *The Immigration Problem.* New York, 1912.
(3) Commons, John R. *Races and Immigrants in America.* New ed. New York, 1920.
(4) Fairchild, Henry P. *Immigration.* A world-movement and its American significance. New York, 1913. [Bibliography.]
(5) Ross, E. A. *The Old World in the New.* The significance of past and present immigration to the American People. New York, 1914.
(6) Abbott, Grace. *The Immigrant and the Community.* With an introduction by Judge Julian W. Mack. New York, 1917.
(7) Steiner, Edward A. *On the Trail of the Immigrant.* New York, 1906.
(8) ———. *The Immigrant Tide, Its Ebb and Flow.* Chicago, 1909.

(9) Brandenburg, Broughton. *Imported Americans.* The story of the experience of a disguised American and his wife studying the immigration question. New York, 1904.

(10) Kapp, Friedrich. *Immigration and the Commissioners of Emigration of the State of New York.* New York, 1880.

(11) Abbott, Edith. *Immigration: Select Documents and Case Records.* Chicago, 1924.

B. *Immigrant Communities*

(1) Faust, Albert B. *The German Element in the United States.* With special reference to its political, moral, social, and educational influence. New York, 1909.

(2) Green, Samuel S. *The Scotch-Irish in America, 1895.* A paper read as the report of the Council of the American Antiquarian Society, at the semi-annual meeting, April 24, 1895, with correspondence called out by the paper. Worcester, Mass., 1895.

(3) Hanna, Charles A. *The Scotch-Irish.* Or the Scot in North Britain, North Ireland, and North America. New York and London, 1902.

(4) Jewish Publication Society of America. *The American Jewish Yearbook.* Philadelphia, 1899.

(5) *Jewish Communal Register, 1917–1918.* 2d ed. Edited and published by the Kehillah (Jewish Community) of New York City. New York, 1919.

(6) Balch, Emily G. *Our Slavic Fellow Citizens.* New York, 1910.

(7) Millis, Harry A. *The Japanese Problem in the United States.* An investigation for the Commission on Relations with Japan appointed by the Federal Council of the Churches of Christ in America. New York, 1915.

(8) Fairchild, Henry P. *Greek Immigration to the United States.* New Haven, 1911.

(9) Burgess, Thomas. *Greeks in America.* An account of their coming, progress, customs, living, and aspirations; with a historical introduction and the stories of some famous American-Greeks. Boston, 1913.

(10) Coolidge, Mary R. *Chinese Immigration.* New York, 1909.

(11) Chen, Ta. *Chinese Migrations.* With special reference to labor conditions. Bulletin of the United States Bureau of Labor Statistics, No. 340. Washington, 1923.

(12) Foerster, Robert F. *The Italian Emigration of Our Times.* Cambridge, Mass., 1919.

(13) Lord, Eliot, Trenor, John J. D., and Barrows, Samuel J. *The Italian in America.* New York, 1905.

(14) DuBois, W. E. Burghardt. *The Philadelphia Negro, A Social Study.* Together with a special report on domestic service by Isabel Eaton. "Publications of the University of Pennsylvania, Series in Political Economy and Public Law," No. 14. Philadelphia, 1899.

(15) Williams, Daniel J. *The Welsh of Columbus, Ohio.* A study in adaptation and assimilation. Oshkosh, Wis., 1913.

(16) Taft, Donald R. *Two Portuguese Communities in New England.* New York, 1923.
(17) Hitti, Philip K. *The Syrians in America.* New York, 1924.
(18) Davis, Jerome. *The Russian Immigrant.* New York, 1922.
(19) Wargelin, John. *The Americanization of the Finns.* Hancock, Mich., 1924.

C. *Americanization*

(1) Drachsler, Julius. *Democracy and Assimilation.* The blending of immigration heritages in America. New York, 1920. [Bibliography.]
(2) Dushkin, Alexander M. *Jewish Education in New York City.* New York, 1918.
(3) Thompson, Frank V. *Schooling of the Immigrant.* New York, 1920.
(4) Daniels, John. *America via the Neighborhood.* New York, 1920.
(5) Park, Robert E., and Miller, Herbert A. *Old World Traits Transplanted.* New York, 1921.
(6) Speek, Peter A. *A Stake in the Land.* New York, 1921.
(7) Davis, Michael M. *Immigrant Health and the Community.* New York, 1921.
(8) Breckinridge, Sophonisba P. *New Homes for Old.* New York, 1921.
(9) Leiserson, William M. *Adjusting Immigrant and Industry.* New York, 1924.
(10) Gavit, John P. *Americans by Choice.* New York, 1922.
(11) Claghorn, Kate H. *The Immigrant's Day in Court.* New York, 1923.
(12) Park, Robert E. *The Immigrant Press and Its Control.* New York, 1922.
(13) Miller, Herbert A. *The School and the Immigrant.* Cleveland Education Survey. Cleveland, 1916.
(14) Kallen, Horace M. "Democracy versus the Melting-Pot, a Study of American Nationality." *Nation,* C (1915), 190–94, 217–20.
(15) Gulick, Sidney L. *American Democracy and Asiatic Citizenship.* New York, 1918.
(16) Talbot, Winthrop, editor. *Americanization.* Principles of Americanism; essentials of Americanization; technic of race-assimilation. New York, 1917. [Annotated bibliography.]
(17) Stead, W. T. *The Americanization of the World.* Or the trend of the twentieth century. New York and London, 1901.
(18) Aronovici, Carol. *Americanization.* St. Paul, 1919. [Also in *American Journal of Sociology,* XXV (1919–20), 695–730.]

D. *Personal Documents*

(1) Bridges, Horace. *On Becoming an American.* Some meditations of a newly naturalized immigrant. Boston, 1919.
(2) Riis, Jacob A. *The Making of an American.* New York, 1901.
(3) Rihbany, Abraham Mitrie. *A Far Journey.* Boston, 1914.

(4) Hasanovitz, Elizabeth. *One of Them.* Chapters from a passionate autobiography. Boston, 1918.

(5) Cohen, Rose. *Out of the Shadow.* New York, 1918.

(6) Ravage, M. E. *An American in the Making.* The life-story of an immigrant. New York, 1917.

(7) Cahan, Abraham. *The Rise of David Levinsky.* A novel. New York, 1917.

(8) Antin, Mary. *The Promised Land.* New York, 1912.

(9) ———. *They Who Knock at Our Gates.* A complete gospel of immigration. New York, 1914.

(10) Washington, Booker T. *Up from Slavery.* An autobiography. New York, 1901.

(11) Steiner, Edward A. *From Alien to Citizen.* The story of my life in America. New York, 1914.

(12) Lewisohn, Ludwig. *Up Stream.* An American chronicle. New York, 1922.

(13) Stern, Mrs. Elizabeth Gertrude (Levin). *My Mother and I.* New York, 1919.

(14) DuBois, W. E. Burghardt. *Darkwater: Voices from within the Veil.* New York, 1920.

(15) ———. *The Souls of Black Folk.* Essays and sketches. Chicago, 1903.

(16) Hapgood, Hutchins. *The Spirit of the Ghetto.* Studies of the Jewish quarter in New York. Rev. ed. New York, 1909.

TOPICS FOR WRITTEN THEMES

1. Race and Culture, and the Problem of the Relative Superiority and Inferiority of Races

2. The Relation of Assimilation to Amalgamation

3. The Mulatto as a Cultural Type

4. Language as a Means of Assimilation and a Basis of National Solidarity

5. History and Literature as Means for Preserving National Solidarity

6. Race Prejudice and Segregation in Their Relations to Assimilation and Accommodation

7. Domestic Slavery and the Assimilation of the Negro

8. A Study of Historical Experiments in Denationalization; the Germanization of Posen, the Russianization of Poland, the Japanese Policy in Korea, etc.

9. The "Melting-Pot" versus "Hyphen" in Their Relation to Americanization

10. A Study of Policies, Programs, and Experiments in Americanization from the Standpoint of Sociology

11. The Immigrant Community as a Means of Americanization

12. The Process of Assimilation as Revealed in Personal Documents, as Antin, *The Promised Land;* Rihbany, *A Far Journey;* Ravage, *An American in the Making;* etc.

13. Foreign Missions and Native Cultures
14. The Rôle of Assimilation and Accommodation in the Personal Development of the Individual Man
15. Assimilation and Accommodation in Their Relations to the Educational Process

QUESTIONS FOR DISCUSSION

1. What do you understand Simons to mean by the term "assimilation"?
2. What is the difference between amalgamation and assimilation?
3. How are assimilation and amalgamation interrelated?
4. What do you consider to be the difference between Trotter's explanation of human evolution and that of Crile?
5. What do you understand Trotter to mean by the gregarious instinct as a mechanism controlling conduct?
6. Of what significance is the distinction made by Trotter between (a) the three individual instincts, and (b) the gregarious instincts?
7. What is the significance of material and non-material cultural elements for the study of race contact and intermixture?
8. How do you explain the difference in rapidity of assimilation of the various types of cultural elements?
9. What factors promoted and impeded the extension of Roman culture in Gaul?
10. What social factors were involved in the origin of the French language?
11. To what extent does the extension of a cultural language involve assimilation?
12. In what sense do the cultural languages compete with each other?
13. Do you agree with the prediction that within a century English will be the vernacular of a quarter of the people of the world? Justify your position.
14. Does Park's definition of assimilation differ from that of Simons?
15. What do you understand Park to mean when he says, "Social institutions are not founded in similarities any more than they are founded in differences, but in relations, and in the mutual interdependence of the parts"? What is the relation of this principle to the process of assimilation?
16. What do you understand to be the difference between the type of assimilation (a) that makes for group solidarity and corporate action, and (b) that makes for formal like-mindedness? What conditions favor the one or the other type of assimilation?
17. What do you understand by the term "Americanization"?
18. Is there a difference between Americanization and Prussianization?

19 With what programs of Americanization are you familiar? Are they adequate from the standpoint of the sociological interpretation of assimilation?

20. In what way is language both a means and a product of assimilation?

21. What is meant by the phrases "apperception mass," "universes of discourse," and "definitions of the situations"? What is their significance for assimilation?

22. In what way does assimilation involve the mediation of individual differences?

23. Does the segregation of immigrants make for or against assimilation?

24. In what ways do primary and secondary contacts, imitation and suggestion, competition, conflict and accommodation, enter into the process of assimilation?

CHAPTER XII

SOCIAL CONTROL

I. INTRODUCTION

1. Social Control Defined

Social control has been studied, but, in the wide extension that sociology has given to the term, it has not been defined. All social problems turn out finally to be problems of social control. In the introductory chapter to this volume social problems were divided into three classes: Problems (a) of administration, (b) of policy and polity, (c) of social forces and human nature.[1] Social control may be studied in each one of these categories. It is with social forces and human nature that sociology is mainly concerned. Therefore it is from this point of view that social control will be considered in this chapter.

In the four preceding chapters the process of interaction, in its four typical forms, competition, conflict, accommodation, and assimilation, has been analyzed and described. The community and the natural order within the limits of the community, it appeared, are an effect of competition. Social control and the mutual subordination of individual members to the community have their origin in conflict, assume definite organized forms in the process of accommodation, and are consolidated and fixed in assimilation.

Through the medium of these processes, a community assumes the form of a society. Incidentally, however, certain definite and quite spontaneous forms of social control are developed. These forms are familiar under various titles: tradition, custom, folkways, mores, ceremonial, myth, religious and political beliefs, dogmas and creeds, and finally public opinion and law. In this chapter it is proposed to define a little more accurately certain of these typical mechanisms through which social groups are enabled to act. In the chapter on "Collective Behavior" which follows, materials will be presented to exhibit the group in action.

[1] Chap. i, pp. 46-47.

It is in action that the mechanisms of control are created, and the materials under the title "Collective Behavior" are intended to illustrate the stages, (a) social unrest, (b) mass movements, (c) institutions in which society is formed and reformed. Finally, in the chapter on "Progress," the relation of social change to social control will be discussed and the rôle of science and collective representations in the direction of social changes indicated.

The most obvious fact about social control is the machinery by which laws are made and enforced, that is, the legislature, the courts, and the police. When we think of social control, therefore, these are the images in which we see it embodied and these are the terms in which we seek to define it.

It is not quite so obvious that legislation and the police must, in the long run, have the support of public opinion. Hume's statement that governments, even the most despotic, have nothing but opinion to support them, cannot be accepted without some definition of terms, but it is essentially correct. Hume included under opinion what we would distinguish from it, namely, the mores. He might have added, using opinion in this broad sense, that the governed, no matter how numerous, are helpless unless they too are united by "opinion."

A king or a political "boss," having an army or a political "machine" at his command, can do much. It is possible, also, to confuse or mislead public opinion, but neither the king nor the boss will, if he be wise, challenge the mores and the common sense of the community.

Public opinion and the mores, however, representing as they do the responses of the community to changing situations, are themselves subject to change and variation. They are based, however, upon what we have called fundamental human nature, that is, certain traits which in some form or other are reproduced in every form of society.

During the past seventy years the various tribes, races, and nationalities of mankind have been examined in detail by the students of ethnology, and a comparison of the results shows that the fundamental patterns of life and behavior are everywhere the same, whether among the ancient Greeks, the modern Italians, the Asiatic Mongols, the Australian blacks, or the African Hottentots. All have a form of family life, moral and legal regulations, a religious system, a form of government, artistic practices, and so forth. An examination of the moral code of any given group, say the African Kaffirs, will disclose many identities with that of any other given group, say the Hebrews. All groups have such "commandments" as "Honor thy father and mother," "Thou shalt not kill," "Thou shalt not steal." Formerly it was assumed that this similarity was the result of borrowing between groups. When Bastian recorded a Hawaiian myth resembling the one of Orpheus and Eurydice, there was speculation as to how this story had been carried so far from Greece. But it is now recognized that similarities of culture are due, in the main, not to imitation, but to parallel development. The nature of man is everywhere essentially the same and tends to express itself everywhere in similar sentiments and institutions.[1]

There are factors in social control more fundamental than the mores. Herbert Spencer, in his chapter on "Ceremonial Government," has defined social control from this more fundamental point of view. In that chapter he refers to "the modified forms of action caused in men by the presence of their fellows" as a form of control "out of which other more definite controls are evolved." The spontaneous responses of one individual to the presence of another which are finally fixed, conventionalized, and transmitted as social ritual constitute that "primitive undifferentiated kind of government from which political and religious government are differentiated, and in which they continue immersed."

In putting this emphasis upon ceremonial and upon those forms of behavior which spring directly and spontaneously out of the innate and instinctive responses of the individual to a social situation, Spencer is basing government on the springs of action which are fundamental, so far, at any rate, as sociology is concerned.

2. Classification of the Materials

The selections on social control have been classified under three heads: (a) elementary forms of social control, (b) public opinion, and (c) institutions. This order of the readings indicates the development of control from its spontaneous forms in the crowd, in ceremony, prestige, and taboo; its more explicit expression in gossip, rumor, news, and public opinion; to its more formal organization in law,

[1] Robert E. Park and Herbert A. Miller, *Old World Traits Transplanted*, pp. 1-2. (New York, 1921.)

dogma, and in religious and political institutions. Ceremonial, public opinion, and law are characteristic forms in which social life finds expression as well as a means by which the actions of the individual are co-ordinated and collective impulses are organized so that they issue in behavior, that is, either (a) primarily expressive—play, for example—or (b) positive action.

A very much larger part of all human behavior than we ordinarily imagine is merely expressive. Art, play, religious exercises, and political activity are either wholly or almost wholly forms of expression, and have, therefore, that symbolic and ceremonial character which belongs especially to ritual and to art, but is characteristic of every activity carried on for its own sake. Only work, action which has some ulterior motive or is performed from a conscious sense of duty, falls wholly and without reservation into the second class.

a) *Elementary forms of social control.*—Control in the crowd, where rapport is once established and every individual is immediately responsive to every other, is the most elementary form of control.

Something like this same direct and spontaneous response of the individual in the crowd to the crowd's dominant mood or impulse may be seen in the herd and the flock, the "animal crowd."

Under the influence of the vague sense of alarm, or merely as an effect of heat and thirst, cattle become restless and begin slowly moving about in circles, "milling." This milling is a sort of collective gesture, an expression of discomfort or of fear. But the very expression of the unrest tends to intensify its expression and so increases the tension in the herd. This continues up to the point where some sudden sound, the firing of a pistol or a flash of lightning, plunges the herd into a wild stampede.

Milling in the herd is a visible image of what goes on in subtler and less obvious ways in human societies. Alarms or discomforts frequently provoke social unrest. The very expression of this unrest tends to magnify it. The situation is a vicious circle. Every attempt to deal with it merely serves to aggravate it. Such a vicious circle we witnessed in our history from 1830 to 1861, when every attempt to deal with slavery served only to bring the inevitable conflict between the states nearer. Finally there transpired what had for twenty years been visibly preparing and the war broke.

Tolstoi in his great historical romance, *War and Peace*, describes, in a manner which no historian has equaled, the events that led up to the Franco-Russian War of 1812, and particularly the manner in which Napoleon, in spite of his efforts to avoid it, was driven by social forces over which he had no control to declare war on Russia, and so bring about his own downfall.

The condition under which France was forced by Bismarck to declare war on Prussia in 1870, and the circumstances under which Austria declared war on Serbia in 1914 and so brought on the world-war, exhibit the same fatal circle. In both cases, given the situation, the preparations that had been made, the resolutions formed and the agreements entered into, it seems clear that after a certain point had been reached every move was forced.

This is the most fundamental and elementary form of control. It is the control exercised by the mere play of elemental forces. These forces may, to a certain extent, be manipulated, as is true of other natural forces; but within certain limits, human nature being what it is, the issue is fatally determined, just as, given the circumstances and the nature of cattle, a stampede is inevitable. Historical crises are invariably created by processes which, looked at abstractly, are very much like milling in a herd. The vicious circle is the so-called "psychological factor" in financial depressions and panics and is, indeed, a factor in all collective action.

The effect of this circular form of interaction is to increase the tensions in the group and, by creating a state of expectancy, to mobilize its members for collective action. It is like attention in the individual: it is the way in which the group prepares to act.

Back of every other form of control—ceremonial, public opinion, or law—there is always this interaction of the elementary social forces. What we ordinarily mean by social control, however, is the arbitrary intervention of some individual—official, functionary, or leader—in the social process. A policeman arrests a criminal, an attorney sways the jury with his eloquence, the judge passes sentence; these are the familiar formal acts in which social control manifests itself. What makes the control exercised in this way social, in the strict sense of that term, is the fact that these acts are supported by custom, law, and public opinion.

The distinction between control in the crowd and in other forms of society is that the crowd has no tradition. It has no point of reference in its own past to which its members can refer for guidance. It has therefore neither symbols, ceremonies, rites, nor ritual; it imposes no obligations and creates no loyalties.

Ceremonial is one method of reviving in the group a lively sense of the past. It is a method of reinstating the excitements and the sentiments which inspired an earlier collective action. The savage war dance is a dramatic representation of battle and as such serves to rouse and reawaken the warlike spirit. This is one way in which ceremonial becomes a means of control. By reviving the memories of an earlier war, it mobilizes the warriors for a new one.

Ernst Grosse, in *The Beginnings of Art*, has stated succinctly what has impressed all first-hand observers, namely, the important rôle which the dance plays in the lives of primitive peoples.

The dances of the hunting peoples are, as a rule, mass dances. Generally the men of the tribe, not rarely the members of several tribes, join in the exercises, and the whole assemblage then moves according to one law in one time. All who have described the dances have referred again and again to this "wonderful" unison of the movements. In the heat of the dance the several participants are fused together as into a single being, which is stirred and moved as by one feeling. During the dance they are in a condition of complete social unification, and the dancing group feels and acts like a single organism. *The social significance of the primitive dance lies precisely in this effect of social unification.* It brings and accustoms a number of men who, in their loose and precarious conditions of life, are driven irregularly hither and thither by different individual needs and desires, to act under one impulse with one feeling for one object. It introduces order and connection, at least occasionally, into the rambling, fluctuating life of the hunting tribes. It is, besides wars, perhaps the only factor that makes their solidarity vitally perceptible to the adherents of a primitive tribe, and it is at the same time one of the best preparations for war, for the gymnastic dances correspond in more than one respect to our military exercises. It would be hard to overestimate the importance of the primitive dance in the culture development of mankind. All higher civilization is conditioned upon the uniformly ordered co-operation of individual social elements, and primitive men are trained to this co-operation by the dance.[1]

[1] Ernst Grosse, *The Beginnings of Art*, pp. 228–29. (New York, 1897.)

The dance, which is so characteristic and so universal a feature of the life of primitive man—at once a mode of collective expression and of collective representation—is but a conventionalized form of the circular reaction, which in its most primitive form is represented by the milling of the herd.

b) Public opinion.—We ordinarily think of public opinion as a sort of social weather. At certain times, and under certain circumstances, we observe strong, steady currents of opinion, moving apparently in a definite direction and toward a definite goal. At other times, however, we note flurries and eddies and countercurrents in this movement. Every now and then there are storms, shifts, or dead calms. These sudden shifts in public opinion, when expressed in terms of votes, are referred to by the politicians as "landslides."

In all these movements, cross-currents and changes in direction which a closer observation of public opinion reveals, it is always possible to discern, but on a much grander scale, to be sure, that same type of circular reaction which we have found elsewhere, whenever the group was preparing to act. Always in the public, as in the crowd, there will be a circle, sometimes wider, sometimes narrower, within which individuals are mutually responsive to motives and interests of one another, so that out of this interplay of social forces there may emerge at any time a common motive and a common purpose that will dominate the whole.

Within the circle of the mutual influence described, there will be no such complete rapport and no such complete domination of the individual by the group as exists in a herd or a crowd in a state of excitement, but there will be sufficient community of interest to insure a common understanding. A public is, in fact, organized on the basis of a universe of discourse, and within the limits of this universe of discourse, language, statements of fact, news will have, for all practical purposes, the same meanings. It is this circle of mutual influence within which there is a universe of discourse that defines the limits of the public.

A public, like a crowd, is not to be conceived as a formal organization like a parliament or even a public meeting. It is always the widest area over which there is conscious participation and consensus in the formation of public opinion. The public has not only a circumference, but it has a center. Within the area within which there is participation and consensus there is always a focus of attention around which the opinions of the individuals which compose the public seem to revolve. This focus of attention, under ordinary circumstances, is constantly shifting. The shifts of attention of the public constitute what is meant by the changes in public opinion. When these changes take a definite direction and have or seem to have a definite goal, we call the phenomenon a social movement. If it were possible to plot this movement in the form of maps and graphs, it would be possible to show movement in two dimensions. There would be, for example, a movement in space. The focus of public opinion, the point namely at which there is the greatest "intensity" of opinion, tends to move from one part of the country to another.[1] In America these movements, for reasons that could perhaps be explained historically, are likely to be along the meridians, east and west, rather than north and south. In the course of this geographical movement of public opinion, however, we are likely to observe changes in intensity and changes in direction (devagation).

Changes in intensity seem to be in direct proportion to the area over which opinion on a given issue may be said to exist. In minorities opinion is uniformly more intense than it is in majorities and this is what gives minorities so much greater influence in proportion to their numbers than majorities. While changes in intensity have a definite relation to the area over which public opinion on an issue may be said to exist, the devagations of public opinion, as distinguished from the trend, will probably turn out to have a direct relation to the character of the parties that participate. Area as applied to public opinion will have to be measured eventually in terms of social rather than geographical distance, that is to say, in terms of isolation and contact. The factor of numbers is also involved in any such calculation. Geographical area, communication, and the number of persons involved are in general the factors that would determine the concept "area" as it is used here. If party spirit is strong the general direction or trend of public opinion will probably be intersected by shifts and sudden transient changes in direction, and these shifts will be in proportion to the intensity of the party spirit. Charles E. Merriam's recent study of political parties indicates that the minority parties formulate most of the legislation in the United States.[2] This is because there is not very great

[1] See A. L. Lowell, *Public Opinion and Popular Government*, pp. 12–13. (New York, 1913.)

[2] *The American Party System*, chap. viii. (New York, 1922.) [In press.]

divergence in the policies of the two great parties and party struggles are fought out on irrelevant issues. So far as this is true it insures against any sudden change in policy. New legislation is adopted in response to the trend of public opinion, rather than in response to the devagations and sudden shifts brought about by the development of a radical party spirit.

All these phenomena may be observed, for example, in the Prohibition Movement. Dicey's study of *Law and Public Opinion in England* showed that while the direction of opinion in regard to specific issues had been very irregular, on the whole the movement had been in one general direction. The trend of public opinion is the name we give to this general movement. In defining the trend, shifts, cross-currents, and flurries are not considered. When we speak of the tendency or direction of public opinion we usually mean the trend over a definite period of time.

When the focus of public attention ceases to move and shift, when it is fixed, the circle which defines the limits of the public is narrowed. As the circle narrows, opinion itself becomes more intense and concentrated. This is the phenomenon of crisis. It is at this point that the herd stampedes.

The effect of crisis is invariably to increase the dangers of precipitate action. The most trivial incident, in such periods of tension, may plunge a community into irretrievable disaster. It is under conditions of crisis that dictatorships are at once possible and necessary, not merely to enable the community to act energetically, but in order to protect the community from the mere play of external forces. The manner in which Bismarck, by a slight modification of the famous telegram of Ems, provoked a crisis in France and compelled Napoleon III, against his judgment and that of his advisers, to declare war on Germany, is an illustration of this danger.[1]

[1] "On the afternoon of July 13, Bismarck, Roon, and Moltke were seated together in the Chancellor's Room at Berlin. They were depressed and moody; for Prince Leopold's renunciation had been trumpeted in Paris as a humiliation for Prussia. They were afraid, too, that King William's conciliatory temper might lead him to make further concessions, and that the careful preparations of Prussia for the inevitable war with France might be wasted, and a unique opportunity lost. A telegram arrived. It was from the king at Ems, and described his interview that morning with the French ambassador. The king had met Benedetti's request for the guarantee required by a firm but courteous refusal; and when the ambassador had sought to renew the interview, he had sent a polite

It is this narrowing of the area over which a definite public opinion may be said to exist that at once creates the possibility and defines the limits of arbitrary control, so far as it is created or determined by the existence of public opinion.

Thus far the public has been described almost wholly in terms that could be applied to a crowd. The public has been frequently described as if it were simply a great crowd, a crowd scattered as widely as news will circulate and still be news.[1] But there is this difference. In the heat and excitement of the crowd, as in the choral dances of primitive people, there is for the moment what may be described as complete fusion of the social forces. Rapport has, for the time being, made the crowd, in a peculiarly intimate way, a social unit.

No such unity exists in the public. The sentiment and tendencies which we call public opinion are never unqualified expressions of emotion. The difference is that public opinion is determined by conflict and discussion, and made up of the opinions of individuals not wholly at one. In any conflict situation, where party spirit is aroused, the spectators, who constitute the public, are bound to take sides. The

---

message through his aide-de-camp informing him that the subject must be considered closed. In conclusion, Bismarck was authorized to publish the message if he saw fit. The Chancellor at once saw his opportunity. In the royal despatch, though the main incidents were clear enough, there was still a note of doubt, of hesitancy, which suggested a possibility of further negotiation. The excision of a few lines would alter, not indeed the general sense, but certainly the whole tone of the message. Bismarck, turning to Moltke, asked him if he were ready for a sudden risk of war; and on his answering in the affirmative, took a blue pencil and drew it quickly through several parts of the telegram. Without the alteration or addition of a single word, the message, instead of appearing a mere 'fragment of a negotiation still pending,' was thus made to appear decisive. In the actual temper of the French people there was no doubt that it would not only appear decisive, but insulting, and that its publication would mean war.

"On July 14 the publication of the 'Ems telegram' became known in Paris, with the result that Bismarck had expected. The majority of the Cabinet, hitherto in favour of peace, were swept away by the popular tide; and Napoleon himself reluctantly yielded to the importunity of his ministers and of the Empress, who saw in a successful war the best, if not the only, chance of preserving the throne for her son. On the evening of the same day, July 14, the declaration of war was signed."—W. Alison Phillips, *Modern Europe, 1815-1899*, pp. 465-66. (London, 1903.)

[1] G. Tarde, *L'opinion et la foule.* (Paris, 1901.)

impulse to take sides is, in fact, in direct proportion to the excitement and party spirit displayed. The result is, however, that both sides of an issue get considered. Certain contentions are rejected because they will not stand criticism. Public opinion formed in this way has the character of a judgment, rather than a mere unmeditated expression of emotion, as in the crowd. The public is never ecstatic. It is always more or less rational. It is this fact of conflict, in the form of discussion, that introduces into the control exercised by public opinion the elements of rationality and of fact.

In the final judgment of the public upon a conflict or an issue, we expect, to be sure, some sort of unanimity of judgment, but in the general consensus there will be some individual differences of opinion still unmediated, or only partially so, and final agreement of the public will be more or less qualified by all the different opinions that co-operated to form its judgment.

In the materials which follow a distinction is made between public opinion and the mores, and this distinction is important. Custom and the folkways, like habit in the individual, may be regarded as a mere residuum of past practices. When folkways assume the character of mores, they are no longer merely matters of fact and common sense, they are judgments upon matters which were probably once live issues and as such they may be regarded as the products of public opinion.

Ritual, religious or social, is probably the crystallization of forms of behavior which, like the choral dance, are the direct expression of the emotions and the instincts. The mores, on the other hand, in so far as they contain a rational element, are the accumulation, the residuum, not only of past practices, but of judgments such as find expression in public opinion. The mores, as thus conceived, are the judgments of public opinion in regard to issues that have been settled and forgotten.

L. T. Hobhouse, in his volume, *Morals in Evolution*, has described, in a convincing way, the process by which, as he conceives it, custom is modified and grows under the influence of the personal judgments of individuals and of the public. Public opinion, as he defines it, is simply the combined and sublimated judgments of individuals.

Most of these judgments are, to be sure, merely the repetition of old formulas. But occasionally, when the subject of discussion touches us more deeply, when it touches upon some matter in which we have had a deeper and more intimate experience, the ordinary patter that passes as public opinion is dissipated and we originate a moral judgment that not only differs from, but is in conflict with, the prevailing opinion.   In that case "we become, as it were, centers from which judgments of one kind or another radiate and from which they pass forth to fill the atmosphere of opinion and take their place among the influences that mould the judgments of men."

The manner in which public opinion issues from the interaction of individuals, and moral judgments are formed that eventually become the basis of law, may be gathered from the way in which the process goes on in the daily life about us.

No sooner has the judgment escaped us—a winged word from our own lips—than it impinges on the judgment similarly flying forth to do its work from our next-door neighbor, and if the subject is an exciting one the air is soon full of the winged forces clashing, deflecting or reinforcing one another as the case may be, and generally settling down toward some preponderating opinion which is society's judgment on the case.   But in the course of the conflict many of the original judgments are modified. Discussion, further consideration, above all, the mere influence of our neighbour's opinion reacts on each of us, with a stress that is proportioned to various mental and moral characteristics of our own, our clearness of vision, our firmness, or, perhaps, obstinacy of character, our self-confidence, and so forth.   Thus, the controversy will tend to leave its mark, small or great, on those who took part in it.   It will tend to modify their modes of judgment, confirming one, perhaps, in his former ways, shaping the confidence of another, opening the eyes of a third.   Similarly, it will tend to set a precedent for future judgments.   It will affect what men say and think on the next question that turns up.   It adds its weight, of one grain it may be, to some force that is turning the scale of opinion and preparing society for some new departure.   In any case, we have here in miniature at work every day before our eyes the essential process by which moral judgments arise and grow.[1]

c) *Institutions.*—An institution, according to Sumner, consists of a concept and a structure.   The concept defines the purpose, interest, or function of the institution.   The structure embodies the idea of the institution and furnishes the instrumentalities through which the

[1] L. T. Hobhouse, *Morals in Evolution, A Study in Comparative Ethics*, pp. 13-14.   (New York, 1915.)

idea is put into action. The process by which purposes, whether they are individual or collective, are embodied in structures is a continuous one. But the structures thus formed are not physical, at least not entirely so. Structure, in the sense that Sumner uses the term, belongs, as he says, to a category of its own. "It is a category in which custom produces continuity, coherence, and consistency, so that the word 'structure' may properly be applied to the fabric of relations and prescribed positions with which functions are permanently connected." Just as every individual member of a community participates in the process by which custom and public opinion are made, so also he participates in the creation of the structure, that "cake of custom" which, when it embodies a definite social function, we call an institution.

Institutions may be created just as laws are enacted, but only when a social situation exists to which they correspond will they become operative and effective. Institutions, like laws, rest upon the mores and are supported by public opinion. Otherwise they remain mere paper projects or artefacts that perform no real function. History records the efforts of conquering peoples to impose upon the conquered their own laws and institutions. The efforts are instructive, but not encouraging. The most striking modern instance is the effort of King Leopold of Belgium to introduce civilization into the Congo Free State.[1]

Law, like public opinion, owes its rational and secular character to the fact that it arose out of an effort to compromise conflict and to interpret matters which were in dispute.

To seek vengeance for a wrong committed was a natural impulse, and the recognition of this fact in custom established it not merely as a right but as a duty. War, the modern form of trial by battle, the vendetta, and the duel are examples that have survived down to modern times of this natural and primitive method of settling disputes.

In all these forms of conflict custom and the mores have tended to limit the issues and define the conditions under which disputes might be settled by force. At the same time public opinion, in passing judgment on the issues, exercised a positive influence on the outcome of the struggle.

[1] E. D. Morel, *King Leopold's Rule in Africa.* (London, 1904.)

Gradually, as men realized the losses which conflicts incurred, the community has intervened to prevent them.   At a time when the blood feud was still sanctioned by the mores, cities of refuge and sanctuaries were established to which one who had incurred a blood feud might flee until his case could be investigated.   If it then appeared that the wrong committed had been unintentional or if there were other mitigating circumstances, he might find in the sanctuary protection.   Otherwise, if a crime had been committed in cold blood, "lying in wait," or "in enmity," as the ancient Jewish law books called it, he might be put to death by the avenger of blood, "when he meeteth him."[1]

Thus, gradually, the principle became established that the community might intervene, not merely to insure that vengeance was executed in due form, but to determine the facts, and thus courts which determined by legal process the guilt or innocence of the accused were established.

It does not appear that courts of justice were ever set up within the kinship group for the trial of offenses, although efforts were made there first of all, by the elders and the headmen, to compromise quarrels and compose differences.

Courts first came into existence, the evidence indicates, when society was organized over wider areas and after some authority had been established outside of the local community.   As society was organized over a wider territory, control was extended to ever wider areas of human life until we have at present a program for international courts with power to intervene between nations to prevent wars.[2]

Society, like the individual man, moves and acts under the influence of a multitude of minor impulses and tendencies which mutually interact to produce a more general tendency which then dominates all the individuals of the group.   This explains the fact that a group, even a mere casual collection of individuals like a crowd, is enabled to act more or less as a unit.   The crowd acts under the influence of such a dominant tendency, unreflectively, without

[1] L. T. Hobhouse, *op. cit.*, p. 85.

[2] The whole process of evolution by which a moral order has been established over ever wider areas of social life has been sketched in a masterly manner by Hobhouse in his chapter, "Law and Justice," *op. cit.*, pp. 72–131.

definite reference to a past or a future. The crowd ·has no past and no future. The public introduces into this vortex of impulses the factor of reflection. The public presupposes the existence of a common impulse such as manifests itself in the crowd, but it presupposes, also, the existence of individuals and groups of individuals representing divergent tendencies. These individuals interact upon one another *critically*. The public is, what the crowd is not, a discussion group. The very existence of discussion presupposes objective standards of truth and of fact. The action of the public is based on a universe of discourse in which things, although they may and do have for every individual somewhat different value, are describable at any rate in terms that mean the same to all individuals. The public, in other words, moves in an objective and intelligible world.

Law is based on custom. Custom is group habit. As the group acts it creates custom. There is implicit in custom a conception and a rule of action, which is regarded as right and proper in the circumstances. Law makes this rule of action explicit. Law grows up, however, out of a distinction between this rule of action and the facts. Custom is bound up with the facts under which the custom grew up. Law is the result of an effort to frame the rule of action implicit in custom in such general terms that it can be made to apply to new situations, involving new sets of facts. This distinction between the law and the facts did not exist in primitive society. The evolution of law and jurisprudence has been in the direction of an increasingly clearer recognition of this distinction between law and the facts. This has meant in practice an increasing recognition by the courts of the facts, and a disposition to act in accordance with them. The present disposition of courts, as, for example, the juvenile courts, to call to their assistance experts to examine the mental condition of children who are brought before them and to secure the assistance of juvenile-court officers to advise and assist them in the enforcement of the law, is an illustration of an increasing disposition to take account of the facts.

The increasing interest in the natural history of the law and of legal institutions, and the increasing disposition to interpret it in sociological terms, from the point of view of its function, is another evidence of the same tendency.

II. MATERIALS

A. ELEMENTARY FORMS OF SOCIAL CONTROL

1. Control in the Crowd and the Public[1]

In August, 1914, I was a cowboy on a ranch in the interior of British Columbia. How good a cowboy I would not undertake to say, because if there were any errands off the ranch the foreman seemed better able to spare me for them than anyone else in the outfit.

One ambition, and one only, possessed me in those days. And it was not to own the ranch! All in the world I wanted was to accumulate money enough to carry me to San Francisco when the Panama exposition opened in the autumn. After that I didn't care. It would be time enough to worry about another job when I had seen the fair.

Ordinarily I was riding the range five days in the week. Saturdays I was sent on a 35-mile round trip for the mail. It was the most delightful day of them all for me. The trail lay down the valley of the Fraser and although I had been riding it for months it still wove a spell over me that never could be broken. Slipping rapidly by as though escaping to the sea from the grasp of the hills that hemmed it in on all sides, the river always fascinated me. It was new every time I reached its edge.

An early Saturday morning in August found me jogging slowly along the trail to Dog Creek. Dog Creek was our post-office and trading-center. This morning, however, my mind was less on the beauties of the Fraser than on the Dog Creek hotel. Every week I had my dinner there before starting in mid-afternoon on my return to the ranch, and this day had succeeded one of misunderstanding with "Cookie" wherein all the boys of our outfit had come off second-best. I was hungry and that dinner at the hotel was going to taste mighty good. Out there on the range we had heard rumors of a war in Europe. We all talked it over in the evening and decided it was another one of those fights that were always starting in the Balkans. One had just been finished a few months before and we thought it was about time another was under way, so we gave the matter no particular thought. But when I got within sight of Dog Creek I knew some-

[1] From Lieutenant Joseph S. Smith, *Over There and Back*, pp. 9–22. (E. P. Dutton & Co., 1917.)

thing was up. The first thing I heard was that somebody had retreated from Mons and that the Germans were chasing them. So, the Germans were fighting anyway. Then a big Indian came up to me as I was getting off my pony and told me England's big white chief was going to war, or had gone, he wasn't certain which, but he was going too. Would I?

I laughed at him. "What do you mean, go to war?" I asked him.

I wasn't English; I wasn't Canadian. I was from the good old U.S.A. and from all we could understand the States were neutral. So, I reasoned, I ought to be neutral too, and I went in to see what there might be to eat.

There was plenty of excitement in the dining-room. Under its influence I began to look at the thing in a different light. While I was an alien, I had lived in Canada. I had enjoyed her hospitality. Much of my education was acquired in a Canadian school. Canadians were among my dearest friends. Some of these very fellows, there in Dog Creek, were "going down" to enlist.

All the afternoon we argued about it. Politics, economics, diplomacy; none of them entered into the question. In fact we hadn't the faintest idea what the war was all about. Our discussion hinged solely on what we, personally, ought to do. England was at war. She had sent out a call to all the Empire for men; for help. Dog Creek heard and was going to answer that call. Even if I were an alien I had been in that district for more than a year and I owed it to Dog Creek and the district to join up with the rest. By that time I wanted to go. I was crazy to go! It would be great to see London and maybe Paris and some of the other famous old towns— if the war lasted long enough for us to get over there. I began to bubble over with enthusiasm, just thinking about it. So I made an appointment with some of the boys for the next evening, rode back to the ranch and threw the mail and my job at the foreman.

A week later we were in Vancouver. Then things began to get plainer—to some of the fellows. We heard of broken treaties, "scraps of paper," "Kultur," the rights of nations, big and small, "freedom of the seas," and other phrases that meant less than nothing to most of us. It was enough for me, then, that the country which had given me the protection of its laws wanted to help England. I trusted the government to know what it was doing. Before we were in town an hour we found ourselves at a recruiting office. By the simple expedient of moving my birthplace a few hundred miles north I became a Canadian and a member of the expeditionary force—a big word with a big meaning. Christmas came and I was in a well-trained battalion of troops with no more knowledge of the war than the retreat from Mons, the battles of the Marne and the Aisne, and an occasional newspaper report of the capture of a hundred thousand troops here and a couple of hundred thousand casualties somewhere else. We knew, at that rate, it couldn't possibly last until we got to the other side, but we prayed loudly that it would. In April we heard of the gassing of the first Canadians at Ypres. Then the casualty lists from that field arrived and hit Vancouver with a thud. Instantly a change came over the city. Before that day, war had been a romance, a thing far away about which to read and over which to wave flags. It was intangible, impersonal. It was the same attitude the States exhibited in the autumn of '17. Then suddenly it became real. This chap and that chap; a neighbor boy, a fellow from the next block or the next desk. Dead! Gassed! This was war; direct, personal, where you could count the toll among your friends. Personally, I thought that what the Germans had done was a terrible thing and I wondered what kind of people they might be that they could, without warning, deliver such a foul blow. In a prize ring the Kaiser would have lost the decision then and there. We wondered about gas and discussed it by the hour in our barracks. Some of us, bigger fools than the rest, insisted that the German nation would repudiate its army. But days went by and nothing of the kind occurred. It was then I began to take my soldiering a little more seriously. If a nation wanted to win a war so badly that it would damn its good name forever by using means ruled by all humanity as beyond the bounds of civilized warfare, it must have a very big object in view. And I started—late it is true—to obtain some clue to those objects.

May found us at our port of embarkation for the voyage to England. The news of the "Lusitania" came over the wires and that evening our convoy steamed. For the first time, I believe, I fully realized I was a soldier in the greatest war of all the ages.

Between poker, "blackjack," and "crown and anchor" with the crew, we talked over the two big things that had happened in our soldier lives—gas and the "Lusitania." And to these we later added liquid fire.

Our arguments, our logic, may have been elemental, but I insist they struck at the root. I may sum them up thus: Germany was not using the methods of fighting that could be countenanced by a civilized nation. As the nation stood behind its army in all this barbarism, there must be something inherently lacking in it despite its wonderful music, its divine poetry, its record in the sciences. It, too, must be barbarian at heart. We agreed that if it should win this war it would be very uncomfortable to belong to one of the allied nations, or even to live in the world at all, since it was certain German manners and German methods would not improve with victory. And we, as a battalion, were ready to take our places in France to back up our words with deeds.

A week or so later we landed in England. A marked change had come over the men since the day we left Halifax. Then most of us regarded the whole war, or our part in it, as more or less of a lark. On landing we were still for a lark, but something else had come into our consciousness. We were soldiers fighting for a cause—a cause clear cut and well defined—the saving of the world from a militarily mad country without a conscience. At our camp in England we saw those boys of the first division who had stood in their trenches in front of Ypres one bright April morning and watched with great curiosity a peculiar looking bank of fog roll toward them from the enemy's line. It rolled into their trenches, and in a second those men were choking and gasping for breath. Their lungs filled with the rotten stuff, and they were dying by dozens in the most terrible agony, beating off even as they died a part of the "brave" Prussian army as it came up behind those gas clouds; came up with gas masks on and bayonets dripping with the blood of men lying on the ground fighting, true, but for breath. A great army, that Prussian army! And what a "glorious" victory! Truly should the Hun be proud! So far as I am concerned, Germany did not lose the war at the battle of the Marne, at the Aisne, or at the Yser. She lost it there at Ypres, on April 22, 1915. It is no exaggeration when I say our eagerness to work, to complete our training, to learn how to kill, so we could take our places in the line, and help fight off those mad people, grew by the hour. *They* stiffened our backs and made us fighting mad. We saw what they had done to our boys from Canada; they and their gas. The effect on our battalion was the effect on the whole army, and, I am quite sure, on the rest of the world. They put themselves beyond the pale. They compelled the world to look on them as mad dogs, and to treat them as mad dogs. We trained in England until August, when we went to France. To all outward appearances we were still happy, carefree soldiers, all out for a good time. We were happy! We were happy we were there, and down deep there was solid satisfaction, not on account of the different-colored books that were issuing from every chancellory in Europe, but from a feeling rooted in white men's hearts, backed by the knowledge of Germany's conduct, that we were there in a righteous cause. Our second stop in our march toward the line was a little village which had been occupied by the Boches in their mad dash toward Paris. Our billet was a farm just on the edge of the village. The housewife permitted us in her kitchen to do our cooking, at the same time selling us coffee. We stayed there two or three days and became quite friendly with her, even if she did scold us for our muddy boots. Two pretty little kiddies played around the house, got in the way, were scolded and spanked and in the next instant loved to death by Madame. Then she would parade them before a picture of a clean-cut looking Frenchman in the uniform of the army, and say something about "après la guerre." In a little crib to one side of the room was a tiny baby, neglected by Madame, except that she bathed and fed it. The neglect was so pronounced that our curiosity was aroused. The explanation came through the *estaminet* gossip, and later from Madame herself. A Hun captain of cavalry had stayed there a few days in August, '14, and not only had he allowed his detachment full license in the village, but had abused his position in the house in the accustomed manner of his bestial class. As Madame told us her story; how her husband had rushed off to his unit with the first call for reserves, leaving her alone with two children, and how the blond beast had come, our fists clenched and we boiled with rage. That is German war! but it is not all. What will be the stories that come out of what is now occupied France? This Frenchwoman's story was new to us then, but, like other things in the war, as we moved through the country it became common enough, with here and there a revolting detail more horrible than anything we had heard before.

Now and then Germany expresses astonishment at the persistence of the British and the French. They are a funny people, the Germans. There are so many things they do not, perhaps cannot, understand. They never could understand why Americans, such as myself, who enlisted in a spirit of adventure, and with not a single thought on the justice of the cause, could experience such a marked change of feeling as to regard this conflict as the most holy crusade in which a man could engage. It is a holy crusade! Never in the history of the world was the cause of right more certainly on the side of an army than it is today on the side of the allies: We who have been through the furnace of France know this. I only say what every other American who has been fighting under an alien flag said when our country came in: "Thank God we have done it. Some boy, Wilson, believe me!"

2. Ceremonial Control[1]

If, disregarding conduct that is entirely private, we consider only that species of conduct which involves direct relations with other persons; and if under the name government we include all control of conduct, however arising; then we must say that the earliest kind of government, the most general kind of government, and the government which is ever spontaneously recommencing, is the government of ceremonial observance. This kind of government, besides preceding other kinds, and besides having in all places and times approached nearer to universality of influence, has ever had, and continues to have, the largest share in regulating men's lives.

Proof that the modifications of conduct called "manners" and "behavior" arise before those which political and religious restraints cause is yielded by the fact that, besides preceding social evolution, they precede human evolution: they are traceable among the higher animals. The dog afraid of being beaten comes crawling up to his master clearly manifesting the desire to show submission. Nor is it solely to human beings that dogs use such propitiatory actions. They do the like one to another. All have occasionally seen how, on the approach of some formidable Newfoundland or mastiff, a small spaniel, in the extremity of its terror, throws itself on its back with

[1] From Herbert Spencer, *The Principles of Sociology*, II, 3–6. (Williams & Norgate, 1893.)

legs in the air. Clearly then, besides certain modes of behavior expressing affection, which are established still earlier in creatures lower than man, there are established certain modes of behavior expressing subjection.

After recognizing this fact, we shall be prepared to recognize the fact that daily intercourse among the lowest savages, whose small loose groups, scarcely to be called social, are without political or religious regulation, is under a considerable amount of ceremonial regulation. No ruling agency beyond that arising from personal superiority characterizes a horde of Australians; but every such horde has imperative observances. Strangers meeting must remain some time silent; a mile from an encampment approach has to be heralded by loud *cooeys;* a green bough is used as an emblem of peace; and brotherly feeling is indicated by exchange of names. Ceremonial control is highly developed in many places where other forms of control are but rudimentary. The wild Comanche "exacts the observance of his rules of etiquette from strangers," and "is greatly offended" by any breach of them. When Araucanians meet, the inquiries, felicitations, and condolences which custom demands are so elaborate that "the formality occupies ten or fifteen minutes."

That ceremonial restraint, preceding other forms of restraint, continues ever to be the most widely diffused form of restraint we are shown by such facts as that in all intercourse between members of each society, the decisively governmental actions are usually prefaced by this government of observances. The embassy may fail, negotiation may be brought to a close by war, coercion of one society by another may set up wider political rule with its peremptory commands; but there is habitually this more general and vague regulation of conduct preceding the more special and definite. So within a community acts of relatively stringent control coming from ruling agencies, civil and religious, begin with and are qualified by this ceremonial control which not only initiates but in a sense envelops all other. Functionaries, ecclesiastical and political, coercive as their proceedings may be, conform them in large measure to the requirements of courtesy. The priest, however arrogant his assumption, makes a civil salute; and the officer of the law performs his duty subject to certain propitiatory words and movements.

Yet another indication of primordialism may be named. This species of control establishes itself anew with every fresh relation among individuals. Even between intimates greetings signifying continuance of respect begin each renewal of intercourse. And in the presence of a stranger, say in a railway carriage, a certain self-restraint, joined with some small act like the offer of a newspaper, shows the spontaneous rise of a propitiatory behavior such as even the rudest of mankind are not without. So that the modified forms of action caused in men by the presence of their fellows constitute that comparatively vague control out of which other more definite controls are evolved— the primitive undifferentiated kind of government from which the political and religious governments are differentiated, and in which they ever continue immersed.

3. Prestige[1]

Originally *prestige*—here, too, etymology proves to be an *enfant terrible*—means delusion. It is derived from the Latin *praestigiae* (*-arum*)—though it is found in the forms *praestigia* (*-ae*) and *praestigium* (*-ii*) too: the juggler himself (dice-player, rope-walker, "strong man," etc.) was called *praestigiator* (*-oris*). Latin authors and mediaeval writers of glossaries took the word to mean "deceptive juggling tricks," and, as far as we know, did not use it in its present signification. The *praestigiator* threw dice or put coins on a table, then passed them into a small vessel or box, moved the latter about quickly and adroitly, till finally, when you thought they were in a certain place, the coins turned up somewhere else: "The looker-on is deceived by such innocent tricks, being often inclined to presume the sleight of hand to be nothing more or less than magic art."

The practice of French writers in the oldest times was, so far as we have been able to discover, to use the word *prestige* at first in the signification above assigned to the Latin "praestigiae" (*prestige, prestigiateur, -trice, prestigieux*). The use of the word was not restricted to the prestige of prophets, conjurers, demons, but was transferred by analogy to delusions the cause of which is not regarded any longer as supernatural. Diderot actually makes mention of the prestige of harmony. The word "prestige" became transfigured, ennobled, and writers and orators refined it so as to make it applicable to analogies of the remotest character. Rousseau refers to the prestige of our passions, which dazzles the intellect and deceives wisdom.

[1] Adapted from Lewis Leopold, *Prestige*, pp. 16–62. (T. Fisher Unwin, 1913.)

Prestige is the name continually given to every kind of spell, the effect of which reminds us of "prestige" ("cet homme exerce une influence que rassemble à une prestige"—Littré), and to all magic charms and attractive power which is capable of dulling the intellect while it enhances sensation. We may read of the prestige of fame, of the power which, in default of prestige, is brute force; in 1869 numberless placards proclaimed through the length and breadth of Paris that Bourbeau, Minister of Public Instruction, though reputed to be a splendid lawyer, "lacked prestige"—"Bourbeau manque de prestige." The English and German languages make use of the word in the latter meaning as opposed to the imaginary virtue of the conjurer; the same signification is applied, generally speaking, to the Italian and Spanish *prestigio*, only that the Italian *prestigiáo* and the Spanish *prestigiador*, just like the French *prestigiateur*, have, as opposed to the more recent meaning, kept the older significance; neither of them means anything more or less than conjurer or juggler.

The market clown, the rope-walker, the sword-swallower, the reciter of long poems, the clever manipulator who defies imitation—all possess prestige: but on the other hand, prestige surrounds demoniacal spells, wizardry, and all effectiveness not comprehensible by logic.

We state something of someone when we say that he possesses prestige; but our statement is not clear, and the predicate cannot be distinguished from the subject. Of what is analysable, well-known, commonplace, or what we succeed in understanding thoroughly, in attaining or imitating, we do not say that it possesses prestige.

What is the relation between *prestige* and *prejudice?* When what is unintelligible, or mysterious, is at one time received with enthusiasm, at another with indignation, *what renders necessary these two extreme sentiments of appreciation* which, though appearing under apparently identical circumstances, are diametrically opposed to one another?

The most general form of social prejudice is that of race. A *foreigner* is received with prejudice, conception, or prestige. If we put "conception" aside we find prejudice and prestige facing one another. We see this split most clearly demonstrated if we observe the differences of conduct in the reception of strangers by primitive peoples. In Yrjö Hirn's *Origins of Art* we are told that those travellers who have learned the tongues of savages have often observed that their persons were made the subjects of extemporized poems by the respective savages. Sometimes these verses are of a derisive character; at other times they glorify the white man. When do they deride, when glorify?

Where strong prejudice values are present, as in the case of Negroes, every conception of equality and nationalism incorporated in the statute-book is perverted. All that *appears* permanently divergent is made the subject of damnatory prejudice; and the more apparent and seeming, the more primitive the impression that restrains the more general the prejudice; smell affects more keenly than form, and form more than mode of thought. If a member of a nation is not typical, but exercises an exclusive, personal impression on us, he possesses prestige; if he is typical, he is indifferent to us, or we look down upon him and consider him comical. To sum up: the stranger whom we feel to be divergent as compared with ourselves is indifferent or the object of prejudice; the stranger whom we feel ourselves unable to measure by our own standard, whose measure—not his qualities— we feel to be different, we receive with prestige. We look with prejudice on the stranger whom we dissociate, and receive with prestige the stranger who is dissociated.

Even in the animal world we come across individuals consistently treated with deference, of which, in his work on the psychical world of animals, Perty has plenty to tell us: "Even in the animal world," he says, "there are certain eminent individuals, which in comparison with the other members of their species show a superiority of capability, brain power, and force of will, and obtain a *predominance* over the other animals." Cuvier observed the same in the case of a buck which had only one horn; Grant tells us of a certain ourang-outang which got the upper hand of the rest of the monkeys and often threatened them with the stick; from Naumann we hear of a clever crane which ruled over all the domestic animals and quickly settled any quarrels that arose among them. Far more important than these somewhat obscure observations is the peculiar social mechanism of the animal world to be found in the mechanical following of the leaders of flocks and herds. But this obedience is so conspicuously instinctive, so genuine, and so little varying in substance and intensity, that it can hardly be identified with prestige. Bees are strong royalists; but the extent to which their selection of a queen is instinctive and strictly exclusive is proved by the fact that the smell of a strange queen forced on them makes them hate her; they kill her or torture her—though the same working bees prefer to die of hunger rather than allow their own queen to starve.

Things are radically changed when animals are brought face to face with man. Some animals sympathize with men, and like to take part in their hunting and fighting, as the dog and the horse; others subject themselves as a result of force. Consequently men have succeeded in *domesticating* a number of species of animals. It is here that we find the first traces, in the animal world, of phenomena, reactions of conduct in the course of development, which, to a certain extent, remind us of the reception of prestige. The behaviour of a dog, says Darwin, which returns to its master after being absent—or the conduct of a monkey, when it returns to its beloved keeper—*is far different from what these animals display towards beings of the same order as themselves*. In the latter case the expressions of joy seem to be somewhat less demonstrative, and all their actions evince a feeling of equality. Even Professor Braubach declares that *a dog looks upon its master as a divine person*. Brehm gives us a description of the tender respect shown towards his children by a chimpanzee that had been brought to his home and domesticated. "When we first introduced my little six-weeks-old daughter to him," he says, "at first he regarded the child with evident astonishment, as if desirous to convince himself of its human character, then touched its face with one finger with remarkable gentleness, and amiably offered to shake hands. This trifling characteristic, which I observed in the case of all chimpanzees reared in my house, is worthy of particular emphasis, because it seems to prove that *our man-monkey descries and pays homage to that higher being, man, even in the tiniest child. On the other hand, he by no means shows any such friendly feelings towards creatures like himself—not even towards little ones*."

In every stage of the development of savage peoples we come across classical examples of mock kings—of the "primus inter pares," "duces ex virtute," *not* "ex nobilitate reges"—of rational and valued leaders. The savages of Chile elect as their chief the man who is able to carry the trunk of a tree farthest. In other places, military prowess, command of words, crafts, a knowledge of spells are the causal sources of the usually extremely trifling homage due to the chieftain. "Savage hordes in the lowest stage of civilization are organized, like troops of monkeys, on the basis of authority. The strongest old male by virtue of his strength acquires a certain ascendancy, which lasts as long as his physical strength is superior to that of every other male. . . . ."

Beyond that given by nature, primitive society recognizes no other prestige, for the society of savages lacks the subjective conditions of prestige—settlement in large numbers and permanency. The lack of distance compels the savage to respect only persons who hold their own in his presence: this conspicuous clearness of the estimation of primitive peoples is the cause that has prevailed on us to dwell so long on this point. That the cause of this want of prestige among savages is the lack of concentration in masses, not any esoteric peculiarity, is proved by the profound psychological appreciation of the distances created by nature, and still more by the expansion of tribal life into a barbarian one. The tenfold increase of the number of a tribe renders difficult a logical, ethical, or aesthetic selection of a leader, as well as an intuitive control of spells and superstitions.

The dramatic *mise en scène* of human prestige coincides with the first appearance of this concentration in masses, and triumphs with its triumph.

4. Prestige and Status in South East Africa[1]

In no other land under the British flag, except, perhaps, in the Far East, certainly in none of the great self-governing colonies with which we rank ourselves, is the position of white man *qua* white man so high, his status so impugnable, as in South East Africa. Differing in much else, the race instinct binds the whites together to demand recognition as a member of the ruling and inviolable caste, even for the poorest, the degraded of their race. And this position connotes freedom from all manual and menial toil; without hesitation the white man demands this freedom, without question the black man accedes and takes up the burden, obeying the race command of one who may be his personal inferior. It is difficult to convey to one who has never known this distinction the way in which the very atmosphere is charged with it in South East Africa. A white oligarchy, every

[1] Adapted from Maurice S. Evans, *Black and White in South East Africa,* pp. 15-35. (Longmans, Green & Co., 1911.)

member of the race an aristocrat; a black proletariat, every member of the race a server; the line of cleavage as clear and deep as the colours. The less able and vigorous of our race, thus protected, find here an ease, a comfort, a recognition to which their personal worth would never entitle them in a homogeneous white population.

When uncontaminated by contact with the lower forms of our civilization, the native is courteous and polite. Even to-day, changed for the worse as he is declared to be by most authorities, a European could ride or walk alone, unarmed even with a switch, all through the locations of Natal and Zululand, scores of miles away from the house of any white man, and receive nothing but courteous deference from the natives. If he met, as he certainly would, troops of young men, dressed in all their barbaric finery, going to wedding or dance, armed with sticks and shields, full of hot young blood, they would still stand out of the narrow path, giving to the white man the right of way and saluting as he passed. I have thus travelled alone all over South East Africa, among thousands of blacks and never a white man near, and I cannot remember the natives, even if met in scores or hundreds, ever disputing the way for a moment. All over Africa, winding and zigzagging over hill and dale, over grassland and through forest, from kraal to kraal, and tribe to tribe, go the paths of the natives. In these narrow paths worn in the grass by the feet of the passers, you could travel from Natal to Benguela and back again to Mombasa. Only wide enough for one to travel thereon, if opposite parties meet one must give way; cheerfully, courteously, without cringing, often with respectful salute, does the native stand on one side allowing the white man to pass. One accepts it without thought; it is the expected, but if pondered upon it is suggestive of much.

5. Taboo[1]

Rules of holiness in the sense just explained, i.e., a system of restrictions on man's arbitrary use of natural things, enforced by the dread of supernatural penalties, are found among all primitive peoples. It is convenient to have a distinct name for this primitive institution, to mark it off from the later developments of the idea of holiness in advanced religions, and for this purpose the Polynesian term "taboo"

[1] From W. Robertson Smith, *The Religion of the Semites*, pp. 152–447.   (Adam and Charles Black, 1907.)

has been selected. The field covered by taboos among savage and half-savage races is very wide, for there is no part of life in which the savage does not feel himself to be surrounded by mysterious agencies and recognise the need of walking warily. Moreover all taboos do not belong to religion proper, that is, they are not always rules of conduct for the regulation of man's contact with deities that, when taken in the right way, may be counted on as friendly, but rather appear in many cases to be precautions against the approach of malignant enemies—against contact with evil spirits and the like. Thus alongside of taboos that exactly correspond to rules of holiness, protecting the inviolability of idols and sanctuaries, priest and chiefs, and generally of all persons and things pertaining to the gods and their worship, we find another kind of taboo which in the Semitic field has its parallel in rules of uncleanness. Women after childbirth, men who have touched a dead body, and so forth, are temporarily taboo and separated from human society, just as the same persons are unclean in Semitic religion. In these cases the person under taboo is not regarded as holy, for he is separated from approach to the sanctuary as well as from contact with men; but his act or condition is somehow associated with supernatural dangers, arising, according to the common savage explanation, from the presence of formidable spirits which are shunned like an infectious disease. In most savage societies no sharp line seems to be drawn between the two kinds of taboo just indicated, and even in more advanced nations the notions of holiness and uncleanness often touch. Among the Syrians, for example, swine's flesh was taboo, but it was an open question whether this was because the animal was holy or because it was unclean. But though not precise, the distinction between what is holy and what is unclean is real; in rules of holiness the motive is respect for the gods, in rules of uncleanliness it is primarily fear of an unknown or hostile power, though ultimately, as we see in the Levitical legislation, the law of clean and unclean may be brought within the sphere of divine ordinances, on the view that uncleanness is hateful to God and must be avoided by all that have to do with Him.

The fact that all the Semites have rules of uncleanness as well as rules of holiness, that the boundary between the two is often vague, and that the former as well as the latter present the most startling agreement in point of detail with savage taboos, leaves no reasonable doubt as to the origin and ultimate relations of the idea of holiness. On the other hand, the fact that the Semites—or at least the northern Semites—distinguish between the holy and the unclean, marks a real advance above savagery. All taboos are inspired by awe of the supernatural, but there is a great moral difference between precautions against the invasion of mysterious hostile powers and precautions founded on respect for the prerogative of a friendly god. The former belong to magical superstition—the barrenest of all aberrations of the savage imagination—which, being founded only on fear, acts merely as a bar to progress and an impediment to the free use of nature by human energy and industry. But the restrictions on individual licence which are due to respect for a known and friendly power allied to man, however trivial and absurd they may appear to us in their details, contain within them germinant principles of social progress and moral order. To know that one has the mysterious powers of nature on one's side so long as one acts in conformity with certain rules, gives a man strength and courage to pursue the task of the subjugation of nature to his service. To restrain one's individual licence, not out of slavish fear, but from respect for a higher and beneficent power, is a moral discipline of which the value does not altogether depend on the reasonableness of sacred restrictions; an English schoolboy is subject to many unreasonable taboos, which are not without value in the formation of character. But finally, and above all, the very association of the idea of holiness with a beneficent deity, whose own interests are bound up with the interests of a community, makes it inevitable that the laws of social and moral order, as well as mere external precepts of physical observance, shall be placed under the sanction of the god of the community. Breaches of social order are recognised as offences against the holiness of the deity, and the development of law and morals is made possible, at a stage when human sanctions are still wanting, or too imperfectly administered to have much power, by the belief that the restrictions on human licence which are necessary to social well-being are conditions imposed by the god for the maintenance of a good understanding between himself and his worshippers.

Various parallels between savage taboos and Semitic rules of holiness and uncleanness will come before us from time to time; but it may be useful to bring together at this point some detailed evidences that the two are in their origin indistinguishable.

Holy and unclean things have this in common, that in both cases certain restrictions lie on men's use of and contact with them, and that the breach of these restrictions involves supernatural dangers. The difference between the two appears, not in their relation to man's ordinary life, but in their relation to the gods. Holy things are not free to man, because they pertain to the gods; uncleanness is shunned, according to the view taken in the higher Semitic religions, because it is hateful to the god, and therefore not to be tolerated in his sanctuary, his worshippers, or his land. But that this explanation is not primitive can hardly be doubted when we consider that the acts that cause uncleanness are exactly the same which among savage nations place a man under taboo, and that these acts are often involuntary, and often innocent, or even necessary to society. The savage, accordingly, imposes a taboo on a woman in childbed, or during her courses, and on the man who touches a corpse, not out of any regard for the gods, but simply because birth and everything connected with the propagation of the species on the one hand, and disease and death on the other, seem to him to involve the action of superhuman agencies of a dangerous kind. If he attempts to explain, he does so by supposing that on these occasions spirits of deadly power are present; at all events the persons involved seem to him to be sources of mysterious danger, which has all the characters of an infection and may extend to other people unless due precautions are observed. This is not scientific, but it is perfectly intelligible, and forms the basis of a consistent system of practice; whereas, when the rules of uncleanness are made to rest on the will of the gods, they appear altogether arbitrary and meaningless. The affinity of such taboos with laws of uncleanness comes out most clearly when we observe that uncleanness is treated like a contagion, which has to be washed away or otherwise eliminated by physical means. Take the rules about the uncleanness produced by the carcases of vermin in Lev. 11:32 ff.; whatever they touch must be washed; the water itself is then unclean, and can propagate the contagion; nay, if the defilement affect an (unglazed) earthen pot, it is supposed to sink into the pores, and cannot be washed out, so that the pot must be broken. Rules like this have nothing in common with the spirit of Hebrew religion; they can

only be remains of a primitive superstition, like that of the savage
who shuns the blood of uncleanness, and such like things, as a supernatural and deadly virus.   The antiquity of the Hebrew taboos, for
such they are, is shown by the way in which many of them reappear
in Arabia;   cf. for example Deut. 21:12, 13, with the Arabian ceremonies for removing the impurity of widowhood.   In the Arabian
form the ritual is of purely savage type;   the danger to life that made
it unsafe for a man to marry the woman was transferred in the most
materialistic way to an animal, which it was believed generally died
in consequence, or to a bird.

B.   PUBLIC OPINION

1.   The Myth[1]

There is no process by which the future can be predicted scientifically, nor even one which enables us to discuss whether one hypothesis about it is better than another;   it has been proved by too many
memorable examples that the greatest men have committed prodigious
errors in thus desiring to make predictions about even the least
distant future.

And yet, without leaving the present, without reasoning about
this future, which seems forever condemned to escape our reason, we
should be unable to act at all.   Experience shows that the *framing of
a future, in some indeterminate time*, may, when it is done in a certain way, be very effective, and have very few inconveniences;   this
happens when the anticipations of the future take the form of those
myths, which enclose with them all the strongest inclinations of a
people, of a party, or of a class, inclinations which recur to the mind
with the insistence of instincts in all the circumstances of life;   and
which give an aspect of complete reality to the hopes of immediate
action by which, more easily than by any other method, men can
reform their desires, passions, and mental activity.   We know, moreover, that these social myths in no way prevent a man profiting by
the observations which he makes in the course of his life, and form no
obstacle to the pursuit of his normal occupations.

The truth of this may be shown by numerous examples.

[1] From Georges Sorel, *Reflections on Violence*, pp. 133–37.   (B. W. Huebsch,
1912.)

The first Christians expected the return of Christ and the total ruin of the pagan world, with the inauguration of the kingdom of the saints, at the end of the first generation. The catastrophe did not come to pass, but Christian thought profited so greatly from the apocalyptic myth that certain contemporary scholars maintain that the whole preaching of Christ referred solely to this one point. The hopes which Luther and Calvin had formed of the religious exaltation of Europe were by no means realised; these fathers of the Reformation very soon seemed men of a past era; for present-day Protestants they belong rather to the Middle Ages than to modern times, and the problems which troubled them most occupy very little place in contemporary Protestantism. Must we for that reason deny the immense result which came from their dreams of Christian renovation? It must be admitted that the real developments of the Revolution did not in any way resemble the enchanting pictures which created the enthusiasm of its first adepts; but without those pictures, would the Revolution have been victorious? Many Utopias were mixed up with the Revolutionary myth, because it had been formed by a society passionately fond of imaginative literature, full of confidence in the "science," and very little acquainted with the economic history of the past. These Utopias came to nothing; but it may be asked whether the Revolution was not a much more profound transformation than those dreamed of by the people who in the eighteenth century had invented social Utopias. In our own times Mazzini pursued what the wiseacres of his time called a mad chimera; but it can no longer be denied that, without Mazzini, Italy would never have become a great power, and that he did more for Italian unity than Cavour and all the politicians of his school.

A knowledge of what the myths contain in the way of details which will actually form part of the history of the future is then of small importance; they are not astrological almanacs; it is even possible that nothing which they contain will ever come to pass—as was the case with the catastrophe expected by the first Christians. In our own daily life, are we not familiar with the fact that what actually happens is very different from our preconceived notion of it? And that does not prevent us from continuing to make resolutions. Psychologists say that there is heterogeneity between the ends in view and the ends actually realised: the slightest experience of life reveals this law to us, which Spencer transferred into nature, to extract therefrom his theory of the multiplication of effects.

The myth must be judged as a means of acting on the present; any attempt to discuss how far it can be taken literally as future history is devoid of sense. *It is the myth in its entirety which is alone important:* its parts are only of interest in so far as they bring out the main idea. No useful purpose is served, therefore, in arguing about the incidents which may occur in the course of a social war, and about the decisive conflicts which may give victory to the proletariat; even supposing the revolutionaries to have been wholly and entirely deluded in setting up this imaginary picture of the general strike, this picture may yet have been, in the course of the preparation for the revolution, a great element of strength, if it has embraced all the aspirations of socialism, and if it has given to the whole body of revolutionary thought a precision and a rigidity which no other method of thought could have given.

To estimate, then, the significance of the idea of the general strike, all the methods of discussion which are current among politicians, sociologists, or people with pretensions to political science, must be abandoned. Everything which its opponents endeavour to establish may be conceded to them, without reducing in any way the value of the theory which they think they have refuted. The question whether the general strike is a partial reality, or only a product of popular imagination, is of little importance. All that it is necessary to know is, whether the general strike contains everything that the socialist doctrine expects of the revolutionary proletariat.

To solve this question, we are no longer compelled to argue learnedly about the future; we are not obliged to indulge in lofty reflections about philosophy, history, or economics; we are not on the plane of theories, and we can remain on the level of observable facts. We have to question men who take a very active part in the real revolutionary movement amidst the proletariat, men who do not aspire to climb into the middle class and whose mind is not dominated by corporative prejudices. These men may be deceived about an infinite number of political, economical, or moral questions; but their testimony is decisive, sovereign, and irrefutable when it is a question of knowing what are the ideas which most powerfully move them and their comrades, which most appeal to them as being identical with their socialistic conceptions, and thanks to which their reason, their hopes, and their way of looking at particular facts seem to make but one indivisible unity.

Thanks to these men, we know that the general strike is indeed what I have said: the *myth* in which socialism is wholly comprised, i.e., a body of images capable of evoking instinctively all the sentiments which correspond to the different manifestations of the war undertaken by socialism against modern society. Strikes have engendered in the proletariat the noblest, deepest, and most moving sentiments that they possess; the general strike groups them all in a co-ordinated picture, and, by bringing them together, gives to each one of them its maximum of intensity; appealing to their painful memories of particular conflicts, it colours with an intense life all the details of the composition presented to consciousness. We thus obtain that intuition of socialism which language cannot give us with perfect clearness—and we obtain it as a whole, perceived instantaneously.

2. The Growth of a Legend[1]

Hardly had the German armies entered Belgium when strange rumors began to circulate. They spread from place to place, they were reproduced by the press, and they soon permeated the whole of Germany. It was said that the Belgian people, instigated by the clergy, had intervened perfidiously in the hostilities; had attacked by surprise isolated detachments; had indicated to the enemy the positions occupied by the troops; that women, old men, and even children had been guilty of horrible atrocities upon wounded and defenseless German soldiers, tearing out their eyes and cutting off fingers, nose, or ears; that the priests from their pulpits had exhorted the people to commit these crimes, promising them as a reward the Kingdom of Heaven, and had even taken the lead in this barbarity.

Public credulity accepted these stories. The highest powers in the state welcomed them without hesitation and indorsed them with their authority. Even the Emperor echoed them, and, taking them for a text, advanced, in the famous telegram of September 8, 1914, addressed to the President of the United States, the most terrible accusations against the Belgian people and clergy.

[1] Adapted from Fernand van Langenhove, *The Growth of a Legend*, pp. 5–275. (G. P. Putnam's Sons, 1916.)

At the time of the invasion of Belgium, it was the German army which, as we have seen, constituted the chief breeding ground for legendary stories. These were disseminated with great rapidity among the troops; the *liaison* officers, the dispatch riders, the food convoys, the victualling posts assured the diffusion of them.

These stories were not delayed in reaching Germany. As in most wars, it was the returning soldiery who were responsible for the transmission of them.

From the first day of hostilities in enemy territory the fighting troops were in constant touch with those behind them. Through the frontier towns there was a continual passage of convoys, returning empty or loaded with prisoners and wounded. These last, together with the escorting soldiers, were immediately surrounded and pressed for news by an eager crowd. It is they who brought the first stories.

As a silent listener, seated on the boulevards, I have noticed how curious people, men and women, question the wounded who are resting there, suggesting to them answers to inquiries on the subject of the battles, the losses, and the atrocities of war; how they interpret silence as an affirmative answer and how they wish to have confirmed things always more terrible. I am convinced that shortly afterward they will repeat the conversation, adding that they have heard it as the personal experience of somebody present at the affair.

In their oral form stories of this kind are not definite, their substance is malleable; they can be modified according to the taste of the narrator; they transform themselves; they evolve. To sum up, not only do the soldiers, returned from the field of battle, insure the transmission of the stories, they also elaborate them.

The military post links the campaigning army directly with Germany. The soldiers write home, and in their letters they tell of their adventures, which people are eager to hear, and naturally they include the rumors current among the troops. Thus a soldier of the Landsturm writes to his wife that he has seen at Liège a dozen priests condemned to death because they put a price on the heads of German soldiers; he had also seen there civilians who had cut off the breasts of a Red Cross nurse. Again, a Hessian schoolmaster tells in a letter how his detachment had been treacherously attacked at Ch——— by the inhabitants, with the curé at their head.

Submitted to the test of the German military inquiry these stories are shown to be without foundation. Received from the front and narrated by a soldier who professes to have been an eyewitness, they are nevertheless clothed in the public view with special authority.

Welcomed without control by the press, the stories recounted in letters from the front appear, however, in the eyes of the readers of a paper clothed with a new authority—that which attaches to printed matter. They lose in the columns of a paper their individual and particular character. Those who send them have, as the *Kölnische Volkszeitung* notes, usually effaced all personal allusions. The statements thus obtain a substance and an objectivity of which they would otherwise be devoid. Mixed with authentic news, they are accepted by the public without mistrust. Is not their appearance in the paper a guaranty of accuracy?

Besides imposing itself on public credulity, the printed story fixes itself in the mind. It takes a lasting form. It has entered permanently into consciousness, and more, it has become a source of reference.

All these pseudo-historical publications are, however, only one aspect of the abundant literary production of the Great War. All the varieties of popular literature, the romances of cloak and sword, the stories of adventure, the collections of news and anecdotes, the theater itself, are in turn devoted to military events. The great public loves lively activity, extraordinary situations, and sensational circumstances calculated to strike the imagination and cause a shiver of horror.

So one finds in this literature of the lower classes the principal legendary episodes of which we have studied the origin and followed the development; accommodated to a fiction, woven into a web of intrigue, they have undergone new transformations; they have lost every indication of their source; they are transposed in the new circumstances imagined for them; they have usually been dissociated from the circumstances which individualize them and fix their time and place. The thematic motives from which they spring nevertheless remain clearly recognizable.

The legendary stories have thus attained the last stage of their elaboration and completed their diffusion. They have penetrated not only into the purlieus of the cities but into distant countries;

into centers of education as among the popular classes. Wounded convalescents and soldiers on leave at home for a time have told them to the city man and to the peasant. Both have found them in letters from the front; both have read them in journals and books, both have listened to the warnings of the government and to the imperial word. The schoolteacher has mixed these episodes with his teaching; he has nourished with them infantile imaginations. Scholars have read the text of them in their classbooks and have enacted them in the games inspired by the war; they have told them at home in the family circle, giving them the authority attached to the master's word.

Everywhere these accounts have been the subject of ardent commentaries; in the village, in the councils held upon doorsteps, and in the barrooms of inns; in the big cafés, the trams, and the public promenades of towns. Everywhere they have become an ordinary topic of conversation, everywhere they have met with ready credence. The term *franc tireur* has become familiar. Its use is general and its acceptance widespread.

A collection of prayers for the use of the Catholic German soldiers includes this incredible text: "Shame and malediction on him who wishes to act like the Belgian and French, perfidious and cruel, who have even attacked defenseless wounded."

3. Ritual, Myth, and Dogma[1]

The antique religions had for the most part no creed; they consisted entirely of institutions and practices. No doubt, men will not habitually follow certain practices without attaching a meaning to them; but as a rule we find that while the practice was rigorously fixed, the meaning attached to it was extremely vague, and the same rite was explained by different people in different ways, without any question of orthodoxy or heterodoxy arising in consequence. In ancient Greece, for example, certain things were done at a temple, and people were agreed that it would be impious not to do them. But if you had asked why they were done, you would probably have had several mutually contradictory explanations from different persons, and no one would have thought it a matter of the least reli-

[1] From W. Robertson Smith, *The Religion of the Semites*, pp. 16–24. (Adam and Charles Black, 1907.)

gious importance which of these you chose to adopt. Indeed, the explanations offered would not have been of a kind to stir any strong feeling; for in most cases they would have been merely different stories as to the circumstances under which the rite first came to be established, by the command or by the direct example of the god. The rite, in short, was connected not with a dogma but with a myth.

In all the antique religions, mythology takes the place of dogma; that is, the sacred lore of priests and people, so far as it does not consist of mere rules for the performance of religious acts, assumes the form of stories about the gods; and these stories afford the only explanation that is offered of the precepts of religion and the prescribed rules of ritual. But, strictly speaking, this mythology was no essential part of ancient religion, for it had no sacred sanction and no binding force on the worshippers. The myths connected with individual sanctuaries and ceremonies were merely part of the apparatus of the worship; they served to excite the fancy and sustain the interest of the worshipper; but he was often offered a choice of several accounts of the same thing, and, provided that he fulfilled the ritual with accuracy, no one cared what he believed about its origin. Belief in a certain series of myths was neither obligatory as a part of true religion, nor was it supposed that, by believing, a man acquired religious merit and conciliated the favour of the gods. What was obligatory or meritorious was the exact performance of certain sacred acts prescribed by religious tradition. This being so, it follows that mythology ought not to take the prominent place that is too often assigned to it in the scientific study of ancient faiths. So far as myths consist of explanations of ritual, their value is altogether secondary, and it may be affirmed with confidence that in almost every case the myth was derived from the ritual, and not the ritual from the myth; for the ritual was fixed and the myth was variable, the ritual was obligatory and faith in the myth was at the discretion of the worshipper. The conclusion is, that in the study of ancient religions we must begin, not with myth, but with ritual and traditional usage.

Nor can it be fairly set against this conclusion, that there are certain myths which are not mere explanations of traditional practices, but exhibit the beginnings of larger religious speculation, or of an attempt to systematise and reduce to order the motley variety of local worships and beliefs.   For in this case the secondary character of the myths is still more clearly marked.   They are either products of early philosophy, reflecting on the nature of the universe; or they are political in scope, being designed to supply a thread of union between the various worships of groups, originally distinct, which have been united into one social or political organism; or, finally, they are due to the free play of epic imagination.   But philosophy, politics, and poetry are something more, or something less, than religion pure and simple.

There can be no doubt that, in the later stages of ancient religions, mythology acquired an increased importance.   In the struggle of heathenism with scepticism on the one hand and Christianity on the other, the supporters of the old traditional religions were driven to search for ideas of a modern cast, which they could represent as the true inner meaning of the traditional rites.   To this end they laid hold of the old myths, and applied to them an allegorical system of interpretation.   Myth interpreted by the aid of allegory became the favourite means of infusing a new significance into ancient forms. But the theories thus developed are the falsest of false guides as to the original meaning of the old religions.

Religion in primitive times was not a system of belief with practical applications; it was a body of fixed traditional practices, to which every member of society conformed as a matter of course. Men would not be men if they agreed to do certain things without having a reason for their action; but in ancient religion the reason was not first formulated as a doctrine and then expressed in practice, but conversely, practice preceded doctrinal theory.   Men form general rules of conduct before they begin to express general principles in words; political institutions are older than political theories, and in like manner religious institutions are older than religious theories. This analogy is not arbitrarily chosen, for in fact the parallelism in ancient society between religious and political institutions is complete. In each sphere great importance was attached to form and precedent, but the explanation why the precedent was followed consisted merely of a legend as to its first establishment.   That the precedent, once established, was authoritative did not appear to require any proof. The rules of society were based on precedent, and the continued existence of the society was sufficient reason why a precedent once set should continue to be followed.

I say that the oldest religious and political institutions present a close analogy. It would be more correct to say that they were parts of one whole of social custom. Religion was a part of the organised social life into which a man was born, and to which he conformed through life in the same unconscious way in which men fall into any habitual practice of the society in which they live. Men took the gods and their worship for granted, just as they took the other usages of the state for granted, and if they reasoned or speculated about them, they did so on the presupposition that the traditional usages were fixed things, behind which their reasonings must not go, and which no reasoning could be allowed to overturn. To us moderns religion is above all a matter of individual conviction and reasoned belief, but to the ancients it was a part of the citizen's public life, reduced to fixed forms, which he was not bound to understand and was not at liberty to criticise or to neglect. Religious nonconformity was an offence against the state; for if sacred tradition was tampered with the bases of society were undermined, and the favour of the gods was forfeited. But so long as the prescribed forms were duly observed, a man was recognised as truly pious, and no one asked how his religion was rooted in his heart or affected his reason. Like political duty, of which indeed it was a part, religion was entirely comprehended in the observance of certain fixed rules of outward conduct.

From the antique point of view, indeed, the question what the gods are in themselves is not a religious but a speculative one; what is requisite to religion is a practical acquaintance with the rules on which the deity acts and on which he expects his worshippers to frame their conduct—what in II Kings 17:26 is called the "manner" or rather the "customary law" (*mishpat*) of the god of the land. This is true even of the religion of Israel. When the prophets speak of the knowledge of God, they always mean a practical knowledge of the laws and principles of His government in Israel, and a summary expression for religion as a whole is "the knowledge and fear of Jehovah," i.e., the knowledge of what Jehovah prescribes, combined with a reverent obedience.

The traditional usages of religion had grown up gradually in the course of many centuries, and reflected habits of thought characteristic of very diverse stages of man's intellectual and moral development. No one conception of the nature of the gods could possibly afford the clue to all parts of that motley complex of rites and ceremonies which the later paganism had received by inheritance, from a series of ancestors in every state of culture from pure savagery upwards. The record of the religious thought of mankind, as it is embodied in religious institutions, resembles the geological record of the history of the earth's crust; the new and the old are preserved side by side or rather layer upon layer. The classification of ritual formations in their proper sequence is the first step towards their explanation, and that explanation itself must take the form, not of a speculative theory, but of a rational life-history.

4. The Nature of Public Opinion[1]

"*Vox populi* may be *vox Dei*, but very little attention shows that there has never been any agreement as to what *vox* means or as to what *populus* means." In spite of endless discussions about democracy, this remark of Sir Henry Maine is still so far true that no other excuse is needed for studying the conceptions which lie at the very base of popular government. In doing so one must distinguish the form from he substance; for the world of politics is full of forms in which the spirit is dead—mere shams, but sometimes not recognized as such even by the chief actors, sometimes deceiving the outside multitude, sometimes no longer misleading anyone. Shams, are, indeed, not without value. Political shams have done for English government what fictions have done for English law. They have promoted growth without revolutionary change. But while shams play an important part in political evolution, they are snares for the political philosopher who fails to see through them, who ascribes to the forms a meaning that they do not really possess. Popular government may in substance exist under the form of a monarchy, and an autocratic despotism can be set up without destroying the forms of democracy. If we look through the forms to observe the vital forces behind them; if we fix our attention, not on the procedure, the extent of the franchise, the machinery of elections, and such outward things, but on the essence of the matter, popular government, in one important

[1] Adapted from A. Lawrence Lowell, *Public Opinion and Popular Government*, pp. 3-14. (Longmans, Green & Co., 1913.)

aspect at least, may be said to consist of the control of political affairs by public opinion.

If two highwaymen meet a belated traveler on a dark road and propose to relieve him of his watch and wallet, it would clearly be an abuse of terms to say that in the assemblage on that lonely spot there was a public opinion in favor of a redistribution of property. Nor would it make any difference, for this purpose, whether there were two highwaymen and one traveler, or one robber and two victims. The absurdity in such a case of speaking about the duty of the minority to submit to the verdict of public opinion is self-evident; and it is not due to the fact that the three men on the road form part of a larger community, or that they are subject to the jurisdiction of a common government. The expression would be quite as inappropriate if no organized state existed; on a savage island, for example, where two cannibals were greedy to devour one shipwrecked mariner. In short, the three men in each of the cases supposed do not form a community that is capable of a public opinion on the question involved. May this not be equally true under an organized government, among people that are for certain purposes a community?

To take an illustration nearer home. At the time of the Reconstruction that followed the American Civil War the question whether public opinion in a southern state was or was not in favor of extending the suffrage to the Negroes could not in any true sense be said to depend on which of the two races had a slight numerical majority. One opinion may have been public or general in regard to the whites, the other public or general in regard to the Negroes, but neither opinion was public or general in regard to the whole population. Examples of this kind could be multiplied indefinitely. They can be found in Ireland, in Austria-Hungary, in Turkey, in India, in any country where the cleavage of race, religion, or politics is sharp and deep enough to cut the community into fragments too far apart for an accord on fundamental matters.

In all these instances an opinion cannot be public or general with respect to both elements in the state. For that purpose they are as distinct as if they belonged to different commonwealths. You may count heads, you may break heads, you may impose uniformity by force; but on the matters at stake the two elements do not form a community capable of an opinion that is in any rational sense public or general. If we are to employ the' term in a sense that is significant for government, that imports any obligation moral or political on the part of the minority, surely enough has been said to show that the opinion of a mere majority does not by itself always suffice. Something more is clearly needed.

But if the opinion of a majority does not of itself constitute a public opinion, it is equally certain that unanimity is not required. Unanimous opinion is of no importance for our purpose, because it is perfectly sure to be effective in any form of government, however despotic, and it is, therefore, of no particular interest in the study of democracy. Legislation by unanimity was actually tried in the kingdom of Poland, where each member of the assembly had the right of *liberum veto* on any measure, and it prevented progress, fostered violence, and spelled failure. The Polish system has been lauded as the acme of liberty, but in fact it was directly opposed to the fundamental principle of modern popular government; that is, the conduct of public affairs in accord with a public opinion which is general, although not universal, and which implies under certain conditions a duty on the part of the minority to submit.

A body of men are politically capable of a public opinion only so far as they are agreed upon the ends and aims of government and upon the principles by which those ends shall be attained. They must be united, also, about the means whereby the action of the government is to be determined, in a conviction, for example, that the views of a majority—or it may be some other portion of their numbers—ought to prevail, and a political community as a whole is capable of public opinion only when this is true of the great bulk of the citizens. Such an assumption was implied, though usually not expressed in all theories of the social compact; and, indeed, it is involved in all theories that base rightful government upon the consent of the governed, for the consent required is not a universal approval by all the people of every measure enacted, but a consensus in regard to the legitimate character of the ruling authority and its right to decide the questions that arise.

One more remark must be made before quitting the subject of the relation of public opinion to the opinion of the majority. The late Gabriel Tarde, with his habitual keen insight, insisted on the importance of the intensity of belief as a factor in the spread of opinions.

There is a common impression that public opinion depends upon and is measured by the mere number of persons to be found on each side of a question; but this is far from accurate. If 49 per cent of a community feel very strongly on one side, and 51 per cent are luke-warmly on the other, the former opinion has the greater public force behind it and is certain to prevail ultimately, if it does not at once.

One man who holds his belief tenaciously counts for as much as several men who hold theirs weakly, because he is more aggressive and thereby compels and overawes others into apparent agreement with him, or at least into silence and inaction. This is, perhaps, especially true of moral questions. It is not improbable that a large part of the accepted moral code is maintained by the earnestness of a minority, while more than half of the community is indifferent or unconvinced. In short, public opinion is not strictly the opinion of the numerical majority, and no form of its expression measures the mere majority, for individual views are always to some extent weighed as well as counted.

Without attempting to consider how the weight attaching to in-tensity and intelligence can be accurately gauged, it is enough for our purpose to point out that when we speak of the opinion of a majority we mean, not the numerical, but the effective, majority.

5. Public Opinion and the Mores[1]

We are interested in public opinion, I suppose, because public opinion is, in the long run, the sovereign power in the state. There is not now, and probably there never has been, a government that did not rest on public opinion. The best evidence of this is the fact that all governments have invariably sought either to *control* or, at least, to inspire and direct it.

The Kaiser had his "official" and his "semiofficial" organs. The communists in Russia have taken possession of the schools. It is in the schoolroom that the bolshevists propose to complete the revolu-tion. Hume, the English historian, who was also the greatest of English philosophers, said:

As force is always on the side of the governed, the governors have nothing to support them but opinion. It is therefore on opinion only that government is founded; and this maxim extends to the most despotic and the most military governments as well as to the most free and popular.

[1] From Robert E. Park, *The Crowd and the Public*. (Unpublished manu-script.)

The soldan of Egypt, or the emperor of Rome, might drive their helpless subjects, like brute beasts, against their sentiments and inclinations, but he must at least have led his mameluks, or praetorian bands, like men, by their opinions.

Hume's statement is too epigrammatic to be true. Governments can and do maintain themselves by force rather than consent. Public opinion to be effective must be organized. The policy of divide and conquer succeeds not merely when directed against the enemy's battalions, but especially when directed against his morale. Cortez in Mexico, the Belgians in the Congo, the English in India, have shown how the thing can be done. More highly organized peoples are governed "against their sentiments and inclinations" in subtler ways.

Caspar Schmidt, "Max Stirner," the most consistent of anarchists, said the last tyranny is the tyranny of the idea. The last tyrant, in other words, is the propagandist, the individual who gives a "slant" to the facts in order to promote his own conception of the welfare of the community.

We use the word public opinion in a wider and in a narrower sense. The public, the popular mind, is controlled by something more than opinion, or public opinion, in the narrower sense. It is controlled, for example, by fashion and by advertising.

We are living today under the subtle tyranny of the advertising man. He tells us what to wear, and makes us wear it. He tells us what to eat, and makes us eat it. We do not resent this tyranny. We do not feel it. We do what we are told; but we do it with the feeling that we are following our own wild impulses. This does not mean that, under the inspiration of advertisements, we act irrationally. We have reasons; but they are sometimes after-thoughts. Or they are supplied by the advertiser.

Advertising, like propaganda, is a form of social control. The difference is that propaganda aims to form opinion. Advertising, on the other hand, does not, ordinarily, form opinions. It does not, at any rate, get its results by provoking discussion. Public opinion, on the contrary, is the product of discussion. Where there are no issues and no discussion there is no opinion, certainly no public opinion.

Fashion is one of the subtler forms of control to which we all bow. We all follow the fashions at a greater or less distance. Some of us fall behind the fashions, but no one ever gets ahead of them. No one ever can get ahead of the fashions because we never know what they are, until they arrive.

Fashion, in the broad sense, comes under the head of what Herbert Spencer called ceremonial government. Ceremony, he said, is the most primitive and the most effective of all forms of government. There is no rebellion against fashion; no rebellion against social ritual. At least these rebellions never make martyrs or heroes. Dr. Mary Walker, who defied custom and the police, and for years valiantly paraded the streets of Washington in men's clothes, was a heroine no doubt, but she never achieved martyrdom.

So far as ceremonial government finds expression in a code it is etiquette, social ritual, form. We do not realize how powerful an influence social form is. There are breaches of etiquette that any ordinary human being would rather die than be guilty of.

We often speak of social usages and the dictates of fashion as if they were imposed by public opinion. This is not true, if we are to use public opinion in the narrower sense. Social usages are not matters of opinion; they are matters of custom. They are fixed in habits. They are not matters of reflection, but of impulse. They are parts of ourselves.

There is an intimate relation between public opinion and social customs or the mores, as Sumner calls them. But there is this difference: Public opinion fluctuates. It wobbles. Social customs, the mores, change slowly. Prohibition was long in coming; but the custom of drinking has not disappeared. The mores change slowly; but they change *in one direction* and they change *steadily*. Mores change as fashion does; as language does; by a law of their own.

Fashions must change. It is in their nature to do so. As the existing thing loses its novelty it is no longer stimulating; no longer interesting. It is no longer the fashion.

What fashion demands is not something new; but something different. It demands the old in a new and stimulating form. Every woman who is up with the fashion wants to be in the fashion; but she desires to be something different from everyone else, especially from her best friend.

Language changes in response to the same motives and according to the same law. We are constantly seeking new metaphors for old ideas; constantly using old metaphors to express new ideas. Consider the way that slang grows!

There is a fashion or a trend in public opinion. A. V. Dicey, in his volume on *Law and Opinion in England*, points out that there has been a constant tendency, for a hundred years, in English legislation, from individualism to collectivism. This does not mean that public opinion has changed constantly in one direction. There have been, as he says, "cross currents." Public opinion has veered, but the changes in the mores have been steadily in one direction.

There has been a change in the fundamental attitudes. This change has taken place in response to changed conditions. Change in mores is something like change in the nest-building habits of certain birds, the swallows, for example. This change, like the change in bird habits, takes place without discussion—without clear consciousness—in response to changed conditions. Furthermore, changes in the mores, like changes in fashion, are only slightly under our control. They are not the result of agitation; rather they are responsible for the agitation.

There are profound changes going on in our social organization today. Industrial democracy, or something corresponding to it, is coming. It is coming not entirely because of social agitation. It is coming, perhaps, in spite of agitation. It is a social change, but it is part of the whole cosmic process.

There is an intimate relation between the mores and opinion. The mores represent the attitudes in which we agree. Opinion represents these attitudes in so far as we do not agree. We do not have opinions except over matters which are in dispute.

So far as we are controlled by habit and custom, by the mores, we do not have opinions. I find out what my opinion is only after I discover that I disagree with my fellow. What I call my opinions are for the most part invented to justify my agreements or disagreements with prevailing public opinion. The mores do not need justification. As soon as I seek justification for them they have become matters of opinion.

Public opinion is just the opinion of individuals plus their differences. There is no public opinion where there is no substantial agreement. But there is no public opinion where there is not disagreement. Public opinion presupposes public discussion. When a matter has reached the stage of public discussion it becomes a matter of public opinion.

Before war was declared in France there was anxiety, speculation. After mobilization began, discussion ceased. The national ideal was exalted. The individual ceased to exist. Men ceased even to think. They simply obeyed. This is what happened in all the belligerent countries except America. It did not quite happen here. Under such circumstances public opinion ceases to exist. This is quite as true in a democracy as it is in an autocracy.

The difference between an autocracy and a democracy is not that in one the will of the people finds expression and in the other it does not. It is simply that in a democracy a larger number of the citizens participate in the discussions which give rise to public opinion. At least they are supposed to do so. In a democracy everyone belongs, or is supposed to belong, to one great public. In an autocracy there are perhaps many little publics.

What rôle do the schools and colleges play in the formation of public opinion? The schools transmit the tradition. They standardize our national prejudices and transmit them. They do this necessarily.

A liberal or college education tends to modify and qualify all our inherited political, religious, and social prejudices. It does so by bringing into the field of discussion matters that would not otherwise get into the public consciousness. In this way a college education puts us in a way to control our prejudices instead of being controlled by them. This is the purpose of a liberal education.

The emancipation which history, literature, and a wider experience with life give us permits us to enter sympathetically into the lives and interests of others; it widens that area over which public opinion rather than force exercises control.

It makes it possible to extend the area of political control. It means the extension of democratic participation in the common life. The universities, by their special studies in the field of social science, are seeking to accumulate and bring into the view of public opinion a larger body of attested fact upon which the public may base its opinion.

It is probably not the business of the universities to agitate reforms nor to attempt directly to influence public opinion in regard to current issues. To do this is to relax its critical attitude, lessen its authority in matters of fact, and jeopardize its hard-won academic freedom. When a university takes over the function of a political party or a church it ceases to perform its function as a university.

6. News and Social Control[1]

Everywhere today men are conscious that somehow they must deal with questions more intricate than any that church or school had prepared them to understand. Increasingly they know that they cannot understand them if the facts are not quickly and steadily available. Increasingly they are baffled because the facts are not available; and they are wondering whether government by consent can survive in a time when the manufacture of consent is an unregulated private enterprise. For in an exact sense the present crisis of western democracy is a crisis in journalism.

I do not agree with those who think that the sole cause is corruption. There is plenty of corruption, to be sure, moneyed control, caste pressure, financial and social bribery, ribbons, dinner parties, clubs, petty politics. The speculators in Russian rubles who lied on the Paris Bourse about the capture of Petrograd are not the only example of their species. And yet corruption does not explain the condition of modern journalism.

Mr. Franklin P. Adams wrote recently:

Now there is much pettiness—and almost incredible stupidity and ignorance—in the so-called free press; but it is the pettiness, etc., common to the so-called human race—a pettiness found in musicians, steamfitters, landlords, poets, and waiters. And when Miss Lowell [who had made the usual aristocratic complaint] speaks of the incurable desire in all American newspapers to make fun of everything in season and out, we quarrel again. There is an incurable desire in American newspapers to take things much more seriously than they deserve. Does Miss Lowell read the ponderous news from Washington? Does she read the society news? Does she, we wonder, read the newspapers?

Mr. Adams does read them, and when he writes that the newspapers take things much more seriously than they deserve, he has, as the mayor's wife remarked to the queen, said a mouthful. Since the war, especially, editors have come to believe that their highest duty is not to report but to instruct, not to print news but to· save civilization, not to publish what Benjamin Harris calls "the Circumstances of Publique Affairs, both abroad and at home," but to keep

[1] Adapted from Walter Lippmann, *Liberty and the News*, pp. 4–15. (Harcourt, Brace & Howe, 1920.)

the nation on the straight and narrow path. Like the kings of England, they have elected themselves Defenders of the Faith. "For five years," says Mr. Cobb of the *New York World*, "there has been no free play of public opinion in the world. Confronted by the inexorable necessities of war, governments conscripted public opinion. They goose-stepped it. They taught it to stand at attention and salute. It sometimes seems that, after the armistice was signed, millions of Americans must have taken a vow that they would never again do any thinking for themselves. They were willing to die for their country but not willing to think for it." That minority, which is proudly prepared to think for it, and not only prepared but cocksure that it alone knows how to think for it, has adopted the theory that the public should know what is good for it.

The work of reporters has thus become confused with the work of preachers, revivalists, prophets, and agitators. The current theory of American newspaperdom is that an abstraction like the truth and a grace-like fairness must be sacrificed whenever anyone thinks the necessities of civilization require the sacrifice. To Archbishop Whately's dictum that it matters greatly whether you put truth in the first place or the second, the candid expounder of modern journalism would reply that he put truth second to what he conceived to be the national interest. Judged simply by their product, men like Mr. Ochs or Viscount Northcliffe believe that their respective nations will perish and civilization decay unless their idea of what is patriotic is permitted to temper the curiosity of their readers.

They believe that edification is more important than veracity. They believe it profoundly, violently, relentlessly. They preen themselves upon it. To patriotism, as they define it from day to day, all other considerations must yield. That is their pride. And yet what is this but one more among myriad examples of the doctrine that the end justifies the means? A more insidiously misleading rule of conduct was, I believe, never devised among men. It was a plausible rule as long as men believed that an omniscient and benevolent Providence taught them what end to seek. But now that men are critically aware of how their purposes are special to their age, their locality, their interests, and their limited knowledge, it is blazing arrogance to sacrifice hard-won standards of credibility to some special purpose. It is nothing but the doctrine that I want what I want when I want it.

Its monuments are the Inquisition and the invasion of Belgium. It is the reason given for every act of unreason, the law invoked whenever lawlessness justifies itself. At bottom it is nothing but the anarchical nature of man imperiously hacking its way through.

Just as the most poisonous form of disorder is the mob incited from high places, the most immoral act the immorality of a government, so the most destructive form of untruth is sophistry and propaganda by those whose profession it is to report the news. The news columns are common carriers. When those who control them arrogate to themselves the right to determine by their own consciences what shall be reported and for what purpose, democracy is unworkable. Public opinion is blockaded. For when a people can no longer confidently repair "to the best fountains for their information," then anyone's guess and anyone's rumor, each man's hope and each man's whim, become the basis of government. All that the sharpest critics of democracy have alleged is true if there is no steady supply of trustworthy and relevant news. Incompetence and aimlessness, corruption and disloyalty, panic and ultimate disaster, must come to any people which is denied an assured access to the facts. No one can manage anything on pap. Neither can a people.

Few episodes in recent history are more poignant than that of the British prime minister, sitting at the breakfast table with that morning's paper before him, protesting that he cannot do the sensible thing in regard to Russia because a powerful newspaper proprietor has drugged the public. That incident is a photograph of the supreme danger which confronts popular government. All other dangers are contingent upon it, for the news is the chief source of the opinion by which government now proceeds. So long as there is interposed between the ordinary citizen and the facts a news organization determining by entirely private and unexamined standards, no matter how lofty, what he shall know, and hence what he shall believe, no one will be able to say that the substance of democratic government is secure. The theory of our constitution, says Mr. Justice Holmes, is that truth is the only ground upon which men's wishes safely can be carried out. In so far as those who purvey the news make of their own beliefs a higher law than truth, they are attacking the foundations of our constitutional system. There can be no higher law in journalism than to tell the truth and shame the devil.

In a few generations it will seem ludicrous to historians that a people professing government by the will of the people should have made no serious effort to guarantee the news without which a governing opinion cannot exist. "Is it possible," they will ask, "that at the beginning of the twentieth century nations calling themselves democracies were content to act on what happened to drift across their doorsteps; that apart from a few sporadic exposures and outcries they made no plans to bring these common carriers under social control, that they provided no genuine training schools for the men upon whose sagacity they were dependent; above all, that their political scientists went on year after year writing and lecturing about government without producing one single, significant study of the process of public opinion?" And then they will recall the centuries in which the church enjoyed immunity from criticism, and perhaps they will insist that the news structure of secular society was not seriously examined for analogous reasons.

7. The Psychology of Propaganda[1]

Paper bullets, according to Mr. Creel, won the war. But they have forever disturbed our peace of mind. The war is long since over, all but saying so; but our consciousness of the immanence of propaganda bids fair to be permanent. It has been discovered by individuals, by associations, and by governments that a certain kind of advertising can be used to mold public opinion and control democratic majorities. As long as public opinion rules the destinies of human affairs, there will be no end to an instrument that controls it.

The tremendous forces of propaganda are now common property. They are available for the unscrupulous and the destructive as well as for the constructive and the moral. This gives us a new interest in its technique, namely, to inquire if anywhere there is an opportunity for regulative and protective interference with its indiscriminate exploitation.

Until recently the most famous historical use of the term propaganda made it synonymous with foreign missions. It was Pope Gregory XV who almost exactly three centuries ago, after many years of preparation, finally founded the great Propaganda College

[1] From Raymond Dodge, "The Psychology of Propaganda," *Religious Education*, XV (1920), 241-52.

to care for the interests of the church in non-Catholic countries. With its centuries of experience this is probably the most efficient organization for propaganda in the world. Probably most apologetics is propaganda. No religion and no age has been entirely free from it.

One of the classical psychoanalytic case histories is that of Breuer's water glass and the puppy dog. A young lady patient was utterly unable to drink water from a glass. It was a deep embarrassment. Even under the stress of great thirst in warm weather and the earnest effort to break up a foolish phobia, the glass might be taken and raised, but it couldn't be drunk from. Psychoanalysis disclosed the following facts. Underlying this particular phobia was an intense antipathy to dogs. The young lady's roommate had been discovered giving a dog a drink from the common drinking-glass. The antipathy to the dog was simply transferred to the glass.

The case is a commonplace in the annals of hysteria. But let us examine the mechanism. Suppose that I had wanted to keep that drinking-glass for my own personal use. A perfectly simple and effective expedient it would have been in the absence of other good motives to capitalize that antipathy by allowing her to see the dog drink out of the glass. The case would then have been a perfect case of propaganda. All propaganda is capitalized prejudice. It rests on some emotional premise which is the motive force of the process. The emotional transfer is worked by some associative process like similarity, use, or the causal relationship. The derived sympathetic antipathy represents the goal.

The great self-preservative, social, and racial instincts will always furnish the main reservoir of motive forces at the service of propaganda. They will have the widest and the most insistent appeal. Only second to these in importance are the peculiar racial tendencies and historical traditions that represent the genius of a civilization. The racial-superiority consciousness of the Germans operated as a never-ending motive for their "Aushalten" propaganda. We Americans have a notable cultural premise in our consideration for the underdog. Few things outside our consciousness of family will arouse us as surely and as universally as this modification of the protective instinct.

In addition to the group tendencies that arise from a community of experience, individual propaganda may use every phase of individual experience, individual bias and prejudice. I am told that first-class salesmen not infrequently keep family histories of their customers, producing a favorable attitude toward their merchandise by way of an apparent personal interest in the children. Apparently any group of ideas with an emotional valence may become the basis for propaganda.

There are three limitations to the processes of propaganda. The first is emotional recoil, the second is the exhaustion of available motive force, the third is the development of internal resistance or negativism.

The most familiar of the three is emotional recoil. We know only too well what will happen if we tell a boy all the things that he likes to do are "bad," while all the things that he dislikes are "good." Up to a certain point the emotional value of bad and good respectively will be transferred to the acts as we intend. But each transfer has an emotional recoil on the concepts good and bad. At the end a most surprising thing may happen. The moral values may get reversed in the boy's mind. Bad may come to represent the sum total of the satisfactory and desirable, while good may represent the sum total of the unsatisfactory and the undesirable. To the pained adult such a consequence is utterly inexplicable, only because he fails to realize that all mental products are developments. There is always a kind of reciprocity in emotional transfer. The value of the modified factor recoils to the modifying factor.

The whole mechanism of the transfer and of the recoil may best be expressed in terms of the conditioned reflex of Pavlov. The flow of saliva in a dog is a natural consequence to the sight and smell of food. If concurrently with the smelling of food the dog is pinched, the pinch ceases to be a matter for resentment. By a process of emotional transfer, on being pinched the dog may show the lively delight that belongs to the sight and smell of food. Even the salivary secretions may be started by the transfigured pinch. It was the great operating physiologist Sherrington who exclaimed after a visit to Pavlov that at last he understood the psychology of the martyrs. But it is possible so to load the smell of food with pain and damage that its positive value breaks down. Eating-values may succumb to the pain values instead of the pain to the eating-values. This is the prototype of the concept bad when it gets overloaded with the emotional value of the intrinsically desirable.   The law of recoil seems to be a mental analogue of the physical law that action and reaction are equal and in opposite directions.

The second limitation to propaganda occurs when the reciprocal effects of transfer exhaust the available motive forces of a mind. Propaganda certainly weakens the forces that are appealed to too often.   We are living just now in a world of weakened appeals. Many of the great human motives were exploited to the limit during the war.   It is harder to raise money now than it was, harder to find motives for giving that are still effective.   One of my former colleagues once surprised and shocked me by replying to some perfectly good propaganda in which I tried to tell him that certain action was in the line of duty, to the effect that he was tired of being told that something was his duty, and that he was resolved not to do another thing because it was his duty.   There seems to be evidence that in some quarters, at least, patriotism, philanthropy, and civic duty have been exploited as far as the present systems will carry.   It is possible to exhaust our floating capital of social-motive forces.   When that occurs we face a kind of moral bankruptcy.

A final stage of resistance is reached when propaganda develops a negativistic defensive reaction.   To develop such negativisms is always the aim of counterpropaganda.   It calls the opposed propaganda, prejudiced, half-truth, or, as the Germans did, "Lies, All Lies."   There is evidence that the moral collapse of Germany under the fire of our paper bullets came with the conviction that they had been systematically deceived by their own propagandists.

There are two great social dangers in propaganda.   Great power in irresponsible hands is always a social menace.   We have some legal safeguards against careless use of high-powered physical explosives.   Against the greater danger of destructive propaganda there seems to be little protection without imperiling the sacred principles of free speech.

The second social danger is the tendency to overload and level down every great human incentive in the pursuit of relatively trivial ends.   To become *blasé* is the inevitable penalty of emotional exploitation.   I believe there may well be grave penalties in store for the reckless commercialized exploitation of human emotions in the cheap sentimentalism of our moving pictures.   But there are even graver penalties in store for the generation that permits itself to grow morally *blasé*. One of our social desiderata, it seems to me, is the protection of the great springs of human action from destructive exploitation for selfish, commercial, or other trivial ends.

The slow constructive process of building moral credits by systematic education lacks the picturesqueness of propaganda. It also lacks its quick results. But just as the short cut of hypnotism proved a dangerous substitute for moral training, so I believe we shall find that not only is moral education a necessary precondition for effective propaganda, but that in the end it is a safer and incomparably more reliable social instrument.

C. INSTITUTIONS

1. Institutions and the Mores[1]

Institutions and laws are produced out of mores. An institution consists of a concept (idea, notion, doctrine, interest) and a structure. The structure is a framework, or apparatus, or perhaps only a number of functionaries set to co-operate in prescribed ways at a certain conjuncture. The structure holds the concept and furnishes instrumentalities for bringing it into the world of facts and action in a way to serve the interests of men in society. Institutions are either crescive or enacted. They are crescive when they take shape in the mores, growing by the instinctive efforts by which the mores are produced. Then the efforts, through long use, become definite and specific.

Property, marriage, and religion are the most primary institutions. They began in folkways. They became customs. They developed into mores by the addition of some philosophy of welfare, however crude. Then they were made more definite and specific as regards the rules, the prescribed acts, and the apparatus to be employed. This produced a structure and the institution was complete. Enacted institutions are products of rational invention and intention. They belong to high civilization. Banks are institutions of credit founded on usages which can be traced back to barbarism. There came a time when, guided by rational reflection on experience, men systematized and regulated the usages which had

[1] From William G. Sumner, *Folkways*, pp. 53-56. (Ginn & Co., 1906.)

become current, and thus created positive institutions of credit, defined by law and sanctioned by the force of the state. Pure enacted institutions which are strong and prosperous are hard to find. It is too difficult to invent and create an institution, for a purpose, out of nothing. The electoral college in the Constitution of the United States is an example. In that case the democratic mores of the people have seized upon the device and made of it something quite different from what the inventors planned. All institutions have come out of mores, although the rational element in them is sometimes so large that their origin in the mores is not to be ascertained except by a historical investigation (legislatures, courts, juries, joint-stock companies, the stock exchange). Property, marriage, and religion are still almost entirely in the mores. Amongst nature men any man might capture and hold a woman at any time, if he could. He did it by superior force which was its own supreme justification. But his act brought his group and her group into war, and produced harm to his comrades. They forbade capture, or set conditions for it. Beyond the limits, the individual might still use force, but his comrades were no longer responsible. The glory to him, if he succeeded, might be all the greater. His control over his captive was absolute. Within the prescribed conditions, "capture" became technical and institutional, and rights grew out of it. The woman had a status which was defined by custom and was very different from the status of a real captive. Marriage was the institutional relation, in the society and under its sanction, of a woman to a man, where the woman had been obtained in the prescribed way. She was then a "wife." What her rights and duties were was defined by the mores, as they are today in all civilized society.

Acts of legislation come out of the mores. In low civilization all societal regulations are customs and taboos, the origin of which is unknown. Positive laws are impossible until the stage of verification, reflection, and criticism is reached. Until that point is reached there is only customary law, or common law. The customary law may be codified and systematized with respect to some philosophical principles, and yet remain customary. The codes of Manu and Justinian are examples. Enactment is not possible until reverence for ancestors has been so much weakened that it is no longer thought wrong to interfere with traditional customs by positive enactment. Even then there is reluctance to make enactments, and there is a stage of transition during which traditional customs are extended by interpretation to cover new cases and to prevent evils. Legislation, however, has to seek standing ground on the existing mores, and it soon becomes apparent that legislation, to be strong, must be consistent with the mores. Things which have been in the mores are put under police regulation and later under positive law. It is sometimes said that "public opinion" must ratify and approve police regulations, but this statement rests on an imperfect analysis. The regulations must conform to the mores, so that the public will not think them too lax or too strict. The mores of our urban and rural populations are not the same; consequently legislation about intoxicants which is made by one of these sections of the population does not succeed when applied to the other. The regulation of drinking-places, gambling-places, and disorderly houses has passed through the above-mentioned stages. It is always a question of expediency whether to leave a subject under the mores, or to make a police regulation for it, or to put it into the criminal law. Betting, horse racing, dangerous sports, electric cars, and vehicles are cases now of things which seem to be passing under positive enactment and out of the unformulated control of the mores. When an enactment is made there is a sacrifice of the elasticity and automatic self-adaptation of custom, but an enactment is specific and is provided with sanctions. Enactments come into use when conscious purposes are formed, and it is believed that specific devices can be framed by which to realize such purposes in the society. Then also prohibitions take the place of taboos, and punishments are planned to be deterrent rather than revengeful. The mores of different societies, or of different ages, are characterized by greater or less readiness and confidence in regard to the use of positive enactments for the realization of societal purposes.

2. Common Law and Statute Law[1]

It probably would have surprised the early Englishman if he had been told that either he or anybody else did not know the law—still more that there was ever any need for any parliament or assembly to tell him what it was. They all knew the law, and they all

[1] Adapted from Frederic J. Stimson, *Popular Law-Making*, pp. 2-16. (Charles Scribner's Sons, 1912.)

knew that they knew the law, and the law was a thing that they knew as naturally as they knew fishing and hunting. They had grown up into it. It never occurred to them as an outside thing.

So it has been found that where you take children, modern children, at least boys who are sons of educated parents, and put them in large masses by themselves, they will, without apparently any reading, rapidly invent a notion of law; that is, they will invent a certain set of customs which are the same thing to them as law, and which indeed are the same as law. They have tried in Johns Hopkins University experiments among children, to leave them entirely alone, without any instruction, and it is quite singular how soon customs will grow up, and it is also quite singular, and a thing that always surprises the socialist and communist, that about the earliest concept at which they will arrive is that of private property! They will soon get a notion that one child owns a stick, or toy, or seat, and the others must respect that property. This I merely use as an illustration to show how simple the notion of law was among our ancestors in England fifteen hundred years ago, and how it had grown up with them, of course, from many centuries, but in much the same way that the notion of custom or law grows up among children.

The "law" of the free Anglo-Saxon people was regarded as a thing existing by itself, like the sunlight, or at least as existing like a universally accepted custom observed by everyone. It was five hundred years before the notion crept into the minds, even of the members of the British Parliaments, that they could make a new law. What they supposed they did, and what they were un stood by the people to do, was merely to declare the law, as it was then and as it had been from time immemorial; the notion always being—and the farther back you go and the more simple the people are, the more they have that notion—that their free laws and customs were something which came from the beginning of the world, which they always held, which were immutable, no more to be changed than the forces of nature; and that no Parliament, under the free Anglo-Saxon government or later under the Norman kings who tried to make them unfree, no king could ever make a law but could only declare what the law was. The Latin phrase for that distinction is *jus dare*, and *jus dicere*. In early England, in Anglo-Saxon times, the Parliament never did anything but tell what the law was; and, as I have said, not only what it was then but what it had been, as they supposed, for thousands of years before. The notion of a legislature to make new laws is an entirely modern conception of Parliament.

The notion of law as a statute, a thing passed by a legislature, a thing enacted, made new by representative assembly, is perfectly modern, and yet it has so thoroughly taken possession of our minds, and particularly of the American mind (owing to the forty-eight legislatures that we have at work, besides the national Congress, every year, and to the fact that they try to do a great deal to deserve their pay in the way of enacting laws), that statutes have assumed in our minds the main bulk of the concept of law as we formulate it to ourselves.

Statutes with us are recent, legislatures making statutes are recent everywhere; legislatures themselves are fairly recent; that is, they date only from the end of the Dark Ages, at least in Anglo-Saxon countries. Representative government itself is supposed, by most scholars, to be the one invention that is peculiar to the Anglo-Saxon people.

I am quite sure that all the American people when they think of law in the sense I am now speaking of, even when they are not thinking necessarily of statute law, do mean, nevertheless, a law which is enforced by somebody with power, somebody with a big stick. They mean a law, an ordinance, an order or dictate addressed to them by a sovereign, or at least by a power of some sort, and they mean an ordinance which if they break they are going to suffer for, either in person or in property. In other words, they have a notion of law as a written command addressed by the sovereign to the subject, or at least by one of the departments of government to the citizen. Now that, I must caution you, is in the first place rather a modern notion of law, quite modern in England; it is really Roman, and was not law as it was understood by our Anglo-Saxon ancestor. He did not think of law as a thing written, addressed to him by the king. Neither did he necessarily think of it as a thing which had any definite punishment attached or any code attached, any "sanction," as we call it, or thing which enforces the law; a penalty or fine or imprisonment. There are just as good "sanctions" for law outside of the sanctions that our people usually think of as there are inside of them, and often very much better; for example, the sanction of a strong custom. Take any example you like; there are many states where marriage between blacks and whites is not made unlawful but where practically it is made tremendously unlawful by the force of public opinion [mores]. Take the case of debts of honor, so called, debts of gambling; they are paid far more universally than ordinary commercial debts, even by the same people; but there is no law enforcing them—there is no sanction for the collection of gambling debts. And take any custom that grows up. We know how strong our customs in college are. Take the mere custom of a club table; no one dares or ventures to supplant the members at that table. That kind of sanction is just as good a law as a law made by statute and imposing five or ten dollars' penalty or a week's imprisonment. And judges or juries recognize those things as laws, just as much as they do statute laws; when all other laws are lacking, our courts will ask what is the "custom of the trade." These be laws, and are often better enforced than the statute law; the rules of the New York Stock Exchange are better enforced than the laws of the state legislature. Now all our early Anglo-Saxon law was law of that kind. For the law was but universal custom, and that custom had no sanction; but for breach of the custom anybody could make personal attack, or combine with his friends to make attack, on the person who committed the breach, and then, when the matter was taken up by the members of both tribes, and finally by the witenagemot as a judicial court, the question was, what the law was. That was the working of the old Anglo-Saxon law, and it was a great many centuries before the notion of law changed from that in their minds. And this "unwritten law" perdures in the minds of many of the people today.

3. Religion and Social Control[1]

As a social fact religion is, indeed, not something apart from mores or social standards; it is these as regarded as "sacred." Strictly speaking there is no such thing as an unethical religion. We judge some religions as unethical because the mores of which they approve are not our mores, that is, the standards of higher civilization. All religions are ethical, however, in the sense that without exception

[1] From Charles A. Ellwood, "Religion and Social Control," in the *Scientific Monthly*, VII (1918), 339-41.

they support customary morality, and they do this necessarily because the values which the religious attitude of mind universalizes and makes absolute are social values. Social obligations thus early become religious obligations. In this way religion becomes the chief means of conserving customs and habits which have been found to be safe by society or which are believed to conduce to social welfare.

As the guardian of the mores, religion develops prohibitions and "taboos" of actions of which the group, or its dominant class, disapproves. It may lend itself, therefore, to maintaining a given social order longer than that order is necessary, or even after it has become a stumbling-block to social progress. For the same reason it may be exploited by a dominant class in their own interest. It is in this way that religion has often become an impediment to progress and an instrument of class oppression. This socially conservative side of religion is so well known and so much emphasized by certain writers that it scarcely needs even to be mentioned. It is the chief source of the abuses of religion, and in the modern world is probably the chief cause of the deep enmity which religion has raised up for itself in a certain class of thinkers who see nothing but its negative and conservative side.

There is no necessity, however, for the social control which religion exerts being of a non-progressive kind. The values which religion universalizes and makes absolute may as easily be values which are progressive as those which are static. In a static society which emphasizes prohibitions and the conservation of mere habit or custom, religion will also, of course, emphasize the same things; but in a progressive society religion can as easily attach its sanctions to social ideals and standards beyond the existing order as to those actually realized. Such an idealistic religion will, however, have the disadvantages of appealing mainly to the progressive and idealizing tendencies of human nature rather than to its conservative and reactionary tendencies. Necessarily, also, it will appeal more strongly to those enlightened classes in society who are leading in social progress rather than to those who are content with things as they are. This is doubtless the main reason why progressive religions are exceedingly rare in human history, taking it as a whole, and have appeared only in the later stages of cultural evolution.

Nevertheless, there are good reasons for believing that the inevitable evolution of religion has been in a humanitarian direction, and that there is an intimate connection between social idealism and the higher religions. There are two reasons for this generalization. The social life becomes more complex with each succeeding stage of upward development, and groups have therefore more need of commanding the unfailing devotion of their members if they are to maintain their unity and efficiency as groups. More and more, accordingly, religion in its evolution has come to emphasize the self-effacing devotion of the individual to the group in times of crisis. And as the complexity of social life increases, the crises increase in which the group must ask the unfailing service and devotion of its members. Thus religion in its upward evolution becomes increasingly social, until it finally comes to throw supreme emphasis upon the life of service and of self-sacrifice for the sake of the group; and as the group expands from the clan and the tribe to humanity, religion necessarily becomes less tribal and more humanitarian until the supreme object of the devotion which it inculcates must ultimately be the whole of humanity.

III.   INVESTIGATIONS AND PROBLEMS

1.   Social Control and Human Nature

Society, so far as it can be distinguished from the individuals that compose it, performs for those individuals the function of a mind. Like mind in the individual man, society is a control organization. Evidence of mind in the animal is the fact that it can make adjustments to new conditions. The evidence that any group of persons constitutes a society is the fact that the group is able to act with some consistency, and as a unit. It follows that the literature on social control, in the widest extension of that term, embraces most that has been written and all that is fundamental on the subject of society. In chapter ii, "Human Nature," and the later chapters on "Interaction" and its various forms, "Conflict," "Accommodation," and "Assimilation," points of view and literature which might properly be included in an adequate study of social control have already been discussed. The present chapter is concerned mainly with ceremonial, public opinion, and law, three of the specific forms in which social control has universally found expression.

Sociology is indebted to Edward Alsworth Ross for a general term broad enough to include all the special forms in which the solidarity of the group manifests itself. It was his brilliant essay on the subject published in 1901 that popularized the term social control. Sumner published in 1907 his *Folkways*. This volume, in spite of its unsystematic character, must still be regarded as the most subtle analysis and suggestive statement about human nature and social relations that has yet been written in English.

A more systematic and thoroughgoing review of the facts and literature, however, is Hobhouse's *Morals in Evolution*. After Hobhouse the next most important writer is Westermarck, whose work, *The Origin and Development of the Moral Ideas*, published in 1906, was a pioneer in this field.

2. Elementary Forms of Social Control

Literature upon elementary forms of social control includes materials upon ceremonies, taboo, myth, prestige, and leadership. These are characterized as elementary because they have arisen spontaneously everywhere out of original nature. The conventionalized form in which we now find them has arisen in the course of their repetition and transmission from one generation to another and from one culture group to another. The fact that they have been transmitted over long periods of time and wide areas of territory is an indication that they are the natural vehicle for the expression of fundamental human impulses.

It is quite as true of leadership, as it is of myth and prestige, that it springs directly out of an emotional setting. The natural leaders are never elected and leadership is, in general, a matter that cannot be rationally controlled.

The materials upon ceremony, social ritual, and fashion are large in comparison with the attempts at a systematic study of the phenomena. Herbert Spencer's chapter on "Ceremonial Government," while it interprets social forms from the point of view of the individual rather than of the group, is still the only adequate survey of the materials in this special field.

Ethnology and folklore have accumulated an enormous amount of information in regard to primitive custom which has yet to be interpreted from the point of view of more recent studies of human nature and social life. The most important collections are Frazer's *Golden Bough* and his *Totemism and Exogamy.* Crawley's *The Mystic Rose* is no such monument of scholarship and learning as Frazer's *Golden Bough*, but it is suggestive and interesting.

Prestige and taboo represent fundamental human traits whose importance is by no means confined to the life of primitive man where, almost exclusively hitherto, they have been observed and studied.

The existing literature on leadership, while serving to emphasize the importance of the leader as a factor in social organization and social process, is based on too superficial an analysis to be of permanent scientific value. Adequate methods for the investigation of leadership have not been formulated. In general it is clear, however, that leadership must be studied in connection with the social group in which it arises and that every type of group will have a different type of leader. The prophet, the agitator, and the political boss are types of leaders in regard to whom there already are materials available for study and interpretation. A study of leadership should include, however, in addition to the more general types, like the poet, the priest, the tribal chieftain, and the leader of the gang, consideration of leadership in the more specific areas of social life, the precinct captain, the promoter, the banker, the pillar of the church, the football coach, and the society leader.

3. Public Opinion and Social Control

Public opinion, "the fourth estate" as Burke called it, has been appreciated, but not studied. The old Roman adage, *Vox populi, vox dei,* is a recognition of public opinion as the ultimate seat of authority. Public opinion has been elsewhere identified with the "general will." Rousseau conceived the general will to be best expressed through a plebiscite at which a question was presented without the possibilities of the divisive effects of public discussion. The natural impulses of human nature would make for more uniform and beneficial decisions than the calculated self-interest that would follow discussion and deliberation. English liberals like John Stuart Mill, of the latter half of the nineteenth century, looked upon freedom of discussion and free speech as the breath of life of a free society, and that tradition has come down to us a little shaken by recent experience, but substantially intact.

The development of advertising and of propaganda, particularly during and since the world-war, has aroused a great many misgivings, nevertheless, in regard to the traditional freedom of the press. Walter Lippmann's thoughtful little volume, *Liberty and the News*, has stated the whole problem in a new form and has directed attention to an entirely new field for observation and study.

De Tocqueville, in his study of the early frontier, *Democracy in America*, and James Bryce, in his *American Commonwealth*, have contributed a good deal of shrewd observation to our knowledge of the rôle of political opinion in the United States. The important attempts in English to define public opinion as a social phenomenon and study it objectively are A. V. Dicey's *Law and Opinion in England in the Nineteenth Century* and A. Lawrence Lowell's *Public Opinion and Popular Government*. Although Dicey's investigation is confined to England and to the nineteenth century, his analysis of the facts throws new light on the nature of public opinion in general. The intimate relation between the press and parliamentary government in England is revealed in an interesting historical monograph by Michael Macdonagh, *The Reporters' Gallery*.

4. Legal Institutions and Law

Public law came into existence in an effort of the community to deal with conflict. In achieving this result, however, courts of law invariably have sought to make their decisions first in accordance with precedent, and second in accordance with common sense. The latter insured that the law would be administered equitably; the former that interpretations of the law would be consistent. Post says:

Jural feelings are principally feelings of indignation as when an injustice is experienced by an individual, a feeling of fear as when an individual is affected by an inclination to do wrong, a feeling of penitence as when the individual has committed a wrong. With the feeling of indignation is joined a desire for vengeance, with the feeling of penitence a desire of atonement, the former tending towards an act of vengeance and the latter towards an act of expiation. The jural judgments of individuals are not complete judgments; they are based upon an undefined sense of right and wrong. In the consciousness of the individual there exists no standard of right and wrong under which every single circumstance giving rise to the formation of a jural judgment can be subsumed. A simple instinct impels the individual to declare an action right or wrong.[1]

If these motives are the materials with which the administration of justice has to deal, the legal motive which has invariably controlled the courts is something quite different. The courts in the administration of law have invariably sought, above all else, to achieve consistency. It is an ancient maxim of English law that "it is better that the law should be certain than that the law should be just."[2]

The conception implicit in the law is that the rule laid down in one case must apply in every similar case. In the effort to preserve this consistency in a constantly increasing variety of cases the courts have been driven to the formulation of principles, increasingly general and abstract, to multiply distinctions and subtleties, and to operate with legal fictions. All this effort to make the law a rationally consistent system was itself inconsistent with the conception that law, like religion, had a natural history and was involved, like language, in a process of growth and decay. It is only in recent years that comparative jurisprudence has found its way into the law schools. Although there is a vast literature upon the subject of the history of the law, Maine's *Ancient Law*, published in 1861, is still the classic work in this field in English.

More recently there has sprung up a school of "legal ethnology." The purpose of these studies is not to trace the historical development of the law, but to seek in the forms in use in isolated and primitive societies materials which will reveal, in their more elementary expressions, motives and practices that are common to legal institutions of every people. In the Preface to a recent volume of *Select Readings on the Origin and Development of Legal Institutions*, the editors venture

[1] Albert H. Post, *Evolution of Law: Select Readings on the Origin and Development of Legal Institutions*, Vol. II, "Primitive and Ancient Legal Institutions," compiled by Albert Kocourek and John H. Wigmore; translated from the German by Thomas J. McCormack. Section 2, "Ethnological Jurisprudence," p. 12. (Boston, 1915.)

[2] Quoted by James Bryce, "Influence of National Character and Historical Environment on Development of Common Law," annual address to the American Bar Association, 1907, *Reports of the American Bar Association*, XXXI (1907), 447.

the statement, in justification of the materials from sociology that these volumes include, that "contrary, perhaps, to legal tradition, the law itself is only a social phenomenon and not to be understood in detachment from human uses, necessities and forces from which it arises." Justice Holmes's characterization of law as "a great anthropological document" seems to support that position.

Law in its origin is related to religion. The first public law was that which enforced the religious taboos, and the ceremonial purifications and expiations were intended to protect the community from the divine punishment for any involuntary disrespect or neglect of the rites due the gods which were the first crimes to be punished by the community as a whole, and for the reason that failure to punish or expiate them would bring disaster upon the community as a whole.

Maine says that the earliest conceptions of law or a rule of life among the Greeks are contained in the Homeric words *Themis* and *Themistes*.

When a king decided a dispute by a sentence, the judgment was assumed to be the result of direct inspiration. The divine agent, suggesting judicial awards to kings or to gods, the greatest of kings, was *Themis*. The peculiarity of the conception is brought out by the use of the plural. *Themistes*, Themises, the plural of Themis, are the awards themselves, divinely dictated to the judge. Kings are spoken of as if they had a store of "Themistes" ready to hand for use; but it must be distinctly understood that they are not laws, but judgments. "Zeus, or the human king on earth," says Mr. Grote, in his *History of Greece*, "is not a law-maker, but a judge." He is provided with Themistes, but, consistently with the belief in their emanation from above, they cannot be supposed to be connected by any thread of principle; they are separate, isolated judgments.[1]

It is only in recent times, with the gradual separation of the function of the church and the state, that legal institutions have acquired a character wholly secular. Within the areas of social life that are represented on the one hand by religion and on the other by law are included all the sanctions and the processes by which society maintains its authority and imposes its will upon its individual members.[2]

[1] Henry S. Maine, *Ancient Law*. Its connection with the early history of society and its relation to modern ideas, pp. 4–5. 14th ed. (London, 1891.)

[2] For the distinction between the cultural process and the political process see *supra*, pp. 52–53.

SELECTED BIBLIOGRAPHY

I. SOCIAL CONTROL AND HUMAN NATURE

(1) Maine, Henry S. *Dissertations on Early Law and Custom.* New York, 1886.
(2) Kocourek, Albert, and Wigmore, John H., editors. *Evolution of Law.* Select readings on the origin and development of legal institutions. Vol. I, "Sources of Ancient and Primitive Law." Vol. II, "Primitive and Ancient Legal Institutions." Vol. III, "Formative Influences of Legal Development." Boston, 1915.
(3) Sumner, W. G. *Folkways.* A study of the sociological importance of usages, manners, customs, mores, and morals. Boston, 1906.
(4) Letourneau, Ch. *L'Évolution de la morale.* Paris, 1887.
(5) Westermarck, Edward. *The Origin and Development of the Moral Ideas*, 2 vols. London, 1906-8.
(6) Hobhouse, L. T. *Morals in Evolution.* New ed. A study in comparative ethics. New York, 1915.
(7) Durkheim, Émile. *The Elementary Forms of the Religious Life.* A study in religious sociology. Translated from the French by J. W. Swain. London, 1915.
(8) Novikow, J. *Conscience et volonté sociales.* Paris, 1897.
(9) Wallas, Graham. *Our Social Heritage.* New Haven, 1921.
(10) Ross, Edward A. *Social Control.* A survey of the foundations of order. New York, 1901.
(11) Bernard, Luther L. *The Transition to an Objective Standard of Social Control.* Chicago, 1911.
(12) Sadler, G. T. *The Relation of Custom to Law.* London, 1919.

II. ELEMENTARY FORMS OF SOCIAL CONTROL

A. *Leadership*

(1) Woods, Frederick A. *The Influence of Monarchs.* Steps in a new science of history. New York, 1913.
(2) Smith, J. M. P. *The Prophet and His Problems.* New York, 1914.
(3) Walter, F. *Die Propheten in ihrem sozialen Beruf und das Wirtschaftsleben ihrer Zeit.* Ein Beitrag zur Geschichte der Sozialethik. Freiburg-in-Brisgau, 1900.
(4) Vierkandt, A. "Führende Individuen bei den Naturvölkern," *Zeitschrift für Sozialwissenschaft,* XI (1908), 542-53, 623-39.
(5) Dixon, Roland B. "Some Aspects of the American Shaman," *The Journal of American Folk-Lore,* XXI (1908), 1-12.
(6) Kohler, Josef. *Philosophy of Law.* (Albrecht's translation.) "Cultural Importance of Chieftainry." "Philosophy of Law Series," Vol. XII. [Reprinted in the *Evolution of Law,* II, 96-103.]
(7) Fustel de Coulanges. *The Ancient City,* Book III, chap. ix, "The Government of the City. The King," pp. 231-39. Boston, 1896.
(8) Leopold, Lewis. *Prestige.* A psychological study of social estimates. London, 1913.
(9) Clayton, Joseph. *Leaders of the People.* Studies in democratic history. London, 1910.

(10) Brent, Charles H. *Leadership*. New York, 1908.
(11) Bogardus, Emory S. *Fundamentals of Social Psychology*. Part IV. "Leadership and Interstimulation." Pp. 371–471. New York, 1924.
(12) Chapin, F. Stuart. "Leadership and Group Activity," *Journal of Applied Sociology*, VIII (1923–24), 141–45.
(13) Rothschild, Alonzo. *Lincoln: Master of Men*. A study in character. Boston, 1906.
(14) Mumford, Eben. *The Origins of Leadership*. Chicago, 1909.
(15) Ely, Richard T. *The World War and Leadership in a Democracy*. New York, 1918.
(16) Terman, L. M. "A Preliminary Study of the Psychology and Pedagogy of Leadership," Pedagogical Seminary, XI (1904), 413–51.
(17) Miller, Arthur H. *Leadership*. A study and discussion of the qualities most to be desired in an officer. New York, 1920.
(18) Gowin, Enoch B. *The Executive and His Control of Men*. A study in personal efficiency. New York, 1915.
(19) Cooley, Charles H. "Genius, Fame and the Comparison of Races," *Annals of American Academy*, IX (1897), 317–58.
(20) Odin, Alfred. *Genèse des grands hommes, gens de lettres français modernes*. Paris, 1895. [See Ward, Lester F., *Applied Sociology*, for a statement in English of Odin's study.]
(21) Kostyleff, N. *Le Mécanisme cérébral de la pensée*. Paris, 1914. [This includes a study of the mechanism of the inspiration of poets and writers of romance.]
(22) Chabaneix, Paul. *Physiologie cérébrale*. Le subconscient chez les artistes, les savants, et les écrivains. Bordeaux, 1897–98.
(23) Follett, M. P. *Creative Experience*. New York, 1924. [See bibliography, "Invention," p. 431.]

B. *Ceremony, Rites, and Ritual*

(1) Spencer, Herbert. *The Principles of Sociology, Part IV*, "Ceremonial Institutions." Vol. II, pp. 3–225. London, 1893.
(2) Tylor, Edward B. *Primitive Culture*. Researches into the development of mythology, philosophy, religion, language, art, and custom. Chap. xviii, "Rites and Ceremonies," pp. 362–442. New York, 1874.
(3) Frazer, J. G. *Totemism and Exogamy*. A treatise on certain early forms of superstition and society. 4 vols. London, 1910.
(4) Freud, Sigmund. *Totem and Taboo*. Resemblances between the psychic life of savages and neurotics. Authorized translation from the German by A. A. Brill. New York, 1918.
(5) James, E. O. *Primitive Ritual and Belief*. An anthropological essay. With an introduction by R. R. Marett. London, 1917.
(6) Brinton, Daniel G. *The Religious Sentiment: Its Source and Aim*. A contribution to the science and philosophy of religion. Chap. vi, "The Cult, Its Symbols and Rites," pp. 197–227. New York, 1876.

(7) Frazer, J. G. *Golden Bough.* A study in magic and religion. Part VI, "The Scapegoat." 3d ed. London, 1913.

(8) Nassau, R. H. *Fetichism in West Africa.* Forty years' observation of native customs and superstitions. New York, 1907.

(9) Hubert, H., and Mauss, M. "Essai sur la nature et la fonction de sacrifice," *L'Année sociologique,* II (1897–98), 29–138.

(10) Farnell, L. R. *The Higher Aspects of Greek Religion.* New York, 1912.

(11) Farnell, L. R. *The Cults of the Greek States.* 5 vols. Oxford, 1896–1909.

(12) ———. "Religious and Social Aspects of the Cult of Ancestors and Heroes," *Hibbert Journal,* VII (1909), 415–35.

(13) Harrison, Jane E. *Prolegomena to the Study of Greek Religion.* Cambridge, 1903.

(14) De-Marchi, A. *Il Culto privato di Roma antica.* Milano, 1896.

(15) Oldenberg, H. *Die Religion des Veda.* Part III, "Der Cultus," pp. 302–523. Berlin, 1894.

C. *Taboo*

(1) Thomas, N. W. Article on "Taboo" in *Encyclopaedia Britannica,* XXVI, 337–41.

(2) Frazer, J. G. *The Golden Bough.* A study in magic and religion. Part II, "Taboo and the Perils of the Soul." London, 1911.

(3) Kohler, Josef. *Philosophy of Law.* "Taboo as a Primitive Substitute for Law." "Philosophy of Law Series," Vol. XII. Boston, 1914. [Reprinted in *Evolution of Law,* II, 120–21.]

(4) Crawley, A. E. "Sexual Taboo," *Journal of Anthropological Institute,* XXIV (London, 1894), 116–25, 219–35, 430–45.

(5) Gray, W. "Some Notes on the Tannese," *Internationales Archiv für Ethnographie,* VII (1894), 232–37.

(6) Waitz, Theodor, und Gerland, Georg. *Anthropologie der Naturvölker,* VI, 343–63. 6 vols. Leipzig, 1862–77.

(7) Tuchmann, J. "La Fascination," *Mélusine,* II (1884–85), 169–175, 193–98, 241–50, 350–57, 368–76, 385–87, 409–17, 457–64, 517–24; III (1886–87), 49–56, 105–9, 319–25, 412–14, 506–8.

(8) Durkheim, É. "La prohibition de l'inceste et ses origines," *L'Année sociologique,* I (1896–97), 38–70.

(9) Crawley, A. E. "Taboos of Commensality," *Folk-Lore,* VI (1895), 130–44.

(10) Hubert, H., and Mauss, M. "Le Mana," *L'Année sociologique,* VII (1902–3), 108–22.

(11) Codrington, R. H. *The Melanesians.* Studies in their anthropology and folk-lore. "Mana," pp. 51–58, 90, 103, 115, 118–24, 191, 200, 307–8. Oxford, 1891.

D. *Myths*

(1) Sorel, Georges. *Reflections on Violence.* Chap. iv, "The Proletarian Strike," pp. 126–67. Translated from the French by T. E. Hulme. New York, 1912.

(2) Smith, W. Robertson. *Lectures on the Religion of the Semites.* "Ritual, Myth and Dogma," pp. 16–24, New ed. London, 1907.
(3) Harrison, Jane E. *Themis.* A study of the social origins of Greek religion. Cambridge, 1912.
(4) Clodd, Edward. *The Birth and Growth of Myth.* Humboldt Library of Popular Science Literature. New York, 1888.
(5) Gennep, A. van. *La Formation des légendes.* Paris, 1910.
(6) Langenhove, Fernand van. *The Growth of a Legend.* A study based upon the German accounts of *francs-tireurs* and "atrocities" in Belgium. With a preface by J. Mark Baldwin. New York, 1916.
(7) Case, S. J. *The Millennial Hope.* Chicago, 1918.
(8) Abraham, Karl. *Dreams and Myths.* Translated from the German by W. A. White. "Nervous and Mental Disease Monograph Series," No. 15. Washington, 1913.
(9) Pfister, Oskar. *The Psychoanalytic Method.* Translated from the German by C. R. Payne. Pp. 410–15. New York, 1917.
(10) Jung, C. G. *Psychology of the Unconscious.* A study of the transformations and symbolisms of the libido. A contribution to the history of the evolution of thought. Authorized translation from the German by Beatrice M. Hinkle. New York, 1916.
(11) Brinton, Daniel G. *The Religious Sentiment: Its Source and Aim.* A contribution to the science and philosophy of religion. Chap. v, "The Myth and the Mythical Cycles," pp. 153–96. New York, 1876.
(12) Rivers, W. H. R. "The Sociological Significance of Myth," *Folk-Lore,* XXIII (1912), 306–31.
(13) Rank, Otto. *The Myth of the Birth of the Hero.* A psychological interpretation of mythology. "Nervous and Mental Disease Monograph Series," No. 18. Translated from the German by Drs. F. Robbins and Smith E. Jelliffe. Washington, 1914.
(14) Freud, Sigmund. "Der Dichter und das Phantasieren," *Sammlung kleiner Schriften zur Neurosenlehre.* 2d ed. Wien, 1909.

III. PUBLIC OPINION AND SOCIAL CONTROL

A. *Materials for the Study of Public Opinion*

(1) Lippmann, Walter. *Public Opinion.* New York, 1922.
(2) Lowell, A. Lawrence. *Public Opinion and Popular Government.* New York, 1913.
(3) ———. *Public Opinion in War and Peace.* Cambridge, 1923.
(4) Tönnies, Ferdinand. *Kritik der öffentlichen Meinung.* Berlin, 1922.
(5) Tarde, Gabriel. *L'Opinion et la foule.* Paris, 1901.
(6) Le Bon, Gustave. *Les Opinions et les croyances; genèse-évolution.* Paris, 1911. [Discusses the formation of public opinion, trends, etc.]

(7) Bauer, Wilhelm. *Die öffentliche Meinung und ihre geschichtlichen Grundlagen*. Tübingen, 1914.

(8) Dicey, A. V. *Lectures on the Relation between Law and Public Opinion in England during the Nineteenth Century.* 2d ed. London, 1914.

(9) Shepard, W. J. "Public Opinion," *American Journal of Sociology*, XV (1909), 32–60.

(10) Tocqueville, Alexius de. *The Republic of the United States of America.* Book IV. "Influence of Democratic Opinion on Political Society," pp. 306–55. 2 vols. in one. New York, 1858.

(11) Bryce, James. *The American Commonwealth*, Vol. II, Part IV, "Public Opinion," pp. 239–64. Chicago, 1891.

(12) ———. *Modern Democracies.* 2 vols. New York, 1921.

(13) Lecky, W. E. H. *Democracy and Liberty.* New York, 1899.

(14) Godkin, Edwin L. *Unforeseen Tendencies of Democracy.* Boston, 1898.

(15) Sageret, J. "L'opinion," *Revue philosophique*, LXXXVI (1918), 19–38.

(16) Bluntschli, Johann K. Article on "Public Opinion," *Lalor's Cyclopaedia of Political Science, Political Economy and of the Political History of the United States.* Vol. III, pp. 479–80.

(17) Lewis, George C. *An Essay on the Influence of Authority in Matters of Opinion.* London, 1849.

(18) Jephson, Henry. *The Platform.* Its rise and progress. 2 vols. London, 1892.

(19) Junius. (Pseud.) *The Letters of Junius.* Woodfall's ed., revised by John Wade. 2 vols. London, 1902.

(20) Woodbury, Margaret. *Public Opinion in Philadelphia, 1789–1801.* "Smith College Studies in History." Vol. V. Northampton, Mass., 1920.

(21) Krock, Arthur. *The Editorials of Henry Watterson.* New York, 1923.

(22) Heaton, John L. *The Story of a Page.* Thirty years of public service and public discussion in the editorial columns of *The New York World.* New York, 1913.

(23) *Editorials from the Hearst Newspapers.* New York, 1906.

(24) Harrison, Shelby M. *Community Action through Surveys.* A paper describing the main features of the social survey. Russell Sage Foundation. New York, 1916.

(25) Millioud, Maurice. "La propagation des idées," *Revue philosophique*, LXIX (1910), 580–600; LXX (1910), 168–91.

(26) Scott, Walter D. *The Theory of Advertising.* Boston, 1903.

[See bibliography, "Discussion," pp. 1649–50.]

B. *The Newspaper as an Organ of Public Opinion*

(1) Dana, Charles A. *The Art of Newspaper Making.* New York, 1895.

(2) Irwin, Will. "The American Newspaper," *Colliers*, XLVI and XLVII (1911). [A series of fifteen articles beginning in the issue of January 21 and ending in the issue of July 29, 1911.]

(3) Park, Robert E. *The Immigrant Press and Its Control.* New York, 1922.

(4) ———. "The Natural History of the Newspaper," *American Journal of Sociology,* XXIX (Nov., 1923), 273–89.

(5) Sinclair, Upton. *The Brass Check.* A study of American journalism. Pasadena, 1919.

(6) Salmon, Lucy M. *The Newspaper and the Historian.* New York, 1923.

(7) ———. *The Newspaper and Authority.* New York, 1924.

(8) Stead, W. T. "Government by Journalism," *Contemporary Review,* XLIX (1886), 653–74.

(9) Blowitz, Henri G. S. A. O. de. *Memoirs of M. de Blowitz.* New York, 1903.

(10) Cook, Edward. *Delane of the Times.* New York, 1916.

(11) Trent, William P. *Daniel Defoe: How to Know Him.* Indianapolis, 1916.

(12) Stevens, David H. *Party Politics and English Journalism, 1702–1742.* Menasha, Wis., 1916.

(13) Oberholtzer, E. P. *Die Beziehungen zwischen dem Staat und der Zeitungspresse im Deutschen Reich.* Nebst einigen Umrissen für die Wissenschaft der Journalistik. Berlin, 1895.

(14) Macdonagh, Michael. *The Reporters' Gallery.* London, 1913.

(15) Lippmann, Walter. *Liberty and the News.* New York, 1920.

(16) O'Brien, Frank M. *The Story of the Sun, New York, 1883–1918.* With an introduction by Edward Page Mitchell, editor of *The Sun.* New York, 1918.

(17) Stone, Melville E. *Fifty Years a Journalist.* Garden City, 1921.

(18) Nevins, Allan. *The Evening Post.* A century of journalism. New York, 1922.

(19) Davis, Elmer H. *History of the New York Times, 1851–1921.* New York, 1921.

(20) Hudson, Frederic. *Journalism in the United States, from 1690 to 1872.* New York, 1873.

(21) Villard, Oswald G. *Some Newspapers and Newspapermen.* New York, 1923.

(22) Bourne, H. R. Fox. *English Newspapers.* London, 1887.

(23) Andrews, Alexander. *The History of British Journalism.* 2 vols. London, 1859.

(24) Lee, James Melvin. *A History of American Journalism.* Boston, 1917.

(25) Harris, Emerson P. and Florence H. *The Community Newspaper.* New York, 1923.

(26) Detweiler, F. G. *The Negro Press in the United States.* Chicago, 1922.

(27) *Christian Literature in Moslem Lands.* Joint committee appointed by the Committee of Reference and Counsel of the Foreign Mission Conference of North America and the Committee on Social and Religious Surveys. New York, 1923.

[See bibliography, "Language and the Printing Press," p. 428.]

IV. LAW AND SOCIAL CONTROL

A. *The Sociological Conception of Law*

(1) Kelsen, Hans. *Der soziologische und der juristische Staatsbegriff.* Kritische Untersuchung des Verhältnisses von Staat und Recht. Tübingen, 1922.

(2) Ehrlich, Eugen. *Grundlegen der Soziologie des Rechts.* München, 1913.

(3) Post, Albert H. "Ethnological Jurisprudence." Translated from the German by Thomas J. McCormack. *Open Court*, XI (1897), 641–53, 718–32. [Reprinted in *Evolution of Law*, II, 10–36.]

(4) Vaccaro, M. A. *Les Bases sociologiques.* Du droit et de l'état. Translated by J. Gaure. Paris, 1898.

(5) Duguit, Léon. *Law in the Modern State.* With introduction by Harold Laski. Translated from the French by Frida and Harold Laski. New York, 1919. [The inherent nature of law is to be found in the social needs of man.]

(6) Picard, Edmond. *Le Droit pur.* Secs. 140–54. Paris, 1908. [Translated by John H. Wigmore, under the title "Factors of Legal Evolution," in *Evolution of Law*, III, 163–81.]

(7) Pound, Roscoe. *Interpretations of Legal History.* New York, 1923.

(8) Pound, Roscoe. *The Spirit of the Common Law.* Boston, 1921.

(9) Laski, Harold J. *Studies in the Problem of Sovereignty.* New Haven, 1917.

(10) ———. *Authority in the Modern State.* New Haven, 1919.

(11) ———. *The Problem of Administrative Areas.* An essay in reconstruction. Northampton, Mass., 1918.

(12) Commons, John R. *Legal Foundations of Capitalism.* New York, 1924.

(13) *Rational Basis of Legal Institutions.* By various authors with an editorial preface by John H. Wigmore and Albert Kokurek. New York, 1923.

(14) Follett, M. P. *The New State.* Group organization the solution of popular government. New York, 1918.

B. *Ancient and Primitive Law*

(1) Maine, Henry S. *Ancient Law.* 14th ed. London, 1891.

(2) Fustel de Coulanges. *The Ancient City.* A study on the religion, laws, and institutions of Greece and Rome. Boston, 1894.

(3) Kocourek, Albert, and Wigmore, J. H., editors. *Sources of Ancient and Primitive Law.* "Evolution of Law Series." Vol. I. Boston, 1915.

(4) Steinmetz, S. R. *Rechtsverhältnisse von eingeborenen Völkern in Afrika und Oceanien.* Berlin, 1903.

(5) Sarbah, John M. *Fanti Customary Law.* A brief introduction to the principles of the native laws and customs of the Fanti and Akan districts of the Gold Coast with a report of some cases thereon decided in the law courts. London, 1904. [Reprinted in *Evolution of Law*, I, 326–82.]

(6) McGee, W J. "The Seri Indians," *Seventeenth Annual Report of the Bureau of American Ethnology, 1895-96*. Part I, pp. 269-95. [Reprinted in *Evolution of Law*, I, 257-78.]

(7) Dugmore, H. H. *Compendium of Kafir Laws and Customs*. Grahamstown, South Africa, 1906. [Reprinted in *Evolution of Law*, I, 292-325.]

(8) Spencer, Baldwin, and Gillen, F. J. *The Northern Tribes of Central Australia*. London, 1904. [Reprinted in *Evolution of Law*, I, 213-326.]

(9) Seebohm, Frederic. *Tribal Custom in Anglo-Saxon Law*. Being an essay supplemental to (1) "The English Village Community," (2) "The Tribal System in Wales." London, 1902.

(10) Goitein, H. *Primitive Ordeal and Modern Law*. London, 1923.

[See bibliography, "The Dual and Ordeal of Battle," p. 656.]

C. *The History and Growth of Law*

(1) Wigmore, John H. "Problems of the Law's Evolution," *Virginia Law Review*, IV (1917), 247-72. [Reprinted, in part, in *Evolution of Law*, III, 153-58.]

(2) Robertson, John M. *The Evolution of States*. An introduction to English Politics. New York, 1913.

(3) Jhering, Rudolph von. *The Struggle for Law*. Translated from the German by John J. Lalor. 1st ed. Chicago, 1879. Chap. i, reprinted in *Evolution of Law*, III, 440-47.]

(4) Nardi-Greco, Carlo. *Sociologia giuridica*. Chap. viii, pp. 310-24. Torino, 1907. [Translated by John H. Wigmore under the title "Causes for the Variation of Jural Phenomena in General," in *Evolution of Law*, III, 182-97.]

(5) Bryce, James. *Studies in History and Jurisprudence*. Oxford, 1901.

(6) ———. "Influence of National Character and Historical Environment on the American Law." Annual address to the Bar Association, 1907. *Reports of American Bar Association*, XXXI (1907), 444-59. [Abridged and reprinted in *Evolution of Law*, III, 369-77.]

(7) Pollock, Frederick, and Maitland, Frederic W. *The History of English Law before the Time of Edward I*. 2d ed. Cambridge, 1899.

(8) Jenks, Edward. *Law and Politics in the Middle Ages*. With a synoptic table of sources. London, 1913.

(9) Holdsworth, W. S. *A History of English Law*. 3 vols. London, 1903-9.

(10) *The Modern Legal Philosophy Series*. Edited by a committee of the Association of American Law Schools. 13 vols. Boston, 1911-.

(11) *Continental Legal History Series*. Published under the auspices of the Association of American Law Schools. 11 vols. Boston, 1912-.

(12) *Select Essays in Anglo-American Legal History.* Compiled and edited by a committee of the Association of American Law Schools. 3 vols. Boston, 1907–9.

TOPICS FOR WRITTEN THEMES

1. Social Interaction and Social Control
2. Social Control as the Central Fact and the Central Problem of Sociology
3. Social Control, Collective Behavior, and Progress
4. Manipulation and Participation as Forms of Social Control
5. Social Control and Self-Control
6. Accommodation as Control
7. Elementary Forms of Social Control: Ceremony, Fashion, Prestige, and Taboo, etc.
8. Traditional Forms of Control, as Folkways, Mores, Myths, Law, Education, Religion, etc.
9. Rumors, News, Facts, etc., as Forms of Control
10. Case Studies of the Influence of Myths, Legends, "Vital Lies," etc., on Collective Behavior
11. The Newspaper as Controlling and as Controlled by Public Opinion
12. Gossip as Social Control
13. Social Control in the Primary Group in the Village Community as Compared with Social Control in the Secondary Group in the City
14. An Analysis of Public Opinion in a Selected Community
15. The Politician and Public Opinion
16. The Social Survey as a Mechanism of Social Control
17. A Study of Common Law and Statute Law from the Standpoint of Mores and Public Opinion
18. A Concrete Example of Social Change Analyzed in Terms of Mores, the Trend, and Public Opinion, as Woman's Suffrage, Prohibition, the Abolition of Slavery, Birth Control, etc.
19. The Life History of an Institution from the Standpoint of Its Origin and Survival as an Agency of Control
20. Unwritten Law; a Case Study
21. Legal Fictions and Their Function in Legal Practice
22. The Sociology of Authority in the Social Group and in the State
23. Maine's Conception of Primitive Law
24. The Greek Conception of Themistes and Their Relation to Code of Solon

QUESTIONS FOR DISCUSSION

1. What do you understand by social control?
2. What do you mean by elementary social control? How would you distinguish it from control exercised by public opinion and law?

3. How does social control in human society differ from that in animal society?

4. What is the natural history of social control in the crowd and the public?

5. What is the fundamental mechanism by which control is established in the group?

6. How do you explain the process by which a crisis develops in a social group? How is crisis related to control?

7. Under what conditions is a dictatorship a necessary form of control? Why?

8. In what way does the crowd control its members?

9. Describe and analyze your behavior in a crowd. Were you conscious of control by the group?

10. What is the mechanism of control in the public?

11. In what sense is ceremony a control?

12. How do music, rhythm, and art enter into social control?

13. Analyze the mechanism of the following forms of ceremonial control: the salute, the visit, the decoration, forms of address, presents, greetings. What other forms of ceremonial control occur to you?

14. What is the relation of fashions to ceremonial control?

15. What is the meaning to the individual of ceremony?

16. What are the values and limitations of ceremonial control?

17. What do you understand by "prestige" in interpreting control through leadership?

18. In what sense is prestige an aspect of personality?

19. What relation, if any, is there between prestige and prejudice?

20. How do you explain the prestige of the white man in South East Africa? Does the white man always have prestige among colored races?

21. What is the relation of taboo to contact? (See pp. 291-93.)

22. Why does taboo refer both to things "holy" and things "unclean"?

23. How does taboo function for social control?

24. Describe and analyze the mechanism of control through taboo in a selected group.

25. What examples do you discover of American taboos?

26. What is the mechanism of control by the myth?

27. "Myths are projections of our hopes and of our fears." Explain with reference to the Freudian wish.

28. How do you explain the growth of a legend? Make an analysis of the origin and development of the legend.

29. Under what conditions does the press promote the growth of myths and legends?

30. Does control by public opinion exist outside of democracies?

31. What is the relation of the majority and the minority to public opinion?

32. What is the distinction made by Lowell between (a) an effective majority, and (b) a numerical majority, with reference to public opinion?

33. What is the relation of mores to public opinion?

34. How do you distinguish between public opinion, advertising, and propaganda as means and forms of social control?

35. What is the relation of news to social control?

36. "The news columns are common carriers." Discuss the implications of this statement.

37. How do you explain the psychology of propaganda?

38. What is the relation between institutions and the mores?

39. What is the nature of social control exerted by the institution?

40. What is the relation of mores to common law and statute law?

41. "Under the free Anglo-Saxon government, no king could ever make a law, but could only declare what the law was." Discuss the significance of this fact.

42. In what different ways does religion control the behavior of the individual and of the group?

43. Is religion a conservative or a progressive factor in society?

CHAPTER XIII

COLLECTIVE BEHAVIOR

I. INTRODUCTION

1. Collective Behavior Defined

A collection of individuals is not always, and by the mere fact of its collectivity, a society. On the other hand, when people come together anywhere, in the most casual way, on the street corner or at a railway station, no matter how great the social distances between them, the mere fact that they are aware of one another's presence sets up a lively exchange of influences, and the behavior that ensues is both social and collective. It is social, at the very least, in the sense that the train of thought and action in each individual is influenced more or less by the action of every other. It is collective in so far as each individual acts under the influence of a mood or a state of mind in which each shares, and in accordance with conventions which all quite unconsciously accept, and which the presence of each enforces upon the others.

The amount of individual eccentricity or deviation from normal and accepted modes of behavior which a community will endure without comment and without protest will vary naturally enough with the character of the community. A cosmopolitan community like New York City can and does endure a great deal in the way of individual eccentricity that a smaller city like Boston would not tolerate. In any case, and this is the point of these observations, even in the most casual relations of life, people do not behave in the presence of others as if they were living alone like Robinson Crusoe, each on his individual island. The very fact of their consciousness of each other tends to maintain and enforce a great body of convention and usage which otherwise falls into abeyance and is forgotten. Collective behavior, then, is the behavior of individuals under the influence of an impulse that is common and collective, an impulse, in other words, that is the result of social interaction.

2.   Social Unrest and Collective Behavior

The most elementary form of collective behavior seems to be what is ordinarily referred to as "social unrest." Unrest in the individual becomes social when it is, or seems to be, transmitted from one individual to another, but more particularly when it produces something akin to the milling process in the herd, so that the manifestations of discontent in A communicated to B, and from B reflected back to A, produce the circular reaction described in the preceding chapter.

The significance of social unrest is that it represents at once a breaking up of the established routine and a preparation for new collective action. Social unrest is not of course a new phenomenon; it is possibly true, however, that it is peculiarly characteristic, as has been said, of modern life. The contrast between the conditions of modern life and of primitive society suggests why this may be true.

The conception which we ought to form of primitive society, says Sumner, is that of small groups scattered over a territory. The size of the group will be determined by the conditions of the struggle for existence and the internal organization of each group will correspond (1) to the size of the group, and (2) to the nature and intensity of the struggle with its neighbors.

Thus war and peace have reacted on each other and developed each other, one within the group, the other in the intergroup relation. The closer the neighbors, and the stronger they are, the intenser is the warfare, and then the intenser is the internal organization and discipline of each. Sentiments are produced to correspond. Loyalty to the group, sacrifice for it, hatred and contempt for outsiders, brotherhood within, warlikeness without—all grow together, common products of the same situation. These relations and sentiments constitute a social philosophy. It is sanctified by connection with religion. Men of an others-group are outsiders with whose ancestors the ancestors of the we-group waged war. The ghosts of the latter will see with pleasure their descendants keep up the fight, and will help them. Virtue consists in killing, plundering, and enslaving outsiders.[1]

The isolation, territorial and cultural, under which alone it is possible to maintain an organization which corresponds to Sumner's description, has disappeared within comparatively recent times from

[1] W. G. Sumner, *Folkways.* A study of the sociological importance of usages, manners, customs, mores, and morals, pp. 12-13. (Boston, 1906.)

all the more inhabitable portions of the earth. In place of it there has come, and with increasing rapidity is coming, into existence a society which includes within its limits the total population of the earth and is so intimately bound together that the speculation of a grain merchant in Chicago may increase the price of bread in Bombay, while the act of an assassin in a provincial town in the Balkans has been sufficient to plunge the world into a war which changed the political map of three continents and cost the lives, in Europe alone, of 8,500,000 combatants.

The first effect of modern conditions of life has been to increase and vastly complicate the economic interdependence of strange and distant peoples, i.e., to destroy distances and make the world, as far as national relations are concerned, small and tight.

The second effect has been to break down family, local, and national ties, and emancipate the individual man.

When the family ceases, as it does in the city, to be an economic unit, when parents and children have vocations that not only intercept the traditional relations of family life, but make them well nigh impossible, the family ceases to function as an organ of social control. When the different nationalities, with their different national cultures, have so far interpenetrated one another that each has permanent colonies within the territorial limits of the other, it is inevitable that the old solidarities, the common loyalties and the common hatreds that formerly bound men together in primitive kinship and local groups should be undermined.

A survey of the world today shows that vast changes are everywhere in progress. Not only in Europe but in Asia and in Africa new cultural contacts have undermined and broken down the old cultures. The effect has been to loosen all the social bonds and reduce society to its individual atoms. The energies thus freed have produced a world-wide ferment. Individuals released from old associations enter all the more readily into new ones. Out of this confusion new and strange political and religious movements arise, which represent the groping of men for a new social order.

3. The Crowd and the Public

Gustave Le Bon, who was the first writer to call attention to the significance of the crowd as a social phenomenon,[1] said that

[1] Scipio Sighele, in a note to the French edition of his *Psychology of Sects*, claims that his volume, *La Folla delinquente*, of which the second edition was

mass movements mark the end of an old régime and the beginning of a new.

"When the structure of a civilization is rotten, it is always the masses that bring about its downfall."[1] On the other hand, "all founders of religious or political creeds have established them solely because they were successful in inspiring crowds with those fanatical sentiments which have as result that men find their happiness in worship and obedience and are ready to lay down their lives for their idol."[2]

The crowd was, for Le Bon, not merely any group brought together by the accident of some chance excitement, but it was above all the emancipated masses whose bonds of loyalty to the old order had been broken by "the destruction of those religious, political, and social beliefs in which all the elements of our civilization are rooted." The crowd, in other words, typified for Le Bon the existing social order. Ours is an age of crowds, he said, an age in which men, massed and herded together in great cities without real convictions or fundamental faiths, are likely to be stampeded in any direction for any chance purpose under the influence of any passing excitement.

Le Bon did not attempt to distinguish between the crowd and the public. This distinction was first made by Tarde in a paper entitled "Le Public et la foule," published first in *La Revue de Paris* in 1898, and included with several others on the same general theme under the title *L'Opinion et la foule* which appeared in 1901. The public, according to Tarde, was a product of the printing press. The limits of the crowd are determined by the length to which a voice will carry or the distance that the eye can survey. But the public presupposes a higher stage of social development in which suggestions are transmitted in the form of ideas and there is "contagion without contact."[3]

---

published at Turin in 1895, and his article "Physiologie du succès," in the *Revue des Revues*, October 1, 1894, were the first attempts to describe the crowd from the point of view of collective psychology. Le Bon published two articles, "Psychologie des foules" in the *Revue scientifique*, April 6 and 20, 1895. These were later gathered together in his volume *Psychologie des foules*, Paris, 1895. See Sighele *Psychologie des sectes*, pp. 25, 39.

[1] Gustave Le Bon, *The Crowd*. A study of the popular mind, p. 19. (New York, 1900.)

[2] *Ibid.*, p. 83.   [3] *L'Opinion et la foule*, pp. 6–7. (Paris, 1901.)

The fundamental distinction between the crowd and the public, however, is not to be measured by numbers nor by means of communication, but by the form and effects of the interactions. In the public, interaction takes the form of discussion. Individuals tend to act upon one another critically; issues are raised and parties form. Opinions clash and thus modify and moderate one another.

The crowd does not discuss and hence it does not reflect. It simply "mills." Out of this milling process a collective impulse is formed which dominates all members of the crowd. Crowds, when they act, do so impulsively. The crowd, says Le Bon, "is the slave of its impulses."

"The varying impulses which crowds obey may be, according to their exciting causes, generous or cruel, heroic or cowardly, but they will always be so imperious that the interest of the individual, even the interest of self-preservation, will not dominate them."[1]

When the crowd acts it becomes a mob. What happens when two mobs meet? We have in the literature no definite record. The nearest approach to it are the occasional accounts we find in the stories of travelers of the contacts and conflicts of armies of primitive peoples. These undisciplined hordes are, as compared with the armies of civilized peoples, little more than armed mobs. Captain S. L. Hinde in his story of the Belgian conquest of the Congo describes several such battles. From the descriptions of battles carried on almost wholly between savage and undisciplined troops it is evident that the morale of an army of savages is a precarious thing. A very large part of the warfare consists in alarms and excursions interspersed with wordy duels to keep up the courage on one side and cause a corresponding depression on the other.[2]

[1] *The Crowd*, p. 41.

[2] Sidney L. Hinde, *The Fall of the Congo Arabs*, p. 147. (London, 1897.) Describing a characteristic incident in one of the strange confused battles Hinde says: "Wordy war, which also raged, had even more effect than our rifles. Mahomedi and Sefu led the Arabs, who were jeering and taunting Lutete's people, saying that they were in a bad case, and had better desert the white man, who was ignorant of the fact that Mohara with all the forces of Nyange was camped in his rear. Lutete's people replied: 'Oh, we know all about Mohara; we ate him the day before yesterday.'" This news became all the more depressing when it turned out to be true. See also Hirn, *The Origins of Art*, p. 269, for an explanation of the rôle of threats and boastings in savage warfare.

Gangs are conflict groups. Their organization is usually quite informal and is determined by the nature and imminence of the conflicts with other groups. When one crowd encounters another it either goes to pieces or it changes its character and becomes a conflict group. When negotiations and palavers take place as they eventually do between conflict groups, these two groups, together with the neutrals who have participated vicariously in the conflict, constitute a public. It is possible that the two opposing savage hordes which seek, by threats and boastings and beatings of drums, to play upon each other's fears and so destroy each other's morale, may be said to constitute a very primitive type of public.

Discussion, as might be expected, takes curious and interesting forms among primitive peoples. In a volume, *Iz Derevni: 12 Pisem* ("From the Country: 12 Letters"), A. N. Engelgardt describes the way in which the Slavic peasants reach their decisions in the village council.

In the discussion of some questions by the *mir* [organization of neighbors] there are no speeches, no debates, no votes. They shout, they abuse one another—they seem on the point of coming to blows; apparently they riot in the most senseless manner. Some one preserves silence, and then suddenly puts in a word, one word, or an ejaculation, and by this word, this ejaculation, he turns the whole thing upside down. In the end, you look into it and find that an admirable decision has been formed and, what is most important, a unanimous decision. . . (In the division of land) the cries, the noise, the hubbub do not subside until everyone is satisfied and no doubter is left.[1]

4. Crowds and Sects

Reference has been made to the crowds that act, but crowds do not always act. Sometimes they merely dance or, at least, make expressive motions which relieve their feelings. "The purest and most typical expression of simple feeling," as Hirn remarks, "is that which consists of mere random movements."[2] When these motions assume, as they so easily do, the character of a fixed sequence in time, that is to say when they are rhythmical, they can be and inevitably are, as

[1] Robert E. Park and Herbert A. Miller, *Old World Traits Transplanted*. Document 23, pp. 32–33. (New York, 1921.)

[2] Yrjö Hirn, *The Origins of Art*. A psychological and sociological inquiry, p. 87. (London, 1900.)

by a sort of inner compulsion, imitated by the onlookers. "As soon as the expression is fixed in rhythmical form its contagious power is incalculably increased."[1]

This explains at once the function and social importance of the dance among primitive people. It is the form in which they prepare for battle and celebrate their victories. It gives the form at once to their religious ritual and to their art. Under the influence of the memories and the emotions which these dances stimulate the primitive group achieves a sense of corporate unity, which makes corporate action possible outside of the fixed and sacred routine of ordinary daily life.

If it is true, as has been suggested, that art and religion had their origin in the choral dance, it is also true that in modern times religious sects and social movements have had their origin in crowd excitements and spontaneous mass movements. The very names which have been commonly applied to them—Quakers, Shakers, Convulsionaires, Holy Rollers—suggest not merely the derision with which they were at one time regarded, but indicate likewise their origin in ecstatic or expressive crowds, the crowds that *do not act.*

All great mass movements tend to display, to a greater or less extent, the characteristics that Le Bon attributes to crowds. Speaking of the convictions of crowds, Le Bon says:

> When these convictions are closely examined, whether at epochs marked by fervent religious faith, or by great political upheavals such as those of the last century, it is apparent that they always assume a peculiar form which I cannot better define than by giving it the name of a religious sentiment.[2]

Le Bon's definition of religion and religious sentiment will hardly find general acceptance but it indicates at any rate his conception of the extent to which individual personalities are involved in the excitements that accompany mass movements.

> A person is not religious solely when he worships a divinity, but when he puts all the resources of his mind, the complete submission of his will, and the whole-souled ardour of fanaticism at the service of a cause or an individual who becomes the goal and guide of his thoughts and actions.[3]

[1] *Ibid.*, p. 89.   [2] Le Bon, *op. cit.*, p. 82.
[3] *Ibid.*, p. 82.

Just as the gang may be regarded as the perpetuation and permanent form of "the crowd that acts," so the sect, religious or political, may be regarded as a perpetuation and permanent form of the orgiastic (ecstatic) or expressive crowd.

"The sect," says Sighele, "is a crowd *triée*, selected, and permanent; the crowd is a transient sect, which does not select its members. The sect is the *chronic* form of the crowd; the crowd is the *acute* form of the sect."[1] It is Sighele's conception that the crowd is an elementary organism, from which the sect issues, like the chick from the egg, and that all other types of social groups "may, in this same manner, be deduced from this primitive social protoplasm." This is a simplification which the facts hardly justify. It is true that, implicit in the practices and the doctrines of a religious sect, there is the kernel of a new independent culture.

5.   Sects and Institutions

A sect is a religious organization that is at war with the existing mores. It seeks to cultivate a state of mind and establish a code of morals different from that of the world about it and for this it claims divine authority. In order to accomplish this end it invariably seeks to set itself off in contrast with the rest of the world. The simplest and most effective way to achieve this is to adopt a peculiar form of dress and speech. This, however, invariably makes its members objects of scorn and derision, and eventually of persecution. It would probably do this even if there was no assumption of moral superiority to the rest of the world in this adoption of a peculiar manner and dress.

Persecution tends to dignify and sanctify all the external marks of the sect, and it becomes a cardinal principle of the sect to maintain them. Any neglect of them is regarded as disloyalty and is punished as heresy. Persecution may eventually, as was the case with the Puritans, the Quakers, the Mormons, compel the sect to seek refuge in some part of the world where it may practice its way of life in peace.

Once the sect has achieved territorial isolation and territorial solidarity, so that it is the dominant power within the region that it occupies, it is able to control the civil organization, establish schools

[1] Scipio Sighele, *Psychologie des sectes*, p. 46. (Paris, 1898.)

and a press, and so put the impress of a peculiar culture upon all the civil and political institutions that it controls. In this case it tends to assume the form of a state, and become a nationality. Something approaching this was achieved by the Mormons in Utah. The most striking illustration of the evolution of a nationality from a sect is Ulster, which now has a position not quite that of a nation within the English empire.

This sketch suggests that the sect, like most other social institutions, originates under conditions that are typical for all institutions of the same species; then it develops in definite and predictable ways, in accordance with a form or entelechy that is predetermined by characteristic internal processes and mechanisms, and that has, in short, a nature and natural history which can be described and explained in sociological terms. Sects have their origin in social unrest to which they give a direction and expression in forms and practices that are largely determined by historical circumstances; movements which were at first inchoate impulses and aspirations gradually take form; policies are defined, doctrine and dogmas formulated; and eventually an administrative machinery and efficiencies are developed to carry into effect policies and purposes. The Salvation Army, of which we have a more adequate history than of most other religious movements, is an example.

A sect in its final form may be described, then, as a movement of social reform and regeneration that has become institutionalized. Eventually, when it has succeeded in accommodating itself to the other rival organizations, when it has become tolerant and is tolerated, it tends to assume the form of a denomination. Denominations tend and are perhaps destined to unite in the form of religious federations— a thing which is inconceivable of a sect.

What is true of the sect, we may assume, and must assume if social movements are to become subjects for sociological investigation, is true of other social institutions. Existing institutions represent social movements that survived the conflict of cultures and the struggle for existence.

Sects, and that is what characterizes and distinguishes them from secular institutions, at least, have had their origin in movements that aimed to reform the mores—movements that sought to renovate and renew the inner life of the community. They have wrought upon

society from within outwardly. Revolutionary and reform movements, on the contrary, have been directed against the outward fabric
and formal structure of society. Revolutionary movements in
particular have assumed that if the existing structure could be
destroyed it would then be possible to erect a new moral order upon
the ruins of the old social structures.

A cursory survey of the history of revolutions suggests that the
most radical and the most successful of them have been religious. Of
this type of revolution Christianity is the most conspicuous example.

6. Classification of the Materials

The materials in this chapter have been arranged under the
headings: (*a*) social contagion, (*b*) the crowd, and (*c*) types of mass
movements. The order of materials follows, in a general way, the
order of institutional evolution. Social unrest is first communicated, then takes form in crowd and mass movements, and finally
crystallizes in institutions. The history of almost any single social
movement—woman's suffrage, prohibition, protestantism—exhibits in
a general way, if not in detail, this progressive change in character.
There is at first a vague general discontent and distress. Then a
violent, confused, and disorderly, but enthusiastic and popular movement arises. Finally the movement takes form; develops leadership,
organization; formulates doctrines and dogmas. Eventually it is
accepted, established, legalized. The movement dies, but the
institution remains.

a) *Social contagion.*—The ease and the rapidity with which a
cultural trait originating in one cultural group finds its way to other
distant groups is familiar to students of folklore and ethnology. The
manner in which fashions are initiated in some metropolitan community, and thence make their way, with more or less rapidity, to the
provinces is an illustration of the same phenomenon in a different
context.

Fashion plays a much larger rôle in social life than most of us imagine.
Fashion dominates our manners and dress but it influences also our sentiments and our modes of thought. Everything in literature, art or philosophy that was characteristic of the middle of the nineteenth century, the
"mid-Victorian period," is now quite out of date and no one who is intelligent now-a-days practices the pruderies, defends the doctrines, nor shares

the enthusiasms of that period. Philosophy, also, changes with the fashion and Sumner says that even mathematics and science do the same. Lecky in his history of Rationalism in Europe describes in great detail how the belief in witches, so characteristic of the Middle Ages, gradually disappeared with the period of enlightenment and progress.[1] But the enlightenment of the eighteenth century was itself a fashion and is now quite out of date. In the meantime a new popular and scientific interest is growing up in obscure mental phenomena which no man with scientific training would have paid any attention to a few years ago because he did not believe in such things. It was not good form to do so.

But the changes of fashion are so pervasive, so familiar, and, indeed, universal phenomena that we do not regard the changes which they bring, no matter how fantastic, as quite out of the usual and expected order. Gabriel Tarde, however, regards the "social contagion" represented in fashion (imitation) as the fundamental social phenomenon.[2]

The term social epidemic, which is, like fashion, a form of social contagion, has a different origin and a different connotation. J. F. C. Hecker, whose study of the Dancing Mania of the Middle Ages, published in 1832, was an incident of his investigation of the Black Death, was perhaps the first to give currency to the term.[3] Both the Black Death and the Dancing Mania assumed the form of epidemics and the latter, the Dancing Mania, was in his estimation the sequel of the former, the Black Death. It was perhaps this similarity in the manner in which they spread—the one by physical and the other by psychical infection—that led him to speak of the spread of a popular delusion in terms of a physical science. Furthermore, the hysteria was directly traceable, as he believed, to the prevailing conditions of the time, and this seemed to put the manifestations in the world of intelligible and controllable phenomena, where they could be investigated.

It is this notion, then, that unrest which manifests itself in social epidemics is an indication of pathological social conditions, and the

[1] W. E. H. Lecky, *History of the Rise and Influence of the Spirit of Rationalism in Europe.* 2 vols. (Vol. I.) (New York, 1866.)

[2] See Gabriel Tarde, *Laws of Imitation.*

[3] J. F. C. Hecker, *Die Tanzwuth, eine Volkskrankheit im Mittelalter.* (Berlin, 1832.) See Introduction of *The Black Death and the Dancing Mania.* Translated from the German by B. G. Babington. Cassell's National Library. (New York, 1888.)

further, the more general, conception that unrest does not become social and hence contagious except when there are contributing causes in the environment—it is this that gives its special significance to the term and the facts. Unrest in the social organism with the social ferments that it induces is like fever in the individual organism, a highly important diagnostic symptom.

b) The crowd.—Neither Le Bon nor any of the other writers upon the subject of mass psychology has succeeded in distinguishing clearly between the organized or "psychological" crowd, as Le Bon calls it, and other similar types of social groups. These distinctions, if they are to be made objectively, must be made on the basis of case studies. It is the purpose of the materials under the general heading of "The 'Animal' Crowd," not so much to furnish a definition, as to indicate the nature and sources of materials from which a definition can be formulated. It is apparent that the different animal groups behave in ways that are distinctive and characteristic, ways which are predetermined in the organism to an extent that is not true of human beings.

One other distinction may possibly be made between the so-called "animal" and the human crowd. The organized crowd is controlled by *a common purpose* and acts to achieve, no matter how vaguely it is defined, a common end. The herd, on the other hand, has apparently no common purpose. Every sheep in the flock, at least as the behavior of the flock is ordinarily interpreted, behaves like every other. Action in a stampede, for example, is collective but it is not concerted. It is very 'difficult to understand how there can be concerted action in the herd or the flock unless it is on an instinctive basis. The crowd, however, responds to collective representations. The crowd does not imitate or follow its leader as sheep do a bellwether. On the contrary, the crowd *carries out the suggestions of the leader*, and even though there be no division of labor each individual acts more or less in his own way to achieve a common end.

In the case of a panic or a stampede, however, where there is no common end, the crowd acts like a flock of sheep. But a stampede or a panic is not a crowd in Le Bon's sense. It is not a psychological unity, nor a "single being," subject to "the mental unity of crowds."[1] The panic is the crowd in dissolution. All effective methods of

[1] Le Bon, *op. cit.*, p. 26.

dispersing crowds involve some method of distracting attention, breaking up the tension, and dissolving the mob into its individual units.

c) *Types of mass movements.*—The most elementary form of mass movement is a mass migration. Such a mass movement displays, in fact, many of the characteristics of the "animal" crowd. It is the "human" herd. The migration of a people, either as individuals or in organized groups, may be compared to the swarming of the hive. Peoples migrate in search of better living conditions, or merely in search of new experience. It is usually the younger generation, the more restless, active, and adaptable, who go out from the security of the old home to seek their fortunes in the new. Once settled on the new land, however, immigrants inevitably remember and idealize the home they have left. Their first disposition is to reproduce as far as possible in the new world the institutions and the social order of the old. Just as the spider spins his web out of his own body, so the immigrant tends to spin out of his experience and traditions, a social organization which reproduces, as far as circumstances will permit, the organization and the life of the ancestral community. In this way the older culture is transplanted and renews itself, under somewhat altered circumstances, in the new home. That explains, in part, at any rate, the fact that migration tends to follow the isotherms, since all the more fundamental cultural devices and experience are likely to be accommodations to geographical and climatic conditions.

In contrast with migrations are movements which are sometimes referred to as crusades, partly because of the religious fervor and fanaticism with which they are usually conducted and partly because they are an appeal to the masses of the people for direct action and depend for their success upon their ability to appeal to some universal human interest or to common experiences and interests that are keenly comprehended by the common man.

The Woman's Christian Temperance Crusade, referred to in the materials, may be regarded, if we are permitted to compare great things with small, as an illustration of collective behavior not unlike the crusades of the eleventh and twelfth centuries.

Crusades are reformatory and religious. This was true at any rate of the early crusades, inspired by Peter the Hermit, whatever may have been the political purposes of the popes who encouraged them. It was the same motive that led the people of the Middle Ages to make pilgrimages which led them to join the crusades. At bottom it was an inner restlessness, that sought peace in great hardship and inspiring action, which moved the masses.

Somewhat the same widespread contagious restlessness is the source of most of our revolutions. It is not, however, hardships and actual distress that inspire revolutions but hopes and dreams, dreams which find expression in those myths and "vital lies," as Vernon Lee calls them,[1] which according to Sorel are the only means of moving the masses.

The distinction between crusades, like the Woman's Temperance Crusade, and revolutions, like the French Revolution, is that one is a radical attempt to correct a recognized evil and the other is a radical attempt to reform an existing social order.

II. MATERIALS

A. SOCIAL CONTAGION

1. An Incident in a Lancashire Cotton Mill[2]

At a cotton manufactory at Hodden Bridge, in Lancashire, a girl, on the fifteenth of February, 1787, put a mouse into the bosom of another girl, who had a great dread of mice. The girl was immediately thrown into a fit, and continued in it with the most violent convulsions for twenty-four hours. On the following day three more girls were seized in the same manner; and on the seventeenth, six more. By this time the alarm was so great that the whole work, in which 200 or 300 were employed, was totally stopped, and an idea prevailed that a particular disease had been introduced by a bag of cotton opened in the house. On Sunday, the eighteenth, Dr. St. Clare was sent for from Preston; before he arrived three more were seized, and during that night and the morning of the nineteenth, eleven more, making in all twenty-four. Of these, twenty-one were young women, two were girls of about ten years of age, and one man, who had been much fatigued with holding the girls. Three of the number lived

---

[1] Vernon Lee [pseud.], *Vital Lies*. Studies of some varieties of recent obscurantism. (London, 1912.)

[2] Taken from *Gentleman's Magazine*, March, 1787, p. 268.

about two miles from the place where the disorder first broke out, and three at another factory in Clitheroe, about five miles distant, which last and two more were infected entirely from report, not having seen the other patients, but, like them and the rest of the country, strongly impressed with the idea of the plague being caught from the cotton. The symptoms were anxiety, strangulation, and very strong convulsions; and these were so violent as to last without any intermission from a quarter of an hour to twenty-four hours, and to require four or five persons to prevent the patients from tearing their hair and dashing their heads against the floor or walls. Dr. St. Clare had taken with him a portable electrical machine, and by electric shocks the patients were universally relieved without exception. As soon as the patients and the country were assured that the complaint was merely nervous, easily cured, and not introduced by the cotton, no fresh person was affected. To dissipate their apprehension still further, the best effects were obtained by causing them to take a cheerful glass and join in a dance. On Tuesday, the twentieth, they danced, and the next day were all at work, except two or three, who were much weakened by their fits.

2. The Dancing Mania of the Middle Ages[1]

So early as the year 1374, assemblages of men and women were seen at Aix-la-Chapelle who had come out of Germany and who, united by one common delusion, exhibited to the public both in the streets and in the churches the following strange spectacle. They formed circles hand in hand and, appearing to have lost all control over their senses, continued dancing, regardless of the by-standers, for hours together in wild delirium, until at length they fell to the ground in a state of exhaustion. While dancing they neither saw nor heard, being insensible to external impressions through the senses, but were haunted by visions, their fancies conjuring up spirits whose names they shrieked out; and some of them afterward asserted that they felt as if they had been immersed in a stream of blood, which obliged them to leap so high. Others, during the paroxysm, saw the heavens open and the Saviour enthroned with

[1] Adapted from J. F. C. Hecker, *The Black Death, and the Dancing Mania*, pp. 106–11. (Cassell & Co., 1888.)

the Virgin Mary, according as the religious notions of the age were strangely and variously reflected in their imaginations.

Where the disease was completely developed, the attack commenced with epileptic convulsions. Those affected fell to the ground senseless, panting and laboring for breath. They foamed at the mouth, and suddenly springing up began their dance amid strange contortions. Yet the malady doubtless made its appearance very variously, and was modified by temporary or local circumstances, whereof non-medical contemporaries but imperfectly noted the essential particulars, accustomed as they were to confound their observation of natural events with their notions of the world of spirits.

It was but a few months ere this demoniacal disease had spread from Aix-la-Chapelle, where it appeared in July, over the neighboring Netherlands. Wherever the dancers appeared, the people assembled in crowds to gratify their curiosity with the frightful spectacle. At length the increasing number of the affected excited no less anxiety than the attention that was paid to them. In towns and villages they took possession of the religious houses, processions were everywhere instituted on their account, and masses were said and hymns were sung, while the disease itself, of the demoniacal origin of which no one entertained the least doubt, excited everywhere astonishment and horror. In Liège the priests had recourse to exorcisms and endeavored by every means in their power to allay an evil which threatened so much danger to themselves; for the possessed, assembling in multitudes, frequently poured forth imprecations against them and menaced their destruction.

A few months after this dancing malady had made its appearance at Aix-la-Chapelle, it broke out at Cologne, where the number of those possessed amounted to more than five hundred; and about the same time at Metz, the streets of which place are said to have been filled with eleven hundred dancers. Peasants left their plows, mechanics their workshops, housewives their domestic duties, to join the wild revels, and this rich commercial city became the scene of the most ruinous disorder. Secret desires were excited and but too often found opportunities for wild enjoyment; and numerous beggars, stimulated by vice and misery, availed themselves of this new complaint to gain a temporary livelihood. Girls and boys quitted their parents, and servants their masters, to amuse themselves at the dances of those possessed, and greedily imbibed the poison of mental infection.   Above a hundred unmarried women were seen raving about in consecrated and unconsecrated places, and the consequences were soon perceived.   Gangs of idle vagabonds, who understood how to imitate to the life the gestures and convulsions of those really affected, roved from place to place seeking maintenance and adventures, and thus, wherever they went, spreading this disgusting spasmodic disease like a plague; for in maladies of this kind the susceptible are infected as easily by the appearance as by the reality.   At last it was found necessary to drive away these mischievous guests, who were equally inaccessible to the exorcisms of the priests and the remedies of the physicians.   It was not, however, until after four months that the Rhenish cities were able to suppress these impostures, which had so alarmingly increased the original evil.   In the meantime, when once called into existence, the plague crept on and found abundant food in the tone of thought which prevailed in the fourteenth and fifteenth centuries, and even, though in a minor degree, throughout the sixteenth and seventeenth, causing a permanent disorder of the mind, and exhibiting, in those cities to whose inhabitants it was a novelty, scenes as strange as they were detestable.

B.   THE CROWD

1. The "Animal" Crowd

a.   The Flock[1]

Understand that a flock is not the same thing as a number of sheep.   On the stark, wild headlands of the White Mountains, as many as thirty Bighorn are known to run in loose, fluctuating hordes; in fenced pastures, two to three hundred; close-herded on the range, two to three thousand; but however artificially augmented, the flock is always a conscious adjustment.   There are always leaders, middlers, and tailers, each insisting on its own place in the order of going. Should the flock be rounded up suddenly in alarm it mills within itself until these have come to their own places.

There is much debate between herders as to the advantage of goats over sheep as leaders.   In any case there are always a few goats

[1] From Mary Austin, *The Flock*, pp. 110–29.   (Houghton Mifflin Co., 1906.)

in a flock, and most American owners prefer them; but the Frenchmen choose bell-wethers. Goats lead naturally by reason of a quicker instinct, forage more freely, and can find water on their own account. But wethers, if trained with care, learn what goats abhor, to take broken ground sedately, to walk through the water rather than set the whole flock leaping and scrambling; but never to give voice to alarm, as goats will, and call the herder.

It appears that leaders understand their office, and goats particularly exhibit a jealousy of their rights to be first over the stepping-stones or to walk the teetering log-bridges at the roaring creeks. By this facile reference of the initiative to the wisest one, the shepherd is served most. The dogs learn to which of the flock to communicate orders, at which heels a bark or a bite soonest sets the flock in motion. But the flock-mind obsesses equally the best-trained, flashes as instantly from the meanest of the flock.

By very little the herder may turn the flock-mind to his advantage, but chiefly it works against him. Suppose on the open range the impulse to forward movement overtakes them, set in motion by some eager leaders that remember enough of what lies ahead to make them oblivious to what they pass. They press ahead. The flock draws on. The momentum of travel grows. The bells clang soft and hurriedly; the sheep forget to feed; they neglect the tender pastures; they will not stay to drink. Under an unwise or indolent herder the sheep going on an unaccustomed trail will overtravel and underfeed, until in the midst of good pasture they starve upon their feet. So it is on the Long Trail you so often see the herder walking with his dogs ahead of his sheep to hold them back to feed. But if it should be new ground he must go after and press them skilfully, for the flock-mind balks chiefly at the unknown.

In sudden attacks from several quarters, or inexplicable man-thwarting of their instincts, the flock-mind teaches them to turn a solid front, revolving about in the smallest compass with the lambs in their midst, narrowing and indrawing until they perish by suffocation. So they did in the intricate defiles of Red Rock, where Carrier lost 250 in '74, and at Poison Springs, as Narcisse Duplin told me, where he had to choose between leaving them to the deadly waters, or, prevented from the spring, made witless by thirst, to mill about until they piled up and killed threescore in their midst. By no urgency of the dogs could they be moved forward or scattered until night fell with coolness and returning sanity. Nor does the imperfect gregariousness of man always save us from ill-considered rushes or strangulous in-turnings of the social mass. Notwithstanding there are those who would have us to be flock-minded.

It is doubtful if the herder is anything more to the flock than an incident of the range, except as a giver of salt, for the only cry they make to him is the salt cry. When the natural craving is at the point of urgency, they circle about his camp or his cabin, leaving off feeding for that business; and nothing else offering, they will continue this headlong circling about a bowlder or any object bulking large in their immediate neighborhood remotely resembling the appurtenances of man, as if they had learned nothing since they were free to find licks for themselves, except that salt comes by bestowal and in conjunction with the vaguely indeterminate lumps of matter that associate with man. As if in fifty centuries of man-herding they had made but one step out of the terrible isolation of brute species, an isolation impenetrable except by fear to every other brute, but now admitting the fact without knowledge, of the God of the Salt. Accustomed to receiving this miracle on open bowlders, when the craving is strong upon them, they seek such as these to run about, vociferating, as if they said, In such a place our God has been wont to bless us, come now, let us greatly entreat Him. This one quavering bleat, unmistakable to the sheepman even at a distance, is the only new note in the sheep's vocabulary, and the only one which passes with intention from himself to man. As for the call of distress which a leader raised by hand may make to his master, it is not new, is not common to flock usage, and is swamped utterly in the obsession of the flock-mind.

b. The Herd[1]

My purpose in this paper is to discuss a group of curious and useless emotional instincts of social animals, which have not yet been properly explained. Excepting two of the number, placed first and last in the list, they are not related in their origin; consequently they are here grouped together arbitrarily, only for the reason that

[1] From W. H. Hudson, "The Strange Instincts of Cattle," in *Longman's Magazine*, XVIII (1891), 389-91.

we are very familiar with them on account of their survival in our domestic animals, and because they are, as I have said, useless; also because they resemble each other, among the passions and actions of the lower animals, in their effect on our minds. This is in all cases unpleasant, and sometimes exceedingly painful, as when species that rank next to ourselves in their developed intelligence and organized societies, such as elephants, monkeys, dogs, and cattle, are seen under the domination of impulses, in some cases resembling insanity, and in others simulating the darkest passions of man.

These instincts are:

(1) The excitement caused by the smell of blood, noticeable in horses and cattle among our domestic animals, and varying greatly in degree, from an emotion so slight as to be scarcely perceptible to the greatest extremes of rage or terror.

(2) The angry excitement roused in some animals when a scarlet or bright red cloth is shown to them. So well known is this apparently insane instinct in our cattle that it has given rise to a proverb and metaphor familiar in a variety of forms to everyone.

(3) The persecution of a sick or weakly animal by its companions.

(4) The sudden deadly fury that seizes on the herd or family at the sight of a companion in extreme distress. Herbivorous mammals at such times will trample and gore the distressed one to death. In the case of wolves, and other savage-tempered carnivorous species, the distressed fellow is frequently torn to pieces and devoured on the spot.

To take the first two together. When we consider that blood is red; that the smell of it is, or may be, or has been, associated with that vivid hue in the animal's mind; that blood, seen and smelt, is, or has been, associated with the sight of wounds and with cries of pain and rage or terror from the wounded or captive animal, there appears at first sight to be some reason for connecting these two instinctive passions as having the same origin—namely, terror and rage caused by the sight of a member of the herd struck down and bleeding, or struggling for life in the grasp of an enemy. I do not mean to say that such an image is actually present in the animal's mind, but that the inherited or instinctive passion is one in kind and in its working with the passion of the animal when experience and reason were its guides.

But the more I consider the point, the more am I inclined to regard these two instincts as separate in their origin, although I retain the belief that cattle and horses and several wild animals are violently excited by the smell of blood for the reason just given—namely, their inherited memory associates the smell of blood with the presence among them of some powerful enemy that threatens their life.

The following incident will show how violently this blood passion sometimes affects cattle, when they are permitted to exist in a half-wild condition, as on the Pampas. I was out with my gun one day, a few miles from home, when I came across a patch on the ground where the grass was pressed or trodden down and stained with blood. I concluded that some thievish Gauchos had slaughtered a fat cow there on the previous night, and, to avoid detection, had somehow managed to carry the whole of it away on their horses. As I walked on, a herd of cattle, numbering about three hundred, appeared moving slowly on to a small stream a mile away; they were traveling in a thin, long line, and would pass the blood-stained spot at a distance of seven to eight hundred yards, but the wind from it would blow across their track. When the tainted wind struck the leaders of the herd they instantly stood still, raising their heads, then broke out into loud, excited bellowings; and finally turning, they started off at a fast trot, following up the scent in a straight line, until they arrived at the place where one of their kind had met its death. The contagion spread, and before long all the cattle were congregated on the fatal spot, and began moving round in a dense mass, bellowing continually.

It may be remarked here that the animal has a peculiar language on occasions like this; it emits a succession of short, bellowing cries, like excited exclamations, followed by a very loud cry, alternately sinking into a hoarse murmur and rising to a kind of scream that grates harshly on the sense. Of the ordinary "cow-music" I am a great admirer, and take as much pleasure in it as in the cries and melody of birds and the sound of the wind in trees; but this performance of cattle excited by the smell of blood is most distressing to hear.

The animals that had forced their way into the center of the mass to the spot where the blood was, pawed the earth, and dug it up with their horns, and trampled each other down in their frantic excitement. It was terrible to see and hear them. The action of those on the border of the living mass, in perpetually moving round in a circle with dolorous bellowings, was like that of the women in an Indian village when a warrior dies, and all night they shriek and howl with simulated grief, going round and round the dead man's hut in an endless procession.

c. The Pack[1]

Wolves are the most sociable of beasts of prey. Not only do they gather in bands, but they arrange to render each other assistance, which is the most important test of sociability. The most gray wolves I ever saw in a band was five. This was in northern New Mexico in January, 1894. The most I ever heard of in a band was thirty-two that were seen in the same region. These bands are apparently formed in winter only. The packs are probably temporary associations of personal acquaintances, for some temporary purpose, or passing reason, such as food question or mating-instinct. As soon as this is settled, they scatter.

An instance in point was related to me by Mr. Gordon Wright of Carberry, Manitoba. During the winter of 1865 he was logging at Sturgeon Lake, Ontario. One Sunday he and some companions strolled out on the ice of the lake to look at the logs there. They heard the hunting-cry of wolves, then a deer (a female) darted from the woods to the open ice. Her sides were heaving, her tongue out, and her legs cut by the slight crust of the snow. Evidently she was hard pressed. She was coming toward them, but one of the men gave a shout which caused her to sheer off. A minute later six timber wolves appeared galloping on her trail, heads low, tails horizontal, and howling continuously. They were uttering their hunting-cry, but as soon as they saw her they broke into a louder, different note, left the trail and made straight for her. Five of the wolves were abreast and one that seemed much darker was behind. Within half a mile they overtook her and pulled her down, all seemed to seize her at once. For a few minutes she bleated like a sheep in distress; after that the only sound was the snarling and the crunching of the wolves as they feasted. Within fifteen minutes nothing was left of the deer but hair and some of the larger bones, and the wolves fighting among themselves for even these. Then they scattered, each going a quarter of a

[1] From Ernest Thompson Seton, "The Habits of Wolves," in *The American Magazine*, LXIV (1907), 636.

mile or so, no two in the same direction, and those that remained in view curled up there on the open lake to sleep. This happened about ten in the morning within three hundred yards of several witnesses.

2. The Psychological Crowd[1]

In its ordinary sense the word "crowd" means a gathering of individuals of whatever nationality, profession, or sex, and whatever be the chances that have brought them together. From the psychological point of view the expression "crowd" assumes quite a different signification. Under certain given circumstances, and only under those circumstances, an agglomeration of men presents new characteristics very different from those of the individuals composing it. The sentiments and ideas of all the persons in the gathering take one and the same direction, and their conscious personality vanishes. A collective mind is formed, doubtless transitory, but presenting very clearly defined characteristics. The gathering has thus become what, in the absence of a better expression, I will call an organized crowd, or, if the term is considered preferable, a psychological crowd. It forms a single being, and is subjected to the law of the mental unity of crowds.

It is evident that it is not by the mere fact of a number of individuals finding themselves accidentally side by side that they acquire the character of an organized crowd. A thousand individuals accidentally gathered in a public place without any determined object in no way constitute a crowd, from the psychological point of view. To acquire the special characteristics of such a crowd, the influence is necessary of certain predisposing causes, of which we shall have to determine the nature.

The disappearance of conscious personality and the turning of feelings and thoughts in a definite direction, which are the primary characteristics of a crowd about to become organized, do not always involve the simultaneous presence of a number of individuals on one spot. Thousands of isolated individuals may acquire at certain moments, and under the influence of certain violent emotions—such, for example, as a great national event—the characteristics of a psychological crowd. It will be sufficient in that case that a mere

[1] Adapted from Gustave Le Bon, *The Crowd*, pp. 1–14. (T. Fisher Unwin, 1897.)

chance should bring them together for their acts at once to assume the characteristics peculiar to the acts of a crowd. At certain moments half a dozen men might constitute a psychological crowd, which may not happen in the case of hundreds of men gathered together by accident. On the other hand, an entire nation, though there may be no visible agglomeration, may become a crowd under the action of certain influences.

It is not easy to describe the mind of crowds with exactness, because its organization varies not only according to race and composition but also according to the nature and intensity of the exciting causes to which crowds are subjected. The same difficulty, however, presents itself in the psychological study of an individual. It is only in novels that individuals are found to traverse their whole life with an unvarying character. It is only the uniformity of the environment that creates the apparent uniformity of characters. I have shown elsewhere that all mental constitutions contain possibilities of character which may be manifested in consequence of a sudden change of environment. This explains how it was that among the most savage members of the French Convention were to be found inoffensive citizens who, under ordinary circumstances, would have been peaceable notaries or virtuous magistrates. The storm past, they resumed their normal character of quiet, law-abiding citizens. Napoleon found amongst them his most docile servants.

It being impossible to study here all the successive degrees of organization of crowds, we shall concern ourselves more especially with such crowds as have attained to the phase of complete organization. In this way we shall see what crowds may become, but not what they invariably are. It is only in this advanced phase of organization that certain new and special characteristics are superposed on the unvarying and dominant character of the race; then takes place that turning, already alluded to, of all the feelings and thoughts of the collectivity in an identical direction. It is only under such circumstances, too, that what I have called above the psychological law of the mental unity of crowds comes into play.

The most striking peculiarity presented by a psychological crowd is the following: Whoever be the individuals that compose it, however like or unlike be their mode of life, their occupations, their character, or their intelligence, the fact that they have been transformed into a crowd puts them in possession of a sort of collective mind which makes them feel, think, and act in a manner quite different from that in which each individual of them would feel, think, and act, were he in a state of isolation.   There are certain ideas and feelings which do not come into being or do not transform themselves into acts except in the case of individuals forming a crowd.   The psychological crowd is a provisional being formed of heterogeneous elements, which for a moment are combined, exactly as the cells which constitute a living body form by their reunion a new being which displays characteristics very different from those possessed by each of the cells singly.

Contrary to an opinion which one is astonished to find coming from the pen of so acute a philosopher as Herbert Spencer, in the aggregate which constitutes a crowd there is in no sort a summing-up of or an average struck between its elements.   What really takes place is a combination followed by the creation of new characteristics, just as in chemistry certain elements, when brought into contact— bases and acids, for example—combine to form a new body possessing properties quite different from those of the bodies that have served to form it.

It is easy to prove how much the individual forming part of a crowd differs from the isolated individual, but it is less easy to discover the causes of this difference.   To obtain, at any rate, a glimpse of them it is necessary in the first place to call to mind the truth established by modern psychology that unconscious phenomena play an altogether preponderating part not only in organic life but also in the operations of the intelligence.   The conscious life of the mind is of small importance in comparison with its unconscious life. The most subtle analyst, the most acute observer, is scarcely successful in discovering more than a very small number of the unconscious motives that determine his conduct.

The greater part of our daily actions are the result of hidden motives which escape our observation.   It is more especially with respect to those unconscious elements that all the individuals belonging to it resemble each other, while it is principally in respect to the conscious elements of their character—the fruit of education, and yet more of exceptional hereditary conditions—that they differ from each other.   Men most unlike in the matter of their intelligence possess instincts, passions, and feelings that are very similar. In the case of everything that belongs to the realm of sentiment—religion, politics, morality, the affections and antipathies, etc.—the most eminent men seldom surpass the standard of the most ordinary individuals. From the intellectual point of view an abyss may exist between a great mathematician and his bootmaker, but from the point of view of character the difference is most often slight or non-existent.

It is precisely these general qualities of character, governed by forces of which we are unconscious, and possessed by the majority of the normal individuals of a race in much the same degree, it is precisely these qualities that in crowds become common property. In the collective mind the intellectual aptitudes of the individuals, and in consequence their individuality, are weakened. The heterogeneous is swamped by the homogeneous, and the unconscious qualities obtain the upper hand.

This very fact that crowds possess in common ordinary qualities explains why they can never accomplish acts demanding a high degree of intelligence. The decisions affecting matters of general interest come to by an assembly of men of distinction, but specialists in different walks of life, are not sensibly superior to the decisions that would be adopted by a gathering of imbeciles. The truth is, they can only bring to bear in common on the work in hand those mediocre qualities which are the birthright of every average individual. In crowds it is stupidity and not mother-wit that is accumulated. It is not all the world, as is so often repeated, that has more wit than Voltaire, but assuredly Voltaire that has more wit than all the world, if by "all the world" crowds are to be understood.

If the individuals of a crowd confined themselves to putting in common the ordinary qualities of which each of them has his share, there would merely result the striking of an average, and not, as we have said is actually the case, the creation of new characteristics. How is it that these new characteristics are created? This is what we are now to investigate.

Different causes determine the appearance of these characteristics peculiar to crowds and not possessed by isolated individuals. The first is that the individual forming part of a crowd acquires, solely from numerical considerations, a sentiment of invincible power which allows him to yield to instincts which, had he been alone, he would perforce have kept under restraint. He will be the less disposed to check himself from the consideration that, a crowd being anonymous and in consequence irresponsible, the sentiment of responsibility which always controls individuals disappears entirely.

The second cause, which is contagion, also intervenes to determine the manifestation in crowds of their special characteristics, and at the same time the trend they are to take. Contagion is a phenomenon of which it is easy to establish the presence, but which it is not easy to explain. It must be classed among those phenomena of a hypnotic order. In a crowd every sentiment and act is contagious, and contagious to such a degree that an individual readily sacrifices his personal interest to the collective interest. This is an aptitude very contrary to his nature, and of which a man is scarcely capable except when he makes part of a crowd.

A third cause, and by far the most important, determines in the individuals of a crowd special characteristics which are quite contrary at times to those presented by the isolated individual. I allude to that suggestibility of which, moreover, the contagion mentioned above is neither more nor less than an effect.

The most careful observations seem to prove that an individual immerged for some length of time in a crowd in action soon finds himself—either in consequence of the magnetic influence given out by the crowd or from some other cause of which we are ignorant— in a special state, which much resembles the state of fascination in which the hypnotized individual finds himself in the hands of the hypnotizer.

Such also is approximately the state of the individual forming part of a psychological crowd. He is no longer conscious of his acts. In his case, as in the case of the hypnotized subject, at the same time that certain faculties are destroyed, others may be brought to a high degree of exaltation. Under the influence of a suggestion, he will undertake the accomplishment of certain acts with irresistible impetuosity. This impetuosity is the more irresistible in the case of crowds than in that of the hypnotized subject, from the fact that, the suggestion being the same for all the individuals of the crowd, it gains in strength by reciprocity. The individualities in the crowd who might possess a personality sufficiently strong to resist the suggestion are too few in number to struggle against the current. At the utmost, they may be able to attempt a diversion by means of different suggestions. It is in this way, for instance, that a happy expression, an image opportunely evoked, have occasionally deterred crowds from the most bloodthirsty acts.

We see, then, that the disappearance of the conscious personality, the predominance of the unconscious personality, the turning by means of suggestion and contagion of feelings and ideas in an identical direction, the tendency to immediately transform the suggested ideas into acts; these, we see, are the principal characteristics of the individual forming part of a crowd. He is no longer himself, but has become an automaton who has ceased to be guided by his will.

Moreover, by the mere fact that he forms part of an organized crowd, a man descends several rungs in the ladder of civilization. Isolated, he may be a cultivated individual; in a crowd, he is a barbarian—that is, a creature acting by instinct. He possesses the spontaneity, the violence, the ferocity, and also the enthusiasm and heroism of primitive beings.

An individual in a crowd is a grain of sand amid other grains of sand, which the wind stirs up at will. It is for these reasons that juries are seen to deliver verdicts of which each individual juror would disapprove, that parliamentary assemblies adopt laws and measures of which each of their members would disapprove in his own person. Taken separately, the men of the Convention were enlightened citizens of peaceful habits. United in a crowd, they did not hesitate to give their adhesion to the most savage proposals, to guillotine individuals most clearly innocent, and, contrary to their interest, to renounce their inviolability and to decimate themselves.

The conclusion to be drawn from what precedes is that the crowd is always intellectually inferior to the isolated individual, but that, from the point of view of feelings and of the acts these feelings provoke, the crowd may, according to circumstances, be better or worse than the individual. All depends on the nature of the suggestion to which the crowd is exposed. This is the point that has been completely misunderstood by writers who have only studied crowds from the criminal point of view. Doubtless a crowd is often criminal, but also it is often heroic. It is crowds rather than isolated individuals that may be induced to run the risk of death to secure the triumph of a creed or an idea, that may be fired with enthusiasm for glory and honor, that are led on—almost without bread and without arms, as in the age of the Crusades—to deliver the tomb of Christ from the infidel, or, as in '93, to defend the fatherland. Such heroism is without doubt somewhat unconscious, but it is of such heroism that history is made. Were peoples only to be credited with the great actions performed in cold blood, the annals of the world would register but few of them.

3. The Crowd Defined[1]

A crowd in the ordinary sense of that term is any chance collection of individuals. Such a collectivity becomes a crowd in the sociological sense only when a condition of *rapport* has been established among the individuals who compose it.

Rapport implies the existence of a mutual responsiveness, such that every member of the group reacts immediately, spontaneously, and sympathetically to the sentiments and attitudes of every other member.

The fact that A responds sympathetically toward B and C implies the existence in A of an attitude of receptivity and suggestibility toward the sentiments and attitudes of B and C. Where A, B, and C are mutually sympathetic, the inhibitions which, under ordinary circumstances, serve to preserve the isolation and self-consciousness of individuals are relaxed or completely broken down. Under these circumstances each individual, in so far as he may be said to reflect, in his own consciousness and in his emotional reactions, the sentiments and emotions of all the others, tends at the same time to modify the sentiments and attitudes of those others. The effect is to produce a heightened, intensified, and relatively impersonal state of consciousness in which all seem to share, but which is, at the same time, relatively independent of each.

The development of this so-called "group-consciousness" represents a certain amount of loss of self-control on the part of the individual. Such control as the individual loses over himself is thus automatically transferred to the group as a whole or to the leader.

What is meant by *rapport* in the group may be illustrated by a somewhat similar phenomenon which occurs in hypnosis. In this case a relation is established between the experimenter and his subject

[1] From Robert E. Park, *The Crowd and the Public.* (Unpublished manuscript.)

such that the subject responds automatically to every suggestion of the experimenter but is apparently oblivious of suggestions coming from other persons whose existence he does not perceive or ignores. This is the condition called "isolated rapport."[1]

In the case of the crowd this mutual and exclusive responsiveness of each member of the crowd to the suggestions emanating from the other members produces here also a kind of mental isolation which is accompanied by an inhibition of the stimuli and suggestions that control the behavior of individuals under the conditions of ordinary life. Under these conditions impulses long repressed in the individual may find an expression in the crowd. It is this, no doubt, which accounts for those so-called criminal and atavistic tendencies of crowds, of which Le Bon and Sighele speak.[2]

The organization of the crowd is only finally effected when the attention of the individuals who compose it becomes focused upon some particular object or some particular objective. This object thus fixed in the focus of the attention of the group tends to assume the character of a *collective representation*.[3] It becomes this because it is the focus of the collectively enhanced emotion and sentiment of the group. It becomes the representation and the symbol of what the crowd feels and wills at the moment when all members are suffused with a common collective excitement and dominated by a common and collective idea. This excitement and this idea with the meanings that attach to it are called collective because they are a product of the interactions of the members of the crowd. They are not individual but corporate products.

Le Bon describes the organization thus effected in a chance-met collection of individuals as a "collective mind," and refers to the group, transitory and ephemeral though it be, as a "single being."

The positive factors in determining the organization of the crowd are then:

(1) A condition of *rapport* among the members of the group with a certain amount of contagious excitement and heightened suggestibility incident to it.

[1] Moll, *Hypnotism*, pp. 134–36.

[2] Sighele, *Psychologie des Auflaufs und der Massenverbrechen* (translated from the Italian), p. 79.

[3] Durkheim, *The Elementary Forms of Religious Life*, pp. 432–37.

(2) A certain degree of mental isolation of the group following as a consequence of the *rapport* and sympathetic responsiveness of members of the group.

(3) Focus of attention; and finally the consequent

(4) Collective representation.

C. TYPES OF MASS MOVEMENTS

1. Crowd Excitements and Mass Movements: The Klondike Rush[1]

It was near the middle of July when the steamer *Excelsior* arrived in San Francisco from St. Michael's, on the west coast of Alaska, with forty miners, having among them seven hundred and fifty thousand dollars' worth of gold, brought down from the Klondike. When the bags and cans and jars containing it had been emptied and the gold piled on the counters of the establishment to which it was brought, no such sight had been seen in San Francisco since the famous year of 1849.

On July 18 the *Portland* arrived in Seattle, on Puget Sound, having on board sixty-eight miners, who brought ashore bullion worth a million dollars. The next day it was stated that these miners had in addition enough gold concealed about their persons and in their baggage to double the first estimate. Whether all these statements were correct or not does not signify, for those were the reports that were spread throughout the states. From this last source alone, the mint at San Francisco received half a million dollars' worth of gold in one week, and it was certain that men who had gone away poor had come back with fortunes. It was stated that a poor blacksmith who had gone up from Seattle returned with $115,000, and that a man from Fresno, who had failed as a farmer, had secured $135,000.

The gold fever set in with fury and attacked all classes. Men in good positions, with plenty of money to spend on an outfit, and men with little beyond the amount of their fare, country men and city men, clerks and professional men without the faintest notion of the meaning of "roughing it," flocked in impossible numbers to secure a passage. There were no means of taking them. Even in distant New York, the offices of railroad companies and local agencies were

[1] Adapted from T. C. Down, "The Rush to the Klondike," in the *Cornhill Magazine*, IV (1898), 33–43.

besieged by anxious inquirers eager to join the throng. On Puget Sound, mills, factories, and smelting works were deserted by their employees, and all the miners on the upper Skeena left their work in a body. On July 21 the North American Transportation Company (one of two companies which monopolized the trade of the Yukon) was reincorporated in Chicago with a quadrupled capital, to cope with the demands of traffic. At the different Pacific ports every available vessel was pressed into the service, and still the wild rush could not be met. Before the end of July the *Portland* left Seattle again for St. Michael's, and the *Mexico* and *Topeka* for Dyea; the *Islander* and *Tees* sailed for Dyea from Victoria, and the *G. W. Elder* from Portland; while from San Francisco the *Excelsior*, of the Alaska Company, which had brought the first gold down, left again for St. Michael's on July 28, being the last of the company's fleet scheduled to connect with the Yukon river boats for the season. Three times the original price was offered for the passage, and one passenger accepted an offer of $1,500 for the ticket for which he had paid only $150.

This, however, was only the beginning of the rush. Three more steamers were announced to sail in August for the mouth of the Yukon, and at least a dozen more for the Lynn Canal, among which were old tubs, which, after being tied up for years, were now overhauled and refitted for the voyage north. One of these was the *Williamette*, an old collier with only sleeping quarters for the officers and crew, which, however, was fitted up with bunks and left Seattle for Dyea and Skagway with 850 passengers, 1,200 tons of freight, and 300 horses, men, live stock, and freight being wedged between decks till the atmosphere was like that of a dungeon; and even with such a prospect in view, it was only by a lavish amount of tipping that a man could get his effects taken aboard. Besides all these, there were numerous scows loaded with provisions and fuel, and barges conveying horses for packing purposes.

A frightful state of congestion followed as each successive steamer on its arrival at the head of the Lynn Canal poured forth its crowds of passengers and added to the enormous loads of freight already accumulated. Matters became so serious that on August 10 the United States Secretary of the Interior, having received information that 3,000 persons with 2,000 tons of baggage and freight were then waiting to cross the mountains to Yukon, and that many more were preparing to join them, issued a warning to the public (following that of the Dominion Government of the previous week) in which he called attention to the exposure, privation, suffering, and danger incident to the journey at that advanced period of the season, and further referred to the gravity of the possible consequences to people detained in the mountainous wilderness during five or six months of Arctic winter, where no relief could reach them.

To come now to the state of things at the head of the Lynn Canal, where the steamers discharged their loads of passengers, horses, and freight. This was done either at Dyea or Skagway, the former being the landing-place for the Chilcoot Pass, and the latter for the White Pass, the distance between the two places being about four miles by sea. There were no towns at these places, nor any convenience for landing except a small wharf at Skagway, which was not completed, the workmen having been smitten with the gold fever. Every man had to bring with him, if he wanted to get through and live, supplies for a year: sacks of flour, slabs of bacon, beans, and so forth, his cooking utensils, his mining outfit and building tools, his tent, and all the heavy clothing and blankets suitable for the northern winter, one thousand pounds' weight at least. Imagine the frightful mass of stuff disgorged as each successive vessel arrived, with no adequate means of taking it inland!

Before the end of September people were preparing to winter on the coast, and Skagway was growing into a substantial town. Where in the beginning of August there were only a couple of shacks, there were in the middle of October 700 wooden buildings and a population of about 1,500. Businesses of all kinds were carried on, saloons and low gaming houses and haunts of all sorts abounded, but of law and order there was none. Dyea also, which at one time was almost deserted, was growing into a place of importance, but the title of every lot in both towns was in dispute. Rain was still pouring down, and without high rubber boots walking was impossible. None indeed but the most hardy could stand existence in such places, and every steamer from the south carried fresh loads of people back to their homes.

Of the 6,000 people who went in this fall, 200 at the most got over to the Dawson Route by the White Pass, and perhaps 700 by the Chilcoot. There were probably 1,000 camped at Lake Bennett, and all the rest, except the 1,500 remaining on the coast, had returned home to wait till midwinter or the spring before venturing up again. The question of which was the best trail was still undecided, and men vehemently debated it every day with the assistance of the most powerful language at their command.

As to the crowds who had gone to St. Michael's, it is doubtful whether any of them got through to Dawson City, since the lower Yukon is impassable by the end of September, and, at any rate, in view of the prospects of short rations, it would have been rash to try. The consequence would be that they would have to remain on that desolate island during nine months of almost Arctic winter, for the river does not open again till the end of June. Here they would be absolutely without employment unless they chose to stack wood for the steamboat companies, and their only amusements (save the mark) would be drinking bad rye-whiskey—for Alaska is a "prohibition" country—and poker-playing. For men with a soul above such delights, the heart-breaking monotony of a northern winter would be appalling, and it is only to be understood by those who have had to endure similar experiences themselves on the western prairies.

2. Mass Movements and the Mores: The Woman's Temperance Crusade[1]

On the evening of December 23, 1873, there might have been seen in the streets of Hillsboro, Ohio, persons singly or in groups wending their way to Music Hall, where a lecture on temperance was to be delivered by Dr. Dio Lewis, of Boston, Massachusetts.

Hillsboro is a small place, containing something more than 3,000 people. The inhabitants are rather better educated than is usually the case in small towns, and its society is indeed noted in that part of the country for its quietude, culture, and refinement.

But Hillsboro was by no means exempt from the prevailing scourge of intemperance. The early settlers of Hillsboro were mostly from Virginia, and brought with them the old-fashioned ideas of hospitality. For many years previous to the crusade the professional men, and especially of the bar, were nearly all habitual drinkers, and many of them very dissipated. When a few earnest temperance men, among

[1] Adapted from Mrs. Annie Wittenmyer, *History of the Woman's Temperance Crusade* (1878), pp. 34–62.

whom was Governor Allen Trimble, initiated a total-abstinence movement in or about the year 1830, the pulpit took up arms against
them, and a condemnatory sermon was preached in one of the
churches.

Thus it was that, although from time to time men, good and true,
banded themselves together in efforts to break up this dreadful state
of things and reform society, all endeavors seemed to fail of any
permanent effect.

The plan laid down by Dr. Lewis challenged attention by its
novelty at least. He believed the work of temperance reform might
be successfully carried on by women if they would set about it in the
right manner—going to the saloon-keeper in a spirit of Christian love,
and persuading him for the sake of humanity and his own eternal
welfare to quit the hateful, soul-destroying business. The doctor
spoke with enthusiasm; and seeing him so full of faith, the hearts
of the women seized the hope—a forlorn one, 'tis true, but still a
hope—and when Dr. Lewis asked if they were willing to undertake
the task, scores of women rose to their feet, and there was no lack of
good men who pledged themselves to encourage and sustain the women
in their work.

At a subsequent meeting an organization was effected and Mrs.
Eliza J. Thompson, a daughter of ex-Governor Trimble of Ohio, was
elected chairman. Mrs. Thompson gives the following account of
the manner in which the crusade was organized:

My boy came home from Dr. Dio Lewis' lecture and said, "Ma,
they've got you into business"; and went on to tell that Dio Lewis had
incidentally related the successful effort of his mother, by prayer and
persuasion, to close the saloon in a town where he lived when a boy, and
that he had exhorted the women of Hillsboro to do the same, and fifty had
risen up to signify their willingness, and that they looked to me to help
them to carry out their promise. As I'm talking to you here familiarly,
I'll go on to say that my husband, who had retired, and was in an adjoining
room, raised up on his elbow and called out, "Oh! that's all tomfoolery!"
I remember I answered him something like this: "Well, husband, the men
have been in the tomfoolery business a long time; perhaps the Lord is going
to call us into partnership with them." I said no more. The next morning
my brother-in-law, Colonel ———, came in and told me about the meeting,
and said, "Now, you must be sure to go to the women's meeting at the
church this morning; they look to see you there." Our folks talked it all

over, and my husband said, "Well, we all know where your mother'll take this case for counsel," and then he pointed to the Bible and left the room.

I went into the corner of my room, and knelt down and opened my Bible to see what God would say to me. Just at that moment there was a tap on the door and my daughter entered. She was in tears; she held her Bible in her hand, open to the 146th Psalm. She said, "Ma, I just opened to this, and I think it is for you," and then she went away, and I sat down and read

THIS WONDERFUL MESSAGE FROM GOD

"Put not your trust in princes, nor in the son of man, in whom there is no help. Happy is he that hath the God of Jacob for his help, whose hope is in the Lord his God; which keepeth truth forever; which executeth judgment for the oppressed; the Lord looseth the prisoners; the Lord openeth the eyes of the blind; the Lord raiseth them that are bowed down; the Lord loveth the righteous; the Lord relieveth the fatherless and the widow—*but the way of the wicked he turneth upside down.* The Lord shall reign forever, even thy God, O Zion, unto all generations. Praise ye the Lord!"

I knew that was for me, and I got up, put on my shoes, and started. I went to the church, in this town where I was born. I sat down quietly in the back part of the audience room, by the stove. A hundred ladies were assembled. I heard my name—heard the whisper pass through the company, "Here she is!" "She's come!" and before I could get to the pulpit, they had put me "in office"—I was their leader.

Many of our citizens were there, and our ministers also. They stayed a few minutes, and then rose and went out, saying, "This is your work—we leave it with the women and the Lord." When they had gone, I just opened the big pulpit Bible and read that 146th Psalm, and told them the circumstance of my selecting it. The women sobbed so I could hardly go on. When I had finished, I felt inspired to call on a dear Presbyterian lady to pray. She did so without the least hesitation, though it was the first audible prayer in her life. I can't tell you anything about that prayer, only that the words were like fire.

When she had prayed, I said—and it all came to me just at the moment —"Now, ladies, let us file out, two by two, the smallest first, and let us sing as we go, 'Give to the winds thy fears.' "

We went first to John ———'s saloon. Now, John was a German, and his sister had lived in my family thirteen years, and she was very mild and gentle, and I hoped it might prove a family trait, but I found out it wasn't. He fumed about dreadfully and said, "It's awful; it's a sin and a shame to pray in a saloon!" But we prayed right on just the same.

Next day the ladies held another meeting, but decided not to make any visitations, it being Christmas day, and the hotel-keepers more than usually busy and not likely to listen very attentively to our proposition.

On the twenty-sixth, the hotels and saloons were visited; Mrs. Thompson presenting the appeal. And it was on this morning, and at the saloon of Robert Ward, that there came a break in the established routine. "Bob" was a social, jolly sort of fellow, and his saloon was a favorite resort, and there were many women in the company that morning whose hearts were aching in consequence of his wrong-doing. Ward was evidently touched. He confessed that it was a "bad business," said if he could only "afford to quit it he would," and then tears began to flow from his eyes. Many of the ladies were weeping, and at length, as if by inspiration, Mrs. Thompson kneeled on the floor of the saloon, all kneeling with her, even the saloonist, and prayed, pleading with indescribable pathos and earnestness for the conversion and salvation of this and all saloon-keepers. When the amen was sobbed rather than spoken, Mrs. Washington Doggett's sweet voice began, "There is a fountain," etc., in which all joined; the effect was most solemn, and when the hymn was finished the ladies went quietly away, and that was the first saloon prayer meeting.

There was a saloon-keeper brought from Greenfield to H—— to be tried under the Adair law. The poor mother who brought the suit had besought him not to sell to her son—"her only son." He replied roughly that he would sell to him "as long as he had a dime." Another mother, an old lady, made the same request, "lest," she said, "he may some day fill a drunkard's grave." "Madam," he replied, "your son has as good a right to fill a drunkard's grave as any other mother's son." And in one of the Hillsboro saloons a lady saw her nephew. "O, Mr. B——," said she, "don't sell whiskey to that boy: if he has one drink he will want another, and he may die a drunkard." "Madam, I will sell to him if it sends his soul to hell," was the awful reply. The last man is a peculiarly hard, stony sort of man; his lips look as if chiseled out of flint, a man to be afraid of. One morning, when the visiting band reached his door, they found him in a very bad humor. He locked his door and seated himself on the horse block in front in a perfect rage, clenched his fist, swore furiously, and ordered us to go home. Some gentlemen, on the opposite side of the street, afterward said that they were watching the scene, ready to rush over and defend the ladies from an attack, and they were sure it would come; but one of the ladies, a sweet-souled woman, gentle and placid, kneeled just at his feet, and poured out such a tender, earnest prayer for him, that he quieted down entirely, and when she rose and offered him her hand in token of kind feeling, he could not refuse to take it.

During the Crusade, a saloon-keeper (at Ocean Grove) consented to close his business. There was a great deal of enthusiasm and interest, and we women decided to compensate the man for his whiskey and make a bonfire of it in the street. A great crowd gathered about the saloon, and the barrels of whiskey were rolled out to the public square where we were to have our bonfire. Myself and two other little women, who had been chosen to knock in the heads, and had come to the place with axes concealed under our shawls, went to our work with a will.

I didn't know I was so strong, but I lifted that axe like a woodman and brought it down with such force that the first blow stove in the head of a barrel and splashed the whiskey in every direction. I was literally baptized with the noxious stuff. The intention was to set it on fire, and we had brought matches for that purpose, *but it would not burn!* It was a villainous compound of some sort, but we had set out to have a fire, and were determined by some means or other to make it burn, so we sent for some coal oil and poured it on and we soon had a blaze. The man who could sell such liquors would not be likely to keep the pledge. He is selling liquors again.

The crusade began at Washington C.H. only two days later than at Hillsboro. And Washington C.H. was the first place where the crusade was made prominent and successful.

On Friday morning, December 26, 1873, after an hour of prayer in the M.E. Church, forty-four women filed slowly and solemnly down the aisle, and started forth upon their strange mission with fear and trembling, while the male portion of the audience remained at the church to pray for the success of this new undertaking; the tolling of the church-bell keeping time to the solemn march of the women, as they wended their way to the first drug-store on the list. (The number of places within the city limits where intoxicating drinks were sold was fourteen—eleven saloons and three drug-stores.) Here, as in every place, they entered singing, every woman taking up the sacred strain as she crossed the threshold. This was followed by the reading of the appeal and prayer; then earnest pleading to desist from their soul-destroying traffic and sign the dealer's pledge.

Thus, all the day long, they went from place to place, without stopping even for dinner or lunch, till five o'clock, meeting with no marked success; but invariably courtesy was extended to them; not even their reiterated promise, "We will call again," seeming to offend.

No woman who has ever entered one of these dens of iniquity on such an errand needs to be told of the heartsickness that almost overcame them as they, for the first time, saw behind those painted windows or green blinds, or entered the little stifling "back room," or found their way down winding steps into the damp, dark cellars, and realized that into *such places* those they loved best were being landed, through the allurements of the brilliantly lighted drug-store, the fascinating billiard table, or the enticing beer gardens, with their siren attractions. A crowded house at night, to hear the report of the day's work, betrayed the rapidly increasing interest in this mission.

On the twenty-seventh the contest really began, and, at the first place, the doors were found locked. With hearts full of compassion, the women knelt in the snow upon the pavement, to plead for the divine influence upon the heart of the liquor-dealer, and there held their first street prayer meeting.

At night the weary but zealous workers reported at a mass meeting of the various rebuffs, and the success in having two druggists sign the pledge not to sell, except upon the written prescription of a physician.

The Sabbath was devoted to union mass meeting, with direct reference to the work in hand; and on Monday the number of ladies had increased to near one hundred. That day, December 29, is one long to be remembered in Washington, as the day upon which occurred the first surrender ever made by a liquor-dealer, of his stock of liquors of every kind and variety, to the women, in answer to their prayers and entreaties, and by them poured into the street. Nearly a thousand men, women, and children witnessed the mingling of beer, ale, wine, and whiskey, as they filled the gutters and were drunk up by the earth, while the bells were ringing, men and boys shouting, and women singing and praying to God who had given the victory. But on the fourth day, "stock sale-day," the campaign had reached its height, the town being filled with visitors from all parts of the county and adjoining villages. Another public surrender, and another pouring into the street of a larger stock of liquors than on the previous day, and more intense excitement and enthusiasm.

Mass meetings were held nightly, with new victories reported constantly, until on Friday, January 21, one week from the beginning of the work, at the public meeting held in the evening, the secretary's report announced the unconditional surrender of every liquor-dealer, some having shipped their liquors back to wholesale dealers, others having poured them into the gutters, and the druggists as all having signed the pledge. Thus a campaign of prayer and song had, in eight days, closed eleven saloons, and pledged three drug-stores to sell only on prescription. At first men had wondered, scoffed, and laughed, then criticized, respected, and yielded.

Morning prayer and evening mass meetings continued daily, and the personal pledge was circulated till over one thousand signatures were obtained. Physicians were called upon to sign a pledge not to prescribe ardent spirits when any other substitute could be found, and in no case without a personal examination of the patient.

Early in the third week the discouraging intelligence came that a new man had taken out a license to sell liquor in one of the deserted saloons, and that he was backed by a whiskey house in Cincinnati, to the amount of $5,000, to break down this movement. On Wednesday, the fourteenth, the whiskey was unloaded at his room. About forty women were on the ground and followed the liquor in, and remained holding an uninterrupted prayer meeting all day and until eleven o'clock at night. The next day, bitterly cold, was spent in the same place and manner, without fire or chairs, two hours of that time the women being locked in, while the proprietor was off attending a trial. On the following day, the coldest of the winter of 1874, the women were locked out, and stood on the street holding religious services all day long.

Next morning a tabernacle was built in the street, just in front of the house, and was occupied for the double purpose of *watching* and prayer through the day; and before night the sheriff closed the saloon, and the proprietor surrendered; thus ended the third week.

A short time after, on a dying-bed, this four days' liquor-dealer sent for some of these women, telling them their songs and prayers had never ceased to ring in his ears, and urging them to pray again in his behalf; so he passed away.

Thus, through most of the winter of 1874 no alcoholic drinks were publicly sold as a beverage in the county.

During the two intervening years weekly temperance-league meetings have been kept up by the faithful few, while frequent union mass meetings have been held, thus keeping the subject always before the people. Today the disgraceful and humiliating fact exists that there are more places where liquors are sold than before the crusade.

3. Mass Movements and Revolution

a. The French Revolution[1]

The outward life of men in every age is molded upon an inward life consisting of a framework of traditions, sentiments, and moral influences which direct their conduct and maintain certain fundamental notions which they accept without discussion.

Let the resistance of this social framework weaken, and ideas which could have had no force before will germinate and develop. Certain theories whose success was enormous at the time of the Revolution would have encountered an impregnable wall two centuries earlier.

The aim of these considerations is to recall to the reader the fact that the outward events of revolutions are always a consequence of invisible transformations which have slowly gone forward in men's minds. Any profound study of a revolution necessitates a study of the mental soil upon which the ideas that direct its courses have to germinate.

Generally slow in the extreme, the evolution of ideas is often invisible for a whole generation. Its extent can only be grasped by comparing the mental condition of the same social classes at the two extremities of the curve which the mind has followed.

The actual influence of the philosophers in the genesis of the Revolution was not that which was attributed to them. They revealed nothing new, but they developed the critical spirit which no dogma can resist, once the way is prepared for its downfall.

[1] Adapted from Gustave Le Bon, *The Psychology of Revolution*, pp. 147–70. (G. P. Putnam's Sons, 1913.)

Under the influence of this developing critical spirit things which were no longer very greatly respected came to be respected less and less. When tradition and prestige had disappeared, the social edifice suddenly fell. This progressive disaggregation finally descended to the people, but was not commenced by them. The people follow examples, but never set them.

The philosophers, who could not have exerted any influence over the people, did exert a great influence over the enlightened portion of the nation. The unemployed nobility, who had long been ousted from their old functions and who were consequently inclined to be censorious, followed their leadership. Incapable of foresight, the nobles were the first to break with the traditions that were their only *raison d'être*. As steeped in humanitarianism and rationalism as the *bourgeoisie* of today, they continually sapped their own privileges by their criticisms. As today, the most ardent reformers were found among the favorites of fortune. The aristocracy encouraged dissertations on the social contract, the rights of man, and the equality of citizens. At the theater it applauded plays which criticized privileges, the arbitrariness and the incapacity of men in high places, and abuses of all kinds.

As soon as men lose confidence in the foundations of the mental framework which guides their conduct, they feel at first uneasy and then discontented. All classes felt their old motives of action gradually disappearing. Things that had seemed sacred for centuries were now sacred no longer.

The censorious spirit of the nobility and of the writers of the day would not have sufficed to move the heavy load of tradition but that its action was added to that of other powerful influences. We have already stated, in citing Bossuet, that under the *ancien régime* the religious and civil governments, widely separated in our day, were intimately connected. To injure one was inevitably to injure the other. Now even before the monarchical idea was shaken, the force of religious tradition was greatly diminished among cultivated men. The constant progress of knowledge had sent an increasing number of minds from theology to science by opposing the truth observed to the truth revealed.

This mental evolution, although as yet very vague, was sufficient to show that the traditions which for so many centuries had guided men had not the value which had been attributed to them, and that it would soon be necessary to replace them.

But where discover the new elements which might take the place of tradition? Where seek the magic ring which would raise a new social edifice on the remains of that which no longer contented men?

Men were agreed in attributing to reason the power that tradition and the gods seemed to have lost. How could its force be doubted? Its discoveries having been innumerable, was it not legitimate to suppose that by applying it to the construction of societies it would entirely transform them? Its possible function increased very rapidly in the thoughts of the more enlightened, in proportion as tradition seemed more and more to be distrusted.

The sovereign power attributed to reason must be regarded as the culminating idea which not only engendered the Revolution but governed it throughout. During the whole Revolution men gave themselves up to the most persevering efforts to break with the past and to erect society upon a new plan dictated by logic.

Slowly filtering downward, the rationalistic theories of the philosophers meant to the people simply that all the things which had been regarded as worthy of respect were now no longer worthy. Men being declared equal, the old masters need no longer be obeyed. The multitude easily succeeded in ceasing to respect what the upper classes themselves no longer respected. When the barrier of respect was down the Revolution was accomplished.

The first result of this new mentality was a general insubordination. Mme. Vigée Lebrun relates that on the promenade at Longchamps men of the people leaped on the footboards of the carriages, saying, "Next year you will be behind and we shall be inside."

The populace was not alone in manifesting insubordination and discontent. These sentiments were general on the eve of the Revolution. "The lesser clergy," says Taine, "are hostile to the prelates; the provincial gentry to the nobility of the court; the vassals to the seigneurs; the peasants to the townsmen, etc."

This state of mind, which had been communicated from the nobles and clergy to the people, also invaded the army. At the moment the States General were opened, Necker said: "We are not sure of the troops." The officers were becoming humanitarian and philosophical. The soldiers, recruited from the lowest class of the population, did not philosophize, but they no longer obeyed. In their feeble minds the ideas of equality meant simply the suppression of all leaders and masters, and therefore of all obedience. In 1790 more than twenty regiments threatened their officers, and sometimes, as at Nancy, threw them into prison.

The mental anarchy which, after spreading through all classes of society, finally invaded the army was the principal cause of the disappearance of the *ancien régime.* "It was the defection of the army affected by the ideas of the Third Estate," wrote Rivarol, "that destroyed royalty."

The genesis of the French Revolution, as well as its duration, was conditioned by elements of a rational, affective, mystic, and collective nature, each category of which was ruled by a different logic. The rational element usually invoked as an explanation exerted in reality but very slight influence. It prepared the way for the Revolution, but maintained it only at the outset, while it was still exclusively middle class. Its action was manifested by many measures of the time, such as the proposals to reform the taxes, the suppression of the privileges of a useless nobility, etc.

As soon as the Revolution reached the people, the influence of the rational elements speedily vanished before that of the affective and collective elements. As for the mystic elements, the foundation of the revolutionary faith, they made the army fanatical and propagated the new belief throughout the world.

We shall see these various elements as they appeared in events and in the psychology of individuals. Perhaps the most important was the mystic element. The Revolution cannot be clearly comprehended—we cannot repeat it too often—unless it is considered as the formation of a religious belief. What I have said elsewhere of all beliefs applies equally to the Revolution. They impose themselves on men apart from reason and have the power to polarize men's thoughts and feelings in one direction. Pure reason had never such a power, for men were never impassioned by reason.

The religious forms rapidly assumed by the Revolution explain its power of expansion and the prestige which it possessed and has retained. Few historians have understood that this great monument ought to be regarded as the foundation of a new religion. The penetrating mind of Tocqueville, I believe, was the first to perceive as much. He wrote:

The French Revolution was a political revolution which operated in the manner of and assumed something of the aspect of a religious revolution. See by what regular and characteristic traits it finally resembled the latter; not only did it spread itself far and wide like a religious revolution, but, like the latter, it spread itself by means of preaching and propaganda. A political revolution which inspires proselytes, which is preached as passionately to foreigners as it is accomplished at home: consider what a novel spectacle was this.

Although the mystic element is always the foundation of beliefs, certain affective and rational elements are quickly added thereto. A belief thus serves to group sentiments and passions and interests which belong to the affective domain. Reason then envelops the whole, seeking to justify events in which, however, it played no part whatever.

At the moment of the Revolution everyone, according to his aspirations, dressed the new belief in a different rational vesture. The peoples saw in it only the suppression of the religious and political despotisms and hierarchies under which they had so often suffered. Writers like Goethe and thinkers like Kant imagined that they saw in it the triumph of reason. Foreigners like Humboldt came to France "to breathe the air of liberty and to assist at the obsequies of despotism." These intellectual illusions did not last long. The evolution of the drama soon revealed the true foundations of the dream.

b. Bolshevism[1]

Great mass movements, whether these be religious or political, are at first always difficult to understand. Invariably they challenge existing moral and intellectual values, the revaluation of which is, for the normal mind, an exceedingly difficult and painful task. Moreover the definition of their aims and policies into exact and comprehensive programs is generally slowly achieved. At their inception and during the early stages of their development there must needs be many crude and tentative statements and many rhetorical exaggerations. It is safe to assert as a rule that at no stage of its history

[1] Adapted from John Spargo, *The Psychology of Bolshevism*, pp. 1–120. (Harper & Brothers, 1919.)

can a great movement of the masses be fully understood and fairly interpreted by a study of its formal statements and authentic expositions only. These must be supplemented by a careful study of the psychology of the men and women whose ideals and yearnings these statements and expositions aim to represent. It is not enough to know and comprehend the creed: it is essential that we also know and comprehend the spiritual factors, the discontent, the hopes, the fears, the inarticulate visionings of the human units in the movement. This is of greater importance in the initial stages than later, when the articulation of the soul of the movement has become more certain and clear.

No one who has attended many bolshevist meetings or is acquainted with many of the individuals to whom bolshevism makes a strong appeal will seriously question the statement that an impressively large number of those who profess to be Bolshevists present a striking likeness to extreme religious zealots, not only in the manner of manifesting their enthusiasm, but also in their methods of exposition and argument. Just as in religious hysteria a single text becomes a whole creed to the exclusion of every other text, and instead of being itself subject to rational tests is made the sole test of the rationality of everything else, so in the case of the average Bolshevist of this type a single phrase received into the mind in a spasm of emotion, never tested by the usual criteria of reason, becomes not only the very essence of truth but also the standard by which the truth or untruth of everything else must be determined. Most of the preachers who become pro-Bolshevists are of this type.

People who possess minds thus affected are generally capable of, and frequently indulge in, the strictest logical deduction and analysis. Sometimes they acquire the reputation of being exceptionally brilliant thinkers because of this power. But the fact is that their initial ideas, upon which everything is pivoted, are derived emotionally and are not the results of a deliberate weighing of available evidence. The initial movement is one of feeling, of emotional impulse. The conviction thereby created is so strong and so dominant that it cannot be affected by any purely rational functional factors.

People of this type jump at decisions and reach very positive convictions upon the most difficult matters with bewildering ease. For them the complexities and intricacies which trouble the normal mind do not exist. Everything is either black or white: there are no perplexing intervening grays. Right is right and wrong is wrong; they do not recognize that there are doubtful twilight zones. Ideas capable of the most elaborate expansion and the most subtle intricacies of interpretation are immaturely grasped and preached with naïve assurance. Statements alleged to be facts, no matter what their source, if they seem to support the convictions thus emotionally derived, are received without any examination and used as conclusive proof, notwithstanding that a brief investigation would prove them to be worthless as evidence.

If we take the group of American intellectuals who at present are ardent champions of bolshevism we shall find that, with exceptions so few as to be almost negligible, they have embraced nearly every "ism" as it arose, seeing in each one the magic solvent of humanity's ills. Those of an older generation thus regarded bimetallism, for instance. What else could be required to make the desert bloom like a garden and to usher in the earthly Paradise? The younger ones, in their turn, took up anarchist-communism, Marxian socialism, industrial unionism, syndicalism, birth control, feminism, and many other movements and propagandas, each of which in its turn induced ecstatic visions of a new heaven and a new earth. The same individuals have grown lyrical in praise of every bizarre and eccentric art fad. In the banal and grotesque travesties of art produced by cubists, futurists, *et al.*, they saw transcendent genius. They are forever seeking new gods and burying old ones.

It would be going too far to say that these individuals are all hystericals in the pathological sense, but it is strictly accurate to say that the class exhibits marked hysterical characteristics and that it closely resembles the large class of over-emotionalized religious enthusiasts which furnish so many true hystericals. It is probable that accidents of environment account for the fact that their emotionalism takes sociological rather than religious forms. If the sociological impetus were absent, most of them would be religiously motived to a state not less abnormal.

To understand the spread of bolshevist agitation and sympathy among a very considerable part of the working class in this country, we must take into account the fact that its logical and natural nucleus is the I.W.W. It is necessary also to emancipate our minds from the obsession that only "ignorant foreigners" are affected. This is not a true estimate of either the I.W.W. or the bolshevist propaganda as a whole. There are indeed many of this class in both, but there are also many native Americans, sturdy, self-reliant, enterprising, and courageous men. The peculiar group psychology which we are compelled to study is less the result of those subtle and complex factors which are comprehended in the vague term "race" than of the political and economic conditions by which the group concerned is environed.

The typical native-born I.W.W. member, the "Wobbly" one frequently encounters in our mid-western and western cities, is very unlike the hideous and repulsive figure conjured up by sensational cartoonists. He is much more likely to be a very attractive sort of man. Here are some characteristics of the type: figure robust, sturdy, and virile; dress rough but not unclean; speech forthright, deliberate, and bold; features intelligent, frank, and free from signs of alcoholic dissipation; movements slow and leisurely as of one averse to over-exertion. There are thousands of "wobblies" to whom the specifications of this description will apply. Conversation with these men reveals that, as a general rule, they are above rather than below the average in sobriety. They are generally free from family ties, being either unmarried or, as often happens, wife-deserters. They are not highly educated, few having attended any school beyond the grammar-school grade. Many of them have, however, read a great deal more than the average man, though their reading has been curiously miscellaneous in selection and nearly always badly balanced. Theology, philosophy, sociology, and economics seem to attract most attention. In discussion—and every "Wobbly" seems to possess a passion for disputation—men of this type will manifest a surprising familiarity with the broad outlines of certain theological problems, as well as with the scriptural texts bearing upon them. It is very likely to be the case, however, that they have only read a few popular classics of what used to be called rationalism—Paine's *Age of Reason*, Ingersoll's lectures in pamphlet form, and Haeckel's *Riddle of the Universe* are typical. A surprisingly large number can quote extensively from Buckle's *History of Civilization* and from the writings of Marx. They quote statistics freely—statistics of wages, poverty, crime, vice, and so on—generally derived from the radical press and implicitly believed because so published, with what they accept as adequate authority.

Their most marked peculiarity is the migratory nature of their lives. Whether this is self-determined, a matter of temperament and habit, or due to uncontrollable factors, it is largely responsible for the contempt in which they are popularly held. It naturally brings upon them the reproach and resentment everywhere visited upon "tramps" and "vagabonds." They rarely remain long enough in any one place to form local attachments and ties or anything like civic pride. They move from job to job, city to city, state to state, sometimes tramping afoot, begging as they go; sometimes stealing rides on railway trains, in freight cars—"side-door Pullmans"—or on the rods underneath the cars. Frequently arrested for begging, trespassing, or stealing rides, they are often victims of injustice at the hands of local judges and justices. The absence of friends, com-·bined with the prejudice against vagrants which everywhere exists, subjects them to arbitrary and high-handed injustice such as no other body of American citizens has to endure. Moreover, through the conditions of their existence they are readily suspected of crimes they do not commit; it is all too easy for the hard-pushed police officer or sheriff to impute a crime to the lone and defenseless "Wobbly," who frequently can produce no testimony to prove his innocence, simply because he has no friends in the neighborhood and has been at pains to conceal his movements. In this manner the "Wobbly" becomes a veritable son of Ishmael, his hand against the hand of nearly every man in conventional society. In particular he becomes a rebel by habit, hating the police and the courts as his constant enemies.

Doubtless the great majority of these men are temperamentally predisposed to the unanchored, adventurous, migratory existence which they lead. Boys so constituted run away to sea, take jobs with traveling. circuses, or enlist as soldiers. The type is familiar and not uncommon. Such individuals cannot be content with the prosaic, humdrum, monotonous life of regular employment. As a rule we do not look upon this trait in boy or man as criminal.

Many a hardworking, intelligent American, who from choice or from necessity is a migratory worker, following his job, never has an opportunity to vote for state legislators, for governor, for congressman or president.   He is just as effectively excluded from the actual electorate as if he were a Chinese coolie, ignorant of our customs and our speech.

We cannot wonder that such conditions prove prolific breeders of bolshevism and similar "isms."   It would be strange indeed if it were otherwise.   We have no right to expect that men who are so constantly the victims of arbitrary, unjust, and even brutal treatment at the hands of our police and our courts will manifest any reverence for the law and the judicial system.   Respect for majority rule in government cannot fairly be demanded from a disfranchised group. It is not to be wondered at that the old slogan of socialism, "Strike at the ballot-box!"—the call to lift the struggle of the classes to the parliamentary level for peaceful settlement—becomes the desperate, anarchistic I.W.W. slogan, "Strike at the ballot-box with an ax!"   Men who can have no family life cannot justly be expected to bother about school administration.   Men who can have no home life but only dreary shelter in crowded work-camps or dirty dosshouses are not going to bother themselves with municipal housing reforms.

In short, we must wake up to the fact that, as the very heart of our problem, we have a bolshevist nucleus in America composed of virile, red-blooded Americans, racy of our soil and history, whose conditions of life and labor are such as to develop in them the psychology of reckless, despairing, revengeful bolshevism.   They really are little concerned with theories of the state and of social development, which to our intellectuals seem to be the essence of bolshevism. They are vitally concerned only with action.   Syndicalism and bolshevism involve speedy and drastic action—hence the force of their appeal.

Finally, if we would understand why millions of people in all lands have turned away from old ideals, old loyalties, and old faiths to bolshevism, with something of the passion and frenzy characteristic of great messianic movements, we must take into account the intense spiritual agony and hunger which the Great War has brought into the lives of civilized men.   The old gods are dead and men are everywhere expectantly waiting for the new gods to arise.   The aftermath of the war is a spiritual cataclysm such as civilized mankind has never before known.   The old religions and moralities are shattered and men are waiting and striving for new ones. It is a time suggestive of the birth of new religions. Man cannot live as yet without faith, without some sort of religion. The heart of the world today is strained with yearning for new and living faiths to replace the old faiths which are dead. Were some persuasive fanatic to arise proclaiming himself to be a new Messiah, and preaching the religion of action, the creation of a new society, he would find an eager, soul-hungry world already predisposed to believe.

4. Mass Movements and Institutions: Methodism[1]

The corruption of manners which has been general since the Restoration was combated by societies for "the reformation of manners, which in the last years of the seventeenth century acquired extraordinary dimensions. They began in certain private societies which arose in the reign of James II, chiefly under the auspices of Beveridge and Bishop Horneck. These societies were at first purely devotional, and they appear to have been almost identical in character with those of the early Methodists. They held prayer meetings, weekly communions, and Bible-readings; they sustained charities and distributed religious books, and they cultivated a warmer and more ascetic type of devotion than was common in the Church. Societies of this description sprang up in almost every considerable city in England and even in several of those in Ireland. In the last years of the seventeenth century we find no less than ten of them in Dublin. Without, however, altogether discarding their first character, they assumed, about 1695, new and very important functions. They divided themselves into several distinct groups, undertaking the discovery and suppression of houses of ill fame, and the prosecution of swearers, drunkards, and Sabbath-breakers. They became a kind of voluntary police, acting largely as spies, and enforcing the laws against religious offenses. The energy with which this scheme was carried out is very remarkable. As many as seventy or eighty persons were often prosecuted in London and Westminster for cursing and swearing, in a single week. Sunday markets, which had hitherto been not uncommon, were effectually suppressed. Hundreds of disorderly houses were closed. Forty or fifty night-walkers were

[1] Adapted from William E. H. Lecky, *A History of England in the Eighteenth Century*, III, 33–101. (D. Appleton & Co., 1892.)

sent every week to Bridewell, and numbers were induced to emigrate to the colonies. A great part of the fines levied for these offenses was bestowed on the poor. In the fortieth annual report of the "Societies for the Reformation of Manners" which appeared in 1735, it was stated that the number of prosecutions for debauchery and profaneness in London and Westminster alone, since the foundation of the societies, had been 99,380.

The term Methodist was a college nickname bestowed upon a small society of students at Oxford, who met together between 1729 and 1735 for the purpose of mutual improvement. They were accustomed to communicate every week, to fast regularly on Wednesdays and Fridays, and on most days during Lent; to read and discuss the Bible in common, to abstain from most forms of amusement and luxury, and to visit sick persons and prisoners in the gaol. John Wesley, the future leader of the religious revival of the eighteenth century, was the master-spirit of this society. The society hardly numbered more than fifteen members, and was the object of much ridicule at the university; but it included some men who afterward played considerable parts in the world. Among them was Charles, the younger brother of John Wesley, whose hymns became the favorite poetry of the sect, and whose gentler, more submissive, and more amiable character, though less fitted than that of his brother for the great conflicts of public life, was very useful in moderating the movement, and in drawing converts to it by personal influence. Charles Wesley appears to have originated the society at Oxford; he brought Whitefield into its pale, and besides being the most popular poet he was one of the most persuasive preachers of the movement.

In the course of 1738 the chief elements of the movement were already formed. Whitefield had returned from Georgia, Charles Wesley had begun to preach the doctrine with extraordinary effect to the criminals in Newgate and from every pulpit into which he was admitted. Methodist societies had already sprung up under Moravian influence. They were in part a continuation of the society at Oxford, in part a revival of those religious societies that have been already noticed as so common after the Revolution. The design of each was to be a church within a church, a seedplot of a more fervent piety, the center of a stricter discipline and a more energetic propagandism than existed in religious communities at large. In these societies the old Christian custom of love-feasts was revived. The members sometimes passed almost the whole night in the most passionate devotions, and voluntarily submitted to a spiritual tyranny that could hardly be surpassed in a Catholic monastery. They were to meet every week, to make an open and particular confession of every frailty, to submit to be cross-examined on all their thoughts, words, and deeds. The following among others were the questions asked at every meeting: "What known sin have you committed since our last meeting? What temptations have you met with? How were you delivered? What have you thought, said, or done of which you doubt whether it be sin or not? Have you nothing you desire to keep secret?"

Such rules could only have been accepted under the influence of an overpowering religious enthusiasm, and there was much truth in the judgment which the elder brother of John Wesley passed upon them in 1739. "Their societies," he wrote to their mother, "are sufficient to dissolve all other societies but their own. Will any man of common sense or spirit suffer any domestic to be in a band engaged to relate to five or ten people everything without reserve that concerns the person's conscience how much soever it may concern the family? Ought any married persons to be there unless husband and wife be there together?"

From this time the leaders of the movement became the most active of missionaries. Without any fixed parishes they wandered from place to place, proclaiming their new doctrine in every pulpit to which they were admitted, and they speedily awoke a passionate enthusiasm and a bitter hostility in the Church.

We may blame, but we can hardly, I think, wonder at the hostility all this aroused among the clergy. It is, indeed, certain that Wesley and Whitefield were at this time doing more than any other contemporary clergymen to kindle a living piety among the people. Yet before the end of 1738 the Methodist leaders were excluded from most of the pulpits of the Church, and were thus compelled, unless they consented to relinquish what they considered a Divine mission, to take steps in the direction of separation.

Two important measures of this nature were taken in 1739. One of them was the creation of Methodist chapels, which were intended not to oppose or replace, but to be supplemental and ancillary to, the churches, and to secure that the doctrine of the new birth should be faithfully taught to the people. The other and still more important event was the institution by Whitefield of field-preaching. The idea had occurred to him in London, where he found congregations too numerous for the church in which he preached, but the first actual step was taken in the neighborhood of Bristol. At a time when he was himself excluded from the pulpits at Bristol, and was thus deprived of the chief normal means of exercising his talents, his attention was called to the condition of the colliers at Kingswood. He was filled with horror and compassion at finding in the heart of a Christian country, and in the immediate neighborhood of a great city, a population of many thousands, sunk in the most brutal ignorance and vice, and entirely excluded from the ordinances of religion. Moved by such feelings, he resolved to address the colliers in their own haunts. The resolution was a bold one, for field-preaching was then utterly unknown in England, and it needed no common courage to brave all the obloquy and derision it must provoke, and to commence the experiment in the center of a half-savage population. Whitefield, however, had a just confidence in his cause and in his powers. Standing himself upon a hillside, he took for his text the first words of the sermon which was spoken from the Mount, and he addressed with his accustomed fire an astonished audience of some two hundred men. The fame of his eloquence spread far and wide. On successive occasions, five, ten, fifteen, even twenty thousand were present. It was February, but the winter sun shone clear and bright. The lanes were filled with carriages of the more wealthy citizens, whom curiosity had drawn from Bristol. The trees and hedges were crowded with humbler listeners, and the fields were darkened by a compact mass. The voice of the great preacher pealed with a thrilling power to the outskirts of that mighty throng. The picturesque novelty of the occasion and of the scene, the contagious emotion of so great a multitude, a deep sense of the condition of his hearers and of the momentous importance of the step he was taking, gave an additional solemnity to his eloquence. His rude auditors were electrified. They stood for a time in rapt and motionless attention. Soon tears might be seen forming white gutters down cheeks blackened from the coal mine. Then sobs and groans told how hard hearts were melting at his words. A fire was kindled among the outcasts of Kingswood which burnt long and fiercely, and was destined in a few years to over-spread the land.

But for the simultaneous appearance of a great orator and a great statesman, Methodism would probably have smouldered and at last perished like the very similar religious societies of the preceding century. Whitefield was utterly destitute of the organizing skill which could alone give a permanence to the movement, and no talent is naturally more ephemeral than popular oratory; while Wesley, though a great and impressive preacher, could scarcely have kindled a general enthusiasm had he not been assisted by an orator who had an unrivaled power of moving the passions of the ignorant. The institution of field-preaching by Whitefield in the February of 1739 carried the impulse through the great masses of the poor, while the foundation by Wesley, in the May of the same year, of the first Methodist chapel was the beginning of an organized body capable of securing and perpetuating the results that had been achieved.

From the time of the institution of lay preachers Methodism became in a great degree independent of the Established Church. Its chapels multiplied in the great towns, and its itinerant missionaries penetrated to the most secluded districts. They were accustomed to preach in fields and gardens, in streets and lecture-rooms, in market places and churchyards. On one occasion we find Whitefield at a fair mounting a stage which had been erected for some wrestlers, and there denouncing the pleasures of the world; on another, preaching among the mountebanks at Moorfields; on a third, attracting around his pulpit ten thousand of the spectators at a race course; on a fourth, standing beside the gallows at an execution to speak of death and of eternity. Wesley, when excluded from the pulpit of Epworth, delivered some of his most impressive sermons in the churchyard, standing on his father's tomb. Howell Harris, the apostle of Wales, encountering a party of mountebanks, sprang into their midst exclaiming, in a solemn voice, "Let us pray," and then proceeded to thunder forth the judgments of the Lord. Rowland Hill was accustomed to visit the great towns on market day in order that he might address the people in the market place, and to go from fair to fair preaching among the revelers from his favorite text, "Come out from among them." In this manner the Methodist preachers came in contact with the most savage elements of the population, and there were few forms of mob violence they did not experience.   In 1741 one of their preachers named Seward, after repeated ill treatment in Wales, was at last struck on the head while preaching at Monmouth, and died of the blow.   In a riot, while Wheatley was preaching at Norwich, a poor woman with child perished from the kicks and blows of the mob.   At Dublin, Whitefield was almost stoned to death. At Exeter he was stoned in the very presence of the bishop.   At Plymouth he was violently assaulted and his life seriously threatened by a naval officer.

Scenes of this kind were of continual occurrence, and they were interspersed with other persecutions of a less dangerous description. Drums were beaten, horns blown, guns let off, and blacksmiths hired to ply their noisy trade in order to drown the voices of the preachers. Once, at the very moment when Whitefield announced his text, the belfry gave out a peal loud enough to make him inaudible.   On other occasions packs of hounds were brought with the same object, and once, in order to excite the dogs to fury, a live cat in a cage was placed in their midst.   Fire engines poured streams of fetid water upon the congregation.   Stones fell so thickly that the faces of many grew crimson with blood.   At Hoxton the mob drove an ox into the midst of the congregation.   At Pensford the rabble, who had been baiting a bull, concluded their sport by driving the torn and tired animal full against the table on which Wesley was preaching.   Sometimes we find innkeepers refusing to receive the Methodist leaders in their inns, farmers entering into an agreement to dismiss every laborer who attended a Methodist preacher, landlords expelling all Methodists from their cottages, masters dismissing their servants because they had joined the sect.   The magistrates, who knew by experience that the presence of a Methodist preacher was the usual precursor of disturbance and riot, looked on them with the greatest disfavor, and often scandalously connived at the persecutions they underwent.

It was frequently observed by Wesley that his preaching rarely affected the rich and the educated.   It was over the ignorant and the credulous that it exercised its most appalling power, and it is difficult to overrate the mental anguish it must sometimes have produced. Timid and desponding natures unable to convince themselves that they had undergone a supernatural change, gentle and affectionate natures who believed that those who were dearest to them were descending into everlasting fire, must have often experienced pangs compared with which the torments of the martyr were insignificant. The confident assertions of the Methodist preacher and the ghastly images he continually evoked poisoned their imaginations, haunted them in every hour of weakness or depression, discolored all their judgments of the world, and added a tenfold horror to the darkness of the grave. Sufferings of this description, though among the most real and the most terrible that superstition can inflict, are so hidden in their nature that they leave few traces in history; but it is impossible to read the journals of Wesley without feeling that they were most widely diffused. Many were thrown into paroxysms of extreme, though usually transient, agony; many doubtless nursed a secret sorrow which corroded all the happiness of their lives, while not a few became literally insane. On one occasion Wesley was called to the bedside of a young woman at Kingswood. He tells us:

> She was nineteen or twenty years old, but, it seems, could not write or read. I found her on the bed, two or three persons holding her. It was a terrible sight. Anguish, horror, and despair above all description appeared in her pale face. The thousand distortions of her whole body showed how the dogs of hell were gnawing at her heart. The shrieks intermixed were scarce to be endured. But her stony eyes could not weep. She screamed out as soon as words could find their way, "I am damned, damned, lost forever: six days ago you might have helped me. But it is past. I am the devil's now. . . . . I will go with him to hell. I cannot be saved." They sang a hymn, and for a time she sank to rest, but soon broke out anew in incoherent exclamations, "Break, break, poor stony hearts! Will you not break? What more can be done for stony hearts? I am damned that you may be saved!" . . . . She then fixed her eyes in the corner of the ceiling, and said, "There he is, ay, there he is! Come, good devil, come! Take me away." . . . . We interrupted her by calling again on God, on which she sank down as before, and another young woman began to roar out as loud as she had done.

For more than two hours Wesley and his brother continued praying over her. At last the paroxysms subsided and the patient joined in a hymn of praise.

In the intense religious enthusiasm that was generated, many of the ties of life were snapped in twain. Children treated with contempt the commands of their parents, students the rules of their colleges, clergymen the discipline of their Church. The whole structure of society, and almost all the amusements of life, appeared criminal. The fairs, the mountebanks, the public rejoicings of the people, were all Satanic. It was sinful for a woman to wear any gold ornament or any brilliant dress. It was even sinful for a man to exercise the common prudence of laying by a certain portion of his income. When Whitefield proposed to a lady to marry him, he thought it necessary to say, "I bless God, if I know anything of my own heart, I am free from that foolish passion which the world calls love." "I trust I love you only for God, and desire to be joined to you only by His commands, and for His sake." It is perhaps not very surprising that Whitefield's marriage, like that of Wesley, proved very unhappy. Theaters and the reading of plays were absolutely condemned, and Methodists employed all their influence with the authorities to prevent the erection of the former. It seems to have been regarded as a divine judgment that once, when *Macbeth* was being acted at Drury Lane, a real thunderstorm mingled with the mimic thunder in the witch scene. Dancing was, if possible, even worse than the theater. "Dancers," said Whitefield, "please the devil at every step"; and it was said that his visit to a town usually put "a stop to the dancing-school, the assemblies, and every pleasant thing." He made it his mission to "bear testimony against the detestable diversions of this generation"; and he declared that no "recreations, considered as such, can be innocent."

Accompanying this asceticism we find an extraordinary revival of the grossest superstition. It was a natural consequence of the essentially emotional character of Methodism that its disciples should imagine that every strong feeling or impulse within them was a direct inspiration of God or Satan. The language of Whitefield—the language in a great degree of all the members of the sect—was that of men who were at once continually inspired and the continual objects of miraculous interposition. In every perplexity they imagined that, by casting lots or opening their Bibles at random, they could obtain a supernatural answer to their inquiries.

In all matters relating to Satanic interference, Wesley was especially credulous. "I cannot give up to all the Deists in Great Britain the existence of witchcraft till I give up the credit of all history, sacred and profane." He had no doubt that the physical contortions into which so many of his hearers fell were due to the direct agency of Satan, who tore the converts as they were coming to Christ. He had himself seen men and women who were literally possessed by devils; he had witnessed forms of madness which were not natural, but diabolical, and he had experienced in his own person the hysterical affections which resulted from supernatural agency.

If Satanic agencies continually convulsed those who were coming to the faith, divine judgments as frequently struck down those who opposed it. Every illness, every misfortune that befell an opponent, was believed to be supernatural. Molther, the Moravian minister, shortly after the Methodists had separated from the Moravians, was seized with a passing illness. "I believe," wrote Wesley, "it was the hand of God that was upon him." Numerous cases were cited of sudden and fearful judgments which fell upon the adversaries of the cause. A clergyman at Bristol, standing up to preach against the Methodists, "was suddenly seized with a rattling in his throat, attended with a hideous groaning," and on the next Sunday he died. At Todmorden a minister was struck with a violent fit of palsy immediately after preaching against the Methodists. At Enniscorthy a clergyman, having preached for some time against Methodism, deferred the conclusion of the discourse to the following Sunday. Next morning he was raging mad, imagined that devils were about him, "and not long after, without showing the least sign of hope, he went to his account." At Kingswood a man began a vehement invective against Wesley and Methodism. "In the midst he was struck raving mad." A woman, seeing a crowd waiting for Wesley at the church door, exclaimed, "They are waiting for their God." She at once fell senseless to the ground, and next day expired. "A party of young men rowed up to Richmond to disturb the sermons of Rowland Hill. The boat sank, and all of them were drowned." At Sheffield the captain of a gang who had long troubled the field-preachers, was bathing with his companions. "Another dip," he said, "and then for a bit of sport with the Methodists." He dived, struck his head against a stone, and appeared no more. By such anecdotes and by such beliefs a fever of enthusiasm was sustained.

But with all its divisions and defects the movement was unquestionably effecting a great moral revolution in England. It was essentially a popular movement, exercising its deepest influence over

the lower and middle classes.   Some of its leaders were men of real
genius, but in general the Methodist teacher had little sympathy with
the more educated of his fellow-countrymen.   To an ordinarily
cultivated mind there was something extremely repulsive in his tears
and groans and amorous ejaculations, in the coarse and anthropo-
morphic familiarity and the unwavering dogmatism with which he
dealt with the most sacred subjects, in the narrowness of his theory of
life and his utter insensibility to many of the influences that expand
and embellish it, in the mingled credulity and self-confidence with
which he imagined that the whole course of nature was altered for
his convenience.   But the very qualities that impaired his influence
in one sphere enhanced it in another.   His impassioned prayers and
exhortations stirred the hearts of multitudes whom a more decorous
teaching had left absolutely callous.   The supernatural atmosphere
of miracles, judgments, and inspirations in which he moved, invested
the most prosaic life with a halo of romance.   The doctrines he
taught, the theory of life he enforced, proved themselves capable of
arousing in great masses of men an enthusiasm of piety which was
hardly surpassed in the first days of Christianity, of eradicating
inveterate vice, of fixing and directing impulsive and tempestuous
natures that were rapidly hastening toward the abyss.   Out of the
profligate slave-dealer, John Newton, Methodism formed one of the
purest and most unselfish of saints.   It taught criminals in Newgate
to mount the gallows in an ecstasy of rapturous devotion.   It planted
a fervid and enduring religious sentiment in the midst of the most
brutal and most neglected portions of the population, and whatever
may have been its vices or its defects, it undoubtedly emancipated
great numbers from the fear of death, and imparted a warmer tone
to the devotion and a greater energy to the philanthropy of every
denomination both in England and the colonies.

III.   INVESTIGATIONS AND PROBLEMS

1.   Social Unrest

The term collective behavior, which has been used elsewhere to
include all the facts of group life, has been limited for the purposes
of this chapter to those phenomena which exhibit in the most obvious
and elementary way the processes by which societies are disintegrated

into their constituent elements and the processes by which these elements are brought together again into new relations to form new organizations and new societies.

Some years ago John Graham Brooks wrote a popular treatise on the labor situation in the United States. He called the volume *Social Unrest*. The term was, even at that time, a familiar one. Since then the word unrest, in both its substantive and adjective forms, has gained wide usage. We speak in reference to the notorious disposition of the native American to move from one part of the country to another, of his restless blood, as if restlessness was a native American trait transmitted in the blood. We speak more often of the "restless age," as if mobility and the desire for novelty and new experience were peculiarly characteristic of the twentieth century. We use the word to describe conditions in different regions of social life in such expressions as "political," "religious," and "labor" unrest, and in every case the word is used in a sense that indicates change, but change that menaces the existing order. Finally, we speak of the "restless woman," as of a peculiar modern type, characteristic of the changed status of women in general in the modern world. In all these different uses we may observe the gradual unfolding of the concept which seems to have been implicit in the word as it was first used. It is the concept of an activity in response to some urgent organic impulse which the activity, however, does not satisfy. It is a diagnostic symptom, a symptom of what Graham Wallas calls "balked disposition." It is a sign that in the existing situation some one or more of the four wishes—security, new experience, recognition, and response—has not been and is not adequately realized. The fact that the symptom is social, that it is contagious, is an indication that the situations that provoke it are social, that is to say, general in the community or the group where the unrest manifests itself.

The materials in which the term unrest is used in the sense indicated are in the popular discussions of social questions. The term is not defined but it is frequently used in connection with descriptions of conditions which are evidently responsible for it. Labor strikes are evidences of social unrest, and the literature already referred to in the chapter on "Conflict"[1] shows the conditions under which unrest

[1] *Supra*, pp. 652–53; 657–58.

arises, is provoked and exploited in labor situations. The relation of unrest to routine and fatigue has been the subject of a good deal of discussion and some investigation. The popular conception is that labor unrest is due to the dull driving routine of machine industry. The matter needs further study. The actual mental experiences of the different sexes, ages, temperamental and mental types under the influence of routine would add a much needed body of fact to our present psychology of the worker.

2. Psychic Epidemics

If social unrest is a symptom of disorganization, then the psychic epidemics, in which all the phenomena of social unrest and contagion are intensified, is evidence positive that disorganization exists. Social disorganization must be considered in relation to reorganization. All change involves a certain amount of disorganization. In order that an individual may make new adjustments and establish new habits it is inevitable that old habits should be broken up, and in order that society may reform an existing social order a certain amount of disorganization is inevitable. Social unrest may be, therefore, a symptom of health. It is only when the process of disorganization goes on so rapidly and to such an extent that the whole existing social structure is impaired, and society is, for that reason, not able to readjust itself, that unrest is to be regarded as a pathological symptom.

There is reason to believe, contrary to the popular conception, that the immigrant in America, particularly in the urban environment, accommodates himself too quickly rather than too slowly to American life. Statistics show, particularly in the second generation, a notable increase in juvenile delinquency, and this seems to be due to the fact that in America the relation between parents and children is reversed. Owing to the children's better knowledge of English and their more rapid accommodation to the conditions of American life, parents become dependent upon their children rather than the children dependent upon their parents.

Social epidemics, however, are evidence of a social disintegration due to more fundamental and widespread disorders. The literature has recorded the facts but writers have usually interpreted the phenomena in medical rather than sociological terms. Stoll, in his very interesting but rather miscellaneous collection of materials upon primitive life, disposes of the phenomena by giving them another name. His volume is entitled *Suggestion and Hypnotism in Folk Psychology*.[1] Friedmann, in his monograph, *Über Wahnideen im Völkerleben*, is disposed as a psychiatrist to treat the whole matter as a form of "social" insanity.

3. Mass Movements

In spite of the abundance of materials on the subject of mass movements no attempt has been made as yet to collect and classify them. There have been a number of interesting books in the field of collective psychology, so called mainly by French and Italian writers—Sighele, Rossi, Tarde, and Le Bon—but they are not based on a systematic study of cases. The general assumption has been that the facts are so obvious that any attempt to study systematically the mechanisms involved would amount to little more than academic elaboration of what is already obvious, a restatement in more abstract terms of what is already familiar.

On the other hand, shepherds and cowboys, out of their experience in handling cattle and sheep, have learned that the flock and the herd have quite peculiar and characteristic modes of collective behavior which it is necessary to know if one is to handle them successfully. At the same time, practical politicians who make a profession of herding voters, getting them out to the polls at the times they are needed and determining for them, by the familiar campaign devices, the persons and the issues for which they are to cast their ballots, have worked out very definite methods for dealing with masses of people, so that they are able to predict the outcome with considerable accuracy far in advance of an election and make their dispositions accordingly.

Political manipulation of the movements and tendencies of popular opinion has now reached a point of perfection where it can and will be studied systematically. During the world-war it was studied, and all the knowledge which advertisers, newspaper men, and psychologists possessed was used to win the war.

---

[1] Otto Stoll, *Suggestion und Hypnotismus in der Völkerpsychologie.* 2d ed. (Leipzig, 1904.)

Propaganda is now recognized as part of the grand strategy of war. Not only political and diplomatic victories, but battles were won during the world-war by the aid of this insidious weapon. The great victory of the Austrian and German armies at Caporetto which in a few days wiped out all the hard-won successes of the Italian armies was prepared by a psychic attack on the morale of the troops at the front and a defeatist campaign among the Italian population back of the lines.

In the battle of Caporetto the morale of the troops at the front was undermined by sending postal cards and letters to individual soldiers stating that their wives were in illicit relations with officers and soldiers of the allies. Copies of Roman and Milanese newspapers were forged and absolute facsimiles of familiar journals were secretly distributed or dropped from Austrian aeroplanes over the Italian lines. These papers contained sensational articles telling the Italians that Austria was in revolt, that Emperor Charles had been killed. Accompanying these were other articles describing bread riots throughout Italy and stating that the Italian government, unable to quell them with its own forces, had sent British and French re-enforcing troops and even Zulus into the cities, and that these troops were shooting down women and children and priests without mercy.

This attack upon the morale of the troops was followed by an unforeseen assault upon a quiet sector, which succeeded in piercing the line at numerous points. In the confusion that followed the whole structure of the defense crumbled, and the result was disastrous.

When the final history of the world-war comes to be written, one of its most interesting chapters will be a description of the methods and devices which were used by the armies on both sides to destroy the will to war in the troops and among the peoples behind the lines. If the application of modern science to war has multiplied the engines of destruction, the increase of communication and the interpenetration of peoples has given war among civilized peoples the character of an internal and internecine struggle. Under these circumstances propaganda, in the sense of an insidious exploitation of the sources of dissension and unrest, may as completely change the character of wars of peoples as they were once changed by the invention of gunpowder.

In this field there is room for investigation and study, for almost all attempts thus far made to put advertising on a scientific basis have been made by students of individual rather than social psychology.

4. Revivals, Religious and Linguistic

For something more than a hundred years Europe has experienced a series of linguistic and literary revivals, that is to say revivals of the folk languages and the folk cultures. The folk languages are the speech of peoples who have been conquered but not yet culturally absorbed by the dominant language group. They are mostly isolated rural populations who have remained to a large extent outside of the cosmopolitan cultures of the cities. These people while not wholly illiterate have never had enough education in the language of the dominant peoples of the cities to enable them to use this alien speech as a medium of education. The consequence is that, except for a relatively small group of intellectuals, they have been cut off from the main current of European life and culture. These linguistic revivals have not been confined to any one nation, since every nation in Europe turns out upon analysis to be a mosaic of minor nationalities and smaller cultural enclaves in which the languages of little and forgotten peoples have been preserved. Linguistic revivals have, in fact, been well-nigh universal. They have taken place in France, Spain, Norway, Denmark, in most of the Balkan States, including Albania, the most isolated of them all, and in all the smaller nationalities along the Slavic-German border—Finland, Esthonia, Letvia, Lithuania, Poland, Bohemia, Slovakia, Roumania, and the Ukraine. Finally, among the Jews of Eastern Europe, there has been the Haskala Movement, as the Jews of Eastern Europe call their period of enlightenment, a movement that has quite unintentionally made the Judeo-German dialect (Yiddish) a literary language.

At first blush, it seems strange that the revivals of the folk speech should have come at a time when the locomotive and the telegraph were extending commerce and communication to the uttermost limits of the earth, when all barriers were breaking down, and the steady expansion of cosmopolitan life and the organization of the Great Society, as Graham Wallas has called it, seemed destined to banish all the minor languages, dialects, and obsolescent forms of speech, the last props of an international provincialism, to the limbo of forgotten things. The competition of the world-languages was already keen; all the little and forgotten peoples of

Europe—the Finns, Letts, Ukrainians, Russo-Carpathians, Slovaks, Slovenians, Croatians, the Catalonians of eastern Spain, whose language, by the way, dates back to a period before the Roman Conquest, the Czechs, and the Poles—began to set up presses and establish schools to revive and perpetuate their several racial languages.

To those who, at this time, were looking forward to world-organization and a universal peace through the medium of a universal language, all this agitation had the appearance of an anachronism, not to say a heresy. It seemed a deliberate attempt to set up barriers, where progress demanded that they should be torn down. The success of such a movement, it seemed, must be to bring about a more complete isolation of the peoples, to imprison them, so to speak, in their own languages, and so cut them off from the general culture of Europe.[1]

The actual effect has been different from what was expected. It is difficult, and for the masses of the people impossible, to learn through the medium of a language that they do not speak. The results of the efforts to cultivate Swedish and Russian in Finland, Polish and Russian in Lithuania, Magyar in Slovakia and at the same time to prohibit the publication of books and newspapers in the mother-tongue of the country has been, in the first place, to create an artificial illiteracy and, in the second, to create in the minds of native peoples a sense of social and intellectual inferiority to the alien and dominant race.

The effect of the literary revival of the spoken language, however, has been to create, in spite of the efforts to suppress it, a vernacular press which opened the gates of western culture to great masses of people for whom it did not previously exist. The result has been a great cultural awakening, a genuine renaissance, which has had profound reverberations on the political and social life of Europe.

The literary revival of the folk speech in Europe has invariably been a prelude to the revival of the national spirit in subject peoples. The sentiment of nationality has its roots in memories that attach to the common possessions of the people, the land, the religion, and the language, but particularly the language.

Bohemian patriots have a saying, "As long as the language lives, the nation is not dead." In an address in 1904 Jorgen Levland, who was afterward Premier of Norway, in a plea for "freedom with self-government,

[1] Robert E. Park, *Immigrant Press and Its Control*, chap. ii, "Background of the Immigrant Press." (New York, 1921. In press.)

home, land, and our own language," made this statement: "Political freedom is not the deepest and greatest. Greater is it for a nation to preserve her intellectual inheritance in her native tongue."

The revival of the national consciousness in the subject peoples has invariably been connected with the struggle to maintain a press in the native language. The reason is that it was through the medium of the national press that the literary and linguistic revivals took place. Conversely, the efforts to suppress the rising national consciousness took the form of an effort to censor or suppress the national press. There were nowhere attempts to suppress the spoken language as such. On the other hand, it was only as the spoken language succeeded in becoming a medium of literary expression that it was possible to preserve it under modern conditions and maintain in this way the national solidarity. When the Lithuanians, for example, were condemned to get their education and their culture through the medium of a language not their own, the effect was to denationalize the literate class and to make its members aliens to their own people. If there was no national press, there could be no national schools, and, indeed, no national church. It was for this reason that the struggle to maintain the national language and the national culture has always been a struggle to maintain a national press.

European nationalists, seeking to revive among their peoples the national consciousness, have invariably sought to restore the national speech, to purge it of foreign idioms, and emphasize every mark which serves to distinguish it from the languages with which it tended to fuse.[1]

Investigation of these linguistic revivals and the nationalist movement that has grown out of them indicates that there is a very intimate relation between nationalist and religious movements. Both of them are fundamentally cultural movements with incidental political consequences. The movement which resulted in the reorganization of rural life in Denmark, the movement that found expression in so unique an institution as the rural high schools of Denmark, was begun by Bishop Grundtvig, called the Luther of Denmark, and was at once a religious and a nationalist movement. The rural high schools are for this reason not like anything in the way of education with which people outside of Denmark are familiar. They are not technical schools but cultural institutions in the narrowest, or broadest, sense of that term.[2] The teaching is "scientific," but at the same

[1] *Ibid.*

[2] Anton H. Hollman, *Die dänische Volkshochschule und ihre Bedeutung für die Entwicklung einer völkischen Kultur in Dänemark.* (Berlin, 1909.)

time "inspirational." They are what a Sunday school might be if it were not held on Sunday and was organized as Mr. H. G. Wells would organize it and with such a bible as he would like to have someone write for us.[1]

The popular accounts which we have of religious revivals do not at first suggest any very definite relations, either psychological or sociological, between them and the literary revivals to which reference has just been made. Religious revivals, particularly as described by dispassionate observers, have the appearance of something bizarre, fantastic, and wild, as indeed they often are.

What must strike the thoughtful observer, however, is the marked similarity of these collective religious excitements, whether among civilized or savage peoples and at places and periods remote in time and in space. Frederick Morgan Davenport, who has collected and compared the materials in this field from contemporary sources, calls attention in the title of his volume, *Primitive Traits in Religious Revivals*, to this fundamental similarity of the phenomena. Whatever else the word "primitive" may mean in this connection it does mean that the phenomena of religious revivals are fundamentally human.

From the frantic and disheveled dances of the Bacchantes, following a wine cart through an ancient Greek village, to the shouts and groans of the mourners' bench of an old-time Methodist camp-meeting, religious excitement has always stirred human nature more profoundly than any other emotion except that of passionate love.

In the volume by Jean Pélissier, *The Chief Makers of the National Lithuanian Renaissance* (*Les Principaux artisans de la renaissance nationale lituanienne*), there is a paragraph describing the conversion of a certain Dr. Kudirka, a Lithuanian patriot, to the cause of Lithuanian nationality. It reads like a chapter from William James's *The Varieties of Religious Experience*.[2]

It is materials like this that indicate how close and intimate are the relations between cultural movements, whether religious or literary and national, at least in their formal expression. The question that remains to be answered is: In what ways do they differ?

[1] H. G. Wells, *The Salvaging of Civilization*, chaps. iv–v, "The Bible of Civilization," pp. 97–140. (New York, 1921.)

[2] See *The Immigrant Press and Its Control*, chap. ii, for a translation of Dr. Kudirka's so-called "Confession."

5. Fashion, Reform and Revolution

A great deal has been written in recent times in regard to fashion. It has been studied, for example, as an economic phenomenon. Sombart has written a suggestive little monograph on the subject. It is in the interest of machine industry that fashions should be standardized over a wide area, and it is the function of advertising to achieve this result. It is also of interest to commerce that fashions should change and this also is largely, but not wholly, a matter of advertising. Tarde distinguishes between custom and fashion as the two forms in which all cultural traits are transmitted. "In periods when custom is in the ascendant, men are more infatuated about their country than about their time; for it is the past which is pre-eminently praised. In ages when fashion rules, men are prouder, on the contrary, of their time than of their country."[1]

The most acute analysis that has been made of fashion is contained in the observation of Sumner in *Folkways*. Sumner pointed out that fashion though differing from, is intimately related to, the mores. Fashion fixes the attention of the community at a given time and place and by so doing determines what is sometimes called the Spirit of the Age, the *Zeitgeist*. By the introduction of new fashions the leaders of society gain that distinction in the community by which they are able to maintain their prestige and so maintain their position as leaders. But in doing this, they too are influenced by the fashions which they introduce. Eventually changes in fashion affect the mores.[2]

Fashion is related to reform and to revolution, because it is one of the fundamental ways in which social changes take place and because, like reform and revolution, it also is related to the mores.

Fashion is distinguished from reform by the fact that the changes it introduces are wholly irrational if not at the same time wholly unpredictable. Reform, on the other hand, is nothing if not rational. It achieves its ends by agitation and discussion. Attempts have been made to introduce fashions by agitation, but they have not succeeded. On the other hand, reform is itself a fashion and has

[1] Gabriel Tarde, *The Laws of Imitation*. Translated from the 2d French ed. by Elsie Clews Parsons, p. 247. (New York, 1903.)

[2] Sumner, *Folkways*, pp. 200–201.

largely absorbed in recent years the interest that was formerly bestowed on party politics.

There has been a great deal written about reforms but almost nothing about *reform*. It is a definite type of collective behavior which has come into existence and gained popularity under conditions of modern life. The reformer and the agitator, likewise, are definite, temperamental, and social types. Reform tends under modern conditions to become a vocation and a profession like that of the politician. The profession of the reformer, however, is social, as distinguished from party politics.

Reform is not revolution. It does not seek to change the mores but rather to change conditions in conformity with the mores. There have been revolutionary reformers. Joseph II of Austria and Peter the Great of Russia were reformers of that type. But revolutionary reforms have usually failed. They failed lamentably in the case of Joseph II and produced many very dubious results under Peter.

A revolution is a mass movement which seeks to change the mores by destroying the existing social order. Great and silent revolutionary changes have frequently taken place in modern times, but as these changes were not recognized at the time and were not directly sought by any party they are not usually called revolutions. They might properly be called "historical revolutions," since they are not recognized as revolutions until they are history.

There is probably a definite revolutionary process but it has not been defined. Le Bon's book on the *Psychology of Revolution*, which is the sequel to his study of *The Crowd*, is, to be sure, an attempt, but the best that one can say of it is that it is suggestive. Many attempts have been made to describe the processes of revolution as part of the whole historical process. This literature will be considered in the chapter on "Progress."

SELECTED BIBLIOGRAPHY

I. DISORGANIZATION, SOCIAL UNREST, AND PSYCHIC EPIDEMICS

A. *Social Disorganization*

(1) Cooley, Charles H. *Social Organization*. Chap. xxx, "Formalism and Disorganization," pp. 342–55; chap. xxxi, "Disorganization: the Family," pp. 356–71; chap. xxxii, "Disorganization: the Church," pp. 372–82; chap. xxxiii, "Disorganization: Other Traditions," pp. 383–92. New York, 1909.

(2) Thomas, W. I., and Znaniecki, Florian. *The Polish Peasant in Europe and America.* Monograph of an immigrant group. Vol. IV, "Disorganization and Reorganization in Poland." Boston, 1920.

(3) ———. *The Polish Peasant in Europe and America.* Vol. V, "Organization and Disorganization in America," Part II, "Disorganization of the Immigrant," pp. 165–345. Boston, 1920.

(4) Friedländer, Ludwig. *Darstellungen aus der Sittengeschichte Roms in der Zeit von August bis zum Ausgang der Antonine.* 9th ed. Leipzig, 1922. Translation by L. A. Magnus from the 7th rev. ed. under the title "Roman Life and Manners under the Early Empire." 4 vols. London, 1908–13.

(5) Lane-Poole, S. *The Mohammedan Dynasties.* Charts showing "Growth of the Ottoman Empire" and "Decline of the Ottoman Empire," pp. 190–91. London, 1894.

(6) Taine, H. *The Ancient Régime.* Translated from the French by John Durand. New York, 1896.

(7) Nordau, Max. *Degeneration.* Translated from the 2d ed. of the German work. New York, 1895.

(8) Patrick, George T. W. *The Psychology of Social Reconstruction.* Chap. vi, "Our Centripetal Society," pp. 174–98. Boston, 1920.

(9) Tyau, M. T. Z. *China Awakened.* New York, 1922.

(10) Spengler, Oswald. *Der Untergang des Abendlandes.* Umrisse einer Morphologie der Weltgeschichte. Rev. ed., 2 vols. München, 1922.

(11) *The Taint in Politics.* A study in the evolution of parliamentary corruption. New York, 1920.

(12) Steiner, Jesse F. "Community Disorganization," *Journal of Social Forces*, II, 1924, 177–87.

(13) Webb, Sidney and Beatrice. *The Decay of Capitalist Civilization.* New York, 1923.

[See bibliography, "Parties," pp. 659–60.]

B. *Social Unrest*

(1) Brooks, John Graham. *The Social Unrest.* Studies in labor and socialist movements. London, 1903.

(2) Fuller, Bampfylde. *Life and Human Nature.* Chap. ii, "Change," pp. 24–45. London, 1914.

(3) Wallas, Graham. *The Great Society.* A psychological analysis. Chap. iv, "Disposition and Environment," pp. 57–68. New York, 1914. [Defines "the baulked disposition," see also pp. 172–74.]

(4) Healy, William. *The Individual Delinquent.* A textbook of diagnosis and prognosis for all concerned in understanding offenders. "Hypomania, Constitutional Excitement," pp. 609–13. Boston, 1915.

(5) Janet, Pierre. *The Major Symptoms of Hysteria.* Fifteen lectures given in the medical school of Harvard University. New York, 1907.

(6) Barr, Martin W., and Maloney, E. F. *Types of Mental Defectives.*
"Idiot Savant," pp. 128–35. Philadelphia, 1920.

(7) Thomas, Edward. *Industry, Emotion and Unrest.* New York,
1920.

(8) Parker, Carleton H. *The Casual Laborer and Other Essays.*
Chap. i, "Toward Understanding Labor Unrest," pp. 27–59.
New York, 1920.

(9) *The Cause of World Unrest.* With an introduction by the editor
of *The Morning Post* (of London). New York, 1920.

(10) Stoddard, Lothrop. *The Revolt against Civilization.* The menace
of the under man. New York, 1922.

(11) Ross, Edward A. *The Russian Bolshevik Revolution.* New York,
1921.

(12) ———. *The Russian Soviet Republic.* New York, 1923.

(13) Ghent, W. J. *The Reds Bring Reaction.* Princeton, 1923.

(14) Ferrero, Guglielmo. *Ancient Rome and Modern America.* A
comparative study of morals and manners. New York, 1914.

(15) Veblen, Thorstein. "The Instinct of Workmanship and the
Irksomeness of Labor," *American Journal of Sociology*, IV (1898–
99), 187–201.

(16) Lippmann, Walter. "Unrest," *New Republic*, XX (1919), 315–22.

(17) Tannenbaum, Frank. *The Labor Movement.* Its conservative
functions and social consequences. New York, 1921.

(18) Baker, Ray Stannard. *The New Industrial Unrest.* Its reason
and remedy. New York, 1920.

(19) Stoddard, Lothrop. *The New World of Islam.* Chapter ix, "Social
Unrest and Bolshevism," pp. 323–54. New York, 1921.

(20) MacCurdy, J. T. "Psychological Aspects of the Present Unrest,"
Survey, XLIII (1919–20), 665–68.

(21) Myers, Charles S. *Mind and Work.* The psychological factors
in industry and commerce. Chap. vi, "Industrial Unrest,"
pp. 137–69. New York, 1921.

(22) Adler, H. M. "Unemployment and Personality—a Study of
Psychopathic Cases," *Mental Hygiene*, I (1917), 16–24.

(23) Chirol, Valentine. *Indian Unrest.* A reprint, revised and enlarged,
from *The Times*, with an introduction by Sir Alfred Lyall. London,
1910.

(24) Münsterberg, Hugo. *Social Studies of Today.* Chap. ii, "The
Educational Unrest," pp. 25–57. London, 1913.

(25) ———. *American Problems.* From the point of view of a psychologist. Chap. v, "The Intemperance of Women," pp. 103–13.
New York, 1912.

(26) Corelli, Marie. "The Great Unrest," *World Today*, XXI (1912),
1954–59.

(27) Ferrero, Guglielmo. *The Women of the Caesars.* New York, 1911.

(28) Myerson, Abraham. *The Nervous Housewife.* Boston, 1920.

(29) Mensch, Ella. *Bilderstürmer in der Berliner Frauenbewegung.*
2d ed. Berlin, 1906.

[See bibliography, "Industrial Conflict," pp. 652–53.]

C. *Psychic Epidemics*

(1) Hecker, J. F. C. *The Black Death and the Dancing Mania.* Translated from the German by B. G. Babington. Cassell's National Library. New York, 1888.

(2) Stoll, Otto. *Suggestion und Hypnotismus in der Völkerpsychologie.* 2d ed. Leipzig, 1904.

(3) Friedmann, Max. *Über Wahnideen im Völkerleben.* Wiesbaden, 1901.

(4) Regnard, P. *Les maladies épidémiques de l'esprit.* Sorcellerie, magnétisme, morphinisme, délire des grandeurs. Paris, 1886.

(5) Meyer, J. L. *Schwärmerische Greuelscenen oder Kreuzigungsgeschichte einer religiösen Schwärmerin in Wildensbuch, Canton Zürich.* Ein merkwürdiger Beytrag zur Geschichte des religiösen Fanatismus. 2d ed. Zürich, 1824.

(6) Gowen, B. S. "Some Aspects of Pestilences and Other Epidemics," *American Journal of Psychology*, XVIII (1907), 1–60.

(7) Weygandt, W. *Beitrag zur Lehre von den psychischen Epidemien.* Halle, 1905.

(8) *Histoire des diables de Loudun.* Ou de la possession des Religieuses Ursulines et de la condamnation et du supplice d'Urbain Grandier, curé de la même ville, cruels effets de la vengeance du Cardinal de Richelieu. Amsterdam, 1740.

(9) Finsler, G. "Die religiöse Erweckung der zehner und zwanziger Jahre unseres Jahrhunderts in der deutschen Schweiz," *Züricher Taschenbuch auf das Jahr 1890.* Zürich, 1890.

(10) Fauriel. M. C. *Histoire de la croisade contre les hérétiques Albigeois.* Écrite en vers provençaux par un poète contemporain. (Aiso es la consos de la crozada contr els ereges Dalbeges.) Paris, 1837.

(11) Mosiman, Eddison. *Das Zungenreden, geschichtlich und psychologisch untersucht.* Tübingen, 1911. [Bibliography.]

(12) Vigouroux, A., and Juquelier, P. *La contagion mentale.* Paris, 1905.

(13) Kotik, Dr. Naum. "Die Emanation der psychophysischen Energie," *Grenzfragen des Nerven- und Seelenlebens.* Wiesbaden, 1908.

(14) Aubry, P. "De l'influence contagieuse de la publicité des faits criminels," *Archives d'anthropologie criminelle*, VIII (1893), 565–80.

(15) Achelis, T. *Die Ekstace in ihrer kulturellen Bedeutung.* Kulturprobleme der Gegenwart. Berlin, 1902.

(16) Cadière, L. "Sur quelques Faits religieux ou magiques, observés pendant une épidémie de choléra en Annam," *Anthropos*, V (1910), 519–28, 1125–59.

(17) Hansen, J. *Zauberwahn, Inquisition und Hexenprozess im Mittelalter und die Entstehung der grossen Hexenverfolgung.* München, 1900.

(18) Hansen, J. *Quellen und Untersuchungen zur Geschichte des Hexenwahns und der Hexenverfolgung im Mittelalter.* Bonn, 1901.

(19) Rossi, P. *Psicologia collettiva morbosa.* Torino, 1901.

(20) Despine, Prosper. *De la Contagion morale.* Paris, 1870.

(21) Moreau de Tours. *De la Contagion du suicide à propos de l'épidémie actuelle.* Paris, 1875.

(22) Aubry, P. *La Contagion du meutre.* Étude d'anthropologie criminelle. 3d ed. Paris, 1896.

(23) Rambosson, J. *Phénomènes nerveux, intellectuels et moraux, leur transmission par contagion.* Paris, 1883.

(24) Dumas, Georges. "Contagion mentale, épidémies mentales, folies collectives, folies grégaires," *Revue philosophique*, LXXI (1911), 225–44, 384–407.

II. MUSIC, DANCE, AND RITUAL

(1) Wallaschek, Richard. *Primitive Music.* An inquiry into the origin and development of music, songs, instruments, dances, and pantomines of savage races. London, 1893.

(2) Combarieu, J. *La Musique et le magic.* Étude sur les origines populaires de l'art musical; son influence et sa fonction dans les sociétés. Paris, 1908.

(3) Simmel, Georg. "Psychologische und ethnologische Studien über Musik," *Zeitschrift für Völkerpsychologie und Sprachwissenschaft*, XIII (1882), 261–305.

(4) Boas, F. "Chinook Songs," *Journal of American Folk-Lore*, I (1888), 220–26.

(5) Densmore, Frances. "The Music of the Filipinos," *American Anthropologist*, N.S., VIII (1906), 611–32.

(6) Fletcher, Alice C. *Indian Story and Song from North America.* Boston, 1906.

(7) ———. "Indian Songs and Music," *Journal of American Folk-Lore*, XI (1898), 85–104.

(8) Grinnell, G. B. "Notes on Cheyenne Songs," *American Anthropologist*, N.S., V (1903), 312–22.

(9) Matthews, W. "Navaho Gambling Songs," *American Anthropologist*, II (1889), 1–20.

(10) Hearn, Lafcadio. "Three Popular Ballads," *Transactions of the Asiatic Society of Japan*, XXII (1894), 285–336.

(11) Ellis, Havelock. "The Philosophy of Dancing," *Atlantic Monthly*, CXIII (1914), 197–207.

(12) Hirn, Yrjö. *The Origins of Art.* A psychological and sociological inquiry. Chap. xvii, "Erotic Art," pp. 238–48. London, 1900.

(13) Pater, Walter. *Greek Studies.* A series of essays. London, 1911.

(14) Grosse, Ernst. *The Beginnings of Art.* Chap. viii, "The Dance," pp. 207–31. New York, 1898.

(15) Vogt, von Ogden. *Art and Religion.* New Haven, 1921.

(16) Bücher, Karl. *Arbeit und Rhythmus.* 3d ed. Leipzig, 1902.

(17) Lhérisson, E. "La Danse du vaudou," *Semaine médicale*, XIX (1899), lxxiv.

(18) Reed, V. Z. "The Ute Bear Dance," *American Anthropologist*, IX (1896), 237–44.

(19) Gummere, F. B. *The Beginnings of Poetry.* New York, 1901.

(20) Prescott, Frederick C. *The Poetic Mind.* New York, 1922.

(21) Fawkes, J. W. "The Growth of the Hopi Ritual," *Journal of American Folk-Lore,* XI (1898), 173–94.
(22) Crawley, A. E. "Processions and Dances," *Encyclopaedia of Religion and Ethics,* X, 356–62.
(23) Cabrol, F. *Les origines liturgiques.* Paris, 1906.
(24) Gennep, A. van. *Les Rites de passage.* Paris, 1909.
(25) Pitre, Giuseppe. *Feste patronali in Sicilia.* Palermo, 1900.
(26) Murray, W. A. "Organizations of Witches in Great Britain," *Folk-Lore,* XXVIII (1917), 228–58.
(27) Taylor, Thomas. *The Eleusinian and Bacchic Mysteries.* New York, 1891.
(28) Tippenhauer, L. G. *Die Insel Haiti.* Leipzig, 1893. [Describes the Voudou Ritual.]
(29) Wuensch, R. *Das Frühlingsfest der Insel Malta.* Ein Beitrag zur Geschichte der antiken Religion. Leipzig, 1902.
(30) Loisy, Alfred. *Les mystères païens et le mystère chrétien.* Paris, 1919.
(31) Lummis, Charles F. *The Land of Poco Tiempo.* Chap. iv, "The Penitent Brothers," pp. 77–108. New York, 1893.
(32) "Los Hermanos Penitentes," *El Palacio,* VIII (1920), 3–20, 73–74.

III. THE CROWD AND THE PUBLIC

A. *The Crowd*

(1) Le Bon, Gustave. *The Crowd.* A study of the popular mind. London, 1920.
(2) Tarde, G. *L'Opinion et la foule.* Paris, 1901.
(3) Sighele, S. *Psychologie des Auflaufs und der Massenverbrechen.* Translated from the Italian by Hans Kurella. Leipzig, 1897.
(4) ————. *La foule criminelle.* Essai de psychologie collective. 2d ed., entièrement refondue. Paris, 1901.
(5) Tarde, Gabriel. "Foules et sectes au point de vue criminel," *Revue des deux mondes,* CXX (1893), 349–87.
(6) Miceli, V. "La Psicologia della folla," *Rivista italiana di sociologia,* III (1899), 166–95.
(7) Tayler, J. Lionel. *Social Life and the Crowd.* Boston, 1923.
(8) Conway, M. *The Crowd in Peace and War.* New York, 1915.
(9) Martin, E. D. *The Behavior of Crowds.* New York, 1920.
(10) Christensen, A. *Politics and Crowd-Morality.* New York, 1915.
(11) Park, R. E. *Masse und Publikum.* Bern, 1904.
(12) Freud, Sigmund. *Masspsychology and Ego-analysis.* New York, 1923.
(13) Clark, H. "The Crowd." "University of Illinois Studies." *Psychological Monograph,* No. 92, XXI (1916), 26–36.
(14) Tawney, G. A. "The Nature of Crowds," *Psychological Bulletin,* II (1905), 329–33.
(15) Rossi, P. *Le suggesteur et la foule, psychologie du meneur.* Paris, 1904.
(16) ————. *I suggestionatori e la folla.* Torino, 1902.
(17) ————. "Dell'Attenzione colletiva e sociale," *Manicomio,* XXI (1905), 248 ff.

B. *Political Psychology*

    (1) Beecher, Franklin A. "National Politics in Its Psychological Aspect," *Open Court*, XXXIII (1919), 653–61.

    (2) Boutmy, Émile. *The English People*. A study of their political psychology. London, 1904.

    (3) Palanti, G. "L'Esprit de corps. (Remarques sociologiques.)" *Revue philosophique*, XLVIII (1899), 135–45.

    (4) Gardner, Chas. S. "Assemblies," *American Journal of Sociology* XIX (1914), 531–55.

    (5) Bentham, Jeremy. *Essay on Political Tactics.* Containing six of the principal rules proper to be observed by a political assembly, in the process of forming a decision: with the reasons on which they are grounded; and a comparative application of them to British and French practice. London, 1791.

    (6) Tönnies, Ferdinand. "Die grosse Menge und das Volk," *Schmollers Jahrbuch*, XLIV (1920), 317–45. [Criticism of Le Bon's conception of the crowd.]

    (7) Botsford, George W. *The Roman Assemblies.* From their origin to the end of the Republic. New York, 1909.

    (8) Crothers, T. D. "A Medical Study of the Jury System," *Popular Science Monthly*, XLVII (1895), 375–82.

    (9) Coleman, Charles T. "Origin and Development of Trial by Jury," *Virginia Law Review*, VI (1919–20), 77–86.

    (10) Kent, Frank R. *The Great Game of Politics.* An effort to present the elementary human facts about politics, politicians, and political machines, candidates and their ways, for the benefit of the average citizen. New York, 1923.

    (11) Merriam, Charles E. and Gosnell, Harold F. *Non-Voting: Causes and Methods of Control.* Chicago, 1924.

C. *Collective Psychology in General*

    (1) Rossi, P. *Sociologia e psicologia collettiva.* 2d ed. Roma, 1909.

    (2) Straticò, A. *La Psicologia collettiva.* Palermo, 1905.

    (3) Worms, René. "Psychologie collective et psychologie individuelle," *Revue internationale de sociologie*, VII (1899), 249–74.

    (4) Brönner, W. "Zur Theorie der kollektiven-psychischen Erscheinungen," *Zeitschrift für Philosophie und philosophische Kritik*, CXLI (1911), 1–40.

    (5) Newell, W. W. "Individual and Collective Characteristics in Folk-Lore," *Journal of American Folk-Lore*, XIX (1906), 1–15.

    (6) Campeano, M. *Essai de psychologie militaire individuelle et collective.* Avec une préface de M. Th. Ribot. Paris, 1902.

    (7) Hartenberg, P. "Les émotions de Bourse. (Notes de psychologie collective)." *Revue philosophique*, LVIII (1904), 163–70.

    (8) Scalinger, G. M. *La Psicologia a teatro.* Napoli, 1896.

    (9) Burckhard, M. "Das Theater." Die Gesellschaft. *Sammlung Sozial-Psychologische Monographien*, 18. Frankfurt-am-Main, 1907.

(10) Woolbert, C. H. "The Audience." "University of Illinois Studies." *Psychological Monograph*, No. 92, XXI (1916), 36–54.
(11) Howard, G. E. "Social Psychology of the Spectator," *American Journal of Sociology*, XVIII (1912), 33–50.
(12) Peterson, J. "The Functioning of Ideas in Social Groups," *Psychological Review*, XXV (1918), 214–26.
(13) Moede, Walther. *Experimentelle Massenpsychologie.* Leipsic, 1920.

IV. MASS MOVEMENTS

(1) Bryce, James. "Migrations of the Races of Men Considered Historically," *Contemporary Review*, LXII (1892), 128–49.
(2) Mason, Otis T. "Migration and the Food Quest: A Study in the Peopling of America," *American Anthropologist*, VII (1894), 275–92.
(3) Pflugk-Harttung, Julius von. *The Great Migrations.* Translated from the German by John Henry Wright. Philadelphia, 1905.
(4) Bradley, Henry. *The Story of the Goths.* From the earliest times to the end of the Gothic dominion in Spain. New York, 1888.
(5) Jordanes. *The Origin and Deeds of the Goths.* English version by Charles C. Mierow. Princeton, 1908.
(6) Archer, T. A., and Kingsford, C. L. *The Crusades.* New York, 1894.
(7) Ireland, W. W. "On the Psychology of the Crusades," *Journal of Mental Science*, LII (1906), 745–55; LIII (1907), 322–41.
(8) Groves, E. R. "Psychic Causes of Rural Migration," *American Journal of Sociology*, XXI (1916), 623–27.
(9) Woodson, Carter G. *A Century of Negro Migrations.* Washington, 1918. [Bibliography.]
(10) Fleming, Walter L. "'Pap' Singleton, the Moses of the Colored Exodus," *American Journal of Sociology*, XV (1909–10), 61–82.
(11) Bancroft, H. H. *History of California.* Vol. VI, 1848–59. Chaps. ii–ix, pp. 26–163. San Francisco, 1888. [The discovery of gold in California.]
(12) Down, T. C. "The Rush to the Klondike," *Cornhill Magazine*, IV (1898), 33–43.
(13) Ziegler, T. *Die geistigen und socialen Strömungen des neunzehnten Jahrhunderts.* Berlin, 1899.
(14) Zeeb, Frieda B. "Mobility of the German Woman," *American Journal of Sociology*, XXI (1915–16), 234–62.
(15) Anthony, Katharine S. *Feminism in Germany and Scandinavia.* New York, 1915. [Bibliography.]
(16) Croly, Jane (Mrs.). *The History of the Woman's Club Movement in America.* New York, 1898.
(17) Taft, Jessie. *The Woman Movement from the Point of View of Social Consciousness.* Chicago, 1916.
(18) Harnack, Adolf. *The Mission and Expansion of Christianity in the First Three Centuries.* Translated from the 2d rev. German ed. by James Moffatt. New York, 1908.

(10) Buck, S. J. *The Agrarian Crusade*. A chronicle of the farmer in politics. New Haven, 1920.

(20) McVey, Frank L. "The Populist Movement," *Economic Studies*, I (1896), 135–209. [Bibliography.]

(21) *Labor Movement*. The last six volumes of *The Documentary History of American Industrial Society*. Vols. V–VI, 1820–40, by John R. Commons and Helen L. Sumner; Vols. VII–VIII, 1840–60, by John R. Commons; Vols. IX–X, 1860–80, by John R. Commons and John B. Andrews. Cleveland, 1910.

(22) Begbie, Harold. *The Life of General William Booth*. The Founder of the Salvation Army. 2 vols. New York, 1920.

(23) Wittenmyer, Annie (Mrs.). *History of the Woman's Temperance Crusade*. A complete official history of the wonderful uprising of the Christian women of the United States against the liquor traffic which culminated in the Gospel Temperance Movement. Introduction by Frances E. Willard. Philadelphia, 1878.

(24) Gordon, Ernest. *The Anti-alcohol Movement in Europe*. New York, 1913.

(25) Cherrington, Ernest H. *The Evolution of Prohibition in the United States of America*. A chronological history of the liquor problem and the temperance reform in the United States from the earliest settlements to the consummation of national prohibition. Westerville, Ohio, 1920.

(26) Rainwater, Clarence E. *The Play Movement in the United States*. A study of community recreation. Chicago, 1921. [Bibliography.]

(27) Woods, Robert A. *English Social Movements*. New York, 1891.

(28) Zimand, Savel. *Modern Social Movements*. Descriptive summaries and bibliographies. New York, 1921.

V. REVIVALS, RELIGIOUS AND LINGUISTIC

A. *Religious Revivals and the Origin of Sects*

(1) Meader, John R. Article on "Religious Sects," *Encyclopaedia Americana*, XXIII, 355–61. [List of nearly 300 denominations and sects.]

(2) Articles on "Sects," *Encyclopaedia of Religion and Ethics*, XI, 307–47. [The subject and author of the different articles are "Sects (Buddhist)," T. W. Rhys Davids; "Sects (Chinese)," T. Richard; "Sects (Christian)," W. T. Whitley; "Sects (Hindu)," W. Crooke; "Sects (Jewish)," I. Abrahams; "Sects (Russian)," K. Grass and A. von Stromberg; "Sects (Samaritan)," N. Schmidt; "Sects (Zoroastrian)," E. Edwards. Bibliographies.]

(3) United States Bureau of the Census. *Religious Bodies, 1906*. 2 vols. Washington, 1910.

(4) ———. *Religious Bodies, 1916*. 2 vols. Washington, 1919.

(5) Davenport, Frederick M. *Primitive Traits in Religious Revivals*. A study in mental and social evolution. New York, 1905.

(6) Mooney, James. "The Ghost-Dance Religion and the Sioux Outbreak of 1890." *14th Annual Report of the Bureau of American Ethnology* (1892–93), 653–1136.

(7) Shonle, Ruth. "The Christianizing Process among Preliterate Peoples," *Journal of Religion*, IV (1924), 261–80.

(8) Stalker, James. Article on "Revivals of Religion," *Encyclopaedia of Religion and Ethics*, X, 753–57. [Bibliography.]

(9) Burns, J. *Revivals, Their Laws and Leaders*. London, 1909.

(10) Tracy, J. *The Great Awakening*. A history of the revival of religion in the time of Edwards and Whitefield. Boston, 1842.

(11) Finney, C. G. *Autobiography*. London, 1892.

(12) Hayes, Samuel P. "An Historical Study of the Edwardean Revivals," *American Journal of Psychology*, XIII (1902), 550–74.

(13) Maxon, C. H. *The Great Awakening in the Middle Colonies*. Chicago, 1920. [Bibliography.]

(14) Gibson, William. *Year of Grace*. Edinburgh, 1860. [Irish revival, 1859.]

(15) Moody, W. R. *The Life of Dwight L. Moody*. New York, 1900.

(16) Bois, Henri. *Le Réveil au pays de Galles*. Paris, 1906. [Welsh revival of 1904–6.]

(17) ———. *Quelques réflexions sur la psychologie des réveils*. Paris, 1906.

(18) Cartwright, Peter. *Autobiography of Peter Cartwright, the Backwoods Preacher*. Cincinnati, 1859.

(19) MacLean, J. P. "The Kentucky Revival and Its Influence on the Miami Valley," *Ohio Archaeological and Historical Publications*, XII (1903), 242–86. [Bibliography.]

(20) Cleveland, Catharine C. *The Great Revival in the West, 1797–1805*. Chicago, 1916. [Bibliography.]

(21) Rogers, James B. *The Cane Ridge Meeting-House*. To which is appended the autobiography of B. W. Stone. Cincinnati, 1910.

(22) Stchoukine, Ivan. *Le Suicide collectif dans le Raskol russe*. Paris, 1903.

(23) Bussell, F. W. *Religious Thought and Heresy in the Middle Ages*. London, 1918.

(24) Gebhart, Émile. *Mystics and Heretics in Italy*. A history of the religious revival in the Middle Ages. Translated from the French and with an introduction by E. M. Hulme. New York, 1923.

(25) Campbell, Thomas J. *The Jesuits, 1534–1921*. A history of the Society of Jesus from its foundation to the present time. New York, 1921.

(26) Egli, Emil. *Die Züricher Wiedertäufer zur Reformationszeit*. Zürich, 1878.

(27) Bax, Ernest Belfort. *Rise and Fall of the Anabaptists*. New York, 1903.

(28) Schechter, S. *Documents of Jewish Sectaries.* 2 vols. Cambridge, 1910.

(29) Graetz, H. *History of the Jews.* 6 vols. Philadelphia, 1891–98.

(30) Jost, M. *Geschichte des Judenthums und seiner Sekten.* 3 vols. Leipzig, 1857–59.

(31) Farquhar, J. N. *Modern Religious Movements in India.* New York, 1915.

(32) Selbie, W. B. *English Sects.* A history of non-conformity. Home University Library. New York, 1912.

(33) Barclay, Robert. *The Inner Life of the Religious Societies of the Commonwealth.* London, 1876. [Bibliography.]

(34) Jones, Rufus M. *Studies in Mystical Religion.* London, 1909.

(35) Braithwaite, W. C. *Beginnings of Quakerism.* London, 1912.

(36) Jones, Rufus M. *The Quakers in American Colonies.* London, 1911.

(37) ———. *The Later Periods of Quakerism.* London, 1921.

(38) Evans, F. W. *Shakers.* Compendium of the origin, history, principles, rules and regulations, government, and doctrines of the United Society of Believers in Christ's Second Appearing. With biographies of Ann Lee, William Lee, James Whittaker, J. Hocknell, J. Meacham, and Lucy Wright. New York, 1859.

(39) Train, J. *The Buchanites from First to Last.* Edinburgh, 1846.

(40) Miller, Edward. *The History and Doctrines of Irvingism.* Or of the so-called Catholic and Apostolic Church. 2 vols. London, 1878.

(41) Neatby, W. Blair. *A History of the Plymouth Brethren.* London, 1901.

(42) Lockwood, George B. *The New Harmony Movement.* "The Rappites." Chaps. ii–iv, pp. 7–42. [Bibliography.]

(43) Shambaugh, Berta. *Amana.* The community of true inspiration. Iowa City, 1908.

(44) James, B. B. *The Labadist Colony of Maryland.* Baltimore, 1899.

(45) Dixon, W. H. *Spiritual Wives.* 2 vols. London, 1868.

(46) Randall, E. O. *History of the Zoar Society from Its Commencement to Its Conclusion.* Columbus, 1899.

(47) Loughborough, J. N. *The Great Second Advent Movement.* Its rise and progress. Nashville, Tenn., 1905. [Adventists.]

(48) Harlan, Rolvix. *John Alexander Dowie and the Christian Catholic Apostolic Church in Zion.* Evansville, Wis., 1906.

(49) Smith, Henry C. *Mennonites of America.* Mennonite Publishing House, Scottdale, Pa., 1909. [Bibliography.]

(50) La Rue, William. *The Foundations of Mormonism.* A study of the fundamental facts in the history and doctrines of the Mormons from original sources. With introduction by Alfred Williams Anthony. New York, 1919. [Bibliography.]

B. *Language Revivals and Nationalism*

(1) Dominian, Leon. *Frontiers of Language and Nationality in Europe.* New York, 1917.

(2) Bourgoing, P. de. *Les Guerres d'idiome et de nationalité.* Paris, 1849.

(3) Meillet, A. "Les Langues et les nationalités," *Scientia,* XVIII (1915), 192–201.

(4) Tegnér, Esaias. *Ur språkens värld.* Especially article, "Om språk och nationalitet," pp. 95–164. Stockholm, 1922.

(5) Rhys, John, and Brynmor-Jones, David. *The Welsh People.* Chap. xii, "Language and Literature of Wales," pp. 501–50. London, 1900.

(6) Dinneen, P. S. *Lectures on the Irish Language Movement.* Delivered under the auspices of various branches of the Gaelic League. London, 1904.

(7) Montgomery, K. L. "Some Writers of the Celtic Renaissance," *Fortnightly Review,* XCVI (1911), 545–61.

(8) ———. "Ireland's Psychology: a Study of Facts," *Fortnightly Review,* CXII (1919), 572–88.

(9) Dubois, L. Paul. *Contemporary Ireland.* With an introduction by T. M. Kettle, M. P. London, 1908.

(10) *The Teaching of Gaelic in Highland Schools.* Published under the auspices of the Highland Association. London, 1907.

(11) Fedortchouk, Y. "La Question des nationalités en Autriche-Hongrie: les Ruthenes de Hongrie," *Annales des nationalités,* VIII (1915), 52–56.

(12) Seton-Watson, R. W. [Scotus Viator, *pseud.*] *Racial Problems in Hungary.* London, 1908. [Bibliography.]

(13) Samassa, P. "Deutsche und Windische in Südösterreich," *Deutsche Erde,* II (1903), 39–41.

(14) Wace, A. J. B., and Thompson, M. S. *The Nomads of the Balkans.* London, 1914.

(15) Tabbé, P. *La vivante Roumanie.* Paris, 1913.

(16) Louis-Jarau, G. *L'Albanie inconnue.* Paris, 1913.

(17) Brancoff, D. M. *La Macédoine et sa population Chrétienne.* Paris, 1905.

(18) Fedortchouk, Y. *Memorandum on the Ukrainian Question in Its National Aspect.* London, 1914.

(19) Vellay, Charles. "L'Irredentisme hellénique," *La Revue de Paris,* XX (Juillet-Août, 1913), 884–86.

(20) Sands, B. *The Ukraine.* London, 1914.

(21) Auerbach, B. "La Germanization de la Pologne Prussienne. La loi d'expropriation," *Revue Politique et Parlementaire.* LVII (1908), 109–125.

(22) Bernhard, L. *Das polnische Gemeinwesen im preussischen Staat.* Die Polenfrage. Leipzig, 1910.

(23) Henry, R. "La Frontière linguistique en Alsace-Lorraine," *Les Marches de l'Est,* 1911–1912, pp. 60–71.

(24) Nitsch, C. "Dialectology of Polish Languages," *Polish Encyclopaedia*, Vol. III. Cracow, 1915.
(25) Witte, H. "Wendische Bevölkerungsreste in Mecklenburg," *Forschungen zur deutschen Landes- und Volkskunde*, XVI (1905), 1–124.
(26) Kaupas, A. "L'Église et les Lituaniens aux États-Unis d'Amérique," *Annales des Nationalités*, II (1913), 233 ff.
(27) Pélissier, Jean. *Les Principaux artisans de la renaissance nationale lituanienne*. Hommes et choses de Lituanie. Lausanne, 1918.
(28) Jakstas, A. "Lituaniens et Polonais." *Annales des nationalités*, VIII (1915), 219 ff.
(29) Headlam, Cecil. *Provence and Languedoc*. Chap. v, "Frédéric Mistral and the Félibres." London, 1912.
(30) Belisle, A. *Histoire de la presse franco-américaine*. Comprenant l'historique de l'émigration des Canadiens-Français aux États-Unis, leur développement, et leur progrès. Worcester, Mass., 1911.

VI. ECONOMIC CRISES

(1) Wirth, M. *Geschichte der Handelskrisen*. Frankfurt-am-Main, 1890.
(2) Jones, Edward D. *Economic Crises*. New York, 1900.
(3) Gibson, Thomas. *The Cycles of Speculation*. 2d ed. New York, 1909.
(4) Bellet, Daniel. *Crises économiques*. Crises commerciales. Crises de guerre. Leurs caractères, leurs indices, leurs effets. Paris, 1918.
(5) Clough, H. W. "Synchronous Variations in Solar and Terrestrial Phenomena," *Astrophysical Journal*, XXII (1905), 42–75.
(6) Clayton, H. H. "Influence of Rainfall on Commerce and Politics," *Popular Science Monthly*, LX (1901–2), 158–65.
(7) Mitchell, Wesley C. *Business Cycles*. Berkeley, Cal., 1913.
(8) ———. "Business Cycles," *Business Cycles and Unemployment*. Report and recommendations of a committee of the President's Conference on Unemployment. Pp. 5–18. New York, 1923.
(9) Moore, Henry L. *Economic Cycles: Their Law and Cause*. New York, 1914.
(10) Hurry, Jamieson B. *Vicious Circles in Sociology and Their Treatment*. London, 1915.
(11) Thiers, Adolphe. *The Mississippi Bubble*. A memoir of John Law. To which are added authentic accounts of the Darien expedition and the South Sea scheme. Translated from the French by F. S. Fiske. New York, 1859.
(12) Wiston-Glynn, A. W. *John Law of Lauriston*. Financier and statesman, founder of the Bank of France, originator of the Mississippi scheme, etc. London, 1907.

(13) Mackay, Charles. *Memoirs of Extraordinary Popular Delusions and the Madness of Crowds.* 2 vols. in one. London, 1859. [Vol. I, the Mississippi scheme, the South Sea bubble, the tulipomania, the alchymists, modern prophecies, fortune-telling, the magnetisers, influence of politics and religion on the hair and beard. Vol. II, the crusades, the witch mania, the slow prisoners, haunted houses, popular follies of great cities, popular admiration of great thieves, duels and ordeals, relics.]

VII. FASHION, REFORM, AND REVOLUTION

A. *Fashion*

(1) Spencer, Herbert. *Principles of Sociology.* Part IV, chap. xi, "Fashion," II, 205–10. London, 1893.

(2) Tarde, Gabriel. *Laws of Imitation.* Translated from the 2d French ed. by Elsie Clews Parsons. Chap. vii, "Custom and Fashion," pp. 244–365. New York, 1903.

(3) Simmel, G. *Philosophie der Mode.* Berlin, 1905.

(4) ———. "The Attraction of Fashion," *International Quarterly,* X (1904), 130–55.

(5) Sumner, W. G. *Folkways.* "Fashion," pp. 184–220. Boston, 1906.

(6) Sombart, Werner. "Wirtschaft und Mode," *Grenzfragen des Nerven- und Seelenlebens.* Wiesbaden, 1902.

(7) Clerget, Pierre. "The Economic and Social Rôle of Fashion," *Annual Report of the Smithsonian Institution,* 1913, pp. 755–65. Washington, 1914.

(8) Squillace, Fausto. *La Moda.* L'abito è l'uomo. Milano, 1912.

(9) Shaler, N. S. "The Law of Fashion," *Atlantic Monthly,* LXI (1888), 386–98.

(10) Patrick, G. T. W. "The Psychology of Crazes," *Popular Science Monthly,* LVII (1900), 285–94.

(11) Linton, E. L. "The Tyranny of Fashion," *Forum,* III (1887), 59–68.

(12) Bigg, Ada H. "What is 'Fashion'?" *Nineteenth Century,* XXXIII (1893), 235–48.

(13) Foley, Caroline A. "Fashion," *Economic Journal,* III (1893), 458–74.

(14) Aria, E. "Fashion, Its Survivals and Revivals," *Fortnightly Review,* CIV (1915), 930–37.

(15) Thomas, W. I. "The Psychology of Woman's Dress," *American Magazine,* LXVII (1908–9), 66–72.

(16) Schurtz, Heinrich. *Grundzüge einer Philosophie der Tracht.* Stuttgart, 1871.

(17) Wechsler, Alfred. *Psychologie der Mode.* Berlin, 1904.

(18) Stratz, Carl H. *Die Frauenkleidung und ihre natürliche Entwicklung.* Stuttgart, 1904.

948 INTRODUCTION TO THE SCIENCE OF SOCIOLOGY

(19) Holmes, William H. "Origin and Development of Form and Ornament in Ceramic Art," *Fourth Annual Report of the U.S. Bureau of American Ethnology, 1882–83*, pp. 437–65. Washington, 1886.

(20) Kroeber, A. L. "On the Principle of Order in Civilization as Exemplified by Changes of Fashion," *American Anthropologist*, N.S., XXI (1919), 235–63.

B. *Reform*

(1) Sumner, W. G. *Folkways.* "Reform and Revolution," pp. 86–95. Boston, 1906.

(2) Patrick, G. T. W. *The Psychology of Social Reconstruction.* Chaps. i–ii, "Psychological Factors in Social Reconstruction," pp. 27–118. Boston, 1920.

(3) Jevons, William S. *Methods of Social Reform.* And other papers. London, 1883.

(4) Pearson, Karl. *Social Problems.* Their treatment, past, present, and future. London, 1912.

(5) Mallock, W. H. *Social Reform as Related to Realities and Delusions.* An examination of the increase and distribution of wealth from 1801 to 1910. New York, 1915.

(6) Matthews, Brander. "Reform and Reformers," *North American*, CLXXXIII (1906), 461–73.

(7) Miller, J. D. "Futilities of Reformers," *Arena*, XXVI (1901), 481–89.

(8) Lippmann, Walter. *A Preface to Politics.* Chap. v, "Well Meaning but Unmeaning: The Chicago Vice Report," pp. 122–58. New York, 1913.

(9) Stanton, Henry B. *Sketches of Reforms and Reformers, of Great Britain and Ireland.* 2d rev. ed. New York, 1850.

(10) Gibbins, Henry de B. *English Social Reformers.* London, 1892.

(11) Stoughton, John. *William Wilberforce.* London, 1880.

(12) Field, J. *The Life of John Howard.* With comments on his character and philanthropic labours. London, 1850.

(13) Hodder, Edwin. *The Seventh Earl of Shaftesbury, K. G., as Social Reformer.* New York, 1898.

(14) Atkinson, Charles M. *Jeremy Bentham, His Life and Work.* London, 1905.

(15) Morley, John. *The Life of Richard Cobden.* Boston, 1890.

(16) Bartlett, David W. *Modern Agitators.* Or pen portraits of living American reformers. New York, 1855.

(17) Greeley, Horace. *Hints toward Reforms.* In lectures, addresses, and other writing. New York, 1850.

(18) Austin, George L. *The Life and Times of Wendell Phillips.* New ed. Boston, 1901.

(19) Hill, Georgiana. *Women in English Life.* From medieval to modern times. Period III, chap. v, "The Philanthropists," Vol. II, pp. 59–74; Period IV, chap. xi, "The Modern Humanitarian Movement," Vol. II, pp. 227–36. 2 vols. London, 1896.

(20) Yonge, Charlotte M. *Hannah More.* Famous women. Boston, 1888.

(21) Besant, Annie. *An Autobiography.* 2d ed. London, 1908.

(22) Harper, Ida H. *The Life and Work of Susan B. Anthony.* Including public addresses, her own lectures and many from her contemporaries during fifty years. A story of the evolution of the status of woman. 3 vols. Indianapolis, 1898–1908.

(23) Whiting, Lilian. *Women Who Have Ennobled Life.* Philadelphia, 1915.

(24) Willard, Frances E. *Woman and Temperance.* Or the work and workers of the Woman's Christian Temperance Union. 3d ed. Hartford, Conn., 1883.

(25) Gordon, Anna A. *The Beautiful Life of Frances E. Willard.* A memorial volume. Introduction by Lady Henry Somerset. Chicago, 1898.

(26) Lasker, Bruno. "What Has Become of Social Reform?" *American Journal of Sociology*, XXVIII (1922), 129–59.

C. *Revolution*

(1) Le Bon, Gustave. *The Psychology of Revolution.* Translated from the French by Bernard Miall. New York, 1913.

(2) Petrie, W. M. F. *The Revolutions of Civilisation.* London, 1912.

(3) Hyndman, Henry M. *The Evolution of Revolution.* London, 1920.

(4) Adams, Brooks. *The Theory of Social Revolutions.* New York, 1913.

(5) Bauer, Arthur. *Essai sur les révolutions.* Paris, 1908.

(6) Landauer, G. *Die Revolution.* "Die Gesellschaft, Sammlung sozial-psychologischer Monographien." Frankfurt-am-Main, 1907.

(7) Thomas, W. I. *Source Book for Social Origins.* "Crisis and Control," pp. 13–22. Chicago, 1909.

(8) Ellwood, Charles A. "A Psychological Theory of Revolutions," *American Journal of Sociology*, XI (1905–6), 49–59.

(9) ———. *Introduction to Social Psychology.* Chap. viii, "Social Change under Abnormal Conditions," pp. 170–87. New York, 1917.

(10) Edwards, Lyford P. "Mechanics of Revolution," *St. Stephen's College Bulletin*, LXIV (May, 1923), 17–24.

(11) King, Irving. "The Influence of the Form of Social Change upon the Emotional Life of a People," *American Journal of Sociology*, IX (1903–4), 124–35.

(12) Toynbee, Arnold. *Lectures on the Industrial Revolution of the Eighteenth Century in England.* New ed. London, 1908.

(13) Taine, H. A. *The French Revolution.* Translated from the French by John Durand. 3 vols. New York, 1878–85.

(14) Olgin, Moissaye J. *The Soul of the Russian Revolution.* Introduction by Vladimir G. Simkhovitch. New York, 1917.

(15) Kropotkin, P. *Memoirs of a Revolutionist.* Boston, 1899.

(16) Spargo, John. *The Psychology of Bolshevism.* New York, 1919.

(17) Khoras, P. "La Psychologie de la révolution chinoise," *Revue des deux mondes*, VIII (1912), 295–331.

(18) Szende, Paul. *Die Krise der mitteleuropäischen Revolution.* Ein massenpsychologischer Versuch. Tübingen, 1921.

(19) Toller, Ernst. *Masse Mensch.* Ein Stück aus der sozialen Revolution des 20 Jahrhunderts. Potsdam, 1921.

(20) Stoddard, Lothrop. *The Revolt against Civilization.* The menace of the under man. New York, 1922.

(21) Le Bon, Gustave. *The World in Revolt.* A psychological study of our times. Translated from the French by Bernard Miall. New York, 1921.

(22) Lombroso, Cesare. *Le Crime politique et les révolutions par rapport au droit, à l'anthropologie criminelle et à science du gouvernement.* Translated by A. Bouchard. Paris, 1912.

(23) Prince, Samuel H. *Catastrophe and Social Change.* Based upon a sociological study of the Halifax disaster. "Columbia University Studies in Political Science." New York, 1920.

TOPICS FOR WRITTEN THEMES

1. Collective Behavior and Social Control
2. Unrest in the Person and Unrest in the Group
3. The Agitator as a Type of the Restless Person
4. A Study of Adolescent Unrest: the Runaway Boy and the Girl Who Goes Wrong
5. A Comparison of Physical Epidemics with Social Contagion
6. Case Studies of Psychic Epidemics: the Mississippi Bubble, Gold Fever, War-Time Psychosis, the Dancing Mania in Modern Times, etc.
7. Propaganda as Social Contagion: an Analysis of a Selected Case
8. A Description and Interpretation of Crowd Behavior: the Orgy, the Cult, the Mob, the Organized Crowd
9. The "Animal" Crowd: the Flock, the Herd, the Pack
10. A Description of Crowd Behavior on Armistice Day
11. The Criminal Crowd
12. The Jury, the Congenial Group, the Committee, the Legislature, the Mass Meeting, etc., as Types of Collective Behavior
13. Crowd Excitements and Mass Movements
14. A Study of Mass Migrations: the Barbarian Invasions, the Settlement of Oklahoma, the Migrations of the Mennonnites, the Treks of the Boers, the Rise of Mohammedanism, the Mormon Migrations, etc.
15. Crusades and Reforms: the Crusades, the Abolition Movement, Prohibition, the Woman's Temperance Crusades, Moving-Picture Censorship, etc.
16. Fashions, Revivals, and Revolutions

17. The Social Laws of Fashions
18. Linguistic Revivals and the Nationalist Movements
19. Religious Revivals and the Origin of Sects
20. Social Unrest, Social Movements, and Changes in Mores and Institutions

QUESTIONS FOR DISCUSSION

1. What do you understand by collective behavior?
2. Interpret the incident in a Lancashire cotton factory in terms of sympathy, imitation, and suggestion.
3. What simple forms of social contagion have you observed?
4. In what sense may the dancing mania of the Middle Ages be compared to an epidemic?
5. Why may propaganda be interpreted as social contagion? Describe a concrete instance of propaganda and analyze its *modus operandi*.
6. What are the differences in behavior of the flock, the pack, and the herd?
" Is it accurate to speak of these animal groups as "crowds"?
8. What do you understand Le Bon to mean by "the mental unity of crowds"?
9. Describe and analyze the behavior of crowds which you have observed.
10. "The crowd is always intellectually inferior to the isolated individual." "The crowd may be better or worse than the individual." Are these statements consistent? Elaborate your position.
11. In what sense may we speak of sects, castes, and classes as crowds?
12. What do you mean by a social movement?
13. What is the significance of a movement?
14. Why is movement to be regarded as the fundamental form of freedom?
15. How does crowd excitement lead to mass movements?
16. What were the differences in the characteristics of mass movements in the Klondike Rush, the Woman's Crusade, Methodism, and bolshevism?
17. What are the causes of social unrest?
18. What is the relation of social unrest to social organization?
19. How does Le Bon explain the mental anarchy at the time of the French Revolution?
20. What was the nature of this mental anarchy in the different social classes? Are revolutions always preceded by mental anarchy?
21. What was the relative importance of belief and of reason in the French Revolution?
22. What are the likenesses and differences between the origin and development of bolshevism and of the French Revolution?

23. Do you agree with Spargo's interpretation of the psychology (*a*) of the intellectual Bolshevists, and (*b*) of the I.W.W.?
24. Are mass movements organizing or disorganizing factors in society? Illustrate by reference to Methodism, the French Revolution, and bolshevism.
25. Under what conditions will a mass movement (*a*) become organized, and (*b*) become an institution?

CHAPTER XIV

PROGRESS

I. INTRODUCTION

1. Popular Conceptions of Progress

It seems incredible that there should have been a time when mankind had no conception of progress. Ever since men first consciously united their common efforts to improve and conserve their common life, it would seem there must have been some recognition that life had not always been as they found it and that it could not be in the future what it then was. Nevertheless, it has been said that the notion of progress was unknown in the oriental world, that the opposite conception of deterioration pervaded all ancient Asiatic thought. In India the prevailing notion was that of vast cycles of time "through which the universe and its inhabitants must pass from perfection to destruction, from strength and innocence to weakness and depravity until a new mahá-yuga begins."[1]

The Greeks conceived the course of history in various ways, as progress and as deterioration, but in general they thought of it as a cycle. The first clear description of the history of mankind as a progression by various stages, from a condition of primitive savagery to civilization, is in Lucretius' great poem *De Rerum Natura*. But Lucretius does not conceive this progress will continue. On the contrary he recognizes that the world has grown old and already shows signs of decrepitude which foreshadow its ultimate destruction.

It is only in comparatively recent times that the world has sought to define progress philosophically, as part of the cosmic process, and has thought of it abstractly as something to be desired for its own sake. Today the word progress is in everyone's mouth; still there is no general agreement as to what progress is, and particularly in recent years, with all the commonly accepted evidences of progress about

[1] Robert Flint, *The Philosophy of History in Europe*, I, 29-30. (London, 1874.)

them, skeptics have appeared, who, like the farmer who saw for the first time a camel with two humps, insisted "there's no such animal."

The reason there is no general understanding in regard to the meaning of progress, as it has been defined by the philosophers, is not because there is no progress in detail, but because the conception of progress in general involves a balancing of the goods against the ills of life. It raises the question whether the gains which society makes as a whole are compensation for the individual defeats and losses which progress inevitably involves. One reason why we believe in progress, perhaps, is that history is invariably written by the survivors.

In certain aspects and with people of a certain temperament, what we ordinarily call progress, considering what it costs, will always seem a very dubious matter. William Ralph Inge, Dean of St. Paul's Cathedral, London, seems to be the most eminent modern example of the skeptic.

> Human nature has not been changed by civilization. It has neither been leveled up nor leveled down to an average mediocrity. Beneath the dingy uniformity of international fashions in dress, man remains what he has always been—a splendid fighting animal, a self-sacrificing hero, and a bloodthirsty savage. Human nature is at once sublime and horrible, holy and satanic. Apart from the accumulation of knowledge and experience, which are external and precarious acquisitions, there is no proof that we have changed much since the first stone age.[1]

It must be remembered in this connection that progress, in so far as it makes the world more comfortable, makes it more complicated. Every new mechanical device, every advance in business organization or in science, which makes the world more tolerable for most of us, makes it impossible for others. Not all the world is able to keep pace with the general progress of the world. Most of the primitive races have been exterminated by the advance of civilization, and it is still uncertain where, and upon what terms, the civilized man will let the remnant of the primitive peoples live.

It has been estimated that, in the complicated life of modern cities, at least one-tenth of the population is not competent to maintain an independent, economic existence, but requires an increasing amount

[1] W. R. Inge, *Outspoken Essays*, i, "Our Present Discontents," p. 2. (London, 1919.)

of care and assistance from the other nine-tenths.[1]   To the inferior, incompetent, and unfortunate, unable to keep pace with progress, the more rapid advance of the world means disease, despair, and death. In medicine and surgery alone does progress seem wholly beneficent, but the eugenists are even now warning us that our indiscriminate efforts to protect the weak and preserve the incompetent are increasing the burdens of the superior and competent, who are alone fit to live.

On the other hand, every new invention is a response to some specific need.   Every new form of social control is intended to correct some existing evil.   So far as they are successful they represent progress.   Progress in the concrete has reference to recognized social values.   Values, as Cooley points out, have no meaning except with reference to an organism.

"The organism is necessary to give meaning to the idea [value]; there must be worth *to* something.   It need not be a person; a group, an institution, a doctrine, any organized form of life will do; and that it be conscious of the values that motivate it is not at all essential."[2]

Any change or adaptation to an existing environment that makes it easier for a person, group, institution, or other "organized form of life" to live may be said to represent progress.   Whether the invention is a new plow or a new six-inch gun we accept it as an evidence of progress if it does the work for which it is intended more efficiently than any previous device.   In no region of human life have we made greater progress than in the manufacture of weapons of destruction.

Not everyone would be willing to admit that progress in weapons of warfare represents "real" progress.   That is because some people do not admit the necessity of war.   Once admit that necessity, then every improvement is an evidence of progress, at least in that particular field.   It is more easy to recognize progress in those matters where there is no conflict in regard to the social values.   The following excerpt from Charles Zueblin's preface to his book on American progress is a concrete indication of what students of society usually recognize as progress.

Already this century has witnessed the first municipalized street railways and telephones in American cities; a national epidemic of street

[1] Charles Booth, *Labour and Life of the People*, I, 154–55, 598.   2d ed.   (London, 1889.)

[2] Charles Cooley, *The Social Process*, p. 284.   (New York, 1918.)

paving and cleaning; the quadrupling of electric lighting service and the national appropriation of display lighting; a successful crusade against dirt of all kinds—smoke, flies, germs,—and the diffusion of constructive provisions for health like baths, laundries, comfort stations, milk stations, school nurses and open air schools; fire prevention; the humanizing of the police and the advent of the policewomen; the transforming of some municipal courts into institutions for the prevention of crime and the cure of offenders; the elaboration of the school curriculum to give every child a complete education from the kindergarten to the vocational course in school or university or shop; municipal reference libraries; the completion of park systems in most large cities and the acceptance of the principle that the smallest city without a park and playground is not quite civilized; the modern playground movement giving organized and directed play to young and old; the social center; the democratic art museum; municipal theaters; the commission form of government; the city manager; home rule for cities; direct legislation—a greater advance than the whole nineteenth century compassed.[1]

2. The Problem of Progress

Sociology inherited its conception of progress from the philosophy of history. That problem seems to have had its origin in the paradox that progress at retail does not insure progress at wholesale. The progress of the community as individuals or in specific directions may, for example, bring about conditions which mean the eventual destruction of the community as a whole. This is what we mean by saying that civilizations are born, grow, and decay. We may see the phenomenon in its simplest form in the plant community, where the very growth of the community creates a soil in which the community is no longer able to exist. But the decay and death of one community creates a soil in which another community will live and grow. This gives us the interesting phenomenon of what the ecologists call "succession." So individuals build their homes, communities are formed, and eventually there comes into existence a great city. But the very existence of a great city creates problems of health, of family life, and social control which did not exist when men lived in the open, or in villages. Just as the human body generates the poisons that eventually destroy it, so the communal life, in the very process of

[1] Charles Zueblin, *American Municipal Progress*, pp. xi–xii. New and rev. ed. (New York, 1916.)

growth and as a result of its efforts to meet the changes that its growth involves, creates diseases and vices which tend to destroy the community. This raises the problem in another form. Communities may and do grow old and die, but new communities profiting by the experience of their predecessors are enabled to create social organizations, more adequate and better able to resist social diseases and corrupting vices. But in order to do this, succeeding communities have had to accumulate more experience, exercise more forethought, employ more special knowledge and a greater division of labor. In the meantime, life is becoming constantly more complex. In place of the simple spontaneous modes of behavior which enable the lower animals to live without education and without anxiety, men are compelled to supplement original nature with special training and with more and more elaborate machinery, until life, losing its spontaneity, seems in danger of losing all its joy.

Knowledge accumulates apace and its applications threaten the very existence of civilized man. The production of the flying machine represented a considerable advance in mechanical knowledge; but I am unaware of any respect in which human welfare has been increased by its existence; whereas it has not only intensified enormously the horrors of war, and, by furnishing criminal and other undesirable characters with a convenient means of rapid and secret movement, markedly diminished social security, but it threatens, by its inevitable advance in construction, to make any future conflict virtually equivalent to the extermination of civilized man. And the maleficent change in the conditions of human life which the flying machine has produced from the air, the submarine parallels from the depths of the sea; indeed, the perception of this truth has led to the very doubtfully practicable suggestion that the building of submarines be made illegal. . . . .
Moreover if life itself is more secure, there is at the present moment a distinct tendency towards a diminution of personal liberty. The increasing control by the state over the conduct and activities of the individual; the management of his children, the details of his diet and the conduct of his ordinary affairs; tend more and more to limit his personal freedom. But the restriction of his liberty amounts to a reduction of his available life just as complete loss of liberty differs little from complete loss of life.[1]

[1] R. Austin Freeman, *Social Decay and Regeneration.* With an introduction by Havelock Ellis. Pp. 16-17. (Boston, 1921.)

It is this condition which, in spite of progress in details, has raised in men's minds a question whether there is progress in general, and if there is, whether the mass of mankind is better or worse because of it.

3. History of the Concept of Progress

The great task of mankind has been to create an organization which would enable men to realize their wishes. This organization we call civilization. In achieving this result man has very slowly at first, but more rapidly in recent times, established his control over external nature and over himself. He has done this in order that he might remake the world as he found it more after his own heart.

But the world which man has thus remade has in turn reacted back upon man and in doing so has made him human. Men build houses to protect them from the weather and as places of refuge. In the end these houses have become homes, and man has become a domesticated animal, endowed with the sentiments, virtues, and lasting affections that the home inevitably cultivates and maintains.

Men made for themselves clothing for ornament and for comfort, and men's, and especially women's, clothes have become so much a part of their personalities that without them they cease to be persons and have no status in human society. Except under very exceptional circumstances a man who appeared without clothing would be treated as a madman, and hunted like a wild animal.

Men have built cities for security and for trade, and cities have made necessary and possible a division of labor and an economic organization. This economic organization, on the other hand, has been the basis of a society and a social order which imposes standards of conduct and enforces minute regulations of the individual life. Out of the conditions of this common life there has grown a body of general and ruling ideas: liberty, equality, democracy, fate, providence, personal immortality, and progress.

J. B. Bury, who has written a history of the idea of progress, says that progress is "the animating and controlling idea of western civilization." But in defining progress he makes a distinction between ideas like progress, providence, and fate and ideas like liberty, toleration, and socialism. The latter are approved or condemned because they are good or bad. The former are not approved or condemned. They are matters of fact, they are true or false. He says:

When we say that ideas rule the world, or exercise a decisive power in history, we are generally thinking of those ideas which express human aims and depend for their realisation on the human will, such as liberty, toleration, equality of opportunity, socialism. Some of these have been partly realised, and there is no reason why any of them should not be fully realised, in a society or in the world, if it were the united purpose of a society or of the world to realise it. They are approved or condemned because they are held to be good or bad, not because they are true or false. But there is another order of ideas that play a great part in determining and directing the course of man's conduct but do not depend on his will—ideas which bear upon the mystery of life, such as Fate, Providence, or personal immortality. Such ideas may operate in important ways on the forms of social action, but they involve a question of fact and they are accepted or rejected not because they are believed to be useful or injurious, but because they are believed to be true or false.

The idea of the progress of humanity is an idea of this kind, and it is important to be quite clear on the point.[1]

All of the ideas mentioned are of such a general nature, embody so much of the hopes, the strivings, and the sentiments of the modern world, that they have, or did have until very recently, something of the sanctity and authority of religious dogmas. All are expressions of wishes, but there is this difference: ideas, like liberty, toleration, etc., reflect the will of the people who accept them; ideas like providence and progress, on the contrary, represent their hopes. The question of the progress of humanity like that of personal immortality is, as Bury points out, a question of fact. "It is true or false but it cannot be proved whether true or false. Belief in it is an act of faith." When we hypostatize our hopes and wishes and treat them as matters of fact, even though they cannot be proved to be either true or false, they assume a form which Sorel describes as myth. The progress of humanity, as Herbert Spencer and the other Victorians understood it, is such a myth. Dean Inge calls it a "superstition" and adds: "To become a popular religion, it is only necessary for a superstition to enslave a philosophy. The superstition of progress had the singular good fortune to enslave at least three philosophies—those of Hegel, of Comte, and of Darwin."[2]

[1] J. B. Bury, *The Idea of Progress.* An inquiry into its origin and growth, p. 1. (London, 1921.)

[2] W. R. Inge, *The Idea of Progress*, p. 9. The Romanes Lecture, 1920. (Oxford, 1920.)

The conception of progress, if a superstition, is one of recent origin. It was not until the eighteenth century that it gained general acceptance and became part of what Inge describes as the popular religion. The conception which it replaced was that of providence. But the Greeks and Romans knew nothing of providence. They were under the influence of another idea of a different character, the idea, namely, of nemesis and fate. And before them there were more primitive peoples who had no conception of man's destiny at all. In a paper, not yet published, Ellsworth Faris has sketched the natural history of the idea of progress and its predecessors and of a new conception, control, that is perhaps destined to take its place.

The idea of progress which has been so influential in modern times is not a very old conception. In its distinctive form it came into existence in the rationalistic period which accompanied the Renaissance. Progress, in this sense, means a theory as to the way in which the whole cosmic process is developing. It is the belief that the world as a whole is growing better through definite stages, and is moving "to one far-off divine event."

The stages preceding this idea may be thought of under several heads. The first may be called "cosmic anarchy," in which we find "primitive people" now living. It is a world of chaos, without meaning, and without purpose. There is no direction in which human life is thought of as developing. Death and misfortune are for the most part due to witchcraft and the evil designs of enemies; good luck and bad luck are the forces which make a rational existence hopeless.

Another stage of thinking is that which was found among the Greeks, the conception of the cosmic process as proceeding in cycles. The golden age of the Greeks lay in the past, the universe was considered to be following a set course, and the whole round of human experience was governed and controlled by an inexorable fate that was totally indifferent to human wishes. The formula which finally arose to meet this situation was "conformity to nature," a submission to the iron laws of the world which it was vain to attempt to change.

This idea was succeeded in medieval Europe by the idea of providence, in which the world was thought of as a theater on which the drama of human redemption was enacted. God has created man free, but man was corrupted by the fall, given an opportunity to be redeemed by the gospel, and the world was soon to know the final triumph and happiness of the saved. Most of the early church fathers expected the end of the world very soon, many of them in their own lifetime. This is distinctly different from the preceding two ideas. All life had meaning to them, for the evil in the world was but God's way to accomplish his good purposes. It was man's duty to submit, but submission was to take the form of faith in an all-wise beneficent and perfect power, who was governing the world and who would make everything for the best.

The idea of progress arose on the ruins of this concept of providence. In the fourteenth century, progress did not mean merely the satisfaction of all human desires either individual or collective. The idea meant far more than that. It was the conviction that the world as a whole was proceeding onward indefinitely to greater and greater perfection. The atmosphere of progress was congenial to the construction of utopias and schemes of perfection which were believed to be in harmony with the nature of the world itself. The atmosphere of progress produced also optimists who were quite sure everything was in the long run to be for the best, and that every temporary evil was sure to be overcome by an ultimate good.

The difficulty in demonstrating the fact of progress has become very real as the problem has been presented to modern minds. It is possible to prove that the world has become more complex. It is hardly possible to prove that it has become better, and quite impossible to prove that it will continue to do so. From the standpoint of the Mohammedan Turks, the last two hundred years of the world's history have not been years of marked progress; from the standpoint of their enemies, the reverse statement is obviously true.

The conception which seems to be superseding the idea of progress in our day is that of control. Each problem whether personal or social is thought of as a separate enterprise. Poverty, disease, crime, vice, intemperance, or war, these are definite situations which challenge human effort and human ingenuity. Many problems are unsolved; many failures are recorded. The future is a challenge to creative intelligence and collective heroism. The future is thought of as still to be made. And there is no assurance that progress will take place. On the contrary, there is every reason to believe that progress will not take place unless men are able by their skill and devotion to find solutions for their present problems, and for the newer ones that shall arise.

The modern man finds this idea quite as stimulating to him as the idea of progress was to his ancestor of the Renaissance or the idea of providence to his medieval forebears. For while he does not blindly believe nor feel optimistically certain things will come about all right, yet he is nerved to square his shoulders, to think, to contrive, and to exert himself to the utmost in his effort to conquer the difficulties ahead, and to control the forces of nature and man. The idea of providence was not merely a generalization on life, it was a force that inspired hope. The idea of progress was likewise not merely a concept, it was also an energizing influence in a time of great intellectual activity. The idea that the forces of nature can be controlled in the service of man, differs from the others, but is also a dynamic potency that seems to be equally well adapted to the twentieth century.

The conception that man's fate lies somehow in his own hands, if it gains general acceptance, will still be, so far as it inspires men to work and strive, an article of faith, and the image in which he pictures the future of mankind, toward which he directs his efforts, will still have the character of myth. That is the function of myths. It is this that lends an interest to those ideal states in which men at different times have sought to visualize the world of their hopes and dreams.

4. Classification of the Materials

The purpose of the materials in this chapter is to exhibit the variety and diversity of men's thought with reference to the concept of progress. What they show is that there is as yet no general agreement in regard to the meaning of the term. In all the special fields of social reform there are relatively definite conceptions of what is desirable and what is not desirable. In the matter of *progress in general* there is no such definition. Except for philosophical speculation there is no such thing as "progress in general." In practice, progress turns out to be a number of special tasks.

The "progress of civilization" is, to be sure, a concept in good standing in history. It is, however, a concept of appreciation rather than one of description. If history has to be rewritten for every new generation of men, it is due not merely to the discovery of new historical materials, but just to the fact that there is a new generation. Every generation has its own notion of the values of life, and every generation has to have its own interpretation of the facts of life.

It is incredible that Strachey's *Life of Queen Victoria* could have been written forty years ago. It is incredible that the mass of men should have been able to see the Victorian Age, as it is here presented, while they were living it.

The materials in this chapter fall under three heads: (*a*) the concept of progress, (*b*) progress and science, (*c*) progress and human nature.

a) The concept of progress.—The first difficulty in the study of progress is one of definition. What are the signs and symptoms, the criteria of progress? Until we have framed some sort of a definition we cannot know. Herbert Spencer identified progress with evolution. The law of organic progress is the law of all progress. Intelligence, if we understand by that the mere accumulations of knowledge, does not represent progress. Rather it consists in "those internal modifications of which this larger knowledge is an expression." In so far, Spencer's conception is that of the eugenists. Real progress is in the breed—in the germ plasm. For men like Galton, Karl Pearson, and Madison Grant,[1] what we call civilization is merely the efflorescence of race. Civilizations may pass away, but if the racial stock is preserved, civilization will reproduce itself. In recent years, a school of political philosophy has sprung up in Europe and in the United States, which is seeking to define our social policy toward the "inner enemies," the dependents, the defectives, and the delinquents, and a foreign policy toward immigrant races and foreign peoples, on the general conception that the chief aim of society and the state is to preserve the germ plasm of the Nordic race.[2] For Spencer, however, the conception that all values were in the organism was modified by the conviction that all life was involved in an irreversible process called evolution which would eventually purge the race and society of the weak, the wicked, and the unfit.

In contrast, both with the views of Spencer and of the eugenists, Hobhouse, voicing a conviction that was first expressed by Huxley, believes that man is bound to intervene in the beneficent law of natural selection. He insists, in fact, that social development is something quite distinct and relatively independent of the organic changes in the individual. It is, in other words, a sociological rather than a biological product. It is an effect of the interaction of individuals and is best represented by organized society and by the social tradition in which that organization is handed on from earlier to later generations.

[1] Author of *The Passing of a Great Race, or the Racial Basis of European History.* (New York, 1916.)

[2] See Lothrop Stoddard, *The Rising Tide of Color against White World-Supremacy* (New York, 1920); and William McDougall, *Is America Safe for Democracy?* (New York, 1921.)

[3] Thomas H. Huxley, *Evolution and Ethics and Other Lectures*, Lecture ii pp. 46–116. (New York, 1894.)

b) *Progress and science.*—In contrast with other conceptions of progress is that of Dewey, who emphasizes science and social control, or, as he puts it, the "problem of discovering the needs and capacities of collective human nature as we find it aggregated in racial or national groups on the surface of the globe." The distinction between Hobhouse and Dewey is less in substance than in point of view. Hobhouse, looking backward, is interested in progress itself rather than in its methods and processes. Dewey, on the other hand, looking forward, is interested in a present program and in the application of scientific method to the problems of social welfare and world-organization.

Arthur James Balfour, the most intellectual of the elder statesmen of England, looking at progress through the experience of a politician, speaks in a less prophetic and authoritative tone, but with a wisdom born of long experience with men. For him, as for many other thoughtful minds, the future of the race is "encompassed with darkness," and the wise man is he who is content to act in "a sober and a cautious spirit," seeking to deal with problems as they arise.

c) *Progress and human nature.*—Progress, which is much a matter of interpretation, is also very largely a matter of temperament. The purpose of the material upon human nature and progress is to call attention to this fact. Progress is with most people an article of faith, and men's faiths, as to their content, at least, are matters of temperament. The conservative who perhaps takes a mild interest in progress is usually "a sober and cautious" person, fairly content with the present and not very sure about the future. The radical, on the other hand, is usually a naturally hopeful and enthusiastic individual, profoundly pessimistic about the present, but with a boundless confidence in even the most impossible future.

Philosophy, like literature, is, in the final analysis, the expression of a temperament, more or less modified by experience. The selections from Schopenhauer and Bergson may be regarded, therefore, as the characteristic reactions of two strikingly different temperaments to the conception of progress and to life. The descriptions which they give of the cosmic process are, considered formally, not unlike. Their interpretations and the practical bearings of these interpretations are profoundly different.

It is not necessary for the students of sociology to discuss the merits of these different doctrines. We may accept them as human documents. They throw light, at any rate, upon the idea of progress, and upon all the other fundamental ideas in which men have sought to formulate their common hopes and guide their common life.

II. MATERIALS

A. THE CONCEPT OF PROGRESS

1. The Earliest Conception of Progress[1]

The word "progress," like the word "humanity," is one of the most significant.. It is a Latin word, not used in its current abstract sense until after the Roman incorporation of the Mediterranean world. The first writer who expounds the notion with sufficient breadth of view and sufficiently accurate and concrete observation to provide a preliminary sketch was the great Roman poet, Lucretius.

He begins by describing a struggle for existence in which the less well-adapted creatures died off, those who wanted either the power to protect themselves or the means of adapting themselves to the purposes of man. In this stage, however, man was a hardier creature than he afterward became. He lived like the beasts of the field and was ignorant of tillage or fire or clothes or houses. He had no laws or government or marriage and, though he did not fear the dark, he feared the real danger of fiercer beasts. Men often died a miserable death, but not in multitudes on a single day as they do now by battle or shipwreck.

The next stage sees huts and skins and fire which softened their bodies, and marriage and the ties of family which softened their tempers. And tribes began to make treaties of alliance with other tribes. Speech arose from the need which all creatures feel to exercise their natural powers, just as the calf will butt before his horns protrude. Men began to apply different sounds to denote different things, just as brute beasts will do to express different passions, as anyone must have noticed in the cases of dogs and horses and birds. No one man set out to invent speech.

Fire was first learned from lightning and the friction of trees, and cooking from the softening and ripening of things by the sun. Then men of genius invented improved methods of life, the building of

[1] Adapted from F. S. Marvin, *Progress and History*, pp. 8-10. (Oxford University Press, 1916.)

cities and private property in lands and cattle. But gold gave power to the wealthy and destroyed the sense of contentment in simple happiness. It must always be so whenever men allow themselves to become the slaves of things which should be their dependents and instruments.

They began to believe in and worship gods, because they saw in dreams shapes of preterhuman strength and beauty and deemed them immortal; and as they noted the changes of the seasons and all the wonders of the heavens they placed their gods there and feared them when they spoke in the thunder.

Metals were discovered through the burning of the woods, which caused the ores to run. Copper and brass came first and were rated above gold and silver. And then the metals took the place of hands, nails, teeth, and clubs, which had been men's earliest arms and tools. Weaving followed the discovery of the use of iron. Sowing, planting, and grafting were learned from nature herself, and gradually the cultivation of the soil was carried farther and farther up the hills.

Men learned to sing from the birds, and to blow on pipes from the whistling of the zephyr through the reeds; and those simple tunes gave as much rustic jollity as our more elaborate tunes do now.

Then, in a summary passage at the end, Lucretius enumerates all the chief discoveries which men have made in the age-long process—ships, agriculture, walled cities, laws, roads, clothes, songs, pictures, statues, and all the pleasures of life—and adds, "These things practice and the experience of the unresting mind have taught mankind gradually as they have progressed from point to point."

It is the first definition and use of the word in literature.

2.   Progress and Organization[1]

The current conception of progress is shifting and indefinite. Sometimes it comprehends little more than simple growth—as of a nation in the number of its members and the extent of territory over which it spreads. Sometimes it has reference to quantity of material products—as when the advance of agriculture and manufactures is the topic. Sometimes the superior quality of these products is contemplated; and sometimes the new or improved appliances by which they are produced. When, again, we speak of moral or intel-

[1] Adapted from Herbert Spencer, *Essays*, I, 8–10.   (D. Appleton & Co., 1899.)

lectual progress, we refer to states of the individual or people exhibiting it; while, when the progress of science or art is commented upon, we have in view certain abstract results of human thought and action.

Not only, however, is the current conception of progress more or less vague, but it is in great measure erroneous. It takes in not so much the reality of progress as its accompaniments—not so much the substance as the shadow. That progress in intelligence seen during the growth of the child into the man, or the savage into the philosopher, is commonly regarded as consisting in the greater number of facts known and laws understood; whereas the actual progress consists in those internal modifications of which this larger knowledge is the expression. Social progress is supposed to consist in the making of a greater quantity and variety of the articles required for satisfying men's wants; in the increasing security of person and property; in widening freedom of action; whereas, rightly understood, social progress consists in those changes of structure in the social organism which have entailed these consequences. The current conception is a teleological one. The phenomena are contemplated solely as bearing on human happiness. Only those changes are held to constitute progress which directly or indirectly tend to heighten human happiness; and they are thought to constitute progress simply because they tend to heighten human happiness. But rightly to understand progress, we must learn the nature of these changes, considered apart from our interests. Ceasing, for example, to regard the successive geological modifications that have taken place in the earth as modifications that have gradually fitted it for the habitation of man, and as therefore constituting geological progress, we must ascertain the character common to these modifications—the law to which they all conform. And similarly in every other case. Leaving out of sight concomitants and beneficial consequences, let us ask what progress is in itself.

In respect to that progress which individual organisms display in the course of their evolution, this question has been answered by the Germans. The investigations of Wolff, Goethe, and von Baer have established the truth that the series of changes gone through during the development of a seed into a tree, or an ovum into an animal, constitute an advance from homogeneity of structure to heterogeneity of structure. In its primary stage, every germ consists of a substance that is uniform throughout, both in texture and chemical composition. The first step is the appearance of a difference between two parts of this substance; or, as the phenomenon is called in physiological language, a differentiation. Each of these differentiated divisions presently begins itself to exhibit some contrast of parts; and by and by these secondary differentiations become as definite as the original one. This process is continuously repeated—is simultaneously going on in all parts of the growing embryo; and by endless differentiations of this sort there is finally produced that complex combination of tissues and organs constituting the adult animal or plant. This is the history of all organisms whatever. It is settled beyond dispute that organic progress consists in a change from the homogeneous to the heterogeneous.

Now, we propose to show that this law of organic progress is the law of all progress. Whether it be in the development of the earth, in the development of life upon its surface, in the development of society, of government, of manufactures, of commerce, of language, literature, science, art—this same evolution of the simple into the complex, through successive differentiations, holds throughout. From the earliest traceable cosmic changes down to the latest results of civilization, we shall find that the transformation of the homogeneous into the heterogeneous is that in which progress essentially consists.

3. The Stages of Progress[1]

If we regard the course of human development from the highest scientific point of view, we shall perceive that it consists in educing more and more the characteristic faculties of humanity, in comparison with those of animality; and especially with those which man has in common with the whole organic kingdom. It is in this philosophical sense that the most eminent civilization must be pronounced to be fully accordant with nature, since it is, in fact, only a more marked manifestation of the chief properties of our species, properties which, latent at first, can come into play only in that advanced state of social life for which they are exclusively destined. The whole system of biological philosophy indicates the natural progression. We have seen how, in the brute kingdom, the superiority

[1] Adapted from Auguste Comte, *Positive Philosophy*, II, 124. (Trübner & Co., 1875.)

of each race is determined by the degree of preponderance of the animal life over the organic. In like manner we see that our social evolution is only the final term of a progression which has continued from the simplest vegetables and most insignificant animals, up through the higher reptiles to the birds and the mammifers, and still on to the carnivorous animals and monkeys, the organic characteristics retiring and the animal prevailing more and more, till the intellectual and moral tend toward the ascendancy which can never be fully obtained, even in the highest state of human perfection that we can conceive of. This comparative estimate affords us the scientific view of human progression, connected, as we see it is, with the whole course of animal advancement, of which it is itself the highest degree. The analysis of our social progress proves indeed that, while the radical dispositions of our nature are necessarily invariable, the highest of them are in a continuous state of relative development, by which they rise to be preponderant powers of human existence, though the inversion of the primitive economy can never be absolutely complete. We have seen that this is the essential character of the social organism in a statical view; but it becomes much more marked when we study its variations in their gradual succession.

4. Progress and the Historical Process[1]

The conclusion which these reflections suggest is that the uncritical application of biological principles to social progress results in an insuperable contradiction. The factors which determine the survival of physical organism, if applied as rules for the furtherance of social progress, appear to conflict with all that social progress means. A sense of this conflict is no doubt responsible for the further reconstruction which the biological view has in recent years undergone. Biologists now begin to inquire seriously whether "natural" selection may not be replaced by a rational selection in which "fitness for survival" would at length achieve its legitimate meaning, and the development of the race might be guided by reasoned conceptions of social value. This is a fundamental change of attitude, and the new doctrine of eugenics to which it has given rise requires careful examination. Before proceeding to this examination, however, it will be well

[1] Adapted from Leonard T. Hobhouse, *Social Evolution and Political Theory*, pp. 29–39. (The Columbia University Press, 1911.)

to inquire into the causes of the contrast on which we have insisted between biological evolution and social progress. Faced by this contradiction, we ask ourselves whether social development may not be something quite distinct from the organic changes known to biology, and whether the life of society may not depend upon forces which never appear in the individual when he is examined merely as an individual or merely as a member of a race.

Take the latter point first. It is easily seen in the arguments of biologists that they conceive social progress as consisting essentially in an improvement of the stock to which individuals belong. This is a way of looking at the matter intelligible enough in itself. Society consists of so many thousand or so many million individuals, and if, comparing any given generation with its ancestors, we could establish an average improvement in physical, mental, or moral faculty, we should certainly have cause to rejoice. There is progress so far. But there is another point of view which we may take up. Society consists of individual persons and nothing but individual persons, just as the body consists of cells and the product of cells. But though the body may consist exclusively of cells, we should never understand its life by examining the lives of each of its cells as a separate unit. We must equally take into account that organic interconnection whereby the living processes of each separate cell co-operate together to maintain the health of the organism which contains them all. So, again, to understand the social order we have to take into account not only the individuals with their capabilities and achievements but the social organization in virtue of which these individuals act upon one another and jointly produce what we call social results; and whatever may be true of the physical organism, we can see that in society it is possible that individuals of the very same potentialities may, with good organization, produce good results, and, with bad organization, results which are greatly inferior.

The social phenomenon, in short, is not something which occurs in one individual, or even in several individuals taken severally. It is essentially an interaction of individuals, and as the capabilities of any given individual are extraordinarily various and are only called out, each by appropriate circumstances, it will be readily seen that the nature of the interaction may itself bring forth new and perhaps unexpected capacities, and elicit from the individuals contributing to it forces which, but for this particular opportunity, might possibly remain forever dormant. If this is so, sociology as a science is not the same thing as either biology or psychology. It deals neither with the physical capacities of individuals as such nor with their psychological capacities as such. It deals rather with results produced by the play of these forces upon one another, by the interaction of individuals under the conditions imposed by their physical environment. The nature of the forces and the point of these distinctions may be made clear by a very simple instance.

The interplay of human motives and the interaction of human beings is the fundamental fact of social life, and the permanent results which this interaction achieves and the influence which it exercises upon the individuals who take part in it constitute the fundamental fact of social evolution. These results are embodied in what may be called, generically, tradition. So understood, tradition —its growth and establishment, its reaction upon the very individuals who contribute to building it up, and its modifications by subsequent interactions—constitutes the main subject of sociological inquiry.

Tradition is, in the development of society, what heredity is in the physical growth of the stock. It is the link between past and future, it is that in which the effects of the past are consolidated and on the basis of which subsequent modifications are built up. We might push the analogy a little further, for the ideas and customs which it maintains and furnishes to each new generation as guides for their behavior in life are analogous to the determinate methods of reaction, the inherited impulses, reflexes, and instincts with which heredity furnishes the individual. The tradition of the elders is, as it were, the instinct of society. It furnishes the prescribed rule for dealing with the ordinary occasions of life, which is for the most part accepted without inquiry and applied without reflection. It furnishes the appropriate institution for providing for each class of social needs, for meeting common dangers, for satisfying social wants, for regulating social relations. It constitutes, in short, the framework of society's life which to each new generation is a part of its hereditary outfit.

But of course in speaking of tradition as a kind of inheritance we conceive of it as propagated by quite other than biological methods.

In a sense its propagation is psychological, it is handed on from mind to mind, and even though social institutions may in a sense be actually incorporated in material things, in buildings, in books, in coronation robes, or in flags, still it need not be said that these things are nothing but for the continuity of thought which maintains and develops their significance. Yet the forces at work in tradition are not purely psychological; at least they are not to be understood in terms of individual psychology alone. What is handed on is not merely a set of ideas but the whole social environment; not merely certain ways of thinking or of acting but the conditions which prescribe to individuals the necessity for thinking or acting in certain specific ways if they are to achieve their own desires. The point is worth dwelling on, because some writers have thought to simplify the working of tradition by reducing it to some apparently simple psychological phenomenon like that of imitation. In this there is more than one element of fallacy.

Now the growth of tradition will in a sense gravely modify the individual members of the society which maintains it. To any given set of institutions a certain assemblage of qualities, mental and physical, will be most appropriate, and these may differ as much as the qualities necessary for war differ from those of peaceful industry. Any tradition will obviously call forth from human beings the qualities appropriate to it, and it will in a sense select the individuals in which those qualities are the best developed and will tend to bring them to the top of the social fabric, but this is not to say that it will assert the same modification upon the stock that would be accomplished by the working of heredity. The hereditary qualities of the race may remain the same, though the traditions have changed and though by them one set of qualities is kept permanently in abeyance, while the other is continually brought by exercise to the highest point of efficiency.

We are not to conclude that physical heredity is of no importance to the social order; it must be obvious that the better the qualities of the individuals constituting a race, the more easily they will fit themselves into good social traditions, the more readily they will advance those traditions to a still higher point of excellence, and the more stoutly they would resist deterioration. The qualities upon which the social fabric calls must be there, and the more readily they are forthcoming, the more easily the social machine will work. Hence social progress necessarily implies a certain level of racial development, and its advance may always be checked by the limitations of the racial type. Nevertheless, if we look at human history as a whole, we are impressed with the stability of the great fundamental characteristics of human nature and the relatively sweeping character and often rapid development of social change.

In view of this contrast we must hesitate to attribute any substantial share in human development to biological factors, and our hesitation is increased when we consider the factors on which social change depends. It is in the department of knowledge and industry that advance is most rapid and certain, and the reason is perfectly clear. It is that on this side each generation can build on the work of its predecessors. A man of very moderate mathematical capacity today can solve problems which puzzled Newton, because he has available the work of Newton and of many another since Newton's time. In the department of ethics the case is different. Each man's character has to be formed anew, and though teaching goes for much, it is not everything. The individual in the end works out his own salvation. Where there is true ethical progress is in the advance of ethical conceptions and principles which can be handed on; of laws and institutions which can be built up, maintained, and improved. That is to say, there is progress just where the factor of social tradition comes into play and just so far as its influence extends. If the tradition is broken, the race begins again where it stood before the tradition was formed. We may infer that, while the race has been relatively stagnant, society has rapidly developed, and we must conclude that, whether for good or for evil, social changes are mainly determined, not by alterations of racial type, but by modifications of tradition due to the interactions of social causes. Progress is not racial but social.

B.   PROGRESS AND SCIENCE

1.   Progress and Happiness[1]

Human progress may be properly defined as that which secures the *increase of human happiness*. Unless it do this, no matter how great a civilization may be, it is not progressive. If a nation rise,

[1] From Lester F. Ward, *Dynamic Sociology*, II, 174–77. (D. Appleton & Co., 1893.)

and extend its sway over a vast territory, astonishing the world with its power, its culture, and its wealth, this alone does not constitute progress. It must first be shown that its people are happier than they would otherwise have been. If a people be seized with a rage for art, and, in obedience to their impulses or to national decrees, the wealth of that people be laid out in the cultivation of the fine arts, the employment of master artists, the decoration of temples, public and private buildings, and the embellishment of streets and grounds, no matter to what degree of perfection this purpose be carried out, it is not to progress unless greater satisfaction be derived therefrom than was sacrificed in the deprivations which such a course must occasion. To be progressive in the true sense, it must work an increase in the sum total of human enjoyment. When we survey the history of civilization, we should keep this truth in view, and not allow ourselves to be dazzled by the splendor of pageantry, the glory of heraldry, or the beauty of art, literature, philosophy, or religion, but should assign to each its true place as measured by this standard.

It cannot be denied that civilization, by the many false practices which it has introduced, by the facilities which its very complexity affords to the concealment of crime, and by the monstrous systems of corruption which fashion, caste, and conventionality are enabled to shelter, is the direct means of rendering many individuals miserable in the extreme; but these are the necessary incidents to its struggles to advance under the dominion of natural forces alone.

It would involve a great fallacy to deduce from this the conclusion that civilization begets misery or reduces the happiness of mankind. Against this gross but popular mistake may be cited the principle before introduced, which is unanimously accepted by biologists, that an organism is perfect in proportion as its organs are numerous and varied. This is because, the more organs there are, the greater is the capacity for enjoyment. For this enjoyment is quantitative as well as qualitative, and the greater the number of faculties, the greater is the possible enjoyment derivable from their normal exercise. To say that primitive man is happier than enlightened man, is equivalent to saying that an oyster or a polyp enjoys more than an eagle or an antelope. This could be true only on the ground that the latter, in consequence of their sensitive organisms, suffer more than they enjoy; but if to be happy is to escape from all feeling, then it were better to be stones or clods, and destitute of conscious sensibility. If this be the happiness which men should seek, then is the Buddhist in the highest degree consistent when he prays for the promised *Nirvâna*, or annihilation. But this is not happiness—it is only the absence of it. For happiness can only be increased by increasing the capacity for feeling, or emotion, and, when this is increased, the capacity for suffering is likewise necessarily increased, and suffering must be endured unless sufficient sagacity accompanies it to prevent this consequence. And that is the truest progress which, while it indefinitely multiplies and increases the facilities for enjoyment, furnishes at the same time the most effective means of preventing discomfort, and, as nearly all suffering is occasioned by the violation of natural laws through ignorance of or error respecting those laws, therefore that is the truest progress which succeeds in overcoming ignorance and error.

Therefore, we may enunciate the principle that progress is in proportion to the opportunities or facilities for exercising the faculties and satisfying desire.

2. Progress and Prevision[1]

We have confused rapidity of change with progress. We have confused the breaking down of barriers by which advance is made possible with advance itself.

We had been told that the development of industry and commerce had brought about such an interdependence of peoples that war was henceforth out of the question—at least upon a vast scale. But it is now clear that commerce also creates jealousies and rivalries and suspicions which are potent for war. We were told that nations could not long finance a war under modern conditions; economists had demonstrated that to the satisfaction of themselves and others. We see now that they had underrated both the production of wealth and the extent to which it could be mobilized for destructive purposes. We were told that the advance of science had made war practically impossible. We now know that science has not only rendered the machinery of war more deadly but has also increased the powers of

[1] Adapted from John Dewey, "Progress," in the *International Journal of Ethics*, XXVI (1916), 312–18.

resistance and endurance when war comes. If all this does not demonstrate that the forces which have brought about complicated and extensive changes in the fabric of society do not of themselves generate progress, I do not know what a demonstration would be. Has man subjugated physical nature only to release forces beyond his control?

The doctrine of evolution has been popularly used to give a kind of cosmic sanction to the notion of an automatic and wholesale progress in human affairs. Our part, the human part, was simply to enjoy the usufruct. Evolution inherited all the goods of divine Providence and had the advantage of being in fashion. Even a great and devastating war is not too great a price to pay for an awakening from such an infantile and selfish dream. Progress is not automatic; it depends upon human intent and aim and upon acceptance of responsibility for its production. It is not a wholesale matter, but a retail job, to be contracted for and executed in sections.

Spite of the dogma which measures progress by increase in altruism, kindliness, peaceful feelings, there is no reason that I know of to suppose that the basic fund of these emotions has increased appreciably in thousands and thousands of years. Man is equipped with these feelings at birth, as well as with emotions of fear, anger, emulation, and resentment. What appears to be an increase in one set and a decrease in the other set is, in reality, a change in their social occasions and social channels. Civilized man has not a better endowment of ear and eye than savage man; but his social surroundings give him more important things to see and hear than the savage has, and he has the wit to devise instruments to reinforce his eye and ear—the telegraph and telephone, the microscope and telescope. But there is no reason for thinking that he has less natural aggressiveness or more natural altruism—or will ever have—than the barbarian. But he may live in social conditions that create a relatively greater demand for the display of kindliness and which turn his aggressive instincts into less destructive channels.

There is at any time a sufficient amount of kindly impulses possessed by man to enable him to live in amicable peace with all his fellows; and there is at any time a sufficient equipment of bellicose impulses to keep him in trouble with his fellows. An intensification of the exhibition of one may accompany an intensification of the display of the other, the only difference being that social arrangements cause the kindly feelings to be displayed toward one set of fellows and the hostile impulses toward another set. Thus, as everybody knows, the hatred toward the foreigner characterizing peoples now at war is attended by an unusual manifestation of mutual affection and love within each warring group. So characteristic is this fact that that man was a good psychologist who said that he wished that this planet might get into war with another planet, as that was the only effective way he saw of developing a world-wide community of interest in this globe's population.

The indispensable preliminary condition of progress has been supplied by the conversion of scientific discoveries into inventions which turn physical energy, the energy of sun, coal, and iron, to account. Neither the discoveries nor the inventions were the product of unconscious physical nature. They were the product of human devotion and application, of human desire, patience, ingenuity, and mother-wit. The problem which now confronts us, the problem of progress, is the same in kind, differing in subject-matter. It is a problem of discovering the needs and capacities of collective human nature as we find it aggregated in racial or national groups on the surface of the globe, and of inventing the social machinery which will set available powers operating for the satisfaction of those needs.

We are living still under the dominion of a laissez faire philosophy. I do not mean by this an individualistic, as against a socialistic, philosophy. I mean by it a philosophy which trusts the direction of human affairs to nature, or Providence, or evolution, or manifest destiny—that is to say, to accident—rather than to a contriving and constructive intelligence. To put our faith in the collective state instead of in individual activity is quite as laissez faire a proceeding as to put it in the results of voluntary private enterprise. The only genuine opposite to a go-as-you-please, let-alone philosophy is a philosophy which studies specific social needs and evils with a view to constructing the special social machinery for which they call.

3. Progress and the Limits of Scientific Prevision[1]

Movement, whether of progress or of retrogression, can commonly be brought about only when the sentiments opposing it have been designedly weakened or have suffered a natural decay. In this

[1] From *The Mind of Arthur James Balfour*, by Wilfrid M. Short, pp. 293–97. (Copyright 1918, George H. Doran Company, publishers.)

destructive process, and in any constructive process by which it may be followed, reasoning, often very bad reasoning, bears, at least in western communities, a large share as cause, a still larger share as symptom; so that the clatter of contending argumentation is often the most striking accompaniment of interesting social changes. Its position, therefore, and its functions in the social organism are frequently misunderstood. People fall instinctively into the habit of supposing that, as it plays a conspicuous part in the improvement or deterioration of human institutions, it therefore supplies the very basis on which they may be made to rest, the very mold to which they ought to conform; and they naturally conclude that we have only got to reason more and to reason better in order speedily to perfect the whole machinery by which human felicity is to be secured.

Surely this is a great delusion. A community founded upon argument would soon be a community no longer. It would dissolve into its constituent elements. Think of the thousand ties most subtly woven out of common sentiments, common tastes, common beliefs, nay, common prejudices, by which from our very earliest childhood we are all bound unconsciously but indissolubly together into a compacted whole. Imagine these to be suddenly loosed and their places taken by some judicious piece of reasoning on the balance of advantage, which, after taking all proper deductions, still remains to the credit of social life. These things we may indeed imagine if we please. Fortunately, we shall never see them. Society is founded —and from the nature of the human beings which constitute it, must, in the main, be always founded—not upon criticism but upon feelings and beliefs, and upon the customs and codes by which feelings and beliefs are, as it were, fixed and rendered stable. And even where these harmonize, so far as we can judge, with sound reason, they are in many cases not consciously based on reasoning; nor is their fate necessarily bound up with that of the extremely indifferent arguments by which, from time to time, philosophers, politicians, and, I will add, divines have thought fit to support them.

We habitually talk as if a self-governing or free community was one which managed its own affairs. In strictness, no community manages its own affairs, or by any possibility could manage them. It manages but a narrow fringe of its affairs, and that in the main by deputy. It is only the thinnest surface layer of law and custom, belief and sentiment, which can either be successfully subjected to destructive treatment, or become the nucleus of any new growth—a fact which explains the apparent paradox that so many of our most famous advances in political wisdom are nothing more than the formal recognition of our political impotence.

As our expectations of limitless progress for the race cannot depend upon the blind operation of the laws of heredity, so neither can they depend upon the deliberate action of national governments. Such examination as we can make of the changes which have taken place during the relatively minute fraction of history with respect to which we have fairly full information shows that they have been caused by a multitude of variations, often extremely small, made in their surroundings by individuals whose objects, though not necessarily selfish, have often had no intentional reference to the advancement of the community at large. But we have no scientific ground for suspecting that the stimulus to these individual efforts must necessarily continue; we know of no law by which, if they do continue, they must needs be co-ordinated for a common purpose or pressed into the service of a common good. We cannot estimate their remoter consequences; neither can we tell how they will act and react upon one another, nor how they will in the long run affect morality, religion, and other fundamental elements of human society. The future of the race is thus encompassed with darkness; no faculty of calculation that we possess, no instrument that we are likely to invent, will enable us to map out its course, or penetrate the secret of its destiny. It is easy, no doubt, to find in the clouds which obscure our paths what shapes we please: to see in them the promise of some millennial paradise, or the threat of endless and unmeaning travel through waste and perilous places. But in such visions the wise man will put but little confidence, content, in a sober and cautious spirit, with a full consciousness of his feeble powers of foresight and the narrow limits of his activity, to deal as they arise with the problems of his own generation.

4. Eugenics as a Science of Progress[1]

Eugenics is the science which deals with all influences that improve the inborn qualities of a race; also with those that develop them to the utmost advantage.

[1] From Francis Galton, "Eugenics: Its Definition, Scope, and Aims," in the *American Journal of Sociology*, X (1904–5), 1–6.

What is meant by improvement? There is considerable differ-ence between goodness in the several qualities and in that of the character as a whole. The character depends largely on the *proportion* between qualities whose balance may be much influenced by educa-tion. We must therefore leave morals as far as possible out of the discussion, not entangling ourselves with the almost hopeless diffi-culties they raise as to whether a character as a whole is good or bad. Moreover, the goodness or badness of character is not absolute, but relative to the current form of civilisation. A fable will best explain what is meant. Let the scene be the Zoölogical Gardens in the quiet hours of the night, and suppose that, as in old fables, the animals are able to converse, and that some very wise creature who had easy access to all the cages, say a philosophic sparrow or rat, was engaged in collecting the opinions of all sorts of animals with a view of elaborat-ing a system of absolute morality. It is needless to enlarge on the con-trariety of ideals between the beasts that prey and those they prey upon, between those of the animals that have to work hard for their food and the sedentary parasites that cling to their bodies and suck their blood and so forth. A large number of suffrages in favour of maternal affection would be obtained, but most species of fish would repudiate it, while among the voices of birds would be heard the musical protest of the cuckoo. Though no agreement could be reached as to absolute morality, the essentials of Eugenics may be easily defined. All creatures would agree that it was better to be healthy than sick, vigorous than weak, well fitted than ill fitted for their part in life. In short, that it was better to be good rather than bad specimens of their kind, whatever that kind might be. So with men. There are a vast number of conflicting ideals of alternative characters, of incompatible civilisations; but all are wanted to give fulness and interest to life. Society would be very dull if every man resembled the highly estimable Marcus Aurelius or Adam Bede. The aim of Eugenics is to represent each class or sect by its best specimens; that done, to leave them to work out their common civilisation in their own way.

The aim of Eugenics is to bring as many influences as can be reasonably employed, to cause the useful classes in the community to contribute *more* than their proportion to the next generation.

The course of procedure that lies within the functions of a learned and active Society such as the Sociological may become, would be somewhat as follows:

1. Dissemination of a knowledge of the laws of heredity so far as they are surely known, and promotion of their further study. Few seem to be aware how greatly the knowledge of what may be termed the *actuarial* side of heredity has advanced in recent years. The average closeness of kinship in each degree now admits of exact definition and of being treated mathematically, like birth- and death-rates, and the other topics with which actuaries are concerned.

2. Historical inquiry into the rates with which the various classes of society (classified according to civic usefulness) have contributed to the population at various times, in ancient and modern nations. There is strong reason for believing that national rise and decline is closely connected with this influence. It seems to be the tendency of high civilisation to check fertility in the upper classes, through numerous causes, some of which are well known, others are inferred, and others again are wholly obscure. The latter class are apparently analogous to those which bar the fertility of most species of wild animals in zoölogical gardens. Out of the hundreds and thousands of species that have been tamed, very few indeed are fertile when their liberty is restricted and their struggles for livelihood are abolished; those which are so and are otherwise useful to man becoming domesticated. There is perhaps some connection between this obscure action and the disappearance of most savage races when brought into contact with high civilisation, though there are other and well-known concomitant causes. But while most barbarous races disappear, some, like the Negro, do not. It may therefore be expected that types of our race will be found to exist which can be highly civilised without losing fertility; nay, they may become more fertile under artificial conditions, as is the case with many domestic animals.

3. Systematic collection of facts showing the circumstances under which large and thriving families have most frequently originated; in other words, the *conditions* of Eugenics. The names of the thriving families in England have yet to be learnt, and the conditions under which they have arisen. We cannot hope to make much advance in the science of Eugenics without a careful study of facts that are now accessible with difficulty, if at all. The definition of a thriving family, such as will pass muster for the moment at least, is one in which the children have gained distinctly superior positions to those who were their classmates in early life. Families may be considered "large"

that contain not less than three adult male children.   The point to be ascertained is the *status* of the two parents at the time of their marriage, whence its more or less eugenic character might have been predicted, if the larger knowledge that we now hope to obtain had then existed.   Some account would, of course, be wanted of their race, profession, and residence; also of their own respective parentages, and of their brothers and sisters.   Finally, the reasons would be required why the children deserved to be entitled a "thriving" family, to distinguish worthy from unworthy success.   This manuscript collection might hereafter develop into a "golden book" of thriving families.   The Chinese, whose customs have often much sound sense, make their honours retrospective.   We might learn from them to show that respect to the parents of noteworthy children, which the contributors of such valuable assets to the national wealth richly deserve.

4. Influences affecting Marriage.   The passion of love seems so overpowering that it may be thought folly to try to direct its course. But plain facts do not confirm this view.   Social influences of all kinds have immense power in the end, and they are very various. If unsuitable marriages from the eugenic point of view were banned socially, or even regarded with the unreasonable disfavour which some attach to cousin marriages, very few would be made.   The multitude of marriage restrictions that have proved prohibitive among uncivilised people would require a volume to describe.

5. Persistence in setting forth the national importance of Eugenics.   There are three stages to be passed through.   *Firstly*, it must be made familiar as an academic question, until its exact importance has been understood and accepted as a fact; *secondly*, it must be recognised as a subject whose practical development deserves serious consideration; and *thirdly*, it must be introduced into the national conscience, like a new religion.   It has, indeed, strong claims to become an orthodox religious tenet of the future, for Eugenics co-operates with the workings of Nature by securing that humanity shall be represented by the fittest races.   What Nature does blindly, slowly, and ruthlessly, man may do providently, quickly, and kindly. I see no impossibility in Eugenics becoming a religious dogma among mankind, but its details must first be worked out sedulously in the study.   The first and main point is to secure the general intellectual acceptance of Eugenics as a hopeful and most important study.   Then

let its principles work into the heart of the nation, who will gradually give practical effect to them in ways that we may not wholly foresee.

C. PROGRESS AND HUMAN NATURE
1. The Nature of Man[1]

Man is certainly an animal that, when he lives at all, lives for ideals. Something must be found to occupy his imagination, to raise pleasure and pain into love and hatred, and change the prosaic alternative between comfort and discomfort into the tragic one between happiness and sorrow. Now that the hue of daily adventure is so dull, when religion for the most part is so vague and accommodating, when even war is a vast impersonal business, nationality seems to have slipped into the place of honor. It has become the one eloquent, public, intrepid illusion—illusion, I mean, when it is taken for an ultimate good or a mystical essence, for of course nationality is a fact. It is natural for a man to like to live at home, and to live long elsewhere without a sense of exile is not good for his moral integrity. It is right to feel a greater kinship and affection for what lies nearest to one's self. But this necessary fact and even duty of nationality is accidental; like age or sex it is a physical fatality which can be made the basis of specific and comely virtues; but it is not an end to pursue or a flag to flaunt or a privilege not balanced by a thousand incapacities. Yet of this distinction our contemporaries tend to make an idol, perhaps because it is the only distinction they feel they have left.

Everywhere in the nineteenth century we find a double preoccupation with the past and with the future, a longing to know what all experience might have been hitherto, and on the other hand to hasten to some wholly different experience, to be contrived immediately with a beating heart and with flying banners. The imagination of the age was intent on history; its conscience was intent on reform.

2. Progress and the Mores[2]

What now are some of the leading features in the mores of civilized society at the present time? Undoubtedly they are monogamy,

[1] Adapted from G. Santayana, *Winds of Doctrine*, pp. 6–8. (Charles Scribner's Sons, 1913.)

[2] Adapted from W. G. Sumner, "The Mores of the Present and the Future," in the *Yale Review*, XVIII (1909–10), 235–36. (Quoted by special permission of the *Yale Review*.)

anti-slavery, and democracy.   All people now are more nervous than anybody used to be.   Social ambition is great and is prevalent in all classes.   The idea of class is unpopular and is not understood.   There is a superstitious yearning for equality.   There is a decided preference for city life, and a stream of population from the country into big cities.   These are facts of the mores of the time.   Our societies are almost unanimous in their response if there is any question raised on these matters.

Medieval people conceived of society under forms of status as generally as we think of it under forms of individual liberty.   The mores of the Orient and Occident differ from each other now, as they apparently always have differed.   The Orient is a region where time, faith, tradition, and patience rule.   The Occident forms ideals and plans, and spends energy and enterprise to make new things with thoughts of progress.   All details of life follow the leading ways of thought of each group.   We can compare and judge ours and theirs, but independent judgment of our own, without comparison with other times or other places, is possible only within narrow limits.

Let us first take up the nervous desire and exertion which mark the men of our time in the western civilized societies.   There is a wide popular belief in what is called progress.   The masses in all civilized states strain toward success in some adopted line.   Struggling and striving are passionate tendencies which take possession of groups from time to time.   The newspapers, the popular literature, and the popular speakers show this current and popular tendency.   This is what makes the mores.

3.   War and Progress[1]

Let us see what progress means.   It is a term which covers several quite different things.

There is material progress, by which I understand an increase in wealth, that is, in the commodities useful to man, which give him health, strength, and longer life, and make his life easier, providing more comfort and more leisure, and thus enabling him to be more physically efficient, and to escape from that pressure of want which hampers the development of his whole nature.

[1] Adapted from James Bryce, *Essays and Addresses in War Time*, pp. 84–102. (Published by The Macmillan Co., 1918.   Reprinted by permission.)

There is intellectual progress—an increase in knowledge, a greater abundance of ideas, the training to think, and to think correctly, the growth in capacity for dealing with practical problems, the cultivation of the power to enjoy the exercise of thought and the pleasures of letters and art.

There is moral progress—a thing harder to define, but which includes the development of those emotions and habits which make for happiness—contentment and tranquility of mind; the absence of the more purely animal and therefore degrading vices (such as intemperance and sensuality in all its other forms); the control of the violent passions; good will and kindliness toward others—all the things which fall within the philosophical conception of a life guided by right reason. People have different ideas of what constitutes happiness and virtue, but these things are at any rate included in every such conception.

A further preliminary question arises. Is human progress to be estimated in respect to the point to which it raises the few who have high mental gifts and the opportunity of obtaining an education fitting them for intellectual enjoyment and intellectual vocations, or is it to be measured by the amount of its extension to and diffusion through each nation, meaning the nation as a whole—the average man as well as the superior spirits? You may sacrifice either the many to the few—as was done by slavery—or the few to the many, or the advance may be general and proportionate in all classes.

Again, when we think of progress, are we to think of the world as a whole, or only of the stronger and more capable races and states? If the stronger rise upon the prostrate bodies of the weaker, is this clear gain to the world, because the stronger will ultimately do more for the world, or is the loss and suffering of the weaker to be brought into the account? I do not attempt to discuss these questions; it is enough to note them as fit to be remembered; for perhaps all three kinds of progress ought to be differently judged if a few leading nations only are to be regarded, or if we are to think of all mankind.

It is undeniable that war has often been accompanied by an advance in civilization. If we were to look for progress only in time of peace there would have been little progress to discover, for mankind has lived in a state of practically permanent warfare. The Egyptian and Assyrian monarchs were always fighting. The author of the Book of Kings speaks of spring as the time when kings go forth to war, much as we should speak of autumn as the time when men go forth to shoot deer. "War is the natural relation of states to one another," said Plato. The fact has been hardly less true since his day, though latterly men have become accustomed to think of peace as the normal, war as the abnormal or exceptional, relation of states to one another. In the ancient world, as late as the days of Roman conquest, a state of peace was the rare exception among civilized states as well as barbarous tribes. But Carthage, like her Phoenician mother-city, went on building up a mighty commerce till Rome smote her down, and the Hellenic people, in its many warring cities, went on producing noble poems and profound philosophical speculations, and rearing majestic temples and adorning them with incomparable works of sculpture, in the intervals of their fighting with their neighbors of the same or other races. The case of the Greeks proves that war and progress are compatible.

The capital instance of the association of war with the growth and greatness of a state is found in Prussia. One may say that her history is the source of the whole thesis and the basis of the whole argument. It is a case of what, in the days when I learned logic at the University of Oxford, we used to call the induction from a single instance. Prussia, then a small state, began her upward march under the warlike and successful prince whom her people call the Great Elector. Her next long step to greatness was taken by Frederick II, again by favor of successful warfare, though doubtless also by means of a highly organized, and for those days very efficient, administration. Voltaire said of Frederick's Prussia that its trade was war. Another war added to her territory in 1814–15. Three successful wars—those of 1864, 1866, and 1870–71—made her the nucleus of a united German nation and the leading military power of the Old World.

Ever since those victories her industrial production, her commerce, and her wealth have rapidly increased, while at the same time scientific research has been prosecuted with the greatest vigor and on a scale unprecedentedly large. These things were no doubt achieved during a peace of forty-three years. But it was what one may call a belligerent peace, full of thoughts of war and preparations for war. There is no denying that the national spirit has been carried to a high point of pride, energy, and self-confidence, which have stimulated effort in all directions and secured extraordinary efficiency in civil as well as in military administration. Here, then, is an instance in which a state has grown by war and a people has been energized by war.

Next, let us take the cases which show that there have been in many countries long periods of incessant war with no corresponding progress in the things that make civilization. I will not speak of semi-barbarous tribes, among the more advanced of which may be placed the Albanians and the Pathans and the Turkomans, while among the more backward were the North American Indians and the Zulus. But one may cite the case of the civilized regions of Asia under the successors of Alexander, when civilized peoples, distracted by incessant strife, did little for the progress of arts or letters or government, from the death of the great conqueror till they were united under the dominion of Rome and received from her a time of comparative tranquillity.

The Thirty Years' War is an example of long-continued fighting which, far from bringing progress in its train, inflicted injuries on Germany from which she did not recover for nearly two centuries. In recent times there has been more fighting in South and Central America, since the wars of independence, than in any other civilized countries. Yet can anyone say that anything has been gained by the unending civil wars and revolutions, or those scarcely less frequent wars between the several republics, like that terrible one thirty years ago in which Peru was overcome by Chile? Or look at Mexico. Except during the years when the stern dictatorship of Porfirio Diaz kept order and equipped the country with roads and railways, her people have made no perceptible advance and stand hardly higher today than when they were left to work out their own salvation a hundred years ago. Social and economic conditions have doubtless been against her. All that need be remembered is that warfare has not bettered those conditions or improved the national character.

If this hasty historical survey has, as I frankly admit, given us few positive and definite results, the reason is plain. Human progress is affected by so many conditions besides the presence or absence of fighting that it is impossible in any given case to pronounce that it has been chiefly due either to war or to peace. Two conclusions, however, we may claim to have reached, though they are rather negative than positive. One is that war does not necessarily arrest progress. Peoples may advance in thought, literature, and art while they are fighting. The other is that war cannot be shown to have been a cause of progress in anything except the wealth or power of a state which extends its dominions by conquest or draws tribute from the vanquished.

What, then, are the causes to which the progress of mankind is due? It is due partly, no doubt, if not to strife, to competition. But chiefly to thought, which is more often hindered than helped by war. It is the races that know how to think, rather than the far more numerous races that excel in fighting rather than in thinking, that have led the world. Thought, in the form of invention and inquiry, has given us those improvements in the arts of life and in the knowledge of nature by which material progress and comfort have been obtained. Thought has produced literature, philosophy, art, and (when intensified by emotion) religion—all the things that make life worth living. Now the thought of any people is most active when it is brought into contact with the thought of another, because each is apt to lose its variety and freedom of play when it has worked too long upon familiar lines and flowed too long in the channels it has deepened. Hence isolation retards progress, while intercourse quickens it.

The great creative epochs have been those in which one people of natural vigor received an intellectual impulse from the ideas of another, as happened when Greek culture began to penetrate Italy, and thirteen centuries later, when the literature of the ancients began to work on the nations of the medieval world.

Such contact, with the process of learning which follows from it, may happen in or through war, but it happens far oftener in peace; and it is in peace that men have the time and the taste to profit fully by it. A study of history will show that we may, with an easy conscience, dismiss the theory of Treitschke—that war is a health-giving tonic which Providence must be expected constantly to offer to the human race for its own good.

The future progress of mankind is to be sought, not through the strifes and hatreds of the nations, but rather by their friendly co-operation in the healing and enlightening works of peace and in the growth of a spirit of friendship and mutual confidence which may remove the causes of war.

4. Progress and the Cosmic Urge

a. The "Élan Vitale"[1]

All life, animal and vegetable, seems in its essence like an effort to accumulate energy and then to let it flow into flexible channels, changeable in shape, at the end of which it will accomplish infinitely varied kinds of work. That is what the *vital impetus*, passing through matter, would fain do all at once. It would succeed, no doubt, if its power were unlimited, or if some reinforcement could come to it from without. But the impetus is finite, and it has been given once for all. It cannot overcome all obstacles. The movement it starts is sometimes turned aside, sometimes divided, always opposed; and the evolution of the organized world is the unrolling of this conflict. The first great scission that had to be effected was that of the two kingdoms, vegetable and animal, which thus happen to be mutually complementary, without, however, any agreement having been made between them. To this scission there succeeded many others. Hence the diverging lines of evolution, at least what is essential in them. But we must take into account retrogressions, arrests, accidents of every kind. And we must remember, above all, that each species behaves as if the general movement of life stopped at it instead of passing through it. It thinks only of itself, it lives only for itself. Hence the numberless struggles that we behold in nature. Hence a discord, striking and terrible, but for which the original principle of life must not be held responsible.

It is therefore conceivable that life might have assumed a totally different outward appearance and designed forms very different from those we know. With another chemical substratum, in other physical conditions, the impulsion would have remained the same, but it would have split up very differently in course of progress; and the whole would have traveled another road—whether shorter or longer who can tell? In any case, in the entire series of living beings no term would have been what it now is.

---

[1] From Henri Bergson, *Creative Evolution*, translated by Arthur Mitchell, pp. 253–71. (Henry Holt & Co., 1913.)

There are numerous cases in which nature seems to hesitate between the two forms, and to ask herself if she shall make a society or an individual. The slightest push is enough, then, to make the balance weigh on one side or the other. If we take an infusorian sufficiently large, such as the Stentor, and cut it into two halves each containing a part of the nucleus, each of the two halves will generate an independent Stentor; but if we divide it incompletely, so that a protoplasmic communication is left between the two halves, we shall see them execute, each from its side, corresponding movements; so that in this case it is enough that a thread should be maintained or cut in order that life should affect the social or the individual form. Thus, in rudimentary organisms consisting of a single cell, we already find that the apparent individuality of the whole is the composition of an *undefined* number of potential individualities potentially associated. But, from top to bottom of the series of living beings, the same law is manifested. And it is this that we express when we say that unity and multiplicity are categories of inert matter, that the vital impetus is neither pure unity nor pure multiplicity, and that if the matter to which it communicates itself compels it to choose one of the two, its choice will never be definitive: it will leap from one to the other indefinitely. The evolution of life in the double direction of individuality and association has therefore nothing accidental about it: it is due to the very nature of life.

Essential also is the progress to reflexion. If our analysis is correct, it is consciousness, or rather supra-consciousness, that is at the origin of life. Consciousness, or supra-consciousness, is the name for the rocket whose extinguished fragments fall back as matter; consciousness, again, is the name for that which subsists of the rocket itself, passing through the fragments and lighting them up into organisms. But this consciousness, which is a *need of creation*, is made manifest to itself only where creation is possible. It lies dormant when life is condemned to automatism; it wakens as soon as the possibility of a choice is restored. That is why, in organisms unprovided with a nervous system, it varies according to the power of locomotion and of deformation of which the organism disposes. And in animals with a nervous system, it is proportional to the complexity of the switchboard on which the paths called sensory and the paths called motor intersect—that is, of the brain.

Consciousness corresponds exactly to the living being's power of choice; it is coextensive with the fringe of possible action that surrounds the real action: consciousness is synonymous with invention and with freedom.   Now, in the animal, invention is never anything but a variation on the theme of routine.   Shut up in the habits of the species, it succeeds, no doubt, in enlarging them by its individual initiative; but it escapes automatism only for an instant, for just the time to create a new automatism.   The gates of its prison close as soon as they are opened; by pulling at its chain it succeeds only in stretching it.   With man, consciousness breaks the chain.   In man, and in man alone, it sets itself free.   The whole history of life until man has been that of the effort of consciousness to raise matter, and of the more or less complete overwhelming of consciousness by the matter which has fallen back on it.   The enterprise was paradoxical, if, indeed, we may speak here otherwise than by metaphor of enterprise and of effort.   It was to create with matter, which is necessity itself, an instrument of freedom, to make a machine which should triumph over mechanism, and to use determinism of nature to pass through the meshes of the net which this very determinism had spread.   But, everywhere except in man, consciousness has let itself be caught in the net whose meshes it tried to pass through: it has remained the captive of the mechanisms it has set up.   Automatism, which it tries to draw in the direction of freedom, winds about it and drags it down.   It has not the power to escape, because the energy it has provided for acts is almost all employed in maintaining the infinitely subtle and essentially unstable equilibrium into which it has brought matter.   But man not only maintains his machine, he succeeds in using it as he pleases.   Doubtless he owes this to the superiority of his brain, which enables him to build an unlimited number of motor mechanisms, to oppose new habits to the old ones unceasingly, and, by dividing automatism against itself, to rule it. He owes it to his language, which furnishes consciousness with an immaterial body in which to incarnate itself and thus exempts it from dwelling exclusively on material bodies, whose flux would soon drag it along and finally swallow it up.   He owes it to social life, which stores and preserves efforts as language stores thought, fixes thereby a mean level to which individuals must raise themselves at the outset, and by this initial stimulation prevents the average man from slumbering and drives the superior man to mount still higher. But our brain, our society, and our language are only the external and various signs of one and the same internal superiority. They tell, each after its manner, the unique, exceptional success which life has won at a given moment of its evolution. They express the difference of kind, and not only of degree, which separates man from the rest of the animal world. They let us guess that, while at the end of the vast springboard from which life has taken its leap, all the others have stepped down, finding the cord stretched too high, man alone has cleared the obstacle.

It is in this quite special sense that man is the "term" and the "end" of evolution. Life, we have said, transcends finality as it transcends the other categories. It is essentially a current sent through matter, drawing from it what it can. There has not, therefore, properly speaking, been any project or plan. On the other hand, it is abundantly evident that the rest of nature is not for the sake of man: we struggle like the other species, we have struggled against other species. Moreover, if the evolution of life had encountered other accidents in its course, if, thereby, the current of life had been otherwise divided, we should have been, physically and morally, far different from what we are. For these various reasons it would be wrong to regard humanity, such as we have it before our eyes, as prefigured in the evolutionary movement. It cannot even be said to be the outcome of the whole of evolution, for evolution has been accomplished on several divergent lines, and while the human species is at the end of one of them, other lines have been followed with other species at their end. It is in a quite different sense that we hold humanity to be the ground of evolution.

From our point of view, life appears in its entirety as an immense wave which, starting from a centre, spreads outwards, and which on almost the whole of its circumference is stopped and converted into oscillation: at one single point the obstacle has been forced, the impulsion has passed freely. It is this freedom that the human form registers. Everywhere but in man, consciousness has had to come to a stand; in man alone it has kept on its way. Man, then, continues the vital movement indefinitely, although he does not draw along with him all that life carries in itself. On other lines of evolution there have traveled other tendencies which life implied, and of which, since everything interpenetrates, man has, doubtless, kept something, but of which he has kept only very little. *It is as if a vague and formless being, whom we may call, as we will,* man *or* super-man, *had sought to realize himself, and had succeeded only by abandoning a part of himself on the way.* The losses are represented by the rest of the animal world, and even by the vegetable world, at least in what these have that is positive and above the accidents of evolution.

From this point of view, the discordances of which nature offers us the spectacle are singularly weakened. The organized world as a whole becomes as the soil on which was to grow either man himself or a being who morally must resemble him. The animals, however distant they may be from our species, however hostile to it, have none the less been useful traveling companions, on whom consciousness has unloaded whatever encumbrances it was dragging along, and who have enabled it to rise, in man, to heights from which it sees an unlimited horizon open again before it.

Consciousness is distinct from the organism it animates, although it must undergo its vicissitudes. As the possible actions which a state of consciousness indicates are at every instant beginning to be carried out in the nervous centres, the brain underlies at every instant the motor indications of the state of consciousness; but the inter-dependency of consciousness and brain is limited to this; the destiny of consciousness is not bound up on that account with the destiny of cerebral matter. Finally, consciousness is essentially free; it is freedom itself; but it cannot pass through matter without settling on it, without adapting itself to it: this adaptation is what we call intellectuality; and the intellect, turning itself back towards active, that is to say, free, consciousness, naturally makes it enter into the conceptual forms into which it is accustomed to see matter fit. It will therefore always perceive freedom in the form of necessity; it will always neglect the part of novelty or of creation inherent in the free act; it will always substitute for action itself an imitation artificial, approximative, obtained by compounding the old with the old and the same with the same. Thus, to the eyes of a philosophy that attempts to reabsorb intellect in intuition, many difficulties vanish or become light. But such a doctrine does not only facilitate speculation; it gives us also more power to act and to live. For, with it, we feel ourselves no longer isolated in humanity, humanity no longer seems isolated in the nature that it dominates. As the smallest grain of dust is bound up with our entire solar system, drawn along with it in that undivided movement of descent which is materiality itself, so all organized beings, from the humblest to the highest, from the first origins of life to the time in which we are, and in all places as in all times, do but evidence a single impulsion, the inverse of the movement of matter, and in itself indivisible. All the living hold together, and all yield to the same tremendous push. The animal takes its stand on the plant, man bestrides animality, and the whole of humanity, in space and in time, is one immense army galloping beside and before and behind each of us in an overwhelming charge able to beat down every resistance and clear the most formidable obstacles, perhaps even death.

b.   The "Dunkler Drang"[1]

Every glance at the world, to explain which is the task of the philosopher, confirms and proves that *will to live*, far from being an arbitrary hypostasis or an empty word, is the only true expression of its inmost nature. Everything presses and strives towards *existence*, if possible *organized existence*, i.e., *life*, and after that to the highest possible grade of it. In animal nature it then becomes apparent that *will to live* is the keynote of its being, its one unchangeable and unconditioned quality. Let anyone consider this universal desire for life, let him see the infinite willingness, facility, and exuberance with which the will to live presses impetuously into existence under a million forms everywhere and at every moment, by means of fructification and of germs, nay, when these are wanting, by means of *generatio aequivoca*, seizing every opportunity, eagerly grasping for itself every material capable of life: and then again let him cast a glance at its fearful alarm and wild rebellion when in any particular phenomenon it must pass out of existence; especially when this takes place with distinct consciousness. Then it is precisely the same as if in this single phenomenon the whole world would be annihilated forever, and the whole being of this threatened living thing is at once transformed

[1] From Arthur Schopenhauer, *The World as Will and Idea*, III, 107–18. (Paul, Trench, Trübner & Co., 1909.)

into the most desperate struggle against death and resistance to it. Look, for example, at the incredible anxiety of a man in danger of his life, the rapid and serious participation in this of every witness of it, and the boundless rejoicing at his deliverance. Look at the rigid terror with which a sentence of death is heard, the profound awe with which we regard the preparations for carrying it out, and the heartrending compassion which seizes us at the execution itself. We would then suppose there was something quite different in question than a few less years of an empty, sad existence, embittered by troubles of every kind, and always uncertain: we would rather be amazed that it was a matter of any consequence whether one attained a few years earlier to the place where after an ephemeral existence he has billions of years to be. In such phenomena, then, it becomes visible that I am right in declaring that *the will to live* is that which cannot be further explained, but lies at the foundation of all explanations, and that this, far from being an empty word, like the absolute, the infinite, the idea, and similar expressions, is the most real thing we know, nay, the kernel of reality itself.

But if now, abstracting for a while from this interpretation drawn from our inner being, we place ourselves as strangers over against nature, in order to comprehend it objectively, we find that from the grade of organized life upwards it has only one intention— that of the *maintenance of the species*. To this end it works, through the immense superfluity of germs, through the urgent vehemence of the sexual instinct, through its willingness to adapt itself to all circumstances and opportunities, even to the production of bastards, and through the instinctive maternal affection, the strength of which is so great that in many kinds of animals it even outweighs self-love, so that the mother sacrifices her life in order to preserve that of the young. The individual, on the contrary, has for nature only an indirect value, only so far as it is the means of maintaining the species. Apart from this, its existence is to nature a matter of indifference; indeed nature even leads it to destruction as soon as it has ceased to be useful for this end. Why the individual exists would thus be clear; but why does the species itself exist? That is a question which nature when considered merely objectively cannot answer. For in vain do we seek by contemplating her for an end of this restless striving, this ceaseless pressing into existence, this anxious care for the maintenance of the species. The strength and the time of the individuals are consumed in the effort to procure sustenance for themselves and their young, and are only just sufficient, sometimes even not sufficient, for this. The whole thing, when regarded thus purely objectively, and indeed as extraneous to us, looks as if nature was only concerned that of all her (Platonic) *Ideas*, i.e., permanent forms, none should be lost. For the individuals are fleeting as the water in the brook; and Ideas, on the contrary, are permanent, like its eddies: but the exhaustion of the water would also do away with the eddies. We would have to stop at this unintelligible view if nature were known to us only from without, thus were given us merely *objectively*, and we accepted it as it is comprehended by knowledge, and also as sprung from knowledge, i.e., in the sphere of the idea, and were therefore obliged to confine ourselves to this province in solving it. But the case is otherwise, and a glance at any rate is afforded us into the *interior of nature;* inasmuch as this is nothing else than *our own inner being*, which is precisely where nature, arrived at the highest grade to which its striving could work itself up, is now by the light of knowledge found directly in self-consciousness. Thus the subjective here gives the key for the exposition of the objective. In order to recognize, as something original and unconditioned, that exceedingly strong tendency of all animals and men to retain life and carry it on as long as possible—a tendency which was set forth above as characteristic of the subjective, or of the will—it is necessary to make clear to ourselves that this is by no means the result of any objective *knowledge* of the worth of life, but is independent of all knowledge; or, in other words, that those beings exhibit themselves, not as drawn from in front, but as impelled from behind.

If with this intention we first of all review the interminable series of animals, consider the infinite variety of their forms, as they exhibit themselves always differently modified according to their element and manner of life, and also ponder the inimitable ingenuity of their structure and mechanism, which is carried out with equal perfection in every individual; and finally, if we take into consideration the incredible expenditure of strength, dexterity, prudence, and activity which every animal has ceaselessly to make through its whole life; if, approaching the matter more closely, we contemplate the untiring diligence of wretched little ants, the marvellous and ingenious industry of the bees, or observe how a single burying-beetle (*Necro-phorus vespillo*) buries a mole of forty times its own size in two days in order to deposit its eggs in it and insure nourishment for the future brood (Gleditsch, *Physik. Bot. Oekon. Abhandl.*, III, 220), at the same time calling to mind how the life of most insects is nothing but ceaseless labour to prepare food and an abode for the future brood which will arise from their eggs, and which then, after they have consumed the food and passed through the chrysalis state, enter upon life merely to begin again from the beginning the same labour; then also how, like this, the life of the birds is for the most part taken up with their distant and laborious migrations, then with the building of their nests and the collection of food for their brood, which itself has to play the same rôle the following year; and so all work constantly for the future, which afterwards makes bankrupt—then we cannot avoid looking round for the reward of all this skill and trouble, for the end which these animals have before their eyes, which strive so ceaselessly—in short, we are driven to ask: What is the result? What is attained by the animal existence which demands such infinite preparation? And there is nothing to point to but the satisfaction of hunger and the sexual instinct, or in any case a little momentary comfort, as it falls to the lot of each animal individual, now and then in the intervals of its endless need and struggle. Take, for example, the mole, that unwearied worker. To dig with all its might with its enormous shovel claws is the occupation of its whole life; constant night surrounds it; its embryo eyes only make it avoid the light. It alone is truly an *animal nocturnum;* not cats, owls, and bats, who see by night. But what, now, does it attain by this life, full of trouble and devoid of pleasure? Food and the begetting of its kind; thus only the means of carrying on and beginning anew the same doleful course in new individuals. In such examples it becomes clear that there is no proportion between the cares and troubles of life and the results or gain of it. The consciousness of the world of perception gives a certain appearance of objective worth of existence to the life of those animals which can see, although in their case this consciousness is entirely subjective and limited to the influence of motives upon them. But the *blind* mole, with its perfect organiza-tion and ceaseless activity, limited to the alternation of insect larvae and hunger, makes the disproportion of the means to the end apparent.

Let us now add the consideration of the human race. The matter indeed becomes more complicated, and assumes a certain seriousness of aspect; but the fundamental character remains unaltered. Here also life presents itself by no means as a gift for enjoyment, but as a task, a drudgery to be performed; and in accordance with this we see, in great and small, universal need, ceaseless cares, constant pressure, endless strife, compulsory activity, with extreme exertion of all the powers of body and mind. Many millions, united into nations, strive for the common good, each individual on account of his own; but many thousands fall as a sacrifice for it. Now senseless delusions, now intriguing politics, incite them to wars with each other; then the sweat and the blood of the great multitude must flow, to carry out the ideas of individuals, or to expiate their faults. In peace industry and trade are active, inventions work miracles, seas are navigated, delicacies are collected from all ends of the world, the waves engulf thousands. All strive, some planning, others acting; the tumult is indescribable. But the ultimate aim of it all, what is it? To sustain ephemeral and tormented individuals through a short span of time in the most fortunate ease with endurable want and comparative freedom from pain, which, however, is at once attended with ennui; then the reproduction of this race and its striving. In this evident disproportion between the trouble and the reward, the will to live appears to us from this point of view, if taken objectively, as a fool, or subjectively, as a delusion, seized by which everything living works with the utmost exertion of its strength for something that is of no value. But when we consider it more closely, we shall find here also that it is rather a blind pressure, a tendency entirely without ground or motive.

The law of motivation only extends to the particular actions, not to willing *as a whole and in general*. It depends upon this, that if we conceive of the human race and its action *as a whole and universally*, it does not present itself to us, as when we contemplate the particular actions, as a play of puppets who are pulled after the ordinary manner by threads outside them; but from this point of view, as puppets that are set in motion by internal clockwork. For if, as we have done above, one compares the ceaseless, serious, and laborious striving of men with what they gain by it, nay, even with what they ever can gain, the disproportion we have pointed out becomes apparent, for one recognizes that that which is to be gained, taken as the motive power, is entirely insufficient for the explanation of that movement and that ceaseless striving. What, then, is a short postponement of death, a slight easing of misery or deferment of pain, a momentary stilling of desire, compared with such an abundant and certain victory over them all as death? What could such advantages accomplish taken as actual moving causes of a human race, innumerable because constantly renewed, which unceasingly moves, strives, struggles, grieves, writhes, and performs the whole tragi-comedy of the history of the world, nay, what says more than all, *perseveres* in such a mock-existence as long as each one possibly can? Clearly this is all inexplicable if we seek the moving causes outside the figures and conceive the human race as striving, in consequence of rational reflection, or something analogous to this (as moving threads), after those good things held out to it, the attainment of which would be a sufficient reward for its ceaseless cares and troubles. The matter being taken thus, everyone would rather have long ago said, "Le jeu ne vaut pas la chandelle," and have gone out. But, on the contrary, everyone guards and defends his life, like a precious pledge entrusted to him under heavy responsibility, under infinite cares and abundant misery, even under which life is tolerable. The wherefore and the why, the reward for this, certainly he does not see; but he has accepted the worth of that pledge without seeing it, upon trust and faith, and does not know what it consists in. Hence I have said that these puppets are not pulled from without, but each bears in itself the clockwork from which its movements result. This is *the will to live*, manifesting itself as an untiring machine, an irrational tendency, which has not its sufficient reason in the external world. It holds the individuals firmly upon the scene, and is the *primum mobile* of their movements; while the external objects, the motives, only determine their direction in the particular case; otherwise the cause would not be at all suitable to the effect. For, as every manifestation of a force of nature has a cause, but the force of nature itself none, so every particular act of will has a motive, but the will in general has none: indeed at bottom these two are one and the same. The will, as that which is metaphysical, is everywhere the boundary-stone of every investigation, beyond which it cannot go. We often see a miserable figure, deformed and shrunk with age, want, and disease, implore our help from the bottom of his heart for the prolongation of an existence, the end of which would necessarily appear altogether desirable if it were an objective judgment that determined here. Thus instead of this it is the blind will, appearing as the tendency to life, the love of life, and the sense of life; it is the same which makes the plants grow. This sense of life may be compared to a rope which is stretched above the puppet show of the world of men, and on which the puppets hang by invisible threads, while apparently they are supported only by the ground beneath them (the objective value of life). But if the rope becomes weak the puppet sinks; if it breaks the puppet must fall, for the ground beneath it only seemed to support it: i.e., the weakening of that love of life shows itself as hypochondria, spleen, melancholy: its entire exhaustion as the inclination to suicide. And as with the persistence in life, so is it also with its action and movement. This is not something freely chosen; but while everyone would really gladly rest, want and ennui are the whips that keep the top spinning. Therefore everything is in continual strain and forced movement, and the course of the world goes on, to use an expression of Aristotle's (*De coelo* ii. 13), "οὐ φύσει, ἀλλὰ βίᾳ" (*motu, non naturali sed violento*). Men are only apparently drawn from in front; really they are pushed from behind; it is not life that tempts them on, but necessity that drives them forward. The law of motivation is, like all causality, merely the form of the phenomenon.

In all these considerations, then, it becomes clear to us that the will to live is not a consequence of the knowledge of life, is in no way a *conclusio ex praemissis*, and in general is nothing secondary. Rather, it is that which is first and unconditioned, the premiss of all premisses, and just on that account that from which philosophy must *start*, for the will to live does not appear in consequence of the world, but the world in consequence of the will to live.

III. INVESTIGATIONS AND PROBLEMS

1. ·Progress and Social Research

The problem of progress comes back finally to the problem of the ultimate good. If the world is getting better, measured by this ultimate standard, then there is progress. If it is growing worse, then there is retrogression. But in regard to the ultimate good there is no agreement. What is temporary gain may be ultimate loss. What is one man's evil may be, and often seems to be, another man's good. In the final analysis what seems evil may turn out to be good and what seems good may be an eventual evil. But this is a problem in philosophy which sociology is not bound to solve before it undertakes to describe society. It does not even need to discuss it. Sociology, just as any other natural science, accepts the current values of the community. The physician, like the social worker, assumes that health is a social value. With this as a datum his studies are directed to the discovery of the nature and causes of diseases, and to the invention of devices for curing them. There is just as much, and no more, reason for a sociologist to formulate a doctrine of social progress as there is for the physician to do so. Both are concerned with specific problems for which they are seeking specific remedies.

If there are social processes and predictable forms of change in society, then there are methods of human intervention in the processes of society, methods of controlling these processes in the interest of the ends of human life, methods of progress in other words. If there are no intelligible or describable social processes, then there may be progress, but there will be no sociology and no *methods of progress*. We can only hope and pray.

It is not impossible to formulate a definition of progress which does not assume the perfectibility of mankind, which does not regard progress as a necessity, and which does not assume to say with finality what has happened or is likely to happen to humanity as a whole.[1]

Progress may be considered as the addition to the sum of accumulated experience, tradition, and technical devices organized for social

[1] Scientific optimism was no doubt rampant before Darwin. For example, Herschel says: "Man's progress towards a higher state need never fear a check, but must continue till the very last existence of history." But Herbert Spencer asserts the perfectibility of man with an assurance which makes us gasp. "Progress is not an accident, but a necessity. What we call evil and immorality must disappear. It is certain that man must become perfect." "The ultimate development of the ideal man is certain—as certain as any conclusion in which we place the most implicit faith; for instance, that all men will die." "Always towards perfection is the mighty movement—towards a complete development and a more unmixed good."—W. R. Inge, *The Idea of Progress*, p. 9. (Oxford, 1920.)

efficiency. This is at once a definition of progress and of civilization, in which civilization is the sum of social efficiencies and progress consists of the units (additions) of which it is composed. Defined in these terms, progress turns out to be a relative, local, temporal, and secular phenomenon. It is possible, theoretically at least, to compare one community with another with respect to their relative efficiency and their relative progress in efficiency, just as we can compare one institution with another in respect to its efficiency and progress. It is even possible to measure the progress of humanity in so far as humanity can be said to be organized for social action.

This is in fact the point of view which sociologists have adopted as soon as progress ceased to be, for sociology, a matter of definition and became a matter of observation and research. Score cards for neighborhoods and for rural communities have already been devised.[1]

2. Indices of Progress

A few years ago, Walter F. Willcox, in an article "A Statistician's Idea of Progress," sought to define certain indices of social progress which would make it possible to measure progress statistically. "If progress be merely a subjective term," he admitted, "statistics can throw no light upon it because all such ends as happiness, or self-realization, or social service are incapable of statistical measurement." Statistics works with indices, characteristics which are accessible to measurement but are "correlated with some deeper immeasurable characteristic." Mr. Willcox took as his indices of progress:

1. Increase in population.
2. Length of life.
3. Uniformity in population.
4. Racial homogeneity.
5. Literacy.
6. Decrease of the divorce rate.

Certainly these indices, like uniformity, are mere temporary measures of progress, since diversity in the population is not per se an evil. It becomes so only when the diversities in the community

[1] "Scale for Grading Neighborhood Conditions," *Publications of the Whittier State School, Research Bulletin, No. 5*, Whittier, Cal., May, 1917. "Guide to the Grading of Neighborhoods," *Publications of the Whittier State School, Research Bulletin, No. 8*, Whittier, Cal., April, 1918. Nat T. Frame, "The Country Community Score Card," *West Virginia University Agricultural Extension Circular 240*, Morgantown, W.Va., 1919.

are so great as to endanger its solidarity.   Applying his indices to the United States, Mr. Willcox sums up the result as follows:

The net result is to indicate for the United States a rapid increase of population and probable increase in length of life, and increase in racial uniformity and perhaps in uniformity of other sorts connected with immigration, and at the same time a decrease in uniformity in the stability and social serviceability of family life.   Some of these indications look towards progress, others look towards retrogression.   As they cannot be reduced to any common denominator, the statistical method is unable to answer the question with which we started.[1]

The securing of indices which will measure satisfactorily even such social values as are generally accepted is difficult.   The problem of giving each index in the series a value or weight in proportion to the value of all the others is still more difficult.   This statement, at any rate, illustrates the procedure and the method.

The whole subject of numerical indices for the measurement of civilization and progress has recently been discussed in a little volume by Alfredo Niceforo,[2] professor in the School of Criminal Law at Rome.   He proposes as indices of progress:

1. The increase in wealth and in the consumption of goods, and the diminution of the mortality rate.   These are evidences of material progress.

2. The diffusion of culture, and "when it becomes possible to measure it," the productivity of men of genius.   This is the measure of intellectual superiority.

3. Moral progress he would measure in terms of crime.

4. There remains the social and political organization, which he would measure in terms of the increase and decrease of individual liberty.

In all these attempts to measure the progress of the community the indices have invariably shown progression in some direction, retrogression in others.

From the point of view of social research the problem of progress is mainly one of getting devices that will measure all the different factors of progress and of estimating the relative value of different factors in the progress of the community.

[1] "A Statistician's Idea of Progress," *International Journal of Ethics*, XVIII (1913), 296.

[2] *Les indices numériques de la civilisation et du progrès.*   (Paris, 1921.)

SELECTED BIBLIOGRAPHY

I. THE DEFINITION OF PROGRESS

(1) Dewey, John. "Progress," *International Journal of Ethics*, XXVI (1916), 311–22.

(2) Bury, J. B. *The Idea of Progress*. An inquiry into its origin and growth. London, 1921.

(3) Bryce, James. "What is Progress?" *Atlantic Monthly*, C (1907), 145–56.

(4) Todd, A. J. *Theories of Social Progress*. A critical attempt to formulate the conditions of human advance. New York, 1918.

(5) Woods, E. B. "Progress as a Sociological Concept," *American Journal of Sociology*, XII (1906–7), 779–821.

(6) Cooley, Charles H. *The Social Process*. Chap. xxvii, "The Sphere of Pecuniary Valuation," pp. 309–28. New York, 1918.

(7) Mackenzie, J. S. "The Idea of Progress," *International Journal of Ethics*, IX (1899), 195–213.

(8) Bergson, H. *Creative Evolution*. New York, 1911.

(9) Frobenius, L. *Die Weltanschauung der Naturvölker*. Weimar, 1899.

(10) Inge, W. R. *The Idea of. Progress*. The Romanes Lecture, 1920. Oxford, 1920.

(11) Balfour, Arthur J. *Arthur James Balfour, as Philosopher and Thinker*. A collection of the more important and interesting passages in his non-political writings, speeches, and addresses, 1879–1912. Selected and arranged by Wilfrid M. Short. "Progress," pp. 413–35. London and New York, 1912.

(12) Carpenter, Edward. *Civilization, Its Cause and Cure*. And other essays. New and enlarged ed. London and New York, 1917.

(13) Nordau, Max S. *The Interpretation of History*. Translated from the German by M. A. Hamilton. Chap. viii, "The Question of Progress." New York, 1911.

(14) Sorel, Georges. *Les Illusions du progrès*. 2d ed. Paris, 1911.

(15) Allier, R. "Pessimisme et civilisation," *Revue Encyclopédique*, V (1895), 70–73.

(16) Simmel, Georg. "Moral Deficiencies as Determining Intellectual Functions," *International Journal of Ethics*, III (1893), 490–507.

(17) Delvaile, Jules. *Essai sur histoire de l'idèe de progrès jusqu'à la fin du 18ième siècle*. Paris, 1910.

(18) Sergi, G. "Qualche idea sul progresso umano," *Rivista italiana di sociologia*, XVII (1893), 1–8.

(19) Barth, Paul. "Die Frage des sittlichen Fortschritts der Menschheit," *Vierteljahrsschrift für wissenschaftliche Philosophie*, XXIII (1899), 75–116.

(20) Lankester, E. Ray. *Degeneration*. A chapter in Darwinism, and parthenogenesis. Humboldt Library of Science. New York, 18—.

(21) Lloyd, A. H. "The Case of Purpose against Fate in History," *American Journal of Sociology*, XVII (1911–12), 491–511.

(22) Case, Clarence M. "Religion and the Concept of Progress," *Journal of Religion*, I (1921), 160–73.

(23) Reclus, E. "The Progress of Mankind," *Contemporary Review*, LXX (1896), 761–83.

(24) Bushee, F. A. "Science and Social Progress," *Popular Science Monthly*, LXXIX (1911), 236–51.

(25) Shafer, Robert. *Progress and Science*. Essays in criticism. New Haven, 1922.

(26) Jankelevitch, S. "Du Rôle des idées dans l'évolution des sociétés," *Revue philosophique*, LXVI (1908), 256–80.

(27) Small, Albion W. "The Category 'Progress' as a Tool of Research in Social Science," *American Journal of Sociology*, XXVIII (1922–23), 554–76.

II. HISTORY, THE PHILOSOPHY OF HISTORY AND PROGRESS

(1) Condorcet, Marquis de. *History of the Progress of the Human Mind*. London, 1795.

(2) Comte, Auguste. *The Positive Philosophy of Auguste Comte*. (Translated from the French by Harriet Martineau) Book VI, chap. ii, vi. 2d ed. 2 vols. London, 1875–90.

(3) Caird, Edward. *The Social Philosophy and Religion of Comte*. 2d ed. Glasgow and New York, 1893.

(4) Buckle, Henry Thomas. *History of Civilization in England*. 2 vols. From 2d London ed. New York, 1903.

(5) Condorcet, Marie J. A. C. *Esquisse d'un tableau historique des progrès de l'esprit humain*. 2 vols. in one. Paris, 1902.

(6) Harris, George. *Civilization Considered as a Science*. In relation to its essence, its elements, and its end. London, 1861.

(7) Lamprecht, Karl. *Alte und neue Richtungen in der Geschichtswissenschaft*. Berlin, 1896.

(8) ———. "Individualität, Idee und sozialpsychische Kraft in der Geschichte," *Jahrbücher für National-Ökonomie und Statistik*, XIII (1897), 880–900.

(9) Barth, Paul. *Philosophie der Geschichte als Sociologie*. Erster Teil, "Einleitung und kritische Übersicht." Leipzig, 1897.

(10) Rickert, Heinrich. *Die Grenzen der naturwissenschaftlichen Begriffsbildung*. Leipzig, 1902.

(11) Simmel, Georg. *Die Probleme der Geschichtsphilosophie*. Eine erkenntnistheoretische Studie. 2d ed. Leipzig, 1905.

(12) Mill, John Stuart. *A System of Logic, Ratiocinative and Inductive*. Being a connected view of the principles of evidence and the methods of scientific investigation. 8th ed. New York and London, 1900.

(13) Letelier, Valentin. *La Evoluçion de la historia*. 2d ed. 2 vols. Santiago de Chile, 1900.

(14) Teggart, Frederick J. *The Processes of History*. New Haven, 1918.

(15) Znaniecki, Florian. *Cultural Reality*. Chicago, 1919.

(16) Hibben, J. G. "The Philosophical Aspects of Evolution," *Philosophical Review*, XIX (1910), 113–36.

(17) Bagehot, Walter. *Physics and Politics.* Or thoughts on the application of the principles of "natural selection" and "inheritance" to political society. Chap. vi, "Verifiable Progress Politically Considered," pp. 205–24. New York, 1906.

(18) Crawley, A. E. "The Unconscious Reason in Social Evolution," *Sociological Review*, VI (1913), 236–41.

(19) Froude, James A. "Essay on Progress," *Short Studies on Great Subjects.* 2d Ser. II, 245–79, 4 vols. New York, 1888–91.

(20) Morley, John. "Some Thoughts on Progress," *Educational Review*, XXIX (1905), 1–17.

(21) Ogburn, William F. *Social Change.* With respect to culture and original nature. New York, 1922.

III. EVOLUTION AND PROGRESS

(1) Spencer, Herbert. "Progress, Its Law and Cause," *Westminster Review*, LXVII (1857), 445–85. [Reprinted in Everyman's edition of his *Essays*, pp. 153–97. New York, 1866.]

(2) Federici, Romolo. *Les Lois du Progrès.* II, 32–35, 44, 127, 136, 146–47, 158 ff.; 223, etc. 2 vols. Paris, 1888–91.

(3) Baldwin, James Mark. *Development and Evolution.* Including psychophysical evolution, evolution by orthoplasy, and the theory of genetic modes. New York, 1902.

(4) Adams, Brooks. *The Law of Civilization and Decay.* An essay on history. New York and London, 1903.

(5) Kidd, Benjamin. *Principles of Western Civilization.* London, 1902.

(6) ———. *Social Evolution.* New ed. New York and London, 1896.

(7) Müller-Lyer, F. *The History of Social Development.* Translated from the German by Elizabeth C. and H. A. Lake. London, 1920.

(8) McGee, W J. "The Trend of Human Progress," *American Anthropologist*, N.S., I (1899), 401–47.

(9) Carver, Thomas N. *Sociology and Social Progress.* A handbook for students of sociology. Boston, 1905.

(10) Weber, L. *Le Rythme du progrès.* Étude sociologique. Paris, 1913.

(11) Baldwin, J. Mark. *Social and Ethical Interpretations in Mental Development.* Chap. xiv, "Social Progress," pp. 537–50. New York, 1906.

(12) Bernard, L. L. "The Conditions of Social Progress," *American Journal of Sociology*, XXVIII (1922–23), 21–48.

(13) ———. "Invention and Social Progress," *American Journal of Sociology*, XXIX (July, 1923), 1–33.

(14) Wallace, Alfred R. *Social Environment and Moral Progress.* London and New York, 1913.

(15) Freeman, R. Austin. *Social Decay and Regeneration.* With an introduction by Havelock Ellis. Boston, 1921.

(16) Hobhouse, L. T. *Social Development.* New York, 1924.

IV. EUGENICS AND PROGRESS

(1) Galton, Francis, and others. "Eugenics, Its Scope and Aims," *American Journal of Sociology*, X (1904–5), 1–25.

(2) Saleeby, Caleb W. *The Progress of Eugenics*. London, 1914.

(3) Ellis, Havelock. *The Problem of Race Regeneration*. New York, 1911.

(4) Pearson, Karl. *National Life from the Standpoint of Science*. 2d ed. London, 1905.

(5) Saleeby, Caleb W. *Methods of Race Regeneration*. New York, 1911.

(6) Davenport, C. B. *Heredity in Relation to Eugenics*. New York, 1911.

(7) Demoor, Jean, Massart, J., et Vandervelde, É. *L'Évolution régressive en biologie et en sociologie*. Paris, 1897.

(8) Thomson, J. Arthur. "Eugenics and War," *Eugenics Review*, VII (1915–16), 1–14.

(9) Southard, E. E. "Eugenics *vs.* Cacogenics," *Journal of Heredity*, V (1914), 408–14.

(10) Conn, Herbert W. *Social Heredity and Social Evolution*. The other side of eugenics. Cincinnati, 1914.

(11) Popenoe, Paul, and Johnson, R. H. *Applied Eugenics*. New York, 1918.

(12) Kelsey, Carl. "Influence of Heredity and Environment upon Race Improvement," *Annals of American Academy*, XXXIV (1909), 3–8.

(13) Ward, L. F. "Eugenics, Euthenics and Eudemics," *American Journal of Sociology*, XVIII (1912–13), 737–54.

(14) Holmes, S. J. *The Trend of the Race*. A study of present tendencies in the biological development of civilized mankind. New York, 1921.

V. PROGRESS AND THE MORAL ORDER

(1) Harrison, Frederic. *Order and Progress*. London, 1875.

(2) Hobhouse, Leonard T. *Social Evolution and Political Theory*. Chaps. i, ii, vii, pp. 1–39; 149–65. New York, 1911.

(3) ———. *Morals in Evolution*. A study in comparative ethics. 2 vols. New York, 1906.

(4) Alexander, Samuel. *Moral Order and Progress*. An analysis of ethical conceptions. 2d ed. London, 1891.

(5) Chapin, F. S. "Moral Progress," *Popular Science Monthly*, LXXXVI (1915), 467–71.

(6) Keller, Albert G. *Societal Evolution*. New York, 1915.

(7) Dellepiane, A. "Le Progrès et sa formule. La lutte pour le progrès," *Revue internationale de sociologie*, XX (1912), 1–30.

(8) Burgess, Ernest W. *The Function of Socialization in Social Evolution*. Chicago, 1916.

(9) Ellwood, C. A. "The Educational Theory of Social Progress," *Scientific Monthly*, V (1917), 439–50.

(10) Bosanquet, Helen. "The Psychology of Social Progress," *International Journal of Ethics*, VII (1896–97), 265–81.

(11) Perry, Ralph Barton. *The Moral Economy*. Chap. iv, "The Moral Test of Progress," pp. 123–70. New York, 1909.

(12) Patten, S. N. "Theories of Progress," *American Economic Review*, II (1912), 61–68.
(13) Alexander, H. B. "The Belief in God and Immortality as Factors in Race Progress," *Hibbert Journal*, IX (1910–11), 169–87.

VI. UTOPIAS

(1) Plato. *The Republic of Plato*. Translated into English by Benjamin Jowett. 2 vols. Oxford, 1908.
(2) More, Thomas. *The "Utopia" of Sir Thomas More*. Ralph Robinson's translation, with Roper's "Life of More" and some of his letters. London, 1910.
(3) *Ideal Commonwealths*. Comprising More's "Utopia," Bacon's "New Atlantis," Campanella's "City of the Sun," and Harrington's "Oceana," with introductions by Henry Morley. Rev. ed. New York, 1901.
(4) Kaufmann, Moritz. *Utopias, or Schemes of Social Improvement*. From Sir Thomas More to Karl Marx. London, 1879.
(5) Bacon, Francis. *New Atlantis*. Oxford, 1915.
(6) Campanella, Tommaso. *La città di sole e aforasmi politici*. Lanciana, Carabba, 19—.
(7) Andreä, Johann V. *Christianopolis*. An ideal state of the seventeenth century. Translated from the Latin by F. E. Held. New York, 1916.
(8) Harrington, James. *The Oceana of James Harrington*. London, 1700.
(9) Mandeville, Bernard de. *Fable of the Bees*. Or private vices, public benefits. Edinburgh, 1772. [First published in 1714.]
(10) Cabet, Étienne. *Voyage en Icarie*. 5th ed. Paris, 1848.
(11) Butler, Samuel. *Erewhon: or over the Range*. New York, 1917. [First published in 1872.]
(12) ———. *Erewhon Revisited Twenty Years Later*. New York, 1901.
(13) Lytton, Edward Bulwer. *The Coming Race*. London, 1871.
(14) Bellamy, Edward. *Looking Backward, 2000–1887*. Boston, 1898.
(15) Morris, William. *News from Nowhere*. Or an epoch of rest, being some chapters from a utopian romance. New York, 1910. [First published in 1891.]
(16) Hertzka, Theodor. *Freeland*. A social anticipation. New York, 1891.
(17) Wells, H. G. *A Modern Utopia*. New York, 1905.
(18) ———. *New Worlds for Old*. New York, 1908.
(19) Mumford, Lewis. *The Story of Utopias*. New York, 1922.
(20) Hertzler, Joyce O. *The History of Utopian Thought*. New York, 1923.

VII. PROGRESS AND SOCIAL WELFARE

(1) Crozier, John B. *Civilization and Progress*. 3d ed., pp. 366–440. London and New York, 1892.
(2) Obolensky, L. E. ["Self-Consciousness of Classes in Social Progress"] *Voprosy filosofii i psichologuii*, VII (1896), 521–51. [Short review in *Revue philosophique*, XLIV (1897), 106.]

(3) Mallock, William H. *Aristocracy and Evolution*. A study of the rights, the origin, and the social functions of the wealthier classes. London, 1898.

(4) Tenney, E. P. *Contrasts in Social Progress*. New York, 1907.

(5) Hall, Arthur C. *Crime in Its Relations to Social Progress*. New York, 1902.

(6) Hughes, Charles E. *Conditions of Progress in a Democratic Government*. New Haven, 1910.

(7) Parmelee, Maurice. *Poverty and Social Progress*. Chaps. vi–vii. New York, 1916.

(8) George, Henry. *Progress and Poverty*. Book X, chap. iii. New York, 1899.

(9) Nasmyth, George. *Social Progress and the Darwinian Theory*. New York, 1916.

(10) Harris, George. *Inequality and Progress*. New York, 1897.

(11) Irving, L. "The Drama as a Factor in Social Progress," *Fortnightly Review*, CII (1914), 268–74.

(12) Salt, Henry S. *Animal Rights Considered in Relation to Social Progress*. New York, 1894.

(13) Delabarre, Frank A. "Civilisation and Its Effects on Morbidity and Mortality," *Journal of Sociologic Medicine*, XIX (1918), 220–23.

(14) Knopf, S. A. "The Effects of Civilisation on the Morbidity and Mortality of Tuberculosis," *Journal of Sociologic Medicine*, XX (1919), 5–15.

(15) Giddings, Franklin H. "The Ethics of Social Progress," in the collection *Philanthropy and Social Progress*. Seven essays . . . . delivered before the School of Applied Ethics at Plymouth, Mass., during the session of 1892. With introduction by Professor Henry C. Adams. New York and Boston, 1893.

(16) Morgan, Alexander. *Education and Social Progress*. Chaps. vi, ix–xxi. London and New York, 1916.

(17) Butterfield, K. L. *Chapters in Rural Progress*. Chicago, 1908.

(18) Robertson, John M. *The Economics of Progress*. New York, 1918.

(19) Willcox, Walter F. "A Statistician's Idea of Progress," *International Journal of Ethics*, XXIII (1913), 275–98.

(20) Zueblin, Charles. *American Municipal Progress*. Rev. ed. New York, 1916.

(21) Niceforo, Alfredo. *Les Indices numériques de la civilisation et du progrès*. Paris, 1921.

(22) Todd, A. J. *Theories of Social Progress*. Chap. vii, "The Criteria of Progress," pp. 113–53. New York, 1918.

TOPICS FOR WRITTEN THEMES

1. The History of the Concept of Progress
2. Popular Notions of Progress
3. The Natural History of Progress: Evolution of Physical and Mental Traits, Economic Progress, Moral Development, Intellectual Development, Social Evolution

4. Stages of Progress: Determined by Type of Control over Nature, Type of Social Organization, Type of Communication, etc.
5. Score Cards and Scales for Grading Communities and Neighborhoods
6. Progress as Wish-Fulfilment: an Analysis of Utopias
7. Criteria or Indices of Progress: Physical, Mental, Intellectual, Economic, Moral, Social, etc.
8. Progress as an Incident of the Cosmic Process
9. Providence versus Progress
10. Happiness as the Goal of Progress
11. Progress as Social Change
12. Progress as Social Evolution
13. Progress as Social Control
14. Progress and the Science of Eugenics
15. Progress and Socialization
16. Control through Eugenics, Education, and Legislation

QUESTIONS FOR DISCUSSION

1. What do you understand by progress?
2. How do you explain the fact that the notion of progress originated?
3. What is the relation of change to progress?
4. What is Spencer's law of evolution? Is it an adequate generalization? What is its value?
5. Why do we speak of "stages of progress"?
6. To what extent has progress been a result (a) of eugenics, (b) of tradition?
7. What do you understand by progress as (a) a historical process, and (b) increase in the content of civilization?
8. What is the relation of progress to happiness?
9. "We have confused rapidity of change with progress." Explain.·
10. "Progress is not automatic." Elaborate your position with reference to this statement.
11. What is the relation of prevision to progress?
12. Do you believe that mankind can control and determine progress?
13. "Our expectations of limitless progress cannot depend upon the deliberate action of national governments." Contrast this statement of Balfour with the statement of Dewey.
14. "A community founded on argument would dissolve into its constituent elements." Discuss this statement.
15. What is Galton's conception of progress?
16. What would you say to the possibility or the impossibility of the suggestion of eugenics becoming a religious dogma as suggested by Galton?

17. What is the relation, as conceived by the eugenists, as between germ plasm and culture?
18. Is progress dependent upon change in human nature?
19. How are certain persistent traits of human nature related to progress?
20. What is meant by the statement that progress is in the mores?
21. What are the different types of progress analyzed by Bryce? Has advance in each of them been uniform in the last one thousand years?
22. Does war make for or against progress?
23. What is the relation of freedom to progress?
24. What place has the myth in progress?
25. To what extent is progress as a process of realizing values a matter of temperament, of optimism, and of pessimism?

INDEX OF NAMES

[Page numbers in italics refer to selections or short extracts]

Abbott, Edith, 222, 570, 780
Abbott, Grace, 779
Abraham, Karl, 857
Abrahams, I., 942
Achelis, T., 937
Adams, Brewster, 646, 657
Adams, Brooks, 949, 1006
Adams, Charles C., 218, 555
Adams, Charles F., 760
Adams, Franklin P., 834
Adams, Henry, 5, 14, 15, 565
Addams, Jane, 329, 331, 335
Addison, Joseph, 66
Adler, Alfred, 147, 153, 497, 500, 641, 648, 649
Adler, H. M., 936
Alexander, H. B., 1008
Alexander, Samuel, 1007
Alexander the Great, 987
Alfred [pseud.], see Kydd, Samuel
Allier, R., 1004
Ambrosio, M. A. d', 567
Ames, Edward S., 426
Amiel, H., 154
Ammon, Dr. O., 534
Amsden, G. S., 155
Anderson, Nels, 731
Anderson, Wilbert L., 334
Andreä, Johann V., 1008
Andrews, Alexander, 859
Andrews, John B., 942
Anthony, Alfred W., 944
Anthony, Katharine S., 154, 941
Anthony, Susan B., 949
Antin, Mary, 774, 782
Antony, Marc, 386
Arc, Jeanne d', 419
Archer, T. A., 941
Aria, E., 947
Aristotle, 11, 29, 30, 32, 61, 143, 147, 158, 223, 226, 231, 261, 371, 373, 600, 640, 1000
Aronovici, Carol, 218, 781
Atkinson, Charles M., 948
Aubry, P., 937, 938
Audoux, Marguerite, 154
Auerbach, Bertrand, 274, 660, 778, 945

Augustinus, Aurelius (Saint Augustine), 125-26, 147, 154
Aurousseau, M., 218
Austin, George L., 948
Austin, John, 109
Austin, Mary, 881-83

Bab, Julius, 731
Babbitt, Eugene H., 275, 754-56
Babinsky, J. F., 650
Bachofen, J. J., 214, 219
Bacon, Lord Francis, 66, 233-34, 277, 1008
Baden-Powell, H., 219
Baer, Karl Ernst von, 518, 967
Bagehot, Walter, 423, 430, 495-96, 564, 565, 649, 1006
Bailey, Thomas P., 654, 728
Bailey, W. F., 778
Bailie, William, 566
Baillie, J. B., 151
Bain, A., 371
Bakeless, John, 651
Baker, Ray Stannard, 646, 654, 658, 936
Balch, Emily G., 780
Baldwin, J. Mark, 41, 88, 152, 153, 390, 423, 426, 430, 431, 649, 663-64, 719, 725, 727, 775, 1006
Balfour, Arthur James, 964, 977-79, 1004
Ballagh, James C., 857
Balzac, H. de, 145, 429
Bancroft, H. H., 941
Bang, J. P., 652
Barbellion, W. N. P. [pseud.], see Cummings, B. F.
Barclay, Robert, 944
Baring-Gould, S., 273
Barnes, Harry E., 660
Barr, Martin W., 936
Barrère, Albert, 428
Barrow, Sir John, 274
Barrows, Samuel J., 780
Barth, Paul, 3, 4, 217, 1004, 1005
Bartlett, D. W., 948
Bastian, A., 673, 787
Bastiat, Frédéric, 504-5, 552-53, 565, 573

Bates, Jean V., 778
Bauer, Arthur, 728, 949
Bauer, Otto, 777
Bauer, Wilhelm, 858
Bax, Ernest B., 943
Beard, Charles A., 498, 659
Beaulieu, P. Leroy-, see Leroy-Beaulieu, P.
Bechterew, W. v, 126-28, 153, 160, 345, 408-12, 415-20, 424, 431, 434, 494, 500
Beck von Mannagetta, G., 181
Beddoe, Dr. John, 535
Beecher, Franklin A., 940
Beer, M., 567
Beers, C. W., 155
Beethoven, Ludwig van, 228
Begbie, Harold, 727, 942
Behn, Dr., 366
Belisle, A., 946
Bell, Alexander G., 276
Bell, Sir Charles, 421
Bellamy, Edward, 1008
Bellet, Daniel, 946
Belloc, Hilaire, 654
Bennett, Arnold, 216
Bentham, Jeremy, 109, 500, 940, 948
Bentley, A. F., 458-61, 501, 503
Bergson, Henri, 373, 374, 422, 427, 964, 989-94, 1004
Bernard, Luther, L., 854, 1006
Bernhard, L., 275, 770, 945
Bernheim, A., 430
Bernheim, Hyppolyte, 265
Bertillon, Jacques, 265
Besant, Annie, 123, 124, 569, 949
Besant, Walter, 335
Best, Harry, 276, 568
Bevan, Edwyn R., 660
Beveridge, W. H., 568
Bhattacharya, Jogendra N., 728
Bigg, Ada H., 947
Binet, Alfred, 116-20, 148, 153, 157, 424, 431, 496
Bing, Alexander M., 652
Bismarck, Prince, 238, 239, 789, 793, 794
Björkman, Edwin A., 154

Blackmar, F. W., 499, 770
Blair, R. H., 362, 366
Blanchard, Phyllis, 649
Blanchard, R. H., 658
Bloch, Iwan, 221, 333
Blondel, H., 728
Blowitz, Henri de, 859
Blumenbach, J. F., 243
Bluntschli, Johann K., 659, 858
Blyden, Edward W., 654
Boas, Franz, 19, 156, 332, 660, 725, 730, 770, 776, 938
Bodenhafer, Walter B., 48
Bogardus, Emory S., 855
Böhme, Margarete, 652
Bohannon, E. W., 273
Bois, Henri, 943
Bonger, W. A., 563, 569
Bonnaterre, J. P., 276
Boodin, J. E., 426
Booth, Charles, 44, 45, 58, 212, 219, 335, 955
Booth, William, 942
Borght, R. van der, 428
Bosanquet, Bernard, 217
Bosanquet, Helen, 215, 222, 1007
Bossuet, J. B., 906
Botsford, George W., 940
Bouglé, C., 728
Bourde, Paul, 656
Bourgoing, P. de, 275, 945
Bourne, Rev. Ansel, 472, 473
Bourne, H. R. Fox, 565, 859
Boutmy, Émile, 940
Boutroux, Pierre, 652
Bovet, Pierre, 650
Bradford, Gamaliel, Jr., 731
Bradlaugh, Charles, 560
Bradley, F. H., 109
Bradley, Henry, 941
Braid, James, 424
Brailsford, H. N., 654
Braithwaite, W. C., 944
Brancoff, D. M., 945
Brandenburg, Broughton, 780
Brandes, Georg, 144, 498, 778
Braubach, W., 810
Breckinridge, Sophonisba P., 221, 222, 570, 781
Brehm, A. E., 810
Brent, Charles H., 855
Brentano, Lujo, 500, 659
Breuer, J., 838
Bridges, Horace, 781
Bridges, J. H., 58
Bridges, J. W., 148
Bridgman, Laura, 244, 366

Bright, John, 447
Brill, A. A., 273
Brinton, Daniel G., 666, 671–74, 725, 855, 857
Brissenden, Paul Frederick, 567, 658
Bristol, Lucius M., 718, 725
Brönner, W., 940
Bronner, Augusta F., 59, 155, 563
Brooks, John Graham, 567, 658, 925, 935
Browne, Crichton, 366
Browne, Sir Thomas, 65, 131
Bruhl, S. Lévy-. see Lévy-Bruhl, S.
Bruner, F. G., 156
Brunhes, Jean, 270, 274
Bryan, William J., 734
Bryce, James, 653, 655, 659, 726, 759, 779, 851, 852 n., 858, 861, 941, 984–89, 1004, 1011
Brynmor-Jones, David, 152, 945
Buchanan, J. R., 731
Buck, Carl D., 660
Buck, S. J., 942
Buckle, Henry Thomas, 4, 5, 270, 493, 498, 912, 1005
Bücher, Karl, 385–89, 428, 528–32, 728, 938
Bullock, Edward, 332
Bunyan, John, 125
Burckhard, M., 940
Burgess, Ernest W., 334, 426, 1007
Burgess, John, 741
Burgess, John S., 219
Burgess, Thomas, 780
Burgess, T. H., 366, 367, 368
Burke, Edmund, 449, 850
Burnell, A. C., 275
Burns, Allen T., 59, 335, 498, 773, 782
Burns, J., 943
Burr, Anna R., 727
Burton, Richard F., 152
Bury, J. B., 333, 958–59, 1004
Busch, Paul, 414
Bushee, F. A., 1005
Bussell, F W., 943
Buswell, Leslie, 651
Butler, Joseph, 430
Butler, Ralph, 660
Butler, Samuel, 1008
Butterfield, K. L., 1009
Buzzard, E. F., 650

Cabet, Étienne, 1008
Cabrol, F., 939

Cadière, L., 937
Caelius, 386
Caesar, 147, 238, 386, 387, 751
Cahan, Abraham, 782
Caird, Edward, 1005
Cairnes, J. E., 547, 548, 549
Calhoun, Arthur W., 215, 222, 726
Calvin, 817
Campanella, Tommaso, 1008
Campbell, John C., 274, 656
Campbell, Thomas J., 943
Campeano, M., 940
Canat, René, 273
Cannon, Walter B., 422, 427
Cardan, Jerome, 147
Carlile, Richard, 560
Carlton, Frank T., 658
Carlyle, Thomas, 494
Carnegie, Andrew, 670
Carpenter, Edward, 1004
Carr-Saunders, A. M., 564
Carter, George R., 565
Cartwright, Peter, 943
Carver, Thomas N., 1006
Case, Clarence M., 653, 1005
Case, S. J., 857
Castle, W. E., 131, 150
Caxton, William, 237
Cellini, Benvenuto, 154
Chabeneix, Paul, 855
Chapin, F. Stuart, 59, 855, 1007
Chapin, Robert C., 215, 221
Chapman, 298
Charcot, J. M., 147, 415, 424
Charlemagne, 238
Chen, T. A., 780
Cherrington, Ernest H., 942
Chevillon, André, 652
Chevreul, M. E., 462
Cheyney, Edward P., 499
Cheysson, E., 728
Chirol, Valentine, 96, 936
Chrestus, 386
Christensen, A., 939
Churchill, William, 275
Cicero, 386, 387
Ciszewski, S., 775
Claghorn, Kate H., 781
Clarendon, Earl of, 65
Clark, H., 939
Clark, John B., 545–51
Clark, Thomas A., 731
Claudius, Emperor, 598, 752
Clayton, H. H., 946
Clayton, Joseph, 854

Clemens, Samuel L., (Mark Twain, *pseud.*), 154, 314
Clements, Frederic E., 217, *525-27*, 555, 571
Clerget, Pierre, 947
Cleveland, Catharine C., 943
Clibborn, Edward, 542
Clodd, Edward, 857
Clough, H. W., 946
Cobb, Irvin, *835*
Cobden, Richard, 447, 948
Coblenz, Felix. 153
Codrington, R. H., 856
Coe, George Albert, *235-37*, 726
Coffin, Ernest W., 779
Cohen, Rose, 774, 782
Coicou, M., 728
Colcord, Joanna, 223
Coleman, Charles T., 940
Coleridge, Samuel T., 368
Collier, John, 731
Combarieu, J., 938
Commons, John R., 647, 658, 659, 776, 779, 860, 942
Comte, Auguste, 1, 2, 3, 4, 5, 6, 12, 24, 25, 39, 43, 44, 57, 60, 61, 68, 143, 210, 496, *716*, 959, *968-69*, 1005
Condorcet, Marie J. A. C., 3, 554, 1005
Conn, Herbert W., 1007
Connor, Dr. Bernard, 241
Constantin, A., 651
Conway, M., 939
Cook, Edward, 859
Cooley, Charles H., 56, 58, 67, *67-68*, *70-71*, 151, 157, 158, 159, 216, 285, 330, 421, 426, 431, 500, 649, *665*, *708-12*, *723*, 728, 729, 855, 934, 955, 1004
Coolidge, Mary R., 786
Corelli, Marie, 936
Cornish, Vaughan, 218
Cornyn, John H., *751-54*
Corot, Jean Baptiste Camille, 129
Cory, H. E., 731
Coulter, J. M., 131, 150
Crafts, L. W., *254-57*
Crawley, A. Ernest, 221, 282, *291-93*, 330, 332, 654, 850, 856, 939, 1006
Creel, George, 837
Creighton, Louise, 778
Crile, George W., *521-25*, 564, 572, 644, 783
Croce, Benedetto, 10
Croly, Jane (Mrs.), 941
Crooke, William, 276, 728, 777, 942

Crosby, Oscar T., 651
Crothers, Samuel M., 333
Crothers, T. D., 940
Crowell, John F., 565
Crozier, John B, 1008
Culin, Stewart, 656, 657
Cummings, B. F., 154
Cunningham, William, 565, 778
Cutler, James E., 655
Cutrera, A., 656
Cuvier, Georges, 809

D'Aeth, F. G., 729
D'Ambrosio, Manlio A., 566
Damiron, J. Ph., 649
Dana, Charles A., 858
Dana, Richard H., Jr., 275
Daniels, John, 781
Danielson, F. H., 150, 254
Dargun, L. von, 220
Darwin, Charles, 4, 7, 146, 167, 214, 329, 342, *361-65*, *365-70*, 421, 422, 425, 426, 433, 511, 512, 513, *514-18*, *518-21*, 555, 558, 564, 571, 644, 650, 663, 768, 810, 959, 1001
Daudet, Alphonse, 123
Daudet, Ernest, 651
Dauzat, Albert, 429
Davenport, C. B., 71, *131-36*, 150, 254, 569, 1007
Davenport, Frederick M., 932, 942
Davids, T. W. Rhys, 942
Davis, Elmer H., 859
Davis, H., 655
Davis, Jerome, 781
Davis, Katharine B., 570
Davis, Michael M., 781
Dawley, Almena, 570
Dealey, J. Q., 222
Deane, W. J., 238
DeGreef, Guillaume. 58
Delabarre, Frank A., 1009
Delbet, E., 728
Delbrück, H., 273, 777
Delesalle, Georges, 429
Dellepaine, A., 1007
Delvaille, Jules, 1004
De-Marchi, A., 856
Demolins, Edmond, 152, 333
Demoor, Jean, 1007
Demosthenes, 641
Densmore, Frances, 938
Desagher, Maurice, 276
Descartes, René, 372, 463, 465
Despine, Prosper, 937
Detweiler, F. G., 859
Devine. Edward T., 333, 491, 498, 568, 731

Devon, J., 570
Dewey, John *36*, *37*, *38*, *75-79*, 151, 152, 166, *184-87*, 202, 224, 424, 427, 430, 508, 964, *975-77*, 1004, 1010
Diaz, Porfirio, 987
Dibblee, G. Binney, 428
Dicey, A. V., *445-51*, 558, 793, 831, 851, 858
Dickinson, Z. C., 500
Diderot, Denis, 807
Dilich, Wilhelm, 241
Dinneen, P. S., 945
Disraeli, Benjamin, 721
Ditchfield, P. H., 333
Dixon, Roland B., 777, 854
Dixon, W. H., 944
Dobschütz, E. von, 333
Dodge, Raymond, *837-41*
Doll, E. A., *254-57*
Dominian, Leon, 274, 648, 945
Donovan, Frances, 570
Dorsey, J. Owen, 656, 711
Dostoévsky, F., 145, 273
Dowie, John Alexander, 944
Down, T. C., *895-98*, 941
Downey, June E., 149, 156
Drachsler, Julius, 774, 776, 781
Draghicesco, D., 728
Draper, J. W., 644, 649
Dubois, L. Paul, 945
Du Bois, W. E. Burghardt, 155. 222, 780, 782
Dugas, L., *370-75*, 422, 427
Dugdale, Richard L., 146, 150, 254
Dugmore, H. H., 861
Duguit, Léon, 860
Dumas, Georges, 938
Dunbar, Paul Lawrence, 630
Duncan, Sara Jeannette, 655
Durand, E. Dana, 652
Durkheim, Émile, 18, 33, 34, *35*, 36, 37, 38, *39*, 40, 58, 166, *195-98*, 217, 220, 222, 267, *268*, 343, 671, *714-18*, 723, 729, 854, 856, 894
Dushkin, Alexander M., 774, 781
Dutaillis, C. E. Petit-, *see* Petit-Dutaillis, C. E.

East, E. M., 131, 150
Eastman, R. S., 731
Eaton, Isabel, 780
Eddy, Arthur J., 566
Edie, Lionel D., 498
Edman, Irwin, 151
Edwards, Bryan, 727
Edwards, E., 942

Edwards, Lyford P., 940
Edwards, Milne, 518
Effertz, Otto, 564
Egerton, Charles E., 652
Egli, Emil, 943
Ehrenfels, Chrn. v., 500
Ehrlich, Eugen, 860
Elderton, Ethel M., 567, 569
Eliot, George, 145. 231
Eliot, Thomas D., 501
Elliott, A. M., 275
Ellis, Havelock, 151, 156, 215, 221, 223, 660, 726, 938, 957, 1007
Ellwood, Charles A., 41, 58, 567, 846-48, 949, 1007
Elsing, W. T., 567
Elster, Alexander, 567
Elworthy, F. T., 332
Ely, Richard T., 444-45, 502, 649, 855
Empedocles, 292
Empey, Arthur Guy, 429
Engel, Ernst, 215, 221
Engelgardt, A. N., 870
Engels, Frederick, 566, 568
Espinas, Alfred, 165, 167-68, 217, 223, 224, 407.
Estabrook, A. H., 150, 254
Eubank, Earle E., 222
Evans, F. W., 944
Evans, Maurice S., 646, 654, 811-12

Faber, Geoffrey, 660
Fadl, Said Memum Abul, 651
Fahlbeck, Pontus, 218
Fairchild, Henry P., 779, 780
Faria, Abbé, 424
Faris, Ellsworth, 150, 960-62
Farmer, John S., 428, 429
Farnell, L. R., 856
Farnam, Henry W., 569
Farquhar, J. N., 944
Faunce, W. H. P., 778
Fauriel, M. C., 937
Faust, Albert B., 780
Fawkes, J. W., 939
Fay, Edward A., 276
Federici, Romolo, 1006
Federtchouk, Y., 945
Féré, Ch., 405, 431
Ferguson, G. O., Jr., 156
Fernald, Mabel R., 570
Ferrari, G. C., 118
Ferrero, Guglielmo, 936
Feuerbach, Paul J. A. von, 276
Fichte, Johann G., 106-7

Field, J., 948
Field, James A., 567
Fielding-Hall, H., 651
Finck. Henry T., 221
Finlavson, Anna W., 150
Finney, C. G., 943
Finot, Jean, 654
Finsler, G., 937
Fischer, Eugen, 776
Fishberg, Maurice, 152, 271, 274, 431, 778
Fisher, H. A., 660
Flaten, Nils, 275
Fleming, Daniel J., 779
Fleming, Walter L., 730, 941
Fletcher, Alice C., 938
Flexner, Abraham, 570
Flint, Robert, 567, 953
Florian, Eugenio, 333
Fluegel, John Carl, 222
Flynt, Josiah [pseud.], see Willard, Josiah Flynt
Foerster, Robert F., 780
Foley, Caroline A., 947
Follett, M. P, 855, 860
Forel, A., 171, 172
Fornarsi di Verce, E., 570
Fosbroke, Thomas D., 274
Fosdick, H. E., 237
Foster William Z., 653
Fouillée, Alfred, 152, 155, 461-64, 499
Frame, Nat T., 1002
Francke, Kuno, 493, 498. 660
Frankfurter, Felix, 59
Frazer, J. G., 151, 220, 330, 850, 855. 856
Frederick the Great, 631, 986
Freeman, Edward A., 3, 10, 23
Freeman, R. Austin, 957, 1006
Freud, Sigmund, 41, 147, 154, 236, 329, 475, 478, 479, 482, 486, 487, 497, 500, 503, 641, 855, 857, 939
Friedländer, L., 935
Friedmann, Max, 927, 937
Friesen, P. M., 658
Frobenius, Leo, 643, 651, 730, 776, 1004
Froebel, F. W. A., 85
Froment, J., 650
Froude, James A., 1006
Fuller, Bampfylde, 935
Fustel de Coulanges, 854, 860

Gall, F. J., 148
Galpin, Charles J., 212, 218, 232, 247-49, 274, 278, 724, 731

Galton, Francis, 726 963, 979-83, 1007, 1010
Gamble, Sidney D., 219
Gardner, Charles S., 940
Gavit, John P., 781
Gebhart, Émile, 943
Geddes, P., 59, 156
Gehlke, Charles E., 39
Gehring, Johannes, 658
Gennep, A. van, 857, 939
George, Henry, 1009
Gerland, Georg, 270, 274, 856
Gesell, A. L., 150
Ghent, W. J., 936
Gibbins, Henry de B., 948
Gibbon, Edward, 711
Gibson, Thomas, 946
Gibson, William, 943
Giddings, Franklin H., 32, 33, 36, 40, 58, 498, 545, 613-19, 662, 735, 740, 1009
Gilbert, William S., 65
Gillen, F. J., 152, 220, 861
Gillin, J. L., 499, 568, 658
Ginsberg, M., 214, 220
Gladden, Washington, 491, 498
Glotz, Gustave, 656
Glynn, A. W. Wiston-, see Wiston-Glynn
Gobineau, Arthur de, 769
Goddard, Henry H., 134. 146, 148, 150, 155, 254, 568
Godkin, Edwin L., 858
Godwin, William, 554, 560
Goethe, Johann Wolfgang von, 129, 909, 967
Goitein, H., 861
Goldenweiser, A. A., 151, 777
Goltz, E. von der, 273
Goncourt, Edmond de, and Jules de, 405
Goodhart, S. P., 468
Goodsell, Willystine, 222
Gordon, Anna A., 949
Gordon, Ernest. 942
Goring, Charles, 148, 156
Gosnell, H. F., 660, 940
Gould, S. Baring-, see Baring-Gould, S.
Gowen, B. S., 937
Gowin, Enoch B., 855
Graebner, F., 777
Graetz, H., 944
Grant, Madison. 963
Gras, N. S. B., 543-45, 565
Grass, K., 658, 942
Grasserie, R. de la, see La Grasserie, R. de
Gratiolet, Pierre, 421

Gray, Thomas, 314
Gray, W., 856
Greco, Carlo Nardi-, *see* Nardi-Greco, Carlo
Greeley, Horace, 948
Green, Alice S. A., 334
Green, Samuel S., 780
Gregoire, *Abbé*, 451
Gregory XV, 837
Greig, J. Y. T., 427
Grenfell, George, 779
Grierson, *Sir* G., 687
Grierson, P. J. H., 565
Griffiths, Arthur, 273
Grinnell, G. B., 938
Groat, George G., 658
Groos, Karl, 427, 642, 643, 649
Grosse, Ernst, 221, *790*, 938
Grote, George, 233, *260–64*, 853
Grotjahn, Alfred, 567
Groves, E. R., 941
Grundtvig, N. F. S., *Bishop*, 931
Gulick, J. T., 227
Gulick, Sidney L., 431, 781
Gummere, Amelia M., 274
Gummere, F. B., 938
Gumplowicz, Ludwig, 212, 341, *346–48*, 420, 426, 432, 645, 648, 776
Guyot, Edouard, 567

Hadley, Arthur T., 659
Haeckel, Ernst, 912
Hagens, J. von, 171
Haines, Lynn, 659
Haldane, *Viscount*, *105–11*
Hall, Arthur C., 1009
Hall, Frederick S., 652
Hall, G. Stanley, 80, 153, 427, 650
Hall, H. Fielding-, *see* Fielding-Hall, H.
Hall, W. P., 565
Hammer, von, 380
Hammond, Barbara, 334
Hammond, John L., 334
Haney, Lewis H., 566
Hanford, Benjamin, 653
Hanna, Charles A., 780
Hanna, *Rev.* Thomas C., 468, 469
Hansen, F. C. C., 431, 534
Hansen, J., 937
Hanson, William C., 569
Hapgood, Hutchins, 154, 731, 782
Harlan, Rolvix, 944
Harnack, Adolf, **941**

Harper, Ida H., 949
Harrington, James, 1008
Harris, Benjamin, 834
Harris, Emerson P. and Florence H., 859
Harris, George, 1005, 1009
Harrison, Frederic, 1007
Harrison, James A., 275
Harrison, Jane E., 17, *18*, 856, 857
Harrison, Shelby M., 59, 219, 858
Hart, A. B., 498
Hart, Joseph K., 731
Hartenberg, P., 940
Harttung, Pflugk-, *see* Pflugk-Harttung
Hasanovitz, Elizabeth, 782
Hasbach, Wilhelm, 495
Hassert, Kurt, 218
Hauser, Caspar, 239
Hawthorne, Nathaniel, 237
Hayes, A. W., 731
Hayes, Edward C., 499
Hayes, Mary H., 570
Hayes, Samuel P., 943
Haynes, E. S. P., 650
Haynes, Frederick E., 659
Headlam, Cecil, 946
Healy, William, 59, 155, 273, 563, 648, 935
Hearn, Lafcadio, 938
Heaton, John L., 858
Hecker, J. F. C., 875, *879–81*, 937
Heckethorn, C. W., 274, 729
Hegel, G. W. F., 69, 159, 959
Heidenhain, R., 415
Heijningen, Hendrik M. K. van, 656
Hellpach, W., 152
Helps, Sir Arthur, *66*, 727
Hempl, George, 275
Henderson, Charles R., 567
Henderson, Ernest N., 424, 430
Henry, R., 945
Héricourt, J., 118
Hermann, F. B. W. v., 499
Heron, David, 561, 567
Herschel, *Sir* J. F. W., 1001
Hertzka, Theodor, 1008
Hertzler, Joyce O., 1008
Hess, Grete Meisel-, *see* Meisel-Hess
Hibben, J. G., 1006
Hichborn, Franklin, 659
Hicks, Mary L., 731

Higgs, Henry, *557*
Hill, Georgiana, 948
Hinde, Sidney L., *869* n.
Hinds, William A., 334
Hirn, Yrjö, 344, *401–7*, 427, 430, 434, 808, 869, 870, 938
Hirt, Eduard, 155
Hitti, Philip K., 781
Hobbes, Thomas, 25, 29, 30, 61, 109, 143, 158, 223, 511, 645
Hobhouse, Leonard T., 56, *192–95*, 214, 220, 224, 728, 795, *796*,*798* n., 849, 854, 963, 964, *969–73*, 1006, 1007
Hobson, John A., 568
Hocart, A. M., 749
Hoch, A., 155, 273
Hocking, W. E., *98–100*, 151, *207–9*
Hodder, Edwin, 948
Hogarth, William, 402
Holdsworth, W. S., 861
Hollingworth, Leta S., 155, 156
Hollman, Anton H., 931
Holmes, O. W., Jr., 836, 853
Holmes, S. J., 1007
Holmes, William H., 948
Holt, Edward B., *478–82*, 500, 503
Home, H., *Lord Kames*, 402
Homer, 264
Hooper, Charles E., 332
Horn, Paul, 429
Hotten, John C., 429
Howard, G. E., 214, 222, 941
Howard, John, 948
Howells, William Dean, 630
Hoxie, Robert F., 647, 658
Hoyt, C. F., 657
Hubert, H., 856
Hudson, Frederic, 859
Hudson, W. H., *245–47*, 278, 332, *604–5*, *883–86*
Hughes, Charles E., 1009
Hughes, Henry, 430
Hugo, Victor, 429
Hulme, E. M., 943
Humboldt, Alexander von 673, 909
Hume, David, 3, 430, 554, 786, *829–30*
Hunter, Robert, 653
Huntington, Ellsworth, 328, *666*, 726
Huot, Louis, 650
Hupka, S. von, 333
Hurry, Jamieson B., 946
Huxley, Thomas H . 963

Hyde, 749
Hyndman, Henry M., 949

Inge, William R., *954*, 959, *1001*, 1004
Ingersoll, Robert, 912
Ingram, John K., 565, 675
Ireland, W. W., 941
Irving, L., 1009
Irwin, Will, 858
Itard, *Dr.* Jean E. M. G., 242, *271-72*, 276
Iyer, L. K. A. K., 728

Jacobowski, L., 221
Jakstas, A., 946
James, B. B., 944
James, E. O., 855
James, William, 80, *122-26*, 151, 153, 421, 427, 472, 473, 486, 598, 662, 669, 726, 736, 932
Janes, George M., 652
Janet, Pierre, 147, 430, 474, 935
Jankelevitch, S., 1005
Jannasch, R., 726
Jarau, G. Louis-, *see* Louis-Jarau
Jarrett, Mary C., 569, 648
Jastrow, J., 335
Jefferson, Thomas, 40
Jellinek, Georg, 725
Jenks, Albert, 211, 219, 775
Jenks, Edward, 861
Jenks, Jeremiah, 779
Jennings, Hargrave, 730
Jennings, H. S., 150, 285, 488
Jephson, Henry, 858
Jespersen, Otto, 428
Jevons, William S., 500, 948
Jhering, Rudolph von, 861
Johnson, James W., 154
Johnson, John H., 657
Johnson, R. H., 568, 1007
Johnson, Samuel, 451
Johnson, W., 777
Johnston, C., 655
Johnston, Harry H., 779
Johnston, R. M., 730
Jones, David Brynmor-, *see* Brynmor-Jones
Jones, Edward D., 946
Jones, Rufus M., 944
Jonson, Ben, 239
Jordanes, 941
Joseph II, of Austria, 934
Jost, M., 944
Jouffroy, T. S., 402
Judd, Charles H., *381-84*, *390-91*

Jung, Carl G., 77, 147, 236, 497, 500, 857
Junius [*pseud.*], 858
Juquelier, P., 411, 412, 937

Kaindl, Raimund F., 770, 778
Kalb, Ernst, 658
Kallen, Horace M., 778, 781
Kammerer, Percy G., 223
Kan, J. van, 570
Kant, Immanuel, 85, 111, 420, 909
Kapp, Friedrich, 780
Kaufmann, Moritz, 1008
Kaupas, H., 946
Kautsky, Karl, 333
Kawabé, Kisaburo, 428
Keith, Arthur, 660
Keller, Albert G., 72, *137-38*, 160, 651, 719, 725, 1007
Keller, Helen, 154, 231, *243-45*, 278
Kellogg, Paul U., 59, 219
Kellogg, Walter G., 731
Kelly, J. Liddell, 778
Kelsen, Hans, 860
Kelsey, Carl, 1007
Kelynack, T. N., 569
Kemble, Frances A., 728
Kennedy, Albert J., 731
Kenngott, G. F., 219
Kent, Frank R., 940
Kerlin, Robert T., 660
Kerner, R. J., 777
Kerr, Norman S., 569
Kerschensteiner, Georg, 90
Kettle, T. M., 945
Key, Ellen, 214, 221
Key, Wilhelmina, 254
Khoras, P, 950
Kidd, Benjamin, 1096
Kidd, D., 152
Kilpatrick, James A., 651
King, Irving, 153, 949
Kingsbury, J. E., 428
Kingsford, C. L., 941
Kingsley, Charles, 273
Kingsley, Mary H., 770
Kipling, Rudyard, 67
Kirchhoff, G. R., 13
Kirkpatrick, E. A., 153
Kistiakowski, *Dr.* Th., 217
Kite, Elizabeth S., 150, 254
Klein, Henri F., 730
Klenz, Heinrich, 429
Kline, L. W., 221
Kluge, F., 429
Knapp, G. F., 217, 564, 729

Kneeland. George J., 570
Knopf, S. A. 1009
Knortz, Karl, 275
Knowles, L. C. A., 565
Knowlson, T. Sharper, *237-30*
Kober, George M., 569
Kobrin, Leon, 219
Kocourek, Albert, 852, 854, 860
Kohle, Josef, 566, 854, 856
Kolthamer, F. W., 559
Koren, John, 569
Kostir, Mary S., 150, 254
Kostyleff, N., 500, 855
Kotik, *Dr.* Naum, 937
Kovalewsky, M., 220, 728
Kowalewski, A., 156
Kraepelin, E., 149, 155
Krauss, F. S., 152
Kreibig, Josef K., 500
Kroch, Arthur. 858
Kroeber, A. L., 948
Kropotkin, P., 566, 949
Kudirka, *Dr.* V., 932
Kydd, Samuel (Alfred, *pseud.*), 568

La Bruyère, Jean de, 147, 154
Lacombe, Paul, 498
Lafargue, G., 728
Lagorgette, Jean, 651
La Grasserie, R. de, 650, 728
La Hodde. Lucien de, 730
Laidler, Harry W., 653
Lamarck, J. B., 146
Lamprecht, Karl, 493, *494*, 498, 1005
Landauer, G., 949
Lane, W. D., 657
Lane-Poole, S., 935
Lang, Andrew, 276
Lang, Lewis J., 659
Lang, R., 152
Lange, C. G., 421
Langenhove, Fernand van, *819-22*, 857
Lankester, E. Ray, 1004
Lapouge, V., 266
La Rochefoucauld, François de, 371
La Rue, William, 944
Lasch, R., 221
Lasker, Bruno, 568, 949
Laski, Harold, 860
Laubach, Frank C., 333
Lauck, William J., 779
Law, John, 946
Lay, Wilfrid, 649
Lazarus, Moritz, 21, 217, 428

Lea, Henry C., 656, 658
Le Bon, Gustave, 33, 34, 41, 58, 156, 166, *202-3*, 213, 218, 225, 660, 857, 867, *868*, 869, *871*, 876, *887-93*, 894, *905-9*, 927, 934, 939, 949, 950, 951
Lebrun, Mme. Vigée, 907
Lecky, W. E. H., 644, 650, 858, 875, *915-24*
Lee, Ann, 944
Lee, James Melvin, 859
Lee, Vernon (*pseud.*), 402, 878
Le Gouix. M., 728
Lehmann, A., 431
Leibnitz, Gottfried W., 396
Leiserson, William M., 781
Leland, C. G., 429
Leonard, O., 655
Leopold III, 797
Leopold, Lewis, *807-11*, 854
Le Play, P. G. Frédéric, 59, 215, 221
Leroy-Beaulieu, P., 726
Lester, J. C., 730
Letelier, Valentin, 1005
Letourneau, Ch., 220, 643, 650, 727, 854
Letzner, Karl, 275
Levine, Louis, 657, 658
Levland, Jorgen, 930
Lévy-Bruhl, L., 24, 151, 332
Levy, Hermann, 565
Lewis, George C., 858
Lewis, Matthew, G., *677-81*
Lewis, Sinclair, 213, 219
Lewisohn, Ludwig, 782
Lhérisson, E., 938
Lhermitte, J., 650
L'Houet, A., 334
Lichtenberger, J. P., 222
Lilienfeld, Paul von, 28, 58, 567
Lillehei, Ingebrigt, 660
Limousin, Ch., 728
Lindeman, Eduard, 59, 731
Linnaeus, 515
Linton, E. L., 947
Lippert, Julius, 151
Lippmann, Walter, 151, *834-37*, 851, 857, 859, 936, 948
Lisch, R., 428
Lloyd, A. H., 1004
Lockwood, George B., 944
Loeb, Jacques, 82, 83, 84, 150, 467, 494
Löwenfeld, L., 155, 410
Loisy, Alfred, 939
Lombroso, Cesare, 148, 155, 563, 950
Lord, Eliot, 780

Lord, Herbert Gardiner, 650
Loria, A., 498
Lotze, Hermann, 420, 426
Loughborough, J. N., 944
Louis-Jarau, G., 945
Loutschisky, I., 728
Love, Albert G., 569
Lowell, Amy. 834
Lowell, A. Lawrence, 659, 792, *826-29*, 851, 857, 864
Lowie, Robert H., 18, *19*, 220, 723, 729, 777
Lubbock, J., 182, 396
Lucretius, 953, 965, 966
Ludwig, E., 651
Lummis, Charles F., 939
Luther, Martin, 817
Lyall, Sir Alfred, 108
Lyell, Charles, 768
Lyer, F. Müller-, *see* Müller-Lyer
Lytton, Edward-Bulwer. 1008

Macaulay, T. B., 142
Macbeth, A., 153
McCormac, E. I., 727
M'Culloch, O. C., 146, 150
MacCurdy, J. T., 936
Macdonagh, Michael, 851, 859
McDougall, William, 58, 426, 441, *464-67*, 496, 501, 655, 721, 726, 963
McGee, W J, 211, 219, 777, 861, 1006
Mach, Ernst, 13
Machiavelli, 100, 143
Maciver, R. M., 426
McIver, J., 569
Mackay, Charles, 947
Mackay, R. W., 649
MacKay, Thomas, 558, 566
McKenzie, F. A., 775
Mackenzie, J. S., 1004
McKenzie, R. D., 218, 498
McLaren, A. D., 660
MacLean, J. P., 943
McLennan, J. F., 220
McMurtrie, Douglas C., 560
McVey, Frank L., 942
Macrosty, Henry W., 565
Mahomet, 419
Maine, Sir Henry S., 219, 220. 556, 565, 710, 826, 852, *853*. 854, 860, 862
Maitland, Frederic W., 861
Malinowski, Bronislaw, 220
Mallery, Garrick, 422, 427
Mallock, W. H., 729, 948, 1009
Maloney, E. F., 936

Malthus, T. R., *7*, 515, 554, 555, 560, 562, 564
Mandeville, Bernard de, 1008
Marchi, A. De-, *see* De-Marchi, A.
Marot, Helen, 658
Marpillero, G., 335
Marshall, Alfred, 499, 564
Marshall, Henry R., 426, *600-3*
Martin, E. D., 939
Martineau, Harriet, 1, 2, 57, 562
Marvin, Francis S., 778, *965-66*
Marx, Karl, 77, 343, 562. 566, 568, 912, 1008
Mason, Otis T., 302, 428, 431, 941
Mason, William A., 428
Massart, J., 218, 1007
Mathiez, Albert, 658
Matthews, Brander, 948
Matthews, W., 938
Maublanc, René, 651
Mauss, M., 856
Maxon, C. H., 943
Mayer, Émile, 652
Mayer, J. R., 768
Mayo-Smith, Richmond, 741. 776, 778
Mazzini, 817
Mead, G. H., 424, 426
Meader, John R., 942
Means, Philip A., 654
Mecklin, John M., 654, 730
Medlicott, H. B., *377*
Meillet, A., 275, 945
Meinong, Alexius, 500
Meisel-Hess, Grete, 214, 221
Mendel, G., 71. 146, 157
Menger, Karl, 499
Mensch, Ella, 936
Mercier, C. A., 500
Meredith, George, 145
Merker, *Polizeirat*, 240
Merriam, Charles E., 659, 792, 940
Mesmer, F. A., 424
Metcalf, H. C., 152
Meumann, Ernst, 89
Meyer, Adolph, 285, 488
Meyer, J. L., 937
Miceli, V., 939
Michels, Robert, 647, 659
Michiels, A., 373, 374
Miklosich, Franz, 655
Mill, James, 451
Mill, John Stuart, 547. 561, 850, 1005
Miller, Arthur H., 855

Miller, Edward, 944
Miller, Herbert A., 335, 656, 660, 781, 786–87, 870
Miller, J. D., 948
Miller, Kelly, 140, 251, 654
Millingen, J. G., 656
Millioud, Maurice, 858
Millis, Harry A., 780
Milmine, Georgine, 658
Miner, Maude, 570
Minin, 415
Mirabeau, Octave, 154
Mitchell, P. Chalmers, 172–75
Mitchell, Wesley C., 946
Moede, Walther, 941
Moll, Albert, 88–92, 332, 412–15, 430, 894
Moltke, Count von, 670, 793–94 n.
Monin, H., 728
Montague, G., 7
Montague, Helen, 156
Montesquieu, Baron de, 3, 270
Montgomery, K. L., 945
Moody, Dwight L., 945
Moody, W. R., 943
Mooney, James, 943
Moore, Edward C., 778
Moore, Henry L., 946
Moore, William H., 777
More, Hannah, 949
More, Thomas, 1008
Moreau de Tours, 938
Morel, E. D., 779, 797
Morgan, Alexander, 1009
Morgan, C. Lloyd, 150, 188, 189, 342, 375–79, 431, 494, 725
Morgan, E. L., 731
Morgan, Lewis H., 214, 740
Morgan, W. T., 659
Morley, John, 725, 948, 1006
Morris, Lloyd R., 660
Morris, William, 1008
Morrison, W. D., 92
Morrow, Prince A., 223
Morse, Josiah, 156, 655
Morselli, Henry, 266, 272
Mosiman, Eddison, 937
Mouromtzeff, Mme. de, 728
Müller, F. Max, 342, 379–81, 395, 433
Müller, Fritz, 520
Müller-Lyer, F., 1006
Mumford, Eben, 855
Mumford, Lewis, 1008
Münsterberg, Hugo, 424, 428, 431, 668, 688–92, 726, 936
Murray, W. A., 939

Myers, C. S., 92–95, 936
Myers, Gustavus, 659
Myerson, Abraham, 223, 936

Napoleon I, 28, 207, 238, 241, 419, 631, 698, 789
Napoleon III, 698, 793
Nardi-Greco, Carlo, 861
Nasmyth, George, 1009
Nassau, R. H., 856
Naumann, Friedrich, 652, 809
Neatby, W. Blair, 944
Necker, J., 907
Neill, Charles P., 653
Neilson, George, 656
Nesbitt, Florence, 221
Nesfield, John C., 218, 681–84
Neter, Eugen, 273
Nevins, Allan, 859
Nevinson, Margaret W., 568
Newell, W. W., 940
Newton, Sir Isaac, 13, 973
Niceforo, Alfredo, 568, 1003, 1009
Nicolai, G. F., 644
Nieboer, Dr. H. J., 674–77, 727, 732
Nietzsche, F. W., 599
Nims, Harry D., 566
Nitsch, C., 946
Noiré, L., 395
Nordau, Max, 935, 1004
Nordhoff, Charles, 334, 657
Norlie, O. M., 775
Novicow, J., 212, 426, 645, 649, 740, 741, 775, 854

Oakesmith, John, 648, 660
Oberholtzer, E. P., 859
Obolensky, L. E., 1008
O'Brien, Frank M., 859
O'Brien, Frederick, 657
Odin, Alfred, 855
Odum, Howard, 152
Oertel, Hans, 22
Ogburn, W. F., 215, 498, 1006
Ogden, C. K., 427
Oldenburg, H., 856
Older, Fremont, 659
Olgin, Moissaye J., 949
Oliver, Frederick S., 651
Oliver, Thomas, 568
Olmsted, F. L., 727
Oncken, August, 565
Oppenheimer, Franz, 50, 647
Ordahl, George, 642, 649
Ormond, Alexander T., 340, 420, 426

Orth, Samuel P., 659
Osborne, T. M., 563
Osten, von, 413, 414, 430
Osterhausen, Dr., 240
Ostrogorskii, Moisei, 659
Otto the Great, 591
Owen, Richard, 768
Owen, Robert Dale, 560
Paget, Sir James, 366
Pagnier, Armand, 156, 333
Paine, Thomas, 912
Palanti, G., 940
Pandian, T. B., 333 .
Park, Robert E., 1–57, 79–84, 138–42, 157, 158, 187–91, 200–202, 218, 224, 252–54, 311–15, 315–17, 335, 430, 467–78, 619–26, 626–34, 655, 656, 712–14 756–62, 775, 781, 783, 786–87, 829–33, 859, 870, 893–95, 930, 934, 939
Parker, Carleton H., 152, 494, 936
Parkman, Francis, 777, 778
Parmelee, Maurice, 217, 568, 570, 1009
Parsons, Elsie Clews, 220
Parton, James, 654
Partridge, G. E., 569, 726
Pascal, B., 463
Pascoe, C. F., 778
Pasteur, Louis, 44
Pater, Walter, 938
Patetta, F., 656
Paton, Stewart, 150
Patrick, G. T. W., 593–600, 643, 644, 650, 935, 947, 948
Patten, Simon N., 498, 1008
Patterson, M. R., 727
Patterson, R. J., 727
Paulhan, Fr., 332, 730
Pavlov, I. P., 494, 830
Payne, George Henry, 428
Pearson, Karl, 13, 14, 948, 963, 1007
Pélissier, Jean, 932, 946
Pennington, Patience, 334
Percin, Alexandre, 650
Periander, 67
Pericles, 261
Perry, Bliss, 40
Perry, Ralph B., 426, 1007
Perty, M., 809
Peter the Great, 419, 934
Peter the Hermit, 877
Peterson, J., 150, 941
Petit-Dutaillis, C. E., 651
Petman, Charles, 275
Petrie, W. M. F., 940
Pfister Ch., 275

Pfister, Oskar, 500, 857
Pfleiderer, Otto, 730
Pflugk-Harttung, Julius von, 941
Pfungst, Oskar, 430
Philippe, L., 728
Phillips, Ulrich B., 727
Phillips, W. Alison, 793-94 n.
Phillips, Wendell, 948
Picard, Edmond, 860
Piderit, T., 421, 427
Pillsbury, W. B., 648, 650, 654
Pinet, G., 728
Pintner, Rudolf, 155, 568
Pitre, Giuseppe, 939
Place, Francis, 560
Plato, 99, 108, 238, 261, 607, 986, 1008
Platt, Thomas G., 659
Ploss, H., 220
Plunkitt, G. W., 660
Pollock, Frederick, 861
Pope, Alexander, 283 n.
Popenoe, Paul, 568, 1007
Porter, W. T., 650
Post, Albert H., 851-52, 860
Pound, Arthur, 335
Pound, Roscoe, 59, 860
Powell, H. Baden-, see Baden-Powell, H.
Poynting, J. H., 13
Prescott, Frederick C., 938
Preuss, Hugo, 334
Preyer, W., 87
Price, Dr., 554
Price, G. F., 569
Price, Maurice T., 779
Prince, Morton, 70, 113-16, 153, 474, 477, 648, 720, 777
Prince, Samuel H., 950
Probst, Ferdinand, 147, 154
Proudhon, P. J., 566
Puchta, G. F., 677
Puffer, J. Adams, 646, 657

Rainwater, Clarence E., 731, 942
Ralph, Julian, 275
Rambosson, J., 938
Randall, E. O., 944
Rank, Otto, 857
Rastall, B. M., 653
Ratzel, Friedrich, 151, 270, 274, 298-301, 728, 770, 776
Ratzenhofer, Gustav, 36, 58, 212, 421, 496, 645, 648, 775
Rauber, August, 241, 242, 243, 276
Ravage, M. E., 774, 782

Ray, P. O., 659
Reclus, E., 1005
Reed, V. Z., 938
Regnard, P., 937
Reich, Emil, 777
Reinheimer, H., 218
Reuter, E. B., 567, 770, 776
Rhodes, J. F., 657
Rhŷs, John, 152, 945
Ribot, Th. A., 111-13, 127, 147, 153, 344, 394-97, 427, 430, 431, 433, 465, 496, 501, 940
Ribton-Turner, Charles J., 333
Ricardo, David, 545, 547, 559
Rice, Stuart A., 498
Richard, T., 942
Richards, Caroline C., 305-11
Richards, I. A., 427
Richet, Ch., 116, 118, 430
Richmond, Mary E., 59, 215, 221, 491, 498
Rickert, Heinrich, 10, 1005
Rihbany, Abraham M., 774, 781, 782
Riis, Jacob A., 568, 781
Riley, I. W., 154
Riordan, William L., 660
Ripley, William Z., 264-68, 274, 533-37, 572, 725, 776
Risley, Herbert H., 681-84, 684-88, 728
Ritchie, David G., 725
Rivarol, Antoine, 908
Rivers, W. H. R., 211, 219, 220, 723, 729, 738, 746-50, 776, 857
Roberts, Peter, 219
Robertson, John M., 644, 649, 861, 1009
Roberty, E. de, 728
Robinson, Charles H., 778
Robinson, James Harvey, 5, 6, 498
Robinson, Louis, 85
Roepke, Dr. Fritz, 652
Rogers, Edward S., 566
Rogers, James B., 943
Rohde, Erwin, 658
Romanes, G. J., 227, 379
Roosevelt, Theodore, 659, 776
Rosanoff, A. J., 135
Roscher, W., 726
Ross, Edward A., 58, 213, 499, 725, 779, 849, 854, 936
Rossi, Pasquale, 658, 927, 937, 939, 940
Rothschild, Alonzo, 855
Rousiers, Paul de, 731
Rousseau, Jean Jacques, 110, 142, 223, 231, 234-35, 241, 278, 807, 850

Roussy, G., 650
Routledge, Mrs. Scoresby, 274
Rowntree, B. Seebohm, 59, 567, 568, 569
Royce, Josiah, 153, 390, 426, 427, 430, 431, 655
Rubinow, I. M., 569
Rudolph, Heinrich, 427
Rudolphi, K. A., 243
Ruml, Beardsley, 570
Russell, B. A. W., 566
Russell, J. H., 727
Ryckère, Raymond de, 570

Sabine, Lorenzo, 656
Sadler, G. T., 854
Sageret, J., 858
Săineanu, Lazar, 429
Saint-Simon, C. H. comte de, 3, 4
Saleeby, Caleb W., 1007
Salmon, Lucy M., 859
Salt, Henry S., 1009
Salz, Arthur, 729
Samassa, P., 945
Sandburg, Carl, 655
Sands, B., 945
Santayana, G., 983
Sapper, Karl, 779
Sarbah, John M., 860
Sartorius von Walterhausen, August, 727
Saunders, F. H., 427
Scalinger, G. M., 940
Schaeffle, Albert, 28, 58
Schatz, Albert, 564
Schechter, S., 944
Schmidt, Caspar, 566, 830
Schmidt, N., 942
Schmoller, Gustav, 428, 728
Schmucker, Samuel M. (ed.), 334
Schoell, Frank L., 655
Schopenhauer, Arthur, 964, 994-1000
Schurtz, Heinrich, 723, 729, 947
Schuster, G., 730
Schwartz, 85
Schwittau, G., 652
Scott, Walter D., 858
Seager, Henry R., 653
Secrist, Frank K., 428
Seebohm, Frederic, 219, 861
Seguin, Edward, 276
Selbie, W. B., 944
Seligman, E. R. A., 564
Seligmann, H. J., 655
Séménoff, E., 728

Semple, Ellen C., *268–69*, 274, *289–91*, *301–5*

Sergi, G., 1004

Seton, Ernest Thompson, *886–87*

Seton-Watson, R. W., 945

Shafer, Robert, 1005

Shaftesbury, *Seventh Earl of*, 948

Shakespeare, William, 238, 239

Shaler, N. S., 151, 233, *257–59*, 283, *294–98*, 330, 337, 654, 726, 947

Shambaugh, Berta, 944

Shand, A. F., 153, 465, 477, 496, 497, 501

Sheldon, H. D., 657

Shepard, W. J., 858

Sherrington, C. S., 839

Shinn, Milicent W., *85–88*, 153

Shonle, Ruth, 943

Short, Wilfrid M., *977–79*, 1004

Sicard, *Abbé*, 242

Sidis, Boris, *415–16*, 424, 431, 468

Sighele, Scipio, 41, 58, *202–7*, 213, 218, 647, 722, 867, 872, 894, 927, 939

Simkhovitch, (Mrs.) Mary K., 331, 335

Simmel, Georg, 10, 36, 58, 154, 217, 218, 221, 286, *322–27*, 331, 332, 341, 342, *348–56*, *356–61*, 421, 426, 432, 434, 500, *553–54*, 560, 564, *582–86*, *586–94*, 642, 648, 661, 668, 670, *695–97*, *697–703*, *703–6*, *706–8*, 720, 725, 726, 729, 733, 938, 947, 1004, 1005

Simon, Th., 148, 157

Simons, A. M., *443–44*, 502

Simons, Sarah E., *740–41*, 775, 783

Simpson, Bertram L., 653

Sims, George R., 568

Sims, Newell L., 218, 334

Sinclair, Upton, 859

Skeat, Walter W., 275

Small, Albion W., 36, 58, *198–200*, *288–89*, 332, 348, 421, 426, *451–54*, *454–58*, 496, 499, 502, 582, 586, 648, 660, 695, 697, 703, 706, 726, 1005

Small, Maurice H., *239–43*

Smedes, Susan D., 334, 727

Smith, Adam, 344, *397–401*, 401, 430, 432, 433, 447, 449, 495, 504, *551–52*, 554, 555, 557, 559, 573

Smith, Arthur H., 334

Smith, G. Elliot, 776

Smith, Henry C., 944

Smith, J. M. P., 854

Smith, *Lieut.* Joseph S., *800–805*

Smith, Lorenzo N., 429

Smith, Richmond Mayo-, *see* Mayo-Smith, Richmond

Smith, W. Robertson, 16, *812–16*, *822–26*, 857

Smyth, C., 655

Socrates, 108, 143, 646

Solon, 261

Sombart, Werner, *317–22*, 335, 568, 651, 933, 947

Somló, F., 728

Sorel, Georges, 648, *816–19*, 856, 959, 1004

Southard, E. E., 648, 1007

Spadoni, D., 730

Spargo, John, *909–15*, 949, 952

Speek, Peter A., 781

Speer, Robert E., 778

Spencer, Baldwin, 152, 220, 861

Spencer, Herbert, 24, 25, 26, 27, 28, 43, 44, 58, 60, 61, 144, 210, 217, 396, 402, 495, 558, 566, 787, *805–7*, 818, 831, 849, 855, 889, 947, 959, 963, *966–68*, 1001, 1006, 1010

Spengler, Oswald, 335, 935

Spiller, G. (ed.), *92–95*, 654

Spranger, Eduard, 153

Spurzheim, J. F. K., 148

Spykman, N. J., 58

Squillace, Fausto, 947

Stalker, James, 943

Stanhope, Philip Henry (Fourth Earl), 276

Stanley, H. M., 427

Stanley, L. L., 569

Stanton, Henry B., 948

Starbuck, Edwin D., 332, 726

Starcke, C. N., 220

Stchoukine, Ivan, 943

Stead, W. T., 781, 859

Steffens, Lincoln, 331

Stein, L., 566

Steiner, Edward A., 779, 782

Steiner, Jesse F., 335, 619, 624, 625, 646, 654, 731, 935

Steinmetz, Andrew, 656, 657

Steinmetz, S. R., 651, 656, 860

Steinthal, H., 21, 217

Stephen, Sir Leslie, 649

Stephenson, Gilbert T., 654

Stern, B., 89, 90, 152, 153

Stern, (Mrs.) Elizabeth G., 774, 782

Stern, W., 155

Stevens, David H., 859

Stevens, W. H. S., 566

Stewart, Dugald, 402, 430

Stillson, Henry L., 730

Stimson, Frederic J., *843–46*

Stirner, Max [*pseud.*], *see* Schmidt, Caspar

Stoddard, Lothrop, 654, 936, 950, 963

Stoker Bram 731

Stoll, Otto, 221, 332, 431, 926 f., 937

Stone, Alfred H., *634–40*, 654

Stone, B. W., 943

Stone, Melville E., 859

Stoughton, John, 948

Stout, G. F., 344, *391–94*, 424

Stow, John, 219

Strachey, Lytton, 721, 962

Straticò, A., 940

Stratton, George M., 650

Stratz, Carl H., 947

Strausz, A., 152

Stromberg, A. von, 942

Strong, Anna L., 273

Stubbs, William, 353, 354

Stumpf, C., 413, 414

Su, S. G., 222

Sugenheim, S., 727

Sullivan, Anne, 243, 244

Sully, J., 153, 332, 422, 427

Sumner, Helen L., 942

Sumner, William G., 36, 37, 46, *100–103*, 146, 151, 283, *293–94*, 333, 643, 650, 759, 779, 796, 797, 831, *841–43*, 849, 854, 866, 875, 933, 947, 948, *953–84*

Swift, Jonathan, 67

Szende, Paul, 950

Tabbé, P., 945

Taft, Donald R., 781

Taft, Jessie, 941

Taine, H. A., 144, *493*, 498, 907, 935, 949

Talbot, Marion, 221

Talbot, Winthrop, 781

Tannenbaum, Frank, *49*, 936

Tanner, Amy E., 431

Tarde, Gabriel, 21, 22, 32, 33, 36, 37, 41, 58, 202, 204, 213, 218, 332, 390, 418, 423, 430, 563, 570, 728, 729, 777, 794 n., 828, 857, 868, 875, 927, 933, 939, 947

Tardieu, É., 725

Taussig, F. W., 731

Tawney, G. A., 726, 939

Tawney, Richard H., 565

Tayler, J. Lionel, 939

Taylor, F. W., 152

Taylor, Graham R., 219

Taylor, Thomas, 939

Tead, Ordway, 152, 494
Teggart, Frederick J., 1005
Tegnér, Esaias, 945
Tenney, E. P., 1009
Terman, L. M., 148, 855
Theophrastus, 147, 154
Thiers, Adolphe, 946
This, G., 275
Thomas, Edward, 936
Thomas, N. W., 220, 856
Thomas, William I., 47, 52, 57, 38, 59, 147, 149, 151, 154, 156, 215, 222, 249-52, 278, 285, 332, 335, 438, 442, 488-90, 497, 501, 563, 579-82, 643, 654, 655, 657, 718, 728, 729, 730, 774, 777, 935, 947, 949
Thompson, Anstruther, 402
Thompson, Frank V., 781
Thompson, Helen B., 156
Thompson, M. S., 945
Thompson, Warren S., 567
Thompson, W. Gilman, 569
Thomson, J. Arthur, 13, 71, 129-31, 150, 156, 218, 227, 512-14, 564, 1007
Thorndike, Edward L., 68, 71, 73-75, 80, 81, 95-98, 150, 153, 155, 157, 189, 190, 424, 430, 494, 650, 721, 726
Thorndike, Lynn, 152
Thoreau, H. D., 229
Thurston, Henry W., 657
Thwing, Charles F., and Carrie F. B., 222
Tippenhauer, L. G., 939
Tocqueville, Alexius de, 851, 858, 909
Todd, Arthur J., 220, 1004, 1009
Toller, Ernst, 950
Tolstoy, Count Leon, 154, 789
Tönnies, Ferdinand, 103-5, 857, 940
Toops, Herbert A., 568
Topinard, Paul, 182, 536
Tosti, Gustavo, 426
Tower, W. L., 131, 150
Towns, Charles B., 569
Toynbee, Arnold, 334, 940
Tracy, J., 943
Train, Arthur, 657
Train, J., 944
Tredgold, A. F., 155, 276
Treitschke, Heinrich von, 988
Trenor, John J. D., 780
Trent, William P., 859
Tridon, André, 500
Triplett, Norman, 649
Trotter, W., 31, 650, 742-45, 783
Tuchmann, J., 856

Tufts, James H., 152
Tulp, Dr., 241
Turner, Charles J. Ribton-, see Ribton-Turner, Charles J.
Turner, Frederick J., 498
Twain, Mark [pseud.], see Clemens, Samuel L.
Tyau, M. T. Z., 935
Tylor, Edward B., 19, 151, 220, 674, 855

Urban, Wilbur M., 500

Vaccaro, M. A., 860
Valentinelli, 388
Vallaux, Camille, 274, 333
Van Beneden, 177
Vandervelde, É., 218, 333, 1007
Van Hise, Charles R., 566
Varendonck, J., 273
Vavin, P., 728
Veblen, Thorstein, 71, 287, 501, 644, 721, 729, 936
Vellay, Charles, 945
Vendryes, J., 428
Vierkandt, Alfred, 151, 333, 723, 729, 776, 854
Vignes, J.-B.-Maurice, 59
Vigouroux, A., 411, 412, 937
Villard, Oswald G., 859
Villatte, Césare, 429
Villon, François, 429
Vincent, George E., 58, 605-10, 649
Virchow, Rudolph, 536, 725
Vischer, F. T., 402
Vogt, Paul, 731
Vogt, von Ogden, 938
Voivenel, Paul, 650
Voltaire, 890, 986
Von Kolb, 240
Vries, Hugo de, 146

Wace, A. J. B., 945
Wagener, C., 651
Wagner, Adolf, 564
Wagner, J. M., 243
Waitz, Theodor, 856
Wald, Lillian, 331
Walford, Cornelius, 565
Walker, Charles R., 152
Walker, Francis A., 490, 507, 538-43, 565, 572
Walker, Mary, 831
Wallace, 554
Wallace, Alfred R., 555, 564, 725, 1006
Wallace, D. Mackenzie, 333
Wallas, Graham, 151, 164, 335, 422, 432, 494, 854, 925, 929, 935

Wallaschek, Richard, 938
Walling, W. E., 655
Wallon, H., 727
Walter, F., 854
Ward, E. J., 331, 731
Ward, James, 775
Ward, Lester F., 48, 58, 497, 499, 512, 718, 855, 973-75, 1007
Ward, Robert De C., 726
Ware, J. Redding, 428
Wargelin, John, 781
Warming, Eugenius, 175-82, 218, 555
Warne, Frank J., 653
Warneck, Gustav, 778
Warren, H. C., 777
Warren, Josiah, 566
Washburn, Margaret F., 150
Washington, Booker T., 155, 607, 632, 782
Wasmann, Eric, 171
Watterson, Henry, 858
Watson, Elkanah, 539, 542
Watson, John B., 84, 150, 285, 482-88, 488 494
Watson, R. W. Seton-. see Seton-Watson, R. W.
Waxweiler, E., 218
Weatherly, U. G., 776
Webb, Sidney and Beatrice, 59, 565, 647, 658, 935
Weber, Adna F., 334
Weber, John L., 727
Weber, L., 1006
Weber, Max, 13, 217, 332
Webster, Hutton, 274, 730
Wechsler, Alfred, 947
Weeks, Arland D., 649
Wehrhan, K., 652
Weidensall, C. J., 156
Weigall, A., 333
Weismann, August, 146, 227, 514, 564
Weller, Charles F., 731
Wells, H. G., 154, 496, 498, 932, 1008
Wendland, Walter, 652
Wermert, Georg, 656
Wesley, Charles, 916
Wesley, John 154, 916 ff.
Wesnitsch, Milenko R., 656
West, Arthur Graeme, 652
Westermarck, Edward, 16, 17, 61, 151, 214, 215, 220, 643, 778, 849, 854
Weygandt, W., 937
Whately, Richard, 835
Wheeler, G. C., 220

Wheeler, William M., *169–72, 182–84*, 214, 217, 555
White, A. K., 153
White, Andrew D., 650
White, F. M., 656
White, W. A., 500, *594–98*
Whitefield, George, 916 ff.
Whitley, Opal S., 273
Whiting, Lilian, 949
Whitley, W. T., 942
Wigmore, John H., 852, 854, 860, 861
Wilberforce, William, 948
Wilbert, Martin I., 569
Wilde, Oscar, 154
Willard, Frances E., 942, 949
Willard, Josiah Flynt, 154
Willcox, Walter F., 222, *1002–3*, 1009
Willey, Malcolm M., 498
Williams, Daniel J., 780
Williams, J. M., 212, 219, 222
Willoughby, W. W., 566
Wilmanns, Karl, 156
Wilson, D. L., 730
Wilson, *Captain* H. A., 640
Wilson, Warren H., 219

Windelband, Wilhelm. *8–10*, 286, 649
Windisch, H., 775
Winship, A. E., 150
Winston, L. G., *120–22*
Wirth, M., 946
Wishart, Alfred W., 274
Wissler, Clark, 59
Wiston-Glynn, A. W., 946
Witte, H., 946
Wittenmyer, (Mrs.) Annie, *898–905*, 942
Wolff, C. F., 967
Wolman, Leo, 653
Wood, Walter (ed.), 651
Woodbury, Margaret, 858
Woodhead, T. W., 181
Woods, A., 656
Woods, E. B., 1004
Woods, Frederick A., 499, 854
Woods, Robert A. 219, 331, 335, 567, *610–13*, 656 (ed.), 731, 942
Woodson, Carter G., 941
Woodworth, R. S., 156
Woolbert, C. H., 941
Woolman, John, 154
Woolston, Howard B., 570

Wordsworth, William, 66
Worms, René, 28, *29*, 58, 61 426, 651 (ed.), 728, 940
Wright, Arnold 653
Wright, Gordon, 886
Wuensch, R., 939
Wundt, Wilhelm, **21**, **22**, 421 422, 428, 775, 777
Wuttke, Heinrich, 428

Yerkes, R. M., 148
Yonge, Charlotte M., 949
Yule, Henry, 275

Zangwill, Israel, 734
Zeeb, Frieda B., 941
Zenker, E V., 566
Ziegler, T., 941
Zimand, Savel, 942
Zimmermann, Johann G., 271, 273
Zimmern, Alfred E., 660, 729
Znaniecki, Florian, *47*, *52*, *57*, 58, 147, 154, 222, 335, 501, 730, 774, 935, 1005
Zola, Émile, *144–45*, 266, 334
Zollschan, Ignaz, 152
Zueblin, Charles, *955–56*, 1009

GENERAL INDEX

ACCLIMATIZATION: *bibliography*, 725–26; as a form of accommodation, 666, 671–74, 719

ACCOMMODATION: *chap. x*, 663–733; *bibliography*, 725–32; and adaptation, 663–65; and assimilation, 735–36; and competition, 664–65; and compromise, 706–8; and conflict, 634–40, 669–70, 703–8; creates social organization, 510; defined, 663–64; distinguished from assimilation, 510; facilitated by secondary contacts, 736–37; in the form of domination and submission, 440–41; in the form of slavery, 674–77, 677–81; forms of, 666–67, 671–88, 718–20; and historic forms of the organization of society, 667; investigations and problems, 718–25; natural issue of conflict, 665; and the origin of caste in India, 681–84, 684–88; and peace, 703–6; in relation to competition, 509–10; in relation to conflict, 510, as subordination and superordination, 667–69. *See* Subordination and superordination

ACCOMMODATION GROUPS, classified, 50, 721–23

ACCULTURATION: *bibliography*, 776–77; defined, 138; problems of, 771–72; and tradition, 72; transmission of cultural elements, 737

ADAPTATION, and accommodation, 663–65

ADVERTISING, *see* Publicity

AGGREGATES, SOCIAL: composed of spatially separated units, 26; and organic aggregates, 25

AMALGAMATION: *bibliography*, 776; and assimilation, 740–41, 769–71; fusion of races by intermarriage, 737–38; result of contacts of races, 770. *See* Miscegenation

AMERICANIZATION: *bibliography*, 781–82; as assimilation, 762–63; and immigration, 772–75; as participation, 762–63; as a problem of assimilation, 739–40, 762–69; Study of Methods of, 739, 773–74; surveys

and studies of, 772–75. *See* Immigration

ANARCHISM: *bibliography*, 566–67; economic doctrine of, 559

ANARCHY, of political opinion and parties, 2

ANGER: analyzed, 76–77

ANIMAL CROWD. *See* Crowd, animal

ANIMAL SOCIETY: bee and ant community, 742; prestige in, 809–10

ANTHROPOLOGY, 10

APPRECIATION: in relation to imitation, 344, 401–7; and sense impressions, 356–57

ARCHAEOLOGY, as a new social science, 5

ARGOT, *bibliography*, 428–29

ART: as expressive behavior, 787–88; origin in the choral dance, 871

ASSIMILATION: *chap. xi*, 734–84; *bibliography*, 775–82; and accommodation, 735–36; and amalgamation, 740–41, 769–71; Americanization as, 762–63; based on differences, 735; biological aspects of, 737–38, 740–45; conceived as a "Melting Pot," 734; defined, 756, 761; and democracy, 734; distinguished from accommodation, 510; facilitated by primary contacts, 736–37, 739, 761–62; final product of social contact, 736–37; in the formation of nationalities, 756–58; fusion of cultures, 737; of the Germans in the Carpathian lands, 770; instinctive basis of, 742–45; investigations and problems, 769–75; as like-mindedness, 735, 741; and mediation of individual differences, 766–69; natural history of, 774; in personal development, 510; popular conceptions of, 734–45; a problem of secondary groups, 761; a process of prolonged contact, 741; of races, 756–62; and racial differences, 769–70; sociology of, 735–37. *See* Amalgamation, Americanization, Cultures, conflict and fusion of, Denationalization.

ATTENTION, in relation to imitation, 344, 391–94

ATTITUDES: *bibliography*, 500–501; as behavior patterns, 439–42; complexes of, 57; polar conception of, 441–42; as the social element, 438–39; as social forces, 467–78; in subordination and superordination, 692–95; and wishes, 442–43; wishes as components of, 439

BALKED DISPOSITION, a result of secondary contacts, 287

BEHAVIOR: defined, 187–88; expressive and positive, 787–88

BEHAVIOR, COLLECTIVE. *See* Collective behavior

BEHAVIOR PATTERNS, and culture, 72

BLUSHING, communication by, 365–70

BOLSHEVISM, 909–15

BUREAU OF MUNICIPAL RESEARCH, of New York City, 46, 315

CARNEGIE REPORT UPON MEDICAL EDUCATION, 315

CASTE: *bibliography*, 728; as an accommodation of conflict, 584; defined, 205–6; a form of accommodation group, 50; interpreted by superordination and subordination, 684–88; its origin in India, 681–84; and the limitation of free competition, 623–25; study of, 722–23

CATEGORIC CONTACTS. *See* Sympathetic contacts

CEREMONY: *bibliography*, 855–56; as expressive behavior, 787–88; fundamental form of social control, 787

CHARACTER: defined, 84; inherited or acquired, 130–31; and instinct, 192–95; as the organization of the wishes of the person, 490; related to custom, 194–95

CIRCLE, VICIOUS. *See* Vicious circle

CIRCULAR REACTION. *See* Reaction, circular

CITY: an area of secondary contacts, 285–87; aversion, a protection of the person in the, 584–85; and the evolution of individual types, 712–14; growth of, 533–34; physical human type of, 534–37; planning, studies of, 328–29; studies of, 331

CIVILIZATION: and historical continuity, 298–301; life of, 956–57; and mobility, 303–5; a part of nature, 3; an organization to realize wishes, 958; and permanent settlement, 528–29

CLASS CONSCIOUSNESS, 40

CLASSES, SOCIAL: *bibliography*, 728–29; defined, 206–7; as a form of accommodation groups, 50; patterns of life of, 46; separated by isolation, 230; study of, 722

CLEVER HANS, case of, 412–15

COLLECTIVE BEHAVIOR: *chap. xiii*, 865–952; *bibliography*, 58, 934–50; defined, 865; investigations and problems, 924–34; and the origin of concerted activity, 32; and social control, 785–86; and social unrest, 866–67. *See* Crowd, Herd, Mass movements, Public

COLLECTIVE CONSCIOUSNESS: defined, 197; of society, 28

COLLECTIVE FEELING, and collective thinking, 17

COLLECTIVE MIND, and social control, 36–43

COLLECTIVE REPRESENTATION: application of Durkheim's conception of, 18; contrasted with sensation, 195; in the crowd, 894–95; defined, 166–67, 197–98; and intellectual life, 195–98; and public opinion, 38

COLLECTIVISM: and the division of labor, 718

COLONIZATION: *bibliography*, 725–26; a form of accommodation, 719; and mobility, 302

COMMON PURPOSE, as ideal, wish, and obligation, 33

COMMUNISM, economic doctrine of, 559

COMMUNITY ORGANIZATION: *bibliography*, 731; study of, 724–25

COMMUNICATION: *bibliography*, 275–76, 427–29; and art, 37; basis of participation in community life, 763–66; basis of society, 185–87; basis of world-society, 343; by blushing, 365–70; concept, the medium of, 379–81; extension of, by human invention, 343, 385–89; a form of social interaction, 36; and interstimulation, 37; by laughing, 370–75; in the lower animals, 375–79; as the medium of social interaction, 341–43; natural forms of, 356–75; newspaper as medium of, 316–17; rôle of the book in, 343; study of, 421–23; through the expression of the emotions, 342, 361–75; through language and ideas, 375–89; through the senses, 342, 356–61; writing as a form of, 381–84. *See* Language, Newspaper, Publicity

COMMUNITIES: *bibliography*, 58–59, 219; animal, 26; defined, 163; local and territorial, 50; plant, *bibliography*, 217–18; plant, organization of, 26, 175–82, 525–27; plant, unity of, 200–1; rural and urban, 56; scale for grading, 1002 n.; studies of, 211–12, 327–29

COMMUNITY, as a constellation of social forces, 436, 493

COMPETITION: *chap. viii*, 504–73; *bibliography*, 564–70; and accommodation, 509–10, 664–65; biological, 554–55; changing forms of, 546–51; and commercial organization, 543–45; conscious, as conflict, 574, 576, 579–94; and control, 508–9; of cultural languages, 754–56, 771; and the defectives, the dependents, and the delinquents, 560–64; destroys isolation, 232; economic, 545–55, 555–59; and the economic equilibrium, 504–5, 510; the elementary process of interaction, 506–10; elimination of, and caste, 623–25; and freedom, 505–6, 508, 512, 552–53; history of theories of, 557–59; and human ecology, 559; and the "inner enemies," 560–64; investigations and problems, 554–64, and laissez faire, 555–59; the "life of trade," 504; makes for progress, 988; makes for specialization and organization, 518–21; and man as an adaptive mechanism, 521–25; and metropolitan economy, 343–45; and mobility, 512; most severe between members of the same species, 516; and the natural harmony of individual interests, 551–52; natural history of, 556–57; and natural selection, 514–18; opposed to sentiment, 508; personal, as conflict, 574, 575–76; personal, and the evolution of individual types, 712–14; personal, and social selection, 708–12; and plant migration, 525–27; popular conception of, 504–6; and race suicide, 538–43; restricted by custom, tradi-

tion, and law, 512; and segregation, 525–43; and social contact, 280–81; and social control, 562–64; and social solidarity, 670–71, 708–18; and the standard of living, 542–43; and status, 540–42, 670–71, 708–18; and the struggle for existence, 504, 511, 512–14, 514–18, 521–25, 546–51; unfair, 505. *See* Competitive co-operation

COMPETITIVE CO-OPERATION: Adam Smith's conception of ·an "invisible hand," 504, 552; in the ant community, 511–12; and competition, 507; complementary association, 181–89; and human ecology, 559; and participation, 767–68; in the plant community, 165

COMPREHENSION, and sense impressions, 357–61

COMPROMISE, a form of accommodation, 706–8

CONCEPTS: as collective representations, 195–97; as medium of communication, 379–81

CONDUCT: as self-conscious behavior, 190–91

CONFLICT: *chap. ix*, 574–662; *bibliography*, 648–60; and accommodation, 510, 634–40, 665, 669–70, 703–8; of beliefs, and the origin of sects, 614–15; concept of, 574–76; as conscious competition, 281, 574, 576, 579–94; cultural, and the organization of sects, 613–19; cultural, and sex differences, 618–19; cultural, and social organization, 577–78; determines the status of the person in society, 574–75, 576; emotional, 475–76; and fusion of cultures, 738–39, 746–62, 771–72; and fusion of cultures and social unity, 202; industrial, *bibliography*, 652–53; of impersonal ideals, 592–94; instinctive interest in, 579–82; investigations and problems, 641–48; natural history of, 579–82; and origin of law, 850–52; as personal competition, 575–76; and the political order, 510; psychology and sociology of, 641–42; race, and social contact, 619–26; and race consciousness, 626–34; racial, 619–40; and the rise of nationalities, 631–34; and repression, 601–2; and social control, 607–8; as

CONFLICT—*continued*
a struggle for status, 574, 578–79; as a type of social interaction, 582–86; types of, 642–44, 586–94; and the unification of personality, 583–84. *See* Feud, Litigation, Mental conflict, Race conflicts, Rivalry, War

CONFLICT GROUPS, classified, 50

CONSCIENCE: as an inward feeling, 106; a manifestation of the collective mind, 33; a peculiar possession of the gregarious animals, 31

CONSCIOUS, 41

CONSCIOUSNESS: national and racial, 40–41; and progress, 990–94

CONSCIOUSNESS, SOCIAL: *bibliography*, 426; of the community, 48; existence of, 28; as mind of the group, 41; in the person, 29; and the social organism, 39

CONSENSUS: defined, 166; social, and solidarity, 24; social, closer than the vital, 25; as society, 163; versus co-operation, 186

CONTACT, maritime, and geographical, 260–64

CONTACTS, PRIMARY: *bibliography*, 333–34; and absolute standards, 285–86; defined, 284, 311; distinguished from secondary contacts, 284–87, 305–27; facilitate assimilation, 736–37, 739; of intimacy and acquaintanceship, 284–85; related to concrete experience, 286; and sentimental attitudes, 319–20; studies of, 329–31; in village life in America, 305–11

CONTACTS, SECONDARY: *bibliography*, 334–35; and abstract relations, 325; accommodation facilitated by, 736–37; and capitalism, 317–22; a cause of the balked disposition, 287; characteristic of city life, 285–87, 311–15; conventional, formal, and impersonal, 56; defined, 284; distinguished from primary contacts, 284–87, 305–27; laissez faire in, 758; modern society based on, 286–87; publicity as a form of, 315–17; and the problems of social work, 287; and rational attitudes, 317–22; sociological significance of the stranger, 286, 322–27; studies of, 331

CONTACTS, SOCIAL: *chap. v*, 280–338; *bibliography*, 332–35; in assimilation,

736–37; avoidance of, 292–93, 330; defined, 329; desire for, 291–92; distinguished from physical contacts, 282; economic conception of, 280–81; extension through the devices of communication, 280–81; as the first stage of social interaction, 280,282; frontiers of, 288–89; intensity of, 282–83; investigations and problems of, 327–31; land as a basis for, 282, 289–91; preliminary notions of, 280–81; and progress, 988–89; and race conflict, 619–26; and racial intermixture, 770; and social forces, 36; sociological concept of, 281–82; spatial conception of, 282; sympathetic versus categoric, 294–98; in the transmission of cultural objects, 746. *See* Communication; Contacts, primary; Contacts, secondary; Continuity; Interaction, social; Mobility; Touch; We-group and others-group

CONTAGION, SOCIAL: *bibliography*, 937–38; and collective behavior, 874–76, 878–81; in fashion, 874–75; and psychic epidemics, 926–27

CONTINUITY: through blood-relationship, 351–52; by continuance of locality, 350; through group honor, 355–56; through the hereditary principle, 353–54; historical, 283–84, 298–301; through leadership, 353–54; through material symbols, 354–55; through membership in the group, 352–53; through specialized organs, 356

CONTROL: aim of sociology, 339; defined, 184; the fundamental social fact, 34; loss of, and unrest, 766–67. *See* Control, social

CONTROL, SOCIAL: *chap. xii*, 785–864; *bibliography*, 854–62; absolute in primary groups, 285–86, 305–11; through advertising, 830; in the animal "crowd," 788–90; as an artefact, 29; central problem of society, 42; and collective behavior, 785–86; and the collective mind, 36–43; and competition, 508–9, 562–64; and conflict, 607–8; and corporate action, 27; in the crowd, 790–91; in the crowd and the public, 800–805; defined, 785–87; and definitions of the situation, 764–65; elementary forms of, 788–91; 800–816, 849–50; and human nature, 785–87, 848–49; and the individual, 52; investigations and problems, 848–53; through laughter, 373–75; mechanisms of, 29; through news, 834–37; through opinion, 193–94; organization of, 29; through prestige, 807–11, 811–12; through propaganda, 837–41; in the public, 791–96, 800–805; through public opinion in cities, 316–17; resting on consent, 29; with the savage, 90; and schools of thought, 27–35; and social problems, 785; as taming, 165. *See* Ceremony, Law, Leadership, Institutions, Mores, Myth, Taboo

CONVERSION: *bibliography*, 726–27; as the mutation of attitudes and wishes, 669; religious, and the social group, 48

CO-OPERATION: of the machine type, 186. *See* Collective behavior, Corporate action

CORPORATE ACTION: problem of, 30; and social consciousness, 41–42; and social control, 27; as society, 165. *See* Collective behavior

CRIME, from the point of view of the primary group, 48, 49. *See* Defectives, dependents, and delinquents

CRISES, ECONOMIC: *bibliography*, 946–47

CRISIS, and public opinion, 793, 794

CROWD: *bibliography*, 930; animal, 788–89, 876, 881–87; characteristics of, 890–93; classified, 202–203; control in the, 790–91, 800–805; defined, 868, 893–95; excitement of, in mass movements, 895–98; homogeneous and heterogeneous, 202–203; "in being," 33; milling in, 869; organized, 33, 34; "psychological," 34, 876–77, 887–93; psychology of, 5; and the public, 867–70; and unreflective action, 798–99

CULTURAL DIFFERENCES, as caused by isolation, 229

CULTURAL PROCESS: the function of, 52–54; and isolation, 233

CULTURAL RESEMBLANCES, interpretation of, 19

CULTURAL TRAITS: *bibliography*, 151–52; independently created, 20; transmission of, 21

CULTURE: and behavior patterns, 72; materials, why diffused, 20; Roman, extension of in Gaul, 751–54

CULTURES: analysis of blended, 746–50; comparative study of, 18; conflict and fusion of, 738–39; 746–62; 771–72; *bibliography*, 776–79; fusions of, nature of the process, 20

CUSTOM: as the general will, 105; and law, 799. *See* Mores

DANCE: *bibliography*, 938–39; and corporate action, 870–71

DANCING MANIA OF THE MIDDLE AGES: 875, 879–81

DEFECTIVES, DEPENDENTS, AND DELINQUENTS: *bibliography*, 150, 567–70; and competition, 560–63; isolated groups, 232–33, 254–57, 271; and progress, 954–55; solution of problems of, 563–64

DEFINITION OF THE SITUATION, 764–65

DENATIONALIZATION: *bibliography*, 777–78; implies coercion, 740–41; as negative assimilation, 734; in the Roman conquest of Gaul, 751–54

DENOMINATIONS: as accommodation groups, 50, 722 distinguished from sects, 873

DESIRES: in relation to interests, 456; as social forces, 437–38, 453–54, 455, 497

DIALECTS: *bibliography*, 275–76, 428–29; caused by isolation, 271; of isolated groups, 423; *lingua franca*, 752–54

DISCOURSE, UNIVERSES OF. *See* Universes of discourse

DISCUSSION, *bibliography*, 649–50

DISORGANIZATION, SOCIAL: *bibliography*, 934–35; and change, 55; disintegrating influences of city life, 312–13; and emancipation of the individual, 867

DIVISION OF LABOR: and collectivism, 718; and co-operation, 42; and individualism, 718; and the moral code, 717–18; physiological, 26; in slavery, 677; and social solidarity, 714–18; and social types, 713–14

DOGMA, as based upon ritual and myth, 822–26

DOMESDAY SURVEY, 436

DOMESTICATION: defined, 165; of animals, 172–75

DOMINATION. See Subordination and superordination

DUEL: bibliography, 656

ECESIS, defined, 525

ECONOMIC COMPETITION. See Competition

ECONOMIC CONFLICT GROUPS: bibliography, 658–59

ECONOMIC CRISES. See Crises, economic

ECONOMIC MAN, as an abstraction to explain behavior, 495–96

ECONOMIC PROCESS, and personal values, 53–54

ECONOMICS: conception of society of, 280–81; and the economic process, 53–54; use of social forces in, 494–96. See Competition

EDUCATION: device of social control, 339; purpose of, 833

EMOTIONS, expressions of: bibliography, 427; study of, 421–22

EPIDEMICS, PSYCHIC OR SOCIAL. See Contagion, social

EQUILIBRIUM, a form of accommodation, 667, 719

ESPRIT DE CORPS: as affective morale, 209; defined, 166; in relation to isolation, 229–30

ETHNOLOGY: and history, 18; as a social science, 5

EUGENICS: bibliography, 150, 1007; and biological inheritance, 136; as human domestication, 165; and progress, 969–73, 979–83; research in, 146

EVOLUTION, SOCIAL: and progress, bibliography, 1006

FAMILY: bibliography, 219–23; government of, 46; outline for sociological study, 216; a primary group, 56; as a social group, 50; study of, 213–16

FASHION: bibliography, 947–48; a form of imitation, 390; as social contagion, 874–75; and social control, 831–32; study of, 933–34

FEAR: not a single instinct, 77–78

FEEBLE-MINDEDNESS. See Defectives, dependents, and delinquents

FERAL MEN: bibliography, 276; result of isolation, 239–43, 271–72

FERMENTATION, SOCIAL, 34

FEUD: bibliography, 655–56; as a form of conflict, 588–90; as the personal settlement of disputes, 581

FIELD STUDIES: bibliography, 59

FLOCK, 881–83

FOLK PSYCHOLOGY: aim of, 21; its origin, 20; and sociology, 5

FOLKLORE, as a social science, 5

FOLKWAYS: not creations of human purpose, 101. See Customs, Mores

FORCES, SOCIAL: chap. vii, 435–504; bibliography, 498–501; in American history, 443–44; attitudes as, 437–42; 467–78; desires as, 437–38, 453–54, 497; gossip as, 452; in history, 436–37, 493–94; history of the concept of, 436–37; idea-forces as, 461–64; and interaction, 451–54; interests as, 454–58, 458–62, 494–96; investigations and problems of, 491–97; organized in public opinion, 35; popular notions of, 491–93; in public opinion in England, 445–51; social pressures as, 458–61; and the social survey, 436; in social work, 435–37; 491–93; sources of the notion of, 435–36; tendencies as, 444–45; trends as, 436–37. See Attitudes, Desires, Interests, Sentiments, and Wishes

FREEDOM: bibliography, 564–65; and competition, 505–6, 508, 552–53; and laissez faire, 561–62; as the liberty to move, 323; of thought and speech, 643–44

FRENCH REVOLUTION, 905–9

GALTON LABORATORY FOR NATIONAL EUGENICS, 146, 561

GAMES AND GAMBLING: bibliography, 656–57; study of, 640

GANGS: bibliography, 657; as a form of conflict groups, 50, 722, 870; develop into clubs, 611–12; permanent form of crowd that acts, 872; and political organization, 610–13

GENERAL EDUCATION BOARD, 315

GENIUS, among civilized peoples, 95

GEOGRAPHY: and history, 8; as a science, 7

GOVERNMENT, a technical science, 1. *See* Politics

GREGARIOUSNESS, regarded as an instinct, 30, 742–45

GROUP, PRIMARY, defined, 50, 56

GROUP SELF-CONSCIOUSNESS, 51

GROUPS, SECONDARY: in relation to conflict and accommodation, 50. *See* Contacts, secondary

GROUPS, SOCIAL: *bibliography*, 218–23, 274, 333–35; accommodation type of, 721–23; centers of new ideas, 21; and character, 57; classification of, 50, 200–205, 722; concept of, 47; cooperation in, 22; defined, 45, 198–200; determines types of personality, 606–7; investigations of, 210–16, 270–71; natural, 30; organization and structure of, 51; persistence of, 349–56; a real corporate existence, 33; rivalry of, 605–10; and social problems, 50; study of, 646–48; subordination to, 699–702; types of, 47–51; unit of classification, 163–64; unit of investigation, 212–13; unity of, 200–2. *See* Groups, primary, Groups, secondary, Contacts, primary, Contacts, secondary, also the names of specific groups

GROWTH, SOCIAL, 26

HABIT, as the individual will, 103–5

HERD: behavior of, 30; contagion in, 885–86; homogeneity of, 31; instinct of the, 32, 742–45, 884–86; milling in the, 788–90; simplest type of social group, 30

HEREDITY AND EUGENICS: *bibliography*, 150. *See* Eugenics

HERITAGES, SOCIAL: complex of stimuli, 72; of the immigrant, 765; investigation of, 51; transmission of, 72

HINTERLAND, an integral part of metropolitan unit, 543–44

HISTORICAL FACT, 7

HISTORICAL PROCESS, and progress, 969–73

HISTORICAL RACES: as products of isolation, 257–60

HISTORY: a catalogue of facts, 14; defined by Karl Pearson, 14; and geography, 15; as group memory, 51–52; mother science of all the social sciences, 42, 43; as a natural science, 23; and the natural sciences, 6; scientific, 4, 14; and sociology, 5, 1–12, 16–24

HOMOGENEITY: and common purpose, 32; and like-mindedness, 32

HOUSING, and zoning studies, 328–29

HUMAN BEINGS, as artificial products, 98

HUMAN ECOLOGY, and competition, 558

HUMAN NATURE: *chap. ii*, 64–158; *bibliography*, 151–56; adaptability of, 98–100; Aristotle's conception of, 143; defined, 65–68; described in literature, 144–46; description and explanation of, 82; founded on instincts, 77–78; and the four wishes, 442–43; Hobbes's conception, 143; human interest in, 64–65; investigations and problems, 142–49; and law, 12–16; Machiavelli's conception, 143; and the mores, 100–3; political conceptions, 143–44; problems of, 47; product of group life, 67; product of social intercourse, 47; product of society, 161; and progress, 954, 957–58, 964–65, 983–1000; religious conceptions of, 142; and social control, 785–87; 848–49; and social life, 69; Spencer's conception, 144; and war, 594–98

HUMAN NATURE AND INDUSTRY: *bibliography*, 152

HUMAN SOCIETY: contrasted with animal societies, 201–2; and social life, 184–87

HYPNOTISM: a form of dissociation of memory, 472; post-hypnotic suggestion, 477. *See* Suggestion

IDEA-FORCES, 461–64. *See* Sentiment, Wishes

IMITATION: *bibliography*, 430; active side of sympathy, 394–95; and appropriation of knowledge, 403–4; and art, 401–7; circular reaction, 390–91; communication by, 72; defined, 344, 390–91, 391–94; in emotional communcation, 404–7; and fashion, 390; and the imitative process, 392–93; internal, 404–5; and like-mindedness, 33; as a process of learning, 344, 393–94; and rapport, 344; in relation to attention

IMITATION·—*continued*
and interest, 344, 391–94; in relation to trial and error, 344–45;
and the social inheritance, 390–91;
as the social process, 21; study of,
423–24; and suggestion, differentiated, 346; and suggestion, inner
relation between, 688–89; and the
transmission of tradition, 391–92

IMMIGRATION: *bibliography*, 779–80;
and Americanization, 772–75; involves accommodation, 719. *See*
Migration

IMMIGRATION COMMISSION, REPORT OF,
772–73

INBORN CAPACITIES, defined, 73–74

INDIVIDUAL: *bibliography*, 59, 149–50,
155–56; an abstraction, 24; isolated,
55; and person, 55; subordination to,
697–98

INDIVIDUAL DIFFERENCES: *bibliography*,
155–56, 276; assimilation and the
mediation of, 766–69; cause of isolation, 228–29; described, 95–97;
developed by city life, 313–15;
measurement of, 148–49; in primitive and civilized man, 93; and sex
differences, 90

INDIVIDUAL REPRESENTATION, 37,195

INDIVIDUALISM, and the division of
labor, 718

INDUSTRIAL ORGANIZATION: *bibliography*, 565–66; impersonality of, 287

IN-GROUP. *See* We-group

INHERITANCE, BIOLOGICAL: *bibliography*, 150

INHERITANCE, SOCIAL: through imitation, 390–91. *See* Heritages, social

"INNER ENEMIES." *See* Defectives,
dependents, and delinquents.

INSPIRATION, and public sentiment,
34, 35

INSTINCTS: *bibliography*, 150, 155–56;
and character, 192–95; in conflict, 576–77, 579–82; defined, 73–74;
gregarious, 742–45; in the human
baby, 85–88; instinctive movements
as race movements, 85; no separate,
75–79; physiological bases of assimilation, 742–45. *See* Human nature,
Original nature

INSTITUTIONS: defined, 796–97, 841;
investigations of, 51; and law, 797–

99; and mass movements, 915–24;
and mores, 841–43; natural history
of, 16; and sects, 872–74; and social
control, 796–99, 841–48, 851–53

INTERACTION, SOCIAL: *chap. vi*, 339–
434; *bibliography*, 426–31; in communication, 341–43, 356–89; concept
of, 339–41; in conflict, 582–86; defines the group in time and space, 341,
348–56; history of the concept, 420–
21; imitation as a mechanistic form
of, 344, 390–407; investigations and
problems, 420–24; language, science,
religion, public opinion, and law
products of, 37; and mobility, 341;
Ormond's analysis, 340; as a principal fundamental to all the natural
sciences, 341–42, 346–48; in secondary contacts in the large city, 360–
61; and social forces, 451–54; and
social process, 36, 421; and suggestion, 345–56, 408–12; visual, 356–61.
See Communication, Imitation, Process, social, Suggestion, and Sympathy

INTEREST: in relation to imitation,
344, 391–94

INTERESTS: *bibliography*, 499–500;
classification of, 456–57; defined,
456; and desires, 456; instincts and
sentiments, 30; natural harmony of,
551–52; as social forces, 454–58,
458–61

INTIMACY: *bibliography*, 332–33; and
the desire for response, 329–30; form
of primary contact, 284–85

INVENTION: *bibliography*, 431; as variation, 424–25; in relation to social
change and social control, 425. *See*
Leadership, Progress, Social control

INVERSION, of impulses and sentiments,
283, 292, 329

INVESTIGATION, and research, 45

ISOLATION: *chap. iv*, 226–79; *bibliography*, 273–76; in anthropogeography, 226, 269–70; barrier to invasion in plant communities, 526–27;
in biology, 227–28, 270; cause of
cultural differences, 229; cause of
dialects, 271; cause of mental
retardation, 231, 239–52; cause
of national individuality, 233, 257–
69; cause of originality, 237–39;
cause of personal individuality, 233–
39, 271–73; cause of race prejudice,

250-52; cause of the rural mind, 247-49; circle of, 232; destroyed by competition, 232; disappearance of, 866-67; effect upon social groups, 270-71; feral men, 239-43; geographical, and maritime contact, 260-64; investigations and problems of, 269-73; isolated groups, 270-71; mental effects of, 245-47; and prayer, 235-37; and the processes of competition, selection and segregation, 232-33; product of physical and mental differences, 228-29; result of segregation, 254-57; and secrecy, 230; and segregation, 228-30; and solidarity, 628-29; solitude and society, 243-45; subtler effects of, 249-52

JEW: product of isolation, 271; racial temperament, 139-40; as the sociological stranger, 318-19, 323

KLONDIKE RUSH, 895-98

LABOR ORGANIZATIONS: as conflict groups, 50
LABORING CLASS, psychology of, 40
LAISSEZ FAIRE: bibliography, 564-65; and competition, 554-58; and individual freedom, 560-61; in secondary contacts, 758
LANGUAGE: bibliography, 274-76, 428-29, 945-46; as condition of Americanization, 765-66; gesture, 362-64; and participation, 763-66. See Communication, Speech community
LANGUAGE GROUPS AND NATIONALITIES, 50-51
LANGUAGE REVIVAL AND NATIONALISM: bibliography, 945-46; study of, 930-32
LANGUAGES: comparative study of, and sociology, 5, 22; cultural, competition of, 754-56, 771
LAUGHTER: communcation by, 370-75; essays upon, 422; in social control, 373-75; and sympathy, 370-73, 401
LAW: bibliography, 860-62; based on custom and mores, 799, 843-46; common and statute, 842-46; comparative study of, 5; and conscience, 105-11; and creation of law-making opinion, 451; formation of, 16; and the general will, 105-11; and human nature, 12-16; as influenced

by public opinion, 445-51; and institutions, 797-99; and legal institutions, 851-53; moral, 13; municipal, 13; natural, defined, 11; natural, distinguished from other forms, 12; and public opinion, 446-51; and religion, 853; result of like-mindedness, 717; social, as an hypothesis, 12; "unwritten," 643
LAWS OF NATURE, 13
LAWS OF PROGRESS, 15
LAWS OF SOCIAL EVOLUTION, 18
LEADERSHIP: bibliography, 854-55; in the flock, 881-83; and group continuity, 353-54; interpreted by subordination and superordination, 695-97, 697-98; in Methodism, 916-17; study of, 721, 849-50. See Collective behavior, Invention, Social control, Suggestion, Subordination and superordination
LEGEND: as a form of social control, 819-22; growth of, 819-22; in the growth of Methodism, 922-23. See Myth
LEGISLATION. See Law
LIKE-MINDEDNESS: and corporate action, 42; as an explanation of social behavior, 32-33; formal, in assimilation, 757-60; in a panic, 33-34
LINGUA FRANCA, 752-54
LITERATURE, and the science of human nature, 144-46
LITIGATION, as a form of conflict, 590-92
LYNCHING: bibliography, 655

MAN: an adaptive mechanism, 521-25; economic, 495-96; the fighting animal, 600-3; the natural, 85-88; as a person, 10; a political animal, 10, 32; primitive and civilized, sensory discrimination in, 93. See Human nature, Individual, Person, Personality
MARKETS: bibliography, 565; and the origin of competition, 556-57
MASS MOVEMENTS: bibliography, 941-42; crowd excitements and, 895-98; and institutions, 915-24; and mores, 898-905; and progress, 54; and revolution, 905-15; study of, 927-32; types of, 895-924

MEMORY: associative, Loeb's definition, 467; rôle of, in the control of original nature, 468–71

MENTAL CONFLICT: bibliography, 648–49; and the disorganization of personality, 638; its function in individual and group action, 578; and sublimation, 669

MENTAL DIFFERENCES. See Individual differences

METHODISM, 915–24

METROPOLITAN ECONOMY, defined, 543

MIGRATION: classified into internal and foreign, 530–32; and mobility, 301–5; in the plant community, 525–27; and segregation, 528–32. See Immigration, Mobility

MILLING, in the herd, 788–90

MIND, COLLECTIVE, 887, 889–90

MISCEGENATION: and the mores, 53. See Amalgamation

MISSIONS: bibliography, 778–79; and the conflict and fusion of cultures, 771; and social transmission, 202

MOBILITY: bibliography, 333; and communication, 284; and competition, 512; contrasted with continuity, 286; defined, 283–84; facilitated by city life, 313–14; and instability of natural races, 300–1; of the migratory worker, 912–13; and the movement of the peoples, 301–5; and news, 284; and social interaction, 341; and the stranger, 323–24. See Communication, Contacts, social, Migration

MOBILIZATION, of the individual man, 313

MORALE: defined, 166; and isolation, 229–30; of social groups, 207–9. See Esprit de corps, Collective representation, Consciousness, social

MORES: bibliography, 151–52; as the basis of social control, 786–87; and conduct, 191; and human nature, 100–103; influence of, 30; and institutions, 841–43; and mass movements, 898–905; and miscegenation, 53; not subject of discussion, 52–53; and progress, 983–84; and public opinion, differentiated, 832

MOVEMENTS. See Mass movements

MUSIC: bibliography, 938–39

MYTHOLOGY, comparative study of, 5

MYTHS: bibliography, 856–57; as a form of social control, 816–19; progress as a, 958–62; relation to ritual and dogma, 822–26; revolutionary, 817–19, 909, 911; and socialism, 818–19. See Legend

NATIONAL DEVELOPMENT, as affected by natural or vicinal location, 268–69

NATIONAL DIFFERENCES, explained by isolation, 264–68

NATIONALITIES: bibliography, 274–75, 660; assimilation in the formation of, 756–58; conflict groups, 50, 628–31; defined, 645; and nations, 723; and patterns of life, 46; and racial temperament, 138–42. See Denationalization, Nationalization, Language revivals

NATIONALIZATION: bibliography, 777–78

NATURAL HISTORY: and natural science, 16; of a social institution, 16

NATURAL SCIENCE: defined, 12; and history, 8

NATURALIZATION, SOCIAL: as a form of accommodation, 666–67, 719

NATURE: defined, 11; laws of, 13; and nurture, 129–31

NATURE, HUMAN. See Human nature

NEGRO: accommodation of, in slavery, and freedom, 634–40; assimilation of, 760–62; race consciousness of, 626–34; racial temperament of, 139–40, 762

NEIGHBORHOOD: deterioration of, 252–54; as a local community, 50; as a natural area of primary contacts, 285; as a primary group, 56; scale for grading, 1002 n.

NEO-MALTHUSIAN MOVEMENT, 560–61

NEWS: and social control, 834–37. See Newspaper, Publicity

NEWSPAPER: bibliography, 428, 858–59; historical development of, 385–89; as medium of communication, 316–17. See Public opinion, Publicity

NOMINALISM, and social psychology, 41

NOMINALISTS, and realists in sociology, 36

OPINION. *See* Public opinion

ORDEAL OF BATTLE: *bibliography*, 656

ORGANISM, SOCIAL: and biological, 28; Comte's conception of, 24–25, 39; humanity or Leviathan? 24–27; and the separate organs, 27; Spencer's definition of, 25; Spencer's essay on, 28

ORGANIZATION, ECONOMIC, stages in, 543

ORGANIZATION, POLITICAL, gang as a factor, 610–13

ORGANIZATION, SOCIAL: *bibliography*, 729–31; of groups, 51; and progress, 966–68; and rivalry, 604–19; study of, 723–25

ORGANIZATIONS, sociological and biological, 26

ORIGINAL NATURE: an abstraction, 68; control over, 84; controlled through memory, 468–71; defined, 56, 73–74; and environment, 73; inheritance of, 131–36; of man, 68–69; research in, 146. *See* Individual, Individual differences, Instincts

ORIGINAL TENDENCIES: range of, 74

ORIGINALITY: accumulated commonplaces, 21; in relation to isolation, 237–39

OTHERS-GROUP. *See* We-group

OUT-GROUP. *See* We-group

PACK, 886–87

PARTICIPATION: Americanization as, 762–63; and competitive co-operation, 767–68; language as a means and a product of, 763–66. *See* Americanization, Assimilation, Collective behavior, Social control

PARTIES: *bibliography*, 659–60; as conflict groups, 50

PATTERNS OF LIFE, in nationalities, 46; in social classes, 46

PEACE, as a type of accommodation, 703–6

PERIODICALS, SOCIOLOGICAL: *bibliography*, 60

PERSON: *bibliography*, 152–55, 273; effect of city upon, 329; and his wishes, 488–90; as an individual with status, 55. *See* Personality, Status

PERSONALITY: *bibliography*, 152–55; alterations of, 116–20; classified, 149; as a complex, 69, 113–16; conscious, 490; defined, 70, 115–16; defined in terms of attitude, 490; disorganization of, and mental conflict, 641; dissociation of, 472–75; effect of isolation upon, 233–39, 271–73; and the four wishes, 442–43; and group membership, 609; harmonization of conflict, 583–84; of individuals and peoples, 126–28; investigation of, 146–48; as the organism, 111–13; shut-in type of, 272; and the social group, 48, 52; study of, 271–73; and suggestion, 419–20; types of, determined by the group, 606–7. *See* Individual, Person, Self, Status

PERSONS, defined, 55; as "parts" of society, 36; product of society, 161

PHILOSOPHY, and natural science, 4

PITTSBURGH SURVEY, 315, 724

PLANT COMMUNITIES. *See* Communities

PLAY: as expressive behavior, 787–88

POLITICS: *bibliography*, 940; comparative, Freeman's lectures on, 23; as expressive behavior, 787–88; among the natural sciences, 3; as a positive science, 3; shams in, 826–82

POVERTY. *See* Defectives, dependents, and delinquents

PRESTIGE: with animals, 809–10; defined, 807; and prejudice, 808–9; in primitive society, 810–11, 811–12; in social control, 807–11, 811–12; and status in South East Africa, 811–12. *See* Leadership, Status

PRIMARY CONTACTS. *See* Contacts, primary

PRINTING-PRESS, *bibliography*, 428

PRIVACY: defined, 231; values of, 231

PROBLEMS, ADMINISTRATIVE: practical and technical, 46

PROBLEMS, HISTORICAL: become psychological and sociological, 19

PROBLEMS OF POLICY: political and legislative, 46

PROBLEMS, SOCIAL: classification of, 45, 46; of the group, 47

PROCESS: historical, 51; political, as distinguished from the cultural, 52–54

PROCESS, SOCIAL: defined, 51; and interaction, 36, 346; natural, 346–48, 420–21; and social progress, 51–55

PROGRESS: *chap. xiv*, 953–1011; *bibliography*, 57–58, 1004–9; as the addition to the sum of accumulated experience, 1001–2; concept of, 962–63, 965–73; and consciousness, 990–94; and the cosmic urge, 989–1000; criteria of, 985–86; and the defectives, the dependents, and the delinquents, 954–55; and the *dunkler drang*, 994–1000; earliest conception of, 965–66; and the *élan vitale*, 989–94; and eugenics, 979–83; and happiness, 967, 973–75; and the historical process, 969–73; history of the concept of, 958–62; as a hope or myth, 958–62; and human nature, 954, 957–58, 964–65, 983–1000; indices of, 1002–3; investigations and problems, 1000–3; laws of, 15; and the limits of scientific prevision, 977–79; and mass movements, 54; a modern conception, 960–62; and the mores, 983–84; and the nature of man, 983; and organization, 966–68; popular conceptions of, 953–56; and prevision, 975–77; problem of, 956–58; and providence, in contrast, 960–62; and religion, 846–48; a result of competition, 988; a result of contact, 988–89; and science, 973–83; and social control, 786; and social process, 51–58; and social research, 1000–2; and social values, 955; stages of, 968–69; types of, 984–85; and war, 984–89

PROPAGANDA: in modern nations, 772; psychology of, 837–41

PROVIDENCE: in contrast with progress, 960–62

PSYCHOLOGY, COLLECTIVE, *bibliography*, 940–41

PUBLIC: and the crowd, 867–70; control in, 800–805; a discussion group, 798–99, 870

PUBLIC OPINION: *bibliography*, 59, 857–59; changes in intensity and direction of, 792–93; and collective representations, 38; combined and sublimated judgments of individuals, 795–96; continuity in it development, 449–51; and crises, 793–94; cross currents in, 450–51, 791–93; defined, 38;

and legislation in England, 445–51; and mores, 829–33; nature of, 826–29; opinion of individuals plus their differences, 832–33; organization of, 51; organization of social forces, 35; and schools of thought, 446–49; and social control, 786, 816–41, 850–51; as social weather, 791–93; as a source of social control in cities, 316–17; supported by sentiment, 478

PUBLICITY: as a form of social contact, 315–17; as a form of social control, 830; historical evolution of the newspaper, 385–89; and publication, 38

RACE CONFLICT: *bibliography*, 653–55; and race prejudice, 578–79; study of, 645–46

RACE CONSCIOUSNESS: and conflict, 626–34; in relation to literature and art, 629–32

RACE PREJUDICE: and competition of peoples with different standards of living, 622–26; as a defense-reaction, 623; a form of isolation, 250–52; a phenomenon of social distance, 440; and prestige, 808–9; and primary contacts, 330; and race conflicts, 578–79

RACE SUICIDE, and inter-racial competition, 538–43

RACES: assimilation of, 756–62; defined, 634–36

RACIAL DIFFERENCES: *bibliography*, 156, 776; and assimilation, 769–70; basis of race prejudice and conflict, 634–36; in primitive and civilized man, 92–95

RAPPORT: in the crowd, 893–94; in hypnotism, 345; in imitation, 344; in suggestion, 345

REACTION, CIRCULAR: in collective behavior and social control, 788–92; in imitation, 390–91; in social unrest, 866

REALISM, and collective psychology, 41

REALISTS, and nominalists in sociology, 43

REFLEX: defined, 73; as response toward an object, 479–82; Watson's definition of, 81

REFORM: *bibliography*, 948–50; method of effecting, 47; study of, 934

RELIGION: as an agency of social control, 846–48; comparative study of, 5; as expressive behavior, 787–88; as the guardian of mores, 847; and law, 853; Methodism, 915–24; origin in the choral dance, 871; and revolutionary and reform movements, 873–74, 908–9

RELIGIOUS REVIVALS, AND THE ORIGIN OF SECTS: bibliography, 942–44; study of, 932–33

RESEARCH, SOCIAL: and progress, 1000–2; and sociology, 43–57

RESEARCH, sociological, defined, 44

RESPONSE, MULTIPLE, and multiple causation, 75

REVIVALS. See Language revivals, Religious revivals

REVOLUTION: bibliography, 949–50; bolshevism, 909–15; French, 905–9; and mass movements, 905–15; moral, and Methodism, 923–24; and religion, 873–74, 908–9; study of, 934

RITES. See Ritual

RITUAL: bibliography, 855–56, 938–39; as a basis of myth and dogma, 822–26

RIVALRY: bibliography, 649; animal, 604–5; and national welfare, 609–10; of social groups, 605–10; and social organization, 577–78, 604–19; sublimated form of conflict, 577–78

ROCKEFELLER MEDICAL FOUNDATION, 670

RURAL COMMUNITIES: as local groups, 50. See Communities

RURAL MIND, as a product of isolation, 247–49

RUSSELL SAGE FOUNDATION, social surveys, 46, 315, 724

SALVATION ARMY, 873

SCIENCE: and concrete experience, 15; and description, 13; and progress, 973–83

SCIENCES, ABSTRACT, instrumental character of, 15

SCIENTIFIC EXPLANATION, and common sense, 83

SECONDARY CONTACTS. See Contacts, secondary

SECRET SOCIETIES, bibliography, 729–30

SECTS: bibliography, 657–58; as conflict groups, 50, 722; defined, 204–5; distinguished from denomination, 873; and institutions, 872–74; origin in conflict of beliefs, 614–15; origin in the crowd, 870–72; permanent form of expressive crowd, 872. See Religious revivals

SEGREGATION: and competition, 525–45; and isolation, 228–30, 254–57; and migration, 528–32; in the plant community, 525–27; as a process, 252–54; and social selection, 533–37

SELECTION, SOCIAL: and demographic segregation, 533–37; personal competition and status, 708–12

SELF: conventional, versus natural person, 120–22; divided, and moral consciousness, 122–26; as the individual's conception of his rôle, 116–20; "looking-glass," 70–71. See Individual, Person, Personality

SENSES, SOCIOLOGY OF, bibliography, 332–33

SENSORIUM, SOCIAL, 27, 28

SENTIMENTS: bibliography, 500–1; of caste, 684–88; and competition, 507; classification of, 466–67; and idea-forces, 463–64; of loyalty, as basis of social solidarity, 759; McDougall's definition, 441, 465; mutation of, 441–42; related to opinion, 478; as social forces, 464–67

SEX DIFFERENCES: bibliography, 156; and cultural conflicts, 618–19; described, 88–92

SITTLICHKEIT: defined, 105–7

SITUATION: definition of, 764–65; and response, 73

SLANG, bibliography, 428–29

SLAVERY: bibliography, 727–28; defined, 674–77; and the division of labor, 677; interpreted by subordination and superordination, 676, 677–81

SOCIAL ADVERTISING. See Publicity

SOCIAL AGGREGATES. See Aggregates, social

SOCIAL CHANGES, and disorganization, 55

SOCIAL CLASSES. See Classes, social

SOCIAL CONSCIOUSNESS. See Consciousness, social

SOCIAL CONTACT. See Contact, social

SOCIAL CONTROL. See Control, social

SOCIAL DISORGANIZATION. See Disorganization, social

SOCIAL DISTANCE: graphic representation of, 282; maintained by isolation, 230; as psychic separation, 164; and race prejudice, 440

SOCIAL FACT: classification of, 51; imitative, 21

SOCIAL FORCES. See Forces, social

SOCIAL GROUPS. See Groups, social

SOCIAL HERITAGES. See Heritages, social

SOCIAL INTERACTION. See Interaction, social

SOCIAL LIFE: defined, 185–87; and human nature, 184–87

SOCIAL MOVEMENTS. See Mass movements

SOCIAL ORGANISM. See Organism, social

SOCIAL ORGANIZATION. See Organization, social

SOCIAL PHENOMENA: causes of, 17; as susceptible of prevision, 1

SOCIAL PRESSURES, as social forces, 458–61

SOCIAL PROBLEMS. See Problems, social

SOCIAL PROCESS. See Process, social

SOCIAL REFORM. See Problems, social, Reform

SOCIAL SENSORIUM. See Sensorium, social

SOCIAL SOLIDARITY. See Solidarity, social

SOCIAL SURVEYS. See Surveys, social

SOCIAL TYPES. See Types, social

SOCIAL UNIT PLAN, 724

SOCIAL UNITY, as a product of isolation, 229–30

SOCIAL UNREST. See Unrest, social

SOCIALISM: bibliography, 566–67; economic doctrines of, 559; function of myth in, 818–19

SOCIALIZATION: the goal of social effort, 496; as the unity of society, 348–49

SOCIETY: bibliography, 217–23; animal, bibliography, 217–18; in the animal colony, 24; ant, 182–84; an artefact, 30; based on communication, 185–86; collection of persons, 158; collective consciousness of, 28; "collective organism," 24; as consensus, 163; defined, 161–64, 167–68, 348–49; differentiated from community and social group, 163–64; as distinct from individuals, 27; exists in communication, 36; an extension of the individual organism, 161–62; and the group, chap. iii, 161–225; bibliography, 217–23; from an individualistic and collectivistic point of view, 41, 42; investigations and problems of, 210–16; mechanistic interpretation of, 346–48; metaphysical science of, 2; as part of nature, 29; product of nature and of design, 30; scientific study of, 210–11; and social distance, 164; as social interaction, 341, 348; and the social process, 211; and solitude, 233–34, 234–45; as the sum total of institutions, 161; and symbiosis, 167–75

SOCIOLOGY: aims at prediction and control, 339–40; in the classification of the sciences, 6; as collective psychology, 342; Comte's program, 1; a description and explanation of the cultural process, 35; an experimental science, 6; a fundamental science, 6; and history, 1–12, 16–24; as an independent science, 1; origin in history, 23; origin of, 5, 6; and the philosophy of history, 44; positive science of society, 3; representative works in, bibliography, 57–59; rural and urban, 40; schools of, 28; a science of collective behavior, 24; a science of humanity, 5; and social research, 43–57; and the social sciences, chap. i, 1–63

SOCIOLOGICAL INVESTIGATION: methods of, bibliography, 58–59

SOCIOLOGICAL METHOD, 23

SOCIOLOGICAL POINT OF VIEW, 16

SOLIDARITY, SOCIAL: and the division of labor, 714–18; and loyalty, 759; and status and competition, 670–71, 708–18

SOLITUDE. See Isolation

SPEECH COMMUNITY, changes in, 22. See Language

STATE, sociological definition of, 50

STATISTICS, as a method of investigation, 51

STATUS: and competition, 540–42, 670–71, 708–18; determined by conflict, 574–75, 576; determined by members of a group, 36; of the person in the city, 313; and personal competition and social selection, 708–12; and prestige in South East Africa, 811–12; and social solidarity, 670–71, 708–18. *See* Prestige

STRANGER, sociology of, 317–22, 322–27

STRIKES, *bibliography*, 652–53

STRUCTURE, SOCIAL, permanence of, 746–50

STRUGGLE FOR EXISTENCE: and competition, 504, 511, 512–14, 521–25; and natural selection, 514–18. *See* Competition

STRUGGLE: for struggle's sake, 585–86

SUBLIMATION: the accommodation of mental conflict, 669; defined, 79; rivalry as, 577–78; of war, 598

SUBMISSION. *See* Subordination and superordination

SUBORDINATION AND SUPERORDINATION, *bibliography*, 726; in accommodation, 667–68; in animal rivalry, 604–5; in caste, 684–88; in leadership, 695–97; literature of, 721; psychology of, 688–92; reciprocal character of, 695–97; in slavery, 676, 677–81; social attitudes in, 692–95; three types of, 697–703

SUGGESTION: *bibliography*, 430–31; basis of social change, 22; case of Clever Hans, 412–15; and contra-suggestion, 419; in the crowd, 415–16; defined, 408; distinguished from imitation, 345–46; in hypnotism, 345, 412, 424, 471–72; and idea-forces, 461–64; and imitation, inner relation between, 688–89; and leadership, 419–20; and mass or corporate action, 415–20; as a mechanistic form of interaction, 344–46, 408–20; and perception, active and passive, 345, 408–12; personal and general consciousness, 409–12; and personality, 419–20; as psychic infection, 410–12; in social life, 345–46, 408–20, 424; study of, 424; subtler forms of, 412–15. *See* Hypnotism

SUPERORDINATION. *See* Subordination and superordination

SUPPRESSION, not annihilation, 79

SURVEY, SOCIAL: as a type of community study, 436; types of, 46

SYMBIOSIS: in the ant community, 169–72; in the plant community, 177–82

SYMPATHETIC CONTACTS, versus categoric contacts, 294–98

SYMPATHY: and imagination, 397–98; imitation its most rudimentary form, 394–95; intellectual or rational, 396–97, 397–401; the "law of laughter," 370–73, 401; psychological unison, 395; Ribot's three levels of, 394–97

TABOO: *bibliography*, 856; and religion, 847; and rules of holiness and uncleanness, 813–16; as social control, 812–16; and touch, 291–93. *See* Touch

TAMING, of animals, 172–75

TEMPERAMENT: *bibliography*, 155–56; divergencies in, 94; of Negro, 139–40, 762; racial and national, 138–42

TOUCH: as most intimate kind of contact, 280; and social contact, 282–83, 291–93; study of, 329–30; and taboo, 291–93

TRADITION: and inheritance of acquired nature, 137–38; and temperament, 138–42; versus acculturation, 72. *See* Heritages, social

TRANSMISSION: by imitation and inculcation, 72, 138; and society, 185; Tarde's theory of, 21

TYPES, SOCIAL: *bibliography*, 730–31; in the city, 313–15; and the division of labor, 713–14; result of personal competition, 712–14

UNIVERSES OF DISCOURSE: *bibliography*, 428–29; and assimilation, 737, 764; "every group has its own language," 423. *See* Communication, Language, Publicity

UNREST, MORAL, 57

UNREST, SOCIAL: *bibliography*, 935–36; and circular reaction, 866; and collective behavior, 866–67; increase of Bohemianism, 57; in the I.W.W., 911–15; like milling in the herd, 788;

UNREST—*continued*
manifest in discontent and mental anarchy, 907–8; product of the artificial conditions of city life, 287, 329; result of mobility, 320–21; sign of lack of participation, 766–67; and social contagion, 875–76; studies of, 924–26; and unrealized wishes, 442–43

URBAN COMMUNITIES: as local groups, 50. *See* Communities

UTOPIAS, *bibliography*, 1008

VALUES: *bibliography*, 500; object of the wish, 442; personal and impersonal, 54; positive and negative, 488; and progress, 955

VICIOUS CIRCLE, 788–89

VOCATIONAL GROUPS, as a type of accommodation groups, 50

WANTS AND INTERESTS, *bibliography*, 499–500

WAR: *bibliography*, 650–52; as an exciting game, 580; as a form of conflict, 575–76, 576–77, 586–88, 703–6; and the "Great Society," 600–601; and human nature, 594–98; literature of, 644–45; and man as the fighting animal, 600–603; and possibility of its sublimation, 598; the preliminary process of rejuvenescence, 596–97; and progress, 984–89; in relation to instincts and ideals, 576–77, 594–603; as relaxation, 598–603; and social utopia, 599

WE-GROUP: and collective egotism, 606; and others-group defined, 283, 293–94; ethnocentrism, 294

WILL: common, 109; general, 110–11; general, in relation to law and conscience, 105–11; individual, 104; social, 105

WISH, the Freudian, 438, 442, 478–80, 482–88, 497

WISHES: *bibliography*, 500–501; and attitudes, 442–43; civilization organized to realize, 958; as components of attitudes, 439; and growth of human nature and personality, 442–43; as libido, 442; organized into character, 490; of the person, 488–90; as psychological unit, 479; and the psychic censor, 484–88; and the reflex, 479–82; repressed, 482–83; as the social atoms, 478–82; Thomas' classification of, 438, 442, 488–90, 497; and values, 442, 488

WOMAN'S TEMPERANCE CRUSADE, 898–905

WRITING: as form of communication, 381–84; pictographic forms, 381; by symbols, 382–83

DATE DUE

APR 2 1981			